FOR REFERENCE

Do Not Take From This Room

D1616160

Ben Hodges / Scott Denny

THEATRE WORLD®

VOLUME 66 / 2009–2010

R
792
T374

APPLAUSE
THEATRE & CINEMA BOOKS

An Imprint of Hal Leonard Corporation

COLLEGE OF THE SEQUOIAS
LIBRARY

THEATRE WORLD®
Volume 66
Copyright © 2011 by Ben Hodges

All rights reserved. No part of this book may be reproduced in any form, without written permission,
except by a newspaper or magazine reviewer who wishes to quote brief passages in connection with a review.

Published in 2011 by Applause Theatre & Cinema Books
An Imprint of Hal Leonard Corporation
7777 West Bluemound Road
Milwaukee, WI 53213

Trade Book Division Editorial Offices
33 Plymouth Street, Montclair, NJ 07042

Printed in the United States of America
Book design by Tony Meisel

ISBN 978–1–4234–9271–9
ISSN 1088–4564

www.applausepub.com

To Alec Baldwin

Whose talent as a performer is matched only by his steadfast commitment to *Theatre World*, the Theatre World Awards, and personal dedication to our late editor, John Willis. His ability to maintain a successful career as a stage and screen performer alongside an unwavering mission of dedicating himself to the preservation of the history of theatre and film is unprecedented and a testament to his love of life and to his life's work.

PAST EDITORS	Daniel Blum (1945–1963)
	John Willis (1963–2007)
EDITOR IN CHIEF	Ben Hodges (1998–present)
CO-EDITOR	Scott Denny (2005-present)
ASSOCIATE OFF-OFF BROADWAY EDITOR	Shay Gines
CONTRIBUTING BROADWAY EDITOR	Adam Feldman
CONTRIBUTING OFF-BROADWAY EDITOR	Linda Buchwald
CONTRIBUTING REGIONAL EDITOR	Nicole Estvanik Taylor
ASSISTANT EDITORS	Kelley Murphy Perlstein
	Cristina Politano
STAFF PHOTOGRAPHERS	Rommel "Raj" Autencio, Jim Baldassare, Konrad Brattke, Walter McBride, Michael Portantiere, Aubrey Rueben, Michael Riordan, Laura Viade, Michael Viade

Acknowledgements

Theatre World would like to extend a very special thank you to all the New York and regional press agents, theatre marketing departments, and theatre photographers for their constant and steadfast support of this publication as well as for the endless resources that they provide to the editorial staff.

Our gratitude is eternally extended to our contributing photographers: Joan Marcus, Carol Rosegg, Paul Kolnik, Richard Termine, Gerry Goodstein, T. Charles Erickson, Monique Carboni, Dixie Sheridan, Paula Court, Michal Daniel, Robert J. Saferstein, Peter James Zielinski, Dan Acquisto, David Alkire, Richard Anderson, Pavel Antonov, Miranda Arden, Catherine Ashmore, Pier Baccaro, Jim Baldassare, Erin Balino, SuzAnne Barabas, Armin Bardel, Brian Barenio, Stan Barouh, Rachelle Beckerman, Derrick Belcham, Chris Bennion, Stephanie Berger, Kevin Berne, Rick Berubé, Rose Billings, Marc Bovino, Jay Brady, Michael Brosilow, Harry Butler, Nino Fernando Campagna, Owen Carey, Roy Chicas, Jonathan Christman, Meagan Cignoli, Bradley Clements, Larry Cobra, Peter Coombs, Arthur Cornelius, Gregory Costanzo, Sandra Coudert, Lindsey Crane, Amanda Culp, Julie Curry, Whitney Curtis, Ellie D'Eustachio, Blaine Davis, Robert Day, Manuel Navarro de la Fuente, Joe del Tufo, Phile Deprez, Jeff Derose, Henry DiRocco, Lisa Dozier, Erik Ekroth, Aaron Epstein, Eric Y. Exit, Felix Photography, Benoit Fontaine, Joshua Frachisseur, Tim Fuller, Marc Garvin, Drew Geraci, Gili Getz, Gion, Ronald L. Glassman, Jenny Graham, Larry Gumpel, Aric Gunter, Steven Gunther, Raymond Haddad, Sabrina Hamilton, Jeremy Handelman, John Haynes, Murray Head, Susan Helbock, Michael Henninger, Ben Hider, Albert Hirshon, Justin Hoch, Nikola Horejs, Ken Howard, Lyn Hughes, Ken Huth, James David Jackson, Ken Jacques, Ryan Jensen, Rafael Jordan, Kristie Kahns, Thom Kaine, Jon Kandel, Dermot Kelly, Jennifer Maufrais Kelly, Sue Kessler, Ben King, Johnny Knight, Alex Koch, Ed Kreiger, Stephen Kunken, Michael Kwlechinski, Michael Lamont, Liz Lauren, Chang W. Lee, Corky Lee, Kantu Lentz, Stuart Levine, Geraint Lewis, James Leynse, Alexandria Marlin, Roger Mastroianni, Douglas McBride, Dave McCracken, Jeff McCrum, Steve McNicholas, Ari Mintz, Gustavo Monroy, Meghan Moore, David Morgan, Jerry Naunheim Jr., Doug Nuttelman, Erik Pearson, Ry Pepper, Johan Persson, Pierre, Ves Pitts, Eduardo Placer, Stephen Poff, Michael Portantiere, Leah Prater, Jaime Quinoñes, Patrick Redmond, Justin Richardson, Alyssa Ringler, John Roese, Mark Rohna, Suzi Sadler, Craig Schwartz, Darron Setlow, The Shaltzes, Kim T. Sharp, Bev Sheehan, Steve Shevett, Erika Sidor, Michelle Sims, Jonathan Slaff, Richard Hubert Smith, Gil Smith, Owen Smith, Diane Sobolewski, Hong Sooyeon, Squid Ink Creative, Theresa Squire, Marcus Stern, Noah Strone, Ben Strothmann, Scott Suchman, Stephen Sunderlin, Evan Sung, Daniel Talbott, Steve Tanner, Eran Tari, Brandon Thibodeaux, Ned Thorne, Stephen B. Thornton, Shirin Tinat, Ali Tollervey, Dominick Totino, Mark Turek, Sandy Underwood, Goran Veljic, Pascal Victor, Levi Walker, Bree Michael Warner, Sturgis Warner, Jon Wasserman, Lee Wexler, Drew Wingert, Nicholas Woods, Scott Wynn, Jordana Zeldin, and Tom Zuback.

Equally, we are extremely grateful for our New York press agents: *The Acting Company*: Paula Raymond; Janet Appel; Jim Baldassare; *Boneau/Bryan-Brown*: Chris Boneau, Adrian Bryan-Brown, Jim Byk, Brandi Cornwell, Jackie Green, Kelly Guiod, Linnae Hodzic, Jessica Johnson, Kevin Jones, Amy Kass, Emily Meagher, Aaron Meier, Christine Olver, Joe Perrotta, Matt Polk, Heath Schwartz, Michael Strassheim, Susanne Tighe; Jill Bowman; John Capo; Bruce Cohen; *Cohn Dutcher*: Dan Dutcher, Candace Newson; Peter Cromarty; *DARR Publicity*: David Gibbs, *David Gersten and Associates*: David Gersten, Shane Marshall Brown, Bill Evans, Jim Randolph; Helene Davis; Lauren Fitzgerald; Merle Frimark; Karen Greco; *The Hartman Group*: Michael Hartman, Leslie Baden Papa, Michelle Bergmann, Nicole Capatasto, Tom D'Ambrosio, Juliana Hannett, Alyssa Hart, Bethany Larsen, Matt Ross, Frances White, Wayne Wolfe; Ellen Jacobs; Judy Jacksina; *The Karpel Group*: Bridget Klapinski, Aicha Diop, Adam Bricault; *Keith Sherman and Associates*: Keith Sherman, Scott Klein, Bret Oberman, Glenna Freedman, Dan Demello, Logan Metzler; *Jeffrey Richards and Associates*: Irene Gandy, Elon Rutberg, Alana Karpoff, Diana Rissetto; Beck Lee; Jenny Lerner; *Lincoln Center Theater*: Philip Rinaldi, Barbara Carroll, Amanda Dekker; Kevin McAnarney; *Miller Wright and Associates*: Miller Wright, Dan Fortune, Danielle Grabianowski; *Maya PR*: Penny Landau; Emily Owens; *O + M Company*: Rick Miramontez, Dusty Bennett, Molly Barnett, Philip Carrubba, Jaron Caldwell, Sam Corbett, Jon Dimond, Richard Hillman, Yufen Kung, Jillian Lawton, Chelsea Nachman, Patrick O'Neil, Felicia Pollack, Alexandra Rubin, Andy Snyder, Elizabeth Wagner; *Paper Mill Playhouse*: Shayne Austin Miller; Patrick Paris; *Pearl Theatre Company*: Aaron Schwartzbord; *The Public Theater*: Candi Adams, Sam Neuman, Josh Ferri, Julie Danni; *The Publicity Office*: Marc Thibodeau, Michael Borowski, Jeremy Shaffer, Matt Fasano; Scotti Rhodes; Katie Rosin; Audrey Ross; *Richard Kornberg and Associates*: Richard Kornberg, Don Summa, Billy Zavelson, Danielle McGarry; *Rubenstein Communications Inc.*: Howard Rubenstein, Amy Jacobs, Tom Keaney, Elyse Weissman; *Sam Rudy Media Relations*: Sam Rudy, Robert Lasko, Dale Heller; Pete Sanders; Susan L. Schulman; Brett Singer; Jonathan Slaff; *Spin Cycle*: Ron Lasko; *Springer Associates*: Gary Springer, Joe Trentacosta; *Sun Productions*: Stephen Sunderlin; Michelle Tabnick, *Type A Marketing*: DJ Martin; *Walt Disney Theatricals*: Adrianna Douzous, Dennis Crowley; *The Wooster Group*: Clay Hapaz; Blake Zidell; and Lanie Zipoy.

Our gratitude is also eternally extended to our contributing regional theatre staff and press personnel who have contributed time and efforts for their company's listing: Jacquelyn Rardin (ACT- A Contemporary Theatre), John Longenbaugh (5th Avenue Theatre), Meg Lewis (Alabama Shakespeare Festival), Lauren Pelletier (Alley Theatre), Lindsay Hardegree (Alliance Theatre Company), Evren Odciken (American Conservatory Theater), Katalin Mitchell (American Repertory Theatre), Brittany Howard, Erin Read (Arden Theatre Company), Kristin Franko (Arena Stage), David Morden (Arizona Theatre Company), Ashley Pettit (Arkansas Repertory Theatre), Charlie Siedenburg, Laura Roudabush (Barrington Stage Company), Christina Webb (Barter Theatre), Robert Sweibel (Berkeley Repertory Theatre), Jaime Davidson (Berkshire Theatre Festival), Marilyn Langbehn (California Shakespeare Theater), T.J. Gerckens (CATCO), Nancy Hereford, Taylor Johnson (Center Theatre Group), Heather Jackson (CENTERSTAGE), Connie Yeager (Cincinnati Playhouse in the Park), Lisa Craig (Cleveland Play House), Eva Chien (Dallas Theatre Center), Amy Bish (Delaware Theatre Company), Chris Wiger (Denver Center Theatre Company), Jeff Carpenter (Eugene O'Neill Theater Center), Michael Gepner (Florida Stage), Dawn Kellogg (Geva Theatre Center), Carly Leviton (Goodman Theatre), Elisa Hale, Briana Bridgewater (Goodspeed Musicals), Doug Nuttleman (Great Plains Theatre), Lee Henderson, Melodie Bahan

(Guthrie Theater), Paul Marte (Hartford Stage Company), Anne Morgan (Huntington Theatre Company), Jon Billig (Illinois Theatre Center), Kelly Young (Indiana Repertory Theatre), Stephanie Coen (Intiman Theatre), Laura Muir (Kansas City Repertory Theatre), Becky Biegelsen (La Jolla Playhouse), Steven Scarpa (Long Wharf Theatre), Erin Breznitsky (McCarter Theatre), Dan Berube (Merrimack Repertory Theatre), Wayne Bryan (Music Theatre of Wichita), Kristin Buie (North Carolina Theatre), Jeffrey Weiser (The Old Globe), Deb Fiscella (Olney Theatre Center), Amy Richard (Oregon Shakespeare Festival), Shayne Austin Miller (Paper Mill Playhouse), Deborah K. Fleischman, Rachel Knorr; (Philadelphia Theatre Company), Maggie Romero (Pittsburgh Public Theater), Connie Mahan (Playmaker's Repertory Company), Trisha Mead (Portland Center Stage), Katie Puglisi (Repertory Theatre of St. Louis), Michelle Hou (San Jose Repertory Theatre), Diana Fenves (Seattle Repertory Theatre), Amy Scott-Douglas (Shakespeare Theatre Company), Katherine Tucker (Signature Theatre), Jessical Neil (South Coast Repertory), Megan Gibson (Stages St. Louis), Linda Garrison (Steppenwolf Theatre), Pat Patrick (Tennessee Rep), Lauren Lovell (Theatre Under the Stars), Marilyn Busch (Trinity Repertory Company), Patricia Blaufuss (Westport Country Playhouse), Lisa Bender (Williamstown Theatre Festival), Nora Sidoti (Wilma Theater), and Stephen Padla (Yale Repertory).

The editors of *Theatre World* would also like give very special thanks to the staff at Hal Leonard Performing Arts Publishing Group: John Cerullo (Group Publisher), Carol Flannery (Editorial Director), Diane Levinson (Publicity and Marketing Manager), Clare Cerullo (Production Manager), Marybeth Keating, (Associate Editor); the staffs of Accademia di Vino, 'Cesca, and Ouest restaurants; Gerard Alessandrini; Beth Allen, Amelia Alverson; Bob Anderson; Epitacio Arganza; Elvira, Kenneth, Bryan, J.R., Arlene, Daryl, and Kayden Autencio; Joel Banuelos and Justin Cherry; Jason Baruch and Sendroff and Baruch LLP; Seth Barrish, Lee Brock, Eric Paeper, and The Barrow Group Theater Company/The Barrow Group School; Jed Bernstein and the Commercial Theater Institute; Wayne Besen and Truth Wins Out; Micah-Shane Brewer and Drew Ogle; Fred Cantor; Fred Caruso; Ann Cason and East Tennessee Life; Michael Che; Jason Cicci, Monday Morning Productions, and Summer Stage New York; June Clark; Richard Cohen; Sue Cosson; Susan Cosson; Kimberley Courtney Esq.; Robert Dean Davis; Carol and Nick Dawson; Bob and Brenda Denny; Jamie deRoy; Tim Deak; Diane Dixon; Craig Dudley; the staff of the Duplex Cabaret and Piano Bar; Sherry Eaker; Ben Feldman Esq. and Beigelman, Feiner, and Feldman, P.C.; Emily Feldman; David Fritz; Christine and David Grimsby; the estates of the late Charles J. Grant Jr. and Zan Van Antwerp; Helen Guditis and the Broadway Theater Museum; Jason Hadzinikolov; Brad Hampton; Laura and Tommy Hanson; Richard M. Henderson Sr. and Patricia Lynn Henderson; Al and Sherry Hodges; Michael Humphreys Esq.; Charlie and Phyllis Hurt; Leonard Jacobs; Gretchen, Aaron, Eli, and Max Kerr; Jane, Lynn, and Kris Kircher; Andrew Kirtzman, Bobbie Kraus; the staff of Macy's Parade and Entertainment Group; Louis Del Vecchio and The Madison Fire Island Pines; David Lowry; Stuart Marshall; Kenneth Marzin; Joaquin Matias; Michael Messina; Barry Monush and Screen World; Ted Chapin, Howard Sherman and the American Theatre Wing; Jason Bowcutt, Shay Gines, Nick Micozzi, and the staff and respective voting committees of the New York Innovative Theatre Awards; Barbara O'Malley; Petie Dodrill, Craig Johnson, Rob Johnson, Dennis Romer, Katie Robbins, Dean Jo Ann VanSant, Ed Vaughan, the late Dr. Charles O. Dodrill and the staff of Otterbein College/Otterbein College Department of Theatre and Dance, P.J. Owen; William Craver and Paradigm; Hugo Uys and the staff of Paris Commune; Bernadette Peters; John Philip, Esq. and Andrew Resto; Angie and Drew Powell; Kay Radtke; Carolyn, David, Glenna, and Jonas Rapp; Jetaun Dobbs, Sydney Davalos, Todd Haimes, and Roundabout Theatre Company; Bill Schaap; Emmanuel Serrano; Charlotte St. Martin and the League of American Theatres and Producers; Susan Stoller; Henry Grossman, Michael Riordan, John Sala, Mark Snyder, Eleanor Speert; Martha Swope; Renée Isely Tobin and Bob, Kate, Eric, Laura, Anna, and Foster Tobin; Bob Ost and Theater Resources Unlimited Inc.; Laura Viade, Michael Viade, Rachel Werbel, Amanda Flynn, Rob Rokicki, and the staff of Theatre World and the John Willis Theatre World/Screen World Archive; Tom Lynch, Kati Meister, Erin Oestreich, Steven Bloom, Mary Botosan, Randall Hemming, Barry Keating, Jane Stuart, and the board of directors of The Theatre World Awards Inc.; Peter Filichia, Harry Haun, Howard Kissel, Matthew Murray, Frank Scheck, Michael Sommers, Linda Winer, and the voting committee of The Theatre World Awards Inc.; Jack Williams, Barbara Dewey, and the staff of the University of Tennessee at Knoxville; Wilson Valentin; Kathie Packer and the estate of the late Frederic B. Vogel; Sarah and Bill Willis; the estate of John A. Willis; George Wilson; Seth and Adeena Wolfovsky; Shane Frampton Wolters; and Doug Wright.

Contents

Top: *Sean Hayes and the Company in* Promises, Promises

Center: *Maria Dizzia, Wendy Rich Stetson, and Laura Benanti in* In the Next Room or the vibrator play

Bottom: *Jan Maxwell, Tony Shalhoub, and Jay Klaitz in* Lend Me a Tenor

A scene from Burn the Floor. *Opened at the Longacre Theatre August 2, 2009 (photo by Kevin Berne)*

Hugh Jackman and Daniel Craig in A Steady Rain. *Opened at the Gerald Schoenfeld Theatre September 29, 2009 (photo by Joan Marcus)*

Michael McKean and Jon Michael Hill in Superior Donuts. *Opened at the Music Box Theatre October 1, 2009 (photo by Robert J. Saferstein)*

Left: *Rufus Collins, Rosemary Harris, and Reg Rogers in the Manhattan Theatre Club production of* The Royal Family. *Opened at the Samuel J. Friedman Theatre October 8, 2009 (photo by Joan Marcus)*

Bottom left: *Jude Law in* Hamlet. *Opened at the Broadhurst Theatre October 6, 2009 (photo by Johan Persson)*

Bottom right: *Carrie Fisher in* Wishful Drinking. *Opened at the Studio 54 September 25, 2009 (photo by Joan Marcus)*

Julia Stiles and Bill Pullman in Oleanna. *Opened at the John Golden Theatre October 11, 2009 (photo by Craig Schwartz)*

Nolan Gerard Funk and the Company of the Roundabout Theatre Company production of Bye Bye Birdie. *Opened at Henry Miller's Theatre October 15, 2009 (photo by Joan Marcus)*

Jonny Lee Miller and Sienna Miller in the Roundabout Theatre Company production of After Miss Julie. *Opened at the American Airlines Theatre October 22, 2009 (photo by Joan Marcus)*

Montego Glover, Chad Kimball, and the Company in Memphis. *Opened at the Shubert Theatre October 19, 2009 (photo by Joan Marcus)*

(Clockwise from top left) *Noah Robbins, Laurie Metcalf, Alexandra Socha, Jessica Hecht, Santino Fontana, Dennis Boutsikaris, and Gracie Bea Lawrence in* Brighton Beach Memoirs. *Opened at the Nederlander Theatre October 25, 2009 (photo by Joan Marcus)*

(Center) *Cheyenne Jackson, Kate Baldwin, and Jim Norton and the Company of* Finian's Rainbow. *Opened at the St. James Theatre October 29, 2009 (photo by Joan Marcus)*

Top: *The Company of* Ragtime.
*Opened at the Neil Simon
Theatre November 15, 2009
(photo by Joan Marcus)*

Left: *Michael Cerveris and
Laura Benanti in the Lincoln
Center Theater production of*
In the Next Room or the vibrator
play. *Opened at the Lyceum
Theatre November 19, 2009
(photo by Joan Marcus)*

Top left: *Tony Yazbeck and Mara Davi in*
Irving Berlin's White Christmas. *Opened at*
the Marquis Theatre November 22, 2009

Top right: *Catherine Foster, Sahr Ngaujah,*
and Nicole de Weever in Fela! *Opened at*
the Eugene O'Neill Theatre November 23,
2009 (photo by Monique Carboni)

Right: *Kerry Washington, James Spader,*
Richard Thomas, and David Alan Grier
in Race. *Opened at the Barrymore Theatre*
December 6, 2009
(photo by Robert J. Saferstein)

Scarlett Johansson, Jessica Hecht, and Liev Schreiber in A View from the Bridge. *Opened at the Cort Theatre January 24, 2010 (photo by Joan Marcus)*

Victor Garber and Lisa Banes in the Roundabout Theatre Company production of Present Laughter. *Opened at the American Airlines Theatre January 21, 2010 (photo by Joan Marcus)*

Angela Lansbury, Catherine Zeta-Jones, and Keaton Whittaker in A Little Night Music. *Opened at the Walter Kerr Theatre December 13, 2009 (photo by Joan Marcus)*

*Laura Linney and Brian d'Arcy James in the Manhattan Theatre Club
production of* Time Stands Still. *Opened at the Samuel J. Friedman
Theatre January 28, 2010 (photo by Joan Marcus)*

Alison Pill and Abigail Breslin in The Miracle Worker. *Opened at
Circle in the Square Theatre March 3, 2010 (photo by Joan Marcus)*

Christopher Walken and Sam Rockwell in
A Behanding in Spokane. *Opened at the
Gerald Schoenfeld Theatre March 4, 2010
(Photo by Joan Marcus)*

Patrick Heusinger and Patrick Breen in Next Fall. *Opened at the Helen Hayes Theatre March 11, 2010 (photo by Carol Rosegg)*

Dame Edna and Michael Feinstein in All About Me. *Opened at Henry Miller's Theatre March 18, 2010 (photo by Joan Marcus)*

Valerie Harper in Looped. *Opened at the Lyceum Theatre March 14, 2010 (photo by Carol Rosegg)*

John Selya, Holley Farmer, Matthew Stockwell Dibble, and the Company in Come Fly Away. *Opened at the Marquis Theatre March 25, 2010 (photo by Joan Marcus)*

Alfred Molina and Eddie Redmayne in Red. *Opened at the John Golden Theatre April 1, 2010 (photo by Johan Persson)*

Adam Riegler, Jackie Hoffman, Bebe Neuwirth, Nathan Lane, Kevin Chamberlin, Krysta Rodriguez, and Zachary James in The Addams Family. *Opened at the Lunt-Fontanne Theatre April 8, 2010 (photo by Joan Marcus)*

Douglas Hodge in La Cage aux Folles. *Opened at the Longacre Theatre April 18, 2010 (photo by Joan Marcus)*

Hunter Foster, Levi Kreis, Robert Britton Lyons, Eddie Clendening, and Lance Guest in Million Dollar Quartet. *Opened at the Nederlander Theatre April 11, 2010 (photo by Joan Marcus)*

Stark Sands, John Gallagher Jr., Michael Esper and the Company in American Idiot. *Opened at the St. James Theatre April 20, 2010 (photo by Paul Kolnik)*

Anthony LaPaglia, Tony Shalhoub, and Justin Bartha in Lend Me a Tenor. *Opened at the Music Box Theatre April 4, 2010 (photo by Joan Marcus)*

Sherie Rene Scott in the Roundabout Theatre Company production of Everyday Rapture. *Opened at the American Airlines Theatre April 29, 2010 (photo by Carol Rosegg)*

Sean Hayes and Kristin Chenoweth in Promises, Promises. *Opened at the Broadway Theatre April 25, 2010 (photo by Joan Marcus)*

Vanessa Williams, Tom Wopat, Matthew Scott, Erin Mackey, Barbara Cook, Euan Morton, Norm Lewis, and Leslie Kritzer in the Roundabout Theatre Company production of Sondheim on Sondheim. *Opened at Studio 54 April 22, 2010 (photo by Richard Termine)*

Above left: *Viola Davis, Chris Chalk, and Denzel Washington in* Fences. *Opened at the Cort Theatre April 26, 2010 (photo by Joan Marcus)*

Above right: *Norbert Leo Butz in* Enron. *Opened at the Broadhurst Theatre April 27, 2010 (photo by Joan Marcus)*

Linda Lavin and Sarah Paulson in the Manhattan Theatre Club production of Collected Stories. *Opened at the Samuel J. Friedman Theatre April 28, 2010 (photo by Joan Marcus)*

Editor's Note:

Our longtime editor, John Willis, passed away on June 25, 2010, just as this volume was being readied for publication. As his executor as well as close friend, my duties immediately turned to prolonging his legacy, including ensuring that the marquees of Broadway were dimmed in his honor, which they were, on June 30, 2010, thanks to the Broadway League in coordination with the Broadway theatre owners.

As a result of Mr. Willis' untimely passing, I asked Adam Feldman and Linda Buchwald to fill in for me in writing the seasonal reviews of Broadway and Off-Broadway, respectively, for this edition of *Theatre World*, which they agreed to do. To them both, as well as our other estimable editors, I am very grateful.

— Ben Hodges, Editor in Chief

Bernadette Peters, Brenda Smiley, and Alice Playten, on June 30, 2010, as the Broadway marquee lights dimmed in honor of the passing of longtime Theatre World *editor John Willis. They hold a copy of* Theatre World Volume 24: 1967-68, *in which they all three appeared as* Theatre World Award *winners during that season.*

Theatre World *editor in chief Ben Hodges with the late longtime* Theatre World *editor John Willis at the 2001 American Theatre Wing Antoinette Perry "Tony" Awards ceremony, at which, on behalf of* Theatre World, *Mr. Willis was presented with a Special Tony Honor for Excellence in the Theatre.*

West 44th Street in New York City, at sundown on June 30, 2010, as the Broadway marquee lights dimmed in honor of the passing of longtime Theatre World *editor John Willis.*

THE 2009–2010 BROADWAY SEASON: AN OVERVIEW

Adam Feldman

For Broadway theatre lovers, hope springs eternal every fall. No matter how disappointing the previous season, no matter how ominous the trends about what sells to whom and why, there is always the prospect of something coming, something good, just around the corner. On paper, the 2009–2010 Broadway season offered much to whet such dreams: new plays by David Mamet, Tracy Letts, Sarah Ruhl, and Martin McDonagh; daring-sounding original musicals about pop-culture icons; fresh looks at treasures of yesteryear, from *Finian's Rainbow* to *Brighton Beach Memoirs*.

When awards season arrived, however, these could-have-been contenders did not come out on top. The Tony Awards for Best Play and Best Musical went respectively to *Red*, a portrait of the painter Marc Rothko, and *Memphis*, a tuner about racial integration. The Pulitzer Prize for Drama was bestowed on *Next to Normal*, which had opened during the previous season. In its 75th-anniversary year, the New York Drama Critics' Circle gave its Best Play award to Horton Foote's *The Orphans' Home Cycle*, an Off-Broadway production, and withheld its usual prizes for Best Musical and Best Foreign Play; in neither category were there serious Broadway candidates.

In mid-July, members of the so-called First Night Press List—the upper echelon of critics and reporters who cover theatre—had been stripped of their long-held Tony Award votership. Interpreted as a step toward empowering producers at the expense of more impartial voices, this decision was decried in some quarters of the press; in March, the Tonys stanched some of the damage by inviting members of the Drama Critics' Circle to rejoin the voting pool in 2010–2011. But the critical community took further blows during the season with the losses of John Heilpern (who resigned from the *New York Observer*), David Rooney (whose position at *Variety* was eliminated), and the *Associated Press'* Michael Kuchwara (who died unexpectedly in May).

This erosion of critical weight may be symptomatic of a larger drift within the industry. As theatre going becomes a less routine event for average New Yorkers, Broadway productions seem increasingly intended for tourists, whose limited time and attention are more likely to be grabbed by familiar titles and big-name stars than by iffier qualities like originality and artistic merit.

Consider what the season had to offer when it came to the Great White Way's bread and butter: new musicals. The most important story in this department was the big show that couldn't: the massively expensive and ambitious comic-book adaptation *Spider-Man*, featuring a score by U2 rock titans Bono and the Edge, and directed by *The Lion King*'s visionary Julie Taymor. Originally scheduled to begin previews in January, and reported to cost upward of $40 million, the production was caught in a web of financial troubles and—after months of construction work at the Hilton Theatre—was forced to postpone its debut until the fall. Ten productions that could be called new musicals did open in 2009–2010, but little about them was actually new; of the ten, in fact, only two—*Memphis* and *The Addams Family*—had original scores.

Technically, the season began in the summer with the touring *Burn the Floor*, a flashy night of hopped-up ballroom dancing. Those who wanted a dance show with a higher level of artistry—and richer eroticism than *Burn the Floor*'s well-practiced pumping—had to wait for the terpsichorean icon Twyla Tharp's *Come Fly Away* in March. Set to a score of Frank Sinatra classics, Tharp's surprisingly racy spectacle tracked the courtship and coupling of multiple couples at a nightclub, and featured an astonishing company of dancers. (Karine Plantadit earned particular attention for her ferocious charisma and physical daring.)

Memphis opened in October to lukewarm reviews, and seemed destined for a brief run. Few could fault its good intentions, and the production featured a dynamic lead performance by Chad Kimball as a quirky white deejay in 1950s Nashville, as well as strong vocals by the lovely Montego Glover as a black singer whom he champions. The show's book and lyrics (by Joe DiPietro) and music (by Bon Jovi's David Bryan) struck some as simplistic; *Hairspray* had told a similar story with a sense of humor and multiple subplots. But strong word of mouth, especially after its Tony win, helped build the show into a sleeper hit.

Fela!, which opened in November, was much less conventional. Directed and choreographed by modern-dance lion Bill T. Jones, the musical limned the life of Nigerian musician and activist Fela Kuti in a bold explosion of African music, dance, and color. (The riveting Sahr Ngaujah alternated the title role with Kevin Mambo.) The show presented itself as a mid-1970s night at a Lagos nightclub, and used Fela's own music; if the storytelling was often hazy, the energy was galvanizing.

Existing musical catalogs also formed the basis of two new musicals in April. The first, *Million Dollar Quartet*, was a jukebox tuner loosely based on a 1956 jam session among Elvis Presley, Carl Perkins, Johnny Cash, and Jerry Lee Lewis. (The piano-ravaging Levi Kreis made a killer Lewis.) *American Idiot*, a multimedia fantasia based on songs by the punk-pop band Green Day, took a more ambitious approach. Working with Green Day's front man, Billie Joe Armstrong, director Michael Mayer knit the score into an archetypal storyline of self-discovery in a conformist culture; as in *Fela!*, immersive experience was emphasized above strictly linear story, and the youthful cast gave Broadway a rare jolt of contemporary rock energy. Boosted by a rave review in the *New York Times*, *American Idiot* seemed poised to be a front-runner for the Best Musical Tony Award, for which it was nominated; but the Tony nomination committee cut the show off at the knees by snubbing it in all other major categories.

Absent *Spider-Man*, the most eagerly anticipated new musical of the season became *The Addams Family*, based on the macabre clan created by cartoonist Charles Addams (and familiar from TV and film adaptations). The casting could not have been better: the buoyant Nathan Lane as Gomez, the dry-ice Bebe Neuwirth as Morticia, the lovably goony Kevin Chamberlin as Fester. After a troubled tryout in Chicago, the show's directors, who had also helmed the elegantly ghoulish *Shockheaded Peter*, were replaced with veteran Jerry Zaks for the move to New York. The revised *Addams Family* was largely disowned by critics nonetheless.

Rounding out the crop of original musicals were three modest productions in venues run by the not-for-profit Roundabout Theatre Company. The variety show *All About Me*, a platform for Australian hausfrau-diva Dame Edna and Great American Songbook champion Michael Feinstein, shuttered in three weeks. The multimedia revue *Sondheim on Sondheim* careered among performances of songs by Stephen Sondheim—ubiquitous in the year of his 80th birthday—and video interviews with the composer; led by the golden Barbara Cook, the ensemble also featured Vanessa Williams and Tom Wopat, as well as such up-and-comers as Leslie Kritzer and Euan Morton. The enjoyable Sherie Rene Scott showcase *Everyday Rapture*, which had played at Off-Broadway's Second Stage a year earlier, was patched into the American Airlines Theatre at the last minute to replace a scheduled revival of Terrence McNally's *Lips Together Teeth Apart* when that play's star, Megan Mullally, dropped out.

It is worth noting that the conventional wisdom about the increasing import of marquee actors continued to be a non-issue for new book musicals. Of this season's output, only *The Addams Family* had familiar names above its title. Musical revivals, on the other hand, relied more heavily on star power.

Cases in point: the season's first and final musical revivals, a pair of throwbacks to the 1960s. *Bye Bye Birdie*, which opened in October, was hunted mercilessly by critics who found the Roundabout's production tacky and declared Hollywood expats John Stamos and Gina Gershon to be wanting in the leading roles. And director Rob Ashford's *Mad Men*–inflected revival of *Promises, Promises*, starring Emmy winners Sean Hayes and Kristin Chenoweth, received decidedly mixed reviews when it opened in April; although Katie Finneran was singled out for her show-stealing cameo, many considered the formidable Chenoweth miscast. Yet both shows did solid business.

Neither *Bye Bye Birdie* nor *Promises, Promises* was Tony-nominated for Best Revival of a Musical at the end of the season. Their potential slots were filled instead by *Finian's Rainbow* and *Ragtime*—cold comfort for productions that had closed months earlier. Having moved to Broadway after acclaimed debuts elsewhere (the former at City Center's *Encores!* series, the latter at the Kennedy Center), *Finian's Rainbow* and *Ragtime* earned fervent admirers but struggled to lure wider audiences. Did it matter that neither had a pop-culture star attached? Or were these revivals—which both dealt with questions of race in America—more inherently limited in their mass appeal than the frothier 1960s spectacles?

The star wattage of Catherine Zeta-Jones and Angela Lansbury certainly helped light up Trevor Nunn's shadowy revival of 1973's *A Little Night Music*, attracting audiences that might otherwise have been unlikely targets for a Sondheim musical adapted from an Ingmar Bergman film and set in turn-of-the-20th-century Sweden. Although some Sondheim purists found this London transfer somewhat coarse, the production offered a new hearing for the composer's masterfully witty and elegant score.

It was a different stripped-down English import, however, that earned the year's most enthusiastic reviews (and the Tony Award at season's end): Terry Johnson's vividly tawdry and revelatory London revival of Jerry Herman and Harvey Fierstein's 1983 farce *La Cage Aux Folles*, which unfolds in a drag club in Southern France. After its middling 2004 Broadway incarnation, few people expected the show to pop up again—much less at such a rollicking boil—but the third time was a charm, thanks in large measure to its lead actors. As the steadier half of the central gay couple, *Frasier*'s Kelsey Grammer provided name recognition as well as suave ballast for the flighty diva played with superb dithering zest by Broadway newbie Douglas Hodge.

Success was also in the stars for many of 2009–2010's straight plays, both originals and revivals. The season began with a box-office bang in each category. Mediocre notices for the script of the fall's first new play, Keith Huff's monologue-heavy police drama *A Steady Rain*, did little to dampen the drawing power of its bold-faced-name actors: the A-list action-movie stars Hugh Jackman and Daniel Craig, both of whom also had substantial stage backgrounds. And in his kinetic take on the title role of *Hamlet*, Jude Law—another foreign-born cinematic luminary with theatre chops—made Shakespeare's Denmark a tourist destination of choice.

The financial roar of these plays made the implosion of the Neil Simon diptych *Brighton Beach Memoirs* and *Broadway Bound*—nostalgic, semiautobiographical comedies that had been hits in the 1980s—all the more troubling to industry insiders. Directed with sensitivity and insight by David Cromer (fresh from his triumphant Off-Broadway revival of *Our Town*), *Brighton Beach Memoirs* opened in October to mostly glowing reviews, and closed just a week later; *Broadway Bound*, which had been scheduled to run in rep with its predecessor after a December opening, never even began previews. Hand-wringing postmortems ensued: was faulty marketing to blame? Should both plays have opened at once? Did the project, whose cast was led by the multiple Emmy laureate Laurie Metcalf, need bigger names? And was the presumed audience for the show—the largely Jewish, middle-class, local, and suburban theatregoers thought to constitute a major chunk of Broadway attendance—no longer the force that it once had been?

Amid this autumnal soul-searching, other productions came and went without incident. Manhattan Theatre Club's classy revival of George S. Kaufman and Edna Ferber's 1927 comedy *The Royal Family*, about a clan of Barrymore-like thespians, showcased two of New York's most distinguished leading ladies: Rosemary Harris and, as her daughter, Jan Maxwell. (Both earned Tony nominations, with Maxwell earning a rare second nod in the same season for her featured work in *Lend Me a Tenor*.) Less felicitous was an October revival of David Mamet's fraught 1993 two-hander *Oleanna*, starring Bill Pullman as a tenure-track college professor and Julia Stiles as a student who accuses him of sexual misconduct. Reviewers charged that this account of Mamet's inflammatory drama lacked the requisite spark, and audiences agreed; it closed in December, a month ahead of schedule.

A favorite of producers Jeffrey Richards and Jerry Frankel, Mamet has been a Broadway staple in recent years, and the punchy playwright fared better in December with a self-directed new work titled *Race*. James Spader, who had won multiple awards as a loquacious lawyer on TV's *Boston Legal*, starred as a defense attorney deciding whether to represent a wealthy white man who has been charged with raping a black woman; David Alan Grier played his African American partner. Mixed *Race* reviews notwithstanding, Mamet's investigation of white guilt (both literal and figurative) went on to enjoy the longest run of any straight play in the 2009–2010 season.

Tracy Letts, whose *August: Osage County* was the toast of Broadway in 2007, also returned with a new play in the fall: the dark-edged comedy *Superior Donuts*, starring Michael McKean as a burnt-out Chicago donut-shop owner and the engaging Jon Michael Hill as his eager young assistant. Mostly affectionate reviews (many of which mentioned contrivances in the script, then forgave them) didn't help the show find an audience, and it closed after three months. Lincoln Center Theater's production of the fancifully titled *In the Next Room, or The Vibrator Play*—which marked the Broadway debut of MacArthur "genius" grantee Sarah Ruhl—had an even briefer run, opening in November and closing as scheduled in early January. But many critics were stimulated by Ruhl's drawing-room comedy about the inchoate science of sexual pleasure in the late 19th century, noting the sensitivity with which it handled multiple orgasms and praising Laura Benanti's central performance as a woman emerging from erotic stagnation.

The Roundabout's Studio 54 space played host in the fall to Carrie Fisher's one-woman memoir, *Wishful Drinking*, a celebrity tell-some in which the former *Star Wars* princess served a Hollywood martini with a twist of citric humor. The company's main Broadway venue, the American Airlines Theatre, was meanwhile occupied by Patrick Marber's *After Miss Julie*, an adaptation of Strindberg's drama reset in post–World War II England; both the play and film siren Sienna Miller's performance in the title role received wildly varied notices. In January, at the same theatre, critics reacted politely to Victor Garber's suave portrayal of an aging matinee idol in a revival of Noël Coward's *Present Laughter*. Save for *Present Laughter*'s set design, none of these three productions were remembered at Tony time.

New York's other non-for-profit Broadway company, Manhattan Theatre Club, made a bigger impression in January with the premiere of Donald Margulies's *Time Stands Still*, which reunited the playwright with ace director Daniel Sullivan. Margulies's astute drama examined themes of violence, spectatorship, and intimacy through the lens of a tough-minded war photographer, played with steely intelligence by stage-and-screen stalwart Laura Linney; Alicia Silverstone was winning as Linney's bubbly foil. When *Time Stands Still* completed its successful limited run, MTC followed it with another Margulies play: a warmly received revival of 1997's *Collected Stories*, in which the formidable Linda Lavin was lauded for her performance as a writer who feels threatened by her protégée.

But the biggest buzz in 2010 again surrounded famous actors in well-chosen roles. Gregory Mosher's forceful revival of Arthur Miller's neoclassical tragedy *A View from the Bridge*, which opened in January, quickly became the winter's hot ticket, thanks to star turns by Liev Schreiber as a Brooklyn longshoreman and, especially, Scarlett Johansson—in a Tony-winning Broadway debut—as his ripening niece. And in April, Denzel Washington hit *Fences* out of the park, drawing ecstatic reviews as well as sold-out houses in a revival of August Wilson's searing 1985 drama about the limits of the African American dream in the 1950s. The production won Tonys for Best Revival of a Play as well as for Washington and the extraordinary Viola Davis (who also received a special citation from the New York Drama Critics' Circle).

The season's two other play revivals generated less heat. A new account of William Gibson's 1959 Helen Keller drama, *The Miracle Worker*, won solid notices for its two leads, Alison Pill and *Little Miss Sunshine*'s Abigail Breslin, but there was general agreement that the show was ill served by its nebulous, in-the-round staging at Circle in the Square; it closed after just three weeks. And a jaunty new production of Ken Ludwig's 1989 backstage farce *Lend Me a Tenor*, directed by actor Stanley Tucci, had critics singings its praises almost everywhere—except in the still-powerful *New York Times*, where Charles Isherwood's brutal pan may have fried the show's long-term prospects.

Times critic Ben Brantley's enthusiastic gloss on *Red*, by contrast, gave a boost to John Logan's depiction of the tormented abstract-expressionist painter Marc Rothko, which had been brought over from London's Donmar Warehouse with its two-man cast intact: the imposing Alfred Molina as Rothko and Eddie Redmayne as his fictional young assistant. (Unlike *Time Stands Still*, the play was still running at Tony time.) A structurally similar but campier biodrama, Matthew Lombardo's *Looped*—starring *Rhoda* alumna Valerie Harper as the dissolute stage legend Tallulah Bankhead—got the hook after just a month, but Harper was a dragonish hoot. Also shining in unpopular material was the unique Christopher Walken, who played a sinister creep holed up in a run-down motel in Martin McDonagh's *A Behanding in Spokane*. Although critics considered the show a throwaway compared with McDonagh's major work, such as *The Pillowman*, Walken's eccentric rhythms were compelling as always.

Completing the 2009–2010 season were two serious plays that had trouble finding Broadway audiences. *Next Fall*, a thoughtful tragicomedy about a gay couple divided by questions of religious faith, had its Off-Broadway premiere in the summer of 2009, and transferred to the Helen Hayes Theatre in March. But despite lavish praise from the *Times*' Brantley and others, Geoffrey Nauffts's play—which

boasted Elton John as a producer, but no name-brand stars—closed at a loss four months later. *Enron*, English playwright Lucy Prebble's stylish autopsy of a cancerous business culture, fared still worse: critical reception for the show was fiercely divided, with the Times coming down firmly on the con side. Lacking star buoyancy, *Enron* sank in two weeks.

As we bid the season goodbye, let us pause for a moment to remember some of the people we lost along the way. The Broadway League authorized the lights on Broadway to be dimmed eight times during the season, to honor of members of the community who had died: producer George MacPherson; Edison Café restaurateur Harry Edelstein; actor Karl Malden; playwright Larry Gelbart; actor Lynn Redgrave; singer Lena Horne; centenarian Ziegfeld Girl Doris Eaton Travis; and critic Michael Kuchwara. (Among many other lost this year were Gene Barry, Dixie Carter, T. Scott Cunningham, Donal Donnelly, Max Eisen, June Havoc, John Kenley, Patrick Lee, Rue McClanahan, Harve Presnell, Douglas Watt, Joseph Wiseman and Edward Woodward.)

The lights were dimmed eight times; but then the lights went up again. So it goes. How will history judge the 2009-2010 Broadway season? It is impossible, of course, to know. From the perspective of the critics—admittedly, perhaps obsolescent—it was not necessarily a banner year. But although the season may have struck some observers as an awkward one for the Broadway stage, awkward stages can be signs of growth. Here's hoping.

Chad Kimball and the Company in Memphis *(photo by Joan Marcus)*

Burn the Floor

Longacre Theatre; First Preview: July 25, 2009; Opening Night: August 2, 2009; Closed January 10, 2010; 8 previews, 185 performances

Produced by Harley Medcalf, Joe Watson, Richard Levi, Richard Frankel, Thomas Viertel, Steven Baruch, Marc Routh, Raise The Roof One (Elaine Krauss, Jean Doumanian, Harriet Newman Leve, Jennifer Manocherian), Toppall/Stevens/Mills (Lawrence S. Toppall), Tom & Angie Benigno/Sharon Klein, David Caldwell/Chris Allen, Carrpailet/Danzansky (Janet Pailet, Sharon Carr, Danzansky Partners), Bud Martin, The Production Studio (Allan S. Gordon, Elan V. McAllister, Adam S. Gordon), Greg Schaffert/Terry Schnuck, Carrie Ann Inaba; Produced by special arrangement with Dance Partner Inc. (Harley Medcalf, Founder and Producer; Jason Gilkison, Director and Choreographer; Peta Roby, Company Manager; Nic Notley, Executive Producer; Charlie Hull (Music Consultant; Bruce Bolton, PSM); Associate Producers, Dan Frishwasser, Peta Roby, Nic Notley, Brad Bauner; Director/Choreographer, Jason Gilkison; Creative Consultant: Raj Kapoor; Set, Ray Klausen; Costumes, Janet Hine (based on original designs by John Van Gastel); Lighting, Rick Belzer; Sound, Peter J. Fitzgerald; Production Manager, Peter Fulbright/Tech Production Services Inc.; Production Stage Manager, Bruce Bolton; Music Consultant, Charlie Hull; Musical Coordinator, John Miller; General Manager, Frankel Green Theatrical Management, Joe Watson; Company Manager, Sammy Ledbetter/Adam Miller; Assistant Stage Manager, Suzanne Apicella; Company Management Assistant, Andrew Michaelson; Production Crew: Erik Hansen (production carpenter), Michael W. Brown (production electrician), Barbara Bartel (assistant electrician), Wallace Flores (production sound engineer), Penny Davis (wardrobe supervisor), Ginny Hounsell & Laura Totero (dressers); For Frankel Green: Richard Frankel, Laura Green, Joe Watson, Leslie Ledbetter; For Tech Production Services: Mary Duffe, Colleen Houlehen, Kate Baker; Dance Partner, Inc.; Advertising, Serino Coyne; Director of Marketing/Promotions, Allied Live; Marketing, Leanne Schanzer Promotions; Press, Boneau/Bryan-Brown, Chris Boneau, Jackie Green, Kelly Guiod

CAST Special Guest Stars **Karina Smirnoff** & **Maksim Chmerkovskiy**; With **Sharna Burgess**, **Henry Byalikov**, **Kevin Clifton**, **Sasha Farber**, **Jeremy Garner**, **Gordana Grandosek**, **Patrick Helm**, **Sarah Hives**, **Melanie Hooper**, **Peta Murgatroyd**, **Giselle Peacock**, **Nuria Santalucia**, **Sarah Soriano**, **Damon Sugden**, **Rebecca Sugden**, **Trent Whiddon**, **Damian Whitewood**, **Robin Windsor**, and **Ricky Rojas** & **Rebecca Tapia**; Succeeding Cast and Special Guest Stars **MiG Ayesa**, **Artem Chigvintsev**, **Anya Garnis**, **Derek Hough**, **Kym Johnson**, **Pasha Kovalev**, **Mary Murphy**, **Mirko Sciolan**, **Emma Slater**

MUSICIANS Henry Soriano (Conductor/percussion), Roger Squitero (percussion), David Mann (saxophone), Earl Maneein (violin/guitar)

DANCE AND MUSICAL NUMBERS Act I: *Inspirations*: Ballroom Beat, Let's Face the Music and Dance, History Repeating, Magalena, Slip Into Something More Comfortable, Weather Storm/The Ballroom Boys, Fishies, Nights in White Satin, Pastorale; *Things That Swing*: Sway, It Don't Mean a Thing (If It Ain't Got That Swing), I Just Want to Make Love to You, The Dirty Boogie, I'm a Ding Dong Daddy; Act II: *The Latin Quarter*: Cariño, Sit u Supieras, Sing Sing Sing, Tanguera, Matador, España Cañi; *Contemporary*: Burn for You, Club le Narcisse, After All, Proud Mary, Turn the Beat Around

New York premiere of a theatrical ballroom dance and music performance piece presented in two acts.

SYNOPSIS From Harlem's hot nights at The Savoy, where dances such as the Lindy, Foxtrot and Charleston were born, to the Latin Quarter where the Cha-Cha, Rumba and Salsa steamed up the stage, *Burn the Floor* takes the audience on a journey through the passionate drama of dance. The elegance of the Viennese Waltz, the exuberance of Jive, the intensity of the Paso Doble – audiences experience them all, as well as the Tango, Samba, Mambo, Quickstep, and Swing. It's Ballroom dance with a sexy 21st century edge.

A scene from Burn the Floor

A scene from Burn the Floor *(photos by Mark Kitaoka and Kevin Berne)*

A Steady Rain

Gerald Schoenfeld Theatre; First Preview: September 10, 2009; Opening Night: September 29, 2009; Closed December 6, 2009; 21 previews, 81 performances

Written by Keith Huff; Produced by Frederick Zollo, Michael G. Wilson, Barbara Broccoli, Raymond L. Gaspard, Frank Gero, Cheryl Wiesenfeld, Jeffrey Sine, Michael Rose Ltd., The Shubert Organization, and Robert Cole; Director, John Crowley; Sets/Costumes, Scott Pask; Lighting, Hugh Vanstone; Original Music and Sound, Mark Bennett; Production Management, Aurora Productions: Gene O'Donovan & W. Benjamin Heller II; Production Stage Manager, Michael J. Passaro; Company Manager, Lisa M. Poyer; Hair, David Brian Brown; Makeup, Naomi Donne; Casting, Jim Carnahan; Dialect Coach, Jess Platt; Assistant Stage Manager, Pat Sosnow; Assistant Company Manager, Kyle Bonder; General Management, Cole Productions LLC; Associate Design: Orit J. Carroll (set), Daryl A. Stone (costumes), Philip S. Rosenberg (lighting), Tony Smolenski IV (sound); Assistant Set Design, Frank M. McCullough, Lauren M. Alvarez; Guitarist, Brien Brannigan; Production Crew: Tony Menditto (production carpenter), David Cohen (flyman), Dan Coey (production electrician), Laura Frank (electrics programmer), Kathy Fabian/Propstar (prop coordinator), Jennifer Breen (associate prop coordinator), Heidi L. Brown (prop master), Brien Brannigan (production sound engineer), Tony Smolenski IV (sound programmer), Kathleen Gallagher (wardrobe supervisor), Yvonne Jensen & Geoffrey Polischuk (dressers); Assistant to the Producer & General Manager, Gabriel Flateman; Production Assistant, Alison M. Roberts; Assistant to Mr. Jackman, Alexandra Ducocq; Assistant to the Director, Meg Griffiths; Assistant to the Designers, Roman Palyk (Mr. Pask), Isabella F. Byrd (Mr. Vanstone), Phillip Owen (Mr. Bennett); Advertising, SpotCo: Drew Hodges, Jim Edwards, Tom Greenwald, Tom McCann, Josh Fraenkel; Production Management Associates: Rachel Sherbill, Steve Rosenberg, Jarid Sumner, Melissa Mazdra, Amy Merlino Coey, Amanda Raymond, Graham Forden, Lisa Luxenberg; Casting Assistant, Jillian Cimini; Press, The Hartman Group, Michael Hartman, Wayne Wolfe, Matt Ross

CAST Joey **Daniel Craig**; Denny **Hugh Jackman**

UNDERSTUDIES C.J. Wilson (Joey), Danny Mastrogiorgio (Denny)

Daniel Craig and Hugh Jackman

SETTING Chicago. The not-too-distant-past. A new play presented without intermission. First workshopped in July 2006 at New York Stage and Film's Powerhouse Theatre and at the Barrow Group Theatre in February 2007, the play had its world premiere at Chicago Dramatists September 28–October 28, 2007, and was remounted at Chicago's Royal George Studio Theatre February 27–April 27, 2008.

SYNOPSIS *A Steady Rain* tells the story of two Chicago cops who are lifelong friends and their differing accounts of a few harrowing days that changed their lives forever. During a routine domestic disturbance call, the cops return a panic-stricken Vietnamese boy to a man claiming to be the boy's uncle. When the man is revealed to be a cannibalistic serial killer and the boy his latest victim, the men's friendship is put to the test when one of them has to take the fall.

Daniel Craig and Hugh Jackman (photos by Joan Marcus)

Kate Buddeke, Michael McKean, and Jon Michael Hill

Jon Michael Hill and Michael McKean

Jon Michael Hill (photos by Robert J. Saferstein)

Superior Donuts

Music Box Theatre; First Preview: September 16, 2009; Opening Night: October 1, 2009; Closed January 3, 2010; 17 previews, 109 performances

Written by Tracy Letts; Produced by Jeffrey Richards, Jean Doumanian, Jerry Frankel, Awaken Entertainment, Debra Black, Chase Mishkin, Karmichelle Productions (Sharon Karmazin & Michelle Schneider)/Robert G. Bartner, Barry and Carole Kaye/Irv Welzer, Andrew Asnes, Rebecca Gold, Dasha Theatricals Inc. (Dasha Epstein), Kathleen K. Johnson, George Kaufman, Charles McAteer, Terry Schnuck, Michael Gardner/David Jaroslowicz, Roy Gottlieb/Raise the Roof Two (Jennifer Manocherian, Harriet Newman Leve & Elaine Krauss), Dena Hammerstein/Pam Pariseau, Stewart F. Lane & Bonnie Comley; Presented by The Steppenwolf Theatre Company; Director, Tina Landau; Set, James Schuette; Costumes, Ana Kuzmanic; Lighting, Christopher Akerlind; Sound, Rob Milburn and Michael Bodeen; Hair & Wigs, Charles LaPointe; Dramaturg, Edward Sobel; Original Casting, Erica Daniels; New York Casting, Telsey + Company; Fight Director, Rick Sordelet; Production Stage Manager, Arthur Gaffin; Technical Supervisor, Hudson Theatrical Associates; General Management, Richards/ Climan Inc., David R. Richards, Tamar Haimes; Associate Producers, Jeremy Scott Blaustein, Patrick Daly, Susan Jean Steiger, Donna Roehn Ward; Company Manager: Mary Miller; Stage Manager, Lauren Hickman; Assistant Director, Robert Quinlan; Associate Design: Ben Krall (lighting), Jeremy J. Lee (sound); Assistant Design, Jonathan Collins, Andrew Boyce (set), Kristina Lucka (costumes); Production Props Coordinator, Jeremy Chernick; Associate Props Coordinator, Jeremy Lydic; Associate General Manager, Michael Sag; General Management Associate, Jeremy Smith; Management Assistant, Cesar Hawas; Production Crew: Jimmy Maloney (production electrician), Brad Robertson (associate production electrician), Valerie Spradling (production sound), Dennis Maher (house carpenter), William Rowland (house electrician), Kim Garnett (house props), Rob Bevenger (wardrobe supervisor), Amy Neswald (hair & makeup supervisor), Kim Prentice (dresser); Production Assistant, Jamie Greathouse; Advertising: SpotCo, Drew Hodges, Jim Edwards, Stephen Sosnowski, Meghan Wonbey; Press, Jeffrey Richards Associates, Irene Gandy, Alana Karpoff, Elon Rutberg, Diana Rissetto

CAST Max Tarasov **Yasen Peyankov**; Officer Randy Osteen **Kate Buddeke**; Officer James Hailey **James Vincent Meredith**; Lady Boyle **Jane Alderman**; Arthur Przybyszewski **Michael McKean**; Franco Wicks **Jon Michael Hill**; Luther Flynn **Robert Maffia**; Kevin Magee **Cliff Chamberlain**; Kiril Ivakina **Michael Garvey**

UNDERSTUDIES Marilyn Dodds Frank (Lady Boyle, Officer Randy Osteen), Stephen Payne (Arthur Przybyszewski), Sean Patrick Reilly (Kevin Magee, Luther Flynn, Max Tarasov), Michael Rossmy (Kiril Ivakina), Samuel Stricklen (Franco Wicks, Officer James Hailey)

2009–2010 AWARDS Outer Critics Circle Award: Outstanding Featured Actor in a Play (Jon Michael Hill); **Theatre World Award:** Jon Michael Hill

SETTING "Superior Donuts," a small donut shop in Chicago's Uptown neighborhood. New York premiere of a new play presented in two acts. World premiere at Chicago's Steppenwolf Theatre June 19–August 24, 2008 (see *Theatre World* Vol. 64, page 333).

SYNOPSIS Arthur Przybyszewski owns a decrepit donut shop in the Uptown neighborhood of Chicago. Franco Wicks, a black teenager who is his only employee, wants to change the shop for the better. This provocative comedy, set in the heart of one of Chicago's most diverse communities, explores the challenges of embracing the past and the redemptive power of friendship.

Carrie Fisher

Carrie Fisher

Wishful Drinking

Studio 54; First Preview: September 22, 2009; Opening Night: October 4, 2009; Closed January 17, 2010; 15 previews, 133 performances

Created by Carrie Fisher; Produced by the Roundabout Theatre Company (Todd Haimes, Artistic Director; Harold Wolpert, Managing Director; Julia C. Levy, Executive Director) in association with Jonathan Reinis, Jamie Cesa, Eva Price, and Berkeley Repertory Theatre; Director, Tony Taccone; Set/Lighting/Projections, Alexander V. Nichols; Production Stage Manager, Daniel J. Kells; Associate Producer, Garret Edington; Technical Supervisor, Steve Beers; General Manager, Sydney Beers; Director of Marketing/Sales, David B. Steffen; Founding Director, Gene Feist; Associate Artistic Director, Scott Ellis; Assistant Company Manager, Chris Minnick; General Manager for *Wishful Drinking JV*, Cesa Entertainment Inc.; Production Crew: Dan Hoffman (production carpenter), John Wooding (production electrician), Mai-Linh Lofgren (deck electrician), Jennifer Pesce Fagant (spot operator), Josh Weitzman (production consultant), Lawrence Jennino (running props), Markus Fokken (wardrobe supervisor), Francis Elers (sound mixer), Mike Widmer (IATSE Apprentice); Roundabout Staff: Director of Artistic Development/Casting, Jim Carnahan; Director of Education, Greg McCaslin, Director of Finance, Susan Neiman; IT Director, Antonio Palumbo; Director of Ticketing Sales, Charlie Garbowski Jr.; Press, Boneau/Bryan-Brown, Adrian Bryan-Brown, Matt Polk, Jessica Johnson, Amy Kass, Emily Meagher

Performed by **Carrie Fisher**

2009–2010 AWARDS   Outer Critics Circle Award: Outstanding Solo Performance (Carrie Fisher)

New York premiere of a solo performance play presented in two acts. World premiere presented at Geffen Playhouse (Gil Cates, Producing Director; Randall Arney, Artistic Director; Stephen Eich, Managing Director) November 7, 2006–January 14, 2007. Subsequently played a national tour last season prior to the New York engagement, including runs at Arena Stage, Hartford Stage, and Seattle Repertory Theatre (see *Theatre World* Vol. 65, pages 308, 326, and 348).

SYNOPSIS   Carrie Fisher recounts the true and intoxicating tale of her life as a Hollywood legend, told with the same wry wit she poured into bestsellers like *Postcards from the Edge*. The daughter of Eddie Fisher and Debbie Reynolds, Carrie Fisher became a cultural icon when she starred as "Princess Leia" in the first *Star Wars* trilogy at 19 years old. Forever changed, Carrie's life did not stay picture perfect. Fisher is the life of the party in this uproarious and sobering look at her Hollywood hangover

Carrie Fisher (photos by Joan Marcus)

Hamlet

Broadhurst Theatre; First Preview: September 12, 2009; Opening Night: October 6, 2009; Closed December 6, 2009; 25 previews, 72 performances

Written by William Shakespeare; Produced by Arielle Tepper Madover, The Donmar Warehouse, Matthew Byam Shaw, Scott M. Delman, Stephanie P. McClelland, Neal Street Productions/Carl Mollenberg, Ruth Hendel/Barbara Whitman, Philip Morgaman/Frankie J. Grande; Presented by The Donmar Warehouse; Director, Michael Grandage; Sets/Costumes, Christopher Oram; Lighting, Neil Austin; Composer/Sound, Adam Cork; Donmar Executive Producer, James Bierman; Casting, Anne McNulty; Marketing, Eric Schnall; General Management, 101 Productions Ltd.; Production Stage Manager, Frank Lombardi; U.S. Technical Supervisor, Aurora Productions; U.K. Technical Supervisor, Patrick Molony; Company Manager, Beverly Edwards; Wigs and Hair, Richard Mawbey; Stage Manager, Diane DeVita; Associate Director, Sam Yates; Associate Design: Andrew D. Edwards (set), Barry Doss (costumes), Pamela Kupper (lighting), Chris Cronin (sound); U.K. Associate Design, Richard Kent (Set), Rob Halliday (lighting); Production Crew: Jim Cane (production carpenter), Jon Lawson (production electrician), Tom Lawrey (head electrician), Andrew Meeker (props supervisor), Ed Chapman (production sound), Brian McGarty (house carpenter), Brian Bullard (house flyman), Charley DeVerna (house electrician), Ron Vitelli (house properties), Kelly Saxon (wardrobe supervisor), Lyle Jones (star dresser), Meredith Benson, Sandy Binion, Cesar Porto (dressers), Carmel Vargyas (harir supervisor); For 101 Productions: Wendy Orshan, Jeffrey M. Wilson, David Auster, Elie Landua; For Aurora Producitons: Gene O'Donovan, W. Benjamin Heller II, Rachel Sherbill, Steve Rosenberg, Jarid Sumner, Melissa Mazdra, Amy Merlino Coey, Amanda Raymond, Graham Forden, Liza Luxenberg; Press, Boneau/Bryan-Brown, Adrian Bryan-Brown, Jim Byk, Christine Olver

CAST Barnardo, Priest, Captain **Michael Hadley**; Francisco, Fortinbras, 4th Player **Alan Turkington**; Marcellus, 3rd Player, 2nd Gravedigger, English Ambassador **Henry Pettigrew**; Horatio **Matt Ryan**; Claudius **Kevin R. McNally**; Osric **Ian Drysdale**; Laertes **Gwilym Lee**; Polonius, 1st Gravedigger **Ron Cook**; Gertrude **Geraldine James**; Hamlet **Jude Law**; Ophelia **Gugu Mbatha-Raw**; Ghost of Hamlet's Father, Player King **Peter Eyre**; Reynaldo **Sean Jackson**; Rosencrantz **John MacMillan**; Guildenstern **Harry Attwell**; Player Queen **Jenny Funnell**; Cornelius **Ross Armstrong**; Member of the Court **Faye Winter**; Member of the Court **Colin Haigh**; Member of the Court **James Le Feuvre**

UNDERSTUDIES Ross Armstrong (Laertes, Osric, Rosencrantz), Ian Drysdale (Claudius, Polonius), Jenny Funnell (Gertrude), Colin Haigh (Barnardo, Ghost, Gravedigger), Sean Jackson (Captain, Marcellus, Priest), James Le Feuvre (Cornelius, English Ambassador, Francisco, Gravedigger, Guildenstern, Player, Reynaldo), John MacMillan (Horatio), Henry Pettigrew (Fortinbras), Matt Ryan (Hamlet), Alan Turkington (Player King), Faye Winter (Ophelia, Player Queen)

SETTING In and around Elsinore Castle in Denmark. Revival of the play presented in two acts. This production of *Hamlet* was first performed at the Wyndam's Theatre as part of the Donmar West End season on May 29-August 22, 2009. The production then traveled to Kronberg Castle in Elsinore, Denmark from August 25-30, 2009, before coming to Broadway.

SYNOPSIS The King of Denmark is dead. Consumed with grief, Prince Hamlet determines to avenge his father's death with devastating consequences for his family and the kingdom. Michael Grandage's acclaimed Donmar Warehouse production of Shakespeare's definitive tragedy returns to Broadway for a limited engagement featuring Mr. Law and the Donmar Warehouse cast.

Jude Law (photos by Johan Persson)

Gugu Mbatha-Raw and Jude Law

The Royal Family

Samuel J. Friedman Theatre; First Preview: September 15, 2009; Opening Night: October 8, 2009; Closed December 13, 2009; 26 previews, 77 performances

Written by George S. Kaufman and Edna Ferber; Produced by Manhattan Theatre Club (Lynne Meadow, Artistic Director; Barry Grove, Executive Producer); Director, Doug Hughes; Set, John Lee Beatty; Costumes, Catherine Zuber; Lighting, Kenneth Posner; Sound, Darron L West; Original Music, Maury Yeston; Hair & Wigs, Tom Watson; Fight Director, Rick Sordelet; Animals, William Berloni; Production Stage Manager, Rick Steiger; General Manager, Florie Seery; Associate Artistic Director, Mandy Greenfield; Director of Artistic Development, Jerry Patch; Marketing, Debra Waxman-Pilla; Production Manager, Kurt Gardner; Director of Casting, Nancy Piccione; Development, Jill Turner Lloyd; Artistic Consultant, Daniel Sullivan; Artistic Administration/Assistant to Artistic Director, Amy Gilkes Loe; Musical Development, Clifford Lee Johnson III; Finance, Jeffrey Bledsoe; Associate General Manager, Lindsey Brooks Sag; Subscriber Services, Robert Allenberg; Telesales, George Tetlow; Education, David Shookhoff; Associate Production Manager, Joshua Helman; Prop Supervisor, Scott Laule; Costume Supervisor, Erin Hennessy Dean; Company Manager, Seth Shepsle; Stage Manager, Elizabeth Moloney; Assistant Director, David Hilder; Makeup, Angelina Avellone; Ms. Harris' Wig, Paul Huntley; Associate Lighting, Aaron Spivey; Assistant Design: Yoshinori Tanokura (scenic), Brian Hemesath, Nikki Moody, David Newell (costumes), Alex Fogel (lighting), Matt Hubbs (sound); Production Crew: Chris Wiggins (head carpenter), Timothy Walters (head propertyman), Louis Shapiro (sound engineer), Jeff Dodson (master electrician), Angela Simpson (wardrobe supervisor), Natasha Steinhagen (hair/makeup supervisor), Ruth Carsch (assistant hair supervisor), Cathy Prager (assistant props), Virginia Neininger, Eunice Dugan (dressers), Jane Masterson (lightboard programmer), Brian Hoffman (animal handler), Christopher Munnell (production assistant); Theatre Manager, Jim Joseph; Box Office Treasurer, David Dillon; Advertising, SpotCo; Press, Boneau/Bryan-Brown, Aaron Meier, Christine Olver

CAST Perry Stewart **Freddy Arsenault**; Gwen Cavendish **Kelli Barrett**; Della **Caroline Stefanie Clay**; McDermott, Gunga **Rufus Collins**; Kitty Dean **Ana Gasteyer**; Herbert Dean **John Glover**; Jo **David Greenspan**; Fanny Cavendish **Rosemary Harris**; Julie Cavendish **Jan Maxwell**; Chauffeur **Anthony Newfield**; Gilbert Marshall **Larry Pine**; Oscar Wolfe **Tony Roberts**; Tony Cavendish **Reg Rogers**; Miss Peake **Henny Russell**; Hallboy **Cat Walleck**; Hallboy **John Wernke**

UNDERSTUDIES Rufus Collins (Gilbert Marshall, Tony Cavendish), Beth Dixon (Fanny Cavendish), Anthony Newfield (Herbert Dean, Jo, Oscar Wolfe), Henny Russell (Della, Julie Cavendish, Kitty Dean), Cat Walleck (Gwen Cavendish, Hall boy, Miss Peake), John Wernke (Gunga, McDermott, Perry Stewart)

2009–2010 AWARDS Tony Award: Best Costume Design of a Play (Catherine Zuber); Drama Desk Award: Outstanding Actress in a Play (Jan Maxwell)

SETTING The duplex apartment of the Cavendishes, in the East Fifties, New York City, 1927. Act I: A Friday in November, early afternoon. Act II: Saturday, between matinee and night. Act III: A year later. Revival of a play presented in three acts with two intermissions. The original production opened at the Selwyn Theatre December 28, 1927. The play had a minor revival at City Center from January 10-21, 1951 (see *Theatre World* Vol. 7, page 140), and a major revival at the Helen Hayes Theatre (in which Rosemary Harris played "Julie Cavendish") December 30, 1975–July 18, 1976 (see *Theatre World* Vol. 32, page 36).

SYNOPSIS *The Royal Family* follows the lives of the Cavendishes, a famous family of stage stars (patterned after the Barrymores) as they go about the drama of the day: choosing scripts, dashing off to performances, stealing kisses from handsome beaus. But what's the business about the youngest diva wanting to quit the stage for domestic bliss? Never, darling!

Jan Maxwell, Kelli Barrett, and Rosemary Harris

Ana Gasteyer and Reg Rogers

Jan Maxwell and Tony Roberts (photos by Joan Marcus)

Julia Stiles and Bill Pullman (photos by Craig Schwartz))

Bill Pullman and Julia Stiles

Oleanna

John Golden Theatre; First Preview: September 29, 2009; Opening Night: October 11, 2009; Closed December 6, 2009; 15 previews, 65 performances

Written by David Mamet; Produced by Jeffrey Finn, Arlene Scanlan, Jed Bernstein, Ken Davenport, Carla Emil, Ergo Entertainment, Harbor Entertainment, Elie Hirschfeld, Rachel Hirschfeld, Hop Theatricals, Brian Fenty/Martha H. Jones, Center Theatre Group (Michael Ritchie, Artistic Director; Charles Dillingham, Managing Director; Gordon Davidson, Founding Artistic Director); Director, Doug Hughes; Set, Neil Patel; Costumes, Catherine Zuber; Lighting, Donald Holder; Fight Director, Rick Sordelet; Production Stage Manager, Charles Means; Marketing Services; B&B Marketing (Betsy Bernstein, Jed Bernstein); Production Management, Juniper Street Productions (Hillary Blanken, Ana Rose Greene, Kevin Broomell, Guy Kwan); General Management, Alan Wasser, Allan Williams, Mark Shacket; Company Manager, Penelope Daulton; Stage Manager, Marti McIntosh; Assistant to the Director, Jenny Slattery; Associate Design: Caleb Levengood (set), Carolyn Wong (lighting); Assistant to the Lighting Designer, Carla Linton; Production Crew: Dave Fulton (production carpenter), Geoff Vaughn (automation carpenter), Jimmy Maloney (production electrician), Chris Pantuso (production properties), Patrick Bevilacqua (wardrobe supervisor/Mr. Pullman's dresser), Carrie Kamerer (Ms. Stiles' dresser); Advertising, SpotCo, Drew Hodges, Jim Edwards, Tom Greenwald, Stephen Sosnowski, Meghan Ownbey; Website/Internet Marketing, Jamie Lynn Ballard/Davenport Theatrical Enterprises Inc; General Management Associates, Aaron Lustbader, Lane Marsh, Thom Mitchell; Press, The Publicity Office, Marc Thibodeau, Michael S. Borowski, Jeremy Shaffer, Matt Fasano

CAST John **Bill Pullman;** Carol **Julia Stiles**

STANDBYS Blair Baker (Carol), Marty Lodge (John)

SETTING The play takes place in John's office. Broadway premiere and revival of an Off-Broadway play presented without intermission. This production played last season at Center Theatre Group's Mark Taper Forum May 28–July 12, 2009 (see *Theatre World* Vol. 65, page 315). Following a world premiere in May 1992 as the first production of David Mamet's Back Bay Theater Company in Cambridge, Massachusetts and starring William H. Macy and Rebecca Pidgeon, *Oleanna* had its New York premiere Off-Broadway at The Orpheum Theatre on October 23, 1992, directed by Mamet and again starring Mr. Macy and Ms. Pidgeon, playing 513 performances (see *Theatre World* Vol. 49, page 80).

SYNOPSIS Mamet's controversial 1992 drama *Oleanna* receives its Broadway premiere in this production. *Oleanna* is a gripping account of a power struggle between a male university professor and one of his female students who accuses him of sexual exploitation, and by doing so, spoils his chances of being accorded tenure. Written in the heyday of political correctness and culture wars of the early 1990s, *Oleanna* divides audiences at every performance into two camps, compelled to attack or defend either character.

Julia Stiles and Bill Pullman

Bye Bye Birdie

Henry Miller's Theatre; First Preview: September 10, 2009; Opening Night: October 15, 2009; Closed January 22, 2010; 40 previews, 117 performances

Book by Michael Stewart, music by Charles Strouse, lyrics by Lee Adams; Produced by the Roundabout Theatre Company (Todd Haimes, Artistic Director; Harold Wolpert, Managing Director; Julia C. Levy, Executive Director); Director/Choreographer, Robert Longbottom; Music Supervisor/Vocal & Dance Arrangements, David Chase; Orchestrations, Jonathan Tunick; Set, Andrew Jackness; Costumes, Gregg Barnes; Lighting, Ken Billington; Sound, Acme Sound Partners; Projections, Howard Werner; Musical Director, David Holcenberg; Music Coordinator, Howard Joines; Hair & Wigs, David Brian Brown; Makeup, Angelina Avallone; Production Stage Manager, Peter Hanson; Casting, Jim Carnahan, Kate Boka; Associate Director, Tom Kosis; Technical Supervisor, Steve Beers; Executive Producer/General Manager, Sydney Beers; Marketing/Sales Promotion, David B. Steffen; Founding Director, Gene Feist; Associate Artistic Director, Scott Ellis; Director of Artistic Development and Casting, Jim Carnahan; Education, Greg McCaslin; Finance, Susan Neiman; Development Directors, Julie K. D'Andrea, Steve Schaeffer, Joy Pak, Amber Jo Manuel; IT Director, Antonio Palumbo; Sales Operations, Charlie Garbowski Jr.; Company Manager, Denise Cooper; Company Manager Assistant, Ellen Campion; Stage Manager, Jon Krause; Assistant Stage Manager, Rachel Bauder; Associate Choreographer, Pamela Remler; Dance Supervisor/Assistant Choreographer, Chad L. Schiro; Dance Captain, Julia Knitel; Associate Design: Melissa Shakun (set), Matthew Pachtman (costumes), Paul Toben (lighting), Nick Borisjuk (sound), Jason Lindahl (projections); Assistant Design: Sia Balabanova, Veronica Kimmel, Sean Tribble (set), Anthony Pearson (lighting); Assistants to the Designers: David Towlun (set), Mitchell Travers (costume); Costume Assistant, Tescia Seufferlein; Costume Shoppers, Brenda Abbandandolo, Noah Marin; Costume Interns, Alice Garfield, Kathleen Doyle; Production Properties Coordinator, Kathy Fabian/Propstar; Associate Production Properties, Tim Ferro, Scott Keclik; Projection Programmer, Phil Gilbert; Production Crew: Patrick Pummill (production sound engineer), Dan Hoffman (production carpenter), Donald Roberts (carpenter), Steve Jones (flyman), Josh Weitzman (production electrician), Tim Rogers (moving light programmer), Paul Coltoff, Dorion Fuchs, Erica Warmbrunn (follow spots), Jocelyn Smith (deck electrician), Aaron Straus (deck sound), Andrew Forste (house properties), Ben Barnes, Dan Mendeloff, Nelson Vaughn (properties run crew), Nadine Hettel (wardrobe supervisor), Vanessa Anderson (hair & wig supervisor), Tara Delahunt, Joe Godwin, Vincent Grecki, Joe Hickey, Mary Ann Oberpriller, Suzanne Lunney-Delahunt, Kimberly Mark, Stacy Sarmiento (dressers), Joshua First, Jennifer Pendergraft (hair assistants), Lauren J. Benn, Jill Valentine (child wranglers); Production Assistants, Rachel Bauder, McKenzie Murphy; Synthesizer Programmer, Bruce Samuels; Music Copying, Emily Grishman, Katherine Edmonds; Company Management Assistant, Dave Solomon; Advertising, SpotCo; Press, Boneau/Bryan-Brown, Adrian Bryan-Brown, Matt Polk, Jessica Johnson, Amy Kass

CAST Mr. Harry MacAfee **Bill Irwin**; Mrs. MacAfee **Dee Hoty**; Randolph MacAfee **Jake Evan Schwencke***; Kim MacAfee **Allie Trimm**; Conrad Birdie **Nolan Gerard Funk**; Albert Peterson **John Stamos**; Rose Alvarez **Gina Gershon**; The Teenagers **Allison Strong, Julia Knitel, Emma Rowley, Jess LeProtto, Daniel Quadrino, Paul Pilcz, Deanna Cipolla, Kevin Shotwell, Riley Costello, Catherine Blades, Jillian Mueller**; Ursula Merkle **Brynn Williams**; The Fan Club Girls **Allison Strong, Julia Knitel, Emma Rowley, Deanna Cipolla, Catherine Blades, Jillian Mueller**; Mrs. Mae Peterson **Jayne Houdyshell**; Hugo Peabody **Matt Doyle**; Reporters/Parents **Paula Leggett Chase, John Treacy Egan, Colleen Fitzpatrick, Todd Gearhart, Patty Goble, Suzanne Grodner, Natalie Hill, David McDonald, JC Montgomery, Timothy Shew**; Mayor Garfein **Timothy Shew**; Mrs. Edna Garfein **Patty Goble**; Helen **Allison Strong**; Alice **Julia Knitel**; Mrs. Merkle **Suzanne Grodner**; Gloria Rasputin **Paula Leggett Chase**; TV Quartet **Matt Doyle, Jess LeProtto, Daniel Quadrino, Kevin**

Shotwell; TV Stage Manager **David McDonald**; Charles Maude **Jim Walton**; Bar Quartet **John Treacy Egan, David McDonald, JC Montgomery, Timothy Shew**; Ed Sullivan **Will Jordan**; Teen Male Swing **Robert Hager**; Adult Female Swing **Nina Hennessey**; Teen Female Swing **Bethany Ann Tesarck**; Adult Male Swing **Branch Woodman**

* Succeeded by Neil McCaffrey (11/9/09)

UNDERSTUDIES Catherine Blades (Kim MacAfee), Riley Costello (Randolph MacAfee), Colleen Fitzpatrick (Mrs. MacAfee), Todd Gearhart (Albert Peterson), Suzanne Grodner (Mae Peterson), Robert Hager (Conrad Birdie), Nina Hennessey (Gloria Rasputin), Natalie Hill (Rose Alvarez), Julia Knitel (Ursula Merkle), Daniel Quadrino (Hugo Peabody), Jim Walton (Mr. MacAfee)

ORCHESTRA David Holcenberg (Conductor/keyboards); Mat Eisenstein (Associate Conductor/keyboards); Les Scott, Ralph Olsen, Thomas Christensen, Mark Thrasher (reeds); Donald Downs, Stu Satalof, Barry Danielian (trumpets); Vincent Fanuele (trombone); Paul Pizzuti (drums/percussion); Ray Kilday (bass); Scott Kuney (guitar); Kenneth Burward-Hoy, Liuh-Wen Ting (viola); Sarah Seiver, Summer Boggess (cello)

MUSICAL NUMBERS Overture/Prologue: We Love You Conrad; An English Teacher; The Telephone Hour; How Lovely to Be a Woman; Put on a Happy Face; A Healthy, Normal American Boy; One Boy; Honestly Sincere; Hymn for a Sunday Evening; One Last Kiss; What Did I Ever See in Him; Kids; A Lot of Livin' to Do; Baby, Talk to Me; Spanish Rose; Rosie; Bye Bye Birdie

SETTING New York City and Sweet Apple, Ohio; 1960. Revival of a musical presented in eighteen scenes in two acts. Originally presented on Broadway at the Martin Beck Theatre (now the Al Hirschfeld) April 14, 1960 (see *Theatre World* Vol. 16, page 87). The production moved to the 54th Street Theatre, and then to the Shubert Theatre, where it closed October 7, 1961 after 607 performances. This production was the first revival of the 1961 musical and the inaugural production of the newly renovated Henry Miller's Theatre.

SYNOPSIS In *Bye Bye Birdie*, the exuberant rock 'n' roll musical comedy, it's 1960 and hip-swingin' teen idol superstar Conrad Birdie has been drafted into the army. Birdie's manager Albert and his secretary Rosie have cooked up a plan to send him off with a swell new song and one last kiss from a lucky teenage fan… on "The Ed Sullivan Show"!

John Stamos and Gina Gershon

Back Row (l-r): *Emma Rowley, Deanna Cipolla;* Front row: *Julia Knitel, Allison Strong, John Stamos, Jillian Mueller, and Catherine Blades*

John Stamos, Nolan Gerard Funk, Gina Gershon, and the Company

Gina Gershon and John Stamos (photos by Joan Marcus)

Allie Trimm, Dee Hoty, Bill Irwin, Jake Evan Schwencke

Nolan Gerard Funk and the Company

The Company (photos by Joan Marcus)

Chad Kimball

Memphis

Shubert Theatre; First Preview: September 23, 2009; Opening Night: October 19, 2009; 30 previews, 256 performances as of May 31, 2010

Book and lyrics by Joe DiPietro, music and lyrics by David Bryan; Based on a concept by George W. George; Produced by Junkyard Dog Productions (Randy Adams, Kenny Alhadeff, Sue Frost), Barbara and Buddy Freitag, Marleen and Kenny Alhadeff, Latitude Link, Jim and Susan Blair, Demos Bizar Entertainment (Nick Demos & Francine Bizar), Land Line Productions, Apples and Oranges Productions, Dave Copley, Dancap Productions Inc., Alex and Katya Lukianov, Tony Ponturo, 2 Guys Productions, Richard Winkler, in association with Lauren Doll, Eric and Marsi Gardiner, Linda and Bill Potter, Broadway Across America (John Gore, CEO; Thomas B. McGrath, Chairman; Beth Williams, COO & Head of Production), Jocko Productions, Patty Baker, Dan Frishwasser, Bob Bartner/ Scott and Kaylin Union, Loraine Boyle/Chase Mishkin, Remmel T. Dickinson/ Memphis Orpheum Group (Pat Halloran), ShadowCatcher Entertainment/Vijay and Sita Vashee; Director, Christopher Ashley; Choreographer, Sergio Trujillo; Music Producer/Music Supervisor, Christopher Jahnke; Associate Producers, Emily and Aaron Alhadeff, Alison and Andi Alhadeff, Ken Clay, Joseph Craig, Ron and Marjorie Danz, Cyrena Esposito, Bruce and Joanne Glant, Matt Murphy; Sets, David Gallo; Costumes, Paul Tazewell; Lighting, Howell Binkley; Sound, Ken Travis; Projections, David Gallo & Sandy Sagady; Hair & Wigs, Charles G. LaPointe; Fight Director, Steve Rankin; Casting, Telsey + Company; Associate Choreographer, Kelly Devine; Orchestrations, Daryl Waters & David Bryan; Musical Director, Kenny J. Seymour; Dance Arrangements, August Eriksmoen; Music Contractor, Michael Keller; Production Stage Manager, Arturo E. Porazzi; General Manager, Alchemy Production Group, Carl Pasbjerg & Frank Scardino; Production Management, Juniper Street Productions, Hilary Blanken, Guy Kwan, Kevin Broomell, Ana Rose Greene; Marketing Direction, Type A Marketing, Anne Rippey, Nick Pramik, Janette Roush, Nina Bergelson; Company Manager, Jim Brandeberry; Associate Director, Beatrice Terry; Associate Choreographer, Edgar Godineaux; Stage Manager, Gary Mickelson; Assistant Stage Manager, Monica A Cuoco; Assistant Company Manager, Tegan Meyer; Junkyard Dog Associate, Carolyn D. Miller; Associate to the General Managers, Sherra Johnston; Dance/ Fight Captain, Jermaine R. Rembert; Assistant Dance Captain, Dionne Figgins; Assistant Fight Director, Shad Ramsey; Dramaturg, Gabriel Greene; Dialect Coach, Stephen Gabis; Makeup, Angelina Avellone; Associate Design: Steven C. Kemp (set), Rory Powers (costumes), Mark Simpson (lighting), Leah Loukas (hair); Assistant Design: Maria Zamansky (costumes), Alex Hawthorn (sound), Steve Channon (projections); Assistants to Desginers: Kara Harmon (costumes), Amanda Zieve (lighting); Moving Light Programmer, David Arch; Projection Programmer, Florian Mosleh; Production Crew: Hank Hale (production/head carpenter), Erik Hansen (flyman), Scott Poitras (assistant carpenter/automation), James Fedigan (production electrician), Patrick Ainge (head electrician), Mike Pilipski (production property master), John Paull (head property master), Peter Drummond (assistant property master), Philip Lojo (production sound engineer), Ty Lackey (front of house sound), Jens McVoy (assistant sound engineer), Deborah Chereton (wardrobe supervisor), Fred Castner (associate wardrobe supervisor), Michelle Rutter (hair supervisor), Dora Bonialla, Maureen George, Betty Gillespie, James Hodun, Franklin Hollenbeck, Kim Kaldenberg, Franc Weinperl, Kyle Wesson (dressers), Mary Kay Yezerski-Bondoc, Charlene Belmond (hair stylists); Music Copying, Christopher Deschene; Keyboard Programmer, Kenny J. Seymoure; Music Assistant, Clare Cooper; Production Assistants, Megan J. Alvord, Meg Friedman; Scenic/Projection Studio Manager, Sarah Zeitler; Advertising, SpotCo; Press, The Hartman Group, Michael Hartman, Juliana Hannett, Frances White; Cast recording: Rhino 523944

CAST White DJ/Mr. Collins/Gordon Grant **John Jellison**; Black DJ **Rhett George**; Delray **J. Bernard Calloway**; Bobby **Derrick Baskin**; Wailin' Joe/Reverend Hobson **John Eric Parker**; Ethel **LaQuet Sharnell**; Felicia **Montego Glover**; Huey **Chad Kimball**; Mr. Simmons **Michael McGrath**; Clara **Jennifer Allen**; Buck Wiley/Martin Holton **Kevin Covert**; Perry Como/ Frank Dryer **Brad Bass**; Mama **Cass Morgan**; Ensemble **John Jellison, Rhett George, John Eric Parker, Tracee Beazer, Dionne Figgins, Vivian Nixon, LaQuet Sharnell, Ephraim M. Sykes, Danny Tidwell, Daniel J. Watts, Dan'yelle Williamson, Jennifer Allen, Kevin Covert, Hilary Elk, Bryan Fenkart, Cary Tedder, Katie Webber, Charlie Williams, Brad Bass**; Swings **Candice Monet McCall, Sydney Morton, Jermaine R. Rembert**

UNDERSTUDIES Jennifer Allen (Mama), Brad Bass (Huey), Tracee Beazer (Felicia), Bryan Fenkart (Huey), Rhett G. George (Bobby, Delray), John Jellison (Mr. Simmons), John Eric Parker (Bobby, Delray), Jermaine R. Rembert (Gator), Ephraim M. Sykes (Gator), Dan'yelle Williamson (Felicia)

THE *MEMPHIS* BAND Kenny J. Seymour (Conductor/keyboard 1), Shelton Becton (Associate Conductor/keyboard 2), Michael Aarons (guitars), George Farmer (bass), Clayton Craddock (drums), Nicholas Marchione (trumpet), Mike Davis (trombone), Tom Murray & Ken Hitchcock (reeds)

MUSICAL NUMBERS Underground; The Music of My Soul; Scratch My Itch; Ain't Nothin' But a Kiss; Hello, My Name is Huey; Everybody Wants to Be Black on a Saturday Night; Make Me Stronger; Colored Woman; Someday; She's My Sister; Radio; Say a Prayer; Crazy Little Huey; Big Love; Love Will Stand When All Else Falls; Stand Up; Change Don't Come Easy; Tear the House Down; Love Will Stand/ Ain't Nothin' But a Kiss (reprise); Memphis Lives in Me; Steal Your Rock 'n' Roll

2009–2010 AWARDS Tony Award: Best Musical, Best Book of a Musical (Joe DiPietro), Best Original Score (Joe DiPietro and David Bryan), Best Orchestrations (Daryl Waters and David Bryan); Drama Desk Awards: Outstanding Musical, Outstanding Actress in a Musical (Montego Glover – tie with Catherine Zeta-Jones), Outstanding Music (David Bryan), Outstanding Orchestrations; Outer Critics Circle Awards: Outstanding New Broadway Musical, Outstanding New Score, Outstanding Choreography (Sergio Trujilo)

SETTING Time: The 1950s. Place: Memphis, Tennessee and New York City. World premiere produced as a joint venture at North Shore Music Theatre in Beverly, Massachusetts (Jon Kimbell, Executive Producer) September 23–October12, 2003 in and at TheatreWorks in Palo Alto, California (Robert Kelley, Artistic Director; Phil Santora, Managing Director) January 24–February 15, 2004. The show played LaJolla Playhouse (Christopher Ashley Artistic Director; Michael S. Rosenberg, Managing Director) August 19–September 28, 2008 and at 5th Avenue Theatre in Seattle (David Armstrong, Producing Artistic Director; Marilynn Sheldon, Managing Director) from January 27–February 15, 2009 prior to its Broadway debut (see *Theatre World* Vol. 65, pages 319 and 330).

SYNOPSIS Inspired by actual events, *Memphis* takes place in the smoky halls and underground clubs of the segregated 1950s. A young white DJ named Huey Calhoun who wants to change the world falls in love with everything he shouldn't: rock and roll and an electrifying black club singer who is ready for her big break. *Memphis* is an original story about the cultural revolution that erupted when his vision met her voice, and the music changed forever.

Derrick Baskin, Cass Morgan, James Monroe Iglehart, and J. Bernard Calloway

Montego Glover

J. Bernard Calloway and Montego Glover

After Miss Julie

American Airlines Theatre; First Preview: September 18, 2009; Opening Night: October 22, 2009; Closed December 6, 2009; 40 previews, 53 performances

Written by Patrick Marber, inspired by *Miss Julie* by August Strindberg; Produced by the Roundabout Theatre Company (Todd Haimes, Artistic Director; Harold Wolpert, Managing Director; Julia C. Levy, Executive Director) in association with Sonia Friedman Productions and Ostar Productions; Director, Mark Brokaw; Set, Allen Moyer; Costumes, Michael Krass; Lighting, Mark McCullough; Original Music and Sound, David Van Tieghem; Wigs, Paul Huntley; Dialect Coach, Deborah Hecht; Fight Director, Thomas Schall; Production Stage Manager, James FitzSimmons; Casting, Jim Carnahan; Production Management, Aurora Productions (Gene O'Donovan, W. Benjamin Heller II, Rachel Sherbill, Jarid Sumner, Steve Rosenberg, Melissa Mazdra, Amy Merlino Coey, Amanda Raymond, Graham Forden, Liza Luxenberg); General Manager, Rebecca Habel; Marketing/Sales Promotion, David B. Steffen; Founding Director, Gene Feist; Associate Artistic Director, Scott Ellis; Director of Artistic Development and Casting, Jim Carnahan; Finance, Susan Neiman; Education, Greg McCaslin; General Manager, Sydney Beers; Telesales, Marco Frezza; IT Director, Antonio Palumbo; Development Directors, Julie K. D'Andrea, Steve Schaeffer, Joy Pak, Amber Jo Manuel; Sales Operations, Charlie Garbowski Jr.; Company Manager, Carly DiFulvio; Stage Manager, Bryce McDonald; Etiquette/Movement Consultant, Frank Ventura; Assistant Director, Alec Strum; Associate Design: Warren Karp (set), Tracy Christensen (costumes), Driscoll Otto (lighting), Jill BC DuBoff (sound); Assistant Sound, Sam Doerr; Makeup, Angelina Avallone; Production Crew: Peter Sarafin (production properties), Glenn Merwede (production carpenter), Barb Bartel (production electrician), Brian Maiuri (house electrician), Robert W. Dowling II (running properties), Dann Wojnar (sound operator), Susan J. Fallon (wardrobe supervisor), Manuela Laporte (hair and wig supervisor), Kat Martin (dresser), Lauren Galitelli (day wardrobe), Jorge Vargas (assistant makeup artist), Katherine Wallace (production assistant); Music Search Supervisor, Hank Aberle; Advertising, SpotCo; Press, Boneau/Bryan-Brown, Adrian Bryan-Brown, Matt Polk, Jessica Johnson, Amy Kass, Emily Meagher

CAST Christine **Marin Ireland**; John **Jonny Lee Miller**; Miss Julie **Sienna Miller**; Additional Voices **Paul O'Brien, Sandra Shipley, Daniel Stewart**

UNDERSTUDIES Ryan McCarthy (John), Lisa Velten Smith (Miss Julie/Christine)

SETTING Place: The kitchen of a large country estate outside London. Time: July 26, 1945. Night and the morning after. American premiere of play presented without intermission. Originally produced at the Donmar Warehouse November 20, 2003.

SYNOPSIS *After Miss Julie* transposes August Strindberg's 1888 play about sex and class to an English country house on the eve of the British Labour Party's historic landslide election.

Sienna Miller (photos by Joan Marcus)

Jonny Lee Miller and Sienna Miller

Jonny Lee Miller and Marin Ireland

Front: *Noah Robbins, Gracie Bea Lawrence;* Back: *Santino Fontana, Laurie Metcalf, Dennis Boutsikaris, Jessica Hecht, Alexandra Socha*

Noah Robbins *(photos by Joan Marcus)*

Brighton Beach Memoirs

Nederlander Theatre; First Preview: October 2, 2009; Opening Night: October 25, 2009; Closed November 1, 2009; 25 previews, 9 performances

Written by Neil Simon; Produced by Ira Pittelman, Max Cooper, Jeffrey A. Sine, Scott Delman, Ruth Hendel, Roy Furman, Ben Sprecher/Wendy Federman, Scott Landis, Emanuel Azenberg; Director, David Cromer; Set, John Lee Beatty; Costumes, Jane Greenwood; Lighting, Brian MacDevitt; Sound, Fitz Patton & Josh Schmidt; Hair & Wigs, Tom Watson; Technical Supervision, Hudson Theatrical Associates, Neil Mazzella; Casting, Jay Binder & Jack Bowdan; Associate Producer, Sheila Steinberg; General Manager, John E. Gendron; Production Supervisor, Barclay Stiff; Stage Manager, Brandon Kahn; Assistant Company Manager, Chelsea Salyer; Assistant Director, Michael Padden; Associate Design: Kacie Hultgren (set), Jennifer Moeller (costumes), Peter Hoerburger (lighting), David Stollings (sound); Lighting Programmer, Marc Polimeni; Assistant Sound, David Koch; Production Crew: Joe Ferreri Sr. (production carpenter), Richard Beck (production electrician), James Maloney (advance electrician), James van Bergen (production sound engineer), George Wagner (production properties supervisor), Kathryn Guida (wardrobe supervisor), Jill Heller, Gayle Palmieri, Rodd Sovar (dressers), Katie Beatty (hair supervisor), Jessica Azenberg (child wrangler), Kelly Beaulieu (production assistant); Management Assistant, Errolyn Rosa; Management Intern, Nathaniel Hill; Advertising, Serino Coyne Inc.; Interactive Marketing, Situation Marketing; Press, Boneau/Bryan-Brown, Chris Boneau, Jim Byk, Kelly Guiod

CAST Eugene Morris Jerome **Noah Robbins**; Blanche Morton **Jessica Hecht**; Kate Jerome **Laurie Metcalf**; Laurie Morton **Gracie Bea Lawrence**; Nora Morton **Alexandra Socha**; Stanley Jerome **Santino Fontana**; Jack Jerome **Dennis Boutsikaris**

UNDERSTUDIES Adam Grupper (Jack Jerome), Jürgen Hooper (Stanley Jerome), Finnerty Steeves (Blanche), Coby Getzug (Eugene Morris Jerome), Bridget Megan Clark (Nora Morton, Laurie Morton)

SETTING Brighton Beach, Brooklyn, New York; September, late 1930s. Revival of a play presented in two acts. The original production opened on Broadway at the Alvin Theatre (now the Neil Simon Theatre) on March 27, 1983, transferred to the 46th Street Theatre (now the Richard Rodgers Theatre) on February 26, 1985, and closed May 11, 1986 after 1,530 performances (see *Theatre World* Vol. 39, page 41). A revival of Simon's *Broadway Bound*, the third show in his semi-autobiographical trilogy of plays (that also includes the second installment, *Biloxi Blues*) was slated to open November 18, 2009 and run in repertory with *Brighton Beach Memoirs*. However, after slow advance sales, the producers shuttered this production and cancelled *Broadway Bound*.

SYNOPSIS *Brighton Beach Memoirs* centers on young Jewish teen Eugene Morris Jerome and his extended family living in a crowded home in the Brighton Beach section of Brooklyn: his overworked father, Jack; overbearing mother, Kate; his older brother Stanley; Kate's widowed sister Blanche and her daughters, Nora and Laurie. As Eugene spends his time daydreaming about a baseball career, he must also cope with his family's troubles, his awkward discovery of the opposite sex and his developing identity as a writer.

Finian's Rainbow

St. James Theatre; First Preview: October 8, 2009; Opening Night: October 29, 2009; Closed January 17, 2010; 22 previews, 92 performances

Music by Burton Lane, lyrics by Yip Harburg, book by Yip Harburg and Fred Saidy; Based on the 2009 New York City Center *Encores!* Production; Produced by David Richenthal, Jack Viertel, Alan D. Marks, Michael Speyer, Bernard Abrams, David M. Milch, Stephen Moore, Debbie Bisno/Myla Lerner, Jujamcyn Theatres (Jordan Roth, President; Paul Libin, Producing Director; Jack Viertel, Creative Director) in association with Melly Garcia, Jamie deRoy, Jon Bierman, Richard Driehaus, Kevin Spirtas, Jay Binder, StageVentures 2009 Limited Partnership; Director & Choreography, Warren Carlyle; Music Supervision and Vocal Arrangements, Rob Berman; Sets, John Lee Beatty; Costumes, Toni-Leslie James; Lighting, Ken Billington; Sound, Scott Lehrer; Hair/Wigs/Makeup, Wendy Parson; Book Adaptation, Arthur Perlman; Original Adaptation for *Encores!*, David Ives; Casting, Jay Binder, Nikole Vallins; Associate Choreographer, Parker Esse; Production Stage Manager, Tripp Phillips; Original Orchestrations, Robert Russell Bennett and Don Walker; Music Coordinator, Seymour Red Press; General Management, Frankel Green Theatrical Management, Richard Frankel, Laura Green, Joe Watson, Leslie Ledbetter; Technical Supervision, Hudson Theatrical Associates, Neil Mazzella, Sam Ellis, Patrick Sullivan, Irene Wang; Associate Producers, Andrew Hartman, Gail Lawrence; Executive Producer, Nicole Kastrinos; Dance Captain, Elisa Van Duyne; Assistant Dance Captain, Grasan Kingsberry; Original Dance Music Arrangements, Trude Rittman; Original Vocal Arrangements, Lyn Murray; Associate Music Director, David Gursky; Music Preparation, Randy Cohen; Additional Orchestrations, Larry Moore; Keyboard Programmer, Brian Allan Hobbs; Company Manager, Kathy Lowe; Associate Company Manager, Maia Sutton; Stage Manager, Jason Hindelang; Associate Director, Seth Sklar-Heyn; Assistant Choreographer, Angie Canuel; Magic & Illusions Consultant, Matthew Holtzclaw; Dialect Coach, Deborah Hecht; Associate Design: Neno Russell (costumes), Anthony Pearson (lighting); Assistant Design: Kacie Hultgren (set), Nicky Tobolski, Christopher Mueller, Bonnie McCoy (costumes), Jonathan Spencer (lighting), Ashley Hanson (sound), Jorie Mars Malan (hair & wigs); Assistants to Ms. James, Cailin Anderson, Josh Quinn; Company Management Assistant, Katie Pope; Production Crew: Donald J. Oberpriller (production carpenter), Ryan McDonough (deck automation carpenter), Dave Brown (flyman), Scott De Verna (production electrician), Fraser Weir (head electrician), Hillary Knox (moving light programmer), Sandy Paradise (front light head), Susan Pelkofer, Bob Miller (follow spots), Carin Ford (production sound engineer), Joe Lenihan, Emile Lafargue (deck sound technicians), Joseph P. Harris Jr (production property supervisor), Eric Castaldo (head properties), Shana Albery (production wardrobe supervisor), Dolly Williams (assistant wardrobe supervisor), Cailin Anderson, Joshua Burns, Charlie Catanese, Barry Doss, Samantha Lawrence, Del Miskie (dressers), Shanah-Ann Kendall (wig & hair supervisor), Anna Hoffman (assistant wig & hair supervisor), Therese Ducey, Alison Wadsworth (hair stylists); Child Wrangler, Alissa Zulvergold; Rehearsal Musicians, Mark Mitchell (piano), Rich Rosenzweig (drums); Production Assistants, John Bantay, Andrew Zachary Cohen, John Murdock; Marketing, Type A Marketing, Anne Rippey, Nick Pramik, Nina Bergelson; Internet Marketing & Web Design, Art Meets Commerce; Advertising, SpotCo; Press, Richard Kornberg & Associates, Don Summa, Billy Zavelson, Tommy Wesely; Cast recording: PS Classics 1088

The Company

CAST Sunny **Guy Davis**; Dottie **Terri White**; Buzz Collins **William Youmans**; Sheriff **Brian Reddy**; Susan Mahoney **Alina Faye**; Finian McLonergan **Jim Norton**; Sharon McLonergan **Kate Baldwin**; Woody Mahoney **Cheyenne Jackson**; Henry **Christopher Borger**; Diana **Paige Simunovich**; Og **Christopher Fitzgerald**; Howard/Sharecropper Howard **Tyrick Wiltez Jones**; Senator Rawlins **David Schramm**; Black Geologist **Joe Aaron Reid**; White Geologist/Sharecropper Jack **Taylor Frey**; Deputy/Sharecropper Sam **Steve Schepis**; Bill Rawkins **Chuck Cooper**; Preacher/Second Gospeleer/Sharecropper Willie **James Stovall**; Mr. Shears/Sharecropper John **Tim Hartman**; Mr. Robust/Sharecropper Frank **Kevin Ligon**; First Gospeleer/Sharecropper George **Bernard Dotson**; Third Gospeleer/Sharecropper Eugene **Devin Richards**; *Sharecroppers:* Betty **Tanya Birl**; Meg **Meggie Cansler**; Melinda **Leslie Donna Flesner**; Melinda **Sara Jean Ford**; Rose **Lisa Gajda**; Suzanne **Kearran Giovanni**; Charlotte **Monica L. Patton**; Jesse **Joe Aaron Reid**; Dolores **Rashidra Scott**; Swings **Lauren Lim Jackson**, **Grasan Kingsberry**, **Elisa Van Duyne**; Partial Covers **Bernard Dotson**, **Taylor Frey**, **Kevin Ligon**, **Joe Aaron Reid**, **Steve Schepis**

UNDERSTUDIES Aaron Bantum (Diana, Henry), Bernard Dotson (Bill Rawkins), Leslie Donna Flesner (Susan Mahoney), Sara Jean Ford (Sharon McLonergan), Taylor Frey (Woody Mahoney), Lisa Gajda (Susan Mahoney), Tim Hartman (Finian McLonergan), Lauren Lim Jackson (Dottie), Grasan Kingsberry (Sunny), Kevin Ligon (Buzz Collins, Senator Rawkins, Sheriff), Devin Richards (Sunny), Steve Schepis (Og), Rashidra Scott (Dottie), Brian Sears (Buzz Collins, Og, Sheriff, Woody Mahoney), James Stovall (Bill Rawkins), Elisa Van Duyne (Sharon McLonergan), William Youmans (Finian McLonergan)

ORCHESTRA Rob Berman (Conductor); David Gursky (Associate Conductor/keyboards); Joshua Clayton (Assistant Conductor/keyboards); Suxanne Ornstein [Concert Mistress], Maura Giannini, Kristina Musser, Mineko Yajima (violins); Richard Brice, Shelley Holland-Moritz (violas); Roger Shell, Deborah Assael (cellos); Anna Reinersman (harp); Steven Kenyon, Dennis Anderson, James Ercole, Kenneth Adams, John Winder (woodwinds); Dave Stahl, Ken Rampton (trumpets), Wayne Goodman, Robert Suttmann (trombones), Nancy Billmann, Leise Anschuetz Ballou (French horns); John Beal (bass); Billy Miller (drums and percussion)

MUSICAL NUMBERS Overture, This Time of the Year, How Are Things in Glocca Morra?, Look to the Rainbow, Old Devil Moon, How Are Things in Glocca Morra? (reprise), Something Sort of Grandish, If This Isn't Love, Something Sort of Grandish (reprise), Necessity, That Great 'Come-and-Get-It' Day, When the Idle Poor Become the Idle Rich, Old Devil Moon (reprise), Dance of the Golden Crock, The Begat, Look to the Rainbow (reprise), When I'm Not Near the Girl I Love, Finale: How Are Things in Glocca Morra? (reprise)

2009–2010 AWARDS Drama Desk Award: Outstanding Featured Actor in a Musical (Christopher Fitzgerald)

SETTING The mythical state of Missitucky, 1940s. Revival of a musical presented in nine scenes in two acts. This version of the show originally played as part of New York City Center's *Encores!* March 26–29, 2009 with most of this company (see *Theatre World* Vol. 65, page 203). The original production opened at the 46th Street Theatre (now the Richard Rodgers) January 10, 1947–October 2, 1948 playing 725 performances (see *Theatre World* Vol. 3, page 71). City Center Light Opera Company revived the show twice: May 18–29, 1955 (see *Theatre World* Vol. 11, page 113) and April 27–May 8, 1960 (see *Theatre World* Vol. 16, page 106). The second revival transferred briefly to the 46th Street Theatre May 23–June 1, 1960.

SYNOPSIS With a sparkling score of beloved standards and a whimsical story that dances between romance, satire, and fairy tale, *Finian's Rainbow* is a musical theater treasure. *Finian's Rainbow* pits a charming Irish dreamer and his headstrong daughter against the host of complications that await them in their newly adopted land: a bigoted southern Senator, a credit crisis, a pesky leprechaun, and, of course, a complicated love affair that gives birth to some of the most witty, charming and heartfelt songs ever written for the stage.

Kate Baldwin and Cheyenne Jackson (photos by Joan Marcus)

Cheyenne Jackson and the Company

Terri White, Guy Davis, and the Company

Jim Norton and Cheyenne Jackson

Alina Faye anad Christopher Fitzgerald

Paige Simunovich, Christopher Fitzgerald, and Christopher Borger

James Stovall, Chuck Cooper, Bernard Dotson, and Devin Richards

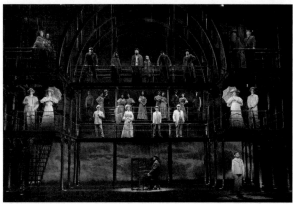

The Company

Christiane Noll, Ron Bohmer, Robert Petkoff, and Sarah Rosenthal

The Company

Ragtime

Neil Simon Theatre; First Preview: October 23, 2009; Opening Night: November 15, 2009; Closed January 10, 2010; 28 previews, 65 performances

Book by Terrence McNally, music by Stephen Flaherty, lyrics by Lynn Ahrens; Based on the novel *Ragtime* by E.L. Doctorow; Produced by Kevin McCollum, Roy Furman, Scott Delman, Roger Berlind, Max Cooper, Tom/Kirdahy/Devlin Elliott, Jeffrey A. Sine, Stephanie McClelland, Roy Miller, Lams Productions, Jana Robbins, Sharon Karmazin, Eric Falkenstein/Morris Berchard, RialtoGals Productions, Independent Producers Network, Held-Haffner Productions, HRH Foundation, Emanuel Azenberg, in association with The John F. Kennedy Center for the Performing Arts (Michael Kaiser, President; Max Woodward, Vice President); Director/Choreography, Marcia Milgrom Dodge; Music Director, James Moore; Orchestrations, William David Brohn; Sets, Derek McLane; Costumes, Santo Loquasto; Lighting, Donald Holder; Sound, Acme Sound Partners; Hair & Wigs, Edward J. Wilson; Vocal Arrangements, Stephen Flaherty; Music Coordinator, John Miller; Casting, Laura Stanczyk Casting; Marketing, Scott A. Moore; Associate Director/Choreographer & Dance Captain, Josh Walden; General Manager, John S. Corker, Lizbeth Cone; Technical Supervisor, Brian Lynch; Production Supervisor, Peter Lawrence; Company Manager, Roeya Banuazizi; Stage Manager, Karen Moore; Assistant Stage Manager, Jim Woolley; Associate Conductor, Jamie Schmidt; Assistant Company Manager, Michael Bolgar; Fight Captain, Aaron Galligan-Stierle; Assistant Dance Captain, Jim Weaver; Assistant to the Director, Josie Bray; Casting Dance Assistant, Anne Cooley-Presley; Associate Design: Shoko Kambara (set), Matthew Pachtman (costumes), Mitchell Bloom (original Broadway costumes), Caroline Chao, Jeanne Koenig (lighting), Giovanna Calabretta (hair & wigs); Assistant Design: Erica Hemminger, Brett Banakis (set), Sophia Lidz (costumes), Michael Jones, Karen Spahn (lighting), Alexander Ritter (sound), Susan Corrado (hair & wigs); Costume Assistant, Noah Marin; Moving Light Programmer, Elfin Lighting/Richard Tyndall; Technical Consultant, Douglas Grekin; Production Crew: Chris Kluth (production carpenter), Justin Garvey (flyman), Michael Shepp (automation), Keith Buchanan (production electrician), Patrick Harrington (follow spot/moving lights), John Dory (sound engineer), Greg Freedman (advance sound engineer), Ron Groomes (production propmaster), Michael D. Hannah (wardrobe supervisor), Christel Murdock (assistant wardrobe supervisor), Edward J. Wilson (hair supervisor), Steven Kirkham (assistant hair supervisor), Alicia Aballi, Christina Ainge, Samanthe Burrow, Alexa K. Burt, Anita Ali Davis, Jackie S. Freeman, Rachael Garrett, Bobby Gerard, Rosemary Keough, Yleana Nunez, Jerome Parker, Danny Paul, Kyle Stewart, Ron Tagert, Arlene Watson, Cheryl Lyn Widner (dressers); Tutor, Priscilla Richardson; Child Guardian, John Mara; Dialect Coach, Anita Maynard-Losh; Rehearsal Pianist, Sue Anschutz; Assistant to Mr. Miller, Nichole Jennino; Music Preparation, Holly Carroll; Keyboard Programming, Synthlink LLC/Jim Harp; Music Assistants, Shawn James Bolduc, Hannah Kohl; Production Assistants, Lisa Chernoff, Bryan Rountree; Assistant to Mr. McCollum, Caitlyn Thomson; Assistant to Mr. Corker, Kim Marie Vasquez; Advertising, SpotCo; Marketing Associate, Joshua Lee Poole; Press, Boneau/Bryan-Brown, Chris Boneau, Joe Perrotta, Michael Strassheim

CAST The Little Boy **Christopher Cox**; Father **Ron Bohmer**; Mother **Christiane Noll**; Mother's Younger Brother **Bobby Steggert**; Grandfather **Dan Manning**; Coalhouse Walker Jr. **Quentin Earl Darrington**; Sarah **Stephanie Umoh**; Booker T. Washington **Eric Jordan Young**; Tateh **Robert Petkoff**; The Little Girl **Sarah Rosenthal**; Harry Houdini **Jonathan Hammond**; J.P. Morgan/Admiral Peary/Train Conductor **Michael X. Martin**; Henry Ford/Trolley Conductor **Aaron Galligan-Stierle**; Emma Goldman **Donna Migliaccio**; Evelyn Nesbit **Savannah Wise**; Matthew Henson **Terence Archie**; Judge **Dan Manning**; Stanford White/Policeman #2/Charles S. Whitman **Mike McGowan**; Harry K. Thaw, Policeman #1 **Josh Walden**; Kathleen, Welfare Official **Jennifer Evans**; "Till We Reach That Day" Soloist/Baron's Assistant **Bryonha Parham**; Willie Conklin/Child Buyer **Mark Aldrich**; Brigit **Tracy Lynn Olivera**; Coalhouse Walker III **Jayden Brockington** or **Kylil Christopher Williams**; New Rochelle Citizens, Harlem Men and Women,

Immigrants, Vaudevillians and Stagehands, Reporters, Ford Workers, Firemen, Millworkers, Strikers, Militia, Bureaucrats and Lawyers, Coalhouse Gang, Spectators, Hotel Staff, Vacationers, Bathing Beauties and Camera Crew **Mark Aldrich, Sumayya Ali, Terence Archie, Corey Bradley, Jennifer Evans, Aaron Galligan-Stierle, Jonathan Hammond, Carly Hughes, Valisia Lekae, Dan Manning, Michael X. Martin, Mike McGowan, Donna Migliaccio, Tracy Lynn Olivera, Bryonha Parham, Mamie Parris, Nicole Powell, Arbender J. Robinson, Benjamin Schrader, Wallace Smith, Josh Walden, Catherine Walker, Savannah Wise, Eric Jordan Young;** Swings **Carey Rebecca Brown, Lisa Karlin, James Moye, Jim Weaver**

UNDERSTUDIES Mike McGowan (Father, Tateh), James Moye (Father), Terence Archie (Coalhouse Walker Jr.), Wallace Smith (Coalhouse Walker Jr.), Eric Jordan Young (Coalhouse Walker Jr.), Mamie Parris (Mother), Catherine Walker (Mother), Jonathan Hammond (Tateh), Benjamin Schrader (Younger Brother), Josh Walden (Younger Brother), Carly Hughes (Sarah), Valisia Lakae (Sarah), Benjamin Cook (Little Boy), Kaylie Rubinaccio (Little Girl)

ORCHESTRA James Moore (Conductor); Jamie Schmidt (Associate Conductor/keyboards); Sue Anschutz (Assistant Conductor/keyboards);Rick Dolan [Concert Master], Elizabeth Lim-Dutton, Cenovia Cummins, Ashley Horn, Una Tone, Kiku Enomoto; (violins); Maxine Roach, Debra Shufelt-Dine (violas); Laura Bontrager, Sarah Hewitt-Roth (celli); Jeff Cooper (bass); Barbara Biggers (harp); Katherine Fink, Lynne Cohen, Jonathan Levine, Todd Groves (woodwinds); Timothy Schadt, Daniel Urness (trumpets); Patrick Pridemore, Will DeVos (French horns); Alan Ferber, Dan Levine (trombones); Marcus Rojas (tuba); Charles Descarfino (percussion); Rich Rosenzweig (drums); Greg Utzig (guitar)

MUSICAL NUMBERS Ragtime; Goodbye, My Love; Journey On; The Crime of the Century; What Kind of Woman; A Shtetl Iz Amereke; Success; Getting' Ready Rag; Henry Ford; Nothing Like the City; Your Daddy's Son; New Music; The Wheels of a Dream; The Night That Goldman Spoke at Union Sqauare; Gliding; Justice; President; Till We Reach That Day; Entr'acte; Coalhouse's Soliloquy; Coalhouse Demands; What a Game!; Atlantic City; New Music (reprise); Atlantic City, Part II; Sarah Brown Eyes; He Wanted to Say; Back to Before; Look What You've Done; Make Them Hear You; Ragtime/The Wheels of a Dream (reprise)

2009–2010 AWARDS Drama Desk Award: Outstanding Sound Design in a Musical (Acme Sound Partners); **Theatre World Award:** Stephanie Umoh

SETTING New York City, New Rochelle, Ellis Island, Atlantic City, and Lawrence, Massachusetts; the early 1900s. Revival of a musical presented in two acts with prologue, eighteen scenes, and epilogue. This version of the show was previously presented at the Kennedy Center April 18–May 17, 2009 with most of this cast and production team. World premiere in Toronto at the Ford Center for the Performing Arts, December 8, 1996. After a pre-Broadway tryout in Los Angeles, the show had its New York premiere at the newly renovated Ford Center for the Performing Arts (now the Hilton Theatre) January 18, 1998–January 16, 2000, playing 834 performances (see *Theatre World* Vol. 54, page 28).

SYNOPSIS At the dawn of the century, everything is changing…and anything is possible. Based on Doctorow's celebrated epic novel and set in the volatile melting pot of turn-of-the-century New York, *Ragtime* weaves together three distinctly American tales: that of a stifled upper-class wife, a determined Jewish immigrant and a daring young Harlem musician– united by their courage, compassion and belief in the promise of the future. Their personal journeys come alive as historic figures offer guidance and diversion – among them escape artist Harry Houdini, auto tycoon Henry Ford, educator Booker T. Washington and infamous entertainer Evelyn Nesbit. Together, their stories celebrate the struggle between tradition and independence all in pursuit of the American dream.

Stephanie Umoh

The Company (photos by Joan Marcus)

In the Next Room or the vibrator play

Lyceum Theatre; First Preview: October 22, 2009; Opening Night: November 19, 2009; Closed January 10, 2010; 31 previews, 60 performances

Written by Sarah Ruhl; Produced by Lincoln Center Theater (André Bishop, Artistic Director; Bernard Gersten, Executive Producer); Director, Les Waters; Sets, Annie Smart; Costumes, David Zinn; Lighting, Russell H. Champa; Sound, Bray Poor; Music, Jonathan Bell; Production Stage Manager, Roy Harris; Wigs & Hair, Paul Huntley; Casting, Daniel Swee; Director of Development, Hattie K. Jutagir; Director of Marketing, Linda Mason Ross; General Manager, Adam Siegel; Production Manager, Jeff Hamlin; Director of Finance, David S. Brown; Director of Education, Kati Koerner; Artistic Directors of Lincoln Center, Graciela Daniele, Nicholas Hytner, Jack O'Brien, Susan Stroman, Daniel Sullivan; Resident Director, Bartlett Sher; Dramaturg/LCT Directors Lab, Anne Cattaneo; Musical Theatre Associate Producer, Ira Weitzman; Director of LCT3, Paige Evans; Associate General Manager, Jessica Niebanck; Associate Production Manager, Paul Smithyman; Company Manager, Matthew Markoff; Assistant Company Manager, Daniel Hoyos; Assistant Director, Sarah Rasmussen; Assistant Stage Manager, Denise Yaney; Makeup, Jon Carter; Props, Susan Barras; Technical Supervisors, William Nagle, Patrick Merryman; Assistant Design: Andrew Kaufman (set), Jacob Climer (costumes), Justin Partier (lighting), Charles Coes (sound); Production Crew: John Weingart (production carpenter), David Karlson (production electrician), Mark Dignam (production propertyman), Wallace Flores (production soundman), Moira MacGregor-Conrad (wardrobe supervisor), Cindy Demand (hair supervisor), Erick Medinilla, Tree Sarvay (dressers), Vanessa Poggioli (production assistant); Poster Art, James McMullan; Advertising, Serino Coyne Inc.; Press, Philip Rinaldi, Barbara Carroll

CAST Mrs. Givings **Laura Benanti**; Dr. Givings **Michael Cerveris**; Annie **Wendy Rich Stetson**; Mr. Daldry **Thomas Jay Ryan**; Mrs. Daldry **Maria Dizzia**; Elizabeth **Quincy Tyler Bernstine**; Leo Irving **Chandler Williams**

UNDERSTUDIES Nathan Darrow (Dr. Givings, Leo Irving), Emily Dorsch (Annie, Mrs. Daldry), Donnetta Lavinia Grays (Elizabeth), Paul Niebanck (Dr. Givings, Mr. Daldry), Erica Sullivan (Annie, Mrs. Givings)

SETTING Place: A prosperous spa town outside of New York City, perhaps Saratoga Springs. Place: The dawn of the age of electricity, and after the Civil War; circa 1880s. New York premiere of a new play presented in two acts. Commissioned and world premiere at Berkeley Repertory Theatre (Tony Taccone, Artistic Director; Susan Medak, Managing Director) January 30–March 15, 2009 (see *Theatre World* Vol. 65, page 312).

SYNOPSIS *In the Next Room or the vibrator play* is a comedy about marriage, intimacy and electricity. Set at the dawn of the age of electricity and based on the bizarre historical fact that doctors used vibrators to treat "hysterical" women (and some men), the play centers on a doctor and his wife and how his new therapy affects their entire household.

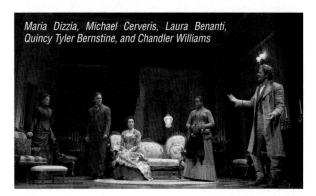
Maria Dizzia, Michael Cerveris, Laura Benanti, Quincy Tyler Bernstine, and Chandler Williams

Chandler Williams and Laura Benanti (photos by Joan Marcus)

Maria Dizzia, Thomas Jay Ryan, Wendy Rich Stetson, and Michael Cerveris

Quincy Tyler Bernstine and Laura Benanti

Irving Berlin's **White Christmas**

Marquis Theatre; First Preview: November 13, 2009; Opening Night: November 22, 2009; Closed January 3, 2010; 12 previews, 52 performances

Music and lyrics by Irving Berlin, book by David Ives and Paul Blake; based upon the Paramount Pictures film written for the screen by Norman Krasna, Norman Panama, and Melvin Frank; Produced by Kevin McCollum, John Gore, Thomas B. McGrath, Paul Blake, The Producing Office (Kevin McCollum, Jeffrey Seller, John S. Corker, Debra Nir, Scott A. Moore, Caitlyn Thomson), Dan Markley, Sonny Everett, Broadway Across America, in association with Paramount Pictures; Director, Walter Bobbie; Choreography, Randy Skinner; Music Supervisor, Rob Berman; Sets, Anna Louizos; Costumes, Carrie Robbins; Lighting, Ken Billington; Sound, Acme Sound Partners; Orchestrations, Larry Blank; Vocal and Dance Arrangements, Bruce Pomahac; Music Coordinator, Seymour Red Press; Music Director, Steven Freeman; Technical Supervisor, Brian Lynch; Production Stage Manager, Peter Wolf; Marketing, Scott A. Moore; Casting, Jay Binder, Nikole Vallins; General Management, John S. Corker, Barbara Crompton; Associate Director, Marc Bruni; Associate Choreographer/Dance Captain, Kelli Barclay; Associate Producers, Richard A. Smith, Douglas L. Meyer, and James D. Stern; Company Manager, Barbara Crompton; Stage Manager, Jay McLeod; Associate Company Manager, Andrew Jones; Assistant Stage Manager, Jim Athens; Associate Music Director, Matthew Perri; Additional Orchestrations, Peter Myers; Assistant Director, David Ruttura; Assistant Choreographer/Assistant Dance Captain, Mary Giattino; Principle Wigs, Paul Huntley; Ensemble Wigs, Howard Leonard; Associate Design: Todd Potter (sets), Ed McCarthy & Jim Milkey (lighting), Jason Badger (automated lighting programmer), Nick Borisjuk (sound), Lee Austin (costumes); Assistant Design: Jonathan Spencer (set), Bridget O'Connor (sound); Production Crew: Lehan Sullivan (production carpenter), Joe Valentino (head carpenter), Jeremy Palmer (flyman), Robert Valli (automation), Chris Doornbos (deck automation), Manuel Becker (production electrician), Craig Caccamise (head electrician), Jason Wilkosz (assistant electricians), Chris Robinson (spot light operator), Dan Robillard (production sound), Brad Gyorgak (sound engineer), Elizabeth Coleman (assistant sound engineer), George Wagner (production props master), Jacob White (prop master), Lee Austin (production wardrobe supervisor), Jessica Worsnop (wardrobe supervisor), Cherie Cunningham (assistant wardrobe), Elisa Acevedo (hair supervisor), Nathaniel Hathaway (assistant hair); Assistant to Mr. McCollum Mr. Seller, Caitlyn Thomson; Assistant to Mr. Blake, Michael Bosner; Assistant to General Manager, Kim Marie Vasquez; Marketing Associate, Joshua Lee Poole; Production Assistants, Danny Sharron, Danielle Teague-Daniels; Music Preparation, Chelsea Music Service/Paul Holderbaum; Synthesizer Programmer, Bruce Samuels; Rehearsal Pianists, Andrew Graham & Paul Masse; Advertising, SpotCo; Press, Boneau/Bryan-Brown, Chris Boneau, Joe Perrotta, Kelly Guiod; Show recording: Sh-K-Boom/Ghostlight Records 7915581225-2

CAST Ralph Sheldrake **Peter Reardon**; Bob Wallace **James Clow**; Phil Davis **Tony Yazbeck**; General Henry Waverly **David Ogden Stiers**; Ed Sullivan Announcer **Remy Auberjonois**; Rita **Kiira Schmidt**; Rhoda **Beth Johnson Nicely**; Tessie **Leah Horowitz**; Betty Haynes **Melissa Errico**; Judy Haynes **Mara Davi**; Jimmy **Matthew LaBanca**; Quintet **Cliff Bemis, Leah Horowitz, Drew Humphrey, Joseph Medeiros, Anna Aimee White**; Mr. Snoring Man/Ezekiel Foster **Cliff Bemis**; Mrs. Snoring Man/Sheldrake's Secretary **Denise Nolin**; Train Conductor **Drew Humphrey**; Martha Watson **Ruth Williamson**; Susan Waverly **Madeleine Rose Yen**; Mike Nulty/Regency Room Announcer **Remy Auberjonois**; "Let Me Sing" Dancers/Regency Room Dancers **Chad Harlow, Drew Humphrey, Ryan Worsing**; "Let Me Sing" Dancer **Joseph Medeiros**; Ensemble **Abby Church, Sara Edwards, Chad Harlow, Leah Horowitz, Drew Humphrey, Matthew LaBanca, Joseph Medeiros, Taryn Molnar, Beth Johnson Nicely, Denise Nolin, Dennis O'Bannion, Con O'Shea-Creal, Kristyn Pope, Kiira Schmidt, Kelly Sheehan, Anna Aimee White, Ryan Worsing, Richard Riaz Yoder**; Swings **Kelli Barclay, Mary Giattino, Matthew J. Kilgore, Jason Luks**

UNDERSTUDIES Peter Reardon (Bob Wallace), Leah Horowitz (Betty Haynes), Drew Humphrey (Phil Davis), Anna Aimee White (Judy Haynes), Cliff Bemis (General Waverly), Tori Heinlein (Susan Waverly), Remy Auberjonois (Ralph Sheldrake), Denise Nolin (Martha Watson), Drew Humphrey (Mr. Snoring Man/Ezekiel Foster), Chad Harlow (Mike McNulty/Ed Sullivan Announcer)

ORCHESTRA Steven Freeman (Conductor); Matthew Perri (Associate Conductor/keyboards); Marilyn Reynolds (violin); Dave Trigg, Anthony Gorruso, Mike Ponella (trumpets); Micah Young (keyboards); Danny Miller (celli); Dave Pietro, Harry Hassell, Aaron Heick, Scott Shachter, Eugene Scholtens (woodwinds); Larry Farrell, Clint Sharman, Jeff Nelson (trombones); David Byrd-Marrow (French horn); Bill Hayes (percussion); Lou Bruno (bass); Eric Halvorson (drums)

MUSICAL NUMBERS Overture, Happy Holiday, White Christmas, Let Yourself Go, Love and the Weather, Sisters, The Best Things Happen While You're Dancing, Snow, What Can You Do With a General?, Let Me Sing and I'm Happy, Count Your Blessings Instead of Sheep, Blue Skies, Entr'acte, I Love a Piano, Falling Out of Love Can Be Fun, Sisters (reprise), Love You Didn't Do Right By Me/How Deep Is the Ocean, We'll Follow the Old Man, Let Me Sing and I'm Happy (reprise), How Deep Is the Ocean (reprise), We'll Follow the Old Man (reprise), White Christmas (reprise), Finale: I've Got My Love to Keep Me Warm

SETTING An army camp in Europe, Christmas Eve, 1944; New York City and the Columbia Inn in Vermont; December, 1954. Revival of a musical presented in seventeen scenes in two acts. World premiere at The Muny (St. Louis) in 2000. The Broadway production team launched this version of the show in San Francisco (Curran Theatre) in 2004. In the fall of 2005 three major productions opened simultaneously in Boston (Wang Theatre), Los Angeles (Pantages Theatre), and again in San Francisco (Orpheum Theatre). In 2006 the production was remounted at the Ordway Theatre in Minneapolis, and also played major engagements in Detroit and Toronto. In addition, the show was licensed and produced at numerous regional and dinner theatres in 2007, prior to its Broadway debut in 2008 at the Marquis Theatre (see *Theatre World* Vol. 65, page 44).

SYNOPSIS Based on the holiday favorite classic 1954 film starring Bing Crosby, Danny Kaye, Rosemary Clooney, and Vera Ellen, *Irving Berlin's White Christmas* tells the story of two showbiz buddies who put on a show in a picturesque Vermont inn, and find their perfect mates — a sister act, no less — in the bargain. The show features some of Berlin's most famous tunes.

James Clow, Melissa Errico, Tony Yazbeck, and Mara Davi (photos by Joan Marcus)

Fela!

Eugene O'Neill Theatre; First Preview: October 19, 2009; Opening Night: November 23, 2009; 34 previews, 215 performances as of May 31, 2010

Book by Jim Lewis & Bill T. Jones, music and lyrics by Fela Anikulapo-Kuti, book, additional lyrics by Jim Lewis, additional music by Aaron Johnson & Jordan McLean; Based on the life of Fela Anikulapo; Conceived by Bill T. Jones, Jim Lewis, & Stephen Hendel; Produced by Shawn "Jay-Z" Carter, Will Smith and Jada Pinkett Smith, Ruth & Stephen Hendel, Roy Gabay, Sony Pictures Entertainment, Edward Tyler Nahem, Salva Smolokowski, Chip Meyrelles/Ken Greiner, Douglas G. Smith, Steve Semlitz/Cathy Glaser, Daryl Roth/True Love Productions, Susan Dietz/Mort Swinsky, Knitting Factory Entertainment; Director/Choreographer, Bill T. Jones; Music Director & Supervision/Orchestrations/Arrangements, Aaron Johnson; Sets/Costumes, Marina Draghici; Lighting, Robert Wierzel; Sound, Robert Kaplowitz; Projections, Peter Nigrini; Wigs, Hair, & Makeup, Cookie Jordan; Production Stage Manager, Jon Goldman; Casting, Mungioli Theatricals, Arnold J. Mungioli; Advertising & New Media Services, Art Meets Commerce; Marketing, HHC Marketing–Hugh Hysell, Walk Tall Girl Productions–Marcia Pendleton; Technical Supervision, Hudson Theatrical Associates, Neil A. Mazzella; Associate Technical Supervision, Jay Janicki, John Tiggeloven, Aduro Productions, Caitlin McInerney; General Manager, Roy Gabay; Music Coordinator, Michael Keller; Associate Producer, Ahmir "Questlove" Thompson; Associate Musical Director & Arranger, Jordan McLean; Music Consultant, Antibalas; Associate Director, Niegel Smith; Associate Choreographer, Maija Garcia; Company Management, Daniel Kuney, Chris Aniello; Stage Manager, Linda Marvel; Assistant Stage Manager, Hilary Austin; Associate Design: Timothy R. Mackabee, Wilson Chin, Katheryn Monthei (set), Amy Clark (costumes), Paul Hackenmueller (lighting), Jessica Paz (sound); Original Mural/Scenic Art, IRLO, Omar and Nuclear Fairy; Assistant Design: Mike Floyd (costumes), G. Benjamin Swope (lighting), John Emmett O'Brien (sound); Assistant to Lighting Designer, Xavier Pierce; Associate Projection Designers, C. Andrew Bauer (content), Dan Scully (system); Additional Projection Content and Editing, Mirit Tal; Props Master, Kathy Fabian/Propstar; Associate Props, Jennifer Breen, Sid King; Props Artisans, Sarah Bird, Corey Shipler, Hanna Davis, Martin Izquierdo Studio, Arianna Zindler, Emily Walsh; Flame Treatment, Turning Star Inc.; Production Crew: Benjamin Keightley (projection programmer), Greg Peeler (production projectionist), Jordan Gable (production carpenter), Kevin Mar (flyman), Mark Diaz, Todd Frank, Jordan Gable (automation operators), Timothy F. Rogers (automated lighting programmer), Todd D'Aiuto (production electrician), Robert Hale (assistant electrician/board operator), Damian Caza-Cleypool (head spot op), James Gardener (spot op), Reid Hall, Shannon Slayton (sound engineers), Sue Stepnik (wardrobe supervisor), Heather Wright (hair supervisor), Tonya Bodsin (hair assistant), Sue Cerceo, Bobby Clifton, Cathy Cline, Mindy Eng, Alessandro Ferdico, Susie Ghebresillassie, Nesreen Mahmoud (dressers), Christopher Beck (house props), Ken Keneally (head props); Interns: Abby Kong (costumes), Ted Pallas (sound), Barbara Samuels (projections); General Management Staff, Chris Aniello, Bobby Driggers, Daniel Kuney, Jennifer Pluff, Mandy Tate; Casting Associates, Alex Hanna, Melanie Lockyer; Production Assistants, Melanie Ganim, Leslie Grisdale, Colleen M. Sherry; Artistic Assistant, Radha Blank; Press, Richard Kornberg & Associates, Billy Zavelson, Don Summa, Tommy Wesely; Off-Broadway Cast recording: Knitting Factory 1103

CAST Fela Anikulapo-Kuti **Kevin Mambo** or **Sahr Ngaujah**; Funmilayo Anikulapo-Kuti **Lillias White**; Sandra Isadore **Saycon Sengbloh**; Ismael/Geraldo Piño/Orisha/Ensemble **Ismael Kouyaté**; J.K. Brahman (Tap Dancer)/Egungun/Ensemble **Gelan Lambert**; Ensemble **Corey Baker, Hettie Barnhill, Lauren De Veaux, Nicole Chantal de Weever, Elasea Douglas, Rujeko Dumbutshena, Talu Green, Shaneeka Harrell, Abena Koomson, Gelan Lambert, Shakira Marshall, Afi McClendon, Adesola Osakalumi, Jeffrey Page, Jill M. Vallery, Daniel Soto, Iris Wilson, Aimee Graham Wodobode**; Swings **Catherine Foster, Chanon Judson, Farai M. Malianga, J.L. Williams**

UNDERSTUDIES Adesola Osakalumi (Fela), Abena Koomson (Funmilayo), Elasea Douglas (Sandra)

BAND Aaron Johnson (Conductor/trombone), Greg Gonzalez (Assistant Conductor/drums/percussion), Jordan McLean (trumpet), Jeremy Wilms (bass/keyboards/percussion), Oren Bloedow (guitar/percussion), Ricardo Quinones (guitar/percussion), Yoshihiro Takemasa (percussion), Alex Harding (baritone saxophone/percussion), Stuart Bogie (tenor saxophone/percussion/featured saxophone soloist), Dylan Fusillo (percussion)

MUSICAL NUMBERS Everything Scatter, Iba Orisa, Hymn, Medzi Medzi, Mr. Syms, Manteca, I Got the Feeling, Originality/Yellow Fever, Trouble Sleep, Teacher Don't Teach Me Nonsense, Lover, Upside Down, Expensive Shit, Pipeline/I.T.T. (International Thief Thief), Kere Kay, Water No Get Enemy, Egbe Mio, Zombie, Trouble Sleep (reprise), Na Poi, Sorrow Tears and Blood, Iba Orisa/Shakara, Rain, Coffin for Head of State, Kere Kay (reprise)

2009–2010 AWARDS Tony Awards: Best Choreography (Bill T. Jones), Best Costume Design of a Musical (Marina Draghici), Best Sound Design of a Musical (Robert Kaplowitz); **Theatre World Award:** Sahr Ngaujah

SETTING Fela's final concert at the Shrine in Lagos, Nigeria; the summer of 1978, six months after the death of Funmilayo, Fela's mother. Transfer of the Off-Broadway musical presented in two acts. The show had its world premiere at 37 Arts Theatre B August 5–October 5, 2008 (see *Theatre World* Vol. 65, page 146).

SYNOPSIS His story inspired a nation. His music inspires the world. *Fela!* tells the true story of the legendary Nigerian musician Fela Kuti, whose soulful Afrobeat rhythms ignited a generation. Motivated by his mother, a civil rights champion, he defied a corrupt and oppressive military government and devoted his life and music to the struggle for freedom and human dignity. *Fela!* is a triumphant tale of courage, passion, and love, featuring Fela Kuti's captivating music (a blend of jazz, funk and African rhythm and harmonies) and Bill T. Jones's imaginative staging.

Lillias White and Kevin Mambo

Kevin Mambo and the Company

The Company (photos by Monique Carboni)

Kevin Mambo

Lauren De Veux, Sahr Ngaujah, and Hettie Barnhill

Sahr Ngaujah

Sahr Ngaujah and the Company

James Spader, Kerry Washington, and Richard Thomas

James Spader (photos by Robert J. Saferstein)

Race

Barrymore Theatre; First Preview: November 17, 2009; Opening Night: December 6, 2009; 23 previews, 201 performances as of May 31, 2010

Written and Directed by David Mamet; Produced by Jeffrey Richards, Jerry Frankel, Jam Theatricals, JK Productions, Peggy Hill & Nicholas Quinn Rosenkranz, Scott M. Delman, Terry Allen Kramer/James L. Nederlander, Mort Swinsky/Joseph Deitch, Bat-Barry Productions, Ronald Frankel, James Fuld Jr., Kathleen K. Johnson, Terry Schnuck, The Weinstein Company, Marc Frankel, Jay & Cindy Gutterman/Stewart Mercer; Associate Producer, Jeremy Scott Blaustein; Set, Santo Loquasto; Costumes, Tom Broecker; Lighting, Brian MacDevitt; Production Stage Manager, Matthew Silver; Casting, Telsey + Company; Technical Supervision, Hudson Theatrical Associates; Company Manager, Bruce Klinger; General Management, Richards/Climan Inc. (David R. Richards and Tamar Haimes); West Coast Casting, Sharon Bialy & Sherry Thomas; Stage Manager, Jillian M. Oliver; Technical Supervisor, Neil A. Mazzella/Hudson Theatrical Associates; Assistant to the Director, Justin Fair; Associate Design, Jenny Sawyers (set), David Withrow (costumes), Driscoll Otto (lighting); Associate General Manager, Michael Sag; General Management Associate, Jeromy Smith; General Management Assistant, Cesar Hawas; Production Assistant, John Ferry; Production Crew: Don Oberpriller (production carpenter), Jimmy Maloney (production electrician), Kathy Fabian/Propstar (production props), Rob Bevenger (wardrobe supervisor), Sandy Binion (dresser), Carrie Mossman (associate props coordinator), Tim Ferro, Sarah Bird (props assistants); Assistant to Mr. Mamet, Pam Susemiehl; Assistant to Mr. Traxler, Brandi Preston; Advertising, Serino Coyne Inc; Press, Jeffrey Richards Associates, Irene Gandy, Alana Karpoff, Elon Rutberg, Diana Rissetto

CAST Jack Lawson **James Spader**; Henry Brown **David Alan Grier**; Susan **Kerry Washington**; Charles Strickland **Richard Thomas**

UNDERSTUDIES Jordan Lage (Jack Lawson, Charles Strickland), Ray Anthony Thomas (Henry Brown), Afton C. Williamson (Susan)

SETTING The law office of Jack Lawson and Henry Brown. World premiere of a new play presented in two acts.

SYNOPSIS *Race*, a play about lies, centers on three attorneys, two black and one white, who are offered a chance to defend a white man charged with a crime against a black woman.

David Alan Grier and James Spader

A Little Night Music

Walter Kerr Theatre; First Preview: November 24, 2009; Opening Night: December 13, 2009; 20 previews, 193 performances as of May 31, 2010

Music and lyrics by Stephen Sondheim, book by Hugh Wheeler; Suggested by a film by Ingmar Bergman; Originally produced and directed on Broadway by Harold Prince; Produced by Tom Viertel, Steven Baruch, Marc Routh, Richard Frankel, The Menier Chocolate Factory, Roger Berlind, David Babani, Sonia Friedman Productions, Andrew Fell, Daryl Roth/Jane Bergère, Harvey Weinstein/ Raise the Roof 3, Beverly Bartner/Dancap Productions Inc., Nica Burns/Max Weitzenhoffer, Erik Falkenstein/Anna Czekaj, Jerry Frankel/Ronald Frankel, James D. Stern/Douglas L. Meyer; Director, Trevor Nunn; Choreography, Lynne Page; Music Supervision, Caroline Humphris; Sets & Costumes, David Farley; Lighting, Hartley T.A. Kemp; Sound, Dan Moses Schreier, Gareth Owen; Wigs & Hair, Paul Huntley; Makeup, Angelina Avallone; Casting, Tara Rubin Casting; Production Stage Manager, Ira Mont; Associate Director, Seth Sklar-Heyn; Associate Choreographer, Scott Taylor; Music Direction, Tom Murray; Orchestrations, Jason Carr; Music Coordinator, John Miller; General Management, Frankel Green Theatrical Management, Richard Frankel, Laura Green, Joe Watson, Leslie Ledbetter; Technical Supervision, Aurora Productions (Gene O'Donovan, Ben Heller, Rachel Sherbill, Jarid Sumner, Melissa Mazdra, Amy Merlino Coey, Amanda Raymond, Graham Forden, Liza Luxenberg); Associate Producers, Broadway Across America, Dan Frishwasser, Dan Frishwasser, Jam Theatricals, Richard Winkler; Company Manager, Sammy Ledbetter; Associate Company Manager, Grant A. Rice; Stage Manager, Julia P. Jones; Assistant Stage Manager/ Dance Captain, Mary MacLeod; U.K. Stage Management Consultant, Ciara Fanning; Associate Design: Josh Zangen (U.K. set), Tracy Christensen (U.S. costumes), Poppy Hall (U.K. costumes), Vivien Leone (lighting), David Bullard (sound); Assistant Design: Machiko Hombu, Cara Newman (U.K. set), Ellan Perry (U.K. costumes), Ben Hagen (lighting); U.K. Set Intern, Vicki Stevenson; U.K Costume Supervisor, Binnie Bowerman; Assistant to the Wig Designer, Giovanna Calabretta; Company Management Assistant, Travis Ferguson; Dialect Coach, Deborah Hecht; Production Crew: Tony Menditto (head carpenter), Scott Anderson (advance electrician), Justin McClintock (head electrician), Michael Hill (moving light programmer), Stephen Allain (assistant electrician), Francis Elers (head sound engineer), William Allen Sanders (assistant sound engineer), Vera Pizzarelli (head props), Peter Sarafin (props shopper), Douglas Petitjean (wardrobe supervisor), Deirdre LaBarre (assistant wardrobe supervisor), Lolly Totero (Ms. Zeta-Jones's dresser), Maeve Fiona Butler (Ms. Lansbury's dresser), Adam Giradet, Tanya Guercy-Blue, John Rinaldi, Mark Trezza (dressers), Ruth Carsch (hair & wig supervisor), Enrique Vega (assistant hair & wig supervisor); Production Assistant, Stuart Shefter; Guardian, Rachel Maier; Music Consultant, Kristen Blodgette; Music Preparation, Emily Grishman (U.S.), Colin Rae (U.K.); Synthesizer Programmer, Bruce Samuels; Music Copying, Katherine Edmonds; Rehearsal Pianists, Paul Staroba, Mathew Eisenstein; Assistant to Mr. Sondheim, Steven Clar; Assistants to the Producers, Tania Senewiratne (Mr. Viertel), Sonja Soper (Mr. Baruch), Katie Adams (Mr. Routh), Jeffrey Hillock (Mr. Berlind); Advertising, Serino Coyne Inc., Sandy Block, Scott Johnson, Robert Jones; Online Advertising & Marketing, Art Meets Commerce; Press, Boneau/Bryan-Brown, Chris Boneau, Heath Schwartz, Michael Strassheim; Cast recording: PS Classics 523488

CAST Henrik Egerman **Hunter Ryan Herdlicka**; Mr. Lindquist **Stephen R. Buntrock**; Mrs. Nordstrom **Jayne Paterson**; Mrs. Anderssen **Marissa McGowan**; Mr. Erlanson **Kevin David Thomas**; Mrs. Segstrom **Betsy Morgan**; Fredrika Armfeldt **Katherine Leigh Doherty** (Tues., Wed. mat, Fri., Sat. mat); **Keaton Whittaker** (Wed. eve., Thurs., Sat. eve., Sun.); Madame Armfeldt **Angela Lansbury**; Frid **Bradley Dean**; Anne Egerman **Ramona Mallory**; Petra **Leigh Ann Larkin**; Desirée Armfeldt **Catherine Zeta-Jones**; Fredrik Egerman **Alexander Hanson**; Count Carl-Magnus Malcolm **Aaron Lazar**; Countess Charlotte Malcolm **Erin Davie**; Swings **Karen Murphy, Erin Stewart, Kevin Vortmann**

UNDERSTUDIES Stephen R. Buntrock (Fredrik Egerman, Frid), Bradley Dean (Count Carl-Magnus Malcolm), Marissa McGowan (Anne Egerman, Petra), Betsy Morgan (Countess Charlotte Malcolm), Karen Murphy (Madame Armfeldt), Jayne Paterson (Desiree Armfeldt), Erin Stewart (Anne Egerman, Countess Charlotte Malcolm, Petra), Kevin David Thomas (Henrik Egerman), Kevin Vortmann (Frid)

ORCHESTRA Tom Murray (Conductor/keyboard), Paul Staroba (Associate Conductor), Matthew Lehmann (Concert Master), David Blinn (viola), Mairi Dorman-Phaneuf (cello), David Young (woodwind), Thomas Sefcovic (bassoon), Susan Jolles (harp), Dick Sarpola (bass)

MUSICAL NUMBERS Overture, Night Waltz, Now, Later, Soon, The Glamorous Life, Remember?, You Must Meet My Wife, Liaisons, In Praise of Women, Every Day a Little Death, A Weekend in the Country, The Sun Won't Set, It Would Have Been Wonderful, Night Waltz II, Perpetual Anticipation, Send in the Clowns, The Miller's Son, Finale

2009–2010 AWARDS Tony Award: Best Actress in a Musical (Catherine Zeta-Jones); Drama Desk Award: Outstanding Actress in a Musical (Catherine Zeta-Jones – tie with Montego Glover)

SETTING Time: Turn of the last century. Place: Sweden. Revival of a musical presented in two acts. Originally opened on Broadway at the Shubert Theatre February 25, 1973, transferred to the Majestic Theatre September 17, 1973, and closed August 3, 1974 after 601 performances (see *Theatre World* Vol. 29, page 56). This version of the show originally played at the London's Menier Chocolate Factory (David Babani, Artistic Director), featuring Mr. Hanson as "Fredrick", November 22, 2008–March 8, 2009. The show transferred to the Garrick Theatre in the West End from March 28–July 25, 2009 for a limited commercial run.

SYNOPSIS *A Little Night Music* is set in a weekend country house in turn of the century Sweden, bringing together surprising liaisons, long simmering passions and a taste of love's endless possibilities. Hailed as witty and wildly romantic, the story centers on the elegant actress Desirée Armfeldt and the spider's web of sensuality intrigue and desire that surrounds her.

Alexander Hanson and Catherine Zeta-Jones

Angela Lansbury

Angela Lansbury, Catherine Zeta-Jones, and Keaton Whittaker

Alexander Hanson, Catherine Zeta-Jones, and Aaron Lazar

The Company

Catherine Zeta-Zones (photos by Joan Marcus)

Victor Garber and Harriet Harris (photos by Joan Marcus)

Present Laughter

American Airlines Theatre; First Preview: January 2, 2010; Opening Night: January 21, 2010; Closed March 21, 2010; 23 previews, 69 performances

Written by Noël Coward; Produced by the Roundabout Theatre Company (Todd Haimes, Artistic Director; Harold Wolpert, Managing Director; Julia C. Levy, Executive Director); Director, Nicholas Martin; Set, Alexander Dodge; Costumes, Jane Greenwood; Lighting, Rui Rita; Sound, Drew Levy; Hair & Wigs, Tom Watson; Dialect Coach, Deborah Hecht; Production Stage Manager, Stephen M. Kaus; Original Casting, Alaine Alldaffer; Additional Casting, Jim Carnahan, Carrie Gardner; Production Management, Aurora Productions (Gene O'Donovan, W. Benjamin Heller II, Rachel Sherbill, Jarid Sumner, Steve Rosenberg, Melissa Mazdra, Amy Merlino Coey, Amanda Raymond, Graham Forden, Liza Luxenberg); General Manager, Rebecca Habel; Marketing/Sales Promotion, David B. Steffen; Founding Director, Gene Feist; Associate Artistic Director, Scott Ellis; Director of Artistic Development and Casting, Jim Carnahan; Finance, Susan Neiman; Education, Greg McCaslin; General Manager, Sydney Beers; Telesales, Marco Frezza; IT Director, Antonio Palumbo; Development Directors, Julie K. D'Andrea, Steve Schaeffer, Joy Pak, Amber Jo Manuel; Sales Operations, Charlie Garbowski Jr.; Company Manager, Carly DiFulvio; Stage Manager, Jamie Greathouse; Assistant Director, Erick Herrscher; Associate Design: Kevin Judge (set), Moira Clinton (costumes), Carl Faber (lighting), Will Pickens (sound); Assistant Design: Melissa Shakun (set), Matthew Taylor (lighting); Production Crew: Peter Sarafin (production properties), Glenn Merwede (production carpenter), Brian Maiuri (house electrician), Robert W. Dowling II (running properties), Dann Wojnar (sound operator), Susan J. Fallon (wardrobe supervisor), Manuela Laporte (hair and wig supervisor), Kat Martin, Lauren Galitelli, Cathy Cline (dressers), Dale Carman (day wardrobe), Morgan R. Holbrook (production assistant); Advertising, SpotCo; Press, Boneau/Bryan-Brown, Adrian Bryan-Brown, Matt Polk, Jessica Johnson, Amy Kass, Emily Meagher

CAST Daphne Stillington **Holley Fain**; Miss Erikson **Nancy E. Carroll**; Fred **James Joseph O'Neil**; Monica Reed **Harriet Harris**; Garry Essendine **Victor Garber**; Liz Essendine **Lisa Banes**; Roland Maule **Brooks Ashmanskas**; Morris Dixon **Mark Vietor**; Henry Lyppiatt **Richard Poe**; Joanna Lyppiatt **Pamela Jane Gray**; Lady Saltburn **Alice Duffy**

UNDERSTUDIES Peter Bradbury (Fred, Henry Lyppiatt, Morris Dixon), Kathleen McElfresh (Daphne Stillington), Robin Moseley (Lady Saltburn, Miss Erikson, Monica Reed), James Joseph O'Neil (Roland Maule), Nicole Orth-Pallavicini (Joanna Lyppiatt, Liz Essendine)

SETTING Late 1930s London. Garry Essendine's flat. Act I: The morning. Act II: Scene 1: Midnight, three days later; Scene 2: The following morning. Act III: Evening, a week later. Revival of a comedy presented in three acts with two intermissions. This production of *Present Laughter* was originally presented by the Huntington Theatre Company May 18–June 17, 2007. Originally presented on Broadway at the Plymouth Theatre, starring Clifton Webb, October 29, 1946–March 15, 1947 (see *Theatre World* Vol. 3, page 82). The play has had three other Broadway revivals: Belasco Theatre, directed by and starring Noël Coward, January 31–February 8, 1958 (see *Theatre World* Vol. 14, page 76); Circle in the Square, starring George C. Scott, July 15, 1982–January 2, 1983 (see *Theatre World* Vol. 39, page 12); Walter Kerr Theatre, starring Frank Langella, November 18, 1996–April 20, 1997 (see *Theatre World* Vol. 53, page 16).

SYNOPSIS In Noël Coward's classic comedy, matinee idol Garry Essendine sits at the center of his own universe. While Garry struggles to plan his upcoming trip to Africa, his elegant London flat is invaded by a love-struck ingénue, an adulterous producer and a married seductress, not to mention Garry's estranged wife and a crazed young playwright. Just before Garry escapes, the full extent of his misdemeanors is discovered and all hell breaks loose.

Brooks Ashmanskas and Victor Garber

A View from the Bridge

Cort Theatre; First Preview: December 28, 2009; Opening Night: January 24, 2010; Closed April 4, 2010; 30 previews, 81 performances

Written by Arthur Miller; Produced by Stuart Thompson, The Araca Group, Jeffrey Finn, Broadway Across America (John Gore, CEO; Thomas B. McGrath, Chairman; Beth Williams, COO & Head of Production), Olympus Theatricals, Marisa Sechrest, The Weinstein Company, Jon B. Platt, Sonia Friedman Productions/Robert G. Bartner, Mort Swinsky/Joseph Deitch, Adam Zotovich/Ruth Hendel/Orin Wolf, Shelter Island Enterprises, The Shubert Organization (Phillip J. Smith, Chairman; Robert E. Wankel, President); Director, Gregory Mosher; Set, John Lee Beatty; Costumes, Jane Greenwood; Lighting, Peter Kaczorowski; Sound, Scott Lehrer; Hair & Wigs, Tom Watson; Casting, Cindy Tolan; Dialect Coach, Stephen Gabis; Production Stage Manager, William Joseph Barnes; Production Management, Hudson Theatrical Associates (Neil Mazzella & Sam Ellis); General Management, Stuart Thompson Productions (Stuart Thompson, David Turner, & James Triner); Company Manager, Nathan Gehan; Marketing, Type A Marketing (Anne Rippey, Nick Pramik, Elyce Henkin); Internet Marketing, The Araca Group; Fight Director, Thomas Schall; Stage Manager, Thea Bradshaw Scott; Associate Design: Kacie Hultgren (set), Wade Laboissonniere (costumes), John Viesta (lighting), Alex Hawthorn (sound); Assistant to Mr. Mosher, Christopher Thomasson; Fight Captain, Corey Stoll; Production Crew: Edward Diaz (production carpenter), Scott Deverna (production electrician), Scott Laule (advance props), Scott Monroe (production props), Jim vanBergen (production sound), Cookie Jordan (makeup consultant), Lyle Jones (wardrobe supervisor), Kelly A. Saxon (Ms. Johansson's dresser), Katie Beatty (hair supervisor), Carrie Kamerer, Claire Verlaet (dressers), Kathryn McKee, Ashley Bigge (production assistants); Casting Associate, Adam Caldwell; General Management Assistants, Geo Karapetyan, Brittany Levasseur; Assistant to Mr. Thompson, Christopher Taggart; Advertising, SpotCo; Press, Boneau/Bryan-Brown, Chris Boneau, Susanne Tighe, Christine Olver

CAST Louis **Robert Turano**; Mike **Joe Ricci**; Alfieri **Michael Cristofer**; Eddie **Liev Schreiber**; Catherine **Scarlett Johansson**; Beatrice **Jessica Hecht**; Marco **Corey Stoll**; Tony **Matthew Montelongo**; Rodolpho **Morgan Spector**; 1st Immigration Officer **Anthony DeSando**; 2nd Immigration Officer **Marco Verna**; Submarines **Matthew Montelongo, Alex Cendese**; Mr. Lipari **Mark Morettini**; Mrs. Lipari **Antoinette LaVecchia**

UNDERSTUDIES Alex Cendese (First Immigration Officer, Second Immigration Officer, Submarine, Tony), Bonnie Dennison (Catherine, Mrs. Lipari), Anthony DeSando (Eddie), Jim Iorio (1st Immigration Officer, Louis, Mike, Mr. Lipari, 2nd Immigration Officer, Submarine), Antoinette LaVecchia (Beatrice), Matthew Montelongo (First Immigration Officer, Marco, Second Immigration Officer, Submarine, Tony), Mark Morettini (Alfieri), Marco Verna (Louis, Marco, Mike)

2009–2010 AWARDS Tony Award: Best Featured Actress in a Play (Scarlett Johansson); Drama Desk Awards: Outstanding Revival of a Play (tie with *Fences*), Outstanding Actor in a Play (Liev Schreiber), Drama League Award: Outstanding Revival of a Play; **Theatre World Award:** Scarlett Johansson

SETTING In the apartment and environment of Eddie Carbone, in Red Hook, on the Bay seaward from Brooklyn Bridge. Revival of a drama presented in two acts. Originally produced on Broadway as a one-act verse drama (on a double bill with Miller's one-act *A Memory of Two Mondays*) at the Coronet Theatre September 29, 1955–February 4, 1956, playing 149 performances (see *Theatre World* Vol. 12, page 20). The full two-act version was first presented at the Comedy Theatre in London in 1956. After a 1961 film version (directed by Sidney Lumet), the full play was produced Off-Broadway at Sheridan Square Playhouse, starring Robert Duval, January 28, 1965–December 11, 1966, playing 780 performances (see *Theatre World* Vol. 21, page 163). The play has had two other Broadway revivals, first at the Ambassador Theatre February 3–June 12, 1983 (see *Theatre World* Vol. 39, page 35). The Roundabout Theatre Company's acclaimed revival starring Anthony LaPaglia, Allison Janney, and Brittany Murphy, which opened at the Criterion Center Stage Right on December 14, 1997, transferred to the Neil Simon Theatre on April 3, 1998, and closed August 30, 1998 after 35 previews and 239 performances (see *Theatre World* Vol. 54, page 27).

SYNOPSIS Eddie Carbone, a Brooklyn longshoreman, is obsessed with his 17-year-old niece Catherine. When Catherine falls in love with a newly arrived immigrant, Eddie's jealousy erupts in a rage that consumes him, his family, and his world.

Scarlett Johansson, Liev Schreiber, and Morgan Spector

Scarlett Johansson and Jessica Hecht

Liev Schreiber and Michael Cristofer

Time Stands Still

Samuel J. Friedman Theatre; First Preview: January 5, 2010; Opening Night: January 28, 2010; Closed March 23, 2010; 28 previews, 67 performances

Written by Donald Margulies; Produced by Manhattan Theatre Club (Lynne Meadow, Artistic Director; Barry Grove, Executive Producer) by special arrangement with Nelle Nugent & Wendy Federman; Director, Daniel Sullivan; Set, John Lee Beatty; Costumes, Rita Ryack; Lighting, Peter Kaczorowski; Sound, Darron L West; Original Music, Peter Golub; Fight Director, Thomas Schall; Production Stage Manager, Robert Bennett; General Manager, Florie Seery; Associate Artistic Director, Mandy Greenfield; Director of Artistic Development, Jerry Patch; Marketing, Debra Waxman-Pilla; Production Manager, Kurt Gardner; Director of Casting, Nancy Piccione; Development, Jill Turner Lloyd; Artistic Consultant, Daniel Sullivan; Artistic Administration/Assistant to Artistic Director, Amy Gilkes Loe; Finance, Jeffrey Bledsoe; Associate General Manager, Lindsey Brooks Sag; Subscriber Services, Robert Allenberg; Telesales, George Tetlow; Education, David Shookhoff; Associate Production Manager, Philip Naudé; Prop Supervisor, Scott Laule; Costume Supervisor, Erin Hennessy Dean; Company Manager, Seth Shepsle; Stage Manager, Shanna Spinello; Drama League-Assistant Director, Mia Rovegno; Makeup Design for Ms. Linney, Mindy Hall; Assistant Design: Katie Hultgren (set), Richard Schurkamp (costumes), Jake DeGroot (lighting), Charles Coes (sound); Video Editor, Rocco DiSanti; Lightboard Programmer, Marc Polimeni; Production Crew: Timothy Coffey (deck crew), Chris Wiggins (head carpenter), Timothy Walters (head propertyman), Louis Shapiro (sound engineer), Jeff Dodson (master electrician), Angela Simpson (wardrobe supervisor), Natasha Steinhagen (hair/makeup supervisor), Virginia Neininger (dresser), Aaron Gonzalez (production assistant); Advertising, SpotCo; Press, Boneau/Bryan-Brown, Chris Boneau, Aaron Meier, Christine Olver, Emily Meagher

CAST Richard Ehrlich **Eric Bogosian**; James Dodd **Brian d'Arcy James**; Sarah Goodwin **Laura Linney**; Mandy Bloom **Alicia Silverstone**

UNDERSTUDIES Tony Carlin (Richard, James), Monica McCarthy (Sarah, Mandy)

SETTING A loft in Williamsburg, Brooklyn. Recently. New York premiere of a new drama presented in two acts. Originally commissioned and produced at the Geffen Playhouse (Gil Cates, Producing Director; Randall Arney, Artistic Director) February 3–March 11, 2009 (see *Theatre World* Vol. 65, page 322). A commercial extension of the play was scheduled for the fall of the 2010.

SYNOPSIS *Time Stands Still* is about two journalists who return home after covering war — only to investigate their own conflicting feelings about life and work. Sarah and James, a photographer and a journalist, have been together for nine years and share a passion for documenting the realities of war. When injuries force them to return home to New York, the adventurous couple confronts the prospect of a more conventional life.

Laura Linney, Briaan d'Arcy James, and Eric Bogosian

Brian d'Arcy James and Laura Linney

Laura Linney and Alicia Silverstone (photos by Joan Marcus)

Alicia Silverstone and Eric Bogosian

The Miracle Worker

Circle in the Square Theatre; First Preview: February 12, 2010; Opening Night: March 3, 2010; Closed April 4, 2010; 21 previews, 38 performances

Written by William Gibson; Produced by David Richenthal, Eric Falkenstein, Randall L. Wreghitt, Barbara & Buddy Freitag/Dan Frishwasser, Joe & Kathy Grano, Mallory Factor, Cheryl Lachowicz, Marta Falkenberg, Bruce J. Carusi & Susan Altamore Carusi, David & Sheila Lehrer, Lynn Shaw in association with Connie Bartlow Kristan, Jamie deRoy/Remmel T. Dickinson; Director, Kate Whoriskey; Sets, Derek McLane; Costumes, Paul Tazewell; Lighting, Kenneth Posner; Original Music & Sound, Rob Milburn & Michael Bodeen; Hair, Charles LaPointe; Physical Coaching & Movement, Lee Sher; Production Stage Manager, J. Philip Bassett; Casting, Jay Binder & Jack Bowdan; Marketing, Type A Marketing (Anne Rippey, Nick Pramik, Janette Roush, Nina Bergelson); Company Manager, Penelope Daulton; Production Management, Juniper Street Productions (Kevin Broomell, Hilary Blanken, Guy Kwan, Ana Rose Greene); Executive Producer, Red Awning; Associate Producers, Rosalind Productions Inc., Patty Baker/Anna Czekaj, Goode Productions; General Manager, Alan Wasser, Allan Williams, Aaron Lustbader; Stage Manager, Amber Wedin; Dialect Coach, Deborah Hecht; Fight Consultant, Ron Piretti; Makeup, Cookie Jordan; Fight Captain, Michael Izquierdo; Sign Language Consultant, Anne Tomasetti; Associate Design, Shoko Kambara (set), Daryl Stone (costumes), Philip Rosenberg (lighting), Christopher Cronin (sound); Assistant Design: Erica Hemminger (set), Valerie Spradling (sound); Production Crew: Anthony Menditto (production carpenter), David Cohen (automation carpenter), Dan Coey (production electrician), Christopher Pantuso (production properties), Eileen Miller (wardrobe supervisor), Laura Beattie, Barry Hoff (dressers), Cory McCutcheon (hair and makeup supervisor), Christina Grant (assistant hair and makeup); Chaperone, Bridget Mills; Advertising, SpotCo; Website & Internet Marketing, Art Meets Commerce; Press, Boneau/Bryan-Brown, Chris Boneau, Adrian Bryan-Brown, Joe Perrotta, Kelly Guiod

CAST Helen Keller **Abigail Breslin**; Jimmie **Lance Chantiles-Wertz**; Percy **Michael Cummings**; Aunt Ev **Elizabeth Franz**; Viney **Yvette Ganier**; Martha **Simone Joy Jones**; Captain Keller **Matthew Modine**; Kate Keller **Jennifer Morrison**; Doctor/Anagnos **Daniel Oreskes**; Annie Sullivan **Alison Pill**; James Keller **Tobias Segal**

UNDERSTUDIES Aru Banks (Martha, Percy), Bill Christ (Anagnos, Captain Keller, Doctor), Sandra Daley (Viney), Katrina Lenk (Annie Sullivan, Kate Keller), Anthony Scarpone-Lambert (Jimmie), Kyra Ynez Siegel (Helen Keller)

SETTING Time: 1880s. Place: In and around the Keller homestead in Tuscumbia, Alabama; also, briefly, the Perkins Institute for the Blind in Boston. Revival of a play presented in three acts with one intermission. Originally produced on Broadway at the Playhouse Theatre (starring Anne Bancroft and Patty Duke) October 19, 1959–July 1, 1961, playing 719 performances (see *Theatre World* Vol. 26, page 16).

SYNOPSIS The 1960 Tony Award-winning *The Miracle Worker* receives a fiftieth anniversary revival, telling the story of real-life blind and deaf Medal of Freedom winner Helen Keller, who suddenly lost her sight and hearing at the age of 19 months, and the extraordinary teacher who taught her to communicate with the world, Annie Sullivan.

Abigail Breslin and Alison Pill

Alison Pill, Jennifer Morrison, Abigail Breslin, and Matthew Modine

Elizabeth Franz, Tobias Segal, Yvette Ganier, Matthew Modine, Jennifer Morrison, Abigail Breslin, and Alison Pill
(photos by Joan Marcus)

Christopher Walken (photos by Joan Marcus)

Christopher Walken, Anthony Mackie, and Zoe Kazan

Zoe Kazan and Anthony Mackiea

A Behanding in Spokane

Gerald Schoenfeld Theatre; First Preview: February 15, 2010; Opening Night: March 4, 2010; 20 previews, 100 performances as of May 31, 2010

Written by Martin McDonagh; Produced by Robert Fox, Carole Shorenstein Hays, Debra Black, Stephanie P. McClelland, Ostar, Roger Berlind, Scott Rudin, Shubert Organization (Philip J. Smith, Chairman; Robert E. Wankel, President) in association with Robert G. Bartner, Lorraine Kirke, Jamie deRoy/Rachel Neubuger; Presented in association with the Atlantic Theater Company (Neil Pepe, Artistic Director; Jeffory Lawson, Managing Director); Director, John Crowley; Sets & Costumes, Scott Pask; Lighting, Brian MacDevitt; Original Music & Sound, David Van Tieghem; Casting, Jim Carnahan; Technical Supervisor, Theatersmith Inc.; General Management, Nina Lannan Associates, Maggie Brohn; Production Stage Manager, Frank Lombardi; Associate Producers, Erich Jungwirth, Richard Jordan; Company Manager, Beverly Edwards; Stage Manager, Lisa Buxbaum; Associate Company Manager, Steve Dow; Assistant Director, JV Mercanti; Production Assistant, Timothy Eaker; Associate Design: Antje Ellerman (set), Valerie Ramshur (costumes), Jennifer Schriever (lighting), David Sanderson (sound); Assistant Set, Lauren Alvarez; Assistant to Mr. Pask, Warren Stiles; Automated Lighting Programmer, Timothy F. Rogers; Makeup, Angelina Avallone; Prosthetic Effects Design, Prosthetic Renaissance Inc., Mike Marino, Hayes Vilandry, Chris Kelly; Production Properties, Kathy Fabian/Propstar; Specialty Prop Artisan, Craig Grigg; Propstar Assistants, Tim Ferro, Carrie Mossman; Production Crew: Timmy McWilliams (house carpenter), Michael Ward (production electrician), Leslie Ann Kilian (house electrician), Neil Rosenberg (head properties) Heidi Brown (house properties), Brien Brannigan (production sound), Kathleen Gallagher (wardrobe supervisor), Rachel Garrett, Geoffrey Polischuk (dressers); Advertising, SpotCo: Drew Hodges, Jim Edwards, Tom Greenwald, Jim Aquino, Stacey Maya; Press, Boneau/Bryan-Brown, Chris Boneau, Susanne Tighe, Christine Olver

CAST Carmichael **Christopher Walken**; Mervyn **Sam Rockwell**; Marilyn **Zoe Kazan**; Toby **Anthony Mackie**

UNDERSTUDIES Glenn Fleshler (Carmichael), Dashiell Eaves (Mervyn), Meredith Forlenza (Marilyn), Tory Kittles (Toby)

SETTING A hotel room in Spokane, Washington; the present. World premiere of a new play presented without intermission.

SYNOPSIS In Irish playwright Martin McDonagh's new dark comedy (and his first set in America) *A Behanding in Spokane*, the title is just the starting point. Take a man searching for his missing hand (Walken), two con artists out to make a few hundred bucks (Mackie and Kazan), and an overly curious hotel clerk (Rockwell), and the rest is up for grabs.

Christopher Walken and Sam Rockwell

Next Fall

Helen Hayes Theatre; First Preview: February 16, 2010; Opening Night: March 11, 2010; 26 previews, 92 performances as of May 31, 2010

Written by Geoffrey Nauffts; Produced by Elton John and David Furnish, Barbara Manocherian, Richard Willis, Tom Smedes, Carole L. Haber/Chase Mishkin, Ostar, Anthony Barrile, Michael Palitz, Bob Boyett, James Spry/ Catherine Schreiber, Probo Productions, Roy Furman in association with Naked Angels (Geoffrey Nauffts, Artistic Director; John Alexander, Managing Director; Andy Donald, Associate Artistic Director; Brittany O'Neill, Producer); Director, Sheryl Kaller; Set, Wilson Chin; Costumes, Jess Goldstein; Lighting, Jeff Croiter; Original Music and Sound, John Gromada; Casting, Howie Cherpakov; Production Stage Manager, Charles Means; Marketing, Promotional and Digital Services, Allied Live; Production Management, Aurora Productions (Gene O'Donovan, Ben Heller, Rachel Sherbill, Jarid Sumner, Melissa Mazdra, Amanda Raymond, Graham Forden, Liza Luxenberg); Executive Producer, Susan Mindell; General Management, Stuart Thompson Productions, David Turner, James Triner; Company Manager, Bobby Driggers; Fight Director, Drew Leary; Stage Manager, Elizabeth Moloney; Associate Director, Joe Langworth; Associate Design: Mikiko Suzuki MacAdams (set), China Lee (costumes), Grant W.S. Yeager (lighting), Christopher Cronin (sound); Assistant Sound Design, Alex Neumann; Production Crew: Doug Purcell (production carpenter), Joe Beck (production electrician), Pete Sarafin (advance props), Roger Keller (production props), Bob Etter (production sound), James Strunk (wardrobe supervisor), Katie Chihaby (dresser), Katrina Herrmann (production assistant), Sam Kramer (production intern); General Management Assistants, Geo Karapetyan, Brittany Levasseur; Advertising, SpotCo. (Drew Hodges, Jim Edwards, Tom Greenwald, Beth Watson, Tim Falotico); Press, Boneau/Bryan-Brown, Chris Boneau, Heath Schwartz, Michael Strassheim

CAST Holly **Maddie Corman**; Brandon **Sean Dugan**; Arlene **Connie Ray**; Adam **Patrick Breen**; Butch **Cotter Smith**; Luke **Patrick Heusinger**

STANDBYS David Adkins (Adam, Butch), Clayton Apgar (Brandon, Luke), Kristie Dale Sanders (Arlene, Holly)

2009–2010 AWARDS Outer Critics Circle Award: John Gassner Playwriting Award (Geoffrey Nauffts)

SETTING A hospital waiting room, an apartment, and various locations in and around New York City and Washington D.C. over the course of five years. Transfer of the Off-Broadway play presented in two acts. World premiere at the Peter Jay Sharp Theatre May 26–August 8, 2009 (see "Off Broadway" section in this volume).

SYNOPSIS *Next Fall* takes a witty and provocative look at faith, commitment and unconditional love, and forces us all to examine what it means to "believe" and what it might cost us not to. Luke believes in God. Adam believes in everything else. *Next Fall* portrays the ups and downs of this unlikely couple's five-year relationship with sharp humor and unflinching honesty. And when an accident changes everything, Adam must turn to Luke's family and friends for support… and answers. *Next Fall* goes beyond a typical love story and paints a beautiful and funny portrait of modern romance.

Patrick Breen, Maddie Corman, and Connie Ray

Patrick Heusinger and Patrick Breen (photos by Carol Rosegg)

Sean Dugan, Patrick Breen, and Maddie Corman

Patrick Heusinger, Cotter Smith, and Patrick Breen

Valerie Harper

Brian Hutchison and Valerie Harper

Looped

Lyceum Theatre; First Preview: February 19, 2010; Opening Night: March 14, 2010; Closed March 27, 2010; 27 previews, 25 performances

Written by Matthew Lombardo; Produced by Tony Cacciotti, Chase Mishkin, Bard Theatricals, Lauren Class Schneider, Lawrence S. Toppall, Leonard Soloway; Director, Rob Ruggiero; Sets, Adrian W. Jones; Costumes, William Ivey Long; Lighting, Ken Billington; Sound, Michael Hooker & Peter Fitzgerald; Wigs, Charles LaPointe; Production Supervision, Arthur Siccardi & Patrick Sullivan; Production Stage Manager, Bess Marie Glorioso; Casting, Jay Binder; Associate Producers, Barbara Freitag, David Mirvish; Marketing, HHC Marketing; General Management, Leonard Soloway; Company Manager, Judith Drasner; Stage Manager, Ana M. Garcia; Production Assistant, Melanie T. Morgan; Assistant Director, Nick Eilerman; Associate Design: Catherine A Parrott (costumes), Anthony Pearson (lighting); Director of William Ivey Long Studios, Donald Sanders; Assistant to Designers, Ann Bartek (set), Megan Henninger (sound); Production Crew: Michael Pilipski (production properties), Adam Braunstein (head carpenter), Leah Nelson (head properties), Neil McShane (production electrician), Jonathan Cohen (head electrician), Wally Flores (production sound), Jesse Galvan (wardrobe supervisor), Erin Brooke Roth (dresser), Cookie Jordan (makeup consultant); Advertising, Eliran Murphy Group/Barbara Eliran, Frank Verlizzo, Elizabeth Findlay, Caraline Sogliuzzo; Website and Interactive Marketing, Bay Bridge Productions/Laura Wagner, Jean Strong; HHC Marketing Team, Hugh Hysell, Michael Redman, Todd Briscoe; Assistant to Mr. Cacciotti, Emily McGill; Press, Boneau/Bryan-Brown, Chris Boneau, Jackie Green, Michael Strassheim

CAST Steve **Michael Mulheren**; Danny **Brian Hutchison**; Tallulah Bankhead **Valerie Harper**

UNDERSTUDIES Tim Altmeyer (Steve, Danny), Glynis Bell (Tallulah Bankhead)

SETTING Time: Summer, 1965. Place: A Recording Studio, Los Angeles, California. New York premiere of a new play presented in two acts. World premiere at Pasadena Playhouse (Sheldon Epps, Artistic Director; Brian Colburn, Managing Director; Tom Ware, Producing Director) June 27–August 3, 2009.

SYNOPSIS *Looped* is loosely based on the true story of when the inebriated Tallulah Bankhead stumbled into a sound studio to re-record ('or loop') one line from her final film *Die, Die, My Darling*. Ms. Bankhead was known for her wild partying and convention-defying exploits that surpassed even today's celebrity bad girls. The session was to have only taken five minutes, but instead lasted well over eight hours. Given her intoxicated state and inability to loop the line properly, what ensues is an uproarious showdown between an uptight film editor, Danny Miller, and the outrageous legend.

Valerie Harper (photos by Carol Rosegg

All About Me

Henry Miller's Theatre; First Preview: February 22, 2010; Opening Night: March 18, 2010; Closed April 4, 2010; 27 previews, 20 performances

Written by Christopher Durang, Michel Feinstein and Barry Humphries; Conceived by Michael Feinstein with Lizzie Spender, Terrence Flannery, and Barry Humphries; Original Music by Matthew Sklar, Chad Beguelin, Nick Rowley, Barry Humphries, Michael Feinstein, Glen Kelly, Wayne Barker; Produced by Jeffrey Richards, Jerry Frankel, Eagle Productions LLC, Jamie deRoy/Remmel T. Dickinson, Richard Winkler/Dan Frishwasser, Mallory Factor, Cheryl Lachowicz, Chris Yegen, Judith Resnick, Jon Bierman, Christopher Hart Productions, CTM Media Group, Stewart F. Lane/Bonnie Comley, Michael Filerman, Barry & Carole Kaye/Irv Welzer, Terry Allen Kramer, Terrie J. Lootens; Stein & Gunderson Productions (Joan Stein & James Gunderson), WenSheJack Productions (Wendy Federman, Sheila Steinberg, & Jacki Barilia Florin), Mickey Conlon; Director, Casey Nicholaw; Music Supervisor, Rob Bowman; Sets & Costumes, Anna Louizos; Lighting, Howell Binkley; Sound, Peter Fitzgerald; Video, Chris Cronin; Production Stage Manager, James W. Gibbs; Orchestrations, John Oddo; Additional Arrangements, Glen Kelly; Music Coordinator, Michael Keller; Casting, Telsey + Company; Technical Supervision, Hudson Theatrical Associates, Neil Mazzella, Sam Elis, Irene Wang; General Management, Stuart Thompson Productions, James Triner, David Turner; Associate Producers, Jeremy Scott Blaustein, Roe Rothfield; Company Manager, Cassidy J. Briggs; Stage Manager, Francesca Russell; Dance Captain, Patrick Wetzel; Assistant Director, Matt Williams; Associate Design: Mike Carnahan (set), Ryan O'Gara (lighting), Heather Dunbar (costumes), Domonic Sack (sound); Assistant Design: Hilary Noxon (set), Aimee M. Dombo (costumes); Props, Kathy Fabian/Propstar; Propstar Associates, Tim Ferro, Carrie Mossman; Propstar Assistants, Jessica Provencale, Edward Morris; Production Assistants, Brian Bogin, Quinn M. Corbin; Moving Light Programmer, Chris Herman; Production Crew: Matt Anderson (animator), Paul Ashton (automation), Jordan Gable (flyman), Dorion Fuchs, Jocelyn Smith (spot operators), Ed Chapman (sound operator), Aaron Straus (deck sound), Jake Hall (assistant sound), Kimberly Baird (wardrobe supervisor), Judy Badame, Cleon Byerly (dressers), Markus Fokken (hair supervisor); Orchestration Team, Bill Elliot, Dick Lieb, Jonathan Tunick, Doug Walter, William Waranoff; Special Media and Creative Consultant, Andy Drachenberg; Assistant to Mr. Humphries and Ms. Spender, Nicola Pedlingham; Assistant to Mr. Feinstein, Andy Brattain; General Management Assistants, Megan Curren, Brittany Levasseur; Assistants to Mr. Richards, Michael Crea, Will Trice; Music Copying, Kaye-Houston Music, Anne Kaye & Doug Houston; Advertising, Serino Coyne; Press, Jeffrey Richards Associates, Irene Gandy, Alana Karpoff, Elon Rutberg, Diana Rissetto

Michael Feinstein and Dame Edna

CAST As Themselves **Michael Feinstein** and **Dame Edna Everage** (a.k.a. Barry Humphries); Stage Manager **Jodi Capeless**; Bruno **Gregory Butler**; Benito **Jon-Paul Mateo**

UNDERSTUDY Patrick Wetzel (Stage Manager, Bruno, Benito)

ORCHESTRA Rob Bowman (Conductor/piano); David Mann, Aaron Heick, Mark Vinci, Ron Jannelli (reeds); Craig Johnson, Brian Pareschi, Kenny Rampton (trumpets); John Fedchock, Birch Johnson (trombones); David Finck (bass); Albie Berk (drums)

ORIGINAL SONGS Make That Piano Sing, Niceness, We Get Along Amazingly Well, I'm Forcing Myself, The Dingo Ate My Baby, The Koala Song, Medley Song, All About Me, The Gladdy Song

World premiere of a new musical comedy entertainment presented without intermission.

SYNOPSIS Michael Feinstein and Dame Edna Everage combine forces in this new show. After advance publicity where both performers announced a return to Broadway in their own similarly titled show *All About Me*, thus instigating a comic warring in the press, the two stars decide to share the stage at last, with the help of a diplomatic stage manager and two back-up dancers, to present a fun evening of new songs and comedy, along with Feinstein's classic tunes and the Dame's signature audience zingers.

Dame Edna

Michael Feinstein (photos by Joan Marcus)

Come Fly Away

Marquis Theatre; First Preview: March 1, 2010; Opening Night: March 25, 2010; 26 previews, 76 performances as of May 31, 2010

Concept, book, direction, and choreography by Twyla Tharp, music by various, vocals by Frank Sinatra; Presented by special arrangement with the Frank Sinatra family and Frank Sinatra Enterprises; Produced by James L. Nederlander, Nicholas Howey, W.A.T. Ltd., Terry Allen Kramer, Patrick Catullo/Jon B. Platt, Jerry Frankel, Ronald Frankel/Marc Frankel, Roy Furman, Allan S. Gordon/Élan McAllister, Jam Theatricals, Stewart F. Lane /Bonnie Comley, Margo Lion/Daryl Roth, Hal Luftig/Yasuhiro Kawana, Pittsburgh CLO/GSFD, Spark Productions, The Weinstein Company and Barry & Fran Weissler; Sets, James Youmans; Costumes, Katherine Roth; Lighting, Donald Holder; Sound, Peter McBoyle; Original Sinatra Arrangements, Nelson Riddle, Don Costa, Gordon Jenkins, Quincy Jones, Johnny Mandel, Neal Hefti, Torrie Zito, Sam Nestico, Emuir Deodato, Ernie Freeman; Additional Orchestrations & Arrangements, Don Sebesky, Dave Pierce; Original Music Supervisor, Sam Lutfiyya; Musical Supervisor & Coordinator, Patrick Vaccariello; Conductor/Pianist, Russ Kassoff; Casting, Stuart Howard, Amy Schecter, Paul Hardt; Marketing, Scott A. Moore; Creative Consultant, Charles Pignone; Production Executive, Randall A. Buck; Resident Director, Kim Craven; Production Stage Manager, Rick Steiger; Technical Supervisor, David Benken; General Management, The Charlotte Wilcox Company (Seth Marquette, Matthew W. Krawiec, Dina S. Friedler, Steve Supeck, Margaret Wilcox); Company Manager, Heidi Neven; Assistant Company Manager, Michael Bolgar; Stage Manager, Lisa Dawn Cave; Assistant Stage Manager, Kevin Bertolacci; Dance Captain, Alexander Brady; Assistant Dance Captain, Colin Bradbury; Assistant to Mr. Nederlander, Ken Happel; Associate Director of W.A.T. Ltd, Ann Tuomey DePiro; Assistant to Ms. Tharp, Roy Chicas; Associate Design: Jerome Martin (set), Amy Clark (costumes), Jeanne Koenig, Caroline Chao (lighting), David Patridge (sound); Assistants to Costume Designer, Mike Floyd, Caitlin Hunt; Assistant Sound, Daniel Fiandaca; Assistant Production Manager, Canara Price; Production Crew: Jeff Zink (head carpenter), Michael Shepp Jr. (automation carpenter), James Maloney (production electrician), Brad Robertson (spot operator), Dillon Cody (head sound), Daniel Hochstine (assistant sound), Jerry L. Marshall (production props), Edmund Harrison (wardrobe supervisor), Jennifer Griggs (assistant wardrobe supervisor), Tim Greer, Kay Gowenlock, Maggie Horkey, Jeannie Naughton (dressers), Sue Hamilton (stitcher), Morgan Hartley, Jennifer O'Byrne (production assistant); Rehearsal Programmer, Joe DeVico; Rehearsal Pianist, Jim Laev; Music Copying, Emily Grishman, Katherine Edmonds; Advertising, SpotCo; Press, The Hartman Group, Michael Hartman, Tom D'Ambrosio, Michelle Bergmann; Additional Press, Ellen Jacobs Company; Cast recording: Reprise Records

CAST *Evening performances*: Betsy **Laura Mead**; Marty **Charlie Neshyba-Hodges**; Vico **Alexander Brady**; Sid **John Selya**; Kate **Karine Plantadit**; Slim **Rika Okamoto**; Hank **Keith Roberts**; Chanos **Matthew Stockwell Dibble**; Babe **Holley Farmer**; Featured Vocalist **Hilary Gardner**; *Matinee performances*: Betsy **Ashley Tuttle**; Marty **Jeremy Cox**; Vico **Alexander Brady**; Sid **Cody Green**; Kate **Marielys Molina**; Slim **Kristine Bendul**; Hank **Joel Prouty**; Chanos **Ron Todorowski**; Babe **Laurie Kanyok**; Featured Vocalist **Rosena M. Hill**; Ensemble **Todd Burnsed, Carolyn Doherty, Heather Hamilton, Meredith Miles, Eric Michael Otto, Justin Peck**

ALTERNATES/SWINGS Kristine Bendul, Colin Bradbury, Jeremy Cox, Amanda Edge, Cody Green, Laurie Kanyok, Marielys Molina, Joel Prouty, Ron Todorowski, Ashley Tuttle

ORCHESTRA Russ Kassoff (Conductor/piano), Jerry Dodgion (reed 1), Jimmy Cozier (reed 2), P.J. Perry (reed 3), Dave Noland (reed 4), Frank Basile (reed 5), Dave Stahl (trumpet 1), Earl Gardner (trumpet 2), Larry Moses (trumpet 3), Richie Vitale (trumpet 4), John Mosca (trombone 1), Mark Miller (trombone 2), Clarence Banks (trombone 3), Jeff Nelson (trombone 4), Jay Anderson (bass), James Chirillo (guitar), Warren Odze(drums), Hilary Gardner/Rosena M. Hill (percussion)

MUSICAL NUMBERS Moonlight Becomes You, Come Fly With Me, I've Got the World on a String, Let's Fall in Love, I've Got You Under My Skin, Summer Wind, Fly Me to the Moon, I've Got a Crush On You, Body and Soul, It's Alright With Me, You Make Me Feel So Young, September of My Years, Witchcraft, Yes Sir, That's My Baby, Learnin' the Blues, That's Life, Nice 'n' Easy, Makin Whoopee, Jumpin' at the Woodside, Saturday Night Is the Loneliest Night, I'm Gonna Live 'Til I Die, Pick Yourself Up, Wave, Let's Face the Music and Dance, Teach Me Tonight, Take Five, Just Friends, Lean Baby, Makin' Whoopee (reprise), One for My Baby, My Funny Valentine, Air Mail Special, My Way, New York, New York, All the Way

2009–2010 AWARDS Drama Desk Award: Outstanding Choreography (Twyla Tharp)

New York premiere of a new dance musical presented in two acts. World premiere (under the title *Come Fly With Me*) at the Alliance Theatre, Atlanta, Georgia (Susan V. Booth, Artistic Director; Thomas Pechar, Managing Director) September 15–October 11, 2009 (see "Regional Theatre" listings in this volume).

SYNOPSIS Based on the songs of Frank Sinatra, *Come Fly Away* follows four couples as they fall in and out of love during one song and dance filled evening at a crowded nightclub. Blending Sinatra's legendary vocals with a live on-stage big band and the world's finest dancers, *Come Fly Away* weaves an unparalleled hit parade of classics into a soaring musical fantasy of romance and seduction.

Keith Roberts and Karine Plantadit

Laura Mead and Charlie Neshyba-Hodges

The Company (photos by Joan Marcus)

Charlie Neshyba-Hodges and Company

Karine Plantadit, Rika Okamoto, Alexander Brady, Keith Roberts and Company

Holle[y Farmer and John Selya

Alexander Brady and Charlie Neshyba-Hodges

Holley Farmer and Matthew Stockwell Dibble (photo by Greg Mooney)

Red

John Golden Theatre; First Preview: March 11, 2010; Opening Night: April 1, 2010; 22 previews, 69 performances as of May 31, 2010

Written by John Logan; Produced by Arielle Tepper Madover, Stephanie P. McClelland, Matthew Byam Shaw, Neal Street Productions, Fox Theatricals, Ruth Hendel/Barbara Whitman, Philip Hagemann/Murray Rosenthal, The Donmar Warehouse; Presented by the Donmar Warehouse; Director, Michael Grandage; Set/Costumes, Christopher Oram; Lighting, Neil Austin; Composer & Sound, Adam Cork; Donmar Warehouse Executive Producer, James Bierman; Casting, Annie McNulty; Marketing Director, Eric Schnall; General Management, 101 Productions Ltd. (Wendy Orshan, Jeffrey M. Wilson, David Auster, Elie Landau); Production Stage Manager, Arthur Gaffin; Production Management, Aurora Productions (Gene O'Donovan, W. Benjamin Heller II, Rachel Sherbill, Jarid Sumner, Steve Rosenberg, Jarid Sumner, Melissa Mazdra, Amy Merlino Coey, Amanda Raymond, Graham Forden, Liza Luxenberg); Company Manager, Barbara Crompton; Stage Manager, Jamie Greathouse; Associate Director, Paul Hart; U.K. Scenic Associate, Richard Kent; Associate Costume Design, Barry Doss; U.K. Associate Lighting Design/Lighting Programmer, Rob Halliday; U.S. Associate Lighting Design, Pamela Kupper; Lighting Design Intern, Kelly Smith; Associate Sound Design, Chris Cronin; Dialect Coach, Kate Wilson; Production Crew: Jon Lawson (production electrician), Vera Pizzarelli (production props supervisor), Brad Gyorjak (production sound), Tom Lawrey (head electrician), Kelly Saxon (wardrobe supervisor), Mark Trezza (star dresser), Mickey Abbate (dresser), Assistant to Ms. Tepper Madover, Holly Ferguson; Advertising, SpotCo; Marketing Associate, Holly Ferguson; Production Assistant, Jenny Kennedy; For Donmar Warehouse: Michael Grandage (Artistic Director), Jo Danvers (General Manager); Press, Boneau/Bryan-Brown, Adrian Bryan-Brown, Jim Byk, Christine Olver

CAST Mark Rothko **Alfred Molina**; Ken **Eddie Redmayne**

UNDERSTUDIES Gabriel Ebert (Ken), Stephen Rowe (Mark Rothko)

2009–2010 AWARDS Tony Awards: Best Play, Best Director (Michael Grandage), Best Featured Actor in a Play (Eddie Redmayne), Best Set Design of a Play (Christopher Oram), Best Lighting Design of a Play (Neil Austin), Best Sound Design of a Play (Adam Cork); Drama Desk Awards: Outstanding Play, Outstanding Director of a Play (Michael Grandage), Outstanding Lighting Design (Neil Austin); Outer Critics Circle Award: Outstanding New Broadway Play; Drama League Awards: Outstanding Play, Performance Award (Alfred Molina); **Theatre World Award:** Eddie Redmayne

SETTING A New York art studio in the Bowery, 1958. New York premiere of a new play presented without intermission. *Red* had its world premiere at the Donmar Warehouse December 8, 2009–February 6, 2010 prior to its Broadway run.

Eddie Redmayne (photos by Johan Persson)

SYNOPSIS New York artist Mark Rothko has received the art world's largest commission to create a series of murals for The Four Seasons restaurant in the new Seagram building on Park Avenue. Under the watchful gaze of his young assistant, Ken, and the threatening presence of a new generation of artists, Rothko faces his greatest challenge yet: to create a definitive work for an extraordinary setting. *Red* is a moving and compelling account of one of the greatest artists of the twentieth century, whose struggle to accept his growing riches and praise became his ultimate undoing.

Alfred Molina and Eddie Redmayne

Alfred Molina

Lend Me a Tenor

Music Box Theatre; First Preview: March 12, 2010; Opening Night: April 4, 2010; 25 previews, 65 performances as of May 31, 2010

Written by Ken Ludwig; Produced by The Araca Group (Matthew Rego, Michael Rego, Hank Unger), Stuart Thompson, Carl Moellenberg, Rodney Rigby, Olympus Theatricals, Broadway Across America (John Gore, CEO; Thomas B. McGrath, Chairman; Beth Williams, COO & Head of Production), The Shubert Organization (Phillip J. Smith, Chairman; Robert E. Wankel, President) in association with Wendy Federman/Jamie deRoy/Richard Winkler, Lisa Cartwright, Spring Sirkin, Scott and Brian Zeilinger; Director, Stanley Tucci; Set, John Lee Beatty; Costumes, Martin Pakledinaz; Lighting, Kenneth Posner; Sound, Peter Hylenski; Wigs & Hair, Paul Huntley; Casting, MelCap/David Caparelliotis, Mele Nagler; Dialect Coach, Stephen Gabis; Production Stage Manager, David O'Brien; Production Management, Juniper Street Productions, Kevin Broomell, Hilary Blanken, Guy Kwan, Ana-Rose Greene, Sue Semaan; General Management, Stuart Thompson Productions, David Turner, James Triner; Executive Producer, Amanda Watkins; Company Manager, Adam J. Miller; Musical Supervisor, Patrick Vaccariello; Makeup, Joe Dulude II; Marketing Direction, Type A Marketing, Anne Rippey, Nick Pramik, Elyce Henkin; Internet Marketing/Merchandising, The Araca Group; Stage Manager Rachel E. Wolff; Assistant Director, Kristin McLaughlin; Associate Design: Kacie Hultgren (set), Sarah Sophia Lidz (costumes), Aaron Spivey (lighting), Keith Caggiano (sound); Production Crew: Erik Hansen (production carpenter), Dan Coey (production electrician), Chris Pantuso (production props supervisor), Simon Matthews (production sound engineer), Paul Delcioppo (sound engineer), Karen L. Eifert (wardrobe supervisor), Edward Wilson (hair supervisor), Dan Foss, Rosemary Keough, Chris Sanders (dressers), Colleen Danaher (production assistant); Costume Assistant, Tescia Seufferlein; Assistant to Mr. Pakledinaz, Inca Kangal; Production Management Assistants, Alexandra Paull; Assistant to Mr. Zeilinger, Robert Wachsberger; Costume Interns, Carly Bradt, Jaime Torres; Advertising, Serino Coyne, Greg Corradetti, Sandy Block, Joaquin Esteve, Lauren D'Elia Pressman; Press, Boneau-Bryan/Brown, Adrian Bryan-Brown, Jackie Green, Emily Meagher

CAST Maggie **Mary Catherine Garrison**; Max **Justin Bartha**; Saunders **Tony Shalhoub**; Tito Merelli **Anthony LaPaglia**; Maria **Jan Maxwell**; Bellhop **Jay Klaitz**; Diana **Jennifer Laura Thompson**; Julia **Brooke Adams**

UNDERSTUDIES Jessie Austrian (Diana, Maggie), Tony Carlin (Saunders, Tito Merelli), Donna English (Julia, Maria), Brian Sears (Bellhop, Max)

2009–2010 AWARDS Outer Critics Circle Award: Outstanding Featured Actress in a Play (Jan Maxwell)

Brooke Adams, Mary Catherine Garrison, Tony Shalhoub, and Jay Klaitz

SETTING A hotel suite in Cleveland, in 1934, an afternoon and evening on a Saturday in September. Revival of a play presented in four scenes in two acts with one intermission. Originally produced on Broadway at the Royale Theatre (now the Bernard B. Jacobs Theatre) February 17, 1989–April 22, 1990, playing 18 previews and 476 performances (see *Theatre World* Vol. 45, page 26). World premiere at the Globe Theatre in London in 1986.

SYNOPSIS *Lend Me a Tenor* is a madcap screwball comedy that takes place when Tito Merelli, the fiery-tempered and world famous Italian superstar, arrives in Cleveland, Ohio to make his debut with the local opera and promptly goes missing. As Saunders, the show's presenter, conspires to cover for Tito's absence, placate his hot-blooded wife, and distract his most passionate fans, chaos on a truly operatic level ensues.

Justin Bartha and Tony Shalhoub (photos by Joan Marcus)

Jennifer Laura Thompson and Justin Bartha

Anthony LaPaglia and Jan Maxwell

The Addams Family

Lunt-Fontanne Theatre; First Preview: March 8, 2010; Opening Night: April 8, 2010; 35 previews, 60 performances as of May 31, 2010

Book by Marshall Brickman & Rick Elice, music by Andrew Lippa; Based on characters created by Charles Addams; Produced by Stuart Oken, Roy Furman, Michael Leavitt, Five Cent Productions, Stephen Schuler, Decca Theatricals, Scott M. Delman, Stuart Ditsky, Terry Allen Kramer, Stephanie P. McClelland, James L. Nederlander, Eva Price, Jam Theatricals (Arny Granat, Jerry Mickelson, Steve Traxler)/Mary Lu Roffe, Pittsburgh CLO/Jay & Cindy Gutterman/Mort Swinsky, Vivek Tiwary/Gary Kaplan, The Weinstein Company/Clarence LLC, Adam Zotovich/Tribe Theatricals (Carl Moellenberg, Wendy Federman, Jamie deRoy, Larry Hirschhorn) in special arrangement with Elephant Eye Theatrical; Direction/ Design, Phelim McDermott & Julian Crouch; Choreography, Sergio Trujillo; Creative Consultant, Jerry Zaks; Lighting, Natasha Katz; Sound, Acme Sound Partners, Puppetry, Basil Twist; Hair, Tom Watson; Makeup, Angelina Avallone; Special Effects, Gregory Meeh; Orchestrations, Larry Hochman; Music Director, Mary-Mitchell Campbell; Dance Arrangements, August Eriksmoen; Vocal Arrangements & Incidental Music, Andrew Lippa; Casting, Telsey + Company; Marketing, Type A Marketing (Anne Rippey, Nick Pramik) Music Coordinator, Michael Keller; Production Supervisor, Beverley Randolph; Production Management, Aurora Productions (Gene O'Donovan, Ben Heller, Rachel Sherbill, Jarid Sumner, Melissa Mazdra, Amanda Raymond, Graham Forden, Liza Luxenberg, Janelle Coats); General Management, 101 Productions Ltd. (Wendy Orshan, Jeffrey M. Wilson, David Auster, Elie Landau); Company Manager, Sean Free; Stage Manager, Scott Taylor Rollison; Assistant Stage Manager, Allison A. Lee; Associate Directors, Heidi Miami Marshal, Steve Bebout; Associate Choreographer, Dontee Kiehn; Associate Company Manager, Chris D'Angelo; Drama League Directing Fellow, David F. Chapman; Associate Design: Frank McCullough (set), MaryAnn D. Smith, David Kaley (costumes), Yael Lubetzky (lighting), Jason Crystal (sound), Jeremy Chernick (special effects), Ceili Clemens (puppets); Automated Lighting, Aland Henderson; Assistant Design: Lauren Alvarez, Jeffrey Hinchee, Christine Peters (set), Sarah Laux (costumes), Joel Shier (lighting), Jorge Vargas (makeup); Costume Assistant, Jennifer A. Jacob; Assistant in Puppetry, Meredith Miller; Production Crew: Paul T. Wimmer (production carpenter), Bill Partello (assistant carpenter/automation), Bryan S. Davis (flyman), J. Michael Pitzer (production electrician), Mike Hyman (head electrician), Jeremy Wahlers (assistant electrician), Stephen R. Long (lead follow spot), Denise J. Grillo (production props), Kevin Crawford (assistant props), David Gotwald (production sound), Scott Silvian (assistant sound), Darin Stillman (advance sound), Linda Lee (wardrobe supervisor), Andrea Gonzalez (assistant wardrobe supervisor), Ken Brown (Mr. Lane's dresser), Paula Davis (Ms. Neuwirth's dresser), Jennifer Barnes, Ceili Clemens, Del Miskie, Ronald Tagert, John Webber (dressers), Barry Enst (hair & makeup supervisor), Suzanne Storey, Whitney Adkins Mvondo (hair dressers); Music Preparation, Kaye-Houston Music Inc., Anne Kaye, Doug Houston; Music Preparation Assistants, Russell Driscoll, Ernst Ebell III; Electronic Music Programmer, James Abbott; Additional Orchestrations, August Eriksmoen, Danny Troob; Additional Drum & Percussion Arrangements, Damien Bassman; Guardian, Katy Lathan; Stage Management Production Assistants, Zac Chandler, CJ LaRoche, Jenn McNeil, Alison Roberts, Deanna Weiner; Company Management Assistants, Johnny Milani, Kathleen Mueller; Lighting Design Production Assistant, Alec Thorne; Producer Assistants: Missy Greenberg (Mr. Oken), Eileen Williams (Mr. Furman), Erlinda Vo (Mr. Leavitt); Assistant to Mr. Lippa, Will Van Dyke; Assistant to Mr. Lane, Andrea Wolfson; Advertising, Serino Coyne, Sandy Block, Angelo Desimini; Interactive Marketing, Situation Interactive; Press, The Publicity Office, Marc Thibodeau, Jeremy Shaffer, Michael S. Borowski, Matthew Fasano; Cast recording: Decca 001428002

CAST *The Addams Family*: Gomez Addams **Nathan Lane**; Morticia Addams **Bebe Neuwirth**; Uncle Fester **Kevin Chamberlin**; Grandma **Jackie Hoffman**; Wednesday Addams **Krysta Rodriguez**; Pugsley Addams **Adam Riegler**; Lurch **Zachary James**; *The Beineke Family*: Mal Beineke **Terrence Mann**; Alice Beineke **Carolee Carmello**; Lucas Beineke **Wesley Taylor**; *The Addams Ancestors*: **Erick Buckley, Rachel de Benedet, Matthew Gumley, Fred Inkley, Morgan James, Clark Johnson, Barrett Martin, Jessica Lea Patty, Liz Ramos, Charlie Sutton, Aléna Watters**; Standby for Gomez Addams and Mal Beineke **Merwin Foard**; Swings **Jim Borstelmann, Colin Cunliffe, Valerie Fagan, Samantha Sturm**

UNDERSTUDIES Jim Borstelmann (Gomez Addams, Uncle Fester), Erick Buckley (Uncle Fester), Colin Cunliffe (Lucas Beineke), Rachel deBenedet (Morticia Addams), Valerie Fagan (Alice Beineke, Grandma), Matthew Gumley (Pugsley Addams), Fred Inkley (Lurch, Mal Beineke), Morgan James (Alice Beineke, Wednesday Addams), Clark Johnson (Lucas Beineke), Barrett Martin (Lurch), Jessica Lea Patty (Morticia Addams, Wednesday Addams)

ORCHESTRA Mary Mitchell Campbell (Conductor), Chris Fenwick (Associate Conductor/keyboard 1), Victoria Paterson (Concert Master/violin), Sean Carney (violin), Hiroko Taguchi (viola), Allison Seidner (cello), Tony Kadleck (lead trumpet), Bud Burridge (trumpet), Randy Andos (trombones/tuba), Erica Von Kleist (reed 1), Charles Pillow (reed 2), Mark Thrasher (reed 3), Zohar Schondorf (French horn), Damien Bassman (drums), Dave Kuhn (bass), Will Van Dyke (keyboard 2), Jim Hershman (guitars), Billy Miller (percussion)

MUSICAL NUMBERS Overture, When You're an Addams, Pulled, Where Did We Go Wrong, One Normal Night, Morticia, What If, Full Disclosure, Waiting, Full Disclosure – Part 2, Entr'acte, Just Around the Corner, The Moon and Me, Happy/ Sad, Crazier Than You, Let's Not Talk About Anything Else But Love, In the Arms, Live Before We Die, Tango de Amor, Move Toward the Darkness

2009–2010 AWARDS Drama Desk Award and Outer Critics Circle Awards: Outstanding Set Design (Phelim McDermott, Julian Crouch, and Basil Twist)

SETTING The Addams Family mansion in Central Park, New York City. New York premiere of a new musical presented in two acts. World premiere (out-of-town tryout) at the Ford Center for the Performing Arts Oriental Theatre in Chicago, Illinois, November 13, 2009–January 10, 2010.

SYNOPSIS Based on the beloved *The New Yorker* cartoon characters created by American cartoonist Charles Addams, *The Addams Family* is a new musical comedy about the ghoulish clan that lives by its own rules in a haunted mansion. The macabre family is put to the test when daughter Wednesday falls for the normal "boy next door," Lucas Beineke. When the Beineke family comes to dinner, Gomez, Morticia, Wednesday, Pugsley, Fester, Grandma, and Lurch are sent headlong into a night that will change the family forever.

Nathan Lane and Bebe Neuwirth (photos by Joan Marcus)

Jackie Hoffman and Adam Riegler

Kevin Chamberlin, Terrence Mann, and Nathaan Lane

Nathan Lane and
Krysta Rodriguez

Nathan Lane and Terrence Mann

Nathan Lane and Company

Adam Riegler,
Krysta Rodriguez,
and Wesley Taylor

Bebe Neuwirth, Nathan Lane, and Company

Million Dollar Quartet

Nederlander Theatre; First Preview: March 13, 2010; Opening Night: April 11, 2010; 34 previews, 57 performances as of May 31, 2010

Book by Colin Escott & Floyd Mutrux; Original concept and direction by Floyd Mutrux; Inspired by Elvis Presley, Johnny Cash, Jerry Lee Lewis, and Carl Perkins; Produced by Relevant Theatricals (Gigi Pritzker and Ted Rawlins), John Cossette Productions, American Pop Anthology, Broadway Across America (John Gore, CEO; Thomas B. McGrath, Chairman; Jennifer Costello, Associate Producer; Sara Skolnick, Associate Producer), James L. Nederlander; Director, Eric Schaeffer; Musical Arrangements and Supervisor, Chuck Mead; Set, Derek McLane; Costumes, Jane Greenwood; Lighting, Howell Binkley; Sound, Kai Harada; Hair & Wigs, Tom Watson; Associate Music Supervisor, August Eriksmoen; Casting, Telsey + Company; Marketing Director, Carol Chiavetta; Marketing, Allied Live LLC; Production Stage Manager, Robert Witherow; Production Manager, Juniper Street Productions, Hilary Blanken, Kevin Broomell, Guy Kwan, Ana Rose Greene, Sue Semaan; General Management, Alan Wasser, Allan Williams, Mark Shacket, Dawn Kusinski; Company Manager, Jolie Gabler; Assistant Director, David Ruttura; U.K. Consulting Producers, Joseph Smith, Michael McCabe; Japan Consulting Producer, TBS Services Inc.; Stage Manager, Carolyn Kelson; Assistant Stage Manager, Erik Hayden; Associate Design: Shoko Kambara (set), Moria Clinton (costumes), Ryan O'Gara (lighting); Assistant Lighting Designers, Amanda Zieve, Sean Beach; Music Contractor, Michael Keller; Additional Arrangements, Levi Kreis; Production Crew: Todd Frank (production carpenter), John Riggins (advance carpenter), Joseph Fererri Sr. (house carpenter), Joseph Fererri Jr. (flyman), Scott "Gus" Poitras (automation carpenter), James J. Fedigan, Randall Zaibek (production electricians), Ron Martin (head electrician), Richard Beck (house electrician), Patrick Pummill (production sound engineer), Will Sweeney (production properties supervisor), William Wright (house properties), David Arch (moving lights programmer), Ryan Rossetto (wardrobe supervisor), Francine Buryiak (dresser), Shanah-Ann Kendall (hair & wig supervisor), Ashley Ryan (makeup consultant), Alexandra Paull, Steve Chazaro, Jennie Bownan (technical production assistants); Advertising, SpotCo; For Allied Live Marketing, Elizabeth Kandel, Tanya Grubich, Victoria Cairl, Sara Rosenzweig; Press, Boneau/Bryan-Brown, Adrian Bryan-Brown, Aaron Meier, Amy Kass

CAST Carl Perkins **Robert Britton Lyons**; Johnny Cash **Lance Guest**; Jerry Lee Lewis **Levi Kreis**; Elvis Presley **Eddie Clendening**; Sam Phillips **Hunter Foster**; Dyanne **Elizabeth Stanley**

UNDERSTUDIES Christopher Ryan Grant (Johnny Cash), Erik Hayden (Elvis Presley, Carl Perkins), Jared Mason (Jerry Lee Lewis, Carl Perkins), Victoria Matlock (Dyanne), James Moye (Sam Phillips)

ORCHESTRA Corey Kaiser (bass), Larry Lelli (drums)

Levi Kreis, Elizabeth Stanley, Eddie Clendening, Hunter Foster, Lance Guest, and Robert Britton Lyons

MUSICAL NUMBERS Blue Suede Shoes, Real Wild Child, Matchbox, Who Do You Love? Folsom Prison Blues, Fever, Memories Are Made of This, That's All Right, Brown Eyed Handsome Man, Down By the Riverside, Sixteen Tons, My Babe, Long Tall Sally, Peace in the Valley, I Walk the Line, I Hear You Knocking, Party, Great Balls of Fire, Down By the Riverside (reprise), Hound Dog, Riders in the Sky, See You Later Alligator, Whole Lotta Shakin' Goin On

2009–2010 AWARDS Tony Award: Best Featured Actor in a Musical (Levi Kreis); Outer Critics Circle Award: Outstanding Featured Actor in a Musical (Levi Kreis)

SETTING Time: December 4, 1956. Place: Sun Records, Memphis, Tennessee. New York premiere of a new musical presented without intermission. World premiere presented at Seaside Music Theater, Daytona Beach, Florida (Tippin Davidson, Producer; Lester Malizia, Artistic Director) November 9–December 10, 2006. Further developed and produced at Village Theatre, Issaquah, Washington (Robb Hunt, Producer; Steve Tomkins, Artistic Director) September 19–November 25, 2007. The show had its Midwest premiere at the Goodman Theatre's Owen Theatre in Chicago September 26–October 26, 2008 with most of this cast, and transferred to Chicago's Apollo Theatre on October 31, 2008 where it is still playing.

SYNOPSIS On December 4, 1956, an auspicious twist of fate brought Johnny Cash, Jerry Lee Lewis, Carl Perkins, and Elvis Presley together. The place was Sun Records' storefront studio in Memphis. The man who made it happen was Sam Phillips, the "Father of Rock and Roll," who discovered them all. The four young musicians united for the only time in their careers for an impromptu recording that has come to be known as one of the greatest rock jam sessions of all time.

Hunter Foster and Levi Kreis

Robert Britton Lyons, Eddie Clendening, and Lance Guest

Robert Britton Lyons and Lance Guest

Levi Kreis, Robert Britton Lyons, Eddie Clendening, and Lance Guest

Levi Kreis, Robert Britton Lyons, Eddie Clendening, and Lance Guest

*Levi Kreis, Robert Britton Lyons,
Corey Kaiser, Lance Guest, and
(kneeling) Eddie Clendening,
(photos by Joan Marcus)*

La Cage aux Folles

Longacre Theatre; First Preview: April 6, 2010; Opening Night: April 18, 2010; 15 previews, 49 performances as of May 31, 2010

Music and lyrics by Jerry Herman, book by Harvey Fierstein; Based on the play *La Cage aux Folles* by Jean Poiret; Presented by the Menier Chocolate Factory; Produced by Sonia Friedman Productions, David Babani, Barry and Fran Weissler, Edwin W. Schloss, Bob Bartner/Norman Tulchin, Broadway Across America (John Gore, CEO; Thomas B. McGrath, Chairman; Beth Williams, COO & Head of Production), Matthew Mitchell, Raise the Roof 4 (Harriet Newman Leve, Jennifer Manocherian, Elaine Krauss), Richard Winkler/Chris Bensinger/Deborah Taylor/Pam Laudenslager/Jane Bergère, Arlene Scanlan/John O'Boyle, Independent Presenters Network, Olympus Theatricals (Liz Timperman, Executive Director), Allen Spivak, Jerry Frankel/Bat-Barry Productions (Robert Masterson & Barry Weisbord), Nederlander Presentations Inc., INC/Harvey Weinstein; Director, Terry Johnson; Choreography, Lynne Page; Music Supervision, Orchestrations, & Dance Arrangements, Jason Carr; Set, Tim Shortall; Costumes, Matthew Wright; Lighting, Nick Richings; Sound, Jonathan Deans; Wigs & Makeup, Richard Mawbey; Associate Choreographer, Nicholas Cunningham; Technical Supervision, Arthur Siccardi & Patrick Sullivan; Production Stage Manger, Kristen Harris; Associate Producers, Carlos Arana, Robert Driemeyer; Music Director, Todd Ellison; Music Coordinator, John Miller; Casting, Duncan Stewart; U.K. General Management, Diane Benjamin, Pam Skinner, Tom Siracusa; General Manager, B.J. Holt; Executive Producer, Alecia Parker; Company Manager, Kimberly Kelly; Stage Manager, Glynn David Turner; Assistant Stage Manager, Neveen Mahmoud; Associate General Manager, Hilary Hamilton; General Management Associates, Dana Sherman, Stephen Spadaro; Assistant Company Manager, Dominic Shiach; Original Set Design, David Farley; Associate Design: Bryan Johnson (set), Vivien Leone (lighting); Assistant Lighting Design, Michael Hill; U.K. Production Consultant, Kristen Turner; Production Crew: Karl Schuberth (head carpenter), James J. Fedigan, Randall Zaibek (production electricians), Eric Norris (head electrician), Robert Presley (head properties), Carin M. Ford (sound engineer), Simon Matthews (advance sound), Brigid Guy (production costume coordinator), Jessica Wornop (wardrobe supervisor), Jason Bishop, Cherie Cunningham, Tracey Diebold, Kimberly Santos Mark, William Hubner, Deborah Black, Anastasya Julia (dressers), John Curtin (hair & makeup supervisor), Wanda Gregory, Jorie Malan (hair & makeup assistants); Production Assistants, Aaron Elgart, Beth Stegman; Assistant to John Miller, David A. Vandervliet; Casting Associate, Benton Whitley; Vice President of Marketing, Todd Stuart; Director of Marketing, Ken Sperr; Advertising, SpotCo; Press, Boneau/Bryan-Brown, Adrian Bryan-Brown, Jim Byk, Michael Strassheim; Cast recording: PS Classics 1094

CAST Georges **Kelsey Grammer**; Angelique (Les Cagelles) **Nick Adams**; Bitelle (Les Cagelles) **Logan Keslar**; Chantal (Les Cagelles) **Sean Patrick Doyle**; Hanna (Les Cagelles) **Nicholas Cunningham**; Mercedes (Les Cagelles) **Terry Lavell**; Phaedra (Les Cagelles) **Sean A. Carmon**; Francis **Chris Hoch**; Babette **Cheryl Stern**; Jacob **Robin De Jesús**; Albin **Douglas Hodge**; Jean-Michel **A.J. Shively**; Anne **Elena Shaddow**; Colette **Heather Lindell**; Etienne **David Nathan Perlow**; Tabarro **Bill Nolte**; Jacqueline **Christine Andreas**; M. Renaud/M. Dindon **Fred Applegate**; Mme. Renaud/Mme. Dindon **Veanne Cox**; Waiter **Dale Hensley**; Swings **Christophe Caballero**, **Todd Lattimore**, **Caitlin Mundth**

UNDERSTUDIES Nick Adams (Jean-Michel), Christophe Caballero (Francis, Jacob), Sean Patrick Doyle (Jacob), Dale Hensley (Albin, Edouard Dindon, Francis, M. Renaud), Chris Hoch (Albin, Georges), Heather Lindell (Anne, Jacqueline, Mme. Dindon, Mme. Renaud), Caitlin Mundth (Anne), Bill Nolte (Edouard Dindon, Georges, M. Renaud), David Nathan Perlow (Jean-Michel), Cheryl Stern (Jacqueline, Mme. Dindon, Mme. Renaud)

ORCHESTRA Todd Ellison (Conductor/keyboards), Antony Geralis ; Associate Conductor/keyboards, Steve Kenyon and Roger Rosenberg (woodwinds), Don Downs (trumpet), Keith O'Quinn (tenor trombone), Marc Schmied (acoustic bass), Sean McDaniel (drums/percussion)

MUSICAL NUMBERS We Are What We Are, A Little More Mascara, With Anne on My Arm, With You on My Arm, Song on the Sand, La Cage aux Folles, I Am What I Am, Song on the Sand (reprise), Masculinity, Look Over There, Cocktail Counterpoint, The Best of Times, Look Over There (reprise), Finale

2009–2010 AWARDS Tony Awards: Best Revival of a Musical, Best Director of a Musical (Terry Johnson), Best Actor in a Musical (Douglas Hodge); Drama Desk Awards: Outstanding Musical Revival, Outstanding Actor in a Musical (Douglas Hodge), Outstanding Costume Design (Matthew Wright); Drama League Award: Best Revival of a Musical; Outer Critics Circle Awards: Outstanding Revival of a Musical; Outstanding Actor in a Musical (Douglas Hodge), Outstanding Director of a Musical (Terry Johnson), Outstanding Costume Design (Matthew Wright)

SETTING Summer, St. Tropez, France; in and around the La Cage aux Folles nightclub. Revival of a musical presented in fourteen scenes in two acts. Originally presented on Broadway at the Palace Theatre August 21, 1983–November 15, 1987, playing 1,761 performances (see *Theatre World* Vol. 40, page 10). The first Broadway revival played the Marquis Theatre December 9, 2004–June 26, 2005, playing 229 performances (see *Theatre World* Vol. 61, page 44). This production premiered at London's Menier Chocolate Factory (David Babani, Artistic Director), starring Mr. Hodge, November 23, 2007–March 8, 2008 and transferred to the Playhouse Theatre October 30, 2008. The show won 2009 Olivier Awards for Best Musical Revival and Best Actor in a Musical for Douglas Hodge. *La Cage aux Folles* made history with this production's Tony Award win for Best Revival, as both the original and first revival productions won the award for Best Musical and Best Musical Revival, respectively, marking the first time a show has won the Best Musical award for every staged production.

SYNOPSIS Jerry Herman and Harvey Fierstein's hilarious musical comedy *La Cage aux Folles* returns to Broadway in this production presented by London's Menier Chocolate Factory. Kelsey Grammar stars as Georges, the owner of a glitzy nightclub in Saint-Tropez, and Douglas Hodges stars as his partner Albin, who moonlights as the glamorous chanteuse "Zaza." When Georges' son Jean-Michele brings his fiancée's conservative parents home to meet the flashy pair, the bonds of family are put to the test and the feather boas fly! In this extraordinary new version, *La Cage aux Folles* solidifies its place in history as a musical comedy classic.

Les Cagelles (photos by Joan Marcus)

Kelsey Grammer

Douglas Hodge

Les Cagelles

Christine Andreas
and Company

Kelsey Grammer and Douglas Hodge

American Idiot

St. James Theatre; First Preview: March 24, 2010; Opening Night: April 20, 2010; 26 previews, 48 performances as of May 31, 2010

Music by Green Day (Billie Joe Armstrong, Mike Dirnt, Tré Cool), lyrics by Billie Joe Armstrong, book by Billie Joe Armstrong and Michael Mayer; Produced by Tom Hulce, Ira Pittelman, Ruth and Stephen Hendel, Vivek J. Tiwary and Gary Kaplan, Aged in Wood and Burnt Umber, Scott M. Delman, Latitude Link, HOP Theatricals and Jeffrey Finn, Larry Welk, Chris Bensinger/Michael Filerman and Carl Moellenberg/Deborah Taylor, Allan S. Gordon and Élan V. McAllister, Berkeley Repertory Theatre, in association with Awaken Entertainment (Jennifer Maloney and Steve Kantor), John Pinckard and John Domo; Director, Michael Mayer; Choreographer, Steven Hoggett; Musical Supervision, Arrangements, and Orchestrations, Tom Kitt; Additional Lyrics, Mike Dirnt & Tré Cool, Set, Christine Jones; Costumes, Andrea Lauer; Lighting, Kevin Adams; Sound, Brian Ronan; Video/Projections, Darrel Maloney; Casting, Jim Carnahan, Carrie Gardner; Production Stage Manager, James Harker; Technical Supervisor, Hudson Theatrical Associates, Neil A. Mazzella, Sam Ellis, Irene Wang; Music Coordinator, Michael Keller; General Management, Abbie M. Strassler; Marketing, Type A Marketing (Anne Rippey, Nick Pramik, Janette Rouch); Music Director, Carmel Dean; Associate Choreographer, Lorin Latarro; Associate Director, Johanna McKeon; Associate Producers, SenovvA (K Lee Harvey, Arianna Knapp, Jon Kimbell), Tix Productions, Tracy Straus and Barney Straus, Lorenzo Thione and Jay Kuo, Pat Magnarella, Christopher Maring; Company Manager, Kimberly Helms; Production Vocal Supervisor, Liz Caplan Vocal Studios LLC; Stage Manager, Freda Farrell; Assistant Stage Manager, Bethany Russell; Assistant Company Manager, Rachel Scheer; Dance Captain, Lorin Latarro; Assistant Dance Captain, Ben Thompson; Assistant Director, Austin Regan; Hair, Brandon Dailey; Wigs, Leah Loukas; Makeup, Amy Jean Wright; Flying, Flying by Foy; Associate Design: Edward Coco (set), Chloe Chapin (costumes), Aaron Sporer (lighting), Ashley Hanson (sound), Dan Scully (video/projections); Assistant Design: Damon Pelletier (set), Janice Lopez (costumes), Benjamin Travis (lighting); Assistant to the Lighting Designer, Barbara Samuels; Assistant Editor, Nico Sarudiansky; Moving Light Programmer, Victor Seastone; Video and Projection Programmer, Jeff Cady/SenovvA; Video and Projection Assistant, Alex Marshall/SenovvA; Production Crew: Donald J. Oberpriller (production carpenter), Dave Brown (flyman), Mark Diaz (flying automation/deck carpenter), Greg Husinko (production electrician), Eric Abbott (head electrician), Sue Pelkofer, Tom Maloney (follow spots), David Dignazio (production sound operator), Cody Spencer (assistant sound), Joe Lenihan (deck sound), Greg Peeler (production video/deck audio), Joseph P. Harris Jr. (production property supervisor), Eric Castaldo (head properties), Angela Simpson (wardrobe supervisor), Jaki Harris (assistant wardrobe supervisor), Meredith Benson, Ryan Oslak, Danny Paul, Julienne Schubert-Blechman, Jack Scott, Yleana Nuñez (dressers), Kevin Maybee (hair supervisor); Craft Artisan, Jennilee Houghton; Costume Interns, Amy Sutton, Matt Allemon, Mikaela Holmes; Costume Shoppers, Paloma Young, Kara Harmon; Assistant Synthesizer Programmer, Bryan Cook; Music Preparation, Colleen Darnall; Management Associate, Scott Armstrong; Assistant to Mr. Hulce, Christopher Maring; Assistant to Mr. Pittelman, Dorothy Evins; Casting Associate, Jillian Cimini; Interns: Clinton Harwood, Katie Klehr White (stage management), Jamie Caplan, Amanda Gagnon (production office); Advertising, Serino Coyne Inc., Tom Callahan, Scott Johnson, Kristina Curatolo; Press, The Hartman Group, Michael Hartman, Leslie Baden, Alyssa Hart; Cast recording: Reprise Records 523724

CAST Johnny **John Gallagher Jr.**; Will **Michael Esper**; Tunny **Stark Sands**; Heather **Mary Faber**; Whatsername **Rebecca Naomi Jones**; St. Jimmy **Tony Vincent**; The Extraordinary Girl **Christina Sajous**; Ensemble **Declan Bennett, Andrew Call, Gerard Canonico, Miguel Cervantes, Joshua Henry, Brian Charles Johnson, Leslie McDonel, Chase Peacock, Theo Stockman, Ben Thompson, Alysha Umphress, Libby Winters**; Standby for Johnny, Will, Tunny **Van Hughes**; Swings **Joshua Kobak, Lorin Latarro, Omar Lopez-Cepero, Aspen Vincent**

UNDERSTUDIES Declan Bennett (Will), Andrew C. Call (St. Jimmy), Joshua Kobak (St. Jimmy), Leslie McDonel (Heather, Whatsername), Chase Peacock (Johnny), Christina Sajous (Whatsername), Ben Thompson (Tunny), Aspen Vincent (The Extraordinary Girl), Libby Winters (Heather, The Extraordinary Girl)

BAND Carmel Dean (Conductor/keyboard/accordion), Trey Files (drums/percussion), Michael Aarons (guitar 1), Alec Berlin (guitar 2), Dan Grennes (bass), Cenovia Cummins (violin), Alissa Smith (viola), Amy Ralske (cello), Jared Stein (Associate Conductor)

MUSICAL NUMBERS American Idiot, Jesus of Suburbia, City of the Damned, I Don't Care, Dearly Beloved, Tales of Another Broken Home, Holiday, Boulevard of Broken Dreams, Favorite Son, Are We the Waiting, St. Jimmy, Give Me Novacaine, Last of the American Girls/She's a Rebel, Last Night on Earth, Too Much Too Soon, Before the Lobotomy, Extraordinary Girl, Before the Lobotomy (reprise), When It's Time, Know Your Enemy, 21 Guns, Letterbomb, Wake Me Up When September Ends, Homecoming, The Death of St. Jimmy, East 12th Street, Nobody Likes You, Rock and Roll Girlfriend, We're Coming Home Again, Whatsername

2009–2010 AWARDS Tony Awards: Best Scenic Design of a Musical (Christine Jones), Best Lighting Design of a Musical (Kevin Adams); Drama Desk Awards: Outstanding Director of a Musical (Michael Mayer), Outstanding Lighting Design (Kevin Adams)

SETTING Time: The Recent Past. Place: Jingletown, U.S.A. New York premiere of a new musical presented without intermission. Developed at Berkeley Repertory Theatre November–December 2008 and New York Stage and Film and the Powerhouse Theater at Vassar, July 2009. World premiere at Berkeley Repertory's Roda Theatre (Tony Taccone, Artistic Director; Susan Medak, Managing Director) September 4–November 15, 2009 prior to its Broadway engagement.

SYNOPSIS Based on Green Day's Grammy® Award-winning rock opera album of the same name, *American Idiot* follows the exhilarating journey of a new generation of young Americans as they strive to find meaning in a post 9/11 world, borne along by Green Day's electrifying score. The musical includes every song from the acclaimed album as well as several songs from the band's Grammy® Award-winning new release, *21st Century Breakdown*.

Christina Sajous and Stark Sands

John Gallagher Jr. (photo by Kevin Berne)

Rebecca Naomi Jones
(photos by Paul Kolnik unless noted)

Michael Esper, Stark Sands, and John Gallagher Jr.

Michael Esper and Mary Faber

Rebecca Naomi Jones and Company

Sondheim on Sondheim

Studio 54; First Preview: March 19, 2010; Opening Night: April 22, 2010; 37 previews, 44 performances as of May 31, 2010

Music and lyrics by Stephen Sondheim; Conceived and directed by James Lapine; Produced by the Roundabout Theatre Company (Todd Haimes, Artistic Director; Harold Wolpert, Managing Director; Julia C. Levy, Executive Director); Musical Staging, Dan Knechtges; Music Direction/Arrangements, David Loud; Sets, Beowulf Boritt; Costumes, Susan Hilferty; Lighting, Ken Billington; Sound, Dan Moses Schreier; Video & Projections, Peter Flaherty; Orchestrations, Michael Starobin; Music Coordinator, John Miller; Conductor/Rehearsal Pianist, Andy Einhorn; Production Stage Manager, Peter Hanson; Casting, Jim Carnahan; Technical Supervisor, Steve Beers; Executive Producer/General Manager, Sydney Beers; Marketing/Sales Promotion, David B. Steffen; Founding Director, Gene Feist; Associate Artistic Director, Scott Ellis; Director of Artistic Development & Casting, Jim Carnahan; Education, Greg McCaslin; Finance, Susan Neiman; Telesales, Marco Frezza; Sales Operations, Charlie Garbowski Jr.; Concept Inspiration, David Kernan; Company Manager, Denise Cooper; Stage Manager, Shawn Pennington; Wigs, Tom Watson; Hair, John Barrett; Company Manager Assistant, David Solomon; Assistant Director, Sarna Lapine; Assistant Musical Stager, DJ Gray; Assistant to Mr. Sondheim, Steve Clar; Assistant Technical Supervisor, Chad Woerner; Associate Design: Jo Winiarski (set), Tricia Barsamian (costumes), John Demous (lighting), David Bullard (sound), Austin Switser (video/video programmer), Joshua Higgason (video); Assistant Design: Jason Lajka, Maiko Chii (set), Jeremy Cunningham (lighting), Daniel Brodie (video); Assistant to Costume Designer, Becky Lasky; Costume Shopper, Brooke Cohen; Production Sound Engineer, Scott Anderson; Lead Video Animator, Michael Bell-Smith; Musical Assistant, David Ben Dabbon; Assistant to John Miller, Nichole Jennino; Production Crew: Dan Hoffman (production carpenter), Ann Cavanaugh (automation carpenter), Steve Jones (flyman), John Wooding (production electrician), Timothy F. Rogers (moving light programmer), Jessica Morton (conventional light programmer), Paul Coltoff, Jenn Fagant (spot operators), T.J. McEvoy (deck sound), Buist Bickley (production properties coordinator), Lawrence Jennino (house properties), Nadine Hettel (wardrobe supervisor), Mary Ann Oberpriller, Suzanne Lunney-Delahunt, Julie Tobia (dressers), John James (hair supervisor), IATSE Apprentice, Michael Widmer; Emmy Frank (production assistant); Synthesizer Programmer, Randy Cohen; Music Copying, Emily Grishman, Katherine Edmonds; Advertising, SpotCo; Press, Boneau/Bryan-Brown, Adrian Bryan-Brown, Matt Polk, Jessica Johnson, Amy Kass Cast recording: PS Classics 1093

CAST Barbara Cook, Leslie Kritzer, Norm Lewis, Erin Mackey, Euan Morton, Matthew Scott, Vanessa Williams, Tom Wopat

UNDERSTUDIES Kyle Harris (Euan Morton, Matthew Scott), N'Kenge (Vanessa Williams, Leslie Kritzer, Erin Mackey)

ORCHESTRA Andy Einhorn (Conductor/piano), Mark Hartman (Assistant Conductor/keyboard), Christian Hebel (Concert Master/violin), Sarah Seiver (cello), Rick Heckman & Alden Banta (woodwinds), R.J. Kelly (French horn), Bill Ellison (bass)

MUSICAL CHRONOLOGY I'll Meet You at the Donut (*By George*); So Many People (*Saturday Night*); Something's Coming (*West Side Story*), Smile, Girls (*Gypsy*); Invocation/Forget War, Love Is in the Air, Comedy Tonight (*A Funny Thing Happened on the Way to the Forum*); Anyone Can Whistle (*Anyone Can Whistle*); Do I Hear a Waltz? (*Do I Hear a Waltz?*); Take Me to the World (*Evening Primrose*); You Could Drive a Person Crazy, The Wedding Is Off, Multitudes of Amys, Happily Ever After, Being Alive, Company (*Company*); Ah, But Underneath, Waiting for the Girls Upstairs, In Buddy's Eyes (*Follies*); Send in the Clowns, A Weekend in the Country (*A Little Night Music*); Entr'acte (*Pacific Overtures*); Epiphany (*Sweeney Todd*); Now You Know, Franklin Shepard Inc., Good Thing Going, Opening Doors, Not a Day Goes By, Old Friends (*Merrily We Roll Along*); Finishing the Hat, Sunday, Beautiful (*Sunday in the Park With George*); Children

Will Listen, Ever After (*Into the Woods*); Something Just Broke, The Gun Song (*Assassins*); Fosca's Entrance (I Read), Is This What You Call Love?, Loving You, Happiness (*Passion*); The Best Thing That Ever Has Happened (*Road Show* formerly titled *Bounce*); God (original number for *Sondheim on Sondheim*)

2009–2010 AWARDS Drama Desk Award: Outstanding Musical Revue; Drama League Award: Outstanding Musical

World premiere of a new musical revue with video presented in two acts.

SYNOPSIS He brought us *Into The Woods, Company, Sweeney Todd, A Little Night Music, Sunday in the Park with George, A Funny Thing Happened On The Way To The Forum, West Side Story* and *Gypsy* (to name a few). By writing songs that reflect the complexity of his characters, he has changed the way we define a great musical. But even though millions of fans know his songs by heart, few know much about Stephen Sondheim himself. Until now. *Sondheim on Sondheim* offers an intimate portrait of the famed composer in his *own* words... and music. Through the use of exclusive interview footage, the revue takes an inside look at Sondheim's personal life and artistic process. With brand-new arrangements of over two dozen Sondheim tunes, ranging from the beloved to the obscure, and helmed by frequent Sondheim collaborator James Lapine, this unique experience takes audiences inside the life and mind of an ordinary New Yorker... with an extraordinary talent.

Norm Lewis, Vanessa Williams, Matthew Scott, Euan Morton (photos by Richard Termine)

Vanessa Williams, Tom Wopat, Matthew Scott, Erin Mackey, Barbara Cook, Euan Morton, Norm Lewis, and Leslie Kritzer

Tom Wopat (front), Euan Morton, Erin Mackey, Matthew Scott, Leslie Kritzer, and Norm Lewis

Euan Morton, Leslie Kritzer, Erin Mackey, and Matthew Scott

Barbara Cook and Vanessa Williams

Erin Mackey, Vanessa Williams, Leslie Kritzer, and Barbara Cook

Promises, Promises

Broadway Theatre; First Preview: March 28, 2010; Opening Night: April 25, 2010; 30 previews, 41 performances as of May 31, 2010

Book by Neil Simon, music by Burt Bacharach, lyrics by Hal David; Based on the screenplay *The Apartment* by Billy Wilder and I.A.L. Diamond; By arrangement with MGM On Stage; Produced by Broadway Across America (John Gore, CEO; Thomas B. McGrath, Chairman; Beth Williams, COO & Head of Production), Craig Zadan, Neil Meron, The Weinstein Company/Terry Allen Kramer, Candy Spelling, Pat Addiss, Bernie Abrams/Michael Speyer, Takonkiet Viravan/Scenario Thailand, Norton Herrick/Barry & Fran Weissler/TBS Service/Laurel Oztemel; Director/Choreographer, Rob Ashford; Orchestrations, Jonathan Tunick; Music Director, Phil Reno; Set, Scott Pask; Costumes, Bruce Pask; Lighting, Donald Holder; Sound, Brian Ronan; Hair and Wigs, Tom Watson; Musical Coordinator, Howard Joines; Dance Music Arrangements, David Chase; Casting, Tara Rubin Casting; Production Stage Manager, Michael J. Passaro; Associate Director/Choreographer, Christopher Bailey; Production Manager, Juniper Street Productions (Hilary Blanken, Guy Kwan, Kevin Broomell, Ana Rose Green); Marketing, Type A Marketing, Anne Rippey; General Manager, Alan Wasser, Allan Williams, Mark D. Shacket; Associate Producers, Michael McCabe/Joseph Smith, Stage Ventures 2009, No. 2 Limited Partnership; Executive Producer, Beth Williams; Company Manager, Laura Kirspel; Fight Director, Thomas Schall; Stage Manager, Pat Sosnow; Assistant Director, Stephen Sposito; SDC Directing Fellow, Gregg Wiggans; Dance Captain, Sarah O'Gleby; Assistant Dance Captain, Matt Wall; Associate Design: Orit Jacoby Carroll (set), Matthew Pachtman (costumes), Karen Spahn, Carolyn Wong (lighting), Joanna Lynne Staub (sound); Assistant Design: Lauren Alvarez (set) Katie Irish, Jessica Pabst (costumes); Assistants to Designers: G. Warren Stiles (set), R. Christopher Stokes (lighting); Makeup, Ashley Ryan; Technical Director, Fred Gallo; Moving Lights Programmer, Richard Tyndall; Production Crew: Jack Anderson (head carpenter), Geoffrey Vaughn (flyman), Hugh Hardyman (automation carpenter), Andrew Elman, Alan Grudzinski, Matty Lynch (assistant carpenters), Randall Zaibek, James Fedigan (production electricians), Michael Cornell (head electrician), Tim Abel (production properties supervisor), David Fulton (head properties supervisor), Christopher Sloan (production sound engineer), Mike Farfalla (deck audio), Jason McKenna (advance audio), Dolly Williams (wardrobe supervisor), Fred Castner (assistant wardrobe supervisor); Barry Hoff (Mr. Hayes' dresser), Jay Woods (Ms. Chenoweth's dresser), Shana Albery, Brendan Cooper, Melanie McClintock, Christopher Murdock, Virginia Neinenger, David Oliver (dressers), Thomas Augustine (hair supervisor), Carmel Vargyas (assistant hair supervisor), Joshua First (hair dresser), Charles Rasmussen (house carpenter), George D. Milne (house electrician), Rick DalCortivo (house properties), Thomas Cole Jr. (house flyman); Music Copying, Emily Grishman, Katherine Edmonds; Synthesizer Programmer, Bruce Samuels; Advertising, Serino Coyne Inc.; Website and Internet Marketing, Art Meets Commerce; Press, The Hartman Group; Cast recording: Masterworks Broadway 773495

CAST Chuck Baxter **Sean Hayes**; J.D. Sheldrake **Tony Goldwyn**; Fran Kubelik **Kristin Chenoweth**; Eddie Roth **Keith Kühl**; Mr. Dobitch **Brooks Ashmanskas**; Sylvia Gilhooley, Miss Polanski **Megan Sikora**; Mike Kirkeby **Peter Benson**; Ginger, Miss Della Hoya, Lum Ding Hostess **Cameron Adams**; Mr. Eichelberger **Seán Martin Hingston**; Vivien, Miss Wong **Mayumi Miguel**; Dr. Dreyfuss **Dick Latessa**; Jesse Vanderhof **Ken Land**; Miss Kreplinski, Helen Sheldrake **Ashley Amber**; Company Doctor, Karl Kubelik **Brian O'Brien**; Miss Olson **Helen Anker**; Kathy, Orchestra Voice **Sarah Jane Everman**; Patsy, Orchestra Voice **Kristen Beth Williams**; Barbara, Orchestra Voice **Nikki Renée Daniels**; Sharon, Orchestra Voice **Chelsea Krombach**; Night Watchman, New Young Executive **Ryan Watkinson**; Lum Ding Waiter **Matt Loehr**; Eugene **Adam Perry**; Marge MacDougall **Katie Finneran**; Swings **Nathan Balser, Wendi Bergamini, Sarah O'Gleby, Matt Wall**

UNDERSTUDIES Ashley Amber (Miss Olson, Miss Polanski), Nathan Balser (Eugene, Jesse Vanderhof, Karl Kubelik, Lum Ding Waiter, Mike Kirkeby, Mr. Dobitch, Mr. Eichelberger, Night Watchman), Wendi Bergamini (Ginger, Helen Sheldrake, Miss Della Hoya, Miss Kreplinski, Miss Olson, Miss Polanski, Miss Wong, Orchestra Voice, Sylvia Gilhooley, Vivien), Sarah Jane Everman (Fran Kubelik), Ken Land (Dr. Dreyfuss, J.D. Sheldrake), Matt Loehr (Chuck Baxter, Mike Kirkeby), Sarah O'Gleby (Ginger, Helen Sheldrake, Miss Della Hoya, Miss Kreplinski, Miss Olson, Miss Polanski, Miss Wong, Orchestra Voice, Sylvia Gilhooley, Vivien), Brian O'Brien (J.D. Sheldrake, Jesse Vanderhof, Mr. Dobitch, Mr. Eichelberger), Megan Sikora (Fran Kubelik, Marge MacDougall), Matt Wall (Eugene, Jesse Vanderhof, Karl Kubelik, Lum Ding Waiter, Mike Kirkeby, Mr. Dobitch, Mr. Eichelberger, Night Watchman), Ryan Watkinson (Karl Kubelik), Kristen Beth Williams (Marge MacDougall)

ORCHESTRA Phil Reno (Conductor); Mat Eisenstein (Associate Conductor/keyboard 2); Les Scott, James Ercole, Kenneth Dybisz, Jacqueline Henderson (reeds); Barry Danielian, David Trigg, Dan Urness (trumpets); Jason Jackson rombone; Perry Cavari (drums); Michael Kuennen (bass), Ed Hamilton (guitar), Bill Hayes (percussion); Rick Dolan (Concert Master/violin); Elizabeth Lim-Dutton (violin), Liuh-Wen Ting (viola), Laura Bontrager (cello), Matthew Perri (keyboard 1)

MUSICAL NUMBERS Half As Big As Life, Grapes of Roth, Upstairs, You'll Think of Someone, Our Little Secret, I Say a Little Prayer, She Likes Basketball, Knowing When to Leave, Where Can You Take a Girl?, Wanting Things, Turkey Lurkey Time, A House Is Not a Home, A Fact Can Be a Beautiful Thing, Whoever You Are, Christmas Day, A House Is Not a Home (reprise), A Young Pretty Girl Like You, I'll Never Fall in Love Again, Promises, Promises, I'll Never Fall in Love Again (reprise)

2009–2010 AWARDS Tony Award: Best Featured Actress in a Musical (Katie Finneran); Drama Desk Award: Outstanding Featured Actress in a Musical (Katie Finneran)

SETTING Manhattan, 1962. Revival of a musical presented in two acts. Originally presented on Broadway at the Shubert Theatre December 1, 1968–January 1, 1972, playing 1,281 performances (see *Theatre World* Vol. 25, page 32). While this production marked the first Broadway revival, New York City Center *Encores!* presented a staged concert of the show March 20-23, 1997, starring Martin Short as "Chuck" and Christine Baranski as "Marge" (see *Theatre World* Vol. 53, page 53). Coincidentally, Dick Latessa played "Dr. Dreyfuss" in that production, the role he recreates in this revival.

SYNOPSIS Based on the 1960 Academy Award-winning Billy Wilder film *The Apartment, Promises, Promises* tells the story of the Consolidated Life Insurance Company and Chuck Baxter, one of its charming young employees. In an effort to advance at the company, Chuck lends executives his apartment for their extramarital romantic trysts. But things become slightly complicated when Fran Kubelik, the object of Chuck's affection, becomes the mistress of one of his executives.

Sean Hayes and Company

Brooks Ashmanskas, Ken Land, Peter Benson, and
Seán Martin Hingston (photos by Joan Marcus)

Kristin Chenoweth, Dick Latessa, and Sean Hayes

Sean Hayes and Katie Finneran

Tony Goldwyn and Kristin Chenoweth

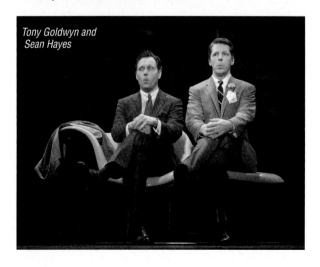

Tony Goldwyn and
Sean Hayes

Kristin Chenoweth and Company

Fences

Cort Theatre; First Preview: April 14, 2010; Opening Night: April 26, 2010; 13 previews, 40 performances as of May 31, 2010

Written by August Wilson; Produced by Carole Shorenstein Hays and Scott Rudin; Director, Kenny Leon; Original Music, Brandford Marsalis; Sets, Santo Loquasto; Costumes, Constanza Romero; Lighting, Brian MacDevitt; Sound, Acme Sound Partners; Production Stage Manager, Narda E. Alcorn; Casting, MelCap Casting, Mele Nagler, David Caparelliotis; Production Management, Aurora Productions, Gene O'Donovan, Ben Heller, Jarid Sumner, Rachel Sherbill, Melissa Mazdra, Amanda Raymond, Graham Forden, Liza Luxenberg; General Management, Stuart Thompson Productions, David Turner, James Triner; Associate Producer, Constanza Romero; Company Manager, Chris Morey; Fight Director, Rick Sordelet; Wigs, Charles LaPointe; Stage Manager, Michael P. Zaleski; Associate Director, Todd Kreidler; Associate Design: Jenny Sawyers (set), Katie Irish (costumes), Jennifer Schriever (lighting), Nick Borisjuk (sound); Assistant Design: Antje Ellerman, Yoki Lai (set), Aaron Parsekian (lighting); Production Crew: Edward Diz (production carpenter), Dan Coey (production electrician), Kathy Fabian/ Propstar (production properties coordinator), Darin Stillman (production sound engineer), Scott DeVerna (house electrician), Lonny Gaddy (house properties), Moira MacGregor (wardrobe supervisor), Anita-Ali Davis, Ginny Hounsell, Laura Ellington (dressers), Amy Neswald (hair supervisor) Alissa Zulvergold (child wrangler), Chelsea Antrim (production assistant); Propstar Associates, Carrie Mossman, Timothy Ferro; Fight Captain, Chris Chalk; Associates for Ms. Hays, Duffy Anderson-Rothe, Pip Ngo; Assistant to Ms. Hays, Paula Miller; Assistants to Mr. Rudin, Tim Kava, David Kennedy, Allie Moore, Matt Nemeth; Assistant to Mr. Thompson, Christopher Taggart; General Management Assistants, Megan E. Curren, Geo Karapetyan, Brittany Levasseur; General Management Interns, Erin Byrne, Andrew Lowy; Stage Management Interns, Erica Gambino, Benjamin Bales Karlin; Advertising, SpotCo; Marketing, Walk Tall Girl Productions, Marcia Pendleton, Jesse Wooden Jr., Kojo Ade, Sharif Colon, Merielin Lopez; Press, Boneau/Bryan-Brown, Chris Boneau, Heath Schwartz, Kelly Guiod

CAST Troy Maxon **Denzel Washington**; Jim Bono, *Troy's friend* **Stephen McKinley Henderson**; Rose, *Troy's wife* **Viola Davis**; Lyons, *Troy's oldest son by a previous marriage* **Russell Hornsby**; Gabriel, *Troy's brother* **Mykelti Williamson**; Cory, *Troy and Rose's son* **Chris Chalk**; Raynell, *Troy's daughter* **Eden Duncan-Smith** or **SaCha Stewart-Coleman**

STANDBYS Jason Dirden (Corey, Lyons), Michael Genet (Gabriel, Jim Bono), Roslyn Ruff (Rose), Keith Randolph Smith (Troy Maxson)

2009–2010 AWARDS Tony Awards: Best Play Revival, Best Actor in a Play (Denzel Washington), Best Actress in a Play (Viola Davis): Drama Desk Awards: Outstanding Revival of a Play (tie with *A View from the Bridge*), Outstanding Featured Actress in a Play (Viola Davis), Outstanding Music in a Play (Branford Marsalis); Outer Critics Circle Awards: Outstanding Revival of a Play, Outstanding Actor in a Play (Denzel Washington), Outstanding Actress in a Play (Viola Davis); New York Drama Critics' Circle Award: Viola Davis (Sustained Excellence); Drama League Award: Kenny Leon (Excellence in Directing); **Theatre World Award:** Chris Chalk

SETTING Pittsburg, 1957. Revival of a play presented in two acts. World premiere at Yale Repertory Theatre in 1985. Originally produced on Broadway at the 46th Street (now the Richard Rodgers) Theatre, starring James Earl Jones, Mary Alice, and Courtney B. Vance, March 17, 1987–June 26, 1988, playing 525 performances (see *Theatre World* Vol. 43, page 35). The play won the Pulitzer Prize for Drama, and Tony Awards for Best Play, Best Director (Lloyd Richards), Best Actor (Mr. Jones), and Best Featured Actress (Ms. Alice). This revival echoed three of those Tony Awards this year with Best Revival of Play win and acting awards for Mr. Washington and Ms. Davis. Coincidentally, Courtney B. Vance won a Theatre World Award for his performance as Cory that year, which Chris Chalk received this year for the same role.

SYNOPSIS Both a monumental drama and an intimate family portrait, *Fences* tells the story of Troy Maxson, a man torn between the glory of his past and the uncertainty of his future. Emboldened by pride and embittered by sacrifice, Troy is determined to make life better for future generations, even as he struggles to embrace the dreams of his own son.

Denzel Washington and Stephen McKinley Henderson

Denzel Washington and Viola Davis (photos by Joan Marcus)

Enron

Broadhurst Theatre; First Preview: April 8, 2010; Opening Night: April 27, 2010; Closed May 9, 2010; 22 previews, 16 performances

Written by Lucy Prebble; Produced by Jeffrey Richards, Jerry Frankel, Matthew Byam Shaw, ACT Productions, Neal Street Productions (Carol Newling), Beverly Bartner & Norman Tulchin, Lee Menzies, Bob Boyett, Scott M. Delman, INFINITY Stages, JK Productions, The Araca Group, Jamie deRoy, Mallory Factor, Michael Filerman, Ian Flooks, Ronald Frankel, James Fuld Jr., Dena Hammerstein, Jam Theatricals, Rodger H. Hess, Sharon Karmazin, Cheryl Lachowicz, Ostar Productions, Parnassus Enterprise, Jon B. Platt, Judith Resnick, Daryl Roth, Stein and Gunderson Company (Joan Stein & James Gunderson), Anita Waxman, The Weinstein Company, Barry & Carole Kaye, Stewart F. Lane & Bonnie Comley, Fran and Barry Weissler and The Shubert Organization (Phillip J. Smith, Chairman; Robert E. Wankel, President); Presented by the Headlong Theatre, Chichester Festival Theatre, and Royal Court Theatre (U.K.); Director, Rupert Goold; Set & Costumes, Anthony Ward; Lighting, Mark Henderson; Composition and Sound, Adam Cork; Video and Projections, Jon Driscoll; Choreography, Scott Ambler; Casting, Telsey + Company; Production Stage Manager, Barclay Stiff; Technical Supervision, Hudson Theatrical Associates, Neil Mazzella, Irene Wang; Associate Producer, Jeremy Scott Blaustein; General Management, Richards/Climan Inc., David R. Richards, Tamar Haimes; Company Manager, Mary Miller; Stage Manager, Matthew Farrell; Associate Director, Sophie Hunter; Assistant Choreographer/Dance Captain, Ben Hartley; Associate Design: Christine Peters (set), Patrick Bevilacqua (costumes), Michael Jones (lighting), Chris Cronin (sound); Video Programmer, Chris Herman; Vocal Coach, David Shrubsole; Production Properties Supervisor, Faye Armon; Assistants to Mr. Richards, Michael Crea, Will Trice; Associate General Managers, Michael Sag, Jeromy Smith; General Management Assistant, Cesar Hawas; Company Management Assistant, Kyle Bonder; Production Assistant, Kelly Beaulieu; Child Supervisor, Allison Sherry; Production Crew: Todd Frank (production carpenter), Fraser Weir (production electrician), Valerie Spradling (production sound), Scott Monroe (production props), Brian McGarty (house carpenter), Charles DeVerna (house electrician), Ronni Vitelli (house props), Brian Bullard (house flyman), Rob Bevenger (wardrobe supervisor), Katie Beatty (hair consultant), Ashley Ryan (makeup consultant), Julian Andres Arango, Victoria Grecki, Jeff Johnson, Tree Sarvay (dressers); Advertising, Serino Coyne; Interactive Marketing, Situation Marketing; Press, Jeffrey Richards Associates, Irene Gandy, Alana Karpoff, Elon Rutberg, Diana Rissetto

CAST Jeffrey Skilling **Norbert Leo Butz**; Kenneth Lay **Gregory Itzin**; Claudia Roe **Marin Mazzie**; Andy Fastow **Stephen Kunken**; Employee/News Reporter/Analyst **Jordan Ballard**; Security Guard/Trader **Brandon J. Dirden**; Lehman Brother/Trader/Employee/Board Member **Rightor Doyle**; Lehman Brother/Trader/Arthur Andersen/Police Officer **Anthony Holds**; Lawyer/Trader **Ty Jones**; Lawyer/Trader **Ian Kahn**; Employee/News Reporter/Hewitt **January LaVoy**; Senator/Trader/Analyst/Judge **Tom Nelis**; Daughter **Madisyn Shipman** or **Mary Stewart Sullivan**; Trader/Analyst/Court Officer **Jeff Skowron**; Sheryl Sloman/Congresswoman/Irene Gant **Lusia Strus**; Trader/Analyst/Ramsay **Noah Weisberg**

UNDERSTUDIES/STANDBYS Ben Hartley, Ellyn Marie Marsh

SETTING Houston, Texas, between 1992 and the present day. American premiere of a new play with music, dance, and video presented in two acts. World premiere at the Minerva Theatre Chichester July 11–August 29, 2009. The play transferred to the Royal Court Theatre September 17–November 7, 2009, and then opened for a West End commercial transfer to the Noel Coward Theatre January 16, 2010.

SYNOPSIS *Enron* explores one of the most infamous real-life scandals in financial history: the bankruptcy of the Enron energy corporation in Houston, Texas. Mixing classic tragedy with savage comedy, *Enron* follows a group of flawed men and women in a narrative of greed and loss which reviews the tumultuous 1990s and casts a new light on the financial turmoil in which the world finds itself in 2009.

Marin Mazzie, Norbert Leo Butz, and Gregory Itzin

Norbert Leo Butz and Stephen Kunken (photos by Joan Marcus)

Sarah Paulson and Linda Lavin

Collected Stories

Samuel J. Friedman Theatre; First Preview: April 6, 2010; Opening Night: April 28, 2010; 22 previews, 38 performances as of May 31, 2010

Written by Donald Margulies; Produced by Manhattan Theatre Club (Lynne Meadow, Artistic Director; Barry Grove, Executive Producer); Director, Lynne Meadow; Set, Santo Loquasto; Costumes, Jane Greenwood; Lighting, Natasha Katz; Original Music & Sound, Obadiah Eaves; Wigs, Paul Huntley; Casting, David Caparelliotis; Production Stage Manager, Laurie Goldfeder; General Manager, Florie Seery; Associate Artistic Director, Mandy Greenfield; Director of Artistic Development, Jerry Patch; Marketing, Debra Waxman-Pilla; Production Manager, Kurt Gardner; Director of Casting, Nancy Piccione; Development, Jill Turner Lloyd; Artistic Consultant, Daniel Sullivan; Artistic Administration/Assistant to Artistic Director, Amy Gilkes Loe; Finance, Jeffrey Bledsoe; Associate General Manager, Lindsey Brooks Sag; Subscriber Services, Robert Allenberg; Telesales, George Tetlow; Education, David Shookhoff; Associate Production Manager, Philip Naudé; Prop Supervisor, Scott Laule; Costume Supervisor, Erin Hennessy Dean; Company Manager, Seth Shepsle; Stage Manager, Timothy R. Semon; Assistant Director, Hilary Adams; Associate Design: Jenny B. Sawyers (set), Wade Laboissonniere (costumes), Aaron Spivey (lighting), Brandon Wolcott (sound); Assistant Set, Yoki Lai; Makeup, Angelina Avallone; Video Design, Rocco DiSanti; Lightboard Programmer, Mark Davidson; Production Crew: Chris Wiggins (head carpenter), Timothy Walters (head propertyman), Louis Shapiro (sound engineer), Jeff Dodson (master electrician), Michael Growler (wardrobe supervisor), Natasha Steinhagen (hair/makeup supervisor), Derek Moreno, Polly Noble (dressers); Advertising, SpotCo; Press, Boneau/Bryan-Brown, Chris Boneau, Aaron Meier, Christine Olver, Emily Meagher

CAST Ruth Steiner **Linda Lavin**; Lisa Morrison **Sarah Paulson**

UNDERSTUDIES Anne Bowles (Lisa Morrison), Kit Flanagan (Ruth Steiner)

SETTING Time: Act 1 – Scene One: September 1990; Scene Two: May 1991; Scene Three: August 1992. Act II – Scene One: December 1994; Scene Two: October 1996; Scene Three: Later that night. Place: The Greenwich Village apartment of Ruth Steiner. Broadway premiere and revival of an Off-Broadway play presented in six scenes in two acts. World premiere at South Coast Repertory in 1996 (see *Theatre World* Vol. 53, page 206). Manhattan Theatre Club produced the original Off-Broadway production at City Center Stage I, starring Maria Tucci and Debra Messing, April 30–July 27, 1997 (see *Theatre World* Vol. 53, page 94). The play was revived at the Lucille Lortel Theatre, starring Uta Hagen and Lorca Simons, July 28, 1998–February 28, 1999 (see *Theatre World* Vol. 55, page 138).

SYNOPSIS *Collected Stories* chronicles the relationship between two female writers – Ruth Steiner, a celebrated New York author and her young protégé, Lisa Morrison. As their fascinating story evolves, and the line between fact and fiction blurs, the twists and turns of this complex relationship weave a play that's as smart and witty as it is powerful.

Linda Lavin (photos by Joan Marcus)

Linda Lavin and Sarah Paulson

Lindsay Mendez, Sherie Rene Scott, and Betsy Wolfe

Sherie Rene Scott (photos by Carol Rosegg)

Everyday Rapture

American Airlines Theatre; First Preview: April 19, 2010; Opening Night: April 29, 2010; 11 previews, 37 performances as of May 31, 2010

Written by Dick Scanlan and Sherie Rene Scott; Produced by the Roundabout Theatre Company (Todd Haimes, Artistic Director; Harold Wolpert, Managing Director; Julia C. Levy, Executive Director); Originally presented by Second Stage (Carole Rothman, Artistic Director; Ellen Richard, Executive Director) Director, Michael Mayer; Choreography, Michele Lynch; Set, Christine Jones; Costumes, Tom Broecker; Lighting, Kevin Adams; Sound, Ashley Hanson, Kurt Eric Fischer, Brian Ronan; Projections, Darrel Maloney; Orchestrations/Arrangements, Tom Kitt; Music Supervisor, Michael Rafter; Musical Director, Marco Paguia; Music Coordinator, Michael Keller; Production Stage Manager, Richard C. Rauscher; Production Management, Aurora Productions (Gene O'Donovan, W. Benjamin Heller II, Rachel Sherbill, Jarid Sumner, Steve Rosenberg, Melissa Mazdra, Amy Merlino Coey, Amanda Raymond, Graham Forden, Liza Luxenberg); Original Casting, MelCap Casting; Additional Casting, Jim Carnahan; General Manager, Rebecca Habel; Marketing/Sales Promotion, David B. Steffen; Founding Director, Gene Feist; Associate Artistic Director, Scott Ellis; Director of Artistic Development and Casting, Jim Carnahan; Finance, Susan Neiman; Education, Greg McCaslin; General Manager, Sydney Beers; Telesales, Marco Frezza; IT Director, Antonio Palumbo; Development Directors, Julie K. D'Andrea, Steve Schaeffer, Joy Pak, Amber Jo Manuel; Sales Operations, Charlie Garbowski Jr.; Company Manager, Carly DiFulvio; Stage Manager, Bryce McDonald; Hair, John Barrett/John Barrett Salon; Makeup, Tiffany Hicks; Assistant Director, Austin Regan; Associate Choreographer, Eric Sean Fogel; Associate Design: John C. Collings (set), David Withrow (costumes), Aaron Sporer, Paul Toben (lighting), Drew Levy (sound), Dan Scully (projections); Dance Captain, Lindsay Mendez; Magic Consultant, Steve Cuiffo; Production Crew: Peter Sarafin (production properties supervisor), Glenn Merwede (production & house carpenter), Brian Maiuri (production & house electrician), Barb Bartel (front light operator), Robert W. Dowling II (running properties), Dann Wojnar (deck sound), Susan J. Fallon (wardrobe supervisor), Manuela Laporte (hair and wig supervisor), Cathy Cline, Mel Hansen (dresser), Lauren Galitelli (day wardrobe), McKenzie Murphy (production assistant); Synthesizer Programmer, Randy Cohen; Music Copying, Colleen Darnall; Music Search Supervisor, Hank Aberle; Advertising, SpotCo; Press, Boneau/Bryan-Brown, Adrian Bryan-Brown, Matt Polk, Jessica Johnson, Amy Kass, Emily Meagher; Cast recording: Sh-K-Boom Records/Ghostlight 82010

CAST **Sherie Rene Scott**, **Lindsay Mendez**, **Betsy Wolfe**, **Eamon Foley**

UNDERSTUDIES Riley Costello, Natalie Weiss

MUSICIANS Marco Paguia (Conductor/piano), Clint De Ganon (drums), Brian Hamm (bass), John Benthall (guitar), Joe Brent (violin/guitar)

MUSICAL NUMBERS The Other Side of This Life (Overture); Got a Thing on My Mind; Elevation; On the Atchison, Topeka, and Santa Fe; Get Happy; You Made Me Love You; Mr. Rodgers Medley (It's Such a Good Feeling, Everybody's Fancy, & I Like to Be Told); It's You I Like; I Guess the Lord Must Be in New York City; Life Line; The Weight; Rainbow Sleeves; Why; Won't You Be My Neighbor; Up the Ladder to the Roof

SETTING Topeka, Kansas and New York City; the past and present. Transfer of the Off-Broadway musical presented without intermission. Originally presented at Second Stage April 7–June 14, 2009 (see *Theatre World* Vol. 64, page 236). A previous version of the show entitled *You May Worship Me Now* was presented as a benefit concert for the Actors Fund Phyllis Newman Women's Health Initiative on March 31, 2008.

SYNOPSIS *Everyday Rapture* tells the true-ish story of a young woman's journey from Mennonite to Manhattanite and from bedroom lip-syncher to Broadway semi-star! Featuring songs by David Byrne, Elton John, Mister Rogers, The Supremes, Tom Waits, U2 and Judy Garland, *Everyday Rapture* is an uplifting and uproarious new musical that asks, is it better to worship...or BE worshipped?

PLAYED THROUGH / CLOSED THIS SEASON

Alfred Hitchcock's **The 39 Steps**

Helen Hayes Theatre; First Preview: April 29, 2008; Opening Night: May 8, 2008; Closed January 10, 2010; 23 previews, 771 performances

Adapted by Patrick Barlow from the film by Alfred Hitchcock and the book by John Buchan; based on an original concept by Simon Corble and Nobby Dimon; Produced by the Roundabout Theatre Company (Todd Haimes, Artistic Director; Harold Wolpert, Managing Director; Julia C. Levy, Executive Director) in association with Bob Boyett, Harriet Newman Leve/Ron Nicynski, Stewart F. Lane/Bonnie Comley, Manocherian Golden Productions, Olympus Theatricals/Douglas Denoff, Marek J. Cantor/Pat Addiss, and the Huntington Theatre Company (Nicholas Martin, Artistic Director; Michael Maso, Managing Director), and Edward Snape for Fiery Angel Ltd.; Director, Maria Aitken; Set/Costumes, Peter McKintosh; Lighting, Kevin Adams; Sound, Mic Pool; Dialect Coach, Stephen Gabis; Original Movement, Toby Sedgewick; Additional Movement, Christopher Bays; Production Manager, Aurora Productions; Production Stage Manager, Nevin Hedley; Casting, Jay Binder, Jack Bowdan; General Manager, Rebecca Habel, Roy Gabay; Associate Producer/Roundabout General Manager, Sydney Beers; Marketing/Sales Promotion, David B. Steffen; Development, Jeffory Lawson; Founding Director, Gene Feist; Associate Artistic Director, Scott Ellis; Artistic Development/Casting, Jim Carnahan; Education, David A. Miller; Telesales, Daniel Weiss; Finance, Susan Neiman; Sales Operations, Charlie Garbowski Jr.; Executive Producer, 101 Productions Ltd.; Associate Producer, Marek J. Cantor; Company Manager, Daniel Kuney; ACM, Carly DiFulvio; Stage Manager, Janet Takami; Wigs, Jason Allen; Assistant Director, Kevin Bigger; Assistant Design: Josh Zangen (set), Aaron Sporer (lighting), Drew Levy (sound); Marketing, HHC Marketing; Advertising, Eliran Murphy Group; Press, Boneau/Bryan-Brown (Adrian Bryan-Brown, Jim Byk, Matt Polk, Jessica Johnson, Amy Kass)

CAST Man #1 **Jeffrey Kuhn**; Man #2 **Arnie Burton**; Richard Hannay **Sean Mahon**; Annabella Schmidt/Pamela/Margaret **Jill Paice**

UNDERSTUDIES Claire Brownell* (Annabella Schmidt/Pamela/Margaret), Cameron Folmar (Man #1/Man #2), Robert Breckenridge (Richard Hannay)

*Succeeded by Nisi Sturgis

SETTING Scotland and London. New York premiere of a new comedy/thriller presented in two acts. Previously presented at the Tricycle Theatre in London in 2006, and at Boston's Huntington Theatre Company, September 14, 2007, prior to this engagement. The Broadway production originally played the American Airlines Theatre January 4–March 29, 2008 (12 previews and 87 performances which are included in the performance count above) before transferring to the Cort Theatre for a commercial run. The show transferred to the Helen Hayes Theatre on January 21, 2009, where it concluded its run. Subsequently, the production opened Off-Broadway at New World Stages later in the season (see Off-Broadway section in this volume).

SYNOPSIS Four cast members play over 150 roles in this hilarious whodunit, part espionage thriller and part slapstick comedy. The story revolves around an innocent man who learns too much about a dangerous spy ring and is then pursued across Scotland and to London. *The 39 Steps* contains every legendary scene from the award-winning movie—the chase on the Flying Scotsman, the escape on the Forth Bridge, the first theatrical bi-plane crash ever staged, and the sensational death-defying finale in the London Palladium.

Sean Mahon, Arnie Burton, Jeffrey Kuhn, and Jill Paice

Jill Paice and Sean Mahon (photos by Joan Marcus)

Sean Mahon, Jill Paice, Arnie Burton, and Jeffrey Kuhn

9 to 5: The Musical

Marquis Theatre; First Preview: April 7, 2009 Opening Night: April 30, 2009; Closed September 6, 2009; 24 previews, 148 performances

Book by Patricia Resnick, music and lyrics by Dolly Parton; based on the motion picture produced by 20th Century Fox (screenplay by Patricia Resnick, screenplay and direction by Colin Higgins); Produced by Green State Productions, Richard Levi, John McColgan/Moya Doherty/Edgar Dobie, James L. Nederlander/Terry Allen Kramer, Independent Presenters Network, Jam Theatricals, Bud Martin, Michael Watt, The Weinstein Company/Sonia Friedman/Dede Harris, Norton Herrick/Matthew C. Blank/Joan Stein, Center Theatre Group (Michael Ritchie, Artistic Director; Charles Dillingham, Managing Director), Toni Dowgiallo, GFour Productions and Robert Greenblatt; Director, Joe Mantello; Choreography, Andy Blankenbuehler; Music Direction/Vocal Arrangements, Stephen Oremus; Sets, Scott Pask; Costumes, William Ivey Long; Lighting, Jules Fisher & Kenneth Posner; Sound, John H. Shivers; Casting, Telsey + Company; Imaging, Peter Nigrini & Peggy Eisenhauer; Hair, Paul Huntley & Edward J. Wilson; Makeup, Angelina Avellone; Technical Supervision, Neil A. Mazzella; Scenic Design Associate, Edward Pierce; Production Supervisor, William Joseph Barnes; Associate Director, Dave Solomon; Associate Choreographer, Rachel Bress; General Management, Nina Lannan Associates, Maggie Brohn; Marketing, Type A Marketing, Situation Interactive; Music Coordinator, Michael Keller; Orchestrator, Bruce Coughlin; Additional Orchestrations & Incidental Music Arrangements, Stephen Oremus & Alex Lacamoire; Dance Music Arrangements, Alex Lacamoire; Additional Music Arrangements, Kevin Stites & Charles duChateau; Company Manager, Kimberly Kelley; Associate Company Manager, Adam Jackson; Pre-Production Stage Manager, C. Randall White; Stage Manager, Timothy R. Semon; Assistant Stage Managers, Chris Zaccardi, Kathryn L. McKee; Assistant Producer, Brian Salb; Dance Captain, Mark Myars; Assistant Dance Captain, Jennifer Balagna; Associate Technical Supervisors, Irene Wang, Frank Illo; Associate Design: Nick Francone (set), Scott Traugott (costumes), Giovanna Calabretta (wigs and hair), Philip Rosenberg (lighting), David Patridge (sound); Assistant Design: Orit Jacoby Carroll, Frank McCullough, Lauren Alvarez (set), Robert J. Martin, Brenda Abbandandolo (costumes), Aaron Spivey, Carl Faber (lighting); Automated Lighting Programmer, David Arch; Imaging Associate, C. Andrew Bauer; Imaging Assistant, Dan Scully; LED Image Wall Programmer, Laura Frank/Luminous FX LLC; Additional Character & Castle Animation, Illum Productions (Jerry Chambless, Creative Director; Joseph Merideth, Animation Director); Keyboard Programming, Randy Cohen; Music Copying, Emily Grishman Music Preparation, Katherine Edmonds; Advertising, SpotCo; Press, The Hartman Group; Cast recording: Dolly Records

CAST Violet Newstead **Allison Janney**; Doralee Rhodes **Megan Hilty**; Dwayne **Charlie Pollock**; Judy Bernly **Stephanie J. Block**; Roz Keith **Kathy Fitzgerald**; Kathy **Ann Harada***; Anita **Maia Nkenge Wilson**; Daphne **Tory Ross**; Franklin Hart Jr. **Marc Kudisch**; Missy **Lisa Howard**; Maria **Iona Alfonso**; Joe **Andy Karl**; Margaret **Karen Murphy**; Josh **Van Hughes**; Dick **Dan Cooney**; Bob Enright **Jeremy Davis**; Tinsworthy **Michael X. Martin**; Ensemble **Ioana Alfonso, Timothy George Anderson, Justin Bohon, Paul Castree, Dan Cooney, Jeremy Davis, Autumn Guzzardi, Ann Harada, Neil Haskell, Lisa Howard, Van Hughes, Michael X. Martin, Michael Mindlin, Karen Murphy, Jessica Lea Patty, Charlie Pollock, Tory Ross, Wayne Schroder, Maia Nkenge Wilson, Brandi Wooten**; Swings **Jennifer Balagna, Mark Myars, Justin Patterson**

UNDERSTUDIES Ann Harada* (Violet, Roz), Lisa Howard (Violet), Gaelen Gilliland (Judy, Doralee, Margaret, Missy), Jessica Lea Patty (Judy, Maria), Tory Ross (Judy, Roz, Kathy, Margaret), Autumn Guzzardi (Doralee), Michael X. Martin (Hart), Wayne Schroder (Hart, Dick, Tinsworthy), Karen Murphy (Roz), Paul Castree (Joe), Justin Patterson (Joe, Dwayne), Justin Bohon (Dwayne, Josh), Jeremy Davis (Dick), Michael Mindlin (Josh), Maia Nkenge Wilson (Kathy), Jennifer Balagna (Maria), Brandi Wooten (Missy), Dan Cooney (Tinsworthy)

*Succeeded by: Jill Abramovitz (6/23/09)

ORCHESTRA Stephen Oremus (Conductor/keyboard 1); Matt Gallagher (Associate Conductor/keyboard 2); Jodie Moore (Assistant Conductor/keyboard 3); Michael Aarons, Jake Ezra Schwartz (guitars); John Putnam (guitars/pedal steel); Dave Phillips (bass); Dean McDaniel (drums); Dave Mancuso (percussion); Vincent Della Rocca, Aaron Heick, Dave Riekenberg (reeds); Bob Millikan, Brian Pareschi (trumpets); Keith O'Quinn, Jennifer Wharton (trombones); Suzy Perelmen, Chris Cardona, Amy Ralske (violins)

MUSICAL NUMBERS 9 to 5, Around Here, Here for You, I Just Might, Backwoods Barbie, The Dance of Death, Cowgirl's Revenge, Potion Notion, Joy to the Girls, Heart to Hart, Shine Like the Sun, Entr'acte, One of the Boys, 5 to 9, Always a Woman, Change It, Let Love Grow, Get Out and Stay Out, Finale: 9 to 5

SETTING Time: 1979. Place: In and around the offices of Consolidated. New York premiere of a new musical presented in two acts. World premiere at the Center Theatre Group's Ahmanson Theatre September 9–October 19, 2008.

SYNOPSIS Violet Newstead (the super-efficient office manager), Judy Bernly (a frazzled divorcee), Doralee Rhodes (the sexy executive secretary) are pushed to their boiling point by their boss, Franklin Hart Jr., and decide to turn the tables on him. The trio hatches a plan to get even with the sexist, egotistical, lying, hypocritical bigot, and that plan quickly spins wildly and hilariously out of control. Parton's original score includes more than 15 new songs as well as the Grammy Award winning, Academy Award nominated, and #1 Billboard title song from the 1980 motion picture upon which the musical is based.

Stephanie J. Block, Allison Janney, and Megan Hilty (photos by Joan Marcus)

Allison Janney, Stephanie J. Block, and Kathy Fitzgerald

Accent on Youth

Mary Catherine Garrison and David Hyde Pierce

Samuel J. Friedman Theatre; First Preview: April 7, 2009 Opening Night: April 29, 2009; Closed June 28, 2009; 24 previews, 71 performances

Written by Samson Raphaelson; Produced by Manhattan Theatre Club (Lynne Meadow, Artistic Director; Barry Grove, Executive Producer) by special arrangement with Daryl Roth, Ostar Productions, Rebecca Gold/Debbie Bisno; Director, Daniel Sullivan; Set, John Lee Beatty; Costumes, Jane Greenwood; Lighting, Brian MacDevitt; Original Music & Sound, Obadiah Eaves; Hair & Wigs, Tom Watson; Production Stage Manager, Roy Harris; General Manager, Florie Seery; Associate Artistic Director, Mandy Greenfield; Director of Artistic Development, Jerry Patch; Marketing, Debra Waxman-Pilla; Production Manager, Kurt Gardner; Director of Casting, Nancy Piccione; Development, Jill Turner Lloyd; Artistic Consultant, Daniel Sullivan; Artistic Administration/Assistant to Artistic Director, Amy Gilkes Loe; Musical Development, Clifford Lee Johnson III; Finance, Jeffrey Bledsoe; Associate General Manager, Lindsey Brooks Sag; Subscriber Services, Robert Allenberg; Telesales, George Tetlow; Education, David Shookhoff; Associate Production Manager, Philip Naudé; Prop Supervisor, Scott Laule; Costume Supervisor, Erin Hennessy Dean; Company Manager, Seth Shepsle; Stage Manager, Denise Yaney; Assistant Director, Rachel Slaven; Makeup, Angelina Avellone; Mr. Pierce's Hair, Paul Huntley; Fight Director, Thomas Schall; Associate Design: Yoshinori Tanokura (set), Jennifer Moeller (costumes), Peter Hoerburger (lighting), Brandon Wolcott (sound); Assistant Design: Anya Klepicov (costumes), Grant Wilcoxen (assistant to Mr. MacDevitt); Production: Vaughn G. Preston (automation operator), Chris Wiggins (head carpenter), Timothy Walters (head propertyman), Marc Polimeni (moving light programmer), Louis Shapiro (sound engineer), Jeff Dodson (master electrician), Angela Simpson (wardrobe supervisor), Natasha Steinhagen (hair/makeup supervisor), Virginia Neininger (dresser), E'bess Greer (production assistant); Theatre Manager, Russ Ramsey; Box Office Treasurer, David Dillon; Advertising, SpotCo; Press, Boneau/Bryan-Brown, Aaron Meier, Christine Olver, Matt Ross

CAST Miss Darling **Lisa Banes**; Genevieve Lang **Rosie Benton**; Butch **Curt Bouril**; Dickie Reynolds **David Furr**; Linda Brown **Mary Catherine Garrison**; Frank Galloway **Byron Jennings**; Flogdell **Charles Kimbrough**; Steven Gale **David Hyde Pierce**; Chuck **John Wernke**

UNDERSTUDIES Ross Bickell (Frank Galloway, Flogdell), Curt Bouril (Chuck), Cynthia Darlow (Miss Darling), Jack Koenig (Steven Gaye, Butch), Karen Walsh (Genevieve Lang, Linda Brown), John Wernke (Dickie Reynolds)

SETTING The New York duplex of Steven Gaye over the course of a year; early 1930s. Revival of a comedy presented in three acts with one intermission. Originally presented on Broadway at the Plymouth Theatre (now the Schoenfeld) December 25, 1934–July 1935.

SYNOPSIS Samson Raphaelson's *Accent on Youth* is a rollicking salute to love's possibilities, both on stage and off. Successful playwright Stephen Gaye is about to abandon his latest script, when his young secretary offers him new inspiration. With her as his muse, he stages the show on Broadway, only to learn, to his dismay, that the show's young leading man is being inspired by her too.

Mary Catherine Garrison and David Hyde Pierce
(photos by Joan Marcus)

Amy Morton and Troy West

August: Osage County

Music Box Theatre; First Preview: October 30, 2007; Opening Night: December 4, 2007; Closed June 28, 2009; 18 previews, 648 performances

Written by Tracy Letts; Originally produced by the Steppenwolf Theatre Company (Martha Lavey, Artistic Director; David Hawkanson, Executive Director); Produced by Jeffrey Richards, Jean Doumanian, Steve Traxler, Jerry Frankel, Ostar Productions, Jennifer Manocherian, The Weinstein Company, Debra Black/Daryl Roth, Ronald & Marc Frankel/Barbara Freitag, Rick Steiner/Staton Bell Group; Director, Anna D. Shapiro; Sets, Todd Rosenthal; Costumes, Ana Kuzmanic; Lighting, Ann G. Wrightson; Sound, Richard Woodbury; Original Music, David Singe; Dramaturg, Edward Sobel; Original Casting, Erica Daniels; New York Casting, Stuart Howard, Amy Schecter, Paul Hardt; Fight Choreography, Chuck Coyl; Dialect Coach, Cecilie O'Reilly; Production Stage Manager, Deb Styer; Production Supervisor, Jane Grey; Technical Supervisor, Theatersmith Inc./ Smitty (Christopher C. Smith); Marketing Services, TMG–The Marketing Group; General Management, Richards/Climan Inc.; Assistant Producers, Mark Barber, Patrick Daly, Ben West; Company Manager, Mary Miller; Assistant Director, Henry Wishcamper; Design Assistants: Kevin Depinet, Matthew D. Jordan, Martin Andrew Orlowicz, Stephen T. Sorenson (sets), Amelia Dombrowski (costumes), Kathleen Dobbins, Kristina Kloss (lighting), Joanna Lynne Staub (sound), Management Associate, Jeromy Smith; Advertising, SpotCo; Press, Jeffrey Richards Associates, Irene Gandy, Judith Hansen, Diana Rissetto, Elon Rutberg

CAST Beverly Weston **John Cullum**; Violet Weston **Phylicia Rashad**; Barbara Fordham **Amy Morton**; Bill Fordham **Frank Wood**; Jean Fordham **Anne Berkowitz**; Ivy Weston **Sally Murphy**; Karen Weston **Mariann Mayberry**; Mattie Fae Aiken **Elizabeth Ashley**; Charlie Aiken **Guy Boyd**; Little Charles **Michael Milligan**; Johnna Monevata **Kimberly Guerrero**; Steve Heidebrecht **Brian Kerwin**; Sheriff Deon Gilbeau **Troy West**

UNDERSTUDIES/STANDBYS Frank Deal (Charlie Aiken, Bill Fordham, Sheriff Deon Gilbeau, Steve Heidebrecht), Susanne Marley (Mattie Fae Aiken, Violet Weston), Stephen Payne (Beverly Weston, Charlie Aiken), Dee Pelletier (Barbara Fordham, Ivy Weston, Karen Weston), Aaron Serotsky (Bill Fordham, Little Charles, Sheriff Deon Gilbeau, Steve Heidebrecht), Kristina Valada-Viars (Johnna Monevata, Ivy Weston, Karen Weston), Emily Watson (Jean Fordham)

SETTING A large country home outside Pawhuska, Oklahoma, 60 miles northwest of Tulsa. New York premiere of a new play presented in three acts with two intermissions. For original production credits see *Theatre World* Vol. 64, page 31.World Premiere presented at the Steppenwolf Theatre Company June 28–August 26, 2007 with most of this cast (see *Theatre World* Vol. 63, page 355).

SYNOPSIS When their patriarch vanishes, the Weston clan must return to their three-story home in rural Oklahoma to get to the heart of the matter. With rich insight and brilliant humor, Letts paints a vivid portrait of a Midwestern family at a turning point.

Phylicia Rashad and Amy Morton (photo by Robert J. Saferstein)

Avenue Q

John Golden Theatre; First Preview: July 10, 2003; Opening Night: July 31, 2003; Closed September 13, 2009; 22 previews, 2,534 performances

Music and lyrics by Robert Lopez and Jeff Marx, book by Jeff Whitty; Produced by Kevin McCollum, Robyn Goodman, Jeffrey Seller, Vineyard Theatre & The New Group; Director, Jason Moore; Choreography, Ken Roberson; Music Supervision/ Orchestrations/Arrangements, Stephen Oremus; Puppets Conception/Design, Rick Lyon; Set, Anna Louizos; Costumes, Mirena Rada; Lighting, Howell Binkley; Sound, Acme Sound Partners; Animation, Robert Lopez; Music Director/Incidental Music, Gary Adler; Music Coordinator, Michael Keller; General Manager, John Corker; Technical Supervisor, Brian Lynch; Production Stage Manager, Beverly Jenkins; Casting, Cindy Tolan; Marketing, TMG–The Marketing Group; Associate Producers, Sonny Everett, Walter Grossman, Mort Swinsky; Stage Manager, Christine M. Daly; Company Manager, Nick Lugo; Resident Director, Evan Ensign; Associate Conductor, Mark Hartman; Assistant Director, Jen Bender; Assistant Stage Manager/Dance Captain, Sharon Wheatley; Associate Design: Todd Potter (set), Timothy F. Rogers (lighting); Music Copying, Emily Grishman and Alex Lacamoire; Animation and Video Production, Noodle Soup Production, Jeremy Rosenberg; Sound and Video Design Effects, Brett Jarvis; Advertising, SpotCo; Press, Sam Rudy Media Relations; Cast recording: RCA 82876-55923-2

CAST Princeton/Rod **Howie Michael Smith**[1]; Brian **Nicholas Kohn**; Kate Monster/Lucy the Slut & others **Carey Anderson**[2]; Nicky/Trekkie Monster/Bad Idea Bear & others **Christian Anderson**; Christmas Eve **Ann Sanders**[3]; Gary Coleman **Carla Renata**[4]; Mrs. T./Bad Idea Bear & others **Jennifer Barnhart**; Ensemble **Minglie Chin**, **Benjamin Schrader**[5]; Swings **Carmen Ruby Floyd**, **Matt Schreiber**, **Sharon Wheatley**

UNDERSTUDIES Jennifer Barnhart (Kate Monster/Lucy), Minglie Chen (Christmas Eve, Kate Monster/Lucy, Mrs. T/Bear), Carmen Ruby Floyd (Gary Coleman, Mrs. T./Bear), Benjamin Schrader[5] (Princeton/Rod, Brian, Nicky/ Trekkie/Bear), Matt Schreiber (Brian, Nicky/Trekkie/Bear, Princeton/Rod), Sharon Wheatley (Kate Monster/Lucy, Mrs. T./Bear, Christmas Eve)

*Succeeded by: 1. Robert McClure (7/6/09) 2. Anika Larson (7/6/09) 3. Danielle K. Thomas (7/6/09) 4. Ann Harada (7/6/09) 5. Seth Rettberg

ORCHESTRA Gary Adler (Conductor/keyboard); Mark Hartman (Associate Conductor/keyboard); Maryann McSweeney (bass); Brian Koonin (guitar); Patience Higgins (reeds); Michael Croiter (drums)

MUSICAL NUMBERS Avenue Q Theme, What Do You Do With a BA in English?/ It Sucks to be Me, If You Were Gay, Purpose, Everyone's a Little Bit Racist, The Internet Is for Porn, Mix Tape, I'm Not Wearing Underwear Today, Special, You Can Be as Loud as the Hell You Want (When You're Making Love), Fantasies Come True, My Girlfriend, Who Lives in Canada, There's a Fine, Fine Line, There Is Life Outside Your Apartment, The More You Ruv Someone, Schadenfreude, I Wish I Could Go Back to College, The Money Song, For Now

SETTING The present, an outer borough of New York City. A musical presented in two acts. For original production credits see *Theatre World* Vol. 60, page 25. Originally presented Off-Broadway March 19, 2003 at the Vineyard Theatre (see *Theatre World* Vol. 59, page 179). In an unprecedented move, *Avenue Q* transferred back to Off-Broadway to New World Stages on October 9, 2009, marking the first time a Broadway musical has moved to an Off-Broadway theatre (see Off-Broadway section in this volume).

SYNOPSIS *Avenue Q* is about real life: finding a job, losing a job, learning about racism, getting an apartment, getting kicked out of your apartment, being different, falling in love, promiscuity, avoiding commitment, and internet porn. Twenty and thirty-something puppets and humans survive life in the big city and search for their purpose in this naughty but timely musical that features "full puppet nudity!"

Anika Larsen and Jennifer Barnhart

The Final Company (photos by Carol Rosegg)

Billy Elliot The Musical

Imperial Theatre; First Preview: October 1, 2008; Opening Night: November 13, 2008; 40 previews, 644 performances as of May 31, 2010

Music by Elton John, book and lyrics by Lee Hall; based on the Universal Pictures/Studio Canal film *Billy Elliot* with screenplay by Lee Hall and direction by Stephen Daldry; Produced by Universal Pictures Stage Productions, Working Title Films, Old Vic Productions, in association with Weinstein Live Entertainment & Fidelity Investments; Director, Stephen Daldry; Choreography, Peter Darling; Associate Director, Julian Webber; Sets, Ian MacNeil; Costumes, Nicky Gillibrand; Lighting, Rick Fisher; Sound, Paul Arditti; Producers, Tim Bevan, Eric Fellner, Jon Fin, Sally Greene; Executive Producers, David Furnish, Angela Morrison; Musical Supervision and Orchestrations, Martin Koch; Music Director, David Chase; Associate Choreographer, Kathryn Dunn; Assistant Choreographer, Nikki Belsher; Hair/Wigs/Makeup, Campbell Young; U.K. Associate Design: Paul Atkinson (set), Claire Murphy (costumes), Vic Smerdon (lighting/programmer), John Owens (sound); Adult Casting, Tara Rubin; Children's Casting, Nora Brennan; Resident Director, B.T. McNicholl; Production Stage Manager, Bonnie L. Becker; Music Contractor, Michael Keller; Production Supervisors, Arthur Siccardi, Patrick Sullivan; General Management, Nina Lannan Associates/Devin Keudell; U.K. Casting, Pippa Ailion; Company Manager, Greg Arst; Associate Company Manager, Carol. M. Oune; Assistant Company Manager, Ashley Berman; Stage Manager, Charles Underhill; Assistant Stage Managers, Scott Rowen, Mary Kathryn Flynt; Supervising Dialect Coach (U.K.), William Conacher; Resident Dialect Coach, Ben Furey; Fight Director, David S. Leong; Dance Captains, Greg Graham & Cara Kjellman; Fight Captain, Grady McLeod Bowman; Choreographic Supervision, Ellen Kane; Staging and Dance Assistant, Lee Proud; Associate Music Director/Conductor, Shawn Gough; U.S. Associate Design: Brian Russman (costumes), Daniel Walker (lighting), Tony Smolenski IV (sound); Assistant Design: Jaimie Todd (sets), Rebecca Lustig (costumes), Kristina Kloss (lighting); Moving Lights, David Arch; Music Copying, Emily Grishman Music Preparation; Ballet Instructors, Finis Jhung, Francois Perron; Acrobat Instructor, Hector Salazar; Rehearsal Pianists, Joseph Joubert, Aron Accurso; Marketing, Allied Live/Laura Matalon, Tanya Grubich, Daya Wolterstorff, Sara Rosenzweig; Advertising, SpotCo; Press, The Hartman Group; London Cast recording: Decca Broadway B0006 130-72

CAST Billy[*1] **David Alvarez** or **Trent Kowalik** or **Kiril Kulish** or **Tommy Batchelor**; Mrs. Wilkinson **Haydn Gwynne**[*2]; Dad **Gregory Jbara**[*3]; Grandma **Carole Shelley**; Tony **Santino Fontana**[*4]; George **Joel Hatch**; Michael **David Bologna**[*5] or **Frank Dolce**[*6]; Debbie **Erin Whyland**[*7]; Small Boy[*8] **Mitchell Michaliszyn** or **Matthew Mindler**; Big Davey **Daniel Oreskes**[*9]; Lesley **Stephanie Kurtzuba**[*10]; Scab/Posh Dad **Donnie Kehr**; Mum **Leah Hocking**[*11]; Mr. Braithwaite **Thommie Retter**; Tracey Atkinson **Casey Whyland**[*12]; Older Billy/Scottish Dancer **Stephen Hanna**[*13]; Mr. Wilkerson **Kevin Bernard**[*14]; Pit Supervisor **Jeff Kready**[*15]; Tall Boy/Posh Boy **Keean Johnson**[*16]; Clipboard Woman **Jayne Patterson**[*17]; "Expressing Yourself" Dancers **Kevin Bernard, Grady McLeod Bowman, Joshua Horner, Jeff Kready, Stephanie Kurtzuba, David Larsen, Darrell Grand Moultrie, Jamie Torcellini**; Ensemble[*18] **Kevin Bernard, Grady McLeod Bowman, Eric Gunhus, Stephen Hanna, Leah Hocking, Joshua Horner, Aaron Kaburick, Donnie Kehr, Jeff Kready, Stephanie Kurtzuba, David Larsen, Merle Louise, Darrell Grand Moultrie, Daniel Oreskes, Jayne Patterson, Jamie Torcellini**; Ballet Girls[*19] **Juliette Allen Angelo, Heather Ann Burns, Eboni Edwards, Meg Guzulescu, Izzy Hanson-Johnston, Caroline London, Marina Micalizzi, Tessa Netting, Corrieanne Stein, Casey Whyland**; Swings[*20] **Maria Connelly, Samantha Czulada, Kyle DesChamps, David Eggers, Brianna Fragomeni, Greg Graham, Cara Kjellman, Kara Klein, David Koch, Liz Pearce**

*Succeeded by: 1. Alex Ko succeeded Kiril Kulish who departed 10/3/09; Liam Redhead and Dayton Tavares replaced Tommy Batchelor who departed 12/13/09 so that five boys alternated the role; Michael Dameski succeeded David Alvarez who departed 1/3/10; Jacob Clemente succeeded Trent Kowalik who departed 3/7/10. 2. Kate Hennig (10/6/09) 3. Philip Whitchurch (1/29/10), Gregory Jbara (5/4/09) 4. Will Chase (7/7/09), Jeff Kready 5. Keean Johnson (9/29/09), Jake Evan Schwencke (1/16/10) 6. Trevor Braun (8/22/09) 7.Maria Connelly, Izzy Hanson-Johnston 8. Seth Fromowitz or Luke Trevisan 9. Rick Hilsabeck 10. Donna Lynne Champlin, Amber Stone 11. Kerry O'Malley (7/28/09), Leah Hocking (9/15/09), Stephanie Kurtzuba 12. Ruby Rakos 13. Easton Smith, Stephen Hanna 14. David Hibbard 15. J. Austin Eyer 16. Kylend Hetherington 17. Liz Pearce 18. Replacement Ensemble: Brad Bradley, Donna Lynne Champlin, C.K. Edwards, J. Austin Eyer, David Hibbard, Rick Hilsabeck, Aaron Kaburick, Liz Pearce, Robbie Roby, Easton Smith, Amber Stone, Matt Trent, Grant Turner 19. Replacement Ballet Girls: Ava DeMary, Georgi James, Maddy Novak, Kara Oates, Ruby Rakos, Rachel Resheff, Kendra Tate, Holly Taylor, Danika Yarosh 20. Tim Federle, Chelsea Galembo, Matthew Serafini, Heather Tepe, Natalie Wisdom

ORCHESTRA David Chase (Conductor); Shawn Gough (Associate Conductor/keyboards); Ed Salkin, Rick Heckman, Mike Migliore, Jay Brandford (reeds); James Dela Garza, John Dent, Alex Holton (trumpets); Dick Clark, Jack Schatz (trombones); Roger Wendt, Eva Conti (French horns); Joseph Joubert (keyboards); JJ McGeehan (guitar); Randy Landau (bass); Gary Seligson (drums); Howard Jones (percussion)

MUSICAL NUMBERS The Stars Look Down, Shine, We'd Go Dancing, Solidarity, Expressing Yourself, Dear Billy (Mum's Letter), Born to Boogie, Angry Dance, Merry Christmas Maggie Thatcher, Deep Into the Ground, He Could Go and He Could Shine, Electricity, Once We Were Kings, Dear Billy (Billy's Reply), Company Celebration

SETTING A small mining town in County Durham, Northeast England, 1984–1985. Act 1: The eve of the Miner's Strike. Act 2: Six months later. American premiere of a musical presented in two acts. World premiere at the Victoria Palace Theatre (London), March 31, 2005 where it is still running.

SYNOPSIS Set behind the political backdrop of England's coal miner strike, *Billy Elliot The Musical* is a funny, heart-warming and feel-good celebration of one young boy's dream to break free from the expectations of his middle class roots. Based on the enormously popular film, this powerful new musical is the story of a boy who discovers he has a special talent for dance.

Dayton Tavares and Company (photo by Carol Rosegg)

Blithe Spirit

Shubert Theatre; First Preview: February 26, 2009 Opening Night: March 15, 2009; Closed July 19, 2009; 20 previews, 145 performances

Written by Noël Coward; Produced by Jeffrey Richards, Jerry Frankel, Steve Traxler, Scott M. Delman, Bat-Barry Productions, Broadway Across America, Ken Davenport, Michael Filerman, Finn Scanlan Productions, Ronald Frankel, JK Productions, Kathleen K. Johnson, Patty Ann McKinnon, Judith Resnick, Terry Schnuck, Jamie deRoy/Alan D. Marks, Zev Buffman, Barbara & Buddy Freitag/ Wendy Federman; Director, Michael Blakemore; Set, Peter J. Davison; Costumes, Martin Pakledinaz; Lighting, Brain MacDevitt; Sound, Peter Fitzgerald; Production Supervisor/Production Stage Manager, Steven Zweigbaum; Wigs & Hair, Paul Huntley; Casting, Telsey + Company; Production Manager, Aurora Productions (Gene O'Donovan, W. Benjamin Heller II, Bethany Weinstein, Melissa Mazdra, Amy Merlino Coey, Laura Archer, Dana Hesch); Company Manager, Bruce Klinger; General Manager, Richards/Climan Inc. (David R. Richards & Tamar Haimes); Stage Manager, Ara Marx; Associate Director, Kim Weild; Associate Design: Ted LeFevre (set), MaryAnn D. Smith (costumes), Caroline Chao (lighting); Makeup, Jason Hayes; Assistant Design: Peter Hoerburger (lighting), Megan Henninger (sound); Assistant to the Costume Designer, Noah Marin; Costume Intern, Sophia Anastasiou; Associate General Manager, John Gendron; General Manager Associate, Jeromy Smith; Production Assistant, Sarah Michele Penland; Production: Jim Kane (production carpenter), Dan Coey (production electrician), Peter Sarafin (production props), Laura McGarty (head props), Ed Chapman (production sound), Karen L. Eifert (wardrobe supervisor), Maeve Butler (Ms. Lansbury's dresser), Jill Frese & Geoffrey Polischuk (dressers), Erin Kennedy Lunsford (hair supervisor); Associate to Mr. Richards, Jeremy Scott Blaustein; Assistant to Mr. Richards, Christopher Taggart; Assistant to Mr. Traxler, Brandi Preston; General Management Assistant, Cesar Hawas; Advertising, Serino Coyne Inc; Press, Jeffrey Richards Associates, Irene Gandy, Elon Rutberg, Alana Karpoff, Shane Marshall Brown, Diana Rissetto

CAST Edith **Susan Louise O'Connor**; Ruth **Jayne Atkinson**; Charles **Rupert Everett**; Dr. Bradman **Simon Jones**; Mrs. Bradman **Deborah Rush**; Madame Arcati **Angela Lansbury**; Elvira **Christine Ebersole**

UNDERSTUDIES Mark Capri (Charles, Dr. Bradman), Elizabeth Norment (Elvira, Ruth, Edith), Sandra Shipley (Madame Arcati, Mrs. Bradman)

SETTING The living room of the Charles and Ruth Condomine's house in Kent, England; late 1930s. Revival of an improbable farce presented in seven scenes in three acts with one intermission. World premiere at the Piccadilly Theatre (London) July 2, 1941. American premiere at the Morosco Theatre November 5, 1941–January 5, 1943, playing 657 performances. The play had a brief return engagement at the Morosco September 6–October 2, 1943, and was revived at the Neil Simon Theatre (starring Blythe Danner, Judith Ivey, Geraldine Page, and Richard Chamberlain) March 10–June 28, 1987 (see *Theatre World* Vol. 43, page 36).

SYNOPSIS In *Blithe Spirit*, one of Coward's biggest successes, novelist Charles Condomine, living with his second wife, Ruth, invites a local medium, Madame Arcati, to his house. His intention is to do some research into the spirit world for his new book. But he gets more than he bargained for when Arcati conjures up the ghost of Elvira, his first wife. Caught between one live wife and one dead wife — both jealous of the other — Charles thinks matters couldn't be worse.

Angela Lansbury, Susan Louise O'Connor, and Rupert Everett

Christine Ebersole (photos by Robert J. Saferstein)

Chicago

Ambassador Theatre; First Preview: October 23, 1996; Opening Night: November 14, 1996; 25 previews, 5,261 performances as of May 31, 2010

Lyrics by Fred Ebb, music by John Kander, book by Fred Ebb and Bob Fosse; based on the play by Maurine Dallas Watkins; Production based on the 1996 City Center *Encores!* production; Original production directed and choreographed by Bob Fosse; Produced by Barry & Fran Weissler/Kardana/Hart Sharp Productions, in association with Live Nation; Director, Walter Bobbie; Choreography, Ann Reinking in the style of Bob Fosse; Supervising Music Director, Rob Fisher; Music Director, Leslie Stifelman; Set, John Lee Beatty; Costumes, William Ivey Long; Lighting, Ken Billington; Sound, Scott Lehrer; Orchestrations, Ralph Burns; Dance Arrangements, Peter Howard; Adaptation, David Thompson; Musical Coordinator, Seymour Red Press; Hair/Wigs, David Brian Brown; Casting, James Calleri/Duncan Stewart (current), Jay Binder (original); Technical Supervisor, Arthur P. Siccardi; Dance Supervisor, Gary Chryst; Production Stage Manager, David Hyslop; Associate Producer, Alecia Parker; General Manager, B.J. Holt; Company Manager, Jean Haring; Stage Managers, Terrence J. Witter, Mindy Farbrother; Assistant Choreographer, Debra McWaters; Dance Captains, Gregory Butler, Bernard Dotson, Gabriela Garcia; Associate General Manager, Hilary Hamilton; General Manager Associate, Stephen Spadaro; Assistant Director, Jonathan Bernstein; Press, The Publicity Office, Jeremy Shaffer; Cast recording: RCA 68727-2

CAST Velma Kelly **Amra-Faye Wright**[1]; Roxie Hart **Charlotte d'Amboise**[2]; Amos Hart **Raymond Bokhour**[3]; Matron "Mama" Morton **Sofia Vergara**[4]; Billy Flynn **Tom Hewitt**[5]; Mary Sunshine **R. Lowe**[6]; Fred Casely **Brian O'Brien**[7]; Sergeant Fogarty **Adam Zotovitch**; Liz **Nicole Bridgewater**; Annie **Dylis Croman**[8]; June **Donna Marie Asbury**; Hunyak **Nili Bassman**; Mona **Jill Nicklaus**[9]; Go-To-Hell-Kitty **Melissa Rae Mahon**; Harry/The Jury **Shawn Emanjomeh**; Aaron/"Me and My Baby" Specialty **James T. Lane**; Doctor/Judge **Jason Patrick Sands**; Martin Harrison/"Me and My Baby" Specialty **Michael Cusumano**[10]; Bailiff/Court Clerk **Dan LoBuono**[11]

UNDERSTUDIES Melissa Rae Mahon (Roxie/Velma), Jill Nicklaus (Roxie), Donna Marie Asbury (Velma, "Mama" Morton), Jason Patrick Sands (Billy), James T. Lane (Amos), Adam Zotovich (Amos), Nicole Bridgewater ("Mama" Morton), David Kent/Brian Spitulnik (Fred Casely, "Me and My Baby"), J. Loeffelholtz (Mary Sunshine); Gabriela Garcia, David Kent, Sharon Moore, Brian Spitulnik (All other roles); Temporary Swing: Pilar Millhollen

*Succeeded by: 1. Deidre Goodwin (9/7/09), Terra C. MacLeod (2/8/10), Amra-Faye Wright (4/5/09), Brenda Braxton (5/3/10) 2. Bryn Dowling (6/15/09), Bonnie Langford (6/29/09), Samantha Harris (7/7/09), Bonnie Langford (9/7/09), Ashlee Simpson-Wentz (11/30/09), Michelle Williams (2/8/10), Bianca Marroquin (4/15/10), Ruthie Henshall (4/26/10) 3. Tom Riis Farrell (6/15/09), Raymond Bokhour (8/10/09) 4. Chandra Wilson (6/8/09), Roz Ryan (7/7/09), Kecia Lewis-Evans (9/7/09), Roz Ryan (11/30/09), Terri White (4/26/10) 5. Brent Barrett (7/7/09), Jerry Springer (8/18/09), Tom Hewitt (9/7/09), Brent Barrett (10/5/09), Obba Babatunde (1/10/10), Brent Barrett (1/18/09), Tom Hewitt (3/29/10), Matthew Settle (4/19/10) 6. D. Vogel 7. Dan LoBuono 8. Solange Sandy 9. Dylis Croman 10. Michael Cusumano 11. Greg Reuter

ORCHESTRA Leslie Stifelman (Conductor); Scott Cady (Associate Conductor/piano); Seymour Red Press, Jack Stuckey, Richard Centalonza (woodwinds); John Frosk, Darryl Shaw (trumpets); Dave Bargeron, Bruce Bonvissuto (trombones); John Johnson (piano/accordion); Jay Berliner (banjo); Ronald Raffio (bass/tuba); Marshall Coid (violin); Ronald Zito (drums/percussion)

MUSICAL NUMBERS All That Jazz, Funny Honey, Cell Block Tango, When You're Good to Mama, Tap Dance, All I Care About, A Little Bit of Good, We Both Reached for the Gun, Roxie, I Can't Do It Alone, My Own Best Friend, Entr'acte, I Know a Girl, Me and My Baby, Mister Cellophane, When Velma Takes the Stand, Razzle Dazzle, Class, Nowadays, Hot Honey Rag, Finale

SETTING Chicago, Illinois. The late 1920s. A musical vaudeville presented in two acts. This production originally opened at the Richard Rodgers Theatre; transferred to the Shubert on February 12, 1997; and transferred to the Ambassador on January 29, 2003. For original production credits see *Theatre World* Vol. 53, page 14. The original Broadway production ran June 3, 1975–August 27, 1977 at the 46th Street Theatre (now the Richard Rodgers Theatre where this revival first played) playing 936 performances (see *Theatre World* Vol. 32, Page 8).

SYNOPSIS Murder, media circus, vaudeville, and celebrity meet in this 1920s tale of two of the Windy City's most celebrated felons and their rise to fame amidst a razzle dazzle trial.

Amra-Faye Wright and Company

Sofia Vergara (photos by Paul Kolnik)

Geoffrey Rush

Exit the King

Barrymore Theatre; First Preview: March 7, 2009 Opening Night: March 26, 2009; Closed June 14, 2009; 21 previews, 93 performances

Written by Eugene Ionesco, adapted by Neil Armfield and Geoffrey Rush; Produced by Stuart Thompson, Robert Fox, Howard Panter, Scott Rudin, Tulchin/Bartner, Jon B. Platt, John Frost, The Weinstein Company/Norton Herrick, Michael Edwards & Carole Winter, Daniel Sparrow/Mike Walsh, and The Shubert Organization; Director, Neil Armfield; Sets & Costumes, Dale Ferguson; Lighting, Damien Cooper; Sound, Russell Goldsmith; Composer, John Rodgers; Production Stage Manager, Evan Ensign; Casting, Daniel Swee; Production Management, Aurora Productions; General Management, Stuart Thompson Productions/Dana Sherman; Associate Producer, Ronnie Planalp; Company Manager, Adam J. Miller; Stage Manager, Jim Woolley; Associate Design: Ted LeFevre (set), Barry Doss (costumes), Dan Walker (lighting), Joanna Lynne Staub (sound); Wig Design Consultant, Paul Huntley; Production: Tony Menditto (production carpenter), Michael Hyman (production electrician), Dylan Foley (production props), Jason McKenna (production sound), Eileen Miller (wardrobe supervisor), Ruth Carsch (hair supervisor), Barry Berger (makeup supervisor), Barry Doss (dresser); Production Assistant, Bryan Rountree; General Management Associates, James Triner, David Turner, Caroline Prugh; Production Management Associates, Gene O'Donovan, W. Benjamin Heller II, Bethany Weinstein, Amy Merlino Coey, Melissa Mazdra, Laura Archer, Dana Hesch; General Management Assistants, Quinn Corbin, Megan Curren, Geo Karapetyan; Management Intern, Brittany Levasseur; Casting Associate, Camille Hickman; Musician Consultant, Michael Keller; Advertising, SpotCo (Drew Hodges, Jim Edwards, Tom Greenwald, Jim Aquino, Stacey Maya); For Company B: Louise Herron (Board Chair), Neil Armfield (Artistic Director), Brenna Hobson (General Manager); For Malthouse: Michael Kantor (Artistic Director), Stephen Armstrong (Executive Producer), Catherine Jones (Associate Producer & General Manager); Press, Boneau/Bryan-Brown, Chris Boneau, Susanne Tighe, Christine Olver

CAST The Guard **Brian Hutchison**; King Berenger **Geoffrey Rush**; Queen Marguerite **Susan Sarandon**; Juliette **Andrea Martin**; The Doctor **William Sadler**; Queen Marie **Lauren Ambrose**; Trumpeter **Shane Endsley/Scott Harrell**

UNDERSTUDIES Michael Hammond (King Berenger, The Doctor), David Manis (King Berenger, The Guard), Erika Rolfsrud (Queen Marguerite, Queen Marie, Juliette)

SETTING Revival of an absurdist play presented in two acts. This production is based on the production produced by Melbourne, Australia's Company B (Belvoir St. Theatre) and Malthouse Theatres. Originally produced on Broadway by the Association of Producing Artists-Phoenix Repertory Company at the Lyceum Theatre January 9–June 22, 1968, in repertory with *The Cherry Orchard*, *Pantagleize*, and *The Show-Off* (see *Theatre World* Vol. 24, page 67).

SYNOPSIS *Exit the King* is a hilarious and poignant comedy about a megalomaniacal ruler, King Berenger, whose incompetence has left his country in near ruin. Despite the efforts of Queen Marguerite and the other members of the court to convince the King he has only 90 minutes left to live, he refuses to relinquish any control.

Susan Sarandon (photos by Joan Marcus)

Original cast members Marcia Gay Harden, Hope Davis, Jeff Daniels, and James Gandolfini

Annie Potts, Ken Stott, Jimmy Smits and Christine Lahti

God of Carnage

Bernard B. Jacobs Theatre; First Preview: February 28, 2009 Opening Night: March 22, 2009; 24 previews, 444 performances as of May 31, 2010[+]

Written by Yasmina Reza, translated by Christopher Hampton; Produced by Robert Fox, David Pugh & Dafydd Rogers, Stuart Thompson, Scott Rudin, Jon B. Platt, The Weinstein Company, and The Shubert Organization; Director, Matthew Warchus; Set and Costumes, Mark Thompson; Lighting, Hugh Vanstone; Music, Gary Yershon; Sound, Simon Baker/Christopher Cronin; Casting, Daniel Swee; Production Stage Manager, Jill Cordle; Production Management, Aurora Productions (Gene O'Donovan, W. Benjamin Heller II, Bethany Weinstein, Melissa Mazdra, Amy Merlino Coey, Laura Archer, Dana Hesch); General Management, Stuart Thompson Productions/David Turner; Company Manager, Chris Morey; Stage Manager, Kenneth J. McGee; Associate Director, Beatrice Terry; Associate Design: Nancy Thun (set), Daryl A. Stone (costumes), Ted Mather (lighting); Vocal Coach, Deborah Hecht; Makeup Consultant, Judy Chin; Production: Randall Zaibek (production electrician), Denise J. Grillo (production properties coordinator), Brien Brannigan (production sound), Kay Grunder (wardrobe supervisor), Derek Moreno (dresser); Casting Associate, Camille Hickman; General Managements Associates, James Triner, Dana Sherman, Caroline Prugh; Assistants: Nathan K. Claus (production), Zack Brown, Michael Megliola (to Mr. Vanstone), Quinn M. Corbin, Megan E. Curren, Geo Karapetyan (general management), Sarah Richardson (to Mr. Fox), Kevin Graham-Caso (to Mr. Rudin), Terrie Lootens (to Mr. Platt); RADA Trainee Assistant Director, Caroline Ranger; General Management Intern, Brittany Levasseur; Advertising, Serino Coyne Inc.; Press, Boneau/Bryan-Brown, Chris Boneau, Susanne Tighe, Christine Olver, Kelly Guiod

CAST Alan **Jeff Daniels**[*1]; Annette **Hope Davis**[*2]; Michael **James Gandolfini**[*3]; Veronica **Marcia Gay Harden**[4]

STANDBYS Bruce McCarty (Alan, Michael), Charlotte Maier (Annette, Veronica)

* Succeeded by: 1. Jimmy Smits (11/17/09), Dylan Baker (3/2/10) 2. Annie Potts (11/17/09), Lucy Liu (3/2/10) 3. Ken Stott (11/17/09), Jeff Daniels (3/2/10) 4. Christine Lahti (11/17/09), Janet McTeer (3/2/10)

SETTING Michael and Veronica's living room; the present. American premiere of a new play presented without intermission. Mr. Warchus directed the English language premiere at the Gielgud Theatre (London) starring Janet McTeer and Ralph Fiennes March 25–June 14, 2008. The play received the 2009 Olivier Award for Best New Comedy. World premiere in Zurich, Switzerland December 8, 2006.

SYNOPSIS God of Carnage is a comedy of manners (without the manners) the deals with the aftermath of a playground altercation between two boys and what happens when their parents meet to talk about it. A calm and rational debate between grown-ups about the need to teach kids how to behave properly? Or a hysterical night of name-calling, tantrums and tears before bedtime? Boys will be boys... but the adults are usually worse... much worse...

[+]The show was on a summer hiatus from July 27–September 7, 2009.

Dylan Baker, Lucy Liu, Janet McTeer, and Jeff Daniels (photos by Joan Marcus)

Guys and Dolls

Nederlander Theatre; First Preview: February 5, 2009 Opening Night: March 1, 2009; Closed June 14, 2009; 28 previews, 121 performances

Music and lyrics by Frank Loesser, book by Jo Swerling and Abe Burrows, based on the stories and characters of Damon Runyon; Produced by Howard Panter for Ambassador Theatre Group, Robert G. Bartner/Norman & Steven Tulchin, Bill Kenwright, Northwater Entertainment, Darren Bagert, and Tom Gregory, with Nederlander Presentations Inc, David Mirvish, Michael Jenkins/Dallas Summer Musicals, Independent Presenters Network, Olympus Theatricals, and Sonia Friedman Productions; Director, Des McAnuff; Choreography, Sergio Trujillo; Music Director/Vocal Arrangements/Incidental Music, Ted Sperling; Sets, Robert Brill; Costumes, Paul Tazewell; Lighting, Howell Binkley; Sound, Steve Canyon Kennedy; Video, Dustin O'Neill; Hair & Wigs, Charles LaPointe; Fight Director, Steve Rankin; Casting, Tara Rubin; Orchestrations, Bruce Coughlin; Dance Arrangements, James Lynn Abbott; Conductor, Jeffrey Klitz; Music Coordinator, Michael Keller; Marketing, Type A Marketing/Anne Rippey; Technical Supervision, Don S. Gilmore; Production Stage Manager, Frank Hartenstein; General Management, Alchemy Production Group (Carl Pasbjerg & Frank Scardino); Associate Producers, Jill Lenhart & Peter Godfrey; Executive Producer, David Lazar; Company Manager, Jim Brandeberry; Makeup, Angelina Avallone; Video Content Production, The Oracle Group/Ari Novak; Associate General Manager, Chris Morey; Stage Manager, Kelly Martindale; Assistant Stage Manager, Alex Lyu Volckhausen; Assistant Company Manager, Sherra Johnston; Associate to the General Managers, Tegan Meyer; Dance Captain, Marcos Santana; Fight Captain, Graham Rowat; Dialect Coach, Stephen Gabis; Dramaturg, James Magruder; Assistant Director, Shelley Butler; Associate Design: Dustin O'Neill (sets), Nancy Palmatier (costumes), Mark Simpson (lighting), Andrew Keister (sound), Leah Loukas (hair); Assistant Set Design, Erica Hemminger, Steve Kemp, Caleb Levengood, Angrette McCloskey, Michael Locher, Daniel Meeker; Assistant Costumes Design, Michael Zecker, Courtney Watson, Maria Zamansky, Caitlin Hunt; Assistant Lighting, Christian DeAngelis; Moving Lights Programmer, David Arch; Video Programmer, Thomas Hague; Sound Programmer, Wallace Flores; Music Copying, Emily Grishman, Katherine Edmonds; Keyboard Programmer, Randy Cohen; Assistant Keyboard Programmers, Jim Mironenik, Bryan Crook; Production Assistants, Jenny Slattery, Andrew Gottlieb, Alissa Zulvergold; Advertising, SpotCo; Press, The Hartman Group

CAST Nicely-Nicely Johnson **Tituss Burgess**; Benny Southstreet **Steve Rosen**; Rusty Charlie **Spencer Moses**; Sarah Brown **Kate Jennings Grant**; Agatha **Andrea Chamberlain**; Martha **Jessica Rush**; Calvin **William Ryall**; Arvide Abernathy **Jim Ortlieb**; Harry the Horse **Jim Walton**; Lt. Brannigan **Adam LeFevre**; Nathan Detroit **Oliver Platt**; Angie the Ox **Graham Rowat**; Society Max **James Harkness**; Liver Lips Louie **Nick Adams**; Damon **Raymond Del Barrio**; The Greek **Joseph Medeiros**; Brandy Bottle Bates **Ron Todorowski**; Scranton Slim **John Selya**; Sky Masterson **Craig Bierko**; Mimi **Lorin Latarro**; Joey Biltmore **Brian Shepard**; Adelaide **Lauren Graham**; General Cartwright **Mary Testa**; Big Jule **Glenn Fleshler**; Carmen **Kearran Giovanni**; Hot Box Girls **Kearran Giovanni, Lorin Latarro, Rhea Patterson, Jessica Rush, Jennifer Savelli, Brooke Wendle**; Ensemble **Nick Adams, Andrea Chamberlain, Raymond Del Barrio, Kearran Giovanni, James Harkness, Lorin Latarro, Joseph Medeiros, Spencer Moses, Rhea Patterson, Graham Rowat, Jessica Rush, William Ryall, Jennifer Savelli, John Selya, Brian Shepard, Ron Todorowski, Jim Walton, Brooke Wendle**; Swings **Melissa Fagan, Benjamin Magnuson, Marcos Santana**

UNDERSTUDIES Graham Rowat (Sky), Adam LeFevre (Nathan), Jim Walton (Nicely-Nicely, Lt. Brannigan), William Ryall (Arvide, Big Jule), Ben Magnuson (Benny), Jessica Rush (Sarah), Andrea Chamberlain (Adelaide, General Cartwright), Lorin Latarro (Adelaide)

ORCHESTRA Jeffrey Klitz (Conductor); Jeff Marder (Associate Conductor/keyboards); Cenovia Cummins [Concertmistress], Lori Miller, Ming Yeh (violins); Mairi Dorman-Phaneuf, Sarah Hewitt-Roth (celli); Don Downs, CJ Camerieri (trumpets); Mike Davis (trombone); Matt Ingman (bass trombone/tuba); Tom Murray, Ken Dubisz, Mark Thrasher (reeds); Greg Utzig (guitar/banjo); Mark Vanderpoel (bass); Steve Bartosik (drums); Javier Diaz (percussion)

MUSICAL NUMBERS Overture, Runyonland, Fugue for Tinhorns, Follow the Fold, The Oldest Established, Follow the Fold (reprise), I'll Know, A Bushel and a Peck, Adelaide's Lament, Guys and Dolls, Havana, If I Were a Bell, My Time of Day, I've Never Been in Love Before, Entr'acte, Take Back Your Mink, Adelaide's Lament (reprise), More I Cannot Wish You, The Crapshooter's Dance, Luck Be a Lady, Sue Me, Sit Down You're Rockin' the Boat, Follow the Fold (reprise), Marry the Man Today, Guys and Dolls (reprise)

SETTING New York City in the time of Damon Runyon. Revival of the musical presented in two acts. Originally produced on Broadway at the 46th Street Theatre (now the Richard Rodgers) November 24, 1950–November 28, 1953, playing 1,200 performances (see *Theatre World* Vol. 7, page 51). New York City Center Light Opera Company revived the show for brief 15 performance runs April 20–May 31, 1955 (see *Theatre World* Vol. 11, page 111), and ten years later April 28–May 9, 1965 (see *Theatre World* Vol. 21, page 143). An all African-American cast revival played the Broadway Theatre July 21, 1976–February 13, 1977 (see *Theatre World* Vol. 33, page 16). The show was revived at the Martin Beck Theatre (now the Al Hirschfeld) April 14, 1992–January 8, 1995, playing 1,143 performances (see *Theatre World* Vol. 48, page 43).

SYNOPSIS Based on "The Idyll of Miss Sarah Brown" and "Blood Pressure" as well as characters and plot elements from other Damon Runyon stories, this musical fable of Broadway concerns a high-stakes gambler who unexpectedly falls for a mission doll, and a the operator of New York's oldest floating crap game who can't commit to marry his showgirl girlfriend after a fourteen-year engagement.

Titus Burgess and the Company (photos by Carol Rosegg)

The Company

Hair: The American Tribal Love-Rock Musical

Al Hirschfeld Theatre; First Preview: March 6, 2009 Opening Night: March 31, 2009; 29 previews, 487 performances as of May 31, 2010

Book and lyrics by Gerome Ragni & James Rado, music and orchestrations by Galt MacDermot; Produced by The Public Theater (Oskar Eustis, Artistic Director; Andrew D. Hamingson, Executive Director), Jeffrey Richards, Jerry Frankel, Gary Goddard Entertainment, Kathleen K. Johnson, Nederlander Productions Inc., Fran Kirmser Productions/Jed Bernstein, Marc Frankel, Broadway Across America, Barbara Manocherian/WenCarLar Productions, JK Productions/Terry Schnuck, Andy Sandberg, Jam Theatricals, The Weinstein Company/Norton Herrick, Jujamcyn Theaters, Joey Parnes, and by special arrangement with Elizabeth Ireland McCann; Director, Diane Paulus; Choreography, Karole Armitage; Music Director, Nadia Digiallonardo; Associate Producers, Arielle Tepper Madover, Debbie Bisno/Rebecca Gold, Christopher Hart, Apples and Oranges, Tony & Ruthe Ponturo, Joseph Traina; Sets, Scott Pask; Costumes, Michael McDonald; Lighting, Kevin Adams; Sound, Acme Sound Partners; Music Coordinator, Seymour Red Press; Casting, Jordan Thaler & Heidi Griffiths; Production Stage Manager, Nancy Harrington; Wigs, Gerard Kelly; Associate Producer (The Public Theater), Jenny Gersten; Marketing, Allied Live Inc.; Sponsorship, Rose Polidoro; General Management, Joey Parnes, John Johnson, S.D. Wagner; Company Manager, Kim Sellon; Stage Manager, Julie Baldauff; Assistant Stage Manager, Elizabeth Miller; Associate Company Manager, Leslie A. Glassburn; Assistant Company Manager, Kit Ingui; Assistant Directors, Allegra Libonati, Shira Milikowsky; Assistant Choreographer, Christine O'Grady; Dance Captain, Tommar Wilson; Associate Design: Orit Jacoby Carroll (set), Aaron Sporer (lighting), Lisa Zinni (costumes); Assistant Design: Jeffrey Hinchee & Lauren Alvarez (set), Joel Silver (lighting), Chloe Chapin (costumes), Alex Hawthorn (sound); Assistants to Designers: Warren Stiles (set), David Mendizabal (costumes); Costume Assistant, Sydney Ledger; Mural Illustration, Scott Pask with Amy Guip; Production: Larry Morley, Steve Cochrane, Richard Mortell, Michael Smanko, Scott Sanders, Brian Dawson, Paul J. Sonnleitner, Jim Wilkinson, John A. Robelen III, Gloria Burke, Cat Dee, Amelia Haywood, Shannon McDowell, Clarion Overmoyer, Gayle Palmieri, Danny Koye; Production Assistant, Johnny Milani; Music Consultant, Tom Kitt; Music Copyist, Rob Baumgardner; Management Associate, Madeline Felix; Director of Communications (The Public Theater), Candi Adams; Director of Marketing (The Public Theater), Ilene Rosen; Advertising, SpotCo; Interactive Marketing, Situation Interactive; Press, O+M Co.; Cast recording: Sh-K-Boom/Ghostlight Records 4467

CAST Dionne **Sasha Allen**; Berger **Will Swenson**; Woof **Bryce Ryness**; Hud **Darius Nichols**; Claude **Gavin Creel**; Sheila **Caissie Levy**; Jeanie **Kacie Sheik**; Crissy **Allison Case**; Mother/Buddhadlirama **Megan Lawrence**; Dad/Margaret Mead **Andrew Kober**; Hubert **Theo Stockman**; Abraham Lincoln **Saycon Sengbloh**; Tribe **Ato Blankson-Wood, Steel Burkhardt, Jackie Burns, Lauren Elder, Allison Guinn, Anthony Hollock, Kaitlin Kiyan, Nicole Lewis, John Moauro, Brandon Pearson, Megan Reinking, Paris Remillard, Saycon Sengbloh, Maya Sharpe, Theo Stockman, Tommar Wilson**; Tribe Swings **Briana Carlson-Goodman, Chasten Harmon, Jay Armstrong Johnson, Josh Lamon, Ryan Link, Michael James Scott**

REPLACEMENT CAST (3/9/2010) Dionne **Jeannette Bayardelle**; Berger **Ace Young**; Woof **Jason Wooten**; Hud **Wallace Smith**; Claude **Kyle Riabko**; Sheila **Diana DeGarmo**; Jeanie **Annaleigh Ashford**; Crissy **Vanessa Ray**; Mother/Buddhadlirama **Rachel Bay Jones**; Dad/Margaret Mead **Josh Lamon**; Hubert **Lee Zarrett**; Abraham Lincoln **Anastacia McCleskey**; Tribe **Justin Badger, Larkin Bogan, Natalie Bradshaw, Catherine Brookman, Ericka Jerry, Jay Armstrong Johnson, Mykal Kilgore, Josh Lamon, Anastacia McClesky, Paris Remillard, Arbender J. Robinson, Kate Rockwell, Cailan Rosenthal, Rashidra Scott, Jen Sese, Lawrence Stallings, Terrance Thomas, Emma Zaks, Lee**

Zarrett; Tribe Swings **Nicholas Belton, Matt DeAngelis, Briana Carlson-Goodman, Antwayn Hopper, Nicole Lewis, Arbender J. Robinson**

MUSICIANS Nadia Digiallonardo (Conductor/keyboard), Lon Hoyt (Assistant Conductor/keyboard), Steve Bargonetti & Andrew Schwartz (guitar), Wilbur Bascomb (bass), Allen Won (woodwinds), Elaine Burt, Ronald Buttacavoli & Christian Jaudes (trumpets), Vincent MacDermot (trombone), Joe Cardello (percussion), Bernard Purdie (drums)

MUSICAL NUMBERS Aquarius, Donna, Hashish, Sodomy, Colored Spade, Manchester England, I'm Black, Ain't Got No, Sheila Franklin, I Believe in Love, Ain't Got No (reprise), Air, The Stone Age, I Got Life, Initials, Going Down, Hair, My Conviction, Easy to Be Hard, Don't Put It Down, Frank Mills, Hare Krishna, Where Do I Go, Electric Blues, Oh Great God of Power, Black Boys, White Boys, Walking in Space, Minuet, Yes I's Finished on Y'alls Farmlands, Four Score and Seven Years Ago/Abie Baby, Give Up All Desires, Three-Five-Zero-Zero, What a Piece of Work Is Man, How Dare They Try, Good Morning Starshine, Ain't Got No (reprise), The Flesh Failures, Eyes Look Your Last, Let the Sun Shine In

SETTING New York City, the late 1960s. Revival of the rock musical presented in two acts. This production was previously presented at the Delacorte Theater July 22–September 14, 2008, and as part of Joe's Pub in the Park September 22-24, 2007, with most of this cast (see *Theatre World* Vol. 64, page 186). Originally produced Off-Broadway at the Public Theater October 17–December 10, 1967; reopened at the midtown discothèque Cheetah December 22, 1968–January 28, 1968. After extensive rewrites and recasting, it transferred to the Biltmore Theatre April 29, 1968, closing July 1, 1972 after 1,750 performances (see *Theatre World* Vol. 24, pages 59 and 11). Briefly revived at the Biltmore August 3–November 6, 1977 (see *Theatre World* Vol. 34, page 14). In a rare scenario on Broadway, 26 members of the original cast went on to open the show in London at the Gielgud Theatre, April 14, 2010, creating one of the largest cast replacements in history.

SYNOPSIS *Hair* depicts the birth of a cultural movement in the 60s and 70s that changed America forever. The musical follows a group of hopeful, free-spirited young people who advocate a lifestyle of pacifism and free-love in a society riddled with intolerance and brutality during the Vietnam War. As they explore sexual identity, challenge racism, experiment with drugs and burn draft cards, the tribe in *Hair* creates an irresistible message of hope that continues to resonate with audiences 40 years later.

Kyle Riabko, Ace Young, and the New Tribe (photo by Joan Marcus)

In the Heights

Richard Rodgers Theatre; First Preview: February 14, 2008; Opening Night: March 9, 2008; 29 previews, 928 performances as of May 31, 2010

Concept, music and lyrics by Lin-Manuel Miranda, book by Quiara Alegría Hudes; Produced by Kevin McCollum, Jeffrey Seller, Jill Furman, Sander Jacobs, Goodman/Grossman, Peter Fine, Everett/Skipper; Director, Thomas Kail; Choreographer, Andy Blankenbuehler; Music Director, Alex Lacamoire; Sets, Anna Louizos; Costumes, Paul Tazewell; Lighting, Howell Binkley; Sound, Acme Sound Partners; Arrangements and Orchestrations, Alex Lacamoire & Bill Sherman; Music Coordinator, Michael Keller; Casting, Telsey + Company; Marketing, Scott A. Moore; Company Manager, Brig Berney; General Manager, John S. Corker, Lizbeth Cone; Technical Supervisor, Brian Lynch; Production Stage Manager, J. Philip Bassett; Associate Producers, Ruth Hendel, Harold Newman; Wigs, Charles LaPointe; Assistant Director, Casey Hushion; Assistant Choreographer, Joey Dowling; Fight Director, Ron Piretti; Latin Assistant Choreographer, Luis Salgado; Fight/Dance Captain, Michael Balderrama; Stage Manager, Amber Wedin; Assistant Stage Manager, Heather Hogan; Associate Design: Donyale Werle, Todd Potter (set), Michael Zecker (costumes), Mark Simpson (lighting), Sten Severson (sound); Assistant Design: Hilary Noxon, Heather Dunbar (set), Caitlin Hunt (costumes), Greg Bloxham, Ryan O'Gara (lighting); Moving Lights, David Arch; Production: McBrien Dunbar, Cheyenne Benson, Keith Buchanan, Dan Robillard, George Wagner, Christopher Kurtz, Brandon Rice, Rick Kelly, Jamie Stewart, Gray Biangone, Jennifer Hohn, Moira MacGregor-Conrad; Music Copying, Emily Grishman; Rehearsal Pianist, Zachary Dietz; Keyboard Programming, Randy Cohen; Advertising, SpotCo; Press, The Hartman Group; Cast recording: Sh-K-Boom/Ghostlight Records 4428

Marcy Harriell, Andrea Burns, Mandy Gonzalez, and Courtney Reed

Corbin Bleu and the Company (photos by Joan Marcus)

CAST Graffiti Pete **Seth Stewart**[1]; Usnavi **Javier Muñoz**[2]; Piragua Guy **Eliseo Román**[3]; Abuela Claudia **Olga Merediz**; Carla **Janet Dacal**[4]; Daniela **Andréa Burns**[5]; Kevin **Rick Negron**; Camila **Priscilla Lopez**; Sonny **Robin De Jesús**[6]; Benny **Christopher Jackson**; Vanessa **Marcy Harriell**; Nina **Mandy Gonzalez**[7]; Ensemble **Danny Bolero, Tony Chiroldes, Dwayne Clark, Rosie Lani Fiedelman, Ruben Flores, Marcus Paul James, Afra Hines**[8]**, Nina Lafarga, Doreen Montalvo, Gabrielle Ruiz, Eliseo Román, Luis Salgado, Shaun Taylor-Corbett**[9]**, Rickey Tripp**; Swings[10] **Michael Balderrama, Blanca Camacho, Stephanie Klemons, José-Luis Lopez, Antuan Raimone, Alejandra Reyes, Jon Rua**

UNDERSTUDIES Michael Balderrama (Usnavi, Graffiti Pete, Piragua Guy), Blanca Camacho (Abuela Claudia, Camila, Daniela), Tony Chiroldes (Kevin, Piragua Guy), Janet Dacal (Vanessa, Nina), Dwayne Clark (Benny), Marcus Paul James (Benny), Stephanie Klemons (Carla), Nina Lafarga (Nina), Doreen Montalvo (Abuela Claudia, Camila, Daniela), Gabrielle Ruiz (Nina, Carla, Vanessa), Eliseo Román (Kevin), Shaun Taylor-Corbett (Usnavi, Sonny, Piragua Guy), Rickey Tripp (Graffiti Pete)

* Succeeded by: 1. William B. Wingfield (8/25/09) 2. Corbin Bleu (1/25/10) 3. Tony Chiroldes (10/26/09), Eliseo Román (11/23/09) 4. Courtney Reed (9/29/09) 5. Justina Machado (6/29/09), Andréa Burns (8/25/09) 6. David Del Rio (2/15/10) 7. Nina Lafarga or Courtney Reed or Gabrielle Ruiz (1/25/10–2/18/10), Janet Dacal (2/19/10) 8. Jennifer Locke 9. Kevin Santos, Noah Rivera 10. Allison Thomas Lee, Marcos Santana

ORCHESTRA Alex Lacamoire (Conductor/keyboard 1); Zachary Dietz (Associate Conductor/keyboard 2); Raul Agraz (lead trumpet); Trevor Neumann (trumpet); Joe Fiedler, Ryan Keberle (trombones); Dave Richards, Kristy Norter (reeds); Andres Forero (drums); Doug Hinrichs, Wilson Torres (percussion); Irio O'Farrill (bass); Manny Moreira (guitars)

MUSICAL NUMBERS In the Heights, Breathe, Benny's Dispatch, It Won't Be Long Now, Inútil (Useless), No Me Diga, 96,000, Paciencia Y Fe (Patience and Faith), When You're Home, Piragua, Siempre (Always), The Club/Fireworks, Sunrise, Hundreds of Stories, Enough, Carnaval del Barrio, Atencíon, Alabanza, Everything I Know, No Me Diga (reprise), Champagne, When the Sun Goes Down, Finale

SETTING Washington Heights, Manhattan. Fourth of July weekend, the present. A new musical presented in two acts. For original production credits see *Theatre World* Volume 64, page 46. Previously presented Off-Broadway at 37 Arts, February 8–July 15, 2007 (see *Theatre World* Vol. 63, page 162).

SYNOPSIS *In the Heights* follows two days in Washington Heights, a vibrant immigrant neighborhood at the top of Manhattan. From the vantage point of Usnavi's corner bodega, we experience the joys, heartbreaks and bonds of a Latino community struggling to redefine home. This original musical features a mix of hip-hop, salsa and meringue music.

Irena's Vow

Walter Kerr Theatre; First Preview: March 10, 2009 Opening Night: March 29, 2009; Closed June 28, 2009; 21 previews, 105 performances

Written by Dan Gordon; Presented by Invictus Theater Company and The Directors Company; Produced by Power Productions/Stan Raiff, Daryl Roth, Debra Black, James L. Nederlander/Terry Allen Kramer, and Peter Fine; Director, Michael Parva; Set, Kevin Judge; Costumes, Astrid Brucker; Lighting, David Castaneda; Projections, Alex Koch; Original Music and Sound, Quentin Chiappetta; Wigs and Hair, Leah J. Loukas; Production Stage Manager, Alan Fox; Technical Supervision, Arthur Siccardi, Patrick Sullivan; Marketing, HHC Marketing; Associate Producers, R. Erin Craig, Alexander Fraser, Roz Goldberg; General Manager, Leonard Soloway; Company Manager, Penelope Daulton; Additional Casting, Jim Carnahan; Stage Manager, Michael Joseph Ormond; Assistant Director, Katherine Heberling; Associate Lighting, Cory Pattak; Assistant Design: Jen Price (set), Josh Liebert (sound), Dragana Vucetic (costumes); Video Programmer, David Tirosh; Dialect Coach, Ralph Zito; Production: George E. Fullum (production carpenter), Vincent J. Valvo Jr. (production electrician), Timothy Bennett (production props), Michael Pilipski (prop supervisor), Penny Davis (wardrobe supervisor), Nathaniel Hathaway (hair supervisor), Ginny Hounsell & Kevin O'Brien (dressers); Marketing Team: Hugh Hysell, Matt Sicoli, Nicole Pando, Michael Redman, Todd Briscoe, Kayla Kuzbel, Paul Zahn; Assistants: Greg Raby (Ms. Roth), Kathleen Ragusa (Ms. Black), Ken Happel (Mr. Nederlander), Sara Shannon (Ms. Kramer), Veronika Crater (Mr. Fine), Sarah Koehler (production); Advertising, Eliran Murphy Group/ Barbara Eliran, Frank Verlizzo, Sasha DeFazio; Press, O+M Co., Rick Miramontez, Molly Barnett

CAST Irena Gut Opdyke **Tovah Feldshuh**; Major Rugemer **Thomas Ryan**; Schultz **Steven Hauck**; Ida Hallar **Maja C. Wampuszyc**; Lazar Hallar **Gene Silvers**; Fanka Silberman **Tracee Chimo**; Sturmbannführer Rokita **John Stanisci**; Helen/Rokita's Secretary **Sandi Carroll**; The Visitor/Polish Worker **Scott Klavan**; Mayor of Jerusalem/SS Officer **Peter Reznikoff**

STANDBYS AND UNDERSTUDIES Tina Benko (Standby for Irena Gut Opdyke), Heather Kenzie (Ida, Fanka, Helen/Rokita's Secretary), Paul O'Brien (Rugemer, Schultz, Mayor/Officer), Kevin O'Donnell (Rokita, Lazar, The Visitor/ Polish Worker)

SETTING An American high school, 1988; Occupied Poland, 1939–1945; Jerusalem, 1988. Transfer of the Off-Broadway play presented without intermission. Previously presented at Baruch Performing Arts Center – Rose Nagelberg Hall from September 7–November 25, 2008.

SYNOPSIS *Irena's Vow* is the riveting, life-affirming story about one of the most courageous and unsung heroines of World War II. During the German occupation of Poland, Irena Gut Opdyke, a Polish Catholic, was forced to work as head housekeeper for a prominent German major. Over a two-year period of service, Irena would risk her own life in order to protect the lives of twelve Jewish refugees whom she secretly took under her care. *Irena's Vow* is the extraordinary true story of one woman's choice and the twelve lives that would ultimately be saved –or lost– by her decision.

Gene Silvers, Maja Wampuszyc, Tracee Chimo, and Tovah Feldshuh

Tovah Feldshuh (photos by Carol Rosegg)

Jersey Boys

August Wilson Theatre; First Preview: October 4, 2005; Opening Night: November 6, 2005; 38 previews, 1,881 performances as of May 31, 2010

Book by Marshall Brickman and Rick Elice, music by Bob Gaudio, lyrics by Bob Crewe; Produced by Dodger Theatricals (Michael David, Edward Strong, Rocco Landesman, Des McAnuff), Joseph J. Grano, Pelican Group, Tamara Kinsella and Kevin Kinsella, in association with Latitude Link, Rick Steiner and Osher/Staton/Bell/ Mayerson Group; Director, Des McAnuff; Choreography, Sergio Trujillo; Musical Director, Vocal Arrangements/Incidental Music, Ron Melrose; Sets, Klara Zieglerova; Costumes, Jess Goldstein; Lighting, Howell Binkley; Sound, Steve Canyon Kennedy; Projections, Michael Clark; Hair/Wigs, Charles LaPointe; Fight Director, Steve Rankin; Assistant Director, West Hyler; Production Supervisor, Richard Hester; Production Stage Manager, Michelle Bosch; Orchestrations, Steve Orich; Music Coordinator, John Miller; Technical Supervisor, Peter Fulbright; Casting, Tara Rubin (East), Sharon Bialy, Sherry Thomas (West); Company Manager, Sandra Carlson; Associate Company Manager, Tim Sulka; Associate Producers, Lauren Mitchell and Rhoda Mayerson; Executive Producer, Sally Campbell Morse; Promotions, HHC Marketing; Stage Manager, Michael T. Clarkston/Jason Brouillard/Michelle Reupert; Assistant Stage Manager, Rachel Wolff/Michelle Reupert/Brendan M. Fay; Dialect Coach, Stephen Gabis; Dance and Fight Captain, Peter Gregus; Music Technical Design, Deborah Hurwitz; Associate General Manager, Jennifer F. Vaughan; Marketing, Dodger Marketing; Advertising, Serino-Coyne; Press, Boneau/Bryan-Brown, Susanne Tighe, Heath Schwartz; Cast recording: Rhino R2 73271

CAST French Rap Star/Detective #1/Hal Miller/Barry Belson/Police Officer/Davis **Kris Coleman**; Stanley/Hank Majewski/Crewe's PA/Joe Long **Matthew Scott**[1]; Bob Crewe/others **Peter Gregus**; Tommy DeVito **Dominic Nolfi**; Nick DeVito/Stosh/Billy Dixon/Norman Waxman/Charlie Calello/others **Miles Aubrey**; Joey/Recording Studio Engineer/others **Russell Fischer**; Gyp De Carlo/others **Mark Lotito**; Mary Delgado/Angel/others **Bridget Berger**; Church Lady/Miss Frankie Nolan/Bob's Party Girl/Angel/Lorraine/others **Heather Ferguson**; Bob Gaudio **Andrew Rannells**[2]; Frankie's Mother/Nick's Date/Angel/Francine/others **Sara Schmidt**; Nick Massi **Matt Bogart**; Frankie Valli **Jarrod Spector** (evenings)/ **Cory Grant** (matinees); Thugs **Ken Dow, Joe Payne**; Swings **Michelle Aravena, Douglas Crawford** (temporary 10/8–10/29), **John Hickman, Katie O'Toole, Jake Speck, Taylor Sternberg**

UNDERSTUDIES Erik Bates (DeVito, Crewe), Russell Fischer (Valli), Miles Aubrey (Massi, Gyp), John Hickman (Gaudio, Massi, Gyp, Crewe), Taylor Sternberg, (Valli), Jake Speck (Gaudio, Massi, DeVito), Douglas Crawford (Gaudio, Massi, DeVito)

*Succeeded by: 1. Erik Bates (7/27/09) 2. Sebastian Arcelus (7/14/09), Drew Gehling (11/20/09), Sebastian Arcelus (1/11/10)

MUSICIANS Adam Ben-David (Conductor/keyboards); Deborah Hurwitz (Associate Conductor/keyboards); Stephen "Hoops" Snyder (keyboards); Joe Payne (guitars); Ken Dow (bass); Kevin Dow (drums); Matt Hong, Ben Kono (reeds); David Spier (trumpet)

MUSICAL NUMBERS Ces Soirées-La (Oh What a Night), Silhouettes, You're the Apple of My Eye, I Can't Give You Anything But Love, Earth Angel, Sunday Kind of Love, My Mother's Eyes, I Go Ape, (Who Wears) Short Shorts, I'm in the Mood for Love/Moody's Mood for Love, Cry for Me, An Angel Cried, I Still Care, Trance, Sherry, Big Girls Don't Cry, Walk Like a Man, December, 1963 (Oh What a Night), My Boyfriend's Back, My Eyes Adored You, Dawn (Go Away), Walk Like a Man (reprise), Big Man in Town, Beggin', Stay, Let's Hang On (To What We've Got), Opus 17 (Don't You Worry 'Bout Me), Bye Bye Baby, C'mon Marianne, Can't Take My Eyes Off of You, Working My Way Back to You, Fallen Angel, Rag Doll, Who Loves You

SETTING New Jersey, New York, and across the U.S., 1950s–now. A new musical presented in two acts. For original production credits see *Theatre World* Vol. 62, page 34. World Premiere produced by La Jolla Playhouse, October 5, 2004.

SYNOPSIS "How did four blue-collar kids become one of the greatest successes in pop music history? You ask four guys, you get four different answers." *Jersey Boys* is the story of the legendary Four Seasons, blue-collar boys who formed a singing group and reached the heights of rock 'n' roll stardom.

Jarrod Spector (photos by Joan Marcus)

Matt Bogart, Jarrod Spector, Sebastian Arcelus, and Dominic Nolfi

Joe Turner's Come and Gone

Belasco Theatre; First Preview: March 19, 2009 Opening Night: April 16, 2009; Closed June 14, 2009; 31 previews, 69 performances

Written by August Wilson; Produced by Lincoln Center Theater (André Bishop, Artistic Director; Bernard Gersten, Executive Producer); Director, Bartlett Sher; Sets, Michael Yeargan; Costumes, Catherine Zuber; Lighting, Brian MacDevitt; Sound, Scott Lehrer & Leon Rothenberg; Music, Taj Mahal; Stage Manager, Narda E. Alcorn; Casting, Daniel Swee; General Manager, Adam Siegel; Production Manager, Jeff Hamlin; Director of Development, Hattie K. Jutagir; Director of Marketing, Linda Mason Ross; Director of Finance, David S. Brown; Director of Education, Kati Koerner; Artistic Directors of Lincoln Center, Graciela Daniele, Nicholas Hytner, Jack O'Brien, Susan Stroman, Daniel Sullivan; Dramaturg/LCT Directors Lab, Anne Cattaneo; Musical Theatre Associate Producer, Ira Weitzman; Director of LCT3, Paige Evans; Associate General Manager, Jessica Niebanck; Associate Production Manager, Paul Smithyman; Company Manager, Matthew Markoff; Assistant Stage Manager, Michael P. Zaleski; Hair & Makeup, Jon Carter; Specialty Makeup, Lou Zakarian; Vocal Coach, Deborah Hecht; Movement, Dianne McIntyre; Movement Assistant, Shireen Dickson; Props, Susan Barras; Associate Design: Mikiko Suzuki McAdams (set), Jennifer Schriever (lighting), David Thomas (sound); Assistant Design: Nicole Moody & David Newell (costumes), Rebecca Eichorn (lighting), Zach Blane (assistant to lighting designer), Ashley Hanson (sound); Production: John Weingart (production carpenter), Graeme McDonnell (production electrician), Mark Dignam (production propertyman), Wayne Smith (production soundman), Moira MacGregor-Conrad (wardrobe supervisor), Yolanda Ramsey (hair supervisor), Tina Marie Clifton, Kevin Andre Dickens (dressers); Assistant to Mr. Sher, Sarna Lapine; Production Assistant, Rosy Garner; Costume Shopper, Lindsey Jones; Guardian, Brooke Engen; Tutoring, On Location Education; Animal Training, William Berloni; Animal Handler, Monica Schaffer; Poster Art, James McMullan; Advertising, Serino Coyne Inc.; Press, Philip Rinaldi, Barbara Carroll

CAST Seth Holly, *owner of the boarding house* **Ernie Hudson**; Bertha Holly, *his wife* **LaTanya Richardson Jackson**; Bynum Walker, *a rootworker* **Roger Robinson**; Rutherford Selig, *a peddler* **Arliss Howard**; Jeremy Furlow, *a resident* **Andre Holland**; Herald Loomis, *a resident* **Chad L. Coleman**; Zonia Loomis, *his daughter* **Amari Rose Leigh**; Mattie Campbell, *a resident* **Marsha Stephanie Blake**; Reuben Scott, *a boy who lives next door* **Michael Cummings**; Molly Cunningham, *a resident* **Aunjanue Ellis**; Martha Pentecost **Danai Gurira**

UNDERSTUDIES Michael Rogers (Seth Holly, Bynum Walker), Brenda Thomas Denmark (Bertha Holly), Christopher McHale (Rutherford Selig), Nyambi Nyambi (Herald Loomis, Jeremy Furlow), Olivia Ford (Zonia Loomis), Afton C. Williamson (Mattie Campbell, Molly Cunningham, Martha Pentecost), Elon Van Buckley (Reuben Scott)

SETTING Time: August 1911. Place: A boardinghouse in Pittsburgh. Revival of a play presented in nine scenes in two acts. World premiere at the Eugene O'Neill Theater Center (Waterford, Connecticut) in 1984. The original Broadway production played the Barrymore Theatre March 27–June 26, 1988, playing 105 performances (see *Theatre World* Vol. 44, page 29).

SYNOPSIS The second play of August Wilson's ten-play Century Cycle, *Joe Turner's Come and Gone* tells the story of Herald Loomis who, after serving seven years hard labor, has journeyed North with his young daughter and arrives at a Pittsburgh boarding house filled with memorable characters who aid him in his search for his inner freedom. The play also examines the conflicts that faced many African-Americans as they struggled to find jobs and security in the years following the emancipation, as many of them migrated North.

Amari Rose Leigh, Chad L. Coleman, and Danai Gurira

Ernie Hudson, Aunjanue Ellis, and Andre Holland

Roger Robinson and Marsha Stephanie Blake
(photos by T. Charles Erickson)

The Lion King

Minskoff Theatre; First Preview: October 15, 1997; Opening Night: November 13, 1997; 33 previews, 5,205 performances as of May 31, 2010

Music by Elton John, lyrics by Tim Rice, additional music and lyrics by Lebo M, Mark Mancina, Jay Rifkin, Julie Taymor, Hans Zimmer; book by Roger Allers and Irene Mecchi, adapted from screenplay by Ms. Mecchi, Jonathan Roberts and Linda Woolverton; Produced by Walt Disney Theatrical Productions (Peter Schneider, President; Thomas Schumacher, Executive VP); Director, Julie Taymor; Choreography, Garth Fagan; Orchestrations, Robert Elhai, David Metzger, Bruce Fowler; Music Director/Conductor, Karl Jurman; Original Music Director, Joseph Church; Sets, Richard Hudson; Costumes/Masks/Puppets, Julie Taymor; Lighting, Donald Holder; Masks/Puppets, Michael Curry; Sound, Tony Meola/Steve Canyon Kennedy; Hair/Makeup, Michael Ward; Projections, Geoff Puckett; Technical Director, David Benken; Casting, Jay Binder; General Manager, Alan Levey; Company Manager, Thomas Schlenk; Assistant Company Manager, Fred Hemminger; Associate Producer, Anne Quart; Project Manager, Nina Essman; Production Stage Manager, Ron Vodicka; Stage Manager, Carmen I Abrazado; Antonia Gianino, Narda Alcorn, Tom Reynolds; Associate Director, Jeff Lee; Resident Director, Darren Katz; Resident Dance Supervisor, Ruthlyn Salomons; Associate Design: Peter Eastman (set), Mary Nemecek Peterson (costumes), Louis Troisi (mask & puppets), John Shivers (sound), Carole Hancock (hair & wigs), Jeanne Koenig (lighting); Assistant Design: Marty Vreeland (lighting), Shane Cook (sound); Executive Music Producer, Chris Montan; Vocal Arrangements, Lebo M; Dance Captains, Garland Days, Willa Noel-Montague; Fight Captain, Ray Mercer; Assistant Choreographers, Norwood J. Pennewell, Natalie Rogers; South African Dialect Coach, Ron Kunene; For *The Lion King* Worldwide: Doc Zorthian (Production Supervisor), Myriah Perkins (Production Manager), John Stefaniuk (Associate Director), Marey Griffith (Associate Choreographer), Clement Ishmael (Music Supervisor), Celise Hicks (Dance Supervisor), Jay Alger (Associate Music Supervisor), Aland Henderson (Automated Lighting), Tara Engler (Production Coordinator), Elizabeth Fine (Management Assistant); Advertising, Serino Coyne Inc.; Interactive Marketing, Situation Marketing, Damian Bazadonna, Lisa Cecchini, Miriam Gardin; Press, Disney Theatricals, Dennis Crowley, Adriana Douzos, Lindsay Braverman; Cast recording: Walt Disney 60802-7

A scene from The Lion King

Jeff Binder (photos by Joan Marcus)

CAST Rafiki **Tshidi Manye**; Mufasa **Nathaniel Stampley**; Sarabi **Jean Michelle Grier**; Zazu **Jeff Binder**[1]; Scar **Derek Smith**; Young Simba **Clifford Lee Dickson**[2] or **Jeremy Gumbs**[3]; Young Nala **Chantylla Johnson**[4] or **Cypress Eden Smith**[5]; Shenzi **Bonita J. Hamilton**; Banzai **James Brown-Orleans**; Ed **Enrique Segura**; Timon **Danny Rutigliano**[6]; Pumbaa **Tom Alan Robbins**; Simba **Dashaun Young**; Nala **Ta'Rea Campbell**; Ensemble[7] Singers: **Alvin Crawford, Charity De Loera, Lindiwe Dlamini, Bongi Duma, Christopher Freeman, Jean Michelle Grier, Joel Karie, Ron Kunene, S'bu Ngema, Selloane Albertina Nkhela, LaQuet Sharnell, Mpume Sikakane, L. Steven Taylor, Rema Webb, Kenny Redell Williams**; Dancers: **Sant'gria Bello, Camille M. Brown, Michelle Brugal, Gabriel Croom, Nicole Adell Johnson, Lisa Lewis, Sheryl McCallum, Ray Mercer, Brandon Christopher O'Neal, Ryan Brooke Taylor, Phillip W. Turner**; Swings[8] **Sean Bradford, Garland Days, Angelica Edwards, Kenny Ingram, Tony James, Dennis Johnston, Sophia N. Stephens, Willa-Noel Montague, Natalie Turner**; Standbys **Jim Ferris**[9] (Timon, Pumbaa, Zazu), **Thom Christopher Warren** (Scar, Pumbaa, Zazu)

*Succeeded by: 1. Cameron Pow 2. Marquis Kofi Rodriguez (9/29/09), Joshua J. Jackson (4/14/10) 3. Alphonso Romero Jones II (10/1/09) 4. Shereen Pimentel (9/29/09) 5. Shannon Skye Tavarez (9/30/09), Khail Toi Bryant (4/14/10) 6. Robert Creighton 7. Brenda Mhlongo, Jacqueline René, Camille Workman 8. Lisa Nicole Wilkerson, Brian M. Love, James A. Pierce III, Kellen Stancil 9. John E. Brady

MUSICAL NUMBERS Circle of Life, Morning Report, I Just Can't Wait to Be King, Chow Down, They Live in You, Be Prepared, Hakuna Matata, One by One, Madness of King Scar, Shadowland, Endless Night, Can You Feel the Love Tonight, King of Pride Rock/Finale

A musical presented in two acts. For original production credits see *Theatre World* Vol. 54, page 20. Originally opened at the New Amsterdam Theatre and transferred to the Minskoff Theatre June 13, 2006.

SYNOPSIS Based on the 1994 Disney animated feature film, *The Lion King* tells the story of the adventures of Simba, a young lion cub, as he struggles to accept the responsibilities of adulthood and his destined role as king.

The Little Mermaid

Lunt-Fontanne Theatre; First Preview: November 3, 2007; Opening Night: January 10, 2008; Closed August 30, 2009; 50 previews, 685 performances

Music by Alan Menken, lyrics by Howard Ashman and Glenn Slater, book by Doug Wright; based on the Hans Christian Anderson story and the Disney film produced by Howard Ashman & John Musker and written and directed by John Musker & Ron Clements; Produced by Walt Disney Theatrical Productions (Peter Schneider, President; Thomas Schumacher, Executive VP); Director, Francesca Zambello; Choreography, Stephen Mear; Music Director/Incidental Music/Vocal Arrangements, Michael Kosarin; Orchestrations, Danny Troob; Sets, George Tsypin; Costumes, Tatiana Noginova; Lighting, Natasha Katz; Sound, John Shivers; Hair, David Brian Brown; Makeup, Angelina Avallone; Projections/Video, Sven Ortel; Dance Arrangements, David Chase; Music Coordinator, Michael Keller; Fight Director, Rick Sordelet; Casting, Tara Rubin; Associate Producer, Todd Lacy; Associate Director, Brian Hill; Associate Choreographer, Tara Young; Technical Director, David Benken; Production Stage Manager/Supervisor, Clifford Schwartz; Aerial Design, Pichón Baldinu; Dialogue/Vocal Coach, Deborah Hecht; Company Manager, Randy Meyer/Eduardo Castro; Asst. Company Manager, Margie Freeswick; Production Manager, Jane Abramson; Stage Manager, Theresa Bailey; ASMs, Robert M. Armitage, Matthew Aaron Stern, Alexis Shorter; Dance Captain, Jason Snow; Fight Captain/Assistant Dance Captain, James Brown III; Associate Design: Peter Eastman (set), Tracy Christensen (costumes), Yael Lubetzky (lighting), David Patridge (sound), Jonathan Carter (hair), Peter Acken, Katy Tucker (projection), Angela Phillips (aerial); Magic/Illusion Design, Joe Eddie Fairchild; Sculptor, Arturs Virtmanis; Automated Lights, Aland Henderson, Joel Shier; Assistant Set Design, Gaetane Bertol, Larry Brown, Kelly Hanso, Niki Hernandez-Adams, Nathan Heverin, Rachel Short Janocko, Jee an Jung, Mimi Lien, Frank McCullough, Arnulfo Maldonado, Robert Pyzocha, Chisato Uno; Assistant Costumes, Brian J. Bustos, Amy Clark; Assistant Lighting, Craig Stelzenmuller, Richard Swan; Assistant Hair, Thomas Augustine; Additional Orchestrations, Larry Hochman, Michael Starobin; Electronic Music Design, Andrew Barrett; Music Preparation, Anixter Rice Music Service; Associate to Mr. Menken, Rick Kunis; Advertising, Serino Coyne; Press, Disney Theatricals; Cast recording: Walt Disney Records D000108102

CAST Pilot **Merwin Foard**; Prince Eric **Sean Palmer**[*1]; Grimsby **Jonathan Freeman**; King Triton **Norm Lewis**; Sebastian **Rogerio Douglas Jr.**; Ariel **Chelsea Morgan Stock**; Flounder **Trevor Braun**[*2] or **Brian D'Addario**; Scuttle **Eddie Korbich**; Gulls **Joe Abraham, Enrique Brown, Tyrone A. Jackson**; Ursula **Faith Prince**; Flotsam **Tyler Maynard**; Jetsam **Eric LaJuan Summers**; Carlotta **Meredith Inglesby**; Chef Louis **Robert Creighton**; Ensemble **Joe Abraham, Cathryn Basile, Megan Campanile, Robert Creighton, Cicily Daniels, Enrique Brown, Merwin Foard, Amy Hall, Ben Hartley, Meredith Inglesby, Tyrone A. Jackson, Michelle Lookadoo, J.C. Montgomery, Alan Mingo Jr., Zakiya Young Mizen, Bret Shuford, Ephraim M. Sykes, Kay Trinidad**; Swings **James Brown III, Joanne Manning, Betsy Morgan, Jason Snow, Price Waldman/,Julie Barnes, J. Austin Eyer, Lyndy Franklin, Courtney Laine Mazza, Michelle Pruiett**

UNDERSTUDIES J.C. Montgomery (King Triton, Grimsby), Meredith Inglesby (Ursula), Robert Creighton (Scuttle), Cicily Daniels (Ursula), Enrique Brown (Jetsam, Scuttle), Merwin Foard (Grimsby, King Triton), Alan Mingo Jr. (Sebastian), J. Austin Eyer (Prince Eric), Bret Shuford (Flotsam, Prince Eric), J.J. Singleton/Cody Hanford (Flounder), Jason Snow (Flotsam, Scuttle), Betsy Morgan, Michelle Pruiett, and Michelle Lookadoo (Ariel), Price Waldman (Flotsam, Grimsby, Jetsam)

*Succeeded by: 1. Drew Seeley (6/9/09) 2. Major Curda (6/30/09)

ORCHESTRA Michael Kosarin (Conductor); Greg Anthony (Associate Conductor/keyboard 2); Suzanne Ornstein (Concert Master); Mineko Yajima (violin); Roger Shell, Deborah Assael (celli); Nicholas Marchione, Frank Greene (trumpets); Gary Grimaldi (trombone); Jeff Caswell (bass trombone/tuba); Steven Kenyon, David Young, Marc Phaneuf (reeds); Zohar Schondorf (French horn); Aron Accurso (keyboard 1); Andrew Grobengieser (keyboard 3); Richard Sarpola (bass); John Redsecker (drums); Joe Passaro (percussion)

MUSICAL NUMBERS Overture, Fathoms Below, Daughters of Triton, The World Above, Human Stuff, I Want the Good Times Back, Part of Your World, Storm at Sea, Part of Your World (reprise), She's in Love, Her Voice, The World Above (reprise), Under the Sea, Sweet Child, Poor Unfortunate Souls, Entr'acte, Positoovity, Beyond My Wildest Dreams, Les Poissons, Les Poissons (reprise), One Step Closer, I Want the Good Times Back (reprise), Kiss the Girl, Sweet Child (reprise), If Only, The Contest, Poor Unfortunate Souls (reprise), If Only (reprise), Finale

World premiere of a new musical presented in two acts. The show had an out-of-town tryout in Denver, Colorado at the Denver Center, July 26, 2007.

SYNOPSIS Based on the 1989 Disney film and the Hans Christian Anderson fairy tale, *The Little Mermaid* is set in a magical kingdom beneath the sea, where a beautiful young mermaid named Ariel longs to leave her ocean home to live in the world above. But first, she'll have to defy her father, the king of the sea, escape the clutches of an evil sea witch and convince a prince that she's the girl with the perfect voice.

Chelsea Morgan Stock (photos by Joan Marcus)

Chelsea Morgan Stock and Drew Seeley

Mamma Mia!

Winter Garden Theatre; First Preview: October 5, 2001: Opening Night: October 18, 2001; 14 previews, 3,568 performances as of May 31, 2010

Book by Catherine Johnson, music, lyrics, and orchestrations by Benny Andersson, Björn Ulvaeus, some songs with Stig Anderson; Produced by Judy Craymer, Richard East and Björn Ulvaeus for Littlestar Services Limited, in association with Universal; Director, Phyllida Lloyd; Sets and Costumes, Mark Thompson; Lighting, Howard Harrison; Sound, Andrew Bruce & Bobby Aitken; Wigs, Paul Huntley; Choreography, Anthony Van Laast; Musical Supervision/Orchestrations, Martin Koch; Associate Musical Director, David Holcenberg; Musical Coordination, Michael Keller; Associate Director, Robert McQueen; Associate Choreographer, Nichola Treherne; Technical Supervisor, Arthur Siccardi; General Manager, Nina Lannan; Associate General Manager/Company Manager, Rina L. Saltzman; Production Stage Manager, Andrew Fenton; Stage Managers, Sherry Cohen, Dean R. Greer; Dance Captain, Janet Rothermel; Resident Director, Martha Banta; Casting, Tara Rubin; Music Coordinator, Michael Keller; Synthesizer Programmer, Nicholas Gilpin; Press, Boneau/Bryan-Brown; London Cast recording: Polydor 543 115 2

Carolee Carmello (photos by Joan Marcus)

Judy McLane, Carolee Carmello, Gina Ferrall

CAST Sophie Sheridan **Brandi Burkhardt**[*1]; Ali **Amina Robinson**[*2]; Lisa **Samantha Eggers**[*3]; Tanya **Judy McLane**; Rosie **Gina Ferrall**[*4]; Donna Sheridan **Carolee Carmello**[*5]; Sky **Chris Peluso**[*6]; Pepper **Ben Gettinger**[*7]; Eddie **Raymond J. Lee**[*8]; Harry Bright **Ben Livingston**[*9]; Bill Austin **Pearce Bunting**[*10]; Sam Carmichael **Sean Allan Krill**[*11]; Father Alexandrios **Bryan Scott Johnson**; Ensemble[*12] **Meredith Akins, Brent Black, Timothy Booth, Allyson Carr, Mark Dancewicz, Meghann Dreyfuss, Lori Haley Fox, Heidi Godt, Corey Greenan, Bryan Scott Johnson, Monica Kapoor, Corinne Melançon, Ian Paget, Courtney Reed, Gerard Salvador, Sharone Sayegh, Britt Shubow, Traci Victoria, Laurie Wells**; Swings[*13] **Lanene Charters, Matthew Farver, Tony Gonzales, Robin Levine, Joi Danielle Price, Janet Rothermel, Ryan Sander, Collette Simmons**

UNDERSTUDIES Brent Black (Bill, Sam, Father Alexandrios), Timothy Booth (Harry, Bill, Sam), Isaac Calpito (Pepper), Lanene Charters (Lisa), Meghann Dreyfuss (Sophie), Samantha Eggers (Sophie), Matthew Farver (Eddie, Father Alexandrios), Lori Haley Fox (Tanya, Rosie, Donna), Heidi Godt (Donna, Tanya, Rosie), Corey Greenan (Sky), Bryan Scott Johnson (Harry, Bill), Monica Kapoor (Lisa), Corinne Melançon (Donna, Tanya), Courtney Reed (Ali), Ryan Sander (Sky, Eddie), Gerard Salvador (Pepper), Leah Zepel (Ali)

*Succeeded by: 1. Alyse Alan Louis (9/22/09) 2. Traci Victoria 3. Halle Morris (9/22/09) 4. Alison Briner (9/22/09), Gina Ferrall 5. Beth Leavel (9/22/09) 6. Corey Greenan 7. Michael Mindlin (9/22/09) 8. Mark Dancewicz 9. David Andrew Macdonald (9/22/09) 10. Patrick Boll (9/22/09) 11. John Dossett (9/22/09) 12. Felicity Claire, Stacia Fernandez, Natalie Gallo, Eric Giancola, Adam Hart, Monette McKay 13. Rachel Frankenthal, Jon-Erik Goldberg

ORCHESTRA Wendy Bobbitt Cavett (Conductor/keyboard); Rob Preuss (Associate Conductor/keyboard 3); Steve Marzullo (keyboard 2); Myles Chase (keyboard 4); Doug Quinn, Jeff Campbell (guitars); Paul Adamy (bass); Gary Tillman (drums); David Nyberg (percussion)

MUSICAL NUMBERS Chiquitita; Dancing Queen; Does Your Mother Know?; Gimme! Gimmie! Gimmie!; Honey, Honey; I Do, I Do, I Do, I Do; I Have a Dream; Knowing Me Knowing You; Lay All Your Love on Me; Mamma Mia; Money Money Money; One of Us; Our Last Summer; Slipping Through My Fingers; S.O.S.; Super Trouper; Take a Chance on Me; Thank You For the Music; The Name of the Game; The Winner Takes All; Under Attack; Voulez-Vous

SETTING Time: A wedding weekend. Place: A tiny Greek island. A musical presented in two acts. For original production credits see *Theatre World* Vol. 58, Page 27.

SYNOPSIS *Mamma Mia!* collects a group of hit songs by the Swedish pop group ABBA and shapes them around the story of a single mother coping with her young daughter's marriage on a picturesque Greek isle. While the daughter plans her future with the love of her life, her mother is haunted by three different men who may or may not be her daughter's father.

Mary Poppins

New Amsterdam Theatre; First Preview: October 14, 2006; Opening Night: November 16, 2006; 30 previews, 1,447 performances as of May 31, 2010

Music and lyrics by Richard M. Sherman and Robert B. Sherman, book by Julian Fellowes, new songs and additional music/lyrics by George Stiles and Anthony Drewe; based on the stories of P.L. Travers and the 1964 Walt Disney Film; Produced and co-created by Cameron Mackintosh; Produced for Disney Theatrical Productions by Thomas Schumacher; Associate Producers, Todd Lacy, James Thane; Director, Richard Eyre; Co-Direction/Choreography, Matthew Bourne; Sets/Costumes, Bob Crowley; Lighting, Howard Harrison; Co-choreographer, Stephen Mear; Music Supervisor, David Caddick; Music Director, Brad Haak; Orchestrations, William David Brohn; Sound, Steve Canyon Kennedy; Dance/Vocal Arrangements, George Stiles; Associate Director, Anthony Lyn; Associate Choreographer, Geoffrey Garratt;; Makeup, Naomi Donne; Casting, Tara Rubin; Technical Director, David Benken; Production Stage Manager, Mark Dobrow; Resident Choreographer, Tom Kosis; Company Manager, Dave Ehle; Assistant Company Manager, Laura Eichholz; Associate GM, Alan Wasser; Stage Manager, Jason Trubitt; Assistant Stage Managers, Valerie Lau-Kee Lai, Michael Wilhoite, Terence Orleans Alexander; Dance Captain, Brian Collier, Suzanne Hylenski, Dialect/Vocal Coach, Deborah Hecht; Wigs, Angela Cobbin; Illusions, Jim Steinmeyer; Technical Director, David Benken; Production Supervisor, Patrick Eviston; Production Manager, Jane Abramson; Flying, Raymond King; Automation, Steve Stackle, David Helk; Properties, Victor Amerling, Tim Abel, Joe Bivone, John Saye; Keyboard Programming, Stuart Andrews; Music Contractor, David Lai; Advertising, Serino-Coyne; Music Copyist, Emily Grisham Music Preparation; Press, Disney Theatricals, Dennis Crowley, Adriana Douzos, Lindsay Braverman; London Cast recording: Disney Theatricals 61391-7

CAST Bert **Adam Fiorentino**[*1]; George Banks **Daniel Jenkins**[*2]; Winifred Banks **Rebecca Luker**[*3]; Jane Banks[*4] **Kelsey Fowler** or **Alison Jaye Horowitz**[*4] or **Cassady Leonard**; Michael Banks **Neil McCaffrey** or **Zach Rand** or **Marlon Sherman**[*5]; Katie Nanna/Annie **Kristine Carbone**; Policeman **Corey Skaggs**; Miss Lark **Jessica Sheridan**; Admiral Boom/Bank Chairman **Jeff Steitzer**[*6]; Mrs. Brill **Jane Carr**[*7]; Robertson Ay **Mark Price**; Mary Poppins **Scarlett Strallen**[*8]; Park Keeper/Mr. Punch **James Hindman**; Neleus **Nick Kepley**; Queen Victoria/Miss Smythe/Miss Andrew **Ruth Gottschall**; Von Hussler/Jack-In-A-Box **Sean McCourt**; Northbrook **Sam Strasfeld**; Bird Woman **Ann Arvia**; Mrs. Corry **Janelle Anne Robinson**; Fannie **Amber Owens**; Annie **Catherine Brunell**; Valentine **Dennis Moench**[*9]; William **T. Oliver Reid**; Glamorous Doll **Catherine Walker**[*10]; Ensemble[*11] **Aaron J. Albano, David Baum, Catherine Brunell, Kristin Carbone, Barrett Davis, James Hindman, Nick Kepley, Melissa Lone, Sean McCourt, Jeff Metzler, Dennis Moench, Kathleen Nanni, Amber Owens, T. Oliver Reid, Janelle Anne Robinson, Laura Schutter, Chad Seib, Jessica Sheridan, Corey Skaggs, Sam Strasfeld, Catherine Walker**; Swings **Pam Bradley, Kathy Calahan, Brian Collier, Suzanne Hylenski, Rommy Sandhu, Jonathan Richard Sandler**[*12]

*Succeeded by: 1. Christian Borle (10/12/09) 2. Jeff Binder (10/12/09), Karl Kenzler (3/1/10) 3. Megan Osterhaus (3/1/10) 4. Juliette Allen Angelo 5. Jeremiah Kissane or Matthew Schechter or Andrew Shipman 6. Michael McCarty (10/12/09), Jonathan Freeman (12/12/09) 7. Jenny Galloway (10/12/09), Valerie Boyle (12/4/09) 8. Laura Michelle Kelly (10/12/09) 9. Aaron J. Albano 10. Elizabeth DeRosa 11. Replacement Ensemble: Brandon Bieber, Barrett Davis, Mark Ledbetter, Tony Mansker 12. James Tabeek

MUSICIANS Brad Haak (Conductor); Dale Rieling (Associate Conductor/2nd keyboard); Milton Granger (Assistant Conductor/piano); Peter Donovan (bass); Dave Ratajczak (drums), Daniel Haskins (percussion), Nate Brown (guitar/banjo/E-Bow), Russell Rizner, Lawrence DiBello (horns); John Sheppard, Jason Covey (trumpets); Marc Donatelle (trombone/euphonium); Randy Andos (bass trombone/tuba); Paul Garment (clarinet); Alexandra Knoll (oboe/English horn); Brian Miller (flutes); Stephanie Cummins (cello)

Laura Michelle Kelly and Christian Borle

Rebecca Luker and Daniel Jenkins (photos by Joan Marcus)

MUSICAL NUMBERS Chim Chim Cher-ee, Cherry Tree Lane (Part 1), The Perfect Nanny, Cherry Tree Lane (Part 2), Practically Perfect, Jolly Holiday, Cherry Tree Lane (reprise), Being Mrs. Banks, Jolly Holiday (reprise), A Spoonful of Sugar, Precision and Order, A Man Has Dreams, Feed the Birds, Supercalifragilisticexpialidocious, Temper, Temper, Chim, Chim, Cher-ee (reprise), Cherry Tree Lane (reprise), Brimstone and Treacle (Part 1), Let's Go Fly A Kite, Good For Nothing, Being Mrs. Banks (reprise), Brimstone and Treacle (Part 2), Practically Perfect (reprise), Chim Chim Cher-ee (reprise), Step in Time, A Man Has Dreams, A Spoonful of Sugar (reprise), Anything Can Happen, A Spoonful of Sugar (reprise), A Shooting Star

SETTING In and around the Banks' household somewhere in London at the turn of the last century. American premiere of a new musical presented in two acts. For original production credits, see *Theatre World* Vol. 63, page 41. Originally opened in London at the Prince Edward Theatre on December 15, 2004.

SYNOPSIS Based on the Walt Disney classic film and the novels by P.L. Travers, *Mary Poppins* is the story of the Banks family and how their lives change after the arrival of nanny Mary Poppins at their home at 17 Cherry Tree Lane in London.

Mary Stuart

Broadhurst Theatre; First Preview: March 30, 2009 Opening Night: April 19, 2009; Closed August 16, 2009; 22 previews, 137 performances

New version written by Peter Oswald, based on the original by Friedrich Schiller; Presented by the Donmar Warehouse (Michael Grandage, Artistic Director; James Bierman, Executive Director; Patrick Gracey, Acting General Manager); Produced by Arielle Tepper Madover, Debra Black, Neal Street Productions/ Matthew Byam Shaw, Scott M. Delman, Barbara Whitman, Jean Doumanian/ Ruth Hendel, David Binder/CarlWend Productions/Spring Sirkin, Daryl Roth/ James L. Nederlander/Chase Mishkin; Director, Phyllida Lloyd; Sets & Costumes, Anthony Ward; Lighting, Hugh Vanstone; Sound, Paul Arditti; Casting, Daniel Swee; U.K. Casting, Anne McNulty; Technical Supervisor, Aurora Productions; Production Stage Manager, Barclay Stiff; Marketing Director, Eric Schnall; General Management, 101 Productions Ltd. (Wendy Orshan, Jeffrey Wilson, David Auster, Ellie Landau); Company Manager, Sean Free; Hair, Campbell Young; Stage Manager, Brandon Kahn; Assistant Director, Seth Sklar-Heyn; Dialect Coach, Kate Wilson; Fight Director, Thomas Schall; Associate Design: Christine Peters (set), Daryl Stone (costumes), Philip Rosenberg & Jake DeGroot (lighting), Jeremy J. Lee (sound), Luc Verschueren (hair); U.K. Associate Costumes, Stephanie Arditti; Casting Associate, Camille Hickman; Aurora Productions: Gene O'Donovan, W. Benjamin Heller II, Bethany Weinstein, Amy Merlino Coey, Melissa Mazdra, Laura Archer, Dana Hesch; Production: Jon Lawson (production electrician), Mike Hill (moving lights programmer), William Lewis (production sound), Andrew Meeker (production props), Denise J. Grillo (prop shopper), Brian McGarty (house carpenter), Charlie DeVerna (house electrician), Brian Bullard (house flyman), Ron Vitelli (house properties), Kelly Saxon (wardrobe supervisor), Carmel Vargyas (hair supervisor), Mickey Abbate & Kristen Gardner (dressers); Production Assistant, Eileen Kelly; Assistant to Ms. Madover, Holly Ferguson; Advertising, SpotCo (Drew Hodges, Jim Edwards, Tom Greenwald, Y. Darius Suyama, Pete Duffy); Press, Boneau/Bryan-Brown, Adrian Bryan-Brown, Jim Byk, Rachel Strange

CAST Hanna Kennedy, *Mary's nurse* **Maria Tucci**; Sir Amias Paulet, *Mary's jailer* **Michael Countryman**; Mary Stuart, *Queen of Scotland* **Janet McTeer**; Mortimer, *Paulet's nephew* **Chandler Williams**; Lord Burleigh **Nicholas Woodeson**; Elizabeth, *Queen of England* **Harriet Walter**; Count Aubespine, *French Ambassador* **Michael Rudko**; Earl of Shrewsbury **Brian Murray**; Earl of Leicester **John Benjamin Hickey**; O'Kelly, *Mortimer's friend* **Adam Greer**; Sir William Davison **Robert Stanton**; Melvil, *Mary's house steward* **Michael Rudko**; Courtiers, Officers and others **Tony Carlin**, **Guy Paul**, **Adam Greer**

UNDERSTUDIES Tony Carlin (Aubespine, Melvil, Courtier, Officer, Earl of Leicester), Monique Fowler (Elizabeth, Hannah Kennedy), Adam Greer (Mortimer, Davison), Guy Paul (Lord Burleigh, Paulet), Michael Rudko (Earl of Shrewsbury), Jacqueline Antaramian (Mary, Hanna Kennedy)

SETTING Between Fotheringhay Castle and Elizabeth's Court at Westminster, 1587. Revival of a drama presented in two acts. This production was previously presented at the Donmar Warehouse (starring Ms. McTeer and Ms. Walter) July 14–September 3, 2005, and then transferred to the West End's Apollo Theatre October 7, 2005–January 14, 2006. The first major New York production opened at the Fifth Avenue Theatre on February 26, 1900. It was revived Off-Broadway at the Phoenix Theatre with Eve LeGallienne and Irene Worth, October 8–November 24, 1957 (see *Theatre World* Vol. 14, page 161). The Repertory Theatre of Lincoln Center revived the show at the Vivian Beaumont Theatre with Nancy Marchand and Salome Jens, October 30–December 18, 1971 (see *Theatre World* Vol. 28, page 70).

SYNOPSIS Seduction, greed and deception lie at the heart of the bitter rivalry between Mary, Queen of Scots, and her cousin, Elizabeth I of England. After being implicated in her husband's murder, Mary turns to Elizabeth for help but finds her cousin distrustful of her motives. Thus begins a bloody feud that will threaten not just their family bond, but the crown of England. *Mary Stuart*, in its first major revival in almost forty years, tells the story of two iconic women whose lust for power reveals one of the most thrilling displays of passion and politics the world has ever seen.

Chandler Williams, Nicholas Woodeson, Tony Carlin, John Benjamin Hickey, Harriet Walter, Robert Stanton, Adam Greer, Brian Murray, Guy Paul and Michael Countryman

Harriet Walter and Janet McTeer (photos by Joan Marcus)

Next to Normal

Booth Theatre; First Preview: March 27, 2009 Opening Night: April 15, 2009; 20 previews, 470 performances as of May 31, 2010

Music by Tom Kitt, book and lyrics by Brian Yorkey; Produced by David Stone, James L. Nederlander, Barbara Whitman, Patrick Catullo, Second Stage (Carole Rothman, Artistic Director; Ellen Richard, Executive Director); Director, Michael Greif; Musical Staging, Sergio Trujillo; Set, Mark Wendland; Costumes, Jeff Mahshie; Lighting, Kevin Adams; Sound, Brian Ronan; Orchestrations, Michael Starobin & Tom Kitt; Vocal Arrangements, AnnMarie Milazzo; Music Director, Charlie Alterman; Music Coordinator, Michael Keller; Casting, Telsey + Company; Production Stage Manager, Judith Schoenfeld; Company Manager, Marc Borsak; Technical Supervisor, Larry Morley; General Management, 321 Theatrical Management (Nina Essman, Nancy Nagel Gibbs, Marcia Goldberg); Stage Manager, Martha Donaldson; Assistant Stage Manager, Sally E. Sibson; Assistant Director, Laura Pietropinto; Associate Choreographer, Dontee Kiehn; Assistant Music Director, Mat Eisenstein; Associate Design: Joel E. Silver (lighting), David Stollings (sound); Assistant Design: Rachel Nemec (set), Paul Toben, Aaron Sporer (lighting), Jon Collin & Shoko Kambara (scenic design assistants); Associate Technical Supervisor, Bradley Thompson; Dance Captain, Jessica Phillips; Writers' Assistant, Brandon Ivie; Production: Bill Craven (production carpenter), Richard Mortell (production electrician), Mike Farfalla (production electrician), Kenneth McDonough (carpenter), Ed White (flyman), Susan Goulet (electrician), James Keane (props), Chris Sloan (sound engineer), Elizabeth Berkeley (assistant sound engineer), Kyle LaColla (wardrobe supervisor), Sara Jane Darneille & Vangeli Kaseluris (dressers); Music Preparation, Emily Grishman; Drum and Percussion Arrangements, Damien Bassman; Additional Guitar Arrangements, Michael Aarons; Assistants: Aaron Glick (to Mr. Stone), Tara Geesaman, Jeanette Norton (to general managers), Stuart Shefter (production); Advertising, Serino Coyne Inc.; Press, The Hartman Group, Michael Hartman, Tom D'Ambrosio, Michelle Bergmann; Cast recording: Sh-K-Boom/Ghostlight Records 4433

CAST Henry **Adam Chanler-Berat**; Natalie **Jennifer Damiano**; Dr. Madden/ Dr. Fine **Louis Hobson**; Diana **Alice Ripley**; Dan **J. Robert Spencer**[*1]; Gabe **Aaron Tveit**[*2]

UNDERSTUDIES Michael Berry (Dan, Dr. Madden/Dr. Fine), Meghann Fahy (Natalie), Jessica Phillips (Diana), Tim Young (Gabe, Henry)

*Succeeded by: 1. Brian d'Arcy James (5/17/10) 2. Kyle Dean Massey (6/9/09), Aaron Tveit (9/7/09), Kyle Dean Massey (1/4/10)

***NEXT TO NORMAL* BAND** Charlie Alterman (Conductor/piano), Yuiko Kamakari (piano/violin), Benjamin Kalb (cello), Eric Davis (guitars), Michael Blanco (bass), Damien Bassman (drums/percussion)

MUSICAL NUMBERS Prelude, Just Another Day, Everything Else, Who's Crazy/My Psychopharmacologist and I, Perfect for You, I Miss the Mountains, Its Gonna Be Good, He's Not Here, You Don't Know, I Am the One, Superboy and the Invisible Girl, I'm Alive, Make Up Your Mind/Catch Me I'm Falling, I Dreamed a Dance, There's a World, I've Been, Didn't I See This Movie?, A Light in the Dark, Wish I Were Here, Song of Forgetting, Hey #1, Seconds and Years, Better Than Before, Aftershocks, Hey #2, You Don't Know (reprise), How Could I Ever Forget?, It's Gonna Be Good (reprise), Why Stay?/A Promise, I'm Alive (reprise), The Break, Make Up Your Mind/Catch Me Im Falling (reprise), Maybe (Next to Normal), Hey #3/Perfect for You (reprise), So Anyway, I Am the One (reprise), Light

SETTING A suburban household; the present. A new musical presented in two acts. World premiere presented at Second Stage February 13–March 16, 2008 (see *Theatre World* Vol. 64, page 190) and subsequently presented at Arena Stage (Molly Smith, Artistic Director), November 21, 2008–January 18, 2009 with this cast (see *Theatre World* Vol. 65, page 308). Originally presented and workshopped (under the title *Feeling Electric*) at the New York Musical Theatre Festival, September 2005, and the Village Theatre (Issaquah Washington), June 21-23, 2005.

SYNOPSIS *Next to Normal* explores how one suburban household copes with its past and future. How does an almost average family navigate today's over-stimulated and over medicated world? This groundbreaking new musical takes a close look at contemporary mental illness and treatment as it shows how far two parents will go to keep themselves sane and their family's world intact.

Jennifer Damiano, Kyle Dean Massey, and Adam Chanler-Berat

The Company (photos by Joan Marcus)

Stephen Mangan (standing) with (clockwise) Ben Miles, Amanda Root, Jessica Hynes, Amelia Bullmore, and Paul Ritter in Table Manners *(photos by Joan Marcus)*

Stephen Mangan (on the floor) with Ben Miles and Paul Ritter in Living Together

The Norman Conquests
Table Manners · Living Together · Round and Round the Garden

Circle in the Square Theatre; First Preview: April 7, 2009 Opening Night: April 23, 2009; Closed July 26, 2009; 18 previews, 109 performances (*Table Manners*: 7 previews, 41 performances; *Living Together*: 5 previews, 28 performances; *Round and Round the Garden*: 6 previews, 40 performances)

Written by Alan Ayckbourn; Presented by The Old Vic Theatre (Kevin Spacey, Artistic Director; Sally Greene, Chief Executive; John Richardson and Kate Pakenham, Producers); Produced by Sonia Friedman Productions, Steven Baruch, Marc Routh, Richard Frankel, Tom Viertel, Dede Harris, Tulchin/Bartner/Lauren Doll, Jamie deRoy, Eric Falkenstein, Harriet Newman Leve, Probo Productions, Douglas G. Smith, Michael Filerman/Jennifer Manocherian, Richard Winkler, in association with Dan Frishwasser, Pam Laudenslager/Remmel T. Dickinson, Jane Dublin/True Love Productions, Barbara Manocherian/Jennifer Isaacson; Director, Matthew Warchus; Set & Costumes, Rob Howell; Lighting, David Howe; Music, Gary Yershon; Sound, Simon Baker; Original Casting, Gabrielle Dawes; Production Stage Manager, Ira Mont; U.S. General Management, Frankel Green Theatrical Management (Richard Frankel, Laura Green, Joe Watson, Leslie Ledbetter); U.K. General Management, Diane Benjamin; Production Manager, Aurora Productions (Gene O'Donovan, Ben Heller, Bethany Weinstein); Company Manager, Kathy Lowe; Associate Company Manager, Townsend Teague; New York Casting, Jim Carnahan; Stage Manager, Julia P. Jones; Associate Director, Annabel Bolton; Assistant Director, Mark Schneider; Video Design, Duncan McLean; Dialect Consultant, Elizabeth A. Smith; Associate Design: Paul Weimer (set), Daryl Stone (costumes), Vivien Leone (lighting), Christopher Cronin (sound); Production Assistant, Nathan K. Claus; Wardrobe Supervisor, Sue Stepnik; Dressers, Bobby Clifton, Jessica Worsnop; Management Assistant, Andrew Michaelson; Circle in the Square Staff: Theodore Mann and Paul Libin (Directors), Susan Frankel (General Manager), Cheryl Dennis (house manager), Anthony Menditto (head carpenter), Stewart Wagner (head electrician), Owen E. Parmele (prop master), Jim Bay (sound engineer); Advertising, SpotCo; Press, Boneau/Bryan-Brown, Adrian Bryan-Brown, Jim Byk, Aaron Meier, Rachel Strange

CAST Ruth **Amelia Bullmore**; Annie **Jessica Hynes**; Norman **Stephen Mangan**; Tom **Ben Miles**; Reg **Paul Ritter**; Sarah **Amanda Root**

UNDERSTUDIES Cassie Beck (Annie), Peter Bradbury (Norman), Angela Pierce (Ruth, Sarah), Tony Ward (Tom, Reg)

SETTING A Victorian house in England during a weekend in July; mid-1970s. *Table Manners*: the dining room (Act I Scene 1: Saturday, 6 p.m.; Act I Scene II: Sunday, 9 a.m.; Act II Scene I: Sunday, 8 p.m.; Act II Scene II: Monday, 8 a.m.); *Living Together:* the sitting room (Act I Scene 1: Saturday, 6:30 p.m.; Act I Scene II: Saturday, 8 p.m.; Act II Scene I: Sunday, 9 p.m.; Act II Scene II: Monday, 8 a.m.); *Round and Round the Garden:* the garden (Act I Scene 1: Saturday, 5:30 p.m.; Act I Scene II: Saturday, 9 p.m.; Act II Scene I: Sunday, 11 a.m.; Act II Scene II: Monday, 9 a.m.). Revival of three full-length plays presented in repertory, each play presented in four scenes in two acts. Prior to the Broadway engagement, the trilogy was produced by The Old Vic Theatre Company (London) September 11–December 20, 2008 (opened October 6) with this cast. The trilogy was first produced on Broadway at the Morosco Theatre December 5, 1975–June 19, 1976 (see *Theatre World* Vol. 32, page 28.)

SYNOPSIS *The Norman Conquests* comprises of three full-length plays—*Table Manners*, *Living Together*, and *Round and Round the Garden*. Each individual play offers a view of one comically catastrophic weekend, shared by six spouses and in-laws, at the family house in the country. And while each play is complete on its own terms, by viewing all three plays (in any order), the audience is able, detective-like, to piece together all of the hidden secrets and lies, the outrageous, hilarious and shocking interactions, which occurred over the weekend. Desperate lothario Norman, an assistant librarian, attempts to seduce his sister-in-law Annie, charm his brother-in-law's wife Sarah and woo his estranged wife Ruth, during a disastrously hilarious weekend of eating, drinking and misunderstanding.

The Phantom of the Opera

Majestic Theatre; First Preview: January 9, 1988. Opening Night: January 26, 1988; 16 previews, 9,292 performances as of May 31, 2010

Music and book by Andrew Lloyd Webber, lyrics by Charles Hart; additional lyrics and book by Richard Stilgoe; based on the novel by Gaston Leroux; Produced by Cameron Mackintosh and The Really Useful Theatre Company; Director, Harold Prince; Musical Staging/Choreography, Gillian Lynne; Orchestrations, David Cullen, Mr. Lloyd Webber; Design, Maria Björnson; Lighting, Andrew Bridge; Sound, Martin Levan; Original Musical Director and Supervisor, David Caddick; Musical Director, David Lai; Production Supervisor, Peter von Mayrhauser; Casting, Tara Rubin; Original Casting, Johnson-Liff Associates; General Manager, Alan Wasser; Production Dance Supervisor, Denny Berry; Associate Musical Supervisor, Kristen Blodgette; Associate General Manager, Allan Williams; Technical Production Managers, John H. Paull III, Jake Bell; Company Manager, Steve Greer; Stage Managers, Craig Jacobs, Bethe Ward, Brendan Smith; Assistant Company Manager, Cathy Kwon; Press, The Publicity Office, Marc Thibodeau, Michael S. Borowski, Jeremy Shaffer; London Cast recording: Polydor 831273

CAST The Phantom of the Opera **Howard McGillin**[1]; Christine Daaé **Jennifer Hope Wills**; Christine Daaé (alt.) **Elizabeth Loyacano**[2]; Raoul, Vicomte de Chagny **Ryan Silverman**; Carlotta Giudicelli **Patricia Phillips**; Monsieur André **George Lee Andrews**[3]; Monsieur Firmin **David Cryer**[4]; Madame Giry **Rebecca Judd**[5]; Ubaldo Piangi **Evan Harrington**[6]; Meg Giry **Heather McFadden**; Monsieur Reyer/Hairdresser **Geoff Packard**[7]; Auctioneer **John Kuether**; Jeweler (Il Muto) **Frank Mastrone**; Monsieur Lefevre/Firechief **Kenneth Kantor**; Joseph Buquet **Richard Poole**; Don Attilio **John Kuether**; Passarino **Jeremy Stolle**; Slave Master & Solo Dancer/Flunky/Stagehand (roles rotate weekly) **Anton Harrison LaMon**[8] or **Jack Hayes**[9]; Page **Satomi Hofmann**[10]; Porter/Fireman **Chris Bohannon**[11]; Spanish Lady **Kimilee Bryant**; Wardrobe Mistress/Confidante **Rayanne Gonzales**[12]; Princess **Susan Owen**[13]; Madame Firmin **Melody Rubie**[14]; Innkeeper's Wife **Cristin J. Hubbard**[15]; Marksman **Paul A. Schaefer**; Ballet Chorus of the Opera Populaire **Dara Adler, Gianna Loungway, Mabel Modrono, Jessica Radetsky, Carly Blake Sebouhian, Dianna Warren**[16]; Ballet Swing **Laurie V. Langdon**; Swings[17] **Scott Mikita, James Romick, Janet Saia, Jim Weitzer**

*Succeeded by: 1. John Cudia (7/27/09) 2. Marni Rabb (6/22/09), Susan Owen (1/18/10 during leave), Kimilee Bryant (2/4/10 during leave), Marni Raab (2/22/10) 3. Scott Mikita, Frank Mastrone, Richard Poole, James Romick, Ted Keegan (all during leave) 4. Bruce Winant (vacations only) 5. Cristin J. Hubbard (7/13/09) 6. Jimmy Smagula (vacations only) 7. Kyle Barisich, Jim Weitzer, Ted Keegan, Jim Weitzer 8. Mykal D. Laury II, James Zander, Mykal D. Laury II 9. James Zander, Jack Hayes, Justin Peck, Mykal D. Laury II, James Zander 10. Cristin J. Hubbard, Wren Marie Harrington, Julie Schmidt, Tonna Miller, Kris Koop 11. Stephen Tewskbury, Jimmy Smagula, Chris Bohannon 12. Kristie Dale Sanders, Michele McConnell 13. Julie Hanson 14. Sarah Anne Lewis, Kris Koop 15. Wren Marie Harrington, Mary Illes 16. (at various times) Emily Adonna, Polly Baird, Amanda Edge, Jessy Hendrickson, Kara Klein, Anna Laghezza, Janice Niggeling 17. (at various times) Kyle Barisich, Tonna Miller, Julie Schmidt, Stephen Tewksbury

ORCHESTRA David Caddick, Kristen Blodgette, David Lai, Tim Stella, Norman Weiss (Conductors); Joyce Hammann (Concert Master), Alvin E. Rogers, Gayle Dixon, Kurt Coble, Jan Mullen, Karen Milne (violins); Stephanie Fricker, Veronica Salas (violas); Ted Ackerman, Karl Bennion (cellos); Melissa Slocum (bass); Henry Fanelli (harp); Sheryl Henze, Ed Matthew, Melanie Feld, Matthew Goodman, Atsuko Sato (woodwinds); Lowell Hershey, Francis Bonny (trumpets); William Whitaker (trombone); Daniel Culpepper, Peter Reit, David Smith (French horn); Eric Cohen, Jan Hagiwara (percussion); Tim Stella, Norman Weiss (keyboards)

MUSICAL NUMBERS Think of Me, Angel of Music, Little Lotte/The Mirror, Phantom of the Opera, Music of the Night, I Remember/Stranger Than You Dreamt It, Magical Lasso, Notes/Prima Donna, Poor Fool He Makes Me Laugh, Why Have You Brought Me Here?/Raoul I've Been There, All I Ask of You, Masquerade/Why So Silent?, Twisted Every Way, Wishing You Were Somehow Here Again, Wandering Child/Bravo Bravo, Point of No Return, Down Once More/Track Down This Murderer, Finale

SETTING In and around the Paris Opera House, 1881–1911. A musical presented in two acts with nineteen scenes and a prologue. For original production credits see *Theatre World* Vol. 44, page 20. The show became the longest running show in Broadway history on January 9, 2006. Howard McGillin ended his record-breaking run on July 25, 2009 with a total of 2,544 performances, making him the World's Longest-Running "Phantom." On September 17, 2009, *Phantom* became the first show in Broadway history to reach and surpass 9,000 performances.

SYNOPSIS A disfigured musical genius haunts the catacombs beneath the Paris Opera and exerts strange control over a lovely young soprano.

John Cudia and Jennifer Hope Wills photos by Joan Marcus)

Ryan Silverman and Jennifer Hope Wills

Jennifer Mudge and Matthew Broderick

Jonathan Cake, Matthew Broderick and Steven Weber

Anna Madeley and Matthew Broderick (photos by Joan Marcus)

The Philanthropist

American Airlines Theatre; First Preview: April 10, 2009 Opening Night: April 26; 2009; Closed June 28, 2009; 19 previews, 73 performances

Written by Christopher Hampton; Produced by the Roundabout Theatre Company (Todd Haimes, Artistic Director; Harold Wolpert, Managing Director; Julia C. Levy, Executive Director); Director, David Grindley; Set, Tim Shortall; Costumes, Tobin Ost; Lighting, Rick Fisher; Sound, Gregory Clarke; Dialects, Gillian Lane-Plescia; Production Stage Manager, Arthur Gaffin; Casting, Carrie Gardner; Production Management, Aurora Productions (Gene O'Donovan, W. Benjamin Heller II, Bethany Weinstein, Amy Merlino Coey, Laura Archer, Dana Hesch, Melissa Mazdra); General Manager, Rebecca Habel; Marketing/Sales Promotion, David B. Steffen; Founding Director, Gene Feist; Associate Artistic Director, Scott Ellis; Director of Artistic Development and Casting, Jim Carnahan; Finance, Susan Neiman; Education, Greg McCaslin; General Manager, Sydney Beers; Telesales, Marco Frezza; Sales Operations, Charlie Garbowski Jr.; Company Manager, Carly DiFulvio; Stage Manager, Jamie Greathouse; Assistant Director, Lori Wolter; Hair & Wigs, Ashley Ryan; Makeup, James Vincent; Associate Design: Tobin Ost (set), Daniel Walker (lighting); Assistant Design: Sean Tribble (costumes), Emma Belli, William Fricker, Jason Southgate (assistants to Mr. Shortall); Production Properties, Denise J. Grillo; U.K. Properties, Kate McDowell; Assistant to Production Properties, Constance Sherman; Production: Glenn Merwede (production carpenter), Brian Maiuri (production electrician), Andrew Forste (running properties), Dann Wojnar (sound operator), Susan J. Fallon (wardrobe supervisor), Manuela Laporte (hair & wig supervisor), Brittany Jones-Pugh, Kat Martin (dressers), Lauren Gallitelli (day wardrobe), Shelley Miles (production assistant); Advertising, SpotCo; Press, Boneau/Bryan-Brown, Adrian Bryan-Brown, Matt Polk, Jessica Johnson, Amy Kass

CAST John **Tate Ellington**; Philip **Matthew Broderick**; Donald **Steven Weber**; Celia **Anna Madeley**; Braham **Jonathan Cake**; Araminta **Jennifer Mudge**; Elizabeth **Samantha Soule**

UNDERSTUDIES Janie Brookshire (Celia, Elizabeth, Araminta), Matthieu Cornillon (John, Braham), Quentin Maré (Don, Philip)

SETTING The rooms of an English university professor in October, 1970. Revival of a play presented in two acts. Originally presented on Broadway at the Barrymore Theatre March 11–May 15, 1971 (see *Theatre World* Vol. 27, page 39). The Donmar Warehouse (Michael Grandage, Artistic Director; James Bierman, Executive Producer) produced a production of the show in 2005, directed by Mr. Grindley, and featuring Ms. Madeley.

SYNOPSIS Written as a response to Moliére's classic play *The Misanthrope*, Christopher Hampton's biting bourgeois comedy *The Philanthropist* examines the empty, insular lives of university intellectuals. At the center of the story is Philip, a professor who seems almost absurdly removed from the political turmoil surrounding him, including the assassination of the Prime Minister and his cabinet.

reasons to be pretty

Lyceum Theatre; First Preview: March 13, 2009 Opening Night: April 2, 2009; Closed June 14, 2009; 21 previews, 85 performances

Written by Neil LaBute; Presented by Manhattan Class Company (MCC) Theater; Produced by Jeffrey Richards, Jerry Frankel, MCC Theater, Gary Goddard Entertainment, Ted Snowdon, Doug Nevin/Erica Lynn Schwartz, Ronald Frankel/Bat-Barry Productions, Kathleen Seidel, Kelpie Arts, Jam Theatricals and Rachel Helson/Heather Provost; Director, Terry Kinney; Set, David Gallo; Costumes, Sarah J. Holden; Lighting, David Weiner; Original Music and Sound, Rob Millburn & Michael Bodeen; Casting, Telsey + Company; Technical Supervisor, Hudson Theatrical Associates; Production Stage Manager, Christine Lemme; Fight Director, Manny Siverio; General Manager, Daniel Kuney, Christopher D'Angelo; Associate Technical Supervisor, B.D. White; Stage Manager, Matthew Farrell; Fight Captain, Michael D. Dempsey; Associate Design: Steven C. Kemp (set), Lauren Phillips (costumes), David Stollings (sound); Assistant Costume Design, Maggie Lee-Burdorff; Lighting Programmer, Marc Polimeni; Dramaturg, Stephen Williams; Vocal Coach, Deborah Hecht; Production: Adam Braunstein (head carpenter), Brian GF McGarity (electrician supervisor), Jonathan Cohen (head electrician), Jeremy Chernick (production props supervisor), Leah Nelson (head properties), Wallace Flores (sound supervisor), Sandy Binion (wardrobe supervisor), Susan Checklick (dresser), Alexis Qualis (production assistant); Advertising, SpotCo; Press, O+M Co., Rick Miramontez, Jon Dimond, Amanda Dekker

CAST Steph **Marin Ireland**; Kent **Steven Pasquale**; Carly **Piper Perabo**; Greg **Thomas Sadoski**

UNDERSTUDIES Ann Bowles (Carly, Steph), Michael D. Dempsey (Greg, Kent)

SETTING The outlying suburbs. Not long ago. Transfer of the Off-Broadway comic drama presented in two acts. World premiere produced by MCC Theater (Robert LuPone, Bernard Telsey, Artistic Directors; William Cantler, Associate Artistic Director; Blake West, Executive Director) at the Lucille Lortel Theatre May 14–July 5, 2008 (opened June 2; see *Theatre World* Vol. 64, page 173).

SYNOPSIS America's obsession with physical beauty is confronted headlong in this brutal and exhilarating new play. In *reasons to be pretty*, Greg's tight-knit social circle is thrown into turmoil when his offhanded remarks about a female coworker's pretty face (and his girlfriend's lack thereof) get back to said girlfriend. But that's just the beginning. Greg's best buddy Kent, and Kent's wife Carly also enter into the picture and the emotional equation becomes exponentially more complicated. As their relationships crumble, the four friends are forced to confront a sea of deceit, infidelity and betrayed trust in their journey to answer that oh-so-American question: How much is pretty worth?

Thomas Sadoski and Marin Ireland

Thomas Sadoski and Marin Ireland

Thomas Sadoski and Piper Perabo
(photos by Robert J. Saferstein)

Rock of Ages

Brooks Atkinson Theatre; First Preview: March 20, 2009 Opening Night: April 7, 2009; 22 previews, 480 performances as of May 31, 2010

Book by Chris D'Arienzo; Produced by Matthew Weaver, Carl Levin, Barry Habib, Scott Prisand, Corner Store Fund, in association with Janet Billig Rich, Hillary Weaver, Toni Habib, Paula Davis, Simon & Stefany Bergson/Jennifer Maloney, Charles Rolecek, Susanne Brook, Israel Wolfson, Sara Katz/Jayson Raitt, Max Gottlieb/John Butler, David Kaufman/Jay Franks, Michael Wittlin, Prospect Pictures, Laura Smith/Bill Bodnar; Director, Kristin Hanggi; Choreography, Kelly Devine; Music Supervision, Arrangements & Orchestrations, Ethan Popp; Music Director, Henry Aronson; Music Coordinator, John Miller; Original Arrangements, David Gibbs; Set, Beowulf Boritt; Costumes, Gregory Gale; Lighting, Jason Lyons; Sound, Peter Hylenski; Projections, Zak Borovay; Hair & Wigs, Tom Watson; Makeup, Angelina Avallone; Casting, Telsey + Company; Production Stage Manager, Claudia Lynch; Vocal Coach, Liz Caplan Vocal Studios; Associate Choreographer, Robert Tatad; Associate Director/Stage Manager, Adam John Hunter; Associate Producer, David Gibbs; General Management, Frankel Green Theatrical Management (Richard Frankel, Laura Green, Joe Watson, Leslie Ledbetter); Technical Supervisor, Peter Fulbright/Tech Production Services Inc. (Colleen Houlehen, Mary Duffe, Miranda Wigginton); Company Management, Tracy Geltman (Manager), Susan Keappock (Assistant); Associate General Manager, Aliza Wassner; Assistant Stage Managers, Marisha Ploski & Matthew Dicarlo; Associate Design, Jo Winiarski (set), Karl Ruckdeschel (costumes), Austin Switser (projections & programming); Assistant Design: Julia Broer & Colleen Kesterson (costumes), Driscoll Otto (lighting), Barbara Samuels (assistant to lighting designer), Keith Caggiano (sound), Daniel Brodie (projections); Creative Advisor, Wendy Goldberg; Production: Brian Munroe, Ray Harold, Mike LoBue, Brent Oakley, Phillip Lojo, Jesse Stevens, Mike Pilipski, Jacob White, Buist Bickly, Robert Guy, Joshua Speed Schwartz, Renee Borys, Michael Louis, Danny Mura, Arlene Watson, Susan Cook, Marisa Lerette; Production Assistant, Samantha Saltzman; Script Supervisor, Justin Mabardi; Synthesizer Programmer, Randy Cohen; Music Copying/Preparation, Firefly Music Service/Brian Hobbs; Rehearsal Pianist, Keith Cotton; Dance Captain, Bahiyah Sayyed Gaines; Advertising, Serino Coyne Inc.; Marketing, Leanne Schanzer Promotions & The Pekoe Group; Internet Marketing, Art Meets Commerce; Press, The Hartman Group; Cast recording: New Line Records

CAST Lonny/Record Company Man **Mitchell Jarvis**; Justice/Mother **Michele Mais**; Dennis/Record Company Man **Adam Dannheisser**; Drew **Constantine Maroulis**; Sherrie **Amy Spanger**[*1]; Father/Stacee Jaxx **James Carpinello**; Regina/Candi **Lauren Molina**; Mayor/Ja'Keith Gill/Ensemble **André Ward**; Hertz **Paul Schoeffler**[*2]; Franz **Wesley Taylor**[*3]; Waitress/ Ensemble **Savannah Wise**[*4]; Reporter/Ensemble **Katherine Tokarz**; Sleazy Producer/Joey Primo/Ensemble **Jeremy Woodard**; Young Groupie/Ensemble **Angel Reed**; Offstage Voices **Ericka Hunter, Tad Wilson**[*5]; Swings[*6] **Jeremy Jordan, Bahiyah Sayyed Gaines, Michael Minarik**

UNDERSTUDIES Ericka Hunter (Sherrie), Jeremy Jordan (Drew, Franz, Stacee Jaxx), Michael Minarik (Dennis, Hertz, Lonny, Stacee Jaxx), Bahiyah Sayyed Gaines (Justice), Katherine Tokarz (Justice, Regina), Tad Wilson[*5] (Dennis, Hertz, Lonny), Savannah Wise[*4] (Sherrie), Jeremy Woodard (Drew, Franz, Stacee Jaxx); Additional this season: Jennifer Foote (Justice, Regina), Geoff Packard (Drew)

* Succeeded by: 1. Savannah Wise (6/7/09), Kerry Butler (9/18/09), Emily Padgett (3/15/10) 2. Don Stephenson (8/17/09), Paul Schoeffler (10/26/09) 3. Tom Lenk (9/18/09), Derek St. Pierre (3/22/10) 4. Emily Padgett (6/7/09), Katie Webber (3/22/10) 5. Matthew Stocke 6. Callie Carter, Jennifer Foote, Geoff Packard, Eric Sciotto, Becca Tobin

ROCK OF AGES BAND Henry Aronson (Conductor/keyboard), Joel Hoekstra (guitar 1), David Gibbs or Tommy Kessler (guitar 2), Jon Weber (drums), Winston Roye (bass)

MUSICAL NUMBERS We Built This City, Nothin' but a Good Time, Keep on Loving You, Just Like Paradise, I Wanna Rock, Too Much Time on My Hands, Renegade, I Hate Myself for Loving You, Oh Sherrie, Waiting for a Girl Like You, Shadows of the Night, Don't Stop Believing, Heaven, The Search is Over, We're Not Gonna Take It, High Enough, The Final Countdown, I Want to Know What Love Is, Harden My Heart, Here I Go Again, To Be With You, Every Rose Has Its Thorn, Hit Me With Your Best Shot, Can't Fight This Feeling, Wanted Dead or Alive, Cum on Feel the Noize, Any Way You Want It, Heat of the Moment, Sister Christian, More Than Words

SETTING Los Angeles and Hollywood, 1987. Transfer of the Off-Broadway musical presented in two acts. Previously presented at New World Stages October 1, 2008–January 4, 2009. World premiere at the Vanguard Hollywood January 26–February 18, 2006.

SYNOPSIS *Rock of Ages* is an explosive new musical with a heart as big as 80's rock hair. In 1987 on the Sunset Strip, as a legendary rock club faces its demise at the hands of eager developers, a young rocker hoping for his big break falls for a small town girl chasing big dreams of her own, and they fall in love to the greatest songs of the era. An arena-rock love story, *Rock of Ages* is told through the hits of some of the 80's greatest rockers including Journey, Bon Jovi, Styx, Reo Speedwagon, Pat Benatar, Joan Jett, Warrant, Night Ranger, Extreme, Foreigner, Survivor, Quarterflash, Damn Yankees, Twisted Sister, Poison, Asia and Whitesnake.

Constantine Maroulis and Company (photo by Joan Marcus)

Shrek The Musical

Broadway Theatre; First Preview: November 8, 2008; Opening Night: December 14, 2008; Closed January 3, 2010; 37 previews, 441 performances

Book and lyrics by David Lindsay-Abaire, music by Jeanine Tesori; based on the DreamWorks Animation motion picture and the book by William Steig; Produced by DreamWorks Theatricals and Neal Street Productions; Director, Jason Moore; Choreography, Josh Prince; Music Direction/Incidental Music Arrangements, Tim Weil; Orchestrations, Danny Troob; Sets/Costumes/Puppet Design, Tim Hatley; Lighting, Hugh Vanstone; Sound, Peter Hylenski; Hair/Wigs, David Brian-Brown; Makeup, Naomi Donne; Prosthetics, Michael Marino/Prosthetic Renaissance; Casting, Tara Rubin; Illusions Consultant, Marshall Magoon; Associate Director/Production Stage Manager, Peter Lawrence; Replacement PSM, Beverly Jenkins; Production Management, Aurora Productions; Dance Arrangements, Matthew Sklar; Vocal Arrangements, Jeanine Tesori & Tim Weil; Associate Orchestrator, John Clancy; Music Coordinator, Michael Keller; Marketing, Clint Bond Jr.; General Management, Stuart Thompson Productions, James Triner; Electronic Music Design, Andrew Barrett; Company Manager, Roeya Banuazizi; Stage Manager, Rachel A. Wolff; Assistant Stage Manager, Chad Lewis/Stacey Zaloga; Assistant Company Manager, Scott Armstrong; Assistant Director, Stephen Sposito; Associate Choreographer, Sloan Just; Dance Captain, Justin Greer; Puppet Captain, John Tartaglia; Assistants to Stage Managers, Stacey Zaloga & Bryan Rountree; Associate Design: Paul Weimer (set), Andrew Edwards (U.K. scenic), Tracy Christensen, Brian J. Bustos, Jack Galloway (costumes), Philip Rosenberg (lighting), Keith Caggiano (sound), Susan Corrado (hair/wigs), Dave Presto (prosthetics); Assistant Design: Derek Stenborg, Zhanna Gervich (U.S. set), Tim Blazdell (U.K. scenic), Ben Davies & Paul Tulley (U.K. model makers), Jessica Wegener, Sarah Laux (costumes), Anthony Pearson (lighting), Angela L. Johnson (makeup), Leon Dobkowski, Katie Irish, Roxana Ramseur (costume department); Moving Lights Programmer, Sharon Huizinga; Media Associate and Programmer, Laura Frank; Media Assistant, Joshua Fleitell; Dialect Coach, Stephen Gabis; Electronic Music Design Associate, Jeff Marder; Rehearsal Pianists, Jodie Moore, Matt Perri, John Deley; Rehearsal Percussionist, Warren Odze; Music Copying, Kaye-Houston Music (Anne Kaye & Doug Houston); Production Assistant, Jacqueline Prats; Music Department Assistant, Michael Gacetta; For Aurora Productions: Gene O'Donovan, W. Benjamin Heller II, Bethany Weinstein, Melissa Mazdra, Amy Merlino Coey, Laura Archer, Dana Hesch; For Stuart Thompson: David Turner, Caroline Prugh; For Renaissance Prosthetics: Hayes Vilandry, Roland Blancafor, Chris Kelly, Paul Komoda; Management Assistants, Megan Curren, Geo Karapetyan, Quinn Corbin; Wrangler, Bridget Walders; Advertising, SpotCo; Press, Boneau/Bryan-Brown; Cast recording: Decca Broadway B0012627-02

CAST Shrek **Brian d'Arcy James**[*1]; Princess Fiona **Sutton Foster**; Lord Farquaad **Christopher Sieber**; Donkey **Daniel Breaker**; Pinocchio **John Tartaglia**[*2]; Ensemble **Cameron Adams**; Sugar Plum Fairy/Gingy **Haven Burton**; Shoemaker's Elf/Duloc Performer/Blind Mouse **Jennifer Cody**; Sticks/Bishop **Bobby Daye**; Bricks **Ryan Duncan**; Ugly Duckling/Blind Mouse **Sarah Jane Everman**; Mama Bear **Aymee Garcia**; Young Fiona (Wed., Fri., Sun.) **Leah Greenhaus**; Baby Bear/Blind Mouse **Lisa Ho**; King Harold/Big Bad Wolf/Captain of the Guard **Chris Hocn**; Fairy Godmother/Magic Mirror Assistant/Bluebird **Danette Holden**[*3]; Ensemble **Marty Lawson**; Papa Ogre/Straw **Jacob Ming-Trent**[*4]; Teen Fiona **Marissa O'Donnell**; Peter Pan **Denny Paschall**; Young Fiona (Tues., Thurs., Sat.) **Rachel Resheff**; Gnome/Pied Piper **Greg Reuter**[*5]; Young Shrek/Dwarf **Adam Riegler**; White Rabbit **Noah Rivera**[*6]; Queen Lillian/Wicked Witch/Magic Mirror Assistant **Jennifer Simard**; Mama Ogre/Humpty Dumpty **Rachel Stern**; Barker/Papa Bear/Thelonius **Dennis Stowe**; Swings **Justin Greer, Carolyn Ockert-Haythe, Heather Jane Rolff, David F.M. Vaughn, Ryan Worsing**; Standby for Shrek **Ben Crawford**; Alternate for Young Fiona **Rozi Baker**

* Succeeded by: 1. Ben Crawford (11/10/09) 2. Robb Sapp (8/18/09), John Tartaglia (12/15/09) 3. Colleen Hawks 4. Eric Petersen 5. Kevin Quillon 6. Frankie Paparone

UNDERSTUDIES Jacob Ming-Trent/Eric Petersen (Shrek), Haven Burton and Sarah Jane Everman (Princess Fiona), Bobby Daye and Ryan Duncan (Donkey), Chris Hoch and Greg Reuter/David F.M. Vaughn (Lord Farquaad), Denny Paschall and Noah Rivera/Justin Greer (Pinocchio), Haven Burton (Teen Fiona), Leah Greenhaus and Rachel Resheff (Young Shrek)

ORCHESTRA Tim Weil/Eric Stern (Conductor); Jason DeBord (Associate Conductor/keyboards); Antoine Silverman (Concertmaster); Jonathan Dinklage, Entcho Todorov, Sean Carney (violins), Jeanne LeBlanc, Anja Wood (celli); Bill Ellison (acoustic bass); Anders Bostrom (flutes); Charles Pillow, Jack Bashkow, Ron Jannelli (reeds); Anthony Kadleck, Bud Burridge (trumpets); Bruce Eidem, Morris Kainuma/Michael Christianson (trombones); Adam Krauthamer (French horn); John Delay (keyboards); Ken Brescia, Bob Baxmeyer (guitars); Luico Hopper (electric bass); Warren Odze (drums); Shane Shanahan (percussion)

MUSICAL NUMBERS Big Bright Beautiful World, Story of My Life, The Goodbye Song, Don't Let Me Go, I Know It's Today, What's Up, Duloc?, Travel Song, Donkey Pot Pie, This Is How a Dream Comes True, Who I'd Be, Morning Person, I Think I Got You Beat, The Ballad of Farquaad, Make a Move, When Words Fail, Morning Person (reprise), Build a Wall, Freak Flag, Big Bright Beautiful World (reprise), Finale

New York premiere of a new musical presented in two acts. World Premiere at Seattle's 5th Avenue Theatre August 15, 2008, prior to its Broadway engagement.

SYNOPSIS *Shrek The Musical* follows the adventures of Shrek, a lovable swamp-dwelling ogre, his wisecracking sidekick, Donkey, the lovely Princess Fiona, the vertically challenged Lord Farquaad, and a chorus of everybody's favorite fractured fairytale creatures. In order to regain his peaceful neighborhood, the fearsome ogre makes a deal with the wanna-be king to rescue his intended, a damsel in distress. But surprises are in store in this funny, fractured fairy tale.

Brian d'Arcy James and Daniel Breaker (photo by Joan Marcus)

South Pacific

Vivian Beaumont Theatre; First Preview: March 1, 2008; Opening Night: April 3, 2008; 37 previews, 901 performances as of May 31, 2010

Music by Richard Rodgers, lyrics and book by Oscar Hammerstein II, book and original staging by Joshua Logan, adapted from the novel "Tales of the South Pacific" by James A. Michener; Produced by Lincoln Center Theater (André Bishop, Artistic Director; Bernard Gersten, Executive Producer) in association with Bob Boyett; Director, Bartlett Sher; Musical Staging, Christopher Gattelli; Music Director, Ted Sperling; Sets, Michael Yeargan; Costumes, Catherine Zuber; Lighting, Donald Holder; Sound, Scott Lehrer; Orchestrations, Robert Russell Bennett; Dance & Incidental Music Arrangements, Trude Rittmann; Casting, Telsey + Company; Production Stage Manager, Michael Brunner; Musical Theatre Associate Producer, Ira Weitzman; General Manager, Adam Siegel; Production Manager, Jeff Hamlin/Rolt Smith; Development, Hattie K. Jutagir; Marketing, Linda Mason Ross; Finance, David S. Brown; Education, Kati Koerner; Dramaturg, Anne Cattaneo; Vocal Coach, Deborah Hecht; Company Manager, Matthew Markoff, Jessica Perlmeter Cochrane/Josh Lowenthal; Assistant Company Manager, Daniel Hoyos; Assistant Stage Managers, David Sugarman, Samantha Greene, Dana Williams; Dance Captain, Wendy Bergamini/George Psomas; Assistant Dance Captain, George Psomas/Margot de la Barre; Assistant Director, Sarna Lapine; Associate Choreographer, Joe Langworth; Associate Design: Lawrence King (sets), Karen Spahn (lighting), Leon Rothenberg (sound); Assistant Design: Mikiko Suzuki (sets), Holly Cain, David Newell, Court Watson (costumes), Caroline Chao (lighting); Rehearsal Pianist, Jonathan Rose; Wigs and Hair, Tom Watson; Makeup, Cookie Jordan; Properties Coordinator, Kathy Fabian; Music Coordinator, David Lai; Press, Philip Rinaldi, Barbara Carroll; Cast recording: Sony BMG – Masterworks Broadway 88697-30457-2

CAST Ensign Nellie Forbush **Laura Osnes**[*1]; Emile de Becque **Paulo Szot**[*2]; Ngana **Laurissa Romain**; Jerome **Luka Kain**; Henry **Helmar Augustus Cooper**; Bloody Mary **Loretta Ables Sayre**; Liat **Li Jun Li**; Bloody Mary's Assistants **MaryAnn Hu, Deborah Lew, Kimber Monroe**; Luther Billis **Danny Burstein**; Stewpot **Eric Anderson**; Professor **Matt Kaplan**[*3]; Lt. Joseph Cable, USMC **Andrew Samonsky**; Capt. George Bracket, USN **Murphy Guyer**[*4]; Cmdr. William Harbison, USN **Sean Cullen**; Lt. Buzz Adams **George Merrick**; Yeoman Herbert Quale **Christian Delcroix**[*5]; Radio Operator Bob McCaffrey **Peter Lockyer**; Seabee Morton Wise **Genson Blimline**[*6]; Seabee Richard West **Nick Mayo**; Seabee Johnny Noonan **Michael Arnold**; Seabee Billy Whitmore **Robert Lenzi**; Sailor Tom O'Brien **Mike Evariste**[*7]; Sailor James Hayes **Jerold E. Solomon**; Sailor Kenneth Johnson **Christian Carter**; Petty Officer Hamilton Steeves **Craig Bennett**[*8]; Seaman Thomas Hassinger **Zachary James**[*9]; Shore Patrolman Lt. Eustis Carmichael **Rob Gallagher**; Lead Nurse Lt. Genevieve Marshall **Liz McCartney**; Ensign Dinah Murphy **Laura Marie Duncan**; Ensign Janet MacGregor **Wendy Bergamini**[*10]; Ensign Connie Walewska **Margot de la Barre**; Ensign Sue Yaeger **Garrett Long**; Ensign Cora MacRae **Marla Mindelle**[*11]; Islanders, Sailors, Seabees, Party Guests: **Michael Arnold, Genson Blimline**[*6], **Craig Bennett**[*8], **Wendy Bergamini**[*10], **Christian Carter, Helmar Augustus Cooper, Margot de la Barre, Christian Delcroix**[*5], **Laura Marie Duncan, Mike Evariste**[*7], **Rob Gallagher, MaryAnn Hu, Zachary James**[*9], **Robert Lenzi, Deborah Lew, Garrett Long, Nick Mayo, Liz McCartney, George Merrick, Marla Mindelle**[*11], **Kimber Monroe, Jerold E. Solomon**; Swings **Julie Foldesi, Greg Roderick, Eric L. Christian**[*12], **George Psomas**

*Succeeded by: 1. Kelli O'Hara (10/13/09), Laura Osnes (1/5/10) 2. William Michael (6/1/09), Paulo Szot (7/6/09), William Michael (1/28/10), David Pittsinger (2/1/10), William Michael (3/23/10), Paulo Szot (3/31/10), William Michael (4/13/10), Paulo Szot (4/15/10) 3. Christian Delcroix (7/7/10) 4. Skipp Sudduth 5. Jason Michael Snow (7/7/10) 6. Matt Wall (5/19/09), Todd Cerveris (12/22/09) 7. Alfie Parker Jr. 8. Taylor Frey 9. Craig Bennett 10. Samantha Shafer 11. Becca Ayers 12. Correy West

ORCHESTRA Ted Sperling/James Moore (Conductor); Fred Lassen (Associate Conductor); Belinda Whitney (concertmistress), Antoine Silverman, Karl Kawahara, Katherine Livolsi-Landau, Lisa Matricardi, Jim Tsao, Michael Nicholas, Rena Isbin, Louise Owen (violins); David Blinn, David Creswell (violas); Peter Sachon, Caryl Paisner (celli); Charles du Chateau (Assistant Conductor/cello); Lisa Stokes-Chin (bass); Liz Mann (flute/piccolo); Todd Palmer, Shari Hoffman (clarinet); Matt Dine/Kelly Perai (oboe/English horn); Damian Primis (bassoon): Robert Carlisle, Chris Komer, Shelagh Abate, Daniel Grabois (French horns); Dominic Derasse, Gareth Flowers, Wayne Dumaine (trumpets); Mark Patterson, Mike Boschen, Nate Mayland (trombones); Marcus Rojas/Andrew Rodgers (tuba); Grace Paradise (harp); Bill Lanham (drums/percussion)

MUSICAL NUMBERS Overture, Dites-Moi, A Cockeyed Optimist, Twin Soliloquies, Some Enchanted Evening, Dites-Moi (reprise), Bloody Mary, There Is Nothin' Like a Dame, Bali Ha'i, My Girl Back Home, I'm Gonna Wash That Man Right Outa My Hair, Some Enchanted Evening (reprise), A Wonderful Guy, Bali Ha'i (reprise), Younger Than Springtime, Finale Act I, Entr'acte, Happy Talk, Honey Bun, You've Got to Be Carefully Taught; This Nearly Was Mine, Some Enchanted Evening (reprise), Finale Ultimo

SETTING The action takes place on two islands in the South Pacific during World War II. Revival of a musical presented in two acts.

SYNOPSIS Rodgers and Hammerstein's classic receives its first major New York revival, almost sixty years after its debut. The story centers on the romance between a southern nurse and a French planter who find love on a small tropical island amidst a backdrop of war and racism.

Laura Osnes and Paulo Szot (Photo by Joan Marcus)

Waiting for Godot

Studio 54; First Preview: April 10, 2009 Opening Night: April 30, 2009; Closed July 12, 2009; 32 previews, 85 performances

Written by Samuel Beckett; Produced by the Roundabout Theatre Company (Todd Haimes, Artistic Director; Harold Wolpert, Managing Director; Julia C. Levy, Executive Director) by special arrangement with Elizabeth McCann; Director, Anthony Page; Sets, Santo Loquasto; Costumes, Jane Greenwood; Lighting, Peter Kaczorowski; Sound, Dan Moses Schreier, Hair & Wigs, Tom Watson; Fight Director, Thomas Schall; Production Stage Manager, Peter Hanson; Casting, Jim Carnahan, Kate Boka; Technical Supervisor, Steve Beers; Executive Producer/General Manager, Sydney Beers; Marketing/Sales Promotion, David B. Steffen; Founding Director, Gene Feist; Associate Artistic Director, Scott Ellis; Director of Artistic Development & Casting, Jim Carnahan; Education, Greg McCaslin; Finance, Susan Neiman; Telesales, Marco Frezza; Sales Operations, Charlie Garbowski Jr.; Company Manager, Denise Cooper; Stage Manager, Jon Krause; Assistant Director; Wes Grantom; Makeup, Angelina Avellone; Associate Design: Jenny Sawyers (set), MaryAnn D. Smith (costumes), David Bullard (sound); Assistant Design/Design Assistants: Anya Klepikov (Ms. Greenwood), Keri Thibodeau (lighting); Production: Dan Hoffman (production carpenter), Josh Weitzman (production electrician), John Wooding (assistant production electrician), Kathy Fabian (production properties), Carrie Mossman (assistant production properties), Lawrence Jennino (house properties), Dan Schultheis (Local One apprentice), David Gotwald (production sound engineer), Nadine Hettel (wardrobe supervisor), Joe Hickey (dresser), Elisa Acevedo (hair & wig supervisor), Rachel Bauder (production assistant), Jill Valentine (child wrangler), Chris Minnick (company manager intern); Advertising, SpotCo; Press, Boneau/Bryan-Brown, Adrian Bryan-Brown, Matt Polk, Jessica Johnson, Amy Kass

CAST Estragon **Nathan Lane**; Vladimir **Bill Irwin**; Pozzo **John Goodman**; Lucky **John Glover**; A Boy **Cameron Clifford** or **Matthew Schechter**

UNDERSTUDIES John Ahlin (Estragon, Pozzo), Anthony Newfield (Vladimir, Lucky)

SETTING Place: A country road. A tree. Time: Act I – Evening; Act II – Next day, same time. Revival of a play presented in two acts. Originally produced on Broadway at the John Golden Theatre April 19–June 9, 1956 (see *Theatre World* Vol. 12, page 107). The show had a brief revival at the Ethel Barrymore Theatre January 21-26, 1957.

SYNOPSIS *Waiting for Godot* remains Samuel Beckett's most magical and beautiful allegory. The story revolves around two seemingly homeless men waiting for someone – or something – named Godot. Vladimir and Estragon wait near a tree on a barren stretch of road, inhabiting a drama spun from their own consciousness. The result is a comical wordplay of poetry, dreamscapes and nonsense, which has been interpreted as a somber summation of mankind's inexhaustible search for meaning.

Nathan Lane and Bill Irwin (photos by Joan Marcus)

Nathan Lane, John Goodman and Bill Irwin

John Glover, Bill Irwin, Nathan Lane and John Goodman

West Side Story

Palace Theatre; First Preview: February 23, 2009 Opening Night: March 19, 2009; 27 previews, 500 performances as of May 31, 2010

Book and direction by Arthur Laurents, music by Leonard Bernstein, lyrics by Stephen Sondheim; Conception, original direction and choreography by Jerome Robbins; Produced by Kevin McCollum, James L. Nederlander, Jeffrey Seller, Terry Allen Kramer, Sander Jacobs, Roy Furman/Jill Furman Willis, Freddy DeMann, Robyn Goodman/Walt Grossman, Hal Luftig, Roy Miller, The Weinstein Company, and Broadway Across America; Choreography Reproduction, Joey McKneely; Music Supervisor/Music Director, Patrick Vaccariello; Set, James Youmans; Costumes, David C. Woolard; Lighting, Howell Binkley; Sound, Dan Moses Schreier; Wigs & Hair, Mark Adam Rampmeyer; Makeup, Angelina Avallone; Casting, Stuart Howard, Amy Schecter, Paul Hardt; Associate Director, David Saint; Associate Choreographer, Lori Werner; Associate Producer, LAMS Productions; Translations, Lin-Manuel Miranda; Orchestrations, Leonard Bernstein with Sid Ramin and Irwin Kostal; Music Coordinator, Michael Keller; Production Stage Manager, Joshua Halperin; Original Broadway Production Co-Choreography, Peter Gennaro; Technical Supervisor, Brian Lynch; Marketing, Scott A. Moore; General Management, The Charlotte Wilcox Company (Seth Marquette, Matthew W. Krawiec, Dina S. Friedler, Margaret Wilcox); Company Manager, James Lawson; Assistant Company Manager, Erica Ezold; Stage Manager, Lisa Dawn Cave; Assistant Stage Manager, Jason Brouillard; Assistant to the Director, Isaac Klein; Fight Director, Ron Piretti; Dance Captain, Marina Lazzaretto; Assistant Dance Captain, Michaeljon Slinger; Fight Captain, Joshua Buscher; Keyboard Programmer, Randy Cohen; Associate Design: Jerome Martin (set), Ryan O'Gara (lighting), David Bullard (sound); Assistant Design: Robert Martin, Daryl A. Stone, Maria Zamansky (costumes), Carrie Wood (lighting); Assistants to Designers: Sara James, Yuri Cataldo, Angela Harner (costume), Lazaro Arencibia (makeup); Moving Light Programmer, David Arch; Assistant Keyboard Programmers, Bryan Cook, Jim Mironchik; Advertising/Website, SpotCo; Press, The Hartman Group; Cast recording: Sony Masterworks 88697-52391-2

CAST *The Jets:* Action **Curtis Holbrook**[*1]; Anybodys **Tro Shaw**[*2]; A-Rab **Kyle Coffman**; Baby John **Ryan Steele**; Big Deal **Eric Hatch**[*3]; Diesel **Joshua Buscher**; Graziella **Pamela Otterson**; Hotsie **Marina Lazzaretto**; Kiddo *(evenings and Sundays)* **Nicholas Barasch**[*4]; Kiddo *(Wed. & Sat. matinees)* **Kyle Brenn**; Mugsy **Amy Ryerson**; Riff **Cody Green**[*5]; Snowboy **Mike Cannon**; Tony **Matt Cavenaugh**[*6]; Velma **Lindsay Dunn**[*7]; Zaza **Kaitlin Mesh**; 4H **Sam Rogers**; *The Sharks:* Alicia **Yanira Marin**; Anita **Karen Olivo**; Bebecita **Mileyka Mateo**; Bernardo **George Akram**; Bolo **Peter Chursin**[*8]; Chino **Joey Haro**[*9]; Consuela **Danielle Polanco**[*10]; Federico **Michael Rosen**[*11]; Fernanda **Kat Nejat**; Inca **Isaac Calpito**; Indio **Manuel Santos**; Lupe **Tanairi Sade Vazquez**; Maria **Josefina Scaglione**; Pepe **Manuel Herrera**[*12]; Rosalia **Jennifer Sanchez**; Tio **Yurel Echezarreta**[*13]; *The Adults:* Doc **Greg Vinkler**; Glad Hand **Michael Mastro**; Krupke **Lee Sellars**; Lt. Schrank **Steve Bassett**; Swings[*14] **Haley Carlucci, Madeline Cintron, John Arthur Greene, Chase Madigan, Angelina Mullins, Christian Elán Ortiz, Michaeljon Slinger**

STANDBYS AND UNDERSTUDIES Standbys: (Tony), Mark Zimmerman (Doc, Gladhand, Krupke, Lt. Schrank), Natalie Cortez (Anita) Understudies: Joshua Buscher (Big Deal), Mike Cannon (Riff, Tony), Haley Carlucci (Fernanda, Maria), Lindsay Dunn (Graziella), John Arthur Greene/Colt Prattes (Action, Diesel, Riff), Wes Hart (Riff), Eric Hatch (Action), Manuel Herrera (Bernardo), Chase Madigan (A-Rab, Baby John, Snowboy), Yanira Marin (Anita, Consuela, Fernanda), Michael Mastro (Doc, Krupke, Lt. Schrank), Kaitlin Mesh (Anybodys), Kat Nejat (Anita, Maria, Rosalia), Pamela Otterson (Anybodys), Sam Rogers (A-Rab, Baby John, Big Deal), Michael Rosen (Chino), Amy Ryerson (Graziella), Jennifer Sanchez (Anita), Manuel Santos & Phillip Spaeth (Bernardo, Chino), Michaeljon Slinger/Alex Ringler (Diesel, Gladhand, Snowboy), Brendon Stimson (A-Rab, Baby John, 4H, Snowboy, Action), Tanairi Sade Vazquez (Consuela)

* Succeeded by: 1. Wes Hart (12/15/09) 2. Sara Dobbs (12/15/09) 3. Mickey Winslow (12/15/09) 4. Michael Kleeman (12/15/09) 5. John Arthur Greene (8/4/09) 6. Matthew Hydzik (12/15/09) & Jeremy Jordan (12/15/09 –Wed. Eve. and Sun. Mat. performances only) 7. Jessica Bishop 8. Stephen Diaz 9. Michael Rosen 10. Shina Ann Morris 11. Phillip Spaeth 12. Sean Ewing 13. Jesus Pacheco, Jess Coronado 14. Kristine Covillo, Colt Prattes, Alex Ringler, Brendon Stimson, Michael Williams

ORCHESTRA Patrick Vaccariello Conductor); Maggie Torre (Associate Conductor/piano); Martin Agee (Concertmaster/violin); Paul Woodiel, Robert Shaw, Victoria Paterson, Fritz Krakowski, Dana Ianculovici, Philip Payton (violins); Peter Prosser, Vivian Israel, Diane Barere, Jennifer Lang (celli); Bill Sloat (bass); Lawrence Feldman, Lino Gomez, Dan Willis, Adam Kolker, Gilbert DeJean (reeds); John Chudoba [lead], Trevor Neumann, Matthew Peterson (trumpets); Tim Albright (trombone); Jeff Nelson (bass trombone); Chris Komer, Theresa MacDonnell (French horns); Jim Laev (keyboard); Eric Poland (drums); Dan McMilla, Pablo Rieppi (percussion)

MUSICAL NUMBERS Prologue; Jet Song; Something's Coming; Dance at the Gym; Maria; Tonight; America; Cool; One Hand, One Heart; Tonight (Quintet); The Rumble; Me Siento Hermosa (I Feel Pretty); Somewhere; Gee, Officer Krupke; Un Hombre Asi (A Boy Like That)/I Have a Love

SETTING Upper West Side of New York City during the last days of summer, 1957. Revival of the musical presented in fifteen scenes in two acts. This production played a pre-Broadway engagement December 15, 2008–January 17, 2009 at Washington, DC's National Theatre, where the musical made its world premiere in 1957. Originally presented on Broadway at the Winter Garden Theatre September 26, 1957–June 27, 1959, playing 732 performances (see *Theatre World* Vol. 14, page 11).

SYNOPSIS *West Side Story* transports the achingly beautiful tale of Shakespeare's *Romeo and Juliet* to the turbulent streets of the Upper West Side in 1950s New York City. Two star-crossed lovers, Tony and Maria, find themselves caught between the rival street gangs of different ethnic backgrounds, the 'Jets' and the 'Sharks.' Their struggle to exist together in a world of violence, hate and prejudice is one of the most heart-breaking, relevant and innovative musical masterpieces of our time.

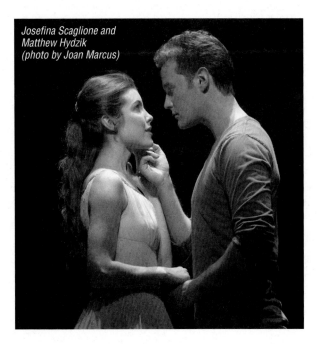

Josefina Scaglione and Matthew Hydzik (photo by Joan Marcus)

Wicked

Gershwin Theatre; First Preview: October 8, 2003; Opening Night: October 30, 2003; 25 previews, 2,726 performances as of May 31, 2010

Book by Winnie Holzman, music and lyrics by Stephen Schwartz; based on the novel by Gregory Maguire; Produced by Marc Platt, Universal Pictures, The Araca Group, Jon B. Platt and David Stone; Director, Joe Mantello; Musical Staging, Wayne Cilento; Music Supervisor, Stephen Oremus; Orchestrations, William David Brohn; Sets, Eugene Lee; Costumes, Susan Hilferty; Lighting, Kenneth Posner; Sound, Tony Meola; Projections, Elanie J. McCarthy; Wigs/Hair, Tom Watson; Technical Supervisor, Jake Bell; Arrangements, Alex Lacamoire, Stephen Oremus; Dance Arrangements, James Lynn Abbott; Music Coordinator, Michael Keller; Special Effects, Chic Silber; Production Supervisor, Thom Widmann; Dance Supervisor, Mark Myars; Associate Director, Lisa Leguillou; Casting, Bernard Telsey; Production Stage Manager, Marybeth Abel; Stage Manager, Jennifer Marik; Assistant Stage Managers, Christy Ney, J. Jason Daunter; General Management, 321 Theatrical Management; Executive Producers, Marcia Goldberg and Nina Essman; Company Management, Susan Sampliner, Robert Brinkerhoff; Fight Director, Tom Schall; Flying, Paul Rubin/ZFX Inc.; Dressing/Properties, Kristie Thompson; Makeup, Joe Dulude II; Assistant Choreography, Corinne McFadden-Herrera; Music Preparation, Peter R. Miller; Synthesizer Programming, Andrew Barrett; Advertising, Serino-Coyne; Press, The Hartman Group; Cast recording: Decca B 0001 682-02

CAST Glinda **Alli Mauzey**[*1]; Witch's Father/Ozian Official **Michael DeVries**; Witch's Mother **Kristen Leigh Gorski**; Midwife **Kathy Santen**; Elphaba **Nicole Parker**[*2]; Nessarose **Cristy Candler**[*3]; Boq **Alex Brightman**; Madame Morrible **Rondi Reed**; Doctor Dillamond **Timothy Britten Parker**; Fiyero **Kevin Kern**[*4]; The Wonderful Wizard of Oz **P.J. Benjamin**; Chistery **Sam J. Cahn**[*5]; Ensemble[*6] **Nova Bergeron, Sarah Bolt, Jerad Bortz, Sam J. Cahn, Michael DeVries, Maia Evwaraye-Griffin, Kristina Fernandez, Adam Fleming, Kristen Leigh Gorski, Chelsea Krombach, Kenway Hon Wai K. Kua, Kyle Dean Massey, Jonathan McGill, Lindsay K. Northen, Eddie Pendergraft, Adam Perry, Alexander Quiroga, Charlie Sutton, Kathy Santen, Heather Spore, Brian Wanee, Robin Wilner**; Standbys **Jennifer Dinoia** (Elphaba), **Laura Woyasz** (Glinda); Swings[*7] **Anthony Galde, Brenda Hamilton, Lindsay Janisse, Jonathan Warren, Briana Yacavone**

Mandy Gonzalez (photos by Joan Marcus)

*Succeeded by: 1. Erin Mackey (8/11/09), Katie Rose Clarke (1/14/10) 2. Dee Roscioli (7/21/09), Mandy Gonzalez (3/23/10) 3. Michelle Federer (8/18/09), Jenny Fellner (1/14/10) 4. Andy Karl (2/2/10) 5. Mark Shunkey 6. Succeeding Ensemble: David Hull, Manuel Herrera, Rhea Patterson, Nathan Peck, Amanda Rose, Mark Shunkey, Stephanie Torns, Brian West 7. Brian Munn, Samantha Zack

ORCHESTRA Dominick Amendum (Conductor); David Evans (Associate Conductor/keyboards); Ben Cohn (Assistant Conductor/keyboards); Christian Hebel (Concertmaster); Victor Schultz (violin); Kevin Roy (viola); Dan Miller (cello); Konrad Adderly (bass); John Moses, John Campo, Tuck Lee, Helen Campo (woodwinds); Jon Owens, Tom Hoyt (trumpets); Dale Kirkland, Douglas Purviance (trombones); Theo Primis, Chad Yarbrough (French horn); Paul Loesel (keyboards); Ric Molina, Greg Skaff (guitars); Andy Jones (percussion); Matt VanderEnde (drums); Laura Sherman (harp)

MUSICAL NUMBERS No One Mourns the Wicked, Dear Old Shiz, The Wizard and I, What Is This Feeling?, Something Bad, Dancing Through Life, Popular, I'm Not That Girl, One Short Day, A Sentimental Man, Defying Gravity, No One Mourns the Wicked (Reprise), Thank Goodness, The Wicked Witch of the East, Wonderful, I'm Not That Girl (Reprise), As Long as You're Mine, No Good Deed, March of the Witch Hunters, For Good, Finale

SETTING The Land of Oz. A musical presented in two acts. World premiere presented in San Francisco at the Curran Theatre May 28–June 29, 2003. For original production credits see *Theatre World* Vol. 60, page 34.

SYNOPSIS *Wicked* explores the early life of the witches of Oz, Glinda and Elphaba, who meet at Shiz University. Glinda is madly popular and Elphaba is green. After an initial period of mutual loathing, the roommates begin to learn something about each other. Their life paths continue to intersect, and eventually their choices and convictions take them on widely different paths.

Alex Brightman and Jenny Fellner

Andy Karl, Katie Rose Clarke, and Rondi Reed

SPECIAL EVENTS

Broadway Bares 19.0: Click It!

Roseland Ballroom; June 21, 2009

Produced by Broadway Cares/Equity Fights AIDS, Michael Graziano, Scott Tucker; Production Supervisor, Michael Clarkston; Production Manager, Nathan Hurlin; Production Stage Manager, Jennifer Rogers; Presenting Sponsor, M•A•C Viva Glam; Executive Producer, Jerry Mitchell; Conception and Director, Peter Gregus; Lighting, Paul Miller, Philip S. Rosenberg; Set, Mary Houston; Projections, Michael Clark, Brian Beasley, Aaron King; Sound, Acme Sound Partners; Costume Coordinator, David Kaley; Hair Design/Coordination, Danny Koye; Makeup Design/Coordination, The M•A•C Pro Team; The Living Art of Armando Artistic Director, Armando Farfan Jr.; Choreographers, Michael Balderrama, Enrique Brown, Tammy Colucci, Connor Gallagher, Steve Konopelski, Ray Mercer, Rhonda Miller, Barry Morgan, Rachelle Rak, Josh Rhodes, Michael Lee Scott, Shea Sullivan, Lee Wilkins; Associate Director, Connor Gallagher; Assistant Director, Enrique Brown; Assistant to the Director, Christopher Berens; Stage Managers, Michael Alifanz, Hilary Austin, Connie Baker, Andrea Jess Berkey, Jared T. Carey, Zac Chandler, Alix Claps, Casey Cook, Richard Costabile, Kimothy Cruse, Matthew DiCarlo, Chris Economakos, Colyn W. Fiendel, Theresa Flanagan, Melanie Ganim, Marci Glotzer, Bradley Harder, Michail Haynes, Cynthia M. Hennon, Samuel-Moses Jones, Matthew S. Karr, Terri Kohler, Talia Krispel, Melissa Magliula, Rachel Maier, Kelly McGrath, Frances Eric Montesa, Chris Munnell, Andrew Polizzi, Jason A. Quinn, Megan Schneid, Lisa Schwartz, Justin Scribner, Daniel Seth, Colleen M. Sherry, Dave Soloman, Ray Wetmore, Michael Willhoite; Opening Number ("Click It!"): Music, Lyrics and arrangement by David Nehls, vocals by Heidi Blickenstaff; Choreography by Peter Gregus, Enrique Brown, Connor Gallagher; Press, Boneau/Bryan Brown

THE COMPANY Joe Abraham, Cameron Adams, Nick Adams, Scott Ahearn, Monique Alhaddad, John Alix, Matthew Anctil, Timothy Anderson, Michael Apuzzo, Ashley Arcement, Piper Arpan, Dave August, Sol Baird, Sean Baptiste, Jim Becker, Jen Bender, Kristine Bendul, John Bitley, Michael Blatt, Heidi Blickenstaff, Patrick Boyd, Thomas Bradfield, Kevin Bradford, Sean Bradford, Steve Bratton, Nancy Renee Braun, Amy Brewer, Jessica Leigh Brown, Michael Buchanan, Larry Bullock, Joshua Buscher, Holly Ann Butler, Daniel C. Byrd, Danny Calvert, Allyson Carr, John Carroll, Adam Cassel, Lou Castro, Anthony CeFala, Andrew Cheng, Jen Cody, Shaun Colledge, Brian Collier, Rosie Colosi, Anne Cooke, Kristine Coville, Gavin Creel, Gabriel Croom, Chris Crowthers, Holly Cruz, Beth Curry, Michael Cusumano, Suzy Darling, Barrett Davis, Desireé Davis, Joshua Dean, Tom Deckman, Christopher deProphetis, Kyle DesChamps. Michael DiMartino, Michelle Dowdy, Yurel Echezarreta, Tracy Edwards, Trevor Efinger, Hilary Elliot, Lynann Escatel, J. Austin Eyer, Armando Farfan, Jr., Rosie Lani Fiedelman, Russell Fisher, Eric Sean Fogel, Lisa Gajda, Stephanie Gibson, Anthony Giorgio, Andrew Glaszek, Frankie James Grande, Jonathan Grant, Jessica Green, Guy Greene, Lindsay Grieshaber, Jenny Gruby, Tony Guerrero, Autumn Guzzardi, Adam Michael Hart, Mair Heller, Dennis Henriquez, Sarah Hicks, Afra Hines, Lisa Ho, Deirdre Hoetmer, Joshua Horner, Rory Hughes, Ryan Jackson, Tyrone A. Jackson, Lisa Kassay, Laura Keller, Stephanie Klemons, Joe Komara, Nina LaFarga, Leah Landau, Nikka Graff Lanzarone, John Paul LaPorte, Norm Lewis, Sabra Lewis, Spencer Liff, Colby Q. Lindeman, Michelle Lookadoo, Jose-Luis Lopez, Giselle Lorenz, Craig Lowry, Ryan Lyons, Erin Maguire, Melissa Rae Mahon, Christopher Mai, Timothy John Mandala, Nicole Mangi, Tyler Marcum, Michael Mastro, Gina Mazarella, Sheryl McCollum, Emily McNamara, Stephanie Meade, Wilson Mendieta, Jeff Metzler, Brant Michaels, Michael Mindlin, Takushi Minami, Travis Nesbitt, Darius Nichols, Jill Nicklaus, Kristin Olness, Whitney Osentoski, Ian Paget,

Alison Paterson, William Michael Peters, Brandon Pereyda, John Pinto, Elizabeth Polito, Eric Potter, Michelle Pruiett, Eddie Rabon, Autuan Raimone, John Raterman, Angel Reed, Madeline Reed, Daniel Reichard, Ariel Reid, Jermaine Rembert, Paul Riner, Daniel Robinson, Mo Rocca, Constantine Rousouli, Jon Rua, Celia Mei Rubin, Naomi Rusalka, Ben Ryan, Bryce Ryness, Valerie Salgado, Gerard Salvador, Siobhan Santapaola, Kevin Santos, Manuel Santos, Kimberly Schafer, Curtis Schroeger, Michael Scirrotto, Tommy Scrivens, Erika Shannon, LaQuet Sharnell, Tro Shaw, Laura Sheehy, Laurie Sheppard, Joseph J. Simeone, Michael Skrincosky, Michaeljon Slinger, Alexandra C. Smith, Leslie Spencer Smith, Beau Speer, Dani Spieler, Brian Spitulnik, Kia Standard, Taylor Sternberg, Jennifer Stetzler, Dennis Stowe, Sarrah Strinek, Eric LaJuan Summers, Marty Thomas, Whitney Thompson, Matt Trent, Kat Ventura, Jason Walker, Shonté Walker, Franklyn Warfield, Seth Watsky, Brooke Wendle, Kristen Beth Williams, Jake Wilson, Sidney Erik Wright, Jessica Wu, Paul Zahn

FUNDRAISING $808,819

SYNOPSIS A variety burlesque show presented without intermission. Since its inception in 1992, choreographer and director Jerry Mitchell – then in the ensemble of *The Will Rogers Follies* – put six of his fellow dancers up on the bar at an infamous "watering hole" in New York City's Chelsea district and raised $8,000 for Broadway Cares, the 19 editions of Broadway Bares have grown beyond all expectations, raising more than $6.5 million for Broadway Cares/Equity Fights AIDS.

John Carrol and the Company of Broadway Bares 19.0: Click It *(photo by Thomas Vrzala)*

Chance and Chemistry: A Centennial Celebration of Frank Loesser

Minskoff Theatre; October 26, 2009

Music and lyrics by Frank Loesser, Remo Blondi, Gene Krupa, Jimmy McHugh, Jule Styne, Joseph Meyer and Frederick Hollander; Presented by The Actors Fund of America and Tim Pinckney; Director/Choreographer, Christopher Gattelli; Music Director, Brad Haak; Scenic Consultant, Paul Weimer; Lighting, Jeff Croiter; Sound, Scott Stauffer; Costume Supervisor, Bobby Pearce; Hair & Makeup Supervisor, Nathan Johnson; Program Design, Tina Benanav; Online Event Communications, Daniel Scholz; PSM, Stephen R. Gruse; Stage Managers, Sherry Cohen, Colleen Danaher, Chad Lewis, Marisa Merrigan, Justin Scribner, Andrew Tucker, Alex Volchausen; Line Producer, Patrick Weaver; Consulting Producer, Stephen Yuhasz; Additional Choreography, James Kinney, Mark Stuart Eckstein, Noah Racey, Christopher Chadman, Wayne Cilento; Event Co-Chairs, Jo Sullivan Loesser, Sir Paul McCartney; Press, Boneau/Bryan-Brown

CAST Laura Benanti, John Bolton, Ashley Brown, Charles Busch, Liz Callaway, Alan Campbell, Mario Cantone, Ana Gasteyer, Debbie

Gravitte, Hugh Jackman, Ramona Keller, Lauren Kennedy, Tom Kitt, Marc Kudisch, Judy Kuhn, Michele Lee, Liz Larsen, Emily Loesser, Jo Sullivan Loesser, Sir Paul McCartney, Audra McDonald, John McMartin, Brian Stokes Mitchell, Julia Murney, Phyllis Newman, Steven Pasquale, Noah Racey, Chita Rivera, Christopher Sieber, John Stamos, Nia Vardalos, Gerry Vichi, Brynn Williams, Patrick Wilson, Maury Yeston; With Ioana Alfonso, Kristine Bendul, Wendi Bergamini, Colin Bradbury, Kimilee Bryant, John Carrol, Paul Castree, Lou Castro, Alison Cimmet, Pamela Dayton, Margot de la Barre, Mark Stuart Eckstein, Michael Hunsaker, Sarah Jenkins, Telly Leung, Michelle Lookadoo, Tyler Maynard, Mayumi Miguel, Christine Mild, Marla Mindelle, Mark Myars, Sarah O'Gleby, Ariel Reid, Jermaine Rembert, Jeffrey Schecter, Tommy Scrivens, Ron Todorowski, David Turner, Tommar Wilson

MUSICAL NUMBERS Overture from *How to Succeed*, I'll Know/Somebody Somewhere, Some Like It Hot, I Wish I Didn't Love You So, Can't Stop Talking, Once in Love with Amy, Murder He Says, Never Will I Marry, In Your Eyes, The Inch Worm, You Understand Me, Two Sleepy People, Sit Down You're Rockin the Boat, Big D, Joey Joey Joey, Rumble Rumble Rumble, What Are You Doing New Year's Eve?, Baby It's Cold Outside, The Crapshooter's Dance/Luck Be a Lady, Standing on the Corner, Junk Man, The Boys in the Backroom, I Believe in You, Adelaide's Lament, My Heart Is So Full of You, Spring Will Be a Little Late This Year, Brotherhood of Man

A benefit concert presented in two acts.

SYNOPSIS This benefit for the Actors Fund celebrated the heralded composer and lyricist Frank Loesser, featuring dozens of Broadway's best performing numbers from the Loesser Broadway catalogue, including *Guys and Dolls*, *How to Succeed in Business Without Really Trying*, *The Most Happy Fella*, *Where's Charley*, *Greenwillow*, as well as many of his standards from feature films such as *Hans Christian Anderson*, *Neptune's Daughter*, *Some Like It Hot*, and *The Perils of Pauline*.

Brian Stokes Mitchell and the Company of Chance and Chemistry: A Centennial Celebration of Frank Loesser *(photo by Lyn Hughes)*

Bernadette Peters: A Special Concert

For Broadway Barks Because Broadway Cares

Minskoff Theatre; November 9, 2009

Produced by Broadway Cares/Equity Fights AIDS (Tom Viola, Executive Producer; Patty Saccente, Scott T. Stevens, and Scott Tucker, Producers); Director, Richard Jay-Alexander; Musical Director, Marvin Laird; Production Managers, Michael Flowers, Nathan Hurlin; Production Stage Manager, Richard Hester; Sound, Tom Sorce; Lighting, Lenny Cowles; Ms. Peters' Gowns, Bob Mackie; Ms. Peters' Hair, Maury Hopson; Stage Managers, Pamela Remler, Kimberly Russell, Andrew Serna, Rachel Wolff; Music Contractor, David Lai; Marketing, Bobby McGuire; Graphics, Brian Schaaf; BC/EFA Website, Roy Palijaro; Associate Production Manager, Michael Palm; Assistant Director, Christopher J. Berens; Ms. Peters & Broadway Barks Web Design, David Risley; Press, Judy Katz, Boneau/Bryan-Brown

Bernadette Peters (photo by Peter James Zielinski)

CAST Bernadette Peters; Featuring **Kyle Barisich**, **Joy Franz**, **Merle Louise**, **Kay McClelland**, **Michael McGowan**, **Greg Mills**, **Lauren Mitchell**, **Matthew Tweardy-Torres**; Special Appearance **Mary Tyler Moore**

ORCHESTRA Marvin Laird (Conductor); Christian Hebel (Concertmaster); Katherine Livolsi-Landau, Sean Carney, Christopher Cardona, Maura Giannini, Lisa Steinberg (violins); David Blinn, Richard Brice (violas); Peter Prosser, Mairi Dorman-Phaneuf (cellos); Ralph Olsen, Mort Silver, Chris MacDonnell, Bob Magnuson, Ron Janelli (woodwinds); Bruce Eidem, Bob Suttman (trombones); Morris Kainuma (bass trombone/tuba); Matt Peterson, Dominic, Derasse, CJ Camerieri (trumpets); Russ Rizner, Bob Carlisle (horns); Bill Ellison (bass);

Barbara Biggers (harp); Joseph Thalken (piano); David Shoup (guitar); Deane Prouty (percussion); Cubby O'Brien (drums)

A benefit concert presented without intermission.

SYNOPSIS Bernadette Peters, Broadway's beloved star and tireless crusader for several causes (especially animal adoption) presented this special one-night-only concert as a fundraiser for Broadway Barks and Broadway Cares/Equity Fights AIDS. The concert featured material from her Broadway career and recordings, as well as popular songs and personal favorites by Rodgers & Hammerstein, Stephen Sondheim, and Jerry Herman among them. She also recreated the opening number from *Into the Woods* with four of her original cast members: Merle Louise, Joy Franz, Kay McClelland, and Lauren Mitchell.

The 24 Hour Plays on Broadway

American Airlines Theatre; November 10, 2009

Produced by Kevin Chinoy, Francesca Silvestri, Sarah Bisman, Lindsay Bowen, Tina Fallon, Kurt Gardner, Loius Moreno, Philip Naudé; Presented by Montblanc as a benefit for Urban Arts Partnership; Benefit Director, Anna Strout; Stage Manager, Mike Alifanz; ASMs, Bertie Michaels, Hanna Woodward; Lighting, Zack Murphy; Props, Julie Sandy, Xaq Webb; Production Management, Philip Naudé, Kelcie Beene; Volunteer Coordinators, Lou Moreno, Kathryn Pierroz; Writer's Assistants, Tony Shaff, Donald Stewart; Tech Staff, Mizell, Martin Perrin; Musical Guests, A Camp (Sweden): Nina Persson and Nathan Larson, directed by Mark Armstrong

Daily Bread by Warren Leight; Director, Lucie Tiberghien; Assistant Directors, Michelle Slonim, Rory Lipide; Cast: **Emmy Rossum, Claudie Blakley, Rosie Perez, Rachel Dratch, Billy Crudup**

Pen Play by Theresa Rebeck; Director, Peter Ellenstein; Assistant Directors, Michael Mood, Sarah Ries; Cast: **Jeremy Sisto, Gaby Hoffman, Julia Stiles, Demi Moore**

Second Option by Tina Howe; Director, Lynne Meadow; Assistant Directors, Colette Robert, Roarke Walker; Cast: **Diane Neal** (Maddy), **Leslie Bibb** (Maggie), **Liev Schreiber** (Randy), Fisher Stevens (Rusty)

Ramen Noodle by Stephen Belber; Director, Leigh Kilton-Smith; Assistant Directors, Sherri Barber, Bobby Moreno; Cast: **Jennifer Aniston** (Danielle), **David Cross** (Bing), **Brooke Shields** (Vita), **Anthony Mackie** (Mack)

And It Seems To Me A Very Good Sign... by Harrison Rivers; Director, Jessica Bauman; Assistant Directors, Alli Maxwell, Julia Grob; Cast: **Amber Tamblyn, John Krasinski, Naomi Watts, Sam Rockwell**

Furry Little Angel by Nathan Louis Jackson; Director, Josie Rourke; Assistant Directors, Lauren Keating, Amanda Joshi; Cast: **Ashton Kutcher** (Mitcher), **Michael Ealy** (Chris), **Rosario Dawson** (Olivia), **Tracie Thoms** (Alisha), **Eva Mendes** (Nikki)

Ninth annual evening of brief plays interspersed with musical performances presented in two acts.

SYNOPSIS *The 24 Hour Plays* calls for creative types to write, direct, and perform six original short plays in just under a day. The process begins at 10PM the night before the show when six writers, six directors, 24 actors, two musical guests, and a production staff gather. After casts and crews have been briefed, writers compose a ten-minute play by 7 AM the following morning, then directors return to read and select their piece. The casts meet for the first time at 8 AM and, over the next 12 hours the plays are rehearsed and produced for a live presentation at 8:00 PM, ink barely dry. The star-studded event benefited Urban Arts Partnership, which provides arts programs for New York public schools.

Gypsy of the Year Competition

Minskoff Theatre; December 7 & 8, 2009

Presented by Broadway Cares/Equity Fights AIDS; Producers, Michael Graziano, Scott Tucker, Tom Viola; Director, Kristin Newhouse; Lighting, Ryan O'Gara; Sound, Lucas Indelicato; Production Manger, Nathan Hurlin; Production Stage Manager, Jason Brouillard; Hosts: Seth Rudetsky and Julie White; Judges: Michael Cerveris, Ana Gasteyer, John Glover, Montego Glover, Paul Libin, Marcia Milgrom Dodge, Jim Norton, Marion Duckworth Smith; Judge Introductions: Daniel Craig, Hugh Jackman; Awards Presentation: Bernadette Peters, Michael McKean; Sponsors, Continental Airlines and *The New York Times*

Kenway Kua and Samantha Zack from the cast of Wicked *present a number in the 21st Annual Gypsy of the Year (photo by Peter James Zielinski)*

HIGHLIGHTS Opening Number created by Melissa Mahon, Sean McKnight and Seth Farber, a parody of "So You Think You Can Dance", featuring Christopher Sieber, Mary Birdsong and Bernie Telsey; *Newsical* ("Boy In The Balloon"); *Naked Boys Singing* ("Something Better Than Naked"); *Mary Poppins* ("Colors For A Cause"); The cast of *Jersey Boys;* Dancers Responding To AIDS; Classical Action featuring pianist Natasha Paremski; National Tours Presentation ("Your Side"); *Mamma Mia!* ("Mamma Mia Goes Acoustic"); *Chicago* ("9th Avenue Story"); *Hair* ("The Trip"); *Rock of Ages* ("Heartless"); *Wicked* ("In Your Own Grace"); The cast of *Bye Bye Birdie; Superior Donuts* ("Pigs-Malion"); *In The Heights/Avenue Q* ("Shafrika, The White Girl"); *Billy Elliot* ("Good Night and Thank You"); *West Side Story* ("Gypsy Nation")

COMPETITION Winner: *Chicago*; Runner-up: *West Side Story*

FUNDRAISING Total for 60 participating Broadway, Off-Broadway, and National Touring Companies: **$4,630,695** (All time record total); All Time Top Fundraiser: *A Steady Rain* ($1,549,952); Broadway Top Fundraiser: *The Phantom of the Opera* ($161,060); First Runner-up: *Billy Elliot The Musical* ($153,677); Second Runner-up: *Hair* ($153,648); Third Runner-up: *Wicked* ($147,611); Top Broadway Play: *Superior Donuts* ($76,309); Off-Broadway Top Fundraiser: *Avenue Q* ($27,917); National Touring Shows Top Fundraiser: *Rent* ($242,383); First Runner-up: *Wicked* – Emerald City Tour ($237,000); Second Runner-up: *Jersey Boys*–Sherry Tour ($225,225); Third Runner-up: *Jersey Boys*–Chicago ($190,466)

SYNOPSIS 21st annual talent and variety show presented without intermission. The *Gypsy of the Year Competition* is the culmination of a period of intensive fundraising where New York's most talented "gypsies," chorus members from Broadway and Off-Broadway shows, join in a competition variety show as six weeks of intensive fundraising by the community comes to a close. Since 1989, 21 editions of the *Gypsy of the Year* have raised a combined total of $35,730,000 for Broadway Cares/Equity Fights AIDS.

Broadway Backwards 5

Vivian Beaumont Theatre; February 22, 2010

Created, written and directed by Robert Bartley, with special material written by Danny Whitman; Presented by The Lesbian, Gay, Bisexual & Transgender Community Center and Broadway Cares/Equity Fights AIDS; Executive Producer, Tom Viola; Producers, Scott Tucker, Michael Graziano, Danny Whitman; Associate Producer, Trisha Doss; Music Director, Wayne Barker; Associate Director & Choreographer, Penny Ayn Maas; Lighting, Paul D. Miller; Costumes, David Withrow; Sound, Marc Salzberg; Production Manager, Nathan Hurlin; Associate Production Manager, Michael Palm; Production Stage Manager, Justin Scribner; Stage Manager, David Sugarman; Arrangements/Orchestrations, Wayne Barker, Fred Barton, Jeffrey Biering, Joshua Clayton, Chris Kong, Larry Moore, Kim Scharnberg, Jeffrey Thomson, Chris Tilley; Assistant Stage Managers, Michael Alifanz, Nathan K. Claus, Susan Davison, Matt DiCarol, Jonathan Donahue, Colyn Fiendel, Mary Kathryn Flynt, Thomas J. Gates, Kelly Glasow, Jamie Greathouse, Richard Hester, Bart Kahn, Angela F. Kiessel, Andrea Jo Martin, Kelly McGrath, Kathryn L. McKee, Shelley Miles, John Murdock, Jessica Pollack, Liz Reddick, Sara Sahin, Anna Trachtman, Katherine Wallace, Chris Zaccardi; Assistant to the Director, Ward Billeisen, Lisa Raze; Guest Choir, Youth Pride Chorus (Wes Webb, Artistic Director; Matthew Fetbrandt, Associate Musical Director); Production Assistant, Brianne Mavis; Dance Captains, Ward Billeisen, Antoinette DiPietropolo, Patrick O'Neill, Jeff Siebert; Fight Choreographer, Joshua Buscher; Fight Captain, Philip D'Amore; Voice of Goddess, Sue Gilad; Contractor, David Lai; Assistant Lighting, Cory Pattak; Associate Costumes, Samantha Burrows;

CAST Host **Florence Henderson**; Starring **Nick Adams, Martine Allard, Gary Beach, Timothy W. Bish, Tituss Burgess, Dan Butler, Mario Cantone, Len Cariou, Robert Cuccioli, Raul Esparza, Tony Goldwyn, Ann Harada, Valerie Harper, Hunter Ryan Herdlicka, Richard Kind, Aaron Lazar, Michele Lee, Julia Murney, Becki Newton, Anthony Nunziata, Will Nunziata, Adam Perry, Tonya Pinkins, Eve Plumb, Lee Roy Reams, Marion Ross, Seth Rudetsky, Lea Salonga, Douglas Sills, Roma Torre and Bruce Vilanch** ; With **Kristi Ambrosetti, Beckley Andrews, Barbara Angeline, Danny Beiruti, Ward Billeisen, Michelle Blakely, Tiffan Borelli, Adam Brozowski, Jason Michael Butler, Richard Costa, Allison Couture, Brendan Cyrus, Philip D'Amore, Amy Deckerm Veronica DiPerna, Antoinette DiPietropolo, Jennifer Evans, Kelli Gautreau, Hollye Gilbert, Ashley Puckett Gonzales, Aaron Hamilton, Scott McLean Harrison, Lindsey Holloway, Carly Hughes, Aaron Kaburick, John-Charles Kelly, Kurt Kleinmann, Stephanie Klemons, Charis Leos, Sabra Lewis, Kevin Loreque, Kristin Maloney, Tim McGarrigal, Marla Mindelle, Rachael Nelson, Patrick O'Neill, Masaya Palmer, Alfie Parker, Elizabeth Racanelli, Antuan Raimone, Thomas Rainey, Lisa Raze, Jody Reynard, Danielle Erin Rhodes, Greg Roderick, Kiira Schmidt, Dan Stone, Shonte Walker, Correy West**

ORCHESTRA Wayne Barker (Conductor/piano), Kerry Meads (drums), Kris Rogers (bass), Fred Rose (cello), Christine MacDonnell, Mikki Ryan & Rick Walburn (reeds), Colin Brigstocke & John Trombetta (trumpets), Mike Engstrom (trombone), Barbara Biggers (harp), Deanna Prouty (percussion)

MUSICAL NUMBERS "Paris Original" (*How to Succeed in Business Without Really Trying*): Robert Cuccioli and Valerie Harper (with Ann Harada and Anthony and Will Nunziata); "Shipoopi" (*The Music Man*): Florence Henderson, Richard

Kind; "Marian the Librarian" (*The Music Man*): Becki Newton; "What Is It About Her?" (*The Wild Party*): Julia Murney; "Come Up to My Place" (*On the Town*): Dan Butler and Hunter Ryan Herdlicka; "I'm Not At All In Love" (*The Pajama Game*): Gary Beach; "I Remember It Well" (*Gigi*): Len Cariou and Lee Roy Reams; "Too Many Mornings" (*Follies*): Tonya Pinkins; "Conga" (*Wonderful Town*): Tony Goldwyn; "As Long As He Needs Me" (*Oliver!*): Aaron Lazar; "My Gentle Young Johnny" (*Tenderloin*): Nick Adams, Danny Beiruti; "There's Gotta Be Something Better Than This" (*Sweet Charity*): Nick Adams, Timothy W. Bish; "Waltz" Kristi Ambrosetti, Beckley Andrews; "I Could Have Danced All Night" (*My Fair Lady*): Douglas Sills; "Johanna" (*Sweeney Todd*): Martine Allard; "Tom, Dick or Harry" (*Kiss Me, Kate*): Bruce Vilanch; "Secret Love"/"The Girl Next Door" (*Calamity Jane/Meet Me in St. Louis*): Michele Lee; "The Man That Got Away" (*A Star Is Born*): Raul Esparza; "Out There" (*The Hunchback of Notre Dame*): Lea Salonga; "Where You Are" (*Kiss of the Spider Woman*): Mario Cantone; "Luck Be a Lady" (*Guys and Dolls*): Florence Henderson; "Children Will Listen" (*Into the Woods*): Tituss Burgess

SYNOPSIS Fifth annual benefit concert presented in two acts; dedicated to . Conceived by Robert Bartley in 2006, *Broadway Backwards* features men singing women's songs, women singing men's songs, and same sex duets.

Florence Henderson in Broadway Backwards 5
(photo by Peter James Zielinski)

Sondheim 80

Studio 54 and New York Hilton; March 22, 2010

Presented by Roundabout Theatre Company (Todd Haimes, Artistic Director); Director, Paul Gemignani; Original Tribute Songs by Tom Kitt, Brian Yorkey, Michael John LaChiusa, Andrew Lippa, Lin-Manuel Miranda, Duncan Sheik, Robert Lopez, Kristen Anderson-Lopez, Jeanine Tesori, David Lindsay-Abaire; Technical Director, John J. Gordon; Sound Consultant, Dan Moses Schreier; Stage Manager, Beverly Jenkins; Gala Honorary Chairs, Barry Diller and Diane von Furstenberg, Bernadette Peters; Gala Chairs, Michael T. Cohen, Martin and Perry Granoff, Tom and Diane Tuft; Vice Chairs, Edward and Betsy Cohen, Micke and Pilar de Graffenried, Mark R. Fetting and Georgia D. Smith, Ted and Mary Jo Shen

CAST *Sondheim on Sondheim*: **Barbara Cook**, **Vanessa Williams**, **Tom Wopat**, **Leslie Kritzer**, **Norm Lewis**, **Euan Morton**, **Erin Mackey**, **Matthew Scott**; Dinner Birthday Tribute Performers **Bernadette Peters**, **Kelli O'Hara**, **Rita Moreno**

SYNOPSIS Legendary composer Stephen Sondheim turned 80 on Monday, March 22, 2010 and celebrated the occasion with Roundabout's 2010 Spring Gala: *Sondheim 80* that began with an early preview performance of *Sondheim on Sondheim*. From his first Broadway shows such as *West Side Story* and *Gypsy*, to his genre-defying work such as *Company*, *Sweeney Todd* and *Into the Woods*, to his complex later work like *Passion* and *Road Show*, Sondheim has redefined the possibilities of musical theatre. At Artists from across the spectrum of his career gathered to pay tribute to this musical giant at birthday dinner with special performances by some of Broadway's greatest talent. Roundabout has had a long relationship with Stephen Sondheim having produced five Tony Award nominated Sondheim revivals including *Company* (1995), *Follies* (2001), Tony Award winning *Assassins* (2004), *Pacific Overtures* (2004) and *Sunday in the Park with George* (2008), a concert reading of *A Little Night Music* (2009) starring Natasha Richardson, Victor Garber and Vanessa Redgrave at Studio 54, and the the current production of *Sondheim on Sondheim*. In 2005, Roundabout honored Sondheim with the Jason Robards Award for Excellence in Theatre for the indelible impact his life's work has made on the theatre world. At the curtain call of this event, Mr. Sondheim was brought onstage with longtime collaborators James Lapine and John Weidman who announced that in September 2010 the Henry Miller's Theatre would be renamed the Stephen Sondheim Theatre.

Vanessa Williams, Stephen Sondheim, and Barbara Cook at the Sondheim 80 *benefit for the Roundabout Theatre Company (photo by Peter James Zielinski)*

Corbin Bleu and the cast of In the Heights *present a number in the 24th Annual* Easter Bonnet Competition *(photo by Peter James Zielinski)*

Easter Bonnet Competition

Minskoff Theatre; April 26 & 27, 2010

Written by Jody O'Neil and Eric Kornfeld; Presented by Broadway Cares/Equity Fights AIDS; Executive Producer, Tom Viola; Producers, Michael Graziano, Scott Tucker; Director, Kristin Newhouse; Sound, Alain Van Achte; Lighting, Martin E. Vreeland; Production Manager, Nathan Hurlin; Production Stage Manager, Valerie Lau-Kee Lai; Stage Managers, Terry Alexander, Christine Daly, Thom Gates, Bess M. Glorioso, Bart Kahn, Jennifer Rodgers, David Sugarman, Jason Trubitt, Nancy Wernick; Associate Producer, Trisha Doss; Hosts: Dylan Baker, Corbin Bleu, Colman Domingo, Chad Kimball, Ron Kunene, Leigh Ann Larkin, Tshidi Manye, Constantine Maroulis, Jan Maxwell, Laura Osnes, Emily Padgett, Loretta Ables-Sayre, Michael Urie; Award Presentations: Nathan Lane, Bebe Neuwirth, Catherine Zeta-Jones; Judge Introductions: Hunter Foster, Robert Britton Lyons, Elizabeth Stanley; Sponsored by The New York Times and Continental Airlines

HIGHLIGHTS Opening Number ("Broadway Goes Gaga"): Director, Nick Demos, Choreographer, Shea Sullivan, Associate Choreographer and Director, Pamela Remler, Musical Director, Ben Cohn; Lyrics by Bill Russell; Additional Lyrics, The Creative Team; Featuring 106 year old Ziegfield Follies dancer, Doris Eaton Travis; *La Cage Aux Folles* ("The Notorious and Dangerous Cagelles"); *The Phantom of the Opera* ("Phantom Phantom Bang Bang"); *Mamma Mia!* ("Spice Up Your Life!"); *In The Heights* ("Heights Cool Musical"); The company of *Wicked* paid tribute to Broadway Green Alliance with "Lets Recycle"; The National Tour Bonnet presentation "Broadway Cares Love Affair" featured choreography by Melissa Mahon and Sean McKnight, music by Stephen Sills; *R.evolución* ("Daring to say Thank You"); Leslie Jordan's *My Trip Down the Pink Carpet*; *Next Fall* ("Next Fall Goes Down"); *Zero Hour* ("The Bonnet"); The Cast of *Fela!*; *South Pacific* ("All I Really Need To Know I Learned On Broadway"); *Million Dollar Quartet* ("Peace in the Valley"); Dancers Responding to AIDS ("Charlie's Angels"); *Billy Elliot* ("The Stars Look Down…in West Virginia"); *Memphis* ("Love Terrorists"); *The Lion King* ("Stringing Up Conkers"); Closing Number/Finale: Montego Glover ("Help Is On the Way," the official anthem of BC/EFA) with the finale bonnet presentation

BONNET PRESENTATION Winner: *Memphis*; First Runner-up: *Next Fall*

BONNET DESIGN AWARD *Fela!* (Created by Alfi McClendon, Chon Judson, Jill Vallery, Rujeko Dumbutshena and Catherine Foster)

FUNDRAISING Total for 64 participating Broadway, Off-Broadway, and National Touring Companies: **$3,265,700**; Top Fundraising Award: *Wicked*-Munchkinland Tour ($251,332); Broadway Top Fundraiser: *Wicked* ($208,880); First Runner-up: *The Phantom of the Opera* ($153,444); Second Runner-up: *Billy Elliot The Musical* ($34,642); Third Runner-up: *In the Heights* ($117,660); Fourth Runner-up: The Lion King (114,684); Broadway Play: Next Fall ($49,946); Off-Broadway Top Fundraiser: *Avenue Q* ($22,326); National Touring Shows Top Fundraiser: *Wicked*- Emerald City Tour ($239,883) First Runner-up: *Jersey Boys* – Sherry Tour ($142,434); Second Runner-up: *Wicked*-San Francisco ($131,815); Third Runner-up: *Mary Poppins* ($128,553)

SYNOPSIS Twenty-forth annual talent and variety show presented without intermission. The *Easter Bonnet Competition* is the two-day Broadway spectacular that features the companies of more than 20 Broadway, Off-Broadway and touring productions singing, dancing, comedic sketches and donning hand-crafted original Easter bonnets. This annual Broadway tradition is the culmination of six intensive weeks of fundraising efforts by Broadway, Off-Broadway, and national touring productions. Since 1987, 24 editions of the *Easter Bonnet Competition* have raised over $42,000,000 for Broadway Cares/Equity Fights AIDS, which, in turn, has supported programs at the Actors Fund including the AIDS initiative, The Phyllis Newman Women's Health Initiative, as well as over 400 AIDS and family service organizations across the country.

Original Ziegfeld Follies Chorus Girl Doris Eaton Travis opens the Easter Bonnet Competition *(photo by Peter James Zielinski)*

OFF-BROADWAY

June 1, 2009–May 31, 2010

Top: *Tyne Daly, Rosie O'Donnell, Samantha Bee, Katie Finneran, and Natasha Lyonne* in Love, Loss, and What I Wore. *Opened at the Westside Theatre (Downstairs) October 1, 2009 (photo by Carol Rosegg)*

Center: *The Cast of* Dreamgirls. *Opened at the Apollo Theatre November 22, 2009 (photo by Joan Marcus)*

Bottom: *Nick Westrate and Jonathan Hammond in the Transport Group's* The Boys in the Band. *Opened at 37 W. 26th Street Penthouse February 21, 2010 (photo by Carol Rosegg)*

A Transcendent Off-Broadway Season

Linda Buchwald

For proof of the strength of the 2009–2010 Off-Broadway season, one can begin by looking at the 2010–2011 Broadway season, which began by resembling the previous Off-Broadway season. *The Scottsboro Boys* transferred to the Lyceum Theatre in the fall of 2010 after a sold-out Vineyard Theatre run in March and April. *Bloody Bloody Andrew Jackson* opened to rave reviews at the Bernard B. Jacobs Theatre after three extensions at the Public Theatre, where it ran from April to June 2010. *Brief Encounter* played St. Ann's Warehouse in December 2009 before moving to Studio 54 as part of Roundabout Theatre Company's fall Broadway season.

In what most critics considered to be a weak season for Broadway musicals, two new Off-Broadway musicals made the biggest impression. John Kander and Fred Ebb's final collaboration, *The Scottsboro Boys*, a minstrel musical about the 1931 Scottsboro case, received mostly positive reviews and went on to win Lucille Lortel Awards for outstanding musical and choreographer (Susan Stroman), a Drama Desk Award for outstanding lyrics, and tied with *Bloody Bloody Andrew Jackson* for the Outer Critics Circle Award for outstanding new Off-Broadway musical.

The irreverent *Bloody Bloody Andrew Jackson*—an emo take on our seventh president, with music and lyrics by Michael Friedman and book by Alex Timbers—was embraced by critics with Ben Brantley calling it "the most entertaining and perceptive political theater of the season." It also won the 2010 Drama Desk Award for outstanding book of a musical.

Kneehigh Theatre Company's *Brief Encounter* (Emma Rice's adaptation of Noel Coward's *Still Life* and the screenplay of *Brief Encounter*) charmed critics with its whimsical staging, combining film projections, live action, and puppets. In Joe Dziemianowicz's review for the *Daily News*, he wrote, "The most blissfully entertaining and inventive show in town isn't running on or off Broadway. Or anywhere near it for that matter. It's in DUMBO at St. Ann's Warehouse."

Rumors of other Off-Broadway transfers have yet to come to fruition. In March, the *New York Times* reported that producer Robert Fox was interested in transferring Classic Stage Company's *Venus in Fur* to Broadway, but talks of that transfer have not resurfaced. The two-hander by David Ives, which ran from January to March 2010, took place at an audition where the upper hand switched between playwright and actress. The show was most notable for launching the career of Nina Arianda, who received rapturous reviews, one of the most talked-about debuts of the season, and a Theatre World Award.

Signature Theatre Company's *The Orphans' Home Cycle* was one of the best-received Off-Broadway plays of the year. Horton Foote's nine-play (in three installments) epic about growing up in Texas ran from November 2009 to May 2010 (after multiple extensions). Though the show was rumored for Broadway, Hallie Foote recently announced that a Broadway transfer will definitely not occur during the 2010-2011 season, citing the economic risk of theatre marathons in these still difficult times as the primary reason, but an eventual Broadway run is not out of the question. The play won a Lucille Lortel Award for outstanding play, a New York Drama Critics Circle Award for best play, a special Drama Desk citation for "the theatrical event of the season," Outer Critics Circle Awards for outstanding new Off-Broadway play and outstanding director of a play (Michael Wilson), and a Theatre World Award for Bill Heck, who is starring in Signature Theatre Company's next hot-ticket marathon event *Angels in America*, part of its 2010–2011 season.

Though a 2010-2011 Broadway transfer was announced for York Theatre Company's *Yank!* with David Cromer at the helm, it has been postponed until at least the 2011–2012 season. The musical, with music by Joseph Zellnik and book and lyrics by his brother David Zellnik, opened in February 2010. With its story about a gay relationship between two American soldiers during World War II, *Yank!* was one of a string of Off-Broadway productions with gay themes.

In the February 22, 2010 *New York Times* article "New Gay Theater Has More Love Than Politics," Patrick Healy wrote, "A new breed of plays and musicals this season is presenting gay characters in love stories, replacing the direct political messages of 1980s and '90s shows like *The Normal Heart* and *Angels in America* with more personal appeals for social progress . . . The politics of these shows—there are seven of them opening in New York in the next several weeks—are subtler, more nuanced: they place the everyday concerns of Americans in a gay context, thereby pressing the case that gay love and gay marriage, gay parenthood and gay adoption are no different from their straight variations." Though *Yank!* proved to be timely with the imminent repeal of Don't Ask Don't Tell, it wasn't overtly political, instead focusing on the sweet love story at its heart.

As *Yank!* gave audiences a glance at life for gay men during World War II, *The Temperamentals* by Jon Marans shed light on a little-known aspect of gay history, the Mattachine Society, founded by Harry Hay and Rudi Gernreich in the '50s. The play sold out its run in 2009 at the Barrow Group's Theater's Black Box Studio and later TBG's larger space. It began its New World Stages run in February 2010 and closed in May. Michael Urie won a Lucille Lortel Award for outstanding lead actor and a Theatre World Award, and the cast was awarded a Drama Desk for outstanding ensemble performances.

MCC Theatre's *The Pride* by Alexi Kaye Campbell also offered a historical perspective on gay life as it shifted between two stories, one in 1958 and the other in 2008. Adam James won the Lucille Lortel Award for outstanding featured actor, and Andrea Riseborough won a Theatre World Award.

In another domestic portrayal of a gay couple, the New Group presented the musical *The Kid*, with music by Andy Monroe, book by Michael Zam, and lyrics by Jack Lechner. Based on Dan Savage's experience adopting a son, the musical presented the story with humor and sweetness, making it a universal story rather than one overtly about gay rights.

The Transport Group's acclaimed revival of Mart Crowley's groundbreaking 1970 play *The Boys in the Band*, which Jack Cummings III set in a site-specific apartment in Chelsea, can be seen as a counterpoint to these new depictions of gay romance with the anger and fear at the forefront of the characters' interactions. Jonathan Hammond received an Obie Award for his performance in that production.

The Boys in the Band was one of many notable revivals, starting with *Twelfth Night* as part of the Public Theater's Shakespeare in the Park season. Daniel Sullivan's balanced production with an all-star cast including Anne Hathaway, Raul Esparza, and Audra McDonald had folks camped out from early the night before to score tickets. Next, Irish Repertory Theatre's production of Eugene O'Neill's *The Emperor Jones*, with a star turn from John Douglas Thompson, ran from October to December and then transferred to the SoHo Playhouse. One of the most talked-about performances of the year also came from an Off-Broadway revival—Cate Blanchett's as the iconic Blanche DuBois in *A Streetcar Named Desire* at BAM, another tough-to-get ticket, owing to a very limited run in November and December.

The New Group's revival of Sam Shepard's *A Lie of the Mind* ran from January to March and garnered much praise for director Ethan Hawke and his cast, which featured Keith Carradine, Laurie Metcalf, Josh Hamilton, Marin Ireland, Alessandro Nivola, Maggie Siff, Frank Whaley, and Karen Young. Metcalf received an Obie Award. Though a few critics were down on Gordon Edelstein's staging of Tennessee Williams's *The Glass Menagerie* at Roundabout in a seedy hotel room, it received a mostly loving reception, especially for its cast—Judith Ivey, Patch Darragh, Keira Keeley, and Michael Mosley. It won Lucille Lortel Awards for outstanding revival and lead actress (Ivey) and a Theatre World Award for Keeley.

As for notable new works, *Circle Mirror Transformation* is certainly at the top of the list. Annie Baker's quiet play about an acting class was somewhat of a surprise hit for Playwrights Horizons, where it opened in October. The play was awarded the Obie for best new American play, Sam Gold received an Obie for direction, and the entire cast (Reed Birney, Tracee Chimo, Peter Friedman, Deirdre O'Connell, and Heidi Schreck) were awarded Obies. The cast also received a Drama Desk for outstanding ensemble performance, and Schreck earned a Theatre World Award.

Kristoffer Diaz's *The Elaborate Entrance of Chad Deity*, exploring such issues as race in America within the world of pro wrestling, was a Pulitzer finalist. After its Chicago premiere, it opened at Second Stage in May. In her *Village Voice* review, Alexis Soloski wrote about Diaz, "His language is overblown, his pop-culture references exhausting, and his comprehensive knowledge of wrestling suggests a wildly misspent youth. But his hyperactive prose dazzles, and there are some very clever ideas—about race, about cultural hegemony, about narrative—nestled just underneath that sparkle."

Critics were struck not only by the writing but by the design elements—Brian Sidney Bembridge's sets, Jesse Klug's lighting, Mikhail Fiskel's sound design, and Peter Nigrini's video projections combined to create the feel of a wrestling match, and David Woolley's fight direction made it feel all the more realistic (for a sport that is not at all real).

Another talented voice emerged, also tackling the subject of race—Tarell McCraney. His two-part *The Brother/Sister Plays* opened at the Public Theater in November and showcased his unique voice, having characters narrate in third person. In his *New York Times* review, Ben Brantley wrote, "Watching them, you experience the excited wonder that comes from witnessing something rare in the theater: a new, authentically original vision. It's what people must have felt during productions of the early works of Eugene O'Neill in the 1920s or of Sam Shepard in the 1960s." Marc Damon Johnson received an Obie Award for his performance.

As impressive as the season was, there were of course a few misses. The worst-received show of the season was *Othello*, presented by LAByrinth Theater and the Public Theatre in September 2009, directed by Peter Sellars and starring Phillip Seymour Hoffman and John Ortiz. In his zero-star review, John Simon wrote that this production "offends Shakespeare, common sense, and decency." Douglas Carter Beane's *Mr. and Mrs. Fitch*, presented by Second Stage and starring John Lithgow and Jennifer Ehle as a pair of married gossip columnists, failed to amuse critics. Playwrights Horizons' melodramatic *The Retributionists,* by Daniel Goldfarb, about Jews plotting revenge against the Germans after World War II, was also among the slammed shows.

As these shows that sound promising on paper prove, new interpretations of classics and new works can be equally risky. As Off-Broadway theatres still struggled with the aftermath of the recession, solo shows continued to be a cheap solution. The Vineyard Theatre opened its season with Colman Domingo's *A Boy and His Soul*. Although coming-of-age stories like Domingo's have been seen before, critics and audiences were captivated by his performance, which won a Lucille Lortel Award for outstanding solo show. The Second Stage presented

Anna Deavere Smith's play on health care *Let Me Down Easy*, which opened in October and was extended through January. The late Lynn Redgrave explored her family tree in *Nightingale*, presented by the Manhattan Theatre Club from October to December, and while perhaps the reviews weren't quite as glowing, it was well received. Charlayne Woodard drew in audiences and critics with her *The Night Watcher*, about the children in her life despite her lack of biological children, presented by Primary Stages at 59E59. Mike Daisey's *The Last Cargo Cult* explored the American financial system at the Public. Finally, though critics found some flaws in the writing of *Zero Hour* by Jim Brochu, they could not deny the accuracy of his depiction of Zero Mostel. It opened at St. Clement's Theatre in November and moved to DR2 for an open-ended run and then transferred again to the Actors Temple Theater, where it continues to run. The play was the Drama Desk winner for outstanding solo performance.

Another long-running Off-Broadway show, *Love, Loss, and What I Wore* by Nora and Delia Ephron, was meant to be a limited run at the Westside Theatre, but due to its popularity and critical reception, it is now an open run with a rotating cast. It won a Drama Desk Award for unique theatrical experience.

The Fantasticks, still the world's longest-running musical, celebrated its 50th anniversary in May 2010. The show, with music by Harvey Schmidt and book and lyrics by Tom Jones, is currently in the fourth year of its revival at the Snapple Theater Center.

Two long-running Broadway shows transferred to commercial Off-Broadway runs. *Avenue Q*, by Robert Lopez, Jeff Marx, and Jeff Whitty, played the Vineyard Theatre in March 2003. When it began its Broadway run in July 2003, it became the little show that could, beating *Wicked* for the Tony and selling out houses. When it closed on September 13, 2009, producer Kevin McCollum surprised audiences by announcing that the show would be moving back Off-Broadway to New World Stages. It again opened to rave reviews and continues to play today.

The 39 Steps, adapted by Patrick Barlow from the Hitchcock movie, also had an interesting trajectory. The London transfer was part of Roundabout's season when it opened at the American Airlines Theatre in January 2008. It moved from the American Airlines to the Cort Theatre in April 2008 and then finally to the Helen Hayes, where it ran from January 2009 to January 2010. When it finished its Broadway run, it too transferred to New World Stages. Time will tell whether Off-Broadway transfers become more of a trend, but it is a promising indicator that the end of a Broadway run does not necessarily signal the end of a show's New York life, and that Off-Broadway is a viable source for profitable runs.

Patrick Heusinger and Patrick Breen in the Naked Angels production of *Next Fall*. Opened at the Peter Jay Sharp Theater June 4, 2009 (photo by Carol Rosegg)

Gretchen Bieber, Kristy Cates, and Michael Thomas Holmes in the TheatreworksUSA production of Click, Clack, Moo. Opened at the Lucille Lortel Theatre July 28, 2009 (photo by Joan Marcus)

Mandy Moore and James Kautz in the Amoralists Theatre Company's
*The Pied Pipers of the Lower East Side. Opened at Theatre 80
September 10, 2009 (photo by Larry Cobra)*

The Company in Groovaloo Freestyle. *Opened at the Joyce Theatre
September 16, 2009 and reopened at the Union Square Theatre
December 8, 2009 (photo by Levi Walker)*

Malcolm Gets and Helen Stenborg in Vigil. *Opened at DR2 September
29, 2009 (photo by Carol Rosegg)*

Maggie Lakis, Cullen Titmas, Nicky, Rod, and Seth Rettberg in
Avenue Q. *Opened at New World Stages October 21, 2009
(photo by Carol Rosegg)*

Judith Ivey in The Lady With All the Answers. *Opened at the Cherry
Lane Theatre October 14, 2009 (photo by Carol Rosegg)*

Robert Stanton and Daniel Jenkins in Love Child. Opened at New World Stages October 31, 2009 (photo by Carol Rosegg)

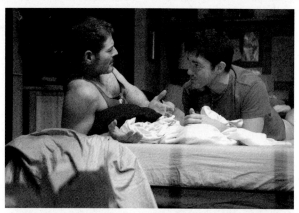

Kevin Spirtas and Scott Kerns in Loaded. Opened at the Lion Theatre on Theatre Row November 15, 2009 (photo by David Morgan)

Michael West, Christine Pedi, Rory O'Malley, and Christina Bianco in NEWSical the Musical. Opened at the 47th Street Theatre December 9, 2009 (photo by Bradley Clements)

Jim Brochu in Zero Hour. Opened at the Theatre at St. Clement's November 22, 2009 (photo by Michael Lamont)

Craig Alan Edwards in The Man in Room 306. Opened at 59E59 Theater B January 20, 2010 (photo by Pier Baccaro)

Liza Van, Sally Mayes, and Lauren Kennedy in Good Ol' Girls. *Opened at the Black Box Theatre at the Steinberg Center February 14, 2010 (photo by Carol Rosegg)*

Carol Halstead and Christina Rouner in the Red Bull Theater production of The Duchess of Malfi. *Opened at the Theatre at St. Clement's February 27, 2010 (photo by Carol Rosegg)*

Michael Urie and Thomas Jay Ryan in The Temperamentals. *Opened at New World Stages February 28, 2010 (photo by Joan Marcus)*

Brian Henson in Stuffed and Unstrung. *Opened at Union Square Theatre April 1, 2010 (photo by Carol Rosegg)*

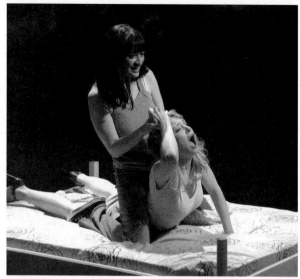

Marielle Heller and Nell Mooney in the New Georges and The Essentials production of The Diary of a Teenage Girl. *Opened at 3LD Art & Technology Center March 28, 2010 (photo by Jim Baldassare)*

Jamie Jackson, Kate MacCluggage, Cameron Folmar, and John Behlmann in Alfred Hitchcock's The 39 Steps. *Opened at New World Stages April 15, 2010 (photo by Carol Rosegg)*

Leslie Jordan in My Trip Down the Pink Carpet. *Opened at the Midtown Theatre April 19, 2010 (photo by Gustavo Monroy)*

MK Lawson and Eric William Morris in Bloodsong of Love. *Opened at Ars Nova April 15, 2010 (photo by Peter James Zielinski)*

Michael Shawn Lewis and Rachel Mouton in This Side of Paradise. *Opened at the Theatre at St. Clement's April 21, 2010 (photo by Lee Wexler)*

Max McLean in The Screwtape Letters. *Opened at the Westside Theatre (Upstairs) May 3, 2010 (photo by Johnny Knight)*

(Clockwise from top left) Rena Strober, Andrea Grano, Betty Buckley Christy Carlson Romano and Tuc Watkins in White's Lies. *Opened at New World Stages May 6, 2010 (photo by Ken Howard)*

Kate Turnbull, Hale Appleman, and Nicole Wiesner in Epic Theatre Ensemble's Passion Play. *Opened at the Irondale Center for the Arts May 12, 2010 (photo by Carol Rosegg)*

Michael Zegen and Johanna Day in stageFARM's Oliver Parker! *Opened at the Cherry Lane Theatre May 17, 2010 (photo by The Shaltzes)*

A scene from Cirque du Soleil's Banana Shpeel. *Opened at the Beacon Theatre May 21, 2010 (photo by Kristie Kahns)*

Girls Night: The Musical

Downstairs Cabaret Theatre at Sofia's; Opening Night: June 2, 2009; Closed November 22, 2009; 97 performances; Reopened January 7–February 13, 2010; 35 performances; Reopened May 6, 2010; Closed August 1, 2010; 52 performances (Weekend performances only)

Written by Louise Roche, adaptation by Betsy Kelso; Presented by Entertainment Events (Tim Flaherty, President); Original U.K. production presented by Goodnights Entertainment Ltd.; Director, Jack Randle; Production Consultant, Kurt Stamm; Musical Director, Joseph Thalken; Set, Shaun L. Motley; Costumes, Karl Ruckdeschel; Technical Advisor, Jennifer Kules; Sound/Track Design, Steve Brightwell, Douglas Oberhamer; Associate Choreography, Emily Morgan; Associate Music Director, Amy Jones; Stage Manager, Rachel Harpham/Andrew Schneider; Producing Partner, Robert Dragotta; Business Manager, Ken Flaherty; Production Supervisor, Sonya Carter; Sound Engineer, Matt Sloan; Sales Manager, Amy Payne; Marketing, Dottie Peterson; Press, David Gersten

CAST Liza **Sonya Carter**[1]; Anita **Justine Hall**[2]; Sharon **Renee Colvert**[3]; Kate **Laurie Gardner**[4]; Carol **Carly Sakolove**[5]

*Succeeded by: 1. Yvette Clark (6/23/09), Laura Saenz (1/7/10) 2. Deb Radloff (1/7/10), Christina Cataldo (1/28/10) 3. Georgia Hair (1/7/10), Priscilla Fernandez or Wilma Cespedes-Rivera (1/28/10), Tina Mallon (5/6/10) 4. Chelsea Minton (1/7/10), Laurie Gardner (5/6/10) 5. Kerrin Clark (1/7/10), Debra Toscano (1/28/10), Tina Jensen (5/6/10)

MUSICAL NUMBERS At Seventeen, Cry Me a River, Don't Cry Out Loud, Girls Just Wanna Have Fun, Holding Out for a Hero, I Am What I Am, I'm Every Woman, It's Raining Men, Lady Marmalade, The Love of My Man, Man I Feel Like a Woman, We Are Family, Young Hearts Run Free

Off-Broadway premiere of a new musical presented in two acts.

SYNOPSIS *Girls Night: The Musical* follows five friends in their 30s and 40s during a wild and outrageous girls night out at a karaoke bar. Friends since their teens, they have all had their fair share of heartache and tragedy, joy and success. Together, they reminisce about their younger days, celebrate their current lives and look to the future, all the while belting out an array of classic tunes.

Night Sky

Baruch Performing Arts Center – Rose Nagelberg Theatre; First Preview: May 22, 2009; Opening Night: June 2, 2009; Closed June 20, 2009; 12 previews, 17 performances

Written by Susan Yankowitz; Produced by Power Productions New York/Stan Raiff and the National Aphasia Association; Director, Daniella Topol; Sets, Cameron Anderson; Costumes, Katherine Roth; Lighting, Peter West; Sound/Original Music/Music Direction, Daniel Baker and Aaron Meicht/Broken Chord Collective; Casting, Geoff Josselson; PSM, Carlos Maisonette; Technical Supervisor, Randall Etheredge; General Manager, La Vie Productions/R. Erin Craig; Company Manager, Beth Reisman; Assistant Director, Chris Masullo; ASM, Jamie Rog; Props, Susanna Harris; Assistant Set, Laura Fabian; Production Manager, James Cleveland; Advertising, Eliran Murphy Group; Press, Sam Rudy Media Relations

CAST Anna **Jordan Baker**; Jennifer **Lauren Ashley Carter**; Daniel **Jim Stanek**; Bill **Tuck Milligan**; Speech Therapist/Acquaintance/Woman Friend **Maria-Christina Oliveras**; Aphasic Patient/Waiter/Ticket Seller/et al **Dan Domingues**

SETTING Present Day. Revised version of a play presented in two acts. The original version of the play premiered at the Judith Anderson Theater May 14–June 9, 1991 (see *Theatre World* Vol. 47, page 78).

SYNOPSIS *Night Sky* explores what the great physicist Stephen Hawking called the two remaining mysteries — the brain and the cosmos. The play looks at what happens to a brilliant, articulate astronomer when she is struck by a car and loses her ability to speak, a condition known as "aphasia." What emerges from her mouth is a hodgepodge of disconnected words alternately poetic, funny, confusing and profound. Anna, her loved ones, and colleagues face challenges of mind and spirit as they learn new ways to communicate, and realize what it really means to listen.

Maria-Christina Oliveras and Jordan Baker in Night Sky
(photo by Carol Rosegg)

The Cast of Girls Night: The Musical *(photo by Mark Rohna)*

Next Fall

Peter Jay Sharp Theater at Playwrights Horizons; First Preview: May 26, 2009; Opening Night: June 3, 2009; Closed August 8, 2009; 9 previews, 70 performances

Written by Geoffrey Nauffts; Presented by Naked Angels (Geoffrey Nauffts, Artistic Director; Brittany O'Neill, Managing Director); Produced by Barbara Manocherian in association with Jeff Davis and Anthony Barrile; Director, Sheryl Kaller; Sets, Wilson Chin; Costumes, Jessica Wegener; Lighting, Jeff Croiter; Sound, Bart Fasbender; PSM, Katrina Renee Hermann; ASM, Rebecca Spinac; Production Manager, David Nelson; Casting, Howie Cherpakov; Assistant Director, Andrew Neisler; Carpenter, Will Duty; Wardrobe, James Strunk; Assistant Set, Grant Yeager; Assistant Sound, Dave Sanderson; Writer's Assistant, Chris Clar; Marketing, Art Meets Commerce; Press, O+M Company, Rick Miramontez, Amanda Dekker, Elizabeth Wagner

CAST Holly **Maddie Corman**; Brandon **Sean Dugan**; Arlene **Connie Ray**; Adam **Patrick Breen**; Butch **Cotter Smith**; Luke **Patrick Heusinger**

2009–2010 AWARDS Outer Critics Circle Award: John Gassner Playwriting Award (Geoffrey Nauffts)

SETTING A hospital waiting room, an apartment, and various locations in and around New York City and Washington D.C. over the course of five years. World premiere of a new play presented in two acts. The play was extended three times from its original closing date of June 21, and transferred to Broadway February 16, 2010 (see Broadway section in this volume).

SYNOPSIS In this witty and provocative urban romance, a Christian gives an Atheist the Heimlich, and dislodges more than they bargained for. *Next Fall* chronicles the five-year relationship of Adam and Luke as they grapple with their respective demons. Timely and compelling, the play places the current Prop 8 controversy in a human context by examining what it means to "believe" in this day and age, and what it might cost us not to.

Patrick Heusinger and Patrick Breen in Next Fall
(photo by Carol Rosegg)

The Cast of An Evening at the Carlyle *(photo by Pierre)*

An Evening at the Carlyle

Algonquin Theater; Opening Night: June 8, 2009; Closed January 5, 2010; 90 performances (Sundays, Mondays, and Tuesday evenings)

Music and lyrics by Albert M. Tapper; Presented by Tony Sportiello and Algonquin Theater Productions; Director, Tom Herman; Music Director/Arrangements, David Wolfson; Choreography, Rachelle Rak; Set, John McDermott; Costumes, Cathy Small; Lighting, Brant Thomas Murray; Sound, Josh Liebert; Stage Manager, Amanda Cynkin; Assistant Director, Melinda Prom; General and Production Management, Pierre Weidemann, Jason Hewitt; Casting, Ten Grand Productions; ASM, Kelly McGrath; Music Copying & Preparation, Brett Macias

CAST Roommate/Carlyle Girl/Ann/Barbara/Lover/Liza **Amanda Gabbard**; Tommy **Dennis Holland**; Barfly **Kelli Maguire**; Roommate/CEO/Lover/Sinatra Wannabe **Michael F. McGuirk**; Herself **Rachelle Rak**; Yoke/The Donald/Yankee Fan **Jason Rowland**

SETTING The Present. Bemelmans Bar at the Hotel Carlyle, New York City. World premiere of a new musical revue presented without intermission. Presented as an Off-Off-Broadway showcase June 8–30, but immediately extended under an Off-Broadway contract.

SYNOPSIS During an evening at the Carlyle Hotel's famed Bemelmans Bar, veteran bartender Tommy encounters an eclectic, humorous, and occasionally infuriating variety of New Yorkers: neurotic barflies, frustrated renters, Sondheim haters and Sinatra fanatics, ex-con executives, thwarted lovers, and even a surprise celebrity or two.

The Temperamentals

TBG Theater; Opening Night: June 10, 2009; Closed August 23, 2009; 76 performances

Written by Jon Marans; Produced by ManUnderdog LLC and Daryl Roth with production support provided by The Barrow Group; Director, Jonathan Silverstein; Set and Costumes, Clint Ramos; Lighting, Josh Bradford; Sound, Daniel Kluger; Musical Consultant, Aaron Dai; Fight Director, Ron Piretti; Dialect Coach, Diego Daniel Pardo; Graphic Design, Adrian Sie; PSM, Samone B. Weissman; ASM, Paloma Pilar; Company Manager, Porter Pickard; Assistant Director, James Stover; Assistant Set, Craig Napoliello; Assistant Costumes, Nicole Wee; Board Operator, Stephen Fontana; Press, Kevin P. McAnarney/KPM Associates

CAST Harry Hay **Thomas Jay Ryan**; Rudi Gernreich **Michael Urie**; Chuck Rowland and others **Tom Beckett**; Bob Hull and others **Matthew Schneck**; Dale Jennings and others **Sam Breslin Wright**

2009–2010 AWARDS Lucille Lortel Award: Outstanding Lead Actor in a Play (Michael Urie); **Theatre World Award**: Michael Urie

SETTING Time: Early 1950s; Place: Various locations around Los Angeles. Transfer of a new Off-Off Broadway play presented in two acts. Previously presented in TBG Studio Theater April 30–May 18 (Opened May 4 playing 5 previews and 11 performances –see *Theatre World* Vol. 65, page 255), and due to overwhelming demand, the play announced the transfer to the larger theatre. The show reopened at New World Stages for a commercial run on February 28, 2010 (see additional listing in this section).

SYNOPSIS *The Temperamentals* tells the story of two men –the communist Harry Hay and the Viennese refugee and designer Rudi Gernreich–who fall in love while building the first gay rights organization in the U.S. (The Mattachine Society) long before the Stonewall Riots. The play weaves together the personal and political to tell a relatively unknown chapter in gay history and explores the love between the two complex men, as their impossible dream of forming such an unheard of organization becomes a realities. The characters are based on the actual founders of the Society who overcame epic struggles to make history.

Front: David Ryan Smith; rear: Kevin Townley, Gilad Ben-Zvi, and Hannah Cheek in #9 *(photo by Ryan Jensen)*

#9

59E59 Theater C; First Preview: June 5, 2009; Opening Night: June 11, 2009; Closed June 28, 2009; 17 performances

Devised and presented by Waterwell as part of the 2009 Americas Off-Broadway Festival; Produced by 59E59 (Elizabeth Kleinhans, President and Artistic Director; Peter Tear, Executive Producer); Director, Tom Ridgely; Music, Lauren Cregor; Choreography, Monica Bill Barnes; Set, Nick Benacerraf; Lighting, Stacey Boggs; Sound, Chris Rummel; Costumes, Elizabeth Payne; Video, Alex Koch; Titles, Brian McMullen; Stage Manager, Robert Signom III; Company Interns, Marianne Broome, Jenna Mannix; Press, Karen Greco

CAST Hanna Cheek, **Matt Dellapina**, **David Ryan Smith**, **Kevin Townley**; Musicians **Lauren Cregor**, **Gilad Ben-Zvi**

World premiere of a new theatrical multimedia piece with music presented without intermission.

SYNOPSIS Brilliant innovations allow people to give and get information, share opinions and express feelings in ways that were unimaginable six years ago. In some ways this is great progress. In other ways it is massive regression. *#9* explores these web 2.0 technologies and how they transform identities and relationships. Music, movement and text combine to convey the experiences of four friends in a strange, bewildering world of cyber-immersion.

Thomas Jay Ryan and Michael Urie in The Temperamentals *(photo by Michael Portantiere/FollowSpotPhoto.com)*

Dov and Ali

Cherry Lane Studio Theatre; First Preview: June 5, 2009; Opening Night: June 12, 2009; Closed June 27, 2009; 6 previews, 15 performances

Written by Anna Ziegler; Presented by The Playwrights Realm; Director, Katherine Kovner; Sets, Steven C. Kemp; Costumes, Oana Botez-Ban; Lighting, Traci Klainer; Composer/Sound, Daniel Kluger; Stage Manager, Joanne E. McInerney; ASM, Denise Cadarelli; Casting, Stephanie Klapper; Production Manager, Janio Marrero; Press, Sam Rudy Media Relations

CAST Ali **Utkarsh Ambudkar**; Sonya **Heidi Armbruster**; Sameh **Anitha Gandhi**; Dov **Adam Green**

SETTING A high school classroom in Detroit; the present. American premiere of a new play presented without intermission. World premiere in London at Theatre503 June 10, 2008.

SYNOPSIS Once upon a time, in the middle of a school, in the middle of Detroit, in the middle of the United States of America, there was a confused teacher and a precocious student. When Dov, an orthodox Jew and Ali, a strict Muslim, get caught in a cultural crossfire, both are confronted with the same choice: will they stand by their beliefs or face the devastating consequences?

Anitha Gandhi and Utkarsh Ambudkar in Dov and Ali
(photo by Erik Pearson)

FUBAR, or Interesting, Incredible, Amazing, Fantastic

59E59 Theater B; First Preview: June 11, 2009; Opening Night: June 16, 2009; Closed June 28, 2009; 13 performances

Written by Karl Gajdusek; Presented by Project Y Theatre Company (Andrew Smith, Producing Artistic Director/Producer; Michole Biancosino, Artistic Director/Producer) as part of the 2009 Americas Off-Broadway Festival; Produced by 59E59 (Elizabeth Kleinhans, President and Artistic Director; Peter Tear, Executive Producer); Director, Larissa Kokernot; Lighting, Ben Hagen; Set, Kevin Judge; Costumes, Emily Pepper; Sound/Composer, Amit Prakash; Projections, Shawn Boyle; Fight Director, Adam Alexander; Production Manager, Christopher Rinaldi; Stage Manager, John Nehlich; ASM, Nicole Rizzo; Assistant Fight Director, Helen McTernan; Assistant Costumes, Melanie Swersey; Casting, Judy Bowman; Marketing/Media, Emily Voorhees; Marketing Assistant, Teresa Stephenson; Press, Karen Greco

CAST Mary **Lisa Velten Smith**; David **Jerry Richardson**; Richard **Ryan McCarthy**; Sylvia **Stephanie Szostak**; DC **Dan Patrick Brady**

SETTING San Francisco; the present. New York premiere of a new play presented in two acts. World premiere at Theatre of Note (Los Angeles) April 24–May 30, 2009.

SYNOPSIS Mary and David live in a small apartment crammed full of boxes her abused mother left behind. When Mary is the victim of random violence, it leads the two of them down different paths of addiction and reconciliation. Meanwhile, Richard is a benevolent drug dealer working on a book while Sylvia uses the internet to lead a double life. These four people try to recognize the people they have become in a time that is totally *FUBAR* (f****d up beyond all recognition).

Jerry Richardson, Lisa Velten Smith, and Stephanie Szostak in FUBAR
(photo by Felix Photography)

Summer Solo Series

Soho Playhouse; Opening Night: June 18, 2009; Closed August 4, 2009; 14 evenings

Produced by Soho Playhouse (Scott Morfee and Darren Lee Cole) and Barrow Street Theater; Series included: *mother load* written and performed by Amy Wilson; Director, Julie Kramer (June 18); *The Tricky Part* written and performed by Martin Moran; Director, Seth Barrish (June 22); *Nocturne* written and directed by Adam Rapp, performed by Dallas Roberts (June 25); *Bukowski from Beyond* written and performed by Stephen Payne, written and directed Leo Farley (June 29); *Tales from the Faucet, and Other Stories, An Evening of Solo Shorts* by Glen Berger (June 30); *The Unbearable Lightness of Being Taylor Negron* written and performed by Taylor Negron, directed by David Schweizer, music by Logan Heftel (July 7); *No Child…* written and performed by Nilaja Sun, directed by Hal Brooks (July 9); *Life in a Marital Institution* written and performed by James Braly, directed Hal Brooks (July 14); *Spalding Gray: Stories Left to Tell* words by Spalding Gray, concept by Kathleen Russo, directed by Lucy Sexton, performed by Ain Gordon, Aasif Mandvi, Carmelita Tropicana, Frank Wood (July 16); *El Conquistador* written and performed by Thaddeus Phillips, directed by Tatiana Mallarino (July 21); *Jamaica Farewell* written and performed Debra Ehrhardt, directed by Wallace Norman (July 23); *Sakina's Restaurant* written and performed by Aasif Mandvi (July 28); *In Concert: Sounds of Desire* A concert adaptation of *Nine Parts of Desire* written and performed by Heather Raffo, co-created and composed by Amir ElSaffar (July 30); *Underneath the Lintel* by Glen Berger (August 4); *That Dorothy Parker* written and performed Carol Lempert, directed by Janice L. Goldberg (August 5)

SYNOPSIS Presented in conjunction with the solo show *Krapp, 39* (written and performed by Michael Laurence and directed by George Demas which played through August 2, 2009 at Soho Playhouse–see *Theatre World* Vol. 65, page 164), the *Solo Summer Series* celebrated the best in solo performance and shows by acclaimed playwrights and performers. The one-night-only each performance series featured new works as well as some recent successful pieces that have been previously performed.

Nilaja Sun in No Child…, part of the Summer Solos Series
(photo by Carol Rosegg)

A scene from Painkillers (photo By Goran Veljic)

Painkillers

Lion Theatre on Theatre Row; Opening Night: June 19, 2009; Closed June 28, 2009; 11 performances

Written by Neda Radulovic; Presented by WorldTree Production (Serbia); Executive Producer, Nikola Ostojic; Director/Producer, Sanja Bestic; Translation, Svetozar Postic; Composer, Ana Milosavljevic; Stylist, Irena Cankovic; Set, Jakub K. Ciesielski; Costumes, Irena Cankovic; Lighting, Zoran Rapajic; Voice Coach, Thana Alexa Pavelic; Choreographer, Nada Vasilijevic; Music Arrangements, Lenart Krecic; Press, AnaMarija Stepanovich, Dejan Mirkovic

CAST The Independent One **Katarina Radivojevic**; The Married One **Tiziana Cosentino**; The Insecure One **Bridget Storm**; The Husband **Toni Naumovski Rotino**; Violinist **Ana Milosavljevic**

SETTING Belgrade, the recent past and present. U.S. premiere of a new play presented without intermission. World premiere at the Serbian National Theatre.

SYNOPSIS *Painkillers* examines the discord between our aspirations and our reality while taking a closer look at the emotional conflict it creates. The drama explores the lives we live versus the lives we want to live as the characters struggle with loneliness, the frustration with conventional and traditional codes of conduct, and understanding themselves, and trying to embrace the best while struggling with the worst of their impulses.

Dance of the Seven Headed Mouse

Beckett Theatre on Theatre Row; First Preview: June 17, 2009; Opening Night: June 23, 2009; Closed July 26, 2009; 7 previews, 35 performances

Written by Carole Gaunt; Produced by Hungry Hill Ltd. and Agustine Welles; Director, Christopher McElroen; Set, Troy Hourie; Costumes, Victoria Gaunt; Lighting, D.M. Wood; Sound, Daniel Erdberg; Props, Morgan Eckert; PSM, Christine Fisichella; ASM, Mary E. Leach; Production Supervision, Autonomous Production Services; Casting, Judy Henderson, Kimberly Graham; Advertising/ Marketing, The Pekoe Group; General Management, Two Step Productions (Cris Buchner, Kate Mott, Amy Dalba, Rachel Merrill Moss); Company Manager, Rachel Merrill Moss; Production Technician, Wheeler B. Kincaid; Production Manager,

Amber Estes; Wardrobe, Heather Davidson; Master Electrician/Programmer, Jessica Simmons; Press, David Gersten

CAST Elly **Laura Bonarrigo**; Kevin **Joseph Adams**; Avril **Lauren Currie Lewis**; Young Molly **Maya Simkowitz**; Juliana **Molly Ephraim**

SETTING Present Day. A Fifth Avenue apartment. Scene I: A mid-September evening. Scene II through End: A weekend in February. Off-Broadway premiere of a new play presented without intermission.

SYNOPSIS The fault lines are exposed when a picture-perfect Upper East Side family faces the death of their daughter. A father turns to work to drown his sorrow, while his wife drifts into a haze of pills and booze. When their surviving child Avril drops out of her boarding school, her roommate Juliana arrives for a visit, determined to lure her back. Acting as a catalyst and witness, Juliana exposes the gaping cracks in the family's façade, forcing them engage with one another and the tragedy they share.

Laura Bonarrigo, Joseph Adams, and Lauren Currie Lewis in
Dance of the Seven Headed Mouse (photo by Carol Rosegg)

Boogie Rican Blvd: The Musical

47th Street Theatre; Opening Night: June 30, 2009; Closed July 26, 2009; 24 performances

Written by Caridad De La Luz; Presented by Urban Lifestyle Media LLC; Produced by The Puerto Rican Traveling Theatre; Director, Nelson Vásquez; Music, Willam Cepeda; Set, Manoli Galanakis; Lighting, Billy DeLace; Costumes, Urban Couture Inc.; Props, Melanie LaTorre; Stage Manager, Lidia Zambrano; Music Engineering, Ed Reed; Sound Technicians, Monica Colon, David Monroy, Kelson Vazquez; Press, Juana Guichardo

CAST Don Jose/Maribella/Pito/Cuca/Lola/Marta/Mama **Caridad De La Luz** (aka "La Bruja"); Papo **Carina De La Luz-Vazquez**; Chico **Amilcar Alfaro-Martell**; Patchy **Patricia Marte**; Eddie **Alejandro Pagan**; Johnny **Dimitri Minucci**

MUSICAL NUMBERS Boogie Rican Blvd., Sugar Papi, Semi-Hard, Lola's Highway, It's Not So Bad, My Little Diamond Baby, God Bless You Girl, Now After All I've Done, Remedio Del Chichon (Voodoo for the Boo-Boo), Cuernophobic, Boogie Rican Blvd. Finale

SETTING The Bronx, New York. Off-Broadway debut of a new musical presented in eighteen scenes without intermission

SYNOPSIS Don Jose, a bodeguero, and his family struggle between the cultural traditions of Puerto Rico traditions and the modern-day values taught on the streets of the boogie-down Bronx. The Pacheco family and their colorful collection of neighborhood friends who become their extended family, examine life, love, and respect through poetry, music and dance, keeping their chins held up, and helping each other through another day. *Boogie Rican Blvd.* explores the modern day ills of the hood, from child abuse, drug addiction and gay bashing, to teen pregnancy, abandonment, and depression in a powerful way, still holding on to the ancestral message of perseverance, spirituality, creativity, and hope.

Caridad De La Luz (at bat) and the Company in Boogie Rican Blvd: The Musical *(photo by Jaime Quiñones)*

Perfect Wedding

Bleecker Street Theatre; First Preview: July 8, 2009; Opening Night: July 12, 2009; Closed August 2, 2009; 4 previews, 21 performances

Written by Robin Hawdon; Presented by Vital Theatre Company (Stephen Sunderlin, Artistic Director; Kerry McGuire, General Manager); Director, Teresa K. Pond; Costumes, Cherie Cunningham; Set, Daniel ZS Jagendorf; Lighting, Perchik Kreilman-Miller; Stage Manager, Kristin Orlando; Fight Choreography, Jeffrey M. Bender; Company Manager, Stephanie Usis; Technical Director, Elle Sunman; Press, Stephen Sunderlin

CAST Bill **Matt Johnson**; Judy **Kristi McCarson**; Tom **Fabio Pires**; Rachel **Amber Bella Muse**; Daphne **Ghana Leigh**; Julie **Dayna Grayber**

New York premiere of a new bedroom farce presented in two acts.

SYNOPSIS *Perfect Wedding* tells the story of a bridegroom who wakes on his wedding morning in his own bridal suite to find an extremely attractive naked girl in bed beside him. But in the depths of his post stag-night hangover, he can't remotely remember her, and his bride-to-be is about to arrive any moment. The chaos that ensues reaches nuclear proportions creating a play that is a rare combination of both riotous comedy and touching love story.

Dayna Grayber, Fabio Pires, Matt Johnson, and Amber Bella Muse in Perfect Wedding *(photo by Sun Productions)*

Levittown

Theatre at St. Clement's; First Preview: July 8, 2009; Opening Night: July 13, 2009; Closed August 1, 2009; 3 previews, 16 performances

Written by Marc Palmieri; Presented by The Cliplight Theatre and the Theatre at St. Clement's; Director, George Demas; Set, Michelle Spadaro; Costumes, Jennifer Bayly; Lighting, Sonia Baidya; Sound, Steve Fontaine; PSM, Dewey Caddell; Assistant Director, Amber Voiles; Master Carpenter, Karl Allen; Casting, Jerry Beaver; Advertising, Eliran Murphy Group/Frank Fraver; Web Design, Stephen Bittrich; ASM, Amanda Martinez; Producer's Assistant, Sean Patrick Monohan; Wardrobe Assistant, Jairy Diaz; Light Board, Melissa Rosado; Sound Board, Hector Martinez; Press, Richard Kornberg

CAST Colleen **Susan Bennett**; Kevin **Tristan Colton**; Richard **Curzon Dobell**; Brian **Todd Lawson**; Joe **Tyler Pierce**; Kathleen **Deborah Tranelli**

SETTING The Levittown homes of Edmund Maddigan and Richard Briggs; 1999. Off-Broadway premiere of a new play presented in two acts. Developed at the Axis Company in 2006.

SYNOPSIS Kevin Briggs returns early from college to learn that his sister Colleen, after some trying times, is about to be married. As the family celebrates the upcoming wedding, Kevin attempts to reconcile his sister with the abusive father who left them years before. Amidst the thin walls of their home, the members of this family are forced to confront a concealed history, the self-destructive nature that has plagued them for generations, and the failure of the tidy truths onto which they have desperately held… in Levittown.

Susan Bennett, Todd Lawson, Tristan Colton, Curzon Dobell in Levittown *(photo Dixie Sheridan)*

Gretchen Bieber, Sarah Katherine Gee, Kristy Cates, Drew McVety, Demond B. Nason, and Michael Thomas Holmes in Click, Clack, Moo *(photo by Joan Marcus)*

Click, Clack, Moo

Lucille Lortel Theatre; First Preview: July 21, 2009; Opening Night: July 28, 2009; Closed August 28, 2009; 9 previews, 56 performances

Book by Billy Aronson, lyrics by Kevin Del Aguila, music by Brad Alexander; Based on the book by Doreen Cronin with illustrations by Betsy Lewin; Produced by Theatreworks USA (Barbara Pasternack, Artistic Director; Ken Arthur, Producing Director); Presented by special arrangement with the Lucille Lortel Theatre Foundation; Director, John Rando; Choreography, Wendy Seyb; Set, Beowulf Boritt; Costumes, Lor LaVon; Lighting, Matthew Richards; Sound, Jeremy Wilson; Associate Director, We Grantom; PSM, Carly J. Price; Orchestrations, Brad Alexander; Music Director/Vocal Arrangements, Justin Hatchimonji; Production Assistant, Alaina Parness; Tech Director, Richard Harrison; Production Electrician, Sheila Donovan; Props Supervisor, Lake Simons; Wardrobe Supervisor, Amy Elizabeth Bravo; Press, The Publicity Office, Jeremy Shaffer

CAST Farmer Brown/Chicken **Drew McVety**; Darlene **Gretchen Bieber**; Loretta **Michael Thomas Holmes** ; Maddie **Kristy Cates**; Duck/Chicken **DeMond B. Nason**; Jenny/Chicken **Sarah Katherine Gee**

UNDERSTUDIES Jason Dula (Farmer Brown, Loretta, Duck), Gwen Hollander (Darlene, Maddie, Jenny)

*Succeeded by Todd Buonopane (8/17/09)

MUSICAL NUMBERS The Farm of Farmer Brown, Cold, Get Down, Cows Type, Mad Cows, Loretta's Anthem, Boiled Chickens, Your Way or the Highway, Negotiation, The Farm of Farmer Brown (reprise)

New York premiere of a new children's musical presented without intermission.

SYNOPSIS All day long Farmer Brown hears "click clack moo, clickety clackety moo..." The cows are typing and protesting their working conditions! *Click, Clack, Moo* is hilariously "moo-ving" new musical about compromise, based on the acclaimed 2005 children's book *Click, Clack, Moo: Cows That Type*.

Slipping

Rattlestick Playwrights Theater; First Preview: July 28, 2009; Opening Night: August 4, 2009; Closed August 15, 2009; 7 previews, 13 performances

Written by Daniel Talbott; Presented by piece by piece productions and Rising Phoenix Repertory (Daniel Talbott, Artistic Director) in association with Rattlestick Playwrights Theater (David Van Asselt, Artistic Director; Brian Long, Managing Director); Director, Kirsten Kelly; Set, Lauren Helpern; Costumes, Chloe Chapin; Lighting, Joel Moritz; Sound/Projections, Brandon Epperson; Props/Assistant Set, Eugenia Furneaux-Arends; Advertising & Marketing, The Pekoe Group; Fight Director, Christian Kelly-Sordelet; PSM, Katrina Herrmann; Production Manager, Travis Walker; General Manager, Snug Harbor Productions; Company Manager, Jill Bernard; ASM, Melissa Gregus; Assistant Costumes, Tristan Raines; Producers, Denis Butkus, Addie Johnson, Julie Kline, Brian Roff, Samantha Soule; Press, Don Summa

CAST Eli **Seth Numrich**; Jan **Meg Gibson**; Jake **MacLeod Andrews**; Chris **Adam Driver**

SETTING A suburb of Des Moines, Iowa, 2006; San Francisco, earlier. New York premiere of a new play presented without intermission. Originally workshopped and developed at The Royal Court Theatre and Rattlestick,; world premiere at The Side Project (Chicago).

SYNOPSIS Alone, numb, and friendless after the violent death of his father, high school senior Eli moves with his mom from San Francisco to a fresh start in Iowa. A new relationship with a boy at school exposes Eli again to the possibility of closeness and the danger of being swallowed by it.

Seth Numrich and MacLeod Andrews in Slipping *(photo by Paula Court)*

The Columbine Project

Actors Temple Theatre; First Preview: July 27, 2009; Opening Night: August 9, 2009; Closed October 29, 2009; 7 previews, 48 performances

Written and directed by Paul Anthony Storiale; Presented by David & Pamela Burrus, Jessimeg Productions, and Bree Pavey; Lighting, Graham Kindred; Scenic Adaptation, Josh Iacovelli; Sound/Costumes, Bree Pavey; Stage Manager, Tristyn Curtiss; General Manager, Jessimeg Productions, Edmund Gaynes, Julia Beardsley; Associate Producer, Scott Jacobs; Graphics, Elnora Keller; Press, David Gersten, Jim Randolph, Shane Marshall Brown

CAST Eric Harris **Artie Ahr**; Crystal **Stacy Allen**; Jake **Will Baker**; Mrs. Harris/Patti Neilson **Kelli Joan Bennett**; Nate/Evan **Alex Bica**; Brooks Brown **Evan Enslow**; Isaiah Shoels **Garland Gregory**; Zach **Jesse Kove**; Mr. Harris/Mr. Sanders **Kelly McCracken**; Rich/Sheriff/Dr. Nice **Derek Meeker**; Rachel Scott **Rya Meyers**; Chris **Bradley Michael**; Dylan Klebold **Justin Mortelliti**; Mrs. Miller/Alice Sparks/Dispatcher **Bree Pavey**; Mrs. Kritch **Karen Praxel**; Seth **Morgan Roberts**; Jen/Becca **Sara Swain**; Sarah **Stephanie Weyant**; Vonda Shoels **Marguerite Wiseman**

SETTING Littleton, Colorado outside of Denver; Spring 1999. New York premiere of a new play presented in two acts. World premiere presented by Fulton Entertainment at the Avery Schreiber Theatre, North Hollywood, California in April 2009 with this cast.

SYNOPSIS On April 20, 1999, the world watched as two young men presumed to be outcasts walked into their high school and attempted to massacre hundreds of their peers. Although failing in their original mission to kill 250 students, the two teens left 12 students and a teacher fatally wounded and many others scarred for life. *The Columbine Project* examines exactly what went through the minds of several students, including the killers who at one time were just normal kids. Pulled straight from journals, diaries and information shared personally with the writer by survivors of the incident, this true story provides insight into who these children were and who may have also had a hand in cultivating the rampage that resulted in bloodshed and destruction.

Penelope Lowder, James Edward Shippy, Steve Greenstein, and Leland Gantt in …Another Man's Poison (photo by Joan Marcus)

…Another Man's Poison

Peter Jay Sharp Theater at Playwrights Horizons; Opening Night: August 12, 2009; Closed August 23, 2009; 15 performances

Written by George O. Brome; Presented by Orielle Creative Company and Broliver Productions; Producer/General Manager, Sheila L. Speller; Director, Passion Hansome; Set, Kevin Lee Allen; Costumes, Ali Turns; Lighting, Burke J. Wilmore; Sound, Sean O'Halloran; Technical Director, Dave McDaniels; Stage Manager, Bayo; ASM, Mutiyat Ade-Salu; Set Construction, Anthony Davidson; Props, Michelle Gray; Wardrobe, Anne Skeete; Press, Katie Rosen/Kampfire PR; PR/Media, Charles Rogers/Rogers Artist Media; Design and Branding, Patrick Florville, Christopher Schrank

CAST Frankie Masters/Wilhelmena **Leland Gantt**; Pauline Phillips **Penelope Lowder**; Alan Phillips **James Edward Shippy**; Mel Stein/The Policeman/TV Director's Voice **Steve Greenstein**; Sarah/Mrs. Baddly/The Assistant/Chili Chuckles/ER Nurse **Toni L. Stanton**; Dick/Mr. Howells/Will Upstage/General Principal/ER Doctor **Dennis Hearn**

SETTING 1970; Hollywood. World premiere of a new play presented in three acts with two intermissions.

SYNOPSIS …*Another Man's Poison* uncovers the irony of success, juxtaposed with the fascinating backdrop of prime time television. When Frankie Masters, a struggling comedian, gets the opportunity to have his own network television show in 1970, his imminent stardom threatens to reveal the hidden conflict and mounting turmoil of his personal life. Taking place prior to the celebrity tabloid when exposés were the norm, it takes a close look at lives intertwined—where each character confronts personal sacrifices that will forever impact them.

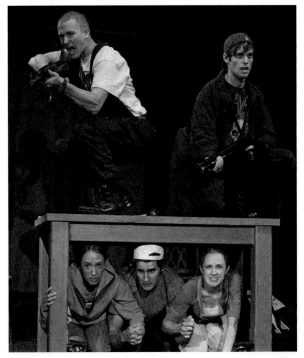

Artie Ahr, Justin Mortelitti, Stacy Allen, Morgan Roberts, and Stephanie Weyant in The Columbine Project (photo by Carol Rosegg)

The Pride of Parnell Street

59E59 Theater B; First Preview: September 1, 2009; Opening Night: September 8, 2009; Closed October 4, 2009; 32 performances

Written by Sebastian Barry; Presented by Fishamble: The New Play Company as part of the 2009 1st Irish Festival and 59E59 Theaters (Elysabeth Kleinhans, Artistic Director; Peter Tear, Executive Producer); Director, Jim Culleton; Producer, Orla Flanagan; Set/Costumes, Sabine Dargent; Lighting, Mark Galione; Composer, Denis Clohessy; PSM, Jenny Deady; Stage Manager, Eavan Murphy; Production Manager, Des Kenny; Assistant Director, Louise Lowe; Literary Manager, Gavin Kostick; Production Coordinator, Eva Scanlan; Hair/Makeup, Val Sherlock; Graphics, Gareth Jones; Press, Karen Greco

CAST Janet **Mary Murray**; Joe **Aidan Kelly**

SETTING September, 1999; Dublin. New York premiere of a new play presented without intermission. World premiere presented by Fishamble at the Tricycle Theatre (London) September 5, 2007, and then transferred to the Tivoli Theatre as part of the Ulster Bank Dublin Theatre Festival. U.S. premiere in 2008 at the International Festival of Arts and Ideas in New Haven, Connecticut.

SYNOPSIS Italy 1-Ireland 0... The score that marked Ireland's demoralizing exit from the World Cup Italia 1990 took its toll. No more so than on Janet and Joe Brady of Parnell Street, who lost far more than the match that night. Some years on, they reveal the intimacies of their love and the rupture of their marriage as well as their enduring love affair with Dublin city itself. *The Pride of Parnell Street* is an intimate, heroic tale of ordinary and extraordinary life on the streets of Dublin.

Aidan Kelly (front) and Mary Murray (back) in The Pride of Parnell Street *(photo by Patrick Redmond)*

The Pied Pipers of the Lower East Side

Theatre 80 St. Marks; Opening Night: September 10, 2009; Closed October 5, 2009; 20 performances

Written and directed by Derek Ahonen; Presented by The Amoralists; Producer, Meghan Ritchie; Set, Alfred Schatz; Lighting, Jeremy Pape; Costumes, Jeremy Pape; Sound, Bart Lucas; Stage Manager, Judy Merrick; Assistant Director, Matt Fraley; Spiritual Advisor, Larry Cobra; Fight Director, Han Mautz; Production Assistant, Rachel Adler; Press, DARR Publicity/David Gibbs

CAST Wyatt **Mathew Pilieci**; Billy **James Kautz**; Dawn **Mandy Moore**; Dear **Sarah Lemp**; Evan **Nick Lawson**; Donovan **Charles Meola**

SETTING Over the course of five days in a Lower East Side apartment/restaurant during a summer heat wave. Off-Broadway transfer of a new play presented in three acts with two intermissions. Originally presented at the Gene Frankel Theatre November 2–25, 2007 (see *Theatre World* Vol. 64, page 227). The show played a return engagement of 51 performances at P.S. 122 June 2–August 23, 2009 prior to this transfer.

SYNOPSIS An extraordinary gathering of young idealists live as a modern day urban tribe above a vegan restaurant in NYC. Billy, Dawn, Dear and Wyatt are an extended sexual family battling their fears and addictions in order to live their utopian dream. *The Pied Pipers of the Lower East Side* is a celebration of love and the search for human grandness.

The Company in The Pied Pipers of the Lower East Side *(photo by Larry Cobra)*

Groovaloo Freestyle

Joyce Theatre; First Preview: September 15, 2009; Opening Night: September 16, 2009; Closed September 27, 2009; 16 performances; Return engagement at Union Square Theatre; First Preview: December 1, 2009; Opening Night: December 8, 2009; Closed January 3, 2010; 38 performances

Conceived and created by Danny Cistone and Bradley Rapier in collaboration with The Groovaloos; Special material written by Charlie Schmidt; Presented by Big League Productions (Dan Sher, Executive Producer); Director, Danny Cistone; Choreography, The Groovaloos/Bradley Rapier; Set Consultant, Laura Fine Hawkes; Lighting, Charlie Morrison; Sound, Lucas Corrubia Jr., Michael H.P. Viveros; Costumes, Mora Stephens; Graffiti Artist, Toons One; Original Music, J. Digzdeep, Stacey Quinealty, Bigwick Entertainment, Trent Dean, Jack Oat, Fan 3, Countre Black, Laurie Anderson, Linney, Siamese Sister, Affion Crockett, Slick Dogg, Keeley Kaukimoce; Performance Audio Track Producer/Designer, Stacey Quinealty; Musical Supervision, Steven Stanton, Bradley Rapier; PSM, Thom Schilling; Associate Producers, Keith Hurd, TJ Young, Levi Walker; Show Supervisor, TJ Young; Production Manager, Pete Frye; Assistant Director, Mercedes Manning; Associate Lighting, Jeremy Rolla; ASM/Assistant Sound, Chris Williams; Original Producer, Joel Viertel; Originating Producer, Frier McCollister; New York Press, Keith Sherman and Associates, Scott Klein

CAST Spee-d **Philip Albuquerque**; Out There **Jessica Rabone**; Poe One **Jesse Brown**; RagDoll **Mary Cebrian Jurado**; LockN'Key **Cristina Benedetti**; Al Star **Kendra Andrews**; JRock **John Nelson**; Shooz **Bradley Rapier**; Kid Rainen **Jon Cruz**; Vzion **Charlie Schmidt**; BoogieMan **Steven Stanton**; Lady Jules **Bonita Lovett**; Steelo **Richard Vazquez**; Double O **Oscar Orosco**; Swings **Jaime Burgos, Anthony Cabaero, D. Sabela Grimes, Gabriel Jaochico, Penelope Vazquez**

New York premiere of a hip-hop freestyle dance theatrical piece with text and music presented without intermission.

SYNOPSIS Based on the troupe's true-to-life experiences as told by the dancers who lived them, *Groovaloo* is driven by intoxicating displays of physicality, a vibrant musical score and powerful spoken word poetry. The show's intertwined stories chronicle the struggles, hopes and triumphs of the 14-member cast. *Groovaloo* celebrates the passion and purpose of life while revealing the heart, soul and artistry of freestyle and hip-hop dance.

The Company in Groovaloo Freestyle *(photo by Levi Walker)*

In the Daylight

McGinn/Cazale Theatre; First Preview: September 8, 2009; Opening Night: September 20, 2009; Closed October 11, 2009; 11 previews, 19 performances

Written by Tony Glazer; Presented by Choice Theatricals in association with Vital Theatre Company; Director, John Gould Rubin; Producer, Summer Crockett Moore; Set, Chris Barreca; Lighting, Thom Weaver; Sound, Elizabeth Rhodes; Casting, McCorkle Casting; General Manager, CJM Productions, Cheryl Dennis; Graphics, George Allison & Michael Logsdon; Marketing, Martian Media/Steven De Luca; Special Effects, Arielle Toelke; Fight Director, Qui Nguyen; Wardrobe/Props, Barbara Janice Kielhofer & Lily Percy; PSM, Meredith Dixon; ASM, Cheryl Rubin; Production Manager, PRF Productions/Peter Feuchtwanger; Press, Springer Associates, Joe Trentacosta

CAST Jessica (Jesse) Feingold **Sharon Maguire**; Charlotte **Ashley Austin Morris**; William Feingold **Jay Patterson**; Elizabeth Feingold **Concetta Tomei**; Martin Feingold **Joe Urla**

SETTING The Feingold home. World premiere of a new play presented in two acts.

SYNOPSIS *In the Daylight* is a darkly comic tale about a well-known writer and his homecoming to a family he has been avoiding for many years. As the play unfolds we discover the true reasons for his extended absence and the dark secrets his family has been keeping.

Joe Urla, Concetta Tomei, and Sharon Maguire in In the Daylight *(photo by Gili Getz)*

The Cambria & Frederick Douglass Now

Donaghy Theatre at the Irish Arts Center; First Previews: September 16 & 17, 2009; Opening Night: September 23, 2009; Closed October 11, 2009; *The Cambria*: 5 previews, 19 performances; *Frederick Douglass Now*: 3 previews, 20 performances

The Cambria written by Donal O'Kelly; *Frederick Douglass Now* written by Roger Guenveur Smith; Presented by the Irish Arts Center (Aidan Connolly, Executive Director) in association with the Classical Theatre of Harlem (Alfred Preisser, Co-Founder/Artistic Director; Christopher McElroen, Co-Founder/Executive Director); Director (*The Cambria*), Raymond Keane; Set (*The Cambria*), Miriam Duffy; Original Music & Sound (*The Cambria*), Trevor Knight; Lighting & Sound, Ronan Fingleton; PSM, Nicole K. Press; Stage Manager, Carol A. Sullivan; Marketing, Marcia Pendelton/Walk Tall Girl Productions, Rachael W. Gilkey, Sydney Snyder, Christine Cullen; Program & Production Manager, Joanna L. Groarke; Master Electrician, Ethan Kaplan; Graphic Design, J. Kyle Manzay, Phillip Shung; Box Office/Front of House, Jen Browne; Education Coordinator, Rachael W. Gilkey; Membership Director, Sydney Snyder; Press, Karen Greco

CAST *The Cambria*: **Donal O'Kelly**, **Sorcha Fox**; *Frederick Douglass Now*: **Roger Guenveur Smith**

Two plays presented in repertory, each presented without intermission. *The Cambria* was presented last season at the Irish Arts Center (see *Theatre World* Vol. 65, page 169).

SYNOPSIS Forced to flee the U.S. after publishing his life story, Frederick Douglass sought refuge in Ireland. With false papers, and a bounty on his head from enraged slaveholders, he boarded the paddle-steamer Cambria out of Boston. *The Cambria* is the thrilling tale of the historic voyage in which Douglass's identity was revealed—placing his life in mortal danger—and how he survived to become the person Abraham Lincoln called "the most impressive man I ever met." *Frederick Douglass Now* brings to life the pioneering abolitionist and orator in a nationally acclaimed solo performance. At the core of Smith's Douglass is the fugitive slave turned statesman, whose quest for an America free of racism, sexism and economic deprivation is still, tragically, relevant.

Donal O'Kelly and Sorcha Fox in The Cambria
(photo by Susan Helbock)

Roger Guenveur Smith in Frederick Douglass Now
(photo by Susan Helbock)

Mahida's Extra Key to Heaven

Peter Norton Space; First Preview: September 16, 2009; Opening Night: September 26, 2009; Closed October 18, 2009; 10 previews, 22 performances

Written by Russell Davis; Presented by Epic Theatre Ensemble (Zak Berkman, Melissa Friedman, Ron Russell, Founding Executive Directors); Director, Will Pomerantz; Sets, Mimi Lien; Costumes, Theresa Squire; Lighting, Justin Townsend; Sound, Katie Down; PSM, Erin Maureen Koster; Stage Manager, Molly Minor Eustis; Casting, Calleri Casting; Production Manager, Jee S. Han; Assistant Production Manager, Chris Connolly; Props, Eric Reynolds; Fight Director, Felix Ivanov; Technical Director, Marshall Miller; Musicians, Matt Darriau (ney), Katie Down (glass percussion), Brandon Terzic (oud); Promo Video Director, Kevan Tucker; Graphics, Another Limited Rebellion Design; Assistant Costumes, Franny Bohar; Press, O+M Company, Rick Miramontez, Jon Dimond, Jaron Caldwell

CAST Mahida **Roxanna Hope**; Thomas **James Wallert**; Edna **Michele Pawk**; Ramin **Arian Moayed**

World premiere of a new play presented in two acts.

SYNOPSIS *Mahida's Extra Key To Heaven* is a poetic, funny and haunting story about crossing borders of all kinds. Thomas is visiting his mother's island home when he encounters Mahida, an Iranian college student stranded after an argument with her brother. The two strangers begin a beautifully awkward search for a common country, but discover that sometimes the smaller the world the bigger the invasions.

Roxanna Hope, Michele Pawk and James Wallert in
Mahida's Extra Key to Heaven *(photo by Carol Rosegg)*

The Buddha Play

Baruch Performing Arts Center – Rose Nagelberg Theatre; First Preview: September 10, 2009; Opening Night: September 26, 2009; Closed October 18, 2009; 13 previews, 27 performances

Conceived by Evan Brenner from the original texts of Siddhartha Gautama; Presented by Ascetic Productions and Baruch Performing Arts Center; Producer/Director, David Fuhrer; Design, Nikki Black; Lighting, Hong Sooyeon

Performed by **Evan Brenner**

SETTING Act I: The Quest. Act II: The Dharma. New York premiere of a new solo performance play presented in thirteen scenes in two acts.

SYNOPSIS The man we know as the Buddha lived in Northern India around 500BC and introduced the teaching known as Buddhism. Approximately 300 years after his death, an extensive oral history of the movement was written down, carried and copied throughout Asia, and this canon became the taproot of the entire Buddhist tradition. Framed in a most unusual and personal context, *The Buddha Play* brings to the stage these authentic texts to enact the extraordinary life of the man, start to finish.

Evan Brenner in The Buddha Play *(photo by Hong Sooyeon)*

Vigil

DR2; First Preview: September 20, 2009; Opening Night: September 29, 2009; Closed November 29, 2009; 9 previews, 49 performances

Written by Morris Panych; Produced by Angelo Fraboni, Daryl Roth, and The Watchful Group; Director, Stephen DiMenna; Set, Andromache Chalfant; Costumes, Ilona Somogyi; Lighting, Ed McCarthy; Original Music & Sound, Greg Pliska; Casting, Lewis and Fox Casting; PSM, Angela Allen; General Manager, Adam Hess; Production Manager, Ricardo Taylor; Associate Producers, Alexander Fraser, Kristine Lewis, Jamie Fox, Jodie Schoenbrun Carter; Advertising, Eliran Murphy Group; Marketing, Leanne Schanzer Promotions; Company Manager, Kyle R. Provost; Production Associate/Wardrobe, Julie DeRossi; Assistant to Ms. Roth, Greg Raby; Assistant Director, Adam Crescenzi; Assistant Set, Jonathan Collins; Assistant Sound, Michael Eisenberg; Props Master, Mallory MacDonald; Associate General Manager, Steven M. Garcia; Press, Richard Kornberg & Associates

CAST Kemp **Malcolm Gets**; Grace **Helen Stenborg**; Understudy for Kemp **Brian Carter**

New York premiere of a dark comedy presented in thirty-seven scenes in two acts. U.S. production originally produced at Westport Country Playhouse in association with Daryl Roth and Angelo Fraboni in February 2008, featuring Ms. Stenborg and Timothy Busfield. Originally produced in Canada in 1995.

SYNOPSIS Written by one of Canada's most acclaimed playwrights, *Vigil* is the much lauded new play that tells the wickedly funny story of a selfish bank drudge who is tending to the wealthy dying aunt he hasn't seen in 30 years. She, however, isn't going anywhere anytime soon.

Malcolm Gets and Helen Stenborg in Vigil *(photo by Carol Rosegg)*

Love, Loss, and What I Wore

Westside Theatre (Downstairs); First Preview: September 21, 2009; Opening Night: October 1, 2009; 11 previews, 232 performances as of May 31, 2010

Written by Nora Ephron and Delia Ephron, based on the book by Ilene Beckerman; Produced by Daryl Roth; Director, Karen Carpenter; Sets, Jo Winiarski; Costumes, Jessica Jahn; Lighting, Jeff Croiter; Sound, Walter Trarbach; Casting, Tara Rubin; Makeup, Maria Verel; PSM, Zoya Kachadurian; ASM, Nancy Elizabeth Vest; Production Manager, Shannon Case; General Manager, Adam Hess; Associate Producer, Alexander Fraser; Associate General Manager, Jodi Schoenbrun Carter; Advertising, Eliran Murphy Group; Marketing, Leanne Schanzer Promotions; Assistant Design: Carla Cruz (set), Sarah James (costumes), Grant Yeager (lighting); Propmaster, Buist Bickley; Wardrobe Supervisor, Ren LaDassor; Production Carpenter, Colin McNamara; Press, O+M Company, Rick Miramontez, Molly Barnett, Andy Snyder

CAST *September 21–October 18:* **Samantha Bee, Tyne Daly, Katie Finneran, Natasha Lyonne, Rosie O'Donnell;** *October 21–November 15:* **Mary Birdsong, Tyne Daly, Lisa Joyce, Jane Lynch, Mary Louise Wilson;** *November 18–December 13:* **Kristin Chenoweth, Lucy DeVito, Capathia Jenkins, Rhea Perlman, Rita Wilson;** *December 14–January 3:* **Lucy DeVito, Katie Finneran, Capathia Jenkins, Carol Kane, Natasha Lyonne;** *January 6–31:* **Katie Finneran, Michele Lee, Debra Monk, Tracee Ellis Ross, Casey Wilson;** *February 3-28:* **Janeane Garafalo, Joanna Gleason, Carol Kane, June Diane Raphael, Caroline Rhea;** *March 3–28:* **Didi Conn, Fran Drescher, Jayne Houdyshell, Carol Kane, Natasha Lyonne;** *March 31–April 25:* **Lucy DeVito, Judy Gold, Melissa Joan Hart, Jayne Houdyshell, Shirley Knight;** *April 28–May 23:* **Anna Chlumsky, Julie Halston, LaTanya Richardson Jackson, Doris Roberts, Brooke Shields;** *May 26–June 27:* **Penny Fuller, Rachel Harris, Diane Neal, Sherri Shepherd, Cobie Smulders**

Off-Broadway commercial transfer of a collection of monologues and scenes presented without intermission. Previously presented last season at the DR2 Theatre. A portion of ticket sales benefited Dress for Success.

SYNOPSIS This collection of vignettes and monologues by Nora and Delia Ephron is based on the best-selling book by Ilene Beckerman, as well as on the recollections of the Ephrons' friends. The production features a five- member all-star rotating cast who will perform the piece in four-week cycles. Like the book it's based on, *Love, Loss, and What I Wore* uses clothing and accessories and the memories they trigger to tell funny and often poignant stories that all women can relate to.

Rosie O'Donnell, Tyne Daly, Samantha Bee, Natasha Lyonne, and Katie Finneran in Love, Loss, and What I Wore *(photo by Carol Rosegg)*

A scene from Homer's Odyssey *(photo by Joshua Frachisseur)*

Homer's Odyssey

Bleecker Street Theatre; Opening Night: October 2, 2009; Closed October 25, 2009; 24 performances

Adapted by Simon Armitage; Presented by Handcart Ensemble in cooperation with Theatres at 45 Bleecker Street; Director, J. Scott Reynolds; Original Music, Nathan Bowen; Fight Director, J. Allen Suddeth; Music Director/Vocal Coach, Matthew Herrick; Costumes, Candida Nichols; Lighting, David Kniep; Set, Tijana Bjelajac; Puppetry/Shadow Effects, Marta Mozelle MacRostie; Stage Manager, Sarah Biesinger; Press, Jonathan Slaff & Associates

CAST Odysseus **David D'Agostini**; Eurybates, Eurycleia **Jeffrey Golde**; Nausicaä, Phemios, Siren **Rachael McOwen**[1]; Zeus, Alcinous, Eumaeus, Tiresias **John Michalski**; Eurymachus, Cyclops, Agamemnon, Sailor **Nicholas Alexiy Moran**; Athena, Circe, Siren **Jane Pejtersen**; Telemachus, Elpenos **Joel Rainwater**; Amphinomous, Polites **Joel Richards**; Penelope, Calypso, Arete, Anticleia **Elizabeth Ruelas**; Antinous, Eurylochus **Javen Tanner**[2]; Hermes, Antiphus, Achilles **Ryan Wood**

*Succeeded by: 1. Rita Markova 2. Torsten Hillhouse Off-Broadway extension of the Off-Off Broadway play presented in two acts. Presented as a showcase in the same space September 3–19, playing 16 performances.

SYNOPSIS *Homer's Odyssey* charts the struggle of the mythical hero Odysseus to return home after ten years' fighting in Troy. Armitage's treatment is masterful yet broadly accessible. It bristles with the economy, wit and guile that we have come to expect from one of the most unique voices of his generation. For New York audiences, the production is a powerful encounter with one of Britain's most gifted and prolific writers.

Penny Penniworth

TADA! Theater; First Preview: October 1, 2009; Opening Night: October 5, 2009; Closed November 8, 2009; 4 previews, 30 performances

Adapted by Chris Weikel from the story by Charles Dickens; Presented by Emerging Artists Theatre (Paul Adams, Artistic Director); Director, Mark Finely; Set, Tim McMath; Costumes, House of Goody; Lighting, Jennifer Granrund; Original Music, Peter Saxe; Sound, Aaron Blank; Set Assistant Helen Jun; Costumer/Wardrobe Mistress, Kate Jansyn Thaw; Costume Assistant, Meredith Neal; Production Manager/Managing Director, Deb Guston; PSM, Terra Vetter; Production Assistant, Alison Jane Carroll; Graphics, Tzipora Kaplan; Associate Artistic Director, Derek Jamison; Literary Manager, Kevin Brofsky; Actors Company Manager, Ron Bopst; Press, Ron Lasko/Spin Cycle

CAST Hotchkiss Spit & Others **Christopher Borg**; Rupert Stryfe, Heir to the House of Stryfe & Others **Jason O'Connell**; Miss Havasnort & Others **Ellen Reilly**; Penny Penniworth & Others **Jamie Heinlein**; Understudies **Lee Kaplan, Karen Stanion**

SETTING The present, but invoking a time early in the reign of Queen Victoria; Place: A stage, but meant to signify Merrie Olde Englande. Revival of a play presented without intermission. Previously presented by Emerging Artists in 2002, and subsequently presented by TOSOSII in the 2003 New York International Fringe Festival.

SYNOPSIS *Penny Penniworth* is Charles Dickens' "lost" epic as mounted by a short-staffed theatre troupe with Royal Shakespeare Company aspirations. The play tells the story of young Penny Penniworth whose childhood love is driven out of town after nearly killing a wealthy businessman. Soon, Penny finds herself penniless, left alone to make her way through a convoluted maze of strange relationships, anonymous benefactors and ultimate justice.

Jamie Heinlein in Penny Penniworth *(photo by Ned Thorne)*

Tanguera: The Tango Musical

New York City Center; First Preview: October 7, 2009; Opening Night: October 8, 2009; Closed October 18, 2009; 2 previews, 14 performances

Story by Diego Romay and Dolores Espeja, lyrics by Eladia Blazques; Presented by Diego Romay Company; Produced by Michael Brenner for BB Group GmbH and Paul Szilard Productions Inc. under the patronage of Daniel Barenboim; Director, Omar Pacheco; Choreography, Mora Goday; Original Music/ Arrangements, Gerardo Gardelin; Tango Arrangements, Lisandro Adrover; Set, Valeria Ambrosia; Costumes, Cecilia Monti; Lighting, Ariel Del Mastro; General Management, Sundance Productions (David Coffman, Managing Director; Robyn Sunderland, Associate General Manager); Technical Directors, Marcello Cuervo, Dieter Brömsen; PSM, Todd Clark; Company Manager, Carlos Marcelo Patane; New York Company Manager, José Esquea; Stage Manager, Edgardo Ariel Alba; Dance Coach, Julio Cesar Di Chiazza; Translations, Dolores Prida, Celia Szew; Advertising, Eliran-Murphy Group; Press, Keith Sherman & Associates, Scott Klein, Brett Oberman, Glenna Freedman

CAST Madam **María Neves**; Lorenzo **Esteban Domenichini**; Giselle **Rocío de Los Santos**; Gaudencio **Oscar Martínez Pey**; Singer **Marianella**; Rengo **Dabel Zanabria**; Ensemble **Maria Sol Alzamora, Leandro Capparelli, Carolina Castiella, Magdalena Cortéz, Norberto Cosentino, Gustavo Fortino, Cristian García, Melina Greco, Albano Jiménez, Gisela Kargel, Carolina Rocchietti, Paola Rodolfo, Fernando Rodriguez, Silvio Sotomayor, Nahuel Gonzalez Yannuci**

UNDERSTUDIES Dabel Zanabria (Guadencio), Luciano Capparelli (Lorenzo), Gabriela Amalfitani (Giselle), Carla Chimento (Madam)

ORCHESTRA Lisandro Adrover (Musical Director/First Bandoneon); Leonardo Suarez-Paz (Music Coordinator/Associate Concert Master); Miguel Angel Bertero, Antoine Silverman (violin); Ron Lawrence (viola); Daniel Miller (cello); Fabian Dario Zylberman (woodwinds); Walther Enrique Cuttini (synthesizer); Hector del Curto, Juan Pablo Jofre Romarion (Bandoneon); Mario Carlos Araolaza (piano); Domingo Jose Diani (double bass); Fernando Alberto Valles (drums)

SETTING Buenos Aries, Argentina. U.S. premiere of a theatrical dance piece presented in without intermission. Originally premiered at El Nacional de Buenos Aries Theatre January 8, 2002.

SYNOPSIS Fresh from Argentina, *Tanguera* explodes onto the stage in a tale of unrequited love in turn-of-the-20th-century Buenos Aires through a unique combination of song, music, and dance. In this erotic and sensual musical, a young French girl, deceived by a prostitution ring arrives in Argentina at the port of Buenos Aires, and meets the dockworker Lorenzo, an idealist and dreamer. Life transforms them: she becomes a cabaret star and he must decide to face destiny and conquer his love.

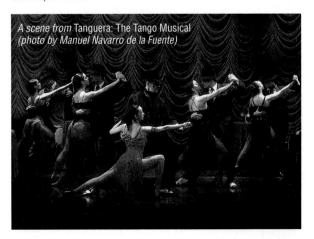

A scene from Tanguera: The Tango Musical
(photo by Manuel Navarro de la Fuente)

Alexander Elisa, Bill Daugherty, Christina Morrell, Deborah Tranelli, Morgan West, and Jennafer Newberry in Brother Can You Spare a Dime *(photo by Ben Strothmann)*

Brother, Can You Spare a Dime?
Songs and Stories from The Great Depression

Triad Theatre; Opening Night: October 9, 2009; Closed January 31, 2010; 33 performances

Conceived and directed by Bill Daugherty; Produced by Thoroughbred Records and Max Weintraub; Music Director/Arrangements, Doyle Newmyer; Musical Staging, Lori Leshner; Lighting, John Anselmo Jr.; Sound, Tonya Pierre; Stage Manager, Gwendolyn M. Gilliam; Sound Engineer/Editor, Chip Fabrizi; Graphics, William Yee; Press, Keith Sherman and Associates

CAST **Bill Daugherty, Alexander Elisa, Christina Morrell, Jennafer Newbery, Deborah Tranelli, Morgan West**

MUSICIANS Doyle Newmyer (piano), John Loehrke (bass), Spiff Wiegand (guitar)

MUSICAL NUMBERS I'm In the Market For You; Let's Have Another Cup of Coffee; As Long As You've Got Your Health; Got the Jitters; I'm an Unemployed Sweetheart; In a One-Room Flat; Brother, Can You Spare a Dime?; My Forgotten Man; Sally Ann; Sweepin' the Clouds Away; Dusty Road; Get Happy; Hallelujah, I'm a Bum!; Sittin' On a Rubbish Can; A Hobo's Lullaby; Love For Sale; Ten Cents a Dance; Cigarettes, Cigars; There's No Depression In Love; We're in the Money; The Clouds Will Soon Roll By; When My Ship Comes In; We're Out of the Red; With Plenty of Money and You; Happy Days Are Here Again; Dawn of a New Day

Return engagement of a new musical revue presented in two acts. Previously presented at the Triad March 6–June 14, 2009, playing 46 performances.

SYNOPSIS *Brother, Can You Spare a Dime: Songs and Stories from The Great Depression* takes audiences on a heartfelt journey from pre-crash mania through to the plight of the Dustbowl "Okies," the folks who rode the rails in search of work, letters to Mrs. Roosevelt and then the eventual recovery of our nation. A timely subject, the revue paints the emotions of a country in economic turmoil and how the music of Hollywood and Tin Pan Alley reflected the commonality of Americans and asked us to look toward better times.

How to Be a Good Italian Daughter
(In Spite of Myself)

Cherry Lane Studio Theatre; First Preview: October 6, 2009; Opening Night: October 12, 2009; Closed December 13, 2009; 4 previews, 40 performances

Written by Antoinette LaVecchia; Presented by Jones Street Productions, Arje Shaw, and Ester Shaw; Director, Ted Sod; Set, Michael V. Moore; Costumes, Daniel James Cole; Lighting, Traci Klainer; Production Manager, Janio Marrero; PSM, Amanda Michaels; ASM, Chris Rinaldi; General Manager, Lisa Dozier; Graphic Designer, James McNeel; Music, Louis Tucci; Assistant Lighting, Laura Schoch; Assistant General Manager, Faiz Osman; Production Assistant, Jessy Grossman; Press, Sam Rudy Media Relations

Performed by **Antoinette LaVecchia**

Off-Broadway premiere of a solo performance play presented without intermission.

SYNOPSIS The actress and writer Antoinette LaVecchia brings her solo show *How to Be a Good Italian Daughter (In Spite of Myself)*, to New York, a funny and touching look at mothers and daughters, centering on the relationship between an immigrant Italian mother and her Americanized daughter.

Antoinette LaVecchia in How to Be a Good Italian Daughter (in Spite of Myself) *(photo by Lisa Dozier)*

Good Bobby

59E59 Theater B; First Preview: October 8, 2009; Opening Night: October 14, 2009; Closed November 8, 2009; 43 performances

Written by Brian Lee Franklin; Presented by Greenway Arts Alliance (Whitney Weston and Pierson Blaetz, Co-Artistic Directors); Produced by Dan Friedman; Associate Producer, Jessica Hanna; For 59E59: Elizabeth Kleinhans, President and Artistic Director; Peter Tear, Executive Producer; Director, Pierson Blaetz; Set, Victoria Bellocq; Lighting, Jeremy Pivnick; Video/Sound, Fritz Davis; Costumes, Naila Aladdin Sanders; Dramaturg, Scott Horstein; PSM, Sanja Kabalin; ASM, Cheryl D. Olszowka; L.A. Production Associate, Cate Cundiff; Press, Karen Greco

CAST Angie Novello **Sila Bermingham**; Bobby Kennedy **Brian Lee Franklin**; CIA Agent **Joe Hindy**; Jimmy Hoffa **Dan Lauria**; Senator John McClellan **William Mahoney**; Nicholas Katzenbach/Governor Patterson **Paul Marius**; Joe Kennedy **Steve Mendillo**; G. Fitzgerald/A. Dobrynin **Barry Primus**; Rose Kennedy **Lisa Richards**

New York premiere of a new play presented in two acts. Previously presented at Greenway Court Theatre in December 2008.

SYNOPSIS *Good Bobby* recounts the formative adult years of Robert F. Kennedy, one of history's great "what ifs". From his battles with Jimmy Hoffa to his stint as Attorney General to the assassination of John Kennedy, RFK struggles to find his own voice and step out of the enormous shadows created by domineering father, a larger-than-life brother and the expectations of a mother who forever believes in the man he ultimately becomes.

Brian Lee Franklin in
Good Bobby
(photo by Ed Krieger)

The Lady with All the Answers

Cherry Lane Theatre; First Preview: October 6, 2009; Opening Night: October 14, 2009; Closed December 6, 2009; 8 previews, 51 performances

Written by David Rambo; Presented by Cherry Lane Theatre (Angelina Fiordellisi, Artistic Director; James King, Managing Director) in association with Northlight Theatre; Director, BJ Jones; Sets, Neil Patel; Costumes, Martin Pakledinaz; Lighting, Nicole Pearce; Sound, Kevin O'Donnell; Wigs, Paul Huntley; PSM, Paige Van Den Burg; Development Consultant, James McNeel; Development Associate, Colleen O'Shea; Production Assistants, Seri Lawrence & Rebecca Leshin; Business Management, Friedman & LaRosa Inc., Joyce Friedman; Production Manager, Janio Marrero; Company Coordinator, Alexander Orbovich; Assistant Lighting, Eric Larson; Assistant Cosutmes, Anna Laclvita; Properties Master, Teralyn Bruketta; Wardrobe, Kate Melvin; Marketing, Art Meets Commerce; Press, Sam Rudy Media Relations

CAST Eppie Lederer **Judith Ivey**

SETTING Place: Eppie Lederer's Lake Shore Drive Apartment, Chicago. Time: Night, June, 1975. New York premiere of a new solo performance play presented in two acts. World premiere at Pasadena Playhouse in 2008.

SYNOPSIS For decades, newspaper columnist and American icon Ann Landers dispensed wit and wisdom to lovelorn teens, confused couples and others in need of advice in her nationally syndicated column. In *The Lady with All the Answers*, Landers finds herself writing a column about a new kind of heartbreak – her own. Drawn from her life and letters, the play is a touching and comic portrait of a wise, funny, no-nonsense woman who was one of the most influential figures in America by virtue of the millions of readers who wrote to her seeking her indispensable advice and controversial opinions on matters ranging from marriage, divorce, life, death and sexuality, to the proper way to hang a roll of toilet paper in the bathroom.

Judith Ivey in The Lady With All the Answers *(photo by Carol Rosegg)*

The Oldsmobiles

Flea Theater; First Preview: October 1, 2009; Opening Night: October 17, 2009; Closed November 14, 2009; 14 previews, 23 performances

Written by Roger Rosenblatt; Produced by the Flea Theater (Jim Simpson; Artistic Director; Carol Ostrow, Producing Director); Director, Jim Simpson; Set, Jerad Schomer; Costumes, Claudia Brown; Lighting, Brian Aldous; Sound, Daniel Kluger; Mikaal Sulaiman; Stage Manager, Lindsay Stares; Assistant to the Director, Joanna Strange; Graphic Design, David Prittie; Scenic Painting, Isaac Ramsey; Casting, Calleri Casting; Managing Director, Beth Dembrow; Technical Director, Zack Tinkelman; Audience Development & Marketing, Sherri Kronfeld; Development Manager, Tiffany Kleeman Baran; Assistant to the Producing Director, Emily Conner; Assistant Technical Director, Tim Pickerill; Press, Ron Lasko/Spin Cycle

CAST Mr. Oldsmobile **Richard Masur**; Mrs. Oldsmobile **Alice Playten**

SETTING The Manhattan Bridge; the present. World premiere of a new play presented without intermission.

SYNOPSIS In *The Oldsmobiles*, Mr. and Mrs. Oldsmobile are perched on the edge contemplating their life together and life hereafter. With the eyes of the NYPD, the fire department, tourists, celebrities, a news anchor, a priest, the mayor, and the Oldsmobile's children upon them, the two relish the attention and ponder the possibilities of life and death.

Richard Masur and Alice Playten in The Oldsmobiles *(photo by Joan Marcus)*

Avenue Q

New World Stages–Stage 3; First Preview: October 9, 2009; Opening Night: October 21, 2009; 14 previews, 256 performances as of May 31, 2010

Music and lyrics by Robert Lopez and Jeff Marx, book by Jeff Whitty; Produced by Kevin McCollum, Robyn Goodman, Jeffrey Seller, Vineyard Theatre & The New Group; Director, Jason Moore; Choreography, Ken Roberson; Music Supervision/Orchestrations/Arrangements, Stephen Oremus; Music Director, Andrew Graham; Puppets Conception/Design, Rick Lyon; Set, Anna Louizos; Costumes, Mirena Rada; Lighting, Howell Binkley; Sound, Acme Sound Partners; Animation, Robert Lopez; Incidental Music, Gary Adler; Casting, Cindy Tolan; General Manager, Davenport Theatrical Enterprises; Production Manager, Travis Walker, Autonomous Production Services; PSM, Christine M. Daly; Marketing, Scott A. Moore; Stage Manager, James Darrah; ASM, Rob Morrison; Company Manager, Ryan Lympus; Resident Director, Evan Ensign; Dance Captain/Puppet Captain, Seth Rettberg; Associate Design: Todd Potter (set), Ryan O'Gara (lighting), Karl Ruckdeschel (costumes); Music Copying, Emily Grishman/Alex Lacamoire; Animation/Video Production, Sound Associates Inc.; Sound & Video Design Effects, Brett Jarvis; Advertising, SpotCo; Press, Sam Rudy Media Relations; Broadway Cast recording: RCA 82876-55923-2

CAST Princeton/Rod **Seth Rettberg**; Brian **Nicholas Kohn**; Kate Monster/Lucy the Slut & others **Anika Larsen**[1]; Nicky/Trekkie Monster/Bad Idea Bear & others **Cullen Titmas**; Christmas Eve **Sala Iwamatsu**[2]; Gary Coleman **Danielle K. Thomas**[3]; Mrs. T./Bad Idea Bear & others **Maggie Lakis**[4]; Ensemble **Ruthie Ann Miles**[5], **Jed Resnick**; Swings **Erica Dorfler, Rob Morrison**

UNDERSTUDIES Jed Resnick and Rob Morrison (Princeton/Rod, Brian, Nicky/Trekkie/Bear), Ruthie Ann Miles[5] (Kate Monster/Lucy, Christmas Eve, Mrs. T./Bear), Maggie Lakis[4] (Kate Monster/Lucy), Erica Dorfler (Kate Monster/Lucy, Gary Coleman, Mrs. T./Bear)

*Succeeded by: 1. Sarah Stiles (1/8/10) 2. Ann Sanders (4/5/10) 3. Haneefah Wood 4. Jennifer Barnhart (5/2/10) 5. Katie Boren (4/19/10)

ORCHESTRA Andrew Graham (Conductor/keyboard); Randy Cohen (Associate Conductor/keyboard); Patience Higgins (reeds); Joe Choroszewski (drums)

MUSICAL NUMBERS Avenue Q Theme, What Do You Do With a BA in English?/It Sucks to be Me, If You Were Gay, Purpose, Everyone's a Little Bit Racist, The Internet Is for Porn, Mix Tape, I'm Not Wearing Underwear Today, Special, You Can Be as Loud as the Hell You Want (When You're Making Love), Fantasies Come True, My Girlfriend, Who Lives in Canada, There's a Fine, Fine Line, There Is Life Outside Your Apartment, The More You Ruv Someone, Schadenfreude, I Wish I Could Go Back to College, The Money Song, For Now

SETTING An outer borough of New York City; the present. A musical presented in two acts. Originally presented Off-Broadway March 19, 2003 at the Vineyard Theatre (see *Theatre World* Vol. 59, page 179). Transferred to Broadway at the John Golden Theatre July 10, 2003 (opened July 31) where it closed this season on September 13, 2010 after 2,534 performances (see *Theatre World* Vol. 60, page 25 for original Broadway credits; for Broadway closing credits see Broadway section in this volume). This unprecedented transfer back to Off-Broadway marked the first time a Broadway musical has moved to an Off-Broadway theatre.

SYNOPSIS *Avenue Q* is about real life: finding a job, losing a job, learning about racism, getting an apartment, getting kicked out of your apartment, being different, falling in love, promiscuity, avoiding commitment, and internet porn. Twenty and thirty-something puppets and humans survive life in the big city and search for their purpose in this naughty but timely musical that features "full puppet nudity!"

Nicholas Kohn, Danielle K. Thomas, Cullen Titmas & Nicky, Seth Rettberg & Princeton, Anika Larsen & Kate Monster, Maggie Lakis & Rod, and Sala Iwamatsu in Avenue Q *(photo by Carol Rosegg)*

Embraceable Me

Kirk Theatre on Theatre Row; First Preview: October 23, 2009; Opening Night: October 28, 2009; Closed November 14, 2009; 5 previews, 24 performances

Written by Victor L. Cahn; Presented by Rachel Reiner Productions; Director, Eric Parness; Set, Sarah B. Brown; Lighting, Carolyn Wong; Costumes, Sidney Shannon; Sound, Nick Moore; PSM, Lyndsey Goode; Assistant Director, Rebecca Kahane; Marketing Coordinator, Christina Fallone; Casting, Stephanie Klapper; Production Manager, Joe Doran; Master Electrician/Associate Production Manager, Flora Vassar; Artwork, Billy Mitchell; Photography, Jon Kandel; Press, Joe Trentacosta/Springer Associates PR

CAST Edward **Scott Barrow**; Allison **Keira Naughton**

World premiere of a new play presented without intermission.

SYNOPSIS Edward is smart, shy, and quirky. Allison is sexy, dramatic, and vulnerable. *Embraceable Me* is a witty and touching "he said-she said" story that traces the journey of these unlikely friends along many surprising detours and byways.

Scott Barrow and Keira Naughton
in Embraceable Me
(photo by Jon Kandel)

Antigone

Dance Theatre Workshop; Opening Night: October 28, 2009; Closed November 1, 2009; 7 performances

Written by Jocelyn Clarke form the original by Sophocles; Created and presented by SITI Company; Director, Anne Bogart; Composer, Christian Fredrickson; Set/Lighting, Brian H. Scott; Costumes, Melissa Trn; PSM, Kris Longley-Postema; Assistant Director, Tina Mitchell; Executive Director, Megan Wanlass Szalla; Associate Producers, Roberta Pereira, David Roberts; Press, Jenny Lerner, Isabelle Doconick

CAST Ismene **Akiko Aizawa**; Chorus/Elder **Will Bond**; Haemon **Leon Ingulsrud**; Tiresias/Elder **Tom Nelis**; Guard **Barney O'Hanlon**; Antigone **Makela Spielman**; Kreon **Stephen Duff Webber**

World premiere of a new play based on a classic presented without intermission. Workshopped at the J. Paul Getty Museum's Getty Villa (California) in May 2009.

SYNOPSIS *Antigone* is a provoking tale of family and loyalty, patriotism and war, and the powers of the state. Adapted by Dublin-based Jocelyn Clarke (SITI's long-time collaborator) the play tells the story of Antigone, the cursed daughter of Oedipus and Jocasta, who defies the King of Thebes for the right to bury her own brother. One of humankind's most enduring and influential stories, it explores conflicts between individual and state and the choices one has to make to either follow one's own beliefs or obey the law.

Akiko Aizawa, Leon Ingulsrud, and Tom Nelis in Antigone
(photo by Michal Daniel)

Love Child

New World Stages–Stage 5; First Preview: October 23, 2009; Opening Night: October 31, 2009; Closed January 3, 2010; 9 previews, 75 performances

Written by Daniel Jenkins and Robert Stanton; Presented by Martin Hummel in association with Primary Stages (Casey Child, Founder & Executive Producer; Andrew Leynse, Artistic Director; Eliot Fox, Managing Director) and The Storyline Project LLC; Director, Carl Forsman; Choreographer, Tracy Bersley; Set, Neil Patel; Lighting, Jeff Croiter & Grant Yeager; Costumes, Kyle LaColla; Sound, Will Pickens; Production Supervisor, PRF Productions/Peter R. Feuchtwanger; PSM, Joanne E. McInerney; General Manager, Cesa Entertainment Inc., Jamie Cesa; Associate General Manager, Gretchen Margaroili; ASM, Andrea Jo Martin; Assistant Set, Gregory Laffey; Assistant Lighting, Austin Smith; Production Electricians, Tom Dyer, Yuriy Nayer; Wardrobe Supervisor, Amy Kaskeski; Light/Sound Board, Barbara Eldredge; Light Board Programmer, Grant Yeager; Production Carpenter, Vadim Malinskiy; Production Audio, David Arnold; "Love Child" Song Arrangement, Steve Fontaine; Press, O+M Company, Rick Miramontez, Philip Carrubba

CAST Daniel Jenkins, Robert Stanton; Understudy **Mark Alhadeff**

SETTING Commercial transfer of an Off-Broadway play presented without intermission. Previously presented last season at Primary Stages October 12–November 19, 2008 (see *Theatre World* Vol. 65, page 227). Developed at New York Stage and Film Company and The Powerhouse Theater at Vassar College July 1–3, 2005.

SYNOPSIS In *Love Child*, it is opening night and the cast is unruly, the crowd is restless, and the play is obscure. Real and theatrical worlds collide in this new madcap comedy about the night a classic play spoke so loudly to its audience that they felt compelled to talk back. Daniel Jenkins and Robert Stanton take you on a wild ride: 2 actors, 22 roles, 85 minutes and heaps of laughs.

Robert Stanton and Daniel Jenkins in Love Child
(photo by Carol Rosegg)

James Tigger Ferguson and Taylor Mac in The Lily's Revenge (photo by Ves Pitts)

The Lily's Revenge

HERE Arts Center; First Preview: October 29, 2009; Opening Night: November 1, 2009; Closed November 22, 2009; 4 previews, 16 performances

Book, lyrics, and concept by Taylor Mac; Presented by HERE Arts Center (Kristin Marting, Artistic Director) and Ethyl Crisp Productions; Dramaturgy, Nina Mankin; Directors, Paul Zimet (Part 1 – *The Deity*), Rachel Chavkin (Part 2 – *Ghost Warrior*), Faye Driscoll (Part 3 – *Love Act*), Aaron Rhyne (Part 4 – *Living Person*), David Drake (Part 5 – *The Mad Demon*), Kristin Marting (Kyogens); Composer, Rachelle Garniez; Set, Nick Vaughn; Lighting, Seth Reiser; Music Director/Arrangements, Matt Ray; Choreography, Julie Atlas Muz (Part 1), Faye Driscoll (Part 3); Video (Part 4), Aaron Rhyne; PSM, Julia Funk; Photography, Karl Giant; Makeup, Derrick Little; Puppets, Emily Decola; ASM, Emily Rea; Assistant Directors, Salty Brine, Stefanie Horowitz, Jennifer Kraus; Rehearsal Stage Managers, Kayla Asbell (Part 2), Randi Rivera (Part 3); Drum Compositions, Stefan Schatz; Director of Photography (Part 4) Ned Stessen-Reuter; Sound Design/Video Programmer (Part 4) Matthew Tennie; Assistant Video Design (Part 4), Linsey Bostwick, Zuzana Godalova; Technical Director, Josh Higgason; Press, Bridget Kaplinski

CAST Prime Love **Vanessa Anspaugh**; Daisy/Bee **Kayla Asbell**; Mary Love Jonathan **Jonathan Bastiani**; Card Girl **World Famous *BOB***; The Tick/Bee **Salty Brine**; Mary/Susan/Stepmother **Heather Christian**; Bride Love **Darlinda Just Darlinda**; Daisy Mattie/Bee/Infectious Disease **Matthew Crosland**; Bee/Kyogen **Mieke Duffly**; The Great Longing **James Tigger! Ferguson**; Master Sunflower **Daphne Gaines**; Tulip **Ikuko Ikari**; Baby's Breath **Barbara Lanciers**; Bride Puppet/White Rose Puppet/Bee **Kristine Haruna Lee**; Time/Stepmother/The Wind **Miss Bianca Leigh**; Lily **Taylor Mac**; Mary Subprime Diety **Ellen Maddow**; Audience Member/Poppy **Glenn Marla**; Mary Deity #2 **Muriel Miguel**; Kyogen/Bee **Una Aya Osato**; Groom Deity **Frank Paiva**; Pony/Bee/Pope **Edith Raw**; Red Rose **Kim Rosen**; Mary Prime Deity **Tina Shepard**; Mary Love #2 **Saeed Siamak**; Groom Love **Phillip Taratula**; The Mary Deity #1 **Rae C. Wright**; Subprime Love **Nikki Zialcita**; Bride Diety **Amelia Zirin-Brown** (aka Lady Rizzo); Video Performances **Cary Curran, Coleman Domingo, David Drake,Bridget Everett, Matt Fraser, Tracey Gilbert, Karen Hartman, Morgan Jenness,Karen Kohlhaas, Lisa Kron, Nina Mankin,Dirty Martini, Julie Atlas Muz, Our Lady J, Mandy Patinkin, James Scruggs, Lucy Thurber**; Voice Over **Justin Bond**

MUSICIANS Jon Natchez (horns), Derek Nievergelt (bass), Matt Ray (pianist), Stefan Schatz (percussion/drums)

World premiere of a new avant-garde theatrical piece with music, media, and dance presented in five parts without intermission.

SYNOPSIS An uprooted lily goes on a quest to wed a human bride and destroy The God of Nostalgia.

Genre squishing Taylor Mac and a company of 40+ unravel our national pastime of melancholy remembrances. *The Lily's Revenge* is a 5 part extravaganza featuring live music, wild costumes, vaudevillian theatrics, macabre entr'actes, a million sequins, and a few flowers.

The New Electric Ballroom

St. Ann's Warehouse; First Preview: October 27, 2009; Opening Night: November 1, 2009; Closed November 22, 2009; 6 previews, 22 performances

Written and directed by Enda Walsh; Presented by Druid (Ireland; Garry Hynes, Artistic Director); Set and Costumes, Sabine Dargent; Lighting, Sinéad McKenna; Sound, Gregory Clark; Casting, Maureen Hughes; For Druid: Bernie Harrigan (Finance), Tim Smith (General Manager), Thomas Conway (Literary Manager), Sinéad McPhillips (Marketing & Development), Ruth Gordon (Administrator); Production Manager, Eamonn Fox; Company Stage Manager, Sarah Lynch; Stage Director, Lee Davis; Technical Manager, Barry O'Brien; Press, Blake Zidell & Associates

CAST Breda **Rosaleen Linehan**; Ada **Catherine Walsh**; Clara **Ruth McCabe**; Patsy **Mikel Murfi**

SETTING A small fishing town on the west coast of Ireland. U.S. premiere of a new play presented in two acts. World premiere (in German) at Kammerspiele Theatre (Munich) September 30, 2004. English-language premiere at the Galway Arts Festival July 14-26, 2008 and the Edinburgh Fringe Festival August 3-24, 2008.

SYNOPSIS Night after night, Breda and Clara, two aging sisters, relive the memories of a single night in the early 1960s when a seductive rock singer at the New Electric Ballroom broke both their fragile hearts. Breda, Clara and their much younger sister, Ada, remain trapped in the story, costumed by their tulle skirts, bolero jackets, pink high heels and lipstick until a lonely fisherman appears as Ada's chance to escape.

Catherine Walsh (left) and Rosaleen Linehan in The New Electric Ballroom (photo by Pavel Antonov)

Creature

Ohio Theatre; First Preview: October 28, 2009; Opening Night: November 2, 2009; Closed November 21, 2009; 4 previews, 20 performances

Written by Heidi Schreck; Presented by Page 73 Productions (Liz Jones and Asher Richelli, Executive Directors) and New Georges (Susan Bernfield, Artistic Director; Sarah Cameron Sunde, Associate Director); Director, Leigh Silverman; Set, Rachel Hauck; Lighting, Matt Frey; Costumes, Theresa Squire; Sound, Kate Down; PSM, Sunneva Stapleton; ASM, Aaron Heflich Shapiro; Props, Sean McArdle; Assistant Director, Lila Neugebauer; Production Manager, Neal Wilkinson; Technical Director, Erik Benson; Casting, Jack Doulin, Jenn Haltman; Producing Associate, Dan Lockhart; Associate Producer, Rehana Mirza; Master Electrician, Stephen Arnold; Design Assistants: Qin Lu (set), Oliver Wason (lighting), Franny Bohar (costumes); Light Programmer, Steve Maturno; Wigs/Makeup, Karine Ivey; Playwright Assistant, Amanda Thompson; Press, Jim Baldassare

CAST Juliana of Norwich **Marylouise Burke**; Margery Kempe **Sofia Jean Gomez**; John Kempe **Darren Goldstein**; Nurse **Tricia Rodley**; Asmodeus/Jacob **Will Rogers**; Father Thomas **Jeremy Shamos**

SETTING 1401. World premiere of a new play presented without intermission. Developed in the Soho Rep Writer/Director Lab and subsequently with New Georges and Teatro de Facto (Los Angeles).

SYNOPSIS A gorgeous young beer-brewer named Margery Kempe sets about trying to become a saint. Seduced by a vision of Jesus Christ in robes of purple – her favorite color – she battles her family, the church, and an intense appetite for earthly pleasures in an improbably bid for salvation. In *Creature*, contemporary and medieval imaginations collide; it's a very funny, a little bit scary new play about faith and its messengers.

Sofia Jean Gomez and Marylouise Burke in Creature (photo by Jim Baldassare)

Made in Heaven

Soho Playhouse; First Preview: October 22, 2009; Opening Night: November 2, 2009; Closed December 6, 2009; 13 previews, 40 performances

Written by Jay Bernzweig; Produced by Barbara Ligeti, Andrew Shaifer, and Victor Syrmis; Director, Andrew Shaifer; Set, Lex Liang; Costumes, Jeffrey Wallach; Lighting, Kia Rogers; Properties, Stephanie Raines; PSM, Fran Rubenstein; ASM, Johanna Weller-Fahy; Production Manager, Amber Estes; Promotions, HHC Marketing; Marketing, Trevor Brown; General Manager, Two Step Productions; Associate Producers, William T. Reid IV, Misty Reid, Steve Wilder; Audience Services Manager, Kevin Sullivan; Casting Coordinator, Rachel Merrill Moss; Consultant, Trevor Brown; Associate Designer, Katie Chiaby; Assistant Production Manager, Becca Ball; Wardrobe, Morgan Blaich; Master Electrician, Jessica Simmons; Carpenter, Pete Fry; Sound Engineer, Joel Wilhelmi; For Two Step: Cris Buchner, Kate Mott, Amy Dalba, Amber Estes, Rachel Merrill Moss, Genevieve Spies; Advertising, Eliran Murphy Group; Press, O+M Company, Rick Miramontez, Elizabeth Wagner, Jaron Caldwell

CAST Max **Kevin Thomas Collins**; Benjie **Alex Anfanger**; Jessica **Maia Madison**; Gilbert **Matthew Bondy**

UNDERSTUDIES David Kenner (Benjie, Gilbert, Max), Johanna Weller-Fahy (Jessica)

SETTING Present day; Max and Benjie's apartment, New York City. Off-Broadway premiere of a new play presented without intermission. Previously presented at the 2009 Midtown International Theatre Festival where it won outstanding production of a play.

SYNOPSIS In *Made in Heaven*, conjoined twins Max and Benjie share everything – a life, a career, even a penis. But when they plan to propose marriage to their mutual girlfriend, Benjie reveals a secret so big it threatens to tear the brothers apart. Family ties are put to the ultimate test in this irreverent comedy about love in all its various forms – and the messy complications that invariably get in its way.

Alex Anfanger and Kevin Thomas Collins in Made in Heaven *(photo by Thom Kaine)*

Persistence of Memory: Three Unforgettable One-Acts

Acorn Theatre on Theatre Row; First Preview: November 1, 2009; Opening Night: November 8, 2009; Closed November 22, 2009; 1 preview, 4 performances (Sundays only)

Written by Christopher Durang, Arthur Miller, and Susan Charlotte; Presented by Cause Célèbre/Part Time Productions in association with The New Group; Directors, Christopher Hart and Antony Marsellis; Assistant Director, Michael Citriniti; Stage Manager, Kelly Hess; Company Manager, Deb Hackenberry; Assistant Company Manager, Brendan Hill; Accounting, Ira Schall; Legal, Nan Bases

CAST *Mrs. Sorken* (by Christopher Durang): Mrs. Sorken **Marian Seldes**; *I Can't Remember Anything* (by Arthur Miller): Lenora **Joan Copeland**; Leo **Bernie McInerney**; *Tango Finish* (by Susan Charlotte): Mary **Tandy Cronyn**; Rose **Rose Gregorio**; **Michael Citriniti**; Dancers **Talia Castro-Pozo**, **Lee Van Bradley**

Three one-act plays presented without intermission. Presented as a benefit for Columbia Psychiatry.

SYNOPSIS Cause Célèbre and Part Time Productions presents a special evening of one-act plays that deal with memory. *Mrs. Sorken* revolves around a woman who seems to be most at home in the theatre and feels most connected when she is with an audience. *I Can't Remember Anything* centers on Leo and Lenora who struggle with their memories of the past, their uneasiness with the present, and their fears of the future. *Tango Finish*, combining theatre and dance, tells the story of Rose and Mary who reconnect to their present when Mary, a former dancer, recalls images of the two dancers who inspired her to be a dancer and teaches Rose to dance the tango and embrace the missing parts of her life.

The Company of Persistence of Memory *(photo by Rose Billings)*

Red Sea Fish

59E59 Theater C; First Preview: November 3, 2009; Opening Night: November 8, 2009; Closed November 22, 2009; 26 performances

Written by Matt Wilkinson; Presented by Two Bins (Brighton, England) as part of the 2009 Brits Off-Broadway Festival; Produced by 59E59 (Elizabeth Kleinhans, President and Artistic Director; Peter Tear, Executive Producer); Directors, Franklyn McCabe and Matt Wilkinson; Design, Jess Wiesner; Set Construction, Vadim Malinskiy; Lighting, Jack Knowles; Sound/Composer, David Benke; Assistant Director, Jett Tattersall; AEA Stage Manager, Trisha Henson; Press, Karen Greco

CAST Ray **Tim Blissett**; Karen **Janna Fox**; Terry **Matthew Houghton**

U.S. premiere of a new play presented in two acts.

SYNOPSIS Ray, a retired thief, sees out his days on the top floor of a tower block on the South Coast. Confined during the day by a rare skin condition, he's cared for by his son Terry. Ray merrily fills the air with accounts of lost love, past misadventure and the daily observations of a bitter old man. When Terry invites a young runaway back to the flat, she ignites long forgotten passions in Ray. *Red Sea Fish* is a darkly funny and ultimately tender story about loss, identity and the folly of trying to control the world.

Matt Houghton, Janna Fox, and Tim Blissett in Red Sea Fish *(photo by Ali Tollervey)*

Talk Like Singing

Skirball Center at Pace University; First Preview: November 12, 2009; Opening Night: November 13, 2009; Closed November 22, 2009; 1 preview, 12 performances

Written and directed by Koki Mitani, English translation by Shin Yamamoto; Produced by Tokyo Broadcasting Systems Inc. and Kyodo Tokyo Inc. in association with Johnny&Associates and Cordly; Music and Musical Direction, Yasuharu Konishi; Choreography, Kaoru Harada; Set, Yukio Horio; Lighting, Motoi Hattori; Sound, Masahiro Inoue; Costumes, Christian Storms; Associate Director, Kiyoko Ogino; Associate Director, Satsuki Watanabe; PSMs, Hiroo Akabane and Tetsuo Matsuzaka; Stage Managers, Matsue Miki, Osamu Hamada, Kazushige Wakamatsu, Shuji Yammamoto; Production Manager, Wendy Luedtke; Associate Music Directors, Chisai Hasebe, Hirotaka Yamazaki; Tap Dance Choreography, Hideboh; Recording Engineer, Toshiya Arai; Associate Set, Yuko Saito; Assistant Choreographer, Ayano Mochizuki; Production Props, Akihiko Horio; Interpreters, Nana Nakayama, Haruku Shinozaki, Jun Kim; Understudy for Rehearsal, Hajime Onodera; Main Visual Design, Hiroomi Hattori; Advertising, Eliran Murphy Group; Press, Cohn Dutcher

CAST Tarlow, *Dyson's Assistant* **Shingo Katori**; Dyson **Jay Kabira**; Nimoy, *Dyson's Assistant* **Keiko Horiuchi**; Brother, *Dyson's Assistant* **Shinya Niiro**

THE BAND *TRI4TH*: Hirotake Kitakata (Conductor/piano), Yusuke Orita (trumpet), Junnosuke Fujita (saxophone), Takao Ito (drums), Tomotaka Sekiya (bass), Shinichi Minami (percussion)

MUSICAL NUMBERS Self-Introduction, Count Soung, Behave Yourself, Dribble Dance, May I Help You?, Social Misfit Monologue, May I? May I?, Dancing Watch, Naruhodo: The Musical; An Eyewitness, Self-Introduction: Reprise, The Nilow's Tonight Show, Always Like This, Scary Typhoon, Social Misfit Monologue: Reprise, Dr. Dyson, the Perfect Psychiatrist, I am Tarlow, Bitter Memories, A.I.U.E.O, Bitter Memories: Reprise, About Singing, 50 States, Resume the Lesson, Hypnotism, Night in the Park, Full of Happiness, My Name Is Brother, Talk Like Singing, Hypnotism: Reprise with Fog, Full of Happiness: Reprise, Extermination Song,

SETTING The action takes place at an international academic psychology conference. World premiere of a new Japanese musical presented in Japanese and English without intermission.

SYNOPSIS In *Talk Like Singing* a unique young man named Tarlow can only communicate through song. His peculiar situation draws the attention of the general public, the media, and most importantly, two respected behavioral specialists. With the help of a speech therapist and psychologist Tarlow is finally able to silence the singing voices in his head and, for the first time in his life, the young man can speak without singing; but what he finds is that he is unhappy and misses the music. The psychologist presents Tarlow as his "success story" at a conference with his fellow colleagues, when all of a sudden the unexpected happens, and Tarlow breaks out into an unforgettable performance for all eyes to see.

Shingo Katori (center) and the Company in Talk Like Singing *(photo by Gion)*

Loaded

Lion Theatre on Theatre Row; First Preview: November 7, 2009; Opening Night: November 15, 2009; Closed January 23, 2010; 9 previews, 64 performances

Written by Elliot Ramón Potts; Produced by Ramoncíto Productions; Director, Michael Unger; Associate Producers, David Santana, Tim Sutton; Set, Adam Koch; Costumes, Steven Schacht; Lighting, Herrick Goldman; Hair & Makeup, David Santana; PSM, Melissa Jernigan; ASM, Joel T. Bauer; Company Manager, Genevieve Spies; Casting, McCorkle Casting Ltd./Joe Lopick; Artists, Mark Beard, Geoff Chadsey; Production Manager, Amber Estes; General Management, Two Step Productions; Assistant Production Manager, Becca Ball; Props, Laura Taber Bacon; Assistant Lighting, Susan Nicholson; Master Electrician/Programmer, Ben Tevelow; Carpenter, Pete Fry; Advertising, Eliran Murphy Group; Graphic Design, Jeff Adkisson; Website, Chad Carano; Marketing, The Karpel Group, Marc Mannino, Vinny Moschetta; Press, The Karpel Group, Bridget Klapinski, Adam Bricault

CAST Patrick **Kevin Spirtas**; Jude **Scott Kerns**

UNDERSTUDIES Joel T. Bauer (Jude), Rik Walter (Patrick)

SETTING Patrick's studio apartment, New York City, present day. New York premiere of a new play presented without intermission.

SYNOPSIS *Loaded* centers on Jude and Patrick, two men exploring whether or not their casual sexual relationship has the potential to be something more. When the generation that separates them sparks a series of misunderstandings and assumptions, their connection is strained and the conversation turns serious. *Loaded* taps into the climate of 21st century gay culture as it seeks to make sense of the bewildering chasm that separates middle-aged and younger gay men.

Kevin Spirtas and Scott Kerns in Loaded *(photo by David Morgan)*

Anna Francolini in Wolves at the Window
(photo by Richard Hubert Smith)

Wolves at the Window
and other Tales of Immorality

59E59 Theater B; First Preview: November 10, 2009; Opening Night: November 15, 2009; Closed December 6, 2009; 35 performances

Written by Toby Davies (after Saki); Presented by Fledgling Theatre in association with Arcola Theatre (London); Produced by 59E59 (Elizabeth Kleinhans, President and Artistic Director; Peter Tear, Executive Producer); Director, Thomas Hescott; Design, Maureen Freedman; Lighting, Richard Howell; Sound/Music, Tim Saward; Costume Supervisor, Dean Burke; Production Manager, Ian McCracken for Support Act Services; AEA Stage Manager, Raynelle Wright; Press, Karen Greco

CAST **Gus Brown**, **Jeremy Booth**, **Anna Francolini**, **Sarah Moyle**

U.S. premiere of a new play presented in two acts.

SYNOPSIS Discover why you must never tell the truth, marvel at why being nice never pays, and understand the complex rules to getting one over your fellow man. Enter the offbeat world of Saki and his biting tales of immorality. This macabre, acid-soaked world taken from ten of Saki's deliciously demented short stories drives a knife into upper class Edwardian life.

Sholom Aleichem: Laughter Through Tears

Baruch Performing Arts Center – Rose Nagelberg Theatre; First Preview: November 8, 2009; Opening Night: November 17, 2009; Closed December 13, 2009; 10 previews, 27 performances

Written by Theodore Bikel; Presented by National Yiddish Theatre Folksbiene (Zalmen Mlotek, Artistic Director; Georgia Buchanan, Managing Director); Presented by special arrangement with National Jewish Theatre (Arnold Mittelman, Producing Artistic Director; Larry Wood, Company Manager); Director, Derek Goldman; Music and Lyrics, E. Lopatnik, A. Sutzkever, Mark Warshafsky, Morris Rosenfeld, Pinkhas Yassinovsky, A. Leyvik, Chava Alberstein; Music Director, Tamara Brooks; Set, Robbie Hayes; Costumes, Gail Cooper-Hecht; Lighting, Dan Covey; Sound, Don Jacobs; Projections, Zachary Borovay; PSM, Marci Skolnick; Production Manager, Jason W.S. Janicki; Wardrobe Supervisor, Dale Carman; Supertitles, Rachel Druck; Company Manager, Julie Congress; Marketing/Promotions, Ashley Bundis, Rock the Stage Inc.; Group Sales, I.W. Firestone; Press, Beck Lee Media Blitz

Performed by **Theodore Bikel**

MUSICIANS Tamara Brooks (piano), Merima Kljuco (accordion)

MUSICAL NUMBERS Ver Vet Blaybbn (Who Will Remain), My Boy, Oyfn Pripetshik, Di Ban (The Train), Der Bal Agole (Coachman), A Sudenyu (The Feast), Zayt Gezunt (Farewell My Friends), Di Mezinke (Our Youngest is Married), Dem Milners Trern (Miller's Tears)

New York premiere of a solo performance play with music presented without intermission. Originally developed in 2008 by Theatre J in Washington D.C. (Ari Roth, Artistic Director; Patricia Jenson, Managing Director).

SYNOPSIS Sholom Aleichem's stories introduced the world to Tevye the Milkman and inspired the landmark Broadway musical, *Fiddler on the Roof*. Theo Bikel played Tevye more than 2,000 performances onstage. Now as playwright and star, Bikel brings back to life one of literature's most beloved authors and a bevy of the unforgettable characters he created.

Yisrael Campbell in Circumcise Me *(photo by Carol Rosegg)*

Circumcise Me

Bleecker Street Theatre; First Preview: November 1, 2009; Opening Night: November 18, 2009; Closed June 27, 2010; 12 previews, 137 performances

Written by Yisrael Campbell; Produced by Evelyn McGee Colbert, Maximum Entertainment, and Daf Alef Productions; Director, Sam Gold; Executive Producer, Eva Price; Scenic/Video Design, Aaron Ryne; Associate Video, Linsey Bostwick; Lighting, Perchik Krelman-Miller; Sound, Drew Fornarola, John Fontein; General Manager, Maximum Entertainment Productions; Marketing, Leanne Schanzer Promotions; Advertising, Hofstetter + Partners/Agency212; Production Supervisor, Matthew Karr; Associate Director, Annie G. Levy; Company Manager, Holly Sutton; Press, Keith Sherman and Associates, Scott Klein

Performed by **Yisrael Campbell**

New York premiere of a new solo performance play presented without intermission.

SYNOPSIS *Circumcise Me* tells the true story of Yisrael Campbell, your average Irish, Italian, Catholic kid from Philly, who became a sober alcoholic, recovering drug addict, husband, father, reform, conservative, unorthodox, orthodox, Jewish comic actor. In his New York theatrical debut, Yisrael (born Christopher) takes the audience on an extraordinary spiritual, creative, and hysterically funny journey including, ouch, three circumcisions along the way.

Theodore Bikel in Sholom Aleichem: Laughter Through Tears *(photo by Stan Barouh)*

My Wonderful Day

59E59 Theater A; First Preview: November 11, 2009; Opening Night: November 18, 2009; Closed December 13, 2009; 34 performances

Written and directed by Alan Ayckbourn; Presented by the Stephen Joseph Theatre Company (Scarborough, England; Chris Monks, Artistic Director) as part of the 2009 Brits Off-Broadway Festival; Produced by 59E59 (Elizabeth Kleinhans, President and Artistic Director; Peter Tear, Executive Producer); Set, Roger Glossop; Lighting, Mick Hughes; Costumes, Jennie Boyer; Sound, Ben Vickers; Stage Manager, Fleur Linden Beeley; ASM, Mark Johnson; AEA Stage Manager, Amy Kaskeski; Touring and Programming Director, Amanda Saunders; Production Manager, Adrian Sweeney; Master Carpenter, Frank Matthews; Press, Karen Greco

CAST Kevin **Terence Booth**; Laverne **Petra Letang**; Winnie **Ayesha Antoine**; Tiffany **Ruth Gibson**; Josh **Paul Kemp**; Paula **Alexandra Mathie**

SETTING Kevin and Paula's home; Tuesday. U.S. premiere of a new comedy/farce presented without intermission. World premiere at the Stephen Joseph Theatre Company. This production, the veteran playwright's 73rd work, marked the first time that an Alan Ayckbourn world premiere transferred to the U.S. prior to a U.K. tour.

SYNOPSIS Winnie lives in a world full of adults. She's off school for the day and has an essay to write, "My Wonderful Day." What better opportunity than quietly seated unnoticed in a corner, whilst mother busies herself at her housekeeping job? What better source of material than the bizarre and increasingly frenetic comings and goings of adults in the weird household in which she finds herself? Enjoy a child's eye view of her "Wonderful" day and prepare to be appalled!

Ayesha Antoine and Petra Letang in My Wonderful Day
(photo by Robert Day)

Dreamgirls

Apollo Theatre; First Preview: November 7, 2009; Opening Night: November 22, 2009; Closed December 6, 2009; 44 performances

Book and lyrics by Tom Eyen, additional material by Willie Reale, music by Henry Krieger; Presented by John Breglio/Vienna Waits Productions in association with Chunsoo Shin, Jake Productions, & Broadway Across America/TBS; Original Broadway production directed and choreographed by Michael Bennett; Director/Choreographer, Robert Longbottom; Co-Choreographer, Shane Sparks; Set, Robin Wagner; Costumes, William Ivey Long; Lighting, Ken Billington; Sound, Acme Sound Partners; Media Design, Howard Werner/Lightswitch; Hair, Paul Huntley; Music Director, Sam Davis; Orchestrations, Harold Wheeler; Vocal Arrangements, David Chase & Cleavant Derricks; PSM, Ray Gin; Stage Manager, Amber Dickerson; ASM, Bob Bones; Technical Supervisor, David Benken; Casting, Jay Binder/Mark Bransdon; General Management, Alan Wasser, Allan Williams, Aaron Lustbader; Press & Marketing, Type A Marketing; Dance Captain, Brittney Griffin; Music Coordinator, Michael Keller; Synthesizer Programmer, Randy Cohen; Music Preparation, Emily Grisham Music Preparation; Musical Contractor, Ray Chew; Booking & Engagement Management, AWA Touring, Alison Spiriti, Matt Chin, Sean Mackey; Production Managers, David Benken, Rose Palombo; Company Manager, Michael Sanfilippo; Associate Director/Choreographer, Courtney Young; Associate Co-Choreographer, Galen Hooks; Assistant Company Manager, Zarinah Washington; Makeup, Angelina Avallone; Associate Design: John Demous (lighting), Daniel Erdberg (sound), Jason Lindahl (media), Giovanna Calabretta (hair & wigs); Assistant Design: David Peterson (set), Rachel Attridge (costumes), Ben Travis (lighting); Costume Production Manager, Tom Beall; Costume Assistant, Tess Sufferlein; Assistant Hair & Wig Production, Lisa Acevedo; William Ivey Long Studio Director, Donald Sanders; Moving Lights, David Arch; LED Programmer, Troy Fujimura; Head Props, Ryan Marquart; National Press Rep, The Hartman Group, Michael Hartman, Wayne Wolf, Matt Ross

CAST M.C./Jerry **Jared Joseph**; Stepp Sisters **Felicia Boswell, Tallia Brinson, Nikki Kimbrough, Kimberly Marable**; Marty **Milton Craig Nealy**; Joann **Talitha Farrow**; Charlene **Brittany Lewis**; Curtis Taylor Jr. **Chaz Lamar Shepherd**; Deena Jones **Syesha Mercado**; Lorrell Robinson **Adrienne Warren**; C.C. White **Trevon Davis**; Effie Melody White **Moya Angela**; Little Albert **Ronald Duncan**; Tru-Tones **Robert Hartwell, Chauncey Jenkins, Douglas Lyons, Jarran Muse**; James "Thunder" Early **Chester Gregory**; Tiny Joe Dixon/Mr. Morgan **James Harkness**; Wayne **Chauncey Jenkins**; Dave **Bret Shuford**; Sweethearts **Emily Ferranti, Stephanie Gibson**; Frank **Jarran Muse**; Michelle Morris **Margaret Hoffman**; Pit Singer **Patrice Covington**; Ensemble **Felicia Boswell, Tallia Brinson, Ronald Duncan, Talitha Farrow, James Harkness, Robert Hartwell, Chauncey Jenkins, Jared Joseph, Nikki Kimbrough, Brittany Lewis, Douglas Lyons, Kimberly Marable, Jarran Muse, Marc Spaulding**; Swings **Brittney Griffin, Eric Jackson, Amaker Smith**

MUSICIANS Sam Davis (Conductor), Alvin Hough (Assistant Conductor/keyboard), Trevor Holder (drums), Jason Langley (bass), Dave Matos (guitar); Local: Jimmy Cozier (reed 1), Patience Higgins (reed 2), Dave Watson (reed 3), James Cage (trumpet 1), Freddie Hendrix (trumpet 2), Scott Harrell (trumpet 3), Danny Hall (trombone 1), Earl McIntyre (trombone 2), Alva Nelson (keyboard 2), Eli Fontaine (percussion)

MUSICAL NUMBERS I'm Lookin' for Something, Goin' Downtown, Takin' the Long Way Home, Move (You're Steppin' on My Heart), Fake Your Way to the Top, Cadillac Car, Steppin' to the Bad Side, Party Party, I Want You Baby, Family, Dreamgirls, Press Conference, Heavy, It's All Over, And I Am Telling You I'm Not Going, What Love Can Do, I Am Changing, One More Picture Please, You Are My Dream, Got to Be Good Times, Ain't No Party, I Meant You No Harm, The Rap, I Miss You Old Friend, One Night Only, I'm Somebody, Listen, Hard to Say Goodbye, Dreamgirls (reprise)

SETTING 1962-1975. Launch of the national touring production of a revival of a musical presented in two acts. Originally produced on Broadway at the Imperial Theatre December 20, 1981–August 11, 1985, playing 1,522 performances, and won six Tony Awards in 1982 (see *Theatre World* Vol. 38, page 20).

SYNOPSIS *Dreamgirls* tells the story of an up-and-coming 1960s girl group from Chicago, and the triumphs and tribulations that come with fame and stardom. This new touring version of the show kicked off at the historic Apollo Theatre (where the opening scene of the musical is set), as part of its seventy-fifth anniversary celebration. The new production incorporated a duet version of the Academy Award nominated song "Listen" which was written for the 2006 DreamWorks film version, as well as a brand new Act Two-opener, "What Love Can Do" written for this version.

Adrienne Warren, Syesha Mercado, and Moya Angela in Dreamgirls *(photo by Joan Marcus)*

*The show concluded its limited engagement at St. Clements on January 31, 2010 and transferred to DR2 for a commercial run on February 23, 2010 (officially reopening March 7). The show closed at DR2 on May 30, 2010 and transferred to the Actors Temple Theater June 19, 2010 to continue its run.

Jim Brochu in Zero Hour *(photo by Stan Barouh)*

Zero Hour

Theatre at St. Clement's; First Preview: November 14, 2009; Opening Night: November 22, 2009; 9 previews, 169 performances as of May 31, 2010*

Written by Jim Brochu; Presented by Kurt Peterson & Edmund Gaynes in association with the Peccadillo Theater Company (Dan Wackerman, Artistic Director; Abigail Rose Solomon, Producing Director; Kevin Kennedy, Managing Director); Director, Piper Laurie; Associate Producer, Richard I. Bloch; Artistic Associate, Steve Schalchlin; Set, Josh Iacovelli; Lighting, Jason Arnold; PSM, Donald William Myers; Marketing, Leanne Schanzer Promotions; General Management, Jessimeg Productions, Edmund Gaynes, Julia Beardsley; Press, David Gersten and Associates

CAST "The Artist" **Jim Brochu**

SETTING An Artist's Studio on West 28th Street, New York City; July 1977. New York premiere of a solo performance play presented in two acts. Originally produced in Los Angeles.

SYNOPSIS In *Zero Hour*, a naïve reporter attempts to interview the famously volatile actor, prompting an explosion of memory, humor, outrage, and juicy backstage lore. The play traces Mostel's early days growing up on the Lower East Side as the son of Orthodox Jewish immigrant parents, through his rise as a stand-up comedian, from the Borscht Belt to Manhattan's most exclusive supper clubs, and from the devastation of the blacklist to his greatest Broadway triumphs, most notably as Tevye in *Fiddler on the Roof* and working through his love-hate relationship with Jerome Robbins. This final interview was made before Mostel left for the pre-Broadway tryout of *The Merchant of Venice* in Philadelphia. Mostel only played one performance as Shylock before his sudden death at the age of 62.

Biography

Theatre 3; First Preview: November 20, 2009; Opening Night: November 24, 2009; Closed December 19, 2009; 4 previews, 23 performances

Written by S.N. Behrman; Presented by Mare Nostrum Elements and Theatre 808 in association with Schoolhouse Theatre; Director, Pamela Moller Kareman; Set, John Pollard; Lighting, David Pentz; Costumes, Kimberly Matela; Sound, Matt Stine; Executive Producers, Quinn Cassavale, Nicola Iervasi, Carey Macaleer, Sherry Stregack; Associate Producers, Evan Sacks, Stephen Moore; Stage Manager, Stephanie Bayliss; ASM, Christina Perry; Technical Director, Ken Larson; House Manager, Jamie Allen; Research Assistant to the Director, Kellie Mecleary; Etiquette Consultant, Ellen Easton; Graphic Design, Kelsey MacMahon; Press, Richard Kornberg and Associates

CAST Richard Kurt **George Kareman**; Minnie **Cheryl Orsini**; Melchior Feydak **Tyne Firman**; Marion Froude **Tracy Shayne**; Leander Nolan **Kevin Albert**; Warwick Wilson **Simon MacLean**; Orrin Kinnicott **Keith Barber**; Slade Kinnicott **Sarah Bennett**

SETTING Marion Froude's West Fifty-Seventh Street atelier. Act 1: 5 pm, early October 1932; Act II: Afternoon, three weeks later; Act III: Afternoon, two weeks later. Revival of a play presented in three acts with two brief intermissions. This production was previously presented at The Schoolhouse Theatre (Croton Falls, NY) March 5–29, 2009.

SYNOPSIS *Biography,* a sophisticated comedy, centers on the heroine and feminist prototype Marian Froude, a gorgeous and promiscuous painter whose subjects include the powerbrokers of the time. She has had many lovers all round the world but not one husband. When she is approached to write her biography, her subjects come running and the comedy explodes into a maddening clash of ethics and ideas.

George Kareman, Tracy Shayne, and Kevin Albert in Biography
(photo by Erik Ekroth)

The Gayest Christmas Pageant Ever!

Actors' Playhouse; First Preview: November 13, 2009; Opening Night: November 29, 2009; Closed January 3, 2010; 10 previews, 19 performances

Written and directed by Joe Marshall; Presented by The Alternative Theatre Company (Joe Marshall, Founder/Artistic Director; Adrian Maynard, Managing Director) and The Actors' Playhouse; Sets/Lighting, Duane Pagano; Sound, Joe Marshall; Costumes, Rachel Dozier-Ezell; Assistant Director, Arlonda Washington; Stage Manager, Jenny Waletzky; Wardrobe Supervisor, Seth M. Gamble; House Manager, Senay Walton; Marketing & Advertising, The Pekoe Group; Press, Springer Associates/Joe Trentacosta

CAST Protesters **Alexandra Dickson**, **Chris von Hoffman**, **Ben Jones**, **Kimberlie Joseph**, **Dorian McGhee**, **Evan Schultz**, **Emily Schramel**, **Heather Shields**, **James Stewart**; Reporter **Rachel Wright**; Actor/Wise Man 3 **Jamey Nicholas**; Actor/Shepherd 2/Manny's Father/Tarquin's Father/Don's Father **John Paul Venuti**; Actor/Spike/Joseph **Bryan Zoppi**; Rod **Jason B. Schmidt**; Manny **Adam Weinstock**; Jim **Ryan Wright**; Don **Blaine Pennington**; Tarquin **Jonathan Chang**; Sam/King Herod/Handsome Man **Ben Jones**; M&M/Shepherd 1/Don's Father **Chris von Hoffman**; Monica **Emily Schramel**; Jesus **Alvaro Sena**; Margie **Crystal Cotton**; Janet **Elyse Beyer**; Martha **Ree Davis**; Tina/Mary/Manny's Mother/Tarquin's Mother/Jim's Mother **Heather Shields**; Tyrone **Kershel Anthony**; Actor 3/Santa/Wise Man 1 **James Stewart**; Ted **Evan Schultz**; Tyrone's Mother **Kymberlie Joseph**; Tyrone's Father/Inn Keeper/Wise Man 2 **Dorian McGhee**; Angel **Alexandra Dickson**

UNDERSTUDIES Michael Munoz (Tarquin, Ted), Ben Jones (Jim)

SETTING The Baron Stage of the Triangle Theatre Company, a small GLBT theatre group in West Hollywood, California near the time for their annual Christmas pageant. New York premiere of a new play presented in two acts.

SYNOPSIS It's time for the annual holiday production for a struggling gay theatre company in West Hollywood. Jim, the pot-smoking straight tech guy, offends M&M, the eclectic playwright, causing him to walk out and take his script with him. Now the crazy and drama-addicted team has just a few weeks to produce the "gayest Christmas pageant ever."

John Paul Venuti, Chris von Hoffman, Bryan Zoppi, Heather Shields, Alexandra Dickson, Dorian McGhee, James Stewart, Jamey Nicholas, and Evan Schultz in The Gayest Christmas Pageant Ever!
(photo by Stuart Levine)

Merrick, the Elephant Man

59E59 Theater C; First Preview: November 24, 2009; Opening Night: December 1, 2009; Closed December 13, 2009; 26 performances

Devised and written by Mary Swan and Saul Jaffé; Presented by Proteus Theatre Company, Basingstoke (Mary Swan, Artistic Director; Ross Harvie, Creative Producer) as part of the 2009 Brits Off-Broadway Festival; Produced by 59E59 (Elizabeth Kleinhans, President and Artistic Director; Peter Tear, Executive Producer); Director, Mary Swan; Design, Sam Pine; Music, Paul Wild; Lighting Design/Production Manager, Simon Beckett; Aerial Choreographer, Lorraine Moynehan; AEA Stage Manager, Trisha Henson; Business/Finance, Anna Tipler; Marketing and Administration Assistant, Samantha Taylor; Press, Karen Greco

CAST Joseph Carey Merrick **Saul Jaffé**

SETTING U.S. premiere of a new solo performance play presented without intermission. Previously presented at Proteus Theatre Company, Basingstoke, England and at the Edinburgh Fringe Festival.

SYNOPSIS Described as a fusion of burlesque, new circus and physical theatre, Jaffé stars in this highly physical, one-man tour-de-force version of this classic story recharged for the 21st Century. Often the most remarkable stories are the true ones, and the story of Joseph Carey Merrick is certainly that. From an object of curiosity and social revulsion to celebrity, Merrick's life and tragic destiny is as relevant today as it ever was.

Saul Jaffe in Merrick, the Elephant Man *(photo by Ben King)*

Sister's Christmas Catechism: The Mystery of the Magi's Gold

Downstairs Cabaret Theatre at Sofia's; First Preview: November 28, 2009; Opening Night: December 3, 2009; Closed January 3, 2010; 3 previews, 35 performances

Written by Maripat Donovan with Jane Morris and Marc Silvia; Presented by Entertainment Events (Tim Flaherty, President); Director/Design, Marc Silvia; Costumes, Catherine Evans; Production Coordinator, Sonya Carter; Producing Partner, Robert Dragotta; Business Manager, Ken Flaherty; Sales Manager, Amy Payne; Sales, Donald Faber; Marketing, Dottie Peterson; Administrative Assistant, Rachel Harpham; *Late Night Catechism* Co-writer, Vicki Quade; Press, David Gersten & Associates

CAST Sister **Maripat Donovan***

*Succeeded by Denise Fennell (12/15–1/3)

Off-Broadway premiere of a play presented in two acts.

SYNOPSIS In this holiday sequel to the hit *Late Night Catechism*, it's "CSI Bethlehem" in this holiday mystery extravaganza as Sister takes on the mystery that has intrigued historians throughout the ages – whatever happened to the Magi's gold? Retelling the story of the nativity, as only Sister can, she poses the burning question, "We know what happened to the myrrh and frankincense – Mary used them as a sort of potpourri. They were in a barn after all. But who was the culprit who made off with the gold coins and left Mary, Joseph, and the infant Jesus in that lousy stable without any chance to upgrade to a suite?" Employing her own scientific tools, assisted by a local choir as well as audience members, Sister creates a living nativity unlike any seen before.

Mary Beth Burns in Sister's Christmas Catechism: The Mystery of the Magi's Gold *(photo courtesy of Theater Mogul)*

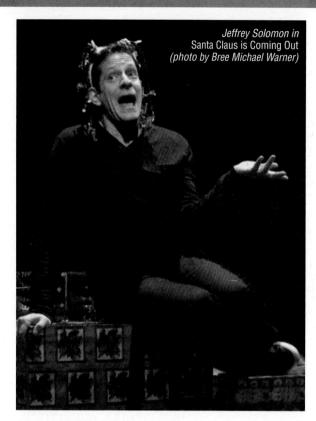

Jeffrey Solomon in
Santa Claus is Coming Out
(photo by Bree Michael Warner)

Santa Claus is Coming Out

Kirk Theatre on Theatre Row; First Preview: November 29, 2009; Opening Night: December 4, 2009; Closed December 20, 2009; 4 previews, 20 performances

Written by Jeffrey Solomon; Presented by Diverse City Theater Company, Penguin Rep Theatre and Shotgun Productions; Director, Joe Brancato; Producers, Andrew M. Horn, Patricia R. Klausner, Victor Lirio; Associate Producer, Martha Zamirski; Set, Michael Schweikardt; Lighting, Jeff Croiter; Costumes, Arnulfo Maldonado; Sound, Jill C DuBoff; PSM, Zachary Spitzer; Technical Director, Vadim Malinskiy; Creative Director, David Derr; Marketing, HHC Marketing; Associate Producer, Martha Zamirski; ASM, Ori Bensimhon; Assistant Set, Ryan Scott; Assistant Lighting, Grant Yeager & David Sexton; Assistant Costumes, Tracy Klein; Assistant Sound, Ien DeNio; Original Music, Andrew Ingavet & Jason Webb; Advertising, D2 Studios Inc.; Press, Janet Appel

Performed by **Jeffrey Solomon**

Off-Broadway premiere of a solo performance play presented without intermission. Previously presented at the Gene Frankel Theatre in 2001 and at the Midtown International Theatre Festival in 2005.

SYNOPSIS *Santa Claus Is Coming Out*, a theatrical mock-u-mentary, is about the worldwide scandal surrounding the outing of Santa Claus. Writer-performer Jeffrey Solomon traces the intensely personal struggle of the great holiday icon, as he tries to reconcile his love relationship with Italian toy maker Giovanni Geppetto with his passion for giving to the world's children. *Santa Claus is Coming Out* features more than a dozen iconic characters. Among them are Sidney Green, the "little Jew who saved Christmas;" nine year-old Gary, who asks Santa for a Sparkle Dream Princess doll; Mary Ellen, who evokes a 21st century Anita Bryant; Rudolph, elves, and many others.

Brief Encounter

St. Ann's Warehouse; First Preview: December 2, 2009; Opening Night: December 6, 2009; Closed January 17, 2010; 5 previews, 38 performances

Written by Noël Coward; Adapted from the play *Still Life* and the screenplay of *Brief Encounter* by Emma Rice; Presented by St. Ann's Warehouse (Susan Feldman, Artistic Director) and Kneehigh Theatre (Emma Rice & Mike Shepherd, Artistic Directors; Paul Crewes, Producer) in association with Piece by Piece Productions and Double M Arts & Events LLC; Original Producers, David Pugh, Dafydd Rogers and Cineworld; Director, Emma Rice; Sets & Costumes, Neil Murray; Lighting, Malcolm Rippeth; Sound, Simon Baker; Projections, Jon Driscoll & Gemma Carrington; Original Music, Stu Barker; U.K. Casting, Sam Jones; Assistant Director, Simon Harvey; U.S. Tour General Manager, Michael Mushalla; Production Manager, Dominic Fraser; Deputy Production Manager, Cath Bates; Wardrobe and Wigs, Nicola Webley; Video Progrmmer, Steve Parkinson; Sound Engineer, Andy Graham; Company Stage Manger, Stephanie Curtis; Deputy Stage Manager, Karen Habens; ASM, Kelly Shaffer; Press, Blake Zidell & Associates

CAST Laura **Hannah Yelland**; Alec **Tristan Sturrock**; Fred/Albert **Joseph Alessi**; Beryl **Dorothy Atkinson**; Myrtle **Annette McLaughlin**; Stanley **Stuart McLoughlin**; Musicians **Edward Jay**, **Adam Pleeth**; Bill/Ensemble **Daniel Canham**

New York premiere of a new adaptation of a 1936 one-act play and 1945 screenplay with music presented without intermission. Previously presented at Kneehigh Theatre (Cornwall) in 2008.

SYNOPSIS Switching seamlessly between live theater and remade film footage, *Brief Encounter* takes audiences back to a bygone age of romance and the silver screen. The production careens around varying moods of clipped, clenched passion heaving under the middle-class restraint of the duty-bound Alec and Laura, and the wild music-hall exuberance of the slap-and-tickle high-jinks of two other clandestine couples among the railway station staff. The lives and loves of the three couples are played out in the train station tearoom as a grand entertainment, using the words (some newly set to original music) and familiar songs of Noël Coward to create a breathtaking, funny and tear-inducing show with live musicians on stage, characters jumping in and out of film screens, and a couple in love floating in mid-air.

Hannah Yelland and Tristan Sturrock in Brief Encounter *(photo by Pavel Antonov)*

Geraint Wyn Davies in Do Not Go Gentle *(photo by Peter James Zielinski)*

Do Not Go Gentle

Clurman Theatre on Theatre Row; First Preview: November 19, 2009; Opening Night: December 6, 2009; Closed January 10, 2010; 15 previews, 29 performances

Written by and original direction by Leon Pownall with original works of Dylan Thomas; Produced by MRK Productions (Marla R. Kaye); Direction Realization, Dean Gabourie; Lighting, Jill Nagle; Stage Manager, D.C. Rosenberg; ASM, Marjorie Golden; Advertising, STEAMcoInc.com; Press, Sam Rudy Media Relations

CAST Dylan Thomas **Geraint Wyn Davies**

SETTING Time: Today. Place: Purgatory. Revival of a solo performance play presented in two acts.

SYNOPSIS *Do Not Go Gentle* finds Dylan Thomas in Purgatory, reflecting on the influences in his life that brought him there. From stories of his childhood, to his marital regrets and his success in America, these reflections run from the tragic to the humorous to the downright fantastic.

NEWSical the Musical

47th Street Theatre; First Preview: November 24, 2009; Opening Night: December 9, 2009; Closed March 21, 2010; 18 previews, 121 performances

Created and written by Rick Crom; Produced by Fred M. Caruso, Tom D'Angora, Elyse Pasquale in association with Annette Niemtzow and Adam Weinstock, Creative Concept Productions; Director, Mark Waldrop; Music Director/Arrangements, Ed Goldenschneider; Set, Jason Courson, Costumes, David Kaley; Lighting, Matthew Gordon; PSM, Scott F. DelaCruz; General Manager, Fred M. Caruso; Assistant Lighting, Josh Starr; Wardrobe Supervisor/Production Assistant, Carolyn Kuether; Production Assistant/Board Operator, Danny Purcell; Wigs and Hair, J. Jared Janas and Rob Greene; Casting Assistant, Ryan Obermeier; Graphics/Photography, Cam Northey; Crew, Wyatt Kuether; Press, John Capo

CAST **Christina Bianco**, **Rory O'Malley**, **Christine Pedi**, **Michael West**; Understudies **Amy Griffin**, **Tommy Walker**

New edition of a musical revue presented in two acts. Previously presented at the John Houseman Studio January 9, 2004 for an eight-week limited engagement. The show reopened as an Off-Broadway production at Upstairs at Studio 54 October 7, 2004–April 17, 2005 playing 215 performances (see *Theatre World* Vol. 61, page 125).

SYNOPSIS No one in the news is safe! The Drama Desk nominated *NEWSical the Musical* is back lampooning current events, headlines, newsmakers, celebrities, and politicians. With songs and material being updated on a regular basis, composer-lyricist Rick Crom's topical musical comedy is an ever-evolving mockery of all the news that is fit to spoof!

(Clockwise from left) Michael West, Christine Pedi, Rory O'Malley, and Christina Bianco in NEWSical the Musical *(photo by Bradley Clements)*

Jack Farthing, William Mannering, Philip Cumbus, and Trystan Gravelle in the Globe Theatre production of Love's Labour's Lost *(photo by John Haynes)*

Love's Labour's Lost

Michael Schimmel Center; First Preview: December 8, 2009; Opening Night: December 10, 2009; Closed December 21, 2009; 2 previews, 14 performances

Written by William Shakespeare; Presented by Shakespeare's Globe Theatre (Dominic Dromgoole, Artistic Director; Conrad Lynch, Executive Producer), 2Luck Concepts (John Luckacovic and Eleanor Oldham), and Pace University; Director, Dominic Dromgoole; Music, Claire van Kampen; Choreography, Siân Williams; Set/Costumes, Jonathan Fensom; Costumes, Lighting, Paul Russell; Text Work, Giles Block; Movement, Glynn MacDonald; Voice Work, Jan Haydn Rowles; Press, Richard Kornberg & Associates

CAST Maria **Jade Anouka**; Ferdinand **Philip Cumbus**; Moth **Seroca Davis**; Dumaine **Jack Farthing**; Sir Nathaniel **Patrick Godfrey**; Holofernes **Christopher Godwin**; Berowne **Trystan Gravelle**; Longaville **William Mannering**; Costard **Fergal McElherron**; Jacquenetta **Rhiannon Oliver**; Rosaline **Thomasin Rand**; Don Armado **Paul Ready**; Katherine **Siân Robins-Grace**; Boyet **Tom Stuart**; Princess of France **Michelle Terry**; Dull **Andrew Vincent**

MUSICIANS Nick Perry, George Bartle, David Hatcher, Arngeir Hauksson, Claire McIntyre, Benjamin Narvey

SETTING Navarre, a province in northern Spain. International touring revival of a classic play presented in two acts.

SYNOPSIS Self-denial is in fashion at the court of Navarre where the young King and three of his noblemen solemnly forswear the company of women in favor of serious study. But the lovely, sharp-tongued Princess of France and her all-too-lovely entourage soon arrive with other ideas and it isn't long before young love, with its flirtations, hesitations and embarrassments, has broken every self-imposed rule set by the young men.

A British Subject

59E59 Theater B; First Preview: December 9, 2009; Opening Night: December 13, 2009; Closed January 3, 2010; 23 performances

Written by Nichola McAuliffe; Presented by Pleasance Theatre Trust (Anthony Alderson, Director) as part of the 2009 Brits Off-Broadway Festival; Produced by 59E59 (Elizabeth Kleinhans, President and Artistic Director; Peter Tear, Executive Producer); Director, Hannah Eidinow; Design, Christopher Richardson; Original Lighting, Mark Jonathan; Original Sound, Tom Lishman; Company Manager (U.K.), Helen Samways; Associate Producer, Louise Chantal; AFA Stage Manager, Raynelle Wright; Press, Karen Greco

CAST Shiv Grewal, Nichola McAuliffe, Tom Cotcher, Kulvinder Ghir

SETTING London and Pakistan, 1988–2006. U.S. premiere of a new play presented without intermission.

U.S. premiere of a new play presented. World premiere at the 2009 Edinburgh Fringe Festival.

SYNOPSIS At the age of 18, Mirza Tahir Hussain, A British Subject, arrived in Pakistan. 24 hours later a taxi driver was dead and Tahir was tried for his murder. Condemned to hang in the Criminal Court, he spent 18 years on Death Row. Don Mackay of the Daily Mirror was the only journalist to visit him in that time. Written by and starring Olivier Award-winning actress (and Mackay's wife) Nichola McAuliffe, A British Subject is their tale that travels from the backstage of a Noel Coward play in the heart of London to the squalid jails of Pakistan as Mackay and McAuliffe race to free this British national from his date with the gallows.

Shivinder Grewal and Nichola McAuliffe in A British Subject *(photo by Geraint Lewis)*

Fascinating Aïda: Absolutely Miraculous!

59E59 Theater A; First Preview: December 16, 2009; Opening Night: December 17, 2009; Closed January 3, 2010; 1 preview, 23 performances

Written and created by Adèle Anderson, Dillie Keane, and Liza Pulman; Presented by Theatre Projects Trust, London in association with Nick Brooke Ltd. as part of the 2009 Brits Off-Broadway Festival; Produced by 59E59 (Elizabeth Kleinhans, President and Artistic Director; Peter Tear, Executive Producer); Director, Frank Thompson; Hair, Vincent Roppatte; Lighting, Ben Hagen; Sound, Ken Hypes; Production Advisor, Carl Ritchie; Press, Karen Greco

CAST Adèle Anderson, Dillie Keane, Liza Pulman

U.S premiere of a musical revue presented in two acts.

SYNOPSIS Fascinating Aida swaggers into New York just in time for some Holiday shenanigans. The three-time Olivier Award nominees make a triumphant return to Brits Off-Broadway direct from another record-breaking, sold-out tour of over 100 cities and towns in the United Kingdom. Having driven New York audiences wild during the first Brits Off-Broadway in 2004, Fascinating Aida returns to entertain sophisticates and cynics prepared to plumb their heights of outrageousness. *Fascinating Aïda: Absolutely Miraculous!* unleashes their wicked humor and sensational musical comedy style at the blizzard of Holiday cheer.

Dillie Keane, Adele Anderson, and Liza Pullman in Fascinating Aida: Absolutely Miraculous *(photo courtesy of Fascinating Aida)*

The Complete Performer

Soho Playhouse Huron Club; Opening Night: December 19, 2009; 22 performances as of May 31, 2010 (Saturday evenings only)

Written by Ted Greenberg, and Mike Motz; Presented by Matt Wayne; Director/Writing Consultant, Steve Rosenfield; Lighting/Stage Manager, Kate August; Production Design, Bestar Mujaj and Matt Wayne; Choreographer, Mike Motz; Website, Stephen Bittrich; Graphics, Jessica Disbrow Talley, Wade Dansby; Technical Director, Bestar Mujaj; Props, Saz Freymann, Ien Denio; Press, Lanie Zipoy

CAST The Complete Performer **Ted Greenberg**; Guest Mascot **Matt Wayne**; Mascot Trainer **Mike Motz**; Audience **Olga Wood, Samantha Chapman**

Return engagement of a mostly one-man comedy presented without intermission. Previously presented at the 2008 New York International Fringe Festival and November 8–December 27, 2008 at Soho Playhouse (see *Theatre World* Vol. 65, page 155.

SYNOPSIS *The Complete Performer* is a mostly one-man comedy show, featuring The Late Show with David Letterman's Emmy Award-winning writer Ted Greenberg and his crowd-rousing mascot. The show combines stand-up, mind reading, magic, a half-time show and full-frontal nudity. *The Complete Performer* is a quintessential New York theatre experience.

Ted Greenberg in The Complete Performer *(photo by Dixie Sheridan)*

Simon Green in Simon Green:
Traveling Light
(photo by Carol Rosegg)

Simon Green: Traveling Light

59E59 Theater C; First Preview: December 15, 2009; Opening Night: December 20, 2009; Closed January 3, 2010; 27 performances

Presented by The Yvonne Arnaud Theatre (Guildford, England) as part of the 2009 Brits Off-Broadway Festival; Created by Simon Green; Produced by 59E59 (Elizabeth Kleinhans, President and Artistic Director; Peter Tear, Executive Producer); Music, lyrics, and text by Walt Whitman, Noel Coward, Howard Dietz, Arthur Schwartz, George Stiles, Anthony Drewe, A.A. Gill, Leslie Bricusse, Kurt Weill, Maxwell Anderson, Tony Hatch, Rudyard Kipling, Robert Frost, Donald Swan, W.H. Auden, Irving Berlin, Richard Rodney Bennett, Betty Comden, Adolph Green, Leonard Bernstein, Stephen Sondheim, Burton Lane, Mark Twain, Leslie Bricusse, John Lennon, Paul McCartney, Ira Gershwin, Jerry Herman, Pam Ayres, David Shrubsole, Henry Charles Beeching, Joni Mitchell, Linda Albert, Blossom Dearie, Bob Hilliard, Dick Miles, Richard Maltby, David Shire, Ivar Novello, Edward Moore, Hapgood Burt, Roy Atwell, Silvio Hein; Press, Karen Greco

CAST Himself **Simon Green**; Piano **David Shrubsole**

U.S. premiere of a musical revue/cabaret with text presented without intermission

SYNOPSIS Simon and David bring their cabaret skills to some of the greatest musical writings of the 20th Century, balancing the heartfelt sentiment of Ivor Novello with the contemporary freshness of Lennon and McCartney, the melodic vigor of Leslie Bricusse with the lyricism of Rudyard Kipling and uncovering an inspired piece of collaboration between J.R.R. Tolkien and the musical magic of Donald Swann. *Simon Green: Traveling Light* touches and alights on special moments and feelings, spontaneously stirred by the anticipation of arrival, of departure, of simply traveling through life.

The Emperor Jones

Soho Playhouse; First Preview: December 15, 2009; Opening Night: December 22, 2009; Closed January 31, 2010; 7 previews, 48 performances

Written by Eugene O'Neill; Presented by the Irish Repertory Theatre (Charlotte Moore, Artistic Director; Ciarán O'Reilly, Producing Director) and Darren Lee Cole Theatricals; Director, Ciarán O'Reilly; Choreography, Barry McNabb; Set, Charlie Corcoran; Costumes, Antonia Ford-Roberts; Lighting, Brian Nason; Original Music & Sound, Ryan Rumery and Christian Frederickson; Puppet & Mask Design, Bob Flannagan; Properties, Deidre Brennan; Dialect Coach, Stephen Gabis; PSM, Pamela Brusoski; ASM, Rebecca C. Monroe; Production Coordinator, Jake McGuire; Set Construction, Ken Larson; Associate Design, Michael J. Barczys; Scenic Artists, Anne Hewett, Sarah Pearline; Assistant to Lighting Designer,, Luamar Ciervejeira; Lighting Programmer, Tyler Coffman; Master Carpenter, Donal O'Reilly; Assistant Costumes, Whitney Locher; Wardrobe, Deirdre Higgins, Cristina Bertocci; Graphics/Marketing, Melissa L. Pelkey; Audience Services, Jared Dawson; Development, Patrick A. Kelsey; Literary Manager, Kara Manning; Press, Shirley Herz Associates, Bob Lasko

CAST Old Native Woman/Ensemble **Sameerah Lugmaan-Harris**; Henry Smithers, *a Cockney Trader* **Peter Cormican**; Brutus Jones, *Emperor* **John Douglas Thompson**; Dandy/Ensemble **Jon Deliz**; Crocodile God/Ensemble **Michael Akil Davis**; Witch Doctor/Ensemble **Sinclair Mitchel**; Lem, *a Native Chief*/Ensemble **David Heron**

SETTING A West Indian island not yet self-determined by white marines. The form of government is, for the moment, an empire. Commercial transfer of a revival of a play presented in eight scenes without intermission. Previously played at Irish Repertory Theatre October 7–December 6, 2009 (see Off-Broadway Company Series listing in this volume).

SYNOPSIS Eugene O'Neill's brilliant groundbreaking play, *The Emperor Jones*, is the story of Brutus Jones, an African-American man who sets himself up as monarch of a Caribbean island following a prison break in the United States. When the Natives rebel after years of exploitation, Jones's mesmerizing journey into darkness becomes a terrifying psychological portrayal of power, fear, and madness. With his demons in heavy pursuit and tom-toms beating, the Emperor is forced to confront the mortal sins of his past in search of forgiveness and salvation.

John Douglas Thompson in The Emperor Jones
(photo by Carol Rosegg)

Little Gem

Flea Theater; First Preview: January 5, 2010; Opening Night: January 7, 2010; Closed January 16, 2010; 2 previews, 11 performances

Written by Elaine Murphy; Presented by Gúna Nua Theatre (Ireland; Paul Meade, Artistic Director; John O'Brien, General Manager) and Civic Theatre Tallaght (Ireland; Bríd Dukes, Artistic Director; Kerry Hendley, General Manager); Co-presented with support from the Carol Tambor Theatrical Foundation, the Flea Theater, and Culture Ireland; Director, Paul Meade; Design, Alice Butler; Lighting, Mark Galione; Music/Sound, Carl Kennedy; AV, Jack Phelan; Production Manager, Mike Burke; Stage Manager, Marella Boschi; Press, Karen Greco

CAST Amber **Sarah Greene**; Lorraine **Hilda Fay**; Kay **Anita Reeves**

U.S. premiere of a new play presented without intermission. Originally presented at the Dublin Fringe Festival in 2008 and at the Traverse Theatre (Edinburgh) on August 6, 2009 as part of the Edinburgh Fringe Festival. The production played London and toured England, Ireland, and Australia following this engagement.

SYNOPSIS Three generations of women. One extraordinary year. *Little Gem* is a magnificent and heart-warming story of courage, comedy and romance as three generations of Dublin women embark on a wild journey through a year of unexpected - and frequently unwanted - events.

Genevieve Hulme Beaman, Anita Reeves, Neill Conroy in Little Gem *(photo by Dermot Kelly)*

David Greenspan in The Myopia *(photo by Jon Wasserman)*

The Myopia & Plays

Atlantic Stage 2; First Preview: January 6, 2010; Opening Night: January 10, 2010; Closed February 7, 2010; *The Myopia*: 4 previews, 21 performances; *Plays*: 2 previews, 8 performances

The Myopia written by David Greenspan, *Plays* based on a lecture by Gertrude Stein, adapted by David Greenspan; Presented by The Foundry Theatre (Melanie Joseph, Artistic Director/Founder); Director, Brian Mertes; Lighting, Peter Ksander; Stage Manger, Casey Llewellyn; Producer, Maedhbh McCullagh; Associate Producer, Anna Hayman; Production Manager/Master Electrician, Christopher Hoyt; Graphics, Ant/Anti; Press, Blake Zidell & Associates

Performed by **David Greenspan**

Two solo performance plays presented in repertory,

SYNOPSIS Playwright and actor David Greenspan performs a double-bill of solo performances. *The Myopia, an epic burlesque of tragic proportion* is a comedy about Barclay, who is secretly writing a play about his father Febus, who is struggling to finish a musical about Warren G. Harding that features Barclay's grandmother, Yetti, his mother, a Jewish Rapunzel named Koreen, Mrs. Harding, 16 U.S. Senators in a smoke-filled room and a cameo performance from Carol Channing. Meanwhile, this entire cavalcade is being performed by one character, who in turn is performed by Greenspan from a single armchair on a bare stage. In *Plays*, Greenspan recreates one of several lectures Gertrude Stein gave throughout her celebrated 1934 U.S. tour, and traces her development as a playwright and makes account of a lifelong investigation into the nature of theater and its audience.

The Man in Room 306

59E59 Theater B; First Preview: January 15, 2010; Opening Night: January 20, 2010; Closed February 14, 2010; 6 previews, 31 performances

Written by Craig Alan Edwards; Presented by Luna Stage (Jane Mandel, Artistic Director; Mona Hennessy, Managing Director); Director, Cheryl Katz; Stage Manager, Paul Whelihan; Lighting, Jill Nagle; Set, Charlie Corcoran; Costumes, Arthur Oliver; Sound, Andy Cohen; Associate Producers, BCOG Productions, Janice C. Bennett, Jeffrey D. Caribou, From the Go Film; General Manager, Jessimeg Productions, Edmund Gayens, Julia Beardsley; Stage Manager, Paul Whelihan; Production Manager, Josh Iacovelli; Assistant Costumes, Christopher Metzger; Props, Jessica Parks; Makeup, Jennifer Snowdon; Advertising, Dewey Moss; Marketing, Aria Arts Consulting, Erin Pauahi Auerbach; Press, Joe Trentacosta, Springer Associates

CAST Dr. Martin Luther King Jr. **Craig Alan Edwards**; Voices **Calvin Grant**, **William J. Ward**, **Fredi Walker-Browne**

SETTING Wednesday, April 3, 1968. 6:30PM. Memphis, Tennessee. The Lorraine Motel, Room 306, and later at the Mason Temple. New York premiere of a new solo performance play presented without intermission. World premiere at Luna Stage Company, Montclair, New Jersey

SYNOPSIS *The Man in Room 306* is an intimate, human portrait Dr. Martin Luther King Jr. set in Memphis on April 3, 1968, the evening before his tragic assassination on the balcony of the Lorraine Motel. Dr. King struggles with himself, his future and the very soul of a non-violent movement shadowed by the rise of Black Power with stunning depth and complexity. Before this night is over, he will change...and so will the country.

Craig Alan Edwards in The Man in Room 306 *(photo by Pier Baccaro)*

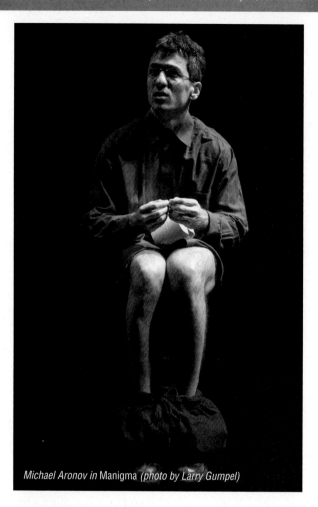

Michael Aronov in Manigma *(photo by Larry Gumpel)*

Manigma

Clurman Theatre on Theatre Row; First Preview: January 15, 2010; Opening Night: January 22, 2010; Closed February 6, 2010; 6 previews, 14 performances

Written by Michael Aranov; Presented by The Process Group Theatre Company and Great Scott Films in association with Artists Empire; Producers, Jack Ballard, Jennifer Makholm and Christopher J. Scott; Director, David Travis; Original Music, David Majzlin and Michael Aranov; Set, Bednark Studios; Lighting, Ben Kato; Stage Manager, Samantha Flint; Press, Sacks & Company

CAST Chaca/Sasha/Frick/T/Pinchy/Rick **Michael Aranov**

Off-Broadway premiere of a new solo performance play presented without intermission. Originally presented Off-Off-Broadway at the 78th Street Theatre Lab in 2006–2007 season.

SYNOPSIS Aranov depicts six distinct characters in *Manigma*: a saucy and resilient cabaret performer embracing her nasty past; a beefy old-world immigrant hungry for a companion; an introverted penny collector who misses his mom; a thug from the streets who demands a revolt; a vulnerable self-helper hunting for courage; and an uninhibited wild man who urges us to abandon and live. These troubled opposites represent extrapolated versions of the actor's own personality. The show highlights the inner conflict of these disparities and then embraces them, celebrating the complexities that make us unique.

The Accidental Pervert

Players Theatre; First Preview: December 14, 2009; Opening Night: January 23, 2010; 13 previews, 44 performances as of May 31, 2010 (weekend and some Monday or Thursday performances only)

Written by Andrew Goffman; Director, Charles Messina; Choreography, Sherri Norige; Audio/Visual Design, Andrew Wingert; Dramaturg, Liza Lentina; Production Coordinator, Gina Ferranti; Lighting, Shannon Epstein; Set/Technical Director, Anthony Augello; Graphic Design, Robert Tallon; Dialogue Coach, Stantley Harrison; Creative Assistant, Christy Benati; House Manager, Carlo Rivieccio; Press, Judy Jacksina

Performed by **Andrew Goffman**

Off-Broadway debut of a solo performance play presented without intermission. Originally workshopped at the 45th Street Theatre and eventually played Off-Off-Broadway at the Triad Theatre.

SYNOPSIS *The Accidental Pervert* is the true accounting of one boy's odyssey to manhood via a childhood dominated by pornography, an addiction accumulated after the boy happens upon his father's collection of XXX-Rated video tapes in a bedroom closet, just to the right of his golf clubs, above the cowboy boots, behind the sweatshirts, all the way up in the top left hand corner. Goffman takes his audience on a hilarious and self-deprecating journey into a world of video vixens, X-Rated fantasies, and really DIRTY movies with no redeeming value whatsoever. He found the tapes at 11 years-of-age. The addiction controlled him until he was 26. THE YEAR HE MET HIS WIFE.

Andrew Goffman in The Accidental Pervert *(photo by Drew Wingert)*

Jamie M. Fox in MazelTov Cocktail *(photo by Carol Rosegg)*

MazelTov Cocktail... an explosive family comedy

McGinn/Cazale Theatre; First Preview: January 26, 2010; Opening Night: February 3, 2010; Closed February 20, 2010; 8 previews, 19 performances

Written by Jamie M. Fox; Presented by Marilyn Ziering; Director, Maria Mileaf; Set, Sandra Goldmark; Costumes, Laurie Churba; Lighting, David Lander; Sound, Nick Borisjuk; Original Music, Casey Geisen; General Manager, Snug Harbor Productions (Steven Chaikelson and Kendra Bator); Website, Brian McGinn; Press, Shane Marshall Brown

Performed by **Jamie M. Fox**

New York premiere of a new solo performance play presented without intermission. West Coast premiere at the Coast Playhouse.

SYNOPSIS *MazelTov Cocktail* follows a Jewish woman as she juggles her job as a personal assistant, her cocaine addicted (and recently jailed) brother and the neurotic parents who spawned them.

The Flying Karamazov Brothers: 4Play

Minetta Lane Theatre; First Preview: February 8, 2010; Opening Night: February 11, 2010; Closed March 7, 2010; 3 previews, 30 performances

Book by Paul Magid & The Flying Karamazov Brothers; Presented by The Flying Karamazov Brothers; Original Music, Mark Ettinger, Doug Wieselman, Howard Patterson; Music Director, Mark Ettinger; Juggling Czar, Rod Kimball; Choreography, Doug Elkins; Set, The Flying Karamazov Brothers; Costumes, Susan Hilferty; Lighting, David Huston; PSM, Emily Cornelius; Assistant Musical Director, Stephen Bent; General Management, Two Step Productions, Cris Buchner, Kate Mott, Amy Dalba, Rachel Merrill Moss; Associate Producer, Highbrow Entertainment; Advertising, Eliran Murphy Group; Marketing, HHC Marketing; Press, Richard Kornberg & Associates, Tommy Wesely

CAST Dmitri **Paul Magid**; Alexei **Mark Ettinger**; Pavel **Roderick Kimball**; Zossima **Stephen Bent**

World premiere of a new theatrical juggling/physical comedy experience with music presented in two acts.

SYNOPSIS A unique blend of music, comedy, dance, theater, and juggling that is sure to dazzle young and old alike, *4Play* features The Flying Karamazov Brothers, New York's favorite multi-faceted new-vaudevillians at the apex of their ambidextrous and alliterative ability. The Flying K's prove with each performance that chaos and unexpected events in our lives are the best part of being human.

Stephen Bent, Mark Ettinger, Paul Magid and Rod Kimball in
The Flying Karamazov Brothers: 4play *(photo by Carol Rosegg)*

Good Ol' Girls

Black Box Theatre at the Steinberg Center; First Preview: February 8, 2010; Opening Night: February 14, 2010; Closed April 11, 2010; 6 previews, 56 performances

Written and adapted by Paul Ferguson from the stories of Lee Smith & Jill McCorkle; Songs by Matraca Berg & Marshall Chapman; Conceived by Matraca Berg; Produced by White Sand Entertainment LLC; Executive Producer, Ken Denison; Director, Randal Myler; Musical Supervisor/Additional Orchestrations, Keith Levenson; Musical Director, Karen Dryer; Set, Timothy R. Mackabee; Costumes, Michael Bevins; Lighting, Brian Nason; Sound, Lew Mead; PSM, Jane Pole; General Management, Aruba Productions/Ken Denison, Eddie Williams, Samantha Schuster; Production Manager/Technical Director, Michael Wade; Casting, Dave Clemmons Casting; ASM, Sandra M. Kroll; Production Assistant, Ellen Mezzera; Associate Technical Director, Joel Krause; Hair & Makeup Consultant, Brenda Bush; Wardrobe Supervisor, Dolores de Crisanti; Sound Mixer, Sebastian Schinkel; Advertising, Eliran Murphy Group; Marketing, Heron Public Relations; Press, Keith Sherman and Associates, Glenna Freedman, Brett Oberman, Dan Demello; Original Cast recording: Sh-K-Boom/Ghostlight Records

CAST Lauren Kennedy, Sally Mayes, Teri Ralston, Gina Stewart, Liza Vann; Understudy Mimi Bessette

BAND Karen Dryer (Conductor/keyboard), Ralph Agresta (guitar), Tom Bradford (percussion), Kelly Lambert (keyboard)

MUSICAL NUMBERS Good Ol' Girl, Appalachian Rain, Lying To The Moon, Late Date With The Blues, Down To My Last Guardian Angel, Booze In Your Blood, Back In The Saddle, All I Want Is Everything, Bad Debt, Betty's Bein' Bad, Happy Childhood, Back When We Were Beautiful, Alice In The Looking Glass, Down To My Last Guardian Angel, Good Ol' Girl (reprise), All I Want Is Everything (reprise)

New York premiere of a new country musical presented without intermission. World premiere at University of North Carolina Chapel Hill in 2000.

SYNOPSIS Two of Nashville's leading singer/songwriters redefine the modern Southern woman in *Good Ol' Girls*, a musical about love, loss and laughter. Through the language of five unique southerners, *Good Ol' Girls* celebrates childhood through old age with big hair and bigger hearts. Great music. Fabulous stories. There's a Good Ol' Girl in all of us. Let yours out.

Liza Vann, Teri Ralston, Gina Stewart, Lauren Kennedy,
and Sally Mayes in Good Ol' Girls *(photo by Carol Rosegg)*

Black Angels Over Tuskegee

St. Luke's Theatre; First Preview: January 29, 2010; Opening Night: February 15, 2010; 6 previews, 74 performances as of May 31, 2010+

Written and directed by Layon Gray; Produced by The Black Gents of Hollywood, Edmund Gaynes, and The Layon Gray Experience; Set, Josh Iacovelli; Costumes, Jason McGee; Lighting, David Boykins & Graham Kindred; Sound, Aidan Cole; General Management, Jessimeg Productions, Julia Beardsley; PSM, Bonnie Hilton; Technical Operator, Jonathon Santos; Choreography/Movement, Layon Gray; Set Dressing/Props, Gayle Lowe; Assistant to Writer, Jackie Coleman; Assistant to Director, Maria Canidy; Casting, Karrie Moore; Advertising, Epstein-Obrien; Press, David Gersten & Associates, Jim Randolph

CAST Man **Antonio D. Charity**[1]; Quenten Dorsey **Layon Gray**; Abraham Dorsey **Thom Scott II**; Theodore Franks **David Wendell Boykins**[2]; Elijah Sams **Lamman Rucker**[3] or **Jay Jones**; Jerimah Jones **Derek Shaun**[4]; Percival Nash **Demetrius Gross**[5]; Sgt. Roberts **Rich Skidmore**[6]

UNDERSTUDIES Stephon Pettyway (Quenten), Reggie Barnes (Jerimah), Jay Jones, Jeantique Oriol (Elijah), Rob Morgan (Man), David Roberts (Abe), Annanias Dixon (Theodore)

*Succeeded by: 1. Thaddeus Daniels 2. Ananias Dixon (alternate) 3. Lawrence Saint-Victor (alternate) 4. Melvin Huffnagle 5. David Roberts or Tobias Truvillion 6. Steve Brustein

New York premiere of a new play presented in two acts. World premiere presented at the Whitmore Lindley Theatre Center in North Hollywood October 10–19, 2008 and January 31–March 1, 2009.

SYNOPSIS In *Black Angels Over Tuskegee*, which is based on true events, six men explore their collective struggle with Jim Crow, their intelligence, patriotism, dreams of an inclusive fair society, and brotherhood as they become the first African American fighter pilots in the U.S. Army Air Forces.

+ The production ended its run at St. Luke's on May 31 and transferred to the Actors Temple Theater on June 5 to continue its run.

(Front): Demetrius Grosse, David Wendell Boykins, Derek Shaun, (back): Thom Scott II, Lamman Rucker, and Layon Gray in Black Angels Over Tuskegee *(photo by Alexandria Marlin)*

Extinction

Cherry Lane Theatre; First Preview: February 13, 2010; Opening Night: February 17, 2010; Closed March 14, 2010; 4 previews, 23 performances

Written by Gabe McKinley; Presented by Red Dog Squadron, Brad Raider, Dulé Hill, and James Roday in association with the Cherry Lane Theatre (Angelina Fiordellisi, Artistic Director; James King, Managing Director); Producer, Breanne Mowdy; Director, Wayne Kasserman; Set, Steve Kemp; Lighting, Mike Durst; Costumes, Gali Noy; PSM, Audra L. Roberson; Marketing, Eliran Murphy Group; Business Manager, Altman, Greenfield & Selvaggi LLP; General Manager, James King; Company Coordinator, Alex Orbovich; Production Manager, Janio Marrero; ASM, Katie Schneller; Press, Sam Rudy Media Relations

CAST Finn **James Roday**; Max **Michael Weston**; Missy **Amanda Detmer**; Victoria **Stefanie E. Frame**

UNDERSTUDIES Michael Hogan (Finn), David Folsom (Max)

SETTING A hotel room in Atlantic City; the present. New York premiere of a new play presented without intermission. Prior to its Off-Broadway engagement the show played at the Elephant Theatre in Hollywood November 21–December 13, 2009.

SYNOPSIS *Extinction* is a darkly funny drama exploring the evolution of friendships – and the lengths to which we go to save them from falling into extinction. College buddies Max and Finn have always spent their vacations in the fast lane, religiously drinking, drugging and chasing women ... but this time something is different. In a hotel room in Atlantic City, the two friends face-off with their indulgent past and take a sober look at their all-too-present future.

Michael Weston, Amanda Detmer, James Roday, and Stefanie E. Frame in Extinction *(photo by Carol Rosegg)*

Palestine

4th Street Theatre (NYTW Space); First Preview: February 5, 2010; Opening Night: February 17, 2010; Closed April 3, 2010; 10 previews, 39 performances

Written by Najla Saïd; Produced by Twilight Theatre Company (Louis Moreno and Sturgis Warner, Co-Artistic Directors; Editha Rosario, Executive Director; Kathryn Pierroz, Managing Producer) in association with New York Theatre Workshop; Director & Dramaturgy, Sturgis Warner; Set & Costumes, Meghan E. Healey; Lighting, Ben Stanton; Original Music, Ray Leslee; Sound, Jeanne Wu; PSM, Molly Minor Eustis; Line Producer, Louis Moreno; Assistant Sound, Alexander Fisher; Draper, Marie Stair; Scenic Artists, Eliza Rankin, Kristen Clare Robinson; Musicians: Ray Leslee (keyboards), Aaron Heick (woodwinds), Rex Benincasa (percussion); Press, Richard Kornberg & Associates

Performed by **Najla Saïd**

World premiere of a new solo performance play with music presented without intermission.

SYNOPSIS In *Palestine*, Saïd makes a case for Palestinian and Arab points of view in ways that truly allow them to be heard. Raised in privilege on NYC's Upper West Side (where many of her best friends were Jewish) Saïd was forced as a teenager to take a family trip to the Middle East to visit her father's homeland. Anorexic and depressed, obsessed with boys and the beach, her experiences nevertheless kindled a life-long exploration of what it means to be both Arab and American. Saïd takes audiences on a whirlwind tour from kissing Jewish boys to what she describes as 'the stench of Gaza,' through two wars, the horrors of 9/11, encounters with world figures including Yasser Arafat, and life with her beloved father. Edward Saïd, was a professor at Columbia University and, until his death in 2003, a worldwide spokesman for Palestine and the Middle East.

Pat Kinevane in Forgotten
(photo by Patrick Redmond)

Najla Saïd in Palestine *(photo by Sturgis Warner)*

Forgotten

Donaghy Theatre at the Irish Arts Center; First Preview: February 14, 2010; Opening Night: February 17, 2010; Closed March 7, 2010; 2 previews, 13 performances

Written by Pat Kinevane; Presented by Irish Arts Center (Aidan Connolly, Executive Director) in association with Georganne Aldrich Heller and Fishamble: The New Play Company (Jim Culleton, Artistic Director; Orla Flanagna, Producer/General Manager); Director, Jim Culleton; Original Music, Brian Byrne; Stylist, Catherine Condell; Costumes, Monica Ennis; PSM, Jenny Deady; Company Manager, Gerard Blanch; Program & Production Manager, Joanna L. Groarke; Master Electrician, Evan Purcell; Marketing, Christine Cullen, Dennis Sherwood, Rachael W. Gilkey, Sydney Snyder; Graphic Design, Betsy Cook; Box Office/Front of House, Jen Browne; Accounts Administrator, Christine Cullen; Education, Rachael W. Gilkey; Fishamble Literary Manager, Gavin Kostick; Press, Karen Greco

CAST Flor/Dora/Gustas/Eucharia **Pat Kinevane**

SETTING Four separate retirement homes and care facilities in Ireland. U.S. premiere of a new solo performance play presented without intermission.

SYNOPSIS *Forgotten* follows four characters, between the ages of 80-100 years old, who reside in retirement homes around Ireland. 1943 was a curious year for this quartet - their lives have never been the same since. This hauntingly dark yet startlingly hilarious play brings to life the heroic challenges, loves and dreams of these people living on the fringe of society.

Romeo and Juliet

Baruch Performing Arts Center – Rose Nagleberg Hall; Opening Night: February 19, 2010; Closed February 27, 2010; 10 performances

Written by William Shakespeare; Presented by The Acting Company (Margot Harley, Producing Director) and the Guthrie Theater (Joe Dowling, Director); Director, Penny Metropulos; Set, Neil Patel; Costumes, Mathew J. LeFebvre; Lighting, Michael Chybowski; Music Composition and Direction, Victor Zupanc; Fight Director, Felix Ivanov; Voice and Text Consultant, Andrew Wade; Sound, Scott W. Edwards; Casting, McCorkle Casting; Text Preparation, Dakin Matthews; Propmaster, Scott Brodsky; PSM, Karen Parlato; Choreography, Marcela Lorca; Production Manager, Scott Palmer; Staff Repertory Director, Corey Atkins; ASM, Nick Tochelli; Development & Communications, Gerry Cornez; General Manager, Nancy Cook; Associate Artistic Director, Ian Belknap; Technical Director, Bobby Edgar; Company Manager, Joseph Parks; Education Director, Justin Gallo; Press, Judy Katz

CAST Abraham/Friar John/Watch **Jesse Bonnell**; Friar Laurence **Raymond L. Chapman**; Juliet **Laura Esposito**; Benvolio **Hugh Kennedy**; Lord Montague/Capulet Guest **Jason McDowell-Green**; Paris/Gregory **Jamie Smithson**; Nurse **Elizabeth Stahlmann**; Mercutio/Prince **William Sturdivant**; Lord Capulet **Chris Thorn**; Perrin **Myxolydia Tyler**; Romeo **Sonny Valicenti**; Lady Capulet **Christine Weber**; Tybalt/Apothecary/Watch **Isaac Woofter**

Revival of the classic play presented in with one intermission. This version of the show premiered at the Guthrie Theater January 9, 2010.

SYNOPSIS *Romeo and Juliet* is the iconic romantic tragedy of innocent young lovers falling victim to family hatred and cruel destiny. This production (which marked the second collaboration of The Acting Company and The Guthrie) toured the United States after its limited engagement at the Guthrie and in New York City.

Laura Esposito and Sonny Valicenti in Romeo and Juliet
(photo by Michal Daniel)

The Boys in the Band

37 W. 26th Street Penthouse; First Preview: February 12, 2010; Opening Night: February 21, 2010; Closed March 28, 2010; 9 previews, 31 performances

Written by Mart Crowley; Presented by the Transport Group (Jack Cummings III, Artistic Director; Lori Fineman, Executive Director); Director, Jack Cummings III; Set, Sandra Goldmark; Costumes, Kathryn Rohe; Lighting, Dane Laffrey; Props, Tessa Dunning; PSM, Wendy Patton; Casting, Alan Filderman; Associate Director, Gregg Wiggans; Technical Director, Joe Cairo; General Manager, Michael Coglan; Dramaturg, Krista Williams; Fight Choreographer, Monica Blaze Leavitt; Development Associate, Michelle Ellis; Assistant Set, Peiyi Wong; Assistant Costumes, Ricardo Fernandez; Hair, Thom Gonzalez; Production Assistants, Michelle Beige, Karen Stern; Wardrobe, Jillian Tully; Graphic Design, Christiaan Rule, Drew Dernavich; Assistant to Mr. Cummings III, Katie Willis; Audience Services, Lauren Scottow; Press, Don Summa

CAST Michael **Jonathan Hammond**; Larry **Christopher Innvar**; Alan **Kevin Isola**; Harold **Jon Levenson**; Bernard **Kevyn Morrow**; Hank **Graham Rowatt**; Cowboy **Aaron Sharff**; Emory **John Wellmann**; Donald **Nick Westrate**

SETTING Michael's Upper East Side apartment; late 1960s. Revival of a play presented without intermission. Originally presented at Theatre Four April 14, 1968, playing 1,000 performances (see *Theatre World* Vol. 24, page 138).

SYNOPSIS *The Boys in the Band* represents a major milestone in American theatre as the first play to openly portray the pleasures, miseries and private lives of gay men. Set during Harold's 32nd birthday party, the evening begins as a hilarious and spirited celebration among friends until unexpected guests and games reveal tensions that unravel these men's souls. Transport Group's production, groundbreaking in its staging, was performed in a penthouse loft that was transformed into the 1960's apartment. The audience was seated around the apartment, enabling them to experience the play in an intimate, three-dimensional environment, allowing a new perspective to the play.

Christopher Innvar, John Wellmann, Kevin Isola, Jon Levenson, Kevyn Morrow, Nick Westrate, Graham Rowat in The Boys in the Band (photo by Carol Rosegg)

Kevin Hart, Catherine Pilafas, and Ami Dayan in Conviction (photo by Eran Tari)

Conviction

59E59 Theater B; First Preview: February 16, 2010; Opening Night: February 23, 2010; Closed March 21, 2010; 35 performances

Written by Oren Neeman, based on the novel *Confession* by Yonathan Ben Nachum; Adapted by Ami Dayan and Mark Williams; Produced by Victory Gardens Theater (Chicago), Maya Productions, and Steve Klein; Director, Jeremy Cole; Original Music, Jon Sousa and Yossi Green; Costumes, Kevin Brainerd; Lighting, Jacob M. Welch; Set Coordination/Gobo Design, Jeremy Cole; Movement Director, Robert Davidson; Properties, Annette Westerby; Stage Manager, Ursula Scriba; General Manager, Brandi Mathis; Marketing, Leanne Schanzer Promotions; Community Outreach Coordinator, Erica Sigmon; Photography, Eran Tari; Associate Producers, Larry Horn, Jeffrey E. Schwarz; Press, Karen Greco

CAST Professor Tal/Andrés González **Ami Dayan**; Director of The National Archives in Spain/Juan de Salamanca **Kevin Hart**; Isabel **Catharine Pilafas**

SETTING 1962 and 1485; Madrid, Spain. New York premiere of a new play presented without intermission. Adaptation commissioned by Denver Center Theatre Company (Kent Thompson, Artistic Director).

SYNOPSIS In *Conviction*, an Israeli scholar is detained and questioned by a Spanish official for stealing a confidential Inquisition file. Together, interrogator and interrogated become drawn to the file's wrinkled yellow pages and unravel the ill-fated love affair between the converted Spanish priest, Andrés González (1446-1486), and his Jewish wife, Isabel.

Patricia Noonan, Allen E. Read, Stuart Zagnit (on the ground), and Nic Cory (back) in Signs of Life *(photo by Joan Marcus)*

Signs of Life

Marjorie S. Deane Little Theatre; First Preview: February 16, 2010; Opening Night: February 25, 2010; Closed March 21, 2010; 9 previews, 26 performances

Book by Peter Ullian, lyrics by Len Schiff, music by Joel Derfner; Presented by Amas Musical Theatre (Donna Trinkoff, Producing Artistic Director) in association with Snap-Two Productions (Virginia Spiegel Criste, President; Maria DiDia, General Manager); Director, Jeremy Dobrish; Musical Staging, Christine O'Grady; Musical Director, Mike Pettry; Set, Alexis Distler; Lighting, Michael Gottlieb; Costumes, Jennifer Caprio; Video, Chris Kateff; Sound, Michael Eisenberg; Technical Director, Cedric Hill; Production Supervisor, Peter F. Feuchtwanger/ PRF Productions; Casting, Carol Hanzel; Marketing, HHC Marketing/Hugh Hysell, Matt Sicoli, Nicole Pando; Orchestrations, Christian Imboden; Associate Producers, Paul Chau, Joan Liman, Bonnie Pederson; Stage Manager, Sunneva Stapleton; ASM, Andrea Jo Martin; Assistant Director, Lisa Marie Morabito; Company Manager, April Armstrong; Fight Choreographer, Jason Collins; Props, Kristine Ayers; Makeup/Hair, Dave Bova; Associate Costumes, Paul Carey; Associate Sound, Veronika Vorel; Production Assistant, Bonnie Hilton; Assistant to the Producer, Lucy Wedderburn; Press, Springer Associates, Joe Trentacosta

CAST Berta Pluhar **Ericka Amato**; Simon Müller **Wilson Bridges**; Kurt Gerard **Jason Collins**; Jonas/Red Cross Inspector/Russian Soldier **Nic Corey**; Wolfie Schumann **Gabe Green**; Lorelei Schumann **Patricia Noonan**; Officer Heindel **Allen E. Read**; Jacob Schumann **Stuart Zagnit**; Commadant Raum **Kurt Zischke**

MUSICIANS Mike Pettry (Conductor/keyboards), Tara Chambers (cello), Joseph Brent (violin), Josh Johnson (reeds)

MUSICAL NUMBERS So Much Life, Signs of Life, Another Picture, Good, The Golemspiel, Home Again Soon, Mourner's Kaddish, Here Today, City for the Jews, Seder, By Your Side, Pieces of Paper, To Make a Man, Pieces of Paper (reprise), Almost, I Will Forget, Find a Way to Live

SETTING Time: WWII. Place: Prague and Terezin, Czechoslovakia. World premiere of a new musical presented in two acts. Originally developed by Village Theatre in Issaquah, Washington (Robb Hunt, Executive Director)

SYNOPSIS *Signs of Life*, a true story of love, defiance and the power of art, is an exploration of life in the Jewish artists' ghetto created by the Nazis in the Czech town of Terezin during World War II. Hitler renamed it Theresienstadt and his propaganda cynically proclaimed it "A City for the Jews". He populated it with prominent artists, composers, scientists, and scholars of Europe. A vibrant community emerged and the ghetto was alive with concerts, plays, and lectures. The Nazi's, for their own propaganda purposes, coerced the prisoners to depict Terezin as a place where they lived free. But hidden from the watchful eyes of their captors, the artists created secret pictures and writings which were concealed and smuggled out to alert the world to what really was happening. They felt that, because of their covert efforts, the truth could survive.

The Duchess of Malfi

Theatre at St. Clement's; First Preview: February 21, 2010; Opening Night: February 27, 2010; Closed March 28, 2010; 4 previews, 35 performances

Written by John Webster, adapted and directed by Jesse Berger; Presented by Red Bull Theater (Jesse Berger, Artistic Director); Sets, Beowulf Boritt; Costumes, Jared B. Leese; Lighting, Jason Lyons; Original Music, Scott Killian; Sound, Nathan Leigh; Fight Director, J. David Brimmer; Choreography, Tracy Bersley; Voice and Speech, Shane Ann Younts; Hair & Makeup, Erin Kennedy Lunsford; Properties, Seán McArdle; Properties, Jessica Scott; Masks, Emily DeCola; Casting, Stuart Howard; PSM, Rebecca C. Monroe; Production Manager, Peter Dean; General Manager, Lisa Dozier; Assistant Director, Damon Krometis; Directorial Assistant, Chantel Pascente; ASM, Rebecca Goldstein-Glaze; Production Assistant, Ashley Crockett; Assistant Set, Buist Bickley; Assistant Costumes, Loren Shaw; Assistant Lighting, Grant Wilcoxen; Dramaturg, Laura Brown; Assistant General Manager, Evan O'Brient; Movement Assistant, Sara-Ashley Bischoff; Marketing, Lisa Dozier; Technical Director, Marshall Miller; Press, David Gersten

CAST Antonio, *Steward to the Duchess* **Matthew Greer**; Delio, *friend to Antonio* **Haynes Thigpen**; Bosola, *formerly in the service of the Cardinal* **Matthew Rauch**; Cardinal of Aragon, *older brother to the Duchess* **Patrick Page**; Ferdinand, Duke of Calabria, *twin brother to the Duchess* **Gareth Saxe**; Roderigo, *a Courtier* **Clark Carmichael**; Grisolan, *a Courtier* **Jason C. Brown**; Castruccio, *a Lord and Doctor* **Eric Hoffmann**; Malateste, *a Count* **Keith Hamilton Cobb**; Duchess of Malfi **Christina Rouner**; Cariola, *her waiting-woman* **Carol Halstead**; Julia, *wife of Castruccio* **Heidi Armbruster**

UNDERSTUDIES Carol Halstead (Julia), Haynes Thigpen (Bosola), Keith Hamilton Cobb (Antonio), Eric Hoffman (Cardinal), Clark Carmichael (Ferdinand, Castruccio), Jason C. Brown (Malateste, Delio), Heidi Armbruster (Cariola, Duchess)

SETTING The court of Malfi, Italy over the period from 1504 to 1510. Revival of a classic play presented in two acts. Red Bull Theater's production is the first New York revival of this Jacobean masterpiece in over 50 years.

SYNOPSIS A great romance turns to horror as the Duchess of Malfi seeks true love in a world of forbidden passions. A play for our time as much as its own, John Webster's *The Duchess of Malfi* examines sexual repression, honor, class, and the true value of the human spirit, in this explosive drama of Italian intrigue.

Heidi Armbruster and Patrick Page in The Duchess of Malfi *(photo by Carol Rosegg)*

The Temperamentals

New World Stages–Stage 5; First Preview: February 18, 2010; Opening Night: February 28, 2010; Closed May 23, 2010; 11 previews, 83 performances

Written by Jon Marans; Produced by Daryl Roth, Stacy Shane, and Martian Entertainment; Director, Jonathan Silverstein; Set and Costumes, Clint Ramos; Lighting, Josh Bradford; Sound, Daniel Kluger; Marketing, HHC Marketing; Graphic Design, Adrian Sie; Casting, Stephanie Klapper; PSM, Tom Taylor; Production Manager, Shannon Case; General Manager, Adam Hess; Associate Producer, Alexander Fraser; Company Manager, Kyle Provost; ASM, Julie DeRossi; Assistant Director, Laura Braza; Assistant Design: Craig Napoliello (set), Ben Tevelow (lighting), Jonathan Reams (sound); Props, Buist Bickley; Musical Consultant, Aaron Dai; Musical Staging Consultant, John Znidarsic; Producer Assistants: Julie DeRossi (Ms. Roth), Greg Raby (Mr. Shane); Press, Kevin P. McAnarney/KPM Associates

CAST Harry Hay **Thomas Jay Ryan**; Rudi Gernreich **Michael Urie**; Chuck Rowland and others **Arnie Burton**; Bob Hull and others **Matthew Schneck**; Dale Jennings and others **Sam Breslin Wright**

UNDERSTUDIES Vince Gatton (Rudi Gernreich/Bob Hull and others/Dale Jennings and others), Robert Gomes (Harry Hay/Chuck Rowland and others)

SETTING Time: Early 1950s; Place: Various locations around Los Angeles. Commercial transfer of a play presented in two acts (for additional production information and synopsis please see previous listing in this section).

Michael Urie and Thomas Jay Ryan in The Temperamentals
photo by Joan Marcus)

A Life in Three Acts

St. Ann's Warehouse; Opening Night: March 4, 2010; Closed March 28, 2010; 22 performances

Written by Bette Bourne and Mark Ravenhill; Presented by London Artists Project (Jeremy Goldstein, Producer) and St. Ann's Warehouse (Susan Feldman, Artistic Director); Director, Mark Ravenhill; Associate Director, Hester Chillingworth; Company Stage Manager, Damon Arrington; Photo Research, Sheila Corr; Internet Film Writer/Director, Helen Wickham; Film Costumes, Maria Jo Garcia; Film Makeup, Paul Shaw; Camera, Graham Cantwell, Richard York, Hannan Majid; "Young Bette" in Film, Chris Cookson; Still Photography, Asa Johannesson; Press, Blake Ziddell & Associates

CAST Bette Bourne, Mark Ravenhill

U.S. premiere of a new play presented in two acts. Previously presented in London at the Soho Theatre; world premiere presented by the Traverse Theatre at the 2009 Edinburgh Fringe Festival.

SYNOPSIS *A Life in Three Acts* is a living, breathing history, edited and adapted for the stage from a series of private conversations between two friends, reminiscing about the life and times of Bette Bourne. The performance is remarkably honest, by turns humorous and angry. The story moves from Bourne's post-war childhood to his first walk across Piccadilly Circus in drag, to his seminal role in the formation of the Gay Liberation Front in Britain. He recalls his life in a drag commune, the creation of the groundbreaking and OBIE Award-winning BLOOLIPS Company, and more – painting an extraordinary portrait of both a life and a movement. To be sure, the work is more than a memoir. It is a moving celebration of the momentous upheavals and transformative achievements of one of the world's greatest liberation struggles in history.

Bette Bourne and Mark Ravenhill in A Life in Three Acts
(photo by Richard Termine)

Finn

Skirball Center at Pace University; Opening Night: March 4, 2010; Closed March 7, 2010; 5 performances

Conceived and directed by Sharon Fogarty, written by Jocelyn Clarke; Produced by Mabou Mines (Julie Archer, Lee Breuer, Sharon Fogarty, Ruth Maleczech, Fred Neumann, and Terry O'Reilly, Co-Artistic Directors) in association with The Skirball Center for the Performing Arts (L. Jay Olivia, Executive Producer); Digital Animation, Misha Films; Music, Phil Cunningham, Manus Lunny; Choreography, Doug Elkins; Set, Milan David; Lighting, Mary Louise Geiger; Costumes, Meganne George; Sound, John Plenge; Production Coordinator, Randy Crabb; Production Manager, Rebecca Josue; PSM, Winnie Y. Lok; ASM, McKenzie Murphy; Projectionists, Shawn Duan, Eamonn Farrell; Assistant Lighting, Greg Goff, Dan Scully; Assistant to the Director, Maggie Bridges; Wardrobe, Meghan Williams; Assistant to the Sound Designer, Anthony Mattana; Production, For Misha Films: Peter Birdsall, Maya Edelman, Dalibor Fencl, Jana Flynn, David Sheahan, Abby Silva, Alisa Stern; Press, Peter Cromarty

CAST Finn Mac Cumhail **Robbie Collier Sublett**; Storyteller One **Jarlath Conroy**; Storyteller Two **Brandon Goodman**; Storyteller Three **Dion Mucciacito**

World premiere of a play with video, animation, music and poetry presented without intermission.

SYNOPSIS Mabou Mines *Finn* offers a sophisticated and engaging interpretation of the Celtic legend of Finn McCool re-imagined for a new generation of theatergoers. *Finn* follows a boy's coming of age quest to avenge his father's death and seize leadership of the clan. Through his journey, he encounters a series of trials testing his moral fortitude. By employing digital animation for a technologically savvy audience, *Finn* explores the nature of violence and ultimately, the nature of morality.

Robbie Collier Sublett in Finn *(photo by Paula Court)*

Defending the Caveman

Downstairs Cabaret Theatre at Sofia's; First Preview: February 23, 2010; Opening Night: March 7, 2010; Closed May 2, 2010; 11 previews, 37 performances

Written by Rob Becker; Produced by Theater Mogul NA Inc. in association with Entertainment Events Inc.; PSM, Alessandra Bono; General Manager, Jill Bowman; Production Supervisor, Jason Rolf Lindhorst; National Booking Director, Michele Gold; Sales Director, Bill Mann; Corporate and Private Events, Eric Sweigard; Press, David Gersten & Associates

Performed by **Paul Perroni**

Revival of a solo performance play presented with one intermission. Originally opened on Broadway at the Helen Hayes Theatre March 26, 1995–January 4, 1997, transferred to the Booth Theatre January 29, 1997 where it closed June 22, 1997 after 25 previews and 674 performances (see *Theatre World* Vol. 51, page 54). The show holds the record for the longest running solo play in Broadway history.

SYNOPSIS *Defending the Caveman* is a hilariously insightful play about the ways men and women relate. This prehistoric look at the battle of the sexes is full of wonderful scenarios that celebrate the differences between men and women. With hilarious insights on contemporary feminism, masculine sensitivity, and the erogenous zone, the show mines the common themes in relationships that go straight through the funny bone and into the heart. *Defending the Caveman* makes the audience laugh at themselves and all the ways that men and women fight, laugh, and love.

Paul Perroni in Defending the Caveman
(photo courtesy of Theater Mogul)

Belfast Blues

Barrow Street Theatre; Opening Night: March 8, 2010; Closed April 26, 2010; 7 performances (Mondays only)

Written by Geraldine Hughes; Presented by Geraldine Hughes in association with Firefly: Theater & Films; Produced by Steven Klein and Nick Micozzi; Director, Carol Kane; Sets/Lighting, Jonathan Christman

Performed by **Geraldine Hughes**

SETTING Belfast, Ireland; 1970s-1980s. Revival of a solo performance play presented without intermission. Previously presented by the Culture Project at the Bleecker Street Theatre January 11–April 24, 2005, playing 10 previews and 91 performances (see *Theatre World* Vol. 61, page 136).

SYNOPSIS One wee girl's story about family, war, Jesus, and Hollywood, Geraldine Hughes's one-woman *Belfast Blues* is a true story told from Hughes' perspective as a little girl coming of age in the warn-torn Belfast of the 1980s. Playwright and performer Hughes depicts over 20 characters in the multi-award-winning performance, which has played to rave reviews in Chicago, Los Angeles, Belfast, London, and New York.

Geraldine Hughes in Belfast Blues
(photo by Jonathan Christman)

Lenin's Embalmers

Ensemble Studio Theatre; First Preview: March 3, 2010; Opening Night: March 8, 2010; Closed March 28, 2010; 5 previews, 22 performances

Written by Vern Thiessen, inspired by the book by Ilya Zbarsky and Samuel Hutchinson; Presented by Ensemble Studio Theatre (William Carden, Artistic Director; Paul Alexander Slee, Executive Director) as part of the Alfred P. Sloan Science and Technology Project (Doron Weber, Vice President of Programs); Producer, Annie Trizna; Director, William Carden; Set, Mikiko Suzuki MacAdams; Costumes, Suzanne Chesney; Lighting, Chris Dallos; Properties, Meghan Buchanan; Original Music & Sound, Shane Rettig; Projections, Alex Koch; Assistant Director, Gerritt Turner; Production Manager/Technical Director, Jack Blacketer; Fight Director, J. Allen Suddeth; PSM, Jeff Davolt; ASM, Michal V. Mendelson; Science Advisor, Bruce Hrnjez; Marketing, Tim Scales; EST/Sloan Project Director, Graeme Gillis; EST/Sloan Project Associate Director, Linsay Firman; Graphic Design, Chrissie Lein; Press, Bruce Cohen

CAST Lenin **Peter Maloney**; Boris **Scott Sowers**; Vlad **Zach Grenier**; Nadia **Polly Lee**; Stalin **Richmond Hoxie**; Krasin **James Murtaugh**; Agent 1 **Steven Boyer**; Trotsky/Agent 2 **Michael Louis Wells**

SETTING Russia, 1924. World premiere of a dark comedy based on a true story presented in two acts.

SYNOPSIS *Lenin's Embalmers* spins the tale of Boris Zbarsky and Vladimir Vorobiov, two scientists who were chosen by The Committee for Immortalization to embalm Vladimir Lenin after his death in 1924. The embalming of the leader of the World Proletariat, which began two months after his death and took almost four months, was a scientific miracle at the time and was hailed by scientists around the world. Lenin's embalmers developed a process which restored the body to a lifelike appearance and is still used for preventive maintenance today. Yet, as so many had during the Great Terror, Lenin's embalmers reached levels of power and influence that ultimately led to their death by a paranoid Stalinist regime.

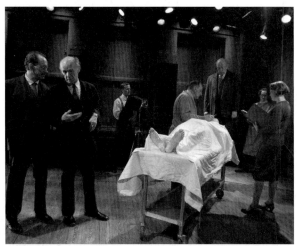

Scott Sowers, James Murtaugh, Steven Boyer, Zach Grenier, Peter Maloney, Michael Louis Wells, and Polly Lee in Lenin's Embalmers (photo by Gerry Goodstein)

Selene Beretta, Rochelle Mikulich, James Kautz, Sarah Lemp, and Matthew Pilieci in Happy in the Poorhouse (photo by Larry Cobra)

Happy In The Poorhouse

Theatre 80 St. Marks; First Preview: March 11, 2010; Opening Night: March 13, 2010; Closed April 26, 2010; 2 previews, 39 performances

Written and directed by Derek Ahonen; Produced by The Amoralists; Assistant Director, Dan Lockhart; Stage Manager, Judy Merrick; Set Design/Fight Choreographer, Al Schatz; Lighting, Jeremy Pape; Sound, The Hernandez Brothers; Costumes, Ricky Lang; Makeup, Lisa K. Hokans; Production Assistants, Rachel Adler, Kelley Swindall; Spiritual Advisor, Larry Cobra; Press, David Gibbs/DARR Publicity

CAST Paulie "The Pug" **James Kautz**; Mary **Sarah Lemp**; Joey **Matthew Pilieci**; Penny **Rochelle Mikulich**; Olga **Selene Beretta**; Flossie **Meghan Ritchie**; Sonny **Morton Matthews**; Sally **Mark Riccadonna**; Petie "The Pit" **William Apps**; Stevie **Nick Lawson**; Larry "The Lab" **Patrick McDaniel**

SETTING Time: Now, but Then. Place: Over a summer afternoon in an apartment on Mermaid Avenue on Coney Island. World premiere of a new play presented in two acts.

SYNOPSIS Paulie "The Pug" is a Coney Island dreamer…just one MMA fight away from the big time. If only he could keep his wife from screwing her ex-husband, his brother-in-law from going to the slammer, and his best friend from taking a bite out of his neck, he'd be on top of the world. A comedy full of weak wrists and strong hearts, *Happy In The Poorhouse* is an unsanitized story of love and sex that will make you think twice about not pulling out!

Sin

Baruch Performing Arts Center – Rose Nagelberg Theatre; First Preview: March 9, 2010; Opening Night: March 17, 2010; Closed March 21, 2010; 9 previews, 6 performances

Based on Isaac Bashevis Singer's *The Unseen*, adapted by Mark Altman; Presented by Tish and Benk Productions; Director, Kent Paul; Set, Michael Locher; Lighting, Matthew McCarthy; Costumes, China Lee; Original Music/Sound, Robert Rees; PSM, Joanne McInerney; Advertising & Marketing, The Pekoe Group; Casting, Alan Filderman; Production Manager, La Vie Productions/James E. Cleveland; General Manager, Cesa Entertainment Inc./Jamie Cesa; Associate General Manager, Gretchen Margaroli; ASM, Emily Levin; Associate Production Manager, Katy Ross; Assistant Director, Mark Stuart; Prop Master, Sven H. Nelson; Technical Director, Joel Howell; Press, Keith Sherman & Associates, Glenna Friedman, Dan Demello, Brett Oberman, Scott Klein

CAST Nosn **Paul Collins**; Rayze Temerl **Suzanne Toren**; Leybish **Grant James Varjas**; Dvoyre Leye **Jessiee Datino**; Shifre Tsirl **Sarah Grace Wilson**; Moyshe Mekheles **Pierre Epstein**

SETTING 16th Century Poland. World premiere of a new play presented in two acts.

SYNOPSIS The devil, demons, and infidelity center stage in *Sin,* a new comedy that pits a happily married couple against the devil himself. On Yom Kippur, the holiest day of the Jewish year, the devil and his demons descend on the tiny town of Frampol. Satan has chosen this most solemn of occasions to test the faith of a happily married couple and in the process ruins their lives. It's a devilish look at two love triangles, one human and one heavenly.

Jessiee Datino, Grant James Varjas, and Sarah Grace Wilson in Sin
(photo by Aaron Epstein)

North Atlantic

Baryshnikov Arts Center;– Jerome Robbins Theatre; First Preview: March 10, 2010; Opening Night: March 23, 2010; Closed April 25, 2010; 11 previews, 29 performances

Written by James Strahs; Presented by Baryshnikov Arts Center and the Wooster Group; Director, Elizabeth LeCompte; Set, Jim Clayburgh; Costumes, The Wooster Group; Lighting, Jennifer Tipton; Sound, Bruce Odland, Matt Schloss, Omar Zubair; Assistant Director, Kate Valk; Production Manager, Bozkurt Karasu; Technical Directors, Geoff Abbas, Aron Deyo; Stage Manager, Teresa Hartmann; Assistant Lighting, Tony Mulanix; Costume Coordinator, Enver Chakartash; Video, Andrew Schneider; Technical Assistant, Daniel Jackson; Original Music & Arrangements, Eddy Dixon; Original Sound Tracks, Bob Cardelli; Additional Music Tracks, Donald DiNicola; Additional Sound Tracks, Bruce Odland; Press, Clay Hapaz

CAST Captain N.I. Roscoe Chizzum **Ari Fliakos**; General Lance "Rod" Benders **Paul Lazar**; Marine Private Walter "Raj" Doberman/Bernice **Steve Cuiffo**; Marine Private Bernard "Gregory" Houlihan **Zachary Oberzan**; Ensign Word-Processor Ann Pusey **Kate Valk**; Master Sergeant Mary Bryzynsky **Frances McDormand**; Nurse Private Wendy-Gwen Clark **Jenny Seastone Stern**; Corporal Nurse Jane Babcock **Maura Tierney**; PFC Med-Tech Kim Buttersworth **Koosil-ja**; Colonel Lloyd "Ned" Lud (A.A.) **Scott Shepherd**; Understudies **Eleanor Hutchins**; **Andrew Schneider**

SETTING Time: 1983 Place: Aboard a U.S. military aircraft carrier, 12 miles off the Dutch coast. Revival of a play with music presented in six scenes without intermission. First presented by the Wooster Group in 1982, the company remounted the show in 1984, 1985, and 1999.

SYNOPSIS *North Atlantic* is a satiric look at the role of the military and the growing influence of technology in American culture during the late Cold War period, after Vietnam, and before the fall of the Berlin Wall. The work follows an international peacekeeping force on an aircraft carrier in the North Atlantic, tracing the cultural and sexual dynamics that rise to the fore as they carry out their top-secret mission. Written expressly for the company by Strahs in 1982, *North Atlantic* joined a series of Wooster Group works rooted in American themes and told in the rhythms of the American vernacular works based on texts by Wilder, Miller, O'Neill, and Gertrude Stein. North Atlantic plays with nostalgia for the analog (pre-digital) 1980s through slang, song and dance.

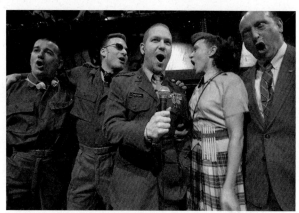

Steve Cuiffo, Zachary Oberzan, Ari Fliakos, Kate Valk, and Paul Lazar in
North Atlantic *(photo by Steven Gunther)*

Looking for Billy Haines

Lion Theatre on Theatre Row; First Preview: March 11, 2010; Opening Night: March 25, 2010; Closed May 22, 2010; 14 previews, 54 performances

Written by Suzanne Brockmann and Will McCabe; Presented by small or LARGE Productions; Director, Suzanne Brockmann; Sets and Props, Meredith Ries; Costumes, Holly Cain; Lighting, Sean Perry; Sound, Amy Altadonna; Music, Barry Singer; Choreography, Joseph Cullinane; Stage Manager, David Craven; ASM, Brandon Davidson; General Manager, Will McCabe; Associate Producer, Jimmy Ferarro; Production Manager, Marshall Miller; Graphic Design, Scott Joseph Fowler and Acting Out Design; Photos, Shirin Tinati; Sets and Props Assistant, Joshua Yocum; Marketing, HHC Marketing; Press, David Gersten & Associates

CAST Jamie Hollis **Jason T. Gaffney**; Mystery Man/Billy Haines **Joseph Cullinane**; Harlan Cavanaugh **Jason Michael Butler**; Lynn Cordero **Apolonia Davalos**; Sugar LaSalle **Annie Kerins**; Alan Zimmerman **Eric Ruben**

UNDERSTUDIES Brandon Davidson (Jamie, Billy), David Covington (Harlan, Alan, Billy), Sarah Ripper (Lynn, Sugar)

SETTING Present day, New York City. Off-Broadway premiere of a new comedy with dance presented in two acts.

SYNOPSIS Jamie Hollis, a struggling actor, scores an audition for a feature film about Billy Haines, a real life gay movie star of the 1920s and '30s who gave up his career to remain in a public relationship with his partner. Billy's story, along with Jamie's rather vibrant imagination and his three colorful roommates, helps him realize that he needs to make some decisions about his own unsatisfying relationship with a closeted man.

Jason T. Gaffney and Joseph Cullinane in Looking for Billy Haines
(photo by Shirin Tinat)

Michael Laurence and Marielle Heller in The Diary of a Teenage Girl
(photo by Jim Baldassare)

The Diary of a Teenage Girl

3LD Art & Technology Center; First Preview: March 15, 2010; Opening Night: March 28, 2010; Closed May 1, 2010; 11 previews, 30 performances

Written by Marielle Heller, adapted from the graphic novel by Phoebe Gloeckner; Directors, Sarah Cameron Sunde and Rachel Eckerling; Produced by Aaron Louis (Producing Director, 3LD Art & Technology Center) in association with New Georges (Susan Bernfield, Artistic Director; Sarah Cameron Sunde, Associate Director) and The Essentials; Set, Lauren Helpern; Video, C. Andrew Bauer; Sound, Marcelo Añez; Lighting, Laura Mroczkowski; Costumes, Emily DeAngelis; Props, Lauren Asta; Composer, Nate Heller; General Manager, Lisa Dozier; Production Manager, Paul DiPietro; PSM, Erin Maureen Koster; ASM, Naomi Anhorn; Casting, Paul Davis/Calleri Casting; Marketing, Melissa Ross; Graphics, David Townsend; Production Consultant, Ralph Capasso; Assistant Video, Piama Habbibullah; Assistant Set, Jacquelyn Marolt; Assistant Lighting, Steve Maturno & Nick Ryckert; Costume Assistant, Teresa Bayer; Video Programmer, James Daher; Fight Choreographer, Jake Witlin; Director of Photography, Jeff Morey; Gaffer, David Tirosh; Sub ASM, Karina Martins; Video Consultant, Jake Witlin; Press, Jim Baldassare

CAST Minnie **Marielle Heller**; Pascal **Jon Krupp**; Monroe **Michael Laurence**; Charlotte **Mariann Mayberry**; Kimmie **Nell Mooney**; Video Actors **Chris Carlone, Mathilde Dratwa**

SETTING San Francisco; the 1970s. World premiere of a new play presented without intermission. Previously presented as an Off-Off-Broadway showcase February 17–March 13 (see Off-Off Broadway section in this volume).

SYNOPSIS *The Diary of a Teenage Girl* is a story about female sexuality and unabashed optimism. Told from the point of view of fifteen-year old Minnie, the play tells the story of her growing up in the chaos of the 1970s, in the haze that is San Francisco. Minnie is incredibly bright and self-reflective. She is gut-wrenchingly honest, and curious about the world around her. And she has just begun an affair with her mother's boyfriend, Monroe.

The Irish Curse

Soho Playhouse; First Preview: March 17, 2010; Opening Night: March 28, 2010; Closed May 30, 2010; 14 previews, 73 performances

Written by Martin Casella; Produced by Craig Zehms and Sarahbeth Grossman in association with Piglet Productions, Anthony George, Lawrence E. Lewis III; Director, Matt Lenz; Set, Lauren Helpern; Costumes, Michael McDonald; Lighting, Traci Klainer; Sound, Walter Trarbach; PSM, Jovon E. Shuck; Production Manager, Amber Estes; Casting, Pat McCorkle, Joe Lopick; General Management, Two Step Productions; Advertising, Eliran Murphy Group; Marketing, HHC Marketing; ASM, Graham Bowen; Dialect Coach, David Wells; Assistant Director, David Rossetti; Properties/Assistant Set, Jacquelyn Marolt; Assistant Costumes, Tristan Raines; Press, David Gersten & Associates

CAST Joseph Flaherty **Dan Butler**; Kieran Reilly **Roderick Hill**; Kevin Shaunessy **Scott Jaeck**; Rick Baldwin **Brian Leahy**; Stephen Fitzgerald **Austin Peck**

UNDERSTUDIES Patrick James Lynch (Rick, Kieran, Stephen), Bill Timoney (Kevin, Joseph)

SETTING A church basement of a Catholic Church in Brooklyn Heights; a Wednesday night. Off-Broadway premiere of a new play presented without intermission. World premiere presented in the 2005 New York International Fringe Festival.

SYNOPSIS Does size matter? It does to the Irish-American guys who meet every Wednesday night in Father Shaunessey's support group…for men with very small penises. All afflicted by the 'Irish Curse' they meet to gossip, fight, moan and share. Sporty student Rick pads his crotch with a rolled up sock; gay cop Stephen has a lot to live up to; lawyer Joseph's wife has walked out; and Father Shaunessy has his own secrets. Fresh-faced Kieran arrives two weeks to his wedding day, and it's the wedding night that's got him terrified. All of them find themselves confronting what it is to be man. *The Irish Curse*, a raucous new comedy, tackles male obsession with body image, masculinity, and sex as it examines the fundamental question on the minds of men since the beginning of time: How do I measure up to the next guy? Five guys…one tiny problem.

Scott Jaeck, Roderick Hill, Dan Butler, Brian Leahy, and Austin Peck in *The Irish Curse* (photo by Carol Rosegg)

David Greenspan and Jennifer Ikeda in Rescue Me (photo by Brian Barenio)

Rescue Me

(A Postmodern Classic with Snacks)

Ohio Theatre; First Preview: March 23, 2010; Opening Night: March 30, 2010; Closed April 18, 2010; 6 previews, 20 performances

Written by Michi Barrall, adapted from Euripides' *Iphigenia in Tauris*; Presented by Ma-Yi Theater Company (Ralph Peña, Artistic Director; Jorge Ortoll, Executive Director); Director, Loy Arcenas; Choreography, Julian Barnett; Set, Loy Arcenas; Costumes, Maiko Matsushima; Lighting, Ben Stanton; Soundscape, Darron L West; Video, Anna Kiraly; PSM, Kat West; ASM, Kristine Ayers; Production Manager, Les Foster; Producer, Suzette Porte; Assistant Director, Dax Valdes; Video Programming, David Tirosh, Alex Koch; Assistant Sound, Matt Hubbs; Prop Supervisor, Emily Lippolis; Wardrobe, Julie Griffith; Greek Tranlation/Coach, Talia Varonos-Pavlopoulos; Voice of Athena, Zoe Anastassiou; Graphics, Noah Scanlin/Another Limited Rebellion; Press, Sam Rudy Media Relations

CAST Artemis/Athena **David Greenspan**; Iphigenia **Jennifer Ikeda**; Orestes **Julian Barnett**; Thoas **Leon Ingulsrud**; Phlades **Ryan King**; Herdsman/Messenger **Paco Tolson**; Sandra **Oni Monifa Renee Brown**; Lydia **Katherine Partington**

SETTING Tauris, a peninsula in the northern Black Sea known today as Crimea. World premiere of a new adaptation of a classic play presented without intermission.

SYNOPSIS In this dance-theatre adaptation of Euripides' *Iphigenia in Tauris*, Iph is 34 and stuck in a dead-end job. Haunted by the past, her present situation is grim – she's at the mercy of a temperamental goddess and a barbarian king with a fondness for human sacrifice. And she's beginning to lose all hope of rescue. *Rescue Me (A Postmodern Classic with Snacks)* is a tragi-comedy about what to do when your Dad tries to kill you, your Mom freaks out, your brother goes crazy and you're surrounded by Barbarians.

ImaginOcean

New World Stages–Stage 5; First Preview: March 17, 2010; Opening Night: March 31, 2010; 11 previews, 48 performances as of May 31, 2010

Book by John Tartaglia, music & lyrics by William Wade; Presented by Philip Katz, Michael Shawn Lewis, and John Tartaglia; Director/Musical Staging, Donna Drake; Set, Robert Andrew Kovach; Puppet Design & Fabrication, The Puppet Kitchen; Music Recording, Yellow Sound Lab/Matthias Winter & Michael Croiter; Recording Engineer, Matthias Winter; Advertising, Hofstetter+Partners/Agency 212; Marketing, HHC Marketing; Casting, Melanie Lockyer; Development Consultant, Georgianna Young; PSM, Emilie Bray Schoenfeld; General Manager, The Splinter Group (Seth A. Goldstein, Heather Schings, William Goldstein); Production Assistant, Beth Rolfs); Creative and Website, Michael Naylor; Assistant to the Director/Producers, Daniel Seth; Study Guide/Educational Outreach, Thru the Stage Door; Press, Betsy Braun

CAST *Puppeteers*: Tank **James W. Wojtal Jr.**; Bubbles **Stacey Weingarten**; Dorsel **Ryan Dillon**; Ripple/Leonard **Lara Maclean**; Baby Jellyfish/Arrows/Others **Carole D'Agostino**; Spirit of Friendship/Jellyfish/Arrow/Others **Nate Begle**; Spirit of Friendship/Jellyfish/Arrows/Others **Jonathan Carlucci**; Puppet Wrangler/Swing **Brian T. Carson**; *Voice*: Tank/Dorsel/Leonard **John Tartaglia**; Bubbles/Arrow **Donna Drake**; Ripple/Baby Jellyfish **Michael Shawn Lewis**; Spirit of Friendship **Meladi Montano** (speaking), **Cathlene Grant** (singing)

RECORDING MUSICIANS Randy Andos (trombone), Michael Croiter (drums), Joe Fiedler (trombone), Brian Koonin (guitar), MaryAnn McSweeney (acoustic/electric bass), Kristy Norter (reeds/winds), Clay Ruede (cello), Denise Stillwell (violin/viola), William Wade (piano/orchestrations); Back-up Vocals: Camilo Castro, Heather Curran, Gavin Esham, Nick Gaswirth, Samantha Grenell-Zaidman, Amy Jones, Tyrick Jones, Ruperta Nelson, Krista Severeid, Michael Yeshion; Children's Chorus: Willow Bennison, Allegra Berman, Nadia Filanovsky, Cathlene Grant, Savannah Henry, Ashley Laird, Meldi Montano, Delainah Perkins, Miranda Powell, Lila Smith-Marooney; "Which Way to Turn" Soloist: Nick Gaswirth

MUSICAL NUMBERS On Our Way, Jellyfish Jive, On Our Way (reprise), Which Way to Turn, Imagination, Just a Stone's Throw Away, The Treasure, Finale

SETTING The Ocean Floor. New York premiere of a puppet theatre musical presented without intermission. A previous version debuted November 20, 2009 on Royal Caribbean International's newest and most revolutionary cruise ship, *Oasis of the Seas.*

SYNOPSIS A one-of-a-kind live black-light puppet show, John Tartaglia's *ImaginOcean* is a magical undersea adventure for kids of all ages. Tank, Bubbles and Dorsel are three best friends who just happen to be fish, and they're about to set out on a remarkable journey of discovery. And it all starts with a treasure map. As they swim off in search of clues, they'll sing, dance, and make new friends, including everyone in the audience. Ultimately they discover the greatest treasure of all: friendship.

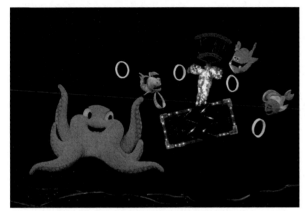

A scene from ImaginOcean *(photo by Aaron Epstein)*

Stuffed and Unstrung

Union Square Theatre; First Preview: March 17, 2010; Opening Night: April 1, 2010; Closed July 3, 2010; 11 previews, 68 performances

Created by Brian Henson and Patrick Bristow; Presented by Henson Alternative and WestBeth Entertainment (Arnold Engleman, President); Director, Patrick Bristow; Lighting, Jen Schriever; Sound, Kerry McDonald; PSM, Jeff Benish/Joe Witt; ASMs, Nicole Brickley, Sarah Koehler, Kyle Jordan; Production Manager, Gregg Bellon; Projections, Jason Seck, Gregg Bellon, Aron Deyo; Puppet Wranglers, Molly Light, Lara McLean, Rebecca Jarrell; Sound Operator, Paul Manley/Kerry McDonald/Jesse Barnes; Light Operator, Ben Tevelow/Shannon Dougherty; Press, Bridget Kaplinski

CAST Host **Patrick Bristow**; Puppeteers (rotating) **Anthony Asbury**, **Jennifer Barnhart**, **Bill Baretta**, **Julianne Buescher**, **Tyler Bunch**, **Leslie Carrara-Rudolph**, **Brian Clark**, **Melissa Creighton**, **Stephanie D'Abruzzo**, **James Godwin**, **Brian Henson**, **Drew Massey**, **Ted Michaels**, **Michael Oosterom**, **Allan Trautman**, **Colleen Smith**, **Victor Yerrid**; Musicians **Willie Etra**, **Dan Ring**

New York premiere of a comedy improv show with puppets and live music presented without intermission.

SYNOPSIS What happens when Henson puppeteers are unleashed? You get a new breed of intelligent nonsense that is *Stuffed and Unstrung*, a live, outrageous, comedy, variety show for adults only. An unpredictable evening ensues when six talented, hilarious, expert puppeteers improvise songs and sketches based on the audience suggestions! With a motley group of characters brought to life by the world renowned puppeteers of The Jim Henson Company, this is not your average night at the improv and it is definitely not for children. But all others are welcome to enjoy the uninhibited anarchy of live puppet performance as never seen before.

Colleen Smith, Brian Henson, and Ted Miachaels in Stuffed and Unstrung *(photo by Carol Rosegg)*

Enjoy

59E59 Theater B; First Preview: March 27, 2010; Opening Night: April 6, 2010; Closed May 1, 2010; 35 performances

Written by Toshiki Okada, translated by Aya Ogawa; Presented by The Play Company (Kate Loewald, Founding Producer; Lauren Weigel, Managing Producer) in association with Japan Society; Director, Dan Rothenberg; Set, Mimi Lien; Costumes, Maiko Matsushima; Lighting, James Clotfelter; Sound, Daniel Kluger; PSM, Dave Polato; Production Manager, James E. Cleveland/La Vie Productions; Casting, Judy Henderson; Associate Producer, Melissa Hardy; Artistic Associate, Linda Bartholomai; Associate Production Manager, Katy J. Ross; ASM, Trisha Henson; Assistant Design: Steve Maturno (lighting), Colin Whitely (sound); Casting Associate, Kimberly Graham; Technical Director, Joel Howell; Assistant Technical Director, Eliot Howell; Graphics, Noah Scalin/Another Limited Rebellion; Press, Sam Rudy Media Relations

CAST Actor 1 **Kris Kling**; Actor 2 **Frank Harts**; Actress 1 **Kira Stenbach**; Actor 4 **Joseph Midyett**; Actor 5 **Alex Torra**; Actress 2 **Stacey Yen**; Actress 3 **Mary McCool**; Actress 4 **Jessica Almasy**; Actor 6 **Joshua Koehn**

SETTING A manga café in Shinjuko, Tokyo's equivalent of Times Square. U.S. premiere and English-language debut of a new play presented in two acts.

SYNOPSIS It's Gen X vs. Gen Y in this slacker comedy of manners that follows the romantic adventures of part-time workers in a Tokyo manga café (a comic and video café). *Enjoy*, a new play from one of Japan's leading theatre artists, reveals a portrait of Japanese youth culture adrift and the current socio-economic rifts that have widened the gap between generations.

Steven Boyer, Joseph Midyett, Kira Sternbach, and Jessica Almasy in Enjoy *(photo by Carol Rosegg)*

The 101 Dalmatians Musical

Theatre at Madison Square Garden; Opening Night: April 7, 2010; Closed April 18, 2010; 16 performances

Book and lyrics by BT McNicholl, music and lyrics by Dennis DeYoung; Based on the book by Dodie Smith; Produced by Magic Arts & Entertainment/Tix Corporation, Troika Entertainment and Luis Alvarez, in association with Allen Spivak and Brad Krassner; Presented by Purina Dog Chow; Director, Jerry Zaks; Choreographer, Warren Carlyle; Sets, Heidi Ettinger; Costumes, Robert Morgan; Lighting, Paul Gallo; Sound, Peter Hylenski; Orchestrations, Danny Troob; Dance Music, Mark Hummel; Music Coordinator, Sam Lutfiyya, Music Services International; Music Director/Additional Arrangements, Don York; Vocal and Music Arrangements, Nadia DiGiallonardo; PSM, John M. Atherlay; Associate Director, Steve Bebout; Associate Choreographer, Parker Esse; Dogs, Joel Slaven Professional Animals; On-Line Producer, Randall A. Buck; Casting, Dave Clemmons; General Manager, Roberta Roberts; Production Manager, Geoff Quart; Creative Services, G Creative Advertising and Design; For Troika Entertainment: Randall Buck (CEO), Don Kindl (CFO), Jennifer Howey (Chief Strategy Officer); Marketing & Press, Type A Marketing, Anne Rippey, DJ Martin, Andrew Cole; Stage Manager, William Gilinsky; ASM, Patricia L. Grabb; Assistant Company Manager, Tracy Blackwell; Dialects, Benjamin Furey; Assistant Choreographer, Sara O'Gleby; Puppet Design, Kelly Tighe; Associate Design: Ann Bartek (set), Nancy Palmatier (costumes), Craig Stelzenmuller (lighting); For Magic Arts & Entertainment: Lee D Marshall and Joe Marsh (Producers), Rita Russo (VP Marketing); Company Manager, George Anthony Agbuya; Dance Captain, Chip Abbott; Assistant Dance Captain, Kristy Cavanaugh

CAST Prince/Bloodhound Miner **Joel Blum**; Pongo **James Ludwig**; Missus **Catia Ojeda**; Mr. Dearly **Mike Masters**; Mrs. Dearly/Tabby Cat **Erin Mosher**; Nanny Cook/Collie Inn Keeper **Erin Maguire**; Nanny Butler **Madeleine Doherty**; Splendid Vet/Tipsy St. Bernard **Joseph Dellger**; Cruella De Vil **Sara Gettelfinger**; Jasper/Gruff Yorkie **Michael Thomas Holmes**; Jinx **Robert Anthony Jones**; Lucky **Sammy Borla**; Patch **Ah-Niyah Ynay Neal**; Cadpig **Lydia Rose Clemente**; Roly-Poly **Piper Curda**; Perdita **Gwen Hollander**; Puli **Jeff Scot Carey**; Beagle **Jose Luaces**; Sheepdog **Kevin C. Loomis**; Ensemble **Chip Abbott, Lkisha Anne Bowen, Jeff Scott Carey, Kristy Cavanaugh, Joseph Dellger, Kevin C. Loomis, Jose Luaces, Clark Kelley Oliver, Paige Simunovich, Kendra Tate, Lynette Toomey, Austin Zambita-Valente**; Swings **Neal Mayer, Molly Sorohan**

MUSICIANS Don York (Conductor/keyboard); John Samorian (Assistant Musical Director/keyboard); Victor Costanzi (violins); Jeanette Stenson (cello); Tansie Mayer, John Summers (woodwinds); Jim Keen (trumpet); John Rutherford III (trombone); Johan Nilson (guitar); Hank Horton (bass); Wayne Dunton (drums); Ed Fast (percussion); Talitha Fehr (Contractor); Karl Mansfield (keyboard programmer

MUSICAL NUMBERS Overture – Koncerto #K-9, Man Is a Dog's Best Friend, A Perfect Family, Hot, There's Always Room for One More, World's Greatest Dad, Hail to the Chef, Twilight Barking, Be a Little Bit Braver, Break Out, Having the Crime of Our Lives, A Perfect Family (reprise), Be a Little Bit Braver (reprise), My Sweet Child, Cruella Always Gets Her Way/Hot Like Me (reprise), 101 Dalmatians

SETTING London, England. 1957. New York premiere of a national touring new musical presented in two acts. The world premiere of the production began its U.S. tour at the Orpheum Theatre (Minneapolis) in October 2009 and ended its run with this limited engagement at Madison Square Garden.

SYNOPSIS Adapted from Dodie Smith's 1957 novel (which is well known due to Disney's beloved animated film version), *101 Dalmatians* revolves around a canine family that must band together to overcome every hurdle and hardship in the most difficult times, including the machinations of Cruella de Vil.

Catia Ojeda, James Ludwig, Kristen Beth Williams, and Mike Masters in The 101 Dalmatians Musical *(photo by Joan Marcus)*

Cirque du Soleil: OVO

Randall's Island; Opening Night: April 9, 2010; Closed June 6, 2010; 71 performances

Presented by Cirque du Soleil; Production Guide, Guy Laliberté; Writer/Director/Choreographer, Deborah Colker; Director of Creation, Chantal Tremblay; Set and Props, Gringo Cardia; Costumes, Liz Vandal; Composer/Musical Director, Berna Ceppas; Lighting, Éric Champoux; Sound, Jonathan Deans; Acrobatic Equipment and Rigging Design, Fred Gérard; Acrobatic Performance Design, Philippe Aubertin; Makeup, Julie Bégin; Press, The Publicity Office, Marc Thibodeau

CAST Lady Bug **Michelle Matlock**; Flipo **Joseph Collard**; Foreigner **François-Guillaume LeBlanc**; Dragonfly of Orvalho (hand balancing) **Vladimir Hrynchenko**; Ants (foot juggling and Icarian games) **Han Jing, Su Shan, Wang Shaohua, Zhu Tingting, Kong Yufei, Pei Xin**; Cocoon (Aerial Silk) **Marjorie Nantel**; Butterflies (Spanish Web Duo) **Maxim Kozlov, Inna Mayorova**; Firefly (Diabolo) **Tony Frebourg**; Creatura **Lee Brearley**; Scarabs Volant (Flying Act) **Roman Khayrullin, Konstantin Kolbin, Maxim Komlev, Yuriy Lukachshuk, Evgeny Mitin, Artem Navalikhin, Sergeï Philippenko, Alexey Runov, Andrey Shapin, Valeri Tomanov, Safarbek Zardakov**; Web Spiders (contortion) **Iuliia Mykhailova, Marjorie**

Nantel, Robyn Houpt; Fleas (acrosport) **Anna Gorbatenko, Natallia Kakhniuk, Khrystsina Maraziuk, Elena Nepytayeva, Olga Varchuk**; Spiderman (slackwire) **Li Wei**; Legs **Anna Gorbatenko, Robyn Houpt, Kong Yufei, Khrystsina Maraziuk, Inna Mayorova**; Crickets (trampo-wall) **Anton Alferov, Grigoriy Alkhov, Michel Boillet, Lee Brearley, Kasper Falkesgaard, Karl L'écuyer, Marjorie Nantel, Ludovic Martin, John Maurer, Zeca Padilha, Gary Smith, Hironori Taniguchi**; Cockroaches (Musicians) **Daniel Baeder, Jean-François Bédard, Robson Cerqueira, Iñaki Dieguez, Caroline Lemay, Marie-Claude Marchand, Renato Martins, Sébastien Savard, Roberto Schilling**

New York premiere of a new theatrical circus with music, dance, and acrobats presented in two acts.

SYNOPSIS *OVO* is a headlong rush into a colorful ecosystem teeming with life, where insects work, eat, crawl, flutter, play, fight and look for love in a non-stop riot of energy and movement. The insects' home is a world of biodiversity and beauty filled with noisy action and moments of quiet emotion. When a mysterious egg appears in their midst, the insects are awestruck and intensely curious about this iconic object that represents the enigma and cycles of their lives. It's love at first sight when a gawky, quirky insect arrives in this bustling community and a fabulous ladybug catches his eye. The hidden, secret world at our feet is revealed as tender and torrid, noisy and quiet, peaceful and chaotic.

A scene from Cirque du Soleil's OVO (photo by Benoit Fontaine)

The Common Air

Bleecker Street Theatre; First Preview: April 7, 2010; Opening Night: April 14, 2010; Closed June 27, 2010; 83 performances

Written by Alex Lyras and Robert McCaskill; Presented by 45 Bleecker Street (Louis S. Salamone, Owner/Creative Director); Director, Robert McCaskill; Original Score, Ken Rich; Costumes, Debra Sugerman; Production Coordinator, Marci Skolnick; Set, Casey Smith; Media Consultant, Matthew Schiffman; Lighting, Perchik Kreisman-Miller; General Manager, Cesa Entertainment Inc.; Associate General Manager, Gretchen Margaroli; Dialect Coach, Robert Easton; Iraqi Language Coach, Munda Razooki; Marketing & Advertising, The Pekoe Group; Press, Keith Sherman Associates, Daniel Demello

CAST The Immigrant/The Dealer/The Champion/The Spinner/The Signifier/The American **Alex Lyras**; Recorded Voices: Concourse Announcements/Donna on cell phone **Celia Schaefer**; Female Reporter **Shayna Padovano**; Male Reporter **Wilbur Edwin Henry**

SETTING JFK Airport; The Present. Off-Broadway premiere of a new solo performance play presented without intermission. Previously ran at the Bleecker Street Theatre on Friday evenings November 6–February 26. Originally produced in Los Angeles in 2008.

SYNOPSIS *The Common Air* links six distinct characters during the mother of all delays at JFK airport. The reason is unknown, and a game of "Telephone" ensues in an effort to find the truth. The show is a comedic/dramatic exploration of the perpetually changing narratives we arrive at and depart from in trying to make sense of life's ever-evolving present tense. What happens when the cell phones and laptops lose their charge? When we're forced to revert to non-high-speed communication, are we even capable anymore, or have our brains devolved into hard drives that crash at the slightest wave of turbulence?

Alex Lyras in The Common Air *(photo by Nicholas Woods)*

Alfred Hitchcock's **The 39 Steps**

New World Stages–Stage 1; First Preview: March 25, 2010; Opening Night: April 15, 2010; 24 previews, 54 performances as of May 31, 2010

Adapted by Patrick Barlow from the film by Alfred Hitchcock and the book by John Buchan; based on an original concept by Simon Corble and Nobby Dimon; Produced by Bob Boyett, Harriet Newman Leve, Richard Winkler/Dan Frishwasser, Pamela Laudenslager/Douglas Denoff, Jane Dubin, Olympus Theatricals, Tim Levy/Jennifer Isaacson, Manocherian Productions, Stewart F. Lane/Bonnie Comely, Remmel T. Dickinson, True Love Productions, Kevin Lyle, John Retsios, Marek J. Cantor/Probo Productions, Lary Brandt/Meredith Lucio in association with the Roundabout Theatre Company (Todd Haimes, Artistic Director; Harold Wolpert, Managing Director; Julia C. Levy, Executive Director), Huntington Theatre Company (Nicholas Martin, Artistic Director; Michael Maso, Managing Director), and Edward Snape for Fiery Angel Ltd.; Director, Maria Aitken; Set/Costumes, Peter McKintosh; Lighting, Kevin Adams; Sound, Mic Pool; Dialect Coach, Stephen Gabis; Original Movement, Toby Sedgwick; Additional Movement, Christopher Bays; Production Manager, Aurora Productions; PSM/Resident Director, Nevin Hedley; Casting, Jay Binder/Jack Bowdan; Marketing, HHC Marketing; Associate Producers, Emily Genduso, Howard Tilkin; General Manager, Roy Gabay; Stage Manager, Rosy Garner; Company Manager, Jennifer Pluff; Assistant Director, Kevin Bigger; Associate Design: Josh Zangen (set), Joel Silver (lighting), Drew Levy (sound); Advertising, SpotCo; Press, Boneau/Bryan-Brown, Adrian Bryan-Brown, Jessica Johnson, Jim Byk, Emily Meagher

CAST Man #1 **Jamie Jackson**; Man #2 **Cameron Folmar**; Richard Hannay **John Behlmann**; Annabella Schmidt/Pamela/Margaret **Kate MacCluggage**

UNDERSTUDIES Greg Jackson (Man #1, Man #2, Richard Hannay), Jane Pfitsch (Annabella Schmidt/Pamela/Margaret)

SETTING Scotland and London. Transfer of the Broadway comedy/thriller presented in two acts. Originally presented at the Tricycle Theatre in London in August 2006, and at Boston's Huntington Theatre Company September 14, 2007 prior its New York engagement. The show opened on Broadway at the American Airlines Theatre January 4–March 29, 2008 (playing 12 previews and 87 performances) and transferred to the Cort Theatre April 29, 2008 for a commercial run (see *Theatre World* Vol. 64, page 38). The show moved to the Helen Hayes Theatre on January 21, 2009, where it concluded its run January 10, 2010 after a total of 771 performances at all venues (see Broadway section in this volume). As with *Avenue Q* this season, the producers prolonged the life of the show in this unprecedented transfer to an Off-Broadway venue.

SYNOPSIS Four cast members play over 150 roles in this hilarious whodunit, part espionage thriller and part slapstick comedy. The story revolves around an innocent man who learns too much about a dangerous spy ring and is then pursued across Scotland and to London. *The 39 Steps* contains every legendary scene from the award-winning movie—the chase on the Flying Scotsman, the escape on the Forth Bridge, the first theatrical bi-plane crash ever staged, and the sensational death-defying finale in the London Palladium.

Jamie Jackson, Cameron Folmar, Kate MacCluggage, and John Behlmann in Alfred Hitchcock's The 39 Steps *(photo by Carol Rosegg)*

666

Minetta Lane Theatre; First Preview: March 30, 2010; Opening Night: April 15, 2010; Closed May 30, 2010; 18 previews, 42 performances

Written and conceived by Yllana; Presented by Psycoductions LLC, Juan Urrutia, Moonglow Productions LLC in association with Producciones Yllana, S.L. (Marcos Ottone, Producer); Director, David Ottone; Set, Juan Ramos Toro; Costumes, Teresa Rodrigo; Lighting, Herrick Goldman; Original Music, Scud Hero; Marketing, Leanne Schanzer Promotions; Advertising, Eliran Murphy Group; Production Manager/Stage Manager, Amber L. Estes; Casting, Scott Wojcik & Gayle Seay; General Management, Theatre Management Associates/Maria Di Dia; Executive Producer, Aldo Scrofani; Company Manager, Bryan K.L. Byrd III; Production Coordinator, Mabel Cañizos; Technical Director, Ismael Garcia; Associate Lighting, Susan Nicholson; Production Assistant, Rochelle Bright; Choreography, German Cabrera; Associate Set, Aitor Casero; Props, Sebastian Sanchez; Scenery Drawings, Amador Rehak; Sound Effects, Jorge Moreno; Press, O+M Company, Rick Miramontez, Philip Carrubba, Andy Snyder

CAST JO **Joseph Michael O'Curneen**; FF **Fidel Fernandez**; JR **Juan Ramos Toro**; RC **Raul Cano**; Replacement Cast **Joel Farrell**, **Jeff LaGreca**, **Lance Windish**

Off-Broadway premiere of a theatrical physical comedy piece presented in ten scenes with no intermission. Originally presented by The Present Company as part of the 2009 New York International Fringe Festival.

SYNOPSIS Created by Spain's internationally acclaimed comedy theatre troupe Yllana, *666* elevates physical comedy (in the grand tradition of Commedia dell'Arte) to its highest form, and sends it screaming into the 21st Century. One of the wildest and most unique productions to hit stages in years, *666* stops short at nothing to astound, shock, and delight its audience with jaw-dropping, sometimes cringe-inducing, and altogether gut-bustingly funny scenes and sketches created out of the most common situations of everyday life.

The Cast of 666 *(photo courtesy of Yllena)*

Bloodsong of Love

Ars Nova; First Preview: April 1, 2010; Opening Night: April 15, 2010; Closed May 9, 2010; 11 previews, 19 performances

Book, music, & lyrics by Joe Iconis; Presented by Ars Nova (Jason Eagan, Artistic Director); Director, John Simpkins; Choreography, Jennifer Werner; Musical Director/Orchestrations/Arrangements, Matt Hinkley; Set, Michael Schweikardt; Costumes, Michelle Eden Humphrey; Lighting, Chris Dallos; Sound, Jon Weston; Props, Eric Reynolds; Production Supervisor, James E. Cleveland; PSM, E. Sara Barnes; ASM, Ashley Rodbro; Associate Conductor, Brian Usifer; Sound Associate, Michael Eisenberg; Production Coordinator, Joshua Kohler; Technical Director, Joel Howell; Scenic Associate, Ryan Scott; Blood Cannon Effect Design, Sean McArdle; Assistant to Costume Designer, Pamela Kupper; Dialect Coach, Evan Mueller; Dance Captain, MK Lawson; Fight Captain, Eric William Morris; Outreach and Promotions, Jennifer Tepper; Press, Sam Rudy Media Relations

CAST The Musician **Eric William Morris**; Banana/Henchman Steve **Lance Rubin**; Santa Violetta/Sofia **MK Lawson**; Lo Cocodrilo/Hick in Overalls **Jeremy Morse**; Whore in Boots/The Crone/The Wife of Banana **Katrina Rose Dideriksen**; The Narrator/Weeping Eduardo/Earl/The Strange Man **Jason 'SweetTooth' Williams**

THE BAND Chris 'Red' Blisset (guitar, harmonica), Matthew Hinkley (Conductor/piano), Danny Stone (bass), Brent Stranathan (drums), Michael James Taylor (guitar, trumpet)

MUSICAL NUMBERS Outlaw, The Musician and Banana, Find the Bastard, Don't Ya Make Me Ask Ya Twice (part 1), The Friendship Song, Turkey Leg, Turkey Leg (reprise), The Bone Bar, Banana's Prayer, Lovesong of Blood (Covered in the Blood of Another), Last on Land, Shoot 'Em Up, The Friendship Song (reprise)

World premiere of a new musical presented in seven chapters with a prologue and epilogue in two acts.

SYNOPSIS In a blood and whiskey-soaked world of shoot 'em ups, stolen brides and kazoo-wielding villains, a rogue musician with a killer guitar is out to set things right. Joe Iconis infuses *Bloodsong of Love* with his infectious musical style, making this rocked out spaghetti western the wildest funeral in town.

The Company in Bloodsong of Love *(photo by Peter James Zielinski)*

Closer Than Ever

Queens Theatre in the Park; First Preview: April 16, 2010; Opening Night: April 17, 2010; Closed April 25, 2010; 2 previews, 8 performances

Lyrics by Richard Maltby Jr., music by David Shire; Conceived by Steven Scott Smith; Presented by Queens Theatre in the Park and Bristol Riverside Theatre (Keith Baker, Artistic Director; Susan D. Atkinson, Founding Director; Amy Kaissar, Managing Director) in association with Adam Friedson/Friedson Enterprises, Leftfield Productions Inc./Neil Berg; Director, Richard Maltby Jr.; Co-Director/Musical Staging, Kurt Stamm; Music Director, Patrick Brady; Set, Roman Tatarowicz; Lighting, Ryan O'Gara; Costumes, Thom Heyer; Sound, Maia Fedderly; Stage Manager, Amy Massari; ASM, Clif Ballard; Casting, Michael Cassara; Original Producers, Janet Brenner, Michael Gill, Daryl Roth; Props, Jennifer Blazek; Assistant Set, Samantha Miller; Production Manager, William S. Crandall

CAST **George Dvorsky**, **Sally Mayes**, **Sal Viviano**, **Lynne Wintersteller**

MUSICIANS Patrick Brady (Conductor/piano), Bob Renino (bass)

MUSICAL NUMBERS Doors; She Loves Me Not; You Want to Be My Friend; What Am I Doin?; The Bear, The Tiger, The Hamster, and The Mole; I'll Get Up Tomorrow Morning; Miss Byrd; Dating Again; One of the Good Guys; There's Nothing Like It; Life Story; Next Time/I Wouldn't Go Back; Three Friends; Fandango; There; Patterns; Something in a Wedding; Another Wedding Song; If I Sing; Back on Base; The March of Time; Fathers of Fathers; It's Never That Easy/I've Been Here Before; Closer Than Ever

Twentieth anniversary revisal of a musical revue presented in two acts. The production also played Bristol Riverside Theatre May 4–23, 2010. Originally conceived as a one-act revue entitled *Next Time Now!* at Eighty-Eights Nightclub, the show was expanded and developed at Williamstown Theatre Festival in the summer of 1989. World premiere at the Cherry Lane Theatre October 17, 1989–July 1, 1990, playing 312 performances (see *Theatre World* Vol. 45, page 57).

SYNOPSIS *Closer Than Ever* is a theatrical revue filled with wise and witty "songs of experience," that reflect on marriage, parents, children, and lasting friendships. In this 20th Anniversary production, original cast members Sally Mayes and Lynn Wintersteller, along with original music director Patrick Brady and bassist Bob Renino reunited with original director and writer, Richard Maltby Jr. As part of their ongoing efforts to update and keep the work relevant to a new generation of theatergoers, Maltby and Shire added new material including a new song called "Dating Again" about the pitfalls and pleasures of being single again, as well as updating outdated lyrics and additional material.

Lynne Wintersteller, Sal Viviano, Sally Mayes, and George Dvorsky in Closer Than Ever *(photo by Dominick Totino)*

The Really Big Once

Ontological Theater at St. Mark's; First Preview: April 13, 2009; Opening Night: April 17, 2009; Closed May 8, 2009; 4 previews, 19 performances

Created and presented by Target Margin Theater (David Herskovits, Artistic Director) and the Ontological-Hysteric Theater Incubator (Richard Foreman, Artistic Director); Director, David Herskovits; Lighting, Lenore Doxsee; Costumes, Carol Bailey; Set, Laura Jellinek; Sound, Jim Breitmeier, David Herskovits, Kate Marvin; Dramaturg, Kathleen Kennedy Tobin; Production Managers, Shannon Case & Neal Wilkinson; PSM, Laura Wilson; Assistant Directors, Heidi Lauren Duke & Maia Karo; Props/Assistant Set, Kate Sinclair Foster; Assistant Lighting, Natalie Robin; Rehearsal ASM, Lily Perlmutter; Production ASM, Joseph Fletcher; Production Electrician, Avery Lewis; Target Margin Theatre Director, John Del Guadio; Target Margin Theatre Marketing & Development, Aimee Davis; Press, O+M Company, Rick Miramontez, Philip Carrubba

CAST McKenna Kerrigan, John Kurzynowski, Maria-Christina Oliveras, Hubert Point-Du Jour, Steven Rattazzi

World premiere of a new play presented without intermission.

SYNOPSIS *The Really Big Once* tells the story of two theatrical giants, Elia Kazan and Tennessee Williams, and how they changed American culture. The show, based on meticulous research of notebooks, letters, and recollections, explores their collaboration on *Camino Real*. Between 1948 and 1953 Williams and Kazan developed one of their most ambitious productions in the context of a crucial moment in their growth as artists and in the life of our country. Target Margin Theater's project incorporates a broad range of documentary sources, as well as selections of dialogue and scenes from the existing versions and drafts of Williams' play- and much of this work has never been revealed or is unpublished. Interviews were conducted by the company with people and artists who saw or were influenced by the original production of *Camino Real*.

Steven Rattazzi (kneeling, left), McKenna Kerrigan, Maria-Christina Oliveras, John Kurzynowski, and Hubert Point-Du Jour (kneeling, right) in The Really Big Once (photo by Sue Kessler)

Leslie Jordan in My Trip Down the Pink Carpet
(photo by Gustavo Monroy)

My Trip Down The Pink Carpet

Midtown Theatre; First Preview: April 14, 2010; Opening Night: April 19, 2010; Closed July 3, 2010; 5 previews, 54 performances

Written by Leslie Jordan; Produced by Lily Tomlin and Jane Wagner, Bruce Robert Harris, Jack W. Batman, Dennis Grimaldi, Jean McFaddin/Susan Falk, Daniel Wallace, D. Michael Dvorchak/Jim McLaughlin; Production Sponsors, Mitchell Gold and Bob Williams; Director, David Galligan; Set, Michael Hotopp; Lighting, Jesse Belsky; Sound, Wallace Flores; PSM, Andrea Wales; Press, O+M Company, Rick Miramontez, Richard Hillman, Jaron Caldwell

Performed by **Leslie Jordan**

New York premiere of a new solo performance play presented without intermission.

SYNOPSIS *My Trip Down The Pink Carpet* tells the unlikely tale of one of America's true gay icons and his journey from small-town USA to the pink carpet of Hollywood. Raised in a conservative family in Chattanooga, Tennessee, Leslie boarded a Greyhound bus bound for L.A. with $1,200 sewn into his underpants and never looked back. His pocket-sized physique and inescapable talent for high camp paved the way to a lucrative and varied career in film, commercials, television, and the stage. But with success came dangerous temptations that threatened his career and life. Filled with comically overwrought childhood agonies, offbeat observations, and revealing celebrity encounters – from Boy George to George Clooney – *My Trip Down The Pink Carpet* delivers a laugh-out-loud take on Hollywood, fame, addiction, gay culture, and learning to love oneself.

End of the Road

St. Ann's Warehouse; Opening Night: April 21, 2010; Closed May 1, 2010; 11 performances

Created by No Theater (Northampton, Massachusetts), Roy Faudree, and Sheena See; Presented by St. Ann's Warehouse (Susan Feldman, Artistic Director); Produced by No Theater, Manchester International Festival, and Young@Heart; Director, Roy Faudree; Chorus Director, Bob Cilman; Music Director, Ken Maiuri; Set, Wim Van de Cappelle; Lighting, Harry Cole; Sound, Melvyn Coote for Tube Uk Ltd.; Associate Sound, Nick Sagar; Costumes, Jill St. Coeur; Video, Jeff Derose; Additional Video, Dana Gentes & Andrew Schneider; Production Designers, Roy Faudree & Sheena See; For St. Ann's Warehouse: Alex Berg (Finance), Inga J. Glodowski (Development), Marilynn Donini (External Affairs), Bill Updegraff (Marketing), Laura Roumanos (General Manager), Owen Hughes (Production Manager), Christopher Heilman (Technical Director); Press, Blake Zidell and Associates

CAST *The Young@Heart Chorus*: **Bob Cilman** (Chorus Director), **Patricia Booth, Helen Boston, Patricia Cady, Louise Canady, Claire Couture, Dick Dragon, Patricia McTee Ervin, Jean Florio, Jeanne Hatch, Arthur Klein, Norma Landry, Patricia Larese, M. Eileen Litke, Brock Lynch, Steve Martin, Grant Milner, Joseph Mitchell, Gloria Parker, Dora B. (Parker) Morrow, Glenda Philips, Liria Petrides, John Rinehart, Evelyn Robb, Fran Saed, Jack Schnepp, Janice St. Laurence, Shirley Stevens, Andrew Walsh**; Bartenders/Hatcheck Girl/EMS/Janitor **Diane Porcella, Jill St. Coeur, Jan Stenson**

***YOUNG@HEART* BAND** Ken Maiuri (Piano/Bass/Ukulele/Autoharp), William E. Arnold, Jr. (drums/percussion), Frederick Alexander Johnson (guitar), Tom Mahnken (saxophone/flute/bass), Bob Cilman (harmonica/bass), Matt Farthing (violin) Emily Dix Thomas (cello)

American premiere of a new theatrical concert presented without intermission. World premiere at Manchester International Festival July 2009, and subsequently Rotterdamse Schouwburg (Netherlands) and the Vooruit Theatre (Ghent, Belgium). Commissioned by Manchester International Festival, St. Ann's Warehouse, Les Ballaet C de la B (Ghent), Rotterdamse Schouwburg, and UCLA Live (Los Angeles).

SYNOPSIS The third part of Young@Heart's musical theatre "road" trilogy, *End of the Road* is an exploration of the power of music to transcend age. The show takes audiences on a journey through the 20th century, with ballads giving way to hardcore rock & roll. Some of the songs are pure fun ("Monkey Gone to Heaven" by The Pixies), while others are tender in the Chorus' hands ("Handle with Care" by The Traveling Wilburys). A core value for Young@Heart can be summed up in one of its famous program notes: "We all have to die. Some of us are lucky enough to grow old first."

The Young@Heart Chorus in End of the Road *(photo by Jeff Derose)*

Rachel Moulton, Michael Shawn Lewis, Clark Carmichael, Mandy Bruno, and Jamie LaVerdiere in This Side of Paradise *(photo by Lee Wexler © 2010)*

This Side of Paradise

Theatre at St. Clement's; First Preview: April 14, 2010; Opening Night: April 21, 2010; Closed May 23, 2010; 7 previews, 40 performances

Music and lyrics by Nancy Harrow, book by Nancy Harrow and Will Pomerantz; Presented by Living Image Arts and Culture Project (Allan Buchman, Producer); Director/Musical Staging, Will Pomerantz; Set, Troy Hourie; Costumes, Devon Painter; Lighting, Cory Pattak; Sound, Steve Fontaine; PSM, Samone B. Weissman; Production Managers, Pete Fry & Amber Estes; Advertising/Marketing, The Pekoe Group; Casting, Jerry Beaver; Associate Producer/Company Manager, Corey Pearlstein; ASM, Lauren McArthur; Associate Company Manager, Jessica Segal; Props, Michael Guagno; Dialect Consultant, Wendy Waterman; Assistant Costumes, Ren LaDassor; Scenic Artist, Michael R. Hetzer; Master Electrician, Laura Schooch; Production Assistants, Zachary Moody & Aaron Jefferson Tindall; Wardrobe Supervisor, Stephanie Pezolano; Website, Stephen Bittrich; Press, Blake Zidell & Associates

CAST Zelda Fitzgerald **Maureen Mueller**; Doctor Cassell **Michael Sharon**; Young Zelda **Rachel Mouton**; F. Scott Fitzgerald **Michael Shawn Lewis**; Ernest Hemmingway/Maxwell Perkins **Clark Carmichael**; Callaghan/Editor's Assistant/Jozan **Jamie LaVerdiere**; Scottie/Honoria/Nurse **Mandy Bruno**

BAND Art Hirahara (piano), Bill Easley (reeds), Calvin Jones (bass), Willie Martinez (drums)

MUSICAL NUMBERS If I Want To, Belle of the Ball, Belle of the Ball (reprise), You May Never Get to East Egg, Winter Dreams, This Side of Paradise, This Side of Paradise (reprise), Oh God I'm Sophisticated, The Old Pro, The Old Pro (reprise), My Lost City, Lost Lady, My Swan, Starting Over, If I Want To (reprise), Dear Max, Until It Comes Up Love, The Extra Mile, Until It Comes Up Love (reprise)

SETTING A hospital outside Baltimore, as well as Paris, the French Riviera, St. Paul, New York City and Montgomery, Alabama - between the years 1918 and 1940. World premiere of a new musical presented in two acts.

SYNOPSIS Zelda and F. Scott Fitzgerald reflected all of the success, glamour and excess of 1920s America. Such a lifestyle would leave Zelda in a mental institution, ultimately. *This Side of Paradise* takes a look into the lives and loves of the Fitzgeralds, from their first meeting in 1918 in Montgomery, Alabama, until Scott's death in Hollywood in 1940. The musical centers on Zelda, looking into her past during sessions with a young doctor, searching to find the true meaning of her life with Scott, one of America's most accomplished writers.

bobrauschenbergamerica

Dance Theater Workshop; Opening Night: April 23, 2010; Closed May 16, 2010; 23 performances

Written by Charles L. Mee; Created and performed by SITI Company; Director, Anne Bogart; Set/Costumes, James Schuette; Lighting, Brian H. Scott; Sound, Darron L West; PSM, Kris Longley-Postema; ASM, Justin Donham; Associate Producers, Roberta Pereira, David Roberts; Executive Director, Megan Wanlass Szalla; Production Management, The Lighting Syndicate; Wigs, Anne Ford-Coates; Dramaturg, Tanya Palmer; Original Props, Jason Szalla; Wardrobe, Melissa Trn; Sound Engineer, Asa Wembler; Original PSM, Elizabeth Moreau; Press, Jenny Lerner, Isabelle Doconinck

CAST Phil's Girl **Akiko Aizawa**; Becker **J. Ed Araiza**; Allen **Will Bond**; Bob, the Pizza Boy **Gian Murray Gianino**; Phil **Leon Ingulsrud**; Susan **Ellen Lauren**; Bob's Mom **Kelly Maurer**; Carl **Barney O'Hanlon**; Wilson **Samuel Stricklen**; Roller Girl **Jen Taher**

Revival of a play presented without intermission. Previously presented at BAM's 2003 Next Wave Festival. World premiere at the 2001 Humana Festival of New American Plays at Actors Theatre of Louisville, and subsequently toured the U.S.

SYNOPSIS Anne Bogart, SITI Company, and Charles L. Mee take us on a wild theatrical road trip through the American landscape as Robert Rauschenberg might have conceived it had he been a playwright instead of a painter. More than a biographical portrait, *bobrauschenbergamerica* is a tribute to one artist's singular vision.

Julianne Nicholson and James Waterston in Parents' Evening *(photo by Carol Rosegg)*

Parents' Evening

Flea Theater; First Preview: April 17, 2010; Opening Night: April 29, 2010; Closed May 29, 2010; 10 previews, 21 performances

Written by Bathsheba Doran; Presented by the Flea Theater (Jim Simpson, Artistic Director; Carol Ostrow, Producing Director); Director, Jim Simpson; Set, Jerad Schomer; Lighting, Brian Aldous; Costumes, Claudia Brown; Stage Manager, Carrie Dell-Furay; Assistant Director, Seth Moore; SDC Observer, Matthew Strother; Box Office Manager, Tommy Crawford; Light Board Operator, Katherine Folk-Sullivan; Managing Director, Beth Dembrow; Technical Director, Zack Tinkelman; Development, Tiffany Kleeman Baran; Audience Development/Marketing, Eric Emch; Assistant to Ms. Ostrow, Sarah Wansley; Assistant Technical Director, Tim Pickerill; Graphics, David Prittie; Press, Ron Lasko/Spin Cycle

CAST Judy **Julianne Nicholson**; Michael **James Waterston**

SETTING Judy and Michael's bedroom; the present. World premiere of a new play presented in two acts.

SYNOPSIS It's that time of year again – *Parents' Evening* at school. Last year's conference ended with the history teacher crying and this year mildly pornographic novels are being passed around fifth grade. One couple finds this seemingly mundane event suddenly revealing their deepest insecurities as lovers and parents. *Parents' Evening* is a play about modern married life – particularly the working woman's struggle to be mother, lover, breadwinner and wife – to be it all and have it all.

Leon Ingulsrud and Akiko Aizawa in bobrauschenbergamerica *(photo by Michael Brosilow)*

Bass for Picasso

Kirk Theatre on Theatre Row; First Preview: April 17, 2010; Opening Night: May 2, 2010; Closed May 23, 2010; 32 performances

Written by Kate Moira Ryan; Presented by Theatre Breaking Through Barriers (Ike Schambelan, Artistic Director); Director, Ike Schambelan; Set/Lighting, Bert Scott; Costumes, Christine Field; Sound, Alden Fulcomer; Fight Director, J. David Brimmer; Fight Captain, Terry Small; PSM, Kimothy Cruse; ASM, Brooke Elsinghorst; Production Manager, Nicholas Lazzaro; Marketing, Michelle Tabnick; Administrator, Joan Duddy; Administrative Assistants, Christina Roussos, Nicholas Viselli; Outreach, Gregg Mozgala; Business Consultant, Sherri Kotimsky; Fundraising, Sue Ferziger; Graphics, Jane O'Wyatt; Press, Shirley Herz Associates, Bob Lasko

CAST Francesca **Anita Hollander**; Kev **Terry Small**; Bricka **Mary Theresa Archbold**; Pilar **Felice Neals**; Joe **Nicholas Viselli**

SETTING Francesca and Pilar's loft on Desbrosses Street, in Tribeca, NYC. World premiere of a new play presented without intermission.

SYNOPSIS In *Bass for Picasso*, a funny, irreverent look at gay and lesbian life in the new millennium, Francesca Danieli, an amputee and food writer for the New York Times, throws a dinner party for her friends recreating recipes (including the titular entrée) from the Alice B. Toklas Cookbook. The guest list includes Pilar, her multilingual art detective lover, who has spent time in Guantanamo for visa problems; Bricka Matson, a lesbian widow with a small child and Republican in-laws who are trying to gain custody; Joe, an OB/GYN whose lover is a geographically challenged crystal meth addict; and Kev, a playwright who has recently fallen off the wagon and written a soon-to-open Off-Broadway play about all of them.

Mary Theresa Archbold, Terry Small, Nicholas Viselli, Felice Neals, and Anita Hollander in Bass for Picasso *(photo by Carol Rosegg)*

Max McClean and Elise Giradin in The Screwtape Letters
(photo by Johnny Knight)

The Screwtape Letters

Westside Theatre (Upstairs); First Preview: April 15, 2010; Opening Night: May 3, 2010; 30 previews, 25 performances as of May 31, 2010

Adapted and directed for the stage by Jeffrey Fiske and Max McLean from the story by C.S. Lewis; Produced by Fellowship for the Performing Arts (Max McLean, President and Artistic Director) and William & Bridget Coughran and Walt & Anne Waldie; Executive Producer, Ken Denison; Set, Cameron Anderson; Costumes, Michael Bevins; Lighting, Jesse Klug; Original Music & Sound, John Gromada; Sound Supervisor, Lew Mead; Production Supervisor, Bill Castellino; Production Manager, Technical Theater Solutions, Rys Williams; General Management, Aruba Productions, Ken Denison, Samantha Schuster, Eddie Williams; Advertising Manager, Aruba Advertising, Robyn Sunderland; PSM, Jane Grey; Casting, Carol Hanzel, Colleen Piquette; Company Manager, Michael Altbaum; Technical Director, Michael East; Marketing & Press, Noreen Heron & Associates

CAST His Abysmal Sublimity Screwtape **Max McLean**; Toadpipe, *Screwtape's personal secretary* **Elise Giradin**

STANDBYS Steven Hauck (Screwtape), Beckley Andrews (Toadpipe)

SETTING A Dining Hall in Hell; The Graduation Banquet at the Tempters' Training College for Young Devils; Screwtape's Office in Hell. New York. Commercial revival of a play presented without intermission. Previously presented at Theatre at St. Clements October 18–December 19, 2007 (see *Theatre World* Vol. 64, page 122).

SYNOPSIS In this inverted and moral universe set in an office in hell, God is called the "Enemy" and the devil is referred to as "Our Father Below." *The Screwtape Letters* follows the clever scheming a high level demon employs to entice a human toward damnation. At his feet is the creature-demon Toadpipe, who transforms into paragons of vice that Screwtape conjures with a flick of his fingers.

Emily Joy Weiner, Jose Aranda, and Carlo D'Amore in DeNovo *(photo by Alyssa Ringler)*

De Novo

59E59 Theater C; First Preview: April 28, 2010; Opening Night: May 4, 2010; Closed May 16, 2010; 15 performances

Written and directed by Jeffrey Solomon; Presented by Houses on the Moon Theater Company in association with Queens Theatre in the Park as part of the 2010 Americas Off-Broadway Festival; Produced by 59E59 (Elizabeth Kleinhans, President and Artistic Director; Peter Tear, Executive Producer); Set, Alex Escalante; Lighting, Michael Kimmel & Lisa Weinshrott; Costumes, Arnulfo Moldanado; Composer/Sound, Andrew Ingkavet; Additional Development, Emily Weiner and Jose Aranada; Translation, Alex Escallante, Jose Aranda, Carlo D'Amore, Paola Poucel; Imagery, Donna Decassare; Associate Producer, Andrew Ronan; Press, Karen Greco

CAST **Jose Aranda**, **Carlo D'Amore**, **Socorro Santiago**, **Emily Joy Weiner**

New York premiere of a new play presented without intermission.

SYNOPSIS *De Novo* is the gripping true story of a fourteen-year old Edgar Chocoy, who fled Guatemala's deadly gangs and his legal struggle to be allowed to stay in the United States. This documentary play, crafted entirely from immigration court transcripts as well as interviews and letters, provides a rare glimpse into the lives of undocumented youth, many thousands of whom make the harrowing journey across the border and the system of justice every year.

White's Lies

New World Stages–Stage 4; First Preview: April 12, 2010; Opening Night: May 6, 2010; Closed June 13, 2010; 26 previews, 46 performances

Written by Ben Andron; Presented by Aaron Grant, Jeremy Handelman, Jana Robbins, Craig Haffner, and Karl E. Held, with Sneaky Pete Productions; Director, Bob Cline; Costumes, Michael Bevins; Set, Robert Andrew Kovach; Sound/Original Music, Nathan Leigh; Lighting, Solomon Weisbard; Props, Seán McArdle; Casting, Daryl Eisenberg; Projections, Pamela Traynor; Co-Producer/Production Manager, Vincent J. DeMarco; PSM, Allison Deutch; ASM, Andrea Jo Martin; Assistant Director, Trey Compton; General Manager, Kelvin Productions LLC; Associate Producer, Carl Mollenberg; Company Manager, Rachel Klein; Video Design, Ron Eyal; Video Footage, Raphael Alvarez; Assistant Lighting, Katharine Lowery; Associate Sound, Aaron Mack; Audio Master, Jessica Bauer; Advertising/Marketing, Allied Live LLC; Press, Maya Public Relations, Penny M. Landau

CAST Joe White **Tuc Watkins**; Various Women **Rena Strober**; Alan **Peter Scolari**; Mark/Frank/Doctor Shuman **Jimmy Ray Bennett**; Mrs. White **Betty Buckley**; Barbara **Andrea Grano**; Michelle **Christy Carlson Romano**

UNDERSTUDIES Josh Adam Davis (Joe White, Alan, Mark/Frank/Doctor Shuman), Jimmy Ray Bennett (Alan), Elyse Mirto (Various Women, Barbara), Rena Strober (Michelle); Standby by for Ms. Buckley: Jana Robbins

SETTING The action takes place in the private office of Joe White's very successful law firm and an upscale martini bar that's about to go under. World premiere of a new comedy presented in two acts.

SYNOPSIS In *White's Lies*, some guys are scared stiff at the prospect of settling down, getting married, having kids – and Joe White is no exception. He's a divorce lawyer, representing one of his many ex-girlfriends and above all else, he's a bachelor who wouldn't have it any other way. So when his mother desperately wants him to start a family, he'll do the next best thing: make one up! What could go wrong?

Tuc Watkins and Rena Strober in White's Lies *(photo by Ken Howard)*

Passion Play

Irondale Center; First Preview: April 27, 2010; Opening Night: May 12, 2010; Closed June 5, 2010; 12 previews, 27 performances

Written by Sarah Ruhl; Presented by Epic Theatre Ensemble (Zak Berkman, Melissa Friedman, Ron Russell, Founding Executive Directors); Director, Mark Wing-Davey; Sets, Allen Moyer & Warren Karp; Costumes, Gabriel Berry & Antonia Ford-Roberts; Lighting, David Weiner; Additional Music, David Van Tieghem; PSM, Iris Dawn O'Brien; ASM, Casey Schmal; Movement, Jim Calder; Dialect Coach, Deborah Hecht; Fight Director, David Anzuelo; Casting, Calleri Casting; Production Manager, Jee S. Han; Associate Director, Scott Illingworth; Assistant Director, Christopher Tadros; Festival Associate, Maryna Harrison; Associate Lighting, Sarah Jakubasz; Technical Director, Marshall Miller; Props Master/Deck Captain, Josh Yocum; Master Electrician, Doug Filomena; Costumer, Whitney Adams; Wardrobe, Samantha Newby; Light Board, Tim Pracher-Dix; Videographer, Kevan Tucker; Graphics, Noah Scalin/Another Limited Rebellion; Press, O+M Company, Rick Miramontez, Jon Dimond, Jaron Caldwell

CAST John the Fisherman/Eric/J **Hale Appleman**; Carpenter #1/Ensemble **Brendan Averett**; Pontius the Fish-gutter/Footsoldier/P **Dominic Fumusa**; Village Idiot/Violet **Polly Noonan**; Visiting Friar/Visiting Englishman/Special Effects/Ensemble **Daniel Pearce**; Machinist/German Officer/Young Director **Alex Podulke**; Director **Keith Reddin**; Carpenter #2/Ensemble **Godfrey L. Simmons Jr.**; Queen Elizabeth/Hitler/Reagan **T. Ryder Smith**; Mary 1/Elsa/Mary 1 **Kate Turnbull**; Mary 2 **Nicole Wiesner**

SETTING Part 1: A village in Northern England, 1575; Part 2: Oberammergau, Bavaria, 1934; Part 3: Spearfish, South Dakota, 1969, 1984, and the present. New York premiere of a new three-play cycle presented with two intermissions. World premiere and development in 2005 at Arena Stage, Washington D.C. Wing-Davey directed highly acclaimed productions of *Passion Play* at the Goodman Theatre in September 2007 (see *Theatre World* Vol. 64, page 307) and at Yale Repertory Theatre in September 2008 (see *Theatre World* Vol. 65, page 354).

SYNOPSIS Inspired by the historic festivals where everyday citizens came together to elevate their communities by staging the life and death of Christ, *Passion Play* transports audiences first to 16th century England, where Queen Elizabeth threatens to shut down a small town's production; then to Nazi Germany, where Adolf Hitler's arrival at the famous Oberammergau Passion Play influences the lives of its cast; and finally to Spearfish, South Dakota in 1984, as a local production becomes a campaign stop for a famous actor-turned-President running for re-election. Wing-Davey re-envisioned the play for the site-specific Irondale Center, a converted Sunday School inside the Lafayette Avenue Presbyterian Church in Fort Greene.

Phoenix Vaughn, Natalie Mosco, and Corey Tazmania in
The Housewives of Mannheim (photo by SuzAnne Barabas)

The Housewives of Mannheim

59E59 Theater B; First Preview: May 6, 2010; Opening Night: May 14, 2010; Closed June 6, 2010; 32 performances

Written by Alan Brody; Presented by New Jersey Repertory Company (Gabor Barabas, Executive Producer; SuzAnne Barabas, Artistic Director; Jane E. Huber, Managing Director) by special arrangement with Pat Addiss and Vasi Laurence as part of the 2010 Americas Off-Broadway Festival; Produced by 59E59 (Elizabeth Kleinhans, President and Artistic Director; Peter Tear, Executive Producer); Director, SuzAnne Barabas; Set/Properties, Jessica L. Parks; Lighting, Jill Nagle; Costumes, Patricia E. Doherty; Sound, Merek Royce Press; Stage Manager, Patrick Ellison Shea; ASM, Kelly Farah; Technical Director, Matthew Campbell; Press, Karen Greco

CAST May Black **Pheonix Vaughn**; Alice Cohen **Wendy Peace**; Billie Friedhoff **Corey Tazmania**; Sophie Birnbaum **Natalie Mosco**

SETTING May Black's kitchen in an apartment house in Brooklyn, New York; spring and summer, 1944. New York premiere of a new play presented in seven scenes in two acts. Previously presented at New Jersey Repertory Company.

SYNOPSIS While War is raging overseas, May, Alice, and Billie are home in Brooklyn marking the days until the men return. Every day has an unhurried rhythm with the women caring for their children, maintaining their households, visiting one another to catch up on gossip, borrowing coffee, trading ration cards and shopping at Loehman's. Into this carefully crafted world enters Sophie, a woman who has fled the Holocaust, and her appearance on the scene threatens the delicate equilibrium that the housewives have so skillfully created.

Hale Appleman (center) and the Company in Passion Play
(photo by Carol Rosegg)

Oliver Parker!

Cherry Lane Theatre; First Preview: May 9, 2010; Opening Night: May 17, 2010; Closed June 6, 2010; 7 previews, 18 performances

Written by Elizabeth Meriwether; Presented by the stageFARM (Carrie Shaltz, Founder & Executive Director; Alex Kilgore, Artistic Director); Director, Evan Cabnet; Set, Lauren Helpern; Lighting, Ben Stanton; Costumes, Jessica Shay; Sound, Zane Birdwell; PSM, Charles M. Turner III; ASM, Courtney James; Props, Faye Armon; Production Manager, La Vie Productions/James E. Cleveland; Technical Director, Joel Howell; Producers, Anthony Francavilla, Brittany O'Neill; Company Manager/Producer, Jen Driscoll; Marketing, Kate Laughlin; Special Events, Jason Shaltz; Casting, Calleri Casting; Press, Sam Rudy Media Relations

CAST Willa Cross **Johanna Day**; Jasper **John Larroquette**; Agnes **Monica Raymond**; Oliver Parker **Michael Zegen**

World premiere of a new play presented without intermission.

SYNOPSIS *Oliver Parker!* is a jet black comedy about hurting the ones you love, and loving the ones that hurt. Oliver is 17 and Jasper is 60. They are best friends. Oliver wants to get laid, and Jasper wants to help. Jasper wants to drink himself to death, and Oliver wants to save him. And they share a secret that could ruin them both... if it hasn't already.

John Larroquette and Michael Zegen in Oliver Parker! *(photo by The Shaltzes)*

Hebrew School Dropout

Actors Temple Theatre; First Preview: April 24, 2010; Opening Night: May 19, 2010; Closed June 17, 2010; 7 previews, 20 performances

Written by Dave Konig; Presented by Edmund Gaynes and What Exit? Theatre; Director, Pamela Hall; Sets & Lighting, Josh Iacovelli; Stage Manager, Lisa Pierucci; General Management, Jessimeg Productions, Julia Beardsley; Press, David Gersten & Associates

Performed by **Dave Konig**

New York premiere of a new solo performance play presented without intermission.

SYNOPSIS In *Hebrew School Dropout, or: Or: How I Converted From Judaism to Catholicism and Back to Judaism and Lost Those Stubborn Last 10 Pounds!*, three time Emmy Award winning comedian Dave Konig takes theatergoers on a journey of faith...with really bad MapQuest directions! In this new comedy, Kong goes from being a "lousy' Jew who doesn't fit in with good Jews, to convert to Catholicism, to national spokesman for the Catholic Church on satellite radio, to, maybe, an ever-so-slightly-better-than-lousy Jew. In between he experiences life-changing encounters with Marisa Tomei, Adam Sandler, Deepak Chopra, and

The Three Stooges! This show is for anyone who has ever had faith, lost it, found new faith, or just had a plain, old mid-life crisis.

Dave Konig in Hebrew School Dropout *(photo by Bev Sheehan)*

Banana Shpeel

Beacon Theatre; First Preview: April 29, 2010; Opening Night: May 21, 2010; Closed June 27, 2010; 28 previews, 32 performances

Written and directed by David Shiner; Presented by Cirque du Soleil (Guy Laliberté, Founder; Danile Lamarre, President & CEO; Aldo Giampaolo, Executive Producer) Director of Creation, Serge Roy; Composer and Arranger, Simon Carpentier; Choreographer, Jared Grimes; Costumes, Dominique Lemieux; Set/Co-Props, Patricia Ruel; Co-Props, Jasmine Catudal; Lighting, Bruno Raie; Sound, Harvey Robitaille; Makeup, Eleni Uranis; Comic Art Design/Assistant to the Director, Stefan Haves; Music Director, Sébastian Laurendeau; Additional Lyrics and Music, Jean François Côté, Scott Price, Christopher Ward; Eccentric Dance Specialist, Betsy Baytos; Magic Consultants, Mark Mitton, Ed Alonzo; Additional Consultants, Bob Martin, Bill Irwin; Casting, Fabrice Becker, Line Giasson; Production Manager, Michel Granger; Creation Technical Director, Matthieu Gourd; Company Manager, Paul Morer; Production Coordinator, Marie-Soleil Gascon; General Artistic Director, Pierre Parisien; Artistic Director, Daniel Ross; General Stage Manager, Claudette Waddle; Stage Manager, Jen Elfverson; ASM, Robert Vézina; Dance Captain, Kassie Brown; Production Technical Director, Phillip Hampton; Contortion Coach, Selenge Tsend-Ochir; Costume/Props Coordinator, Johanne Allaire; Performance Medicine, Tracy Guy (supervisor), Kristen Luby (therapist); Music Coordinator, Julie Beauséjour; Acrobatic Consultant, Danny Zen; Marketing SVP, Mario D'Amico; Press, The Publicity Office, Marc Thibodeau

CAST Foot Juggler **Vanessa Alvarez**; Hand Balancing **Dmitry Bulkin**; Hand to Hand **Preston Jamieson, Kelsey Wiens**; Marty Schmelky **Danny Rutigliano**; Contortion **Tsybenova Ayagma, Tsydendambaeva Imin, Zhambalova Lilia**; Tap Dance Duo **Joseph Wiggan, Josette C. Wiggan**; Juggler **Le Tuan**; Clowns **Claudio Carneiro, Patrick De Valette, Shereen Hickman, Daniel Passer, Gordon White, Wayne Wilson**; Ensemble **Robyn Baltzer, Kassie Brown, Adrienne Jean Fisher, Dewitt Fleming Jr., Karida Griffith, Luke Hawkins, Kathleen Hennessey, Adrienne Reid, Anthony J. Russo, Melissa Schott, Josh Scribner, Alexis Sims, Steven T. Williams**

MUSICIANS Roland Barber (trombone),Bobby Brennan (bass, double bass), Mario Hébert (guitar), Iohann Laliberté (drums, percussion), Jean-François Ouellet (sax, flute), Petros Sakelliou (bandleader, keyboards), Roger Squitero (percussion), Scott Steen (trumpet, flugelhorn, cornet)

New York premiere of a new vaudeville style theatrical production with circus acts presented without intermission. World premiere in Chicago in fall 2009.

SYNOPSIS *Banana Shpeel* is a roller coaster mix of styles that blends intense choreography, crazy comedy and distinctive acrobatic acts. The show offers a diverse spectrum of performances including tap, hip-hop and eccentric dance, slapstick comedy and Cirque du Soleil acrobatic acts – plus madcap characters spreading chaos in all directions.

The Company in Cirque du Soleil's Banana Shpeel *(photo by Kristie Kahns)*

My Big Gay Italian Wedding

St. Luke's Theatre; First Preview: May 5, 2010; Opening Night: May 22, 2010; 11 previews, 5 performances as of May 31, 2010

Written by Anthony J. Wilkinson; Produced by Dina Manzo & Sonia Blangiardo in association with Anndee Productions; Director, Teresa A. Cicala; Choreography, J. Austin Eyer; Original Music, David Boyd; Sets, Rob Santeramo; Costumes, Philip Heckman; Lighting, Graham Kindred; General Manager, Davenport Theatrical Enterprises, Matt Kovich; Marketing, HHC Marketing; Production Manager, Jeramiah Peay; Casting, Daryl Eisnberg; PSM, C.J. Thom III; ASM, Kelly Ice; Wardrobe Supervisor, Megan Opalinski; Original Press, David Gersten; Current Press, Keith Sherman & Associates, Brett Oberman

CAST Anthony **Anthony Wilkinson**; Andrew **Reichen Lehmkuhl**; Lucia **Liz Gerecitano**; Angela **Randi Kaplan**; Rodney **Erik Ransom**; Father Rosalia **Chad Kessler**; ToniAnn **Carla-Marie Mercun**; Gregorio **Fabio Taliercio**; Connie **Meagan Robar**; Joseph **Joe Scanio**; Mario **Adam Zelasko**; Frankie **Bryan Anthony**; Maria **Tricia Burns**; Maurizio **Brett Douglas**; Ensemble/Male Understudy **Kevin McIntyre**; Ensemble/Female Understudy **Leah Gerstel**

SETTING Revised version of a play presented in two acts. Originally presented at the Actors Playhouse November 14, 2003 (see *Theatre World* Vol. 60, page 107).

SYNOPSIS Planning a wedding can be hell… or a hell of a lot of fun! Two handsome grooms, one overbearing Italian mother, a jealous ex-boyfriend, the wedding planner from Hell, and an assortment of kooky family and friends all gather together for Off-Broadway's newest laugh-out-loud comedy with a heart.

The Company in My Big Gay Italian Wedding *(photo by Carol Rosegg)*

Jack's Precious Moment

59E59 Theater C; First Preview: May 21, 2010; Opening Night: May 26, 2010; Closed June 13, 2010; 22 performances

Written by Samuel D. Hunter; Presented by Page 73 Productions (Liz Jones and Asher Richelli, Executive Directors; John Baker, Artistic Associate) as part of the 2010 Americas Off-Broadway Festival; Produced by 59E59 (Elizabeth Kleinhans, President and Artistic Director; Peter Tear, Executive Producer); Director, Kip Fagan; Set, Lee Savage; Costumes, Jessica Ford; Lighting, Matt Frey; Sound, Bart Fasbender; Props, Sean McArdle; PSM, Jamie Rog; Production Manager, James Cleveland/La Vie Productions; Casting, Jack Doulin & Jenn Haltman; Dramaturg, John Baker; Fight Director, Thomas Schall; Assistant Director, Stella Powell-Jones; Production Assistant, Kyle Koszewnik; Technical Director, Joel Howell; Assistant Lighting, Oliver Wason; Assistant Sound, Nicholas Quinn; "Angel" Construction, Jessica Ford, John Leonard Thompson; Business Manager, Melanie Hopkins; Producing Associates, Claire Gresham, Jake McMullen; Press, Karen Greco

CAST Bib **Eddie Kaye Thomas**; Karen **Karen Walsh**; Jim **Tom Bloom**; Chuck **Lucas Papaelias**; The Precious Moments Angel **Danny Ryan**

SETTING Time: The late 2000s; Place: The heartland. World premiere of a new play presented without intermission. Developed at the Lark Play Development Center under the title *God of Meat*, and at the Playwrights Foundation (Mark Rucker, Director; Amy Mueller, Artistic Director) as part of the "In the Rough" series in 2009.

SYNOPSIS A video of insurgents beheading Jack Lewis is released over the Internet. Back home in Idaho, Jack's twin, father and widow are left to pick up the pieces– so to speak. The only solution to this Christian family's grief and mounting spiritual crisis: The Precious Moments Chapel in Carthage, MO.

Lucas Papaelias and Eddie Kaye Thomas in Jack's Precious Moment *(photo by Evan Sung)*

PLAYED THROUGH / CLOSED THIS SEASON

Altar Boyz

New World Stages–Stage 4; First Preview: February 15, 2005; Opening Night: March 1, 2005; Closed January 10, 2010; 16 previews, 2,032 performances

Book by Kevin Del Aguila, music, lyrics, and vocal arrangements by Gary Adler and Michael Patrick Walker, conceived by Marc Kessler and Ken Davenport; Produced by Ken Davenport and Robyn Goodman, in association with Walt Grossman, Ruth Hendel, Sharon Karmazin, Matt Murphy, and Mark Shacket; Director, Stafford Arima; Choreography, Christopher Gattelli; Musical Director/Dance Music and Additional Arrangements, Lynne Shankel; Set, Anna Louizos; Costumes, Gail Brassard; Lighting, Natasha Katz; Sound, Simon Matthews; Orchestrations, Doug Katsaros, Lynne Shankel; Casting, David Caparelliotis; PSM, Sara Jaramillo; Hair, Josh Marquette; Production Manager, Andrew Cappelli; Associate Producer, Stephen Kocis; Press; David Gersten and Associates; General Manager, Martian Entertainment; Company Manager, Ryan Lympus; ASM, Alyssa Stone; Casting, David Petro; Associate Choreographer, Tammy Colucci; Music Programmer, Doug Katsaros; Cast recording: Sh-K-Boom Records 86050

CAST Matthew **Michael Kaden Craig**; Mark **Travis Nesbitt**; Luke **Lee Markham**; Juan **Mauricio Perez**; Abraham **Ravi Roth**; Voice of GOD **Shadoe Stevens**; Understudies **Mitch Dean**, **Joey Khoury**

ALTAR BOYZ BAND Jason Loffredo (Conductor/keyboard), Danny Percefull (keyboard), David Matos (guitar), Clayton Craddock (drums)

MUSICAL NUMBERS We Are the Altar Boyz, Rhythm in Me, Church Rulz, The Calling, The Miracle Song, Everybody Fits, Something About You, Body Mind & Soul, La Vida Eternal, Epiphany, Number 918, Finale: I Believe

SETTING Here and Now. A musical presented without intermission. Originally produced at the New York Musical Theatre Festival, September, 2004. For original production credits see *Theatre World* Volume 61, page 142.

SYNOPSIS A struggling Christian boy band (with one nice Jewish boy), trying to save the world one screaming fan at a time, perform their last tour date at the Dodger Stages. Their pious pop act worked wonders on the home state Ohio bingo-hall-and-pancake breakfast circuit, but will temptation for solo record deals threaten to split the Boyz as take a bite out of the forbidden Big Apple?

The closing cast of Altar Boyz: *Travis Nesbitt, Mauricio Perez, Ravi Roth, Lee Markham, and Michael Kadin Craig* (photo by Michael Portantiere/FollowSpotPhoto.com)

Jason Carden and Jessica West Regan in The Awesome 80's Prom *(photo courtesy of Ken Davenport)*

The Awesome 80s Prom

Webster Hall; First Performance: July 23, 2004 (Friday evenings only); Opening Night: September 10, 2004 (Fridays and Saturdays); 317 performances as of May 31, 2010 (Friday and Saturday evening performances only)

Written and produced by Ken Davenport; Co-Authored by The Class of '89 (Sheila Berzan, Alex Black, Adam Bloom, Anne Bobby, Courtney Balan, Mary Faber, Emily McNamara, Troy Metcalf, Jenna Pace, Amanda Ryan Paige, Mark Shunock, Josh Walden, Noah Weisberg, Brandon Williams, Simon Wong and Fletcher Young); Director, Ken Davenport; Choreography, Drew Geraci; Costumes, Randall E. Klein; Lighting, Martin Postma; Production Stage Manger, Carlos Maisonet; Associate Producers, Amanda Dubois, Jennifer Manocherian; Company Manager, Matt Kovich; ASM, Kathryn Galloway; Casting, Daryl Eisenberg; Press, David Gersten & Associates

CAST Johnny Hughes – The DJ **Dillon Porter**; Lloyd Parker – The Photographer **Daryl Embry**; Dickie Harrington – The Drama Queen **Bennett Leak**; Michael Jay – The Class President **Craig Jorczak**; Mr. Snelgrove – The Principal **Thomas Poarch**; Molly Parker – The Freshman **Lauren Schafler**; Inga Swanson – The Swedish Exchange Student **Annie Ragsdale**[1]; Joshua "Beef" Beefarowski – A Football Player **Michael Barra**; Whitley Whitiker – The Head Cheerleader **Jessica West Regan**; Nick Fender – The Rebel **Brandon Marotta**; Heather #1 – A Cheerleader **Allison Carter Thomas**[2]; Heather #2 – The Other Cheerleader **Kate Wood Riley**; Kerrie Kowalski – The Spaz **Missy Diaz**; Melissa Ann Martin – Head of the Prom Committee **Angie Blocher**; Louis Fensterpock – The Nerd **Nick Austin**; Blake Williams – Captain of the Football Team **Jason Carden**; Mrs. Lascalzo – The Drama Teacher **Andrea Biggs**; Feung Schwey – The Asian Exchange Student **Anderson Lim**; The Mystery Guest **CP Lacey**

*Succeeded by: 1. Lindsay Ryan 2. Jenny Peters

SETTING Wanaget High's Senior Prom, 1989. An interactive theatrical experience presented without intermission

SYNOPSIS The Captain of the Football Team, the Asian Exchange Student, the Geek, and the Head Cheerleader are all competing for Prom King and Queen. The audience decides who wins while moonwalking to retro hits from the decade.

A scene from Blue Man Group
(photo courtesy of Blue Man Productions)

Blue Man Group

Astor Place Theatre; Opening Night: November 7, 1991; 10,060 performances as of May 31, 2010

Created and written by Matt Goldman, Phil Stanton, Chris Wink; Produced by Blue Man Productions; Director, Marlene Swartz and Blue Man Group; Artistic Directors, Caryl Glaab, Michael Quinn; Artistic/Musical Collaborators, Larry Heinemann, Ian Pai; Set, Kevin Joseph Roach; Costumes, Lydia Tanji, Patricia Murphy; Lighting, Brian Aldous, Matthew McCarthy; Sound, Raymond Schilke, Jon Weston; Computer Graphics, Kurisu-Chan; Video, Caryl Glaab, Dennis Diamond; PSM, Patti McCabe; Company Manager, Akia Squitieri; Stage Managers, Bernadette Castro, Jenny Lynch; Resident General Manager, Leslie Witthohn; General Manager of North American Productions, Alison Schwartz; Performing Director, Chris Bowen; Performing Directors, Chris Bowen, Michael Dahlen, Randall Jaynes, Jeffrey Doornbos, Brian Scott; Original Executive Producer, Maria Di Dia; Casting, Deb Burton; Press, Tahra Milan

CAST (rotating) **Kalen Allmandinger, Gideon Banner, Collin Batten, Chris Bowen, Wes Day, Michael Dahlen, Isaac Eddy, Josh Elrod, Matt Goldman, Randall Jaynes, General Judd, Peter Musante, Matt Ramsey, Pete Simpson, Scott Speiser, Phil Stanton, Chris Wink**

MUSICIANS (rotating) Tom Shad, Geoff Gersh, Clem Waldmann, Dan Dobson, Jeff Lipstein, Byron Estep, Matt Hankle, Tommy Kessler, Jerry Kops, Josh Matthews, Jordan Perlson, Jano Rix, Clifton Hyde, Dave Steele

An evening of performance art presented without intermission. For original production credits see *Theatre World* Volume 48, Page 90.

SYNOPSIS The three-man new-vaudeville Blue Man Group combines comedy, music, art, and multimedia to produce a unique form of entertainment.

Danny and Sylvia: The Danny Kaye Musical

St. Luke's Theatre; First Preview: May 6, 2009; Opening Night: May 13, 2009; 5 previews, 199 performances as of May 31, 2010

Book and lyrics by Robert McElwaine, music by Bob Bain; Presented by Hy Juter and Edmund Gaynes; Director, Pamela Hall; Choreographer, Gene Castle; Sets, Josh Iacovelli; Lighting, Graham Kindred; Costumes, Elizabeth Flores; Music Director, David Fiorello; General Manager, Jessimeg Productions; PSM, Josh Iacovelli; Associate General Manager, Julia Beardsley; Props, Robert Pemberton; Press, Susan L. Schulman

CAST Danny Kaye **Brian Childers**; Sylvia Fine **Kimberly Faye Greenberg**

MUSICIANS David Fiorello (piano)

MUSICAL NUMBERS Another Summer, At Liberty, at the Club Versailles, At the London Palladium, Can't Get That Man Off My Mind, Danny Kaminsky, I Can't Live Without You, If I Knew Then, If I Needed a Guy, I'm a Star, Just one Girl, La Vie Paree, Now Look What You Made Me Do, Requiem for Danny Kaminsky, She's Got a Fine Head on My Shoulders, Sylvia's Song, Tummler, We've Closed On Opening Night, We Make a Wonderful Team, What Shall We Say, You Got A Problem With That, Anatole of Paris, The Maladjusted jester, Melody in 4F, One Life to Live, Tchaikovsky, Dinah, Minnie the Moocher, Ballin' the Jack, P.S. One Four Nine

SETTING 1936 to 1948 in New York, Hollywood and London. Off-Broadway premiere of a musical presented in two acts.

SYNOPSIS *Danny and Sylvia* takes a look at the famous couple from the time the young undisciplined comic Danny Kaminsky meets aspiring songwriter Sylvia Fine at an audition in the 1930s. Under Sylvia's guidance as mentor, manager, and eventually, wife, Kaye rises from improvisational comic to international film star. The musical explores their inspired collaboration and the romance and conflict that made them such a volatile and successful couple.

Brian Childers and Kimberly Faye Greenberg in Danny and Sylvia: The Danny Kaye Musical *(photo by Carol Rosegg)*

Don't Leave It All to Your Children!

Actors Temple Theatre; First Preview: May 6, 2009; Opening Night: May 20, 2009; Closed November 22, 2009; 9 previews, 104 performances

Book, music and lyrics by Saul Ilson; Presented by Sausau Productions LLC; Director Saul Ilson; Staging, Rudy Tronto; Music Director, John Bell; Sets, Josh Iacovelli; Lighting, Graham Kindred; Stage Manager, Jana Llynn; General Manager, Jessimeg Productions; Associate General Manager, Julia Beardsley; Photographer, Albert Hirson; Press, Susan L. Schulman

CAST **Barbara Minkus**[1]; **Marcia Rodd**[2], **Steve Rossi**[3], **Ronnie Schell**[4]; Understudies **Alix Elias**, **Rudy Tronto**

*Succeeded by: 1. Cheryl Stern 2. Joy Franz 3. Jay Stuart 4. James Dybas (7/1/09)

MUSICAL NUMBERS The Best Medicine, You're a Boomer, The Golden Years, March in the Parade, Three of You, A Singles Cruise, Old Cronies, I Love You/ Looking Back, My Grandchildren & Me, Where Did the Time Go?, It's the High Cost, A Man Named Mel, Age is Not a Factor, Ed Sullivan, What Do You Think About That?, Another Wrinkle, A Wonderful Life, Why Do We Do It, Don't Leave it All/Have a Good Time, Old Memories, The Best Medicine (reprise)

New York premiere of a musical revue presented without intermission.

SYNOPSIS *Don't Leave It All to Your Children!* is a laugh-filled 90 minutes of music and comedy that celebrates the funny side of the Golden years.

Steve Rossi, Marcia Rodd, Ronnie Schell, and Barbara Minkus in Don't Leave It All to Your Children! *(photo by Albert Hirshon)*

Erik Altemus and Kimberly Whalen in The Fantasticks *(photo by Joan Marcus)*

The Fantasticks

Snapple Theater Center – Jerry Orbach Theater; First Preview: July 28, 2006; Opening Night: August 23, 2006; 27 previews, 1,472 performances as of May 31, 2010+

Book and lyrics by Tom Jones, music by Harvey Schmidt, suggested by the play *Les Romanesques* by Edmond Rostand; Produced by Terzetto LLC, Pat Flicker Addiss, and MARS Theatricals (Amy Danis/Mark Johanness); Director, Tom Jones; Original Staging, Word Baker; Sets and Costumes, Ed Wittstein; Lighting, Mary Jo Dondlinger; Sound, Dominic Sack; Casting, Terzetto LLC; Musical Director, Robert Felstein; Choreography/Musical Staging, Janet Watson; Production Stage Manager, Shanna Spinello/Paul Blankenship; ASMs, Michael Krug, Brandon Kahn, Paul Blankenship; Associate Director, Kim Moore; Associate Producers, Carter-Parke Productions and Patrick Robustelli; Production Supervisor, Dan Shaheen; Press, John Capo–DBS Press; Cast recording: Sh-K-Boom/Ghostlight 84415

CAST The Narrator (El Gallo) **Bradley Dean**[1]; The Boy (Matt) **Jonathan Schwartz**[2]; The Girl (Luisa) **Ramona Mallory**[3]; The Boy's Father (Hucklebee) **Gene Jones**; The Girl's Father (Bellomy) **Steve Routman**; The Old Actor (Henry) **John Thomas Waite**[4]; The Man Who Dies (Mortimer) **Michael Nostrand**; The Mute **Douglas Ullman Jr.**[5]; At the Piano **Robert Felstein**; At the Harp **Jacqueline Kerrod**

STANDBYS Tom Flagg (Hucklebee/Henry/Mortimer), Scott Willis (El Gallo/Hucklebee/Bellomy), Evy Ortiz (The Mute/Luisa), Jordan Nichols (Matt), Richard Roland (Mortimer)

*Succeeded by: 1. Lewis Cleale (6/29/09), Dennis Parlato (7/13/09), Lewis Cleale (8/3/09), Edward Watts (3/22/10) 2. Nick Spangler, Erik Altemus (12/14/09) 3. Addi McDaniel (6/29/09), Kimberly Whalen (11/5/09) 4. Thomas Bruce, MacIntyre Dixon (8/17/09) 5. Matt Leisy (12/28/09)

MUSICAL NUMBERS Overture, Try to Remember, Much More, Metaphor, Never Say No, It Depends on What You Pay, Soon It's Gonna Rain, Abduction Ballet, Happy Ending, This Plum is Too Ripe, I Can See It, Plant a Radish, Round and Round, They Were You, Try to Remember (reprise)

Revival of the musical presented in two acts. *The Fantasticks* is the world's longest running musical and the longest running Off-Broadway production ever. The original production opened at the Sullivan Street Playhouse on May 3, 1960 and closed January 13, 2002 playing over 17,000 performances (see *Theatre World* Volume 16 page 167 for original cast credits). On May 3, 2010, *The Fantasticks* celebrated its fiftieth anniversary with weekend long celebration. Over fifty actors from the original Sullivan Street production and current revival reunited after the curtain call on May 1. The Lucille Lortel Awards featured a photo tribute to the show on May 2, and on May 3, audience members were given a special commemorative program and a reproduction of the original opening night playbill from May 3, 1960.

SYNOPSIS *The Fantasticks* tells the story of a young boy and girl who fall madly in love at the hands of their meddling fathers, but soon grow restless and stray from one another. The audience uses its imagination to follow El Gallo as he creates a world of moonlight and magic, then pain and disillusionment, until the boy and girl find their way back to one another.

⁺The show had a brief hiatus from February 24–June 16, 2008 when new producers took over the production.

A scene from Fuerza Bruta: Look Up (photo courtesy of Fuerzabruta)

Fuerza Bruta: Look Up

Daryl Roth Theatre; First Preview: October 11, 2007; Opening Night: October 24, 2007; 14 previews, 957 performances as of May 31, 2010

Created and directed by Diqui James; Produced by Live Nation Artists Events Group, Fuerzabruta, Ozono, and David Binder; Composer/Musical Director, Gaby Kerpel; Lighting, Edi Pampin; Sound, Hernan Nupieri; Costumes, Andrea Mattio; Automation, Alberto Figueiras; General Coordinator, Fabio D'Aquila; Production, Agustina James; Technical Director, Alejandro Garcia; Marketing, Eric Schnall; Casting, James Calleri; Set-up Technical Supervisor, Bradley Thompson; General Manager, Laura Kirspel; PSM, Jeff Benish; Production Coordinator/ASM, E. Cameron Holsinger; Special Effects, Rick Sordelet; Press, The Karpel Group, Bridget Klapinski, Adam Bricault

CAST **Freddy Bosche**, **Hallie Bulleit**, **Daniel Case**, **Dusty Giamanco**, **John Hartzell**, **Michael Hollick**, **Joshua Kobak**, **Angelica Kushi**, **Gwyneth Larsen**, **Tamara Levinson**, **Rose Mallare**, **Brooke Miyasaki**, **Jon Morris**, **Marlyn Ortiz**, **Kepani Salgado-Ramos**; Swings **Jason Novak**, **Kira Morris**, **Andy Pellick**, **Jeslyn Kelly**, **Ilia Castro**

U.S. premiere of a theatrical experience piece with music presented without intermission. Originally presented in Buenos Aries, and subsequently in Lisbon, London, and Bogata.

SYNOPSIS The creators of the long running hit *De La Guarda* push the boundaries of theatrical creativity, motivation, and innovation in their new work featuring a non-stop collision of dynamic music, visceral emotion, and kinetic aerial imagery. *Fuerza Bruta: Look Up* breaks free from the confines of spoken language and theatrical convention as both performers and audience are immersed in an environment that floods the senses, evoking pure visceral emotion in a place where individual imagination soars.

The Gazillion Bubble Show

New World Stages–Stage 3; Previews: January 17–23, 2007; Opening Night: February 15, 2007; 1,334 performances as of May 31, 2010

Created and staged by Fan Yang; Produced and Set Design by Fan Yang and Neodus Company, Ltd.; Artistic Director, Jamie Jan; Show Director, Steve Lee; Lighting, Jin Ho Kim; Sound, Joon Lee; Gazilllion Bubbles FX, Special Effects, Alex Cheung; Theatrical Special Effects, CITC/Gary and Stephanie Crawford; Original Music, Workspace Co, Ltd.; Laser Design, Abhilash George; Lumalaser, Tim Ziegenbein; Lighting Effects, David Lau; Special Effects Inventor, Dragan Maricic; Production Stage Manager, Yeung Jin Son; Stage Manager, Min Song; Technical Director, Alan Kho; General Manager, New World Stages; Marketing, HHC Marketing; Marketing Director, Chermaine Cho; Press, Springer Associates, Joe Trentacosta, Gary Springer

Performed by **Ana Yang**, **Fan Yang**, or **Jano Yang**

New York premiere of an interactive theatrical event presented without intermission.

SYNOPSIS The first interactive stage production of its kind, complete with fantastic light effects and lasers, Fan Yang blends art and science to dazzle audiences with his jaw-dropping masterpieces of bubble artistry that defy gravity and logic as we know it. He holds Guinness World records for the biggest bubble ever blown, the largest bubble wall ever created (a staggering 156 feet!), most bubbles within a bubble, and in May 2006, was able to encapsulate 22 people inside a single soap bubble on live television. Fan's wife Ana has performed in the New York production the past two seasons. Fan and his brother Jano have made appearances in the show this past year.

Fan Yang in The Gazillion Bubble Show
(photo by Nino Fernando Campagna)

The Marvelous Wonderettes

Westside Theatre (Upstairs); First Preview: August 26, 2008; Opening Night: September 14, 2008; Closed January 3, 2010; 19 previews, 545 performances

Written and directed by Roger Bean; Presented by David Elzer, Peter Schneider and Marvelous NYC LLC; Choreography, Janet Miller; Sets, Michael Carnahan; Costumes, Bobby Pierce; Lighting, Jeremy Pivnick; Sound, Cricket S. Myers; Music Director/Orchestrations, Michael Borth; Music Supervisor/Vocal and Band Arrangements, Brian William Baker; Vocal Arrangements, Roger Bean; PSM, Anita Ross; ASM, Kelly Varley; Props, Kathy Fabian; Company Manager, Jennifer Pluff; Production Manager, Michael Casselli; General Manager, Roy Gabay; Associate Director/Dance Captain, Bets Malone; Associate Wigs, Robert-Charles Vallance; Marketing, HHC Marketing; Casting, Jay Binder & Jack Bowdan; Press, The Karpel Group, Bridget Klapinski, Adam Bricault; Cast recording: PS Classics 874
CAST Missy **Misty Cotton**[1]; Betty Jean **Beth Malone**[2]; Suzy **Bets Malone**[3]; Cindy Lou **Victoria Matlock**[4]

UNDERSTUDIES Leslie Spencer Smith (Suzy/Betty Jean/Cindy Lou); Kristen Beth Williams (Cindy Lou/Missy/Suzy)

*Succeeded by: 1. Courtney Ballan (10/26/09) 2. Lindsay Mendez (6/14/09) 3. Kristen Bracken (6/8/09), Lowe Taylor 4. Christina DeCicco (6/8/09

MUSICIANS Michael Borth (Conductor/keyboards), Brandon Sturiale (keyboard 2), Danny Taylor (drums), Neal Johnson (guitar)

SETTING Springfield High School. Act 1: The 1958 Prom. Act 2: The 1968 ten-year reunion. New York premiere of a new musical with pop standards presented in two acts. World premiere at the Milwaukee Repertory Theatre (Joseph Hanreddy, Artistic Director; Timothy J. Shields, Managing Director).

SYNOPSIS *The Marvelous Wonderettes* is an effervescent musical blast from the past. Set at the Springfield High School prom and later their ten-year reunion, the Wonderettes (Betty Jean, Cindy Lou, Missy and Suzy–four young girls with hopes and dreams as big as their crinoline skirts and voices to match!) tell about their lives and loves, and perform such classic 50's and 60's songs as "Lollipop," "Dream Lover," "Stupid Cupid," "Lipstick on Your Collar," "Hold Me, Thrill Me, Kiss Me," "It's My Party," "It's In His Kiss (The Shoop Shoop Song)" and many more.

Victoria Matlock, Farah Alvin, Bets Malone, and Beth Malone in The Marvelous Wonderettes *(photo by Carol Rosegg)*

My First Time

New World Stages–Stage 5; First Preview: July 12, 2007; Opening Night: July 30, 2007; Closed January 22, 2010; 224 performances (Friday and Saturday evenings)

Written by Ken Davenport and Real People Just Like You; Inspired by the website www.MyFirstTime.com created by Peter Foldy and Craig Stuart; Produced and directed by Ken Davenport; Production Design, Matthew A. Smith; Marketing, HHC Marketing; Casting, Daryl Eisenberg; Associate Producer/Press, David J. Gersten; General Management, DTE, Inc.; PSM, Kathryn Galloway; Associate General Manager, Matt Kovich; Associate to the Producer, Nicole Brodeur; Crew, Allison Hersh; Davenport Theatrical Enterprises: Jamie Lynn Ballard, Amanda Butcher, Matt Kovich; Press, David Gersten

CAST Dana Watkins, Nathan Williams, Kathy Searle, Cyndee Welburn

World premiere of a new play presented without intermission.

SYNOPSIS *My First Time* is a new play in the style of *The Vagina Monologues*, featuring hysterical and heartbreaking stories about first sexual experiences written by real people, just like you. Four actors bring to life confessional monologues about the silly, sweet, absurd, funny, heterosexual, homosexual, awkward, shy, sexy and everything-in-between stories of first times submitted to the website. *My First Time*: I'll tell you mine if, you tell you yours.

Bill Dawes, Cyndee Welburn, Josh Heine and Kathy Searle in My First Time *(photo by Drew Geraci)*

Naked Boys Singing

New World Stages–Stage 4; First Preview: July 2, 1999; Opening Night: July 22, 1999; 2,898 performances as of May 31, 2010 (Weekends only)

Written by Stephen Bates, Marie Cain, Perry Hart, Shelly Markham, Jim Morgan, David Pevsner, Rayme Sciaroni, Mark Savage, Ben Schaechter, Robert Schrock, Trance Thompson, Bruce Vilanch, Mark Winkler; Conceived and directed by Robert Schrock; Produced by Jamie Cesa, Carl D. White, Hugh Hayes, Tom Smedes, Jennifer Dumas; Choreography, Jeffry Denman; Music Director, Jeffrey Biering; Original Musical Director and Arrangements, Stephen Bates; Set/Costumes, Carl D. White; Lighting, Aaron Copp; Production Stage Manager, Heather Weiss/Scott DelaCruz; Assistant Stage Manager, Mike Kirsch/Dave August; Dance Captain, Craig Lowry; Press, David Gersten; Original Press, Peter Cromarty; L.A. Cast recording: Café Pacific Records

CAST Naked Maid **Gregory Stockbridge**; Radio **Eric Dean Davis**; Robert Mitchum **Nimmy Weisbrod**; Entertainer **Russell Saylor**; Bris **Matt Burrow**; Porn Star **Tony Neidenbach**; Muscle Addiction **Trevor Efinger**; Window **Dave August**; Swings: **Craig Lowry**, **Melvin Bell III**; Piano: **Jeffrey Biering**

MUSICAL NUMBERS Gratuitous Nudity, Naked Maid, The Bliss of a Bris, Window to Window, Fight the Urge, Robert Mitchum, Jack's Song, Members Only, Perky Little Porn Star, Kris Look What You've Missed, Muscle Addiction, Nothin' But the Radio On, The Entertainer, Window to the Soul, Finale/Naked Boys Singing!

A musical revue presented in two acts. For original production credits see *Theatre World* Volume 56, page 114. Originally opened at The Actors' Playhouse; transferred to Theatre Four March 17, 2004; transferred to the John Houseman Theater September 17, 2004; transferred to the 47th Street Theatre November 12, 2004; transferred to the Julia Miles Theatre May 6, 2005; transferred to New World Stages October 14, 2005.

SYNOPSIS The title says it all! Caution and costumes are thrown to the wind in this all-new musical revue featuring an original score and a handful of hunks displaying their special charms as they celebrate the splendors of male nudity in comedy, song and dance.

The Cast of Naked Boys Singing *(photo by Joan Marcus)*

Our Town

Barrow Street Theatre; First Preview: February 17, 2009; Opening Night: February 26, 2009; 10 previews, 525 performances as of May 31, 2010

Written by Thornton Wilder; Presented by Scott Morfee, Jean Doumanian, Tom Wirtshafter, Ted Snowdon, Eagle Productions, Dena Hammerstein/Pam Pariseau, The Weinstein Company, Burnt Umber Productions; Director, David Cromer; Sets, Michele Spadaro; Costumes, Alison Siple; Lighting, Heather Gilbert; Original Music/Music Director, Jonathan Mastro; Production Manager, B.D. White; PSM, Richard A. Hodge; ASM, Kate McDoniel; Associate Producers, Patrick Daly & Marc Biales; Assistant Director, Michael Page; General Management, Two Step Productions; Advertising, Eliran Murphy Group; Casting, Pat McCorkle, Joe Lopick, Assistant Director, Michael Page; Press, O+M Company

James McMenamin and Jennifer Grace in Our Town *(photo by Carol Rosegg)*

CAST Stage Manager **Scott Parkinson**[1]; Mrs. Gibbs **Lori Myers**[2]; Mrs. Webb **Kati Brazda**; Dr. Gibbs **Jeff Still**[3]; Joe Crowell Jr. **Adam Hinkle**[4]; Howie Newsome **Robert Beitzel**; George Gibbs **James McMenamin**; Rebecca Gibbs **Ronette Levenson**[5]; Emily Webb **Jennifer Grace**; Wally Webb **Seamus Mulcahy**[6]; Professor Willard **Wilbur Edwin Henry**[7]; Mr. Webb **Ken Marks**[8]; Simon Stimson **Jonathan Mastro**[9]; Mrs. Soames **Donna Jay Fulks**[10]; Constable Warren **George Demas**[11]; Si Crowell **Jason Yachanin**; Joe Stoddard **Jay Russell**[12]; Sam Craig **Jeremy Beiler**[13]; Irma **Dana Jacks**; Citizen **Elizabeth Audley**[14]; Farmer McCarty **Keith Perry**; Citizen **Kathleen Pierce**; Citizen **Mark Shock**

UNDERSTUDIES Elizabeth Audley[14] (Mrs. Soames), Jeremy Beiler (Simon Stimpson), Robert Beitzel (George), George Demas[11] (Dr. Gibbs/Mr. Webb), Donna Jay Fulks[10] (Mrs. Gibbs/Mrs. Webb), Adam Hinkle[4] (Si Cromwell/ Howie), Dana Jacks (Rebecca Gibbs/Emily Webb), Keith Perry (Constable Warren/ Professor Willard/Joe Stoddard), Jay Russell[12] (Stage Manager), Mark Shock (Sam Craig), Jason Yachanin (Joe Crowell, Jr./Wally)

*Succeeded by: 1. David Cromer, Jason Butler Harner, David Cromer (12/22/09), Stephen Kunken (1/5/10), Michael Shannon (2/23/10) 2. Donna Jay Fulks (5/25/10) 3. Mark L. Montgomery, Armand Schultz, Ben Livingston (1/5/10) 4. Will Brill 5. Jacey Powers, Ronette Levenson (1/5/10), Emma Galvin 6. Jake Horowitz (1/5/10), Seamus Mulcahy 7. Ben Livingston, Wilbur Edwin Henry (1/5/10), Mark Hattan (5/25/10) 8. David Manis (1/5/10) 9. Jeremy Beiler (9/5/09), Daniel Marcus (1/5/10) 10. Susan Bennett, Elizabeth Audley 11. Mark Hattan, George Demas 12. Roger DeWitt 13. Nathan Dame 14. Lynn Lawrence

SETTING 1901. Grover's Corners, New Hampshire. Revival of a play presented in three acts with two intermissions. This production was originally presented by The Hypocrites (Chicago) May 1, 2008. On December 17, 2009, this engagement became the longest-running production of the play in its 72-year history with its 337th performance, surpassing the original Broadway run.

SYNOPSIS In David Cromer's staging of Wilder's timeless play, the action takes place in, among and around the audience, creating an intimacy between actors and audience and a powerful encounter with the play's searching questions about family, community and mortality.

Perfect Crime

Snapple Theatre Center – 4th Floor; Opening Night: April 18, 1987; 9,448 performances as of May 31, 2010

By Warren Manzi; Presented by The Actors Collective in association with the Methuen Company; Director, Jeffrey Hyatt; Set, Jay Stone, Warren Manzi; Costumes, Nancy Bush; Lighting, Jeff Fontaine; Sound, David Lawson; PSM, Brian Meister; Press, John Capo–DBS Press

CAST Margaret Thorne Brent **Catherine Russell**; Inspector James Ascher **Richard Shoberg**; W. Harrison Brent **Robert Emmet Lunney**[1]; Lionel McAuley **Michael Brian Dunn**[2]; David Breuer **Patrick Robustelli**; Understudies **Andrea Leigh**, **Don Noble**

*Succeeded by: 1. Randy Kovitz, John Hillner 2. Rob Sedgwick, Erick Parillo, George McDaniel

SETTING Windsor Locks, Connecticut. A mystery presented in two acts. For original production credits see *Theatre World* Volume 43, page 96. Catherine Russell has only missed four performances since the show opened in 1987, and on April 18, 2009, she was inducted into the Guinness Book of Records for "Most Performances by a Theater Actor in the Same Role for not missing a day of work in twenty-two years. The show originally opened at the Courtyard Playhouse (39 Grove Street); transferred to: Second Stage Uptown (now the McGinn-Cazale Theatre) August–October 1987; 47th Street Theatre: October–December 1987; Intar 53 Theater on 42nd Street (now demolished): January–April 1988; Harold Clurman Theatre (now demolished): May 1988–August 1990; 47th Street Theatre: August–December 1990; Theatre Four (now the Julia Miles Theatre): January 1991–September 1993; 47th Street Theatre: September 1993–January 1994; The Duffy Theatre at Broadway and 46th (now demolished): February 1994–May 2006; Snapple Theatre Center–Duffy Theatre: May 22, 2006–present. *Perfect Crime* is the longest running play in the history of New York theatre.

SYNOPSIS Margaret Brent is an accomplished Connecticut psychiatrist and potential cold-blooded killer. When her wealthy husband turns up dead, she gets caught in the middle of a terrifying game of cat and mouse with a deranged patient and the handsome but duplicitous investigator assigned to the case.

Richard Shoberg, David Butler, and Catherine Russell in Perfect Crime (photo courtesy John Capo Public Relations)

Pinkalicious, The Musical

Bleecker Street Theatre; Opening Day: November 1, 2008; 181 performances as of May 31, 2010 (Saturday and Sunday performances)

Book and lyrics by Elizabeth Kann & Victoria Kann, music & lyrics by John Gregor; Produced by Vital Theatre Company (Stephen Sunderlin, Artistic Director; Linda Ames Key, Education Director; Mary Kate Burke, Associate Producer); Director, Teresa K. Pond; Original Director, Suzu McConnell-Wood; Choreography, Dax Valdes; Music Director, Jad Bernardo; Set, Mary Hamrick; Costumes, Colleen Kesterson & Randi Fowler; Props, Dan Jagendorf & Kerry McGuire; PSM, Kara M. Teolis; Stage Manager, Annie Deardorf; Casting, Bob Cline; Company Manager, Cadien Dumas; Press, Stephen Sunderlin

CAST Peter Pinkerton **Jeff Barba**[1] or **Eric Restivo**; Pinkalicious **Kristin Parker** or **Bridget Riley**; Dr. Wink/Alison **Jill Anthony**[2] or **Molly Gilman**; Mr. Pinkerton **John Galas** or **Jace Nichols**[3]; Mrs. Pinkerton **Colleen Fee**[4] or **Rebecca Stavis**[5]

UNDERSTUDY Holly Buczek (Dr. Wink/Alison)

*Succeeded by: 1. Brian Maxsween 2. Rori Nogee 3. Chris Kind 4. Claire McClanahan 5. Chloe Sabin

A musical for young audiences presented without intermission. Previously played at New World Stages January 12–May 25, 2008 (see *Theatre World* Vol. 64, page 268) and encored there August 2–September 21, 2008. Originally presented at the McGinn Cazale Theatre January 13–February 25, 2007, and extended at Soho Playhouse March 3–May 25, 2007 (see *Theatre World* Vol. 63, page 291).

SYNOPSIS Pinkalicious can't stop eating pink cupcakes despite warnings from her parents. Her pink indulgence lands her at the doctor's office with Pinkititis, an affliction that turns her pink from head to toe - a dream come true for this pink loving enthusiast. But when her hue goes too far, only Pinkalicious can figure out a way to get out of this predicament.

The Company in **Pinkalicious** *(photo by Stephen Sunderlin)*

The Quantum Eye – Magic and Mentalism

Bleecker Street Theatre; Opening Night: February 9, 2007; 482 performances as of May 31, 2010

Created by Sam Eaton; Produced and directed by Samuel Rosenthal; Original Music, Scott O'Brien; Art Design, Fearless Design; Assistant Producer, Mimi Rosenthal; Artwork, Glenn Hidlago; House Manger, Janet Oldenbrook; Wardrobe, Larry the Tailer

Performed by **Sam Eaton**

Programme: A Gulity Conscience, One Card, Fourth Dimension, Reading Minds, Animal Instinct, Digimancy, Mental Sketch, Transmission, An Unusual Talent, Mnemoncis, Strange News

A mentalist/magic show presented in 90 minutes without intermission. The show was workshopped and made open to the public from August 2006 through its opening at the WorkShop Theatre's Jewel Box Theatre on January 5, 2007. The show transferred to Soho Playhouse's Huron Club on June 15, 2007, playing Friday nights. The show transferred to the Duffy Theatre on November 24, 2007 playing on Saturday twilights, and last season transferred to the Bleecker Street Theatre Downstairs on February 14, 2009, performing on Saturday twilights and Tuesday evenings.

SYNOPSIS *The Quantum Eye* is Sam Eaton's entertaining and fascinating exploration of mentalism, magic, perception and deception, where extraordinary ability and humor blend with the audience to make for a unique performance every time. His masterful use of prediction, manipulation, memorization and calculation will amaze and entertain audiences. It is an extraordinary blend of 21st Century mentalism and Victorian-era mystery. Join Sam on a journey past the limits of possibility in a show that you will never forget.

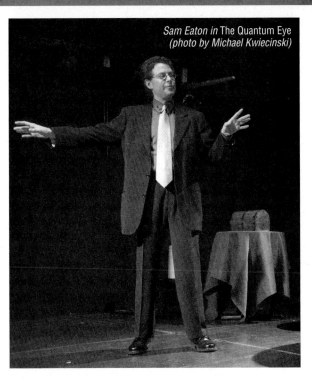

Sam Eaton in The Quantum Eye *(photo by Michael Kwiecinski)*

Sessions

Algonquin Theatre–Kauffman Stage; First Preview: October 28, 2008; Opening Night: January 14, 2009; Closed January 3, 2010; 61 previews, 360 performances

Book, music and lyrics by Albert M. Tapper; Produced by Algonquin Theater Productions and Ten Grand Productions Inc.; Director, Thomas Coté; Choreography, Penny Ayn Mass; Additional Choreography, James Horvath; "Breathe" Choreography, Rachelle Rak; Music Director, Frank Minarik; Sets, John McDermott; Costumes, Michele Pasqua; Lighting, Brant Thomas Murray; Sound, Josh Liebert; Arrangements/Orchestrations/Music Supervisor, Steven Gross; PSM, Lara Maerz; Assistant Director, Cheryl Lynn Swift; General Manager, Jason Hewitt, Joan Pelzer; Executive Producer, Tony Sportiello; Casting, Ten Grand Productions; Production Manager, Chris Johnson; Press, Rogers Artist Media, Charlie Rogers/Keith Sherman Associates, Glenna Friedman

CAST Batxer/Voice **Al Bundonis**[1]; Mary **Natalie Buster**[2]; Leila **Maya Days**[3]; George **Scott Richard Foster**; Dr. Peterson **John Hickok**[4]; Mr. Murphy **Ken Jennings**; Mrs. Murphy **Liz Larsen**[5]; Sunshine **Kelli Maguire**; Dylan **Sky Seals**

UNDERSTUDIES Stephen Ted Beckler, Brittany Graham, Natalie Buster, Robert Koutras,

*Succeeded by: 1. Dennis Holland 2. Trisha Rapier 3. Rachelle Rak 4. Robert Newman 5. Bertilla Baker 6. Marsha Mercant

MUSICIANS Steven Gross and Kim Steiner (piano)

MUSICAL NUMBERS I'm Only Human, It's All on the Record, Wendy, Above the Clouds, Breathe, The Murphy's Squabble, I'm an Average Guy, Feels Like Home, If I Could Just Be Like Pete, I Saw the Rest of My Life, You Should Dance, This Is One River I Can't Cross, Living Out a Lie, I Never Spent Time with My Dad, I Just Want to Hold You, The Sun Shines In, This Is One River I Can't Cross (reprise), This Life of Mine, I Will Never Find Another You, Finale

SETTING The present. In Dr. Peterson's office and waiting room, and various locales in New York City. A new musical presented in two acts. A limited engagement of the show was presented at the Peter Jay Sharp Theatre in June 2007 prior to this engagement (see *Theatre World* Vol. 64, page 99).

SYNOPSIS Dr. Peter Peterson listens, advises and tests his patients. *Sessions* offers a humorous, poignant and relatable look into the familiar worlds of self-help, personal growth and those long hours that many have spent on a therapist's couch.

Robert Newman and Rachelle Rak in Sessions *(photo by Murray Head)*

Stomp

Orpheum Theatre; First Preview: February 18, 1994; Opening Night: February 27, 1994; 6,854 performances as of May 31, 2010

Created/Directed by Luke Cresswell and Steve McNicholas; Produced by Columbia Artists Management, Harriet Newman Leve, James D. Stern, Morton Wolkowitz, Schuster/Maxwell, Galin/Sandler, and Markley/Manocherian; Lighting, Mr. McNicholas, Neil Tiplady; Casting, Vince Liebhart/Scot Willingham; Executive Producers, Richard Frankel Productions/Marc Routh; Associate Producer, Fred Bracken; General Manager, Richard Frankel Productions/Joe Watson; PSM, Paul Botchis; ASM, Elizabeth Grunewald; Technical Director, Joseph Robinson; Company Manager, Tim Grassel; Assistant Company Manager, Maia Watson; Press, Boneau/Bryan-Brown, Jackie Green, Joe Perrotta

CAST (rotating) **Alan Asuncion, Michelle Dorrance, Dustin Elsea, Fritzlyn Hector, Brad Holland, Lance Liles, Stephanie Middleton, Keith Middleton, Jason Mills, Joeseph Russomano, Marivaldo Dos Santos, Carlos Thomas, Fiona Wilkes, Nicholas V. Young**

A percussive performance art piece presented with an intermission. For original production credits see *Theatre World* Vol. 50, page 113.

SYNOPSIS *Stomp* is a high-energy, percussive symphony, coupled with dance, played entirely on non-traditional instruments, such as garbage can lids, buckets, brooms and sticks.

Yako Miyamoto and Carlos "Peaches" Thomas in Stomp
(photo Steve McNicholas)

Tony 'n' Tina's Wedding

Edison Hotel; Opening Night: February 6, 1988; 5,899 performances as of May 31, 2010 (Friday and Saturday evenings only)

Written by Artificial Intelligence; Conceived by Nancy Cassaro; Originally created by Thomas Allen, James Altuner, Mark Campbell, Nancy Cassaro, Patricia Cregan, Elizabeth Dennehy, Chris Fracchiolla, Jack Fris, Kevin Alexander, Mark Nassar, Larry Pellegrini, Susan Varon, Moira Wilson; Produced by Big Apple Entertainment, Raphael Berko, Jeff Gitlin, Sonny Ricciardi, Kim Ricciardi; Director, Larry Pelligrini; Choreography, Hal Simons; Costumes/Hair/Makeup, Juan DeArmas; Stage Manager, Ryan DeLorge; Assistant Stage Manager, Derek Barbara; Wardrobe and Hair, Concetta Rella; Senior Production Coordinator, Drew Seltzer; Production Coordinator, Evan Weinstein; Marketing, Gary Shaffer; Promotions, DeMarcus Reed

CAST Valentina Lynne Vitale Nunzio **Joli Tribuzio**; Anthony Angelo Nunzio Jr. **Craig Thomas Rivela**; Connie Mocogni **Dina Rizzo**; Barry Wheeler **Gregory Allen Bock**; Donna Marsala **Jessica Aquino**; Dominick Fabrizzi **Anthony Augello**; Marina Gulino **Dawn Luebbe**; Johnny Nunzio **Deno Vourderis**[1]; Josephine Vitale **Anita Salvate**; Joseph Vitale **Rhett Kalman**; Sister Albert Maria **Daniela Genoble**; Anthony Angelo Nunzio, Sr. **John DiBenedetto**; Madeline Monore **Emily Rome Mudd**; Michael Just **Matthew Knowland**; Father Mark **Scott Voloshin**[2]; Vinnie Black **Anthony Patellis**[3]; Loretta Black **Cindi Kostello**; Sal Antonucci **Joe Leone**; Donny Dolce **Johnny Tammaro**; Celeste Romano **Sharon Kenny**; Carlo Cannoli **Anthony Ventura**; Rocco Caruso **Ray Grappone**

*Succeeded by: 1. Matthew Cassaro 2. Craig Clary 3. Henry Caplan

SETTING Tony and Tina's wedding and reception. An interactive environmental theatre production. For original production credits see *Theatre World* Volume 44, page 63. Originally played at Washington Square Church and Carmelita's; transferred to St. John's Church (wedding ceremony) and Vinnie Black's Coliseum (reception) until August, 1988; transferred to St. Luke's Church and Vinnie Black's Vegas Room Coliseum in the Edison Hotel. The production closed May 18, 2003, then reopened on October 3, 2003. It closed again May 1, 2004, reopened under new co-producers (Raphael Berko and Jeff Gitlin) on May 15th, 2004. This past season the show was performed on the Circle Line Cruises during the summer of 2009, returned to the Edison Hotel, and transferred to Sweet Caroline's April 10, 2010. On May 21, 2010, the show had alternate Friday performances at Il Cortile restaurant in Little Italy.

SYNOPSIS Tony and Tina are getting hitched. Audience members become part of the exuberant Italian family—attending the ceremony, mingling with relatives and friends, eating, drinking and dancing to the band.

Scott Bielecky and Joli Tribuzio in Tony 'n Tina's Wedding *(photo courtesy of Dan Cochran)*

The Toxic Avenger

New World Stages–Stage 1; First Preview: March 18, 2009; Opening Night: April 6, 2009; Closed January 3, 2010; 21 previews, 309 performances

Book and lyrics by Joe DiPietro, Music and lyrics by David Bryan, based on Lloyd Kaufman's 1985 film *The Toxic Avenger*; Presented by Jean Cheever and Tom Polum; Director, John Rando; Choreographer, Wendy Seyb; Music Director, Doug Katsaros; Sets, Beowulf Boritt; Costumes, David C. Woolard; Lighting, Kenneth Posner; Sound; Kurt Fischer; Hair and Make-up, Mark Adam Rampmeyer; Prosthetics/Special Effects, John Dods; Fight Director, Rick Sordelet & David DeBese; PSM, Scott Taylor Rollison; Stage Manager, Kelly Hance; Production Manager, Robert G. Mahon III & Jeff Wild; Casting, McCorkle Casting; Company Manager, Megan Trice Orchestrations/Arrangements, David Bryan & Christopher Jahnke; General Management, Splinter Group Productions; Advertising & Marketing, Allied Li0ve LLC; N.J. Marketing, Kelly Ryman; Dance Captain, Demond Green; Fight Captain, Nicholas Rodriguez; Assistant Director, Wes Grantom; Assistant Choreography, Keith Coughlin; Associate Set, Alexis Distler; Associate Lighting, Joel Shier; Properties, Karen Cahill; Press O+M Company, Rick Miramontez, Richard Hillman; Cast recording: Time Life 80140-D

CAST White Dude **Matthew Saldivar**[1]; Black Dude **Demond Green**; Mayor Babs Belgoody/Ma Ferd/A Nun **Nancy Opel**; Melvin Ferd the Third **Nick Codero**; Sarah **Sara Chase**[2]

UNDERSTUDIES Nicholas Rodriguez[3] (Melvin/Black Dude/White Dude), Erin Leigh Peck (Nun/Ma/Mayor/Sarah)

Succeeded by: 1. Jonathan Root (7/9/09) 2. Celina Carvajal (6/15/09), Diana DeGarmo (8/14/09) 3. Jason Wooten

MUSICIANS Ian Herman (Conductor/keyboards), Alan Childs (drums), Chris Cicchino (guitars), Dan Grennes (bass)

MUSICAL NUMBERS Who Will Save New Jersey?, Jersey Girl, Get The Geek, Kick Your Ass, My Big French Boyfriend, Thank God She's Blind, Big Green Freak, Choose Me, Oprah, Hot Toxic Love, The Legend of the Toxic Avenger, Evil is Hot, Bitch/Slut/Liar/Whore, Everybody Dies, You Tore My Heart Out, All Men Are Freaks, The Chase, Hot Toxic Love (reprise), A Brand New Day in New Jersey

SETTING Present. Tromaville, Exit 13B on the New Jersey Turnpike. New York premiere of a new musical presented without intermission. World premiere presented by the George Street Playhouse October 10, 2008 (David Saint, Artistic Director; Todd Schmidt, Managing Director).

SYNOPSIS *The Toxic Avenger* is set in the mythical town of Tromaville, Exit 13B off the New Jersey Turnpike. An aspiring earth scientist, Melvin Ferd the Third, is determined to clean up the town's burgeoning toxic waste, until he is tossed into a vat of radioactive goo and emerges as a seven-foot mutant freak and New Jersey's first superhero. Armed with superhuman strength and a heart as big as Newark, he's out to save New Jersey, end global warming and woo Sarah, the prettiest, blindest librarian in town.

Desmond Green, Matthew Saldivar, Nick Codero, Sara Chase, and Nancy Opel in The Toxic Avenger *(photo by Carol Rosegg)*

SPECIAL EVENTS AND PRODUCTIONS

Nothing Like a Dame

New World Stages; June 15, 2009

Produced by Tom Pinckney; Presented by the Actor's Fund; Director, Lorin Latarro; Line Producer, Patrick Weaver; PSM, Marisa Merrigan; Program Design, Tina Benanav; Hair/Make-up Consultant, Nathan Johnson; Sound Design Consultant, Katherine Miller; Lighting Design Consultant, Laura Williams; Press, Judy Katz and Jeremy Shaffer

CAST Host **Seth Rudetsky**; Performers **Stephanie J. Block**, **Betty Buckley**, **Andrea McArdle**, **Audra McDonald**, **Bebe Neuwirth**, **Kelli O'Hara**, **Lynnda Ferguson**, **Barbara Graham**; Special Appearance **Nick Adams**

An interview and performance entertainment presented in two parts.

SYNOPSIS *Nothing Like a Dame* features songs and stories from the women of Broadway, as well as rare video clips from earlier days of their remarkable careers, accompanied by commentary from Rudetsky and the women themselves. Presented as a benefit for the Phyllis Newman Women's Health Initiative.

Seth Rudetsky and Kelli O'Hara in Nothing Like a Dame, *a benefit for the Phyllis Newman Women's Health Initiative and The Actors Fund (photo by Steve Shevett)*

Lincoln Center Festival 2009

July 7–26, 2009

Nigel Redden, Director

Les Ephemeres

Park Avenue Armory; July 7–19; Part 1: 3 performances; Part 2: 3 performances; Full Cycle: 4 performances

Created collectively and presented by Le Théâtre du Soleil; Presented in association with the Park Avenue Armory Director, Ariane Mnouchkine; Director/Concept, Ariane Mnouchkine; Music, Jean-Jacques Lemêtre; Design, Everest Canto de Montserrat; Lighting, Elsa Revol & Hugo Mercier; Costumes, Nathalie Thomas, Marie-Hélène Bouvet, Annie Tran, Cécile Gacon, Chloé Bucas; Sound, Yan Lemêtre, Virginie Le Coënt, and Thérèse Spirli

CAST Delphine Cottu, Serge Nicolaï, Juliana Carneiro da Cunha, Andreas Simma, Olivia Corsini, Astrid Grant, Shaghayegh Beheshti, Duccio Bellugi-Vannuccini, Camille Grandville, Maurice Durozier, Dominique Jambert, Jeremy James, Sébastian Brottet-Michel, Alexandre Michel, Alice Milléquant, Eve Doe-Bruce, Kaveh Kishipour, Vincent Mangado, Virginie Le Coënt, Servane Ducorps, Marie-Louise Crawley, Pauline Poignand, Seietsu Onochi, Galatea Kraghede Bellugi

U.S. premiere of a new play cycle presented in French with English supertitles, shown in two parts, each part with one intermission.

SYNOPSIS Written collectively by the company, this work illuminates the ephemeral quality of human existence in all of its fragility and banality.

Ivanov

Gerald W. Lynch Theater; July 7–11; 5 performances

Written by Anton Chekhov; Presented by Katona Jozsef Theatre in conjunction with Extremely Hungary, a year-long festival of contemporary Hungarian arts; Director, Tamás Ascher; Set, Zsolt Khell; Costumes, Györgyi Szakács; Lighting, Tamás Bányai; Music, Márton Kovács; Dramaturgy, Géza Fodor, Ildikó Gáspár; Assistant Director, György Tiwald

CAST Ivanov **Ern Fekete**; Anna Petrovna **Ildikó Tóth**; Zhinaida **Judit Csoma**; Lebedhev **Zoltán Bezerédi**; Sasha **Anna Szandtner**; Count Shabelsky **Gábor Máté**; Babakina **Ági Szirtes**; Borkin **Ervin Nagy**; Kosih **János Bán**; Avdotha Nazharovna **Éva Olsavszky**; Yegorushka **Vilmos Kun**; Gavrila **Vilmos Vajdai**; Petr **Imre Morvay**; First Guest **Béla Mészáros**; Second Guest **Klára Czakó**; Guests **Réka Pelsoczy**, **Szabina Nemes**, **Anna Pálmai**, **Csaba Eros**, **Tamás Keresztes**, **István Dankó**; Musician **Eszter Horváth**

New York premiere of a new adaptation of a classic play presented in Hungarian with English supertitles in two act.

SYNOPSIS Tamar Ascher's production of Chekhov's *Ivanov* brings Budapest's Katona Jozsef Theater Company to New York for the first time, interpreting this timeless masterpiece in a stark, depressing world, a setting that perfectly reflects the essence of Nikolai Ivanov's soul.

Kalkwerk (The Lime Works)

Gerald W. Lynch Theater; July 14–18; 5 performances

Adapted from the novel by Thomas Bernhard by Krystian Lupa; Presented by Narodowy Stary Teatr; Director/Set, Krystian Lupa; Music, Jacek Ostaszewski; Translation, Ernest Dyczek and Marek Feliks Nowak; Supertitles, Philip Boehm

CAST Konrad **Andrzej Hudziak**; Konrad's Wife **Małgorzata Hajewska-Kryzsztofik**; Councillor Baurat **Zbigniew Kosowski**; Fro/Professor **Piotr Skiba**; Höller **Bolesław Brzozowski**; Bank Director **Paweł Miskiewicz** Moritz **Paweł Kruszelnicki**; Karl **Krzysztof Głuchowski**

U.S. premiere of a new play presented in Polish with English titles with two intermissions.

SYNOPSIS Krystian Lups'a powerful staging explores the psychological complexities of Bernhard's character Konrad, a scientist obsessed with his work and mentally imprisoned by it, along with his captive wife Konradowa.

Peasant Opera

Clark Studio Theater; July 21–26; 7 performances

Devised and directed by Béla Pinter, music by Benedek Darvas; Presented by Béla Pinter and Company in conjunction with Extremely Hungary, a yearlong festival showcasing contemporary Hungarian art)

CAST The Groom **Bela Pinter**; His Bride **Sarolta Nagy-Abonyi**; His Father **Jozsef Toth**; His Mother **Szilvia Baranyi**; His Stepsister **Eva Enyedi**; Her Mother **Tunde Szalontay**; Her Father **Sandor Bencze**; Stationmaster **Szabolcs Thuroczy**; The Stranger **Tamas Deak**

U.S. premiere of a musical melodrama presented in Hungarian with English supertitles without intermission.

SYNOPSIS *The Peasant Opera* encompasses classic theatrical tropes such as incest, secret parentage, and infanticide, fused with distinctly Hungarian folk ballads, recitatives and arias accompanied by cembalo, and baroque recitatives full of musical and linguistic puns.

Life and Fate

Gerald W. Lynch Theater; July 21–26; 5 performances

Written by Vasily Grossman, adapted by Lev Dodin; Presented by Maly Drama Theatre (St. Petersburg); Director, Lev Dodin; Set, Alexey Poray-Koshits; Costumes, Irina Tsvetkova; Lighting, Gleb Filshtinsky; Music Coordinators, Mikhail Alexandrov, Evgeny Davydov; Stage Manager, Vladimir Gladchenko; Assistant Director, Natalia Sollogub

CAST Anna Semyonovna Shtrum **Tatyana Shestakova**; Viktor Pavlovich Shtrum **Sergey Kuryshev**; Lyudmila **Elena Solomonova**; Nadya **Darya Rumyantseva**; Abarchuk **Vladimir Seleznev**; Neulovimov **Alexey Zubarev**; Monidze **Anatoly Kolibyanov**; Kovchenko **Igor Chernevich**; Ugarov **Pavel Gryaznov**; Vershkov **Stanislav Nikolsky**; Orderly **Adrian Rostovsky**; Getmanov **Alexander Koshkarev**; Ikonnikov **Oleg Ryazantsev**; Ershov **Alexey Morozov**; Mostovskoy **Igor Ivanov**; Liss **Oleg Dmitriev**; Osipov **Vladimir Zakhariev**; Special Agent **Maxim Pavlenko**; Security/Driver **Oleg Gayanov**; Prisoners **Anastasia Zabirova, Danila Kozlovsky, Ekaterina Kleopina, Urshula Magdalena Malka, Elizaveta Boyarskaya, Alexander Pulinets**

North American premiere of a new drama presented in Russian with English supertitles without intermission.

SYNOPSIS Adapted from Vasily Grossman's novel of life on the 1940s Eastern Front, *Life and Fate* focuses on a Jewish mother facing death in a Ukranian ghetto, and her physicist son confronted with a moral dilemma while developing a nuclear weapon.

Boris Godunov

Park Avenue Armory; July 22–26; 5 performances

Written by Alexander Pushkin; Presented by the Chekhov International Theatre Festival; Director, Declan Donnellan; Set, Nick Ormerod; Lighting, Judith Greenwood; Music Director, Maxim Gutkin; Movement, Andrey Shchukin; Choreography, Irina Filippova

CAST Prince Vorotynsky **Ilya Ilin**; Prince Vasily Shuisky **Avangard Leontiev**; Shchelkalov, the Duma-Scribe **Alexey Dadonov**; Boris Godunov, the Russian czar **Alexander Feklistov**; Pimen, a monk **Igor Yasulovich**; the monk Grigory Otrepiev/Dmitri **Evgeny Mironov**; Yury Mnisheck, the Polish nobleman **Oleg Vavilov**; Marina **Irina Grineva**

New York premiere of a new adaptation of a classic play with music presented in Russian with English supertitles without intermission.

SYNOPSIS Written by Pushkin in 1825, this Shakespeare-inspired drama relates the bitter power struggle that ensued in Tsarist Russia following Ivan the Terrible's death in 1584.

Trilogia della villeggiatura

Rose Theater; July 22–26; 5 performances

Written by Carlo Goldoni, adapted and directed by Toni Servillo; Presented by Piccolo Teatro di Milano and Teatri Uniti di Napoli; Sets, Carlo Sala; Costumes, Ortensia De Francesco; Lighting, Pasquale Mari; Lighting Realization, Lucio Sabatino; Sound, Daghi Rondanini; Assistant Director, Costanza Boccardi

CAST Leonardo **Andrea Renzi**; Paolino **Francesco Paglino**; Cecco **Rocco Giordano**; Vittoria **Eva Cambiale**; Filippo **Paolo Graziosi**; Guglielmo **Tommaso Ragno**; Giacinta **Anna Della Rosa**; Brigida **Chiara Baffi**; Fulgenzio **Gigio Morra**; Berto **Fiorenzo Madonna**; Sabina **Betti Pedrazzi**; Costanza **Mariella Lo Sardo**; Rosina **Giulia Pica**; Tognino **Marco D'Amore**

SYNOPSIS *Trilogia Della Villeggiatura* follows two families as they embark on a trip for the country, and the comic misadventures that ensue.

Broadway Barks 11

Shubert Alley; July 11, 2009

Written by Julie Halston and Richard Hester; Presented by Shubert Alley and Broadway Cares/Equity Fights AIDS; Produced by Richard Hester, Patty Saccente, and Scott T. Stevens; Executive Producers/Hosts, Mary Tyler Moore and Bernadette Peters; Stage Managers, Brian Bogin, Monica Cuoco, Meg Friedman, Bess Marie Glorioso, Ken McGee, Kim Russell, Sarah Safer, Nancy Wernick, Rachel Wolff; Shelter Coordinator, Barbara Tolan; Sound Equipment, John Grasso; Sound Design and Engineer, Lucas Rico Corrubia; Graphic Design, Carol A. Ingram; Website, David Risley; Program Design, Tracy Lynn Putman; Press, Judy Katz & Associates

CAST Elizabeth Ashley, Jayne Atkinson, Bill Berloni, Stephanie J. Block, David Bologna, Matt Cavenaugh, Michael Cerveris, Gavin Creel, Hope Davis, Christine Ebersole, Rupert Everett, Tovah Feldshuh, Sutton Foster, John Glover, Lauren Graham, Kate Jennings Grant, Zach Grenier, Haydn Gwynne, Dee Hoty, Allison Janney, Gregory Jbara, Carol Kane, Andy Karl, Marc Kudisch, Angela Lansbury, Li Jun Li, Constantine Maroulis, Michael Mastro, Nick Mayo, Audra McDonald, Judy McLane, Becki Newton, Karen Olivo, Michael O'Keefe, David Hyde Pierce, Alice Ripley, Bryce Ryness, Loretta Ables Sayre, Christopher Sieber, Jennifer Smith, J. Robert Spencer, Will Swenson, John Tartaglia, Michael Urie, Harriet Walter, Chandler Williams

A theatrical animal adoption marathon with entertainment.

SYNOPSIS A star-studded dog and cat adopt-a-thon benefiting New York City animal shelters and adoption agencies. The event, produced by Broadway Cares/Equity Fights AIDS and sponsored by the ASPCA and PEDIGREE with additional sponsorship by the New York Times, helps many of New York City's shelter animals find permanent homes by informing New Yorkers about the plight of the thousands of homeless dogs and cats in the metropolitan area.

Mary Tyler Moore and Bernadette Peters at Broadway Barks (photo by Peter James Zielinski)

Kristina

Carnegie Hall; September 23–24, 2009; 2 performances

Music by Göran Bror Benny Andersson, lyrics by Björn Kristian Ulvaeus; Presented by Universal Music & Decca Records; Director, Lars Rudolfsson; Music Director, Paul Gemignani; English Lyrics, Herbert Kretzmer; Press, Boneau/Bryan-Brown

CAST Kristina **Helen Sjöholm**; Karl Oskar **Russel Watson**; Ulrika **Louise Pitre**; Robert **Kevin Odekirk;** Ensemble **Derin Altay, Jane Brockman, Walter Charles, Rebecca Eichenberger, Osborn Focht, Blythe Gruda, Liz Griffith, Joy Hermalyn, David Hess, Michael James Leslie, T. Doyle Leverett, Rob Lorey, Frank Mastrone, Raymond Jaramillo McLeod, Linda Mugleston, Jan Neuberger, Robert Ousley, Sal Sabella, Wayne Schroder, Greg Stone, John Wasiniak, Jessica Vosk, Kathy Voytko**

MUSICAL NUMBERS Overture, Path of Leaves and Needles, Where You Go I Go With You, Stone Kingdom, Down to the Sea, A Bad Harvest, No!, He's Our Pilot, Never, Golden Wheat Fields, All Who Are Grieving, We Open Up the Gateways, Peasants at Sea, Lice, In the Dead of Darkness, A Sunday in Battery Park, Home, American Man, Dreams of Gold, Summer Rose, Emperors and Kings, Twilight Images, Queen of the Prairie, Wild Grass, Gold Can Turn to Sand, Wildcat Money, To the Sea, Miracle of God, Down to the Waterside, Miscarriage, You Have to Be There, Here I Am Again, With Child Again, Rising from the Myth and Legend, I'll Be Waiting There

Concert version and U.S. premiere of the English language version of a musical presented in two acts. World premiere at Malmo Music Theatre (Sweden) in 1995.

SYNOPSIS Based on *The Emigrants*, a series of novels by Swedish author Vilhelm Moberg, *Kristina* tells the epic story of a poor family's migration from Sweden to Minnesota in the 1850s.

Under My Hat

Kaye Playhouse; September 29, 2009; 1 performance

Written and performed by **Sarah Jones**, Hosted and performed by **Glenn Close**

A series of sketches, readings, and scenes presented without intermission.

SYNOPSIS Written and performed for The Fountain House, *Under My Hat* is staged as a benefit for the Fountain House's mission to reduce the debilitating stigma associated with mental illness. The performances feature a series of character sketches based on interviews Ms. Jones conducted with members of Fountain House and other accounts of mental illness researched by Ms. Jones and Ms. Close.

An Evening Without Monty Python

Town Hall; October 6–10, 2009; 5 performances

Created by Eric Idle; Presented by WestBeth Entertainment (Arnold Engelman, President); Co-Directors, Eric Idle and B.T. McNicholl; Composer/Musical Director, John Du Prez; Costumes, Ann Closs-Farley; Lighting, Jen Schriever; Sound, Dennis Moody; Choreography, Peggy Hickey; Technical Director, Gregg Bellón; Production Manager, Joe Witt; Assistant Stage Managers, Nikki Hyde & Ashley Singh; Costumes/Wardrobe, Suzanne Scott & Lauren Opelt: Props, Caroline Klemp; Backdrop Design, Steve Kirwan; Graphic Designer, Sally Cato; Press, L.A.–Davidson & Choy/Tim Choy & Laura Shane; New York– The Karpel Group/Bridget Klapinski, Beth Sorrell, Aicha Diop

CAST **Jeff B. Davis, Rick Holmes, Jane Leeves, Jim Piddock, Alan Tudyk**

An evening of sketches and songs presented without intermission. Previously presented in Los Angeles at the Ricardo Montalban Theatre September 23–October 4 prior to this engagement.

SYNOPSIS From the creators of *Spamalot*, WestBeth Entertainment presents a 40th Anniversary Celebration of the original Monty Python's Flying Circus.

Jim Piddock, Rick Holmes, Alan Tudyk, Jane Leaves, and Jeff B. Davis in An Evening Without Monty Python *(photo by Gil Smith)*

The Laramie Project: Ten Years Later

Alice Tully Hall; October 12, 2009; 1 performance

Written by Tectonic Theater Project members Moisés Kaufman, Leigh Fondakowski, Greg Pierotti, Andy Paris and Stephen Belber; Presented by Tectonic Theater Project (Moisés Kaufman, Artistic Director; Greg Reiner, Executive Director; Dominick Balletta, General Manager; Jeffrey LaHoste, Senior Producer); Director, Moisés Kaufman; Scenic Consultant, Derek McLane; Dramaturg, Jimmy Maize; Event Vice-Chairs, Violy and Company, Jeanne Sullivan; Event Benefactors, Time Warner Inc., HBO, Kevin Jennings, Barbara Whitman; Press, Boneau/Bryan-Brown (Chris Boneau, Aaron Meier, Kelly Guiod) & Renna Communications (Cathy Renna, Leah McElrath, Laura McGinnis)

Host **Glenn Close**; Special Guest **Judy Shepard**; Post-Play Moderator **Neda Ulaby**

CAST **Stephen Belber, Amanda Gronich, Mercedes Herrero, John McAdams, Andy Paris, Greg Pierotti, Barbara Pitts, Kelli Simpkins**

Special presentation and reading of a follow-up to the acclaimed play presented in two acts. *The Laramie Project* was originally presented at the Denver Center Theatre Company in association with Tectonic in 2000, and ran Off-Broadway at the Union Square Theatre March 18–September 2, 2000 (see *Theatre World* Vol. 56, page 164).

SYNOPSIS *The Laramie Project: Ten Years Later, An Epilogue* focuses on the long-term effect of the violent 1998 murder of the gay youth, Matthew Shepard, on the town of Laramie, Wyoming. It includes new interviews with Matthew's mother Judy Shepard and Matthew's murderer Aaron McKinney, who is serving dual life sentences, as well as follow-up interviews with many of the individuals from the original piece. The new piece was performed simultaneously in over 120 theaters across the globe.

Andy Paris, Stephen Belber, and Greg Pierotti in The Laramie Project: Ten Years Later *(photo by Aaron Epstein)*

Hedwig and the Angry Inch

New World Stages; November 2, 2009; 1 performance

Book by John Cameron Mitchell, music and lyrics by Stephen Trask; Produced by Scott Tucker and Trisha Doss; Presented by Broadway Cares/Equity Fights AIDS; Director, Aaron Mark; Musical Director, Daniel Lincoln; Production Managers, Nathan Hurlin and Michael Palm; Sound, Eva Schultz; Lighting, David Lau; PSM, Jennifer Rogers; Stage Manager, Jason Quinn; Multimedia, Kevin Regan & Joel Rickenbach

CAST Hedwig/Tommy Gnosis **David Brian Colbert**; Yitzhak **Petra DeLuca**; The Angry Inch **Tim Cleary** (bass), **Chris Gordon** (guitar), **Daniel Lincoln** (keyboards), **Matt Orlando** (drums)

Benefit concert revival of a musical presented without intermission. The original production was presented at the Jane Street Theatre February 14, 1998–April 9, 2000 playing 857 performances (see *Theatre World* Vol. 54, page 149).

SYNOPSIS *Hedwig and the Angry Inch* tells the story of a young East Berliner who reluctantly submits to a sex change operation in order to marry an American GI and escape to West Berlin, and freedom. After the operation is botched and Hedwig finds herself divorced in a Kansas trailer park, she forms a rock band and encounters a lover/protégé in young Tommy Gnosis. Presented as a benefit for Broadway Cares/Equity Fights AIDS.

The Lover and the Poet, An Evening of Shakespeare

Florence Gould Hall; November 2, 2009; 1 performance

Conceived and directed by Kevin Kline; Presented by The Acting Company (Margot Harley, Artistic Director); Lighting, Greg MacPherson; Sound, Tim Boyce; PSM, Michael J. Passaro; Production Manager, Ian Belknap; Piano, Paul Ford

CAST Meryl Streep, **Kevin Kline**

A presentation of scenes, monologues, and sonnets presented without intermission.

SYNOPSIS This very special evening of selected Shakepearian works starring stage and screen greats Kevin Kline and Meryl Streep benefitted the Acting Company, which promotes theater and literacy by bringing productions, talented young actors and teaching artists into underserved and disadvantaged communities across America.

Wintuk

Theatre at Madison Square Garden; Opening Night: November 11, 2009; Closed January 3, 2010

Presented by Cirque du Soleil, Madison Square Garden Entertainment, and Base Entertainment; Artistic Guide, Guy Laliberté; Composer and Arranger, Simon Carpentier; Lyrics, Jim Corcoran; Director/Director of Creation, Fernand Rainville; Original Director and Writer, Richard Blackburn; Choreographer, Catherine Archambault; Costume and Puppet Visual Design, François Barbeau; Set Designer and Props Co-Design, Patricia Ruel; Images and Projections Designer, Francis Laporte; Sound, Leon Rothenberg, Jonathan Deans; Acrobatic Equipment and Rigging Design, Guy St-Amour; Acrobatic Performance Design, Daniel Cola; Lighting Designer, Yves Aucoin, Matthieu Larivée; Puppetry Design, René Charbonneau; Props and Puppets Design, Michael Curry; Makeup, Eleni Uranis; Senior Artistic Director, Alison Crawford; Artistic Director, James Tanabe; Press, The Hartman Group, Leslie Baden

CAST Jamie Adkins, Keigoh Arizono, Cédric Bélisle, Sébastien Bergeron, René Bibaud, Michael Brunet, Sujana Chaud, Maria Choodu, Rustan Coda, Nathalie Daubard, Lurian Duarte, Alicia Enstrom, Jean-Francois Faber, Tenealle Farragher, Laur Fugère, Danni G., Sylvain Gagnon, Gabrielle Garant, Facundo Gimenez, Alan Miguel Hall, Terrance Harrison, Mario Hébert, Tye Hill, Justine Hubert, Darin Robert Inkster, Igor Issakov, Christopher Jones, Katie Ketchum, Charlotte "Charli K." Martin, Kylee "Ky" Maupoux, Valérie Laplante-Bilodeau, Sébastien Laurendeau, Elena Lev, Mikalai Liubezny, Dzianis Maskalenka, Mark McLauchlan, Alexandre Monteiro, Antonio Moore, Yury Pautau, Audrone Pavloviciene, Alfons Pavlovics, Mark Peterson, Casey Rigney, Petros Sakelliou, Serguei Samoded, Lais Santos Andrade, Huges Sarra-Bournet, Oleg Sharypov, Iana Shkarupa, Roger Squitero, Derek Stangel, Svetlana Suvorova, Terry Synnott, Sébastien Tardif, Alexandre Tessier, Martin Vaillancourt, Anke van Engelshoven

Revival of a theatrical presentation with music and acrobats presented in two acts. Previously presented last season at Madison Square Garden.

SYNOPSIS *Wintuk* is an exciting winter adventure about a boy's quest for snow. The show weaves thrilling acrobatics, breathtaking theatrical effects and memorable songs into an extraordinary journey to an imaginary land called Wintuk. The boy and his companions deliver endless excitement, exhilaration and intrigue.

A scene from Wintuk *(photo by Richard Termine)*

One Evening

Gerald W. Lynch Theater; December 9–11, 2009; 3 performances

Music by Franz Shubert, text by Samuel Beckett; Presented by Lincoln Center Theater with Aldeburgh Music and Southbank Centre; Director, Katie Mitchell; Design, Vicki Mortimer; Lighting, Paule Constable; English Translation, Michael Symmons Roberts

CAST Tenor **Mark Padmore**; Actor **Stephen Dillane**; Piano **Andrew West**

A theatrical concert with text and music presented without intermission.

SYNOPSIS A performance that explores the impact that Franz Schubert's music had on playwright and poet Samuel Beckett. Mark Padmore's expressive vocals account of Schubert's *Winterreise* is juxtaposed with Stephen Dillane's readings of Beckett's poetry and prose on the human condition.

The 24 Hour Musicals

Gramercy Theatre; February 8, 2010; 1 performance

Presented by the Exchange and the 24 Hour Company; Included: *You Can See the East River From Here, Too* Music and lyrics by Jeanine Tesori and Jonathan Bernstein; Director, Ted Sperling; **Cast**: **Dee Roscioli, John Ellison Conlee, Katie Thompson**; *Anti Valentines* Music and lyrics by Jeff Blumenkrantz and Julia Jordan; Director, Moisés Kaufman; **Cast: Celia Keenan-Bolger, Marnie Schulenburg, Michael Winther, Zachary Prince**; *The First of His Heart* music and lyrics by Adam Gwon and Jonathan Marc Sherman; Director, Trip Cullman; **Cast: Julian Fleisher, Nancy Opel, Darius DeHaas**; *What's Wrong with Twinkie?* Music and lyrics by Zina Goldrich, Marcy Heisler and Josh Koenigsberg; Director, Kathleen Turner; **Cast: Alicia Witt, Cady Huffman, Mo Rocca, Raven-Symoné**

An evening of short musicals presented without intermission.

SYNOPSIS The *24 Hour Musicals* are four 15-minute musicals created, rehearsed, and produced in 24 hours that culminate in a one-night-only performance. Proceeds from ticket sales and auctions at the event benefit The Orchard Project.

Recipe for Life

Acorn Theatre on Theatre Row; February 14–March 7, 2010 (Mondays only); 4 performances

Written by Susan Charlotte, Tandy Cronyn, A.R. Gurney, Joseph Stein, and Danny & Neil Simon; Presented by Cause Cèlébre/Part Time Productions and Tina's Wish in association with The New Group; Directors, Christopher Hart & Antony Marsellis; Assistant Director, Michael Citriniti; Stage Manager, Kelly Hess; Company Manager, Deb Hackenberry; Assistant Company Manager, Brendan Hill; Accounting, Ira Schall; Legal, Nan Bases

CAST *Tallulah Finds Her Kitchen* (by Danny & Neil Simon, & Joseph Stein): Tallulah Bankhead **Frances Sternhagen**; *Menu by Jessie* (by Tandy Cronyn)**:** Herself **Tandy Cronyn**; *The Love Course* (by A.R. Gurney): Mrs. Carroway **Maria Tucci;** Professor Burgess **Harris Yulin**; Mike **Jake Robards**; Sally **Miriam Silverman**; *The Hairdresser* by Susan Charlotte: **Kathleen Chalfant, Maria Tucci**

An evening of short plays presented in two acts.

SYNOPSIS Cause Cèlébre/Part Time Productions present their third Off-Broadway production (and second in this series) with short plays that explore the Recipe for Life: Good Cooking, Good Writing, Good Friends, Good Health, and Great Haircuts. Presented as a benefit for Tina's Wish, a non-profit organization supporting research to create an early and effective test for ovarian cancer and education for diagnosis and treatment.

Broadway Bears XIII

B.B. Kings; February 14, 2010

Presented by Scott T. Stevens for Broadway Cares/Equity Fights AIDS; Director,

Production Manager, Michael Palm; Music Director, Michael Lavine; Opening Number Lyrics, Douglas Braverman; Stage Manager, Bess Marie Glorioso; Program/Poster, Carol A. Ingram; Press, Boneau/Bryan-Brown

TALENT Host **John Bolton**; Auctioneer **Lorna Kelly**; Performers **Felicia Finley, John Bolton**; Bear Presenters **Loretta Ables Sayre, Ann Harada, Christopher Sieber, Michael Dameski, Alex Ko, Liam Redhead, Jim Caruso**,

HIGHEST BIDS **Mrs. Wilkinson** from *Billy Elliott*, the musical ($8,000), created by D. Barak Stribling and signed by Haydn Gwynne, Stephen Daldry, and Sir Elton John; **Lord Farquaad** from *Shrek, the Musical* ($8,000), created by Zoë Morsette and signed by Christopher Sieber; **Griddlebone** from *Cats* ($6,000), created by Therese Stadelmeier-Tresco and signed by Betty Buckley; **Liza Minnelli** from *Liza's at the Palace* ($4,000), created by Donna Langman Costumes and signed by Liza Minnelli; **Drew** from *Rock of Ages* ($6,000), created by Karl Ruckdeschel and D. Barak Stribling and signed by Constantine Maroulis; **Doralee Rhodes** from *9 to 5* ($3,750), created by Julie Song and signed by Megan Hilty and Dolly Parton; **Song Liling** from *M. Butterfly* ($3,000), created by Brionna McMahon and signed by B.D. Wong and John Lithgow

A Grand Auction of Broadway inspired teddy bears presented with special entertainment.

SYNOPSIS A total of 42 teddy bears, donated by the North American Bear Company and transformed into uniquely costumed, handmade, one-of-a-kind, collectibles, raised $101,095 through online bids, telephone bids, and, of course, live bids. Proceeds went to Broadway Cares/Equity Fights AIDS. $1,740,072 has been raised so far from twelve editions of this favorite event.

Ann Harada at Broadway Bears *(photo by Peter James Zielinski)*

Valley of the Dolls

Gerald W. Lynch Theatre; March 15, 2010; 1 performance

Music by André Previn, lyrics by Dory Previn; Based on the novel by Jacqueline Susann and the original screenplay by Helen Deutsch and Dorothy Kingsley; Presented by the Actor's Fund and Tim Pinckney by special arrangement with Tiger LLC, in association with Lisa Bishop and Whitney Robinson; Director, Carl Andress; Musical Director, Steve Marzullo; Set, Brian T. Whitehill; Lighting, Kirk Bookman; Costume Supervisor, Carol Sherry; Sound, Patrick Weaver; Makeup and Hair, Nathan Johnson; Wigs, Katherine Carr; PSM, Stage Manager, Don Myers; Consulting Producer, Stephen Yuhasz; Event Marketing, Adam Jay; On-line Marketing, Daniel Scholz; Program Design, Tina Benanav; Press, The Publicity Office, Jeremy Shaffer

CAST Anne Welles **Martha Plimpton**; The Singer **Julia Murney**; Miss Steinberg and others **Julie Halston**; Mr. Bellamy and others **Brad Oscar**; Helen Lawson **Charles Busch**; Neely O'Hara **Heidi Blickenstaff**; Lyon Burke **Craig Bierko**; Jennifer North **Nancy Anderson**; Mel Harris/Ted Casablanca **Hunter Bell**; Tony Polar **Troy Britton Johnson**; Miriam Polar **Tovah Feldshuh**; Kevin Gilmore and others **Ed Watts**;

MUSICIANS Steve Marzullo (piano), Mary Ann McSweeney (bass), Ray Marchica (drums)

Staged concert version of a new musical presented in two acts.

SYNOPSIS *Valley of the Dolls* follows the lives of three women as they strive to achieve fame and fortune in show business, and the world full of pitfalls and heartbreak they discover on the way. Presented as a benefit for The Actor's Fund.

The Company of the Actors Fund performance of Valley of the Dolls *(photo by Jay Brady)*

ABC Daytime & SoapNet Salute to Broadway Cares

Town Hall; March 21, 2010; 1 performance

Produced by Trisha Doss and Scott Tucker; Presented by Broadway Cares/Equity Fights AIDS; Director, John Dietrich; Musical Directors, Steven Freeman and Shawn Gough; Lighting, John Torres; Production Manager/Set Design, Nathan Hurlin; Sound, Sound Associates; Associate Producers, Jody O'Neil, Frank Conway; Stage Managers, Casey Cook, Jennifer Rogers, Jeffrey Wain, Colyn Fiendel, Michelle Abesamis, Christopher Davis, Andy Halliday; Associate Lighting, Jay Woods; Costume Coordinator, Jeff Johnson-Doherty; Company Manager, Keith Bullock; Music Preparation, Emily Grishman; Marketing for BC/EFA, Bobbie McGuire

Host **Cameron Mathison** (*All My Children*); Guest Host **Lee Cummings**

CAST *All My Children*: **Brittany Allen, Bobbie Eakes, Natalie Hall, Adam Mayfield, Cornelius Smith Jr., Walt Willey**; *One Life to Live*: **Kristen Alderson, Melissa Archer, Brandon Buddy, Kassie DePaiva, David Gregory, Mark Lawson, Kelley Missal, Jason Tam, Bree Williamson**; *General Hospital*: **Bradford Anderson, Brandon Barash, Anthony Geary, Jonathan Jackson, Nathan Parsons**; *The View*: **Sherri Shepherd**; Additional Cast **Nina Hudson, Tim McGarrigal, Jackie Meyers, Cody Smith, Jill Wolins, Cole Burden, DJ Daw, James Jackson, Kelly Carpenter, Christine LaDuca, Mary Catherine McDonald, BethAnn Bonner**

ORCHESTRA Steven Freeman & Shawn Gough (Conductors/keyboards), Howard Joines (Contractor/percussion), Justin Smith (violin), Dan Wieloszynski (reed 1), Ken Hitchcock (reed 2), Glenn Drewes (trumpet), Chris Olness (trombone), Joe Nero Jr. (drums), Randall Klitz (bass), Kevin Kuhn (guitar)

Sixth annual evening of musical entertainment and comedy presented in two acts.

SYNOPSIS Over the past six years, this event featuring performances from the stars of ABC's daytime dramas has raised over $1,605,000 in ticket sales, auction bids, and online fundraising donations benefiting Broadway Cares/Equity Fights AIDS. This year's highlights included songs from *9 to 5, The Wild Party, High Fidelity, Rent, Young Frankenstein, Mamma Mia, Dirty Rotten Scoundrels, Rent, Wicked,* and *Miss Saigon,* along with Sherrie Sheppard's rousing rendition of "Proud Mary."

An Enemy of the People

Skirball Center; March 30, 2010; 1 performance

Written by Henrik Ibsen; Presented by the Aquila Theatre Company (Peter Meineck, Founder and Artistic Director); Director, Peter Meineck; Lighting/Technical Director, Kevin Shaw; Projections, Rufus Lusk; Costumes/Assistant Artistic Director, Kimberly Pau Donato; Production Manager, Nate Terracio

CAST Dr. Thomas Stockmann **Damian Davis**; Katrine Stockmann **Leandra Ashton**; Peter Stockmann **James Lavender**; Petra Stockmann **Lauren Davis**; Aslaksen **Howard Crossley**; Hovstad **Owen Young**; Mortine Kiil **Lucy Black**

Touring version of a revival of a classic play presented in two acts.

SYNOPSIS A new production of Henrik Ibsen's classic, *An Enemy of the People* explores the impact of severe environmental issues on a small town, and the consequences to one man seeking to uncover the truth. When Dr. Stockmann discovers that the town spa, the main source of local income, is toxic, he must stand up against the financial interests of his brother the mayor in order to protect the people from a deadly threat.

Lauren Davis & Leandra Ashton in the Aquila Theatre's
An Enemy of the People *(photo by Erika Sidor)*

As You Like It

Skirball Center; March 31, 2010; 1 performance

Written by William Shakespeare; Presented by the Aquila Theatre Company (Peter Meineck, Founder and Artistic Director); Director, Kenn Sabberton; Design, Peter Meineck and Kenn Sabberton; Lighting, Peter Meineck; Movement, Desiree Sanchez; Assistant Artistic Director, Kimberly Pau Donato; Production Manager, Nate Terracio; Technical Director, Kevin Shaw

CAST Oliver/Adam **James Lavender**; Orlando **Owen Young**; Charles/Le Beau/Amiens/Silvius/Sir Oliver Mar-Tex/William/Priest **Damian Davis**; Celia **Lauren Davis**; Rosalind **Leandra Ashton**; Touchtone **James Lavender**; Duke Frederick/Duke Senior/Corin **Howard Crossley**; Jaques/Audrey/Phoebe **Lucy Black**

Touring version of a revival of a classic play presented in two acts.

SYNOPSIS Shakespeare's comedy classic *As You Like It* tells a story of power and exile, of deceit and unexpected romance. Set in a period of revolution in France, Aquila infuses this production with their unique blend of fun and entertaining theatricality, faithful to Shakespeare and relevant and accessible to a modern audience

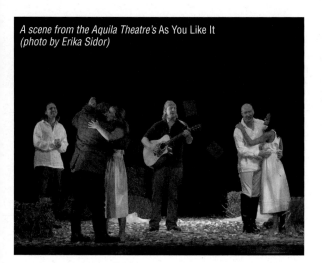

A scene from the Aquila Theatre's As You Like It
(photo by Erika Sidor)

Stars Give LOVE

Angel Orensanz Foundation; April 19, 2010; 1 performance

Written by Julia Cho, Laura Eason, Susanal Fogel & Joni Lefkowitz, Megan Mostyn-Brown, Sarah Treem; Produced by Sasha Eden and Victoria Pettibone; Director, Abby Epstein; Event Designer, Bryant Keller; Music, DJ Blue; Assistant Producers, Ashley Eichhorn Thompson, Amy DePaola; Special Awards: Lynda Obst & Maria Zuckerman; Awards Presenter: Nora Ephron

CAST Emmanuelle Chriqui, Rosemarie DeWitt, Carla Gugino, Mamie Gummer, Ron Livingston, Jennifer Carpenter, Hamish Linlater, Maulik Pancholy, Zachary Quinto, Michael Stuhlbarg, Jennifer Westfeldt, Glennis McMurray, Rachel Dratch

A benefit featuring short plays and awards presentation presented without intermission.

SYNOPSIS This one-night only performance of short plays on the subject of LOVE benefiting the nonprofit WET Productions' fight to end gender inequality and their unique leadership and media-literacy program for NYC teenage girls.

Charlie Williams (Mr. Memphis), Wes Hart (Mr. West Side Story), Eddie Pendergraft (Mr. Wicked), Daniel Soto (Mr. Fela) and Rickey Tripp (Mr. In The Heights), the contestants of the Broadway Beauty Pageant *(photo by Carol Rosegg)*

Broadway Beauty Pageant

Symphony Space; April 19, 2010

Written and conceived by Jeffery Self; Produced by the Ali Forney Center, Ryan J. Davis, Jeffrey Self and Wil Fisher in association with Tim Hur;; Director, Ryan J. Davis; Original Music, Rick Crom; Musical Director, Christopher Denny; Host: Tovah Feldshuh; Judges: Charles Busch, Christine Ebersole, Michael Musto; Press, O+M Company, Jaron Caldwell

CONTESTANTS Wes Hart (Mr. *West Side Story*), **Eddie Pendergraft** (Mr. *Wicked*), **Daniel Soto** (Mr. *Fela!*), **Rickey Tripp** (Mr. *In the Heights*), **Charlie Williams** (Mr. *Memphis*–**WINNER**)

SYNOPSIS The fourth annual *Broadway Beauty Pageant*, formerly titled *Mr. Broadway*, features male cast members representing their respective Broadway shows, competing for the title crown through talent, interview, and swimsuit competitions. The contestants go head to head in front of a panel of celebrity judges, but the final vote is in the audience's hands. Presented as a benefit for the Ali Forney Center, the nation's largest and most comprehensive organization dedicated to LGBT youth.

Honor

Baruch Performing Arts Center–Engelman Recital Hall; April 25, 2010; 1 performance

Book, music and lyrics by Peter Mills and Cara Reichel; Presented by the Prospect Theater Company; Director, Cara Reichel; Managing Director, Melissa Huber; Musical Director, Daniel Feyer

CAST Alan Ariano, Billy Bustamante, Steven Eng, Ariel Estrada, Ali Ewoldt, Christine Toy Johnson, Brian Jose, Austin Ku, Whitney Kam Lee, Jose Llana, Jason Ma, Jaygee Macapugay, Mel Maghuyop, Paolo Montalban, Romney Piamonte, Diane Phelan, Dave Shlh, Toshiji Takeshima, Robert Torigoe

Concert version of a new musical presented in two acts. Previously presented at the Hudson Guild Theatre April 19–May 18, 2008.

SYNOPSIS This one-night-only concert transplants Shakespeare's *As You Like It* to feudal Japan, in a passionate tale of romance and redemption of family honor. Presented as a benefit for the Prospect Theater Company, a non-profit organization whose goal is to connect communities of artists and audiences through re-interpretation of classic plays and musicals.

OFF-BROADWAY Company Series

Top: *Kimberly Hebert Gregory and Andre Holland in* Marcus; or The Secret Of Sweet, *part of* The Brother/Sister Plays. *Opened at the Public Theater's Anspacher Theater November 17, 2009 (photo by Joan Marcus)*

Center: *Kristen Johnston, John Windsor-Cunningham, Ned Noyes, Kevin O'Donnell, Catherine Curtin (seated), and Anna Chlumsky in the Mint Theatre Company's* So Help Me God! *Opened at the Lucille Lortel Theatre December 7, 2009 (photo by Richard Termine)*

Bottom: *Susan Blackwell, Christopher Sieber, and Lucas Steele in The New Group production of* The Kid. *Opened at the Acorn Theatre on Theatre Row May 10, 2010 (photo by Monique Carboni)*

Cate Blanchett and Joel Edgerton in A Streetcar Named Desire, *presented at BAM (photo by Richard Termine)*

Nina Arianda in the Classic Stage Company production of Venus in Fur *at (photo by Joan Marcus)*

Benjamin Walker (center) and the Company in the Public Theater's Bloody Bloody Andrew Jackson *(photo by Joan Marcus)*

(Clockwise from left) Bill Heck, Maggie Lacey, Hallie Foote, Bryce Pinkham, and Dylan Riley Snyder in Signature Theatre Company's The Orphans' Home Cycle, Part 3 *(photo by Gregory Costanzo)*

Zach Grenier and Lisa Emery in Ages of the Moon at the Atlantic Theater Company *(photo by Ari Mintz)*

Michael Mosley and Keira Keeley in the Roundabout Theatre Company production of The Glass Menagerie *(photo by Joan Marcus)*

Derrick Cobey, Julius Thomas III, Brandon Victor Dixon, and Josh Breckenridge in The Scottsboro Boys *at the Vineyard Theatre (photo by Carol Rosegg)*

Victoria Clark and Rod McLachlan in When the Rain Stops Falling *at Lincoln Center Theater (photo by T. Charles Erickson)*

John Douglas Thompson in The Emperor Jones *at the Irish Repertory Theatre (photo by Carol Rosegg)*

Bobby Steggert and Jeffry Denman in Yank! *at the* York Theatre Company *(photo by Carol Rosegg)*

Andrea Riseborough and Hugh Dancy in MCC Theater's The Pride *(photo by Joan Marcus)*

Abingdon Theatre Company

Seventeenth Season

Artistic Director, Jan Buttram; Managing Director, Samuel Bellinger; General Manager, Danny Martin; Associate Artistic Director & Literary Manager, Kim T. Sharp; Marketing, Doug DeVita; Development Associate, Piper Gunnarson; Play Development Advisor, Pamela Paul; Casting, William Schill; Facilities Manager, John Trevellini; Resident Production Manager, Ian Gurnes; Resident Dramaturg, Julie Hegner; Cabaret Producer, David Flora, Playwright Group Coordinator, Frank Tangredi; Playwright Outreach Coordinator, Bara Swain; Press, Shirley Herz Associates

Inventing Avi (and other theatrical maneuvers) by Robert Cary and Benjamin Feldman; Presented in association with Sharon Carr, Dan Frishwasser, Richard Winkler, Demos Bizar Entertainment, and Anna Ryan; Director, Mark Waldrop; Sets, Ray Klausen; Costumes, Matthew Hemesath; Lighting, Brian Nason; Sound, David Margolin Lawson; Wigs, Daniel Koe; PSM, Joshua R. Pilote; **CAST:** Alix Korey (Judy Siff), Emily Zacharias (Mimi/Mother), Stanley Bahorek (David Smith), Havilah Brewster (Amy/Young Mimi), Lori Gardner (Astrud/Young Judy), Juri Henley-Cohn (Avi Aviv)

Setting: New York City; the present. World premiere of a new farce presented in two acts; June Havoc Theatre; October 2–November 1, 2009 (Opened October 14); 12 previews, 20 performances.

Alix Korey, Havilah Brewster, Stanley Bahorek, Emily Zacharias, and Lori Gardner *in* Inventing Avi *(photos by Kim T. Sharp)*

Phantom Killer by Jan Buttram; Director, Jules Ochoa; Sets, David B. Ogle; Costumes, Kimberly Matela; Lighting, Travis McHale; Sound, David Margolin Lawson; Fight Choreography, Rick Sordelet; PSM, Genevieve Ortiz; **CAST:** Wrenn Schmidt (Jessie), Jon McCormick (Luke), Denny Bess (Randy)

Setting: A rural town in Texas, 1946. World premiere of a new thriller presented in without intermission; Dorothy Strelsin Theatre; January 22–February 14, 2010 (Opened January 31); 9 previews, 13 performances.

Jon McCormick, Wrenn Schmidt, and Denny Bess *in* Phantom Killer

Engaging Shaw by John Morogiello; Director, Jackob G. Hofmann; Sets, The Ken Larson Company; Costumes, Deborah Caney; Lighting, Matthew McCarthy; Music, Larry Spivack; Stage Manager, Mickey McGuire; Cast: Warren Kelley (George Bernard Shaw), Claire Warden (Charlotte Payne-Twonshend), Victoria (Jamee) Vance (Beatrice Webb), Marc Geller (Sidney Webb)

Setting: A cottage in Stratford, England, Shaw's office, Fitzroy Square, London, and other European locations; 1896–1897. New York premiere of a new comedy presented in two acts; Dorothy Strelsin Theatre; April 9–May 2, 2010 (Opened April 18); 9 previews, 13 performances.

Sister Myotis's Bible Camp by Steve Swift, additional material by Jerre Dye; Director & Sets, Jerre Dye; Costumes, Ashley Whitten Kopera & Kim Yeager; Lighting, Travis McHale; Sound, David Newsome; PSM, Genevieve Ortiz; **CAST:** Todd Berry (Sister Velma Needlemeyer), Jenny Odle Madden (Sister Ima Lone), Steve Swift (Sister Myotis)

Setting: A bunker, disguised as a theatre on West 36th Street, New York City; the present. New York premiere of a play presented in two acts; Dorothy Strelsin Theatre; June 11–July 4, 2010 (Opened June 20); 9 previews, 13 performances.

Claire Warden, Victoria (Jamee) Vance, Marc Geller, and Warren Kelley in Engaging Shaw

The Actors Company Theatre (TACT)

Seventeenth Season

Co-Artistic Directors, Scott Alan Evans, Cynthia Harris, & Simon Jones; General Manager, Cathy Bencivenga; Associate Producer, Jenn Thompson; Development Manager, Erin Carney; Casting, Stephanie Klapper; Press, O+M Company, Richard Hilman

The Late Christopher Bean by Sidney Howard, based upon *Prenez Garde a la Peinture* by Rene Fauchois; Director, Jenn Thompson; Set, Charlie Corcoran; Costumes, Martha Hally; Lighting, Ben Stanton; Sound, Stephen Kunken; Original Music, Mark Berman; Technical Director, Patrick Cecala; Master Electrician, John Anselmo; PSM, Meredith Dixon; ASM, Jane Clausen; Wardrobe, Amanda Jenks; **CAST:** James Murtaugh (Dr. Haggett), Cynthia Darlow (Mrs. Haggett), Jessiee Datino (Susan Haggett), Mary Bacon (Abby), Hunter Canning (Warren Creamer), Kate Middleton (Ada Haggett), Greg McFadden (Tallant), Bob Ari (Rosen), James Prendergast (Maxwell Davenport)

Setting: Dining room of the Haggetts' house, not far from Boston; early 1930s. Revival of a comedy in three acts presented with one intermission; Beckett Theatre on Theatre Row; November 1–December 12, 2009 (Opened November 11); 8 previews, 33 performances. Originally presented at Ford's Opera House in Baltimore on October 24, 1932 and subsequently at Henry Miller's Theatre on Broadway October 31, 1932–May 1933, playing 224 performances. This production marked the play's first New York revival in seventy-seven years.

Cynthia Darlow, James Murtaugh (seated), Kate Middleton, Greg McFadden, James Prendergast, and Bob Ari in The Late Christopher Bean *(photo by Stephen Kunken)*

The Cocktail Party by T.S. Eliot; Director, Scott Alan Evans; Sets, Andrew Lieberman & Laura Jellnek; Costumes, David Toser; Lighting, Aaron Copp; Sound, Jill BC DuBoff; Original Music, Joseph Trapanese; Props, Lily Fairbanks; PSM, Meredith Dixon; ASM, Kelsey Daye Lutz; Assistant Director, Andrew Block; **CAST:** Mark Alhadeff (Alexander MacColgie Gibbs), Cynthia Harris (Julia Schttlethwaite), Jeremy Beck (Peter Quilpe), Lauren English (Celia Coplestone), Simon Jones (An Uninvited Guest), Jack Koenig (Edward Chamberlayne), Ericka Rolfsrud (Lavinia Chamberlayne), Celia Smith (Miss Barraway), Ben Beckley (A Carterer's Man)

Setting: The Chamberlayne's flat in London and a Consulting Room in Harley Street; late 1940s. Revival of a play presented in two acts; Beckett Theatre on Theatre Row; March 7–April 10, 2010 (Opened March 17); 8 previews, 33 performances. Originally produced at the Edinburgh Festival in 1949 and in London in 1950. The play debuted in New York on January 21, 1950 at Henry Miller's Theatre (winning the 1950 Tony Award for Best Play), and closed January 13, 1951 after 409 performances (see *Theatre World* Vol. 6, page 68).

Simon Jones and Cynthia Harris in The Cocktail Party *(photo by Carol Rosegg)*

Salon Series – Staged Readings at TACT Studio

The Devil Passes by Benn W. Levy; Director, Scott Alan Evans; PSM, Christine Massoud; Original Music, David Broome; **CAST:** Jack Koenig (D.C. Magnus), Harry Barandes (Cosmo Penny), Richard Ferrone (Louis Kisch), Scott Schafer (Rev. Herbert Messiter), Robert Krakovski (Rev. Nicholas Lucy), Mackenzie Meehan (Paul Robinson), Melissa Miller (Dorothy Lister), Cynthia Darlow (Mrs. Beatrice Messiter); October 2–5, 2009.

Waters of the Moon by N.C. Hunter; Director, Victor Pappas; PSM, Kelsey Daye Lutz; Music, Amir Khosrowpour; **CAST:** Matthew Carlson (John Daly), Simon Jones (Colonel Selby), Gregory Salata (Julius Winterhalter), Ron McClary (Robert Lancaster), Margaret Nichols (Evelyn Daly), Delphi Harrington (Mrs. Whyte), Nora Chester (Mrs. Daly), Darrie Lawrence (Mrs. Ashworth), Francesca Di Mauro (Helen Lancaster), Justine Salata (Tonetta Landi); December 18–21, 2009.

Candle-light by Sigfried Geyer, adapted by P.G. Wodehouse; Director, Gregory Salata; Stage Manager, Mel McCue; Music, Ayanna Witter-Johnston; **CAST:** Scott Schafer (Josef), Mark Alhadeff (Prince Rudolf), Richard Ferrone (Chauffeur/Baron/Waiter), Margaret Nichols (Marie), Lynn Wright (Liserl/Baroness); January 10–12, 2010.

The Amazing Doctor Clitterhouse by Barre Lyndon; Director, Drew Barr; PSM, Kelsey Daye Lutz; Original Music, Wally Gunn; Pianist, Youngwoo Yoo; **CAST:** Angel Desai (Nurse Ann), Gregory Salata (Dr. Clitterhouse), James Prendergast (Inspector Charles/Tug Wilson), Scott Schafer (Benny Kellerman), Mackenzie Meehan (Daisy), Jeffrey Mawkins (Pal Green), Jamie Bennett (Sgt. Bates), James Murtaugh (Oakie), Simon Jones (Sir William Grant); May 14–17, 2010.

Atlantic Theater Company

Twenty-fourth Season

Artistic Director, Neil Pepe; Managing Director, Jeffory Lawson; General Manager, Jamie Tyrol; Associate Artistic Director, Christian Parker; School Executive Director, Mary McCann; Development Director, Cynthia Flowers; Development Associates, Cameron Shreve (Institutional Giving), Catherine Williams (Individual Giving & Special Events); Capital Giving Director, Julia Lazarus; Production Managers, Michael Wade (Linda Gross Theatre) & Gabriel Evansohn (Stage 2 & Atlantic School); Marketing, Ryan Pointer; Business Manager, Mara Ditchfield; Artistic Leadership Associate, Jaime Castañeda; Audience Services, Sara Montgomery; Operations, Ian Crawford; Literary Associate, Abigail Katz; Company Manager, Aaron Thompson; School Associate Directors, Steven Hawley & Kate Blumberg; Education/Box Office Treasurer, Frances Tarr; School Artistic Director, Allison Beatty; Casting, Telsey + Company; Press, Boneau/Bryan-Brown, Chris Boneau, Joe Perrotta, Kelly Guiod

OOHRAH! by Bekah Brunstetter; Director, Evan Cabnet; Sets, Lee Savage; Costumes, Jessica Wegener; Lighting, Tyler Micoleau; Sound, Broken Chord Collective; Casting, MelCap Casting; PSM, Jullian M. Olliver; Fight Director, J. David Brimmer; ASM, Jason T. Vanderwoude; Military Advisor, James Hutchison; Properties, Eric Reynolds; Technical Director, Brian Kalin; **CAST:** Jennifer Mudge (Sara), Cassie Beck (Abby), Darren Goldstein (Ron), Sami Gayle (Lacey), Maximilian Osinski (Chip), Lucas Near-Verbrugghe (Christopher), JR Horne (Pop Pop)

Setting: Fayetteville, North Carolina; the present. World premiere of a new play presented in two acts; Atlantic Stage 2; September 1–27, 2009 (Opened September 10); 9 previews, 19 performances.

Maximilian Osinski, Cassie Beck (standing), Sami Gayle, J.R. Horne, Darren Goldstein, and Jennifer Mudge in OOHRAH! (photos by Ari Mintz)

Two Unrelated Plays by David Mamet: *Keep Your Pantheon* and *School* Director, Neil Pepe; Sets, Takeshi Kata; Costumes, Ilona Somogyi; Lighting, Christopher Akerlind; Sound, Obadiah Eaves; PSM, Gregory T. Livoti; ASM, Paige D. Causey; Assistant Director, Jaime Castañeda; Sound Consultant, Obadiah Eaves; Properties, Desiree Maurer; **CAST:** *School*: John Pankow (A), Rod McLachlan (B); *Keep Your Pantheon*: Steven Hawley (Herald), Brian Murray (Strabo), John Pankow (Pelargon), Michael Cassidy (Philius), Jack Wallace (Ramus), Todd Weeks (Quintus Magnus), Rod McLachlan (Messenger/Ensemble), Jonathan Rossetti (Ensemble), J.J. Johnston (Titus), Jordan Lage (Lupus Albus), Jeffrey Addiss (Ensemble)

Setting: An actor's studio in Ancient Rome. New York premiere (*Keep Your Patheon*) and world premiere (*School*) of a two new one-act plays presented without intermission; Linda Gross Theater; September 9–November 1, 2009 (Opened September 30); 24 previews, 39 performances. *Keep Your Pantehon* was originally produced by Center Theater Group Mark Taper Forum (Michael Ritchie Artistic Director; Charles Dillingham, Managing Director) May 11–June 8, 2008 (see *Theatre World* Vol. 64, page 298).

Jack Wallace, Michael Cassidy, Brian Murray, John Pankow, and Todd Weeks in Keep Your Pantheon

Rod McLachlan and John Pankow in School

Ages of the Moon by Sam Shepard; Presented by the Abbey Theatre (Dublin, Ireland) in association with True Love Productions; Director, Jimmy Fay; Sets, Brien Vahey; Costumes, Joan Bergin; Lighting, Paul Keogan; Sound, Phillip Stewart; U.S. Fight Consultant, J. David Brimmer; PSM, Alison DeSantis; ASM, Lauren Kurinskas; Assistant Director/Fight Director, Paul Burke; Properties, Desiree Maurer; **CAST**: Stephen Rea (Ames), Seán McGinley (Byron)

U.S. premiere of a new play presented without intermission; Linda Gross Theater; January 12–March 21, 2010 (Opened January 27); 17 previews, 62 performances. World premiere at the Abbey Theatre (Fiach Mac Conghail, Director) March 23, 2009.

Stephen Rea and Sean McGinley in Ages of the Moon

Zach Grenier, Patricia Connolly, Lisa Emery, Samantha Soule, and Libby Woodbridge in Gabriel

Gabriel by Moira Buffini; Director, David Esbjornson; Sets, Riccardo Hernandez; Costumes, Martin Pakledinaz; Lighting, Scott Zielinski; Sound, Obadiah Eaves; Fight Consultant, J. David Brimmer; Dialect Coach, Ben Furey; Wigs, Paul Huntley; PSM, Alison DeSantis; ASM, Lauren Kurinskas; Technical Director, Brian Kalin; Properties, Seán Mcardle; **CAST**: Patricia Conolly (Margaret Lake), Lisa Emery (Jeanne Becquet), Zach Grenier (Major Von Pfunz), Lee Aaron Rosen (Gabriel), Samantha Soule (Lilian Becquet), Libby Woodbridge (Estelle Becquet)

Setting: An island on the edge of a foreign occupation; February 1943. U.S. premiere of a new play presented in two acts; Linda Gross Theater; April 23–June 20, 2010 (Opened May 13); 23 previews, 45 performances. World premiere at London's Soho Theatre Company in 1997.

Dusk Rings a Bell by Stephen Belber; Director, Sam Gold; Set, Takeshi Kata; Costumes, Theresa Squire; Lighting, Ben Stanton; Sound, Jill BC DuBoff; Projections, Peter Nigrini; Casting, MelCap Casting; PSM, Erin Maureen Koster; ASM, Molly Minor Eustis; Assistant Director, Craig Baldwin; Properties, Teralynn Bruketta; **CAST**: Paul Sparks (Ray), Kate Walsh (Molly)

World premiere of a new play presented without intermission; Atlantic Stage 2; May 19–June 26, 2010 (Opened May 27); 8 previews, 33 performances.

Paul Sparks and Kate Walsh in Dusk Rings a Bell

Brooklyn Academy of Music

Founded in 1861

Chairman of the Board, Alan H. Fishman; Vice Chairmen of the Board, William I. Campbell & Adam E. Max; President, Karen Brooks Hopkins; Executive Producer, Joseph V. Melillo

2009 Next Wave Festival (27th Annual)

In-I Directed and performed by Juliette Binoche and Akram Khan; Co-produced by Hermès Foundation, National Theatre (London), Théâtre de la ville, (Paris), Grand Théâtre de Luxembourg, Romaeuropa Festival and Accademia Filarmonica Romana (Rome), La Monnaie (Brussels), Sydney Opera House (Sydney), Curve (Leicester); Set, Anish Kapoor; Lighting, Michael Hulls; Music, Philip Sheppard; Costumes, Alber Elbaz, Kei Ito; Sound, Nicolas Faure

U.S. premiere of a new dance play presented without intermission; Harvey Theater; September 15–26; 11 performances.

Juliette Binoche and Akram Khan in IN-I

Lipsynch by the Cast, Marie Gignac, and Robert Lepage; Created and presented by Ex Machina/Théâtre Sans Frontières; Presented in association with Cultural Industry Ltd. and Northern Stage; Co-produced by Arts 276/Automne en Normandie; Barbicanbite08, Cabildo Insular de Tenerife, Chekhov International Theatre Festival, Festival de Otoño, Festival TransAmériques, La Comète (Scène Nationale de Châlons-en-Champagne), Le Théâtre Denise-Pelletier, Le Volcan - Scène Nationale du Havre, Luminato, Toronto Festival of Arts & Creativity, The Sydney Festival, Director, Robert Lepage; Set, Jean Hazel; Costumes, Yasmina Giguère; Lighting, Étienne Boucher; Sound, Jean-Sébastien Côté; Props, Virginie Leclerc; Assistant Director, Félix Dagenais; American Stage Manager, Caroline Dufresne; Dramaturgy Consultant, Marie Gignac; Costume Assistant, Jeanne

Frédérike Bédard and Rick Miller in
Lipsynch (photo by Chang W. Lee)

Lapierre; Images Producer, Jacques Collin; Wigs, Richard Hansen; Creative Collaboration, Sophie Martin; Production and Touring Manager, Louise Roussel; Production Assistant, Marie-Pierre Gagné; Technical Director, Paul Bourque; Stage Manager, Judith Saint-Pierre; Lighting Manager, Catherine Guay; Sound Manager, Stanislas Elie; Video Manager, David Leclerc; Costume Manager Sylvie Courbron; Set Design Collaborator, Carl Fillion; **CAST**: Frédérike Bédard (Marie & others), Carlos Belda (Sebastian & others), Rebecca Blankenship (Ada & others), Lise Castonguay (Michelle & others), John Cobb (Jackson & others), Nuria Garcia (Lupe & others), Sarah Kemp (Sarah & others), Rick Miller (Jeremy & others), Hans Piesbergen (Thomas & others)

U.S. premiere a new theatrical piece with music, text, and movement presented in nine acts in three parts (each part with one intermission on performance days where only one part presented) performed in multiple languages with English titles; Four weekend performances presented as marathons with four intermissions and a dinner break; Harvey Theater; October 3–11; 7 performance days (5 performances of each part).

Decreation Choreography, set, and lighting by William Forsythe; Inspired by the writing of Anne Carson; Presented by the Forsythe Company; Co-Lighting, Jan Walter; Music, David Morrow; Costumes, Claudia Hill; Dramaturgy, Rebecca Groves; Video, Philip Bußmann; Sound, Bernhard Klein, Dietrich Krüger, Niels Lanz; Camera, Ursula Maurer; **CAST**: Yoko Ando, Cyril Baldy, Esther Balfe, Dana Caspersen, Amancio Gonzalez, David Kern, Fabrice Mazliah, Roberta Mosca, Tilman O'Donnell, Nicole Peisl, George Reischl, Christopher Roman, Jone San Martin, Parvaneh Scharafali, Yasutake Shimaji, Richard Siegal, Elizabeth Waterhouse, Ander Zabala

U.S. premiere of a dance theatrical piece presented without intermission; Howard Gilman Opera House; October 7–10; 4 performances.

Imaginary City Written and performed by Sō Percussion (Josh Quillen, Adam Sliwinski, Jason Treuting, Eric Beach); Director, Rinde Eckert; Lighting, Aaron Copp; Sound, Lawson White; Video, Jenise Treuting

World premiere of a percussion and video theatrical piece presented without intermission; Harvey Theater; October 14–17; 4 performances.

Songs of Ascension Music, direction, and choreography by Meredith Monk, video by Ann Hamilton; Lighting, Elaine Buckholtz, Costumes, Yoshio Yabara, Gary Graham; Sound, Jody Eff; Score Preparation/Music Director, Allison Sniffin; Choral Director, Cynthia Powell; Production Manager, Michael Casselli; Stage Manager, Courtney Golden; ASM, Lily Perlmutter; Visual Consultant, Debby Lee Cohen; **CAST**: Meredith Monk & Vocal Ensemble: Ellen Fisher, Katie Geissinger, Ching Gonzalez, Bruce Rameker, Allison Sniffin (voices), Bohdan Hilash (winds), John Hollenbeck (percussion), Allison Sniffin (violin); The Todd Reynolds String Quartet: Todd Reynolds (violin, viola), Matt Albert (violin), Nadia Sirota (viola), Ha-Yang Kim (cello); Chorus: Members of the Stonewall Chorale and The M6

World premiere of a music, dance, and video piece presented without intermission; Harvey Theater; October 21–25; 5 performances.

The Long Count by Bryce Dessner, Aaron Dessner, and Matthew Ritchie; Music Director, Rob Moose; Audio, David Sheppard; Costumes, Rabi Troncelliti; Vocalists: Kim Deal, Kelley Deal, Shara Worden, Matt Beminger

World premiere of a music and art piece presented without intermission; Howard Gilman Opera House; October 28–31; 3 performances.

Quartett by Heiner Müller, based on Les Liasisons Dangereuses by Choderlos de Laclos; Conceived and directed by Robert Wilson; Presented by Odéod-Théâtre de l'Europe; Co-produced by La Comédie De Genève and Théâtre du Gymnase/Marseille; Co-Director, Ann-Christin Rommen; Music, Michael Galasso; Set and Lighting, Robert Wilson; Translators, Jean Jourdheuil, Béatrice Perregaux; Costumes, Frida Parmeggiani; Co-Lighting, A.J. Weissbard; Makeup, Luc Verschueren; Co-Set, Stephanie Engein; **CAST**: Isabelle Huppert (Merteuil), Ariel Garcia Valdès (Valmont), Louis Beyler, Rachel Eberhart, Benoît Maréchal

Revival of a performance and theatrical piece presented without intermission; Harvey Theater; November 4–14; 10 performances. Previously presented at Theatre for the New City in 1986.

Rachel Eberhart, Benoît Maréchal, Ariel Garcia Valdès, and Isabelle Huppert in Quartett *(photo by Richard Termine)*

Itutu Choreographed by Karole Armitage; Presented by Armitage Gone! Dance; Music, Burkina Electric and Lukas Ligeti; Costumes, Peter Speliopoulos; Set, Philip Taaffe; Lighting, Clifton Taylor

U.S. premiere of a dance piece presented without intermission; Howard Gilman Opera House; November 4–7; 3 performances.

Inside Out Created and presented by Cirkus Cirkör; Director, Tilde Björfors; Live Music, Irya's Playground; Composers, Irya Gmeyner and Pange Öberg; Set and Costumes, Sigyn Stenqvist; Dramaturgy/Circus Script, Mia Winge; Choreography, Dag Andersson; Lighting, Jenny Larsson; Circus Choreography, Christian "Vippen" Vilppola; Makeup, Helena Andersson

U.S. premiere of a circus and theatrical piece presented without intermission; Howard Gilman Opera House; November 12–15; 5 performances.

Really Real Choreographed and directed by Wally Cardona; Presented by Wally Cardona and Company; Original Music, Phil Kline; Lighting, Roderick Murray; Other Music, Darby R. Slick, June Carter and Merle Kilgore, Jack Bruce and Peter Brown; Costume Consultant, Stephanie Sleeper; Assistant to the Choreographer, Joanna Kotze; Live Music, Brooklyn Youth Chorus; **CAST**: Julian Barnett, Wally Cardona, Kana Kimura, Joanna Kotze, Omagbitse Omagbemi, Stuart Singer, Francis Stansky

World premiere of a multimedia dance piece presented without intermission; Harvey Theater; November 17–21; 4 performances.

Kepler Music and lyrics by Philip Glass, libretto by Martina Winkel; Conductor, Dennis Russell Davies; Performed by Bruckner Orchestra Linz and soloists and choir of the Upper Austrian State Theatre, Linz

U.S. premiere of a concert staging of a new opera presented without intermission in German and Latin with English titles; Howard Gilman Opera House; November 18–21; 3 performances.

Terra Nova: Sinfonia Antarctica Conceived and composed by DJ Spooky That Subliminal Kid (Paul D. Miller); Produced by Change Performing Arts with Music+Art Management; Executive Producer, CRT Artificio; Director, Bob McGrath; Visual Design, A.J. Weissbard; Image Research/Video Editing, V-Factory and Jim Findlay; Performed by DJ Spooky and members of the International Contemporary Ensemble; Musicians, Jen Curtis, Erik Carlson (violin), Kivie Cahn-Lipman (cello), Jacob Greenberg (piano)

World premiere of a multimedia music and drama piece presented without intermission; Howard Gilman Opera House; December 2–5; 3 performances.

Mortal Engine Created by Chunky Move (Australia); Director/Choreography, Gideon Obarzanek; Interactive System Design, Frieder Weiss; Laser and Sound, Robin Fox; Composer, Ben Frost; Costumes, Paula Levis; Lighting, Damien Cooper; Set, Richard Dinnen and Gideon Obarzanek; **CAST**: Kristy Ayer, Sara Black, Amber Haines, Lee Serle, James Shannon, Jorijn Vriesendorp

U.S. premiere of an interactive dance, music, laser, and video performance piece presented without intermission; Howard Gilman Opera House; December 9–12; 4 performances.

The Good Dance - dakar/brooklyn Created and presented by Fist & Heel Performance Group (Brooklyn), and Compagnie 1 er Temps (Dakar, Senegal); Choreography, Reggie Wilson & Andréya Ouamba; Costumes, Naoko Nagata; Lighting, Jonathan Belcher

World premiere of a dance piece presented without intermission; Howard Gilman Opera House; December 16–19; 3 performances.

Fall/Winter Season

A Streetcar Named Desire by Tennessee Williams; Presented by Sydney Theatre Company (Cate Blanchett and Andrew Upton, Artistic Directors); Director, Liv Ullmann; Sets, Ralph Myers; Costumes, Tess Schofield; Lighting, Nick Schlieper; Sound, Paul Charlier; Assistant to the Director, Einar Bjorge; Assistant to the Director, Einar Bjorge; Piano Arrangements and Recording, Alan John; Voice and Text Coach, Charmian Gradwell; American Stage Manager, R. Michael Blanco; Production Manager, Annie Eves-Boland; Company Manager, Rhys Holden; Stage Manager, Georgia Gilbert; Deputy Stage Manager, Jamie Twist; Assistant Stage Manager, Victoria Marques; Wig & Wardrobe Supervisor, Lauren A. Proietti; For Sydney Theatre Company: Tom Wright (Associate Director), Rob Brookman (General Manager), Jo Dyer (Executive Producer), Sally Noonan (Development), Annie Eves-Boland (Production), Serena Hill (Casting), Rani Haywood (Marketing), Tim McKeough (Media Relations); **CAST**: Sara Zwangobani (Rosetta), Mandy McElhinney (Eunice Hubbell), Robin McLeavy (Stella Kowalski), Joel Edgerton (Stanley Kowalski), Tim Richards (Mitch), Cate Blanchett (Blanche Dubois), Michael Denkha (Steve Hubbell), Jason Klarwein (Pablo Gonzales), Morgan David Jones (A Young Collector), Gertraud Ingeborg (A Mexican Woman), Elaine Hudson (A Strange Woman), Russell Kiefel (A Strange Man)

Robin McLeavy and Cate Blanchett in A Streetcar Named Desire *(photo by Richard Termine)*

New York debut of a new revival of a drama presented in two acts; Harvey Theater; November 24–December 20, 2009; 28 performances. This production premiered at the Sydney Theatre Company September 1–October 17, and played the Kennedy Center October 29–November 21, prior to its BAM presentation. Originally premiered on Broadway at the Barrymore Theatre (starring Jessica Tandy, Marlon Brando, and Kim Hunter) December 3, 1947–December 17, 1949, playing 855 performances (see *Theatre World* Vol. 4, page 47). The play has had seven major New York revivals, most recently at Studio 54 (starring Natasha Richardson, John C. Reilly, and Amy Ryan) April 26–July 3, 2005 (see *Theatre World* Vol. 61, page 74).

Spring Season

The Bridge Project: *As You Like It* and *The Tempest* (Second Season) by William Shakespeare; Produced by BAM, The Old Vic (Sally Greene, Chief Executive; Kevin Spacey Artistic Director) and Neal Street Productions (Caro Newling, Producer); Co-commissioned and produced in association with Holland Festival, Hong Kong Arts Festival, Singapore Repertory Theatre, and Théâtre Marigny-Paris; Director, Sam Mendes; Sets, Tom Piper; Costumes, Catherine Zuber; Lighting, Paul Pyant; Sound, Simon Baker for Autograph; Music, Mark Bennett; Casting, Nancy Piccione & Maggie Lunn; Hair & Wigs, Tom Watson; Fight Director, Rick Sordelet; Music Director, Stephen Bentley-Klein; Choreography, Josh Prince; International Tour Producer, Claire Béjanin; PSM, Richard Clayton; ASMs, Jenefer Tait, Sarah Elizabeth Ford; Associate Director, Gaye Taylor Upchurch; U.S. Press, Boneau/Bryan-Brown; Dialects, Deborah Hecht; Singing Instructor, Andrew Byrne; Associate Set, Christine Peters (*As You Like It*); Assistant Set, Caleb Levengood (*The Tempest*); Associate Lighting, Dan Large; Associate Sound, Jeremy Lee; Assistant Costumes, Nicole V. Moody; Props, Faye Armon; Makeup, Ashley Ryan; Production Manager, Dominic Fraser; Musician, Shane Shanahan; **CAST**: *As You Like It*: Christian Camargo (Orlando, *youngest son of Sir Roland de Boys*), Alvin Epstein (Adam, *servant in the de Boys household*/Sir Oliver Martext, *a country vicar*), Edward Bennett (Oliver, *eldest brother to Orlando*), Ross Waiton (Dennis, *Oliver's servant*/William, *a country youth*), Ron Cephas Jones (Charles, *Duke Frederick's wrestler*), Juliet Rylance (Rosalind, *daughter of Duke Senior*), Michelle Beck (Celia, *daughter of Duke Frederic*), Thomas Sadoski (Touchstone, *a clown*), Jonathan Lincoln Fried (Le Beau, *a courtier*), Michael Thomas (Duke Frederick, *the usurping Duke*/Duke Senior, *the exiled Duke banished by his brother*), Richard Hansell (Amiens, *a lord and follower of Duke Senior*/Jacques de Boys, *second son of Sir Roland de Boys*), Ron Cephas Jones (First Lord, *companion of Duke Senior*), Anthony O'Donnell (Corin, *a shepherd*), Aaron Krohn (Silvius, *a shepherd*), Stephen Dillane (Jaques, *a melancholy gentleman*), Jenni Barber (Audrey, *a country girl*), Ashlie Atkinson (Phoebe, *a country girl*); Understudies: Ashlie Atkinson (Celia), Jenni Barber (Phoebe), Michelle Beck (Rosalind), Edward Bennett (Orlando, Amiens), Jonathan Lincoln Fried (Jaques, Jacques de Boys), Ron Cephas Jones (Duke Frederick, Duke Senior), Richard Hansell (Oliver, William, Sir Oliver Martext), Aaron Krohn (Touchstone, Le Beau), Ross Waiton (Charles the Wrestler, Silvius, Corin, Audrey); Revival of a classic play presented in two acts; Harvey Theater; January 3–March 13, 2010 (Opened January 26); 12 previews, 20 performances; *The Tempest*: Stephen Dillane (Prospero, *the right Duke of Milan*), Christian Camargo (Ariel, *a Spirit*), Ron Cephas Jones (Caliban, *a Slave*), Ross Waiton (Boatswain), Jonathan Lincoln Fried (Alonso, *King of Naples*), Alvin Epstein (Gonzalo, *an honest old Counsellor*), Richard Hansell (Sebastian, *brother of the King of Naples*), Michael Thomas (Antonio, *Prospero's brother, the usurping Duke of Milan*), Juliet Rylance (Miranda, *daughter to Prospero*), Edward Bennett (Ferdinand, *son to the King of Naples*), Aaron Krohn (Adrian, *a Lord*), Anthony O'Donnell (Trinculo, *a Jester*), Thomas Sadoski (Stephano, *a drunken Butler*), Michelle Beck (Iris), Jenni Barber (Ceres), Ashlie Atkinson (Juno); Understudies: Ashlie Atkinson (Trinculo, Ceres), Jenni Barber (Iris), Michelle Beck (Miranda, Juno), Aaron Krohn (Ferdinand, Sebastian, Stephano, Boatswain), Michael Thomas (Prospero), Richard Hansell (Ariel), Ross Waiton (Caliban, Gonzalo, Alonso, Antonio); Revival of a play presented without intermission; Harvey Theater; February 14–March 13, 2009 (Opened February 25); 9 previews, 12 performances.

Uncle Vanya by Anton Chekov; Presented by Maly Drama Theatre of St. Petersburg (Russia); Director, Lev Dodin; Set, David Borovsky; Lighting, Igor Tupikin, Ekaterina Dorofeeva; Sound, Yury Vavilov; Props, Svetlana Tretiakova; Wardrobe, Maria Fomina, Natalia Selezneva; Stage Manager, Olga Dazidenko; Technical Director, Evgeny Nikiforov; Makeup, Alla Nudel; **CAST**: Igor Ivanov (Professor Serebriakov), Ksenya Rappoport (Elena, *his wife*), Elena Kalinina (Sonia, *his daughter from his first marriage*), Tatyana Schuko (Madame Voinitskaia, *Professor's first wife's mother*), Sergey Kuryshev (Voinitskiy Ivan or Uncle Vanya, *her son*), Igor Chernevich (Doctor Astrov), Alexander Zavyalov (Telegin Ilia or Waffles, *an impoverished gentry*), Vera Bykova (Marina, *an old nurse*), Alexander Koshkarev (Servant)

Setting: Serebriakov's country house. Revival of a play presented in four acts with one intermission; Harvey Theater; April 7–11, 2010; 5 performances.

Edward Bennett, Stephen Dillane, and Juliet Rylance in The Tempest, *part of The Bridge Project (photo by Joan Marcus)*

Creditors by August Strindberg, in a new version by David Greig; Presented by The Donmar Warehouse (Michael Grandage, Artistic Director; James Bierman, Executive Producer; Jo Danvers, General Manager); Director, Alan Rickman; Set, Ben Stones; Costumes, Fotini Dimou; Lighting, Howard Harrison; Composer and Sound, Adam Cork; Lighting, Associate, Paul Miller; Sound Associate, Chris Cronin; Production Manager, Lucy Tory; Deputy Production Manager, Kate West; Casting, Anne McNulty; Marketing, Jonathan Aplin; Press, Kate Morley; Company Stage Manager, Kristi Warwick; American Stage Manager, Peter Wolf; ASM, Laura Sully; Deputy Production Manager, Kate West; Costume Supervisors, Byrony Fayers, Lynette Mauro; Wardrobe Supervisor, Tansy Blaik-Kelly; Production Carpenter, Dave Skelly; **CAST**: Tom Burke (Adolph), Owen Teale (Gustav), Anna Chancellor (Tekla)

U.S. premiere of a revival of a play in a new translation presented without intermission; Harvey Theater; April 16–May 16, 2010; 28 performances.

Owen Teale and Tom Burke in Creditors *(photo by Stephanie Berger)*

City Center Encores!

Artistic Director, Jack Viertel; President & CEO of City Center, Arlene Shuler; Senior Vice President & Managing Director, Mark Litvin; *Encores!* General Manager, Stephanie Overton; Season Music Director, Rob Berman; Concert Adaptation, David Ives; Scenic Consultant, John Lee Beatty; Music Coordinator, Seymour Red Press; Company Manager, Michael Zande; Casting; Jay Binder, Jack Bowdan; Press, Helene Davis; *Encores!* Artistic Associates: John Lee Beatty, Jay Binder, Walter Bobbie, David Ives, Kathleen Marshall

2009 Summer Stars (Third Season)

The Wiz Book by William F. Brown, music and lyrics by Charlie Smalls; Based on *The Wonderful Wizard of Oz* by L. Frank Baum; Director, Thomas Kail; Choreography, Andy Blankenbuehler; Music Director, Alex Lacamoire; Sets, David Corins; Costumes, Paul Tazewell; Lighting, Ken Billington; Sound, Acme Sound Partners; Casting, Jay Binder, Sara Schatz; Hair & Wigs, Charles G. LaPointe; Makeup, Cookie Jordan; PSM, Karen Moore; Animal Trainer & Handler, Bill Berloni; Original Orchestrations, Harold Wheeler; Associate Music Director, Shelton Becton; Music Associate, Joshua Clayton; Stage Manager, Rachel S. McCutchen; ASM, Karen Evanouskas; Assistant Director, David Ruttura; Associate Choreographer, Joey Dowling; Associate Design: Rod Lemmond (set), Nick Borisjuk (sound), Leah Loukas (wigs and hair); Assistant Design: Maria Zamansky, Caitlin Hunt (costumes), John Demous (lighting); Assistant Company Manager, Katherine McNamee; Production Assistants, Miranda Widdinton, Sarah Trieckel; Rehearsal Musicians: Matt Perri (piano), Brian Brake (drums); Keyboard Programmer, Randy Cohen; Props Coordinator, Scott Laule; Ashanti's Hair, Yusef; Ashanti's Makeup, JJ; Moving Lights, David Arch; Wardrobe Supervisor, Rory Powers; Wig & Hair Supervisor, Mia Neal; Sound Mixer, David Gotwald; Dance Captain, Tanya Bril; **CAST:** LaChanze (Aunt Em/Glinda, *The Good Witch of the South*), Ashanti (Dorothy), John Eric Parker (Uncle Henry), Nigel (Toto), Asmeret Ghebremichael, Angela Grovey, Levensky Smith, Adrienne Warren, Juson Williams (Munchkins), Dawnn Lewis (Addaperle, *The Good Witch of the North*), Christian Dante White (Scarecrow), Raymond Lamar Bennett, Tanya Birl, Lauren Lim Jackson, Carl Lation (Crows), Joshua Henry (Tinman), James Monroe Iglehart (Lion), Tanya Birl, Ebony Haswell, Lauren Lim Jackson, Jennifer Locke, Amy McClendon, Kenna Michelle Morris (Poppies), Daniel J. Watts, Levensky Smith (Field Mice), Juson Williams (Gatekeeper), Orlando Jones (The Wiz), John Eric Parker (Lord High Underling), Tichina Arnold (Evillene, *The Wicked Witch of the West*), Kevin-Anthony (Messenger), William B. Wingfield (Winged Monkey Leader); Ensemble *(Yellow Brick Road, Kalidahs, Winged Monkeys, Quadlings, and Citizens of Emerald City)*: Raymond Lamar Bennett, Tanya Birl, Darlesia Cearcy, Asmeret Ghebremichael, Angela Grovey, Ebony Haswell, Lauren Lim Jackson, Kevin-Anthony, Carl Lation, Jennifer Locke, Amy McClendon, Kenna Michelle Morris, John Eric Parker, Herman Payne, Ryan H. Rankine, Levensky Smith, Ephraim M. Sykes, Adrienne Warren, Daniel J. Watts, Juson Williams, William B. Wingfield; Understudies: Darlesia Cearcy (Aunt Em/Glinda), Adrienne Warren (Dorothy), Angela Grovey (Addaperle, Evillene), Ephraim M. Sykes (Scarecrow), John Eric Parker (The Wiz, Tinman), Juson Williams (Lion); Orchestra: Alex Lacamoire (Conductor); Antoine Silverman (Concertmaster), Maura Giannini, Kristina Musser, Christoph Franzgrote (violins); Anja Wood, Mairi Dorman (cello); Konrad Adderley (bass); Carl Burnett (guitar); Shelton Becton (keyboards); Brian Brake (drums); Steven Kenyon, Todd Groves, Charles Pillow, Jay Brandford (woodwinds); David Byrd-Marrow (French horn); David Stahl, Ken Rampton, Earl Gardner (trumpets); Bruce Bonvissuto, Jack Schatz (trombones); Wilson Torres, Javier Diaz (percussion)

Musical Numbers: Overture, The Feeling We Once Had, Tornado Ballet, He's The Wizard, Soon As I Get Home, I Was Born on the Day Before Yesterday, Ease on Down the Road, Slide Some Oil to Me, Ease on Down the Road (reprise), Mean Ole Lion, Ease on Down the Road (reprise), Kalidah Battle, Be a Lion, Lion's Dream,

Emerald City Ballet, So You Wanted to Meet the Wizard, What Would I Do If I Could Feel?, Entr'acte, No Bad News, Funky Monkeys, Everybody Rejoice (Brand New Day), Who Do You Think You Are?, Brand New Day (reprise), Y'all Got It!, A Rested Body Is a Rested Mind, Believe in Yourself, Home

Revival of the musical presented in fourteen scenes and two acts; June 12–July 5, 2009 (Opened June 18); 6 previews, 21 performances. The original production opened at the Majestic Theatre January 5, 1975, transferred to the Broadway Theatre May 25, 1977, and closed January 28, 1979 after 1,672 performances (see *Theatre World* Vol. 31, page 35).

Christian White, Ashanti, Joshua Henry in The Wiz *(photo by Robert J. Saferstein)*

Dawnn Lewis and Ashanti in The Wiz *(photo by Robert J. Saferstein)*

Fall and Spring Series (Seventeeth Season)

Girl Crazy Music and lyrics by George Gershwin and Ira Gershwin, book by Guy Bolton and Jack McGowan; Director, Jerry Zaks; Guest Musical Director, Rob Fisher; Choreography, Warren Carlyle; Costume Consultant, William Ivey Long; Lighting, Peter Kaczorowski; Sound, Scott Lehrer; Original Orchestrations, Robert Russell Bennett; PSM, Adam John Hunter; Stage Manager, Andrea O. Saraffian; Associate Director, Steve Bebout; Associate Choreography, Parker Esse; Associate Musical Director, Ben Whiteley; Assistant Consultants: Hannah Davis (scenic), Cathy Parrott (costumes); Assistant to the Costume Consultant, Donald Sanders; Assistant Lighting, John Viesta; Photoshop Artisan, Mark Mongold; Music Assistant, Karlan Judd; Rehearsal Pianists, Milton Granger, Matt Gallagher; Music Restoration, Jim Stenborg; Production Assistants, Shelley Miles, Amanda Tamny; Casting Assistants, Karen Young, Patrick Bell; **CAST**: Glenn Seven Allen, Benjamin Howes, Jack Doyle, Carson Church (Cowboy Quaretette), Richard Poe (Jake Howell/Hotel Porter/Policeman), Chris Diamantopoulos (Danny Churchill), Wayne Knight (Gieber Goldfarb), Daniel Stewart Sherman (Lank Sanders), Jeremy Beck (Pete), Becki Newton (Molly Gray), Mylinda Hull (Patsy West), Heather Ayers (Tess Parker), Robin Campbell (Flora Best), Ana Gasteyer (Frisco Kate Follicle), Marc Kudisch (Slick Follicle), Gregory Wooddell (Tom Mason), Emilee Dupré (First Mexican Girl, Bree Branker (Second Mexican Girl); Ensemble (*Cowboys and Dudeens, Caballaeros y Señoritas*): Glenn Seven Allen, Heather Ayers, Ward Billeisen, Colin Bradbury, Bree Branker, James Brown III, Robin Campbell, Carson Church, Jack Doyle, Emilee Dupre, Leah Edwards, Andrew Fitch, Jennifer Frankel, Neil Haskell, Benjamin Howes, Michelle Lookadoo, Sean McKnight, Patricia Noonan, Lauren Pastorek, Sam Prince, Hilary Michael Thompson; Orchestra: Rob Fisher (Conductor); Suzanne Ornstein (Concertmistress), Christoph Franzgrote, Lisa Matricardi, Eric De Gioia, Fritz Krakowski, Karl Kawahara, Robert Zubrycki, Conrad Harris, Lorra Bayliss (violins); Richard Brice, Adria Benjmamin, Sally Shumway, Crystal Garner (violas); Roger Shell, Frances Rowell (celli); Jeffrey Carney (double bass); Susan Rotholtz, Rob Ingliss, Lawrence Feldman, Steve Kenyon, Edward Salkin (woodwinds); Tony Kadleck, Glenn Drewes, Kamau Adilifu (trumpets); Bruce Bonvissuto, Randy Andos (trombones); John Redsecker (drums/percussion); Nick Archer (piano)

Musical Numbers: Overture, Bidin' My Time, The Lonesome Cowboy Won't Be Lonesome Now, Could You Use Me?, Bidin' My Time (reprise), Broncho Busters, Barbary Coast, Embraceable You, Finaletto: Goldfarb! That's I'm!, Embraceable You (reprise), I Got Rhythm, Sam and Delilah, Finale Act I, Entr'acte, Land of the Gay Caballero, But Not for Me, Treat Me Rough, Boy! What Love Has Done to Me!, When It's Cactus Time in Arizona, Bidin' My Time (reprise), Finale

Setting: Custerville, Arizona, and San Luz and Los Pegos, Mexico; 1930s. Concert version revival of the musical presented in seven scenes in two acts; November 19–22, 2009; 5 performances. The original production opened at the Alvin (now the Neil Simon) Theatre October 14, 1930, and closed June 6, 1931, after 272 performances.

Ana Gasteyer, Wayne Knight, Chris Diamantopoulos, Becki Newton, and Mark Kudisch in Girl Crazy *(photo by Joan Marcus)*

Chris Diamantopoulos and Becki Newton in Girl Crazy
(photo by Joan Marcus)

Fanny Music and lyrics by Harold Rome, book by S.N. Behrman and Joshua Logan, based on the trilogy of plays *Marius*, *Fanny*, and *César* by Marcel Pagnol; Director, Marc Bruni; Choreography, Lorin Latarro; Costume Consultant, Martin Pakledinaz; Lighting, Ken Billington; Sound, Scott Lehrer; Original Orchestrations, Philip J. Lang; PSM, Karen Moore; Additional Casting, Mark Brandon; Stage Manager, Rachel S. McCutchen; Associate Director, David Ruttura; Associate Choreographer, Lee A. Wilkins; Associate Music Director, James Lowe; Music Associate, Josh Clayton; Assistant to the Choreographer, Pamela Remler; Associate Lighting, John Demous; Assistant Design Consultants: Hannah Davis (set), Tescia Seufferlein (costumes); Hair Consultant, Carole Morales; Rehearsal Pianists, Mark Mitchell, James Cunningham; Wardrobe Supervisor, Karen Eifert; Costume Assistant, Mitchell Travers; Sound Mixer, Kurt Fisher; Moving Lights, Tim Rogers; Prop Shopper, Brian Howard; Production Assistants, Sara Cox Bradley, Karen Evanouskas; Wrangler, John Mara Jr.; Original Music Continuity, Trude Rittman; Original Vocal Arrangements, Lehman Engel; **CAST**: David Patrick Kelly (The Admiral, *an eccentric waterfront character*), James Snyder (Marius, *the son of Cesar*), Priscilla Lopez (Honorine, *Fanny's mother, a fish-stall keeper*), Elena Shaddow (Fanny), Rebecca Eichenberger (Customer), Megan Sikora (Claudette), Shannon Lewis (Claudine), Fred Applegate (Panisse, *a wealthy sailmaker*), George Hearn (Cesar, *the proprietor of a café on the waterfront*), Michael McCormick (Escartifique, *a ferryboat captain*), Jack Doyle (Brun, *a customs inspector recently returned from Paris*), Nina Lafarga (Belly Dancer), Martín Solá (Hakim), Grasan Kingsberry (Second Mate), Ted Sutherland (Cesario), Jay Lusteck (Louis, *the garage owner*); Ensemble (*Customers, Vendors, Sailors, Fishermen, Townspeople, and Circus Performers*): Adam Alexander, Jack Doyle, Rebecca Eichenberger, Sean Ewing, Leslie Donna Flesner, Margaret Ann Gates, Constantine Germanacos, Miles Johnson, Grasan Kingsberry, Nina Lafarga, Shannon Lewis, Jay Lusteck, Christine Nolan, Monica L. Patton, Rebecca Robbins, Eric Sciotto, Megan Sikora, Martín Solá, Brandon Tyler; Orchestra: Rob Berman (Conductor); Belinda Whitney (Concertmistress), Eric DeGioia, Maura Giannini, Laura Seaton, Christoph Franzgrote, Robert Zubrycki, Fritz Krakowski, Cenovia Cummins (violins); Richard Brice, David Blinn (violas); Roger Shell, Deborah Assael (celli); Richard Sarpola (double bass); Cenovia Cummins (mandolin); Art Bailey (accordion/concertina); Susan Jolles (harp); Susan Rotholtz, Melanie Feld, Lino Gomez, Steve Kenyon, John Winder (woodwinds); Russ Rizner, David Byrd-Marrow (French horns); Tony Kadleck, James De La Garza, John Dent (trumpets); Bruce Bonvissuto, Randy Andos (trombones); Richard Rosenzweig (drums); Thad Wheeler (percussion); David Gursky (piano/celeste)

Musical Numbers: Overture; Octopus Song; Restless Heart; Never Too Late for Love; The Cold-Cream Jar Song; Restless Heart (reprise); Why Be Afraid to Dance?; Never Too Late for Love (reprise); Shika, Shika; Welcome Home, I Like You, I Have to Tell You, Fanny, Montage, Oysters, Cockles, and Mussels; Panisse and Son; Wedding Dance; Act I Finale; Entr'acte; Birthday Song; To My Wife; The Thought of You (Reprise: I Have to Tell You); Love Is a Very Light Thing; Reprise: Fanny (Other Hands, Other Hearts); Be Kind to Your Parents; Cesario's Party (Cirque Français); The Cold-Cream Jar Song; Welcome Home

Setting: In and around the Old Port of Marseilles, over a period of years; many years ago. Concert version revival of the musical presented in thirteen scenes in two acts; February 4–7, 2010; 5 performances. The original production opened at the Majestic Theatre November 4, 1954; it transferred to the Belasco Theatre December 4, 1956, and closed December 16, 1956 after 888 performances (see *Theatre World* Vol. 11, page 34).

James Snyder and the Company in Fanny *(photo by Joan Marcus)*

Donna Murphy in Anyone Can Whistle *(photo by Carol Rosegg)*

Anyone Can Whistle Book by Arthur Laurents, music and lyrics by Stephen Sondheim; Director & Choreography, Casey Nicholaw; Costume Consultant, Gregg Barnes; Lighting, Ken Billington; Sound, Scott Lehrer & Leon Rothenberg; Original Orchestrations, Don Walker; Original Dance Arrangements, Betty Walberg; PSM, Karen Moore; Stage Manager, Rachel S. McCutchen; Associate Director, Casey Hushion; Associate Choreographer, Josh Rhodes; Associate Musical Director, David Gursky; Assistant Design Consultants: Hannah Davis (scenic), Sarah Sophia Lidz (costumes); Hair Design, Richard Orton; Rehearsal Pianists, Paul Ford, Mark Mitchell; Wardrobe Supervisor, Joby Horrigan; Sound Mixer, Kurt Fischer; Moving Lights, Josh Weitzman; Props Shopper, Brian Howard; Production Assistants, Sara Cox Bradley, Karen Evanouskas; Assistant to Mr. Nicolar, Seth Sikes; SSDC Observer, Matthew Hamel; **CAST:** Tally Sessions (First Narrator/George), Sara Jean Ford (Second Narrator/June), Brian Shepard (Third Narrator), Linda Griffin (Fourth Narrator/Mrs. Schroeder), Patrick Wetzel (Dr. Detmold), Donna Murphy (Cora Hoover Hooper), Clyde Alves, Grasan Kingsberry, Eric Sciotto, Anthony Wayne (The Boys), Edward Hibbert (Comptroller Schub), Jeff Blumenkrantz (Treasurer Cooley), Dana Steingold (Baby Joan), John Ellison Conlee (Poice Chief Magruder), Sutton Foster (Fay Apple), Raúl Esparza (J. Bowden Hapgood), Michael Marcotte (John), Max Kumangai (Martin), Holly Ann Butler (Jane Borden Osgood); Ensemble (*Cookies, Nurses, Deputies, Townspeople, Pilgrims, and Tourists):* Clyde Alves, Tanya Bril, Holly Ann Butler, J. Austin Eyer, Sara Jean Ford, Lisa Gajda, Stephanie Gibson, Linda Griffin, Karen Hyland, Natalie King, Grasan Kingsberry, Max Kumangai, Michael Marcotte, Joseph Medeiros, Denny Paschall, Monica L. Patton, Steve Schepis, Eric Sciotto, Tally Sessions, Brian Shepard, Dana Steingold, Brandon Tyler, Anthony Wayne, Patrick Wetzel; Orchestra: Rob Berman (Conductor); Roger Shell, Summer Boggess, Anja Wood, Annabelle Hoffman, Robert Burkhart (violins); John Beal (double bass); Susan Rotholtz, David Young, Andrew Sterman, Todd Groves, John Winder (woodwinds); William Schimmel (accordion); Scott Cady (piano); Russ Rizner, David Byrd-Marrow (French horns); James De La Garza, Glenn Drewes, Ken Rampton (trumpets); Bruce Bonvissuto, Jack Schatz (trombones); Richard Rosenzweig (drums); Erik Charlston (percussion).

Musical Numbers: Prelude Act I, I'm Like the Bluebird, Me and My Town, Miracle Song, There Won't Be Trumpets, Simple, Prelude Act II, A-1 March, Come Play Wiz Me, Anyone Can Whistle, A Parade in Town, Everybody Says Don't, I've Got You to Lean On, See What It Gets You, The Cookie Chase, With So Little to Be Sure Of, Reprise: I've Got You to Lean On, Finale

Setting: The present. A not too distant town. Concert version revival of the musical presented in twelve scenes in two acts; April 8–11, 2010; 5 performances. The original production opened at the Majestic Theatre on April 4, 1964 and closed a week later after only 12 previews and 9 performances (see *Theatre World* Vol. 20, page 100).

Sutton Foster and Raul Esparza in Anyone Can Whistle *(photo by Carol Rosegg)*

Classic Stage Company

Forty-second Season

Artistic Director, Brian Kulick; Executive Director, Jessica R. Jenen; General Manager, Jeff Griffin; Development, Audrey Carmeli; Associate Artistic Director, Tony Speciale; Audience Services, John C. Hume; Assistant General Manager, Meredith Lynsey Schade; Artistic Assistant, Greg Taubman; Education Outreach Coordinator, Jeffrey Feola; Casting, James Calleri; Art Direction and Design, Michael Yuen; Advertising, Eliran Murphy Group; Press, The Publicity Office, Marc Thibodeau

The Age of Iron Adapted from William Shakespeare's *Troilus & Cressida* and Thomas Heywood's *Iron Age*; Adaptor/Director, Brian Kulick; Set, Mark Wendland; Costumes, Oana Botez-Ban; Lighting, Brian H. Scott; Original Music & Sound, Christian Frederickson; Associate Director, Tony Speciale; PSM, Jenifer Shenker; ASM, Kara Teolis; Production Manager, Jack Blacketer; Fight Director, Adam Rihacek; Assistant Fight Director, Casey Robinson; Assistant Lighting, Steve O'Shea; Assistant Production Manager/Board Operator, Megan Caplan; Assistant Costumes, Abby Walton; Props Master, Alexandra Morton; **CAST**: Michael Potts (Homer); *Greeks*: Luis Moreno (Menelaus, *King of Sparta*), Tina Benko (Helen, *wife of Menelaus*), Mark H. Dold (Diomedes, *King of Argos*), Steven Rattazzi (Tersites, *a railer*), Graham Winton (Agamemnon, *King of Mycenae, Greek General*), Dion Mucciacito (Achilles), Bill Christ (Ajax), Steven Skybell (Ulysses, *King of Ithaca*), Xanthe Elbrick (Patroclus, *friend of Achilles*); *Trojans*: Andrew McGinn (Aeneas, *Trojan ally*), Craig Bladwin (Paris, *Prince of Troy*), Elliot Villar (Hector, *Prince of Troy, Trojan Commander*), Finn Wittrock (Troilus, *Prince of Troy*), Michael Potts (Priam, *King of Troy*), Dylan Moore (Cressida, *daughter of Calchas*), Xanthe Elbrick (Andromache, *wife of Hector*)

Craig Baldwin, Elliot Villar, Steven Skybell, and Finn Wittrock in The Age of Iron *(photo by T. Charles Erickson)*

Setting: Greece, during the Trojan War. World premiere of the melding of two classic plays presented in two acts; East 13th Street Theatre; November 6–December 13, 2009 (Opened November 22); 17 previews, 23 performances.

Xanthe Elbrick, Luis Moreno, Graham Winton, Elliot Villar, Bill Christ, Craig Baldwin, and Finn Wittrock in The Age of Iron *(photo by T. Charles Erickson)*

Venus in Fur by David Ives; Inspired by the novel by Leopold Scher-Masoch; Director, Walter Bobbie; Set, John Lee Beatty; Lighting, Peter Kaczorowski; Costumes, Anita Yavich; Sound, Acme Sound Partners; PSM, Christina Lowe; Production Manager, La Vie Productions/James E. Cleveland; Assistant Production Manager, Megan Caplan; Assistant Design: Kacie Hultgren (set), Gina Scherr (lighting), David Sanderson (sound), Nicky Smith (costumes); Technical Director, Joel Howell Jr.; Wardrobe, Kate Mincer; Scenic Artist, Hannah Davis; Tailor, Martin Prelle-Tworek; Props Master, Sarah Bird; **CAST**: Wes Bentley (Thomas); Nina Arianda (Vanda)

Setting: A rehearsal room in Manhattan; the present. World premiere of a comedy-drama presented without intermission; East 13th Street Theatre; January 13–March 28, 2010 (Opened January 26); 13 previews, 63 performances. **2010 Theatre World Award**: Nina Arianda

Wes Bentley and Nina Arianda in Venus in Fur *(photo by Joan Marcus)*

Nina Arianda and Wes Bentley in Venus in Fur *(photo by Joan Marcus)*

The Forest by Alexander Ostrovsky, adapted by Kathleen Tolan; Director, Brian Kulick; Set, Santo Loqusto; Lighting, Peter Kaczorowski; Costumes, Marco Piemontese; Original Music and Sound, Christian Frederickson, Ryan Rumery; Hair, Paul Huntley; Associate Director, Tony Speciale; PSM, Terry K. Kohler; Production Manager, La Vie Productions/James E. Cleveland; ASM, Kara Marie Teolis; Assistant Production Manager, Megan Caplan; Props Master, Sarah Bird; Associate Costume Design, Michelle Bohn; Assistant Design: Jennifer Sawyer (set), John Viesta (lighting), Luana Busetti (costumes); Technical Director, Joel Howell; Production Assistant, Alice Tolan Mee; **CAST**: Lisa Joyce, (Aksyucha), John Christopher Jones (Karp), Adam Driver (Bulanov), Lizbeth MacKay (Ulita), Dianne Wiest (Raisa), Herb Foster (Milonov), George Morfogen (Bodaev), Sam Tsoutsouvas (Vosimbratov), Quincy Dunn-Baker (Pyotr), John Douglas Thompson (Gennady), Tony Torn (Arkady)

Setting: Raisa's estate in Russia; 1870s. Revival of a period comedy of presented in two acts; East 13th Street Theatre; April 24–May 30, 2010 (Opened May 6); 11 previews, 27 performances. The Pearl Theatre produced the first New York production of the play October 31–November 30, 1997 (see *Theatre World* Vol. 54, page 99).

Dianne Wiest, John Douglas Thompson, and the Company in The Forest *(photo by Joan Marcus)*

Additional Events

First Look Festival: Pirandello November 16–30, 2009; Staged reading and workshop series of the works of Luigi Pirandello; November 16: *Six Characters in Search of an Author* directed by Tony Speciale; November 23: *Right You Are If You Think So* directed by Craig Baldwin; November 29–30: *Henry IV* directed by Brian Kulick, featuring John Turturro.

Monday Night Much Ado December 7 & 14, 2009, January 18 & 25, 2010; Open rehearsal series of the play by William Shakespeare; Presented in association with The Shakespeare Society; Directed by Michael Sexton, featuring Mandy Patinkin, Laila Robbins, and Kate Mulgrew.

The Young Company: Twelfth Night by William Shakespeare; Presented by the Graduate Acting Program of the Columbia University School for the Arts; Director, Tony Speciale; **CAST**: Grant Boyd (Toby Belch), Stacy Davidowitz (Maria), Justin Gilman (Fabian), Meera Rohit Kumbhani (Olivia), Jason Martin (Feste), Kelly McCrann (Viola), Brent Yoshikami (Antonio), Paul Caccamise, Christian T. Chan, Jabari Amir Jones, Erin Alexis, Jon Luke, Elizabeth Lee Malone, Amira Nader, Anjili J. Pal, Bari K. Robinson, Monica Santana; East 13th Street Theatre; February 22–March 5, 2010; 15 performances.

Books on Stage: *War and Peace* and *Anna Karenina* April 26, May 3 & 10, 2010; Second installment of a new series of staged readings of adaptations of the novels by Leo Tolstoy; featuring Michael Stuhlbarg and Marin Ireland.

Dianne Wiest in The Forest *(photo by Joan Marcus)*

Irish Repertory Theatre

Twenty-second Season

Artistic Director, Charlotte Moore; Producing Director, Ciarán O'Reilly; Audience Services, Jared Dawson; Business Manager, Dave Friedman; Development, Patrick A. Kelsey; Membership Manager, Abigail Lynn; Literary Manager, Kara Manning; Marketing, Melissa L. Pelkey; Box Office Manager, Jeffrey Wingfield; Casting, Deborah Brown; Dialect Coach, Stephen Gabis; Production Coordinator, Jake McGuire; Press, Shirley Herz Associates, Dan Demello

The Emperor Jones by Eugene O'Neill; Director, Ciarán O'Reilly; Choreography, Barry McNabb; Set, Charlie Corcoran; Costumes, Antonia Ford-Roberts; Lighting, Brian Nason; Original Music & Sound, Ryan Rumery and Christian Frederickson; Puppet & Mask Design, Bob Flannagan; Properties, Deidre Brennan; PSM, Pamela Brusoski; ASM, Rebecca C. Monroe; Assistant Costumes, Whitney Locher; Assistant to Lighting Designer, Luamar Ciervejeira; Lighting Programmer, Tyler Cofman; Set Construction, Ken Larson; Scenic Artists, Anne Hewett, Sarah Pearline; Master Carpenter, Donal O'Reilly; Master Electrician, Michael J. Barczys; Wardrobe, Deirdre Higgins; Graphics, Melissa L. Pelkey; **CAST:** Sameerah Lugmaan-Harris (Old Native Woman, Ensemble), Rick Foucheux (Henry Smithers, a Cockney Trader), John Douglas Thompson (Brutus Jones, Emperor), Jon Deliz (Ensemble, Dandy), Michael Akil Davis (Ensemble, Crocodile God), Sinclair Mitchel (Ensemble, Witch Doctor), David Heron (Lem, a Native Chief, Ensemble)

Setting: A West Indian island not yet self-determined by white marines. The form of government is, for the moment, an empire. Revival of a play presented without in eight scenes without intermission; Francis J. Greenburger Mainstage; October 7–December 6, 2009 (Opened October 18); 13 previews, 50 performances. The production transferred to Soho Playhouse for a commercial extension December 15, 2009–January 31, 2010 (see Off-Broadway section in this volume). The Provincetown Players presented the world premiere of the play at the Playwrights Theater (the Neighborhood Playhouse) November 1, 1920, and transferred the show to the Selwyn Theatre then later to the Princess Theatre, where it closed in April 1921 after 204 performances. It had three brief revivals in 1925, 1926, and 1927, and the Federal Theatre Project (part of the W.P.A.) launched several productions in cities across the U.S. in the 1930s. The Wooster Group recently revived the play at St. Ann's Warehouse March 11, 2006 (see *Theatre World* Vol. 62, page 121).

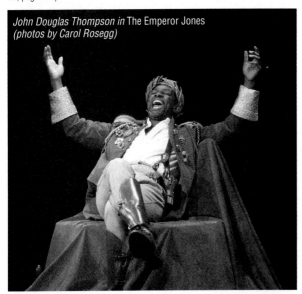

John Douglas Thompson in The Emperor Jones *(photos by Carol Rosegg)*

Noah Racey and Ian Holcomb in Ernest in Love

Ernest in Love Book and lyrics by Anne Croswell, music by Lee Pockriss, based on *The Importance of Being Ernest* by Oscar Wilde; Director, Charlotte Moore; Music Director, Mark Hartman; Choreography, Barry McNabb; Set, James Morgan; Costumes, Linda Fisher; Lighting, Brian Nason; Wigs & Hair, Robert-Charles Vallance; Props Master, Rich Murray; PSM, Christine Lemme; ASM, Kelly Glasgow; Production Assistant, Dug Baker; Assistant to Ms. Moore, Ellen Orchid; Set Construction, Daddy O Productions; Scenic Artist, Maura Kelly; Assistant to Mr. Nason, Luamar Ciervejeira; Lighting Programmer, Tyler Coffman; Master Carpenter, Donal O'Reilly; Master Electrician, Michael J. Barczys; Wardrobe, Deirdre Higgins; Assistant to Mr. Vallance, Sara Bender; Assistant to Mr. Morgan, Matt Allamon; Digital Graphics, Jeb Knight, Scott Dela Cruz; Music Assistant, Matthew Webb; **CAST:** Noah Racey (Jack Worthing), Brad Bradley (Merriman/Lane), Annika Boras (Gwendolen Fairfax), Kerry Conte (Alice/Effie), Ian Holcomb (Algernon Moncrieff), Beth Fowler (Lady Augusta Bracknell), Kristin Griffith (Miss Prism), Katie Fabel (Cecily Cardew), Peter Maloney (Dr. Chasuble); Musicians: Mark Hartman (Conductor/keyboard), Karen Lindquist (harp), Matthew Herren (cello), Vonnie Quinn (violin)

Musical Numbers: How Do You Find the Words?, The Hat, Mr. Bunbury, Perfection, A Handbag Is Not a Proper Mother, Mr Bunbury (reprise), A Wicked Man, Metaphorically Speaking, A Wicked Man (reprise), You Can't Make Love, Lost, My Very First Impression, The Muffin Song, Couples Waltz, A Handbag Is Not a Proper Mother (reprise), The Muffin Song (reprise), Finale (Ernest In Love)

Setting: 1890s; Midsummer in London and Hertfordshire in Jack's flat, Gwendolyn's room, Algy's flat, the gardens and morning room of the Manor House. Revival of a musical presented in eight scenes in two acts; Francis J. Greenburger Mainstage; December 12, 2009–February 14, 2010 (Opened December 20); 9 previews, 57 performances. World premiere May 4, 1960 at the Grammercy Arts Theatre where it closed after 103 performances (see *Theatre World* Vol. 16, page 168).

Candida by George Bernard Shaw; Director/Design, Tony Walton; Lighting, Richard Pilbrow; Associate Set, Heather Wolensky; Sound, Zach Williamson & Jana Hoglund; Wigs & Hair, Robert-Charles Vallance; Properties, Deidre Brennan; PSM, April A. Kline; ASM, Rosie Goldman; Co-Producer, Alexis Doyle; Associate Lighting, Michael Gottlieb; Production Coordinator, Jake McGuire; Assistant to Mr. Vallance, Sara Bender; Production Scenic, Ann Keebaugh; Scenery Construction, The Ken Larson Company; Master Carpenter, Donal O'Reilly; Master Electrician, Michael J. Barczys; Wardrobe Supervisor, Deirdre Higgins; Alterations, Mariko Tokushige; Assistant Props, Rich Murray; Assistant to Ms. Brennan, Stephanie Shannon; Set Model Assistance, Matt Allamon, David Towlun; **CAST:** Ciarán O'Reilly (The Rev. James Morell, *Candida's husband*), Xanthe Elbrick (Miss Proserpine Garnett, *Morrell's typist*), Josh Grisetti (The Rev. Alexander Mill, *Morrell's curate*), Brian Murray (Mr. Burgess, *Candida's father*), Melissa Errico (Candida), Sam Underwood (Eugene Marchbanks, *a shy, poetic youth*)

Setting: October 1894; The Morrell's Home, off Victoria Park in the northeast suburbs of London. Revival of a comedy presented in two acts; Francis J. Greenburger Mainstage; February 24–April 25, 2010 (Opened March 7); 13 previews, 50 performances. The first American production of the play was presented at the Princess Theatre in New York December 9, 1903–April 1904. The play has had thirteen major revivals; the Roundabout Theatre Company produced the most recent revival at Criterion Center Stage Right March 25–May 2, 1993 (see *Theatre World* Vol. 49, page 32). Katherine Cornell starred as "Candida" in the 1924, 1942, and 1946 revivals, the later featuring a young Marlon Brando as "Eugene" (see *Theatre World* Vol. 2, page 87).

Ciarán O'Reilly and Melissa Errico in Candida

Greg Mullavey, Charlie Hudson III, Gordon Stanley, Evan Zes, and Stephen Payne in White Woman Street

Projections, Graham Johnson; Lighting Programmer, Megan Peti; Scenic Artist, Matt Allamon; Master Electrician, Tom Dyer; Master Carpenter, Donal O'Reilly; Carpenter, Rory Duffy; Wardrobe Supervisor, Deirdre Higgins; Intern, Hannah Goldstein; **CAST**: Kerry Conte (Ensemble), Terry Donnelly (Ensemble), Ciarán Sheehan (Ensemble), Patrick Shields (Violin, Mandolin, Bodhran), Gary Troy (Ensemble), Kevin B. Winebold (Piano, Accordion, Ensemble)

Musical Numbers: Opening Medley [The Rose of Tralee, Believe Me If All Those Endearing Young Charms, The Holy Ground, Galway Bay, Carrickfergus, I'll Take You Home Again Kathleen, If You're Irish, Too-Ra-Loo-Ra-Loo-Ra, Come Back Paddy Reilly], Mrs. McGrath, Mother Machree, The Rare Ould Times, The Fields of Athenry, Skibbereen, Shores of Amerikay, Anchors Aweigh, No Irish Need Apply, An Irish Washerwoman, No Irish Need Apply (reprise), Erie Canal, Give My Regards to Broadway, Yankee Doodle Dandy, I've Got Rings On My Fingers, Has Anybody Here Seen Kelly?, Give My Regards to Broadway (reprise), Paddy on the Railway, Moonshiner, Danny Boy, Who Threw the Overalls in Mrs. Murphy's Chowder?, Finnegan's Wake, Dixie, Ireland Boys Hurray, The Ghost of Molly McGuire; You're a Grand Old Flag/Over There, I'll Be Home for Christmas, Johnny I Hardley Knew Ye, I Still Haven't Found What I'm Looking For

Revival of a musical revue presented in two acts; Francis J. Greenburger Mainstage; July 14–September 26, 2010 (Opened July 22); 9 previews, 66 performances. World premiere (featuring Ms. Donnelly and Mr. Sheehan) at the Irish Repertory Theatre June 22–September 7, 1997 (see *Theatre World* Vol. 54, page 85).

White Woman Street by Sebastian Barry; Director, Charlotte Moore; Set, Hugh Landwehr; Costumes, David Toser; Lighting, Clifton Taylor; Sound, Zachary Williamson; Properties, Deirdre Brennan; Guitar Recording, Michael Gomez; PSM, Elis C. Arroyo; ASM, Rebecca C. Monroe; Scenic Artist, Sarah Brown; Assistant to Mr. Landwehr, Caleb Levenwood; Master Electrician, Jared Welsh; Master Carpenter, Donal O'Reilly; Wardrobe Supervisor, Deirdre Higgins; Assistant to Mrs. Brennan, Stephanie Shannon; **CAST**: Stephen Payne (Trooper O'Hara), Greg Mullavey (Blakely), Gordan Stanley (Mo Mason), Evan Zes (Nathaniel Yeshov), Charlie Hudson III (James Miranda), Ron Crawford (Clarke)

Setting: 1916, Ohio. U.S. premiere of a 1992 play presented in thirteen scenes in two acts; Francis J. Greenburger Mainstage; May 7–June 27, 2010 (Opened May 16); 10 previews, 43 performances.

The Irish...and How They Got That Way by Frank McCourt; Director, Charlotte Moore; Music Director, Kevin B. Winebold; Choreography, Barry McNabb; Original Musical Arrangements, Rusty Magee; Sets and Projections, Shawn Lewis; Costumes, David Toser; Lighting, Michael Gottlieb; PSM, Christine Lemme; ASM, Megan J. Alvord; Assistant Director, Teddy Eck; Associate

Patrick Shields, Gary Troy, Kerry Conte, Terry Donnelly, Ciaran Sheehan, and Kevin B. Winebold in The Irish... and How They Got That Way

Keen Company

Tenth Season

Artistic Director, Carl Forsman; Executive Director, Wayne Kelton; Education Director, Blake Lawrence; Resident Director, Jonathan Silverstein; Company Manager, Laura Braza; Production Manager, Josh Bradford; Casting, Judy Bowman; Press, Richard Kornberg & Associates, Billy Zavelson

Such Things Only Happen in Books Short plays and playlets by Thorton Wilder: *Cement Hands*, *Such Things Only Happen in Books*, *The Angel That Troubled the Water*, *Now the Servant's Name Was Malchus*, *In Shakespeare and the Bible*; Directors, Carl Forsman & Jonathan Silverstein; Set, Sandra Goldmark; Costumes, Theresa Squire; Lighting, Josh Bradford; Music Director, Brian Cimmet; PSM, Jess Johnston; **CAST**: Clayton Apgar, Pepper Binkley, Kathleen Butler, Sue Cremin, Kevin Hogan, Paul Niebanck

New York professional premiere of five short plays presented without intermission; Clurman Theatre on Theatre Row; October 6–November 14, 2009 (Opened October 18); 13 previews, 28 performances.

Clayton Apgar, Pepper Binkley, and Kathleen Butler in Such Things Only Happen in Books *(photo by Theresa Squire)*

Paul Niebanck and Sue Cremin in Such Things Only Happen in Books *(photo by Theresa Squire)*

I Never Sang for My Father by Robert Anderson; Presented in association with Wiltsie Bridge Productions; Director, Jonathan Silverstein; Sets, Bill Clarke; Costumes, Theresa Squire; Lighting, Josh Bradford; Sound, Will Pickens; Stage Manager, Jess Johnston; Keir Dullea (Tom Garrison), Marsha Mason (Margaret Garrison), Matt Savitto (Gene Garrison), Rose Courtney (Alice), Melissa Miller (Mary/Nurse Halsey), Hal Robinson (Porter/Reverend Pell/Marvin Scott/Dr. Mayberry)

Setting: New York City and a town in Westchester County. Late 1960s and the past. Revival of a play presented in two acts; Clurman Theatre on Theatre Row; March 23–May 1, 2010 (Opened April 4); 13 previews, 29 performances. Originally produced on Broadway at the Longacre Theatre January 24–May 11, 1968 (see *Theatre World* Vol. 24, page 39).

Keir Dullea, Matt Servitto, Marsha Mason, and Melissa Miller in I Never Sang for My Father *(photo by Suzi Sadler)*

Matt Servitto, Rose Courtney, and Keir Dullea in I Never Sang for My Father *(photo by Suzi Sadler)*

Special Events

The Good Thief by Conor McPherson; Director, Carl Forsman; **CAST**: Brian d'Arcy James

Revival of a solo performance play presented without intermission as a benefit for Keen Company; Lucille Lortel Theatre; November 2, 2009; 1 performance.

Keen Teens Three plays written and performed by teens; Clurman Theatre on Theatre Row; May 28–May 30, 2010.

And Then I Wrote 'The Music Man' based on Meredith Willson's book *But He Doesn't Know the Territory*; Director, Carl Forsman; Music Director/Accompaniment, Brian Cimmet; **CAST**: Brian d'Arcy James (Meredith Willson), Kelli O'Hara (Rini Willson)

World premiere of a reading of a new play presented without intermission as part of Keen Company's Tenth Annual Benefit; Lucille Lortel Theatre; June 16, 2010; 1 performance.

LAByrinth Theater

Eighteenth Season

Artistic Director, Stephen Adly Guirgis, Mimi O'Donnell, and Yul Vázquez; Producing Director, Marieke Gaboury; Development, Veronica R. Bainbridge; Company Manager, Kristina Poe; Literary Manager, Monique Carboni; Bookkeeper/Office Manager, Nicola Hughes; Marketing Consultant, Amada Woods; Marketing Coordinator, Willie Orbison; Social Media Associate, Laura Ramadei; Founding Artistic Directors, John Ortiz, Philip Seymour Hoffman; Press, O+M Company, Rick Miramontez, Philip Carrubba

Othello by William Shakespeare; Co-presented by the Public Theater (Oskar Eustis, Artistic Director; Andrew D. Hamingson, Executive Director) in association with Wienner Festwochen (Vienna), Schauspielhaus Bochum, and by special arrangement with NYU Skirball Center; Director, Peter Sellers; Sets, Gregor Holzinger; Costumes, Mimi O'Donnell; Lighting, James F. Ingalls, Original Music and Sound, Mark Grey; Technical Artist, Cath Brittan; PSM, Pamela Salling; Stage Manager, Ruth E. Sternberg; Dramaturgy, Barry Edelstein; Production Manager, C. Townsend Olcott II; Associate Director, Robert Castro; Assistant Lighting, Seth Reiser; Sunday Speaker Series Coordinator, Avery T. Willis; Production Assistant, Dave Polato; Front of House Engineer, Jake Scudder; Audio Load-In Crew, Yusuke Hama, Matthew Gibney; Wardrobe Supervisor, Kimberly Baird; Master Electrician/Board Operator, Jon Grenay; Light Board Programmer, Stephanie Palmer; Electricians, Andy Knapp, Alex Taylor, Heather Berg; Prop Shopper, Natalie Taylor Hart; Set Construction/Load-In, Mary Elizabeth Barnes, Joe Powell; Video, Georg Eisnecker, Gert Tschuden; Video Operator, Brandon Epperson; Production Crew, Jorge Cortes, Sean Kelso, Matt Micucci, Loren Pratt; **CAST**: Julian Acosta (Roderigo, *a Venetian gentleman*), Gaius Charles (Duke of Venice), Jessica Chastain (Desdemona, *Othello's wife and daughter of the Venetian senator Brabantio*), Liza Colón-Zayas (Emilia, *Iago's wife*), Saidah Arrika Ekulona (Bianca Montano, *Governor of Cyprus who is replaced by Othello*), Philip Seymour Hoffman (Iago, *Othello's ensign*), Leroy McClain (Cassio, *an honorable lieutenant in Othello's service*), John Ortiz (Othello, *a Moor in the service of the Venetian state*)

Revival of a play presented in two acts; Jack H. Skirball Center for the Performing Arts; September 12–October 4, 2009 (Opened September 27); 13 previews, 10 performances.

Workshops and Readings

Barn Series 2009 and **Live Nude Plays 2009** Tenth annual reading series (Barn Series) and fourth annual reading series (Live Nude Plays); Shiva Theater; October 6–30, 2009 (Barn Series), October 31–November 3, 2010 Live Nude Plays); **Barn Series** included: *Love Sick* by Kristina Poe, directed by Mimi O'Donnell (October 6 &7); *Ninth and Joanie* written and directed by Brett C. Leonard (October 8); *Lights Up on the Fade Out* by Padraic Lillis, directed by Marieke Gaboury (October 9 & 14); *Its Hers Now* by Bob Glaudini, directed by Mimi O'Donnell (October 10 & 11); *Pirate* written and directed by John Patrick Shanley (October 12); *Single Mom* by Rebecca Cohen, directed by Marieke Gaboury (October 15 & 17); *The Hard Sell* by Andrea Ciannavei, directed by Scott Illingsworth (October 16 & 18); *Dutch Masters* by Greg Keller, directed by Brian Roff (October 19 & 26); *Paradox of the Urban Cliché* by Craig "muMs" Grant, directed by Sarah Sidman (October 22 & 24); *The Atmosphere of Memory* by David Bar Katz, directed by Peter DuBois (October 23 & 27); *Conservative Right and You're Wrong* by Ed Vassallo, directed by Brian Roff (October 25 & 28); *Cynthia and the Dreadful Kite* by Webb Wilcoxen, music by Jonathan Comisar, directed by Jill DeArmon (October 29 & 30)**; Live Nude Plays** included: *'68* conceived and directed by John Gould Rubin (October 31); *Beautiful* by David Anzuelo, directed by Louis Moreno (October 31); *Handball* by Seth Svi Rosenfeld, directed by Terry Kinny (November 1); *girl in window* by Florencia Lozano, directed by Pedro Pascal (November 1); *The Halal Brothers* by Alladin Ullah (November 2); *The Talk* by

Frank Pugliese, directed by Fisher Stevens (November 2); *Neurotica* by David Deblinger, directed by Padraic Lillis (November 3); *Frequently Unasked Questions* by Daphne Rubin-Vega, directed by John Gould Rubin (November 3); **CAST** (both series): Julian Acosta, Betsy Aidem, Cara Akselrad, Carlo Alban, Eric Bogosian, Maggie Burke, Elizabeth Canavan, Bobby Cannavale, Samrat Chakrabarti, Chris Chalk, Andrea Ciannavei, Beth Cole, J. Eric Cook, Kevin Corrigan, David Deblinger, Jamie Dunn, Danelle Eliav, Nia Fairweather, Marieke Gaboury, Lola Glaudini, Charles Goforth, Yetta Gottesman, Craig "muMs" Grant, Nic Grelli, Scott Hudson, Salvatore Inzerillo, Russell G. Jones, Jinn S. Kim, Jamie Klassel, Angela Lewis, Trevor Long, Florencia Lozano, Eric T. Miller, Tomoko Miyagi, Nyambi Nyambi, Kelley Rae O'Donnell, Pedro Pascal, Richard Petrocelli, Michael Puzzo, Justin Reinsilber, Joselin Reyes, Elizabeth Rodriguez, Gerry Rodriguez, Melissa Ross, Daphne Rubin-Vega, Matthew Stadelman, Alladin Ullah, Carlos Valencia, Ed Vassallo, Yul Vázquez, Katherine Waterston, Aaron Weiner, Sid Williams, Max Woertendyke, David Zayas.

Celebrity Charades Annual benefit for the company; Charade Host, Eric Bogosian; Auction Host, John Patrick Shanley; **CAST**: Julia Roberts, Philip Seymour Hoffman, Bobby Cannavale, Kristen Wiig, Sam Rockwell, Daphne Rubin-Vega, Jesse L. Martin, Julia Stiles, Christopher Meloni, David Zayas, Padma Lakshmi, Billy Crudup, John Ortiz, Cynthia Rowley, Tom Colicchio, Shannon Elizabeth, Yul Vázquez, Bob Balaban and Ian Astbury; The Chuch of Saint Paul the Apostle; December 7, 2009.

The 29 Hour Development Workshop Three new plays by LAByrinth members from the Live Nude Plays series receiving 29 hours of rehearsal and table work, then presented as staged readings; Included: *Lights Up On the Fade Out* by Padraic Lillis, directed by Stephen Adly Guirgis, with Trevor Long, Richard Petrocelli, Daphne Rubin-Vega, Sidney Williams (April 7, 2010); *Love Sick* by Kristina Poe, directed by Mimi O'Donnell, with Julian Acosta, Cara Akselrad, Maggie Burke, Elizabeth Canavan, Charles Goforth, Scott Hudson, Michael Stuhlbarg (April 26, 2010); *FUQ (frequently unasked questions)* by Daphne Rubin-Vega, directed by John Gould-Rubin, with Carlo Alban, Raúl Castillo, Larua Ramadei, Daphne Rubin-Vega and her band: Tony Cruz, Robert Morris, Steven Morris, Joe Passaro, Dan Weiss (June 2010).

Dutch Masters and **Paradox of the Urban Cliché** Co-Producers, Carlo Alban, Kelley Rae O'Donnell, Andre Royo; *Dutch Masters* by Greg Keller; Director, Brian Roff; **CAST**: Amari Cheatom, Seth Numrich; *Paradox of the Urban Cliché* by Craig "muMs" Grant; Director, Sarah Sidman; **CAST**: Sheldon Best, Suzette Azariah Gunn, Warner Miller, Sidney Williams

Two new plays in development presented in repertory; The Cherry Pit Theater; May 14–30, 2010; 14 performances each.

The Monkey Show Book, lyrics and direction by John Patrick Shanley, music by Henry Krieger; Hosts, Jackie Judd and Peter Picard; Co-Hosts, Jeffrey A. Horwitz and Debbie Ohanian; **CAST**: Carlo Alban, Ivette Dumeng, Bill Evans, Ivan Hernandez, Sal Inzerillo, Andy Karl, Angela Lewis, Mark Linn-Baker, Orfeh, Ina Marie Smith, Mary Testa

A musical safari into the fevered hearts of apes in love presented as the company's spring benefit; Lucille Lortel Theatre; May 10, 2010.

Liza Colon-Zayas and Jessica Chastain in Othello (*photos by Armin Bardel*)

Lincoln Center Theater

Twenty-fifth Season

Artistic Director, André Bishop; Executive Producer, Bernard Gersten; General Manager, Adam Siegel; Production Manager, Jeff Hamlin; Development, Hattie K. Jutagir; Finance, David S. Brown; Marketing, Linda Mason Ross; Education, Kati Koerner; Associate Directors, Graciela Danielle, Nicholas Hytner, Jack O'Brien, Susan Stroman, Daniel Sullivan; Resident Director, Bartlett Sher; Dramaturg and Director of Director of LCT Directors Lab, Anne Cattaneo; Musical Theatre Associate Producer, Ira Weitzman; LCT3 Director, Paige Evans; Casting, Daniel Swee; House Manager, William Cannon; Advertising, Serino Coyne; Principal Poster Art, James McMullen; Press, Philip Rinaldi, Barbara Carroll

Broke-ology by Nathan Louis Jackson; Director, Thomas Kail; Set, Donyale Werle; Costumes, Emily Rebholz; Lighting, Jason Lyons; Sound, Jill BC DuBoff; Stage Manager, Rachel S. McCutchen; ASM, Andrea O. Saraffian; Company Manager, Jessica Perlmeter Cochrane; Assistant Company Manager, Daniel Hoyos; Assistant Director, Anika Chapin; Associate Set, Grady Barker; Assistant Design: Mira Veikley (costumes), Grant Wilcoxsen (lighting), David Sanderson, Brandon Wollcott (sound); Assistant to Sound Designer, Daniel Carlyon; Props, Susan Barras; Props Assistant, Meredith Ries; Draftsman, Todd Porter; Crew: Josh Rich (light board), Adam Smolenski (sound), Sheri Maher (wardrobe supervisor), Elizabeth Strader (dresser), Sara Cox Bradley (production assistant); **CAST**: Wendell Pierce (William King), Crystal A. Dickinson (Sonia King), Francois Battiste (Ennis King), Alano Miller (Malcolm King); Understudies: Wiley Moore (William), Larry Powell (Ennis and Malcolm), Lisa Strum (Sonia)

Time/Place: 1982 and 2009; Kansas City, Kansas. New York premiere of a new play presented in two acts; Mitzi E. Newhouse Theatre; September 10–November 22, 2009 (Opened October 5); 28 previews, 56 performances. World premiere produced by the Williamstown Theatre Festival (Nicholas Martin, Artistic Director) July 9–20, 2008.

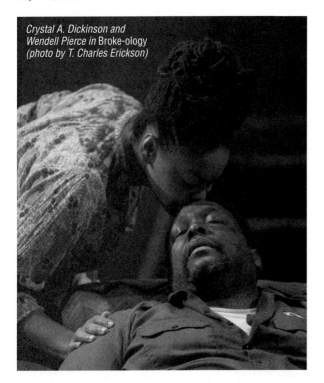

Crystal A. Dickinson and Wendell Pierce in Broke-ology *(photo by T. Charles Erickson)*

Francois Battiste, Wendell Pierce, and Alano Miller in Broke-ology *(photo by T. Charles Erickson)*

When the Rain Stops Falling by Andrew Bovell; Director, David Cromer; Sets, David Korins; Costumes, Clint Ramos; Lighting, Tyler Micoleau; Sound, Fitz Patton; Original Music, Josh Schmidt; Stage Manager, Richard A. Hodge; Hair and Wigs, Jon Carter; Makeup, Angelina Avallone; Dialect Coach, Stephen Gabis; Fight Director, Thomas Schall; Company Manager, Matthew Markoff; Associate Company Manager, Josh Lowenthal; Assistant Company Manager, Daniel Hoyos; Assistant to Mr. Cromer, Michael Padden; Associate Set, Rod Lemmond; Assistant Design: Luke Brown (costumes), Shawn Boyle (lighting); Assistant to Sound Designer, Bridget O'Connor; Props, Faye Armon; Prop Assistant, Kate Costin; Running Crew: Chelsea Roth (hair & makeup supervisor), Josh Rich (light board), Adam Smolenski (sound board), Sheri Maher (wardrobe supervisor), Elizabeth Strader (dresser), Danny Sharron (production assistant); **CAST**: Kate Blumberg (Elizabeth Law, *younger*), Richard Topol (Henry Law), Mary Beth Hurt (Elizabeth Law, *older*), Will Rogers (Gabriel Law), Susan Pourfar (Gabrielle York, *younger*), Victoria Clark (Gabrielle York, *older*), Rod McLachlan (Joe Ryan), Michael Siberry (Gabriel York), Henry Vick (Andrew Price); Understudies: Morgan Hallett (Elizabeth Law, *younger*/Gabrielle York, *younger*), Greg McFadden (Henry Law), Lee Roy Rogers (Elizabeth Law, *older*/Gabrielle York, *older*), Ben Graney (Gabriel Law/Andrew Price), Guy Paul (Joe Ryan/Gabriel York)

Time/Place: Back and forth in time between 1959 and 2039 in London, England and Adelaide, Alice Springs, Ayres Rock, and the Coorong on the Southern Coast of Australia. U.S. premiere of a new play presented without intermission; Mitzi E. Newhouse Theatre; February 11–April 18, 2010 (Opened March 8); 28 previews, 48 performances. Commissioned and originally produced by Brink Productions in Australia in 2008.

Victoria Clark, Kate Blumberg, Mary Beth Hurt, and Susan Pourfar in When the Rain Stops Falling *(photo by T. Charles Erickson)*

Michael Siberry (standing), Victoria Clark, and Richard Topol in When the Rain Stops Falling *(photo by T. Charles Erickson)*

The Grand Manner by A.R. Gurney; Director, Mark Lamos; Sets, John Arnone; Costumes, Ann Hould Ward; Lighting, Russell H. Champa; Original Music and Sound, John Gromada; Hair and Wigs, Paul Huntley; Stage Manager, M.A. Howard; ASM, Sara Cox Bradley; Company Manager, Matthew Markoff; Assistant Company Manager, Daniel Hoyos; Assistant Director, Michael Chamberlin; Associate Set, James Fenton; Assistant Design: Christopher Vergara (costumes), Justin Partier (lighting), Matthew Walsh (sound), Props Coordinator, Faye Armon; Props Assistants, Marina Guzman, Flora Kogan; Makeup, Cindy Demand; Running Crew: Josh Rich (light board), Adam Smolenski (sound board), Sheri Maher (wardrobe supervisor), Katherine White (production assistant); **CAST**: Bobby Steggert (Pete), Brenda Wehle (Gertrude Macy), Kate Burton (Katharine Cornell), Boyd Gaines (Guthrie McClintic); Understudies: Stephen James Anthony (Pete), Susan Wilder (Gertrude Macy, Katharine Cornell), Jack Koenig (Guthrie McClintic)

Time/Place: February, 1948. New York City. World premiere of a new play presented without intermission; Mitzi E. Newhouse Theatre; June 2–August 1, 2010 (Opened June 27); 29 previews, 41 performances.

Boyd Gaines and Kate Burton in The Grand Manner *(photo by Joan Marcus)*

LCT3 Series – The Steinberg New Works Program

What Once We Felt by Ann Marie Healy; Director, Ken Rus Schmoll; Set, Kris Stone; Costumes, Linda Cho; Lighting, Japhy Weideman; Sound, Leah Gelpe; Stage Manager, Jane Pole; ASM, Megan Schwarz; Company Manager, Josh Lowenthal; Assistant Director, Mia Rovegno; Assistant Design: Alexis Distler (set), Kerry Gibbons (costumes), Tamora Wilson (lighting), David Roy (sound); Projections, Leah Gelpe; Prop Master, Faye Armon; Assistant Props, Deborah Mangrum-Price; Running Crew: Kate Conover (light board), Bill Grady (sound board), Alex Bartlett (wardrobe supervisor), Liz Goodrum (dresser), Sandi Kroll, Kelsey Robinson (deck crew); **CAST**: Ronete Levenson (Violet), Lynn Hawley (Cheryl/Benita/Paulina Petrovsky), Mia Barron (Macy), Ellen Parker (Astrid/Yarrow), Opal Alladin (Female Server/Claire/Joan) Marsha Stephanie Blake (Franny/Laura/Bourder Guard)

World premiere of a new play presented in two acts; Duke on 42nd Street; October 26–November 21, 2009 (Opened November 9); 16 previews, 16 performances.

Graceland by Ellen Fairy; Director, Henry Wishcamper; Sets, Robin Vest; Costumes, Anne Kenney; Lighting, Matthew Richards; Sound, Bart Fasbender; Projections, Aaron Rhyne; Stage Manager, Janet Takami; ASM, Dan Barnhill; Company Manager, Josh Lowenthal; Assistant Director, Jenny Mercein; Associate Costumes, Scott Dougan; Associate Sound, Dave Sanderson; Assistant Lighting, Wilburn Bonnell, Steven Maturno; Assistants to Designers: Nicholas Quinn

Bobby Steggert, Brenda Wehle, and Kate Burton (reclining) in The Grand Manner *(photo by Joan Marcus)*

(sound), Linsey Bostwick (projections); Fight Director, Mark Olsen; Prop Master, Faye Armon; Running Crew: Kate Conover (light board), Bill Grady (sound board), Alex Bartlett (wardrobe supervisor), Marina Guzman, Flora Kogan (prop assistants), Ernie Johns (deck crew); **CAST**: Matt McGrath (Sam), Marin Hinkle (Sara), Brian Kerwin (Joe), David Gelles Hurwitz (Miles), Polly Lee (Anna)

Setting: Chicago's Graceland Cemetary. The living/dining room of a low-end high rise. The roof of the high-rise. New York premiere of a new play presented without intermission; Duke on 42nd Street; May 3–29, 2010 (Opened May 17); 15 previews, 16 performances.

Mia Barron and Opal Alladin in What Once We Felt
(photo by Gregory Costanzo)

Brian Kerwin and Marin Hinkle in Graceland
(photo by Gregory Costanzo)

On the Levee Conceived and directed by Lear deBessonet, play by Marcus Gardley, music and lyrics by Todd Almond; Sets, Peter Ksander; Costumes, Emily Rebholz; Lighting, Justin Townsend; Sound, Leon Rothenberg; Music Director/Orchestrations/Vocal Arrangements, Todd Almond; Movement, Tracy Bersley; Projections, Ryan Holsopple; Casting, MelCap Casting; Stage Manager, Jane Pole; Art, Kara Walker; ASM, Marisa Levy; Company Manager, Josh Lowenthal; Vocal Coach, Deborah Hecht; Assistant Director, Charlotte Brathwaite; Playwright's Assistant, Anne Erbe; Assistant Design: Andreea Mincic (set), Mira Veikley, Denise Maroney (costumes), Kristen Opstad, Juliana Beecher (lighting), Bill Grady (sound); Designer Assistants: Ann Perdita (costumes), Molly Spier (sound); Wigs, Leah Loukas; Dance Captain, Harriett D. Foy; Master Carpenter, Adam Shive; Master Electrician, Nathan Winner; Prop Master, Sarah Bird; Running Crew: Kate Conover (light board), Bill Grady (sound board), Alex Bartlett (wardrobe and hair supervisor), Joseph Armon, Elizabeth Goodrum (dressers), Ian Jurgensen, Adam Shive (deck crew), Maggie Swing (production assistant); **CAST**: Brian D. Coats (Buford, *a levee man*), Jacob Ming-Trent (Cephus, *another levee man*), Chuck Cooper (Old Lucas, *a town elder*), Dion Graham (Joe Gooden, *the Percy's bootblack*), Harriett D. Foy (Queen Black, *the Percy's housekeeper*), Michael Siberry (LeRoy Percy, *former senator, the wealthiest man in town*), Maria Couch (Petulia Croserie, *a socialite*), Seth Numrich (Will Percy, *LeRoy's son, a poet and former soldier*), Stephen Plunkett (L'Amour Mason, *a local bachelor*), Amari Cheatom (James Gooden, *Joe's son and proprietor of The Sugar Shack, a juke joint*), Shelley Thomas (Nana Pearson, *James' girlfriend*), April Matthis (Puddin Birdsong, *Rev. Booker's daughter*), Chuck Cooper (Rev. Booker, *a town preacher*)

Setting: 1927, Greenville, Mississippi. World premiere of a new play with music presented in three acts with one intermission and one brief pause; Duke on 42nd Street; June 14–July 10, 2010 (Opened June 28); 15 previews, 16 performances.

(Foreground) Stephen Plunkett, Chuck Cooper, and April Mathis in
On the Levee *(photo by Erin Baino)*

MCC Theater (Manhattan Class Company)

Twenty-fourth Season

Artistic Directors, Robert LuPone & Bernard Telsey; Associate Artistic Director, William Cantler; Executive Director, Blake West; General Manager, Ted Rounsaville; Company Manager/Assistant General Manager, Kristina Bramhall/ Ann Mundorff; Literary Manager/Dramaturg, Stephen Willems; Development, Erica Lynn Schwartz; Development Associate, Jennifer Udden; Marketing, Ian Allen; Marketing Associate, Isabel Sinistore; Education/Outreach, John Michael DiResta; Youth Company Artistic Director, Stephen DiMenna; Production Manager, B.D. White; Resident Playwright, Neil LaBute; Technical Director, Joe Reddington; Producing Special Arrangements, The Lucille Lortel Theatre Foundation; Casting, Telsey + Company; Press, O+M Company, Rick Miramontez, Jon Dimond, Molly Barnett

Still Life by Alexander Dinelaris; Director, Will Frears; Set, David Cornis; Costumes, Sarah J. Holden; Lighting, David Weiner; Sound, Fitz Patton; Original Music, Michael Freidman; PSM, Christine Lemme; Assistant Director, Portia Krieger; Stage Manager, Shanna Spinello; Production Assistant, Tim Kava; Properties, Jeremy Lydic; Onstage Photo Photography, Tamara Staples; Video Coordinator, Aron Deyo; Associate Design: Rod Lemmond (set), Amelie Chunleau (costumes), Lauren Phillips (lighting); **CAST**: Dominic Chianese (Theo), Halley Feiffer (Jessie, Lena, Nina, Sandra), Ian Kahn (Sean), Adriane Lenox (Joanne), Kelly McAndrew (Mary, Al, Michaeline), Sarah Paulson (Carrie Ann), Matthew Rauch (Terry), Frederick Weller (Jeffrey); Bill Camp (Voice of Commercial)

World premiere of a new play presented in two acts; Lucille Lortel Theatre; September 16–November 1, 2009 (Opened October 5); 21 previews, 27 performances. World premiere at the Royal Court Theatre Upstairs (London) December 1, 2008.

Kelly McAndrew, Sarah Paulson, Frederick Weller, and Ian Kahn in Still Life *(photo by Robert J. Saferstein)*

The Pride by Alexi Kaye Campbell; Director, Joe Mantello; Set, David Zinn; Costumes, Mattie Ullrich; Lighting, Paul Gallo; Original Music, Justin Ellington; Sound, Jill BC DuBoff; PSM, James FitzSimmons; ASM, Katherine Wallace; Production Assistant, Kate Fergeson; Fight Choreography, Tom Schall; Properties, Jeremy Lydic; Associate Lighting, Craig Stelzenmuller; Assistant Design: Tim McMath (set), Joshua James Marsh (costumes), John Emmett O'Brien (sound); Assistant Technical Director, Ernie Johns; Scenic Artist, Patrick Mann; Hair & Makeup, Jennifer Donovan; **CAST**: Hugh Dancy (Philip), Adam James (The Man/ Peter/The Doctor), Andrea Riseborough (Sylvia), Ben Whishaw (Oliver)

Setting: London in the year 1958 and the year 2008. American premiere of a new play presented in two acts; Lucille Lortel Theatre; January 28–March 28, 2010 (Opened February 16); 23 previews, 47 performances. **2010 Theatre World Award**: Andrea Riseborough

Ben Whishaw, Hugh Dancy, and Andrea Riseborough in The Pride *(photo by Joan Marcus)*

Family Week by Beth Henley; Presented in association with Marc Platt and by special arrangement with the Lucille Lortel Foundation Director, Jonathan Demme; Set, Derek McLane; Costumes, Mimi O'Donnell; Lighting, Kenneth Posner; Sound, Rob Milburn & Michael Bodeen; Original Music, Dan Bern; PSM, Lisa Porter; Stage Manager, Kelly Glasow; Assistant to the Director, Terell Richardson; Props, Michele Spadar; Wigs, Charles LaPointe; Fight Choreographer, Rick Sordelet; Assistant Design: Zach Blane (lighting), Dave Sanderson (sound); Musicians for Original Music, Dan Bern, Paul Kuhn, Common Rotation; **CAST**: Quincy Tyler Bernstine (Rickey), Kathleen Chalfant (Lena), Rosemarie DeWitt (Claire), Sami Gayle (Kay), Daisy J. Oliver (Jessica), Paul T. Ridgely (Jim)

Setting: The Present. July. World premiere of a play presented without intermission; Lucille Lortel Theatre; April 9–May 23, 2010 (Opened May 4); 25 previews, 21 performances.

Kathleen Chalfant, Rosemarie DeWitt, and Sami Gayle in Family Week *(photo by Carol Rosegg)*

Manhattan Theatre Club

Thirty-eighth Season

Artistic Director Lynne Meadow; Executive Producer, Barry Grove; General Manager, Florie Seery; Associate Artistic Director, Mandy Greenfield; Director of Artistic Development, Jerry Patch; Artistic Consultant, Daniel Sullivan; Director of Artistic Administration/Assistant to the Artistic Director, Amy Gilkes Loe; Casting, Nancy Piccione; Director of Musical Theatre, Clifford Lee Johnson III; Development, Jill Turner Lloyd; Marketing, Debra Waxman-Pilla; Finance, Jeffrey Bledsoe; Associate General Manager, Lindsey Brooks Sag; Subscriber Services, Robert Allenberg; Telesales, George Tetlow; Education, David Shookhoff; Production Manager, Kurt Gardner; Company Manager, Erin Moeller; Properties Supervisor, Scott Laule; Costume Supervisor, Erin Hennessy Dean; Press, Boneau/Bryan-Brown, Chris Boneau, Aaron Meier, Christine Olver.

Nightingale Written and performed by Lynn Redgrave; Director, Joseph Hardy; Sets, Tobin Ost; Costumes, Alejo Vietti; Lighting, Rui Rita; Original Music and Sound, John Gromada; PSM, C.A. Clark; Jonathan Alper Directing Fellow, Rachel Dart; Associate Lighting, Jake DeGroot; Assistant Design: Daniel Zimmerman (set), Matthew Taylor (lighting), Alex Neuman (sound); Understudy: Cynthia Mace

Lynn Redgrave in Nightingale *(photos by Joan Marcus)*

New York premiere of a new solo performance play presented without intermission; City Center Stage I; October 15–December 13, 2009 (Opened November 3); 21 previews, 48 performances. Originally produced by The New End Theatre (Hampstead, London) January 17–February 19, 2006. The play had its American debut at Center Theater Group's Mark Taper Forum (Michael Ritchie, Artistic Director; Charles Dillingham, Managing Director) for one night only on February 27, 2006, and was subsequently produced as part of their following season October 4–November 19, 2006 (see *Theatre World* Vol. 63, page 317).

Equivocation by Bill Cain; Director, Garry Hynes; Sets & Costumes, Francis O'Connor; Lighting, David Weiner; Sound, David Van Tieghem & Brandon Wolcott; Fight Director, J. David Brimmer; PSM, David H. Lurie; Stage Manager, Eileen Ryan Kelly; Jonathan Alper Directing Fellow, Rachel Slaven; Dialect Coach, Charlotte Fleck; Associate Design: Jesse Poleshuck (set), Terese Wadden (costumes), Lauren Phillips (lighting); Assistant Design: Samuel Froeschle (set), Ruth Hall (set & costumes); Assistant Fight Director, Michael Yahn; **CAST**: Charlotte Parry (Judith), John Pankow (Shag), David Pittu (Sir Robert Cecil/Nate/Thomas Percy), David Furr (Sharpe/Thomas Wintour/King James I), Michael Countryman (Richard/Father Henry Garnet), Remy Auberjonois (Armin/Robert Catesby/Sir Edward Coke); Understudies: Mark H. Dold (Armin/Catesby/Coke, Cecil/Nate/Percy, Sharpe/Wintour/King James I), Mattie Hawkinson (Judith), Neal Lerner (Richard/Garnet, Shag)

David Furr, Charlotte Parry, Michael Countryman, David Pittu, Remy Auberjonois, and John Pankow in Equivocation

Place and Time: London, 1606. New York premiere of a new play presented City Center Stage I; February 10–March 28, 2010 (Opened March 2); 24 previews, 32 performances. Originally produced by Oregon Shakepeare Festival (Bill Rauch, Artistic Director; Paul Nicholson, Executive Director) April 15–October 31, 2009 (see Regional Theatre listings in this volume).

That Face by Polly Stenham; Director, Sarah Benson; Sets & Costumes, David Zinn; Lighting, Tyler Micoleau; Sound, Matt Tierney; Fight Director, J. David Brimmer; Dialect Coach, Ben Furey; PSM, Hannah Cohen; Stage Manager, Kyle Gates; Jonathan Alper Directing Fellow, Meghan Finn; SDC Observer, Brendan Clifford; Makeup, Angelina Avallone; Assistant Design, Kirsten Ellert, Tim McMath (set), Jacob Climer (costumes), Natalie Robin (lighting); **CAST**: Christopher Abbott (Henry), Maïté Alina (Alice), Betty Gilpin (Izzy), Cristin Milioti (Mia), Laila Robins (Martha), Victor Slezak (Hugh); Understudies: Maïté Alina (Mia/Izzy), John Bolger (Hugh), Jeff Ward (Henry/Alice)

Setting: Present day London. American premiere of a new play presented in two acts; City Center Stage I; April 29–June 27, 2010 (Opened May 18); 21 previews, 48 performances. Originally presented at the Royal Court Jerwood Theatre Upstairs (London) April 20, 2007, and transferred to the Duke of York's Theatre May 1, 2008.

Laila Robins and Christopher Abbot in That Face

Mint Theater Company

Eighteenth Season

Artistic Director, Jonathan Bank; General Manager, Sherri Kotimsky; Box Office Manager, Martha Graebner; Assistant to the Artistic Director, Hunter Kaczorowski; Development Consultant, Ellen Mittenthal; Dramaturg, Heather J. Violanti; Casting, Stuart Howard, Amy Schecter, and Paul Hardt; Press, David Gersten & Associates, Jim Randolph

Is Life Worth Living? by Lennox Robinson; Presented as a part of the 1st Irish Theater Festival; Director, Jonathan Bank; Set, Susan Zeeman Rogers; Costumes, Martha Hally; Lighting, Jeff Nellis; Sound, Jane Shaw; Properties, Deborah Gaouette; Dialects & Dramaturgy, Amy Stoller; Stage Managers, Rebecca C. Monroe & Samone B. Weissman; ASM, Lauren McArthur; Illustration, Stefano Imbert; Graphics, Hunter Kaczorowski; Assistant Director, Betsy Holt; Assistant Production Manager, Kristina Vnook; Assistant Design: Kathleen McAllister (costumes), Kathleen Dobbins (lighting); Wardrobe Supervisor, Natasha Ticotin; Master Electrician, Keith A. Truax; Technical Director/Master Carpenter, Carlo Adinolfi; **CAST**: Margaret Daly (Lizzie Twohig), Erin Moon (Helena), Leah Curney (Christine Lambert), Graham Outerbridge (Eddie Twohig), Paul O'Brien (John Twohig), Jordan Baker (Constance Constantia), Kevin Kilner (Hector de la Mare), Bairbre Dowling (Annie Twohig), Jeremy Lawrence (Peter Hurley), John Keating (Michael/William Slattery), Grant Neale (John Hegarty), John O'Creagh (Tom Mooney)

Setting: A small room in the Seaview Hotel at Inish, a small resort in Ireland; July. American premiere of a play presented in four scenes in three acts with one intermission; Mint Theater Space; August 19–October 18, 2009 (Opened September 14); 27 previews, 36 performances.

Jordan Baker and Kevin Kilner in Is Life Worth Living? *(photos by Richard Termine)*

So Help Me God! by Maurine Dallas Watkins; Director, Jonathan Bank; Set, Bill Clarke; Costumes, Clint Ramos; Lighting, Robert Wierzel; Sound, Jane Shaw; Props, Deborah Gaouette; Hair & Makeup, Jon Carter; PSM, Samone B. Weissman; ASM, Lauren McArthur; Associate Production Manager, Wayne Yeager; Fight Director, J. David Brimmer; Dialect Coach, Amy Stoller; Production Assistant, Katie Fergerson; Dog Owner, Michelle Bosser; Technical Director, Carlo Adinolfi; Master Electrician, Sheila Donovan; Wardrobe Supervisor, Natasha Ticotin; **CAST**: Kristen Johnston (Lily Darnley, *the Star*), Allen Lewis Rickman (Mose Jason, *her producer*), Brad Bellamy (Dave Hobart, *her director in Act*

I), Kraig Swartz (Glenn, *her director in Act II*), Ned Noyes (Geroge Herrick, *her author*), Peter Van Wagner (Goby, *her press agent*), Jeremy Lawrence (Blake, *her stage manager*); *Members of Lily's Company off and on, now and then*: Catherine Curtin (Belle), John G. Preston (Bart Henley), John Windsor-Cunningham (Mr. Chester Burleigh), Kevin O'Donnell (Jules Meredith), Matthew Waterson (Desmond Armstrong), Margot White (Judith Hudson), Anna Chlumsky (Kerren-Heppuch Lane, *her understudy*), Amy Fitts (Eloise, *her maid and dresser*), Velma or Roxie (Frou-Frou, *her dog*), Matthew Waterson (An electrician)

Setting: The Regent Theatre on Broadway and the living room of a hotel suite at the Ritz Hotel in Philadelphia, early Autumn 1929. World premiere of a forgotten play presented in three acts with one intermission; Lucille Lortel Theatre; November 18–December 20, 2009 (Opened December 7); 19 previews, 14 performances. Originally slated for Broadway in the fall of 1929, *So Help Me God* was never published and was forgotten for more than 75 years. The Mint Theater presented a one-night-only reading of the play starring Ms. Johnston on June 8, 2009.

Ned Noyes, Kristen Johnston, and Allen Lewis Rickman in So Help Me God!

Doctor Knock, or the Triumph of Medicine by Jules Romains; Director, Gus Kaikkonen; Set, Charles Morgan; Costumes, Sam Fleming; Lighting, William Armstrong; Sound, Jane Shaw; Properties, Deborah Gaouette; Hair & Wigs, Gerard James Kelly; Assistant Director, Jenny Lord; PSM, Melissa M. Spengler; ASM, Andrewa Hayward; Illustration, Stefano Imbert; Graphics, Hunter Kaczorowski; Assistant Production Manager, Wayne Yeager; Assistant Design: Eric Larson (lighting), Nick Gorczynski (sound); Production Assistant, Jennifer Sullivan; Wardrobe Supervisor, Karle J. Meyers; Scenic Charge, Julia Hahn; Music, The Knights (Eric Jacobsen, Conductor; Jan Vogler, Cello); **CAST**: Thomas M. Hammond (Dr. Knock), Patrick Husted (Dr. Parpalaid), Patti Perkins (Madame Parpalaid/The Lady in Violet/The Maid), Scott Barrow (Jean/ M. Bernard, *the teacher*/First Farmer), Chris Mixon (Town Crier/ M. Mousquet, *the pharmacist*/Second Farmer), Jennifer Harmon (The Lady in Black/Madame Remy)

Setting: Act I: On the road to St. Maurice. October, 1923. Act II: Knock's consulting-room. The following Monday. Act III: The Key Hotel. January, 1924. Revival of a play presented in three acts with one intermission; April 14–June 6, 2010 (Opened May 10); 20 previews, 36 performances. The play premiered in Paris in 1923, in London in 1924, and in New York in 1928. This production marked the first New York production in seventy-two years.

The New Group

Fourteenth Season

Artistic Director, Scott Elliott; Executive Director, Geoffrey Rich; Managing Director, Development, Oliver Dow; Associate Artistic Director, Ian Morgan; General Manager, Elisabeth Bayer; Artistic Associate, James Gittins; Director of Special Events/Individual Giving, Cristina Galeano; Marketing/Company Manager, Jenna Lauren Freed; Production Supervisor, Peter R. Feuchtwanger/PRF Productions; Casting, Judy Henderson; Press, The Karpel Group, Bridget Klapinski, Beth Sorrell

The Starry Messenger Written and directed by Kenneth Lonergan; Sets, Derek McLane; Costumes, Mattie Ullrich; Lighting, Jason Lyons; Sound, Shane Rettig; Projections, Austin Switser; Assistant Director, Marie Masters; ASM, Stephanie Cali; Properties Supervisors, Matt Hodges, Jeremy Lydic; Wardrobe Supervisor, Kristi Koury; Vocal Coach, Gillian Lane-Plescia; Assistant Design: Erica Hemminger (set), Kate Melvin (costumes), Peter Hoergurger (lighting), Alex Hawthorn (sound); **CAST**: Matthew Broderick (Mark Williams), Stephanie Cannon (Mrs. Pysner), Kieran Culkin (Ian/Adam Williams), Merwin Goldsmith (Norman Ketterly), Catalina Sandino Moreno (Angela Vasquez), Grant Shaud (Arnold Samson), J. Smith-Cameron (Anne Williams), Missy Yager (Doris Ketterly-Welles)

Setting: New York City, September–December, 1995. World premiere of a new play presented in two acts; Acorn Theatre on Theatre Row; October 26–December 19, 2009 (Opened November 23); 21 previews, 54 performances.

J. Smith-Cameron, Matthew Broderick, and Grant Shaud in *The Starry Messenger* *(photos by Monique Carboni)*

A Lie of the Mind by Sam Shepard; Director, Ethan Hawke; Sets, Derek McLane; Costumes, Catherine Zuber; Lighting, Jeff Croiter; Sound, Shane Rettig; Music, Latham Gaines & Shelby Gaines; PSM, Valerie A. Peterson; Assistant Directors, Sam Creely, Azar Kazemi; ASM, Stephanie Cali; Properties Supervisor, Matt Hodges; Wardrobe Supervisor, Kristi Koury; Assistant Design: Erica Hemminger (set), Haley Lieberman, Nicole V. Moody, Ryan Park (costumes), Nicolas Houfek (lighting); Casting Associate, Kimberly Graham; **CAST**: Keith Carradine (Baylor), Josh Hamilton (Frankie), Marin Ireland (Beth), Laurie Metcalf (Meg), Alessandro Nivola (Jake), Maggie Siff (Sally), Frank Whaley (Mike), Karen Young (Lorraine)

Revival of a play presented in two acts; Acorn Theatre on Theatre Row; January 29–March 20, 2010 (Opened February 18); 20 previews, 32 performances. Originally presented Off-Broadway at the Promenade Theatre December 5, 1985–June 1, 1986 (see *Theatre World* Vol. 42, page 67).

Laurie Metcalf, Josh Hamilton, and Marin Ireland in A Lie of the Mind

The Kid Book by Michael Zam, lyrics by Jack Lechner, music by Andy Monroe; Based on the book *The Kid: What Happened After My Boyfriend and I Decided to Go Get Pregnant* by Dan Savage; Director, Scott Elliott; Musical Staging, Josh Prince; Sets, Derek McLane; Costumes, Jeff Mahshie; Lighting, Howell Binkley; Sound, Ken Travis; Animation, Jeff Scher; Video, Aron Deyo; Music Supervision/Orchestrations/Arrangements, Dominick Amendum; Music Director/Orchestrations/Additional Arrangements, Boko Suzuki; PSM, Valerie A. Peterson; Assistant Director, Marie Masters; ASM, Stephanie Cali; Dance Captain, Tyler Maynard; Properties Supervisors, Joe Cairo, Matt Hodges; Assistant Design: Erica Hemminger (set), Kyle Lacolla (costumes), Ryan O'Gara, Amanda Zieve (lighting), Benjamin Furiga (sound); Assistant Animation, William J. Hopper; Reheasal Pianist/Band Sub, Rachel Kaufman; Production Audio, David Arnold; Production Carpenters, Thomas Goehring, John A. Martinez; Production Electrician, Robert Murray; Casting Associate, Kimberly Graham; **CAST**: Kevin Anthony (Reg/Others), Susan Blackwell (Anne/Others), Jill Eikenberry (Dan's Mother), Jeannine Frumess (Melissa), Ann Harada (Ruth/Others), Tyler Maynard (Chad/Others), Brooke Sunny Moriber (Susan/Others), Justin Patterson (Josh/Others), Christopher Sieber (Dan), Lucas Steele (Terry), Michael Wartella (Bacchus); Understudies: Justin Patterson (Dan), Tyler Maynard (Terry), Brooke Sunny Moriber (Melissa), Zachary Berger (Bacchus/Male Ensemble), Jane Brockman (Judy/Female Ensemble), Jeannine Frumess (Swing for "If You Give Us Your Baby"; Orchestra: Boko Suzuki (Conductor/keyboards/acoustic guitar), Danny Percefull (Associate Conductor/keyboards), Ed Levy (electric, acoustic and lap steel guitars), Steve Gilewski (electric and acoustic bass), Kevin Rice (drums/percussion), Randy Cohen (keyboard programmer)

Musical Numbers: I'm Asking You, The Kid, Terry…, They Hate Us, The Kid (reprise), Nice, Gore Vidal, If You Give Us Your Baby, Seize the Day, Her Name is Melissa, Spare Changin, What Do You Say?, We're Not Asking You, It's Not Your Baby, When They Put Him in Your Arms, It Gets Better, Behind the Wheel, I Knew, Beautiful, 42 Hours, What About Him?, My Kid

World premiere of a new musical presented in in two acts; Acorn Theatre on Theatre Row; April 16–May 29, 2010 (Opened May 10); 21 previews, 45 performances.

Special Event

A Battle of Wills: Internal and External Three one-act plays exploring issues related to mental health; Presented in association with Part-Time Productions, a division of Cause Célèbre (Susan Charlotte, Founding Artistic Director); *This Is on Me* by Tom Fontana, directed by Antony Marsellis; *Ashes to Ashes* by Harold Pinter, directed by Christopher Hart; *Love Divided* by Susan Charlotte, directed by John Shea; Featuring: Delphi Harrington, Tasha Lawrence, Lizbeth MacKay, Carolyn McCormick, Larry Pine, Marian Seldes, John Shea, Kevin Stapleton, Frances Sternhagen

An evening of three one-acts presented as a benefit for the Lieber Recovery and Rehabilitation Clinic for Psychotic Disorders; Acorn Theatre on Theatre Row; Sundays, May 31–June 21, 2010; 5 performances. This event was the inaugural event for Part-Time Productions.

New Victory Theater

Fourteenth Season

President, Cora Cahan; Executive VP, Lisa Lawer Post; VP of Operations, Jarret M. Haynes; Curatorial/Progamming, Mary Rose Lloyd; Development SVP, Cheryl Kohn; Education Director, Edie Demas; Finance VP, Kim Dobbie Neuer; NVT Director of Theater Operations, Melinda Berk; Director of Production, David Jensen; NVT Technical Director, Robert Leach, NVT Production Coordinator, Colleen Davis; Public Relations Director, Laura Kaplow-Goldman; Marketing Director, Lauren P. Fitzgerald; IT Director, Michael Reisman; Facilities Manager, Benno van Noort; Ticket Services, Robin Leeds; New 42nd Street Studios/The Duke on 42nd Street Director of Operations, Alma Malabanan- McGrath

Cinderella Conceived, designed, and performed by Shona Reppe, co-codevised and directed by Ian Cameron and Gill Robertson, with Shona Reppe; Presented by Shona Reppe Puppets as part of the New Victory Scottish Festival; Costumes, Katie Hall; Production Manager, Tamlin Wiltshire; Sound, John Williamson; Set Construction, Paul Wright/Collumcile Centre

A puppet theater presentation performed without intermission; Duke on 42nd Street; September 18–28, 2009; 10 performances.

Shona Reppe in Cinderella *(photo by Douglas McBride)*

The Man Who Planted Trees Adapted from Jean Giono's story by Ailie Cohen, Richard Medrington, and Rick Conte; Presented by Puppet State Theatre Company as part of the New Victory Scottish Festival; Director/Set & Puppet Design, Alice Cohen; Sound, Barney Strachan; Lighting/Stage Manager, Elspeth Murray; Tour Manager, Jennifer Williams; Music, Johannes Kasberger, Charles Trénet; Music Performer, Orphénica Lyra; **CAST**: Richard Medrington (Jean), Rick Conte (Jean's Colleague)

A theatrical piece with puppetry performed without intermission; Duke on 42nd Street; October 2–11, 2009; 12 performances.

My House Created, directed, and performed by Andy Manley; Presented by Andy Manley in association with Starcatchers as part of the New Victory Scottish Festival; Composer, Danny Krass; Set, Claire Halleran; Producer, Rhona Matheson; Stage Manager, Rob Evans

New York premiere of a strorytelling/puppetry show performed without intermission; New 42nd Street Studios; October 2–18, 2009; 21 performances.

Hansel and Gretel by Catherine Wheels Theatre Company; Presented by Catherine Wheels Theatre Company (Gill Robertson, Artistic Director; Paul Fitzpatrick, Producer) in association with Brunton Theatre as part of the New Victory Scottish Festival; Director, Gill Robertson; Design, Karen Tennent;

Lighting, Jeanine Davies; Composer, Steve Kettley; Costumes, Alison Brown; Sound, Tom Zwitserlood; Technical Manager, Liam Boucher; Stage Manager, David Young; Deuputy Stage Manager, Lindsey Knight; ASM, Emma McKie; Video, Jonathan Charles/D Fie Foe; Original Sound Design, Mark Sondergren; New Victory Stage Manager, Mary-Susan Gregson; Production Manager, Craig Fleming; Project Manager, Louise Gilmour-Wills; Finance and Admin Assistant, Ian Cheyne; **CAST**: Tommy Joe Mullins, Ashley Smith, Cath Whitefield, Steve Kettley, Joel Sanderson

An interactive promenade theatre presentation performed without intermission; New Victory Theater; October 15–November 1, 2009; 20 performances.

Peter and the Wolf Conceived and directed by Anne Geenen, music and text by Sergei Prokofiev; Presented by In the Wings; New Music Composer, Philip Feeney; Choreography, Didi Veldman; Music Supervisor, Keith Levenson; Conductor, Craig Barna; Music Coordinator, Brian Cassier; Set, Paul Gallis; New Text, Abi Brown after an original story by Jan Geenen; Sound, Bart Bakker; Lighting, David W. Kidd; Costumes, Yan Tax, Marie Lauwers; Stage Manager, Elsbeth Godeschalk; Deputy Stage Manager, Gemma Hauptmeyer; Associate Conductor, Bruce Barnes; **CAST**: Brian Blessed (Narrator); Daniel Rosseel (Bodgan/Grandfather), Maurizio Montis (Peter), Eva Grieco (Masja/Bird), Christian Celini (Boris/Duck), Alessandra Cito (Dina/Cat), Joanne Meredith (Ivana), James Mackie (Lucas/Hunter), Marco Chiodo (Wolf), Lewis Fox (Hunter); Swings: Paul Rooney, Elisa Petrolo

A theatrical piece with dance and music presented in two acts; New Victory Theatre; November 13–29, 2009; 17 performances.

Chestnuts Roasting on The Flaming Idiots Written, directed, produced by Rob Williams, Kevin Hunt, and Jon O'Connor; Composer, Allen Robertson; Set, Heyd Fontenot; Original Costumes, Leslie Bonnel; Stage Manager, Shelli Aderman; Technical Director, Mark Guinn; **CAST**: Rob Williams (Gyro), Jon O'Connor (Pyro), Kevin Hunt (Walter)

A variety show performed without intermission; New Victory Theatre; December 4, 2009–January 3, 2010; 28 performances.

Once and For All We're Gonna Tell You Who We Are So Shut Up and Listen Conceived and designed by Alexander Devriendt, Joeri Smet, and the Cast; Presented by Ontroerend Goed, Kopergietery, and Richard Jordan Productions as part of the Under the Radar Festival 2010; Director/Choreography, Alexander Devriendt; Lighting, Jeroen Doise; Set and Costumes, Sophie De Somere; Sound, Stijn Degezelle; New Victory Stage Manager, Mary-Susan Gregson; Production Manager/Company Manager, Eva Van Den Hove; Dramaturg, Mieke Versyp; Master Technician, Geert Willems; **CAST**: Charlotte De Bruyne, Edith De Bruyne, Febe De Geest, Jorge De Geest, Aaron De Keyzer, Christophe De Poorter, Edouard Devriendt, Dina Dooreman, Ian Ghysels, Barbara Lefebure, Fée Roels, Koba Ryckewaert, Elies Van Renterghem, Verona Verbakel, Nathalie Verbeke

A theatrical piece performed without intermission; Duke on 42nd Street; January 8–17, 2010; 9 performances.

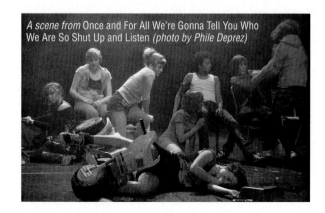

A scene from Once and For All We're Gonna Tell You Who We Are So Shut Up and Listen *(photo by Phile Deprez)*

The Enchanted Pig Music by Jonathan Dove, libretto by Alasdair Middleton; Presented by The Opera Group, ROH2 at the Royal Opera House, and The Young Vic; Director, John Fulljames; Conductor, Brad Cohen; Set and Costumes, Dick Bird; Lighting, Bruno Poet; Movement, Philippe Giraudeau; Music Director, Tim Murray; Orchestra Manager, Sato Moughalian; Production Manager, Bob Holmes; Company Stage Manager, Rupert Carlile; Deputy Stage Manager, Kate Astbury; ASM, Daisy Gladstone; Technical Stage Manager, Andy Stubbs; Tour Lighting, Sally Ferguson; Wardrobe, Morag Hood; **CAST**: Jo Servi (King Hildebrand), Kate Nelson (Mab), Michelle Cornelius (Dot), Susan Boyd or Karina Lucas (Flora), Beverley Klein (The Book of Fate), Terel Nugent (King of the West), Tom Solomon (King of the East), Simon Wilding (The Pig), Jo Servi (The North Wind), Beverley Klein (Mrs. Northwind), Tom Solomon (The Moon), Terel Nugent (Sun), Michelle Cornelius (Day), Beverley Klein (Old Woman), Kate Nelson (Adelaide); Swing: Derek Welton; Orchestra: Michelle Gott (harp), John Hadfield (percussion), Will Holshouser (accordion/piano), Thomas Hutchison (trombone), Troy Rinker (double bass), Aron Zelkowicz (cello)

An opera/musical presented in two acts; New Victory Theatre; February 5–21, 2010; 14 performances.

A scene from The Enchanted Pig *(photo by Catherine Ashmore)*

The Complete Works of William Shakespeare (Abridged) by Adam Long, Daniel Singer, and Jess Winfield, additional material by Reed Martin; Presented by The Reduced Shakespeare Company; Revisions, Daniel Singer & Jess Winfield; Director, Reed Martin & Austin Tichenor; Stage Manager, Elaine Randolph; Set, S.W. Wellen; Props & Costumes, Susan Brooks, Nicole Donery, Dancing Barefoot Productions; U.S. Tour Direction, Opus 3 Artists; Wardrobe Supervisor, Alli Bostedt; **CAST**: Reed Martin, Matt Rippy, Austin Tichenor

Revival of a play presented presented in two acts; New Victory Theatre; March 5–14, 2010; 10 performances.

46 Circus Acts in 45 Minutes Conceived and directed by Yaron Lifschitz; Presented by Circa; Music, David Carberry; Lighting/Production Manager, Jason Organ; Costumes, Amanda Fairbanks; **CAST**: Darcy Grant, Emma McGovern, Emma Serjeant, Lewis West; Understudy: Scott Grove

A theatrical circus presentation performed without intermission; New Victory Theatre; March 19–April 4, 2010; 18 performances.

Time Step Created and choreographed by Ryan Kasprzak, Mark Lonergan, Brent McBeth, Derek Roland; Additional material, dramaturgy, and voiceovers by Joel Jeske; Presented by Parallel Exit; Director, Mark Lonergan; Lighting/Production Manager, Keith Truax; Sound, Duane McKee; Projectins, Ron Amato; Tuxedos, Juliet Jeske; Stage Manager, Oliva O'Brien; Publicity, Michelle Tabnick; **CAST**: Mike Dobson (Drummer/Landlord/EMT/Marco the Mesmerist/Lloyd Ditmars/Passerby), Danny Gardner (Curtis), Joel Jeske (MC/Mailman/EMT/Seniors MC/Policeman), Brent McBeth (Lester), Derek Roland (Max); Standby: John Scacchetti (Max and Lester)

A theatre/tap dance presentation performed without intermission; New Victory Theatre; April 9–18, 2010; 10 performances.

Elephant Conceived, designed, and directed by Ozzie Riley; Presented by Dodgy Clutch in association with The Market Theatre (Malcolm Purkey, Artistic Director); Music, Brendan Murphy, John Alder, and the cast; Choreography, Zamuxolo Mgoduka, Thabank Ramiaila, Tim Rubridge; Puppets, Jane Robinson, Adam Riley, Sarah Riley; Set, Adam Riley, Sarah Riley; Lighting, Declan Randall; Sound, John Alder; Stage Manager, Mary-Susan Gregson; Production Manager, Elaine Beard; **CAST**: Nhlanhla Mahlangu (Chief Zanenvula), Thabang Ramaila (Young Chief), Zamuxolo Mgoduka (Chief's Brother), Pady O'Connor (Lucky Louis), Sarah Riley (Dancer/Performer/Baby Elephant), Unathi Nondumo, Xolisile Bongwana, Wandiswa Gogela, Nosikhunbuzo Mgoduka (Dancers/Performers)

A puppet theatre presentation with dance performed without intermission; New Victory Theatre; April 23–May 28, 2010; 10 performances.

PaGAGnini Presented, conceived and designed, Ara Malikaian & Company, co-conceived, book, direction, and design by Yllana; Music Arrangements, Ara Makikian, Eduardo Ortega, Gartxot Ortiz, Thomas Potiron; Choreography, Carlos Chamorro; Set, Ana Garay; Lighting, Diego Domínguez, Juanjo Llorens; Sound, Luis López De Segovia Perez, Jorge Moreno; Costumes, Maribel Rodríguez; Props, Arte Y Ficción; Music Director, Aara Malikian; Executive Producer, Marcos Ottone; Technical Director, Ismael García; Production Manager, Mabel Caínzos; Artistic Directors, David Ottone, Juan Francisco Ramos; **MUSICIANS/CAST**: Ara Malikian (violin), Eduardo Ortega (violin), Fernando Clemente (violin), Gartxot Ortiz (cello)

A music and comedy presentation performend without intermission; New Victory Theatre; May 7–23, 2010; 15 performances.

The Butterfly Garden Conceived and directed by Francesco Gandi, Davide Venturini; Presented by Teatro di Piazza o d'Occasione (T.P.O. Company); Set and Props, Gregory Petitquex, Valerio Calonego; Costumes, Loretta Mugnai; Digital Design, Elsa Mersi; Sound, Spartaco Cortesi; Technical Direction, Niccolo Gallio, Francesco Taddei; Production Manager, Jason Janicki; Collaborator, Stefania Zampiga; Tour Manager, Valentina Martini, Valerie Castellaneta; Executive Producer of U.S. Tour, Thomas O. Kriegsmann; **CAST**: Paola Carlucci, Stefania Rossetti, Barbara Stimoli

A sensory theatre presentation with dance performed without intermission; New 42nd Street Studios; May 14–23, 2010; 13 performances.

A scene from The Butterfly Garden *(photo courtesy of T.P.O. Company)*

New York Gilbert & Sullivan Players

Thirty-fifth Season*

Artistic Director & General Manager, Albert Bergeret; Managing Director, David Wannen; Administrative Assistant, Amy Maude Helfer; Technical Director/PSM, David Sigafoose; Lighting, Sally Small & Brian Presti; Assistant Music Director, Andrea Stryker-Rodda; Assistant Stage Manager, Annette Dieli; Head of Wardrobe, Corey Groom; Orchestra Manager, Larry Tietze; Promotions, Leanne Schanzer; Press, Peter Cromarty

The Mikado *or, The Town of Titipu* Libretto by Sir William S. Gilbert, music by Sir Arthur Sullivan; Stage Direction, Albert Bergeret & David Auxier; Music Director/Conductor/Set, Albert Bergeret; Costumes, Gail J. Wofford & Kayko Nakamura; **CAST**: Keith Jurosko (The Mikado of Japan), Cameron Smith (Nanki-Poo), David Macaluso (Ko-Ko), Louis Dall'Ava (Pooh-Bah), Richard Alan Holmes (Pish-Tush), Laurelyn Watson Chase (Yum-Yum), Melissa Attebury (Pitti-Sing), Rebecca O'Sullivan (Peep-Bo), Joyce Campana (Katisha) , Lucy Rosenberg (Axe Coolie); Ensemble: David Auxier, Cáitlín Burke, Michael J. Connolly, Lindsey Falduto, Lauren Frankovich, Michael Galante, Katie Hall, Amy Maude Helfer, Susan Hutchison, Daniel Lockwood, James Mills, Jenny Millsap, Marcie Passley, Monique Pelletier, Natalie Ross, Chris Ian-Sanchez, Paul Sigrist, Angela Smith, Sarah Caldwell Smith, Joseph Torello, Matthew Wages, Chris White, William Whitefield, Adam Yankowy

Setting: A Japanese Garden. An operetta presented in two acts; City Center; January 8–16, 2010; 3 performances.

The Company of The Mikado *(photo by Noah Strone)*

The Pirates of Penzance *or, The Slave of Duty* Libretto by Sir William S. Gilbert, music by Sir Arthur Sullivan; Stage Direction/Music Director/Conductor, Albert Bergeret; Choreography, Bill Fabris; Set, Lou Anne Gilleland; Costumes, Gail J. Wofford; Dance Captain, David Auxier; **CAST**: Stephen Quint (Major-General Stanley), David Wannen (The Pirate King), David Macaluso (Samuel), Colm Fitzmaurice (Frederic), David Auxier (Sergeant of Police), Michele McConnell (Mabel), Cáitlín Burke (Edith), Amy Maude Helfer (Kate), Betina Hershey (Isabel), Angela Smith (Ruth); Ensemble: Sarah Best, Paul Betz, Elisabeth Cernadas, Michael Connolly, Louis Dall'Ava, Victoria Devany, Katie Hall, Alan Hill, Sarah Hutchison, Daniel Lockwood, Duane McDevitt, James Mills, Rebecca O'Sullivan, Quinto Ott, Marcie Passley, Monique Pelletier, Jennifer Piacenti, Natalie Ross, Chris-Ian Sanchez, Paul Sigrist, Sarah Caldwell Smith, Eric Werner, William Whitefield, Emily Wright, Adam Yankowy; Understudies: Paul Betz (Frederic), Sarah Caldwell Smith (Mabel), Jennifer Piacenti (Isabel)

Setting: Act I: A Rocky Seashore on the Coast of Cornwall; Act II: A ruined Chapel by Moonlight. An operetta presented in two acts, City Center; January 9 & 15, 2010; 2 performances.

Chris-Ian Sanchez, Rebecca O'Sullivan, David Wannen, Dianna Dollman, Stephen Quint, James Mills, and Sarah Caldwell Smith in The Pirates of Penzance *(photo by Traci J. Brooks)*

H.M.S. Pinafore *or, The Lass That Loved A Sailor* Libretto by Sir William S. Gilbert, music by Sir Arthur Sullivan; Stage Direction/Music Director/Conductor/Sets, Albert Bergeret; Choreography, Bill Fabris; Costumes, Gail Wofford; Dance Captain, David Auxier; **CAST**: Stephen Quint (The Rt. Hon. Sir Joseph Porter, K.C.B.), Keith Jurosko (Captain Corcoran), Colm Fitzmaurice (Ralph Rackstraw), Louis Dall'Ava (Dick Deadeye), William Whitefield (Bill Bobstay), Quinto Ott (Bob Becket), Michele McConnell (Josephine), Victoria Devany (Cousin Hebe), Angela Smith (Little Buttercup), Paul Sigrist (Sergeant of Marines); Lucy Attebury (Midshipmite); Ensemble: Melissa Attebury, David Auxier, Cáitlín Burke, Jonathan Cable, Brooke Collins, Michael Galante, Dan Greenwood, Katie Hall, Amy Maude Helfer, Alan Hill, James LaRosa, Duane McDevitt, Jenny Millsap, Rebecca O'Sullivan, Marcie Passley, Monique Pelletier, Natalie Ross, Chris-Ian Sanchez, Paul Sigrist, Sarah Caldwell Smith, Joseph Torello, Matthew Wages, Emily Wright; Understudy: Dan Greenwood (Ralph Rackstraw)

Setting: Quarterdeck of H.M.S. Pinafore. An operetta presented in two acts; City Center; January 10 & 12, 2010; 2 performances.

Ruddigore *or, The Witch's Curse* Libretto by Sir William S. Gilbert, music by Sir Arthur Sullivan; Stage Direction, Albert Bergeret & David Auxier; Choreography, David Auxier; Music Director/Conductor/Set, Albert Bergeret; Original Set Concept, Edward Gorey; Costumes, Jan Holland; Dance Captains, Lance Olds, Marcie Passley; **CAST**: David Macaluso (Sir Ruthven Murgatroyd), Dan Greenwood (Richard Dauntless), Richard Alan Holmes (Sir Despard Murgatroyd), Ted Bouton (Old Adam Goodheart), Sarah Caldwell Smith (Rose Maybud), Cáitlín Burke (Mad Margaret), Erika Person (Dame Hannah), Jennifer Piacenti (Zorah), Katie Hall (Ruth), David Wannen (Sir Roderic Murgatroyd); Ensemble: Sarah Best, Paul Betz, Jonathan Cable, Elisabeth Cernadas, Laurelyn Watson Chase, Brooke Collins, Michael Connolly, Louis Dall'Ava, Victoria Devany, Michael Galante, Amy Maude Helfer, Betina Hershey, Alan Hill, James Mills, Lance Olds, Rebecca O'Sullivan, Quinto Ott, Marcie Passley, Chris-Ian Sanchez, Angela Smith, Chris White, Emily Wright, Adam Yankowy; Understudies: James Mills (Robin Oakapple), Paul Betz (Richard), Adam Yankowy (Despard), Angela Smith (Dame Hannah), Quinto Ott (Roderic)

Setting: Act I: The Fishing Village of Reddering, in Cornwall; Act II: The Picture Gallery in Ruddigore Castle; Time: Early in the 19th Century. An operetta presented in two acts; City Center; January 14–17, 2010; 3 performances.

*The Gilbert and Sullivan Players were on a hiatus during the 2008–2009 Season

New York Theatre Workshop

Twenty-seventh Season

Artistic Director, James C. Nicola; Managing Director, William Russo; Associate Artistic Director, Linda S. Chapman; General Manager, Harry J. McFadden; Casting, Jack Doulin; Literary Associate, Geoffrey Jackson Scott; Artistic Administrator, Bryn Thorsson; Artistic Associates, Michael Greif, Michael Friedman, Alex Lewin, Ruben Polendo; Development, Alisa Schierman; Finance and Administration, Rachel McBeth; Education, Caroline Reddick Lawson; Marketing Associate Rebekah Paine; Production/Facilities Manager, Julie M. Mason; Technical Director, Brian Garber; Press, Richard Kornberg, Don Summa

Aftermath by Jessica Blank and Erik Jensen; Director, Jessica Blank; Set, Richard Hoover; Costumes, Gabriel Bery; Lighting, David Lander; Sound and Original Music, David Robbins; PSM, Larry K. Ash; ASM, Annette Adamska; Assistant Director, Jake Hart; Production Electrician, John Anselmo Jr.; Prop Master, Jeffrey Wallach; Assistant Design: Casey Smith (set), Andrea Hood (costumes), Justin A. Partier, Ben Pilat (lighting); Dialect Coach, Fajer Al-Kaisi; Scenic Artist, Laura Mroczkowski; Sound Engineer, David Fowler; **CAST**: Fajer Al-Kaisi (Shahid, *a translator*), Amir Arison (Yassar, *a dermatologist*), Leila Buck (Basima, *wife and mother*), Maha Chehlaoui (Fadilah, *an artist*), Demosthenes Chrysan (Abdul-Aliyy, *an imam*), Daoud Heidami (Asad, *a theatre director*), Omar Koury (Fouad, *a cook*), Laith Nakli (Rafiq, *a pharmacist*), Rasha Zamamiri (Naimah, *a cook*); Understudy: Sevan Greene

World premiere of a new play presented without intermission; September 1–October 18, 2009 (Opened September 15); 16 previews, 40 performances. Developed in part during a residency with the Theatre Department at Dartmouth College, in collaboration with Dartmouth's Hopkins Center for the Arts.

Jenny Allen in I Got Sick Then I Got Better

Fajer Al-Kaisi, Rasha Zamamiri, and Omar Koury in Aftermath
(photos by Joan Marcus)

I Got Sick Then I Got Better by Jenny Allen; Directors, James Lapine & Darren Katz; Lighting, David Lander; Assistant Lighting, Ben Pilat; Production Electrician, John Anselmo Jr.; Stage Manager, Laura Arnett; Light Board Programmer, Rebecca McCoy; Light Board Operator, Desiree Fischer; **CAST**: Jenny Allen

Off-Broadway premiere of a solo performance play presented without intermission; September 14–October 19, 2009 (Monday evenings only); Extended run October 23–November 15, 2009; 30 performances. Previously presented at Long Wharf Theatre in April 2009 and at Barrington Stage Company May 15–17, 2009.

The Heart Is a Lonely Hunter by Rebecca Gilman, based on the novel by Carson McCullers; Co-produced by The Acting Company (Margot Harley, Artistic Director); Director, Doug Hughes; Set, Neil Patel; Lighting, Michael Chybowski; Original Music and Sound, David Van Tieghem; Projections, Jan Hartley; Fight Director, Rick Sordelet; PSM, Winnie Y. Lok; ASM, Annette Adamska; Casting, Liz Woodman, Jack Doulin; Assistant Director, Ian Belknap; Production Electrician, John Anselmo Jr.; Sound & Video Supervisor, Jamie McElhinney; Costume Shop Manager, Jeffrey Wallach; Prop Master, Tessa Dunning; Production Assistant, Danielle Buccino; Assistant Design: Greg Laffey (set), Nikki Moody (costumes), Dale Knoth (lighting), Brandon Wolcott (sound); Dialect Coach, Kate Wilson; Harmonica Coach, Jonny Rosch; Wigs, Jon Carter; Assistant Props, Maggie Pilat; Assistant Technical Director, Ben Williams; For the Acting Company: Gerry Cornez (Development and Communications), Nancy Cook (General Manager), Ian Belknap (Associate Artistic Director), Justin Gallo (Education), Bernard Rashbaum (Finance), Joseph Parks (Producing Assistant), Paula Raymond (Design and Communications Coordinator); **CAST**: Bob Braswell (Harry), Jimonn Cole (Willie/Hospital Attendant), Michael Cullen (Charles Parker/Mr. Kelly/Mill Worker/Asylum Patient/Deputy/Doctor), James McDaniel (Dr. Copeland), Cristin Milioti (Mick Kelly), Randall Newsome (Riff), Roslyn Ruff (Portia), I.N. Sierros (Antonapoulous/Preacher/Mill Worker/Deputy), Andrew Weems (Jake)

New York premiere of a new play presented in two acts; November 13–December 20, 2009 (Opened December 3); 22 previews, 21 performances.

James McDaniel, Andrew Weems (sitting), Randall Newsome, Henry Stram, and Cristin Milioti in The Heart Is a Lonely Hunter

Top Secret: The Battle for the Pentagon Papers by Geoffrey Cowan and Leroy Aarons; Co-produced by L.A. Theatre Works and Affinity Collaborative Theater; Director, John Rubinstein; Set & Lighting, David Lander; Costumes, Holly Poe Durbin; PSM, Jennifer Grutza; ASM, Rebecca S. Fleming; Production Electrician, John Anselmo Jr.; Sound Supervisor, Jamie McElhinney; Costume Supervisor/Props, Jeffrey Wallach; Assistant Design: Jessica Mueller (costumes), Justin Partier (lighting); Assistant Technical Director, Ben Williams; Scenic Artists, Laura Mroczkowski, Jennifer Blazek; Light Board Programmer, Bob Going; For L.A. Thetare Works: Susan Albert Loewenberg (Producing Director), Maggie Bourque (Education/Development Associate), Jennifer Brooks (Associate Producer/Casting), Christina Montano (Associate Producer), James Ott (Finance), Lucy Pollak (Publicist); For Affinity Collaborative Theater: John Dias, Diane Morrison, Sheila Schwartz; **CAST**: Diane Adair (Meg Greenfield), Larry Bryggman (John Mitchell/Chal Roberts/Lamont Vanderhall), John Getz (Ben Bagdikian/Robert Mardian), James Gleason (Murry Marder/Judge Martin Peel), Jack Gilpin (Brian Kelly), Kathryn Meisle (Katharine Graham), Matt McGrath (George Wilson/Eugene Patterson), Larry Pine (Richard Nixon/Dennis Doolin), Russell Soder (Soldier/Darryl Cox/Clerk & Bailiff/Ron Ziegler), Peter Strauss (Ben Bradlee), Peter Van Norden (Fritz Beebe/Henry Kissinger)

New York premiere of a new play presented in two acts; February 24–March 28, 2010 (Opened March 9); 15 previews, 24 performances.

Restoration by Claudia Shear; Produced in association with La Jolla Playhouse; Director, Christopher Ashley; Sets, Scott Pask; Lighting, David Lander; Costumes, David C. Woolard; Original Music & Sound, Dan Moses Schreier; Video, Kristin Ellert; Wigs, Mark Adam Rampmeyer; Dramaturgy, Gabriel Greene; PSM, James FitzSimmons; Stage Manager, Katherine Wallace; Assistant Director, Michael Finkle; Script Supervisor, Jeremiah Matthew Davis; Production Electrician, John Anselmo Jr.; Sound/Video Supervisor, Jamie McElhinney; Costume Shop Manager, Jeffrey Wallach; Prop Master, Matt Hodges; Assistant Design: Warren Stiles (set), Thomas Charles Legalley, Amanda Seymour (costumes), Toby Jaguar Algya (sound), Justin Partier (lighting); Wardrobe, Cailin Anderson; Video Programmer, Ryan Holsopple; **CAST**: Tina Benko (Dapne), Jonathan Cake (Max), Alan Mandell (Professor), Natalija Nogulich (Marciante/Beatrice/Nonna), Claudia Shear (Giulia)

New York premiere of a new play presented without intermission; April 30–June 13, 2010 (Opened May 19); 20 previews, 29 performances. Originally commissioned and world premiere produced by La Jolla Playhouse (Christopher Ashley, Artistic Director; Michael S. Rosenberg, Managing Director) June 23–July 19, 2009.

Claudia Shear and Jonathan Cake in Restoration

Jack Gilpin, Matt McGrath, Kathryn Meisle, Peter Van Norden, and Peter Strauss in Top Secret

Pan Asian Repertory Theatre

Thirty-third Season

Artistic Producing Director, Tisa Chang; Producing Associate, Abby Felder; Artistic Associate, Ron Nakahara; Marketing/Education Associate, Steven Osborn; Workshop Instructor, Ernest Abuba; Fight Coordinator, Michael G. Chin; Outreach Associate/House Manager, Danny Gomez; Intern, Jonathan Lim; Webmaster, Auric Abuba; Production Manager, Jay Janicki; Box Office Manager, Monet Hurst-Mendoza; Bookkeeper, Rosemary Kahn; Graphics, Ramon Gil & Chris Loh; Advertising, Miller Advertising; Photo Archivist, Corky Lee; Press, Keith Sherman and Associates

Imelda, A New Musical Book by Sachi Oyama, music by Nathan Wang, lyrics by Aaron Coleman; Presented in association with East West Players; Director, Tim Dang; Choreography, Reggie Lee; Set, Kaori Akazawa; Costumes, Ivy Chou; Lighting, Victor En Yu Tan; Hair & Makeup, Leslie F. Espinosa; Stage Manager, Elis C. Arroyo; ASM, Elyzabeth Gorman; Musical Director, Devin Ilaw; Projection Coordinator, Rocco D'Santi; Dance Captain, Billy Bustamante; Sound Coordinator, Claire L. Bacon; Lighting Assistant, Marciel Irene Greene; Wig Assistant, Christina Lomauro; Assistant to the Costume Designer, Stephanie Petagno; Wardrobe, Dawn Luna; Set Execution, Daddy-O; **CAST**: Jaygee Macapugay (Imelda Marcos), Angelica-Lee Aspiras (Muse 1 Ulli), Sacha Iskra (Muse 2 Verti), Jonelle Margallo (Muse 3 Luz), Brian Jose (Ninoy Aquino), Romney Piamonte (Beauty Pageant Announcer/Various), Billy Bustamante (Mayor/Various), Mel Sagrado Maghuyop (Ferdinand Marcos), Loresa Lanceta (Peasant Mother/Various), Alan Ariano (Peasant Father/Various), Leanne Cabrera (Peasant Daughter/Dovey/Various), Liz Casasola (Corazon Aquino); Musicians: Devin Ilaw (keyboards), Raymund Golamco (guitar), Bradley Lovelace (bass), Pete Lewis (percussion)

Musical Numbers: Forever Part of You, 3,000 Pairs of Shoes, Dreaming of a Dance, Wear a Pretty Bow, Wear a Pretty Bow (reprise), Maharlika, The Education of Imelda, East West, A Beautiful Place, Like God, Philippine Origins, Martial Law...With a Smile, If I Had Raised the Butterfly, Imeldific, Flight Back to the Philippines, Myself My Heart, People Power, Finale/Like God (reprise)

New York premiere of a new musical presented in two acts; Julia Miles Theater; September 22–October 18, 2009 (Opened September 30); 6 previews, 21 performances. World premiere at East West Players (Los Angeles) May 5–June 5, 2005.

Jaygee Macapugay, Mel Sagrado, and the Company in Imelda *(photos by Corky Lee)*

Newworks 2010 Project Director, Ernest Abuba; Lighting, Rocco D'Santi; Stage Manager, A.J. Dobbs; Program A (March 4 & 6): *The Women of Tu-Na House* written and performed by Nancy Eng; *A True Asian Hottie* by Jo Shui, directed by Allen Hope Sermonia, with Eileen Rivera; *Air and Angels* (excerpts from a multi-cast full play) written and directed by Anne Noelani Miyamoto, with Nancy Eng and Kaipo Schwab; Program B (March 5 & 7): *American Mix Tape* written and performed by Allen Hope Sermonia; *Iris* written and performed by Jen Yip; *Whaler* (excerpt from a longer play) written and directed by Snehal Desai, with Una Osato

Two evenings of new solo performance plays and excerpts from full length plays presented in repertory; West End Theatre; March 4–7, 2010; 4 performances.

Allen Hope Sermonia in American Mix-Tape, *part of Newworks 2010*

Ching Chong Chinaman by Lauren Yee; Director, May Adrales; Lighting, Ji-Youn Chang; Costumes, Kate Mincer; Set, Gian Marco Lo Forte; Sound and Original Music, Robert Murphy; Stage Manager, Courtney James; ASM, Amy Scura; Sound Operator, Claire L. Bacon; Master Electrician, Rocco D'Santi; Assistant Director, Alex Mallory; Assistant to Designers: Jesse Belsky (lighting), Michelle Bohn (costumes); Wardrobe Assistant, Keiko Obremski; Props, Jenni Marks; Set Execution, Mark Tambella; **CAST**: Ron Nakahara (Ed), Jennifer Lim (Desdemona), Jon Norman Schneider (Upton), Fay Ann Lee (Grace), James Chen (Jinqiang), Angela Lin (The Chinese Woman)

Off-Broadway premiere of a new play presented in two acts; West End Theatre; March 19–April 11, 2010 (Opened March 24); 7 previews, 20 performances. Previously presented by The Present Company in the 2007 New York International Fringe Festival; world premiere at Mu Performing Arts (Minneapolis, Minnesota) February 13–March 1, 2009.

Pearl Theatre Company

Twenty-sixth Season

Artistic Director, J.R. Sullivan; Managing Director, Shira Beckerman; Production Manager/Technical Director, Gary Levinson; Dramaturg, Kate Farrington; Marketing & Press, Aaron Schwartzbord; Interim Development Director, Angi Taylor; Audience Services Manager, Courtney Breslin; Assistant to the Artistic Director, Sarah Wozniak; Management Associate, Michael Levinton; Costume Shop Manager, Niki Hernandez-Adams; Education, Carol Schultz

The Playboy of the Western World by J.M. Synge; Director, J.R. Sullivan; Set, Henry Feiner; Costumes, Rachel Laritz; Lighting, Stephen Petrilli; Sound, M.L. Dogg; Fight Director, Rod Kinter; Voice, Speech, and Dialect Direction, Dudley Knight & Philip Thompson; Property Master, Lillian Clements; Stage Manager, Lisa Ledwich; Production Assistant, Stephanie Larson; Fight Captain, Michael Brusasco; **CAST**: Sean McNall (Christopher Mahon), Bradford Cover (Michael James Flaherty), Lee Stark (Margaret Flaherty), Ryan G. Metzger (Shawn Keough), Dominic Cuskern (Jimmy Farrell), Rachel Botchan (Widow Quin), Ellen Adair (Sara Tansey), Stephanie Bratnick (Susan Brady), Julie Ferrell (Honor Blake), Joe Kady (Old Mahon); Understudies: Ryan G. Metzger (Christopher Mahon), T.J. Edwards (Michael James Flaherty), Ellen Adair (Margaret Flaherty), Michael Brusasco (Shawn Keough), Robin Leslie Brown (Widow Quin), Stephanie Bratnick (Sara Tansey), Julie Ferrell (Susan Brady), Dominic Cuskern (Old Mahon)

Setting: Early 1900s; a rural tavern along the Atlantic coast in County Mayo, Ireland. Revival of a play presented in three acts with two intermissions; City Center Stage II; October 2–November 22, 2009 (Opened October 11); 10 previews, 43 performances. Originally produced in Dublin in 1907. The play was presented on Broadway at the Vivian Beaumont Theatre January 1–February 20, 1971 (see *Theatre World* Vol. 27, page 133).

Joe Kady, Rachel Botchan, and Michael Brusasco in The Playboy of the Western World *(photo by Gregory Costanzo)*

Misalliance by George Bernard Shaw; Director, Jeff Steitzer; Set, Bill Clarke; Costumes, Liz Covey; Lighting, Stephen Petrilli; Sound, Jane Shaw; Fight Director, Rod Kinter; Dialect Direction, Dudley Knight; Property Master, Lillian Clements; PSM, Dale Smallwood; Production Assistant, Cody Renard Richard; Wigs, Amanda Miller; Fight Captain, Michael Brusasco; **CAST**: Bradford Cover (Johnny Tarleton), Steven Boyer (Bentley Summerhays), Lee Stark (Hypatia Tarleton), Robin Leslie Brown (Mrs. Tarleton), Dominic Cuskern (Lord Summerhays), Dan Daily (John Tarleton), Michael Brusasco (Joey Percival), Erika Rolfsrud (Lina Szczepanowska), Sean McNall (The Man); Understudies: Marc LeVasseur (Johnny Tarleton/Bentley Summerhays/Joey Percival), Jolly Abraham (Hypatia Tarleton), T.J. Edwards (Lord Summerhays/The Man), Bradford Cover (John Tarleton), Lee Stark (Lina Szczepanowska)

Setting: The Tarleton country estate in Surrey, on the slope of Hindhead, England; 1910. Revival of a play presented in two acts; City Center Stage II; December 4, 2009–January 24, 2010 (Opened December 13); 10 previews, 42 performances. Originally produced on Broadway at the Broadhurst Theatre September 27–November, 1917. It was revived by the New York City Drama Company at the Barrymore Theatre March 6–June 27, 1953 (see *Theatre World* Vol. 9, page 128).

Hard Times by Charles Dickens, adapted by Stephen Jeffreys; Director, J.R. Sullivan; Set, Jo Winiarski; Costumes, Devon Painter; Lighting, Stephen Petrilli; Sound, Lindsay Jones; Assistant Sound, Will Pickens; Movement Coach/Assistant Director, Kali Quinn; Dialect Coach, Stephen Gabis; PSM, Lisa Ledwich; Production Assistant, Kelli Keith; Property Master, Buist Bickley; **CAST**: T.J. Edwards (Gradgrind, Blackpool, Waiter, Ensemble), Jolly Abraham (Sissy, Mrs. Pegler, Mary Stokes, Ensemble), Bradford Cover (Bitzer Bounderby, Harthouse, Ensemble), Sean McNall (Sleary, Tom, Slackbridge, Ensemble), Rachel Botchan (Louisa, Emma Gordon, Mrs. Blackpool, Chairwoman, Ensemble), Robin Leslie Brown (Mrs. Gradgrind, Rachel, Mrs. Sparsit, Ensemble); Understudies: Dominic Cuskern (Mr. Edwards), Carol Schultz (Ms. Brown); Acting Apprentices: Gina Serghi, Daniel Wolfe

Setting: 1850s; the fictional town of Coketown, England. Revival of a play in two acts; City Center Stage II; February 5–March 28, 2010 (Opened February 14); 10 previews, 43 performances.

The Subject Was Roses by Frank D. Gilroy; Director, Amy Wright; Set, Harry Feiner; Costumes, Barbara A. Bell; Lighting, Stephen Petrilli; Sound, Jane Shaw; Assistant Sound, Nicholas Gorczynski; Fight Director, Rod Kinter; Additional Casting, Stephanie Klapper; PSM, Dale Smallwood; Production Assistant, Lauren Hirsh; Property Master, Mary Houston; Wigs, Amanda Miller; **CAST**: Dan Daily (John Cleary), Carol Schultz (Nettie Cleary), Matthew Amendt (Timmy Cleary)

Setting: The Bronx, a middle class apartment; May 1946. Revival of a play presented in two acts; City Center Stage II; April 9–May 9, 2010 (Opened April 18); 10 previews, 22 performances. Originally presented on Broadway at the Royale (now the Bernard B. Jacobs) Theatre May 25, 1964, featuring Jack Albertson, Irene Dailey, and Martin Sheen (see *Theatre World* Vol. 20, page 115). The production subsequently transferred to the Winthrop Ames Theatre, the Helen Hays Theatre, Henry Miller's Theatre, and finally to the Belasco Theatre where it closed on May 21, 1966 after 832 performances.

Sean McNall and Robin Leslie Brown in Hard Times *(photo by Gregory Costanzo)*

Playwrights Horizons

Thirty-ninth Season

Artistic Director, Tim Sanford; Managing Director, Leslie Marcus; General Manager, Carol Fishman;

Director of Musical Theatre/Literary Associate, Kent Nicholson; Literary Manager, Adam Greenfield; Casting, Alaine Alldaffer; Production Manager, Christopher Boll; Development, Jill Garland; Controller, Jack Feher; Marketing, Eric Winick; Director of Ticket Central, Ross Peabody; School Director, Helen R. Cook; Dramaturg, Christie Evangelisto; Company Manager, Caroline Aquino; Associate Production Manager, Shannon Nicole Case; Technical Director, Brian Coleman; Technical Supervisors: Desirée Maurer (props), Tiia E. Torchia (costumes), Katie Chihaby, Carrie Buettner, Virginia Ohnesorge (wardrobe), Douglas Filomena (lighting), Mel Schmittroth (sound); Scenic Artist, Hannah Davis; Advertising, Eliran Murphy Group; Press, The Publicity Office, Marc Thibodeau, Michael S. Borowski

The Retributionists by Daniel Goldfarb; Presented in association with South Ark Stage (Rhoda Herrick, Producing Artistic Director); Driector, Leigh Silverman; Sets, Derek McLane; Costumes, Susan Hilferty; Lighting, Peter Kaczorowski; Sound, Jill BC DuBoff; Original Music, Tom Kitt; PSM, Bess Marie Glorioso; Stage Management Resident, Lisa Schwartz; Directing Resident, Hondo Weiss-Richmond; Assistant Design: Julia Noulin-Merat, Giao-Chau Ly, Shoko Kambara (set), Jessica Pabst (costumes), Pamela Kupper (lighting), Daniel Carlyon (sound); **CAST**: Margarita Levieva (Anika Stoller), Adam Rothenberg (Jascha Pinsker), Cristin Milioti (Dinchka Fried), Adam Driver (Dov Kaplinsky), Hamilton Clancy (Gustav), Lusia Strus (Ute), Rebecca Henderson (Christine)

Setting: Act One: A Paris hotel room off Quay St. Michel; a train heading into Germany–late winter 1946. Act Two: The Forest–December 1943; A bakery in Nuremberg; the Paris hotel room; A settlement in Palestine–Spring 1946. World premiere of a new play presented in two acts; Mainstage Theater; August 21–October 3, 2008 (Opened September 16); 27 previews, 21 performances.

Adam Driver and Margarita Levieva in The Retributionists
(photos by Joan Marcus)

Circle Mirror Transformation by Annie Baker; Director, Sam Gold; Sets & Costumes, David Zinn; Lighting, Mark Barton; Sound, Leah Gelpe; PSM, Alaina Taylor; ASM, Katrina Hermann; Stage Management Resident, Michael Block; Directing Resident, Morgan Gould; Assistant Design: Tim McMath (set), Jacob Climer (costumes), Derek Wright (lighting), David Roy (sound); **CAST**: Deirdre O'Connell (Marty), Peter Friedman (James), Reed Birney (Schultz), Heidi Schreck (Theresa), Tracee Chimo (Lauren)

Setting: Time: Summer. Place: Shirely, Vermont. World premiere of a new play presented without intermission; Peter Jay Sharp Theater; September 24–November 21, 2009 (Opened October 13); 21 previews, 45 performances; Extended engagement December 15, 2009–January 31, 2010; 52 performances. Developed with assistance from the Sundance Institute Theatre Program. **2010 Theatre World Award**: Heidi Schreck

Deidre O'Connell, Heidi Schreck, Tracee Chimo, and Reed Birney
in Circle Mirror Transformation

This by Melissa James Gibson; Director, Daniel Aukin; Sets, Louisa Thompson; Costumes, Maiko Matsushima; Lighting, Matt Frey; Sound, Matt Tierney; Original Music, Peter Eldridge; PSM, Kasey Ostopchuck; ASM, Kyle Gates; Stage Manager Resident, Lisa Schwartz; Directing Resident, Hondo Weiss-Richmond; Assistant Design: Andrew Boyce (set), Natalie Robin, Oliver Watson (lighting); **CAST**: Julianne Nicholson (Jane), Eisa Davis (Marrell), Darren Pettie (Tom), Glenn Fitzgerald (Alan), Louis Cancelmi (Jean-Pierre)

Setting: Marrell and Tom's New York City apartment; the present. World premiere of a new play presented without intermission; Mainstage Theatre; November 6, 2009–January 3, 2010 (Opened December 2); 30 previews, 34 performances.

Glenn Fitzgerald, Eisa Davis, Darren Pettie, Julianne Nicholson,
and Louis Cancelmi in This

Clybourne Park by Bruce Norris; Director, Pam MacKinnon; Set, Daniel Ostling; Costumes, Ilona Somogyi; Lighting, Allen Lee Hughes; Sound, John Gromada; PSM, C.A. Clark; ASM, Kyle Gates; Stage Manager Resident, Michael Block; Directing Resident, Morgan Gould; SDCF Observer, Javier Molina; Assistant Design: Jessica Shay (costumes), Miriam Crowe, Xavier Pierce (lighting), Matthew Walsh (sound); **CAST**: Christina Kirk (Bev/Kathy), Frank Wood (Russ/Dan), Crystal A. Dickinson (Francine/Lena), Brendan Griffin (Jim/Tom/Kenneth), Damon Gupton (Albert/Kevin), Jeremy Shamos (Karl/Steve), Annie Parisse (Betsy/Lindsey)

Setting: A house at 406 Clybourne Street in Chicago's Clybourne Park area (the fictional home in Lorraine Hansbury's play *A Raisin in the Sun*). Act One – 1959. Act Two – 2009. World premiere of a new play presented in two acts; Mainstage Theater; January 29–March 21, 2010 (Opened February 21); 27 previews, 33 performances.

Christina Kirk, Jeremy Shamos, Annie Parisse, Brendan Griffin, Damon Gupton, and Crystal A. Dickinson in Clybourne Park

A Cool Dip in the Barren Saharan Crick by Kia Corthron; Presented in association with The Play Company (Kate Leowald, Founding Producer; Lauren Weigel, Managing Producer) and Culture Project (Allan Buchman, Artistic Director); Director, Chay Yew; Set, Kris Stone; Costumes, Anita Yavich; Lighting, Ben Stanton; Sound, Darron L West; PSM, Kasey Ostopchuck; ASM, Casrlos Maisonet; Stage Management Resident, Lisa Schwartz; Directing Resident, Hondo Weiss-Richmond; SDCF Observer, Krystal Banzon; Assistant Design: Kina Park, Alexis Distler, Amanda Stephens (set), Nicole Smith (costumes), Carl Faber (lighting), Matt Hubbs (sound); **CAST**: William Jackson Harper (Abebe), Myra Lucretia Taylor (Pickle), Kianné Muschett (H.J.), Joshua King (Tay), Keith Eric Chappelle (Seyoum/Tich)

Setting: Time: 2006, then seven years later, then a year after that. Place: The U.S. and Ethiopia. World premiere of a new play presented in two acts; Peter Jay Sharp Theater; March 4–April 11, 2010 (Opened March 28); 28 previews, 17 performances.

The Burnt Part Boys Book by Mariana Elder, music by Chris Miller, lyrics by Nathan Tysen; Co-produced by Vineyard Theatre (Douglas Aibel, Artistic Director; Jennifer Garvey-Blackwell, Executive Director); Director and Musical Staging, Joe Calarco; Set, Brian Prather; Costumes, Elizabeth Flauto; Lighting, Chris Lee; Sound, Lindsay Jones; Music Director, Vadim Feichtner; Orchestrations, Bruce Coughlin; Music Coordinator, John Miller; PSM, Lori Lundquist; Additional Casting, Jim Carnahan, Carrie Gardner; Co-Press, Sam Rudy Media; Vineyard Associate Artistic Director, Sarah Stern; Vineyard General Manager, Reed Ridgley; ASM, Katrina Herrmann; Stage Management Resident, Michael Block; SDCF Observer, Jay Cohen; Directing Resident, Sara Sahin; Dialect Coach, Carrie Chapter; Dance Captain, Molly Ranson; Assistant Design, Alexander Woodward (set), Caitlin Hunt (costumes), Denise Wilcox (lighting), Will Pickens (sound);

Myra Lucretia Taylor, Keith Eric Chappelle, William Jackson Harper, Kianné Muschett in A Cool Dip in the Barren Saharan Crick

Music Preparation, Emily Grishman, Katherine Edmonds; **CAST**: Michael Park (Miner Twitchell, Sam Houston, Davy Crockett, Jim Bowie), Randy Redd (Miner Boggs), Asa Somers (Miner Taylor), Steve French (Miner Tinns), Al Calderon (Jake), Charlie Brady (Pete), Noah Galvin (Dusty), Andrew Durand (Chet), Molly Ranson (Frances); Musicians: Vadim Feichtner (Conductor/piano), Matt Hinkley (Associate Conductor/guitars), Maxim Moston (violin/mandolin), Todd Low (viola), Mark Vanderpoel (bass), Frank Pagano (drums)

Musical Numbers: God's Eyes, Eight Hours, Man I Never Knew, Houston's Call to Arms, The Burnt Part, Sunrise, Davy Crockett, Good Morning Gun, Little Toy Compass, Climbing Song I, Bowie's Lament, Balancing, Dusty Plays the Saw, Family Tree, Climbing Song II, Disappear, Countdown, I Made That, Finale

Setting: West Virginia. May, 1962. Off-Broadway premiere of new musical presented without intermission; Mainstage Theater; April 30–June 13, 2010 (Opened May 25); 29 previews, 23 performances. World premiere at Barrington Stage Company in Pittsfield, MA (Julianne Boyd, Artistic Director; Michael Perreca, Producing Director; William Finn, Artistic Director of Musical Theatre Program) June 21–July 15, 2006. Previously presented by the Vineyard Theatre as part of the Developmental Lab series May 26–June 6, 2009 (see *Theatre World* Vol. 65, page 241), and subsequently presented by New York Stage and Film Company and the Powerhouse Theatre at Vassar in July 2009.

Special Event

Stories on Five Stories: *The Elephant in the Room* Seven minute plays written by Adam Bock, Randy Courts, Adam Rapp, Jonathan Reynolds, Evan Smith, Kathleen Tolan, Sarah Treem; **CAST**: Diane Wiest, Debra Monk, Jason Butler Harner, Cassie Beck, Mark Blum, Danny Burstein, Bobby Cannavale, Michael Chernus, Scott Cohen, Patch Darragh, Jerry Dixon, Carmen M. Herlihy, Miranda Jackel, Zoe Kazan, Greg Keller, Sue Jean Kim, Stephen Kunken, Cristin Milloti, Kellie Overby

A one-night only-benefit presentation of seven minute plays on a common theme performed throughout the theater's five floor building; November 9, 2009.

Michael Park (center) and the Company in The Burnt Part Boys

Primary Stages

Twenty-fourth Season

Founder and Executive Producer, Casey Childs; Artistic Director, Andrew Leynse; Managing Director, Elliot Fox; Associate Artistic Director, Michelle Bossy; Literary Manager, Tessa LaNeve; Development, Jessica Sadowski Comas; Marketing, Shanta Mali; General Manager, Reuben Saunders; Production Supervisor, Peter R. Feuchtwanger; Casting, Stephanie Klapper; Press, O+M Company, Rick Miramontez, Philip Carrubba

A Lifetime of Burning by Cusi Cram; Director, Pam MacKinnon; Set, Kris Stone; Costumes, Theresa Squire; Lighting, David Weiner; Sound, Broken Chord Collective; PSM, C.S. Clark; ASM, Annette Verga-Laiger; Assistant Director, Tom Bonner; Assistant Design: Alexis Distlen (set), Ciera Wells (costumes), Andy Fritsch (lighting); Props, Matthew Hodges; **CAST**: Christina Kirk (Tess), Jennifer Westfeldt (Emma), Raúl Castillo (Alejandro), Isabel Keating (Lydia Freemantle)

Setting: New York City; the present. World premiere of a new play presented without intermission; 59E59 Theater A; July 28–September 5, 2009 (Opened August 11); 14 previews, 28 performances. Originally developed with LAByrinth Theater Company.

Raul Castillo and
Jennifer Westfeldt in
A Lifetime of Burning
(photos by James Leynse)

The Night Watcher by Charlayne Woodard; Produced by special arrangement with Bruce Ostler, Bret Adams Ltd.; Director, Daniel Sullivan; Set, Charlie Corcoran and Thomas Lynch; Costumes, Jess Goldstein; Lighting, Geoff Korf; Original Music & Sound, Obadiah Eaves; Projections, Tal Yarden; PSM, Kelly Glasgow; ASM, Kelly "Kiki" Hess; Assistant Design: Choloe Chapin (costumes), Yuriy Nayer (lighting), Hannah Wasileski (projections); **CAST**: Charlayne Woodard

Setting: New York premiere of a new solo performance play presented in two acts; 59E59 Theater A; September 22–October 31, 2009 (Opened October 6); 14 previews, 28 performances. Developed at Ojai Playwrights Conference (Robert Egan, Artistic Director) in 2007. La Jolla Playhouse (Christopher Ashley, Artistic Director; Steven Libman, Managing Director) produced a Page to Stage workshop production July 2, 2008, before the show's world premiere at Seattle Repertory Theatre (David Esbjornson, Artistic Director; Benjamin Moore, Managing Director) September 2–October 26, 2008 (see *Theatre World* Vol. 65, page 347).

Charlayne Woodard in The Night Watcher

*Quentin Mare, Mary Bacon, Brian Keane, Kelly AuCoin,
and Kate Arrington in* Happy Now?

Happy Now? by Lucinda Cox; Produced in association with Barbara & Alan D. Marks and Yale Repertory Theatre; Director, Liz Diamond; Set, Narelle Sissons; Costumes, Jennifer Moeller; Lighting, Matt Frey; Sound, David Budries; Projections, Jeff Sugg; Props, Faye Armon; Fight Director, B.H. Barry; Dialect Coach, Pamela Prather; PSM, Matthew Melchiorre; Additional Casting, Laura Schutzel/Tara Rubin Casting; ASM, Amanda Spooner; Assistant Design: Laura Taber Bacon (set), Jennifer Bilbo (costumes), Joshua Benghiat (lighting), Charles Coes (sound), Deborah Mangrum-Price (props); Associate Projections, Daniel Brodie; **CAST**: CJ Wilson (Michael), Mary Bacon (Kitty), Kelly AuCoin (Johnny), Quentin Mare (Miles), Kate Arrington (Bea), Brian Keane (Carl), Joan MacIntosh (June)

Setting: London. Now. New York premiere of a new play presented in two acts; 59E59 Theater A; January 26–March 21, 2010 (Opened February 9); 14 previews, 42 performances. Originally presented at London's National Theatre January 24, 2008.

Inner Voices: Solo Musicals—*Mosaic* and *Whida Peru: Resurrection Tangle* Presented by PREMIERES (Paulette Haupt, Artistic Director/Producer) in association with Primary Stages; Director, Jonathan Butterell; Sets/Costumes, Dane Lffrey; Lighting, Jennifer Schriever; Sound, Toby Jaguar Algya; Projections, Rocco D'Santi; Stage Manager, Robert Bennett; ASM, Aaron Gonzalez; Production Manager, Robert A. Sherrill; Producing Associate, Susan Elliott; *Mosaic*: Book and lyrics by Cheri Steinkellner, music by Georgia Stitt; Music Director/Pianist, Steve Marzullo; Guitarist, Simon Kafka; **CAST**: Heidi Blickenstaff (Ruth); *Whida Peru: Resurrection Tangle*: Book and lyrics by David Simpatico, music by Josh Schmidt; Music Director/Pianist, Andy Boroson; Music Director/Vocal Coach, J. O'Coner Navarro; **CAST**: Judith Blazer (Whida Peru)

World premiere of a two new solo performance musicals presented with intermission; 59E59 Theater A; April 2–24, 2010 (Opened April 6); 4 previews, 12 performances. PREMIERES began its first series of Inner Voices: Solo Musicals at the Zipper Factory May 12–30, 2008 with three new solo musicals by Ellen Fitzhugh & Michael John LaChiusa, Laura Harrington & Jenny Giering, and Michele Lowe & Scott Davenport Richards, which featured Victoria Clark, Jennifer Damiano, and Barbara Walsh (see *Theatre World* Vol. 64, page 272).

Judith Blazer in Whida Peru: Resurrection Tangle, *one of the two musicals of* Inner Voices: Solo Musicals

Heidi Blickenstaff in Mosaic, *one of the two musicals of* Inner Voices: Solo Musicals

The Public Theater

Fifty-fourth Season

Artistic Director, Oskar Eustis; Executive Director, Andrew Hamingson; General Manager, Andrea Nellis; Associate Artistic Director, Mandy Hackett; Associate Producer, Jenny Gersten; Development, Casey Reitz; Marketing, Nella Vera; Communications, Candi Adams; Casting, Jordan Thaler, Heidi Griffiths; Capital Projects, Adrienne Dobsovits; Finance, Daniel C. Smith; Director of Joe's Pub, Shanta Thake; Director of Musical Theatre Initiative, Ted Sperling; Director of Shakespeare Initiative, Barry Edelstein; Under the Radar, Mark Russell; Special Projects, Maria Goyanes; Master Writer Chair, Suzan-Lori Parks; Director of Production, Ruth E. Sternberg; Information Technology, Robert Cohn; Ticket Services, Jimmy Goodsey; Joe's Pub Managing Director, Kevin Abbott; Press, Sam Neuman

Twelfth Night by William Shakespeare; Director, Oskar Eustis; Sets, John Lee Beatty; Costumes, Jane Greenwood; Lighting, Peter Kaczorowski; Sound, Acme Sound Partners; Composer, HEM; Fight Director, Rick Sordelet; Choreography, Mimi Lieber; PSM, Stephen M. Kaus; Stage Manager, Buzz Cohen; Assistant Director, Rob Melrose; Vocal Consultant, Shane Ann Younts; Dramaturg, Barry Edelstein; Associate Set, Rod Lemmond; ASM, Ashley B. Delegal; Assistant Director, Laura Savia; Music Supervisor and Arranger, Greg Pliska; Vocal Consultant, Elizabeth Smith; Rehearsal Pianist, Matthew Henning; Assistant Design, Kacie Hultgren (set), Gina Scherr (lighting), Jason Crystal (sound); Associate Costumes, Jennifer Moeller; **CAST**: Raúl Esparza (Orsino, *Duke of Illyria*), Baylen Thomas (Curio/1st Officer, *attendant of the Duke*), Herb Foster (Valentine, *attendant of the Duke*), Anne Hathaway (Viola, *sister of Sebastain*), Kevin Kelly (Sea Captain & Priest), Jay O. Sanders (Sir Toby Belch, *uncle to Olivia*), Julie White (Maria, *Olivia's gentlewoman*), Hamish Linklater (Andrew Aguecheek, *suitor of Olivia*), David Pittu (Feste, *a clown, servant to Olivia*), Audra McDonald (Olivia, *a countess*), Michael Cumpsty (Malvolio, *steward to Olivia*), Charles Borland (Antonio, *sea captain, friend to Sebastian*), Stark Sands (Sebastian, *brother of Viola*), Jon Patrick Walker (Fabian, *servant to Olivia*); Ensemble: Clifton Duncan, Slate Holmgren, David Kenner, Robin LeMon, Dorien Makhloghi, Julie Sharbutt, Zach Villa; Ensemble/Musicians: Andrew Crowe (violin), Steve Curtis (guitar), Leslie Harrison (Irish flutes), Christopher Layer (Uillean & Scottish smallpipes, whistles), Ray Rizzo (percussion); Understudies: Clifton Duncan (Feste, Curio), Slate Holmgren (Toby, Sea Captain), Kevin Kelly (Antonio, Malvolio), David Kenner (Sebastian), Robin LeMon (Olivia, Maria), Dorien Makhloghi (Valentine, Preist, Andrew), Julie Sharbutt (Viola), Baylen Thomas (Orsino), Zach Villa (Fabian); Swings: Andrew Crowe, Ray Rizzo, Leslie Harrison

Setting: Illyria. Revival of the play with live music presented in two acts; Delacorte Theater; June 12–July 12, 2009 (Opened June 25); 13 previews, 17 performances.

The Company in Twelfth Night *(photos by Joan Marcus)*

Raúl Esparza and Anne Hathaway in Twelfth Night

The Bacchae by Euripides; Director, Joanne Akalaitis; Original Music, Philip Glass; Translation, Nicholas Rudall; Set, John Conklin; Costumes, Kaye Voyce; Lighting, Jennifer Tipton; Sound, Acme Sound Partners; Soundscape, Darron L West; Dramaturg, James Leverett; Music Director, Mick Rossi; Music Coordinator, John Miller; Choreography, David Neumann; Line Producer, Maria Goyanes; PSM, Martha Donaldson; Stage Manager, Amy McCraney; Associate Music Director, Sara Jobin; Assistant Director, Jill A. Samuels; Assistant Dramaturg, Greg Taubman; Assistant Choreographer, Colleen Sullivan; ASL Consultant, Stephanie Feyne; Assistant to Mr. Miller, David A. Vandervliet; Assistant Lighting, Gina Scherr; Assistant Sound, Jason Crystal, Matt Hubbs; **CAST**: Jonathan Groff (Dionysus, *god of the vine also called Bacchus*), André De Shields (Teiresias, *a Theben prophet*), George Bartenieff (Cadmus, *grandfather of Pentheus and former king*), Anthony Mackie (Pentheus, *king of Thebes*), Joan Macintosh (Agave, *mother of Pentheus*), Sullivan Corey (Servant), Steven Rishard (Herdsman), Rocco Sisto (Messenger), Karen Kandel (Chorus Leader); Chorus: April Armstrong, Marisa Echeverría, Tara Hugo, Jennifer Ikeda, Jennifer Nikki Kidwell, Alexa Kryzaniwsky, Vella Lovell, Nana Mensah, Ereni Sevasti, Elena Shaddow, Han Tang; Understudy: Nana Mensah (Chorus Leader); Musicians: Mick Rossi (Conductor), Sara Jobin (Associate Conductor/Synth), Russell Johnson & Tim Schadt (trumpets), Michael Christianson (bass trombone), Rachel Drehmann (French horn), Tim McLafferty (drums/percussion)

Setting: Thebes. Revival of the classic play with a new translation and original music presented without intermission; Delacorte Theater; August 11–30, 2009 (Opened August 24); 12 previews, 6 performances.

Jonathan Groff and Anthony Mackie in The Bacchae

Philip Seymour Hoffman and John Ortiz in Othello
(photo by Armin Bardel)

Othello by William Shakespeare; Co-presented by LAByrinth Theater Company in association with Wienner Festwochen (Vienna), and Schauspielhaus Bochum and by special arrangement with NYU Skirball Center; Director, Peter Sellers; Starring John Ortiz and Philip Seymour Hoffman

Revival of a play presented in two acts; Jack H. Skirball Center for the Performing Arts; September 12–October 4, 2009 (Opened September 27); 13 previews, 10 performances. For complete production credits, please see the full listing under The LAByrinth Theater Company in this section.

Idiot Savant by Richard Foreman; Produced in association with Ontological-Hysteric Theater; Director and Sets, Richard Foreman; Costumes, Gabriel Berry; Lighting, Heather Carson; Sound, Travis Just; Associate Set, Peter Ksander; PSM, Elizabeth Moreau; Stage Manager, Melissa Rae Miller; Assistant Director, Brenden Regimbal; Associate Lighting, Lucas Benjaminh Krech; Assistant Costumes, Andrea Hood; Production Audio Engineer, Gabe Wood; A-2, Emma Wilk; Wardrobe Superisor, Anne Wingate; Production Electrician, Zach Murphy; Master Electrician, Jon Grenay; Light Board Programmer/Operator, Tim Kaufman; Properties Master, Meghan Buchanan; Props Artisans, Natalie Taylor Hart, Sara Swansberg; Scene Shop Supervisor, Aaron Treat; Production Carpenter, Jason Paradine; Charge Painter, Hugh Morris-Stan; **CAST**: Willem Dafoe (Idiot Savant), Joel Israel (Servant), Alenka Kraigher (Marie, *in the black dress*), Elina Löwensohn (Olga, *in the riding pants*), Eric Magnus (Servant), Daniel Allen Nelson (Servant)

World premiere of a new wild theatrical odyssey presented without intermission; Martinson Hall; October 27–December 20, 2009 (Opened November 4); 9 previews, 54 performances.

Willem Dafoe and Alenka Kraigher in Idiot Savant

The Brother/Sister Plays Part 1: *In the Red and Brown Water*; Part 2: *The Brothers Size & Marcus; or, The Secret of Sweet* by Tarrell Alvin McCraney; Presented in association with McCarter Theatre (Emily Mann, Artistic Director; Timothy J. Shields, Managing Director); Directors, Tina Landau (Part 1), Robert O'Hara (Part 2); Set, James Schuette; Costumes, Karen Perry; Lighting, Peter Kaczorowski; Sound, Lindsay Jones; Vocal Arrangements, Zane Mark; PSM, Barbara Reo; Stage Managers, Alison Cote, Katrina Lynn Olson; Assistant Directors, Patricia McGregor; Anthony Sanford; Fight Director, Christian Kelly-Sordelet; Assistant Design: Jonathan Collins (set), Janelle Nicole Carothers (costumes), Matthew Walsh (sound); Associate Sound, Will Pickens; Production Assistant/Dance Captain, Smanatha Flint; Production Audio, Gabriel Bennett, Wardrobe Supervisor, Emily Merriweather; Production Electrician, Zach Murphy; Master Electrician, Andy Knapp; Properties Master, R. Jay Duckworth; **CAST**: Part 1: *In the Red and Brown Water*: Sterling K. Brown (Shango); Kimberly Hébert Gregory (Augnt Elegua), Brian Tyree Henry (The Egungun), André Holland (Elegba); Marc Damon Johnson (Ogun Size), Sean Allan Krill (The Man From State/O Li Roon), Nikiya Mathis (Shun), Kianné Muschett (Oya), Heather Alicia

Simms (Mamma Moja/Nia/The Woman Who Reminds You); Part 2: *The Brothers Size* and *Marcus; or The Secret of Sweet*. (*The Brothers Size*): Brian Tyree Henry (Oshoosi Size), André Holland (Elegba), Marc Damon Johnson (Ogun Size); (*Marcus; or The Secret of Sweet*): Sterling K. Brown (Shua), Kimberly Hébert Gregory (Shun /Aunt Elegua), Brian Tyree Henry (Terrell/Oshoosi Size); André Holland (Marcus), Marc Damon Johnson (Ogun Size), Sean Allan Krill (O Li Roon), Nikiya Mathis (Shaunta Iyun), Kianné Muschett (Osha), Heather Alicia Simms (Oba); Understudies: Royce Johnson (Shango, Ogun Size, Shau), Vanessa A. Jones (Aunt Elegua, Mama Moja, Nia, Woman Who Reminds You, Shun, Oba), Kevin Kelly (O Li Roon, Man From State), Angela Lewis (Shun, Oya, Shaunta Iyun, Osha), Hubert Point-Dujour (The Egungun, Elegba, Oshoosi Size, Terrell, Marcus)

Setting: Distant Present. San Pere, Louisiana. New York premiere of a trilogy of plays presented in two parts in repertory with some one-day marathons featuring both parts (each part presented with one intermission); Anspacher Theater; October 21–December 20, 2009 (Opened November 17); 28 previews, 41 performances. World premiere presented at the McCarter Theater Center April 24–June 21, 2009 (see *Theatre World* Vol. 65, page 332). An earlier version of *The Brothers Size* was presented at the Public Theater in 2008 (see *Theatre World* Vol. 64, page 186).

Marc Damon Johnson, Brian Tyree Henry, and Andre Holland in The Brothers Size, *part of* The Brother/Sister Plays

Mike Daisey in The Last Cargo Cult

The Last Cargo Cult Created and performed by Mike Daisey; Director, Jean-Michele Gregory; Set, Peer Ksander; Lighting, Russell H. Champa; Sound, Daniel Erdberg; PSM, Michael D. Domue; Assistant Set, Andreea Mincic; Assistant Sound, Bridget O'Connor; Production Assistant, Johanna Thelin; Audio Engineer, Josh Davis; Front of House Engineer, Jana Hoglund; Wardrobe Supervisor, Sydney Ledger; Production Electrician, Zach Murphy; Master Electrician, John Kirkman; Assistant Electrician, Stephanie Palmer; Light Board, Tim Knapp; Props Master, R. Jay Duckworth; Assistant Props, Eric Hart; Production Carpenter, Mary Elizabeth Barnes

New York premiere of a new solo performance monologue presented without intermission; Newman Theater; December 3–13, 2009 (Opened December 7); 5 previews, 7 performances.

The Book of Grace by Suzan-Lori Parks; Director, James MacDonald; Set, Eugene Lee; Costumes, Susan Hilferty; Lighting, Jean Kalman; Sound, Dan Moses Schreier; Projection/Video, Jeff Sugg; Dramaturg, John Dias; Fight Director, Thomas Schall; PSM, Amy McCraney; Stage Manager, Rachel Motz; Assistant Director, Meiyin Wang; Assistant Design: Tristan Jeffers (set), Patrick Lynch (set), Chris Thielking (lighting), Gabre Wood (sound), Shawn Duan (projections); Associate Costumes, Marina Reti; Production Assistant, Mary Spadoni; Production Audio, Arielle Edwards; Wardrobe Supervisor, Emily Merriweather; Production Electrician, Zach Murphy; Master Electrician, Andy Knapp; Light Board Programmer, Jay Penfield; Properties Master, R. Jay Duckworth; Props Artisan, Nathalie Hart, Sara Swanberg; Production Carpenter, Mary Elisabeth Barnes; Scene Shop Supervisor, Aaron Treat; **CAST**: Amari Cheatom (Buddy), John Doman (Vet), Elizabeth Marvel (Grace)

World premiere of a new play presented without intermission; Anspacher Theater; March 2–April 4, 2010 (Opened March 17); 16 previews, 23 performances.

Amari Cheatom and Elizabeth Marvel in The Book of Grace

Bloody Bloody Andrew Jackson Written and directed by Alex Timbers, music and lyrics by Michael Friedman; Presented in collaboration with Center Theatre Group (Michael Ritchie, Artistic Director) in association with Les Freres Corbusier; Music Director, Justin Levine; Choreography, Danny Mefford; Set, Donyale Werle; Costumes, Emily Rebholz; Lighting, Justin Townsend; Sound, Bart Fasbender; Arrangements/Orchestrations, Gabriel Kahane; Fight Director, Jacob Grigolia-Rosenbaum; Dramaturgs, Anne Davison, Mike Sablone; PSM, Elizabeth Moreau; Stage Managers, Alaina Taylor, Melissa Miller; Production Manager, Bethany Ford; Assistant Directors, Adrienne Campbell-Holt; Assistant Production Manager, Leighann Snyder; Associate Design: Kenneth Grady Barker (set), Dave Sanderson (sound); Assistant Costume Master, Syndey Ledger; Assistant Design: Justin Couchara (set), Andrea Hood, Mira Veikley (costumes), Adrianna Desier Durant (lighting), Chris Thielking (lighting); Production Assistants, Bethany Wood, Amy Groeschel; Draftsman, Todd Potter; Production Audio, Gabriel Benett, Emma Wilk, Wardrobe Supervisor, Abigail Hahn; Production Electrician, Zach Murpy; Master Electrician, Tim Kaufman; Light Board Programmer, Jay Penfield; Props Supervisor, Amelia Freeman-Lynde; Dance Captain, Kate Cullen Roberts; Fight Captain, Benjamin Walker; **CAST**: River Aguirre (Lyncoya), James Berry (James Monroe), Michael Crane (Henry Clay), Michael Dunn (John Calhoun), Greg Hildreth (Red Eagle), Jeff Hiller (John Quincy Adams), Joe Jung (Male Soloist), Lucas Near-Verbrugghe (Martin Van Buren), Maria Elena Ramirez (Rachel), Kate Cullen Roberts (Elizabeth), Benjamin Walker (Andrew Jackson), Colleen Werthmann (The Storyteller), Emily Young (Female Soloist); Musicians: Justin Levine (piano & guitar), Charlie Rosen (bass), Ben Arons (drums); Understudies: Steven Boyer (Clay, Monroe, Male Soloist, Red Eagle, Adams), Heath Calvert (Jackson), Greg Hildreth (Calhouun, Van Buren), Julie Lake (Elizabeth, Storyteller, Female Soloist), Maria Christina Oliveras (Rachel), Xander Trop (Lyncoya)

Musical Numbers: Populism, Yea, Yea!; I'm Not That Guy; Oh, Andrew Jackson; Illness As Metaphor; I'm So That Guy; Ten Little Indians; The Corrupt Bargain; Rock Star; The Great Compromise; Public Life; Crisis Averted; The Saddest Song; Second Nature; The Hunters of Kentucky

Off-Broadway premiere of a new musical presented without intermission; Newman Theater; March 23–June 27, 2010 (Opened April 6); 15 previews, 96 performances. The musical was presented May 5–24, 2009 as part of last season's Public LAB series (see *Theatre World* Vol. 65, page 231) and was slated to transfer to Broadway September 2010. World premiere presented by Center Theatre Group at the Kirk Douglas Theatre January 2008 (see *Theatre World* Vol. 64, page 298).

Benjamin Walker (center) and the Company in
Bloody Bloody Andrew Jackson

Public LAB (Fourth Season)

Vital New Plays in Bare-Bones Productions Presented in Association with the LAByrinth Theater

Juan and John Created, directed, and performed by Roger Guenveur Smith; Sound and Video, Marc Anthony Thompson; Costumes, Emilio Sosa; Lighting, Justin Townsend; Associate Director, Patricia McGregor; PSM, Amy McCraney; Production Manager, Bethan Ford; Assistant Production Manager, Leighann Snyder; Assistant Lighting, Christopher Thielking; Production Assistant, Catherine Lynch

World premiere of solo performance play in development presented without intermission; Shiva Theater; December 1–20, 2009 (Opened December 13); 15 previews, 9 performances.

Neighbors by Branden Jacobs-Jenkins; Director, Niegel Smith; Set, Mimi Lien; Costumes, Gabriel Berry; Lighting, Peter West; Sound, Ryan Rumery and Christian Frederickson; Musical Staging, Maija Garcia; PSM, Emily Park Smith; Stage Manager, Pamela Salling; Fight Choreography, Lisa Kopitsky; Production Manager, Bethany Ford; Assistant Production Manager, Leighann Snyder; Assistant Costumes, Sydney Ledger; Production Assistants, Jessica Chayes, Jess Newman; Properties Master, Jeremy Lydic; **CAST**: Chris McKinney (Richard Patterson), Birgit Huppuch (Jean Patteson), Danielle Davenport (Melody Patterson), Tonye Patano (Mammy Crow), Eric Jordan Young (Zip Coon Crow), Okieriete Onadowan (Sambo Crow), Brandon Gill (Jim Crow), Jocelyn Bioh (Topsy Crow)

Setting: A distorted present. World premiere of a new play in development presented without intermission; Shiva Theater; February 16–March 14, 2010 (Opened March 9); 24 previews, 8 performances.

Additional Events

Courage in Concert A one-night only benefit featuring the songs from Bertolt Brecht's *Mother Courage and Her Children*, translated by Tony Kushner, and music by Jeanine Tesori; Featuring the stars of the 2006 Shakespeare in the Park production (directed by George C. Wolfe): Kevin Kline, Jenifer Lewis, Austin Pendleton, Meryl Streep, Frederick Weller; With: Daniel Craig, Maggie Gyllenhaal, Linda Emond, Mike Nichols, and the Broadway cast of *Hair*; Benefit for American Jewish World Service and Partners in Health; Newman Theater; October 19, 2009.

Under the Radar 2010 January 6–17, 2010; Artistic Director and Producer, Mark Russell; Co-Produced by Public Theater; Executive Producer, The Association of Performing Arts Presenters; Sixth annual festival spotlighting international artists ranging from emerging talents to masters in the field in new works; Productions at the Public included: *John Cassavetes' Husbands* based on his 1970s film; conceived, designed, and directed by Doris Mirescu; Presented by Dangerous Ground Productions; *American Documet* by SITI Company and the Martha Graham Company; *Chautauqua!* created by The National Theater of the United States of America; *Invisible Atom* by 2b theatre company (Canada); *Jollyship the Whiz-Bang* created by Nick Jones with Raja Azar; *Must–The Inside Story* created by Clod Ensemble in collaboration with Peggy Shaw; Produced by Fuel (U.K.); *Silver Stars* by Seán Millar, directed by Brokentalkers (Ireland); *Space Panorama* created and performed by Andrew Dawson (U.K.), presented by Broadway Across America; *The Word Begins* written and performed by Sekou tha Misfit and Steve Connell, developed and directed by Robert Egan; *Versus–In the Jungle of Cities* produced by Teatr Nowy (Poland), directed by Radek Rychcik.

New Work Now! May 7–23, 2010; Reading series of new works by emerging artists; Included: *Wings Of Night Sky, Wings Of Morning Light* written and performed by Joy Harjo, directed by Randy Reinholz; *Ady* by Rhiana Yazzie, directed by Hayley Finn, with Jennifer Rice; *Edith Can Shoot Things and Hit Them* by A. Rey Pamatmat, directed by Lisa Peterson, with Christopher Larkin, Teresa Avia Lim, Will Rogers, Jon Norman Schneider; *Urge for Going* by Mona Mansour, directed by Johanna Gruenhut, with Tala Ashe, Ramsey Faragallah, Sevan Greene, Omar Koury, Mozhan Marno, Laith Nakli, Babak Tafti; The Civilians' *The Great Immensity* written and directed by Steven Cosson, with Blair Baker, Damian Baldet, Hannah Cabell, Christina Kirk, Pedro Pascal, Jeremy Shamos, Rachel Stern; *Mary* by Thomas Bradshaw, directed by May Adrales, with Stephanie Berry, Frankie Faison, Judith Hawking, Scott Jaeck, Steven Boyer, Nic Cory, George Burich; *Our Lady of Kibeho* by Katori Hall, directed by Liesl Tommy, with Lynnette Freeman and Nana Mensah; *Welcome Home, Dean Charbonneau* written and directed by Adam Rapp, with Ehad Berisha and Guy Boyd; *Ameriville* written and performed by Universes (Steven Sapp, Mildred Ruiz, Gamal Abdel Chasten, and William Ruiz), directed and developed by Chay Yew; *Forgotten World* by Deborah Asiimwe, directed by Liesl Tommy; *Jane Says* by Diana Son, directed by Jonathan Rosenberg.

Rattlestick Playwrights Theater

Fifteenth Season

Co-Founder/Artistic Director, David Van Asselt; Managing Director, Brian Long; Gala Chairman/Special Advisor, Sandra Coudert; Production Manager, Eugenia Furneaux-Arends; Literary Managers, Denis Butkus, Julie Kline, Daniel Talbott; House Manager/Marketing Associate, Dana Edwards; Box Office Manager, Ira Lopez; Literary Associate, Brian Miskell, Mary Laws; Marketing & Development Intern, Mary Laws, Sam Horwith, Diana Stahl, Cassandra Stroud; Press, O+M Company, Richard Hillman

Killers and Other Family by Lucy Thurber; Director, Caitriona McLaughlin; Set, John McDermott; Costumes, Emily Rebholz; Lighting, Benjamin Ehrenreich; Sound, Isaac Butler; Props, Eugenia Furneaux-Arends; Fight Director, David Anzuelo; Casting, Jodi Bowman; Assistant Director, John Michael DiResta; Technical Director, Brian Smallwood; PSM, Terri K. Kohler; ASM, Melissa Mae Gregus; **CAST**: Aya Cash (Claire), Dashiell Eaves (Jeff), Shane McRae (Danny), Samantha Soule (Lizzie)

Setting: Rural Massachusettes. Revival of a play presented without intermission; Theatre 224 Waverly; September 17–October 17, 2009 (Opened September 24); 6 previews, 19 performances. World premiere at Rattlestick Playwrights Theatre January 17–February 18, 2001 (see *Theatre World* Vol. 57, page 148).

Samantha Soule, Aya Cash, Shane McRae, and Dashiell Eaves in Killers and Other Family (*photos by Sandra Coudert*)

Post No Bills by Mando Alvarado; Director, Michael Ray Escamilla; Composer, Sandra Rubio; "Give In" written by Shanna Zell; Musician, Andrew Wetzel; Set, Raul Abrego; Costumes, Ren LaDassor; Lighting, Joel Moritz; Sound, Eric Shim; Props, Eugenia, Furneaux-Arends; Assistant Director, Krystal Banzon; Musical Director, Randall Eng; Fight Director, David Anzuelo; PSM, Melissa Mae Gregus; Technical Director, Brian Smallwood; Assistant Lighting Designer/Programmer, Dan O'Brien; Sound Operator, Annie Dalenberg; Assistant Set Designer, Ashley Pridmore; Assistant Technical Director, Ian Heitzman; **CAST**: Wade Allain-Marcus (Eddie Harper), Teddy Cañez (Esteban), Audrey Esparza (Reyna Escondido), John-Martin Green (Sal Deberry)

Setting: The Big City; the present. World premiere of a new play with music presented in two acts; Theatre 224 Waverly; November 11–December 13, 2009 (Opened November 19); 7 previews, 25 performances.

John Martin Green, Teddy Canez, and Audrey Esparza in Post No Bills

Blind by Craig Wright; Director, Lucie Tiberghien; Set, Takeshi Kata; Costumes, Anne Kennedy; Lighting, Matt Richards; Sound, Ryan Rumery; Composer, Christian Frederickson; Props, Eugenia Furneaux-Arends; Fight Director, David Anzuelo; Casting, Calleri Casting; PSM, Melissa Mae Gregus; ASM, Rebecca Spinac; Technical Director, Brian Smallwood; Assistant Technical Director, Ian Heitzman; Assistant to the Playwright, Justin Lillehei; Assistant Lighting, Sarah Tunderman; Lighting Programmer, Chris Theilking; **CAST**: Veanne Cox (Jocasta), Seth Numrich (Oedipus), Danielle Slavick (Maid)

World premiere of a new play presented without intermission; Theatre 224 Waverly; February 17–March 21, 2010 (Opened February 25); 7 previews, 22 performances.

Veanne Cox and Seth Numrich in Blind

The Aliens by Annie Baker; Director, Sam Gold; Set, Andrew Lieberman; Costumes, Bobby Frederick Tilley II; Lighting, Tyler Micoleau; Sound, Bart Fasbender; Original Music, Michael Chernus, Patch Darragh, Erin Gann; Casting, Calleri Casting; Props, Eugenia Furneaux-Arends; PSM, Nicole Bouclier; ASM, Rebecca Spinac; Technical Director, Brian Smallwood; Assistant Technical Director, Ian Heitzman; Assistant Director, Will Wiseheart; Lighting Programmer, Chris Thielking; **CAST**: Michael Chernus (KJ), Dane Dehaan (Evan), Erin Gann (Jasper)

Setting: Outside of a coffee shop in Vermont; the present. World premiere of a new play presented in two acts; Theatre 224 Waverly; April 14–May 29, 2010 (Opened April 22); 7 previews, 33 performances.

Roundabout Theatre Company

Forty-fourth Season

Artistic Director, Todd Haimes; Managing Director, Harold Wolpert; Executive Director, Julia C. Levy; Associate Artistic Director, Scott Ellis; Founding Director, Gene Feist; Artistic Development/Casting, Jim Carnahan; Education, Greg McCaslin; General Manager, Sydney Beers; General Manager of the Steinberg Center, Rachel E. Ayers; Finance, Susan Neiman; Marketing/Sales Promotion, David B. Steffen; Sales, Charlie Garbowski Jr.; IT, Antonia Palumbo; Database Operations, Wendy Hutton; Production Manager, Kai Brothers; Associate Production Manager, Michael Wade; Company Manager at the Steinberg, Nicholas Caccavo; Casting, Mele Nagler; Press, Boneau/Bryan-Brown, Jessica Johnson, Matt Polk, Amy Kass, Emily Meagher

Ordinary Days Music and lyrics by Adam Gwon; Director, Marc Bruni; Set, Lee Savage; Costumes, Lisa Zinni; Lighting, Jeff Croiter; Sound, Daniel Erdberg; PSM, Megan Smith; Orchestrations, Andy Einhorn; Music Director, Vadim Feichtner; Casting, Carrie Gardner; Roundabout Underground Curator, Robyn Goodman; Associate Producers, Jill Rafson, Josh Fiedler; ASM, Ryan C. Durham; Properties Supervisor, Desiree Maurer; Assistant Director, Ross Evans; Associate Lighting, Grant Yeager; Assistant Design: Jason Simms (set), Chloe Chapin (costumes), David Sexton (lighting), Reece Nunez (sound); Wardrobe Supervisor, Ashely Rose Horton; **CAST**: Jared Gertner (Warren), Kate Weatherhead (Deb), Hunter Foster (Jason), Lisa Brescia (Claire); Orchestra: Vadim Feichtner (piano), Bryan Crook (woodwinds)

Musical Numbers: One by One by One, Don't Wanna Be Here, The Space Between, Canceling The Party, Dear Professor Thompson/Life Story, I'm Trying, Saturday at the Met, Favorite Places, Sort-Of Fairy Tale, Fine, Big Picture, Hundred-Story City, Canceling The Party (reprise), Calm, Gotta Get Out, Rofftop Duet/Falling, I'll Be Here, Beautiful

Setting: New York City. New York premiere of a new play musical without intermission; Roundabout Underground–Black Box Theatre; October 2–December 13, 2006 (Opened October 25); 28 previews, 57 performances. Originally developed by New York Theatre Barn in 2007. Originally produced by Pennsylvania Centre Stage at Penn State University, and presented at the National Alliance for Musical Theatre's Festival of New Musicals in 2008.

Hunter Foster, Kate Wetherhead, Jared Gertner, and Lisa Brescia in Ordinary Days (*photos by Joan Marcus*)

The Understudy by Theresa Rebeck; Director, Scott Ellis; Set, Alexander Dodge; Costumes, Tom Broecker; Lighting, Kenneth Posner; Original Music & Sound, Obadiah Eaves; PSM, David H. Lurie; Casting, Carrie Gardner; Stage Manager, Eileen Ryan Kelly; Assistant Director, Tamara Fisch; Writer's Assistant, Tariq Hamami; Vocal Coach, Kate Wilson; Movement Coordinator, Brooks Ashmanskas; Master Technician, Nicholas Wolff Lyndon; Assistant Design: Alexander Woodward (set), Ken Elliot (lighting), Daniel Kluger (sound); Properties, Scott Laule; Assistant Technician, Marc Grimshaw; Wardrobe Supervisor, Amy Kitzhaber; **CAST**: Justin Kirk (Harry), Mark-Paul Gosselaar (Jake), Julie White (Roxanne); Understudies: Josh Casaubon (Harry/Jake), Jenn Harris (Roxanne)

New York premiere of a new play presented without intermission; Laura Pels Theatre; October 9, 2009–January 17, 2010 (Opened November 5); 32 previews, 85 performances. World premiere presented at Williamstown Theatre Festival (Nicholas Martin, Artistic Director) July 23, 2008.

Mark-Paul Gosselaar and Justin Kirk in The Understudy

Jared Gertner and Kate Wetherhead in Ordinary Days

Julie White, Justin Kirk, and Mark-Paul Gosselaar in The Understudy

The Glass Menagerie by Tennessee Williams; Presented in association with Long Wharf Theater; Director, Gordon Edelstein; Sets, Michael Yeargan; Costumes, Martin Pakledinaz; Lighting, Jennifer Tipton; Sound, David Budries; PSM, Robyn Henry; Additional Casting, Carrie Gardner; ASM, Gregory T. Livoti; Assistant Director, Shira Milikowsky; Associate Design: Mikiko Suzuki (set), Mitchell Travers (costumes), Joyce Liao (lighting), Charles Coes (sound); Master Technician, Nicholas Wolff Lyndon; Properties Supervisor, Sarah Bird; Assistant Technician, Marc Grimshaw; Wardrobe Supervisor, Amy Kitzhaber; **CAST**: Patch Darragh (Tom Wingfield), Judith Ivey (Amanda Wingfield), Keira Keeley (Laura Wingfield), Michael Mosley (Jim O'Connor); Understudies: Laurie Kennedy (Amanda Wingfield), Michael Simpson (Tom Wingfield, Jim O'Connor), Monica West (Laura Wingfield)

Setting: A hotel in New Orleans and a tenement in St. Louis; the past. Revival of a play presented in two acts; March 5–June 13, 2010 (Opened March 24); 22 previews, 94 performances. Originally produced on Broadway at the Playhouse Theatre and then the Royale Theatre starring Laurette Taylor March 31, 1945–August 3, 1946, playing 563 performances (see *Theatre World* Vol. 1, page 86). The play has had five major revivals on Broadway, most recently at the Barrymore Theatre March 22, 2005 starring Jessica Lange, Christian Slater, Josh Lucas, and Sarah Paulson (see *Theatre World* Vol. 61, page 60). The Roundabout Theatre Company produced the fourth revival at the Criterion Center Stage Right, starring Julie Harris, Calista Flockhart, Željko Ivanek, and Kevin Kilner, October 29, 1994–January 1, 1995 (see *Theatre World* Vol. 51, page 15).

Keira Keeley and Judith Ivey in The Glass Menagerie

Keira Keeley and Patch Darragh in The Glass Menagerie

Second Stage Theatre

Thirty-first Season

Artistic Director, Carole Rothman; Associate Artistic Director, Christopher Burney; Finance, Janice B. Cwill; General Manager, Don-Scott Cooper; Development, Sarah Bordy; Marketing, Larua DiLorenzo; Sales, Noel Hattem; Marketing Associates, Hector Coris, Nathan Leslie; Ticket Services Manager, Greg Turner; Production Manager, Jeff Wild; Technical Director, Robert G. Mahon III; Literary Manager, Sara Bagley; House Manager, Joshua Schleifer; Advertising, Eliran Murphy Group; Press, The Hartman Group, Tom D'Ambrosio, Michelle Bergmann

Let Me Down Easy Conceived and written by Anna Deavere Smith; Director, Leonard Foglia; Set, Riccardo Hernandez; Costumes, Ann Hould-Ward; Lighting, Jules Fisher & Peggy Eisenhauer; Sound, Ryan Rumery; Dialect Coach, Amy Stoller; Movement Coach, Elizabeth Roxas-Dobrish; Dramaturg, Alisa Solomon; Projections, Zak Borovay; Original Musical Elements, Joshua Reman; PSM, Kelly A. Martindale; Stage Manager, Bethany Russell; Assistant to the Director, Donya K. Washington; Artistic Associates, Marcos Najera, Kimber Riddle; Associate Set, Maruti Evans; Assistant Design: Christopher Vergara (set), Dan Ozminkowski (lighting), M.L. Dogg (sound), Daniel Brodie (projections); Video Consultant, Diane Crespo; Props Master, Susan Barras; Recording Musicians: Joshua Redman (saxophone), Richard Sears (piano), Devin Hoff (bass), Michael Davis (drums), Jeff Cressman (engineer); **CAST**: Anna Deavere Smith

New York premiere of a solo performance play presented without intermission; September 15–December 6, 2009 (Opened October 7); 26 previews, 89 performances. A previous version of the play had its world premiere at Long Wharf Theatre (Gordon Edelstein, Artistic Director) January 16, 2008.

Anna Deavere Smith in Let Me Down Easy *(photos by Joan Marcus)*

Mr. & Mrs. Fitch by Douglas Carter Beane; Director, Scott Ellis; Set, Allen Moyer; Costumes, Jeff Mahshie; Lighting, Kenneth Posner; Sound, Bart Fasbender; Original Music, Lewis Flinn; Associate Director, Evan Cabnet; Casting, MelCap Casting; PSM, Diane DiVita; Stage Manager, Neil Krasnow; Production Assistant, Jenny Kennedy; Prop Master, Susan Barras; Associate Design: Warren Karp (set), Kyle LaColla (costumes), Justin Partier (lighting); Assistant Sound, Dylan Carrow; Assistant Props, Meredith Ries; **CAST**: John Lithgow (Mr. Fitch), Jennifer Ehle (Mrs. Fitch)

World premiere of a new comedy presented in two acts; January 26–April 4, 2010 (Opened February 22); 32 previews, 47 performances.

Jennifer Ehle and John Lithgow in Mr. & Mrs. Fitch

The Elaborate Entrance of Chad Deity by Kristoffer Diaz; Director, Edward Torres; Sets, Brian Sidney Bembridge; Costumes, Christine Pascual; Lighting, Jesse Klug, Sound, Mikhail Fiksel; Projections, Peter Nigrini; Fight Director, David Woolley; PSM, Roy Harris; Stage Manager, Denise Yaney; Assistant Director, Jerry Ruiz; Production Assistant, Ashley Nelson; Audio Master, Mark Huang; Associate Design: Alexis Distler (set), Lauren Phillips (lighting); Assistant Set: Ashley Farra & Gail Kennedy (costumes), M.L. Dogg (sound); Assoicate Fight Director, Mike Yahn; Fight Captain, Christian Litke; Video Director, Paul Bozymowski; Video Producer, Liz Bradley; Projection Associate/1st Editor, C. Andrew Bauer; Projection Programmer, Benjamin Keightly; 2nd Projection Editor, Daniel Vatsky; Props Master, Susan Barras; **CAST**: Desmin Borges (Macedonio Guerra), Michael T. Weiss (Everett K. Olson), Terence Archie (Chad Deity), Usman Ally (Vigneshwar Paduar), Christian Litke (Joe Jabroni/Billy Heartland/Old Glory); Standbys: John Rua (Macedonio Guerra), Utkarsh Ambud-Kar (Vigneshwar Paduar), Luke Sholl (Joe Jabroni/Billy Heartland/Old Glory), Samuel Smith (Chad Deity)

New York premiere of a new play presented in two acts; April 27–June 20, 2010 (Opened May 20); 28 previews, 35 performances. World premiere produced by Chicago's Victory Gardens Theater (Dennis Zacek, Artistic Director; Jan Kallish, Executive Director), in association with Teatro Vista, September 25–November 1, 2009.

Trust by Paul Weitz; Director, Peter DuBois; Sets, Alexander Dodge; Costumes, Emilio Sosa; Lighting, David Weiner; Sound, M.L. Dogg; PSM, Kelly Hance; Stage Manager, Denise A. Wilcox; Production Assistant, Ashley Nelson; Assistant Director, Regeinald L. Douglass; Fight Director, Mike Yahn; Associate Design: Kevin Judge (set), Cathy Parrott (costumes); Assistant Design: Alexander Woodward (set), Austin Smith (lighting), Chris Barlow (sound); Props Master, Susan Barras; **CAST**: Zach Braff (Harry), Sutton Foster (Prudence), Ari Graynor (Aleeza), Bobby Cannavale (Morton); Understudy: Charles Socarides (Harry)

World premiere of a new play presented in two acts; June 30–August 9, 2010 (Opened July 16); 25 previews, 37 performances.

Christian Litke and Terence Archie in
The Elaborate Entrance of Chad Deity

Bobby Cannavale and Sutton Foster in Trust

Sutton Foster, Zach Braff, and Ari Graynor in Trust

Second Stage Uptown Series

Year Zero by Michael Golamco; Director, Will Frears; Set, Robin Vest; Costumes, Jenny Mannis; Lighting, David Weiner; Sound, M.L. Dogg; PSM, Lori Ann Zepp; Stage Manager, Rachel Motz; Artistic/Management Assistant, Andrew Hartman; Assistant Design: Mike Floyd (costumes), Sarah Jakubasz (lighting); Props Master, Susan Barras; **CAST**: Louis Ozawa Changchien (Han), Peter Kim (Glenn), Mason Lee (Vuthy), Maureen Sebastian (Ra)

Setting: Long Beach, California. 2003. New York premiere of a new play presented in two acts; McGinn/Cazale Theater; May 18–June 22, 2010 (Opened May 26); 9 previews, 20 performances. World premiere produced by Chicago's Victory Gardens Theater (Dennis Zacek, Artistic Director; Jan Kallish, Executive Director) September 11–October 18, 2009.

Bachelorette by Leslye Headland; Director, Trip Cullman; Set, Andromache Chalfant; Costumes, Emily Rebholz; Lighting, Ben Stanton; Sound, Jill BC DuBoff; PSM, Lori Ann Zepp; Stage Manager, Rachel Motz; Artistic/Management Assistant, Andrew Hartman; Assistant Design, Jon Collins (set), Mira Veikley (costumes), Adam Lerman (sound); Violence Consultant, Mike Yahn; Props Master, Susan Barras; **CAST**: Tracee Chimo (Regan), Carmen M. Herlihy (Becky), Celia Keenan-Bolger (Katie), Fran Kranz (Joe), Eddie Kaye Thomas (Jeff), Katherine Waterston (Gena)

New York premiere of a new play presented without intermission; McGinn/Cazale Theater; July 12–August 28, 2010 (Opened July 26); 14 previews, 39 performances. World premiere presented by Los Angeles' IAMA Theatre Company in January 2008.

Louis Ozawa Changchien and Maureen Sebastian in Year Zero

Katherine Waterston, Tracee Chimo, and Celia Keenan-Bolger
in Bachelorette

Signature Theatre Company

Nineteenth Season

Founding Artistic Director, James Houghton; Executive Director, Erika Mallin; Associate Artistic Director, Beth Whitaker; General Manager, Adam Bernstein; Development, Katherine Jaeger-Thomas; Marketing, David Hatkoff; Production Manager, Paul Ziemer; Casting, Telsey + Company; Database, Dollye Evans; Box Office, Andy Windle; Press, Boneau/Bryan-Brown, Juliana Hannett, Matt Ross, Jim Byk, Emily Meagher; Legacy Playwright, Horton Foote

The Orphans' Home Cycle Nine plays wrriten and adapted by Horton Foote: *Roots in a Parched Ground*, *Convicts*, *Lily Dale*, *The Widow Claire*, *Courtship*, *Valentine's Day*, *1918*, *Cousins*, and *The Death of Papa*; Produced in association with Hartford Stage (Michael Wilson, Artistic Director; Michael Stotts, Managing Director); Director, Michael Wilson; Sets, Jeff Cowie and David M. Barber; Costumes, David C. Woolard; Lighting, Rui Rita; Original Music and Sound, John Gromada; Projections, Jan Hartley; Wigs and Hair, Mark Adam Rampmeyer; Choreography/Movement, Peter Pucci; Fight Director, Mark Olsen; Vocal and Dialect Coach, Maxwell Williams; PSM, Cole P. Bonenberger; Assistant Stage Managers, Jasmine Amii Harrison, Marissa Levy; Production Dramaturgs, Christopher Baker, Kirsten Bowen; Assistant Director, Christopher Schilder; Script Supervisor/Assistant Director, Christina Pellegrini; Associate Lighting, Wilburn Bonnell; Assistant Design: Thomas Charles LeGalley (costumes), Matthew Taylor (lighting), Matthew Walsh (sound); Vocal/Singing Coach, Ken Clark; Piano Teachers, Gregg Kailor, Barbara Rollins; Production Carpenter, Steve Lorick; Production Electrician, Doug Filomena; Production Sound & Video Supervisor, Graham Johnson; Light Board Programmer/Operator, Bridget Chervenka; Wardrobe Supervisor, Vanessa Watters; Wig Supervisor, Karine Ivey; Deck Carpenter, Kara Aghabekian; Production Assistant/Child Wrangler, Maggie Swing; Casting Associates, Jade King Carroll, Joseph Ward; Dance Captain, Stephen Plunkett

Part One–The Story of a Childhood

Prologue: A railroad car on the way to Houston, Texas, 1910. **CAST**: Bill Heck (Horace Robedaux), Pamela Payton-Wright (Mrs. Coons)

Act I (*Roots in a Parched Ground*)–Setting: 1902–1903, Harrison, Texas; **CAST**: Annalee Jeffries (Mrs. Thornton), Dylan Riley Snyder (Horace Robedaux, at age 12), Virgina Kull (corella Robedaux, as a young woman), Emily Robinson (Lily Dale Robedaux, at age 10), Maggie Lacey (Inez Thornton, as a young woman), Justin Fuller (Albert Thornton), Jenny Dare Paulin (Minnie Robedaux Curtis, at age 17), Mike Boland (Mr. Ritter), Hallie Foote (Mrs. Robedaux), Stephen Plunkett (Terrence Robedaux), Bill Heck (Paul Horace Robedaux), Devon Abner (John Howard), Lucas Caleb Rooney (George Tyler, as a young man), Henry Hodges (Lloyd), Bryce Pinkham (Pete Davenport, as a young man)

Act II (*Convicts*)–Setting: 1904, Floyd's Lane, Texas; **CAST**: Henry Hodges (Horace Robedaux, at age 14), Pat Bowie (Martha Johnson), Mike Boland (Billy Vaughn), Hallie Foote (Asa Vaughn), Charles Turner (Ben Johnson), Gilbert Owuor (Leroy Kendricks), James DeMarse (Soll Gautier), Lucas Caleb Rooney (Sheriff), Leon Addison Brown (Jackson Hall)

Act III (*Lily Dale*)–Setting: 1910, Harrison, Texas; **CAST**: Jenny Dare Paulin (Lily Dale Robedaux), Annalee Jeffries (Corella Davenport), Bill Heck (Horace Robedaux), Devon Abner (Pete Davenport), Stephen Plunkett (Will Kidder), Justin Fuller (Albert Thornton), Pamela Payton-Wright (Mrs. Coons)

World premiere of a three-part theatrical event of adaptations of the first, second, and third plays of a nine play cycle presented in three acts with two intermissions; Peter J. Norton Space; November 5, 2009–May 8, 2010 (Opened November 19); 16 previews, 74 performances.

Bill Heck and Pamela Payton-Wright in The Orphans' Home Cycle Part 1 *(photos by Gregory Costanzo)*

Henry Hodges and Dylan Riley Snyder in The Orphans Home Cycle Part 1

Part Two–The Story of a Marriage

Act I (*The Widow Claire*)–Setting: 1912, Harrison, Texas; **CAST**: Bryce Pinkham (Felix Barclay), Justin Fuller (Ed Cordray), Stephen Plunkett (Archie Gordon), Bill Heck (Horace Robedaux), Virginia Kull (Claire Ratliff), Emily Robinson (Molly), Dylan Riley Snyder (Buddy), Lucas Caleb Rooney (Val Stanton), Devon Abner (Roger Culpepper)

Act II (*Courtship*)–Setting: 1916, The Vaughn House, Harrison, Texas; **CAST**: Maggie Lacey (Elizabeth Vaughn), Pat Bowie (Eliza), Pamela Payton-Wright (Sarah Vaughn), Annalee Jeffries (Lucy Vaughn Stewart), Hallie Foote (Mrs. Vaughn), Jenny Dare Paulin (Laura Vaughn), James DeMarse (Mr. Vaughn), Bill Heck (Horace Robedaux), Stephen Plunkett (Steve Tyler)

Act III (*Valentine's Day*)–Setting: 1917, Harrison, Texas; **CAST**: Maggie Lacy (Elizabeth Robedaux), Virginia Kull (Bessie Stillman), Lucas Caleb Rooney (George Tyler), Devon Abner (Bobby Pate), Pamela Payton-Wright (Ruth Amos), Bill Heck (Horace Robedaux), Stephen Plunkett (Steve Tyler), Hallie Foote (Mrs. Vaughn), Bryce Pinkham (Brother Vaughn), James DeMarse (Mr. Vaughn), Justin Fuller (Dr. Greene)

World premiere of a three-part theatrical event of adaptations of the fourth, fifth, and sixth plays of a nine play cycle presented in three acts with two intermissions; Peter J. Norton Space; December 3, 2009–May 8, 2010 (Opened December 17, 2009); 11 previews, 67 performances.

Bryce Pinkham, Stephen Plunkett, and Bill Heck in The Orphans' Home Cycle Part 2

Jenny Dare Paulin and Maggie Lacey in The Orphans' Home Cycle Part 2

Part Three–The Story of a Family

Act I (*1918*)–Setting: 1918, Harrison, Texas; **CAST**: Bill Heck (Horace Robedaux), Gilbert Owuor (Sam Goldman), Bryce Pinkham (Brother Vaughn), Virginia Kull (Bessie Stillman), Maggie Lacey (Elizabeth Robedaux), Hallie Foote (Mrs. Vaughn), James DeMarse (Mr. Vaughn), Emily Robinson (Irma Sue), Justin Fuller (Dr. Greene), Annalee Jeffries (Mrs. Boone), Henry Hodges (A Boy)

Act II (*Cousins*)–Setting: 1925, Harrison, Texas and Houston, Texas; **CAST**: Justin Fuller (Gordon Kirby), Bill Heck (Horace Robedaux), Lucas Caleb Rooney (Lewis Higgins), Maggie Lacey (Elizabeth Robedaux), Mike Boland (Monty Reeves), Stephen Plunkett (Will Kidder), Hallie Foote (Lola Reeves), Devon Abner (Pee Davenport), Jenny Dare Paulin (Lily Dale Kidder), Annalee Jeffries (Corella Davenport), Pat Bowie (Nurse), Leon Addison Brown (Sylvester Malone), Virginia Kull (Minnie Robedaux Curtis)

Act III (*The Death of Papa*)–Setting: 1928, Harrison, Texas; **CAST**: Dylan Snyder Riley (Horace Jr.), Pat Bowie (Eliza), Jasmine Amii Harrison (Gertrude), Maggie Lacey (Elizabeth Robedaux), Hallie Foote (Mrs. Vaughn), Bryce Pinkham (Brother Vaughn), Annalee Jeffries (Corella Davenport), Pamela Payton-Wright (Inez Thornton Kirby), Bill Heck (Horace Robedaux), Charles Turner (Walter)

World premiere of a three-part theatrical event of adaptations of the seventh, eighth, and ninth plays of a nine play cycle presented in three acts with two intermissions; Peter J. Norton Space; January 7–May 8, 2010 (Opened January 26); 16 previews, 62 performances.

Understudies: Curtis Billing (for Bill Heck, Stephen Plunkett, Bryce Pinkham, Justin Fuller), Stephen Bradbury (for Mike Boland, Devon Abner, Lucas Caleb Rooney, James DeMarse), Phil McGlaston (for Charles Turner, Gilbert Owuor, Leon Addison Brown), Rebecca Nelson (for Annalee Jeffries, Hallie Foote, Pamela Payton-Wright), Leah Walsh (for Virginia Kull, Maggie Lacey, Jenny Dare Paulin)

Prior to its New York engament, the cycle was presented at Hartford Stage August 27–October 17, 2009. Each part of the three-part cycle was staged individually as well as in repertory and one-day marathons. Audicnccs could choose to see the individual parts or the entire triology. The nine plays were originally written as full-length plays; some of the plays had been previously produced and some never before seen. Hartford Stage commissioned Foote in 2007 to adapth the plays in the three-part form.

Set in Foote's fictitious town of Harrison, Texas and based partly on the childhood of Foote's father and the courtship and marriage of his parents, *The Orphans' Home Cycle* is a wide-ranging, intricate work that spans the lives of three families over three decades. Mr. Foote passed away March 4, 2009 at the age of 92, after completing the adaptations but prior to both productions. His daughter, Hallie Foote, and son-in-law, Devon Abner, were a part of the acting ensemble. **2010 Theatre World Award**: Bill Heck

Bill Heck and Maggie Lacey in The Orphans' Home Cycle Part 3

Mike Boland, Justin Fuller, Stephen Plunkett, Bill Heck, Annalee Jefferies, Hallie Foote, and Jenny Dare Paulin in The Orphans' Home Cycle Part 3

Soho Rep

Thirty-fourth Season

Artistic Director, Sarah Benson; Executive Director, Tania Carmargo; Producer, Rob Marcato; Literary & Humanities Manager, Raphael Martin; Production & Facilities Manager, Robbie Saenz de Viteri; Development Assisstant, Leslie Caiola; Management Assistant, Annalisa Mickelson; Producing Assistant, Knud Adams; Writer/Director Lab Co-Chairs, Daniel Manley & Katherine Ryan; Box Office, William Burke; Development Consultant, Jennie Greer; Founding Artistic Directors, Marlene Swarz, Jerry Engelbach; Press, Sam Rudy Media Relations, Dale Heller

Lear Written and directed by Young Jean Lee; Presented by Young Jean Lee's Theater Company (Young Jean Lee, Artistic Director; Caleb Hammons, Producing Director); Set, David Evans Morris; Lighting, Raquel Davis; Costumes, Roxana Ramseur; Sound, Matt Tierney; Choreography & Stage Movement, Dean Moss; Dramaturgy, Mike Farry; PSM, Anthony Cerrato; ASM, Miranda Huba; Associate Director, Lee Sunday Evans; Assistant Directors, Morgan Gould, Joshua Lubin-Levy; Technical Director, Maia Robbins-Zust; Assistant Design: Kate Foster (set), Barbara Samuels (lighting), Mia Bednowitz (costumes), Bobby McElver (sound); Set Construction, Berkshire Production Resources; Costume Construction, Seams Unlimited; Millinery Crafts, Roxana Ramseur; Stitchers; Mia Bednowitz, Teralyn Bruketta, Leyla Pearl; Wigs & Makeup, Amanda Miller; Production Assistant, Abby Sindzinski; Graphíc Design, An Art Service; YJLTC Press Representative, Blake Zidell; **CAST**: Paul Lazar (Edgar), April Matthis (Regan), Okwui Okpokwasili (Goneril), Pete Simpson (Edmund), Amelia Workman (Cordelia).

World premiere of a new play presented without intermission; SoHo Rep at 46 Walker; January 7–February 6, 2010 (Opened January 14); 6 previews, 28 performances.

The Truth: A Tragedy Written and composed by Cynthia Hopkins, co-commissioned by Soho Rep and Les Subsistances Lyons (France); Director/Sound/Voiceovers/Film, DJ Mendel; Design, Jeff Sugg; Choreography, Faye Driscoll; Museum Fabrication/Design Consultant, Tom Fruin, Billy Burns, Joseph Silovsky; Stage Manager, Teddy Nicholas; Run Crew: Tavish Miller; Production Assistants, Brielle Silvestri, Emma Wiseman; Graphic Design, An Arts Service; **CAST**: Cynthia Hopkins

World premiere of a solo performance theatrical piece with song and dance presented without intermission; SoHo Rep at 46 Walker; May 6–30, 2010 (Opened May 13); 6 previews, 16 performances.

Workshops and Readings

Writer/Director Lab Reading Series Downtown's premiere program for new plays; April 12–May10; Included: *I'll Meet You in Tijuana* by Jess Barbagallo, directed by Meghan Finn (April 12); *4000 Miles* by Amy Herzog, directed by Pirronne Yousefzadeh (April 19); *Trigger Warning (NSFW)* by Matthew Korahais, directed by Michael Silverstone (April 26); *Science Is Close* by Kate E. Ryan, directed by Mia Rovegno (May 3); *Welcome to Jesus* by Janine Nabers, directed by Adam Greenfield (May 10).

Cynthia Hopkins in The Truth: A Tragedy *(photo by Paula Court)*

Amelia Workman, Paul Lazar, Okwui Okpokwasili, and April Matthis in Lear *(photo by Blaine Davis)*

Theatre for a New Audience

Thirty-first Season

Artistic Director, Jeffrey Horowitz; Chairman, Theodore Rogers; Managing Director, Dorothy Ryan; General Manager, Theresa von Klug; Education, Joseph Giardina; Finance, Elizabeth Lees; Capital Campaign Director, Rachel Lovett; Associate Artistic Director, Arin Arbus; Associate General Manager, Owen M. Smith; Company Manager, Lee Helms; Assistant to the Artistic & Managing Directors, Rebecca Carton; Grants Manager, David Pasteelnick; Development Associate, Daniel Bayer; Associate Director, of Education, Carie Donnelson; Finance Associate, Andrew Zimmerman; Capital Associate, Elizabeth Carena; Casting, Deborah Brown; Subscriptions Associate, Doug "Diamond" Nyman; Production Manager, Ken Larson; Advertising, Eliran Murphy Group; Press, Bruce Cohen

Orpheus X Written and composed by Rinde Eckert; Director, Robert Woodruff; Video, Denise Marika; Set Design, David Zinn & Denise Marika; Costumes, David Zinn; Lighting, Christopeher Akerlind; Sound, David Remedios; PSM, Peter Dean; ASM, Terri K. Kohler; Properties, Meredith Ties; Technical Director, Marshall Miller; Assistant Design: Tim McMath (set), Burke Brown (lighting), Jacob Climer (costumes), Leah Gelpe (video); Video Consultant, Derek Wiles; Associate Video Consultant, Joe Stoltman; **CAST**: Rinde Eckert (Orpheus), Suzan Hanson (Eurydice), John Kelly (John/Persephone); Musicians: Timothy Feeney (percussion), Gina Leishman (keyboard), Blake Newman (bass), Wendy Richman (viola)

New York premiere of a new play with music based on the Greek myth presented without intermission; Duke on 42nd Street; December 2–20, 2009 (Opened December 3); 2 previews, 19 performances. Originally produced at American Repertory Theatre in Cambridge, Massachusettes (Robert Woodruff, Artistic Director; Robert J. Orchard, Executive Director) March 25–April 23, 2006 with this cast and design team (see *Theatre World* Vol. 60, page 266).

Suzan Hanson and Rinde Eckert in Orpheus X
(photo by T. Charles Erickson)

Measure for Measure by William Shakespeare; Director, Arin Arbus; Set, Peter Ksander; Costumes, David Zinn; Lighting, Marcus Doshi; Sound, Jane Shaw; Composer, Sarah Pickett; Vocal and Text Consultants, Cicely Berry, Robert Neff Williams; Movement Director, John Carrafa; Fight Director, B.H. Barry; PSM, Renee Lutz; ASM, Julie Watson; Literary Advisor, Jonathan Kalb; Technical Director, Marshall Miller; Properties Master, Meghan Buchanan; Assistant to the Director, Tommy Bertelsen; Assistant Design: Jacob Climer (costumes), Austin R. Smith (lighting), Nicholas Gorczynski (sound); Lighting Syndicate/Master Electrician, Doug Filomena; **CAST**: Jefferson Mays (Duke Vincentio), Robert

Langdon Lloyd (Escalus, *an ancient lord*), Rocco Sisto (Angelo, *the deputy*), Denis Butkus (Servant/Second Gentleman/Friar Peter/Froth, *a foolish gentleman*), Joe Forbrich (Justice/First Gentleman/ Barnardine, *a dissolute prisoner*), Alfredo Narciso (Lucio, *a fantastic*), Elisabeth Waterston (Isabella, *sister to Claudio*), John Keating (Pompey, *a clown*), Mary Testa (Mistress Overdone, *a bawd*/Attendant), Samara Bay (Kate Keepdown), Alyssa Bresnahan (First Punk/Francisca, *a nun*/Mariana, *betrothed to Angelo*), Rose Seccareccia (Second Punk/Juliet, *beloved of Claudio*), Leroy McClain (Claudio, *a young gentleman*), Graham Winton (Provost), John Christopher Jones (Elbow, *a simple constable*/Abhorson, *an executioner*)

Setting: Vienna. Revival of the classic drama presented in two acts; Duke on 42nd Street; February 6–March 14, 2010 (Opened February 14); 8 previews, 28 performances.

Elisabeth Waterston, LeRoy McClain (background), and Rocco Sisto in Measure for Measure *(photo by T. Charles Erickson)*

Love Is My Sin Sonnets by William Shakespeare, adapted by Peter Brook; Presented by C.I.C.T./Théâtre des Bouffes du Nord; Musician, Franck Krawczyk; Lighting, Philippe Vialatte; PSM, Christopher C. Dunlop; Production Manager, Jean Dauriac; Production Supervisor, Wilburn Bonnell; C.I.C.T. Collaborator, Marie-Hélène Estienne; Technical Director, Marshall Miller; Lighting Syndicate/Master Electrician, Doug Filomena; Wardrobe/Deck Crew, Rien Schlecht; Light/Projections Operator, Drek Raynor; **CAST**: Natasha Parry, Michael Pennington

A theatrical presentation of thirty-one sonnets presented without intermission; Duke on 42nd Street; March 25–April 17, 2010 (Opened April 1); 7 previews, 20 performances.

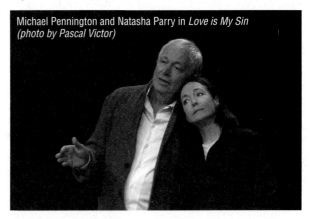

Michael Pennington and Natasha Parry in Love is My Sin
(photo by Pascal Victor)

Urban Stages

Twenty-sixth Season

Founding Artistic Director, Frances Hill; Managing Director, Lauren Schmiedel; Producing Associate, Taryn Anderson; Program Director, Lori Ann Laster; Associate, Aaron Jaros; Financial Admistrator/Wardrobe Supervisor, Olga Devyatisilnaya; Production Manager/Technical Director, Claire Karoff; Master Electrician, Lee Terry; Press, Springer Associates, Joe Trentacosta

ReEntry Written and directed by KJ Sanchez, co-written by Emily Ackerman; Co-presented by Two River Theatre Company (Aaron Posner, Artistic Director; Guy Gsell, Managing Director; Robert M. Rechnitz, Founder & Executive Producer; Joan H. Rechnitz, Associate Producer); Set and Costumes, Marion Williams; Lighting, Thom Weaver; Sound, Zach Williamson; Projections, Alex Koch; Dramaturgy, Ken Cerniglia; PSM, Denise Cardarelli; Assistant Design: Elyse Handelman (set), Jesse Belsky (lighting); Sound Operator, Sean Hagerty; **CAST**: Joseph Harrell (CO), Sameerah Luqmaan-Harris (Mom), Bobby Moreno (Charlie), PJ Sosko (John), Sheila Tapia (Liz)

New York premiere of a new play preseted without intermission; February 6–March 7, 2010 (Opened February 11); 3 previews, 24 performances. World premiere produced by Two River Theater Company (Red Bank, NJ) January 20, 2009.

Sameerah Luqmann-Harris, Sheila Tapia, Bobby Moreno, and PJ Sosko in ReEntry *(photo by Michael Portantiere)*

PJ Sosko and Sameerah Luqmann-Harris in ReEntry *(photo by Michael Portantiere)*

Langston in Harlem Book by Langston Hughes, Walter Marks, and Kent Gash, lyrics by Langston Hughes, music by Walter Marks; Produced by special arrangement with Langston, Ltd.; Executive Producer, Jon Kimbell/SenovvA Inc; Director, Kent Gash; Music Producer, Barry Levitt; Choreography, Byron Easley; Orchestrations, Steve Cohen; Music Director, John DiPinto; Set, Emily Beck; Costumes, Austin K. Sanderson; Lighting, William H. Grant III; Sound, Jason Fitzgerald; Projections, Alex Koch; Associate Choreography, Daniel Watts; Assistant Director, Carl Cofield; PSM, Jonathan Donahue; ASM, Jessa Nicole Pollack; Sound Technician, Sean Hagerty; Property Master, Lillian Clement; Backstage Crew, Erica Holz; Production Assistants, Alyssa Borg, Brendan Naylor; **CAST**: Josh Tower (Langston Hughes), Jordan Barbour (Countee Cullen), Jonathan Burke (Junior Addict), Francesca Harper (Mrs. Pointdexter), LaTrisa Harper (Miss Jefferson/Harlemite), Dell Howlett (Male Harlemite), Krisha Marcano (Mrs. Washington/Harlemite), Kenita Miller (Zora), Okieriete Onaodowan (Cuban Balladeer), Gayle Turner (Mrs. Hughes), Glenn Turner (Simple), C. Kelly Wright (Madame); Orchestra: Robert Kirshoff, John DiPinto, Mitchell Endick, Steven Kroon, Banjamin F. Brown, Shawn Edmonds

Musical Numbers: Between Two Rivers, Beat Me Daddy Seven to the Bar, Who Am I?, Crystal Stair, The Gospel According to Madam-Verse 1, The Weary Blues, Genius Child, You've Taken My Blues, Laughter/Social Dancing, Juke Box Love Song, The Sweet Flypaper of Life, Havana Dreams, Troubled Water, Lullaby, The Negro Mother, The Gospel According to Madame-Verse 2, Dancer, Words Like Freedom, I Am a Negro, The Sweet Flypaper of Life (reprise), The Gospel According to Madame-Verse 3/Life Is Fine, Finale

World premiere of a new musical presented in two acts; April 9–May 9, 2010 (Opened April 15); 6 previews, 25 performances. Workshopped at the National Alliance for Musical Theatre Festival of New Musicals in October 2004.

Kenita Miller, Josh Tower, and Jordan Barbour in Langston in Harlem *(photo by Ben Hider)*

Josh Tower and the Company in Langston in Harlem *(photo by Ben Hider)*

Vineyard Theatre

Twenty-ninth Season

Artistic Director, Douglas Aibel; Executive Director, Jennifer Garvey-Blackwell; General Manager, Reed Ridgley; Associate Artistic Director, Sarah Stern; Development, Scott Pyne; Marketing, Jonathan Waller; Education, Gad Guterman; Production Manager, Ben Morris; Assistant General Manager, Dennis Hruska; Marketing and Development Associate, Eric Emch; Box Office Manager, Literary Fellow, Louise Gough; Development Fellow/Executive Assistant, Erica Mann; Education Instructor, Dax Valdez; Casting, Henry Russell Bergstein; Press, Sam Rudy, Bob Lasko, Dale Heller

A Boy and His Soul by Colman Domingo; Director, Tony Kelly; Choreography, Kenneth L. Roberson; Set, Rachel Hauck; Costumes, Toni-Leslie James; Lighting, Marcus Doshi; Sound, Tom Morse; PSM, Winnie Y. Lok; ASM, Rachel Motz; Properties Manager, Jessica Provenzale; Assistant Design: Nicole Tobolski (costumes), Adam Greene (lighting), Mac Kerr (sound); Light Board Programmer, Austin Smith; Deck Supervisor, Eric Brooks; Wardrobe Supervisor, Ryan Oslak; Production Assistants, Marissa Konstadt, Edward Herman; **CAST**: Colman Domingo (Himself)

Off-Broadway premiere of a new solo performance play with music presented without intermission; Gertrude and Irving Dimson Theatre; September 9–November 1, 2009 (Opened September 24); 15 previews, 40 performances. Previously presented at Joe's Pub February 23, 2009.

Colman Domingo in
A Boy and His Soul
(photos by Carol Rosegg)

The Scottsboro Boys Music and lyrics by John Kander and Fred Ebb, book by David Thompson; Director and Choreography, Susan Stroman; Set, Beowulf Boritt; Costumes, Toni-Leslie James; Lighting, Kevin Adams; Sound, Peter Hylenski; Music Direction/Vocal Arrangements, David Loud; Orchestrations, Larry Hochman; Conductor, Paul Masse; Music Arrangements, Glen Kelly; Music Coordinator, John Monaco; PSM, Megan Smith; Casting, Jim Carnahan and Stephen Kopel; Fight Director, Rick Sordelet; ASM, Ryan C. Durham; Associate Director/Choreographer, Jeff Whiting; Assistant Choreographer, Eric Santagata; Properties Supervisor, Jessica Provenzale; Wig Design, Wendy Parson; Assistant Design: Alexis Distler (set), Nicky Tobolski (costumes), Wilburn Bonnell, Sarah H. Lurie (lighting), Keith Caggiano (sound); Electrics Programmer, Jay Penfield; Master Carpenter/Deck Supervisor, Eric Brooks; Wardrobe Supervisor, Cailin Anderson; Production Assistant, Shane Schnetzler; Music Copying, Kaye-Houston Music; Cast Recording: Jay Records; **CAST**: Sharon Washington (A Lady), Colman Domingo (Mr. Bones), Forrest McClendon (Mr. Tambo), John Cullum (Interlocutor); *The Scottsboro Boys*: Sean Bradford (Ozie Powell), Josh Breckenridge (Olen Montgomery), Kendrick Jones (Willie Roberson), Julius Thomas III (Roy Wright), Christian Dante White (Charles Weems), Rodney Hicks (Clarence Norris), Cody Ryan Wise (Eugene Williams), Derrick Cobey (Andy Wright), Brandon Victor Dixon (Haywood Patterson); *And*: Colman Domingo (Sheriff Bones, Lawyer Bones, Guard Bones, Attorney General, Clerk), Forrest McClendon (Samuel Leibowitz), Christian Dante White (Victoria Price), Sean Bradford (Ruby Bates), John Cullum (Judge, Governor of Alabama), Kendrick Jones (Electrofied Charlie), Julius Thomas III (Electrofied Isaac, Billy, Cook), Rodney Hicks (Preacher), Cody Ryan Wise (Little George); Musicians: Paul Masse (Conductor/piano/harmonium), Ernie Collins (upright bass/tuba), Bruce Doctor (drums/percussion), Donald Downs (trumpet/coronet), Charley Gordon (trombone), Justin Smith (violin), Andrew Sterman (flute/clarinet/piccolo/bass clarinet), Greg Utzig (guitar/banjo/mandolin)

Musical Numbers: Minstrel March, Hey, Hey, Hey, Hey!, Commencing in Chattanooga, Alabama Ladies, Nothin', Electric Chair, Go Back Home, Shout!, Make Friends with the Truth, That's Not The Way We Do Things, Never Too Late, Financial Advice, Southern Days, Alabama Ladies (reprise), It's Gonna Take Time, Zat So, You Can't Do Me, The Scottsboro Boys

Setting: Scottsboro, Alabama; 1931–1937. World premiere of a new musical presented without intermission; Gertrude and Irving Dimson Theatre; February 12–April 18, 2010 (Opened March 10); 25 previews, 41 performances. The show was slated to transfer to Broadway October 7, 2010 after a summer run at the Guthrie Theatre.

The Company in The Scottsboro Boys

Rodney Hicks, John Cullum, Brandon Victor Dixon, and the Company in The Scottsboro Boys

The Burnt Part Boys Book by Mariana Elder, music by Chris Miller, lyrics by Nathan Tysen; April 30–June 13, 2010 (Opened May 25); 29 previews, 23 performances. Co-production with Playwrights Horizons (please see full credits on the Playwrights Horizon pages in this section).

Andrew Durand, Charlie Brady, Al Calderon, and Molly Ranson in The Burnt Part Boys

The Metal Children Written and directed by Adam Rapp; Set, David Korins; Costumes, Jessica Pabst; Lighting, Ben Stanton; Original Music and Sound, David Van Tieghem; Wigs and Makeup, Erin Kennedy Lunsford; PSM, Jennifer Rae Moore; ASM, Emily Glinick; Fight Director, Rick Sordelet; Assistant Director, Joanne Tucker; Properties, Jessica Provenzale; Assistant Design: Amanda Stepehens (set), Evan Prizant (costumes), Austin Smith (lighting), Emma Wilk (sound); Master Carpenter/Deck Supervisor, Eric Brooks; Wardrobe Supervisor, Nicky Tobolski; Production Assistant, Shane Schnetzler; **CAST**: Billy Crudup (Tobin Falmouth), David Greenspan (Bruno Binelli/Father Derby), Halley Wegryn Gross (Kong/Tami Lake/Boy X), Betsy Aidem (Lynne/Roberta Cupp), Susan Blommaert (Edith Dundee), Connor Barrett (Stacey Kinsella), Phoebe Strole (Vera Dundee), Jessy Hodges (Cooper/Nurse/Porky Pig Boy), Guy Boyd (Otto Hurley)

Setting: Early spring and the following winter. An apartment in the West Village, and a small community in the American heartland. World premiere of a new play presented in two acts; Gertrude and Irving Dimson Theatre; May 5–June 13, 2010 (Opened May 19); 14 previews, 26 performances.

Phoebe Strole and Billy Crudup in The Metal Children

Women's Project

Thirty-second Season

Producing Artistic Director, Julie Crosby, PhD.; Associate Artistic Director, Megan E. Carter; Associate Producer, Allison Prouty; Marketing, Deane Brosnan; General Manager, Karron Karr; Grants Manager, Elz Cuya; General Management Fellow/Assistant General Manager, Charity Schubert; Social Media Coordinator, Monet Hurst-Mendoza; Production Manager, Aduro Productions (Carolyn Kelson & Jason Janicki); Facility Coordinator, Seth Morgan; Casting, Alaine Alldaffer & Lisa Donadio; Consultants, Kat Williams, Bruce Cohen; Financial Services, Patricia Taylor; Advertising, Eliran Murphy Group; Press, Bruce Cohen

Or, by Liz Duffy Adams; Director, Wendy McClellan; Set, Zane Pihlstrom; Costumes, Andrea Lauer; Lighting, Deb Sullivan; Sound, Elizabeth Rhodes; Wigs, Charles LaPointe; PSM, Jack Gianino; Stage Manager, Lisa McGinn; Dramaturg, Megan E. Carter; Assistant Production Manager, Seth Morgan; Dialect Coach, Deborah Hecht; Assistant Directors, Joanna Edie, Daliya Karnofsky; Assistant Design: Mar Urrestarazu (set), Ryan Oslak (costumes), Jen Rock (lighting), Jeanne Wu (sound); Props, Zach Roland; **CAST**: Kelly Hutchinson (Nell Gwynne, etc.) Andy Paris (King Charles II, etc.), Maggie Siff (Aphra Behn); Understudy: Gian Murray Gianino (King Charles II, etc.)

World premiere of a new play presented without intermission; Julia Miles Theatre; October 29–December 13, 2009 (Opened November 8); 6 previews, 33 performances.

Smudge by Rachel Axler; Director, Pam MacKinnon; Set, Narelle Sissons; Costumes, Clint Ramos; Lighting, Russell H. Champa; Sound, Asa Wember; PSM, Jack Gianino; Stage Manager, Lisa McGinn; Dramaturg, Megan E. Carter; Assistant Production Manager, Seth Morgan; Props Master, Zach Roland; Pram Fabricator, J & M Special Effects, Jeremy Chernick; Projections, Ryan Holsopple; Assistant Design: Jessica Pabst (costumes), Dani Clifford (lighting); **CAST**: Cassie Beck (Colby), Greg Keller (Nick), Brian Sgambati (Pete)

World premiere of a new play presented without intermission; Julia Miles Theatre; January 3–February 7, 2010 (Opened January 11); 7 previews, 27 performances. Developed at the Eugene O'Neill Theater Center in 2008.

Lascivious Something by Sheila Callaghan; Co-produced by Cherry Lane Theatre (Angelina Fiordellisi, Artistic Director); Director, Daniella Topol; Set, Marsha Ginsberg; Costumes, Theresa Squire; Lighting, Christopher Akerlind; Sound, Broken Chord Collective; PSM, Jack Gianino; Stage Manager, Deanna Weiner; Dramaturg, Megan E. Carter; Assistant Director, Lila Neugebauer; Fight Director, J. David Brimmer; Dialect Coach, Charlotte Fleck; Greek Coach, Valentine Lysikatos; Assistant Design: Brian Ireland & Dimana Lateva (set), Amanda Jenkins (costumes), Sooyeon Hong (lighting); Assistant Dramaturg, Sarah Leonard; Props Master, Zach Roland; **CAST**: Rob Campbell (August), Dana Eskelson (Liza), Ronete Levenson (Boy), Elisabeth Waterston (Daphne)

Setting: A remote Greek Island in 1980; Autumn. World premiere of a new play presented in two acts; Julia Miles Theatre; May 2–June 6, 2010 (Opened May 11); 8 previews, 26 performances. Developed in 2006 as part of Cherry Lane Theatre's Mentor Project.

Top: *Kelly Hutchinson, Maggie Siff, and Andy Paris in* Or,
(photos by Carol Rosegg)

Center: *Cassie Beck and Greg Keller in* Smudge

Bottom: *Rob Campbell & Dana Eskelson in* Lascivious Something

York Theatre Company

Forty-first Season

Artistic Director, James Morgan; Associate Artistic Director, Brian Blythe; Managing Director, Elisa Spencer; Chairman of the Board, W. David McCoy, Founding Director F. Janet Hayes Walker; Directors of External Relations, Bonnie J. Butkas, Michael Perreca; Marketing Manager, Phil Haas; Audience Service Manager, Devin Guinn; Reading Series Coordinator, Leff Landsman; Company Administrator, Jennifer Wills; Development/Box Office Associate, Shahna Sherwood; Graphic Design/Administrative Assistant, Jeb Knight; Casting, Geoff Josselson; Press, David Gersten & Associates

Blind Lemon Blues Created by Alan Govenar and Akin Babatunde; Co-produced by Documentary Arts in association with Central Track Productions; Director/Choreography, Akin Babatunde; Music Arrangements, Akin Babatunde, Cavin Yarbrough, Alisa Peoples Yarbrough; Sets, Russell Parkman; Lighting, Steve Woods; Costumes, Tommy Bourgeois, Choreography Consultant, Norma Miller; Movement Consultant, Janet Watson; Directorial & Dramaturgical Consultant, Obba Babatunde; Producer, Kaleta Doolin; PSM, Sarah Butke; ASM, Jana Llyun; Marketing Consultant, Donna Walker-Kuhne; Production Manager/Technical Director, Scott Dela Cruz; Master Electrician, Chris Robinson; Wardrobe Supervisor, Kiki Bertocci; **CAST**: Cavin Yarbrough (Lead Belly), Inga Ballard (Bessie Tucker/Ensemble), Carmen Ruby Floyd (Hattie Hudson/Ensemble), Timothy Parham (T-Bone Walker/Ensemble), Iisa Peoples Yarbrough (Lillian Miller/Ensemble), Akin Babatunde (Blind Lemon Jefferson); Guitar: Skip Krevens

Musical Numbers: Midnight Special, Shuckin' Sugar Interlude, One Dime Blues, Matchbox Blues, Shuck Suguar Blues (reprise), Gossip Talking Blues, Blind Lemon's Birthing Blues, Gossip Talking Blues (reprise), Steal Away Interlude, Call and Response Jam, Silver City Bound, Indiana Harbor, Doggone My Good Luck Soul, Butcher Shop Blues, Elm Street Blues, Carbolic Acid Blues, Blind Lemon Interlude, Peach Orchard Mama, Bakershop Blues, Deep Ellum Blues, Hambone Talking Blues, Stool Pigeon Blues, Dry Southern Blues, Booster Blues, Blues Hymn, Got The Blues, Long John Work Song And African Chant, Disgusted Blues, Saturday Spender Blues, Fence Breakin' Yellin' Blues, Old Rounder's Blues, Lock Step Blues, Governor Neff Blues, See That My Grave Is Kept Clean, Easin' In, Cravin' A Man Blues, Midnight Special Interlude, Broke And Hungry Blues, Train Blues Sound, Black Snake Dream Blues, Somebody's Calling My Name, Nobody's Fault But Mine, Blood Of Jesus, Motherless Child, Lord, I Want To Be Like Jesus In My Heart, Big Night Blues, Bed Spring Blues, Black Horse Blues, Tick Tock Blues Rap, Rabbit Foot Blues, Rock Island Line, Equality For Negroes, Minstrel Medley, Corinna Blues Medley, In The Midst Of The Blues, Hangman's Blues, Equality For Negroes, Happy New Year Blues, Blind Lemon Jefferson Medley: Piney Woods Mama/Yo-yo Blues/Mosquito Moan Blues/'lectric Chair Blues/War Time Blues/Where Shall I Be/All I Want Is Pure Religion, See That My Grave Is Kept Clean, Midnight Special Epilogue

Setting: A recording session in Lead Belly's New York City apartment in 1948, and various places in the mid-1920s; The Deep Ellum area of Dallas, small East Texas towns, and Chicago. Revival of a biographical musical presented in two acts; Theatre at St. Peter's Church; September 8–October 4, 2009 (Opened September 15); 8 previews, 21 performances. The York Theatre previously presented this show February 15–25, 2007 for a limited ten performance engagement (see *Theatre World* Vol. 63, page 236).

Yank! *A World War II Love Story* Music by Joseph Zellnik, book and lyrics by David Zellnik; Produced in association with Maren Berthelsen/Pamela Koslow/Stuart Wilk, Matt Schicker, Hugh Hayes, Jim Kierstead, Sondra Healy/Shidan Majidi; Director, Igor Goldin; Choreographer/Dance Captain, Jeffry Denman; Music Director, John Baxindine; Set, Ray Klausen; Costumes, Tricia Barsamian; Lighting, Ken Lapham; Wigs and Hair, Ashley Ryan; Musical Arrangements, Joseph Zellnik; Press, O+M Company, Rick Miramontez, Jaron Caldwell; Marketing Consultant, Hugh Hysell/HHC Marketing; PSM, Kimothy Cruse; ASM, Paul O'Toole; Assistant

Akin Babatunde (right) and the Company in Blind Lemon Blues

Choreographer, Erin Denman; Assistant Director/Fight Choreographer, Trey Compton; Production Manager, Scott Dela Cruz; Fight Captain, Andrew Durand; Master Electrician, Chris Robinson; Wardrobe Supervisor, Tim O'Donnell; Crew, Wyatt Kuether, Chris Ford, Lois Catanzaro, Brooke Cohen; General Manager of Yank the Musical LLC, Leonard Soloway; Strategy Consultant, The Tate Group; **CAST**: Bobby Steggert (Stu), Ivan Hernandez (Mitch), Todd Faulkner (Sarge, Scarlett, and Others), Andrew Durand (Tennessee and Others), Tally Sessions (Czechowski and Others), Nancy Anderson (Women), David Perlman (Rotelli and Others), Christopher Ruth (Professor and Others), Joseph Medeiros (India, Dream Stu, and Others), Zak Edwards (Melanie and Others), Denis Lambert (Lieutenant, Dream Mitch, and Others); Orchestra: John Baxindine (Conductor/piano), Adam Wachter (keyboards), Todd Groves (flute/clarinet/alto sax), Allison Seidner (cello), Jay Mack (drums)

Musical Numbers: Rememb'ring You, Yank, Polishing Shoes, Saddest Gal What I Am, Betty, Click, Letters/Rememb'ring You, Blue Twilight, Yank (reprise), A Couple of Regular Guys, Moive Night: The Bright Beyond, Your Squad Is Your Squad, Yank (reprise), Credit To The Uniform, You Boys, Just True, Stuck in a Cell, Ballet, A Couple of Regular Guys (reprise), Finale/Rememb'ring You

Off-Broadway premiere of a new musical presented in two acts; Theatre at St. Peter's Church; February 16–April 4, 2010 (Opened February 24); 9 previews, 40 performances. Originally presented presented September 14–21, 2005 at the second annual New York Musical Theatre Festival (see *Theatre World* Vol. 62, page 242). The Gallery Players presented the show October 20–November 11, 2007, directed by Mr. Goldin, and featuring Mr. Steggert, Mr. Denman, Mr. Faulkner, and Ms. Anderson in the cast (see *Theatre World* Vol. 64, page 227). *Yank!* was slated to transfer to Broadway in the 2010–2011 season. **2010 Dorothy Loudon** ***Starbaby*** **Award**: Bobby Steggert

Tally Sessions, David Perlman, Andrew Durand, Bobby Steggert, Ivan Hernandez, Christopher Ruth, and Zak Edwards in Yank!

Bobby Steggert and Ivan Hernandez in Yank!

Tally Sessions, Joseph Medeiros, David Perlman, Nancy Anderson, Christopher Ruth, and Todd Faulkner in Yank! *(photos by Carol Rosegg)*

Musicals In Mufti—Twenty-fourth Series

Musical Theatre Gems in Staged Concert Performances

The Grand Tour Music and lyrics by Jerry Herman, book by Michael Stewart and Mark Bramble; Based on the original play *Jacobowski and the Colonel* by Franz Werfel and the American play based on the same by S.N. Behrman; Originally produced on Broadway by James M. Nederlander, Diana Shmlin, Jack Schlissel, in association with Carole J. Shorenstein and Stewart F. Lane; Director, Michael Montel; Music Director/Pianist, James Bassi; Musical Staging, Ananda Bena-Weber; Lighting, Chris Robinson; Assistant Director, Jennifer Ashley Tepper; PSM, Sarah Butke; ASM, Emily James Durning; **CAST**: Jason Graae (S.L Jacobowsky), William Thomas Evans (Chauffeur, Undercover Agent), James Barbour (Colonel Tadeusz Boleslav Stjerbinsky), Lorinda Lisitza (Mme. Bouffier, Mme. Manzoni, Bride's Mother), Edwin Cahill (Conductor, Bargeman, Soldier), Sasha Weiss (Bride, Lily), Cynthia Leigh Heim (Mme. Vauclain, Mme. Marville, Yvonne), Roger DeWitt (Papa Clairon), Nicholas Galbraith (Groom, Soldier), Nancy Anderson (Marianne), Daniel Stewart (Captain Meuller)

Musical Numbers: I'll Be Here Tomorrow, For Poland, I Belong Here, Marianne, We're Almost There, Marianne (reprise), More And More/Less And Less, One Extraordinary Thing, One Extraordinary Thing (reprise), Mrs. S.L. Jacobowsky, Wedding Conversation, Mazeltov, I Think, I Think, For Poland (reprise), You I Like, I Belong Here (reprise), I'll Be Here Tomorrow (reprise)

Setting: June 13th to June 18th, 1940, between Paris and the Atlantic Coast of France. Staged concert of a revival of a musical presented in two acts; Theatre at St. Peter's Church; May 29–31, 2009; 5 performances. The original Broadway production played the Palace Theatre (starring Joel Grey) January 11–March 4, 1979, playing 17 previews and 61 performances (see *Theatre World* Vol. 35, page 26).

High Spirits Music, lyrics, and book by Hugh Martin and Timothy Gray, based on *Blithe Spirit* by Noël Coward; Director, Marc Bruni; Music Director/Pianist, Steven Freeman; Musical Staging, Josh Rhodes; Lighting, Chris Robinson; Assistant Music Director/Pianist, Bobby Hirschhorn; Assistant Director, Anna Strasser; PSM, Sarah Butke; ASM, Emily James Durning; **CAST**: Howard McGillin (Charles Condomine), Kirsten Wyatt (Edith), Veanne Cox (Ruth Condomine), Beth Glover (Mrs. Bradman), Daren Kelly (Dr. Bradman), Carol Kane (Madame Arcati), Janine LaManna (Elvira)

Musical Numbers: Was She Prettier Than I?, The Bicycle Song, Go Into Your Trance, You'd Better Love Me, Where Is The Man I Married?, Where Is The Man I Married? (reprise), Forever And A Day, Something Tells Me, I Know Your Heart, Faster Than Sound, If I Gave You, Talking To You, Something is Coming to Tea, Home Sweet Heaven, What In The World Did You Want?

Setting: The Condomine home, Madame Arcati's Place, and the terrace of the Penthouse Club. Hampstead, England; 1964. Staged concert of a revival of a musical presented in two acts; Theatre at St. Peter's Church; June 12–14, 2009; 5 performances. The original Broadway production played the Alvin (now the Neil Simon) Theatre April 7, 1964–February 27, 1965, playing 14 previews and 375 performances (see *Theatre World* Vol. 20, page 104).

Knickerbocker Holiday Music by Kurt Weill, book and lyrics by Maxwell Anderson; Based on Washington Irving's *Father Knickerbocker's History*; Director, Michael Unger; Music Director/Pianist, John Bell; Musical Staging, Jennifer Paulson Lee; Lighting, Chris Robinson; Arrangements/Pianist, William Wade; Assistant Director, Jennifer Ashley Tepper; PSM, Sarah Butke; ASM, Emily James Durning; **CAST**: Josh Grisetti (Washington Irving), Ric Stoneback (Corlear/Schermerhorn/Ensemble), Roland Rusinek (DePeyster/Van Cortlandt/Poffenberg/Ensemble), William Parry (Roosevelt/Ensemble), Jendi Tarde (Van Rensselaer/Ensemble), Cyrilla Baer (Vanderbilt/Mistress Schermerhorn/Ensemble), Ronica Reddick (De Vries/Ensemble), Walter Charles (Tienhoven), Lucia Spina (Van Cortlandt/Ensemble), Nick Gaswirth (Brom Broeck), Kelli Barrett (Tina Tienhoven), Martin Vidnovic (Stuyvesant)

OFF-BROADWAY Company Series • 259

Musical Numbers: Irving Song, Clickety-Clack, Entrance of the Council, Hush Hush, Nowhere To Go But Up, It Never Was You, How Can You Tell An American, Will You Remember Me, One Touch of Alchemy, The One Indispensable Man, Young People Think About Love, September Song, All Hail the Political Honeymoon, Ballad of the Robbers, Sitting in Jail, We Are Cut in Twain, Nowhere To Go But Up (reprise), To War, Our Ancient Liberties, May and January, The Scars, Dirge for a Soldier, We Are Cut in Twain (reprise), Ve Vouldn't Gonto Do It, How Can You Tell An American? (reprise)

Setting: Washington Irving's study in 1809 and in Old New York in 1647. Staged concert of a revival of a musical presented in two acts; Theatre at St. Peter's Church; June 26–28, 2009; 5 performances. The original Broadway production played the Barrymore Theatre October 19, 1938–March 11, 1939, playing 168 performances.

New2NY – Second series

New York Premieres of Musicals in Staged Concert Performances

The Times Book and lyrics by Joe Keenan, music by Brad Ross; Director, Philip Wm. McKinley; Music Director, Brad Ross; Lighting, Chris Robinson; PSM, Eileen F. Haggerty; ASM, Kimothy Cruse; Vocal Coach/Arrangements, Ned Paul Ginsburg; **CAST**: Bill Nolte (John Updike, George, Paper), Mary Gordon Murray (Critic, Fran, Joan, Paper), Jim Stanek (Bob, Paper), Heather Ayers (Meryl Streep, Amy, Columnist, Paper), Sarah Jane Everman (Beth, Paper), Robb Sapp (Critic, Matt, Tom, Paper), Julia Murney (Liz), Jordan Leeds (Ted)

Musical Numbers: The Times/The Same Sad World, If I Never Do Anything Else, A Matter of Time, Help Wanted/Great/Why We Study English, The Great American Novelist, Bob's Review/Great (reprise), The Same Sad World (reprise), Don't Let Me Forget, The Times (reprise)/The Broadway Column, Who Wears These Clothes?, Real Estate, I Didn't Say That, Busy That Night, Running Late, You Choose, The Times (reprise)/New Faces, A Luminous Debut, Watching the Show, Same Sad World (reprise), A Luminous Debut 2, Time, Finale

Setting: New York City over seventeen years. Staged concert of a musical presented without intermission; Theatre at St. Peter's Church; January 15–17, 2010; 5 performances.

Additional Events

The Musical of Musicals (The Musical!) Music and book by Eric Rockwell, lyrics and book by Joanne Bogart; Director and Choreography, Pamela Hunt; Music Director, Matt Castle; Set Supervision, James Morgan; Costumes, John Carver Sullivan; Lighting, Mary Jo Dondlinger; PSM/Production Supervisor, Scott Dela Cruz; ASM, Wyatt Keuther; General Management, Martian Entertainment; Master Electrician, Chris Robinson; Crew, Chris Ford; Press, Helene Davis; Commercial Producer, Melanie Herman; **CAST**: Brent Schindele (Big Willy, Billy-Baby, William, Bill, Villy, Chorus), Kristin Maloney (June, Jeune, Junie Faye, Junita, Juny, Chorus), Matt Castle (Jidder, Jitter, Mr. Jitters, Phantom Jitter, Jütter, Chorus), Joanne Bogart (Mother Abby, Abby, Autie Abby, Abigail Von Schtarr, Fraulein Abby, Chorus)

Revival of a musical presented in two acts presented as a benefit for the York Theatre Company; Theatre at St. Peter's Church; July 8, 2009. Originally presented at the York Theatre Company December 16, 2003–January 25, 2004 (see *Theatre World* Vol. 60, page 111), re-opened June 10–October 24, 2004, and transferred to New World Stages February 2–November 13, 2005, playing a total of 583 performances (see *Theatre World* Vol. 61, pages 112 and 139; Vol. 62, page 146).

Bock & Harnick: A Celebration Continuity and direction by Terry Berliner; Music Director, Mark Janas; PSM, Kimothy Cruse; Stage Manager, Alden Fulcomer; Award Presenter, Alice Hammestein Mathias; **CAST**: Tom Bosley, Jim Brochu, Edwin Cahill, Barbara Cook, Laura Marie Duncan, Jason Graae, Josh Grisetti, Stephen Mo Hanan, Marc Kudisch, Judy Kuhn, Howard McGillin, Christine Pedi, Emily Skinner, Joseph Stein, The Honeybees of Savannah College of Art & Design (Chase Arrington, George Hamilton, Maggie Haren, Derrick Parks, Jenna Paulette, Jasmine Richardson); Musicians: Mark Janas, Kevin Wallace, Matt Ward (piano)

A concert gala and awards presentation for the 2009 Oscar Hammerstein Award for Lifetime Achivement in Musical Theatre; The Racquet & Tennis Club; November 23, 2009.

That Time of Year Concept and lyrics by Laurence Holman and Felicia Needleman, music by Sandford Marc Cohen, Nicholas Levin, Donald Oliver, Kyle Rosen, Brad Ross, Mark Wherry, and Wendy Wilf; Co-produced by Whiskey Down Productions; Director/Choreography, Annette Jolles; Music Director/Pianist, Matt Castle; Orchestrator, Annie Pasqua; Lighting, Chris Robinson; Additional Arrangements, James Mironchik; PSM, Kimothy Cruse; ASM, Brooke Elsinghorst; **CAST**: Bridget Beirne, Kerri Jill Garbis, Josh Grisetti, Ann Harada, Thom Christopher Warren; Orchestra: Matt Castle (Conductor/piano), Chris Pagano (percussion)

Revival of a musical revue (in "Mufti" style) presented in two acts; Theatre at St. Peter's Church; December 18–20, 2010; 5 performances. Previously presented at the York Theatre November 29–December 24, 2006 (see *Theatre World* Vol. 63, page 236).

NEO6 A benefit concert celebrating new, emerging, outstanding music theatre writers; Director, Annette Joelles; Music Director, Matt Castle; PSM, Sarah Butke; ASM, Paul O'Toole; Hosts, Richard Maltby Jr. & Lynne Wintersteller; Featuring the works of Barry Wyner ("Secuity Meltdown from *Calvin Berger*), Michael Ruby & Robert Rokicki ("In the Movies" from *Love, NY*), Matthew Hardy & Randy Klein ("New Jersey" from *Flambé Dreams*), Michael Kooman & Christopher Diamond ("To Excess" from *Homemade Fusion*), Tracy Swallows ("My Point" from *The Preservation of Elizabeth Bottcher*), Daniel Israel & Phoebe Kreutz, & Adam Mathias ("It's the Drugs" from *The Dirty Hippie Jam Band Project*), Deborah Rosentstein & Alex LeFevre ("Doors" from *Cooper Street Rep*), Tina Lear ("Wedding Day"), Gordon Leary & Karlan Judd ("C-H-A-I-R-M-A-N" from *Cheer Wars*), David Holstein & Alan Schmuckler ("Linin' My Ducks in a Row" from *The Emporer's New Clothes*), Katya Stanislavskaya ("Laundry Day" from *Women on Love*), Bomi Lee & Jason Young ("Famous" from *Bradley Cole*); **CAST**: Carey Anderson, Krystal Joy Brown, Tituss Burgess, Donald Corren, Beth Fowler, Jessica Grové, David Hull, Jose Llana, Michael "Tuba" McKinsey, Krysta Rodriguez, Sandie Rosa, Tally Sessions, Dana Steingold, John Tartaglia, Noah Weisberg, Karen Ziemba; With: Thomas Michael Allen, Suzanna Neeley Bridges, Abby Bernbaum, Theresa Burns, Megan Mekjian, Gillian Munsayac; Musicians: Matt Castle, Daniel Israel, Randy Klein, Tina Lear, Alex LeFevre, Alan Schmuckler (piano), Robert Rokicki (guitar)

A benefit concert presented without intermission; Theatre at St. Peter's Church, May 10, 2010

Todd Berry, Steve Swift ,and Jenny Odle Madden in Abingdon Theatre Company's Sister Myotis's Bible Camp (photo by Kim T. Sharp)

Anthony O'Donnell, Thomas Sadoski, and Juliet Rylance in As You Like It, part of The Bridge Project at BAM (photo by Joan Marcus)

Erin Gann, Michael Chernus, and Dane DeHaan in The Aliens at Rattlestick Playwrights Theater (photo by Sandra Coudert)

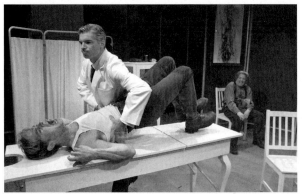

Scott Barrow, Thomas Hammond, and Chris Mixon in Dr. Knock, Or the Triumph of Medicine at the Mint Theatre (photo by Richard Termine)

Christopher Sieber and Lucas Steele in The New Group production of The Kid (photo by Monique Carboni)

Dan Daily, Lee Stark, and Sean McNall in The Pearl Theatre Company's Misalliance (photo by Sam Hough)

OFF-OFF-BROADWAY

June 1, 2009–May 31, 2010

Top: *Annie McGovern, Emma Galvin, and Noah Galvin in* The Power of Birds *presented by 3Graces Theater Co. (photo by Rick Berubé)*

Center: *Harris Yulin and Janet Zarish in* The Glass House *presented by Resonance Ensemble (photo by Jon Kandel)*

Bottom: *Kila Packett, Daniel Cibener, Kai Chapman, Erikamari Rumore, and Lareysa Smith in the Vital Theatre Company production of* Matthew Takes Manhattan *(photo by Dan Acquisto)*

Off-Off Broadway: Theatre of Now

**Shay Gines, Founding Director,
New York Innovative Theatre Awards Foundation**

For years Off-Off-Broadway (OOB) had been disregarded as disposable theatre: easily made and easily dismissed. "Theatre of Now" was an undesirable title because—for decades—most OOB productions were world premieres that had not existed prior to their debut and then, once they closed, were gone forever. Basically they only existed in the present, or the "now." Also, cost and union restrictions prohibited videotaping or recording rehearsals or performances, and media coverage was inconsistent at best, so even archival records are virtually nonexistent.

Though it began as a pejorative, the current generation of OOB artists is redefining the label "Theatre of Now" and embodying it on a number of deeper and more significant levels.

OOB productions rarely have investors or large sponsors. While modest budgets present certain challenges, the lack of commercial obligations allows these artists uninhibited artistic freedom, while creating an environment in which experimentation is encouraged. There is a unique energy and excitement that permeates this community. It is a playground for ideas and creative expression. One artistic experiment spurs on another, building a forward momentum that pushes the boundaries of the art form itself. OOB is at the forefront of developing new American theatre and is consistently ahead of the curve in terms of themes and styles. Perhaps more importantly, it is shaping an entire generation of theatre artists.

Every day, theatre artists from around the world flock to New York City in the hope of finding an artistic home. Nearly all of those artists, at one point or another, work OOB. There are an estimated 40,000 artists working in this sector every year. The independent and entrepreneurial spirit of OOB, where the artists are the producers, appeals to many. It it's also one of the only theatrical communities where emerging and seasoned artists alike are empowered to create their own work and maintain ownership of their creations. Because of this, OOB is producing thousands of new plays every season. It is literally shaping what's happening "now" and inventing what's happening "next" in American theatre.

It is's no coincidence that the qualities of the "Now Generation" are reflected in what is currently happening Off-Off-Broadway. OOB provides a conducive environment for this generation's ambitions, and it is not surprising they are increasingly finding an artistic home in a community uniquely set up to support them. Simultaneously these young artists are infusing the community with the excitement of their sensibilities and aspirations. In essence, the Now Generation is now creating the Theatre of Now.

One of the defining characteristics of the Now Generation is the ubiquity of instant gratification. These artists have grown up being able to fulfill their consumer needs almost immediately, via the internet. Unlike Broadway, or even Off-Broadway, nimble OOB productions can go from an idea to a fully realized presentation within weeks, days, or sometimes even hours.

Another characteristic of this generation is the need for a personal or customizable experience, and for multiple points of entry into that experience. The agility of OOB allows for them to be elastic, to tackle current events, ideas, and issues, providing commentary and catharsis for what is happening right now.

This year's productions eagerly took on political and popular hot button issues from across the country. Wreckio Ensemble's production of *Bail Out: The Musical* pondered what would happen if the government had bailed out the arts the same way it bailed out the nation's largest banks. *Rootless: La No-Nostalgia* took a personal look at immigration in America. In *Hatching: Eat Your Eggs*, playwright Will Porter compared a futuristic American health care system to a prison and questioned the government's responsibility to care for its citizens. Meanwhile, Sauce and Co. brought us *I Can Has Cheezburger: The MusicLOL!*, personifying

the cats of the popular website icanhascheezburger.com that has become such a cultural phenomenon.

You will also find companies such as The New York Neo-Futurists, who perform fifty weeks a year and have made it a part of their mission to present works that have current significance, akin to the "living-newspaper." Every week the ensemble writes and incorporates several new short plays based on current events, while older plays are removed from rotation when they are no longer relevant.

One of the distinguishing attributes of our age is the ever-evolving communications and media landscape. With new technologies being introduced on a daily basis, many in the performing arts find themselves grappling with the question of where they fit in. They wonder how their medium—a live human experience—can remain relevant when technology has pervaded nearly every aspect of our contemporary world.

However, instead of being at odds with new and advancing technology, OOB welcomes and embraces it. The internet has become the great equalizer for many small business endeavors, helping them reach a much larger customer base. They can present a professional appearance, and provide a virtual storefront on a twenty-four24-hour basis with a relatively small financial investment. These kinds of qualities make emerging technology a great match for the OOB community.

With websites now being standard for any legitimate business venture, OOB professionals are always among the first to experiment with new technologies like MySpace, FaceBook, Skype, blogs, YouTube, Twitter, etc. These mediums are ripe for creatively ambitious and technologically savvy artists eager to discover inventive ways to reach audiences.

Artists can now draw people in to productions with online previews, with interviews of the cast and crew through YouTube, or Skyped live. Blogs written by those involved provide a personal window into the experience of creating a production, encouraging audience interaction, and feedback. Performances are broadcast live on the internet, reaching a much larger audience then their physical performance space could accommodate. And links to all of these can be posted on the production website, on FaceBook, and on MySpace pages, sent out to friends and family through personal emails, announced on Twitter, and then forwarded and retweeted again and again.

What is more, where marketing used to be the sole responsibility of the producer, now each of the artists can have their own FaceBook page, website, or Twitter account. Everyone involved can be emissaries of a production, forwarding information to their personal network with the click of a button. These highly advanced marketing methods provide multiple points of contact, can potentially reach tens of thousands of audience members across the world, and none of them cost the producers or the artists themselves a single cent.

With performance, rehearsal, and meeting space at a premium in New York City, these technologies are also becoming essential production tools. Collaborators across the city—or across the country for that matter—can meet, schedule, and share and forward information virtually, without shelling out the cash to rent a room or spending the time or money on travel.

OOB artists are also using the technology to generate more significant media coverage of this sector. Established media sources originally provided coverage, reviews, or listings for OOB productions on a limited, "if space is available" basis. If less editorial space was available, OOB was the first to be cut.

OOB'ers recognized early on that fewer people are reading newspapers and prefer to get their news from online sources. Websites, many of which were developed by OOB artists themselves, such as OffOffOnline.com, Theasy.com, or NYTheatre. com are dedicated to promoting and providing reviews of OOB productions. Artists' blogs are gaining notoriety and helping community members garner new fans and reach like-minded independent theatre practitioners. They also help create a more cohesive sense of community, which in turn strengthens the influence of the community as a whole. As these sites and blogs grow in popularity and gain legitimacy, they encourage more traditional media sources such as the *New York Times* or the *Village Voice* to provide more online coverage of OOB productions.

Furthermore, these innovative artists are not only using these technologies to reach out to the rest of the world, they're actually incorporating them into the theatrical form itself. For example, The Internationalists present works where several artists from different countries simultaneously Skype in to participate in the performance. Gyda Arber's groundbreaking play *Suspicious Package* uses customized portable media players to lead six audience members on an interactive journey. Each audience member takes on a role in the play, and instructions and contextual movies guide them through the production as they solve the mystery, giving each audience member a truly unique and personal theatrical experience that could not have existed without the technology. Kathryn Jones' production *Better Left Unsaid* is performed live in a theatre while simultaneously being live-streamed via the internet.

Off-Off-Broadway is the Theatre of Now. It reflects contemporary American society. It embraces emerging technologies and continually reimagines how they can be integrated into the art form. It provides a home for emerging artists and seasoned professionals to experiment and revolutionize the theatrical experience. It can include re-envisioned Shakespeare, world premieres from new or established playwrights, troupes from around the world, groundbreaking avant-garde theatre, revived American classics from the 1950s, and new musicals. They all have a place in the OOB arena. From thirty-seat black box solo performances to huge outdoor amphitheatres presenting Gilbert and Sullivan; from one-night readings to productions that have been running for years, OOB provides a home for them all. These shows are performed year-round in theatres of all sizes throughout all of NYC's five boroughs. The only universally defining characteristics of this community are its dynamic creative energy, tenacious spirit, modest budgets, and intense devotion to the art.

The tiny independent theatre movement that began over fifty years ago continues to grow in the number of artists, the quality of work, the fearlessness you will find in these intimate venues, and the audiences who discover and rediscover this amazing community every year. It will persist and transform and embody what is happening now in American theatre.

Ian Hyland, Erik Saxvik, and Michael Cullen in Safe Home *presented by Chris Henry & Royal Family Productions at the Women's Interart Center (photo by Alex Koch)*

Carol Hickey, Anthony Crep, and Mark Emerson in Barrier Island *presented by Maieutic Theatre Works at Center Stage NY (photo by Antonio Miniño)*

Karen Eilbacher and Karen Sours in the Working Man's Clothes production of She Like Girls *at the Ohio Theater (photo by Julie Rossman)*

Adam Smith, Erica Livingston, Alicia Harding, Lauren Sharpe and Cara Francis in The New York Neo-Futurists' Too Much Light Makes The Baby Go Blind *at the Kraine Theater (photo by J.M. Pixley)*

Keldrick Crowder, Kipp Lyle, John Rankin in The Task at the Castillo Theatre All Stars Project (photo by Ronald L. Glassman)

Sorah Wadia & Rita Wolf in Chaos Theory, presented by Pulse Ensemble Theatre (photo by Justin Richardson)

Donnie Mather and Mirabelle Ordinaire in WeildWorks' Fêtes de la Nuit (photo by Carol Rosegg)

Chris Ceraso and Halvard Solness in the Resonance Ensemble production of The Master Builder (photo by Jon Kandel)

Phil Cutron, Jay Rohloff, Doug Nyman, Peter Iasillo, and Larry Greenbush in the Clockwork Theatre production of Underground (photo by Owen Smith)

Brit Whittle and Kelly McAndrew in Lyric is Waiting presented by kef theatrical productions and South Ark Stage (photo by Ry Pepper)

Ingrid Nordstrom, Michael Davis, Candice Holdorf, Christina Shipp, and Jason Paradine in the Flux Theatre Ensemble production of The Lesser Seductions of History *(photo by Justin Hoch)*

Tiffany Clementi, Bianca Lavern Jones, and Kelli Holsopple in Jacob's House, *presented by Flux Theatre Ensemble (photo by Justin Hoch)*

Ellen Crawford in the Horizon Theatre Rep production of The Misunderstanding *(photo by Richard Termine)*

Bjorn DuPaty and Gerald McCullouch in Daddy, *presented by DownTownTheatre Company (photo by Eduardo Placer)*

Yvonne Roen and Timothy McCown Reynolds in Rudolf II, *presented by Untitled Theater Company #61 (photo by Arthur Cornelius)*

13P

Executive Producer, Maria Goyanes, General Manager, Barbara Samuels; Sheila Callaghan, Erin Courtney, Madeleine George, Rob Handel, Ann Marie Healy, Julia Jarcho, Young Jean Lee, Winter Miller, Sarah Ruhl, Kate E. Ryan, Lucy Thurber, Anne Washburn, Gary Winter; www.13p.org

Monstrosity by Lucy Thurber; Director, Lear DeBessonet; Set, Peter Ksander; Costumes, Emily Rebholz; Lighting, Justin Townsend; Sound, M.L. Dogg; Stage Manager, Winnie Y. Lok; Movement, Tracy Bersley; Press, Jim Baldassare; Casting, Kelly Gillespie; Associate Producer, Rachel Karpf; Producer, George Spelvin; **Cast:** Carlo Alban, Reyna de Courcy, Frank De Julio, J.D. Goldblatt, Andy Grotelueschen, Ben Hollandsworth, D.J. Mendel, Robert Saietta, Samantha Soule, Kristina Valada-Viars, Michael Warner, The Teen Army; Connelly Theater; July 9–19, 2009

American Treasure by Julia Jarcho; Director, Julia Jarcho; Set, Jason Simms; Costumes, Colleen Werthmann; Lighting, Ben Kato; Sound, Asa Wember; Stage Manager, Jess Chayes; Associate Producer, Rachel Karpf; Press, Blake Zidell; **Cast:** Aaron Landsman, Jenny Seastone Stern; Paradise Factory; November 21–December 12, 2009

13th Street Repertory

Artistic Director and Founder, Edith O'Hara; Producing Artistic Director/Literary Manager, Sandra Nordgren; Set and Costumes, Tom Harlan; Lighting, Jeff Carnell; Graphic Design, Neil Feigeles; www.13thstreetrep.org

The Diary of Anne Frankenstein by Ilya Sapiroe; Presented by Theatre A L'Orange; Director, Elizabeth Elkins; Lighting, Nick Lazzaro; Set, Chesley Allen; Costumes, Mel Kier; Sound, Eben Lillie; Original Music, Kevin Cummines; **Cast:** Mimi Imfurst, Joseph Beuerlein, Geoffrey Borman, Ryan Feyk, Lavinia Co-op, Jessica Caplan, Eric Jaeger; 13th Street Repertory (non-resident); October 4–November 29, 2009

A Christmas Carol by Sondra Nordgren; Director, Lillian Z. King; Choreographer, Joshua M. Feder; Music Director, Shoshana Seid-Green; Lighting, Brian Fortin; Sound, Justin Zalkin; Stage Manager, Erin Person; **Cast:** Ali Levinson, Coby Levinson, Julia Colon, Anthony Michael Stokes, Sam Antar, Ryan Santiago, Ivan Quinonez, Amanda Goodwin, David Zubradt, Elizabeth Bays, Claudia Apicella, Rebecca Spindler, Lucaya Luckey-Bethany, Andy Kirtland, Jessica Bathurst, Allison Paul, Gabriel Zubradt; December 18, 2009–January 10, 2010

3-Legged Dog, Inc. (3LD)

Artistic Director, Kevin Cunningham; Producing Director and Business Development, Aaron Louis; Media Director, Aaron Harrow; Company Manager and Associate Producer, Karina Martins; www.3leggeddog.org

The Diary of a Teenage Girl by Marielle Heller, adapted from the graphic novel by Phoebe Gloeckner; Directors, Sarah Cameron Sunde & Rachel Eckerling; Produced by Aaron Louis in association with New Georges and The Essentials; Set, Lauren Helpern; Video, C. Andrew Bauer; Sound, Marcelo Añez; Lighting, Laura Mroczkowski; Costumes, Emily DeAngelis; Props, Lauren Asta; Composer, Nate Heller; General Manager, Lisa Dozier; Production Manager, Paul DiPietro; PSM, Erin Maureen Koster; ASM, Naomi Anhorn; Press, Jim Baldassare; **Cast:** Marielle Heller, Jon Krupp, Michael Laurence, Mariann Mayberry, Nell Mooney; Video Actors: Chris Carlone, Mathilde Dratwa; February 17–May 1, 2010 (presented under an Off-Broadway contract from April 13—see complete listing under Off-Broadway section in this volume).

Radio Purgatory Written, directed and performed by The Renaldo The Ensemble; Produced by Theatre The; April 22–23, 2010

The Crease Question Written, directed and performed by Kira Onodera; April 27, 2010

New Islands Archipelago Written and directed by Paul Zimet; Presented by The Talking Band; Original Music, Ellen Maddow; Set, Nic Ularu; Lighting, Nan Zhang; Costumes, Olivera Gajic; Video, Simon Tarr; Choreographer, Hilary Easton; Stage Manager, Julia Funk; **Cast:** Todd D'Amour, James Himelsbach, Kristine Haruna Lee, Bianca Leigh, Ellen Maddow, Steven Rattazzi, Tina Shepard; Musicians: Harry Mann and Beth Meyers; May 20–June 6, 2010

3Graces Theater Co.

www.threegracestheater.org

The Power of Birds by Robin Rice Lichtig; Director, Elizabeth Bunnell; Set, Tijana Bjelajac; Costumes, Brooke Cohen; Lighting, Joshua Scherr; Sound, John D. Ivy; Stage Manager, Melissa Nathan; **Cast:** Margot Avery, Emma Galvin, Noah Galvin, Annie McGovern, Jay Potter; Milagro Theatre at the CSV Cultural Center; February 19–March 13, 2010

45th Street Theatre

Dis/Connections 3X Dennis Bush Three plays by Dennis Bush: *Fetal Pig, Below the Belt*, and *Asylum*; Director, Lester Thomas Shane; **Cast:** Justin Anselmi, Kiki Bertocci, Krystal Blackman, Ross Boehringer, Tommy Buck, Jamie Carroll, Nicholas Coleman, Keith Hamilton, Devon Pipars, Sarah Stockton, Melissa Teitel, Kelsey Torstveit; June 17–21, 2009

Crimes of the Heart by Beth Henley; Presented by Michael Chekhov Theatre Company; Director, Christine Sullivan; **Cast:** Julie Garrison, Peter Giser, Kristen Lucas, Duvall O'Steen, Lauren Piselli, Mark Ramsey; July 11–August 18, 2009

Hurlyburly by David Rabe; Presented by Michael Chekhov Theatre Company; Producer, Michael Horn; July 20–28, 2009

Bolt: The Frankenstein Journals Written and directed by Louis Lopardi; Producer Michael Horn; Presented by Michael Chekhov Theatre Company; **Cast:** Stefano Abbruscato, Peter Giser, Goran Ivanovski, Tom Murphy, Steve Peluso, Mark Ramsey, Pam Richard, Zdenko Slobodnik, Ann Van Geson; October 20–November 7, 2009

Holy Ghostly and **Fourteen Hundred Thousand** by Sam Shepard; Presented by Michael Chekhov Theatre Company as part of the Sam Shepard Festival; Producer, Michael Horn; Director, Sally Burtenshaw-Marlowe; Stage Manager, Sarah Culp; Lighting, Joan Racho-Jansen; **Cast:** David Elyha, Ann Van Gieson, Goran Ivanovski, Edward Gregory Jones, Kristen Lucas, Eileen Marlowe, Craig Newman, Mary Ramsey, Tim Swain; January 21–26, 2010

After Easter by Anne Devlin; Presented by Michael Chekhov Theatre Company; Producer, Pink Elephant/Pamela Ehn; Director, Melindia Prom; Lighting, Joan Racho-Jansen; Set, John Jefferies; Sound, Scott Smithelli; Costumes, Dara Fargotstein; Stage Manager, Tom Crockett; **Cast:** Pamela Ehn, Alison Crane, Alexadnra Mingione, Liz De Betta, Tom Crockett, Mary Van Fleet, John Rice, Adam Ewer, Forrest Seamons, Omar Robinson, Anthony Labresco, Stephanie Willing; January 22–February 1, 2010

Psychopatihia Sexualis by John Patrick Shanley; Presented by Michael Chekhov Theatre Company; Director, Christine Sullivan; Producer, Mark Forlenza; **Cast:** Mark Forlenza, Joya Italiano, Goran Ivanovski, Eileen Marlowe, DJ Sharp; January 23–31, 2010

The Reunion: Miles, Bird and Trane by James Marentic; Presented by The Tank as part of the Black History Month Festival; Director, Chuck Patterson; Curator, Suzan Eralslan; Producers, James Marentic, Ellen Martin; Lighting, Joan Racho Jansen; Stage Manager/Sound, Sid Branch; Press, Barbara Sfraga; Cast: Michael Wright, Marcus Naylor, Stacey Dotson, Ellen Martin; February 4–14, 2010

Out of Order by Ray Cooney; Presented by Michael Chekhov Theatre Company; Producer/Director, Peter Giser; Set/Lighting, Joan Racho-Jansen; **Cast:** Bill Barnett, Liz De Betta, Pamela Ehn, Goran Ivanovski, Eileen Marlowe, John Rice, Isaac Scranton, Tim Swain, Luke Tudball, Ann Van Gieson; February 18–26 and May 10–24, 2010

Dog Sees God-Confessions of a Teenage Blockhead by Bert V. Royal; Presented by Michael Chekhov Theatre Company; Producer, Tom Amici; Director, Matt Barbot; Set/Lighting, Joan Racho-Jansen; **Cast:** Adam Ewer, Megan Hartig, Rachel Halper, Rebecca Russell, Tom Amici, Jaqueline Raymond, Joe Mullen, Keith Peruzzi; February 21–March 9

Love's Labor's Lost by William Shakespeare; Presented by Michael Chekhov Theatre Company; Producer/Director, Michael Horn; Lighting, Joan Racho-Jansen; **Cast:** Michael Aiello, Liz De Betta, Rashad Brown, Claudia Cassamassimo, Kim Cichelli, Marc Engberg, Carl Foreman Jr., Laurel Fulcher, Sarah-Jane George, Robert Gilbert, Mia Grottola, Sam Kirk, Olivia Mell, Heather Mingo, Annarosa Mudd, Paul Murillo, Craig Newman, Jimmy Pravasilis, Mark Ramsey, Kimberley Shoniker, Zach Tirone, Linda Wartenweiler, Julia Yoler; April 15–27, 2010

A Midsummer's Nights Dream by William Shakespeare; Presented by Michael Chekhov Theatre Company; Producer, Michael Horn; Director, Katrin Hible; Lighting, Joan Racho-Janson; **Cast:** James Brennan, Elias Buehler, Claudia Casamassimo, Vance Clemente, Amanda Gagnon, Rachel Halper, Matthew Dalton Lynch, Annarosa Fabrizio, Samuel Muniz, Telisha Petteway, Omar Robinson, Miranda Schmidt, Forrest Seamons, Sonia Torres, Kimberly Young, Justin Zacek; April 22–25, 2010

Rock On! Music and lyrics by Robert Stone, book by Robert Stone and Jon Frazier, additional music and lyrics by Gena Ross; Presented by Union Circle Theatre Group; Choreography, Melissa Landreau; April 27–May 18, 2010

59E59

Artistic Director, Elysabeth Kleinhans; Executive Producer, Peter Tear; www.59e59.org

East to Edinburgh 2009 Sixth annual festival; July 14–August 2; included: *A Midsummer Night's Dream, a Rock Musical* by George Griggs, directed by Paul Andrew Perez; Producer, Infinity Repertory Theater; **Cast:** Maxine Builder, Erin Farmer, Elizabeth Campolongo, Matt Rodriguez, Christopher Goodwin; (July 14–22); *No Parole* written and performed by Carlo D'Amore, directed by Margarett Perry (July 14–19); *Miles & Coltrane: Blue (.)* by Concrete Generation, directed by Quentin "Q" Talley; Producer, On Q Productions and Black Butterfly Productions; **Cast:** Sultan Omar El-Amin, Randolph Ward, Quentin "Q" Talley, Chris Pennix, Charles "CP Maze" Perry, Filmore Johnson, Boris "Bluz" Rogers, Kendrea "Mekkah" Griffith, Carlos Robson, Sherry "Swan" Cole, and the Stephen Gordon Quintet (July 16–18); *Jeff Kreisler's Get Rich Cheating* written and performed by Jeff Kreisler; Producer, Up Top Productions (July 16–30); *52 Man Pickup* written and performed by Desiree Burch, directed by Isaac Byrne, with Jessica McVea; Producer, Working Man's Clothes (July 16–18); *West Lethargy* written and directed by Steven Kaliski; Producer, Page 121 Productions; Lighting, Aaron Switzer; Set, Aaron Switzer; Choreographer, Hanley Smith; **Cast:** Joie Bauer, Mikaela Feely-Lehmann, Jeffrey Feola, Graham Halstead, Suzanne Lenz (July 17–25); *Live From New York, It's Jonathan Prager!* written and performed by Jonathan Prager (July 18–26); *Brown Ambition* written and performed by Carolyn Castiglia, directed by Baron Vaughn (July 19–22); *Etty* written and performed by Susan Stein, directed by Austin Pendleton (July 23–26); *Ladybug Warrior* written and performed by Vicki Ferentinos; (July 23–August 1); *The Montana Ranch* by Dylan Dougherty, directed by David Winitsky; Producer, Rhesus Productions; **Cast:** Scott Cagney, Keri Costa (July 28–August 2); *A Longhardt Look at Love With Chad Longhardt* written, produced, and performed by Brianne Berkson, directed by Daniel Kuthner; (July 29–August 2); *Couples Counseling* by Carey Lovelace, directed by Judith Stevens-Ly; Producer, Loose Change Productions; Lights/Sound, Jesse Schoem; Production Manager, Michelle Karem; **Cast:** Kyle Fabel, James Kennedy, Anna Margaret Hollyman (July 3–August 2); Theaters B and C

Summer Shorts 3 Festival of New American short plays; Presented by J.J. Kandel and John McCormack; Sets/Lighting, Maruti Evans; Costumes, Michael Bevins; Sound, Tim Pioppo; Casting, Billy Hopkins & Jessica Kelly; Press, David Gersten; PSM, Michael Alifanz; ASM, Anna Burnham; Production Manager/Props, Aaron Paternoster; included: *Things My Afro Taught Me* written and performed by Nancy Giles; *Death By Chocolate* by John Augustine, directed by Robert Saxner; **Cast:** Mary Joy, Sherry Anderson, Aaron Paternoster; *A Second of Pleasure* by Neil LaBute, directed by Andrew McCarthy; **Cast:** Margaret Colin, Victor Slezak; *The Eternal Anniversary* Book by Bill Connington, music & lyrics by Skip Kennon, directed by Thomas Caruso; **Cast:** Leenya Rideout, Robert W. DuSold; *Don't Say Another Word* by Carole Real, directed by Ian Belknap, **Cast:** Stephanie D'Abruzzo; *The Sin Eater* by Keith Reddin, directed by Billy Hopkins; **Cast:** Clara Hopkins Daniels, Jamie Watkins, Rosalyn Coleman, J.J. Kandel, Teala Dunn, Sheldon Woodley; *If I Had* by Roger Hedden, directed by Billy Hopkins; **Cast:** Shane McRae, Andy Powers, Emily Tremaine; *The Killing* by William Inge, directed by Jose Angel Santana; **Cast:** Neal Huff, J.J. Kandel; Theater B; July 24–August 27, 2009

On the Eighth Day Written and directed by Geoffrey Scheer; Presented by Write Club NYC; Lighting, Cory Pattak; Costumes, Caitlin J. Doukas; **Cast:** Amy Albert, Richard Binder, Adam Sentoni; Theater C in repertory with *Walter Vs. The Water Authority*; August 4–22, 2009

Walter Vs. The Water Authority by Ben T. Scott; Presented by Write Club NYC; Director, Paula D'Alessandris; Lighting, Cory Pattak; Costumes, Caitlin J. Doukas; **Cast:** C.K. Allen, Jenny Burleson, Ron McClary, Abeo Miller, Cody Neeb, Greg Skura; Theater C in repertory with *On the Eighth Day*; August 5–23, 2009

Spinning the Times Five short plays: *The Lemon Tree* by Rosemary Jenkins, *The Luthier* by Lucy Caldwell, *Miracle Conway* by Geraldine Aron, *Gin in a Teacup* by Rosalind Haslett, *Fugue* by Belinda McKeon; Presented by Origin Theatre Company (George C. Heslin, Artistic Director) as part of the 1st Irish Festival; Director, M. Burke Walker; Set, Lex Liang; Costumes, Sandra Alexandre; Lighting, Jonathan Spencer; Sound, Christian Frederickson; Stage Manager, Michael Palmer; Casting, Catherine Lamm; **Cast:** Mark Byrne, Aysan Celik, Rosemary Fine, Jerzy Gwiazdowski, Ethan Hova; Theater C; September 2–20, 2009

Luck Devised by Megan Riordan, Dodd Loomis, and Shawn Sturnick; Produced by Juicy MoMo Productions and Making Strange Theatre Company as part of the 1st Irish Festival; **Cast:** Megan Riordan; Theater C; September 22–October 11, 2009

Ghost Light by Desi Moreno-Penson; Produced by Immediate Theatre Company and Monarch Theater; Director, Jose Zayas; Set, Jason Simms; Lighting, Evan Purcell; Costumes, Carla Bellisio; Sound, John Zalewski; Multimedia, Alex Koch; Stage Manager, Toby Ring Thelin; **Cast:** Kate Benson, Bryant Mason, Hugh Sinclair; Theater C; October 14–31, 2009

Rough Sketch by Shawn Nacol; Produced by rUDE mECHANICALS Theater Company; Director, Ian Morgan; Lighting, Amith A. Chandrashaker; Set, Peter R. Feuchtwanger; Costumes, Angela R. Harner; Sound, Matt Sherwin; Original Music, Matt Sherwin; Props, Matthew J. Fick; Stage Manager, Beth Stegman; Technical Director, Vadim Malinskiy; Producers, Richard C. Aven, Marc Stuart Weitz; **Cast:** Tina Benko, Matthew Lawler; Theater C; January 14–31, 2010

Dog and Wolf by Catherine Filloux; Produced by Watson Arts; Director, Jean Randich; Lighting, Michael Chybowski; Set, Anna Kiraly; Costumes, Alixa Gage Englund; Sound, Robert Murphy; Props, Sam Horwith; PSM, Jes Levine; Dramaturg, Sarah Slight; Assistant Director, Yoni Oppenheim; ASM, Catherine Weingarten; **Cast:** Nadia Bowers, John Daggett, Dale Soules, Daniela Dakich, Traciana Graves; Theater C; February 5–21, 2010

Brack's Last Bachelor Party by Sam Marks; Produced by Babel Theatre Project; Director, Geordie Broadwater; Set, Tristan Jeffers; Costumes, Becky Lasky; Lighting, Simon Cleveland; Sound, Anthony Gabriele; Stage Managers, Caley Clocksin, Pisa Waikwamdee; Props, Eric Reynolds; Technical Director, Vadim Malinskiy; Producer, Miriam Blocker; **Cast:** Alexander Alioto, Josh Barrett, Michael Crane, Crystal Finn; Theater C; February 25–March 14, 2010

John Ball's *In the Heat of the Night* Adapted by Matt Pelfrey; Produced by Godlight Theatre Company; Director, Joe Tantalo; Set/Lighting, Maruti Evans; Costumes, Virginia Monte; Sound, Elizabeth Rhodes; Stage Managers, Christina Hurtado, Derek Shore, Meredith Brown; Fight Director, Rick Sordelet; Choreographer, Hachi Yu; **Cast:** Gregory Konow, Sean Phillips, Nick Paglino, Michael Shimkin, Ryan O'Callaghan, Bryce Hodgson, Sam Whitten, Julianne Nelson, Scarlett Thiele, Adam Kee; Theater C; March 28–April 25, 2010

Abingdon Theatre Complex

Dorothy Strelsin Theatre

This One Girl's Story by Music & lyrics by Dionne McClain-Freeney, book by Bil Wright; Presented by Gayfest NYC Inc.; Director, Devanand Janki; Set, Michael Hotopp; Costumes, T. Michael Hall; Lighting, Jesse Belsky; Music Director, J. Oconer Navarro; **Cast:** Tanesha Gary, Chasten Harmon, Zonya Love Johnson, Lacretta Nicole, Desiree Rodriguez, Charles E. Wallace; May 28–June 6, 2009

Whiskey, Beer and Apple Pie by Rob Egginton, Glenn De Kler, Eli Sands; Presented by Panicked Productions (Directors: Glenn De Kler, Jessica Delbridge, Rob Egginton, Joseph Tomasini) as part of the Midtown Theatre Festival; **Cast:** Maria Smith, Ally Hirschlag, Brian Morvant, Scarlett Thiele, De Kler, Greg Engbrecht, Adam P. Murphy, Amanda Duffy; July 13–August 1, 2009

Fault Lines by Rebecca Louise Miller; Presented by Invisible City Theatre Company; Director, David Epstein; Stage Manager, Alex Cape; Lighting, Joe W. Novak; Set, Ira Haskell; **Cast:** Jenna Doolittle, Anais Alexandra, Rebecca Louise Miller, Tobin Ludwig, Jocelyn Kuritsky; December 9–19, 2009

June Havoc Theatre

Empire of the Trees by Adam Kraar; Presented by Wizard Oil Productions; Director, Sherri Eden Barber; Stage Manager, Jaimie VanDyke; Lighting, S. Benjamin Farrar; Set, Andrew Haserlat; Costumes, Eileen Nober; Sound, Jordan Cooke; Producer, Amanda Kate Joshi; ASM, Jennifer Artesti; Choreographer, Shannon Stowe; Fight Choreographer, Iris McQuillan-Grace; Technical Director, Cynthia Jankowski; **Cast:** Dana Mazzenga, Graham Outerbridge, Kunal Prasad, Rajesh Bose, Taisha Cameron; April 22–30, 2010

Access Theater

www.accesstheater.com

Superhero Celebrity Rehab: The Musical Music & lyrics by William Segal, book by William Segal and Brendan Snow; Presented by Empty Space Productions; Director, Matt Johnston; Production Manager, Mike Salonia; ASM, Elizabeth Bourus; **Cast:** Bill Coyne, Bryce Kemph, Corrie Beula, Jana DeBusk, Melody Moore, Sam Perwin, Will Cooper; Access Theatre; June 5–7, 2009

On The Way Down by Michael Rudez; Presented by Ashberry Productions; Director, Dan Waldron; Set, Jessie Kressen; Costumes, Campbell Ringel; Lighting, Tom Bergeron; Stage Manager, Su Hendrickson; **Cast:** Lindsay Wolf, Steven Todd Smith, Rocco Chierichella; Access Theater Black Box; July 20–August 9, 2009

Greendale, G.P. Written and directed by Brad Saville; Presented by East Wind Theatre; **Cast:** Carmel Amit, Sam Antar, William Apps, Penny Bittone, Amber Bogdewiecz, Matthew Bretschneider, Anne Fidler, Anna Lamadrid, David Marcus, Zoe Metcalfe-Klaw, Jimmy Pravailis, Paul Weissman; Access Gallery; August 2–September 13, 2009

Cymbeline by William Shakespeare; Presented by Fiasco Theater LTD; Directors, Noah Brody & Ben Steinfeld; Costumes, Whitney Locher; Lighting, Tim Cryan; Trunk Design, Jacque Roy; Stage Manager, Casey Schmal; **Cast:** Jessie Austrian, Noah Brody, Paul Coffey, Andy Grotelueschen, Ben Steinfeld, Emily Young; Access Gallery; September 25–October 2, 2009

Below the Belt by Richard Dresser; Presented by The Rock Garden; Director, Larry Preston; Set, Casper De la Torre; Costumes, Jackie Hillenbrand; Lighting, Alan Baron; Choreographer, Kathy Kelly Christos; Stage Manager, Susan Sunday; **Cast:** Chad Brigockas, Ara Shehigian, Larry Preston; Access Theater; October 4–25, 2009

Granada by Avi Glickstein; Presented by Polybe + Seats; Director, Jessica Brater; Set, Peiyi Wong; Costumes, Peiyi Wong; Lighting, Natalie Robin; Sound, John D. Ivy; Stage Manager, Donald Butchko; **Cast:** Elaine O'Brien, Sarah Sakaan, Indika Senanayake, Lindsay Torrey, Jill Usdan, Ari Vigoda; Access Gallery; November 5–22, 2009

Julius Caesar by William Shakespeare; Presented by Bushwick Shakespeare Repertory; Director, Jordan Simmons; Costumes, Megan Sanders; Hair and Makeup, Ashley Chlebus; Stage Manager, Tiffany Baker; **Cast:** Alexis Balaoing, Jordan Boughrum, Rebecca Davis, Whitney Kimball Long, Alexis Robbins, Liz Sklar, Amanda Tudor, Emily Clare Zempel; Access Gallery; February 18–28, 2010

4.48 Psychosis by Sarah Kane; Directed and presented by the Raw Theater Group; Lighting, Christopher Ross Baker; Stage Manager, Lyvann Oum; Producers, J. Edward Cecala & Paula Sapala; **Cast:** Rachel Lynn Wood, Julian Sapala, Michael Jefferson, Emily Ciotti; Access Theater; March 2–28, 2010

Glee Club by Matthew Freeman; Presented by Blue Coyote Theater Group; Director, Kyle Ancowitz; Set, Robert Monaco; Lighting, Wheeler Kincaid; Original Music, Stephen Speights; **Cast:** Bruce Barton, Robert Buckwalter, Steven Burns, David DelGrosso, Carter Jackson, Stephen Speights, Tom Staggs, Matthew Trumbull; Access Theater; March 3–April 3, 2010

Accidental Repertory Theater

Brecht on Brecht by Bertolt Brecht, adapted by George Tabori; Presented by John Strasberg Studios; Director, John Strasberg; Stage Manager, Sean Demers; Music Director, Ross Patterson; **Cast:** Virginia Armitage, Judy Krause, Audrey Lavine, Jerry Marsini, Anne Pasquale, Robert Rowe, Louis Vuolo; November 1–21, 2009

The Active Theater

www.theactivetheater.com

Body Language by Jennie Contuzzi; Director, Nathaniel Shaw; Lighting, Ryan Metzler; Stage Manager, Katie Cheek; **Cast:** Amy Miller Brennan, Jeffrey Trunell, Michael Andrew Daly, David Ojala, Danny Katz; Presented as part of the Midtown International Theater Festival; Dorothy Streslin Theatre; July 4–August 2, 2009

Two Rooms by Lee Blessing; Director, Glory Bowen; Set, Craig Napoliello; Costumes, Laura Catignani; Lighting, Yuriy Nayer; Sound, Jacob Subotnick; Audio/Visual, David Ojala; Stage Manager, Chanda Calentine; **Cast:** Angelica-Lee Aspiras, Raissa Dorff, Andy Kelso, Jason Emanuel; WorkShop Theater; December 3–13 2009

Romance/Romance by Keith Herrmann and Barry Harman; Director, Marc Robin; Set, Craig Napoliello; Costumes, Laura Catignani; Lighting, Paul Black; Sound, Jacob Subotnick; Stage Manager, Katy Moore; **Cast:** Stephanie Youell Binetti, Nathaniel Shaw, Abby Mueller, Nick Dalton, David Strobbe, Alison Solomon; WorkShop Theater; February 18–March 7, 2010

Magnetic North by William Donnelly; Director, Jeremy Dobrish; Set, Alexis Distler; Costumes, Bobby Pearce; Lighting, Michael Gottlieb; Sound, Jacob Subotnick; Stage Manager, Angela Kiessel; **Cast:** Christian Campbell, Sarah Shahinian, Heather Lee Harper, Scott Richard Foster; WorkShop Theater; May 6–16, 2010

Algonquin Productions

Artistic Director, Tony Sportiello; Operations, Mark Sportiello; Box Office, Carly Knight; Youth Theater Director, Liz Amberly; Literary Manager, Thomas Cote; Publicity, Randy Schein; Associate Producers: Sharon Osowski, Joan Pelzer, Robin Rothstein, Dawn Bodrogi, Rick Eisenberg, Kate Konigisor, Steven Petrillo, Greg Skura, John Cerrone; www.algonquintheater.org

Unmitigated Truth: Life, a Lavatory, Loves, and Ladies by Melvin Van Peebles; Music Director, William Patterson; **Cast:** Melvin Van Peebles, William Patterson, Carmen Barika; June 15–July 1, 2009

Slave Shack by Mike Folie; Director, Debra Whitfield; Set, Natalie Taylor Hart; Lighting, Deborah Constantine; Sound, Joel Mofsenson; Fight Director, Rod Kinter; **Cast:** Michael Gnat, Candice LaGia Lenoir, Jeffrey Plunkett, Lizzie Folie; October 19–November 1, 2009

Amas Musical Theatre

Producing Artistic Director, Donna Trinkoff; Managing Director, Jan Hacha; Artist-in-Residence, Marie Torres; www.amasmusical.org

Signs of Life Book by Peter Ullian, lyrics by Len Schiff, music by Joel Derfner; Produced in association with Snap-Two Productions; Director, Jeremy Dobrish; Set, Alexis Distler; Costumes, Jennifer Daprio; Lighting, Mitchael Gottlieb; Sound, Michael Eisenberg; Audio/Visual, Chris Kateff; Stage Manager, Sunny Stapleton; **Cast:** Erika Amato, Wilson Bridges, Jason Collins, Nic Cory, Gabe Green, Patricia Noonan, Allen E. Read, Stuart Zagnit, Kurt Zischke; Marjorie S. Deane Little Theatre; February 16–March 21, 2010

American Bard Theater Company

www.americanbard.org

Witches, Bitches!! Adapted by Jack Herholdt, Damon Kinard, and Raven Peters; Director/Lighting/Sound, Raven Peters; Costumes, Cheri Wicks; Stage Manager, Betty Howe; **Cast:** Bryan L. Cohen, Erin Gilbreth, Tara Henderson, Jack Herholdt, Ross Hewitt, Natalie Doyle Holmes, Betina Joly, Damon Kinard, Mary Riley, Jacob Troy, Cheri Wicks; Nicu's Spoon Theater; October 26–27, 2009

Much Ado About Nothing by William Shakespeare; Director, Jefferson Slinkard; Set, Sheila Phalon; Costumes, Kerry Gibbons; Lighting, Jeff Whitsett; Sound, Mary Riley; Stage Manager, Betty Howe; ASM, Larisa Amaya-Baron; Assistant Director, Kevin P. Joyce; House Manager/Sound Technician, Jennifer Gelber; Box Office Manager, Natalie Piñeiro; **Cast:** Bryan L. Cohen, Andrew Eisenman, Erin Gilbreth, Tara Henderson, Jack Herholdt, Ross Hewitt, Natalie Doyle Holmes, Marcus Denard Johnson, Betina Joly, Damon Kinard, Graciany Miranda, Clint Morris, Mary Riley, Evan Scott Schweitzer, Cheri Wicks; Flamboyan Theater at CSV; April 16–May 1, 2010

American Globe Theatre

Artistic Director, John Basil; Executive Director, Elizabeth Keefe; Development Director, Beth A. Vogel; Education Director, Julia Levo; www.americanglobe.org

Titus Andronicus by William Shakespeare; Director, John Basil; Set, Vincent Masterpaul; Costumes, Jim Parks; Lighting, Mark Hankia; Original Music

& Sound, Scott O'Brien; Choreographer, Jim Parks; Stage Manager, Audrey Marchall; **Cast:** Spencer Bazzano, A.J. Cote, Mike DePaolo, Nick LaMedica, Nick Vorderman; February 25–March 21, 2010

American International Theater, Inc.

Artistic Director, Alix Steel; www.aitheater.org

Ezra Pound: The Poet on Trial Written and directed by William Roetzheim; Lighting, Barbara Samuels; Stage Manager, Kate Erin Gibson; **Cast:** Jeff Berg; Studio Theatre on Theatre Row; May 28–June 30, 2009

Dickinson: The Secret Story of Emily Dickinson by William Roetzheim; Director, Al Germani; Lighting, Barbara Samuels; Stage Manager, Kate Erin Gibson; **Cast:** Rhianna Basore, Diana Sparta, Greg Wittman, Charlie Riendeau; 440 Studios; June 12–20, 2009

American Theatre of Actors

Artistic Director, James Jennings

The Taming of The Shrew by William Shakespeare; Director, James Jennings; Costumes, Christos Fandaros; **Cast:** Charles Baker, Herbert Bennett, Vincent Bivona, Stephanie Casaubon, Nikki Gold, William Greville, William J. Growney, John Paul Harkins, Paul Herbig, Jessica Jennings, Thomas Leverton, Michael Matucci, Hamilton Meadows, Gregory O' Connor, Celeste Sexton, Alex Simmons, Jonathan Reed Wexler, Brian White, Emily Yates; Chernuchin Theatre; March 3–14, 2010

The Libertine by Stephen Jeffreys; Presented by The Fools' Theatre; Director, Eric Tucker; Costumes, Ella Sawtell; Lighting, Drew Vanderburg; Sound, Kristin Worrall; Original Music, Alex Sovrosnsky; Dialect Coach, Claire Warden; Fight Directors, Alexandra Hastings and David Dean Hastings; Choreographer, Sarah Doudna; Stage Manager, Gina Costagliola; **Cast:** Ken Schatz, Rufus Collins, Peter Davenport, Ted Lewis, Simon Pearl, Carey Urban, Andrus Nichols, Garth McCardle, Vivienne Leheny, Olivia Gilliatt, Sarah Doudna, Alison Krauss; May 14–30, 2010

The Amoralists Theatre Company

www.theamoralists.com

The Pied Pipers of the Lower East Side Written and directed by Derek Ahonen; Producer, Meghan Ritchie; Set, Alfred Schatz; Costumes, Ricky Lang; Lighting, Jeremy Pape; Stage Manager, Judy Merrick; Assistant Director, Matt Fraley; **Cast:** James Kautz, Nick Lawson, Sarah Lemp, Malcolm Madera, Mandy Nicole Moore, Matthew Pilieci, Charles Meola; P.S. 122; June 5–October 5, 2009 (presented under an Off-Broadway contract at Theatre 80 St. Marks Place September 10–October 5 – see listing in the Off-Broadway section of this volume).

Happy in the Poorhouse Written and directed by Derek Ahonen; Set, Alfred Schatz; Costumes, Ricky Lang; Lighting, Jeremy Pape; Sound, The Hernandez Brothers; Stage Manager, Judy Merrick; Assistant Director, Dan Lockhart; **Cast:** William Apps, Selene Beretta, James Kautz, Nick Lawson, Sarah Lemp, Morton Matthews, Patrick McDaniel, Rochelle Mikulich, Matthew Pilieci, Mark Riccadonna, Meghan Ritchie; Theatre 80 St. Marks; March 11–April 26, 2010

The Anthropologists

www.theanthropologists.org

Give Us Bread Written, directed, & sound by Melissa F. Moschitto; Set, Maggie Pilat; Costumes, Alexandra H. Rubin; Lighting, Andrew J. Merkel; Stage Manager, Brandi Klein; Dramaturg, Louise Gough; Assistant Costumes, Sarah Biesinger;

Light Board, Joshua Ozro Lucero; Props, Alexandra H. Rubin; **Cast:** Jean Goto, Jennifer Griffee, Jennifer Moses, Shayna Padovano, Katy Rubin, Sonja Sweeney; Milagro Theater at CSV; June 5–21, 2009

For the Love Of... Director/Sound, Melissa F. Moschitto; Lighting, Andrew J. Merkel; Costumes, Alexandra H. Rubin; Stage Manager, Aaron Tindall; Assistant Sound, Aaron Tindall; Assistant Producers, Cherie Roberts, Aisha Jordan; Dramaturg, Louise Gough; **Cast:** Patrick Berger, Petra Denison, Jean Goto, Jennifer Griffee, J.J. Mehren, Karim Muasher, Jennifer Moses, Justin Neal, Katy Rubin, Sonja Sweeney; Flamboyan Theater at CSV; February 4–28, 2010

Readings

Another Place Written and directed by Melissa F. Moschitto; Dramaturg, Louise Gough; **Cast:** John Farrell, Jean Goto, Anna Hayman, Sarena Kennedy, Karim Muasher, Katy Rubin, Sonja Sweeney; May 27, 2010

ArcLight Theatre

Acting Alone by David M. Korn; Produced by Damocles Productions; Director, Lee Gundersheimer; Stage Manager, Michelle Beige; Sound, Noah Aronson; **Cast:** Nick Scoullar, Stephen Graham, Monika Hunken, Vivian Neuwirth; November 12–21, 2009

Goodbye Cruel World by Nikolai Erdman, adapted and directed by Robert Ross Parker; Presented by Roundtable Ensemble; Set, Nick Francone; Costumes, Theresa Squire & Antonia Ford-Roberts; Lighting, Nick Francone; Sound/Original Music, Shane Rettig; **Cast:** Cindy Cheung, Curran Connor, William Jackson Harper, Tami Stronach, Paco Tolson, Aaron Roman Weiner; January 17–February 6, 2010

Franklin by Josh Billig; Produced by Snapped Productions; Director, Larry Singer; Stage Manager, Mark Jesse Swanson; Lighting, Adam Gabel; Set, Jason Simms; Costumes, Keenan Caldwell; Producers, Jon Dalin and Tina Ward; Production Manager, Sarah Painter; Fight Choreographer, Rodriguez; **Cast:** Jon Dalin, Tina Ward, Abraham De Funes, Tim Wersan; May 20–June 5, 2010

art.party.theater.company

Duchess in the Dark by John Webster; Director, Mary Birnbaum; Set, Grace Laubacher; Sound, Chris Rummel; Wigs & Hair, Jojo Karlin; Stage Manager, Jamie Rog; **Cast:** Joe Curnutte, Kyle Davies, Jody Flader, Julia Gwynne, Blake Habermann, Levi Morger, April Palasthy, Michael Schoenfeld; Flamboyan Theater at CSV; November 4–7, 2009

Artistic New Directions

Artistic Co-Directors, Janice L. Goldberg & Kristine Niven; www.artisticnewdirections.org

Eclectic Evening of Shorts - Boxers by Jeffrey Sweet, Robin Goldfin, Tom Shergalis, Joseph Gallo, Demetra Kareman, Susan Middaugh, Jill Melanie Wirth, David Wirth; Directors, Michael Tucker, Eric Nightengale, Robin A. Paterson, Jessica Howell, Ken Talberth, Sarah Bennett; Lighting, Daniel Winters; Stage Manager, Becky Lynn Dawson; **Cast:** Drue Pennella, Isaac Rodriguez, Jacob Moore, Jake Hamilton Lewis, Tawny Sorensen, Niketta Scott, Tai Verley, Marnie Klar, Juri-Henley Cohn, A Ilis Dunbar, Katie Venzia, Rebecca Saathoff Davis, John Calvin Kelly, Bruce Smolanoff, Cheryl Orsini, Michelle Best, Kristine Niven, David Marx, Jill Melanie Wirth, David Wirth; Theatre 54 at Shetler Studios; March 19–28, 2010

Eclectic Evening of Shorts - Briefs by Arlene Hutton, Kristine Niven, Cesi Davidson, Jason Schafer, Drew Larimore, Patrick Nash, Heather Smith; Directors, Janice L. Goldberg, Kathryn Long, Lori Wolter, Nick Stimler, Jay Stern, Chris Lutkin, Mary Hodges; Lighting, Daniel Winters; Stage Manager, Becky Lynn Dawson; **Cast:** Dina Ann Comolli, Kevin T. Collins, Allison Goldberg, Amanda Sykes, Raife Baker, Anita Keal, Jane Marx, Stefan Schick, Joanna Parson, Heather Smith, Chris Lutkin, James Edward Becton, Althea Alexis Vyfhuis; Theatre 54 at Shetler Studios; March 19–28, 2010

The Assembly

theassemblytheater.com

The Dark Heart of Meteorology by Stephen Aubrey; Co-produced by Horse Trade Theater Group; Director, Jess Chayes; Set, Nick Benacerraf; Lighting, Stacey Boggs; Sound, Asa Wember; Video, Alex Koch & Daniel Brodie; Stage Manager, Rachel Silverman; **Cast:** Richard Lovejoy; UNDER St. Marks; September 22–October 14, 2009

The Three Sisters by Anton Chekhov; Co-produced by Horse Trade Theatre Group; Director, Jess Chayes; Set, Nick Benacerraf and The Assembly; Costumes, Justine Lacy; Lighting, Derek Wright; Sound, Brendan McDonough; Audio/Visual, Edward Bauer and The Assembly; Stage Manager, Katy Moore; Translator, Michael Henry Heim; Props, Ben Beckley; Dramaturg, Stephen Aubrey; Producer, Rosalind Grush; **Cast:** Emily Perkins, Kate Benson, Kate MacCluggage, Ben Beckley, Alley Scott, Levi Morger, Christopher Hurt, Moti Margolin, Edward Bauer, Cecil Baldwin, Susan McCallum, Steve Stout, Brendan McDonough, Peter Feliz; The Red Room; January 20–30, 2010

Astoria Performing Arts Center

Executive Director, Taryn Drongowski; Artistic Director, Tom Wojtunik; Production Manager, Annie Jacobs; Marketing, Dave Charest; Press, Katie Rosin/Kampfire PR; Casting, Scott Wojcik & Gayle Seay; Resident Scenic Designer, Michael P. Kramer; www.apacny.org

The Pillowman by Martin McDonagh; Director, Tom Wojtunik; Set, Stephen K. Dobay; Costumes, Emily Morgan DeAngelis; Lighting, Driscoll Otto; Sound, Kristyn Smith; Original Composition: Ryan Homsey; Props, Ashlee Springer; Stage Manager, Paul Brewster; Production Manager, Annie Jacobs; Assistant Director, Rebecca A. Lewis-Whitson; Dramaturg, Katie Courtien; **Cast:** Jordan Bloom, Nathan Brisby, Richard D. Busser, Avery Clark, Seth Duerr, Justin Herfel, Anthony Pierini, Karen Stanion; Good Shepherd United Methodist Church; November 5–21, 2009

Children of Eden by Stephen Schwartz & John Caird; Director, Tom Wojtunik; Choreographer, Christine O'Grady; Musical Director, Lilli Wosk; Set, Michael P. Kramer; Costumes, Hunter Kaczorowski; Lighting, Dan Jobbins; Sound, Kate Northern; Puppets, Hunter Kaczorowski; Props, Nicole Gaignat; Stage Manager, Michelle McDaniel; Associate Set, Laura Taber Bacon; **Cast:** Charissa Bertels, Stacie Bono, Phillip Deyesso, Stephen Gelpi, Jonathan Gregg, Kyle Hines, Zekari Jackson, Terrence Oliver, Shad Olsen, Allyson Pace, Emmy Raver-Lampman, Daniel Henri Luttway, Rachel Rhodes-Devey, Kelly Scanlon, Alan Shaw, Joseph Spieldenn; Good Shepherd United Methodist Church; May 6–29, 2010

Readings

Heartbreak Help by Justin Tanner; Director, Tom Wojtunik; Stage Manager: Jennifer Marie Russo; Stage Directions, Kelly Scanlon; **Cast:** Amy Bizjak, Emily Dorsch, Julie Fitzpatrick, Katherine Folk-Sullivan; September 24, 2009; *The Final Jew* by Alex Goldberg; Director, Seth Soloway; Stage Manager, Jennifer Marie Russo; Stage Directions, Jen Soloway; **Cast:** Richard D. Busser, Kwaku Driskell, Brad Makorowski, Karla Mosley, Kelly Scanlon, Adam Wald; December 10, 2009; *Dead and Buried* by James McLindon; Director, Dominic D'Andrea; Stage Manager, Kristine Schlachter; **Cast:** Margot Bercy, Matt Dickson, Victoria Wylie; March 11, 2010; *Bethany* by Laura Marks; Director, Davis McCallum; Stage Manager, Kristine Schlachter; Stage Directions, Abigail Mankein; **Cast:** Margaret Daly, Kimberly Parker Green, Kathryn Hunter-Williams, Ken Marks, Bob McClure, Allison Weller; May 11, 2010

At Hand Theatre Co.

Producers, Dan Horrigan and Justin Scribner; www.athandtheatre.com

My AiDS Written and performed by Dan Horrigan; Director, Dave Solomon; Set, Shoko Kambara; Lighting, Zach Blane; Stage Manager, Angela Kiessel; Urban Stages; February 13–March 2, 2010

Letters to the End of the World Written and directed by Anton Dudley; Set, Eli Kaplan-Wildmann; Costumes, Nicole Wee; Lighting, Ryan Bauer; Sound, Colin Whitely; Stage Manager, Donald Butchko; **Cast:** Shannon Burkett, Tyrone Mitchell-Henderson, Francesca Choy Kee, Peter O'Connor, Charles Socarides; Studio Theatre on Theatre Row; April 29–May 16, 2010

Lila Cante by Mark Snyder; Director, Sara Sahin; Set, Eli Kaplan-Wildmann; Costumes, Nicole Wee; Lighting, Ryan Bauer; Sound, Julian Mesri; Stage Manager, Melissa Magliula; **Cast:** Danielle Di Vecchio, Rebecca Hart, Matt Shofner, Ryan Spahn; Ted Bardy Acting Studio; October 2–18, 2009

Atlantic Theater Company–Atlantic for Kids

No Dogs Allowed! Book by Sonia Manzano, music by Stephen Lawrence, lyrics by Billy Aronson; Director, Josh Lewis; **Cast:** David Morris, Arielle Siegel, Nicole Spiezio, Ethan Gómez, Josh Lewis, Jessica Gurulé, Mike Smith Rivera, Chloé Wepper; Linda Gross Theater; October 10–November 1, 2009

Books Cook! Written and directed by Liz Swados; Presented by NYU Tisch School of the Arts; Music Director, Kris Kukul; Lighting, Gabriel Evansohn; Costumes/Puppets, Sara Ryer; Props, Travis Boatwright; Artistic Director, Alison Beatty; Stage Manager, Claire Marberg; Assistant Director, Matthew Marberg; Linda Gross Theater; March 6–April 4, 2010

The Attic Theater Company

www.theatticpresents.org

Dark Rapture by Eric Overmyer; Director, Laura Braza; Set, Julia Noulin-Merat; Costumes, Franny Bohar; Lighting, Ben Pilat; Sound, Anthony Spinelli; Stage Manager, Lizz Giorgos; **Cast:** Monica Hammond, Ted Caine, Daniel O'Shae, Nicole Pacent, Sarah Stevens, Rich Dreher, Sam Gooley, Kevin Kane, Thomas Matthews, Victoria Dicce; Connelly Theater; January 22–February 6, 2010

Axis Company

Executive Producer, Jeffrey Resnick; Artistic Director, Randy Sharp; www.axiscompany.org

Glue Trap by Sueli Rocha; Director, Nena Inoue; Lighting, David Zeffren & Amy Harper; Sound, Steve Fontaine; **Cast:** Sueli Rocha; Axis Theatre; October 10–November 22, 2009

Hospital 2009 Written and directed by Randy Sharp; Costumes, Elisa Santiago; Lighting, David Zeffren; Sound, Steve Fontaine; Stage Manager, Edward Terhune; **Cast:** Spencer Aste, Brian Barnhart, Regina Betancourt, David Crabb, Blake DeLong, Britt Genelin, Laurie Kilmartin, Lynn Mancinelli, Matt McGorry, Marc Palmieri, Margo Passalaqua, Brian Sloan, Tom Pennacchini, Edward Terhune, Paul Marc Barnes, Lisa Hickman, Jack; June 11–July 25, 2009

Seven in One Blow, or the Brave Little Kid by Randy Sharp & Axis Company; Director/Original Music, Randy Sharp; Set, Kate Aronsson; Costumes, Elisa Santiago and Kate Aronsson; Lighting, David Zeffren; Sound, Steve Fontaine; Stage Manager, Edward Terhune; **Cast:** Marc Palmieri, Regina Betancourt, Lynn Mancinelli, Jim Sterling, Brian Barnhart, David Crabb, Britt Genelin, Spencer Aste, Edgar Oliver, Laurie Kilmartin, Marlene Berner, Debbie Harry; Eighth annual presentation; December 4–20, 2009

B Productions

My Pal Bette by John Ryan; Director, Kenny Howard; Audio/Visual, Adam Rohrmann & Gerard Kouwhenhoven; Original Music, Rhea Mendoza; Designers, Keith Rogers & Kris Smith; **Cast:** John Ryan, Tammy Kopko, Michael Ell, Reece Scelfo, Sivan Hadari, James Brent Isaacs, PJ Brennan, Cindy Pearlman; Producers Club; June 18–28, 2009

Barefoot Theatre Company

www.barefoottheatrecompany.org

A Christmas Carol: Scrooge and Marley by Israel Horovitz, adapted from Charles Dickens' story; Director, Robert Bruce McIntosh; Sets & Lighting, Francisco Solorzano; Costumes, Victoria Malvagno; Sound, Michael LoPorto; Special Effects, John Harlacher; Choreographer, Victoria Malvagno; Original Music, Aidan Koehler; **Cast:** John Gazzale, Ken Glickfeld, Jeremy Brena, Caitlin Davies, Dan Graff, Steve Weinblatt, Tripp Pettigrew, Gregory Adair, Jennifer Mintzer, Cheryl Dowling, Betty Hudson, Zachary Cohen, Anthony Pierini, Kate Castaneda-Lamar, Victoria Malvagno, Aidan Koehler; Kraine Theater; December 10–23, 2009

70/70 Horovitz Project A year-long, worldwide festival celebrating Israel Horovitz's 70th Birthday with readings and productions of 70 of his plays; Directors included Jo Bonney, Eric Nightengale, Pamela Seiderman, Francisco Solorzano, Nicole Haran, Rose Bonczek, Mimi O'Donell, Ronald Cohen, Terry Kinney, Stephen Adly Guirguis, Israel Horovitz, Paul Russo, Olivia Sklar, Michael LoPorto; Select Casts included Annabella Sciorra, Michael Stuhlbarg, Bobby Cannavale, Francisco Solorzano, Marcia Jean Kurtz, John Doman, Sol Frieder, Michael Aronov, Ashlie Atkinson, John Gazzale, Jeremy Brena, Victoria Malvagno, Anika Solveig, Anna Chlumsky, Dan Graff, Danelle Eliav, Lanna Joffrey, Tala Ashe, Joseph Sousa, Will Allen, Roderick Nash, Betty Hudson, Steven R. Wienblatt, Gil Ron, Kenneth King, Diane Mashburn, Kristin Wheeler, Charles Everett, Christopher Whalen, Lucy Boyle, Marin Ireland, David Nail, Bob Walsh, Gordon McConnell, Chiara Montalto; Cherry Lane Theatre/Theatre For The New City/Bleecker Street Theater/Theatre Row Theatres; March 31, 2009–March 31, 2010

The Barrow Group (TBG Theatre)

Co-Artistic Director/Co-Founder, Seth Barrish; Co-Artistic Director, Lee Brock; www.barrowgroup.org

The Thickness of Skin by Clare McIntyre; Director, Jacob White; Stage Manager, Apolonia Davalos; Production Manager, Porter Pickard; Assistant Director, Kit Bihun; Technical Assistant, Dan Vela; Press, RK/PR; **Cast:** Michael Chenevert, Myles O'Connor, Eli Gelb, Karin Sibrava, Wendy Vanden Heuvel, Alison Wright; October 10–November 9, 2009

Enemy of the People by Henrik Ibsen, adapted by Seth Barrish and K. Lorrel Manning; Director, K. Lorrel Manning; Set, Kate Rance; Costumes, Kate Rance; Stage Manager, Kate Erin Gibson; Production Manager, Porter Pickard; Associate Production Manager, Elizabeth Wipff; Technical Assistants, Joe Williamson and Jason Shoulders; Press, RK/PR; **Cast:** Edward Connors, Jeremy Folmer, Eliza Foss, Larry Mitchell, Katerine Neuman, Myles O'Connor, Herbert Rubens, Clare Schmidt; February 6–March 8, 2010

Phoenix by Scott Organ; Director, Seth Barrish; Lighting, Chrisine Boutin; Production Manager, Porter Pickard; Stage Manager, Kate Erin Gibson; ASMs, Matt Hollerbach, Lori Singleton, Shaka Omari Smith, Marco Torre; Press, RK/PR; **Cast:** Dusty Brown, DeAnna Lenhart; April 3–May 3, 2010

Non-resident Productions

Thunder Above, Deeps Below by A. Rey Pamatmat; Presented by Second Generation Productions Inc.; Director, Pat Diamond; Stage Manager, Lyndsey Goode; Lighting, Scott Bolman; Set, Sandra Goldmark; Costumes, Camille Assaf;

Sound, The Broken Chord Collective; **Cast:** Darian Dauchan, Phyllis Johnson, Rafael Jordan, Rey Lucas, Jon Norman Schneider, Maureen Sebastian; September 8–26, 2009

52nd Street Project Presented by the 52nd Street Project; October 20–24, 2009

…Being Patient Written and performed by Kelly Samara; Presented by The Purpose Theatre; November 4–15, 2009

Daddy by Dan Via; Director, David Hilder; Presented by DownTownTheatre Company; Set, Eugenia Furneaux-Arends; Costumes, Michele Reisch; Lighting, Zakaria M. Al-Alami; Sound, Alexander Neumann; Stage Manager, Michael Palmer; Producer, Samantha Desz; Publicist/Press, DARR Publicity; Casting, Judy Bowman; Fight Director, Galway McCullough; Original Music, Alexander Neumann; Props, Eugenia Furneaux-Arends; Assistant Set/Prop Designer, Ashley Pridmore-Abreg; **Cast:** Gerald McCullouch, Dan Via, Bjorn DuPaty; January 28–February 13, 2010

The Network One-Act Festival Presented by The Network NYC, Paul Michael; March 2–31, 2010

Italian American Reconciliation by John Patrick Shanley; Presented by Passion Play Productions; Director, Suzanne DiDonna; Set, Rohit Kapoor; Lighting, Josh Iacovelli; **Cast:** Michael Basile, Elizabeth Masucci, Brian Murphy, Barbara Speigel, Shirin Tinati; April 15–25, 2010

Baruch Performing Arts Center

December Written and directed by Guillermo Calderon; Presented by Teatro en al Blanco; **Cast:** Jorge Becker, Trinidad Gonzalez, Paula Zuniga; June 26–28, 2009

Third Wing Written and directed by Claudio Tolcachir; Presented by Teatro Timbre 4; **Cast:** Magdalena Grondona, Carlos Hernan Grinstein, Melisa Hermida, Jose Maria Marcos, Daniela Ruth Pal; June 26–28, 2009

Auto Da Fe by Matsuda Masataka, translated by Kameron Steele & Shigeki Morii; Presented by International WOW Company; Director, Josh Fox with Paul Bargetto; Set, Nate Lemoine; Costumes, Cait O'Connor; Lighting, Charles Foster & Jeremy Cunningham; Sound, Julian J. Mesri; Stage Manager, Kate August; Dramaturg, Heather Denyer; **Cast:** Lydia Blaisdell, Adam Boncz, Mike Callaghan, Melissa Chambers, Doug Chapman, Stefani Charitou, Lisa Clair, Herbie Go, Sara Gozalo, Beth Griffith, Ikuko Ikari, Georgia X. Lifsher, Joanna Lu, Tommy McGinn, Mary Notari, Jennifer Oda, Blaire O'Leary, Martina Potratz, Brent Reams, Iracel Rivero, Robert Saietta, Brandon Alan Smith, Carlton Tanis, Evan True, Aya Tucker, Michael Villastrigo, Deborah Wallace, Folami Williams; January 8–24, 2010

Bindlestiff Family Cirkus

www.bindlestiff.org

Buckaroo Bindlestiff's Wild West Jamboree Written and directed by the Company; Set/Costumes, Stephanie Monseu; Lighting/Sound, Keith Nelson; **Cast:** Keith Nelson, Stephanie Monseu; Rocking Horse Ranch; June 20, 2009–April 3, 2010

Bindlestiff Family Cirkus Cabaret by the Company; Directors, Keith Nelson and Stephanie Monseu; Stage Manager, Ellia Bisker; Set, Keith Nelson; Costumes, Stephanie Monseu; **Cast:** Keith Nelson, Stephanie Monseu, Michael Richter, Harvest Moon, Seth, Christina Gelsone, Joel Jeske, Christopher Lueke, Mistress B, Jonathan Nosan, Matt Henry, Josh Edelman, Helium Aeiral Dance, Brian Bielemeier, Tanya Gagne, Michael Karas, Hilary Chaplain; Dixon Place; March 14–April 25, 2010

The New Vaudeville Revue by Frank Cullen; Director, Doug Nielsen; **Cast:** Keith Nelson, Stephanie Monseu, Adam Kuchler, Ariele Ebacher,with the University of Arizona Dance Department; presented at the Stevie Eller Theater (Tuscon School of Dance, University of Arizona); November 11–15, 2010

Bindlestiff Cavalcade of Youth by The Company; Director, Viveca Gardiner; Stage Manager, Viveca Gardiner; **Cast:** The Cavalkids; Coney Island; Ongoing

Bindlestiff Open Stage Variety Show Director/Stage Manager, Keith Nelson; Lighting/Audio-Visual Design/Sound, Kris Anton; Galapagos Art Space; Ongoing

blessed unrest

Artistic Director and Founding Company Member, Jessica Burr; Managing Director and Founding Company Member, Matt Opatrny; www.blessedunrest.org

Nick Adapted by Laura Wickens from Chekhov's *Ivanov*; Director, Jessica Burr; Set/Costumes, Anna-Alisa Belous; Lighting, Benjamin C. Tevelow; Sound, Wei Wang; Audio/Visual, C. Andrew Bauer; Choreographer, Kelly Hayes; **Cast:** Zenzelé Cooper, Anna Kepe, Eunjee Lee, John Peery, Peter Richards, Matthew Sincell, Darrell Stokes, Laura Wickens, Hannah Wilson; Interart Annex; May 28–June 15, 2009

Doruntine by Matt Opatrny and Lirak Celaj; Co-produced with Teatri Oda of Kosova; Directors, Jessica Burr and Florent Mehmeti; Costumes, Anna-Alisa Belous; Sound, Guy Sherman; Stage Manager, Jaimie Van Dyke; **Cast:** Laura Wickens, Matt Opatrny, Dave Edson, Zenzele Cooper, Kelly Hayes, Ilire Celaj, Lirak Celaj, Njomeza Ibraj, Nentor Fetiu; European tour: Kosova, Macedonia, and Albania; August 29–September 20, 2009

A Midsummer Night's Dream by William Shakespeare; adapted and directed by Jessica Burr; Costumes, Evan Prizant; Lighting, Rachel Gilmore; Sound, Joan Jubett; Stage Manager, Jaimie Van Dyke; **Cast:** Scott Barrow, Davina Cohen, Stephen Drabicki, Stephen Pilkington, Damen Scranton, Vaishnavi Sharma, Carlos Alberto Valencia, Laura Wickens, Hannah Wilson; Interart Theatre; March 20–April 5, 2010

BOO-Arts

Founder/Producer/Director, Kathleen O'Neill; Staff: Crystina Wyler, Nany Sirianni, Ed McNameee, Dana Monagan; www.boo-arts.com

Penang by James Larocca; Co-produced with Madison Street Productions; Director, Donya K. Washington; Set, Craig Napoliello; Costumes, David Withrow; Lighting, Zach Blane; Sound, David Schulder; Stage Manager, Michelle Kelleher; ASM, Megan Furnish; PR/Marketing, Antonio Minino; **Cast:** Ray Chao, Andrea Chen, Jacequeline Gregg, Rushi Kota, Chris La Panta, Scott Raker, Peter Sabri, Jeffrey Evan Thomas, Kurt Uy; WorkShop Theater; November 5–22, 2009

The Love List by Norm Foster; Director, Jessica McVea; Set, Ryan Murphy; Costumes, Tracy Klein; Lighting, Morgan Anne Zipf; Sound, Dana Monagan; Stage Manager, Megan Furnish; ASM, London Griffith; PR, Antonio Minino; **Cast:** Jarel Davidow, Kate Goehring, Jake Hart; Manhattan Theatre Source; April 29–May 15, 2010

Readings

A Daughter of Israel by David Stallings based on the true story of co-creator Adi Kurtchik; Director, Kathleen O'Neill; Stage Directions, Sheena Earl; **Cast:** Adi Kurtchik, Shelly Feldman, Lauren Kelston, Maria Makenna Smith, Caroline Tamas; December 6–7, 2009

Boomerang Theatre Company

Artistic Director, Tim Errickson; Managing Director, Francis Kuzler; www.boomerangtheatre.org

The Comedy of Errors by William Shakespeare; Director, Philip Emeott; Costumes, Carolyn Pallister; Fight Director, Carrie Brewer; Assistant Director, Marielle Duke; Stage Manager, Jack Lynch; **Cast:** Steven Beckingham, Emily King Brown, Catherine Dowling, Jon Dykstra, Stuart Green, John Greenleaf,

Sarah Hankins, Walter Hoffman, Uriel Menson, Michael Mraz, Michael Alan Read, Christian Toth, Lillian Wright; Central Park; June 20–July 25, 2009

Readings

The Travel Plays by Greg Romero; Directors, Adriana Baer, Marielle Duke, Jordana Williams, Daniel Talbott, Michael Flanagan, Andrew Merkel; October 10, 2009

The Legacy Reading Series New annual event featuring readings from past seasons; included: *The Monster Tales* by Mary Jett Parsley Wrenn, directed by Cailin Heffernan (February 1); *Burning the Old Man* by Kelly McAllister, directed by Tim Errickson; *The Hot Month* by Taylor Mac, directed by Christopher Thomasson (April 12)

First Flight 2010 Annual new play reading series; included: *Skin Deep* by Rich Orloff, directed by John Greenleaf; *The Barong* by Steven Beckingham, directed by Bob D'Haene; *Attack of the Nearly Dead Russian Children* by Mose Hayward, directed by Marielle Duke; *Dream House* by Zack Calhoun, directed by Daniel Talbott; *Marvelous* by Leslie Bramm, directed by Linda S. Nelson; *Do Geese See God (A Palindrome)* by J.D. Eames, directed by Cailin Heffernan; ART/NY; March 24–28, 2010

Brave New World Repertory Theatre

www.bravenewworldrep.org

The Tempest by William Shakespeare; Director, Claire Beckman; Set, Greg Mitchell; Costumes, Meganne George; Sound, Zach Williamson; Stage Manager, Schwartz; Producer, Claire Beckman; Composer, Milica Paranosic; Choreographer, Sheila Anozier; Technical Director, John Morgan; Lead ASMs, Nataliya Vasilyeva, Sara Swanberg; Associate Producer, Alice Barrett; **Cast:** Jonathan Dewberry, Nixon Cesar, Ezra Barnes, Scott Voloshin, Christopher Salazar, William Brenner, Alvin Hippolyte, John Edmond Morgan, David Frutkoff, John Lederer, Isidore Elias, Margaret Lancaster, Taylor Morgan, Tessa Murphy, Georgeanna Deas, Maeri Hedstrom, Stacey Cervellino, Michael-Alan Read, Bobby Savage, Abigail Drach, Amy Austern, Mike Ramsey, Stanley Mitchell, Kristina Glushkova, Bria Brown, Maria Damachkina, Christina Offley, Crystal Offley, Ryan Raffloer; Coney Island Boardwalk; September 26–27, 2009

The Crucible by Arthur Miller; Director/Lighting, Claire Beckman; Set, Greg Mitchell; Costumes, Dorothy Lawrence; Stage Manager, Nataliya Vasilyeva; Assistant Costumes, Taylor Morgan; ASM, Robert Austern; Properties, Mary Reiser; Music Director, Eleanor Geryk; **Cast:** Ezra Barnes, Tessa Murphy, Sandra Mills Scott, Kira McCarthy, Taylor Morgan, Caroline Ryburn, Kevin Hogan, Dora Friedman, Catherine Mancuso, John Edmond Morgan, Eleanor Ruth, William Brenner, David Frutkoff, Christine Siracusa, Victor Barranca, Edwin Sean; Old Stone House of Brooklyn; March 4–14, 2010

Brian Hampton Productions

www.brianhampton.net

Checking In by Brian Hampton; Director, Richard St. Peter; Stage Manager, Brian Paul Mendoza; Sound, Tommy Gatton; Graphics, Wade Hampton; Company Manager, Roy Chicas; **Cast:** Natalie Buster, Allie Darden, Jennifer Hyman-Zimmerman, Brian Hampton, Beverly Lauchner, Anna Nugent; June Havoc Theatre; July 15–August 1, 2009

The Jungle Fun Room by Brian Hampton; Director, Sam Zalutsky; Stage Manager, Elise Hanley; Company Manger, Roy Chicas; **Cast:** Carter Calvert, Kim S. Goldfeder, Brian Hampton, Beverly Lauchner, Trey Mitchell, Paul Nugent; Actors' Playhouse; August 15–29, 2009

The Brick Theater

Co-Founders, Robert Honeywell and Robert Gardner; www.bricktheater.com

The Tale of the Good Whistleblower of Chaillot's Caucasian Mother... by Stan Richardson; Presented by Theatre Askew (Co-Artistic Directors, Tim Cusack and Jason Jacobs); Original Music, Rachel Peters; Director, Jason Jacobs; Lighting, Ian W. Hill; Sound, Matty Pritchard; Costumes, Bryen Shannon; **Cast:** Tim Cusack, Dennis Courage, Huntleigh Arendt, Bear Matt Steiner, Sara Alvarez, Brandon Uranowitz, Debbie Troché, Joanna Parson; June 5–July 4, 2009

Adventure Quest by Richard Lovejoy; Co-Produced by Sneaky Snake Productions; Director, Adam Swiderski; Set, Timothy McCown Reynolds; Costumes, Marc Borders & Jim Hammer; Lighting, Ian W. Hill; Sound, Chris Chappell; Stage Manager, Kimberly Craven; Art & Projection Design, Jamie Melani Marshall; **Cast:** Kent Meister, Sarah Malinda Engelke, Alley Scott, Danny Bowes, Anne Carlisle, Jesse Wilson, Timothy McCown Reynolds, Richard Lovejoy, Kimberly Craven; June 6–July 25, 2009

Your Lithopedion by Justin Maxwell; Presented by Opium, Fireworks and Lead; Director, Toby Ring Thelin; **Cast:** Lillian Wright, Christian Toth; June 13–30, 2009

Titus Andronicus by William Shakespeare; Co-produced with DMTheatrics; Director/Design, Frank Cwiklik; **Cast:** Kymberly Tuttle, Sean Phillips, Brianna Tyson, Greg Engebrecht, Ann Breitbach, Fred Backus, Ken Simon, Kristin Woodburn, Adam Samtur, Craig Kelton Peterson, Peter Schwartz, Peter Schuyler, Stephanie Wortel; October 9–24, 2009

The Blood Brothers present ... The New Guignol by Danny Bowes, James Comtois, Mac Rogers; Co-produced with Nosedive Productions; Directors, Pete Boisvert, Rebecca Comtois, Stephanie Cox-Williams, Abe Goldfarb, Matt Johnston, Patrick Shearer; Stage Manager, Stephanie Cox-Williams, Dana Rossi; Set, Arnold Bueso; Costumes, Sarah Riffle; Lighting, Daniel Winters; Sound, Patrick Shearer; Original Music, Larry Lees; **Cast:** Ryan Andes, Becky Byers, Rebecca Comtois, Jessi Gotta, Stephen Heskett, Robert Leeds, Marsha Martinez, Ben VandenBoom, Cotton Wright; October 28–31, 2009

Exposition by Matthew Freeman; Director/Lighting, Michael Gardner; **Cast:** Kina Bermudez, Maggie Cino, Sean Kenin, Anna Kull, Alexis Sotile, Moira Stone, Jennifer Gordon Thomas; November 19–21, 2009

Deck the Hallmans! Presented by Ten Directions; Director, Audrey Crabtree; Lighting, Berit Johnson; Fight Choreographer, Adam Swiderski; **Cast:** Audrey Crabtree, Robert Honeywell, Moira Stone, Lauri Berritta, Iracel Rivero, Jonathan Kaplan, Alyssa Simon, Donetta Riley, Lynn Berg; December 6–19, 2009

Power Burn 3 by Alana McNair & Kate Wilkinson; Presented by Cat Fight Productions; Director, Stephen Brackett; Lighting, Eric Southern; Sound, Brandon Wolcott; Fight Director, Carrie Brewer; Stage Manager, E. Sarah Barnes; **Cast:** Rin Allen, Jenna Crawford, Adam Lerman, Rocio Mendez, Amanda O'Callaghan, Angela Sharp, Megan Stern, Becky Yamamoto; December 15–20, 2009

The Ninja Cherry Orchard by Anton Chekhov, adapted and directed by Michael Gardner; Set, Michael Gardner; Costumes/Assistant Director/Stage Manager, Gyda Arber; Lighting, Ian W. Hill; Fight Directors, Qui Nguyen and Alexis Black; **Cast**: Aaron Baker, Alexis Black, Alyssa Simon, Audrey Crabtree, Avery Pearson, Betsy Head, Dina Rose, Eve Udesky, Gyda Arber, Heather Lee Rogers, Jason Liebman, Jorge Cordova, Kelley Rae O'Donnell, Lynn Berg, Maggie Cino, Marguerite French, Mateo Moreno; January 7–9, 2010

A Brief History of Murder by Richard Lovejoy; Co-produced with Sneaky Snake Productions; Director, Ivanna Cullinan; Costumes, Jim Hammer; Lighting, Morgan Anne Zipf; Sound & Original Music, Chris Chappell; Stage Manager, Laura Gomez; Gore and Special Effects, Laura Moss; Choreographer, Becky Byers, Fight Choreographer, Adam Swiderski; **Cast:** David Arthur Bachrach, Danny Bowes, Sal Brienik, Becky Byers, Anne Carlisle, Sarah Malinda Engelke, Justin R.G. Holcomb, Sheila Joon, Gavin Starr Kendall, Kathryn Lawson, Richard Lovejoy, Samantha Mason, Kent Meister, Timothy McCown Reynolds, Adam Swider; January 14–31, 2010

You're Welcome by Paul Thureen & Hannah Bos; Co-produced with The Debate Society; Director, Oliver Butler; Costumes, Sydney Maresca; Lighting, Mike Riggs; Sound, Nathan Leigh; **Cast:** Hannah Bos, Michael Cyril Creighton, Paul Thureen; February 4–27, 2010

Craven Monkey and the Mountain of Fury Written and directed by Jeff Lewonczyk; Co-produced with Piper McKenzie; Costumes, Julianne Kroboth; Lighting, Ian W. Hill; Sound, Jeff Lewonczyk; Stage Manager, Guinevere Pressley; Fight Directors, Qui Nguyen and Adam Swiderski; **Cast:** Fred Backus, Becky Byers, Hope Cartelli, Jessi Gotta, Adrian Jevicki, Mateo Moreno, Jeff Lewonczyk, Melissa Roth, Art Wallace; February 26–March 13, 2010

Samuel and Alasdair: A Personal History of the Robot War by Marc Bovino & Joe Curnutte; Co-produced with The Mad Ones; Director, Lila Neugebauer; Costumes, Evan Prizant; Lighting, Mike Inwood; Sound, Stowe Nelson; Dramaturg, Sarah Lunnie; **Cast:** Marc Bovino, Joe Curnutte, Michael Dalto, Stephanie Wright Thompson; April 1–17, 2010

The Vigil or The Guided Cradle by Crystal Skillman; Co-produced with Impetuous Theater Group; Director, John Hurley; Set, Sylviane Jacobsen; Costumes, Meryl Pressman & Holly Rihn; Lighting, Olivia Harris; Sound, Anthony Mattana; **Cast:** Susan Louise O'Connor, Dion Mucciacito, Christian Rummel, Travis York, Vinnie Penna, Alex Pappas, Joseph Mathers; April 22–May 8, 2010

Dénouement by Matthew Freeman; Director/Lighting, Michael Gardner; **Cast:** Fred Backus, Kina Bermudez, Stephen Burns, Maggie Cino, Ivanna Cullinan, Alexis Sottile, Moira Stone; May 22–28, 2010

Festivals

The Antidepressant Festival June 5–July 4, 2009; included: *Adventure Quest* by Richard Lovejoy, directed by Adam Swiderski, co-produced by Sneaky Snake Productions; **Cast:** Kent Meister, Sarah Engelke, Alley Scott, Danny Bowes, Timothy McCown Reynolds, Anne Carlisle, Jesse Wilson, Richard Lovejoy; *2012: A New Dawn* written, directed and produced by Afternoon Playland; **Cast:** Shawn Wickens, Desiree Nash, Roy Koshy, Gavin Starr Kendall, Eden Gauteron; *...and the fear cracked open* by Lynn Berg & Audrey Crabtree, directed by Audrey Crabtree, co-produced by Ten Directions; **Cast:** Lynn Berg, Becky Byers, Audrey Crabtree, Gavin Starr Kendall; *Big Girls Club (The Happy Happy Dance Princess Show)* written and directed by Leah Winkler, co-produced by Everywhere Theatre Group; **Cast:** Lisa Bierman, Nancy Upton, Katie Hannigan, Joel Israel; *Booze, Sports and Romance* written and performed by Danny Bowes, directed by Chris Connolly; *Cabaret Terrarium* written, directed and performed by Richard Harrington and Chris Kauffman; *Exit, Pursued by Bears* by Casey Wimpee, directed by Julie Rossman, co-produced by The Aztec Economy; **Cast:** Jared Culverhouse, Michael Mason, Richard Saudek, Patrick Vaill, Lucy Kaminsky, Cole Wimpee; *Glee Club* by Matthew Freeman, directed by Kyle Ancowitz, co-produced by Blue Coyote Theater Group; **Cast:** Tom Staggs, Matthew Trumbull, Gary Schrader, David DelGrosso, Robert Buckwalter, Stephen Speights, Bruce Barton, Carter Jackson; *How to Fight Depression When You Don't Even Know its Symptoms?!* by Eduardo Band, co-produced by Five Eduardinos; **Cast:** Dustin X, Jessica Huber, Nick Breeden, Christina Williams, Gretchen Knapp; *Infectious Opportunity* by James Comtois, directed by Pete Boisvert, co-produced by Nosedive Productions; **Cast:** Rebecca Comtois, DR Hanson, Daryl Lathon, David Ian Lee, Ronica Reddick, Andrea Marie Smith, Matthew Trumbull; *Le Mirage* by L'Ordre du Temple Solaire; Presented, translated and minor adaptation by Laboratory Theater; Director, Yvan Greenberg; Original Music, François B. Nouvel- gel; Additional Music, Richard Wagner, Gabriel Fauré; Lighting, Amanda Woodward; **Cast:** Corey Dargel, Sheila Donovan, Oleg Dubson; *Samuel and Alasdair: A Personal History of the Robot War* by Marc Bovino & Joe Curnutte, directed by Lila Neugebauer, co-produced by The Mad Ones; **Cast:** Marc Bovino, Joe Curnutte, Stephanie Thompson; *Schaden, Freude and You: A 3 Clown Seminar* by written and co-produced by Logic Limited Ltd., directed by Jane Nichols; **Cast:** Chris Arruda, Brad Fraizer, Larry Pontius; *Suspicious Package: Rx* by Gyda Arber and Aaron Baker, directed by Gyda Arber, co-produced by The Fifth Wall; *The Tale of the Good Whistleblower of Chaillot's Caucasian Mother and Her Other Children of a Lesser Marriage Chalk*

Circle by Stan Richardson, directed by Jason Jacobs, co-produced by Theatre Askew; *WILM 690: Pirate Radio* created and co-presented by Movementpants Dance, directed by Adrian Jevicki; *Your Lithopedion* by Justin Maxwell, directed by Toby Ring Thelin, co-produced by Opium, Fireworks and Lead; **Cast:** Lillian Wright, Christian Toth

Game Play July 2–25, 2009; included: *Adventure Quest* by Richard Lovejoy, directed by Adam Swiderski; **Cast:** Kent Meister, Sarah Engelke, Alley Scott, Danny Bowes, Timothy McCown Reynolds, Anne Carlisle, Jesse Wilson, Richard Lovejoy; *Suspicious Package: Rx* by Gyda Arber & Aaron Baker, directed by Gyda Arber; *Thank You, But Our Princess Is in Another Castle: Four Live-Action Machinima Theater Pieces* written and directed by Eddie Kim

Amuse Bouche: A NY Clown Theatre Festival Hors D'Oeuvre September 4–27, 2009; Lighting and Sound, James Monahan; included: *And It Feels So Good!* by Happy Hour; **Cast:** Mark Gindick, Ambrose Martos, Matthew Morgan; *Cabaret Terrarium* written, directed and performed by Richard Harrington and Chris Kauffman; *Canarsie Suite: At the Edge of Vaudeville* by Aimee German & Jennifer Sargent; *Icetacles: The Last Chance of a Lifetime* by Lynn Berg, Audrey Crabtree, Jonathan Kaplan, Maria Parra, Jeff Seal, Shawn Wickens; *Viva Evel Knievel* by Lynn Berg; **Cast:** Adam Swiderski, Sarah Engelke, Darius Stone, Brooke Tarnoff, Jenny Harder, Brian Bair; *Schaden, Freude and You: A 3 Clown Seminar* by Logic Limited, Ltd., directed by Jane Nichols; **Cast:** Chris Arruda, Brad Fraizer, Larry Pontius

Fight Fest December 1–20, 2009; included: *The Zombie Project: The Story of Icarus Phoenix* written, directed and performed by Stephanie Cox-Williams; *Butterfly, Butterfly, Kill Kill Kill!* written and directed by Patrick Harrison; **Cast:** Patrick Harrison, Margaret Odette Perkins, Adam Scott Mazer, Alexandra Hellquist, Ian Picco, Dan Rogers, Colin Baker; *The Buccaneer* written and directed by Jacob Grigolia-Rosenbaum; **Cast:** John Gardner, Ryan Karels, Rebecca White, Bonnie Sherman, Nicole Mitzel, Tom Evans; *Craven Monkey and the Mountain of Fury* written and directed by Jeff Lewonczyk; **Cast:** Fred Backus, Becky Byers, Hope Cartelli, Jessi Gotta, Adrian Jevicki, Mateo Moreno, Jeff Lewonczyk, Melissa Roth, Art Wallace; *Deck the Hallmans!* by Ten Directions, directed by Audrey Crabtree; **Cast:** Lynn Berg, Lauri Berritta, Robert Honeywell, Jonathan Kaplan, Donetta Riley, Iracel Rivero, Alyssa Simon, Moira Stone; *Evolution* by Alexandra Hastings and David Dean Hastings, directed by Alexandra Hastings; *Last Life* by Eric Sanders, directed by Timothy Haskell; **Cast:** Taimak Guerriello, Aaron Haskell, Maggie MacDonald, Jo-Anne Lee, Soomi Kim, Alyxx Wilson; *The Ninja Cherry Orchard* by Anton Chekhov, adapted and directed by Michael Gardner; **Cast:** Aaron Baker, Alexis Black, Alyssa Simon, Audrey Crabtree, Avery Pearson, Dina Rose, Eric Bailey, Eve Udesky, Gyda Arber, Heather Lee Rogers, Iracel Rivero, Jason Liebman, Jorge Cordova, Kelley Rae O'Donnell, Lynn Berg, Maggie Cino, Michael Criscuolo, Nikolas Priest, Patrick Pizzolorusso, Rainbow Geffner, Roger Nasser, Samantha Mason, Samantha Tunis, Shelley Ray, Stephanie Willing, Stephen Heskett, Thomas Reid, Trav S.D.; *Power Burn 3* by Alana McNair & Kate Wilkinson, directed by Stephen Brackett; **Cast:** Rin Allen, Jenna Crawford, Adam Lerman, Rocio Mendez, Amanda O'Callaghan, Angela Sharp, Megan Stern, Becky Yamamoto

Tiny Theater 2010 May 14–15, 2010; included: *When You're 97, Laughing Helps* written and directed by David Lawson; *Espionage!* by Gyda Arber and Aaron Baker, directed by Gyda Arber; *Tiny Earnest* by Court Street Group; *Rant* written and directed by Ryan Tracy; *The Lone Starr of Texas* by Gavin Starr Kendall and Afternoon Playland; *A Clever Brain* written and directed by Mian Mian Lu; *Crash Splash* by Callie Kimball, directed by Gyda Arber; *The Plowman's Lunch* written and directed by Art Wallace; *The A-Cake-Ening: Kate Chopin's The Awakening as Performed by Cake* by Kate Wilkinson and Adam Hocke; *Revival* by Ana Isabel Keilson, Jen Leavitt, and Adam Smith; *Roger Nasser Is The One Man-Ten Minute A Streetcar Named Desire* by Roger Nasser and Piper McKenzie; *To Whom* by Robert Kerr, directed by Dominic D'Andrea

Non-resident Productions

The Badass Record Collection presents Taking Liberties: an evening of Elvis Costello Presented by DMTheatrics; July 9–18, 2009

Punkrock/Lovesong Presented by Horse Trade Theater Group; September 30–October 3, 2009

La Spectra Presented by movementpants dance; March 19–20, 2010

The Vigil, Or The Guided Cradle by Crystal Skillman; Presented by Impetuous Theater Group; Director, John Hurley; Lighting, Olivia Harris; Set, Sylvaine Jacobsen; Costumes, Meryl Pressman & Holly Rihn; Sound, Anthony Mattana; **Cast:** Susan Louise O'Connor, Dion Mucciacito, Christian Rummel, Travis York, Vinnie Penna, Alex Pappas, Joseph Mathers; April 22–May 8, 2010

The Bridge Theatre Company

www.thebridgetheatrecompany.com

Readings

Psychomachia by Jennifer Lane; Director, Robin A. Paterson; **Cast:** Ashlie Atkinson, Debra Jo Rupp, Tom Pelphrey, Frank Deal, Jennifer Laine Williams, John Calvin Kelly; October 28–30, 2009

Greenland by Nicolas Billon; Director: Ravi Jain; **Cast:** Susan Louise O'Connor, Peter Lettre and Eryn Murman; February 4–6, 2010

The Swearing Jar by Kate Hewlett; Director: Rosemary Andress; **Cast:** Esther Barlow, Christopher Stanton, Vince Nappo, Mimi Quillin; March 19–20 2010

Broken Watch Theatre Company

Artistic Director, Drew DeCorleto; www.brokenwatch.org

Readings

Look, we are breathing by Laura Jacqmin; Director, Michael Sexton; January 19, 2010; Honey Brown Eyes by Stefanie Zadravec; Director, Martha Banta; January 20, 2010; *Rich Girl* by Victoria Stewart; Director, Thomas Kail; Frederick Loewe Room; January 27, 2010

BrooklynONEtheater

The Heavens of Hell Written and directed by Evan Storey; Set, Kelly Fox; Lighting, Lee Terry; **Cast:** Kelly Fox, Anton Koval, Anthony Marino, Evan Storey; Turtle Shell Theater; June 10–27, 2009

The Bushwick Starr

Artistic Director and Curator, Noel Joseph Allain; Managing Director and Curator, Sue Kessler; Technical Director/Resident Designer, Jay Maury; Associate Artistic Director, Mark Sitko; Development, Erica Rippy; Music Programmer, Ashlyn Davis; Design Consultant, Jared Klein; www.thebushwickstarr.org

New Hope City Written and performed by Pass Kontrol; February 11–27, 2010

Cake Productions

www.cakeproductions.org

Modern Dance for Beginners by Sarah Phelps; Director, Alison Beatty; Lighting, Nick Solyom; Set, Dante Smith; Costumes, Katja Andreiev; Stage Manager, Courtney Ferrell; **Cast:** Marta Kuersten, Charlie Wilson, Sarah Brill, Will Peebles, William Franke, Lucy Rayner, Carter Jackson, Francesca Day; Cherry Lane Theatre; July 16–25, 2009

Psych by Evan Smith; Director, Marta Kuersten; Set, Isaac Ramsey; Costumes, Mark Mears & Brooke Berry; Lighting, Jessica Burgess; Sound, Rick Thompson & Francesca Day; Stage Manager, Courtney Ferrell; **Cast:** Francesca Day, Marta Kuersten, Brooke Berry, Sarah Brill, Jacquleyn Landgraf, Helen Merino, Amir Darvish, Jeremiah Zinger, Matthew J. Nichols; Paradise Factory Theatre; May 8–22, 2010

CAP21

The Trouble With Doug: a Modern-Day Metamorphosis Book and music by Will Aronson, book and lyrics by Daniel Mate; Director, Lawrence Arancio; Music Director, Greg Brown; Set, Gian Marco Lo Forte; Lighting/Sound, Greg Goff; Costumes, Kara Harmon; Stage Manager, Becca Doyle **Cast:** Mary-Pat Green, Adam Heller, Carey McCray, Chuck Rea, Jason Williams; June 9–27, 2009

Castillo Theatre

Managing Director/Director of Production, Diane Stiles; Youth Onstage! Artistic Director/Resident Dramaturg, Dan Friedman; Sales Director, Gail Peck; Technical Director, Kenneth Horgan; Youth Onstage! Managers, Craig Pattison, Craig Bannister; Production Coordinator, Andy Allis; www.castillo.org

The River Crosses Rivers: Short Plays By Women of Color A festival of plays produced in association with the New Federal Theatre and Going to the River; included: *The Kitchen (or 9 1/2 Minutes of Subcontinental Absurdity)* by Naveen Bahar Choudhury; Director, Jamie Richards; **Cast:** Andrew Guilarte, Sakina Jaffrey, Seril James, Yasmin Kazi; *The Step-Mother* by Ruby Dee; Director, Chuck Patterson; **Cast:** Carmen Delavallade, Mary Hodges; *Hot Methuselah* by J.E. Franklin, Director; Imani; **Cast:** Vinie Burrows, Norman Matlock, John Rankin; *Jesse* by P. J. Gibson; Director, Lydia Fort; **Cast:** Christopher Burris, Maya Lynne Robinson; *Banana Beer Bath* by Lynn Nottage, Director, Talvin Wilks; **Cast:** Elain Graham; *His Daddy* by Cori Thomas; Director, Stephen Fried; **Cast:** Matthew Montelongo, Lindsay Smiling; *Rally* by Bridgette Wimberly; Director, Clinton Turner Davis; **Cast:** Venida Evans, Erin Weems; October 8–November 1, 2009

Safe At Third (or Josh Gibson Don't Bunt) Written and directed by Fred Newman; Set/AV Design, Joseph Spirito; Costumes, EmilieCharlotte; Lighting, Kate Ashton; Sound, Michael Klein; Stage Manager, Lisa Oros; Assistant Director, Mary Fridley; Musical Director, Michael Walsh; Scenic Artist, Pei Ying Spirito; Producer, Jessica Massad; **Cast:** Earl Griffin, Gabrielle L. Kurlander, David Nackman, Johanny Paulino; Demonstration Room; October 23–November 22, 2009

The Work/Play by the Company; Director, Dan Friedman; Stage Manager, Martina Vann; Lighting, Kenneth Horgan; Costumes, EmilieCharlotte; Assistant Director, Lorna Ruxton; Producer, Isaac H. Suggs Jr.; Improvisation Coach, Lauren Popper Ellis; Movement Coach, Ruby Lawrence; Vocal Coach, Kristen Manley; **Cast:** Purba Atandrila, Kimarra Cannonier, Andrew Dempster, Wilbenson Eugene, Jessica Garcia, Tamara Jacobs, Aliyyaa Lambert, Shalisha McIntosh, Luz Monica Montanez, Rejinal Simon; December 4, 2009–January 17, 2010

The Task by Heiner Müller; Director, Gabrielle L. Kurlander; Set/Audio Visual Design, Joseph Spirito; Costumes, EmilieCharlotte; Lighting, Antoinette Tynes; Sound, Michael Klein; Stage Manager, Lisa Oros; Translator, Carl Weber; Music and Lyrics, Fred Newman; Assistant Director, Jennifer Fomore; Producer, Jim Horton; Choreographer, Lonné Moretton; Music Producer, Lenny Moore; Music Arranger, David Belmont; **Cast:** Peyton Coles, Keldrick Crowder, Chris Elian, Fulton Hodges, Ava Jenkins, Gabriella Lake, Sylenia Lewis, Kipp Lyle, John Rankin, Sheryl Williams; Downstairs Theatre; January 22–March 7, 2010

Dr. May Edward Chinn by Laurence Holder; Produced by the National Black Touring Circuit; Director, Imani; Set, Tony Davidson; Costumes, Ali Turms; Lighting, Antoinette Tynes; Stage Manager, B.J. Pierce Astwood; **Cast:** Dr. May Edward Chinn, Kim Yancey; February 26–28, 2010

Grapes of Wrath by John Steinbeck, adapted by Frank Galati; Co-Production with City Lights Youth Theatre and Youth Onstage!; Director, Robert Bruce McIntosh; Stage Manager, Michael Palmer; Set, Jen Varbalow; Costumes, Richard Caswell; Lighting, Scott Borowka; Assistant Director, Mary-Jane April; Technical Director, John Sisson; Fight Choreographer, Jacob Grigolia-Rosenbaum; Choreographer, Judith Gelman Myers; **Cast:** Rashad Bashir, Alice Bishop, Jeffrey Carter, Angelo Clement, Lauren Curet, Kevin Drouillard, Francisco Espinoza, Nelson Felix, Brandon Fernandez, Yoshiharu Hewitt, Randy Higgins, Heather Niccollette Lewter, Molly Miller, Anya Opshinksky, Lily Patricof; Demonstration Room; March 12–21, 2010

Che by Mario Fratti; Director, Madclyn Chapman; Set/Audio Visual Design, Joseph Spirito; Lighting, Rachelle Beckerman; Costumes, EmilieCharlotte; Sound, Sean O'Halloran; Stage Manager, Sharon R. Brown; Producer, Jim Horton; Dramaturg, Dan Friedman; Assistant Director, Peter Cook; **Cast:** Purba Atandrila, Randy Higgins, Leticia King, Joneise McCrae, Samantha Randolph, Esteban Rodriguez-Alverio, Rejinal Simon, Faith Vann, Kristina Acheampong, Emily Benitez, Paul Hertel, Hani Omar Khalil, Rao Rampila, Pei Ying Spirito; Demonstration Room; May 7–June 6, 2010

Risky Revolutionary by Fred Newman; Director, David Nackman; Set/Audio Visual Design, Joseph Spirito; Costumes, EmilieCharlotte; Lighting, Rachelle Beckerman; Sound, Sean O'Halloran; Stage Manager, Ellen Korner; Producer, Diane Stiles; Dramaturg, Dan Friedman; **Cast:** Arthur Castro, David Nackman, Chris Triana, Franceli Chapman, Paul Hertel, Mairead Walsh; Demonstration Room; May 7–June 6, 2010

Readings

Let Freedom Ring Written and directed by Ted Lange; Co-presented by the New Federal Theatre as part of The Gurfein Foundation/Ntozake Shange Play Reading Series; Stage Manager, Bayo; **Cast:** Jerome Preston Bates, Lisa Bostnar, Arthur French, Bianca Jones, Chaz Reuben, Count Stovall; March 14, 2010

Dark Meat on a Funny Mind by Wesley Brown; Co-presented by the New Federal Theatre as part of The Gurfein Foundation/Ntozake Shange Play Reading Series; Director, A. Dean Irby; Stage Manager, Bayo; **Cast:** Mark Curry, Ted Lange; May 16, 2010

the cell

Founding Artistic Director, Nancy Manocherian; Artistic Director, Kira Simring; Managing Director, Pat Jones; Director of Development, Garlia Cornelia Jones; Lighting, Lee Terry; P.R. Director, Rick Gomes; Web Director, Chris Gabriel; www.thecelltheatre.com

Leaves of Grass by Walt Whitman, adapted and directed by Jeremy Bloom; Set, Shawn Hollahan; Lighting, Dan Gallagher, Jeanette Yew; Sound and Audio/Visual, Jeremy Bloom; Stage Manager, Amanda K. Acobes; Production Manager, Amanda Thieroff; Web Design, Doug Barron; **Cast:** Kesh Baggan, Scott Barker, LaChrisha Brown, Tjasa Ferme, Ali Khan, Nicole K., Joel Mercedes, Joyce Miller, Dillon Porter; August 14–29, 2009

The Hypochondriac by Moliere, adapted by Matthew A.J. Gregory, Shira Gregory, Chris Harcum and Greg Tito; Director, Matthew Gregory; Set, Justin Couchara; Costumes, Adam Coffia; Lighting, Nick Gonsman; Sound and Audio/Visual, Justin Stasiw; Stage Manager, Katy Moore; **Cast:** Chris Harcum, Vivienne Leheny, Shira Gregory, Cate Bottiglione, Douglas Scott Sorenson, Chris Critelli, Sheila Jones, Kyle Haggerty; November 4–22, 2009

Tosca E Le Altre Due (Tosca and the Two Downstairs) by Franca Valeri; Director, Laura Caparrotti; Set, Lucretia Moroni; Lighting/Sound, Nick Ryckert; Set Assistants, Diego Fernandez, Kathleen Vance; Original Music, Giacomo Puccini; Press, Jonathan Slaff & Associates; Translator, Natasha Lardera; Associate Producer, Donatella Codonesu; Supertitles, Janine White; **Cast:** Laura Caparrotti, Marta Mondelli, Rocco Sisto; February 3–21, 2010

Limonade Tous Les Jours by Charles L. Mee; Director, Diana Basmajian; Set, Hilary Noxon; Costumes, Charles Schoonmaker; Lighting, Kathleen Dobbins; Audio/Visual, Tee McKnight; Stage Manager, Lisa McGinn; Choreographer, Erin Porvaznika; Public Relations, Patrick Paris; Production Manager, Jennifer McKnight; Associate Producer, Moira Boag; Music Director, Cris Frisco; Program Coordinator, Sabrina Cusimano; **Cast:** Eleanor Handley, Austin Pendleton, Anton Briones; April 3–May 9, 2010

Festivals

10 Minutes Deep December 7, 2009; included: *Cleantopia* by Rachael Richman, directed by Elaine Molinaro; **Cast:** Heather Kenzie, Che Lyons; *The Roxys and Bleu* by P.J. Edghill, directed by Pat Jones; **Cast:** Tocarra Cash, Shira Gregory, Kyle Haggerty; *Mets* by Nancy Manocherian, directed by Kira Simring; **Cast:** Almeria Campbell, Rubin Ortiz; *Missed* by Sergei Burbank, directed by Pat Jones; **Cast:** Sarah Elizondo, Brian Patacca; *10 Minutes Deep* by Nancy Manocherian, directed by Kira Simring; **Cast:** Almeria Campbell, Juliana Huestis; *Birthday Duet by* David Bellatoni, directed by Pat Jones; **Cast:** Rubin Ortiz, Corey Triplett; *3-Minute Hamlet* by Matthew Ethan Davis, directed by Kira Simring; **Cast:** Kyle Haggerty, Juliana Huestis, Ruben Ortiz, Brian Patacca, Corey Triplett

Women on the Edge February 25–March 27, 2010; included: *Anchor Woman* by Brian Rady; Director, Jeremy Bloom; **Cast:** Holly Chou, Laila Alj, Eric Dean Wilson, Kaitlin Colombo, Sarah Grace Welbourn, Almeria Campbell, Starr Busby, Ciara Gay; *Blue Skies* by Nancy Manocherian; Director, Kira Simring; **Cast:** Charlotte Cohn, Jim Sands, Kyle Haggerty, Alenka Kraigher; *The Shape of Things* by Neil LaBute; Director, Kathy Gail MacGowan; **Cast:** Dan Gershaw, Kaitlin Colombo, Emily Kenyon Scott, Christopher Scheer; *Bad Evidence* by Terry Quinn; Director, Kira Simring; **Cast:** Patricia Dalen, R. Ward Duffy, Alenka Kraigher, Brian Patacca, Andrew Oswald, Darrell Larson

Readings

Blackboard Reading Series by Deborah Goodwin, Sherry Boon, Sean Jeremy Palmer, Shaun Neblett, Garlia Cornelia Jones, Shawn Harris; September 14; *Tandem Reading Series* October 18; *CCO - Center for Contemporary Opera* by Michael Dellaira, Barbara Kraft, Susan Hurley, Anna Rabinowitz, Elizabeth Isadora Gold, Joan Ross Sorkin, Renzo Oliva; October 22 & 23; *Blue Skies* by Nancy Manocherian; Stage Directions, Kaitlin Colombo; March 5–6; *Bad Evidence* by Terry Quinn; Stage Directions, Kaitlin Colombo; March 26–27

Non-resident Production

The Imaginary Invalid by Moliere, adapted by Matthew A.J. Gregory, Greg Tito, Chris Harcum, Shira Gregory; Presented by Deadline Productions; Director, Matthew A.J. Gregory; Set, Justin Couchara; Costumes, Mary C. Hunt; Lighting, Natalie Robin; Sound, Jason Sebastian; Stage Manager, Katy Moore; **Cast:** Jeremy Lawrence, Tiffany Denise Turner, Cate Bottiglione, Christen Gee, Taryn Turney, Travis Stroessenreuther, Matthew Schatz, Kirsten Anderson, Sheila Jones, Kyle Haggerty, Hailey McCarty, Matt DeCapua; July 23–August 2, 2009

The Chocolate Factory Theatre

Executive Director, Sheila Lewandowski; Artistic Director, Brian Rogers; House Manager, Alexandra Rosenberg; Production Manager, Madeline Best; Bookkeeper, Jodi Bender; Graphic/Web Design, Michael Reardon; THROW Curator, Sarah Maxfield; www.chocolatefactorytheater.org

Liz One - Her Secret Diaries in the Land of 1000 Dances Written and directed by John Jesurun; Lighting, Jeff Nash; Set, Jose Ho; Costumes, Molly Deale; Original Music, Pamelia Kurstin; **Cast:** Black-Eyed Susan, Ben Forster; October 14–31, 2009

Cooler by Gary Winter; Director, Dylan McCullough; Lighting, Ben Kato; Set, Ben Kato; Costumes, Alexandra Gage Englund; Sound, Hillary Charnas; Stage Manager, Jason Weixelman; **Cast:** Havilah Brewster, Crystal Finn, Jocelyn Kuritsky, Michael Tisdale; April 9–24, 2010

Chris Henry & Royal Family Productions

Safe Home by Sean Cullen; Director/Producer/Artistic Director, Chris Henry; Set/Video, Alex Koch; Lighting, David Bengali; Sound, Jeanne Wu; Costumes, Lena Sands; Associate Artistic Director, Katie Avebe; Business Manager, Mary Bernardi; Technical Director, Andy Theodorou; Press, Joe Trentacosta; **Cast:** Michael Cullen, Ian Hyland, Cynthia Mace, Eric T. Miller, Erik Saxvik, Katy Wright Mead; Women's Interart Center; January 8–February 13, 2010

Collective Hole Productions

Co-Founder/Artistic Director, Rebecca V. Nellis; Co-Founder, Edward P. Clapp; www.collectivehole.org

Magnitude of the Slope by Paul Sapp; Co-produced with The Tank; Director, Rebecca V. Nellis; Set/Lighting/Sound, Julia A. Middleton, Rebecca V. Nellis, Paul Sapp; Stage Manager, Julia A. Middleton; Artwork, Kenneth M.T. Beck; Collateral Design and Layout, Stacey C. Rivera; **Cast:** Blythe Coons, Matt Huffman; Upstairs at The Tank; April 3–11, 2010

The Collective Objective

www.collob.com

The Sword Politik by Jon Crefeld; Director, Jon Ciccarelli; Costumes/Stage Manager, Kyle Baxter; Sound, Jon Crefeld; **Cast:** Paul Bellantoni, Jon Crefeld, Kerry Fitzgibbons, Sharon Hunter, Bethany James, Patrick Long, Ryan McCabe, Katherine McDonald, Billy Weimer; Dorothy Strelsin Theatre; Presented as part of the Midtown International Theatre Festival; July, 13– August 1, 2009

I Hate Love by Kyle Baxter & Jon Crefeld; Director, Mark Duncan; Costumes, Susan Slotoroff; Stage Manager, Samantha Gallardo; **Cast:** Elizabeth Allerton, Sarah Barry, Danielle Beckmann, Dan Belmont, Patricia Comstock, Austin Elmore, John Felidi, Anthony Gargano, DR Mann Hanson, Andrew Stephen Johnson, Roi King, Blaine Pennington, Duncan Pflaster, Elizabeth Pickett; Dorothy Strelsin Theatre; July 13 –August 1, 2009

Readings

Never Norman Rockwell by Kyle Baxter; October 3, 2009; *Measure For Measure* by Kyle Baxter; April 12, 2010

Columbia Stages

Lifetime Fairytale by Zhu Yi; Director, Marios Theocharous; Set, Ji- Youn Chang; Costumes, Paul Carey; Lighting, Ji- Youn Chang; Original Music, Stavros Makris; Fight Director, Christian T. Chan; Stage Manager, Pisa Waikwamdee; **Cast:** Anita Anthonj, Jiasi Chen, Mi Sun Choi, Manuel Fihman, R. Paul Hamilton, Kirsten Hopkins, Caitlin Johnston, Jose Kim, James Kwan, Gustavo Obregon, Evangeline Reilly, Sarah Billington Stevens, Andrew Taliano, Moses Villarama; Riverside Theatre; October 21–24, 2009

ComedySportz New York City

www.comedysportznewyork.com

ComedySportz New York City Director, Lynn Marie Hulsman; Musical Director, Frank Spitznagel; Musicians, Doug Nervick, Hector Cortis, Adam Pod; Assistant Director, Glenn Packman; **Cast:** Jill Shely, Lynn Marie Hulsman, Dan Fleming, Sam Cohen, Glenn Packman, Robert Z. Grant, Todd Cowdrey, Tammy Munro, Alicia Barnachetz, Lee Barrett, Kim Weeks, Erin Leigh Schmoyer, AJ Cote, Amelia Fowler, Rebecca Stuard, Scotty Watson, Drew Tarvin, John Woodruff, Julia Frey, Al Dobyns, Michael Rock; Broadway Comedy Club; Ongoing

Company SoGoNo

www.sogono.org

Art of Memory by Lisa Ramirez; Director, Tanya Calamoneri; Set, Sean Breault; Costumes, Mioko Mochizuki; Lighting, Bruce Steinberg; Sound, Miguel Frasconi; Stage Manager, Sarah Nerboso; Video, Matt Tennie and James Short; Choreographer, Tanya Calamoneri; Original Music, Miguel Frasconi; **Cast:** Lisa Ramirez, Cassie Terman, Heather Harpham, Tanya Calamoneri; 3LD Art and Technology Center; July 16–August 2, 2009

Company XIV

www.companyxiv.com

The Judgment of Paris Written and directed by Austin McCormick; Set, Zane Pihlstrom; Costumes, Olivera Gajic; Lighting, Gina Scherr; Sound, Austin McCormick; Choreographer, Austin McCormick; **Cast:** Laura Careless, Nick Fesette, Yeva Glover, Gioia Marchese, Austin McCormick, Davon Rainey; 303 Bond St Theater; December 3, 2009–January 16, 2010

Le Serpent Rouge Written, directed, sound, and choreography by Austin McCormick; Set, Zane Pihlstrom; Costumes, Olivera Gajic; Lighting, Gina Scherr; Laura Careless, Nick Fesette, Yeva Glover, Gioia Marchese, Davon Rainey; 303 Bond Street Theater; December 4, 2009–January 17, 2010

Snow White Director/Sound/Choreography, Austin McCormick; Set/Puppets, Zane Pihlstrom; Costumes, Olivera Gajic; Lighting, Gina Scherr; **Cast:** Laura Careless, Nick Fesette, Yeva Glover, Gioia Marchese, Austin McCormick, Davon Rainey; 303 Bond Street Theater; December 5, 2009–January 17, 2010

Conflict of Interest Theatre Company

www.conflicttheater.com

Wrestling the Alligator by Sergei Burbank; Director, Adam Karsten; Set, Kina Park; Costumes, Daonne Huff; Lighting, Ryan Mueller; **Cast:** James Ware, Sergei Burbank, Amanda Nichols; Robert Moss Theatre; June 13–June 27, 2009

Coyote REP Theatre Company

www.coyoterep.org

Readings

Rated M for Mature by Greg Ayers, directed by Paul Dobie; May 9; *Questions My Mother Can't Answer* by Andrea Caban, directed by Donnetta Lavinia Grays; May 10; *What She Means* by Rebecca Tourino, directed by Michael Lluberes; May 16; *a rhyme for the UNDERground* by Chandra Thomas, directed by Tia Hodge; May 17; *The New Normal* by Donnetta Lavinia Grays, directed by Isaac Byrne; May 24

Cross-Eyed Bear Productions

www.duncanpflaster.com

Suckers Written, directed, and sound by Duncan Pflaster; Costumes, Mark Richard Caswell; Lighting, Emily Gasser; Choreographer, Christopher C. Cariker; **Cast:** Eric C. Bailey, Katherine Damigos, Joe Fanelli, Paula Galloway, Rebecca Hirota, Shawn McLaughlin, Alan McNaney, Jared Morgenstern; The White Box at 440 Studios; June 16–27, 2009

Readings

Mine or Yours by Duncan Pflaster; **Cast:** Jeffery Martin, Kelly Nichols, Alexander Nicosia and Susan Slotoroff; Where Eagles Dare Short Play Lab; January 9–10; *(they kiss)* by Duncan Pflaster; **Cast**: Elisa Abatsis, Christopher Boerger, Don Pflaster; February 27–28; *Fertility Choices* by Duncan Pflaster; **Cast:** Christopher Boerger, Jessica Cermak, Justin Howard, Jeff Martin, Rehmat Qadir, Sam Rosenberg, Laura Yost; April 24–25; *My Perfect Life* by Duncan Pflaster; Director, Clara Barton Green; **Cast:** Lauren Lucksavage, Chrissy Malon, Heather Lee Rogers, Jeffrey Wisniewski; April 24–25

Cuchipinoy Productions

www.cuchipinoy.com

Anonymous by Rodney E. Reyes; Director, Taylor Keith; Set, Mario Corrales; Production Manager, Anna Payumo; Stage Manager, Eileen Gaughan; **Cast:** Thomas Blewitt, Jian Huang, Vanessa Ramalho; 440 Studios; June 13–31, 2010

Dalliance Theater

www.DallianceTheater.com

Refractions by Eliot Stockton; Director, Andy Ottoson; Stage Manager, Aaron Heflich Shapiro; Lighting, Kate Ashton; Set, Joseph Hietman; Costumes, Jennifer Fisher; Sound, Mike Brady; **Cast:** James Allerdyce, W. Tre Davis, Mallory Hawks, Jennifer J. Hopkins, Jose Joaquin Perez, Alisha Soper; Players Theatre; August 19, 2010

Who Is Jordan Bishop by Evan T. Cummings, Ian August, Clayton Smith, Scott Rad Brown, Karly Maurer, Eric Sanders, Andy Ottoson, Patrick Garrigan; Directors, Stephen Tyler Davis, Anne McCormack, Evan Enderle, Noah Racey, Branden Huldeen, Karyn Joy DeYoung, Steven Pierce, Emily Firth; Set/Lighting/Sound, Kent Barrett; Costumes, Jennifer Fisher; Stage Manager, Nathan K. Claus; **Cast:** Liz Ali, Dan McCabe, Stephanie Seward, Sarah Louise Anderson, Daniel Hines, Mallory Hawks, Evan Tyrone Martin, Darin Robert Cabot, Tori Watson, Alisha Soper, Chelsea Jo Pattison, Jessica Palmer, Graciano Nunez, Fred Cabral, Erick Pinnick, Becca Kloha, Kar; TheaterLab; March 5–14, 2010

Readings

Helen and Anne by Andy Ottoson; *Girl in the Park* by Matt Owen; May 5, 2010

Del Valle Productions, Inc.

www.DelValleProductions.com

Brownsville Bred by Elaine Del Valle; Director, Paul J. Michael; Stage Manager, Patrick Woodall; Lighting, Joie Bauer; **Cast:** Elaine Del Valle; Teatro la Tea; June 16–21, 2009

Brownsville Bred...Growing Up Elaine by Elaine Del Valle; Director, Paul J. Michael; Stage Manager, Patrick Woodall; Lighting, Joie Bauer; Producer, Al Eskanazy; **Cast:** Elaine Del Valle; Nuyorican Poets Cafe; November 2–30, 2009

Brownsville Bred...Ghetto to Glamour by Elaine Del Valle; Director, Paul J. Michael; Stage Manager, Patrick Woodall; Lighting, Joie Bauer; **Cast:** Elaine Del Valle; Nuyorican Poets Cafe; January 13–May 12, 2010

Desipina & Company

Artistic Director, Rehana Mirza; Producing Director, Rohi Mirza Pandya; www.desipina.org

Seven.11 Convenience Theatre: The Final Year Written and directed by various artists; Lighting, Jeff McCrum; Set, Jason Simms; Costumes, Jenny Fisher; Sound, Len DeNiro; Producing Director, Rohi Mirza Pandya; Musical Director, Samrat Chakrabarti; Choreographer, Sandhya Jain; **Cast:** Andrew Guilarte, Kavi Ladnier, Cindy Cheung, Sam Ghosh, Tim Cain, Jay Lee, Christopher Larkin; Center Stage NY; June 17–28, 2009

Readings

Out of the Kitchen and Into the Fire by various playwrights including Thelma DeCastro, Jessica Devi Bhargava, Nitika Nagdar, Yasmine Beverly Rana, Lauren D. Yee; December 10–13, 2009

Dixon Place

Founder and Executive Director, Ellie Covan; Managing Director, Emily Morgan; Programming, Leslie Strongwater; Development and Finance, Catherine Porter; Marketing, Tim Ranney; Technical Director, Rob Lariviere; Cultural Education/Community Outreach, Alexis Marnel; Administrative Associate, Christine Fulton; Data Management, Kate Conroy; Tech Goddess, Casey McLain; Marketing Associate, Barry Rowell; www.dixonplace.org

Little Theatre Curated by Mike Taylor and Jeffrey M. Jones; Co-presented by Little Theater in association with the Flea Theater; **Cast:** Scott Adkins, Erin Courney, Erik Ehn, Jeff Jones, Kate E. Ryan, Normandy Sherwood, Anne Washburn, Mac Wellman, Gary Winter, Valerie Work; A benefit for 'Pataphysics Writers Workshops; Ongoing

The Bulldyke Chronicles by Shelly Mars and Kirby; Ongoing

Pebble-and-Cart Cycle Written and co-presented by Terra Incognita Ensemble; Director/Sound/Stage Manager, Polina Klimovitskaya; Lighting, Erik Fox; Set, Jessica Scott; Costumes, Dolly Williams; Puppets, Jessica Scott; Technical Consultant, Joe Rosato; Video, Melissa Clarke, Fly & Horse; Video DP, Isaac Mathes; Video Editor, Deborah Kampmeier; Production Managers, Dolly Williams & Jeremy Goren, Production; **Cast:** Dolly Williams, Natalia Krasnova, Jeremy Goren, Michael Moscoso, Dinne Kopelevich, Ellen Lanese, Anthony Spaldo, David Djambazov; June 16–25, 2009

HOT! Festival: Old Queen Written and performed by Penny Arcade; **Make It Bigger** Written and performed by Jeffrey & Cole; July 1–August 1, 2009

Staying Afloat by Lenora Champagne; Directors, Lenora Champagne and Melissa Kievman; Production Design, Liz Prince; **Cast:** Valda Setterfield, Tricia Rodley; January 25, 2010

The Somnambulist Written and directed by Megan Murtha; Set/Costumes, Kaitlyn Mulligan; January 29–30, 2010

I Am Going to Run Away Written & performed by Bree Benton; Musical Director, Franklin Bruno; February 3–March 3, 2010

Ain't That Good News by The Bengsons; February 5–March 6, 2010

Puppet Blok Curated by Leslie Strongwater; Featuring Papermoon Puppet Theatre, Lone Wolf Tribe, David Michael Friend, Ora Fruchter, Drama of Works; February 10, 2010

Kammerspiel! (a parenthetical drama for the American alcoholic) by Jonny Cigar; **Cast:** Jonny Cigar, Abraham Danz, Max Oglesbee, Phoebe Oglesbee, Bill Chambers, Nick Bennett; February 12–27, 2010

Poet of the Gutter, presents an evening of complacent distractions by Jonny Cigar; **Cast:** Jonny Cigar, Abraham Danz, Max O'Glesbee, Phoebe O'Glesbee, Bill Chambers, Nick Bennett; February 12–27, 2010

Vanishing City Curated by Tim Ranney; February 12–27, 2010

Julian Eltinge by Clay McLeod Chapman; Music by The Venn Diagrams; Director Isaac Butler; **Cast:** Jeffrey Marsh and Rick Sorkin; February 18, 2010

Half Straddle by Tina Satter; February 22, 2010

DoppelGangers: A Love Story Created & performed by Michael Cross Burke, Krys Fox; March, 2010

Family First by Story Pirates; March 2–4, 2010

Bird on a Wire by Chana Porter; March 12–13, 2010

Annette Written, directed, designed, produced, and managed by Regina Nejman; Costumes, Sara James; Sound, Mio Morales; Audio/Visual, Alan McIntyre Smith; **Cast:** Amy Adams, Kristin Licata, Mary Madsen, Regina Nejman, Tomoko Maeda, Gwennaelle Rakotovao, Marcos Vedoveto; March 12–March 27, 2010

Cou-Cou Bijoux: Pour Vous Written and performed by Raquel Cion; Director, Luke Harlan; Musical Director, Brooks Hartell; March 16–18, 2010

5 Story Walk Up: Seven Card Draw by Neil LaBute, John Guare, Clay McLeod Chapman, Quincy Long, Laura Shaine, Daniel Levin, Daniel Gallant; Director, Daniel Gallant; March 19–20, 2010

Love Monster: A Play In 2 Acks Created by Jason Bohon, Corey Sullivan, Hanlon Smith-Dorsey, Emily Zimmer, Prudence Heyert, Andrew Zimmerman; Artists-in-Residence, Lisa Rafaela Clair, Adam Collignon; April 1–3, 2010

Penetrating the Space by Kim Katzberg; Animator, Maia Cruz Palileo; Director, Shelly Mars; April 2, 2010

Von Hottie's Extravaganza: The Dawn of Decadence by Laura Von Holt; Director, Liz Wexler; Choreographer, Diego Funes; April 3, 2010

The Gay Ivy Conceived and directed by Ethan Heard, co-conceived by Thomas Dolan and Megan Stern; Written and composed by Bix Bettwy, Kyle Ewalt, Greg Edwards, Laura Jacqmin, Kyle Jarrow, Haitham Jendoubi, Eric Kubo, Gordon Leary, Deb Margolin, Julia Meinwald, Michael Mitnick, Bradford Proctor, Zak Sandler, Michael Walker, Lauren Yee; April 5, 2010

Money Talks with Citizen Reno Written and performed by Reno; April 5–May 17, 2010

Puppet Blok Hosted and curated by Kate Brehm; **Cast:** Jessica Scott, Maggie Robinson, Jenny Campbell, Jessica Grindstaff, Erik Sanko; John Bell; April 9–10, 2010

Bindlestiff Family Cirkus's 15th annual NYC Winter Cabaret April 11–25, 2010

Asylum Written and Performed by James Braly; Director, Seth Barrish; April 16–May 22, 2010

Plays & Playwrights 2010 Book Launch Hosted by Martin Denton and Rochelle Denton; April 19, 2010

Uncanny Valley Frankenstein by Lucas Crane, Ric Royer, Jackie Milad, Bonnie Jones; April 20, 2010

She's Sleep Created by Kristine Haruna Lee, conceived by Jr Skola; Original Music, Yusuke Namik; Design, Kyle Freeman; **Cast:** Kristine Haruna Lee, Andrew Butler, Greg Manley, Cyndi Perzcek, Lauren Swan-Potras; April 20, 2010

Vanishing City by David Freeland; April 20, 2010

Nothing to Display Written and performed by Jill Pangallo; April 21, 2010

The Barber And The Farmer, a play for computer by Ethan Lipton; Live Animation, Michael Arthur; April 22, 2010

Nuevo Laredo by Gabriella Barnstone; April 22, 2010

Asylum Written and performed by James Braly; April 23–May 22, 2010

Broadway Speaks Out presents "Take the Mic with Marti Gould Cummings" April 26–June 28, 2010

Being Heard: The Lillian Smith Story Created and performed by Lulu Fogarty; Director, Thom Fogarty; Original Music, Gene Tryanny; Visuals, Anja Hitzenberger; May 3, 2010

Captain Ferguson's School for Balloon Warfare by Isaac Rathbone; May 4, 2010

Schaden, Freude & You: Part Deux Written and performed by Chris Arruda, Sandi Carroll, Brad Fraizer, David Jones, Jennifer Kidwell and Jane Nichols; May 7, 2010

Remembrance of Things Pontiac by Kestutis Nakas; May 12, 2010

Carousel Hosted by R. Sikoryak; **Cast:** Ann Decker, Patrick Hambrecht, John Mathias, Jason Little, Neil Numberman, Doug Skinner; May 13, 2010

Crones, Ducks and Babes May 17, 2010

Landscape with the Fall of Icarus Written and performed by Samuael Topiary; Director and Original Music, Miguel Gutierrez; Sound, Peter Kerlin; Costumes, Jocelyn Davis; Video, Samuael Topiary; Aerialist, C. Ryder Cooley; May 18, 2010

Touchscape, An Emotional Striptease Written and performed by James Scruggs; Director, Mark Rayment; Sound, Matt Tennie; Composer Steve Adorno; May 18, 2010

Readings

Page to Stage: *Weep Screed* by Julia Pearlstein; *Tall Tales (and Counterfeit Codices)* by Travis Stewart; *Joycean* by Trav S.D.; February 25; *The Dardy Family Home Movies* by Stephen Sondheim; February 28; *The Rules of Sleepaway Camp* by Valerie Work, directed by Meghan Finn; March 29; *The Obliged: A Post-Play* by Julian Mesri, directed by Andrew Lazarow; April 27

DJM Productions, Inc.

ww.DJMProductions.com

Macbeth In The Other Room by Dave McCracken; Director, Doug Spagnola; Stage Manager, Miriam Hyfler; Production Design, DJM Productions Technical Department; **Cast:** Gregory Casimir, Dale Church, Taliesen Rose; Dionysus Theatre's L'il Peach Theater; July 22–August 8, 2009

Dog Run Rep

The Soap Myth by Jeff Cohen; Director, Larissa Lury; Set, Heather Wolensky; Costumes, Justin Hall; Lighting, Jay Scott; Sound, Matt Rocker; Stage Manager, Donovan Dolan; **Cast:** Katia Asche, Joel Friedman, Louisa Flaningam, Victor Barbella, John Plumpis; @Seaport!; July 13–August 2, 2009

Down Payment Productions

www.downpaymentproductions.org

Pink! by Stacy Davidowitz; Director, Brian Smith; Set, Amanda Stephens; Costumes, Stephanie Alexander; Lighting, Joel Silver; Stage Manager, Johanna Thelin; **Cast:** Kaela Crawford, Julia Giolzetti, Caitlin Mehner, Alison Scaramella, Stephanie Strohm; WorkShop Theater; September 10–20, 2009

The Realm by Sarah Myers; Director, Jessica Fisch; Set, Amanda Stephens; Costumes, Nicole V. Moody; Lighting, Paul Toben; Sound, Daniel Kluger & Charles Koes; Stage Managers, Jamie Lynne Sullivan & Jack F. Lynch; Choreographer, Dax Valdes; **Cast:** Amy Bodnar, Aaron Simon Gross, Timur Kocak, Emily Olson, Jessica Pohly, Amy Temple; Wild Project; April 7–18, 2010

The Dreamscape Theatre

dreamscapetheatre.org

In Fields Where They Lay by Ricardo Perez Gonzalez; Director, Brad Raimondo; Set, Kacie Hultgren; Costumes, Joanne Haas; Lighting, Wilburn Bonnell; Sound, Geoffrey Roecker; **Cast:** Zack Calhoon, Pete Forester, Billy Griffin, Carl Hendrick Louis, Alan McNaney, Jared Sampson, Michael Swartz, Morgan Anne Zipf, Greg McGovern, Daniel Coady; Hudson Guild Theatre; December 12, 2009–January 2, 2010

The Drilling CompaNY Theatre

Producing Artistic Director, Hamilton Clancy; Assistant Artistic Director, David Marantz; General Manager, Aimee Whelan; www.drillingcompany.org

A Midsummer Night's Dream by William Shakespeare; Director, Kathy Curtiss; Stage Manager, Sarah Biesinger; Set, Rebecca Lord; Costumes, Lisa Renee Jordan; Choreographer, Katie Bradley; **Cast:** Adam Fujita, Ron Dreyer, Selena Beretta, Samuel Perwin, JoAnn Sacco, Demetrius Callas, Jasper Stoffer, Jordan Feltner, Christine Dunn, Eileen Townsend, James Davies, David Stadler, William Apps, Aimee Whelan, Garrett Burrseon, Drew Valins, Amanda Dillard, Kelly Zekus, Halima Henderson, Hiroko Tanaka, Maria Niora, Koji Ohashi, Kyle Cheng; Parking lot at Ludlow and Broome Streets; July 9–25, 2009

Measure for Measure by William Shakespeare; Director, Hamilton Clancy; Set, Rebecca Lord; Sound, Chris Rummel; Costumes, Lisa Renee Jordan; **Cast:** Ivory Aquino, Nina Burns, Stephanie Carll, Don Carter, Patricia Chilsen, Sergio Diaz, Amanda Fuller, Michael Gnat, Bill Green, Karla Hendrick, Mark Jeter, Candice Lee Knox, Jonathan Marballi, David Marantz, Cameron Mitchell Mason, Lori Parquet, Joann Sacco, David Sitler, Shaun Bennett Wilson; Parking lot at Ludlow and Broome Streets; July 30–August 15, 2009

Over The Line by P. Seth Bauer; Director, Hamilton Clancy; Stage Manager, Billie Davis; Lighting, Miriam Nilofa Crowe; Set, Jen Varbalow; Costumes, Lisa Renee Jordan; Sound, Christopher Rummel; Audio/Visual, Phillip DeVita; Graphic Artist, Philliip De Vita; Intern, Celeste Sexton; **Cast:** Ivory Aquino, Amanda Dillard, Anwen Darcy, Darren Lipari, Brandon Reilly, David Holmes; November 5–22, 2009

Bird Brain by Vern Thiessen; Director, Hamilton Clancy; Stage Manager, Amy Cruz; Lighting, Miriam Nilofa Crowe; Set, Jen Varbalow; Sound, Christopher Rummel; Assistant Director, Karla Hendrick; Graphics, Phillip De Vita; **Cast:** Hamilton Clancy, Aimee Whelan, Anwen Darcy; January 16, 2010–April 18, 2010

Faith by Brian Dykstra, Jennifer Fawcett, Christine Whitley, Misha Shulman, Scott Baker, Stephen Bittrich, Kate McCamy, C.Denby Dawson, Richard Mover; Directors, Sarah Biesinger, Hamilton Clancy, Richard Harden, Marisa Viola, David Marantz, Kate McCamy; Stage Manager, Billie Davis; Lighting, Miriam Nilofa Crowe; Set, Rebecca Lord; Press, Jonathan Slaff; Graphic Artist, Phillip De Vita; **Cast:** McKey Carpenter, Anwen Darcy, Jordan Feltner, Walter Cline, Ivory Aquino, Darrell Larson, Karla Hendrick, Jane Ray, Amanda Dillard, Amanda C. Fuller, Dan Teachout, Spencer Corona, Elowyn Castle, Billie Davis, Veronica Cruz, Bob Greenberg, Paul Guskin; May 2–23, 2010

The Frog Singer by Laura Strausfeld; Director, Eric Nightengale; Stage Manager, Christina Schildroth; Sound, Eric Nightengale; Press, Jonathan Slaff; Graphic Artist, Phillip De Vita; Onstage Illustrator, Claudia Orenstein; Character Illustrations, Carin Berger; **Cast:** John Heath, JoAnn Sacco; May 15–June 5, 2010

Non-resident Production

Somewhere in Between by Ryan Sprague; Presented by Collaborative Stages; Director, Brian Letchworth; Set, Elyse Handelman; Costumes, Jeni Ahlfeld; Lighting, Michael Megliola; Sound, Jillian Marie Walker; Stage Manager, Griffin Parker; **Cast:** Erik Gullberg, Jeffrey A. Wisniewski. Ariel Woodiwiss; Drilling Company Theatre Lab; March 12–21, 2010

The Dysfunctional Theatre Company

www.dysfunctionaltheatre.org

Arsenic & Old Lace by Joseph Kesselring; Co-produced with Horse Trade Theatre Group; Director.Lighting, Eric Chase; Set, Jason Unfried; Costumes, Amy Overman; Sound, Justin Plowman; Assistant Director, Greg Engbrecht; Producer, Amy Overman; **Cast:** Ron Bopst, Rob Brown, Michael DeRensis, Marilyn Duryea, Greg Engbrecht, Jennifer Gill, Kurt Kingsley, Vivian Meisner, Craig Peterson,

Justin Plowman, Mike Roche, Peter Schuyler, Yanni Walker; Kraine Theater; June 11–27, 2009

The 8: Reindeer Monologues by Jeff Goode; Co-produced with Horse Trade Theatre Group; Directors, Rob Brown, Jennifer Gill, Peter Schuyler; Lighting, Justin Plowman; Set, Jason Unfried; Sound, Justin Plowman; Producer, Amy Overman; **Cast:** Sarah Eliana Bisman, Rob Brown, Danaher Dempsey, Michael DeRensis, Jennifer Gill, Rachel Grundy, Peter Schuyler, Amy Beth Sherman; The Red Room; December 9–19, 2009

A Voluminous Evening of Brevity by F. Scott Fitzgerald, Susan Glaspell, Edna St. Vincent Millay, William Butler Yeats; Directors, Rob Brown, Amy Overman, Justin Plowman, Peter Schuyler; Producer, Amy Overman; **Cast:** Nicole Aiossa, Rob Brown, Danaher Dempsey, Greg Engbrecht, Jennifer Gill, Kurt Kingsley, Tom O'Connor, Amy Overman, Peter Schuyler, Amy Beth Sherman, Theresa Unfried; The Red Room; March 22–31, 2010

E Phoenix Idealis Theater, Inc.

www.ephoenixi.org

The Children's Hour by Lillian Hellman; Directors, Robert Combe and Ben Fabrizi; Set, Tom Kerr; **Cast:** Rachel Alt, Hugh Davies, Sarah Garza, Aimee Hiltz; Poppenhusen Institute; November 13–21, 2009

The Good Doctor by Neil Simon; Director, Ben Fabrizi; Costumes, Annie Wolf; **Cast:** Ethan Aronoff, Charlie Coniglio, Frank Freeman, Emily Garrick, William Longerbeam, Kate Maclauchlan, Emma Peele, April Uhl; Poppenhusen Institute; May 14–22, 2009

EBE Ensemble

www.ebeensemble.com

Pre-Disposal by John Prescod; Director, Joshua Luria; Set, Eric Alba, Josh Luria, Montgomery Sutton; Costumes, Amanda Jenks; Lighting/Sound, Josh Butz; Stage Manager, Mariel Matos; Choreographer, Montgomery Sutton; **Cast:** DK Bowser, Deborah Green, Joe Mullen, Paul Pryce; Access Theater; July 10–25, 2009

Elephants on Parade 2010 Festival performed at Teatro IATI; March 9–20, 2010; included: *Nice Paper* by Isaac Rathbone, directed by Lexie Pregosin; **Cast:** Eve Danzeisen, Hal Fickett; *Leaving Last Night* by Libby Emmons, directed by Charley Layton; **Cast:** Eric Alba, Kate Dearing, Genevieve Hudson-Price, Janet Passanante, Jessica Rothenberg; *Things to do in New Jersey* by Nicole Pandolfo, directed by Kristine Ayers; **Cast:** Jessica Rothenberg, Montgomery Sutton; *Selling Beaver* by Rhea MacCallum, directed by Eric Alba; **Cast:** Eric Alba, Genevieve Hudson-Price, Janet Passanante, Montgomery Sutton; *What if I Don't* by Rebekah Lopata, directed by AJ Heekin; **Cast:** Eve Danzeisen, Kate Dearing; *Buddha Nosh* by Erin Austin, directed by Jonathan Reed Wexler; **Cast:** Eric Alba, Hal Fickett, Genevieve Hudson-Price, Janet Passanante, Montgomery Sutton

Electric Pear Productions

Executive Producer, Melanie Sylvan; Artistic Director, Ashlin Halfnight; Associate Producer, Veronique Ory; www.electricpear.org

Balaton by Ashlin Halfnight; Director, Kristjan Thor; Set, Jennifer de Fouchier; Costumes, Stephanie Alexander; Lighting, Kathleen Dobbins; Sound, Mark Sanders, Joel Bravo; Stage Managers, Kristine Schlachter, Biz Urban; Audio/Visual, Alex Koch, Kate Chumley; Dramaturg, Julie Haverkate; Graphics, Whitney Huhmann; Marketing & Advertising, The Pekoe Group; Press, David Gersten; **Cast:** Jessica Cummings, Kathryn Kates, Daniel O'Brien, Peter O'Connor, Sadie K. Scott, Charlotte Williams; Wild Project; October 17–November 7, 2009

Synesthesia Created by Ari Hest, Jon Morris' The Windmill Factory, Brent Arnold, Mariana Elder & Andrew Elsesser, Thomas Doyle, Meghan Frederick, Brian J. Bustos, Stone Cold Fox, Tarik Cherkaoui, The Mayhem Poets, Joel Bravo, Adam Ramsey; Wild Project; April 21–May 1, 2010

Readings

The Outlet: Fall 2009 by Ross Harris and Winter Miller; Facilitator, Laura Esti Miller; **Cast:** Jessica Browne-White, Michael Criscuolo, Lindy Flowers, Michael Kohn, Stephen Losack, Sarah Matthay, Amy Newhall, Collin Makenzie Smith; October 14– December 9, 2009

The Outlet: Spring 2010 by Melissa Ross and Kathryn Walat; Facilitator, Laura Esti Miller; **Cast:** Jessica Browne-White, Michael Criscuolo, Sarah Kate Jackson, Bret Jaspers, Laura Pruden, Brielle Silvestri, Sara Thigpen, Aaron Weiner; April 5–May 17, 2010

Emerging Artists Theatre (EAT)

Artistic Director, Paul Adams; Managing Director, Deb Guston; Associate Artistic Director, Derek Jamison; Musical Director, Peter Saxe; www.emergingartiststheatre.org

Fall EATFest 2009 Series A: *Organic Mattress* by Gregg Pasternack, directed by Dan Dinero; *Thank You, Nanny Annie* by Mark Finley, directed by Ryan Hilliard; *Labor Day* by Jon Spano, directed by Dan Dinero; *Left Handed Hofner* by Leslie Bramm, directed by Derek Jamison; *Play On* by Emily Mitchell, directed by Andrea Alton; *Sleeping Beauty* by Paul Adams, directed by Ryan Hilliard; *Belle & Angel* by Matt Casarino, directed by Marc Castle; *Unfinished Business* by Marc Castle, directed by Vivian Meisner; Series B: *What's to Become of Poor Father Michael* by David Bell, directed by David Winitsky; *Bone Appetite* by Richard Ploetz, directed by Ian Streicher; *Secret Angel* by Kathleen Warnock, directed by Ian Streicher; *Hard Sparkle* by J. Stephen Brantley, directed by Jonathan Warman; *These Trying Times* by Chris Widney, directed by Deb Guston; *There's No Zombies Like Show Zombies* by Staci Swedeen, directed by Molly Marinik; *The Border of Camelot* by Kevin Brofsky, directed by Aimee Howard; *The Mission* by Joe Godfrey, directed by Ned Thorne; *Wonder Woman! A Cabaret of Heroic Proportions!* by Elizabeth Whitney; TADA! Theater; November 9–22, 2009

Spring EATFest 2010 Series A: *After Ben Alderidge* by Jamie Wylie, directed by Melissa Atteberry; **Cast:** Katia Asche, Andrew Krug, Robert Terell Milner; *To Grandmothers House We Go* by Greg Freier, directed by Barbara Grecki; **Cast:** Michael Cleeff, Brooke Davis, Michael Musi, Meredith Napolitano; *In Flagrante* by Kevin Brofsky, directed by Ian Streicher; **Cast:** Scott Klavan, Tamara Scott; *Horatio & Ismene* by Shannon Reed, directed by Ned Thorne; **Cast:** Enid Cortes, Tommy Day Carey; Series B: *Autumn Quartet* by Emily Mitchell, directed by Deb Guston; **Cast:** Geany Masai, Jeannine Moore, Charles Moss, James Nugent; *Merely Players* by Marc Castle, directed by Tzipora Kaplan; **Cast:** Angus Hepburn, Sally Stockwell; *Broad Daylight* by Alex Goldberg, directed by Mark Finley; **Cast:** Wynne Anders, Patrick Arnheim; *Swans Are Mean* by Mark Finley, directed by David Winitsky; **Cast:** Elizabeth Bell, Matt Boethin, Hunter Gilmore; Series C: *Memory Like a Pale Green Clock* by Richard Ploetz, directed by Paul Adams; **Cast:** Greg Homison, Scott Klavan, Carol Monda, Danielle Quisenberry; *Where's Sheila?* by Janet Burnham, directed by Mark Finley; **Cast:** Joseph Jamrog, Peter Levine, Marie Wallace; *Silencing Ning* by Bil Wright, directed by Ramona Pula; **Cast:** E J An, Andrea Chen, Tommy Day Carey, Antonio Edwards Suarez; *White Baby* by David Lee White, directed by Ron Bopst; **Cast:** Amy Bizjak, Simon Kendall, Rebecca Nyahay; ADA Theatre; March 1–14, 2010

En Garde Entertainment

Evolution Director, Alexandra Hastings; Stage Manager, David Dean Hastings; Fight Director, David Dean Hastings; **Cast:** E. Calvin Ahn, Adam Alexander, Julio Beltron, Tarah Blasi, Joe Brigante, Jenny Brown, Armond Cecere, Chase Cohen, Matt Gordon, Will Gozdziewski, Melinda Hood, Lara Ianni, Scott Key, Randy Kiersnowski, Lisa Kopitsky, Marianna Kozij, Alain Laforest, Pearce Larson, Dave Milo, Ace Nakajima, Emily Rouch, Molly Thomas, Sarah Walsh; Brick Theater; December 11–17, 2009

Ensemble Studio Theatre

Artistic Director, William Carden; Executive Director, Paul Alexander Slee; Youngblood Artistic Directors, Graeme Gillis and R.J. Tolan; www.ensemblestudiotheatre.org

Going to the River 2009: The River Crosses Rivers Tenth anniversary festival of short one-act plays by women playwrights of color; Founders, Curt Dempster (the late EST Founding Director) and Elizabeth Van Dyke (Producing Artistic Director); Series A: *Risen* by France-Luce Benson, directed by Holli Harms; *The Kitchen or 9½ Minutes of Subcontinental Absurdity* by Naveen Bahar Choudhury, directed by Jamie Richards; *Ladybug Gonna Getcha* by Kara Lee Corthron, directed by Pat Golden; *The Step-Mother* by Ruby Dee, directed by Chuck Patterson; *Angels in the Parking Lot* by Nancy Nelson-Ewing, directed by Seret Scott; *Banana Beer Bath* by Lynn Nottage, directed Talvin Wilks; *Rally* by Bridgette Wimberly, directed by Clinton Turner Davis; Series B: *Truth be Told* by Melody Cooper, directed by Petronia Paley; *Dialectic* by Kia Corthron, directed by Chuck Patterson; *Hot Methuselah* by J.e. Franklin, directed by Imani Douglas; *Jesse* by P.J. Gibson, directed by Lydia Fort; *Sloppy Second Chances* by Mrinalini Kamath, directed by Kel Haney; *Spirit Sex: a Paranormal Romance* by Desi Moreno-Penson, directed by Adam Immerwahr; September 9–20, 2009

Graceful Living – The Whole Story by Maria Gabriele; Presented as part of EST's RoughCut Productions; Director, Holli Harms; Lighting, Geoffrey Dunbar; Sound, Goeff Roecker; **Cast:** Julie Fitzpatrick, Maria Gariele, Helen Coxe; March 31–April 3, 2010

First Light 2010 Presented by EST/Alfred P. Sloan Foundation Science and Technology Project; twelfth annual; Program Director, Graeme Gillis; included: *Beautiful Night* by Tommy Smith, directed by Moritz von Stuelpnagel; *Cecilia and the Universe* by Adrienne Campbell-Holt and Emily Conbere, directed by Ms. Campbell-Holt; *Gustie Returns* by Jane Chotard Wheeler, directed by Billy Hopkins; *Isaac's Eyes* by Lucas Hnath, directed by Linsay Firman; *Great Eastern* by Anna Moench, directed by R.J. Tolan; *The Telephone Caveat* by Adam Gwon and Justin Werner; *Notes Toward The Agony and the Ecstasy of Steve Jobs* created and performed by Mike Daisy, directed by Jean-Michele Gregory; *Dark Energy Stuns Universe* by Leah Maddrie; *Progress in Flying* by Lynn Rosen; Youngblood's *Mystery Science Brunch 2010* with plays by Robert Askins, Jon Kern, Anna Kerrigan, Patrick Link, Erica Saleh; April 8–May 2, 2010

EST Marathon 2010 32nd annual festival of new one-act plays; Series A: Sets, Maiko Chi; Costumes, Leslie Bernstein; Lighting, Julie Duro; Sound, Shane Rettig; Props, Renee Williams; included: *Safe* by Ben Rosental, directed by Carolyn Cantor; **Cast:** Gio Perez, Danny Mastrogiorgio; *Wild Terrain* by Adam Kraar, directed by Richmond Hoxie; **Cast:** Jack Davidson, Marcia Jean Kurtz, Catherine Curtin; *Matthew and the Pastor's Wife* by Robert Askins, directed by John Giampietro; **Cast:** Scott Sowers, Geneva Carr; *Turnabout* by Daniel Reitz, directed by Moritz von Stuelpnagel; **Cast:** Lou Liberatore, John-Martin Green, Haskell King; *Where the Children Are* by Maiko Chii, directed by Abigail Zealey Bess; **Cast:** Barbara Andres, Denny Bess, Bill Cwikowski, Freddie Lehne, Melanie Nicholls-King; May 21–June 19, 2010; Series B: Sets, Maiko Chii; Costumes, Arnulfo Maldonado; Lighting, Greg MacPherson; Fight Choreographer, Mark Olson; Stunt Choreographer, Maggie MacDonald; Choreographer, Mimi Quillin; PSM, Danielle Buccino; included: *Airborne* by Laura Jacmin, directed by Dan Bonnell; **Cast:** Edward Boroevich, W. Tre Davis, Brynne Morrice, Amy Staats, Megan Tusing; *Amateurs* by David Auburn, directed by Harris Yulin; **Cast:** Debbie Lee Jones, David Rasche, Diana Ruppe; *Anniversary* by Rachel Bonds, directed by Linsay Firman; **Cast:** Edward Boroevich, Julie Fitzpatrick, Jerry Richardson, Claire Siebers; *Interviewing Miss Davis* by Laura Maria Censabella, directed by Kel Haney; **Cast:** Delphi Harrington, Claire Siebers, Adria Vitlar; *They Float Up* by Jacquelyn Reingold, directed by Michael Barakiva; **Cast:** William Jackson Harper, Kellie Overbey; June 5–26, 2010

Youngblood Company

Asking for Trouble 2009 Two series of short plays; *Series A:* Writers: Jesse Cameron Alick, Nikole Beckwith, Joshua Conkel, Meghan Deans, Michael Lew, Anna Moench, Kyoung H. Park, Sharyn Rothstein, Michael Walek, Emily Chadick Weiss; Directors: Linsay Firman, John Giampetro, Wes Grantom, Kel Haney, Sarah Malkin, Lila Neugebauer, Robert Ross Parker, Tom Rowan, Rachel Slaven, Moritz von Stuelpnagel; **Cast:** Nikole Beckwith, Denny Bess, Lucia Brizzi, Tim Cain, Jackie Chung, Kevin Confoy, Curran Connor, Cathy Curtin, Dane DeHaan, Lucy DeVito, Helen Farmer, Julie Fitzpatrick, Kristen Harlow, Delphi Harrington, Frank Harts, Debbie Lee Jones, Ryan Karels, Shane Kearns, Haskell King, Mordecai Lawner, Julie Leedes, Jason Liehman, Thomas Lyons, Bobby Moreno, Ayesha Nguajah, Patricia Randell, Devere Rogers, Joel Rooks, Diana Ruppe, Risa Sarachan, Scott Sowers, Ann Talman, Michael Louis Wells, Audrey Lynn Weston, Nate Whelden; *Series B:* Writers: Robert Askins, Lucy Boyle, Delaney Britt Brewer, Eliza Clark, Mira Gibson, Jon Kern, Anna Kerrigan, Courtney Brooke Lauria, Patrick Link, Eric March, Erica Saleh; Directors: Eliza Beckwith, Web Begole, Abigail Zealey Bess, Snehal Desai, Christine Farrell, Dylan McCullough, Alexa Polmer, Jamie Richards, R.J. Tolan, Gerritt Turner, Daniel Winerman; **Cast:** Robert Askins, Eddie Boroevich, Steve Boyer, Kelly Ann Burns, Chris Ceraso, Paul Coffey, Alaina Dunn, Bjorn DuPaty, Helen Farmer, Nancy Franklin, Maria Gabriele, Abigail Gampel, Graeme Gillis, Jenny Gomez, William Jackson Harper, Kelli Lynn Harrison, Marcia Haufrecht, Helen Highfield, Dave Hurwitz, Ilene Kristen, Jocelyn Kuritsky, Jared McGuire, Allyson Morgan, Jacob Murphy, Alfredo Narciso, Johnny Pruitt, Shawn Randall, Claire Siebers, Mike Smith-Rivera, Amy Staats, Teresa Stephenson, Megan Tusing, Nitya Vidyasagar, Martina Weber, Susan Willerman; October 8–10, 2009

Princes of Waco by Robert Askins; Director, Dylan McCullough; Set, Maiko Chii; Costumes, Danielle Schembre; Lighting, Ji-youn Chang; Sound, Hillary Charnas; Stage Managers, Jason Weixelman & Michael V. Mendelson; **Cast:** Evan Enderle, Christine Farrell, Scott Sowers, Megan Tusing; January 11–30, 2010

Youngblood Unfiltered Two new plays in studio productions; Producer, Annie Trizna; Lighting, Geoffrey Dunbar; Costumes, Mark Richard Caswell; Sound, Christopher Rummel; PSM, Eliza Jane Bowman; ASM, Flannery Spring-Robinson; Props, Renee Williams; included: *Silver to a Trading Agent* by Sharyn Rothstein, directed by Giovanna Sardelli; **Cast:** Steven Boyer, Bill Cwikowski, Lucy DeVito, Richmond Hoxie, Ilene Kristen, Patricia Randell; February 10–19, 2010; *microcrisis* by Michael Lew, directed by Ralph Peña; **Cast:** Jackie Chung, Graeme Gillis, Jocelyn Kuritsky, Socorro Santiago, Godfrey Simmons, Michael Louis Wells; February 17–26, 2010

Bloodworks 2010 Full length play reading series; included: *Cult of Vultures* by Mira Gibson, directed by Kate Pines; **Cast:** Haskell King, Bill Peden, Grant Shaud, Teresa Stephenson; *Hungry Children* by Michael Walek, directed by Snehal Desai; **Cast:** Pepper Binkley, Evan Enderle, Anthony Johnston, Mike Smith-Rivera; *The Talls* by Anna Kerrigan, directed by Peter Cook; **Cast:** Curzon Dobell, Kristin Griffiths, Matt Harrington, Gayle Rankin, Joanna Simmons; *Internet Famous* by Meghan Deans, directed by Ashley Kelly-Tata; **Cast:** Tenny Cañez, Kate Hamill, Kristen Harlow, Polly Lee, Audrey Lynn Weston; *Sweet Forgotten Flavor* by Patrick Link, directed by Kel Haney; **Cast:** Haskell King, James Murtaugh, Diana Ruppe, Janet Zarish; *Desert Island Days* by Emily Chadick Weiss, directed by Kel Haney; **Cast:** Robert Askins, Steven Boyer, Ryan Karels, Polly Lee, Maureen Sebastian; *The Great American Deli Musical Part 1* by Eric March, directed by Kel Haney; **Cast:** Jessie Barr, Paul Coffey, Emilio Delgado, Stephen Ellis, Liam Rhodes, John Sheehy, Mike Still; *Where Dreams Come True* by Erica Saleh, directed by Kel Haney; **Cast:** Cathy Curtin, Polly Lee, Julie Leedes, Paco Tolson; *Heartbreak/India* written and directed by Kyoung H. Park; **Cast:** Samrat Chakrabarti, Natalia Miranda Guzman, Lanna Joffrey, Hana Moon, Matt Hurley, Chris Larkin, Bobby Moreno; *Modern Terrorism, or They Want to Kill Us and How We Can Learn to Love* by Jon Kern, directed by Kel Haney; **Cast:** Steve Boyer, Vedant Gokhale, Nitya Vidyasagar; Schaeberle Studio at Pace University; June 2–30, 2010

ETC Theatre Co.

Reed in the Wind by Joe McDonald; Director, Tom Holmes; Stage Manager, Steve Fareri; Set, Casper De la Torre; **Cast:** Heather Snow Clark, Nic Tyler, Douglas B. Giorgis, Bob Adrian; Producers Club; June 27–30, 2009

Figment Theatre

www.figmenttheatre.com

Monster Uprising by James DiGiovana, Epidiah Ravachol, Jason Ellis; Directors, Evelyn Sullivan, Jason Ellis, Christine Ann Sullivan; Set, Danny Nuñez; Costumes, Lois Folstein; Lighting, Carol Feeley; Sound, Jim Sullivan; **Cast:** Jason Ellis, Christine Ann Sullivan, Daniel Rockdale, Julia Susman, Jason Keeley, Evelyn Sullivan, Corrie Pond, Jonathan Gissentaner, Aaron Brown, Epidiah Ravachol; Access Theatre; October 29–November 8, 2009

Barbarian! Scrip, original music, and direction by Jason Ellis; Stage Manager, Ryan Roth; **Cast:** Jason Keeley, Johnathan Gissentaner, Ev Sullivan, Monica Murphy, Jason Ellis, Ming Pfeiffer, Anna-Maria Jung; UNDER St. Marks; May 5–June 30, 2010

Firebone Theatre

www.firebonetheatre.com

A Mysterious Way by Steven Walters; Director, Steve Day; Stage Manager, Jon Mark Ponder; Sound, Steve Day; General Manager, Chris Cragin; **Cast:** Christopher Domig, Jared Houseman; NYC Subway Platforms; June 4–21, 2009

Emily, An Amethyst Remembrance by Chris Cragin; Director, Steve Day; Set, Rachelle Beckerman; Costumes, Victoria Depew; Lighting, Rachelle Beckerman; Sound, Josh Leibert; Stage Manager, Alyse Frosch; Choreographer, Kimi Nikaidoh; Assistant Director, Hayli Henderson; House Manager, Becky Branscom; Publicist, Katie Rosin/Kampfire Films PR; **Cast:** Christopher Bonewitz, Jared Houseman, Elizabeth A. Davis, Jenny Ledel, Misti Foster Venters; Kirk Theatre on Theatre Row; September 11– 27, 2009

Readings

The Doll Confessions by Lellund Thompson; Director, Steve Day; April 5, 2010; *St. Francis in Egypt* by Arthur Giron; Director, Steve Day; April 12, 2010; *The Red Flamboyant* by Don Nguyen; April 19, 2010; *Forgiving Typhoid Mary* by Mark St. Germain; Director, Steve Day; April 26, 2010; *Song of the Bow* by Wayne Harrell; Director, Steve Day; May 3, 2010

The Flea Theater

Artistic Directro, Jim Simpson; Producing Director, Carol Ostrow; Managing Director, Beth Dembrow; Technical Director, Zack Tinkerlman; Audience Development and Marketing Manager, Eric Emch; Assistant to the Producing Director, Sarah Wansley; Development Manager, Penn Genthner; Assistant Technical Director, Timothy Pickerill; www.theflea.org

The Great Recession by Adam Rapp, Itamar Moses, Erin Courtney, Sheila Callaghan, Thomas Bradshaw, Will Eno; Directors, Jim Simpson, Kip Fagan, Adam Rapp, Michelle Tattenbaum, Ethan McSweeny, Davis McCallum; Stage Managers, Carrie Dell-Furay and Kara Kaufman; Lighting, Jeanette Yew; Set, John McDermott; Costumes, Becky Lasky and Jessica Pabst; Sound, Nathaniel Putnam; Fight Director, Alexander Sovronsky; Artistic Associate, Sherri Kronfeld; **Cast:** Andy Gershenzon, Anna Greenfield, Anne Elyse Chambers, Ariana Venturi, Betsy Lippitt, Bjorn Dupaty, Brett Aresco, Chloe Wepper, Dominic Spillane, Dorien Makhloghi, Eboni Booth, Emily Simmones, Greg Coughlin, Heidi Niedermeyer, Holly Chou, Ileana Pinyon; November 20–December 30, 2009

Girls in Trouble by Jonathan Reynolds; Director, Jim Simpson; Stage Manager, Rachel Sterner; Set, John McDermott; Costumes, Amanda Bujak; Lighting, Zack Tinkelman; Sound, Jeremy Wilson; Keola Simpson, Assistant Director; **Cast:** Andy Gershenzon, Brett Aresco, Betsy Lippitt, Akyiaa Wilson, Eboni Booth, Laurel Holland, Marshall York, Raul Sigmund Julia, Sarah Ellen Stephens; February 12–April 11, 2010

Flux Theatre Ensemble

www.fluxtheatre.org

The Lesser Seductions of History by August Schulenburg; Director, Heather Cohn; Stage Manager, Jodi Witherell; Lighting, Lauren Parish; Set, Will Lowry; Costumes, Becky Kelly; Sound, Asa Wember; ASM, Doug Faulbourn; Production Manager, Jason Paradine; Dramaturg, Angela Astle; Press, Emily Owens; Assistant Costumes, Jason Tseng; **Cast:** Jake Alexander, Matthew Archambault, Tiffany Clementi, Michael Davis, Candice Holdorf, Ingrid Nordstrom, Kelly O'Donnell, Jason Paradine, Christina Shipp, Raushanah Simmons, Isaiah Tanenbaum; The Cherry Pit; November 6–November 22, 2009

Jacob's House by August Schulenburg; Director, Kelly O'Donnell; Set, Jason Paradine; Costumes, Hannah Rose Peck; Lighting, Kia Rogers; Sound, Elizabeth Rhodes; Stage Manager, Jodi Witherell; Assistant Director, Cat Adler-Josem; Fight Choreographer, Michael Lawrence Eisenstein; **Cast:** Johnna Adams, Matthew Archambault, Zack Calhoon, Tiffany Clementi, Kelli Holsopple, Bianca LaVerne Jones, Jane Lincoln Taylor, Isaiah Tanenbaum, Anthony Wills Jr., Jessica Angleskhan; Access Theater Gallery; April 30–May 22, 2010

Readings

Volleygirls by Rob Ackerman; Director: August Schulenburg; **Cast:** Matt Archambault, Jason Paradine, David Crommett, Jane Taylor, Jaime Robert Carrillo, Catherine Porter, Tiffany Clementi, Candice Holdorf, Kelly O'Donnell, DeWanda Wise, Elise Link, Jessica Angleskhan, Christina Shipp; August 9; *Lickspittles, Buttonholers, and Damned Pernicious Go-Betweens* by Johnna Adams; Director: John Hurley; **Cast:** August Schulenburg, Ryan Quinn, Benjamin Ellis Fine, Tiffany Clementi, Christina Shipp, Katie Hartke, Becky Kelly, Matthew Murumba, Nick Monroy, Michael Poignand, Ryan Andes, Ed Schultz, Isaiah Tanenbaum; February 17; *ForePlay* by several playwrights including Johnna Adams, James Comtois, Kristen Palmer, Brian Pracht, Jeremy Basescu, Bekah Brunstetter, Rob Ackerman, David Ian Lee, Zack Robidas, Christine Evans, Michael John Garces, Bill George, Erin Browne, Fengar Gael, Mac Rogers, Crystal Skill; March 1

The Frog & Peach Theatre Co., Inc.

www.frogandpeachtheatre.org

Much Ado About Nothing by William Shakespeare; Director, Lynnea Benson; Set/Lighting, Jak Prince; Costumes, Laura Taber Bacon; Sound, Lynnea Benson; Composer, Ted Zurkowski; Stage Manager, Jenna Lazar; Assistant Director, Alexandra H. Rubin; Fight Coordinator, Ian Marshall; Choreographer, Tom Knutson; **Cast:** David Arthur Bachrach, Anny Baquero, Ross Beshear, Kyle Cheng, Nick Ciavarella, Lenny Ciotti, Dennis Demitry, Eric Doss, Eric DySart, Vivien Landau, Kaitlin Large, Dan Lendzian, Moti Margolin, Jean-Francois Ogoubiyi, Harry Oram, Hannah Owens, Michael R. Piazza, Joseph W. Rodriguez, Kevin G. Shinnick; West End Theatre; October 1–25, 2009

Tinkerbell Theatre Written and directed by Lynnea Benson, music & lyrics by Ted Zurkowski; Set/Lighting, Jak Prince; Costumes, Laura Taber Bacon; Sound, Lynnea Benson; Stage Manager, Jenna Lazar; Puppets, Spica Wobbe; Assistant Director, Alexandra H. Rubin; Choreographer, Tom Knutson; ASMs, Maria Camilo, Kathryn Turley; **Cast:** Lenny Ciotti, Kaitlin Large, Dan Lendzian, Moti Margolin, Hannah Owens, Michael R. Piazza, Hayley Raphael, Jenna Lazar, William Welles, Lynnea Benson; West End Theatre; November 22, 2009–January 17, 2010; Encore April 17–May 19, 2010

Macbeth by William Shakespeare; Director, Lynnea Benson; Set/Lighting, Jak Prince; Costumes, Laura Taber Bacon; Sound, Lynnea Benson; Stage Manager, Jenna Lazar; Assistant Director, Alexandra H. Rubin; Fight Coordinator, Ian Marchall, Choreographer, Tom Knutson; Press, Kampfire Films PR; **Cast:** Belle Addison, Aaron Bartz, Ariel Bethany, Todd Butera, Lenny Ciotti, Michael Chmiel, Kaitlin Large, Vanessa Weinert Locke, Louis Lourens, Matt Madsen, Moti Margolin, Brandon Morrissey, Jean-Francois Ogoubiyi, Hannah Owens, Amy Frances Quint; West End Theatre; April 15–May 9, 2010

The Gallery Players

Artistic Director, Heather Siobhan Curran; Executive Director, Neal J. Freeman; Director of Family Programming, Dominic Cuskern; www.galleryplayers.com

The 12th annual Black Box New Play Festival Included: *Father Mike* by TJ Edwards, directed by Mark Harborth; *Nobody Does Carpet like Bill* by Edward Versailles, directed by Barrie Gelles; *Given Our Current Fiscal Crisis* by Daniel Damiano, directed by Amanda White; *Unfinished Debasement* by Michael Kevin Baldwin, directed by Andrew Firda; *Bugs* by Rich Espey, directed by Barrie Gelles; *Philosophy 101* by Allan Lefcowitz, directed by Chad Yarborough; *Honey & Candy* by Lauren Cavanaugh, directed by Justine Campbell-Elliot; *Distastefully Yours* by Denis Meadows, directed by Robin Leslie Brown; *Beautiful World* by Kevin Christopher Snipes, directed by Seth Soloway; *Inhale* by Victoria T. Joseph, directed by Taibi Magar; *In the Shadow of the Lighthouse* by Carolina Aguilera, directed by Dev Bondarin; June 4– 28, 2009

The House of Blue Leaves by John Guare; Director, Dev Bondarin; Set, Ann Bartek; Costumes, Brad Scoggins; Lighting, Ryan Bauer; Sound, Chris Rummel; Stage Manager, Jodi Witherell; Producer, Neal J. Freeman; Properties, Virginia Monte; **Cast:** Burke Adams, Victoria Bundonis, Ronn Burton, Tom Cleary, Alex Herrald, Sharon Hunter, David Ojala, Stacey Scotte, Emilie Soffe, Nora Vetter, Elizabeth Wood; September 12–27, 2009

Top of the Heap Music by Jeffrey Lodin, book and lyrics by William Squier; Director, Neal J. Freeman; Set, Ann Bartek; Costumes, Megan Q. Dudley; Lighting, Tsubasa Kamei; Sound, Neal J. Freeman; Stage Manager, Caitlin Orr; Audio/Visual, Nicholas Meyer; Producer, Heather Siobhan Curran; Musical Director, Lili Wosk; Choreographer, Katharine Pettit; Associate Set/Properties, Elyse Handelman; Orchestrations, Bryan Crook; ASM, Janice Acevedo; Assistant Director, Allison Bress; **Cast:** Josh Bates, Ray Bendana, Ronn Burton, John Cardenas, Tina Marie Casamento, Kristin Farrell, Roy Flores, Carolyn Hartvigsen, Greg Horton, Lorinne Lampert, Kenny Wade Marshall, David Perlman, Anette Michelle Sanders, Hollis Scarborough, Natasha Soto-Albors; October 24–November 15, 2009

Mrs. Bob Cratchit's Wild Christmas Binge by Christopher Durang; Director, Trey Compton; Set, Lilia Trenkova; Costumes, Steven Manuel; Lighting, David Roy; Sound, David Roy; Stage Manager, Kyle Atkins; Producer, Robin Mishik-Jett; Associate Producer, Craig Anthony Bannister; Properties, Virgina Monte; Original Music, Michael Friedman; ASM, Emily Louick; Musical Director, Jason Burrow; Assistant Director, Mikey LoBalsamo; **Cast:** Sarah Amandes, Angela Dirksen, Sayfiya Fredericks, Sloan Grenz, Greg Kalafatas, E.C. Kelly, Kyle Metzger, Joanna Parson, Doug Plaut, Douglas Rees, Adam Segaller, Carly Vernon.; December 5– 20, 2009

Caroline, or Change Book and lyrics by Tony Kusher, music by Jeanine Tesori; Director, Jeremy Gold Kronenberg; Musical Director, Nehemiah Luckett; Choreographer, Michael Rice; Set, Edward T. Morris; Costumes, Soule Golden; Lighting, Mike Billings; Sound, Jillian Marie Walker; Producer, Laine Zipoy; Stage Manager, Andrew Zachery; Assistant Director, Allison Bressi; ASM, Marina Steinberg; **Cast:** Gisela Adisa, River Aguirre, Heather Davis, Teisha Duncan, Markeisha Ensley, Peter Gantenbein, Maricie Henderson, Daniel Henri Luttway, Gael Schaefer, Nikki Stephenson, Elyse McKay Taylor, Eileen Tepper, Ellisha Marie Thomas, Frank Viveros, Barrington Wal; January 30–February 21, 2010

The Crucible by Arthur Miller; Director, Heather Siobhan Curran; Set, Lilia Trenkova; Costumes, Megan Q. Dudley; Lighting, David Roy; Sound, Neal J. Freeman; Producer, Graham Mills; Stage Manager, Michael Aaron Jones; Associate Producer, Hannah Mason; Props, Virgina Monte; ASM, Kristine Schlachter; Dramaturg, Amanda White; **Cast:** John Blaylock, Gil Brady, Daniel Damiano, Lisa Darden, Genevieve Gearhart, Emily Hagburg, Justin Herfel, Frederic Heringes, John Isgro, Tom Lawson Jr., Lindsay Mack, Russell Mahrt, Rhyn McLemore, Sofia Munn, Alison Ostergaard, Bob Pritchard, Elisa Pupko; March 20– April 5, 2010

City of Angels Music by Cy Coleman, lyrics by David Zippel, book by Larry Gelbart; Director, Trey Compton; Musical Dirctor, Jeffrcy Campos; Choreographer, Brian Swasey; Set, Eli Kaplan-Wildmann; Costumes, Samantha Guinan; Lighting, John P. Woodey; Sound, Julianne Merrill; Producer, Becca Goland-Van Ryn; Stage Manager, Kyle Atkins; Props, Dustin Moore; Assistant Set, Katherine Fry; ASMs, Liz Bachman and Katy Moore; Follow Spot Operator, Janet Armou; **Cast:** Blair Alexis Brown, Tony Castellanos, Amanda Danskin, Lara Hayhurst, Greg Horton, Matt Malloy, Caitlin Mesiano, Brian Mulay, Danny Rothman, James Ryan Sloan, Abby Stevens, Jared Troilo, Kathleen Watson, John Weigand, J. Tyler Whitmer; May 1– 23, 2010

GeminiCollisionWorks

A Little Piece of the Sun by Daniel McKleinfeld; Co-produced with The Brick Theater; Director/Design, Ian W. Hill; Co-Set and Costumes/Stage Manager, Berit Johnson; **Cast:** David Arthur Bachrach, Fred Backus, Aaron Baker, Olivia Baseman, Adam Belvo, Eric Feldman, Ian W. Hill, Colleen Jasinski, Gavin Starr Kendall, Roger Nasser, Tom Reid, Melissa Roth, Patrick Shearer, Alyssa Simon; Brick Theater; August 7–30, 2009

George Bataille's Bathrobe by Richard Foreman; Co-produced with The Brick Theater; Director/Design, Ian W. Hill; Stage Manager/Co-Set, Berit Johnson; Costumes, Karen Flood; **Cast:** Sarah Malinda Engelke, Liza Wade Green, Justin R.G. Holcomb, Bob Laine, Kathryn Lawson, Patrice Miller, Timothy McCown Reynolds, Bill Weeden; Brick Theater; August 8–29, 2009

Sacrificial Offerings by David Finkelstein & Ian W. Hill; Co-produced with The Brick Theater; Director/Design, Ian W. Hill; Stage Manager/Co-Set, Berit Johnson; Lighting, Ian W. Hill; Audio/Visual, David Finkelstein, Agnes De Garron, Ian W. Hill; **Cast:** Eric C. Bailey, Larry Gutman, Stephen Heskett, Justin R.G. Holcomb, Kirill Khvenkin, Victoria Miller, Ben Robertson, Eve Udesky; Brick Theater; August 8–30, 2009

Blood on the Cat's Neck by Rainer Werner Fassbinder; Co-produced with The Brick Theater; Director/Desing, Ian W. Hill; Stage Manager/Co-Set & Costumes, Berit Johnson; C**ast:** Gyda Arber, Eric C. Bailey, Danny Bowes, V. Orion Delwaterman, Rasheed Hinds, Toya Lillard, Samantha Mason, Amy Overman, Roger Nasser, Shelley Ray; Brick Theater; August 9–29, 2009

Gene Frankel Theatre

Ivanov by Anton Chekhov; adapted by Jacob Knoll & Jeff Barry; Presented by Miscreant Theatre Company; Director, Jacob Knoll; Set, Anya Klepikov; Lighting, Burke Browne; Costumes, Anya Klepikov; Dramaturg, Roweena MacKay; **Cast:** Jonathan Marballi, Tim Martin, Matt Scanlon, Jennifer Regan, Jy Murphy, Stephanie Bratnick, Emily Jon Mitchell, Emily Robin Fink, William Bogert, Lauren Orkus, Jeff Barry, Brad Thomason; June 10–28, 2009

The Pig, the Farmer, and the Artist Book, music and lyrics by David Chesky; Presented by New York City Opera; Director, A. Scott Parry; Music Director, Anthony Aibel; Lighting, Rob Scallan; **Cast:** Tom Blunt, Wendy Buzby, Cory Clines, Michael Dezort, James Kryshak, Melanie Long, Megan Marino, Christopher PrestonThompson, Ami Vice; October 2–17, 2009

The Credeaux Canvas by Keith Bunin; Presented by Aeternalis Theatre; Director, Bryan Radtke; Stage Manager, Matthew Krause; **Cast:** RJ Passetti, Megan Melnyk, Sergey Nagorny, Billie Colobamro; November 4–21, 2009

Closer by Patrick Marber; Presented by Fourdreamers; Director, Eric Tucker; Original Music, Edward Davis; **Cast:** Abbey Dehnert, Amy Hessler, Arash Mokhtar, Joseph R. Rodriquez; December 9–20, 2009

Hostages by Yussef El-Guindi; Presented by Miscreant Theatre Company; Director, Jack Young; Stage Manager, Brad Lee Thomason; Lighting, Cat Starmer; Sound, Ted Pallas; **Cast:** Jacob Knoll, Jeff Barry, Peter Macklin; January 6–24, 2010

Pieces of a Playwright by Matthew Ethan Davis; Presented by Oasis. nyTheatreGroup; Director, Albert Insinnia; Costumes, Sara Minerd, Laura Cleary; Lighting, Teo Solano; Original Music, Hillary Johnson; Stage Manager, Erienne Wredt; **Cast:** Adam Auslander, Laura Michelle Cleary, Adyana De La Torre, Ian Campbell Dunn, Christopher Frederick, Shannon Lower, Sara Minerd, Nick Neglia, Hugo Salazar Jr., Teo Solano, Stefanie Tara, Emilio Paul Tirado, Edward Zimic; January 27–31, 2010

The Average-Sized Mermaid by Jessica Fleitman; Presented by State of Play Productions; Director, Kara-Lynn Vaeni; Stage Manager, Maude Klochendler; Lighting, Jarrod Jahoda; Set, Ryan Palmer; Costumes, Lexi Townsend; Sound, Brendan Barr; Producer, Neal J. Freeman; Properties, Virginia Monte; Original Music, Brenda Barr; **Cast:** Jimmy Allen, Seth Andrew Bridges, Michelle Concha, Starr Kirkland, Christiane Seidel, Joe Sevier; February 3–14, 2010

Gingold Theatrical Group – Project Shaw

Director and Producer, David Staller; Readings of the complete works of George Bernard Shaw; www.projectshaw.com

Six of Calais and **Simpleton of Unexpected Isles** Stage Manager, Nathan K. Claus; Host, David Cote; **Cast:** Jack Berenholtz, John Bolton, Donna Lynne Champlin, Nora Chester, Josh Grisetti, Simon Kendall, James Prendergast, Daphne Robin-Vega, Nathaniel Shaw, Lucy Banks Sheftall, Victor Slezak, Georgia Warner; June 15, 2010

Mrs. Warren's Profession Stage Manager, Nathan K. Claus; Host, Jeremy McCarter; **Cast:** Michael Cristofer, Tyne Daly, Sean Dugan, Xanthe Elbrick, George S. Irving, Howard Kissel, Brian Murray; July 20, 2009

Back to Methuselah. Part One Stage Manager, Nathan K. Claus; Host, David Cote; **Cast:** Tanya Elder, Ariel Estrada, Stephen Mo Hanan, Simon Kendall, Simon Jones, Marc Kudisch, Madeleine Martin, Jeff Steitzer, Diane Stillwell Weinberg; September 21, 2009

Super Shaw Stage Manager, Nathan K. Claus; Host, David Cote; **Cast:** Peter Frechette, Jason Graae, Daniel Jenkins, John McMartin, Charlotte Moore, Liz Morton, Kerry O'Malley, Marian Seldes, Tom Viola; September 29, 2009

Back To Methuselah: Part Two Stage Manager Nathan K. Claus; **Cast:** Harry Barandes, Delphi Herrington, Katharine Houghton, Celia Keenan-Bolger, John Martello, Tyler Maynard, Brian Murray, Ben Rauch, Michael Riedel, Justine Salata, Lenny Wolpe, Oliver Wadsworth, Emily Young; October 19, 2009

On the Rocks Stage Manager Nathan K. Claus; **Cast:** Ezra Barnes, Kelli Barrett, Reed Birney, Carole J. Befford, Ian Gould, Jeffrey Hardy, Jayne Houdyshell, George S. Irving, Tim Jerome, William McCauley, Sal Mistretta, Chirstine Pedi, James Rana, Jeff Steitzer, Joel Van Liew, Diane Stilwell Weinberg, Anatol Yusef; November 16, 2009

The Gadfly and **Why She Would Not** Writers, David Cote, Michael Feingold, Israel Horovitz, Jeremy McCarter, Robert Simonson; Stage Manager, Nathan K. Claus; Host, Jeremy McCarter; **Cast:** Jim Brochu, Donna Lynne Champlin, Mara Davi, Sean Dugan, Josh Grisetti, Simon Jones, Victor Slezak, Tom Viola; December 14, 2009

Arms and the Man Stage Manager, Nathan K. Claus; Host, David Rooney; **Cast:** Kelli Barrett, David Belcher, Michael Cerveris, Rufus Collins, Maria Dizzia, Jayne Houdyshell, George S. Irving, Marc Kudisch; January 25, 2010

The Philanderer Stage Manager, Nathan K. Claus; **Cast:** Cassie Beck, Jim Brochu, Chad Kimball, Liz Morton, Julia Murney, Robert Stanton, Paxton Whitehead; February 15, 2010

GTG Gala on St. Patrick's Day Stage Manager, Nathan K. Claus; **Cast:** Kate Baldwin, Michael Cerveris, Jayne Houdyshell, George S. Irving, Charlotte Moore, Kate Mulgrew, Jane Powell, Michael Riedel, Marian Seldes, Florence Teuscher, Diane Stilwell Weinberg, Tom Viola; March 17, 2010

The Doctor's Dilemma Stage Manager, Nathan K. Claus; Host, Michael Riedel; Narrator, David Cote; Host, Gordon Cox; **Cast:** Rufus Collins, Annie Golden, George S. Irving, Tim Jerome, Simon Kendall, John Martello, Carolyn McCormick, Liz Morton, Brian Murray, Ciaran O'Rielly, Lorenzo Pisoni, Oliver Wadsworth; March 22, 2010

John Bull's Other Island Stage Manager, Nathan K. Claus; **Cast:** Mark Aldrich, Nora Chester, Ed Dixon, Ian Gould, Daniel Jenkins, Tim Jerome, Jimmy Ludwig, Charlotte Parry, Reg Rogers, Alexander Sovronsky, Henry Stram, Dan Truman, Mark Vietor; April 19, 2010

Major Barbara Stage Manager, Nathan K. Claus; Host, Patrick Healy; **Cast:** Ellen Adair, John Bolton, Sidney Burgoyne, Daniel Davis, Adam Greer, Suzanne Grodner, Lianne Kressin, Maryanne Plunkett, Krysta Rodriguez, Jay Rogers, Brian Sgambati, Lindsay Torrey, Jon Patrick Walker, Lenny Wolpe; May 24, 2010

Gnobs Productions

God Bless You, Mister Scrooge! by Janet Hopf; Director, Greg Cicchino; Stage Manager, John Michael Crotty; Design/Sound, R. Allen Babcock; Costumes, T.V. Alexander; **Cast:** Melisa Breiner-Sanders, Marc Geller, Hunter Gilmore, Douglas B. Giorgis, Alexander L. Hill, Jonathan Hinman, Sharon Hunter, Jan-Peter Pedross, Devon Talbott, Caitlyn Elese Williams; La Tea Theater; December 5– 20, 2009

Gorilla Repertory Theatre

Joan of Arc by Robert Steven Ackerman; Director, Christopher Carter Sanderson; Originanl Music, Andre-Philippe Mistier; **Cast:** Aleksandra Yermak, Tim Scott, Greg Petroff, Tim Moore, John Beck, Gregg Adair, Marvin Avila, Dennis Baker, Steven Beckingham, Demetrios Bonaros, Neville Braithwaite, James Chen, Sarah Mollo-Christensen, Richard Cottrell, Marcus Dillon, Ellen DiStasi, Meaghan Bloom Fluitt, Matt Garner, Ken Hailey, Jack Haley, Caitlin Johnston, Zachary Koval, Tom Lapke, Diane Magnuson, Michael Jennings Mahoney, Collin McConnell, Dorian McGhee, Gustavo Obregon, Len Rella, Jessica Ripton, Jack Rondeau, Frances You Sanderson, Nalini Sharma, Ethan Sher, Josh Silverman, Emilio Paul Tirado, Michael Weaver; Pinegrove at Fort Tryon Park; July 9–August 2, 2009

Green Lamp Press

Little Tragedies by Alexander Pushkin, translated by Julian Henry Lowenfeld; Director, Julian Henry Lowenfeld & Natalya Kolotova; **Cast:** Peter Von Berg, Robert Carin, Karen Chapman, Stephen Innocenzi, Nika Leoni, Brandon Ruckdashel, Luiz Simas, John Leonard Thompson; Baryshnikov Arts Center; November 5–14, 2009

Ground UP Productions

www.groundupproductions.org

Barefoot in the Park by Neil Simon; Director, Lon Bumgarner; Set/Lighting, Travis McHale; Costumes, Stacey Berman; Lighting, Travis McHale; Stage Manager, Kate August; Graphic Design, Wade Dansby; Technical Director, Dan Wheeless; **Cast:** Brian Lafontaine, Kate Middleton, Tom Moglia, Guy Olivieri, Eric Purcell, Amelia White; Manhattan Theatre Source; July 8–25, 2009

Readings

Letter from Algeria by Michael Ian Walker, directed by Jordana Williams; November 2; *Avow* by Bill C. Davis, directed by Jerry Less; November 10; *The Other Place* by Sharr White, directed by Ethan McSweeney; November 17; *The Thing About Joe* by Matthew Hardy, directed by West Hyler and Shelley Butler, original music by Randy Klein; November 23

The Group Theatre Too

Artistic Director, Michael Blevins; Executive Producer, Justin Boccitto; www. grouptheatretoo.org

Count To Ten by Michael Blevins, Beth Clary, Scott Knip, Bruce Sacks, David Wollenberger; Director/Choreographer, Michael Blevins; Costumes, Vangeli Kaseluris; Lighting, Christopher Hoyt; Producer, Justin Boccitto; Musical Director, Christine Riley; Stage Manager, Deborah Climo; Fight Choreographer, Dan Renkin; Assistant Director, Jeff Brelvi; Assistant Choreographer, Ryan Schaars; Graphics, Alex Maxwell; Associate Producer, Mary Ann Penzero; **Cast:** Michael Blevins, Nicky Romaniello, Jennifer Avila, Connor Frawley, Lexie Speirs, Jacob Burlas, Ann-Marie Sepe, Hunter Gross, Dylan Paige, Anthony Zas, Cristina Marie, Gillian Beltz-Mohrmann, Cydney Black, Jenna Black, McKenzie Custin, Steven Etienne, Brittany Hoehlein, Chris Kinsey, Nikki Miller, Katelyn Morgan, Erik Schmidt, Mitchell Schneider, Brandon Wiener; Presented as part of NYMF; Theater at St. Clements & The Hudson Guild Theater; October 15–November 1, 2009

The Choreographer's Canvas Director, Justin Boccitto; Stage Manager, Cristina Marie; Lighting, Tim Ruppen; Choreographers: Kyla Barkin, Michael Blevins, Justin Boccitto, Bob Boross, Jessica Chen, Dana Fisch, Bobby Hedglin-Taylor, The Manhattan Youth Ballet, The New York Theatre Ballet, Katrina Phillip, Jonathan Riedel, Sue Samuels, Tracie Stanfield, Michael Su; Manhattan Movement & Arts Center; May 5, 2010

Guerrilla Shakespeare Project

www.guerrillashakespeare.com

Two Noble Kinsmen by William Shakespeare; John Fletcher; Director, Diana Buirksi; Set, Tristan Jeffers; Costumes, James King; Lydia Franz; Lighting, Tom Schwans; Sound, Charles Shell; Stage Manager, Patricia Lynn; Jane Pfitsch; Dramaturg, Haas Regen; **Cast:** Kimiye Corwin, Craig Wesley Divino, Ginger Eckert, Zachary Fine, Jordan Kaplan, Scott Raker, Jordan Reeves, Jacques Roy, Lindsay Torrey; Medicine Show Theater; January 7–17, 2010

King John by William Shakespeare; Director, Jordan Reeves; Set, Jacques Roy, Jordan Reeves; Costumes, Tiffany Baker; Lighting, Melissa Mizell; Sound, Charles Shell; Stage Manager, Darryl Lee VanOudenhove; Dramaturg, Haas Regen; Fight Choreographer, Charles Shell; **Cast:** Ginger Eckert, Jordan Kaplan, Tom Schwans, Jacques Roy, Patricia Lynn, Scott Raker, Lena Hart, Kern McFadden, Jude Sandy; Medicine Show Theater; May 6–23, 2010

Readings

Defiant by George Brant; October 3; *Lathem Prince* by Ashlin Halfnight; February 24

Katy Wright Mead, Michael Cullen, and Cynthia Mace in Safe, *presented by Chris Henry & Royal Family Productions (photo by Alex Koch)*

Leif Huckman, Neil Haskell, Jenna Coker-Jones, Noah Wiseberg, Kate Rockwell, and Liz Larsen in F#@king Up Everything, *presented by Jeremy Handelman and Off The Leash Productions at the New York Musical Theatre Festival (photo by Jeremy Handelman)*

Emmy Raver-Lampman (center) and the Company in Children of Eden *at Astoria Performing Arts Center (photo by Jennifer Maufrais Kelly)*

Lauren Roth and Tyler Hollinger in the Kaleidoscope Theatre Company's Sex & Violence *(photo by Daniel Winters)*

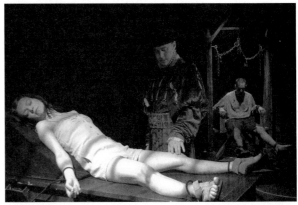

Susan Louise O'Connor, Alex Pappas, and Joseph Mathers in The Vigil, Or The Guided Cradle, *presented by the Impetuous Theatre Group in association with The Brick Theater (photo by James David Jackson)*

Stephanie Wright Thompson, Joe Curnutte and Marc Bovino in Samuel & Alasdair: A Personal History of the Robot War, *presented by The Mad Ones in association with The Brick Theater (photo by Marc Bovino)*

Morgan Lindsey Tachco and Susan Barrett in the John Montgomery Theatre Company production of Benny *(photo by Scott Wynn)*

Taliesen Rose and Gregory Casimir in Macbeth in the Other Room, *presented by DJM Productions (photo by Dave McCracken)*

Kaitlin Large and William Welles in Tinkerbell Theatre, *presented by The Frog & Peach Theatre Company (photo by Kantu Lentz)*

Kavi Ladnier, Sam Ghosh, Andrew Cuilarte, Christopher Larkin, Jay J. Lee, and Tim Cain in Desipina & Company's *final year of* Seven.11 Convenience Theatre *(photo by Jeff McCrum)*

Hamm & Clov Stage Company

Producing Artistic Director, Holly Villaire; www.hammandclov.org

Ardnaglass on the Air by Jimmy Kerr; Co-produced with the New York Irish Center; Director, Geraldine Hughes; Sound, Dan Hamilton; **Cast:** Jimmy Kerr, Jo Kinsella, Jonathan Judge-Russo; New York Irish Center; November 13–22, 2009

Memorial Day by H.H. Hoos; May 22, 2010

Handcart Ensemble

www.handcartensemble.org

Homer's Odyssey (a Retelling) by Simon Armitage; Director, J. Scott Reynolds; Set, Tijana Bjelajac; Costumes, Candida Nichols; Lighting, David Kniep; Original Music, Nathan Bowen; Stage Manager, Sarah Biesinger; Puppetry/Shadow Effects, Marta Mozelle MacRostie; **Cast:** David D'Agostini, Jeffrey Golde, Rachael McOwen, John Michalski, Nicholas Alexiy Moran, Jane Pejtersen, Joel Rainwater, Joel Richards, Elizabeth Ruelas, Javen Tanner, Ryan Wood; The Green Room at 45 Bleecker; September 3–October 18, 2009

Harlem Repertory Theatre

Artistic Director, Kieth Lee Grant; www.harlemrepertorytheatre.org

The Wiz Book by William F. Brown, music & lyrics by Charlie Smalls; Director, Keith Lee Grant; **Cast:** Danyel Fulton, Roderick Warner, Alexandra Bernard, Lynnette Braxton, Natalya Peguero, Eric Myles, Jimmie Mike, Kyria Cameron, Yaritza Pizarro, Mabel Gomez, Tola Sean and Derrick Montalvo; Aaron Davis Hall; July 24–September 5, 2009

Flahooley Book by E.Y. Harburg and Fred Saidy, lyrics by E.Y. Harburg, music by Sammy Fain; Co-Production with Theater for the New City, in conjunction with the Yip Harburg Foundation; Director/Choreography, Keith Lee Grant; Set, Mary Myers; Costumes, Ann-Marie Wright; Lighting, Brian Aldous; Audio/Visual, Daniel Fergus Tamulonis; **Cast:** Alexandra Bernard, Daniel Fergus Tamulonis, Roman Urbanski; Theater for the New City; December 18, 2009–January 3, 2010

HDM Productions

Troubadour Music by Bert Draesel, lyrics by John Martin; Director, John Margulis; Music Director, Paul Stephan; Set, Gian Marco Lo Forte; Costumes, Sarita Fellows; Lighting, Matt Ehlert; Stage Manager, Jaimie Van Dyke; **Cast:** Aaron Davis, Robert A. Felbinger, Charles Kavel, Rob Maitner, Mary Catherine McDonald, Sauel Perwin, John Weigand, Alex Yacovelli; The Theater at The Church of the Epiphany; October 9–November 2, 2009

Heathcliff Entertainment

The House of Yes by Wendy MacLeod; Director, Brandt Reiter; Lighting, Brad Peterson; **Cast:** Hilary Bettis, Marcia Everitt, Tommy Heleringer, Jonathan Blakeley, Zoe Swenson; Access Theatre; April 15–May 2, 2010

The Heights Players

www.heightsplayers.org

Take Me Out by Richard Greenberg; Director/Lighting/Sound, Fabio Taliercio; Set, Carl Tallent; Costumes, Aurora Dreger; Co-Sound, Seth Grugle; Stage Manager, Colleen Finn; **Cast:** Seth Grugle, Ugo Chukwu, Craig Peterson, Ed Healy, Ron Dizon, Miguel Sierra, Jake Krikhan, Mike Basile, Bryant Wingfield, Nathan Richard Wagner, Doua Moua; January 7–24, 2010

HERE Arts Center

Artistic Director, Kristin Marting; Producing Director, Kim Whitener; Associate Producer, Karina Mangu-Ward; Production Manager, Stacey Haggin; Technical Director, Marlon Hurt; www.here.org

machines machines machines machines machines machines machines by Quinn Bauriedel, Geoff Sobelle, and Trey Lyford; Director, Aleksandra Wolska; Set, Hiroshi Iwasaki; Lighting, James Clotfelter; Sound, James Sugg; Machines Design and Set Treatment, Steven Dufala and Billy Blaise Dufala; Stage Managers, Emily Rea and Stacey Haggin; Associate Production Manager, Rachel Moffat; ASM, Anna Abhau Elliott; Technical Director, Derek Cook; **Cast:** Quinn Bauriedel, Geoff Sobelle, Trey Lyford; Mainstage; June 2– 27, 2010

A Night With Walt Whitman Written and performed by Bart Buch & Brian Selznick; Director, Dan Hurlin; Stage Manager/Lighting, George Meyer; Production Coordinator, Lake Simons; Technical Supervisor, Matthew Tennie; Technical Director, Mike Kerns; Dorothy B. Wiliams Theatre; June 3–7, 2009

Los Grumildos Written and Performed by Ety Fefer; Stage Manager, Stacey Haggin; Lighting, Marlon Hurt; Dorothy B. Williams Theatre; July 28–August 2, 2009

The Only Friends We Have by Sarah Petersiel, Josh Matthews, Matt Chapman; Presented by Under the Table; Set, Victoria Bradbury; Original Music, AcHT(eN); **Cast:** Sarah Petersiel, Josh Matthews, Matt Chapman; Dorothy B. Williams Theater; August 4–9, 2009

The Tenement by Jonothon Lyons; Presented by The Associated Mask Ensemble; Director, Daniel Brodie; Set, Jonothon Lyons; Set Consultant/Technical Director, David Ojala; Costumes, Kathy Lyons; Lighting, Wolfram Ott; Sound and Projections, Daniel Brodie; Associate Sound, Patrick Southern; Instrumentation, Tom Tierny; Voice, Kaila McIntyre-Bader; Assistant Director, Caitlin Fraser-Reckard; Press, Zeke Howard; Hair and Makeup, Caitlin Fraser-Reckard; **Cast:** Jonothon Lyons, Allie Avital Tsypin, Joseph Michael Ray Lymous, Bill Mullen; HERE Arts Center–Dorothy B. Williams Theatre (non-resident production); September 3–12, 2009

My Life in a Nutshell by Hanne Tierney; Lighting, Marlon Hurt; Sound, Luke Santy; Composer, Vocalist and Musician, Jane Wang; Projections, Hannah Wasileski; Performers: Shawn Lane, Jamie Ellen Davis, Hanne Tierney; Dorothy B. Williams Theatre; October 8– 25, 2009

The Lily's Revenge Written and performed by Taylor Mac; Mainstage Theatre; October 29–November 22, 2009

Swimming to Spalding by Lian Amaris; Produced by East End Artists in association with Colorado College; Director, Richard Schechner; Stage Manager, Yasmine M. Jahanmir; Set, Angrette McClosky; Lighting, Melissa Mizell; Sound, Lucian Ban; Assistant Director, Joy Brooke Fairfield; **Cast:** Lian Amaris; Mainstage (non-resident production); December 6–19, 2009

Aunt Leaf by Barbara Weichmann; Director, Jeffrey Mousseau; Set, Sarah Edkins; Costumes, Amelia Dombrowski; Lighting, Ayumu Saegusa; Sound & Composer, J. Hagenbuckle; **Cast:** Alan Benditt, Pal Bernstein, Rachael Richman; Dorothy B. Williams Theatre; January 7– 24, 2010

Culturemart 2010 Annual festival, included: *Wooden* by Laura Peterson; *The Venus Riff* by Johari Mayfield; *Sonnambula* by Michael Bodel; *Floating Point Waves* by Ximena Garnica & Shige Moriya; *Lucid Possession* by Toni Dove; *Miranda* by Kamala Sankaram; *Mosheh* by Yoav Gal; *Don Cristobal*, Billy-Club Man by Erin Orr & Rima Fand; *Epyllion* by Lindsay Abromaitis-Smith & Emma Jaster; *At Long Last: Phrase one* by Lake Simons & Chad Lynch; *A Small Leashed Monkey* by Deke Weaver; *Border Towns* by Nick Brooke & Jenny Rohn; Mainstage Theatre & Dorothy B. Williams; January 12–30, 2010

Sounding by Jennifer Gibbs; Director, Kristin Marting; Set, Nick Vaughan; Lighting, Rie Ono; Sound, Jane Shaw; Audio/Visual, Tal Yarden; Stage Manager, Emily Rea; **Cast:** Okwui Okpokwasili, Todd d'amour, Irene Longshore, Ana Kayne, Stephen Reyes, Michael Pemberton, George Tynan Crowley, Rudy Mungaray, Othello Ghartey; Mainstage Theatre; February 17–March 13, 2010

Alice in Slasherland by Qui Nguyen; Presented by Vampire Cowboys Theatre Company; Director, Robert Ross Parker; Stage Manager, Danielle Buccino; Lighting, Nick Francone; Set, Nick Francone; Costumes, Sarah Laux & Jessica Shay; Sound, Shane Rettig; Video, Matt Tennie; Choreographer, Qui Nguyen; Puppets, David Valentine; Original Music; Press, Jim Baldassare; **Cast:** Carlo Alban, Sheldon Best, Tom Myers, Bonnie Sherman, Andrea Marie Smith, Amy Kim Waschke; Mainstage (non-resident production); March 18–April 10, 2010

Horizon Theatre Rep

Managing Producer, Andrew Cohen; Artistic Director, Rafael De Mussa; www.htronline.org

The Misunderstanding by Albert Camus, translated by Jack O'Brien; Director, Alex Lippard; Set, Michael Moore; Costumes, Amanda Bujak; Lighting, Zack Tinkelman; Sound, Amy Altadonna; Stage Manager, Rebekah Hughston; Production Manager, Katherine M. Carter; **Cast:** Wendy Allegaert, Erin Cherry, Ellen Crawford, Rafael De Mussa, Stuart Rudin; Flea Theater Downstairs; October 29–November 22, 2009

Horse Trade Theater Group

Co-Founder and Managing Director, Erez Ziv; Artistic Development, Heidi Grumelot; Technical Director, Elaine Jones; Press, Emily Owens; www.horsetrade.info

Kraine Theater

Arsenic and Old Lace by Joseph Kesselring; Co-Produced with Dysfunctional Theater Company (for detailed listing see Dysfunctional Theater Company in this section); June 11–21, 2009

Waking Up With Strangers by Paul David Young; Co-Produced with Skylight Performances; Director, Mary Beth Smith; **Cast:** Nate Faust, Marco Formosa, Ji-Hye Kwon, David Marshall; June 29–July 2, 2009

Julius Caesar by William Shakespeare; Presented by Pigeon Creek Shakespeare Company; Director, Alisha Huber; **Cast:** Kathleen Bode, Emily Decker, CreeAnn DeWall, Heather Folkvord, Ellie Gramer, Taleah Greve, Kat Hermes, Arielle Leverett, Elle M. Luckstead, Katherine Mayberry, Sarah Stark, Angela Taylor; August 13–16, 2009

Punk Roc/Love Song Based on *Love's Labour's Lost* by William Shakespeare; Directors, Heidi Grumelot with Jaq Bessell; Original Music, Dan Beeman; **Cast:** Nate Faust, Tommy Day Carey, Zak Risinger, Neil Magnuson, Aimée Cucchiaro, Elena Chang, Rashmi, Folake Olowofoyeku, Michael Liscio Jr., Maxwell Eddy, Courtney Shaw, Ian Temple, J. Stephen Brantley; September 30–October 3, 2009

Up For Anything by Marc Spitz; Presented by Bay Bridge Productions and Actionman Productions; Director, Carlo Vogel; Set, Deb O; Costumes, David Tabbert; Lighting, Chris Studley; Sound, Jens McVoy; Stage Manager, Emily Bible; Producers Jonathan Lisecki, Carlo Vogel, Laura Wagner; Associate Producer, Erin Porvanznika; Graphics, David Vertino; **Cast:** Jonathan Marc Sherman, Arthur Aulisi, Ivanna Cullinan, Camille Habacker, James Habacker, Jonathan Lisecki, Leroy Logan, Eva Patton, Brian Reilly, Alyssa Simon, Yuri Skujins, Tom Vaught; Kraine Theater; October 8–31, 2009

The 2009 Burlesque Blitz Co-Produced with The Burlesque Alliance; included: *Fisherman's Island–a Burlesque Hallucination*; **Cast:** Miss Coney Island, GiGi La Femme, Ruby Valentine, Ekaterina; *Bastard Keith Saves Chanukah*; **Cast:** Bastard Keith, Minnie Tonka, Precious Little; *Pinchbottom Burlesque presents*

– How the Pinch Stole Xmas; *Swayze For You: A Tribute to Patrick Swayze* by Casino O'Fortune Cookie; *Revealed's Holiday Bonus* by GiGi La Femme & Doc Wasabassco; December 26–30, 2009

Encores 2010 A festival of past presentations; included: *Hostage Song* by Clay McLeod Chapman, music & lyrics by Kyle Jarrow; **Cast:** Hannah Bos, Hannah Cheek, Abe Goldfarb, Paul Thureen; *The Pumpkin Pie Show: Commencement* by Clay McLeod Chapman; **Cast:** Hanna Cheek; *Frankenstein* written, directed, & composed by Dan Bianchi; January 6–13, 2010

Search and Destroy by Howard Korder; Presented by Strudel Productions; Director, Nick Meo; Stage Manager, Sarah Tickal; Lighting, Josh Starr; Set, Kathryn Kawecki; Sound, Michelangelo Sosnowitz; **Cast:** Kelly Miller, Errickson Wilcox, Tina Jensen, Geoff Lerer, Andrew Kaempfer, Bruce Barton, Stephanie Weyman, Logan Tracey, Ken Hailey, Gustavo Obregon, Kila Packett, Matt Swanston, John Reoli; January 14–23, 2010

Playing Cricket by Andrew Bauer; Director, Eleonore Dyl; Stage Manager, Livia Hill; **Cast:** Nic Tyler, Gabriel Sloyer, Jessica Chazen, Richard Brundage, Scott Glascock, Afton Boggiano, Elizabeth Bove, Tom Batemanbrynne Kraynak; February 4–20, 2010

Price by David Fierro; Produced by Secret Weapon Theatre; Director, Kon Yi; Stage Manager, Christina Najera; Costumes, Stephanie Pope; Sound, Junghoon Pi; Fight Director, Nate Grams; Dramaturg, Erik Grathwohl; **Cast:** Mary Ellen Schneider, David Klasko; February 24–March 6, 2010

Uncorseted by Patrick di Battista and Anne Laffoon; Produced by LaGoDi Productions and the Shark Tank Players; **Cast:** Lobo Logodey, Lacey Carriage, Goober Cemetery, Missy Peyton, Fanny Florida, Phoebe Virgin, Mandy Twin Laurel, Mollie Harvest, Smoky Topaz; February 25–March 6, 2010

Moving Day Written and directed by Helene Montagna; Produced by By & By Productions; Stage Manager, Dorri Aspinwall; Lighting, Ken Conroy; Set, Katherine Fry; Costumes, Sofia Dante; Sound, Sam Dante; **Cast:** Tina Barone, Frank Nigro, Douglas Reid, Christie Zampella; April 22–May 1, 2010

Four Quarters Written and directed by Christopher Heath; Produced by Agony Productions; Lighting, Mark Jeter; Stage Manager, Heather Olmstead; **Cast:** Omer Barnea, Margo Brooke Pellmar, Tamar Pelzig, Solomon Shiv; February 24–March 6, 2010

Two Gentlemen of Lebowski by Adam Bertocci; Co-Produced with DM Theatrics; Director, Frank Cwiklik; Choreographer, Becky Byers; **Cast:** Brianna Tyson, Bob Laine, Stewart Urist, Ed Lane, Josh Mertz, Devin Landin, Kevin Orzechowski, Craig Kelton Peterson, Dan Phai, Shiloh Klein, Kelly McCormack, Melissa Opie, Erin Posanti, Courtni Wilson; March 18–April 4, 2010

The Red Room

Ardor Doody and Big Rock Candy Mountain by Lucille Scott, Jesse Cameron Alick, Julia Holleman, Lucas Cantor; Co-produced with Subjective Theater Company; Director, Steven Gillenwater, Emma Givens; Stage Managers, Allie Connell, Hyatt Michaels; Fight Director, Lisa Kopitsky; Original Music, Lucas Cantor; Set, Jan Stein; Sound, ListenHereNow; Lighting, Vadim Ledvin; **Cast:** Scout Durwood, Peej Mele, John Murdock, Brian Corr, Brianna Hansen, Brian Whisenant; September 8–13, 2009

The Eight: Reindeer Monologues by Jeff Goode; Co-Produced with Dysfunctional Theater Company (for detailed listing see Dysfunctional Theater Companyin this section); December 9–19, 2009

Radio Star by Tanya O'Debra; Director/Lighting, Peter Cook; Costumes, Corinna Mantlo; Sound, Tanya O'Debra & Peter Cook; Composer, Andrew Mauriello; **Cast:** Tanya O'Debra, Lincoln Hallowell; January 7–February 20, 2010

The Fire This Time A festival; included: *By the Banks of the Nile* by Deborah Asiimwe; *Reverb* by Radha Blank; *Poetics of the Creative Process* by Kelley Girod; *The Beyonce Effect* by Katori Hall; *Citizen Jane* by Derek Lee McPhatter; *The Anointed* by Germono Toussaint; *A Goddess Once* by Pia Wilson; February 4–7, 2010

Mechanically Separated Meat by Jeff Belanger and Amanda Sage Comerford; Presented by International BTC; Directors, Dr. E.A. Holstein, Dr. Gates M. Helms, Dr. Petty Shanks, Sean Kenealy; Stage Manager, Sean Kenealy; **Cast:** John Warren, Tim Torres, Amanda Sage Comerford, Jordan Knol, Laura Harrison, Kristopher Swift; February 24–March 7, 2010

Green Man by Don Nigro; Director, Brad Raimondo; Produced by Brad Raimondo and Pageant Wagon Productions; Design, Morgan Anne Zipf; **Cast:** Jared Sampson, Ugo Chukwu, Elizabeth Erwin, Laura Lee Williams, Elizabeth Romanksi; February 25–March 6, 2010

Crack'd Written and performed by Catherine Montgomery; Produced by … performance tube creation; Director, Heather Davies; February 25–March 6, 2010

A Voluminous Evening of Brevity by F. Scott Fitzgerald; Co-Produced with Dysfunctional Theater Company (for detailed listing see Dysfunctional Theater in this section); March 22–31, 2010

The Last Supper by Dan Rosen; Co-Produced with Rising Sun Performance Company (for complete details see listing under Rising Sun Performance Company); April 22–28, 2010

The Drafts Fest: Pre-Existing Condition by Tom Diriwatcher, Kelley Girod, Chris Kipiniak, Paul David Young, Suzanne Dottino, Joshua Conkel, Pia Wilson; Director, Tim Brownell, Randi Rivera, Marybeth Smith, Michael Rau, Heidi Grumelot, Chris Diercksen; Stage Manager, Randi Rivera; **Cast:** JB Rote, Nate Faust, Nick Maccarone, Brittany Bellizeare, Michael Weatherbee, J. Stephen Brantley, Reynaldo Piniella, Laurabeth Breya, Penny Pollack, Yesenia Tromp; May 13–22, 2010

UNDER St. Marks

Bigger Than I by Counting Squares Arts Collective; Director, Nick Sprysenski; Lighting, Jessica M. Burgess; Sound, Joshua Chase Gold; Audio/Visual, Kantarama Gahigiri; Choreographer, John O'Malley; Press, Emily Owens; **Cast:** Michael Barringer, Edward Davis, Matt Greenabaum, Dena Kology, Ryan Nicholoff, Chris Worley; Co-produced with Counting Squares Theater Company; June 4–20, 2009

Boatloads of Shame by Rick Blunt and Robert J. Gibbs; Director, Denis Henry; **Cast:** Rick Blunt; June 25–27, 2009

The Pumpkin Pie Show-In The Margins Written and performed by Clay McLeod Chapman; Co-Produced with The Management; August 5, 2009

MilkMilkLemonade by Joshua Conkel; Produced by The Management; Director, Isaac Butler; Stage Manager, Kelsi Welter; Lighting, Sabrina Braswell; Set, Jason Simms; Costumes, Sydney Maresca; Choreographer, Meredith Steinberg; **Cast:** Andy Phelan, Jess Barbagallo, Nikole Beckwith, Jennifer Harder, Michael Cyril Creighten; September 10–26, 2009

Michael Birch's One Man Hamlet by William Shakespeare; Produced by (a) muse Collective; Director, Bricken Sparacino; Original Music, Eric Chercover; Production Designer, luckydave; **Cast**: Michael Birch; October 11–November 1, 2009

The Pumpkin Pie Show-Commencement by Clay McLeod Chapman; **Cast:** Hanna Cheek; October 15–31, 2009

The Importance of Being Earnest by Oscar Wilde; Presented by Counting Squares Theatre; Director, Jordan Reeves; Set, Edward Davis; Costumes, John O'Malley & Melody Kology; Lighting, Joshua Chase Gold; Sound, Joshua Chase Gold; **Cast:** Tiffany Baker, Edward Davis, Michelle Foytek, Matt Greenbaum, Madeleine Maby, Ryan Nicholoff, Haas Regen, Jacques Roy, Chris Worley; November 5–21, 2009

Bail Out The Musical by Randi Berry, Dechelle Damien, Kimberlea Kressal, Karly Maurer, Benjamin Spradley; Co-Produced with Wreckio Ensemble; Director, Kimberlea Kressal; Music and Lyrics/Music Director, Will Larche; Choreographer, Felicia Blum; Stage Manager, Wayne Petro; Lighting, Pamela Kupper; Costumes,

Kimberlea Kressal; **Cast:** Randi Berry, Dechelle Damien, Anna Lamadrid, Billy Pelt, Benjamin Spradley, Lauren Turner Kiel; December 9–21, 2009

The Three Sisters by Anton Chekhov; Co-Produced with The Assembly Theater Company; Director, Jess Chayes; Dramaturg, Stephen Aubrey; **Cast:** Cecil Baldwin, Ben Beckley, Kate Benson, Christopher Hurt, Kate MacCluggage, Moti Margolin; January 20–30, 2010

Blood Potato by James McManus; Co-Produced with The BE Company; Director, Jordan Young; **Cast:** Dashiell Eaves, Tro Shaw, Ryan King, Ethan Matthews, Jessica Waxman; January 28–February 6, 2010

Tenderpits Produced by sh+sh=gold; Director, Nathan Schwartz; **Cast:** Anthony Johnston; February 24–March 7, 2010

Ramblings of a Gentleman Scumbag by John Murdock; Presented by Sanity Island; Director, JP Schuffman; Audio/Visual, Brian Douglas; **Cast:** John Murdock, Scout Durwood, Sara Gaddis, Sherri Eldin, Paulina Princess of Power, Joe Yoga, Natalie Underwood; February 24–March 7, 2010

Poppycock Written and directed by Jeremy Mather; Co-Produced with No Tea Productions and RadioTheater; Stage Managers, D. Robert Wolcheck, Lisa Nussbaum; Poster, Jeff Sproul; Press, Emily Owens; **Cast:** Alicia Barnatchez, James Patrick Cronin, Daiva Deupree, Sabrina Farhi, Michele McNally, James Richard, Jeff Sproul; April 8–24, 2010

Songs for a Future Generation by Joe Tracz; Director, Meg Sturiano; Set, Tristan Jeffers; Lighting, Grant Wilcox; Sound, Adam Swiderski; Stage Manager, Cristina Knutson; Choreographer, Nicole Beerman; Assistant Choreographer, Charissa Bertels; **Cast:** Cal Shook, Alex Teicheira, Joe Varca, Nick Lewis, Matt Barbot, Tara Giordano, Jennifer Harder, Jenny Gomez, Ronica Reddick, Yesenia Tromp, Joleen Wilkinson, Zoey Martinson, Joshua Conkel; April 29–May 15, 2010

Frigid New York – Fourth Annual Festival – February 24–March 7, 2010

1/4 Life Crisis Written and performed by Alison Lynne Ward; Director, Robert Sterling; UNDER St. Marks

2-Man No-Show by Mark Andrada, Ken Hall, and Isaac Kessler; Director, Mark Andrada; **Cast:** Ken Hall, Isaac Kessler; Kraine Theater

Aurelia and Imago Written and performed by Brianna Stark; Kraine Theater

The Bike Trip Written, directed and performed by Martin Dockery; Kraine Theater

The Bohemians by Aristophanes, adapted by Gabe Miner; Presented by Second Best Bed Productions; Kraine Theater

Bonne Nuit Poo Poo by Kristin Arnesen and Radoslaw Konopka; Presented by Theatre Reverb; **Cast:** Kristin Arnesen, Christopher Thomas Gilkey, Radoslaw Konopka, Daryl Carmen; UNDER St. Marks

Crack'd Written and performed by Catherine Montgomery; Presented by the performance tube; Director, Samantha Madely; Red Room

Fishbowl Written and performed by Mark Shyzer; Director, Evalyn Parry; Red Room

Floundering About (in an age of terror) Written, directed, and performed by David Lawson; Lighting, Mike Rozycki; Under St. Marks

Four Quarters Written and directed by Christopher Heath; Presented by Agony Productions; **Cast:** Omer Barnea, Margo Brooke Pellmar, Tamar Pelzig, Solomon Shiv; Kraine Theater

GREEN MAN by Don Nigro; Presented by Pageant Wagon; Director, Brad Raimondo; **Cast:** Jared Sampson, Ugo Chukwu, Elizabeth Erwin, Laura Lee Williams, Elizabeth Romanski; Red Room

It or Her by Alena Smith; Director, Jessi D. Hill; **Cast:** Brian McManamon; Red Room

Kill the Band by Kelly Dwyer; Director, Lucille Baker Scott; **Cast:** Kelly Dwyer, Mike Milazzo, Joe Yoga, Bamboo Silva; Under St. Marks

LATE NIGHTS WITH THE BOYS: confessions of a leather bar chanteuse Written and performed by Alex Bond with David Carson; UNDER St. Marks

Legs and All Written and performed by Peter Musante and Summer Shapiro; UNDER St. Marks

Let That Sh*t Go Written and presented by Live Blaggard; Kraine Theater

Mechanically Separated Meat by Jeff Belanger and Amanda Sage Comerford; Presented by International BTC; Director, E.A. Holstein; **Cast:** John Warren, Tim Torres, Jordan Knol, Laura Harrison, Kristopher Swift, Amanda Sage Comerford; Red Room

Medea by Euripides; Presented by No. 11 Productions; Director, Ryan Emmons; **Cast:** Willy Appelman, Julie Congress, Mark Ferguson, David Henry Gerson, Haley Greenstein, Nina Meijers, Roger Mulligan, Alison Novelli, Vanessa Wingerwrath; Kraine Theater

My Life of Crime Written and performed by Stephanie Stephenson; Presented by (ral-u-pop) Theatre; Director, Mary Joan Negro; The Red Room

No Traveler Written and performed by Penny Pollak; Presented by (a)muse collective; Director, Samantha Jones; UNDER St. Marks

Nobody's Token Created and performed by Keisha Zollar, Robert King, Jimmy Juste, Keith Cornell, Julia Morales, Lucas Hazlett; Red Room

Onomatopoeia Created and performed by Phillip Gerba, Lisa Soverino, David Ellis; Kraine Theater

pornStar Written and directed by Chris Craddock; Presented by Fancy Molasses; **Cast:** Anne Wyman; Red Room

price by David Fierro; Presented by Secret Weapon Theatre; Director, Kon Yi; **Cast:** Molly Ellen, David Klasko; Kraine Theater

Ramblings of a Gentleman Scumbag Written and performed by John Murdock; presented by (a)muse collective; UNDER St. Marks

Roll With It Written and performed by Maggie Nuttall; Red Room

T-O-T-A-L-L-Y! Written and performed by Kimleigh Smith; Director, Paula Killen; Red Room

Uncorseted by Patrick di Battista with Anne Laffoon; Presented by LaGoDi Productions and Shark Tank Players; Kraine Theater

Vodka Shoes Written and performed by Leslie Goshko; Director, Kyle Erickson; UNDER St. Marks

Readings

Boatloads of Shame by Rick Blunt and Robert J. Gibbs; Director, Denis Henry; June 25–27; *The Hunger Artist* by Nick Fesette, based on works by Franz Kafka; Co-Produced with Human Group; **Cast:** Nick Fesette, William Slater Welles, Stephen Arnoczy, Julia Crockett; July 16–18; *Donnie and The Monsters or the Sock Puppet Play* by Robert Gibbs; Director, Heidi Grumlot; March 25

HQ Rep.

Hound by John Patrick Bray; Director/Costumes, Rachel Klein; Stage Manager, Teressa Maranzano; Sound, Sean Gill; Makeup, Anita Rundles and Emily Taradash; Press, Emily Owens; **Cast:** Cavan Hallman, Ryan Knowles, Grant Boyd, Jack Corcoran, Meredith Dillard, Abigail Hawk, Blaine Peltier, Alyssa Schroeter, Elizabeth Stewart, Jason Stroud; Co-produced by HQ Rep. and Rachel Klein Productions as part of the Planet Connections Theatre Festivity; Robert Moss Theatre at 440 Studios; June 17–25, 2009

Hudson Warehouse

www.hudsonwarehouse.net

The Tempest by William Shakespeare, adapted and directed by Jerrod Bogard; Costumes, Drew Rosene; Choreographer, Maria Colaco; **Cast:** Sydney Stanton, Kym Smith, Kym Smith, Mavis Martin, Joshua David Bishop, Megan Cooper; Soldiers' and Sailors' Monument; June 4–28, 2009

Hamlet by William Shakespeare; Director, Nicholas Martin-Smith; **Cast:** Tyler D. Hall, Chris Behan, Michael C. Freeland; Soldiers' and Sailors' Monument; July 9–August 2, 2009

Human Flight Productions, Inc. & Gramily Entertainment

www.FUCTnyc.com

Cirque du Quoi?!? by FUCT; Director, Jeff Glaser; Choreographer, Lady Circus; **Cast:** Jordann Baker, Lori Barber, Sarah Bell, Kae Burke, Jon Crane, Joe Galan, Tommy Galan, Brian Gillespie, Ian Lassiter, Janio Marrero, Anya Sapozhnikova, Graham Skipper; Skybox at the House of Yes; May 21–June 6, 2009

I MEAN! Productions

The Brokenhearteds by Temar Underwood; Director, Pete Boisvert; Set, Kaitlyn Mulligan; Costumes, Sarah Riffle; Lighting, Daniel Winters; Sound, Kimberly Fuhr; Stage Manager, Saundra Yaklin; Original Music, Temar Underwood and Dan Deming; **Cast:** Mike Mihm, Jon Hoche, Temar Underwood, Andrea Marie Smith, Paco Tolson; Wings Theatre; September 11–26, 2010

Ignited States

Artistic Director, Elyzabeth Gorman; Producers, Martha Goode and Julie Griffith; Artistic Development, Michael Niederman; www.ignitedstates.com

Eli and Cheryl Jump by Daniel McCoy; Director, Nicole Watson; Stage Manager, Rebecca McBee; Lighting, David Bengali; Set, Blair Mielnik; Sound, Martha Goode; Production Manager, Nik Santiago; **Cast:** Charles Linshaw, Cassandra Vincent; Player's Loft; August 14–29, 2009

Don't Do Drugs Festival of short plays produced with Crosstown Playwrights; Stage Manager, Trey Johnson; Lighting, Duane Pagano; Sound, Martha Goode; Projections, David Bengali; Card Design, Hector Coris; Program Design, Eric Rice; Fight Choreography, Ian Roettger; included: *Don't Do Samurai Sword Crime: British Version* by Phlip Wilson, directed by Ilana Becker; **Cast:** Deven Anderson, Jennifer Gartner, Andrew Herzegovich, Anna Mosher, Collin Ware; *Don't Talk to Strangers* by Daniel McCoy, directed by Hondo Weiss-Richmond; **Cast:** Jordan Barbour; *Don't Hold The Doors While The Train is in the Station* by Bronwyn Clark, directed by Brittany Sager; **Cast:** Gwen Eyster, Devin Moriarity, Rob DiSario; *Don't Drink and F*ck* by Michael Niederman, directed by Elyzabeth Gorman; **Cast:** Deborah Radloff, Montgomery Sutton, Sarah Todes; *Don't Write a Bad Play* by Jack Karp, directed by Melissa Annis; **Cast:** Kurt Bantilam, Jennifer Dean, Adrien Saunders, Patrick Woodall; The Red Room; October 16–25, 2009

Immigrants Theatre Project

Sweet Karma by Henry Ong; Director, Marcy Arlin; **Cast:** Jojo Gonzales, Bonna Tek, Brian Hirono, Tina Chilip, Constance Parng; Queens Theatre in the Park; December 4–20, 2009

InProximity Theatre Company

www.InProximituTheatre.org

The Maiden's Prayer by Nicky Silver; Director, Terry Berliner; Set, James J. Fenton; Costumes, Tecsia Seufferlein; Lighting, Cory Pattak; Sound, Amy Altadonna; Stage Manager, Jenna Gottlieb; Producers, Jolie Curtsinger and Laurie Schaefer; ASM, Jasmin Sanchez; Assistant Costumes, Leslie Kelley; Casting Director, Matthew Maisto; Original Music, Amy Altadonna; **Cast:** Jonathan Todd Ross, Jolie Curtsinger, Laurie Schaefer, Josh Clayton, Ari Rossen; Theatre 54 at Shetler Studios; October 1–18, 2009

The Intentional Theatre Group

intentionaltheatregroup.net

NeverCracked by Daniel MacIvor & Gwydion Suilebhan; Director, Emerie Snyder; Lighting, Keith Truax; Costumes, Stacey Berman; Sound, Asa Wember; Co-Producer, Carissa Baker; **Cast:** Daniel Dugan, Candice Holdorf, Grace Kiley, Nick Lewis; Presented as part of The Midtown International Theater Festival; WorkShop Theater Company Main Stage; July 13–August 2, 2009

The International Theatre Laboratory Workshop

Welcome to the Woods by Alex van Warmerdam; Director, Erwin Maas; Lighting, Tim Cryan; Set, Laura Jellinek; **Cast:** Glory Gallo, Jonathan Co Green & Robin Riker; Witzenhausen Gallery (232); November 14–December 10, 2009

Inverse Theater Company

Cycatrix Adaptitude Written and directed by Kirk Wood Bromley; Costumes, Karen Flood; Sound, John Gideon; Original Sound, John Gideon; Masks, Jane Stein; Choreographer, Leah Schrager; **Cast:** Mick O'Brien, Sarah Engelke, Beth Ann Leone, Denice Kondik, Josephine Cashman; Various apartments in Manhattan; October 9–November 21, 2009

InViolet Repertory Theater

Kiss Me on the Mouth by Melanie Angelina Maras; Director, Stephen Adly Guirgis; **Cast:** Ken Matthews, Aubyn Philabaum, Megan Hart, Troy Lococo; Center Stage NY; November 5–21, 2009

Irondale Ensemble Project

alice...Alice...ALICE! Directors, Jim Niesen and Barbara MacKenzie-Wood; Stage Manager, Maria Knapp; Lighting, Randy Glickman; Set, Ken Rothchild; Audio/Visual, The Means of Production; **Cast:** Scarlet Maressa Rivera, Damen Scranton, Elizabeth Woodbury, Michael-David Gordon, Terry Greiss; Irondale Center; January 27–February 20, 2010

John Montgomery Theatre Company

www.jmtcinc.com

Preparation Hex by Bob Brader; Director, Suzanne Bachner; Lighting, Douglas Shearer; Technical Director, Douglas Shearer; Graphics, Michael Koch; **Cast:** Bob Brader; The Directors Studio; June 9–10, 2009

Diving Kitty Written and directed by Suzanne Bachner; Presented by The 34th Annual Samuel French Off-Off-Broadway Short Play Festival; **Cast:** Becky Byers and Bob Brader; The Mainstage Theater; July 14–19, 2009

Benny by Suzanne Bachner; Director, Trish Minskoff; Stage Manager, Douglas Shearer; Lighting, John Tees, III; Set/Costumes, Nadia Volvic; Production Associate, Russ Marisak; Graphics, Michael Koch; Press, Paul Siebold; **Cast:** Susan Barrett, Bob Celli, Tim Smallwood, Morgan Lindsey Tachco, Danny Wiseman; Presented as part of The Midtown International Theatre Festival; June Havoc Theatre; July 14–August 3, 2009

Spitting In The Face Of The Devil by Bob Brader; Director, Suzanne Bachner; Lighting, Douglas Shearer; Technical Director, Douglas Shearer; Graphics, Michael Koch; **Cast:** Bob Brader; Presented as part of The New York International Fringe Festival; Players Loft; August 14–29, 2009

Sex Ed by Suzanne Bachner; Director, Adam David Steele; Technical Director, Russ Marisak; Graphics, Michael Koch; Press, Paul Siebold, Off Off PR; **Cast:** Bob Brader, Judy Krause, Danny Wiseman; Presented as part of the Short Subjects Festival; Where Eagles Dare Studio Blackbird; September 19–30, 2009

Readings

The Raw Show Ongoing performance series of new raw material contributed by participating artists; Creators and Hosts: Suzanne Bachner, Bob Brader, Judy Krause; The Triple Crown Lounge; December 10

Jonathan Alexandratos and Cry Havoc Films

Death in Mozambique by Jonathan Alexandratos; Director, Michael Rutenberg; **Cast:** Matthew Murumba, Dan Pelonis, Namakula, Jan Di Pietro, Jean Neftin, Alex Ferrill; Cherry Pit; July 16–26, 2009

Josiah Theatre Works

The Exchange! Written and directed by Nickolas Long III; Set, Jon Long; Costumes, Michelle Anglin; Lighting, Jessica Harrison; Sound, Jessica Harrison; Stage Manager, Jon Long; House Manager, Lazette Mccants; Press, Black River Dance Studio; **Cast:** Andrew Young, Andria Womack, Sanyika Gray, Christina Ward, Alex Runnels, Chad Tucker, V.R. Small; Black River Center; May 31–June 20, 2009

Harlem Royalty Written and directed by Nickolas Long, III; Set, Michelle Anglin; Costumes, Michelle Anglin; Lighting, Jessica Harrison; Sound, Jon Long; Stage Manager, Jessica Harrison; Musical Director, Lory Dansby; **Cast:** Sanika Gray, Lori Dansby, Michelle Anglin, Nickolas Long III; Black River Center; July 6–August 6, 2009

The Exchange! Written and directed by Nickolas Long III; Sets/Lighting/Sound, Jon Long; Costumes, Michelle Anglin; Stage Manager, Andria Womack; Musical Director, Lori Dansby; **Cast:** Raymond C. Briscoe, Andria Womack, Tangi Guinn, David J. Cork, Sanyika Gray, V.R. Small, Sabrina Bryant, Jhonn De La Puente; Black River Center; December 6, 2009–January 10, 2010

The Unspoken Written and directed by Nickolas Long III; **Cast:** Marcos Luis, Kwasi Osei, Malachi Rivers, V.R. Small, Germaine Williams; Black River Center; May 15–23, 2010

Lena! Written and directed by Nickolas Long III; Costumes, Karl Kackson; Choreographer, Ekiuwa Asemota; Original Music, Nickolas Long III; Stage Manager, Andrea Womack; **Cast:** Dominique Andriese, G.K. Williams, Andrea Womack, Michael Chenervert, Kwasi Osei, V.R. Small, Melvin Mogoli, Colin Toomey, Jhonn De La Puente; Josiah Theatre Works; Reading: March 7–14, 2010; Full production: May 16–23, 2010

Just ASK Productions

What('s) Happen(s)(ed)(ing) in the Elevator... by P. Case Aiken III, Adam Samtur, Matthew Kagen; Director, Tom Berger; Set, Matt Brogan; Costumes, Juan Ibarra; Lighting, Guy Chachkes; Sound, Martha Goode; Stage Manager, Sydney Rais-Sherman; **Cast:** David J. Cork, Heather Lee Harper, Leo Goodman, Matt Pascua, Stephanie Pezolano, Joy Shatz, Reece Scelfo, Ari Vigoda, Miles Warner; The Red Room; May 23–June 15, 2009

Anyone for a Classy Threesome? Written and directed by P. Case Aiken, Matthew Kagen, Adam Samtur; Set/Lighting/Sound, Matt Brogan; Costumes, Juan Jose Ibarra; Stage Manager, Kymberly Tuttle; **Cast:** Dan Belmont, Leilani Drakeford, David Ebert, Greg Engbrecht, Olivia Gilliatt, Sivan Hadari, Katia Hoerning, Ginger Kearns, Lauren Lopez, Pat Reidy, Travis Stroessenreuther, Michael Wetherbee, Steve White, Christopher Williams; Kraine Theater; January 25– February 16, 2010

Kaleidoscope Theatre Company

www.kaleidoscopetheatre.org

Carl & Shelly, Best Friends Forever by Andrea Alton and Allen Warnock; Director, Janice L. Goldberg; Set, Arnold Bueso; Costumes, Anthony Catanzaro; Lighting, Daniel Winters; Sound, Jason Evans; Stage Manager, Seymour; Audio/ Visual, Daryl Lathon; Producing Director, Irwin Kroot; Associate Producer, Alec Stais; Graphics, Donna Heffernan; Composer, Kyle Gordon; ASM, Jessica Forella; Press, Lanie Zipoy; Artistic Director, Marshall Mays; **Cast:** Andrea Alton, Allen Warnock; Theater 3; February 6– February 28, 2010

Sex & Violence by Travis Baker; Director, Marshall Mays; Set, Arnold Bueso; Costumes, Anthony Catanzaro; Lighting, Daniel Winters; Sound, Sharath Patel; Stage Manager, Jessica Forella; Video, Michael Cornelison; Producing Director, Irwin Kroot; Fight Director, Michael Littig; Graphics, Donna Heffernan; Assistant Director, Eva Schelbaum; Press, Lanie Zipoy; **Cast:** Lauren Roth, Tyler Hollinger, Kendall Rileigh, Jake Millgard; Theater 3; February 7–February 28, 2010

kef theatrical productions

Artistic Director, Adam Fitzgerald; Producing Director, Lori Prince; Outreach and Education, Kimberly Strafford; Managing Director, M.J. Menter; General Manager, Dan Kolodny; Associate Producer, Adam Rosen; www.kefproductions.com

Lyric Is Waiting by Michael Puzzo; Co-produced with South Ark Stage; Director, Adam Fitzgerald; Stage Manager, Shannon O'Connor; Set, Joel Sherry; Lighting/Sound, Christopher J. Bailey; Costumes, Jessica Pabst; Associate Producer/Marketing Manager, M.J. Menter; Artistic Associate, Rob Maitner; **Cast:** Joe Masi, Kelly McAndrew, Lori Prince, Britt Whittle; W. Scott McLucas Studio at Irish Repertory Theatre; July 30–August 28, 2009

Killing Women by Marisa Wegrzyn; Co-produced with South Ark Stage; Director, Adam Fitzgerald; Set, Joel Sherry; Lighting/Sound, Christopher J. Bailey; Costumes, Lisa Zinni; Stage Manager, Kelly Hess; Online Marketing, Jim Bredeson; **Cast:** Lisa Brescia, Brian Dykstra, Autumn Hurlbert, Adam Kantor, Lori Prince, Michael Puzzo; Beckett Theatre on Theatre Row; May 13–June 5, 2010

Readings

Interlopers by Gary Lennon, directed by Adam Fitzgerald; **Cast:** Michael Anderson, Liche Ariza, Che Ayende, Tracee Chimo, Dashiell Eaves, Chad Goodridge, Michelle Pawk, Richard Petrochelli; November 2; *Killing Women* by Marisa Wegrzyn, directed by Adam Fitzgerald; **Cast:** Brian Dykstra, Colin Hanlon, Autumn Hurlbert, Kelly McAndrew, Lori Prince, Michael Puzzo; February 2

The Kitchen

www.thekitchen.org

Romeo and Juliet by William Shakespeare, adapted and directed by Pavol Liska and Kelly Copper; Presented by Nature Theatre of Oklahoma; Design, Peter Negrini; **Cast:** Anne Gridley, Robert M. Johanson, Elisabeth Conner; The Kitchen; December 19, 2009–January 16, 2010

Big Eater Created and choreographed by David Neumann; Stage Manager, Amelia Freeman-Lynde; Lighting, Dave Moodey; Costumes, Kaye Voyce; Sound, Katie Down, Kim Fuhr, David Neumann; Audio/Visual, Bryna Lieberman and Richard Sylvarnes; Original Music, Stew; **Cast:** Natalie Agee, Andrew Dinwiddie, Kennis Hawkins, Neal Medlyn, Frederick Neumann, Weena Pauly, Wills Rawls, Dominic, Tom Tancredi; March 4–13, 2010

Bellona, Destroyer of Cities Adapted and directed by Jay Scheib; Set, Peter Ksander; Lighting, Miranda K. Hardy; Costumes, Oana Botez-Ban; Sound, Catherine McCurry; Stage Manager, Kelly Shaffer; Audio/Visual, Carrie Mae Weems, Jay Scheib; **Cast:** Sarita Choudhury, Caleb Hammond, Mikeah Ernest Jennings, Jon Morris, William Nadylam, Kaneza Schaal, Tanya Selvaratnam, April Sweeney, Natalie Thomas; April 3–10, 2010

LaMaMa Experimental Theater Club (E.T.C.)

Executive Director & Artistic Director, Ellen Stewart; www.lamama.org

Days and Nights: Two Chekhovian Interludes Adapted and directed by Byongkoo Ahn; *The Doctor, A Chamber Opera* Music by Martin Herman, libretto by T. F. Curley; *A Joke, A Musical* by Young Hoon Lee; Music Arrangements and Direction, Heesun Hailey Chang; Costumes, Leon Wiebers; Set, Jose Ho; Sound, Curtis Curtis; **Cast:** Young Joon Chai, In Sook Kim, Sook In Em, Steven Sun, Choi Misun; The Annex; September 17–October 4, 2009

Pitch Poems by Gracie Leavitt; Co-produced with East Coast Artists and Richard Schechner; Director, Benjamin Mosse; Set, Kanae Heike; Lighting, Gina Scherr; Costumes, Michael Huang; Production Management, Jennifer Caster; **Cast:** Caleb Bark, Tuomas Hiltunen, Erin Layton, Jennifer Lim, Elka Rodriguez, Joe Tuttle, Wolfgang Zäh; First Floor Theatre; September 18–October 4, 2009

Poetry Electric Festival Curated by William Electric Black; The Club; October 4, 2009

The Traveling Players Present The Women of Troy Written, directed, and set by Theodora Skipitares; Stage Manager, Valerie Elithorpe; Lighting, Jesse Belsky; Costumes, Lara de Bruijn; Sound, Sxip Shirey; Puppets, Jane Catherine Shaw, Cecilia Schiller,Theodora Skipitares; Choreographer, Chris Maresca; Original Music, Sxip Shirey; **Cast:** Quince Marcum, Sheila Dabney, Caroyn Goelzer, Sam Stonefield, Sarah Alden, Alyson Perry, La Vonda Elam, Chris Maresca, Rachel Harrington, Jane Kelton, Catherine Garger, Aaron Long; The Annex; October 8–25, 2009

Radnevsky's Real Magic Original magic by Peter Samelson, text, story and direction by Paul Zimet; Co-produced with The Talking Band; Original Music, Ellen Maddow; Stage Manager, Hannah Woodward; Set, Anna Kiraly; Costumes, Kiki Smith; Lighting, Nan Zhang; Sound, David Wiggall; **Cast:** Dennis Kyriakos, Peter Samelson; First Floor Theatre; October 9–25, 2009

Clown Axioms Created and directed by Kendall Cornell in collaboration with the ensemble, Co-produced and performed by Clowns Ex Machina: Amanda Barron, Christine Bodwitch, Melinda Ferraraccio, Kathie Horejsi, Emily James, Ishah Janssen-Faith, Mona Le Roy, Judi Lewis Ockler, Julie Plumettaz, Maria Smushkovich, Virginia Venk); The Club; October 9–18, 2009

Troop Troupe Created, co-produced, and performed by Anonymous Ensemble: Cory Antiel, Lucrecia Briceno, Kiebpoli Calnek, Liz Davito, Eamonn Farrell, Jessica Weinstein; The Club; October 23–November 1, 2009

A Quarreling Pair: a triptych of small puppet plays by Jane Bowles, Lally Katz, and Cynthia Troup; Co-produced with Aphids Theater Australia; Director, Margaret Cameron; Lighting, Richard Vabre; Set, Margaret Cameron; Sound, Jethro Woodward; Puppetry, Sarah Kriegler; Original Music, Paul Bowles, Jane Bowles, Jethro Woodward; **Cast:** Caroline Lee, Sarah Kriegler; First Floor Theatre; October 29–November 8, 2009

Celebrating Ellen A gala performance to celebrate La MaMa's 48th Season and Ellen's 90th Birthday; Featuring: H.T. Chen and Dancers, Bill Irwin, John Kelly, Potri Ranka Manis, Meredith Monk and Vocal Ensemble, Peggy Shaw, Muna Tseng, Lois Weaver, The Great Jones Repertory; The Annex; November 1, 2009

The Crisp Choreographer by H.T. Chen, music by Fitz Patton; Lighting, Stephen Petrilli; Presented and performed by H.T. Chen and Dancers; The Annex; November 5–8, 2009

Agamemnon by Aeschylus, translated by Alexander Harrington; Co-produced with Eleventh Hour Theatre Company; Director, Alexander Harrington; Stage Manager, A.J. Dobbs; Set/Lighting, Solomon Weisbard; Costumes, Rebecca Bernstein; Choreographer, Renouard Gee; Original Music, Michael Sirotta; **Cast:** Valois Mickens, Robert Ierardi, Jessica Crandall, Sharon-Albertine Dreze, Miguel Edson, Jason Reiff, Patrick James Lynch, Matt Swantson, Peter Tedeschi, Chris Caron, Shigeko Sara Suga, Sarah Vasilas, Gillian Wiggin, Alyssa Wilmoth, Georgia Southern, Margaret O'Connell, Marcie Henderson; The Annex; November 12–29, 2009

Twelfth Night by William Shakespeare; Co-produced with Czechoslovak-American Marionette Theatre and GOH Productions; Director, Vít Horejš; Stage Manager, Nephrii Amenii; Lighting, Federico Restrepo; Set, Emily Wilson; Costumes, Emily Wilson & Michelle Beshaw; Producer, Bonnie Sue Stein; Marionettes, Milos Kasal; **Cast:** Deborah Beshaw, Michelle Beshaw, Vít Horejš; First Floor Theatre; November 12–29, 2009

She Turned on the Light Written and directed by Wendy Woodson; Design, Kathy Couch; **Cast:** Marina Libel; The Club; November 13–22, 2009

Diagnosis of a Faun Inspired by *Afternoon of a Faun*; Co-produced with Tamar Rogoff Performance Project; Creator/Director/Choreographer, Tamar Rogoff; Stage Manager, Sharon Mashihi; Lighting, Tony Giovannetti; Set/Costumes, Robert Eggers; Sound, Leon Rothenberg; Choreographer, Tamar Rogoff; Original Music, Leon Rothenberg; **Cast:** Lucie Baker, Emily Pope-Blackman, Dr. Donald Kollisch, Gregg Mozgala; The Annex/Ellen Stewart Theatre; December 3–20, 2009

Romeo and Juliet by William Shakespeare; Presented by Theatro Patological; Director, Dario D'Ambrosi; Lighting, Federico Restrepo; Set, Aurora Buzzetti; Costumes, Denise Greber; **Cast:** Enrique Esteve, Ashley C. Williams, Neimah Djourabchi, Brian Waters; First Floor Theatre; December 3–13, 2009

Oh, Those Beautiful Weimar Girls! by Mark Altman and Ildiko Nemeth; Co-produced with New Stage Theatre Company; Director, Ildiko Lujza Nemeth; Set, Jason Sturm; Lighting, Federico Restrepo; Costumes, Javier Bone Carbone; Sound, Paul Radelat & Steve Wallace; Choreographers, Julie Atlas Muz & Peter Schmitz; Original Music, Jon Gilbert Leavitt; Music Selection, Ildiko Nemeth; **Cast:** Chris Tanner, Dana Boll, Kaylin Lee Clinton, Gary Hernandez, Markus Hirnigel, Lisa Kathryn Hokans, Madeline James, Denice Kondik, Sarah Lemp, Florencia Minniti, Fabiyan Pemble-Belkin, John Rosania, Christine Ann Ryndak, Jeanne Lauren Smith; The Club; December 4–13, 2009, encored January 29–February 7, 2010

Something to Say Raw Created and performed by Anthony Rodriquez; The Club; December 18–19, 2009

Christmas in Nickyland Holiday cabaret curated by Nicky Paraiso; The Club; December 20, 2009

The Devil You Know Written and directed by Ping Chong; Produced by Ping Chong and Company in association with Phantom Limb Company; Original Music/Marionette Design, Eric Sanko;Set, Jessica Grindstaff; Lighting, Andrew

Hill; Sound, Benjamin Furiga; Projections, Maya Ciarrocchi & Gia Wolff; Stage Manager, Meghan Williams; **Cast:** Sabrina D'Angelo, Oliver Dalzell, Marta Mozelle MacRostie, Ronny Wasserstrom, Anne Posluszny, Jenny Campbell, Matthew Leabo, Edouard Sanko, Michael Schupbach; Ellen Stewart Theatre; December 30, 2009–January 24, 2010

Medea and Its Double Co-produced with Seoul Factory for the Performing Arts from South Korea; First Floor Theatre; January 7–24, 2010

Everyone Who Looks Like You; Created and presented by Hand2Mouth Company (Oregon); The Club; January 8–17, 2010

The Mess You Made Album release party and performance by the Brooklyn producer and emcee duo AbCents and Postell; The Club; January 24, 2010

The Garage by Zdenko Mesaric; Co-produced with Youth Theatre of Croatia; Director, Ivica Buljan; Set, Slaven Tolj; Costumes, Ana Savic Gecan; **Cast:** Ksenija Marinkovic, Frano Maskovic, Sreten Mokrovic, Barbara Prpic, Doris Saric Kukuljica, Nina Violic, Vedran Zivolic, Goran Bogdan, Mladen Badovinac, Sasa Antic; The Annex/Ellen Stewart Theatre; January 28–February 7, 2010

Cocktail Cabaret Conceived and Directed by Pablo Vela; The Club; January 30 &31, February 6 & 7, 2010

Lonely Soldier Monologues by Helen Benedict; Director, William Electric Black; Sets/Lighting, Federico Restrepo; Costumes, Tilly Grimes; Production Coordinator/Manager, Chriz Zaborowski; Sound/Drums, Jim Mussen; Choreography, Jeremy Lardieri; **Cast:** Allison Troesch, Athena Colon, Cara Liander, Julia A. Grob, Kim Weston-Moran, Macah Coates, Verna Hampton and Jamaal Kendall; First Floor Theatre; February 5–7, 2010

Heavy Like the Weight of a Flame by James Gabriel and R. Ernie Silva; **Cast:** R. Ernie Silva; First Floor Theatre; February 11–14, 2010

Shakuntala and the Ring of Recognition by Kalidasa; Co-Produced by Magis Theatre Company; Director, George Drance; Stage Manager, Stephanie Brookover; Lighting, Federico Restrepo; Set, Gian Marco Lo Forte; Costumes, Cathy Shaw; Choreographer, Saju George; **Cast:** Katryna Cordova, George Drance, Josey Flyte, Casey Groves, Erika Iverson, Jarde Jacobs, Walker Lewis, Wendy Mapes, Soneela Nankani, Sajeev Pillai, Margi Sharp, Colista Turner, Taylor Valentine; The Annex; February 11–28, 2010

Kinky & Sweet Presented by Waldo's Gotham City Jazz Masters; The Club; February 12, 2010

Shadow A festival of concert playreading celebrating Black History Month; Curator/Director, George Ferencz; First Floor Theatre; February 18–21, 2010

Hitohira 2010–The Last Golden Bat Created and directed by Yutaka Higashi, music by Itsuro Shimoda; Presented by the Tokyo Kid Brothers; First Floor Theatre; February 25–28, 2010

Don't Peek Created and Performed by Woof Nova: Annie Kunjappy, Daniel Allen Nelson, Morgan van Prelle Pecelli and Carla Bosnjak; The Club; February 26–March 7, 2010

The Realm of Darkness Based on *The Power of Darkness* by Leo Tolstoy, translated by Marvin Kantor with Tanya Tulchinsky; Director/Design, Zishan Ugurlu; **Cast:** Eugene Lang College Students; The Annex/Ellen Stewart Theatre; March 4–7, 2010

La Vie Materielle Created and directed by Irina Brook, based on an interpretation of Marguerite Duras's collection of essays and Virginia Woolf's *A Room of One's Own*; Presented in association with French Institute Alliance Française; Stage Manager, Kiki Bertocci; Lighting, Ben Pilat; Set, Katheryn Monthei; **Cast:** Nicole Ansari, Winsome Brown, Joan Juliet Buck, Sadie Jemmett, Yibin Li; Co-produced with French Institute Alliance Francaise; First Floor Theatre; March 11–21, 2010

Caligula Maximus by Alfred Preisser and Randy Weiner; Director, Christopher McElroen; Set, Evan Collier; Costumes, Laura Clarke; **Cast:** JerZ Short, Justine Joli, Ryan Knowles, Anya Sapozhnikova, Tim DAX, Luqman Brown, Roxanne Edwards, Myra Adams, Jessica Krueger, Miriam Tabb, David King, Andrews

Landsman, Jeff Goldfisher, Aaron Strand, Raheem Green; The Annex/Ellen Stewart Theatre; March 12–April 10, 2010

The Gilded Red Cage Written and performed by Silvester Lavrik and Katarina Morhacova; Presented by BaPoDi (Slovakia); Photography Exhibit, Radek Jahudka; Presented in association with the New York Public Library, the Consulate General of Slovakia in New York and Plus421 Foundation; The Club: March 13–14, 2010

Three One Acts by Mrozek by Slavomir Mrozek; *Enchanted Night* directed by Ruis Woertendyke; *Out at Sea* directed by Grant Kretchik; *Serenade* directed by Cosmin Chivu; Sets, Gian Marco Loforte; Music, George Robson; Sound, Scott O'Brien; **Cast:** Grant Kretchik, Jon Gabrielson, Lilah Shreeve, Kristen Vaphides, Julie Robles, Dorothy James Loechel, Matt Alford, Ruis Woertendyke, Christopher Azara, Steve Lesce, Chelsea Roe, Kehinde Koyejo, Talitha Custer, George Robson, Giacomo Rocchini; The Club; March 19–21, 2010

Thirst: Memory of Water Created and directed by Jane Catherine Shaw; Set, Gian Marco Lo Forte; Costume and Puppet Design, Jane Catherine Shaw; Stage Manager, Jamila Khan; Lighting, Jeff Nash; Choreographer, Hillary Spector; Original Music, David Patterson; **Cast:** Sophia Remolde, Ora Fruchter, Spica Wobbe, Margot Fitzsimmons, Kristine Haruna Lee, Cybele Kaufmann, Sheila Dabney, Eva Lansberry; Voices: Valois Mickens, Karen Kandel, Black-Eyed Susan, Emme Bonilla, Nodoka Yoshida; First Floor Theatre; March 25–April 11, 2010

A Mind The Art Anthology Included: *What if?, DIE,* and *Under the Veil*; Co-produced with Mind the Art Entertainment; March 26–28, 2010

Donald Does Dusty Created and performed by Diane Torr; The Club; April 5, 2010

Too Short To Suck by Carla Bosnjak, Ulrich Fladl, Anna Hendrick, Craig Mungavin and Sarah Murphy; The Club; April 9 & 10, 2010

Scythian Stones Created and directed by Virlana Tkacz, created and presented by Yara Arts Group; Co-director, Watoku Ueno; Design, Watoku Ueno; Stage Manager, Yorie Akikba; Movement, Katja Kolcio, Costume Construction, Keiko Obremski, Original Music, Nurbek Serkebaev and Julian Kytasty; **Cast:** Nina Matvienko, Kenzhegul Satybaldieva, Ainura Kachkynbek kyzy, Tonia Matvienko, Cecilia Arana, Susan Hwang, Maria Sonevytsky, Nurbek Serkebaev, Julian Kytasty; First Floor Theatre; April 16–May 2, 2010

Post Modern Living by Richard Sheinmel; Director, Jason Jacobs; Stage Manager, Heather Olmstead; Lighting, Timothy M. Walsh; Set, John McDermott; Costumes, Jen Caprio; Sound, Tim Schellenbaum; Original Music, Clay Zambo; **Cast:** Frank Blocker, Briana Davis, Mick Hilgers, Wendy Merritt, Chris Orbach, Catherine Porter, Richard Sheinmel; The Club; April 16–May 2, 2010

Powerful Boeyond Power Cabaret benefit for victims of the Haitian earthquake; Co-produced with New York University Tisch School of the Arts; The Club; April 20, 2010

Pandibulan by Kinding Sindaw; Conceived, choreographed and directed by Potri Ranka Manis; Lighting, Federico Restrepo; Sets, Jun Maida; Production Manager, Diane Camino; **Cast:** Amira Aziza, Rose Yapching, Emil Almirante, Nodiah Biruar, Zeana Llamas, Annie Llamas, Cecille de los Santos, Mohamad Zebede Dimaporo, Alex Sarmiento, Jade Enriquez, Shaina Gonzalez, Renia Gardner, Diane Camino, Lisa Parker, Malaika Queano, Guro Frank Ortega and Oliver Torretejo; The Annex; April 22, 2010

Five Days in March by Toshiki Okada, translated by Aya Ogawa; Co-produced with Witness Relocation; Director, Dan Safer; Lighting, Jay Ryan; Set, Jay Ryan; Costumes, Deb O; Sound, Ryan Maeker; Projections, Kaz Phillips; Choreographer, Dan Safer; Original Music, Dave Malloy; **Cast:** Mike Mikos, Sean Donovan, Wil Petre, Heather Christian, Kourtney Rutherford, Chris Giarmo, Laura Berlin Stinger; The Annex/Ellen Stewart Theatre; May 6–23, 2010

Breath on the Mirror Conceived and directed by Beth Skinner; Presented by Triple Shadow; Lighting/Projections, Paul Clay; Set, Jun Maeda; Costumes, Mari Andrejco; Mask and Puppets, Windrose Morris; Original Music, Edward Herbst; **Cast:** Mari Andrejco, Gabrielle Autumn, Andrew Belcher, Lucy Kaminsky & Richard Saudek; First Floor Theatre; May 6–23, 2010

Brazil Nuts by Susan Jeremy & Mary Fulham; Co-produced with Watson Arts; Director, Mary Fulham; Stage Manager, Sarah Rae Murphy; Lighting, Federico Restrepo; Set, Gian Marco Lo Forte; Costumes, Ramona Ponce; Sound, Tim Schellenbaum; Music Editing, Livia Stevenson; **Cast:** Susan Jeremy; The Club; May 7–23, 2010

Leap! Arteon in Motion A multi-media project of Arteon New York Art Foundation Inc.; The Club; May 19, 2010

Kisses, Bites and Scratches Music by Steve Margoshes, libretto and lyrics by Paul Foster; **Cast:** Bertilla Baker; The Club; May 24 & 31, 2010

Great Jones Variations Five short dance pieces; Co-produced with The Great Jones Repertory Company; Directors, George Drance, Ozzie Rodriguez, Elizabeth Swados, Zishan Ugurlu, Perry Young; Original Music by Elizabeth Swados, Ellen Stewart, Michael Sirotta, Yukio Tsuji, Heather Paauwe, Richard Cohen; The Annex/Ellen Stewart Theatre; May 27–30, 2010

Red Mother Written and performed by Muriel Miguel; Presented by Spiderwoman Theater; Director/Choreography, Murielle Borst; Co-produced with Loose Change Productions; First Floor Theatre; May 27, 2010

Laurie Beechman Theater

The Jackie Look Written and performed by Karen Finley; Laurie Beechman Theater; February 6–April 24, 2010

The After Party Weekly series created and hosted by Brandon Cuttrell; Music Director, Ray Fellman; Featuring Becca Johnson and Gabrielle Stravelli; ongoing

Lighthouse Theatre

www.thelighthousetheatre.com

Lunatic: A Love Story by Rachel Adler; **Cast:** Rachel Adler; Center Stage NY; May 27–June 12, 2010

Literally Alive Children's Theatre

www.literallyalive.com

A Christmas Carol by Brenda Bell; Director, Carlo Riviccio; Sets/Lighting, Josh Iacovelli; Costumes, Dustin Cross; Choreographer, Stefanie Smith; Original Music, Michael Sgouros; **Cast:** Dustin Cross, Ryan Cavanaugh, Eric Fletcher, Brianna Hurley, Stefanie Smith, Britney Steele; Players Theatre & Players Loft; November 21– December 30, 2009

The Living Theatre

Founder, Judith Malina; Associate Artistic Director, Brad Burgess; www.livingtheatre.org

Red Noir by Anne Waldman; Director/Set, Judith Malina; Lighting, Richard Retta; Co-Set Design, Ilion Troya and Richard Retta; Music Director, Sheila Dabney; Assistant Director, Brad Burgess; **Cast:** Camilla de Araujo, Brent Barker, Vinie Burrows, Maylin Castro, Ben Cerf, Sheila Dabney, Jay Dobkin, Luis Christian Dilorenzi, Erin Downhour, Eno Edet, Tjasa Ferme, Ondina Frate, Gemma Forbes, Maria Guzman, Home Hynes, Silas Inches Albert Lamont, Jenna Kirk, Celeste Moratti, Martin Munoz, Lucie Pohl, Marie Pohl, Erik Rodriguez, Judi Rymer, Anthony Sisco, Lori Summers, Enoch Wu, Kennedy Yanko; December 7, 2009–January 31, 2009

Non-resident Productions

An Evening with Melba Phelps Belk by James D'Entremont; Presented by A Gathering of the Tribes; Director, David Vining; Original Music, Barry Oremland; **Cast:** Christine Donnelly, Richard Sheinmel, Nomi Tichman; June 28, 2009

Sandy the Dandy and Charlie McGee by Mat Sanders and Guerrin Gardner; Director, Nate Dushku; Choreographer, Alisa Claire; Original Music, Ryland Blackinton and Russel Kirk; **Cast:** Geoffrey Barnes, Jeffrey Cutaiar; July 30–August 1, 2009

Lizzie Borden Music by Steven Cheslik-DeMeyer and Alan Stevens Hewitt, lyrics by Steven Cheslik-DeMeyer and Tim Maner; Book, additional music, and direction by Tim Maner; Presented by Took An Axe Productions; Musical Director, Alan Stevens Hewitt; Set, Caleb Levengood, Costumes, Bobby Frederick Tilley II; Sound, Jamie McElhinney; Lighting, Christian DeAngelis; **Cast:** Marie-France Arcilla, Lisa Birnbaum, Carrie Cimma, Jenny Fellner; September 10–October 17, 2009

Children At Play by Jordan Seavey; Presented by CollaborationTown; Director, Scott Ebersold; Set, David Newell; Costumes, Nikki Moody; Lighting, Scott Bolman; Sound, Brandon Wolcott and Daniel Kluger; Choreographer, Boo Killebrew; **Cast:** Rachel Craw, Geoffrey Decas, John Halbach, Drew Hirschfield, Boo Killebrew, Susan Louise O'Connor, Jay Potter, Jennifer Dorr White; November 5–21, 2009

Manhattanpotamia IV Director/Design, Michael Pauley; Presented by Hyperion Theatre Project; **Cast:** Nina Ashe, Sara Gaddis, Cooper Shaw, Christopher Salazar, Lori Sommer, Barbara Michaels, Michael Pauley, Loren Dunn, Tara Bradway, Jessica Ritacco, Kevin Gilligan, Watts, Brendan Allred, Cory Antiel, Stacy Price, Celeste Moratti, Alex Hill, Edward Weathers; April 19–29, 2010

The Looking Glass Theatre

lookingglasstheatrenyc.com

Ask Someone Else, God by Kenneth Nowell; Director, Shari Johnson; Lighting, David Monroy; Set, Julia Noulin-Mérat; Costumes, Jessica Lustig; Soundscape, Shari Johnson; Original Music, Kenneth Nowell; **Cast:** Adriana Disman, Ricky Dunlop, Will Ellis, Kristen Niché Jeter, Courtney Kochuba, Janelle Mims, Mary Regan, Hanlon Smith-Dorsey; September 9–October 4, 2009

Ready, Set, Story! How Katie Saved the Sneaky Spider's Tales by Emily Paul; Director, Rose Ginsberg; Set, Zane Enloe; Costumes, Rachel Soll; Lighting, David Monroy; **Cast:** Andrew Ash, Renée-Michele Brunet, Lauren Kelly Benson, Andrew S. Davies, Brian Hirono, Elisa Pupko, Emily Tucker; October 10–November 22, 2009

Are You There, Zeus? It's Me, Electra Written and directed by Aliza Shane; Set, Zane Enloe; Costumes, David Moyer; Lighting, David Monroy; Choreographer, Matthew Rini; **Cast:** Elizabeth Bove, Dani Cervone, Carley Colbert, Jan Di Pietro, Marci Koltonuk, Kevin Mitchell, Elisa Pupko, Michael Alan Read, Matthew Rini, Tom Slot; Roy Arias Off Broadway Theatre; October 29–November 22, 2009

Ready, Set, Story! by Emily Paul; Director, Rose Ginsberg; Set, Theresa Rivera; Costumes, Rachel Soll; Lighting, David Monroy; Stage Manager, Melinda Prom; **Cast:** Vinny DiCristo, Stephen Ehrlich, Amanda Hopper, Anthony Labresco, Stacy Osei-Kuffour, Melissa Sussman, Stefanie Tara; March 13–April 25, 2010

70 Million Tons by Terri McKinstry; Director, Chanda Calentine; Set, Theresa Rivera; Costumes, Rachel Soll; Lighting, David Monroy; Stage Manager, Yoleidy Rosario; **Cast:** Ivory Aquino, Chaz Graytok, Dennelle Heidi Clarke, Ben Harrison, Ashley Lovell, Arash Mokhtar, Johanna Perry, Mary Beth Walsh, Jessica Wohlander, Kelly Zekas; April 5–28, 2010

Non-resident Production

The Comedy of Errors by William Shakespeare; Presented by Moses Mogilee; Director, J.M. Holmes; Stage Manager, Graeme Humphrey; Lighting, Brandon Scott Hughes; Set, Brandon Scott Hughes; Costumes, Christine A. Kahler; **Cast:** Brandon Scott Hughes, Steven Bidwell, John Bodycombe, Robert Spaulding, Zoe Sjogerman, Josh Bowen, Jennifer Gartner, Elaine Hayhurst, Nikolai Volkoff, Anna C. Mosher, Kara Townsend, Amy M. Backes, Rachel Kincaid, Morgan Powell, Joe Berardi, Molly Mermelstein, Justin D. Quackenbush, Mark Robert Ryan; May 6–23, 2010

Love Street Theatre

Shining Days Written and directed by Julie S. Halpern; Stage Manager, John Simmons; Lighting, Alison May; Set, Seth Weine; **Cast:** Patricia Duran, Sarah Koestner, Megan O'Leary, Michael Siktberg, Jenne Vath, David Lloyd Walters; Producers Club Royal Theatre; June 17– 28, 2009

Maieutic Theatre Works (MTWorks)

www.mtworks.org

Look After You by Louise Flory; Director, David Stallings; Stage Manager, Howard Tilkin; Lighting, Dan Gallagher; Set, Julie Griffith; Costumes, Vin Victorio; Sound, Martha Goode; Producer, Julie Griffith; Dramaturg, David Stallings; Marketing/PR, Antonio Minino; Graphics, Lindsay Moore; Photographer, Kate Enman; **Cast:** Jason Altman, Lowell Byers, Louise Flory, Adi Kurtchik; Presented as part of the New York International Fringe Festival 2009; The SoHo Playhouse; August 14–29, 2009

Barrier Island by David Stallings; Director, Cristina Alicea; Set, Craig Napoliello; Costumes, David Withrow; Lighting, Dan Gallagher; Sound, Martha Goode; Stage Manager, Carolynn Richer; Producers, Julie Griffith and Martha Goode; Production Manager, Courtenay Drakos; Dialect Coach, Barrie Kreinik; ASM, Nichol C. Rosas-Ullman; Marketing & Press Relations, Antonio Minino; **Cast:** Alex Bond, David L. Carson, Anthony Crep, Mark Emerson, Anne Clare Gibbons-Brown, Carol Hickey, Stu Richel, Frankie Seratch, Jennifer Laine Williams; Center Stage NY; April 30–May 22, 2010

Mainspring Collective

Artistic Director, Hilary Krishnan; Executive Director, Jenna Weinberg; Artistic Associates, Dara Malina, Laine Bonstein, Jimmy Juste; Literary Manager, Hannah Smith; Playwrights: Daniel John Kelley, Bridget Fallen, Alexandria LaPorte, Demetrius Wren; www.mainspringcollective.com

'Twas the Night Before...MONSTERS! by Daniel John Kelley; Directors, Hilary Krishnan and Dara Malina; Production Manager, Laura Archer; Graphic/Video Design, Shawn Rice; Graphic/Art Design, Christian 'Kitty' Schmitt; **Cast:** Jenna Weinberg, Laine Bonstein, Nia Fairweather, Jimmy Juste, Mark DeFrancis, Owen Scott, Aaron Matteson; Brooklyn Lyceum; December 12–20, 2009

Robin Hood: Prince of...MONSTERS! Written and conceived by Daniel John Kelley; Brooklyn Lyceum; February 13–21, 2010

Making Books Sing

Tea with Chachaji Music by Denver Casado, book & lyrics by Gwynne Watkins; Director, Rajendra Ramoon Maharaj; Stage Manager, Ellis C. Arroyo; Lighting, Douglas Cox; Set, Cory Einbinder; Costumes, Leslie Bernstein; Sound, William Grady; Music Director, Tim Rosser; **Cast:** Stephanie Klemons, Tony Mirrcandani, Raja Burrows, Jose Sepulveda, Soneela Nankani; Various locations throughout NYC; January 25–February 11, 2010

Manhattan Children's Theatre

www.mctny.org

Click Clack Moo by James E. Grote; Director, Chris Alonzo; Stage Manager, Chess Venis; Lighting, Christina Watanabe; Set, Cully Long; Costumes, Annie Arthur; Sound/Technical Director, John D. Ivy; Original Music, George Howe; Choreographer, Andrea Steiner; **Cast:** Giselle D'Souza, Devin Elting, Josh Ramos, Sasha Kraichnan, Hannah Jane McMurray; September 19–November 8, 2009

The Snow Queen by Kristin Walter; Director, Bruce Merrill; Stage Managers, Chess Venis, Christie Love Santiago; Lighting, Anjeanette Stokes; Set, Cully Long; Costumes, Sarah Reever; Sound/Technical Director, John D. Ivy; Choreographer, Janel Cooke; Music Director, Nathan Atkinson; **Cast:** Mary Anne Furey, Elias John Ruperto, Kelsey Mahoney, Caroline Kittrell, Martin Glyer, Shanley Pascal, Taryn Turney, Curtis Roth, Megan Kip, Steven Bidwell; November 14, 2009–January 3, 2010

The Little Mermaid by Mike Kenny; Director, Bruce Merrill; Stage Manager, Christie Love Santiago; Lighting, Eli Kaplan-Wildmann; Set, Elisha Shaefer; Costumes, Amy Sutton; Sound/Technical Director, John D. Ivy; Choreographer, Lauren Axelrod; **Cast:** Stephanie Wortel, David Thorton, Angelyn Eve Faust, Adam Patterson; Manhattan Children's Theatre; January 9–February 21, 2010

The Velveteen Rabbit by Chris Alonzo; Director, Chris Alonzo; Stage Manager, Chess Venis; Lighting, Annie Arthur; Set/Drawings, Michael Arthur; Costumes, Cully Long; AV Design/Technical Director/Animator, John D. Ivy; Original Music, Chris Alonzo; **Cast:** Jodie Pfau, Griffin DuBois, Jeffrey Martin, Robyn Buchanan King, Drew Honeywell, John D. Ivy, Curtis Roth, Alyssa Chase; February 27–April 18, 2010

Stanley's Party Book by Caroline Cala, music and lyrics, Seth Bisen-Hersh; Director, Bruce Merrill; Stage Manager, Livia Hill; Lighting, Anjeanette Stokes; Set, Cully Long; Costumes, Nora Gustuson; Sound/Technical Director, John D. Ivy; Choreographer, Erin Porvaznika; Music Director, James Olmstead; Props, Cully Long; **Cast:** Barry Shafrin, Crystal Davidson, Kyra Bromberg, Ryan Makely, Derek Rommel; April 24–May 31, 2010

Manhattan Repertory Theatre

www.manhattanrep.com

Getting Even With Shakespeare by Matt Saldarelli; Director, Laura Konsin; Lighting, Matt Bellas; Costumes, Kelly Honan; Original Music, Will Aronson; Fight Director, Monica Blaze Leavitt; **Cast:** John D'Arcangelo, Martin Glyer, Rachel Halper, Ben Holmes, Eliza Huberth, Ari Jacobson, Patrick Plzzolorusso; January 27–February 6, 2010

Wings of Fire Written and directed by Hayley A. Green; Choreographer, Ashley Peter; **Cast:** Sky Bennett, Chance Blakeley, Peyton Crim, Brent Gobel, Austin Riley Green, Amara Haaksman, Stephanie Joiner, Michael Jones, Melissa McKamie, Ashley Peter, Cecilia Reynoso, Abby C. Smith, Gina-Marie Vincent, Amanda Wertz; March 17–19, 2010

Manhattan Theatre Source

www.theatresource.org

The Roses on the Rocks by Ellen Boscov; Director, Richard Caliban; Stage Manager, Paige Van Den Burg; Lighting, Kia Rogers; Set, Edward Morris; Costumes, Cathy Hirschberg; Sound, Ien DeNio; Original Music, Rana Santacruz; **Cast:** Rachel Jones, Laura Montes, Scott Sowers, Fulvia Vergel; June 4–27, 2009

Caravaggio by Richard Vetere; Co-production with Malet Street Productions; Director, Richard Betere; **Cast:** Andrea Piedimonte-Bodini, Eric Zeisler, Esther Barlow, Dana Pona, Mike Hill, David Barrett; June 14–16, 2009

Broadville by Romy Nordlinger & Adam Burns; Director, Ben Gougeon; Stage Manager, Miriam Hyfler; **Cast:** Nana Mensah, Carmen Rae Meyers, Romy Nordlinger, Megan Simard; November 1–4, 2009

3 Days in the Park by Paul Jordan; Director, Jessica McVea; Stage Manager, Brian Schlanger; Lighting, Christina Hurtado; Audio/Visual, Christina Hurtado; Producing Artist, Jenny D Green; **Cast:** Cindy Keiter, Mark Ellmore, Purva Bedi, Mark Epperson, Paul DiPaula, Libby Collins; November 12–14, 2009

In Loco Parentis by Michael DeVito; Director, Jonathan Warman; **Cast:** Desmond Dutcher, Kristin Katherine Shields, Ali N. Khan, Ralph Pochoda; November 18–21, 2009

Witch Christmas! Written and directed by Sharon Fogarty; Co-produced with Making Light; Stage Manager, Matt Quint; **Cast:** Karen Christie Ward, Susan Secunda, Rachel Korowitz, Amy Evans, Claire Hilton, James Hilton, Natalie Ward, Allison Snyder, Jeff Scherer, Peter Aguero, Sharon Fogarty; December 21–23, 2009

It's A Wonderful (One Man Show) Life! Written and performed by Jason Grossman; Co-production with Funny...Sheesh and Making Light; Director, Sharon Fogarty; December 21–23, 2009

Love (Awkwardly) Written and directed by John Rotondo and Maryann Carolan; Co-production with Fourteen Out of Ten Productions and Union Catholic Performing Arts Company; Stage Manager, Jenna Lloyd; Lighting, Colleen Cassidy; Audio/Visual, Jenna Lloyd; Props, Eric Vollero and Schuyler Peck; Choreographer, Emily Eger; **Cast:** Bobby Dyckman, Greg Gedman, Arielle Gonzalez, Conor McDonough, Sammie Mellina, Taziana Molinara, Jordan Morrisey, Justine Mjuica; January 9–11, 2010

Here We Go Again Written and directed by Alaina Hammond; **Cast:** Seth Lombardi, Kiran Malhotra, Mike Hill, Katie Vaughan, Ali Crosier, David Heidelberger, Johnny Pomatto, Aaron David Kapner; January 13–15, 2010

The Crucible by Arthur Miller; Director, Jessica Solce; Co-production with Coryphaeus Theatre Company; Stage Manager, Gwenevere Sisco; Lighting, Tsubasa Kamei; Costumes, Naomi McDougall Jones and Jenny D. Green; Audio/Visual, Ryan Scammell; Costume Consultant, Catherine Fisher; Props, Amy Bohaker; **Cast:** Krystal Rowley, Ralph Petrarca, Brenda Crawley, Naomi McDougall Jones, Alice Wiesner, Jenny D. Green, Michael W Murray, Lyle Loder Friedman, Amy Bohaker, Seth Duerr, Emily Ward, Ed Schiff, Tony Zazella, Sarah E Mathews, Abe Koogler, Brian Mott, Angus Hepbu; January 27–February 11, 2010

Nobody Written and performed by Antonio Disla; Co-production with 7 Hills Productions; Director, Anita Gonzalez; Stage Manager, Irene Carrol; Lighting, Kia Rogers; Audio/Visual, Mark Parenti; Vocal Consultant, Nancy Saklad; Assistant Director, Khelia Willis; February 7–15, 2010

Dramatizing Dante Written and co-produced by Brooklyn Playwrights Collective; **Cast:** Ashlely Adelman, Angelo Angrisani, Earl Bateman, Ken Coughlin, Flannery Foster, Ben Guralink, Mike Hill, Rachael Palmer Jones, Gavin Starr Kendall, Michelle Kuchuk, Laurel Lockhart, Seth Lombardi, Kiran Malhotra, Nick Palladino, Aubyn Philabaum; March 14–28, 2010

Almost Olive Juice by Nora Vetter; Co-produced wtih ArtEffects Theatre Company Directors, Aimee Todoroff, Alexandra Cremer, Phil Newsom, Zach McCoy, Katherine Carter, Nick Ronan; Stage Manager, Taylor Crampton; **Cast:** Rebecca Servon, Emilie Soffe, Charlie Gorrilla, Joanna Fanizza, Ivan Perez, Laura Yost, Zach McCoy, Bill Bria, Charlie Foster, Doug Rossi, Chris Kind, Kristi McCarson, Simone Zvi, Tim Dowd, Cristina Velez, Oliver Thrun, Lauren Cavanaugh, Kristin Cantwell, Angelyn Faust, Chris Kind, Mary Bailey, Melissa Vogt-Patterson; March 29–31, 2010

The Map of Lost Things Written and directed by Darragh Martin; Co-produced with Invisible Company; Stage Manager, Amy Wowak; Lighting, Buck Wanner; Costumes, Nina Lourie; Puppet Design/Construction, Katey Parker; Composer, Donovan Seidle; Fight Choreographer, Megan Messinger; Assistant Director/Choreographer, Sarah Hartmann; **Cast:** Arla Berman, Rosie DuPont, Courtney D.

Ellis, Ryan Good, Hilary Hanson, Logan McCoy, Katey Parker, Fergus Scully, Evan Sokal, David Speer; April 4–24, 2010

Spalding Gray: Stories Left to Tell Adapted and conceived by Kathleen Russo and Lucy Sexton; Co-produced with actor4hire productions in association with Outrageous Fortune Company; Director, William P Saunders III; **Cast:** Emma Givens, Bernard Bosio, Bill Rapp, Carol Wei, Tracy Winston, Pat Clune; April 7–9, 2010

A Hatful of Rain by Michael V. Gazzo; Co-produced with Clear Muse Productions and Catriona Rubenis-Stevens; Director, Amber Bela Muse; Stage Manager, Kristin Orlando; Lighting, Christina Watanabe; Costumes, Jessica Grable; Assistant Director, Catriona Rubenis-Stevens; ASMs, Rachel Adler and Tammy McNeill; Fight Director, Shad Ramsey; **Cast:** Kenneth Browning, Jordan Tisdale, Amber Bela Muse, Waliek Crandall, Khalipa Oldjohn, David King, Timothy Olin, Kamal Jones, Jennifer Fouche; May 2–4, 2010

Sabra by Julia Rosenfeld; Presented by Squatters Theatre and Isramerica; Director, Samantha Tella; Producer, Sivan Hadari; Associate Producers, Rosie Moss, Jesse Reing, Anna Zicer; Consulting Proudcer, Michelle Slonim; **Cast:** Chris Beier, Noam Haray, Sarah Kaufman, Adam Shiri, Rony Stav, Elian Zach; (Non-resident Production); May 27–June 6, 2010

Non-resident Productions

A Short Wake by Derek Murphy; Presented by Tweiss Productions; Director, Ludovica Villar-Hauser; Lighting, Kia Rogers; Set, CJ Howard; Costumes, Jenny D. Green; **Cast:** Peter Bradbury, Brandon Willliams; September 10–26, 2009

Meg's New Friend by Blair Singer; Presented by The Production Company; Director, Mark Armstrong; Stage Manager, Jeff Meyers; Lighting, Carolyn Wong; Set, April Bartlett; Costumes, Deanna Frieman; Sound, Isaac Butler; Property Design, Jamie Bartlett; Producer, Gabriella Willenz; Associate Set, Laura Taber Bacon; Property Master, Jamie Bressler; Fight Choreographer, Noah Starr; Publicist; **Cast:** Mary Cross, Damon Gupton, Megan McQuillan, Michael Solomon; November 29–December 20, 2009

The Weird by Roberto Aguirre-Sacasa; Presented by Wake Up Marconi! Director, Celine Rosenthal and Erin Gilmore; Stage Manager, Celine Rosenthal; Set, Celine Rosenthal and Mark Rosenthal; Costumes, Emily Lynn; Sound, Celine Rosenthal and Erin Gilmore; **Cast:** Matthew Cohn, Lucky Gretzinger, Allison Hirschlag, Melissa Pinsly, Mark Rosenthal, Mark Stetson, Michael Wolter; February 18–28, 2010

All That Might Happen by John Philip; Presented by 3A Productions; Director, Michael Portantiere; Set, George McGarvey; Lighting, Christina Watanabe; Carpenter, Robert Wisdom; Press, Lanie Zipoy; **Cast:** Barbara Mundy, Brandon Ruckdashel, Andrew Loren Resto, John Philip, Maria Bonner, Natalie Smith; February 19–March 6, 2010

Blood Type Ragu Written and performed by Frank Ingrasciotta; Presented by Flying Machine Productions; Director, Ted Sod; PSM, Katherine Wallace; Set, John McDermott; Lighting, Josh Bradford; Sound, Brandon Wolcott; Video, Joshua Higgason; Co-Producer, Paul Borghese; April 14–18, 2010

Mergatroyd Productions

www.mergatroyd.org

Christmas Blessing Written and directed by N.G. McClernan; **Cast:** Mike Durell, Kymberli McKanna, Amanda Thickpenny, Carolyn Paine, Krista Hasinger; Presented as part of the John Chatterton Playlab; Where Eagles Dare; November 21–22, 2009

Sodom & Gomorrah: The One-Man Show Written and directed by N.G. McClernan; **Cast:** Carolyn Paine, Michael Giorgio, Doug Rossi, Alice Anne English; Presented as part of the John Chatterton Playlab; Where Eagles Dare; February 26–27, 2010

Good Women of Morningside Written and directed by N. G. McClernan; **Cast:** Cat Yudain, Sarah Elizondo, Larissa Adamcyzk; Presented as part of the John Chatterton Playlab; Where Eagles Dare; April 17–18, 2010

New Rules Written and directed by N. G. McClernan; **Cast:** Amanda Thickpenny, Mike Durell, Doug Rossi, Daniel Genalo; Presented as part of the John Chatterton Playlab; Producers Club; May 8–9, 2010

Metropolitan Playhouse

Producing Artistic Director, Alex Roe; Director of Children's Programming, Rachael Kosch; Associate Director, Michael Hardart; Development/Costumes Coordination, Sidney Fortner; Assistant to the Director, Stephen McLarty; www. metropolitanplayhouse.org

The Contrast by Royall Tyler; Director/Set, Alex Roe; Costumes, Sidney Fortner; Lighting, Christopher Weston; Stage Manager, Leone Hanman; **Cast:** Bryan Close, Ali Crosier, Brad Fraizer, George Hosmer, Amanda Jones, Stephen McLarty, Matt Renskers, Maria Silverman, Rob Skolits, Tovah Suttle; October 2–November 1, 2009

Under the Gaslight by Augustin Daly; Director, Michael Hardart; Set, Alex Roe; Costumes, Sidney Fortner; Lighting, Christopher Weston; Stage Managers, Heather Olmstead and Carole A. Sullivan; **Cast:** Richard Cottrell, Maria Deasy, Justin Flagg, Brad Fraizer, Sarah Hankins, Lian-Marie Holmes, Amanda Jones, J. M. McDonough, Ralph Petrarca, Jason Rosoff; November 20–December 19, 2009

Adventure Theater by Kenn Adams; Co-Produced with Freestyle Repertory Theater; Director, Larua Livingston; Stage Manager, Laura Valpey; **Cast:** Michael Durkin, Laura Livingston; December 5–13, 2009

The Festival of the Vegetables by Michael Kosch; Co-produced with The Truly Fooly Children's Theater; Director, Michael Kosch; Set, Michael Kosch; Costumes, Rachael Kosch; Lighting, Maryvel Bergen; Choreographer, Rachael Kosch; Stage Manager, Livia Hill; **Cast:** Preston Burger, Alison Cook Beatty, Diego Carvajal, Jessica Delia, Janna Diamond, Billy Dutton, India Kohn, Hope (Hao-Lun) Kuei, Alessandra Larson, Jenny Levy, Xisko Monroe, Stella Rothfeld, Lily Eugenia Rudd, Miriam-Helene Rudd; February 6–21, 2010

Give and Go: Lerning from Losing to the Harlem Globetrotters by Brandt Johnson; Director, Ron Stetson; Stage Manager, Ian Wehrle; Lighting, Alex Roe; Original Music, Keith Middleton; **Cast:** Brandt Johnson; Co-produced with Syntaxis Productions; February 11–27, 2010

The Return of Peter Grimm by David Belasco; Director/Set, Alex Roe; Costumes, Sidney Fortner; Lighting, Christopher Weston; Stage Manager, Livia Hill; **Cast:** Frank Anderson, Linda Blackstock, Ken Ferrigni, Sidney Fortner, Brad Fraizer, Helen Highfield, George Hosmer, Matthew Hughes, George Taylor, Richard Vernon; March 13–April 11, 2010

Dodsworth by Sinclair Lewis and Sidney Howard; Director, Yvonne Opffer Conybeare; Set, Alex Roe; Costumes, Lena Sands; Lighting, Christopher Weston; Stage Manager, Mahmoud Bawatneh; **Cast:** Oliver Conant, Michael Hardart, D.H. Johnson, Casandera Lollar, Wendy Merritt, Lisa Riegel, Suzanne Savoy, Michael Scott, Brad Thomason; Metropolitan Playhouse; May 15–June 6, 2010

Festivals

Alphabet City VI Directed by Derek Jamison; *My American Style* written and performed by Lisa Barnes; *The Heat* written and performed by Abraham Sparrow; *Nowhere of the Middle* by Jared Houseman; **Cast:** Abraham Sparrow; *Another Kind of Music* written and performed by Teresa Kelsey; *Brother Man Don't Play* written and performed by Danielle Quisenberry; *Don't Stop Me Now* written and performed by Keri Setaro; August 9–23, 2009

East Village Chronicles Vol. 6 Included: *The Alamo* by Michael Bettencourt, directed by Jackob G. Hofmann; **Cast:** Elizabeth Bove and Ethan Sher; *Cheese* by Diane Spodarek, directed by Jacob G. Hofmann; **Cast:** Elizabeth Bove, Jamee Vance; *Day Old Bread* by Robert Anthony, directed by Jackob G. Hofmann; **Cast:**

Laurence Cantor, Alfred Gingold; *The East Fourth Street Years* by M.M. Martell, directed by Laura Livingston; **Cast:** Laurence Cantor, Sarah Hankins, Ethan Sher; *Getting By: The First Five Days* by George Holets, directed by Laura Livingston; **Cast:** Alfred Gingold, Sarah Hankins, Elka Rodriguez, Ethan Sher, Jacqueline van Biene; *Promising* by Pam Dickler, directed by Laura Livingston; **Cast:** Scott Casper, Sarah Hankins, Alejandro Rodriguez, Elka Rodriguez; *Tha Bess Shit* by Chad Beckim, directed by Dan Evans; **Cast:** Alejandro Rodriguez, Jacqueline van Biene; *Tower of Toys* written and directed by Jacob G. Hofmann; **Cast:** Scott Casper, Jacqueline van Biene, Jamee Vance; August 4–23, 2009

Another Sky Co-produced by Lulu Lolo Productions, The Oxy-Morons, Radio Hound Productions, LastMinuteProductions; included *Work* by Yvonne Conybeare, Anthony P. Pennino, and Rob Kendt, directed by Yvonne Conybeare; **Cast:** Branch Fields, Justin Flagg, Rachel Hardin, Lindsey Holloway, Nikita A. Hill, Gia McGlone, Fleur Phillips; *Nellie and the Madhouse* by Laura Livingston, directed by Laura Livingston; **Cast:** Monica Hayes Anderson, John Blaylock, Michael Hardart, Tom Macy, Nalina Mann, Shaundra Noll; *The Straitjacket* by Dan Evans, directed by Dan Evans; **Cast:** Carol Jacobanis, Lulu Lolo, Joel Nagle, Connie Perry, John Rengstorff; *The Real Housewives of the 19th Century* by David Lally, directed by Davil Lally; **Cast:** Trent Carson, Maria Deasy, Andrew Firda, Sue Glausen, Rachael Palmer Jones, Steven Lally, Stephen McLarty, Shaundra Noll, Amy L. Smith, Jason Szamreta; *Oh Dear, Sweet, Bitter Olive* by Trish Harnetiaux and Mary MacLane, directed by Trish Harnetiaux; **Cast:** Emily Davis, Julia Koo, Corey Tazmania; *Men Who Have Made Love to Me* written and directed by Normandy Raven Sherwood; **Cast:** Ilan Bachrach, Anthony Coleman, Juliana Francis-Kelly; *A Brief History of Crossdressing in the Civil War* written and directed by Andrea Pinyan; **Cast:** Maria Alegre, Susan Atwood, Aaron DiPiazza, Theresa Galeani, Tara Henderson, Paige Lussier Johnson, Nick Martorelli, Lindsay Tanner; *When the World Broke in Two–A Visit with Willa Cather* by Toni Schlesinger, directed by Rachel Kerr; **Cast:** Esmé von Hoffman, Rachel Kerr, Toni Schlesinger; *The Bedquilt* by Dorothy Canfield Fisher, directed by Michèle LaRue; **Cast:** Michèle LaRue; January 18–31, 2010

The Midtown International Theatre Festival

Executive Producer, John Chatterton; Managing Producer, Emileena Pedigo; Artistic Director for Plays, Lisa Dozier; Artistic Director for Musicals, Jamibeth Margolis; Artistic Director for Germanic Productions, Daniel Witzke; Marketing, Sarah Kate O'Haver; Artistic Director of English Shows, Joe Walsh; Press, Michelle Tabnick; Festabill Editor, David Lefkowitz; Webmaster, John Michael Villa; www.midtownfestival.org; June 28–August 2, 2009

1812 The Musical Book and lyrics by Ira Shapiro, music by Stacy O'Dell & Michael Murray; Director, Jamibeth Margolis; July 22

The American Black Box by Scott Pardue; Presented by Vincent Scott & Scott Pardue; Dorothy Strelsin Theatre; July 15– 28

Approaching America by James Evans; Presented by Theatre for a Big Country; Dorothy Strelsin Theatre; July 16–August 2

Assholes and Aureoles by Eric Pfeffinger; Presented by InterAction Theater, Inc. & Off the Leash Productions; Jewel Box Theater; July 2–August 2

Bartholomew Fair, NJ Written and directed by Billy Mitchell; Presented by The Theater Company/David Zimmerman; MainStage Theater; July 17–28

Benny by Suzanne Bachner; Director, Trish Minskoff; Technical Director, Douglas Shearer; Presented by John Montgomery Theatre Company; June Havoc Theatre; July 16–August

Bible Stories by Cedric Jones; Director, Alexis M. Hadsall; Presented by Guy Pride Productions; Where Eagles Dare Studio Blackbird; July 25–28

Body Language by Jenny Contuzzi; Director, Nathaniel Shaw; Presented by The Active Theater & Rick Joyce; Dorothy Strelsin Theatre; July 14–August 2

The Broken Jug by Heinrich Von Kleist; Presented by Stephen Wisker; June Havoc Theatre; July 18–August 1

Checking In by Brian Hampton; Director, Richard St. Peter; June Havoc Theatre; July 15–August 1

Christmas Guest by James V. O'Connor; Dorothy Strelsin Theatre; July 25–August 2

Climbing the Ladder by Chuck Orsland; Directors, Lawrence Frank, Ali Ayala, Samantha Dark, Molly Evensky, Michael Selkirk & Tony White; Where Eagles Dare Studio Blackbird; July 16–21

Cock Tales Produced by and book and lyrics by Tjasa Ferme, music by Greg Adair; Director, Carlos D. Gonzalez; Where Eagles Dare Studio Blackbird; July 25–29

Connect/Disconnect Music by Jan-Erik Sääf, English book and lyrics by Owen Robertson, Swedish version by Jan-Erik Sääf and Ola Hörling; Presented by Teater Omen; June Havoc Theatre; July 21–August 2

Cracking the Code by Eren T. Gibson & Jon Freda; Presented by Jon Freda; Where Eagles Dare Studio Blackbird; July 30–August 2

Crossroads by Meri Wallace; Presented by Howling Moon Cab Company; MainStage Theater; July 16–August 2

Dawn by Ralph Diaz; Director, Shelley Titus; Presented by Jen Yip & Seashell Productions; Jewel Box Theater

Disillusioned by Susan Hodara; Director, Noel Neeb; Magician Consultant, Jeff Grow; Presented by Two from the Aisle Productions; Where Eagles Dare Studio Blackbird; July 22–26

Dogs Lie by Ronnie Cohen and Jane Beale; Director, Brian Rhinehart; Presented by Starferry Associates; Jewel Box Theater; July 27–August 2

Eve and Lilith -- Adam's Temptation by Johannes Galli; Presented by Galli Theater NY; Jewel Box Theater; July 15–August 2

Exposed! The Curious Case of Shiloh and Zahara by Kate Gersten; Director, Dan Fogler; Presented by Stage 13, Inc.; WorkShop Mainstage; July 15–July 30

FaceSpace Presented by Lucky Penny Productions; WorkShop Mainstage; July 18–August 1

Family Dinner by Michele Willens; July 29

Family Symmetry Written and directed by Adam Samtur; Jewel Box Theater; July 13–August 19

Forgive Me? by Esther Armah; Director, Trezana Beverley; Presented by Take Wing and Soar Productions; WorkShop Mainstage; July 23–August 1

Gentleman's Wish by Lawson Caldwell; Presented by Lawson Caldwell & Anthony Francavilla; WorkShop Mainstage; July 30–August 2

The Hanged Man by Elisa Abatsis; Director, Samantha Payne; Elisa Abatsis & Shoes For Royalty Productions; Where Eagles Dare Studio Blackbird; July 18–25

Hardware Dreams by Sunilda Caraballo; Director, Eric Greenlund; Choreographer, Sunilda Caraballo; Presented by Eric Greenlund; Where Eagles Dare Studio Blackbird; July 15– 26

Haters Producer, Susan H. Pak; Where Eagles Dare Studio Blackbird; July 14–19

Hello Tomorrow Producers, Ellen Lindsay and Mary Sheridan; Where Eagles Dare Studio Blackbird; July 16–21

How to Make an American Family by Jeff Seabaugh; Presented by Frederick Street Productions; Jewel Box Theater; July 15–August 2

I Hate Love by Kyle Baxter & Jon Crefeld; Director, Mark Duncan; Presented by The Collective Objective; Dorothy Strelsin Theatre; July 13–August 1

In Fireworks Lie Secret Codes by John Guare; Director, Carol Kastendieck; Presented by Park Side Productions & Jack Trinco; Jewel Box Theater; July 15–July 19

Insecurity! Book, music, & lyrics by Mickey Zetts; Presented by Oberon Theatre Ensemble; WorkShop Mainstage; July 14–August 1

Iris and Dawn Director, Elliott George Robinson; Presented by Jen Yip & Seashell Productions; Jewel Box Theater; July 18–22

Keeping It In Retrospect Director, Anna Fosse Wilson; Presented by Writer's State & Judith Fredricks; Where Eagles Dare Studio Blackbird; July 22–24

Las Escenas de la Cruz (Scenes of the Cross) by iDo Theater! and Daniel Carlton; Presented by iDo Theater!; Dorothy Strelsin Theatre; July 17–August 1

Legends by Leslie Lee; Presented by Negro Ensemble Company; July 24

Lesson for Life by Phillip W. Weiss; Presented by Phil's Literary Works LLC; July 21–28

Life Swap: Two Short Solo Shows by Alexis Fedor; Presented by Three Halves Productions; Where Eagles Dare Studio Blackbird; July 31–August 2

The Lincoln Continental by Kathy Kafer; Director, Steven Yuhasz; Presented by Shadow Productions and Kramis Productions; WorkShop Mainstage; July 18–August 2

Love, Humiliation and Karaoke by Enzo Lombard; Presented by DQDI; Jewel Box Theater; July 30–August 1

Lunch by Steven Berkoff; Director, Alan Kinsella; Wallfly Productions; Jewel Box Theater; July 17–21

Made in Heaven by Jay Bernzweig; Director, Dennis Erdman; Presented by Mindful Media LLC; June Havoc Theatre; July 13–August 2

Monroe Bound by Lucile Scott; Director, Steven Gillenwater; Presented by Mighty Little Productions; WorkShop Mainstage; July 13–August 1

My Broken Brain Presented by The Flying Invalid Company; Where Eagles Dare Studio Blackbird; July 17–July 19

NeverCracked by Daniel MacIvor and Gwydion Suilebhan; Presented by Intentional Theater Group and Carissa Baker; WorkShop Mainstage; July 13–August 2

A Night in the Kremlin by Bernard Besserglik and Bob Barton; Presented by AFK Productions; June Havoc Theatre; July 13–August 2

Not My Daughter by Ann Mary Mullane; Presented by No Apology Theatre; WorkShop Mainstage; July 14–August 1

Not My Mother by Robin Amos Kahn; Director, Matt Hoverman; Robin Amos Kahn & Strikingly Different Productions; Where Eagles Dare Studio Blackbird; August 1

Numbers by Kieron Barry; Director, Dan Chen; Presented by Pink Bulb Productions LLC; Where Eagles Dare Studio Blackbird; July 14–August 20

On The Way To O'Neill's: JFK In Ireland by Ann G. Bauer & David Beckett; Presented by David Beckett; June Havoc Theatre; July 23–30

Out of the Sandbox by Jack Sauer; Presented by Richard Humphrey, RedCloud Mobile, Inc., and William Sauer; June Havoc Theatre; July 14–31

Perfectly Natural by Jon Steinhagen; Director, Kevin P. Hale; Presented by Playlab NYC; Where Eagles Dare Studio Blackbird; July 15–July 18

Pizza Man by Darlene Craviotto; Presented by ULU Theatre Collective; Dorothy Strelsin Theatre; July19– 31

A Poisonous Tree Presented by Bruce Colbert; Dorothy Strelsin Theatre; July 14–August 1

Pound: The Poet on Trial Written and directed by William Roetzheim; Artistic Director, Alix Steel; Presented by American International Theatre, Inc.; Jewel Box Theater; July 20–August 2

Prison Theatre by Gabor Harsanyi; Presented by Újpest Theatre; June Havoc Theatre; July 28–August 2

Psycho Therapy by Frank Strausser; Director, Michael Bush; Presented by Mindful Media LLC; June Havoc Theatre; July 15–August 1

Requiem for a Marriage by J.B. Edwards; Director, Linda Selman; Presented by Many Hats Productions & Third Avenue WorkShop Mainstage; July 16–August 2

Run Fast the Fire by Ellen Lindsay; Presented by Ellen Lindsay and Mary Sheridan; Where Eagles Dare Studio Blackbird

Seal Songs by Jennifer Fell Hayes; Presented by Thisbe Productions; Jewel Box Theater; July 13–31

Self-Portrait by Jeff Helgeson; Collage Productions/Gary Ferrar; Jewel Box Theater; July 16–August 1

Shakespeare Saturdays Songs in Concert Written, composed, directed, and adaped by Donna Stearns; Where Eagles Dare Studio Blackbird; July 29–August 2

Southern Man Written and performed by Jeff Pierce, co-written, produced, and directed by Colleen Pierce; Presented by Katzcando Productions; Jewel Box Theater; July 14–August 2

That's Showbiz! Music by Colin Chaston & Tony Clout, book, lyrics, and direction by Colin Chaston; Presented by Janski Productions Limited; June Havoc Theatre; July 14–30

The Play Plays by Jonathan Wallace, Meri Wallace and Duncan Pflaster; Director, Karen Raphaeli, Liz Bove and others; Presented by Howling Moon Cab Company; Where Eagles Dare Studio Blackbird; July 31–August 2

The Real Thing by Mary Sheridan; Presented by Ellen Lindsay and Mary Sheridan; Where Eagles Dare Studio Blackbird

The Sword Politik Written and directed by Jon Crefeld; Fight Choreographer, Nathan Decoux; Presented by Jon Ciccarelli, Hudson Shakespeare Company; Dorothy Strelsin Theatre; July 15–30

The Unanswered Questions Written and directed by Shuga Henry; Presented by Robin Amos Kahn & Strikingly Different Productions; Where Eagles Dare Studio Blackbird; July 30–August 2

Too Much, Too Far, Too Soon Written and directed by Rick Leidenfrost-Wilson; Presented by Off Sides Entertainment; Where Eagles Dare Studio Blackbird; July 19–July 26

Two Girls Written and performed by Gabrielle Maisels; Director, Joey Brenneman; Dramaturgy, Audrey Rosenberg, Presented by Dina Leytes; Dorothy Strelsin Theatre; July 15–August 2

Two-Handers by Martin Fox; Director, Wilson Milam; Presented by Jeffrey Altshuler/Alternative Scenario LLC; June Havoc Theatre; July 13–28

Unanswered Questions ... About My Mother Presented by Robin Amos Kahn & Strikingly Different Productions; July 30–August 2

Up A River/Down the Aisle by Jake Lipman, developed with Mark Hoverman; Director, Brian W. Seibert; Stage Manager, Laura Schuman; Presented by Tongue in Cheek Theater Productions, Pathos Audio Theatre & David Dudley; Where Eagles Dare Studio Blackbird

Whiskey, Beer and Apple Pie by Rob Egginton, Glenn De Kler, and Eli Sands; Presented by Panicked Productions; Dorothy Strelsin Theatre; July 13–August 1

Yo Hot Mama(s)! by Natalie Kim; Presented by Bright Star Productions; Jewel Box Theater; July 14–29

Milk Can Theatre Company

Artistic Director, Julie Fei-Fan Balzer; Marketing/Casting, Lorraine Cink; Development, Bethany Larsen, Cheryl L. Davis; Production Manager, Seth Gamble; Managing Directors, ML Kinney, Riv Massey; www.milkcantheatre.org

Life Among The Natives by ML Kinney; Director, Julie Fei-Fan Balzer; Set, Ann Bartek; Costumes, Sarah Gosnell; Lighting, Wilburn Bonnell; Sound, Chris Larsen; Stage Manager, Ashley Nelson; **Cast:** Tom Cleary, Ashton Heyl, Miranda Jonte, Samuel Muniz, Jacqueline Sydney, Meghan Rose Tonery, JJ von Mehren, Emily Ward; Urban Stages; May 14–29, 2010

The Disorder Plays Set, Ann Bartek; Lighting, Wilburn Bonnell; Costumes, Rachel Dozier-Ezell; Sound, Chris Larsen; included: *BMW* by Cheryl L. Davis; Director, Dev Bondarin; **Cast:** Jed Peterson, Miranda Shields; *Cutting* by Julie Fei-Fan Balzer; Director, Riv Massey; **Cast:** Amanda Nichols, Nate Washburn; *Another Intervention* by Andy Snyder; Director, Kimberly VerSteeg; **Cast:** John J. Isgro, Katherine Nolan Brown, Kyle Minshew; *The Third Date* by Bethany Larsen; Director, Maureen Stanley; **Cast:** John Graham, Courtney Kochuba; *Emilia's Wish* by Lorraine Cink; Director, Riv Massey; **Cast:** Jenny Bennett, Jed Peterson, Douglas Taurel; *What if...* by ML Kinney; Director, Lorraine Cink; **Cast:** Melissa D. Brown; Urban Stages; May 11–30, 2010

Mind The Gap Theatre

www.mindthegaptheatre.com

Durang Durang by Christopher Durang; Director, Alicia Dhyana House; Lighting, Set and Costumes, Ji-Youn Chang; Sound, Simon Thomas; Production Manager, Mishi Bekesi; General Manager, Flavia Fraser-Cannon; **Cast:** Janet Prince, Dan Frost, Stuart Williams, Melanie Machugh; Performed at Gilded Balloon, Scotland in August 2009and at Jermyn Street Theatre, London on February 16–March 6, 2010

BritBits 6 Seven short plays by British playwrights; Stage Manager, Lauren Arneson; Sound, Paula D'Alessandris; included: *Devil May Dare* by Kraig Smith; Director, Paula D'Alessandris; **Cast:** Mia Moreland, Bill Cohen, Anna Frankl-Duval; *The Derelicts* by Darren Murphy; Director, Stephanie Staes; **Cast:** Klemen Novak, Sarah Manton; *Chun Li* by Camilla Maxwell; Director, Camilla Maxwell; **Cast:** Colin Adams-Toomey, Tom Ziebell; *Sleeve Notes* by Duncan Macmillan, Director, Paula D'Alessandris, **Cast:** Camilla Maxwell; *Breaktime* by Philip Gawthorne; Director, Paula D'Alessandris; **Cast:** Stuart Williams, Tom Patrick Stephens; *Omissions* by Stephanie Staes; Director, Stephanie Staes; **Cast:** Daniel Damiano, Fiona Walsh; *Delays* by Dan Remmes; Director, Paula D'Alessandris; **Cast:** Dan Remmes, Mia Moreland, Martin Ewens; Manhattan Theatre Source; November 5–8, 2009

Readings

The Thrill of the Chase by Philip Gawthorne; Director: Paula D'Alessandris, **Cast:** Ben Bergin, Stuart Williams, Camilla Maxwell & Emma Gordon; September 9; *If I Should Go Away* by Owen Sheers; **Cast:** Gwenfair Vaughan, Mia Moreland, Mark Fernandes, Stuart Williams & Ben Bergin; *Father Figures (excerpt)* by Gary Owen; **Cast:** Steve Young; Presented as part of the *Cwmni Theatr Mind The Gap!* An Evening of Welsh Culture, in conjunction with the Welsh Assembly Governmen; September 23

Misfit Toys Repertory Company

Artistic Director, Joe Leo; Advisory Board, Dennis Bush and Ted Kociolek; www.MisfitToysRep.org

Bullied Written and directed by Joe Leo; **Cast:** Richard Brundage, Joseph Franchini, Daniel Henri Luttway, Anna Katherine Montgomery, Ben Prayz; Shell Theatre; June 23, 2009

Willie's Boys Written and directed by Joe Leo; **Cast:** Amanda Renee Baker, Aimee Byers, Kyrian Friedenberg, Joe Leo, Anna Katherine Montgomery, Eric Oleson, John Papais, Davi Santos, David Thompson, and George Trahanis; May 3, 2010

Moose Hall Theatre Company– Inwood Shakespeare Festival

Producing Artistic Director, Ted Minos; www.moosehallisf.org

The Merchant of Venice by William Shakespeare; Director, Ted Minos; Lighting, Catherine Bruce; Set, Ted Minos; Costumes, Catherine Bruce; Sound/Music, Luke St. Francis; Technical Director, Catherine Bruce; Associate Producer, Aaron Simms; Vocal Coach/Casting Assistant, Frank Zilinyi; Assistant Director, Chaya Gordon-Bland; **Cast:** Vandit Bhatt, Christopher Burris, Rebecca Dale, Rick Delaney, Leo Giannopoulos, Emily Vigoda Kurland, Elliot Mayer, Sean MacBride Murray, Jodie Pfau, Ross Pivec, Christopher Salazar, Anna Marie Sell, Steve Unwin, Daniel Vidor, Frank Zilinyi; Inwood Hill Park Peninsula; June 3–20, 2009

Dracula! Written and directed by Ted Minos; Lighting, Catherine Bruce; Set, Ted Minos; Costumes, Catherine Bruce; Sound/Original Music, Luke St. Francis; Technical Director, Catherine Bruce; Associate Producer, Aaron Simms; Fight Choreographer, Ray A. Rodriguez; Vocal Coach/Casting Assistant, Frank Zilinyi; **Cast:** Carla Birkhofer, Roy Brown, Jonathan Craig, Nadia Gan, Michael Hagins, Julia E.C.Jones, Roxann Kraemer, David M. Mead, Sean MacBride Murray, Jessica Ritacco, Ray A. Rodriguez, Kevin G. Shinnick, Ben Trawick-Smith, Nate Washburn, Frank Zilinyi; Inwood Hill Park Peninsula; July 15–August 1, 2009

MultiStages

www.eljallartsannex.com/multistages.htm

New Works Finalist Festival Included: *Dancing with Abandon* by Karen Hartman and Phil Lebovits; Director, Vince Pesce; Music Director Mark Hartman; **Cast:** Sandy Binion, Natalie Ellis, Zachary Clause, Dwayne Boccacio, Danny Beiruti, Debra Cardona, John Haggerty, Karla Mosley, Ronica Reddick, Alison Scaramella; *Ain't Ethiopia* by Michael Bettencourt; Director, Elfin Frederick Vogel; **Cast:** Carlton Byrd, Freedome Bradley, Natasha Yannacañedo, Afton C. Williamson, Douglas Taurel, Bryant Mason, Bruce Faulk, Sandra Berrios, Dennis Fox, David L. Carson; *Empire of the Trees* by Adam Kraar; Director, Giovanna Sardelli; **Cast:** Annie Purcell, Quincy Dunn-Baker, Sanjiv Javeri, David Sajadi, Sarah Garza; Dramatists Guild Frederick Lowe Room; October 6–8, 2009

Hell and High Water, or Lessons for When the Sky Falls by Jamuna Yvette Sirker; Director/Producer, Lorca Peress; Set, Lorca Peress; Costumes, Ellie D'Eustachio; Lighting, Alex Moore; Sound, Josh Allen; PSM, Denise R. Zeiler; Stage Manager, Geoffrey Nixon; Projections, Jan Hartley; Choreographer, Jennifer Chin; Associate Producer, Jaki Silver; **Cast:** Richards Abrams, Frances Chewning, Ross DeGraw, Joyce Griffen, Cary Hite, Russell Jordan, Anna Lamadrid, Frederick Mayer, Paul Christian Mischeshin; Hudson Guild Theatre; April 1–18, 2010

Readings

Shadows by David Sard; Director, Lorca Peress; February 6, 2010; *Temple of the Souls* by Anita Velez-Mitchell; Director, Lorca Peress; Original Music, Anika Paris and Dean Landon; February 20, 2010

Musicals Tonight!

www.musicalstonight.org

Paint Your Wagon Book and lyrics by Alan Jay Lerner, music by Frederick Lowe; Director, Thomas Sabella-Mills; Music Director, James Stenborg; **Cast:** Paul Carlin, Jillian Louis, Paul Woodson, Michielle Pruiett, Crystal Mosser, Gina Milo, Ted Bouton, Jaime Zatrain, Eli Budwill, Roger Rifkin, Bill Coyne, Jacob L. Smith, Andrew Hubacher, Mark Brown, Danny Gardner; McGinn-Cazale Theatre; October 20–November 1, 2009

Silk Stockings Music and lyrics by Cole Porter, book by George S. Kaufman, Leueen MacGrath, Abe Burrows; Director, Thomas Sabella-Mills; Music Director, David Caldwell; **Cast:** Jacob L. Smith, Kevin Kraft, Oakley Boycott, Jody Cook, Jason Simon, Carl Danielsen, T.J. Mannix, John Alban Coughlan, Kate Marrily, Rony Stav, Kristi Roosmaa, Yael Gonen, Sarah Spiegelman, Ethan Sher, Josh Scheer, Matthew Hardy, Mark Brown; Mc-Ginn Cazale Theatre; November 3–15, 2009

Sail Away Book, music and lyrics by Noël Coward; Director, Thomas Sabella-Mills; Music Director, James Stenborg; **Cast:** Beth Glover, Scott Guthrie, Beth McVey, Sarah Knapp, Amber Ward, Erik Keiser, William Ryall, Richard G. Rodgers, Barbara Anne Winn, Patti Perkins, Graham Bailey, Daniel Drewes, Omer Shaish, Jordan Wolfe, Stefan Basti; McGinn-Cazale Theatre; February 23–March 7, 2010

The Rink Book by Terrence McNally, music by John Kander, lyrics by Fred Ebb; Director/Choreography, Thomas Sabella-Mills; Stage Manager, Andrew J. Lonsdale; Music Director, Paul L. Johnson; **Cast:** Mary Jo Mecca, Stacie Perlman, Danny Gardner, David Garry, David Brent Howard, Christian Marriner, Brad Nacht, David Shane, Paige Simunovich; McGinn-Cazale Theatre; March 9–21, 2010

Stop the World…I Want to Get Off Book, music, and lyrics by Leslie Bricusse and Anthony Newley; Director/Choreographer, Thomas Sabella-Mills; Lighting, Andrew J. Lonsdale; Music Director, James Stenborg; **Cast:** Matt Wilson, Stephanie Sine, Lauren Ruff, Sara Sawyer, Kate Campbell, Amy Jackson, Mary Catherine McDonald, Kristin Katherine Shields; McGinn-Cazale Theatre; April 13–25, 2010

NAATCO (National Asian American Theatre Co.)

www.naatco.org

The Seagull by Anton Chekhov; Director, Gia Forakis; Set, Lee Savage; Costumes, Alixandra Gage Englund; Lighting, Stephen Petrilli; Sound, Robert Murphy; AV Design, S. Katy Tucker; Stage Manager, Irena Cumbow; Assistant Director, Tracy Francis; ASM, Jenny Logico; Masks, Kathleen Kennedy Tobin; Props, Alexandra Morton; Technical Director, Jack Blacketer; Assistant Set, Oliver Weson; **Cast:** Rajesh Bose, Cindy Cheung, Jojo Gonzalez, Marcus Ho, Mia Katigbak, Peter Kim, Lavrenti Lopes, Orville Mendoza, Andy Pang, Sophia Skiles, Tiffany Villarin; Theater for the New City; September 26–October 17, 2009

A Play on War by Jenny Connell; Presented collaboration with Theater Mitu; Director, Ruben Polendo; Lighting, Kate Ashton; Set, Justin Nestor; Costumes, Candida K. Nichols; Sound, Adam Cochran; AV Design, Alex Koch; Stage Manager, Irena Cumbow; Bicycles, Justin Nestor; Composer & Musician, Adam Cochran; Musician, Barrie McClain; Assistant Director, Randi Kleiner; ASM, Jenny Logico; Associate Set, Claire Karoff; Assistant Costumes, Judi Olson; **Cast:** Nikki Calonge, Nathan Elam, Brian Hirono, Marcus Ho, Mia Katigbak, Bushra Laskar, Orville Mendoza, Jon Norman Schneider; Connelly Theater; February 13–March 6, 2010

National Comedy Theatre

www.manhattancomedy.com

The National Comedy Theatre Director, Gary Kramer; Producer, Kim Chase; Voice/Sound, Karen Berelsford, Jan Di Pietro, Marcus Lorenzo, James Smith; House Manager, Heather Jewels; **Cast:** JT Arbogast, Kevin Flinn, Dan Guller, Chris Booth, Stephanie Acevedo, Jason Salmon, Jeff Lepine, Gary Cohen, Gary Kramer, Scott Foster, Andrew Kircher, Chris O'Neill, David Weinheimer, Devin Heater, Garrett Willingham, Jeff Cumberlin, Josh Hurley, Katie Jergens, Kevin Laibson, Marian Brock, Paul Valenti, Ron Hill, Sarah Spigelman, Karl Tiedemann; Ongoing

Negro Ensemble Company

Savannah Black & Blue by Raymond Jones; Director, Charles Weldon; Set, Randeil Parsons; Costumes, Matt Caswell; Lighting, Ves Weaver; Sound, Eliot Lanes; Stage Manager, Eliot Lanes; **Cast:** Ohene Cornelius, Kimberlyn Crawford, Chris Johnson, Clinton Lowe, Tomike Ogugua, Ciera Payton, Jammie Patton, Thyais Walsh, Keona Welch; Theatre 54 at Shetler; November 7–22, 2009

The Nerve Tank

www.NerveTank.com

bauhaus the bauhaus by Chance D. Muehleck; Director, Melanie S. Armer; Stage Manager, Nichol C. Rosas-Ullman; Lighting, Solomon Weisbard; Set, Solomon Weisbard; Costumes, Emily Lippolis; Sound, Stephan Moore; Dramaturg, Lutz Kessler; **Cast:** V. Orion Delwaterman, Stacia French, Karen Grenke, Irene Hsi, Anna Konkle, Robin Kurtz, Kevin Lapin, Sandie Luna, James Yu; Brooklyn Lyceum; October 9–November 22, 2009

Live/Feed by Chance D. Muehleck; Director, Melanie S. Armer; Stage Manager, Jennifer Boehm; Lighting, Ryan Metzler; Set, Melanie S. Armer; Costumes, Candida K. Nichols; Sound, Stephan Moore; Choreographers, Chanda Calentine, Melanie S. Armer; **Cast:** Stacia French, Karen Grenke, Robin Kurtz, Mark Lindberg, James Yu; Brooklyn Lyceum; May 7–29, 2010

New Acting Company

Peter Pan by James M. Barrie, adapted by John Caird & Trevor Nunn; Director, Stephen Michael Rondel; Choreographer, Daniella Rabbani; Set, Katya Khellblau; Lighting, Benjamin Tevelow; Costumes, Mark Salinas; Audio/Visual, Justin Warner; Stage Manager, Andrea Ghersetich; Fight Director, Jessica Weis; **Cast:** Zach Zamsky, Synge Maher, Erica Cenci, Alex Demers, Jessica Goldstein, Jeremy Sabol, Kyla Schoer, Elizabeth Ely, Sophie Shuster, Phoebe VanDusen, Charlotte Williams; Philip Coltoff Center; April 9–May 9, 2010

New Georges

Artistic Director, Susan Bernfield; Associate Director, Sarah Cameron Sunde; Literary Manager, Kara-Lynn Vaeni; Creative Outreach Associate, Rehana Mirza; www.newgeorges.org

Creature by Heidi Schreck; Co-produced by Page 73 Productions (for complete details, please see listing in Off-Broadway section); Ohio Theatre; October 27–November 21, 2009

Milk by Emily DeVoti; Co-produced by New Feet Productions; Director, Jessica Bauman; Set, Susan Zeeman Rogers; Costumes, Emily Pepper; Lighting, Leonore Doxsee; Sound, Amy Altadonna; Stage Manager, Kat West; ASM, Emily Paige Ballou; Props, Ashley Gagner; Line Producer, Lisa Dozier; Assistant Director, Samantha Tella; Casting, Paul Davis, Calleri Casting; Associate Producer, Rehana Mirza; Press, Jim Baldassare; **Cast:** Carolyn Baeumler, Jordan Baker, Peter Bradbury, Jon Krupp, Anna Kull, Noah Robbins; HERE Arts Center-Mainstage; April 26–May 22, 2010

New Perspective Theatre Company

Artistic Director, Melody Brooks; General Manager, Catharine Guther; Associate Artistic Director, C. Amanda Maud; Artistic/Marketing Associate, Jenny Greeman; Artistic/ Production Associate, Amanda Johnson; Artistic Associate/ Assistant Director, Apprentice Program, Kerry Watterson; www.newperspectivestheatre.org

Hamlet by William Shakespeare; Director, Melody Brooks; Production Designer, Meganne George; Sound and Video Designer, David L. Schulder; Fight

Choreographer, Ray Rodriguez; **Cast:** Terrell Tilford, Bill Blechingberg, Bernardo Cubria, Jenny Greeman, C. Amanda Maud, Rafael Jordan, Kim Sullivan, James Edward Becton, Amanda Johnson, Mikaela Lynn Johnson, Steve Lynn, Ray Rodriguez and Kerry Watterson; Shetler Studios; May 13–22, 2010

New Play Festival

Presented by the League of Professional Theatre Women; www.theatrewomen.org; Cherry Lane Theatre; November 9, 2009

And Then I Went Inside by Anne Hamilton; Director, Lorca Peress; **Cast:** Kathleen Chalfant

Audition by Shirley Lauro; Director, Melanie Moyer Williams; **Cast:** Laura Anderson, Andrea Mezvinsky

A Chip On My Shoulder by Carol Mack; Director, Tricia McDermott; **Cast:** Kathryn A. Layng

Half Light by Joan Vail Thorne; Director, Elyse Singer; **Cast:** Maryann Plunkett, Nat Cassidy, Frances Sternhagen

I Stood with My Satchel by Leah Kornfeld Friedman; Director, Ludovica Villar-Hauser; **Cast:** Jacqueline Antaramian

The Right Number by Deborah Savadge; Director, Melissa Maxwell; **Cast:** Lyndsay Becker, Brian W. Seibert, Jed Peterson

River Post-Futurist by Paula Cizmar; Director, Melanie Sutherland; **Cast:** Leah Curney, Brandon Jones

Target by Glenda Frank; Director, Edie Cowan; **Cast:** Cady Huffman, Michael Pemberton

The Waiter by Sheilah Rae; Director, Pamela Hunt; **Cast:** Randy Graff, Kristin Maloney, Noah Racey

What's Left by Lee Thuna; Director, Cara Reichel; **Cast:** Anthony Cummings, Kathryn Grody

New Worlds Theatre Project

www.newworldsproject.org

Mentshn by Sholem Aleichem, translated and adapted by Ellen Perecman and Clay McLeod Chapman; Director/Design, Marc Geller; Stage Manager, Scott Matthews; Producer/Dramaturge, Ellen Perecman; **Cast:** Liz Bove, Andrew Dawson, Brent Erdy, Allison Frederick, Stuart Luth, Abby Royle, Clare Schmidt, Laralu Smith, Jamee Vance; Theater 3; May 23–June 13, 2009

Dammerung by Peretz Hirshbein; Director/Set/Costumes/Sound, Marc Geller; Lighting, Sabrina Braswell; Producer/Dramaturge, Ellen Perecman; Stage Manager, Margot Fitzsimmons; **Cast:** Andrew Dawson, Alison Frederick, Jeremy Gender, Nicholas Gorham, Michael Mott, Cally Robertson, Augustus Truhn; Lion Theatre on Theatre Row; January 8– 25, 2009

Displaced Wedding by H. Leivick; Director, Marc Geller; Producer and Dramaturg, Ellen Perecman; January 11, 2010

New Yiddish Rep

www.newyiddishrep.org

The Big Bupkis! A Complete Gentile's Guide to Yiddish Vaudeville by Shane Bertram Baker & Allen Lewis Rickman; Director, Allen Lewis Rickman; Lighting, Nikolas Priest; Set, George Xenos; Costumes, Gail Cooper-Hecht; Music Director, Steve Sterner; **Cast:** Shane Bertram Baker; The Workmen's Circle, 45 East 33rd Street; December 5, 2009–January 30, 2010

New York Classical Theatre

www.newyorkclassical.org

King Lear by William Shakespeare; Director, Stephen Burdman; Costumes, Michelle Bohn; Stage Manager, Kate Croasdale; Casting, Stephanie Klapper; Voice/Speech Coach, Joan Melton; Fight Directors, P.J. Escobio and Shad Ramsey; **Cast:** John-Patrick Driscoll, John Michalski, Torsten Hillhouse, Donald Grody, Amy Landon, Clay Storseth, Kate MacCluggage, Nick Salamone, Heather Wood, Andrew Sellon, David Graham Jones, Travis Blumer, Hunter Canning, Michael Eisenstein, Leon Pease, Shannon Prichard, Vince Nappo, Ryan Krause; Central Park & Battery Park; May 28–July 7, 2009

Hamlet, Prince of Denmark by William Shakespeare; Director, Stephen Burdman; Costumes, Amelia Dombrowski; Stage Manager, Erin Albrecht; Casting, Stephanie Klapper; Voice/Speech Coach, Barbara Adrian; Fight Director, Shad Ramsey; **Cast:** Justin Blanchard, Anthony Reimer, Clay Storseth, Nick Salamone, John-Patrick Driscoll, John Michalski, Rita Rehn, Shad Ramsey, Ian Stuart, Ginny Myers Lee, Alexis Camins, Scott Kerns; World Financial Center; April 1–18, 2010

New York International Fringe Festival

Producing Artistic Director, Elena K. Holy; President of the Board of Directors, Shelley Burch; Festival Administrator, Britt Lafield; Festival Technical Directors, Kevin Bartlett, Gregg Bellon, Scott D. Mancha; Festival Production Manager, Krista Robbins; www.fringenyc.org; Various Venues; Thirteenth Annual; August 14–30, 2009

1-900-SELFPLEX by Alex DeFazio; Director, Jody P. Person; Elixir Productions Theatre Company

38 Witnessed Her Death, I Witnessed Her Love, The Lonely Secret of Mary Ann Zielonko (Kitty Genovese Story) Written and performed by LuLu LoLo; Director/Choreography, Jody Oberfelder; Presented by LuLu LoLo Productions

The 49 Project by Mary Adkins

6 Seconds in Charlack by Brian Golden; Director, Patrick Mills

666 by the Yllana Colective; Director, David Ottone; Presented by Psycoduction Inc. in Association with Produciones Yllana

Abraham Lincoln's Big, Gay Dance Party by Aaron Loeb; Director, Chris Smith; Presented by BlueRare Productions, San Francisco Playhouse, and PlayGround

The Adventures of Alvin Sputnik, Deep Sea Explorer by Tim Watts; Presented by Weeping Spoon Productions

American Jataka Tales by Ed Malin; Director, Mark Duncan; Presented by Temerity Theatre

America's Next Top Bottom, Cycle 5! Created by Efrain Schunior; Presented by Celebration Theatre

And She Said, He Said, I Said Yes by Harrison David Rivers; Director, Eric Louie & Anika Chapin; Presented by DRD Productions

And Sophie Comes Too by Meryl Cohn; Director, Mark Finley; Presented by TOSOS

And Then You Die (How I Ran a Marathon in 26.2 Years) by David Hansen; Director, Alison Garrigan; Presented by Cleveland Public Theatre

The Antarctic Chronicles by Jessica Manuel; Director, Paul Linke; Presented by Sister Fantastic Productions

The Aperture by Sean Christopher Lewis; Director, Craig J. George; Presented by Cleveland Public Theatre

Artifex: The Artistic Life of Emperor Nero by Davide Ambrogi, Original Music by Davide Ambrogi; Director, Velia Viti; Presented by the Artifex Company

Art's Heart Written and performed by Anthony Johnston; Director, Nathan Schwartz

Baby Wants Candy The Improvised Musical with Full Band Improvised and Presented by Baby Wants Candy ensemble

Baking with Bertha, Back to School Special by Michael Bowen and Sam Barber; Director, Sam Barber; Presented by Squeezebox Productions

Bargains & Blood (How To Succeed In Home Shopping!) by Blair Fell with music by Stuart McMeans; Director, Blair Fell; Presented by Burning Boy Theater Company

Be A Man!!! by Exiene Lofgren; Director, Grant Kretchik; Presented by HA! Comedy Corp.

Be The Dog by Emily Kaye Liberis; Director, Jason McDowell-Green; Presented by RyderWorks

Bitch! (The Autobiography of Lady Lawford, as told to Buddy Galon) by Charlotte Booker; Presented by Andsoshedid

The Books by Michael Edison Hayden; Director, Matt Urban; Presented by Imperfect People

Borderline by Rob Benson; Director, Jennifer Lunn; Culturcated Theatre Company

The Boxer Written and directed by Matt Lyle; Choreographer, Nancy Schaeffer; Presented by Bootstraps Comedy Theater

The Boys Upstairs by Jason Mitchell

Breathe... by Tim J. MacMillian; Director, Sally Burtenshaw; Presented by Aim High Productions

Bubs A One Man Musical by Cy Frost & Doug Olson; Presented by MSB Productions LLC

Buddy Becker's Big Uncut Flick by Todd Michael; Director, Walter J. Hoffman; Gracye Productions

Camp Super Friend by Bethany Wallace; Director, Josiah Wallace; Presented by Taproot Theatre Company

Camp Wanatachi, A New Musical Book, music, and lyrics by Natalie Weiss, Conrad Winslow and Travis Stewart; Director, Natalie Weiss; Presented by Mercurial Productions

Candide Americana by Stanton Wood; Director, Edward Elefterion; Presented by Rabbit Hole Ensemble

Cephalopod, A Play Below Sea Level by Kyle Warren; Director, Rebecca Stevens; Presented by Ridge and Davis Presents

The Check is in the Mail by Robert Liebowitz; Director, Mary Elizabeth MiCari; Presented by Genesis Repertory

Circuits Created and directed by Patricia Noworol; Presented by Patricia Noworol Dance Company

Citizen Ruth Music by Michael Brennan, book & lyrics by Mark Leydorf; Director, Howard Shalwitz; Presented by Citizen Ruth LLC

Clemenza And Tessio Are Dead by Gregg Greenberg; Director, Gregg Greenberg & Kate Erin Gibson, Original Staging, Simcha Borenstein

Cock-a-Doodle-Doo! by Danny Ashkenasi and Herman Melville; Director, Nick Martorelli; Presented by Fredrick Byers Productions

Comedogenic by Paul Thomas

Complete by Andrea Kuchlewska; Presented by Open House Performance Project

The Confessional Written and directed by Jayson Akridge; Presented by The Cohort Theatre Company

Confirmation by Vincent Marano; Director, Nat Cassidy; Presented by Teatro Oscuro

A Contemporary American's Guide to a Successful Marriage by Robert Bastron; Director, Dave Solomon; Presented by Sean Bradford Productions

Crazy Good Luck by Karen MacIntyre; Director, Judy Thomas; Choreographer, Karen MacIntyre; Presented by Green Space Arts Collective

Performance Art Crossings Written and directed by Amy Sabin Barrow and Shannon Michael Wamser; Presented by Stages on the Sound

The Crow Mill by Andrew Unterberg

Cut From the Same Cloth by Megan Auster-Rosen; Director, Lindsay Goss; Choreographer, Beth Gill; Presented by Auster-Rosen Company

Daily Sounds by Jay Prasad; Director, Rich Ferraioli; Presented by Trent Productions

Damon and Debra by Judy Chicurel; Presented by B Train Productions

Dances In Funny Presented, written, directed, and choreographed by Ara Fitzgerald, Claire Porter and Collaborators

Dancing with Abandon by Karen Hartman and Phil Lebovits; Presented by Small Pond Entertainment

Dancing With Ghosts by Harley Newman

Dante's Divina Commedia – Inferno by Dante; Director, Rene Migliaccio; Presented by Black Moon Theatre Company

The Death of Evie Avery by Sara Jeanne Asselin; Presented by Fine Feathered Friends

Deathwatch by Jean Genet, Translated by David Rudkin; Director, Aaron Sparks; Presented by The Dialectix Group

Devil Boys from Beyond by Buddy Thomas; Director, Kenneth Elliott; Presented by MadCaP Productions

Diamond Dead Music by Richard Hartley, lyrics by Brian Cooper, book by Andrew Lloyd Baughman, based on the screenplay by Brian Cooper; Director, Melissa Baughman; Presented by The Landless Theatre Company

Dirty Stuff by Jonny McGovern; Director, Presented by Courtney Munch

The Doctor and the Devils by Dylan Thomas, adapted and directed by Daniel Balkin; Presented by Rag 'N Bone Theatre Company

Dolls by Michael Phillis; Director, Andrew Nance; Presented by Bowdashoot Productions

Dominate Yourself! by Amy Heidt; Director, Anthony King

Don't Be Scared! It's Only A Play by Cory Antiel

Don't Step on the Cracks Created by the Ensemble; Director, Eryck Tait; Presented by Five Flights Theater Company

Dream Lovers by Albi Gorn; Director, Albi Gorn, Robin Joseph, Michael Muldoon; Presented by M&M Productions Acting Company, Inc.

e-Station Director, Wang Chong; Presented by Théâtre du Rêve Expérimental

Eat, Drink and Be Merry Book, music, and lyrics by Paul Schult; Presented by Rosetree Productions

Ectospasms by Edmund B. Lingan; Director, Jessica Bonenfant and Edmund B. Lingan; Choreographer, Jessica Bonenfant; Presented by Lola Lola Dance Theatre with the Institute for the Study of Performance and Spirituality

Egg Farm by Bill Heck and Nick Mills; Director, Wes Grantom; Presented by Vitality Productions in Association with Slant Theatre Project

Elephant in the Room by Leah Hendrick; Director, Morgan Goul

Eli and Cheryl Jump by Daniel McCoy; Director, Nicole A. Watson; Presented by Ignited States in Association with Crosstown Playwrights

Eminene by Barton Bishop; Director, Matthew J. Nichols; Zootopia Theatre Company; www.zootopiatheatre.org

Ether Steeds by Jason Williamson; Director, Niegel Smith

Every Love Story Ends in Tears by Nidia Medina, with music by Robert Cowie; Director, Nic Grelli; Presented by Bella Umbrella Theatre

Exiles From The Sun Written and directed by Brent Cirves; Presented by Exiled Productions

Face the Music...and Dance! Created and choreographed by Tina Croll, Heidi Latsky, Maura Nguyen Donohue, Julian Barnett, and Noa Sagie; Presented by the Center for Creative Resources

The Fall of the House of Usher Adapted and directed by Brent Cirves, from the story by Edgar Allan Poe; Music, Mike Johnson; Based on a story by Edgar Allan Poe; Music Director, Mike Johnson; Presented by Exiled Productions

Fancy Footwork by Miriam Gallagher; Director, Rich Johnson; Presented by A Mix Productions

Far Out--the New Sci-Fi Musical Comedy by Brian Breen and Michael Chartier; Director, Kimothy Cruse; Presented by Supreme Eyeball Productions

A Fine Line by Emlyn Morinelli and Jennifer Sanders; Director, Gary Rudoren; Presented by More Sand Company in association with Magnet Theater

Finger Paint by Erin Austin & Ross Evans; Director, Ross Evans; Presented by Plastic Flamingo Theatre Company

first dark Written and directed by Charlotte W. Bence; Presented by CW Productions

Flight Written and directed by Tim Aumiller; Presented by No Hope Productions

Flutterbies by Frank Christopher; Director, Lea DeLaria; Presented by Flutterbies, LLC

For the Love of Christ! Book, music, and lyrics by Ben Knox, additional lyrics & arrangements by Brian J. Nash, additional book by Heather Collis & Karen Weatherwax; Director, Holly-Anne Ruggiero

Forest Maiden Written and directed by Nina Morrison

George and Laura Bush Perform . . . Our Favorite Sitcom Episodes by Ryan Gajewski; Presented by Regular Folks Productions

GirlPower, Voices of a Generation Created by the 2008–2009GirlPower Ensemble; Director, Ashley Marinaccio and Elizabeth Koke; Presented by Girlpower and ManhattanTheatre Source

Graveyard Shift The American Tragedy Musical Written and directed by Ren Casey; Choreographer, Sydney Skybetter; Presented by Renegade Zombie

The Green Manifesto Book and lyrics by Anne Berlin, music by Andy Cohen; Director, Valentina Fratti; Presented by Two Cookies in Association with M2

Groupies by Sharon Lintz; Director, Jonathan Warman

Gutter Star, The Paperback Musical Book by Jack Dyville, music by James Mack Avery, lyrics by David Gillam Fuller; Director, Eric M. Schussel; Choreographer, Jack Dyvill; Presented by Fully Flighted Productions and Linda Wielkotz

Hamlet by William Shakespeare; Director, Kameron Steel; Presented by The South Wing

Harold Pinter Pair by Harold Pinter; Director, Patrick McNult; Presented by Roadworks Productions NYC

Hatching; Eat Your Eggs by Will Porter; Director, Amanda Thompson

Hear What's in the Heart - A Shoemaker's Tale by Steve Scionti; Director, Paul Savas; Presented by The Warehouse Theatre

High Plains by Brian Watkins; Director, Anthony Reimer

Hint by Joe Maloney and Bonnie Milligan, based on the show originally conceived and performed by the Backyard Players

His Greatness by Daniel MacIvor; Presented by Lyric Productions

A History of Cobbling by Justin Klose and Cameron Reed; Presented by Cobbled Productions

Home is the Sailor, Home From Sea Written and directed by Alex Coppola; Presented by WeThree Productions

Hot Air Buffoons by Meredith Jacobs, Alex Wolfson, Shawn Rice, Jarred Baugh; Presented by The Polite Society

How Now, Dow Jones Book by Max Shulman, music by Elmer Bernstein, lyrics by Carolyn Leigh; Director, Ben West; Choreographer, Rommy Sandhu; Presented by UnsungMusicalsCo. Inc.

Hungry by George Kehoe; Director, Christopher J. Schager; Presented by The O'Connor Theatre Project

I Can Has Cheezburger, The MusicLOL! by Kristyn Pomranz and Katherine Steinberg; Additional music by Mike Gillespie; Presented by Sauce and Company

I Will Follow by Barri Tsavaris; Presented by Pennyfield Productions

Imagine Written as part of the Children of Imagine Project workshops; Director, Bill Bartlett; Choreographer, Annie Faulkner; Presented by Imagine Project Inc.

Inferno, The New Rock Musical by Rick Merino; Director, Stephen Innocenzi; Choreographer, Lynn Lesniak Needle; Presented by Varius Productions LLC

Jack and the Soy Beanstalk Book and lyrics by Jerrod Bogard, music by Sky Seals & Jerrod Bogard; Presented by Wide Eyed Productions

Jen & Angie by Laura Bucholz & Christina Casa; Director, Susannah Beckett; Presented by Nobody's Business But Ours, LLC

Jesus Ride by Mike Schlitt; Director, Nancy Keystone; Presented by Deux Ex Productions

John and Greg's High School Reunion by Greg Ayers and John Halbach

The Jungle Fun Room by Brian Hampton; Director, Sam Zalutsky

just don't touch me, amigo by Fernando Gambaroni; Director, Jose Zayas

The K of D, an urban legend by Laura Schellhardt; Director, Braden Abraham; Presented by Pistol Cat Productions

Kaddish (or The Key in the Window) Created & performed by Donnie Mather; Playwright, Allen Ginsberg; Director, Kim Weild

La Ronde by Arthur Schnitzler, Translator, Carl R. Mueller; Director, Larry Biederman; Presented by Big Signature Productions

Live Broadcast by John William Schiffbauer; Producer, Erica Ruff

A Long Walk Home by Lauren Marie Albert

Look After You Presented by Maieutic Theatre Works

Looming the Memory by Thomas Papathanassiou; Director, John Saunders; Presented by Thomas Papathanassiou

Love Money, A Recession Rock Musical Book and lyrics by Lucas Kavner and Willie Orbison, music and lyrics by Thompson Davis; Director, Aaron Gensler; Choreographer, Rishabh Kashyap; Presented by The Zoo

M an adaptation of Shakespeare's Macbeth for three actors by William Shakespeare, adapted by Robert Monaco; Director, Robert Monaco; Presented by Lady M Productions

Mark Storen's A Drunken Cabaret by Mark Storen; Presented by The Moxy Collective

Mars, Population 1 Written and directed by James Allerdyce

May-December with The Nose and Clammy by Jonas Cohen and Naomi McDougall Jones; Presented by The Present Company in association with Mind the Art

The Meaning of Wife by Ailin Conant and Erin Judge; Presented by Theatre Témoin

A Midsummer Night's Dream by William Shakespeare; Director, Peter Macklin; Assistant Director, Erik Andrews; Presented by The BAMA Theatre Company in association with The Figments Theatre Company

MoM - A Rock Concert Musical by Richard Caliban; Director, Richard Caliban; Presented by 5 Mothers

The Most Mediocre Story Never Told! by Jay Sefton; Director, Debra De Liso

The Motherline by Chantal Bilodeau; Director, Jennifer Vellenga; Presented by Ibis Theatre Project

Mr. Sensitivity by Byron Nilsson; Director, David Baecker; Presented by Jollity Farm Productions

Muffin Man Written and directed by Camille Harris; Presented by The Silly Jazz Company

Mutti's After Supper Stories Written and directed by Iris Rose, adapted from the Brothers Grimm; Music and Lyrics by Hugh Hales-Tooke; Presented by Theater of the Grasshopper

Natural History by Ian August; Director, Maura Farver; Presented by Sweeter Theater Productions

Notes on the Land of Earthquake & Fire Written and directed by Jason Schafer; Presented by Goofy Foot

The Office and the Metal Blob Written and directed by Andrew Scoville; Presented by The Centrifuge in Collaboration with the Company

Ones By 2, Fallujah and the Invention of Zero by Rebecca McCarthy & Deepali Gupta; Director, Stephen Stout; Presented by GFA Theatre

Peace Warriors by Doron Ben-Atar with Debbie Pollak; Director, Michael Bahar; Presented by Blue Line Arts

Penumbra by Anthony Fascious Martinez; Director, Shidan Majidi; Presented by Intangible Collective

Photosynthesis by Tim J. MacMillan; Director, Terry Gsell; Presented by Never Assume Productions

Pie-Face! The Adventures of Anita Bryant by David Karl Lee; Director, Kenny Howard; Presented by Kangagirl Productions

Poke Until Wince Written and directed by Matthew Chesmore

Poppy! An Enchanted Evening with Poppy Bulova Written and directed by Lillie Jayne; Presented by Snake In The Boot

Population, 8 by Nicholas Gray; Director, Marc Stuart Weitz; Presented by The Process Group and Purple Man Theater Company
Porn Rock-The Musical Written and directed by Pink Snow; Presented by Pink Snow Productions

Powerhouse by Josh Luxenberg, Joshua Morris and Kali Quinn; Director, Jon Levin; Presented by Sinking Ship Productions

Professor Ralph's Loss of Breath by Professor Ralph; Director, Kevin P. Hale; Presented by Playlab NYC

Refractions by Eliot Stockton; Director, Andy Ottoson; Dalliance Theater

Remission written and directed by Kirk Wood Bromley; Choreographer, Leah Schrager; Presented by Inverse Theater Company

Romeo and Toilet Written and directed by Yu Murai; Presented by Kaimaku and Pennant Race

A Rule of Nines by Brian Kirchner; Director, Christopher Triebel; Presented by BRK Productions

Sadie, Sadie by Ben Izzo; Director, Samantha Shechtman; Presented by BE Theatre Company

Savage International Written and directed by Manny Liyes; Presented by MeanBoy Productions

Scandalous People A Sizzling Jazzical Music by Benny Russell, book and lyrics by Myla Churchill; Director, Fredi Walker- Browne; Presented by My Church Production

Scattered Lives Directed and choreographed by Yoshihisa Kuwayama; Presented by Samurai Sword Soul

The Secret of Our Souls-A Kabalistic Love Story Book and lyrics by Ben Goldstein, music by Phillip Namanworth; Director, Ben Goldstein; Music Director, Kat Sherrell; Choreographer, Kathryn Sullivan; Presented by Filmus Inc.

Series 6.2, Paint on Canvas by Becca Hackett and Katherine Randle; Director, Ilana Becker; Presented by HumanWell Productions

Sex and the Holy Land by Melanie Zoey Weinstein; Director, Jenny Bloom; Presented by Happy Belly Productions

Shelf Life by Molly Goforth; Director, JV Mercanti; Presented by The Arcade

Singin' Wid A Sword in Ma Han' by Vienna Carroll; Director, Keith Johnston

Some Editing and Some Theme Music Director, Jean Ann Douglass

The Songs of Robert by John Crutchfield; Director, Steven Samuels

Sorority Queen in a Mobile Home by Kevin Mahoney and Michael DiGaetano; Presented by The Fundamentally Wrong Co

Spermalot, The Musical by David Brooks, Larry Mahlstedt, Kevin Spire, Karen Swanson, and Thatcher William, music by David Brooks and Karen Swanson; Director, Thatcher Williams, Musical Director, David Brooks; Presented by The Change Co-Operative

Spitting In The Face Of The Devil by Bob Brader; Director, Suzanne Bachner; Presented by John Montgomery Theatre Company

State of Undress by Katie Naka; Director, Katie Naka; Music Director, Alex Knox; Choreographer, Miriam Wasmund; Presented by The Impulse Initiative

Stress Positions by Daniel Sweren-Becker; Presented by Snapping Turtle Productions

Sunday Best by Laura Canty-Samuel, music by Laura Canty-Samuel and Ethan Forrest Wagner; Presented by Azddak Performances

Tales From The Tunnel Written and directed by Troy Diana and James Valletti

Talk Therapy by Thomas Moore; Director, Erick Herrscher; Presented by Thomas Moore and Robert Hawk

The Taming of the Shrew by William Shakespeare; Director, Meghan Farley Astrachan; Presented by Reaching Andromeda Theatre (RAT) NYC

Tearoom Tango by Douglas Holtz; Director, Jessica Jane Witham; Presented by Mercury Players, Inc.

Tell It To Me Slowly by Daniella Shoshan; Director, Jeremiah Matthew Davis; Presented by False Start Productions

Terranova by Pamela Monk and Dennis Loiacono; Director, Irene Carroll; Presented by Monreale Productions in association with StageFace Productions

Testify Choreographer, Elisha Clark Halpin; Presented by ETCH Dance Co.

Thirty Minutes or Less by Jonathan G Galvez; Director, Eliana Meira Rantz; Presented by Scamillante Productions

Thruline by Kevin Horne; Presented by NightWind Productions

A Time To Dance by Libby Skala; Presented by Artistic New Directions

Time's Scream and Hurry by Paul Hoan Zeidler; Presented by Sewer Socialist Productions

Troubles written and directed by Jeremiah Murphy; Presented by Murphy Brothers Productions

Truth Values, One Girl's Romp Through MIT's Male Math Maze by Gioia De Cari; Director, Miriam Eusebio; Presented by Unexpected Theatre

Two on the Aisle, Three in a Van Written and directed by Mary Lynn Dobson; Presented by Tiger Theatricals

Ukrainian Eggs, Terrible Tales of Tragedy and AlleGorey Choreographer, Jonathan Riedel; Presented by Riedel Dance Theater

Union Squared by David S. Singer; Presented by DSE, Inc

The Unlikely Adventure of Race McCloud, Private Eye Written and directed by Tom Hoefner; Presented by Momentum Repertory Company

Venus Written and directed by Jeremy Pickard; Presented by Superhero Clubhouse in association with Odyssey Productions and Upright Egg

Victoria and Frederick for President by Jonathan L. Davidson; Director, Charles Randolph Wright; Presented by Moson Productions

Viral by Mac Rogers; Director, Jordana Williams; Presented by Gideon Productions, LLC

Vote! Book and lyrics by Ryann Ferguson, music and additional lyrics by Steven Jamail; Director, Ryan J. Davis; Choreographer, Rachelle Rak

The W. Kamau Bell Curve, Ending Racism in About an Hour by W. Kamau Bell

White Horses, An Irish Childhood by Owen Dara; Director, Elizabeth Duck & Dan Toscano; Presented by Breaking Tide

Willy Nilly, A Musical Exploitation of the Most Far-Out Cult Murders of the Psychedelic Era by Trav S.D.; Director, Jeff Lewonczyk; Presented by Piper McKenzie

Winnemucca (three days in the belly) by Dan Moyer; Presented by Shelby Company in association with Little Red Square

A World Elsewhere! Arias in the Key of Clown Created and directed by Ben Newman; Presented by Wide Eyed Productions

Woyzeck by Georg Buchner; adapted and directed by Bob McDonald; Presented by the gangbusters theatre company

New York Musical Theatre Festival (NYMF)

Executive Director and Producer, Isaac Robert Hurwitz; Programming, Lily Hung; Operations, Lynn Spector; General Manager, Jennifer Collins; Associate General Manager, Stuart Shefter; Production Manager, Jeremiah Thies; Marketing & Sponsorship, Shane Marshall Brown; Senior Associate Producer, Eric Louie; Associate Producers, Anthony Francavilla, Jason Haft, Melanie Hopkins, Eve Rybnick, Jennifer Ashley Tepper, Liz Ulmer; Festival Press, Keith Sherman & Associates, Scott Klein; Resident Casting, Michael Cassara; Marketing Advisor, Karen Rusch; Graphics, Gabriel Aronson; www.nymf.org; sixth annual; September 28–October 18, 2009

Next Link Productions

Academy Book, music, and lyrics by John Mercurio, conceived and developed by Andrew Kato; Director, John Carafa; TBG Theater; October 6–17

All Fall Down Book by Greg Turner, music and lyrics by Selda Sahin; Directors, Lonny Price and Matt Cowart; 45th Street Theatre; October 9–18

Fantasy Football: The Musical? Book, music, and lyrics by David Ingber; Director, Adam Arian; TBG Theater; October 1-8

Fat Camp Book by Randy Blair and Timothy Michael Drucker, music by Matthew roi Berger, lyrics by Randy Blair; Director, Alex Timbers; Acorn Theatre; September 30–October 8

Marrying Meg Book, music, and lyrics by Mark Robertson; Based on the play *The Lass wi the Muckle Mou* by Alexander Reid; Director, Dave Solomon; Theatre at St. Clements; September 29–October 6

Mo Faya Book and music by Eric Wainaina, additional music by Joshua Mwai, Morris Otis Omollo and Helen Akoth Mtawali; Director, John Sibi-Okumu; TBG Theater; September 29–October 15

My Illustrious Wasteland Book, music, and lyrics by Tod Kimbro; Based on a concept by Jason Bowles; Director, Julia Granacki; American Theatre of Actors-Chernuchin Theatre; October 1–10

Open the Dark Door Book, music, and lyrics by David Lefort Nugent; Director, Susanna Gellert; American Theatre of Actors-Chernuchin Theatre; October 8–17

Plagued - A Love Story Book and lyrics by Vynnie Meli, music by Casey L. Filiaci; Director, Samuel Buggeln; TBG Theater; October 9–18

Rainbow Around the Sun Music and lyrics by Matthew Alvin Brown, book and additional lyrics by Tom Stuart; Director, Nick Demos; 45th Street Theatre; October 5–17

Seeing Stars Book by Shelley McPherson, music by Don Breithaupt, lyrics by Jeff Breithaupt; Director, Jenn Thompson; Theatre at St. Clements; October 7–17

The ToyMaker Book, music, and lyrics by Bryan Putnam; Director, Lawrence Edelson; The Theatre at St. Clements; October 5–18

Invited Productions

Anjou, A Tale of Horror Book, music, and lyrics by Guillermo Mendez and Lupita Sandoval; Director/Choreographer, Edgardo Lar; Theatre at St. Clements; October 8–12

Cross That River Music and lyrics by Allan Harris, book and direction by Andrew Carl Wilk, story by Allan and Pat Harris; TBG Theater; October 12–18

The Cure Story and songs by Mark Weiser; Director, Elizabeth Lucas; American Theatre of Actors-Chernuchin Theatre; September 29–October 11

F#@king Up Everything Music & lyrics by David Eric Davis; book by Sam Forman and David Eric Davis; Director, Stephen Brackett; 45th Street Theatre; October 6–17

Gay Bride of Frankenstein Book by Dane Leeman and Billy Butler; music and lyrics by Billy Butler; Director, Stephen Nachamie; TBG Theater; September 28–October 11

The Happy Embalmer Book, music, and lyrics by Mark Noonan and Nick Oddy; Director/Choreography, Kelly Devine; October 6–10

Hurricane Book, music, and lyrics by Michael Holland, book by Eric Bernat; Director, Michael Bush; Theatre at St. Clements; September 28–October 13

Judas & Me Book and lyrics by Chad Beguelin, music by Matthew Sklar; Director, Jeremy Dobrish; American Theatre of Actors-Chernuchin Theatre; September 28–October 11

The Last Smoker In America Book and lyrics by Bill Russell, music by Peter Melnick; Director, Sheryl Kaller; October 12–18

Lighter Book, music, and lyrics by Monica Bauer, arrangements by Brent-Alan Huffman; Director, Craig J. George; TBG Theater; October 5–17

Lorenzo Book by Judd Woldin and Richard Engquist, music by Judd Woldin, lyrics by Richard Engquist; Director, Christopher Scott; Acorn Theatre; October 5–11

Max Understood Book and lyrics by Nancy Carlin, music and lyrics by Michael Rasbury; Director, David Schweizer; 45th Street Theatre; September 28–October 7

My Scary Girl Book and lyrics by Kyoung-Ae Kang, music by Will Aronson; Director, Jun Joo Byun; Acorn Theatre; October 1–4

Street Lights Music, lyrics and book by Joe Drymala; Director, Ryan J. Davis; American Theatre of Actors-Chernuchin Theatre; October 13–18

Under Fire Book, lyrics and direction by Barry Harman, music by Grant Sturiale; Director, Theatre at St. Clements; September 30–October 12

Whatever Man Book, music, and lyrics by Benjamin Strouse; Director, Hilary Adams; September 29–October 8

Dance Series

Andy Warhol Was Right Book by Sammy Buck, music by Daniel S. Acquisto; Conceived by Melinda Atwood, Sammy Buck, Dan Acquisto, Daryl Gray, Giovanna Sardelli, Darren Lee and Shea Sullivan; Director, Giovanna Sardelli; Choreography, Daryl Gray, Darren Lee, Shea Sullivan; Manhattan Movement & Arts Center; September 30–October 4

Encore Conceived, directed and choreographed by Daniel Gwirtzman; Manhattan Movement & Arts Center; October 1–3

Developmental Series

Live! Nude! Girl! Book and lyrics by Donna Kaz; music by Wayne Barker; Director, Michael O'Donnell; 45th Street Theatre; October 15

Nightingale and the Satin Woman Book by William Kotzwinkle and Elizabeth Gundy, music and lyrics by Jerry Leiber and Mike Stoller; Director, Trevor Alexander; October 2

Punk Princess Book and lyrics by Yasmine Lever, music by Stew and Heidi Rodewald; Director, Jackson Gay; Theatre at St. Clements; October 14

Concerts

The Greenwood Tree Music and concept by Will Reynolds, text by William Shakespeare; 45th Street Theatre; September 30–October 2

Liberty Book and lyrics by Dana Leslie Goldstein, music by Jonathan Goldstein; Stage Direction, Igor Goldin; Acorn Theatre; September 29, 2009

Special Events

Count to Ten Book, music, and lyrics by Michael Blevins, additional lyrics by Beth Clary, additional music by Scott Knipe, Bruce Sacks and David Wollenberger; Theatre at St. Clements; October 15–17, 2009

Deep Cover Book, music, and lyrics by Michael Wolk; October 12–17

Letters to Daddy, Jr. Book by Jill Jaysen, music and lyrics by Mark Shepard, conceived and developed by 4e Productions; October 4

Moisty the Snowman Saves Christmas Book and lyrics by Bradford Scobie, music by Christian Dyas & Bradford Scobie, Additional Music by Paul Leschen; October 8–10

One Night Stand: An Improvised Musical by Quinn Beswick, Adam Cochran, Kobi Libii, Samantha Martin, Josh Margolin, Jonah Platt, Mollie Taxe and Andrew Resnick; American Theatre of Actors-Chernuchin Theatre; October 9–11

R.R.R.E.D: A Secret Musical Book by Adam Jackman, Patrick Livingston and Katie Thompson, music and lyrics by Katie Thompson; October 1–8

In Therapy With Celine Featuring the Music of Celine Dion; Book by Evan Storey; October 13

Rooms A Rock Romance CD Launch Party Music and lyrics by Paul Scott Goodman; Book by Paul Scott Goodman and Miriam Gordon; October 14

Rated RSO: The Music+Lyrics of Ryan Scott Oliver Director, Travis Greisler; American Theatre of Actors-Chernuchin Theatre; October 5

Sing, But Don't Tell Words by Sam Carner, music by Derek Gregor; Director, Igor Goldin; October 18

Partner Events

Argentina Passionate! Created, written and directed by Roi Escudero; October 5–7

Jim Caruso's Cast Party Festival Monday nights at Birdland

Mel and El: Gay Married October 8, 2009

Musicals on Television Paley Center; October 10–11

New York Neo-Futurists

www.nynf.org

Too Much Light Makes The Baby Go Blind Written, directed and performed by the Company; Technical Director, Lauren Parrish; Managing Director, Rob Neill; **Cast:** Adam Smith, Alicia Harding, Christopher Borg, Cara Francis, Christopher Loar, Dan McCoy, Desiree Burch, Eevin Hartsough, Erica Livingston, Jacquelyn Landgraf, Jeffrey Cranor, Jill Beckman, Joey Rizzolo, Kevin R. Free, Lauren Sharpe, Lusia Strus, Rob Neill, Ryan Good; Kraine Theater; June 5, 2009–May 30, 2010

Laika Dog in Space by Eevin Hartsough, Jill Beckman, Rob Neill; Director, Dave Dalton; Stage Manager, Christopher Diercksen; Set/Lightng, Lauren Parrish; Costumes, Meg Bashwiner; Audio/Visual, Timothy Caldwell; Composer, Carl Riehl; Technical Director, Lauren Parrish; Managing Director, Rob Neill; Managing Director, Shannon Sindelar; **Cast:** Eevin Hartsough, Jill Beckman, Rob Neill, Carl Riehl, Kara Ayn Napolitano; Presented as part of the Ontological Incubator Series; Ontological Theater; October 1–17, 2009

The Soup Show by the Company; Director, Lauren Sharpe; Stage Manager, Meg Bashwiner; Set/Lighting, Lauren Parrish; Costumes, Meg Bashwiner; Sound, Erica Livingston; Technical Director, Lauren Parrish; Managing Director, Rob Neill; **Cast:** Erica Livingston, Cara Francis, Desiree Burch; HERE Arts Center; March 4–27, 2010

Nicu's Spoon Theater

www.spoontheater.org

Hiding Behind Comets by Brian Dykstra; Director, John Trevellini; Set, John Trevellini; Costumes, Stephanie Barton-Farcas; Lighting, Steven Wolf; Stage Manager, Michelle Kuchuk; **Cast:** Rebecca Challis, David Tully, Oliver Conant, Kiran Malhotra; Spoon Theater; July 8–26, 2009

23 Coins Book, lyrics, & compositions by Mark Abrahams; Directors, Stephanie Barton-Farcas & Michelle KuchukSet/Costumes, Stephanie Barton-Farcas; Lighting, Steven Wolf; Sound/Arrangements/Music Direction, Michael O'Dell; Stage Manager, Danny Morales; Audio/Visual, Frank Vitale; Poster/Postcard Graphics, Kelly Meyers; Public Relations, Katie Rosin, Kampfire Films PR; **Cast:** Wynne Anders, Margaret Baker, Oliver Conant, Gillian Hurst, Katie Labahn, Rebecca Lee Lerman, Amir Levi, Phrannie Lyons, Michael O'Dell, Tim Romero, Peter Quinones, October 7– 25, 2009

Rumplestiltskin by Katie Labahn; Director, Nick Linnehan; Lighting, Alvarp Sena; Set, Alvaro Sena; Costumes, Alvaro Sena; Stage Manager, Phillip Chavira; **Cast:** Heriska Suthapa, Erin Salm, Sussanah Mcleod, Sammy Mean, Darla Foti, Matt Gaska; January 6– 29, 2010

Erosion: Life on Life's Terms Written and produced by Nicholas Linnehan; Director, Andrew Rothkin; Stage Manager, Phillip Chavira; Lighting, Casper DeLaTorre; Set, Yveyi Yi; Costumes, Phillip Chavira; Sound, Kristopher Pierce; **Cast:** Joane Cajuste, Jimmy Brooks Jr., Diana K. Lee, Daniela Thome, Gillian Hurst, Joe Fanelli; Nicu's Spoon Theater (Non-resident producion); January 13–30, 2010

Wit by Margaret Edson; Director, Alvaro Sena; Set, John Trevellini; Lighting, Steven Wolf; Costumes, Rien Schlecht; Stage Manager, Phillip Chavira; Medical Consultants, Eledryth Barton & Miriam Hernandez; ASL Interpreters, Pamela Mitchell, Gerald Small & Gabrielle Johnson; **Cast:** Stephanie Barton-Farcas, Oliver Conant, Rebecca Challis, Sammy Mena, Wynne Anders; April 7–25, 2010

No Hope Productions

www.nohopeproductions.com

Hello My Name is Billy by Tim Aumiller and Scott Schneider; Director, Tim Aumiller; **Cast:** Casey McClellan, Aaron Kliner, Tush, Robert Maril, Scott Schneider; The Duplex Cabaret Theatre; March 13–April 17, 2010

No.11 Productions

www.no11productions.com

The Elephant Man - The Musical Book, music, and lyrics by Jeff Hylton, co-book by Tim Werenko, co-music by Paul Jones; Director, Julie Congress; Costumes, Jill Hockett; Lighting, Jay Scott; Production Designer, Jen Neads; Choreographer, Simon Gunner; Music Director, Rebecca Greenstein; **Cast:** Ryan Emmons, Haley Greenstein, Roger Mulligan, Ira Sargent; @Seaport!; July 14–28, 2009

Nosedive Productions

Artistic Directors, Pete Boisvert and James Comtois; Company Manager, Stephanie Cox-Williams; Artistic Associates: Rebecca Comtois, Marc Landers, Patrick Shearer, Ben VandenBoom, Christopher Yustin; www.nosediveproductions.com

Infectious Opportunity by James Comtois; Director, Pete Boisvert; Stage Manager, Stephanie Cox-Williams; Lighting, Ian W. Hill; Set, Ben VandenBoom; Sound, Patrick Shearer; Technical Design, Rebecca Comtois; Original Music, Itai Miller; **Cast:** Rebecca Comtois, DR Hanson, Daryl Lathon, David Ian Lee, Ronica Reddick, Andrea Marie Smith, Matthew Trumbull; Brick Theater; June 7–July 21, 2009

The Blood Brothers Present... The New Guignol by Danny Bowes, James Comtois, and Mac Rogers; Directors, Pete Boisvert, Rebecca Comtois, Stephanie Cox-Williams, Abe Goldfarb, Matt Johnston, Patrick Shearer; Set, Arnold Bueso; Lighting, Daniel Winters; Costumes, Sarah Riffle, Madame Rosebud; Sound, Patrick Shearer; Original Music, Larry Lees; Stage Managers, Stephanie Cox-Williams, Dana Rossi; Makeup, Leslie Hughes; Fight Directors, Stephanie Cox-Williams, Patrick Shearer; **Cast:** Ryan Andes, Becky Byers, Rebecca Comtois, Jessi Gotta, Stephen Heskett, Robert Leeds, Marsha Martinez, Ben VandenBoom, Cotton Wright; Brick Theater; October 28–31, 2009

Nutshell Productions

www.noexittheplay.com

No Exit by Jean-Paul Sartres; Director, Robert Haufrecht; Set/Costumes, Craig Napolliello; Lighting/Sound, Eric Nightengale; Stage Manager, Charles Casano; **Cast:** Richard Hymes-Esposito, Geraldine Johns, Katherine Giordano, Etienne Navarro; Turtle Shell Theater; November 19–December 6, 2009

Nuyorican Poets Cafe, Inc.

www.nuyorican.org

The Domestic Crusaders Presented by Before Columbus Foundation; September 10–October 10, 2009

Hee-Haw: It's A Wonderful Lie Presented by LaVie Productions; December 3–20, 2009

Brownsville Bred: Growing Up Elaine! Presented by Del Valle Productions, Inc.; January 10–June 9, 2010

August Wilson's Women Presented by Juneteenth Legacy Theatre; March 25–April 10, 2010

Crossing the BLVD: Strangers, Neighbors, & Aliens in a New America Presented by EarSay; April 16–23, 2010

NYCPlaywrights

www.nycplaywrights.org

Autumn 2009 Reading by Olivia Arietti, Pamela Brown, Aliza Einhorn, Jan Fingland, Alan Glass, Jim Harvey, Peter Nicholls, N.G. McClernan, Walter Thinnes, Pamela Wilson; November 15, 2009

Spring 2010 Reading by Olivia Arieti, Ruth Tyndall Baker, Ruth Beiber, Micharne Cloughley, Rich Docherty, Jan Fingland, Peter Kapsales, Margo Krasne, N. G. McClernan, B. R. Wiggins; April 24, 2010

Ohio Theatre

www.sohothinktank.org

punkplay by Gregory Moss; Presented by Clubbed Thumb; Director, Davis McCallum; Set, Lee Savage; Costumes, Chloe Chapin; Lighting, Miranda K. Hardy; Sound, Dave Malloy; Stage Manager, Danielle Monica Long; Puppets, Kathleen Tobin; Fight Director, Tracy Bersley; **Cast:** Michael Zegen, Alex Anfanger, Matt Burns, Carie Kawa; June 7–13, 2009

Ice Factory Presented by Soho Think Tank; Included: *A Wonderland* by Eamonn Farrell; Produced by Anonymous Ensemble; Director, Eamonn Farrell; **Cast:** Cory Antiel, Kiebpoli Calnek, Liz Davito, Diana Egizi, Julie Foh, Josh Hoglund, Janelle Lannan, Matt Mager, Elisa Pupko, Kelly Shaffer, Jessica Weinstein, Meghan Williams; *Lavaman* by Casey Wimpee; Produced by Aztec Economy; Director, Matthew Hancock; **Cast:** Adam Belvo, Michael Mason, Cole Wimpee; *Babes in Toyland* Produced by The Little Lord Fauntleroys; Directors, Michael Levinton and José Zayas, **Cast:** Eliza Bent, Tonya Canada, David Greenspan, Sofia Jean Gomez, Megan Hill, John Kurzynowski, Michael Levinton, Rodney Pallanck, Sadrina Renee, Julia Sirna-Frest, Laura von Holt. Becky Yamamoto; *Reconstruction* Written and directed by Josh Fox; Producer, International WOW Company; *Conni's Avant-Garde Restaurant* Presented by Conni's Avant-Garde Restaurant; *Space//Space* written and directed by Mallory Catlett, Producer, Banana Bag & Bodice; **Cast:** Jason Craig, Jessica Jelliffe; July 8–August 15, 2009

Lavaman by Casey Wimpee; Presented by Aztec Economy; Director, Matthew Hancock; Lighting, Jake Platt; Sound, Ryan Dorla; Sean Berman; Dramaturg, Laten Willson; **Cast:** Michael Mason, Adam Belvo, Cole Wimpee; July 15–18, 2009

Conni's Avant Garde Restaurant Written, directed and performed by the ensemble; Set, David Barber; Lighting, Jeanette Yew; **Cast:** Justin Badger, Jeffrey Frace, Thomas Gissendanner, Connie Hall, Kelly Hayes, Jerusha Klemperer, Peter Lettre, Rachel Murdy, Deborah Philips, Peter Richards, Melody Bates, Jennifer Caster, Stephanie Dodd, Jesse Gustafson; September 25–26, 2010 (Ongoing at various other locations)

Hip-Hop Theatre Festival October 1–October 18, 2010

She Like Girls by Chisa Hutchinson; Presented by Working Man's Clothes; Director, Jared Culverhouse; Stage Manager, Megan Jupin; Lighting, Jake Platt; Set, Kelly Syring; Costumes, Laura Taber Bacon; Sound, Ryan Dorin; Choreographer, Sabrina Jacob; Artistic Producer, Darcie Champagne; **Cast:**

Amelia Fowler, Karen Eilbacher, Karen Sours, Adam Belvo, Jessica Gist, Ashley Noel Jones, Paul Notcie II, Lavita Shaurice, Chaz Rose; December 2–29, 2009

The Wind-up Bird Chronicle Presented by The Asia Society in association with Bayshnikov Arts Center, the Public Theater's "Under the Radar" Festival; January 12–30, 2010

Fêtes de la Nuit by Charles L Mee; Presented by WeildWorks; Director, Kim Weild; Stage Manager, Victoria Flores; Lighting, Charles Foster; Set, Brian Scott; Costumes, Lisa Renee Jordan; Sound, Christian Frederickson; Video, C. Andrew Bauer; Producer and General Manager, Jamie Forshaw; Documentarian and Photographer, Jill Usdan; Sound Operator, Oriol Muñoz; Press, David Gibbs; Technical Artist, Dave Polato; Marketing Advisor, Stephen J. Elms; American Sign Language Consultant, Lewis Merkin; Assistant to the Director, Matt Wilson; **Cast:** Danyon Davis, Jodi Dick, Corinne Edgerly, Babis Gousias, Jessica Green, Ana Grosse, Christine Rebecca Herzog, Itsuko Higashi, Jubil Khan, Kyle Knauf, Khris Lewin, Donnie Mather, John McGinty, Luis Moreno, Mirabelle Ordinaire, Rumi Oyama, Alexandria Wailes; February 8–27, 2010

Last Life by Eric Sanders; Presented by; Soho Think Tank and Big Time Action Theatre; Director, Timothy Haskell; Set, Paul Smithyman; Costumes, Candice Thompson; Lighting, Garin Marshall; Sound, Ariella Goldstein; Video & Animation, Gino Barzziza; Choreography, Rod Kinter; Stage Manager, Michelle Kelleher; **Cast:** Taimak Guariello, Alyxx Wilson, Aaron Haskell, Soomi Kim, Jo-Anne Lee, Maggie Macdonald; March 4–14, 2010

Rescue Me (A postmodern classic with snacks) Presented by Ma-Yi Theater Company; March 23–April 18, 2010

Short Love Presented by Theatre 4the People and Soho Think Tank; April 21–April 24, 2010

Reconstruction Written and directed by Josh Fox; Presented by International WOW Company; May 3–23, 2010

SummerWorks '10 Presented by Clubbed Thumb; May 31–June 27, 2010

One Armed Man

www.onearmedman.org

The Report of My Death Adapted and directed by Adam Klasfeld from various writings of Mark Twain; Costumes, Katie Falk; Sound, Michael Lemmerling; Stage Manager, Diana Sheivprasad; **Cast:** Michael Graves; Lilac Steamship; July 22–August 22, 2009

Ontological-Hysteric Theatre

www.ontological.com

Trifles by Susan Glaspell; Co-produced with The Theater of a Two-headed Calf; Director, Brooke O'Harra; Lighting, Justin Townsend; Set, Peter Ksander; Costumes, Lambent Flame; Original Music, Yarn/Wire; **Cast:** Mike Mikos, Caitlin McDonough-Thayer, Laryssa Husiak, Becca Blackwell, Daniel Manley; January 28–February 14, 2010

Non-resident Productions

Strangers by Nastaran Ahmadi; Presented by The Shalimar; Director, Shoshona Currier; **Cast:** Joey Williamson, Jen Taher, Kim Gainer, Franny Silverman, Daniel Popa, Brad Love, Peter Stone; Ontological Theatre; June 4–13, 2009

Behind the Bullseye Written and directed by Kevin Doyle; Presented by Sponsored by Nobody; Sound/Audio/Visual, Kevin Doyle; Design, Brendan Regimbal; **Cast:** Michael Carlsen, Mayra Castro, Keith Jamal Downing, Natalie Kim, Sauda Jackson, Sarah Stephens; July 1–11, 2009

I Stand for Nothing Written and directed by Eric Bland; Presented by Old Kent Road Theater; Lighting, Amanda Woodward; Puppets, Abernathy Bland; **Cast:** Anne Carlisle, Siobhan Doherty, Charlie Hewson, Gavin Starr Kendall, Margaret Laney, Jesse Liebman, Richard Lovejoy, Maggie Marion, Timothy John McDonough, Megan McGowan, Iracel Rivero, Joey Ryan, Victoria Tate, Eric Bland, Scott Eckert; July 1–18, 2009

There Will Be Snacks Written and directed by Chris Masullo; Presented by Three Sciences Theatre; Costumes, Dana Covarrubias; Sound, Chris Barlow and Chris Masullo; Production Design, Jonathan Cottle, Barbara Samuels, Chris Masullo; **Cast:** Ronan Babbitt, Emily J. Kunkel, Thomas Pecinka, Joe Hewes Clark, William Callahan; August 5– 8, 2009

Family Written and directed by Tina Satter; Presented by Half Straddle; Set, Nathan Lemoine; Costumes, Normandy Raven Sherwood; Lighting, Zack Tinkelman; Original Music, Chris Giarmo; Stage Manager, D.J. Neal; Choreographer, Chris Giarmo; **Cast:** Eliza Bent, Sara Copeland, Emily Davis, Chris Giarmo, Joseph Keckler, Erin Markey, Katherine Scharhon, Julia Sirna-Frest, Rae C. Wright; August 13–22, 2009

The Importance of Being Earnest Written and performed by Rachel Hynes & Mike Pham; Presented by Helsinki Syndrome; August 27–September 5, 2009

Undine by Created by Faith Helma; Presented by Hand2Mouth Theatre; Director, Jonathan Walters; Music Director, Peter Musselman, DJ Brokenwindow, John Berendzen; Set, Drew Foster; Lighting, Christopher Kuhl; Costumes, Lacey Cassidy, Harmony Arnold; Stage Manager, Liam Kaas-Lentz; **Cast:** Faith Helma; August 27–September 5, 2009

Buddy Cop 2 by Hannah Bos & Paul Thureen; Presented by The Debate Society; Director, Oliver Butler; Set, Laura Jellinek; Costumes, Sydney Maresca; Lighting, Mike Riggs; Sound, Nathan Leigh; **Cast:** Hannah Bos, Paul Thureen, Monique Vukovic, Michael Cyril Creighton; Ontological Theatre; May 20–June 12, 2010

Opening Doors Theater Company

Artistic Director, Suzanne Adams; www.ODTConline.org

Subways Are for Sleeping Music by Jule Styne, book & lyrics by Betty Comden and Adolph Green; Director, Hector Coris; Music Director, Ted Kociolek; Choreography, Diego Funes; Production Manager, Billie Di Stefano; Lighting, Thomas Honeck; **Cast:** Lee Cavellier, Erin Cronican, Scott McLean Harrison, Gregory W. Knotts, Erin McCracken, Spencer Plachy, Lexi Windsor; The Duplex Cabaret Theatre; November 1–11. 2009

Is There Life After High School? Music and lyrics by Craig Carnelia, book by Jeffrey Kindley; Director, Jeremy Gold Kronenberg; Music Director, Andrew Smithson; Choreography, Edward Carnigan; Lighting, Thomas Honeck; Assistant Director, Jennifer Ashley Tepper; Production Manager, Bilie Di Stefano; **Cast:** Doug Chitel, Mark Emerson, Amy Fitts, Marcie Henderson, Leslie Henstock, Autin Ku, Austin Owens, Heather Jane Rolff, Lou Steele; The Duplex Cabaret Theatre; April 6–17, 2010

The Operating Theater

www.operatingtheater.org

The Garden of Forked Tongues Written and directed by Jason Schuler; Set, Gian Marco Lo Forte; Costumes, Jenifer Paar; Lighting, Simon Cleveland; Sound, Matt Szwed & Patrick Murano; Stage Manager, Charles Graytok; Video, Keith Chandler, Jason Schuler; Producers, Dori Ann Scagnelli, Jason Schuler; Consulting Producer, Cynthia Stillwell; Video Consultant, Mike Taylor; Video Editor, Keith Chandler; Photographer, Daniela Sessa; Marketing Consultant, Caroline Burwell; Marketing Associates, Kaira Klueber, Kelly Zekas; Puppets, Jason Schuler; **Cast:** Keith Chandler, Tim Donovan Jr., Alexis Fedor, Adam Hyland, James Rich, Elizabeth Stine, Anna Wilson, Jacqueline LeClaire; Teatro IATI; September 24–October 18, 2009

Transatlantica by Kenny Finkle; Director, Jason Schuler; November 20, 2009

Ordinary Theater

The Joys of Fantasy Written and directed by Mitchell Polin; Lighting, Nick Kolin assisted by Sarah Lurie; Audio/Visual, Jenks Whittenberg; Original Music, Tungsten 74; **Cast:** Susannah Berard, Michael Cross Burke, Caroline Gart, Teri Incampo, Claire Kavanah, Scott Troost; Twelve21; July 8–25, 2009

Orphanage Productions

Walking The Road by Dermot Bolger; Director, John Brant; Stage Manager, Chris Jensen; Lighting, Chris Jensen; Set, Chris Jensen; Sound, Chris Jensen; **Cast:** David Beck, Mark Anthony Noonan; Players Theatre & Players Loft; September 11–October 4, 2009

The Outrageous Fortune Company

www.OutrageousFortuneCompany.com

Dead Man's Cell Phone by Sarah Ruhl; Director, Bernard Bosio; Lighting, Glenn Rivano; Sound, Dayle Vander Sande; Stage Manager, Lydia Scotti; **Cast:** Janice Bishop, Denise Fiore, Ashley Kuske, Ross Pivec, Ben Prayz, Leslie Swanson; Queens Theatre in the Park; November 13–22, 2009

Spalding Gray: Stories Left To Tell by Kathleen Russo & Lucy Sexton; Director, William P. Saunders III; Stage Manager, Lucie Tripon; Lighting, Glenn Rivano; **Cast:** Bernard Bosio, Pat Clune, Emma Givens, Bill Rapp, Carol Wei, Tracy Winston; Queens Theatre in the Park; March 19–27, 2010

The Blue Room by David Hare; Director, Myla Pitt; Set, Theresa Rivera; Lighting, David Monroy; Sound, Lesley Stoller; Stage Manager, Lydia Scotti; **Cast:** Brendan Hunt, Eric Kirchberger, Alain Laforest, Catherine LeFrere, Milada Melli-Jones, Kristen Royal; Queens Theatre in the Park; May 14–23, 2010

A 50-Year Itch by Elyse Nass; Director, Bernard Bosio; **Cast:** Pat Clune, Ronald B. Hellman; May 19, 2010

Packawallop Productions, Inc.

www.packawallop.org

marea by Alejandro Morales; Director, Scott Ebersold; Set, Jo Winiarski; Costumes, Jennifer Paar; Lighting, Scott Bolman; Sound, Brandon Wolcott; Stage Manager, Josh Parkin-Ring; Audio/Visual, Daniel Heffernan; Props, Buist Bickley; Casting, Judy Bowman; Production Manager, Julian Stetkevych; Assistant Director, Laura Pestronk; ASM, Samantha Gallardo; **Cast:** Maria-Christina Oliveras, Polly Lee, Maggie Bofill, Judith Delgado; Presented as part of the HERE Arts Center Supported Artist Program; HERE Arts Center; December 3–6, 2009

The Golden Vanity by Alejandro Morales; Director Scott Ebersold; **Cast:** John Halbach, David Grimm, Julian Stetkevych, Danyon Davis, Sevrin Mason, William Bel; April 20, 2010

The Lounge Series Readings; included**:** *Unblessed* by Kari Bentley-Quinn, directed Laura Pestronk, featuring Gayton Scott, Kat Garson, Polly Lee, Gerald Kimble, Mark Watson, Christina Shipp, Julian Stetkevych; Jimmy's 43; January 12, 2010; *Between Adults* by Josh Sohn, directed by Don Nguyen, featuring Susan Louise O'Connor, Richard Grunn, Joanna Howard, Matthew J. Nichols, Maria Christina Oliveras; 43 E. 7th Street; March 8, 2010; *Mistaken Identity* Nine short plays written and performed by the thirty-five members of The Pack; Robert Moss Theater; May 24, 2010

Page 73 Productions

www.p73.org

Creature by Heidi Schreck; Co-produced with New Georges; Director, Leigh Silverman; Stage Manager, Sunneva Stapleton; Lighting, Matt Frey; Set, Rachel Hauck; Costumes, Theresa Squire; Sound, Katie Down; Sean McArdle; **Cast:** Marylouise Burke, Sofia Jean Gomez, Darren Goldstein, Tricia Rodley, Will Rogers, Jeremy Shamos; (see complete listing in Off-Broadway section of this volume); Ohio Theatre; October 28–November 21, 2009

Jack's Precious Moment by Samuel D. Hunter; Director, Kip Fagan; Presented as part of the Americas Off-Broadway Festival (see complete listing in Off-Broadway section of this volume); 59E59 Theater C; May 21–June 13, 2010

Readings

Love Trapezoid by Matt Schatz; Director, Jordan Young; July 16; *Recall* by Eliza Clark; Director, Kip Fagan; August 3; *House on Stilts* by Sarah Hammond; Director, Ethan McSweeney; October 5; *There Are No More Big Secrets* by Heidi Schreck; Director, Ken Russ Schmoll; December 8; *Special Tonight* by Aaron Landsman; Director, Ken Russ Schmoll; January 28; *Carthage* by Emily Schwend; Director, Davis McCallum; April 12; *Light Years from the Delling Shore* by Sam Marks; Director, Sam Gold; May 24

Pale Fire

www.james-veitch.com

Room 103, Hotel Chelsea Written and directed by James Veitch; Lighting, Jonathan Cottle; Set, Jonathan Cottle; Sound, Melissa Vaughn-Kleppel; Stage Manager, Angela Santillo; Audio/Visual, Gabriel Aronson; Sydney Buchan; **Cast:** Kevin Confoy, Lucia Brizzi, Justin Perkins; Chelsea Hotel Room 103.; March 19–28, 2010

The Panoply Performance Laboratory

The Last Dreams of Helene Weigel or How to Get Rid of The Feminism Once and For All by Brian McCorkle, Esther Neff, and the Panoply Performance Laboratory; Director/Choreographer, Esther Neff; Set, Liz Jenatopolus; Costumes, Lena Sands; Sound/Original Music, Brian McCorkle; Video & Puppet Design, Panoply Design; **Cast:** Andrea Suarez, Tom Swirly, Katie Johnston, Matthew Stephen Smith, Kate Garfield, Loren Barnese, Matthew Gonzalez, Jessica Bathurst; Surreal Estate; July 25–31, 2009

Paradise Factory

Someone in Florida Loves Me Written and directed by Jane Pickett; Set, Adam Brustein; Lighting, John Eckert; Costumes, Leah Piehl; Sound, Peter Zuspan; Stage Manager, Samantha Gallardo; Audio/Visual, Lindsey Bostwick; **Cast:** Lisa Louttit, Ana Perea, T.M. Bergman; June 14–28, 2009

Non-resident Productions

bash by Neil LaBute; Director, Robert Knopf; Presented by Eastcheap Rep; **Cast:** Luke Rosen, Chelsea Lagos; September 9–19, 2009

Hamlet by William Shakespeare; Presented by Organs of State; Director, John Kurzynowski; Stage Manager, Mickey McGuire; Set/Lighting, Natalie Robin; Sound, Kate Marvin; Rehearsal Stage Manager, Cynthia Hennon; Producers, Guy Yedwab and Sydney Matthews; Fire Guard, Sydney Matthews; Assistant Director, Dinah Finkelstein; Electrician, Marika Kent; **Cast:** Jaclyn Backhaus, Jonathan Bock, Matthew Capodicasa, Tommy Heleringer, Stacy Jordan, Anastasia Olowin, Miguel Pinzon, Jon Riddleberger, Eugene Michael Santiago, Tina Shepard, Kyle Williams; February 25–March 6, 2010

Misty Foster Venters and Elizabeth A. Davis in the Firebone Theatre production of Emily, An Amethyst Remembrance *(photo by Rachelle Beckerman)*

Herb Rubens and Larry Mitchell in The Barrow Group's Enemy of the People *(photo by Rafael Jordan)*

A scene from the New York Classical Theatre production of Hamlet, Prince of Denmark *(photo by Miranda Arden)*

Danny Bowes, Shelley Ray, and Gyda Arber in Blood on the Cat's Neck, *presented by Gemini CollisionWorks (photo courtesy of Gemini CollisionWorks)*

Brad Fraizer and J. M. McDonough Under the Gaslilght *at the Metropolitan Playhouse (photo by Aric Gutner)*

A scene from Laughing In The Wind, *presented by Yangtze Repertory Theatre (photo by Jonathan Slaff)*

A scene from !! FreEpLaY !!, presented by *Strike Anywhere Performance Ensemble (photo by Sabrina Hamilton)*

Sean Phillips in the Godlight Theatre Company's production of John Ball's In the Heat of the Night *(photo by Derrick Belcham)*

Members of the Czechoslovak-American Marionette Theatre in Revolution!? *at P.S. 122 (photo by Nikola Horejs)*

Lynn Kenny and Blaine Pennington in the Redd Tale Theatre production of Maddy: A Modern Day *Medea (photo by Ben Strothmann)*

Stacia French and Mark Lindberg in Live/Feed, *presented by The Nerve Tank (photo by Raymond Haddad)*

Pathological Theater Company, Inc.

Night Lights Written and directed by Dario D'Ambrosi, translated by Celeste Moratti; **Cast:** Celeste Moratti, Jarde Jacobs; Washington Street between Spring and Canal; July 6– July 8, 2009

Peculiar Works Project

Directors, Ralph Lewis, Catherine Porter, Barry Rowell; www.peculiarworks.org

At This Site: Houston @ Bowery & Chrystie by various; A site-specific performance written and performed by the students of the Trinity/La Mama Urban Arts Semester program in the Whole Foods Market at Houston & Bowery; November 6, 2009

Readings

Pinky the Pig, and a Few Hallelujahs by Bryn Manion; Director Lauren Keating; Middle Collegiate Church; July 13; *Oneida: Servants of Motion* by Johnna Adams; Director, Connie de Veer; Merchant's House Museum Garden; July 19; *Big Hungry World* by Susan Bernfield; Director, Emma Griffin; Mertz Gilmore Foundation; July 26, 2009; *No One Brings Anything Small into a Bar* by Barry Rowell; Director, Barry Rowell; Jimmy's No. 43 Restaurant; August 2

Performance Lab 115

www.chocolatefactorytheatre.org

Caucasian Chalk Circle by Bertolt Brecht; Director, Alice Reagan; Lighting, Peter Ksander; Set, Peter Ksander; Costumes, Asta Hostetter; Sound, Mark Valadez; Choreographer, Beth Kurkjian; Original Music, Mark Valadez; Translated by Eric Bentley; **Cast:** Justin Badger, Marty Keiser, Jeff Clarke, Rachel Jablin, Sara Buffamanti, Rebecca Lingafelter, Heather Hollingsworth, Liz Eckert, Elizabeth Malone, Chris Richards, Rachel Schwartz, Ben Vershbow; The Chocolate Factory; June 25–July 11, 2009

The Verge by Susan Glaspell; Director, Alice Reagan; Stage Manager, Liz Nielsen; Set, Jennifer de Fouchier; Costumes, Lucrecia Briceno; Sound, Mark Valadez; Jeff Clarke; **Cast:** Sara Buffamanti, B. Brian Argotsinger, Rebecca Lingafelter, Tuomas Hiltunen, Todd d'Amour, Rachel Jablin, Birgit Huppuch; Ontological Theatre; November 5–21, 2009

Performance Space 122 (P.S. 122)

Artistic Director, Vallejo Gantner; Business and Organizational Resources; Winnie Fung; Director of Productions, Derek Lloyd; Marketing, Carleigh Welsh; Development, Morgan von Prelle Pecelli; IT/House Manager, Alex Reeves; Technical Director, Nick Bixby; www.ps122.org

Dark Horse/Black Forest Written, produced, and directed by Yanira Castro; Original Music, Stephan Moore; Costumes, Suzanne Dougan; **Cast:** Heather Olson, Joseph Poulson, Luke Miller, Darrin Wright; The Gershwin Hotel; June 5–28, 2009

Darling Written and choreographed by Sam Kim; Lighting, Justin Sturges; Producer/Sound, Sam Kim; **Cast:** Jodi Bender, Sam Kim, Ryan McNamara, and Liz Santoro; June 24–28, 2009

Spalding Gray: Stories Left to Tell by Spalding Gray; Conceived by Kathleen Russo; Director, Lucy Sexton; Set, David Korins; Lighting, Ben Stanton; Costumes, Michael Krass; Original Music and Sound, Fitz Patton; Presented with Naked Angels Theatre Company; July 16, 2009

Tales from Bordertown (prologue) Written and performed by Eric Dean Scott; Presented by Wax Factory, Ivan Talijancic, Eric Latta; Director/Design, Erika Latta; July 7–10, 2009

Why Won't You Let Me Be Great!!! Conceived by Brendan Kennedy; Producer, Catch, Neal Medlyn, Brendan Kennedy; July 30–August 1, 2009

A Last Supper Written, performed, and produced by The Wau Wau Sisters; August 19, 2009

Braakland (Wasteland) Based on the novels of J.M. Coetzee; Director, Lotte Van den Berg; Producer, Compagnie Dakar/Lotte van der Berg; Governor's Island; September 10–20, 2009

Avant-Garde-Arama Fall 2009 Featuring Karen Therese, Lizzie Thomson, Joey Arias, M. Lamar, Maria Hassabi, Carmelita Tropicana, Maureen Angelos, Carol Lipnik and Spookarama, GoonSquad, Nicole Blackman, Scott Ewalt, Jackie Hoffman, Beadz on Nude Illusion, enemyResearch, Adrienne Truscott, Reggie Watts, Andrew Schneider, Joro-Boro; September 18–19, 2009

Way Out West, the Sea Whispered Me Presented and performed by Cupola Bobber; Technical Consultants, Nat Ward, Michelle Faust; **Cast:** Stephen Fiehn and Tyler B Myers; Producer, Cupola Bobber; September 24–27, 2009

The Archery Contest by John Jahnke; Produced by Hotel Savant; Director, John Jahnke; Lighting, Miranda Hardy; Set, Peter Ksander; Costumes, Carlos Soto; Sound, Kristin Worrall, Jamie Mcelhinney; Andrew Schneider; **Cast:** Richard Toth, Hillary Spector, Carey Urban, Alexander Borinsky, Jeff Worden; October 2–18, 2009

The Assember Dilator by Ryan Holsopple & Shannon Sindelar; Presented by 31 Down Radio Theater; Director, Shannon Sindelar; Set, Andreea Mincic; Costumes, TaraFawn Marek; Lighting, Ryan Holsopple & Jon Luton; Sound, Ryan Holsopple; Mirit Tal; **Cast:** Caitlin McDonough-Thayer, Ryan Holsopple; October 8–18, 2009

Americana Kamikaze written and directed by Kenneth Collins; Presented by Temporary Distortion; Lighting and Set, Kenneth Collins; Costumes, TaraFawn Marek; Sound, John Sully; Audio/Visual, William Cusick and Jon Weiss; Original Music, John Sully; **Cast:** Brian Geer, Yuki Kawahisa, Lorraine Mattox, and Ryosuke Yamada; Upstairs at PS 122; October 24–November 14, 2009; Encored in the COIL Festival January 8–11

Zee Created by Kurt Hentschläger; Produced with FuturePerfect and CPR (Center for Performance Research); 3LD Art & Technology Center; October 28–November 15, 2009

Symphony n.1 Producers, Alterazioni Video and Ragnar Kjartansson; November 5, 2009

Rabih Mroué's Gift to New York Written, directed and performed by Rabih Mroué; Producer, Performa 09; November 7–8, 2009

Terrible Things by Lisa D'Amour; Director/Choreographer, Emily Johnson; Producers, Lisa D'Amour, Katie Pearl and Emily Johnson; **Cast:** Katie Pearl, Emily Johnson, Morgan Thorson, Karen Sherman; December 4–20, 2009; Encored at the COIL Festival January 8–12

Crime or Emergency by Sibyl Kempson; Director, John Collins; Sound, Ben Williams; Musical Accompaniment and Arrangements, Mike Iveson; Production Manager, Brian White; **Cast:** Sibyl Kempson, Mike Iveson Jr.; December 4–20, 2009

Conversations with Culture: Contemporary Performance and the Multiverse Featuring David Z. Albert, Lisa D'Amour, Katie Pearl, Brian Schwartz, DJ Spooky, Richard Easther; Sony Wonder Technology Lab; December 9, 2009

The BodyCartography Project 1/2 Life Presented by BodyCartography Project; Composer and Harpist, Zeena Parkins; Physicist, Bryce Beverlin II; **Cast:** Takemi Kitamura, Sinan Goknur, Becky Olson, Taja Will, Jennifer Arave, Kimberly Lesik, Emma Rainwater, Melissa Birch, Laressa Dickey, Melissa Guerrero, Sharon Mansur, Laura Grant, Nick LeMere; February 10–14, 2010

Whew! Age Written and performed by Marisa Olson; February 12–14, 2010

The Talking Show by Tom Murrin; Director, Lucy Sexton; Lighting, Melissa J. Mendez; Producer, Lori E. Seid; **Cast:** Tom Murrin, Kate Benson, Laurie Berg, Heidi Dorow, Mike Iveson, Salley May, Mimi Goese; Tom Murrin, Lucy Sexton; February 18–March 7, 2010

Whatever, Heaven Allows Written, presented, and directed by the Radiohole Ensemble; Lighting, Michael Casselli; Sound, Jason Sebastian, Raul Vincent Enriquez; Aaron Harrow; **Cast:** Maggie Hoffman, Eric Dyer, Erin Douglass, Mark Jaynes, Joseph "Wedgewood" Silovsky, Kourtney Rutherford; February 20–March 21, 2010

Semiospectacle Curated by Mashinka Firunts; Musical Accompaniment, Grandpa Musselman & His Syncopators; **Cast:** Vaginal Davis, Lord Whimsy, Dr. Lucky, Jeremy JF Thompson, Paolo Javier, Daniel Scott Snelson, The Minsky Sisters, Shonni Enelow; March 22, 2010

Sandra Brown One of Our Ain Written and performed by Sandra Brown; April 8–18, 2010

The Wooster Group's Booty Call Avant-Garde-Arama! Featuring Eric Dyer, Stiven Luka, Jean Coleman, Cynthia Hopkins, Daniel Pettrow, Esra Chelen, Andrew Schneider, Light Asylum, Jibz Cameron, Jamie Poskin, Daniel Jackson, Maurina Lioce, Jim Findlay, Kelley McRae; Producer: Mashinka Firunts, and The Wooster Group; April 16–17, 2010

Gin and "It" Director, Reid Farrington; Stage Manager, Julia Funk; Lighting, Christopher Heilman; Set, Art Domantay; Costumes, Erin Elizabeth Murphy; Sound, Connor Kalista; Dramaturgy, Peter C. von Salis; Script Supervisor, Sara Jeanne Asselin; Fight Choreography, Carrie Brewer; Research Assistant, Sarah Doyle; Best Boy Editor, Thomas Gonzalez; Lead Editor, Paulina Jurzec; Editors, Celina Alarado, Jeanne Angel, Patrick Grizz; **Cast:** Karl Allen, Keith Foster, Christopher Loar, Tim McDonough; Co-presented with Under The Radar in association with 3LD Art & Technology Center, co-produced by the Wexner Center for the Arts at The Ohio State University, 3LD Art & Technology Center; 3LD Art & Technology Center; April 24–May 9, 2010

Performance Space 122 Annual Spring Gala Honorary Chairs, Claire Danes, Baz Luhrmann; Honoring John Leguizamo; Hosts: Carmelita Tropicana, Marga Gomez; Special Guests: Hazelle Goodman, Lenny Kaye, Spike Lee, Rosie Perez, The Wau Wau Sisters, John Turturro, Andrew Andrew, Eric Bogosian; Abrons Arts Center; May 4, 2010

soloNOVA Arts Festival Presented by the terraNOVA Collective; May 5–June 6, 2010; Artistic Director, Jennifer Conley Darling; Associate Artistic Director, James Carter; Managing Director, Diane Alianiello; Producer, Jaimie Mayer; Groundbreakers Program Director, Jessi D. Hill; Press, Emily Owens; included: *Binding* by Jesse Zaritt; Director, Basmat Hazan; Stage Manager, John Murdoch; Lighting, David Tirosh; Set, Daniel Zimmerman; Costumes, Manju Shandler; Sound, Sharath Patel; Puppet Design, David Tirosh; Choreographer, Jesse Zaritt; Original Music, Hillary Charnas; **Cast:** Jesse Zaritt; May 5–29; *It or Her* by Alena Smith; Director, Jessi D. Hill; Set/Costumes, Jennifer Moeller; Sound, David A. Thomas; Choreographer, Alison D'Amato; **Cast:** Brian McManamon; May 13–22; *Monster* by Daniel MacIvor; Director, Steve Cook; Stage Manager, Shannon O'Neill; Lighting, Robin A. Paterson; **Cast:** Avery Pearson; May 5–June 4; *Puppy Love: A Stripper's Tail* by Erin Markey; Director, Travis Chamberlain; Original Music, Rich Campbell; **Cast:** Erin Markey; May 13–June 6; *Remission* by Kirk Wood Bromley; **Cast:** Dan Berkey; May 6–18; *Rootless: La No-Nostalgia* by Karina Casiano; Stage Manager, Miguel Angel Reyes; **Cast:** Karina Casiano; May 11–May 22; *The W. Kamau Bell Curve: Ending Racism in About an Hour* by W. Kamau Bell; Director, Paul Stein; **Cast:** W. Kamau Bell; May 11–June 4; *Wanted* by Shontina Vernon; Director, Kamilah Forbes; Original Music, Shontina Vernon; **Cast:** Shontina Vernon; May 5–15

Vaginal Davis Is Speaking From The Diaphragm Design and production by Jonathan Berger in collaboration with Sarah Marcy Maurer, Joshua Lubin-Levy, Alexander Hollenbach, Julia Rexon; Costumes, Nikko Lencek-Inagaki, Arjuna Balaranjan, Ross Menuez and Rick Owens; Sound, Jason Martin; Audio/Visual, Jean Kim; **Cast:** Carmelita Tropicana, Jennifer Miller, and others; May 15–27, 2010

COIL Festival – January 6–17, 2010

Ads Written and directed by Michael Schmelling and Bozkurt Karasu; Presented by Richard Maxwell/NYC Players; Audio/Visual, Michael Schmelling and Bozkurt Karasu; Technical Director, Bozkurt Karasu; Editor and Projection Operator, Joshua Day; Associate Producer, Allison Lyman; **Cast:** Ramin Bahrani, Lakpa Bhutia, Jerimee Bloemeke, Sophia Chai, Janet Coleman, Keith Connolly, Ginger Corker, Richard Dundy, Bob Feldman, Rosie Goldensohn, Anita Hollander, Rosalie Ann Kaplan, Lou Kuhlmann, Michelle A. Lee, Walid Mohanna, Philip Moore, Farooq Muhammad, Christian Nunez, Nicole, Louis Puopolo, Mark Russell, Katherine Ryan, Rafael Sanchez, Monica de la Torre, Ariana Smart Truman, Kate Valk; Upstairs at PS 122; January 6–17, extended January 20–February 6

Americana Kamikaze Encore presentation (see complete credits in the listing on previous page); Upstairs at PS 122; January 8–11

Blind.ness by Simona Semenic; Director, Ivan Talijancic; Set, Minimart; Sound, Random Logic and Erika Latta; Audio/Visual, Antonio Giacomin; Co-produced by Cankarjev Dom and the WaxFactory; Abrons Arts Center; January 6–12

Chautauqua! Created, presented and performed by the National Theatre of the United States of America; **Cast:** Robert Zukerman, Rollo Romig, Samantha Hunt, Vallejo Gantner, Kathleen Russo, Greta Byrum, Zoe Rosenfeld, Uliana Francis Kelly; The Public Theater; January 7–17

East 10th Street: Self Portrait with Empty House by Edgar Oliver; Presented by Axis Theatre Company; Director, Randy Sharp; Stage Manager, Marc Palmieri; Lighting, David Zeffren; Set, Ian Tooley; Sound, Steve Fontaine; Artistic Director, Randy Sharp; Producing Director, Brian Barnhart; Executive Producer, Jeffrey Resnick; Production Manager, Mr. Tooley; **Cast:** Edgar Oliver; Downstairs at PS 122; January 6–17

Gin and "It" Preview performances at 3LD Art & Technology Center (for complete credits see listing on this page); January 7–16

GuruGuru Written and directed by Ant Hampton; Producer, Rotozaza; Sound, Isambard Khroustaliov; Audio/Visual, Joji Koyama; **Cast:** Joji Koyama, Isambard Khroustaliov; Classroom at PS 122; January 6–12

Heaven Choreographed and performed by Morgan Thorson; Upstairs at PS 122; January 7–12

Jerk by Gisèle Vienne based on text by Dennis Cooper; Director, Gisèle Vienne; **Cast:** Jonathan Capdevielle; Gisèle Vienne, Jonathan Capdeville, Dennis Cooper; Downstairs at PS 122 January 7–17

Mimic Written, produced, music, and performance by Raymond Scannell; Produced and directed by Tom Creed; Upstairs at PS 122; January 8–17

Prima Choreographed by LeeSaar; Presented by LeeSaar The Company; Original Music, DJ Filastine; **Cast:** Jye-Hwei Lin, Hsin-Yi Hsiang, Candice Schnurr, Hyerin Lee; Jewish Community Center; January 7–10

Solo & SoloShow Choreographed, produced and sets by Maria Hassabi; Lighting, Joe Levasseur; Co-Set, Scott Lyall; Costumes, ThreeAsFour; Sound, James Lo; Dramaturg, Marcos Rosales; **Cast:** Maria Hassabi, Hristoula Harakas; Private Studio on W. 27th Street; January 11–12

Terrible Things Encored at the COIL Festival (for complete credits see listing on previous page); Downstairs at PS 122; January 8–12

...within us Choreographer, Megan V. Sprenger; Presented by Producer, Megan Sprenger/mvworks; Lighting, Joe Levasseur; Set, Brad Kisicki; Costumes, Mary McKenzie; Sound, Jason Sebastian; **Cast:** Tara O'Con, Kendra Portier, Alli Ruszkowski, Richert Schonorr; Downstairs at PS 122; January 6–9

Peter and Matt's Production Company

Wait of the World by Peter Dagger; Director, Jeremy Bloom; Set/Original Art, Sean Ward; Special Effects, Jeremy Bloom and Sean Ward; **Cast:** Jenny Checchia, Harry Einhorn, Joyce Miller, Rachel Richman, Joe Tannenbaum; Benefit for the Gynecologic Cancer Foundation; Robert Moss Theatre; June 13–27, 2009

Phoenix Theatre Ensemble

www.phoenixtheatreensemble.org

No Exit by Jean-Paul Sartre; Director, Elise Stone; Stage Manager, Miriam Hyfler; Lighting, Tsubasa Kamei; Set, Tsubasa Kamei; Costumes, Peggy McKowen; Sound, Betsy Rhodes; Technical Director, Vadim Malinskiiy; **Cast:** Joe Menino, Craig Smith, Laura Piquado, Kelli Holsopple; Wild Project; December 3–13, 2009

Goldilocks & The Three Bears by Kathy Menino; Director, Rebecca A. Katzman; Stage Manager, Rebecca A. Katzman; Lighting, Tsubasa Kamei; Set, Justin L. McCormick; Technical Director, Amy Wagner; Graphics, Susan Newman Design Inc.; Original Painting, Meghan Lantzy; **Cast:** Laura Di Certo, Erica Hazel Flory, Brian Hopson, Courtney Kochuba, Diana London, Florence Pape; Wild Project; December 5–12, 2009

The Man of Destiny by George Bernard Shaw; Director, Amy Wagner; Stage Manager, Miriam Hyfler; Set/Lighting, Maruti Evans; Costumes, Suzanne Chesney; Sound, Ellen Mandel; Technical Director, Vadim Maliskiiy, Master Electrician, Melissa Johnson; Assistant Set, Wiki Lo, Graphics, Monty Stilson; **Cast:** Josh Tyson, Craig Smith, Brian A. Costello, Amy Fitts; Wild Project; May 6–16, 2010

The 3 Little Pigs Book by Kathy Menino, original music & lyrics by Ellen Mandel; Director, Kathy Menino; Stage Manager, Peter Cimino; Lighting, Maruti Evans; Set, Jeff Duer; Musical Director, Ellen Mandel; Choreographer, Jeremy Williams; Technical Director, Amy Wagner; Scenic Artist/Props, Erin Duer; Costume Consultant, Florence Pape; Graphics, Meghan Lantzy; **Cast:** Bill Knepper, Madison Celeste James, Leigh Ann Murdaugh, Brian Hopson; Wild Project; May 8–15, 2010

Readings

Suddenly Last Summer by Tennessee Williams; Director, Karen Lordi-Kirkham; **Cast:** Kelli Holsopple, Elise Stone, Josh Tyson, Kathy Menino, Eileen Glenn, Matt Stapleton, Marlene May; September 29–October 4; *A Lovely Sunday for Creve Coeur* by Tennessee Williams; Director, Karen Case-Cook; **Cast:** Laura Piquado, Elise Stone, Angela Vitale, Kathy Menino; November 17–22; *In the Bar of a Tokyo Hotel* by Tennessee Williams; Director, Amy Wagner; **Cast:** John Lenartz, Elise Stone, Craig Smith, Ariel Estrada; December 15–20; *Mary of Magdala: A Gnostic Fable* by Armando Nascimento Rosa; Director, John Giampetro; **Cast:** Elise Stone, Brian Costello, Kelli Holsopple, Josh Tyson, Craig Smith, Kathy Menino, Joe Menino; April 12

Pipeline Theatre Company

Psycho Beach Party by Charles Busch; Director, Daniel Johnsen; Set, Sam Dash; Costumes, Zealan Salemi; Lighting, Rick Hayashi; Sound, Alex Fast; Stage Manager, Kelsey Mills; **Cast:** Jenny Donheiser, Laura Durst, John Early, Janna Emig, Brian Maxsween, Alex Mills, Eric Williams; Green Room Theatre; April 8–17, 2010

Piper McKenzie

Directors, Hope Cartelli and Jeff Lewonczyk; www.pipermckenzie.com

Willy Nilly: A Musical Exploitation of the Most Far-Out Cult Murders of the Psychedelic Era by Trav S.D.; Director, Jeffrey Lewonczyk; Stage Manager, Guinevere Pressley; Lighting, Kia Rogers; Costumes, Julz Kroboth; Sound, Ryan Holsopple; Producer, Hope Cartelli; **Cast:** Becky Byers, Hope Cartelli, Maggie Cino, Michael Criscuolo, Betsy Head, Daryl Lathon, Rich Lovejoy, Mateo Moreno, Avery Pearson, Trav S.D., Esther Silberstein, Adam Swiderski, Elizabeth Hope Williams, Derek Davidson, Oweinama Biu, Darro Sandler, Chris Talsness; Produced as part of the 2009NY International Fringe Festival; Dixon Place; September 17–20, 2009

Craven Monkey and the Mountain of Fury Written and directed by Jeffrey Lewonczyk; Stage Manager, Guinevere Pressley; Lighting, Ian W. Hill; Costumes, Julz Kroboth; Sound, Jeffrey Lewonczyk; Producer, Hope Cartelli; **Cast:** Fred Backus, Becky Byers, Hope Cartelli, Jessi Gotta, Adrian Jevicki, Mateo Moreno, Jeff Lewonczyk, Melissa Roth and Art Wallace; Co-produced with The Brick Theater; Brick Theater; February 26–March 13, 2010

Planet Connections Theatre Festivity

Executive Director, Glory Kadigan; Managing Director, Jenn Boehm; Assistant Managing Director, Chanda Calentine; Associate Directors, Amber Gallery, Amada Anderson; Technical Director, Ryan Metzler; Co-Marketing, Brenden Rogers; Public Relations and Co-Marketing, Katie Rosin; Assistant Managers: Kaira Klueber, Allison Whittinghill, Chaz Graytok; Assistant Associate Directors: Amanda Marino, Nathaniel Kent, Andi Cohen, Carly Robins; 440 Studios and Robert Moss Theatre; June 9–28, 2009

440 Studios

A Play on Words Written and directed by J.C. Svec; Produced by Tribe Productions benefiting City Critters

America: A Problem Play Written and directed by Deborah Wolfson; Set, Zane Robert Enloe; Produced by On the Square Productions benefiting The Woodhull Institute for Ethical Leadership

Café Sustainable & **Instant Happy!** *Café Sustainable* by Corcaigh Irlandese; Director, Nathan Brauner; Original Music, Stephane Wrembel; *Instant Happy!* by Mark William Butler; Director Richard P. Butler; A Corcaigh Irlandese production benefiting EMBARQ and Endometriosis Foundation of America

Chile of Hungry Times Written and performed by Bridget Bailey; Based on the works of Ludmila Petrushevskaya; Produced by The New York Theatre Barn benefiting Broadway Cares/Equity Fights Aids

Dickinson: The Secret Story of Emily Dickinson by William Roetzheim; Director, Al Germani; Stage Manager, Kate Erin Gibson; Lighting, Barbara Samuels; **Cast:** Rhianna Basore; Diana Sparta; Greg Wittman; Charlie Riendeau

Meredith's Ring & **Anonymous** *Meredith's Ring* by Andrew Rothkin; A White Rabbit Theatre production benefiting CEDARS Kids; *Anonymous* by Rodney E. Reyes; Director, Taylor Keith; Stage Manager, Eileen Gaughan; Set, Mario Corrales; Production Manager, Anna Payumo; **Cast:** Thomas Blewitt, Jian Huang, Vanessa Ramalho; Produced by Cuchipinoy Productions benefiting CEDARS Kids

Monetizing Emma by Felipe Ossa; Director, Leah Bonvissuto; **Cast:** Janice Mann, James Arden; A Thackeray Walsh, LLC production benefiting Broadway Cares/Equity Fights AIDS

New Beulah by Dan Moyer; Director, Jordan Fein; Stage Manager, Joie Bauer; Lighting, Chantel Pascente; Set, Chris Ford; Costumes, Dakota Rose; Sound, Chantel Pascente; Audio/Visual, Brian Hedden; **Cast:** Raphael Bob-Waskberg, Hadley Cronk, Emma Galvin, Carl Howell, James B. Kennedy, Nathaniel Kent, Emily Scott, Marisa Lark Wallin; A Shelby Company production benefiting Democracy Now!

Suckers Written and directed by Duncan Pflaster; Lighting, Emily Gasser; Costumes, Mark Richard Caswell; Sound, Duncan Pflaster; Choreographer, Christopher C. Cariker; **Cast:** Eric C. Bailey, Katherine Damigos, Joe Fanelli, Paula Galloway, Rebecca Hirota, Shawn McLaughlin, Alan McNaney, Jared Morgenstern; Produced by Cross-Eyed Bear Productions benefiting the Red Cross Blood Bank

Truth or... Consequences by Brianne Hogan and Carla Lopez; Director, Ashley Beam; A Hogan/Lopez production benefiting The Oasis Project

Robert Moss Theatre

Cleopatra-A Life Unparalleled Book, music, and lyrics by Cheryl E. Kemeny; Directors, Barbara Labbadia and Alexandrea Kemeny; Music Director, Cheryl E. Kemeny; Choreographer, Kari Ann Sweeney; Lighting, Jessica Burgess; **Cast:** Jennifer Van Buskirk, Melissa Labbadia; Produced by Crystal Theatre, Inc. and L2 Entertainment, Inc. benefiting Women for Women International

Designer X, Your Face, What Are You Doing Here? by Maria Alexandria Beech; Director, Oscar A. Mendoza; **Cast:** Danielle Patsakos; Produced by The Mush-Room Performing Design benefiting SOS Children's Villages: Venezuela

Everybody Dies by Molly Rydzel; Director, Russell Dobular; **Cast:** Marek Sapieyevski; Produced by Edible Brains Productions benefiting Play for P.I.N.K.

Her Kind: The Life & Poetry of Anne Sexton by Hannah Wolfe, featuring the poetry of Anne Sexton; Directors, Hannah Wolfe and Shanara Gabrielle; Choreographer, Laurel Tentindo; Sound, Daneil Mintseris; **Cast:** Hannah Wolfe, Laurel Tentindo, Collin Biddle, Debra Kay Anderson; A Wild Child Presents production benefiting Safe Horizon

Hound by John Patrick Bray; Director, Rachel Klein; Stage Manager, Teressa Maranzano; Costumes, Rachel Klein; Sound, Sean Gill; Makeup, Anita Rundles and Emily Taradash; Press, Emily Owens; **Cast:** Cavan Hallman, Ryan Knowles, Grant Boyd, Jack Corcoran, Meredith Dillard, Abigail Hawk, Blaine Peltier, Alyssa Schroeter, Elizabeth Stewart, Jason Stroud; Produced by HQ Rep. in association with Rachel Klein Productions benefiting RAINN at 440 Studios

Our Country Book by Dan Collins, music & lyrics by Tony Asaro; Director, David Taylor Little; Music Director, Eric Day; PSM, Debra Stunich; Associate Producer, Jennifer Ashley Tepper; Orchestrations, Tony Asaro; Set, David Taylor Little; Lighting, Nick Soylum; Sound, Gregory Jacobs-Roseman; Costumes, Gordon Leary; **Cast:** Justin Utley, Jeremy Pasha; Musicians: Eric Day, Matt Hinkley, Jeremy Pasha, Justin Smith, and Arvi Sreenivasan; A Tony Asaro/Dan Collins Production benefiting GLAAD

Resignations by John Kearns; Director, Erin Smiley; A Boann Books and Media LLC production benefiting China Tomorrow Education Foundation

The Imaginary Invalid: By Prescription Only Written and directed by Aliza Shane, based on Le Malade Imaginaire by Molière; Choreographer, Chanda Calentine; **Cast:** Ayelet Blumberg; An Aliza Shane production benefiting Hospice of New York

Those Whistling Lads: The Poetry and Short Stories of Dorothy Parker Adapted for the stage by Maureen Van Trease; Director, Bricken Sparacino; **Cast:** Ethan Angelica; Produced by TimeSpace Theatre Company in association with Third Eye Theatre Company benefiting Safe Horizon

Twin Towers by Damian Wampler; Director, Angela Astle; A Damian Wampler production benefiting ENACT

Wagon Wheel Book and lyrics by Robin Sandusky, music by Erato Kremmyda; Director, Robert Heller; Musical Director, Mark Evans; Choreographer, Claire Cook; **Cast:** Sam Pinkleton; A Sandusky/Kremmyda production benefiting St. Jude Children's Research Hospital

Wait of the World by Peter Dagger; Director, Jeremy Bloom; Set/Art, Sean Ward; Special Effects, Jeremy Bloom, Sean Ward; **Cast:** Jenny Checchia, Harry

Einhorn, Joyce Miller, Rachel Richman and Joe Tannenbaum; Produced by Peter and Matt's Production Company benefiting the Gynecologic Cancer Foundation

Wrestling the Alligator by Sergei Burbank; Director, Adam Karsten; Lighting, Ryan Mueller; Set, Kina Park; Costumes, Daonne Huff; **Cast:** James Ware, Sergei Burbank, Amanda Nichols; A Conflict of Interest Theatre Company production benefiting City Harvest

Readings

Happy New Year, Lady Lou! Written and directed by David Gaard; Presented by The Entertainment Agora benefiting MCC Homeless Youth Service –Sylvia's Place; *Hers* by Ashley Jacobson; Director, Nadine Friedman; An Ashley Jacobson production benefiting Sanctuary for Families; *Howling Hilda* Book and lyrics by Anne Berlin, music by Andrew Bleckner; Director, Travis Greisler; **Cast:** Lucia Spina; A Berlin/Bleckner production benefiting Women's Sport Foundation; *Surfacing* by Julia Stirling Martin; Director, Ellen Orenstein; A Julia Martin production benefiting Food Bank for New York City; *The 40-Foot Tall Jesus Statue* by Glory Bowen & *Hate Myself in the Morning* by Duncan Pflaster; Director, Amber Gallery; Presented by Pistorius Productions benefiting Amnesty International; *The Jamb* by J. Stephen Brantley; Director, Jonathan Worman; A Bowden Square Production benefiting Raising Malawi Academy for Girls

Poiesis Theatre Project

www.wix.com/Poiesis/poiesistheatreproject

[The] Ophelia Landscape A new collaborative work conceived after Hamlet by Shakespeare and Hamletmachine by Heiner Muller; Director, Naum Panovski; **Cast:** Vanessa Bartlett, Nikki Bohm, Annie Chang, Mathilde Dratwa, Andressa Furletti, Megumi Haggerty, Carrie Heitman, Sylvia Milo, Klemen Novak, Julia Peterson, Krystine Summers, Tony Naumovski; Mark Morris Dance Center, 3 Lafayette Street; April 22–May 8, 2010

Point of You Productions

www.pointofyou.org

The Block by Olivia Worden; Director, Jeff Love; Lighting/Sound/Stage Manager, Mary Katherine Hynes; Set, Gerard J. Savoy; Costumes, Jeff Love; Production Coordinator, Johnny Blaze Leavitt; House Manager, Melanie Kuchinski Rodgiguez; **Cast:** Gerard J. Savoy, Alyssa Mann, Morgan White, Gerry Sheridan, Jennifer Grundy, David Holt; The Tank Theatre; June 26–June 28, 2009

A Night of Comedy! Director/Design, Marc Adam Smith; Costumes, The Cast; Stage Manager, Johnny Blaze Leavitt; Production Coordinator, Melanie Kuchinski Rodriguez; House Manager, Sean Rodriguez; **Cast:** Lee Solomon, Jeff Love, Monica Blaze Leavitt, Chris Keating, Marlise Garde, Marc Adam Smith, Gerard J. Savoy, Johnny Blaze Leavitt, Chris Keating, Johnny Blaze Leavitt, Jeff Love, Marc Adam Smith; Gotham City Improv; January 29, 2010

A Midwinter's Tale by Johnny Blaze Leavitt based on a screenplay by Kenneth Branagh; Director, Jeff Love; Stage Manager, Olivia Schlueter-Corey; Set, Gerard J. Savoy; Costumes and Sound, Jeff Love; Lighting, Keri Thibodeau; Assistant Lighting Designer: Christine Boutin; Fight Coordinator: Gerard J. Savoy; Dialect Coach: Monica Blaze Leavitt; House Manager, Melanie Kuchinski Rodriguez; **Cast:** Chris Keating, Tina Trimble Savoy, Lindsay Kitt Wiebe, Olivia Schlueter-Corey, Gerard J. Savoy, Kathleen Rose Fletcher, Lee Solomon, Nick Herbert, Paul Weissman, Christopher Shelton, Johnny Blaze Leavitt, Morgan White, Meghan Love, Leslie Marseglia, Felic; American Theatre of Actors–Sargent Theatre: March 3–13, 2010

Polish Cultural Institute

Wormwood by Theatre of the Eighth Day; Director, Lech Raczak; **Cast:** Ewa Wojciak, Adam Borowski, Tadeusz Janiszewski, Marcin Keszycki; Henry Street Settlement; November 11–15, 2009

Polybe + Seats

www.olybeandseats.org

Granada by Avi Glickstein, Director, Jessica Brater; Stage Manager, Donald Butchko; Lighting, Natalie Robin; Set, Peiyi Wong; Costumes, Peiyi Wong; Sound, John D. Ivy; **Cast:** Elaine O'Brien, Sarah Sakaan, Indika Senanayake, Lindsay Torrey, Jill Usdan, Ari Vigoda; Access Gallery; November 5–22, 2009

A Thousand Thousand Slimy Things by Katya Schapiro; Director, Jessica Brater; **Cast:** Carmel Amit, Elaine O'Brien, Jenni Lerche, Sarah Sakaan, Eugene Santiago, Hilary Thomas, Ari Vigoda; Waterfront Museum and Showboat Barge in Red Hook; April 23–May 9, 2010

Project: Theater

www.projecttheater.org

The Secretaries by The Five Lesbian Brothers; Director, Joe Jung; Set, JJ Bernard and Francois Portier; Sound, Joe Jung; **Cast:** Karis Danish, Brian Frank, Tara Franklin, Laura Dillman, Jenny Schutzman, Jessi Blue Gormezano, Andrew McLeod; 78th Street Theatre Lab, May 25–June 6, 2009

My Custom Van by Michael Ian Black; Director, Joe Jung; Stage Manager, Jacob Seelbach; Lighting, Chad Lefebvre; Set, J.J. Bernard & Francois Portier; Costumes, Jessi Blue Gormezano & Jenny Schutzman; Sound, Joe Jung; Video/Slide Design, Chad Lefebvre; **Cast:** Amanda Byron, Gino Constabile, Laura Dillman, Ruark Downey, Brian Frank, Joe Jung, Andrew McLeod, Brian Sell, Josh Tussin; Drilling Company Theatre Lab; April 1–April 24, 2010

Prose & Content, Inc.

www.proseandcontent.com

Alchemist of Light by Len Fonte and Tom Bisky; Director, Sherry Teitelbaum; Set, Szu-Feng Chen; Costumes, Izzy Fields; Lighting, Christopher Weston; Stage Manager, Arlonda Washington; Audio/Visual, Peter Smith; Technical Director, David Masenheimer; Magic Consultant, Michael Matson; Fight Director, Adam Souza; Hair, Heather Wright; Light Board Operator, Tim Pracher-Dix; Prop Artisan, Ian Grunes; Graphics, Robert Dweck; **Cast:** Peter Reznikoff, Candace Reid, Brian Ray Norris, Lucas Miller, Tom Lock, Annunziata Gianzero, Dared Wright, Colin Chapin, Marcha Everitt; Connelly Theater; August 15–August 29, 2009

PTP/NYC (Potomac Theatre Project)

www.potomactheatreproject.org

The Europeans by Howard Barker; Director, Richard Romagnoli; Lighting, Hallie Zieselman; Set, Mark Evancho; Costumes, Jule Emerson; Sound, Allison Rimmer; Audio/Visual, Hallie Zieselman; Stage Manager, Amy Weissenstein; Producer, Cheryl Faraone; Assistant Costumes, Danielle Nieves; ASM, Alex Mark; Assistants to the Director, Maegan Mishicho and Samantha Collier; Original Music, Peter Hamlin; **Cast:** Aidian Sullivan, Antoinette LaVecchia, Brent Langdon, Robert Emmet Lunney, Megan Byrne, Valerie Leonard, Robert Zukerman, Bill Army, Veracity Butcher, Emily Kron, Judith Dry, Rishabh Kashyap, Jimmy Wong, Samantha Collier; Atlantic Stage 2; June 25–July 26, 2009

Therese Raquin by Neal Bell; Director, Jim Petosa; Set, Mark Evancho; Costumes, Nicole V. Moody; Lighting, Nicholas Houfek; Stage Manager, Lisa McGinn; Producer, Cheryl Faraone; ASM, Becca Poccia; Assistant Costumes, Adrienne Carlisle; Assistants to the Director, Starrett Berry and Sara Swartzfelder; **Cast:** Lily Balsen, Scott Janes, Helen Jean Arthur, Willie Orbison, Peter Schmitz, Stephanie Spencer, Michael Kessler, Jordan Tirrell-Wysocki; Atlantic Stage 2; June 23–July 26, 2009

Readings

Bea, Ned, Maya & Jude by Willie Orbison; July 13; *A Question of Fate* Created by PTP Company; July 17; *Cover me in Humanness* by Jake Jeppson; Director, Caitlin Dennis; July 19; *Kilty* by Michael Wrynn Doyle; July 20; *Ravel* by Samantha Collier; Director, Cheryl Faraone; July 21; *The Spoils* by Stephen Dykes; Director, Cheryl Faraone; July 22; *A Dangerous Electricity/Important People* by Veracity Butcher/Emily Feldman; Director, Leah Day; July 24

Pulse Ensemble Theatre

Executive Artistic Director, Alexa Kelly; Company Manager, Brian Richardson; Literary Manager, Nina daVinci Nichols; New Play Development, Lezley Steele; www.pulseensembletheatre.org

A Midsummer Night's Dream by William Shakespeare; Director, Alexa Kelly; Stage Lighting, Steve O'Shea; Costumes, Kristine Koury; Sound, Louis Lopardi; Manager, Livia Hill; **Cast:** Freddie Bennett, Laura Carbonell, Alvin Chan, Bernardo Cubrio, Mick D'Arcy, Lolita Foster, Chivonne Floyd, Melanie Gretchen, Burt Grinstead, Maria Hurdle, Ryan F. Johnson, Warren Katz, Cara Maltz, Ras McCurdie, Sean McIntire, Michael Gilpin, Brian Richardson, Laura Gaona; Riverbank State Park; August 7–28, 2009

Ladies In Retirement by Edward Percy & Reginald Denham; Director, Amnon Kabatchnik; Set, Zhanna Gurvich; Costumes, Angela Kahler; Lighting, Steve O'Shea; Sound, Louis Lopardi; Stage Manager, Brian Richardson; Producer, Alexa Kelly; **Cast:** Susan Barrett, Hanna Hayes, Burt Grinstead, Carol Lambert, Ashley Taylor, Mikel Sarah Lambert, Camille Mazurek; Theatre 3; March 9–April 3, 2010

Chaos Theory by Anuvab Pal; Director, Alexa Kelly; Set, Zhanna Gurvich; Costumes, Kimberley Glennon; Lighting, Steve O'Shea; Sound, Louis Lopardi; Stage Manager, Brian Richardson; Audio/Visual, Zhanna Gurvich; **Cast:** Rita Wolf, Ranjit Chowdhry, Tony Mirrcandani, Sorab Wadia, Amar Srivastava; TBG Theatre; May 25–June 19, 2010

The Queens Players

www.secrettheatre.com or www.thequeensplayers.com

Macbeth by William Shakespeare; Director/Sound/Original Music, Richard Mazda; Set, Stephanie Stover; Additional Music, Harley Fine, Emily Thomas & Elspeth Turner, Michael Eisenstein; Choreography/Movement, Eric Ragan; **Cast:** Daniel Wolfe, Shelleen Kostabi, Daniel Smith, Elspeth Turner, Rachel Prescott, Alisha Soper, Randy Warshaw, Kryian Friedenberg, Ben Robinson, Alex Stine, Michael Henrici, TJ Clark, Jeni Ahlfeld, Emily Thomas, Kyle Haggerty, Tyler Etheridge, Kimberly Alex Stine, Jesses Kane, Hart Zoe, Anne Roberts, Alex Stein, Perri Yaniv, Ben Prayz, Anthony Martinez, Dmitri Friedenberg; June 11–June 27, 2009

As You Like It by William Shakespeare; Director, Greg Cicchino; Set, Stephanie Stover; Costumes, Jeni Ahlfeld; **Cast:** Michael Henrici, Claire Morrison, and Daniel Smith, with guest actors Jason Basso, Melisa Breiner-Sanders, Matt Cardenes, Timothy J. Cox, Griffin DuBois, Harrison Gibbons, Jonathan Hinman, Chris Kateff, Larissa Laurel, Anthony Martinez, Amy Newhall, Louis Tullo; August 20–September 5, 2009

Henry V by William Shakespeare; Director, Rich Ferraioli; **Cast:** Kirsten Anderson, Jeni Ahlfeld, Alan Kistler and Randy Warsaw, with guest actors Mamoudou Athie, Andy Hassell, Heidi Zenz, Charles Baker, Delano Barbosa, Thom Brown III, Jeff Burroughs, Jennifer Ewing, Kyrian Friedenberg, Adam Griffith, Sean Macbride Murray, Meg Mark, Richard McDonald, Jacquie Militano, Morgan Parpan, Stephanie Rubeo, Jessica Renee Russell, Will Schmincke, Edward Stelz, Charlotte Layne Dunn, Danny Yoerges; September 17–October 3, 2009

Cyrano de Bergerac by Edmond Rostand; Director, Richard Mazda; Stage Manager, Kimberley Miller; **Cast:** Daniel Wolfe, Anthony Martinez, Daniel Smith, Sarah Bonner, Kevin Woods, Tyler Gattoni, Sean MacBride Murray, Delano Barbosa, Jennifer Ewing, Claire Epstein, Alice Bahlke, Elizabeth Seldin; November 18–December 5, 2009

A Midsummer Nights' Dream by William Shakespeare; Co-presented by The Secret Theatre; Director, Katherine M. Carter; Stage Manager, Griffin Parker; Lighting, Lisa Hufnagel; Costumes, Jeni Ahlfeld; Sound, Jillian Marie Walker; **Cast:** Jeni Ahlfeld, Andrew Ash, Charles Baker, Katie Braden, Timothy J. Cox, Angelica Duncan, Charlotte Layne Dunn, Brandon Hillen, Chris Kateff, Sarah King, Miriam Mintz, Joe Mullen, James Parenti, Patricia Phelps, Tiffany D. Turner, Randy Warsaw, Timothy Williams and Heidi Zenz; December 3, 2009–January 3, 2010

Titus Andronicus by William Shakespeare; Director, Rich Ferraioli; Lighting, R. Allen Babcock; Set, R. Allen Babcock; Original Music, Ashley Straw; Fight Director, Elizabeth Seldin; **Cast:** Thom Brown III, Claire Epstein, Meg Mark, Richard McDonald, Sean MacBride Murray, Jonathan Emerson, Brandon Ferraro, Ryan Gorton, James Lentini, Ari Lew, Timothy Olin, Alex Stine, Fred Stuart, Elspeth Turner, Seth Austin, Ed Stelz, Lexie Helgerson; December 10, 2009–January 9, 2010

Romeo and Juliet by William Shakespeare; Director, Greg Cicchino; Stage Manager, Elizabeth Seldin; Set, R. Allen Babcock; Costumes, Jeni Ahlfeld; Sound, Greg Cicchino; Video, Tyler Gattoni; **Cast:** Justin Randolph, Daniel Smith, Fred Stuart, Jessica Russel, Shelleen Kostabi, Katie Braden, Anthony Martinez, David Rysdahl, Charlie Gorilla, Jesse Kane Harnett, Alice bahlke, Danika Wood, Kathryn Browne, Jeni Ahfeld; January 21–February 6, 2010

Servant of Two Masters by Carlo Goldoni; Director, Alberto Bonilla; **Cast:** Mia Borrelli, Adam Feingold, Jennifer Jacobs, Gusta Johnson, Alex Mahgoub, Richard McDonald, Graciany Miranda, Nailini Sharma, Kate Siepert, Joshua Warr, Randy Warshaw; February 4–19, 2010

The Importance of Being Earnest by Oscar Wilde; Director, Ken Hailey; Stage Manager, Catherine Amore; Costumes, Tom Kleinert; Dialect Coach, Pamela Vittorio; **Cast:** Kimberly Miller, John Reoli, Thomas Kleinert, Sarah Pencheff, Arnie Kolodner, Shelleen Kostabi, Michael J. Miller, Gary Lizardo, Zachary Koval; February 10–February 20, 2010

Measure for Measure by Willaim Shakespeare; Director, Rich Ferraioli; Choreographer, Charlotte Layne Dunn; March 4–March 20, 2010

The Tempest by William Shakespeare; Director, Kelly Johnston; Stage Manager, Gabriella Senatore; Lighting, Moses Sandel; Costumes, Jeni Ahlfeld; Sound, Ben Danielowski; Magic, Tempest Production Team; Original Music, Stavros Makris; **Cast:** Jeni Ahlfeld, Sarah Bonner, Katie Braden, Charlotte Layne Dunn, Lexie Helgerson, Anthony Martinez, Richard Mazda, Sean MacBride Murray, Daniel Smith, Heidi Zenz, James Lentini, Jessica Lea Alex, Gina Trebiani, and Kyle Masteller; April 15–April 30, 2010

Queens Shakespeare, Inc

Much Ado About Nothing by William Shakespeare; Director, Jonathan Emerson; Stage Manager, Tara Schmitt; Lighting and Set, Jonathan Emerson and Joseph Sebring; Sound, Justin Asher; **Cast:** Ashley Adelman, Nikki Bohm,

Matthew Coonrod, Timothy J. Cox, Sheira Feuerstein, Andrew Stephen Johnson, Daniel Koenig, Lawrence Lesher, Ari Lew, Zack Locuson, Patrick Mahoney, Alex Simmons, Maria Smith, Antonia Villalon, Heidi Zenz; Bowne Street Community Church; November 5–14, 2009

Rabbit Hole Ensemble

www.rabbitholeensemble.com

Before Your Very Eyes Written, directed, and choreographed by Edward Elefterion; Stage Manager, Brooke Leigh-Barefoot Bell; Lighting, Sam Gordon; Set, Patrick Mills; Costumes, Michael Tester; Sound, David Liao; **Cast:** Bobby Abido, Diana DeLaCruz, Sanam Erfani, Elyse Knight, Damon Pooser; Flamboyan Theatre at CSV Cultural Center; May 20–June 13, 2010

Rachel Klein Productions

www.rachelkleinproductions.com

Hound by John Patrick Bray; Co-Production with HQ Rep and Planet Connections Theatre Festivity; Director/Set/Costumes, Rachel Klein; Stage Manager, Teresa Mazzerano; Lighting, Ryan Metzler; Sound, Sean Gill; Wigs, Rachel Klein; Makeup, Anita Rundles; **Cast:** Ryan Knowles, Cavan Hallman, Abigail Hawk, Blaine Peltier, Jack Corcoran, Meredith Dillard, Elizabeth Stewart, Jason Stroud, Alyssa Schroeter; Robert Moss Theater; June 8–25, 2009

Stage Blood is Never Enough by Sean Gill and Rachel Klein; Director/Costumes, Rachel Klein; Stage Manager, Marina Steinberg; Lighting, Thomas Honeck; Sound, Sean Gill; Makeup, Anita Rundles; **Cast:** Elizabeth Stewart, Michael Porsche, Michele Cavallero, Brian Rubiano, Danielle Marie Fusco, Preston Burger, Veronica Vroom, Meredith Dillard, Megan O'Connor, Kari Warchock, Jillaine Gill, Sapphire Jones, Beau Allulli, Abigail Hawk, Freddy Mancilla, Rob R; The Duplex Cabaret Theatre; October 22–29, 2009

RADIOTHEATRE

Artistic Director, Dan Bianchi; www.radiotheatrenyc.com

Sundays With Poe Adapted and directed by Dan Bianchi based on the writings of Edgar Alan Poe; Co-Produced by Horse Trade Theater Group; Lighting/Stage Manager, Wes Shippee; Set/Sound, Dan Bianchi; **Cast:** Cash Tilton, Frank Zilinyi, Joe Fellman; UNDER St. Marks; January 25– December 27, 2009

Frankenstein Written and directed by Dan Bianchi; Sound, Dan Bianchi; Sound Engineer, Wes Shippee; **Cast:** Frank Zilinyi, Joe Fellman, Dana Mazzenga, Andrea Goldman, Mike Quirk; Kraine Theater; October 11–December 19, 2009

Dracula Written, directed, sound, and original music by Dan Bianchi; **Cast:** Anthony Crep, R. Patrick Alberty, Shelleen Kostabie, Alexandra Loren, Joe Fellman, Frank Zilinyi, Chris Riquinha; Players Theatre & Players Loft; November 11–December 30, 2009

The Haunting of 85 East 4th Street Written and directed by Dan Bianchi; Co-produced with the Horse Trade Theater Group; Sound, Dan Bianchi; Sound Engineer, Wes Shippee; **Cast:** Joe Fellman, Frank Zilinyi; Kraine Theater; April 10–May 23, 2010

Rattapallax, Inc.

Sexual Healing Written and directed by Jonathan Leaf; Set, Craig Napoliello; Costumes, Sarah Shears; Lighting, Maria Cristina Fuste; Stage Manager, Livia Hill; **Cast:** Chuck Montgomery, Judith Hawking, Sayra Player, Ren Matthewson, Sarah Nina Hayon, Peter O'Connor, Hugh Sinclair; Mint Space; January 6–30, 2010

Razors Edge Productions

Selected plays of Joyce Carol Oates by Joyce Carol Oates; Selections from *I Stand Before You Naked*, *The Sacrifice*, *Ontological Proof of My Existence*, *Zombie*; **Cast:** Bill Connington, Jennifer McCabe, Jeff Pagliano, Tony Wolf, Elaine Moran, Emily Tremaine, Colin Sutherland. New York Society Library; October 6–20, 2009

ZOMBIE by Bill Connington, adapted from the novella by Joyce Carol Oates; Director, Thomas Caruso; Lighting, Joel E. Silver; Set, Josh Zangen; Sound, Deirdre Broderick; Production Manager Naomi Anhorn; **Cast:** Bill Connington; Gerald W. Lynch Theater; March 10 March 13, 2010

Rebellious Subjects Theatre

www.rebellioussubjects.org

Henry IV by William Shakespeare; Co-Produced with Seventh Sign Theatre Productions, Inc.; Director, Elyzabeth Gorman; Stage Manager, Grace Gasner; Costumes, Jessica Lustig; Producers, Lauren Ferebee and Patrick Woodall; Associate Producers, Ben Rezendes and Ben Friesen; **Cast:** Tiffany Abercrombie, Bryn Boice, Sutton Crawford, Tarik Davis, Drew de Jesus, Paul Frazee, Ben Friesen, Simone Harrison, Jon Ledoux, Jonathan Levy, Joshua Luria, Kevin Mitchell, Nick Reinhardt, Ben Rezendes, Montgomery Sutton, Eric Rice, Adrien Saunders, Jesse Sells, Steve Viola, Patrick Woodall; The Prospect Park Music Pagoda; August 22–September 6, 2009

(re:) Directions Theatre Company

Artistic Director, Tom Berger; Producing Director, Erin Smiley; Associate Artistic Director, John Bronston; www.redirectionstheatre.com

Epicene by Ben Jonson; Director, Tom Berger; Costumes, David Withrow; Lighting, Tim Kaufman; Stage Manager, Leslie Skalak; **Cast:** Jonathan Cantor, Lucy Gillespie, Robert Gonzales Jr., Gina Marie Jameison, Michael Kirby, Sarah Knittel, Kathryn Elisabeth Lawson, Caitlin McColl, Victoria Miller, Christopher Norwood, Josh Odess-Rubin, Michael-Alan Read; 14th Street Theatre; May 22–June 6, 2010

Red Fern Theatre Company

www.redferntheatre.org

All Through the Night by Shirley Lauro; Director, Melanie Moyer Williams; Stage Manager, Laura Luciano; Lighting, Jessica Greenberg; Set, Adrienne Kapalko; Costumes, Emily DeAngelis; Musical Direction/Arrangements, Kristin Lee Rosenfeld; **Cast:** Theo Allyn, Hana Kalinski, Michelle Lookadoo, Lesley McBurney, Andrea Sooch; Marjorie S. Deane Little Theater; October 2–25, 2009

Redd Tale Theatre Company

Co-Artistic Directors, Will Le Vasseur and James Stewart; www.reddtale.org

Maddy: A Modern Day Medea Written and directed by Will Le Vasseur; Stage Manager, Danny Morales; Set/Lighting, Will Le Vasseur; Sound, Matthew Pritchard; Poster Design, Graeme Offord; Production Photographer/Website Design, Ben Strothmann; **Cast:** Lynn Kenny, Blaine Pennington, Heather Shields, James Stewart, Ben Strothmann, Rainbow Dickerson, Will Le Vasseur; Nicu's Spoon Theater; August 6–August 29, 2009

The Swan Song by Anton Chekhov; Director, Lynn Kenny; Stage Manager, Danny Morales; Set/Lighting, Will Le Vasseur; Poster Design, Graeme Offord; Production Photos and Website Design, Ben Strothmann; **Cast:** Will Le Vasseur, Ben Strothmann; Nicu's Spoon Theater; August 6–August 29, 2009

Repertorio Espanol

Founding President and Producer Emeritus, Gilberto Zaldivar; Artistic Director, René Buch; Executive Director Robert Weber Federico; Associate Producer, José Antonio Cruz; Development, John Mejía; Financial Management, Nieves Vásquez-Ortiz; Special Projects, Allison Astor-Vargas; Production Manager & Assistant to the Artistic Director, Fernando Then; www.repertorio.org

Captain Pantoja and the Special Service Adapted by Jorge Ali Triana & Veronica Triana; Director, Jorge Ali Triana; Set, Robert Weber Federico; Sound, Alfonso Rey; Alex Koch; Original Music, Andres Cabas; Choreographer, Sunilda Caraballo; **Cast:** Anthony Alvarez, Yanko Bakulic, Ricardo Barber, Sunilda Caraballo, Zulema Clares, Raul Duran, Jessica Flori, Ricardo Hinoa, Modesto Lacen, Selenis Leyva, Jesus Martines, Monica Perez-Brandes, Denise Quinones, Eric Robledo, Marcelo Rodriguez, Silvia Sierra; October 14, 2009

Kiss Bessemer Goodbye (El beso del adios) by Tencha Avila; Director, Jerry Ruiz; Misic Director, Jimmy Tanaka; Production Designer, Robert Frederico; **Cast:** Ernesto de Villa Bejjani, Teresa Yenque, Frank Robles, Rosie Berrido, Daniel Isaac, Samantha Dagnino; March 15–August 20, 2010

Retro Productions

Producing Artistic Director, Heather E. Cunningham; www.retroproductions.org

Holy Days by Sally Nemeth; Director, Peter Zinn; Set, Jack and Rebecca Cunningham; Costumes, Debra Krajec; Lighting, Justin Sturges; Sound, Jeanne Travis; Stage Manager, Jeanne Travis; Props, Heather E. Cunningham and Casandera M.J. Lollar; ASM, Jenny Kennedy; Press, Morgan Lindsay Tachco; **Cast:** Lowell Byers, Heather E. Cunningham, Joe Forbrich, Casandera M. J. Lollar; Spoon Theater; November 6–21, 2009

The Desk Set by William Marchant; Director, Tim Errickson; Set, Rebecca Cunningham; Costumes, Viviane Galloway; Lighting, Justin Sturges; Sound/Stage Manager, Jeanne Travis; Props, Heather E. Cunningham and Casandera M.J. Lollar; Computer Design, Justin Sturges; ASM, Jenny Kennedy; Press, Morgan Lindsay Tachco; **Cast:** Heather E. Cunningham, Douglas B. Giorgis, Stuart Green, Anne Shapland Kearns, Ric Sechrest, Alisha Spielmann, Matilda Szydagis, Aubrie Therrien, Matthew Trumbull, Kristen Vaughan; Spoon Theater; May 7–May 22, 2010

Women and War by Jack Hilton Cunningham; Director, Peter Zinn; Stage Manager, Jenny Kennedy; Lighting, Justin Sturges; Set, Jack and Rebecca Cunningham; Costumes, Rebecca Cunningham and Casandera M. J. Lollar; Sound, Jeanne Travis; Press, Morgan Lindsay Tachco; **Cast:** Lowell Byers, Heather E. Cunningham, Lauren Kelston, Casandera M. J. Lollar, Elise Rovinsky; Spoon Theater; May 11, 2010

Riant Theatre

www.therianttheatre.com

Strawberry One-Act Festival Series A: *A Night in Praha* by Steve Capra; *Jumping the Gun* by Kyle Overstreet; *Dreaming of a White House* by Leanna Renee; and *I Do… I Guess* by Michael Musi; Series B: *Another Chance* by Keith R. Higgons; *Business or Pleasure* by Tom Diriwachter; *The Concrete Wall* by J.C. Svec; and *A Broken Barbie* by Ree Merrill; Series C: *The Debt* by Jerry Della Salla; *Melt Into the Sun* by Camilla Maxwell; *How to Be Cute and Break Hearts* by Tommaso Matelli; and *Chrysalis* by Sue Hodara; Series D: *The Baby* by Susan Kaessinger; *Straight Men Are Bitches Too* by Anthony Fusco; *Compubots* by Paul Trupia; and *Prescriptions* by Ellen Orchid; Series E: *Double Fear* by Joseph Lizardi; *Driving: A Lesson* by Lucy Gillespie; *Crime Stoppers* by Paul Schmitt; and *Looking for Talika* by Von H. Washington; Series F: *Joining the Pack* by Will Lenihan; *Liz and Paul* by Jude Hinojosa; *General Admissions* by Crish Barth; and *Introductions* by Laurence C. Schwartz; Series G: *Taming the Bull* by C.C.

Corry; *November Mourning* by Rachel Knowles; and *A Time in South Africa* by Ayanna Nichell; Series H: *Just Like Your Uncle* by Michael Monasterial; *Up A River/Down the Aisle* by Jake Lipman; and *I Just Wish* by Burt Grinstead; Series I: *Bird Watching* by Jeffrey L. Hollman; *The Lifters* by Carol Hollenbeck; *16 Tons* by Adam Harlan; and *Stroller Wars* by Heather Gault; Series J: *Differentiation* by Charlotte Rahn-Lee; *Beastie Buster* by Gretchen O'Halloran; *Deuteranomaly* by Jessica Fleitman; and *Turkey Day* by E.K. Deutsch; The Theatre at St. Clements; August 13–17, 2009

Richmond Shepard Theatre

The Funeral Director's Wife by Beth Gilleland & Kathleen Douglass; Director, Richmond Shepard; Stage Manager, Clinton Schreck; Lighting, Joshua Cohen; Costumes, Leslie Hughes; Music Director, Paul Geiger; **Cast:** Anais Alexandra, Paul Geiger, Lisa Margolin, Sam Platizky; Richmond Shepard Theatre; June 9–27, 2009

A Twelfth Night's Dream About Nothing by William Shakespeare, Gillian Riley and Brett Maughan; Presented by Snorks and Piñs Productions; Director, Gillian Riley and Brett Maughan; Stage Manager, Mary Nogeire; Lighting/Sound, Brett Maughan; Set/Sound, Gillian Riley; Choreography/Graphic Design, Anna Duval; Fight Choreograpy, Michael Hagins; **Cast:** Catherine Corbett, Michael Hagins, Justin Jones, Brian Matthew Landisman, Nick Neglia, Geeta Pereira, Gwenevere Sisco, Marcus Watson, Brian Wicker, Kelly Zekas; Richmond Shepard Theatre; December 11–20, 2009

The Mark Twain You Don't Know by Chris Wallace; Presented by Olentagy Music; Lighting, Brett Maughan; Costumes, Amanda Carr; **Cast:** Chris Wallace; Richmond Shepard Theatre; March 25–April 11, 2010

Rising Phoenix Repertory

Artistic Director, Daniel Talbott; Artistic Associates: Denis Butkus, Addie Johnson, Julie Kline, Brian Roff, Samantha Soule; Artistic Advisors, Jack Doulin, Stephen Willems;www.RisingPhoenixRep.org

Afterclap by Daniel Reitz; Director, Daniel Talbott; **Cast:** Haskell King; Seventh Street Small Stage; February 8–February 22, 2010

Slipping by Daniel Talbott; Produced with piece by piece productions in association with Rattlestick Playwrights Theater; Director, Kirsten Kelly; Lighting, Joel Moritz; Set, Lauren Helpern; Costumes, Chloe Chapin; Sound/Projection Design, Brandon Epperson; PSM, Katrina Renee Herrmann; Properties, Eugenia Furneaux-Arends; Fight Choreographer, Christian Kelly-Sordelet; **Cast:** MacLeod Andrews, Adam Driver, Meg Gibson, Seth Numrish; Rattlestick Playwrights Theater; July 28–August 15, 2009

The Rising Sun Performance Company

www.risingsunnyc.com

Dotty Dot Book and lyrics by Ashley Laverty and Travis Kendrick, music and additional lyrics by John Wascavage and Ryan Cavanaugh; Director/Set, Travis Kendrick; Costumes, Travis Kendrick, Tiffini Minatel; **Cast:** Alexia Tate, Dan Vidor, Flor Bromley, Katherine Stults, Nicole Howard, Nicole Nicastro, Ryan Bowie, Elaine Jones; Touring show in New York City Parks; September 19–27, 2009

Good Night Lovin' Trail by John Patrick Bray; Director, Akia Squitieri; Stage Manager, Lindsey Beecher; Production Design, Akia Squitieri; Props, Elaine Jones; **Cast:** Olivia Roric, Nic Mevoli; Fringe Performance Venue: 423 Market Street, Wilmington, DE; October 1–3, 2009

The Last Supper by Dan Rosen; Co-Produced with Horse Trade Theater Group; Director, Akia Squitieri; Lighting, Dan Jobbins; Set, Jak Prince; Costumes, Tiffini Minatel; Sound, Ryan Kilcourse; Stage Manager, Alexandra Deurr; Audio/Visual, Mathew Kreiner, Nick Micozzi, David Anthony; Production Manager, Lindsey Beecher; Assistant Director and Dramaturg, Tiffany Hogan; Assistant Director, Kelly Hawkins; Original Music, Christopher Bowen; Fight Choreographer, Turner Smith; Props, Alexia Tate; **Cast:** Ariel Heller, Barry Kennedy Jr., Jeff Ronan, Anastasia Peterson, Becky Sterling, Erik Gulberg, Ben Friesen, Matt Riker, Michael Jones, Michael McManus, Leal Vona, Patrick Egan, Alexia Tate, April Bennet, Jessica Ritacco, Christopher Enright, David Anthony, J.L. Reed, Larry Gutman, Lindsay Beecher, Mariana Guillen, Michael Bernardi, Nicole Howard, Susan Burns; Red Room; April 24–25, 2010

Festivals and Readings

Twisted Co-produced by Horse Trade Theater Group; Light and Sound Operators, Elaine Jones, Travis Kendrick, Dan Vidor; Costumes, Katherine Stults; Properties Master/Special Effects Designer/Production Assistant, Elaine Jones; PSM, Howard Tilkin; House Managers/Fireguards, Akia, Tiffini, Mainatel; Travis Kendrick, Dan Vidor; Press, Emily Owens; Marketing, Akia and Ensemble; Photographer/Videographer, David Anthony; Postcard/Poster Designer, Akia; *Teddy Knows Too Much* by Matt Hanf, directed by Joseph McLaughlin; Assistant Director, Cara Liander; **Cast:** Alexia Tate, Nicole Howard, Chris Enright, Peter Aguero; *Nurturing Bond* by Tom Kiesche, directed by Matthew Kreiner; **Cast:** Michael McManus, Melissa Ciesla; *The Kiss* by Mark Harvey Levine, directed by Melissa Farinelli, **Cast:** Flor Bromley, Jonathan Reed Wexler; *Head Games* by Justin Warner, directed by Jason Tyne-Zimmerman; **Cast:** Nicole Howard, Chris Enright, Lindsay Beecher; *Party Girl* by Kitt Lavoie, directed by Ian Quinlan; Sound, Chris Barlow; **Cast:** Becky Sterling, Lindsay Beecher, Billy Fenderson; UNDER St. Marks; July 9–25, 2009

One-Act Reading Series *Part 1*: Director, Jonathan Reed Wexler; Production Manager, Lindsay Beecher; included: *Shark Week* by Matthew Ivan Bennett; *Playing God* by Kristyn Leigh Robinson; *Meet-Up* by Thomas J. Misuraca; *If Nietzche Dated* by Colette Freedman; *Shakespeare Lives* by Mark Harvey Levine; March 16; *Part 2*: Director, Matthew Kreiner; Production Manager, Lindsay Beecher; included: *Via Cruces* by Scott McMorrow; *Blue Tuesday* by Frank Anthony Polito; *Residue* by Stacey Lane; *Nothing* by Elena Naskova; *14th Street* by Laura Rohrman; April 20; *Part 3*: Director, Alexia Tate; Production Manager, Lindsay Beecher; included: *That Good & Juicy* by Barbara Lindsay; *Tenth Muse* by Michael Burgan; *Binge Honeymoon* by Rebecca Stokes; *Prosciutto Sunset* by David Patterson; *At the Public Burning Place* by Molly Goforth; May 18

Rockaway Theatre Company

www.RockawayTheater.com

Rabbit Hole by David Lindsay-Abaire; Director, Frank Caiati; Stage Manager, Nora Coughlin; Set, Frank Caiati; **Cast:** Ryan Max Berman, Jill Cornell, Brandon McCluskey, Valerie O'Hara, Tracy Willet; Post Theater; April 9–April 25, 2010

Roy Arias Studios and Theatres

The Death of A Dream by Nancy Genova; Presented by La Reina Del Barrio Productions; Director, Frank Perez; Stage Manager, T. Pope Jackson; Lighting, T. Pope Jackson; Sound, George Ballard; **Cast:** Frank Perez, Caridad De La Luz, April Lee Hernandez, Rhina Valentin; Off-Broadway Theatre; October 23–November 8, 2009

Hinterland by Benjamin Adair Murphy; Presented by The Living Room Project; Director, Amanda Friou; Costumes, Amanda Friou; Original Music, Amy Baer; **Cast:** Ilana Becker, Jeanette Bonner, Elisabeth Ness, Catriona Rubenis-Stevens, Westley Todd Holiday, Adam Hyland, Adam Laupus; Off-Off-Broadway Playhouse; October 26–November 8, 2009

When Joey Married Bobby by William Wyatt; Director, John William Gibson; Lighting and Sound, Steve Petrilli; **Cast:** Tina McKissick, Lady Bunny, Rebecca Dealy, Deborah Johnstone, Matthew Pender, Collin Biddle, Jennifer Banner Sobers, William Yoder, Richard James Porter, Brett Lannen; February 6–May 29, 2010

The Maids by Jean Genet; Presented by Curious Frog Theatre Company (Director, Reneé Racan Rodriguez; Theatre Administrator, John Lam; Marketing, Nic Musolino; Literary Manager, Gargi Shinde; Movement Director, Marie Morrow; Development/Grant Writer, Rocio Mendez; Marketing/Press, Patrick Doolin; curiousfrog.org); Director, Tracy Cameron Francis; Set, Laura Taber Bacon; Costumes, Emily Lippolis; Lighting, Michael Megliola; Sound, Julian Mesri; Stage Manager, Laura Gomez; **Cast:** Bushra Laskar, Iracel Rivero, and Alex Runnels; Off-Broadway Theatre; April 24–May 8, 2010

Re: Last Night by Steven Alexander, Eden Marryshow, Jesse Wakeman, Bruce Ornstein; Presented by Wednesday Repertory Company (Bruce Ornstein, Acting Artistic Director); Stage Manager, David Comstock; Lighting, David Comstock; Sound, David Comstock; Box Office and Concession Manager, Steve Alexander; **Cast:** Elizabeth Allerton, Nicole Banchevska, Lu Bellini, Ciara Collins-Atkins, Fernando Cordero, Ben Esner, Whitney Harris, Lexie Helgerson, Mike Ivers, Heather Leonard, Amanda Brooke Lerner, Eden Marryshow, Sonja Mauro, Vincent Quintiliani, Annelise Rains, Laurie Schroeder, Shelly Shenoy, Paul David Sibblies, Jesse Wakeman, Dan Lane Williams; Roy Arias Studios; April 29–May 9, 2010

The Sandbox Theatre Company

Quarterlife Cycle Written and performed by Amy Claussen; Director, Henry Fonte; Lafayette Street Theater; August 20–28, 2009

The Seeing Place Theater

www.seeingplacetheater.com

The Credeaux Canvas by Keith Bunin; Director, Lillian Wright; Stage Manager, Casey McLain; Lighting, Christopher Michael Ham; Set/Costumes/Sound, Lillian Wright; **Cast:** Margret Avery, Joseph Mancuso, Jerilyn Sackler, Anna Marie Sell, Brandon Walker; Bridge Theater at Shetler Studios; September 9–October 18, 2009

Hot Cripple by Hogan Gorman; Director, Quin Gordon; Stage Manager, Casey McLain; Lighting, David Sexton; Set, Lillian Wright; Costumes, Hogan Gorman; Sound, Kim Fuhr; **Cast:** Hogan Gorman; American Theater of Actors Sargent Theatre; February 3–21, 2010

When We Have Gone Astray by Brandon Walker; Director, Kaitlin Colombo; Stage Manager, Casey McLain; Lighting, David Sexton; Set/Costumes, Lillian Wright; Sound, Kim Fuhr; **Cast:** Heather Lee Harper, Joseph Mancuso, Joshua Rivedal, Brandon Walker; American Theater of Actors Sargent Theatre; February 4–21, 2010

Waiting for Lefty by Clifford Odets; Directors, Brandon Walker, Reesa Graham; Lighting/Stage Manager, Reesa Graham; Set/Costumes, Lillian Wright; Costumes, Lillian Wright; **Cast:** Margret Avery, David Arthur Bachrach, Steven Beckingham, Christoper Bischoff, Jon Dalin, John Gazzale, John Greenleaf, Norah Elise Johnson, Ned Lynch, Tyler Moss, Dothan Negrin, Gregory Jon Phelps, Adam Reich, Anna Marie Sell, Bonnie Singer, Nick Velkov; American Theater of Actors Sargent Theatre; June 9–26, 2010

Readings

When We Have Gone Astray by Brandon Walker; **Cast:** Heather Lee Harper, Joseph Mancuso, Brandon Walker; July 28; *It's Good to be Home* by Joshua Rivedal; **Cast:** Margret Avery, John Gazzale, Alex Mann, Elliot Mayer, Joshua Rivedal, Anna Marie Sell, Brandon Walker; December 13

Shelby Company

www.shelbycompany.org

New Beulah by Dan Moyer; Director, Jordan Fein; Set, Chris Ford; Costumes, Dakota Rose; Lighting/Sound, Chantel Pascente; Stage Manager, Joie Bauer; Audio/Visual, Brian Hedden; **Cast:** Raphael Bob-Waskberg, Hadley Cronk, Emma Galvin, Carl Howell, James B. Kennedy, Nathaniel Kent, Emily Scott, Marisa Lark Wallin; White Box Theatre, 440 Studios; June 11–27, 2009

My Father Is A Tetris Game by Jonathan A. Goldberg; Director, Alexis Poledouris; Stage Manager, Sunny Stapleton; Lighting, Gina Scherr; Sound, Betsy Rhodes; Audio/Visual, Shaun Rance; **Cast:** Bethany Caputo, Amanda Phillips, Jocelyn Kuritsky, Christina Pumariega, Caroline Tamas; HERE Arts Center; July 15–18, 2009

Say Say Oh Playmate by Raphael Bob-Waksberg, Will Brill, and Dan Moyer; Director, Carl Howell; Audio/Visual, Brian Hedden; **Cast:** Carl Howell, Nathaniel Kent, Dan Moyer; Skull Club; November 11–15, 2009

Winnemucca (three days in the belly) by Dan Moyer; Director, Wren Graves; Stage Manager, Brian Hedden; **Cast:** Will Brill, Grayson DeJesus, and Jenni Putney; Lafayette Street Theatre; August 14–28, 2009

You May Be Splendid Now by Dan Moyer; Director, Will Brill and Emma Galvin; Stage Manager, Alex Mallory; Lighting, Greg Goff; Set, Sean Ward; Costumes, Lizzy Seguin; Sound, Chris Rummel; Production Manager, Shannon O'Neil; **Cast:** Lauren Glover, Nick Lehane, Gabriel Millman, Dan Wohl; Presented as part of Great SCoT: New Plays!, Shelby Company's annual new works series; Access Theatre; January 20–31, 2010

The Luck of the Ibis by Jonathan A. Goldberg; Director, Tom Ridgely; Stage Manager, Christa Boyd; Lighting, Greg Goff; Set, Sean Ward; Costumes, Deanna Frieman; Sound, Chris Rummel; Production Manager, Shannon O'Neil; **Cast:** Brendan Donaldson, Nathaniel Kent, Jocelyn Kuritsky, Amy Landon, Jess Pohly; Presented as part of Great SCoT: New Plays!, Shelby Company's annual new works series; Access Theatre; January 20–31, 2010

The Mike and Morgan Show by Raphael Bob-Waksberg; Director, Lacy Post; Stage Manager, Shannon O'Neil; Lighting, Greg Goff; Set, Sean Ward; Costumes, Deanna Frieman; Sound, Chris Rummel; **Cast:** Emma Galvin, Brian Miskell; Access Theatre; Presented as part of Great SCoT: New Plays!; January 20–31, 2010

Uncle Shelby's Traveling Treasure Trunk by Jonathan A. Goldberg and Dan Moyer; **Cast:** Nathaniel Kent and Dan Moyer; The Complex Theatre, Hollywood; March 24–27, 2010

Shortened Attention Span

www.ShortenedAttentionSpan.com

The Shortened Attention Span Festival *Shelter* by James Fauvell; *Pornophiles* by J Boyett; *Parental Guidance Suggested* by Mim Granahan; *Rockaway* by Alan Gordon; *Fugazy* by Charles Messina; Players Loft; June 2009

The Shortened Attention Span Horror Fest Players Loft; October 2009

The Shortened Attention Span Musical Festival *Sweet Tea and Jesus* by Stephen Elkins; Players Loft; April 2010

Slant Theatre Project

Mine by Bekah Brunstetter; Director, Wes Grantom; Lighting, Derek Wright; Set, Grady Barker; Costumes, Whitney Locher; Sound, P.K. Pickens; Original Music, Joe Pug; Stage Manager, Adam Dworkin; **Cast:** Lucas Kavner, Amelia McClain, Zach Shaffer; Sanford Meisner Theatre; November 12–22, 2009

Sonnet Repertory Theatre

Artistic Directors, Todd Loyd, Tiffany Little Canfield; Executive Director & Founding Member, Katrina Kent; Founding Artistic Director & Associate Executive Director, Robyne Parrish; Development, Sharon Albert; Education, Julianna Jaffe; Curriculum Development, Sean Kent; www.sonnetrepertorytheatre.org

Richard 2 by Willaim Shakespeare; Director, Steven Cole Hughes; Lighting, Ryan O'Gara; **Cast:** Kiebpoli Calnek, Mat Hostetler, Khris Lewin, Eileen Little, Daniel Loeser, Vince Nappo, Brent Rose and Danielle Slavick; Co-Produced by Matchbook Productions; The Tank; May 7–24, 2010

One Music and lyrics by Wade McCollum, book by Kristin Steele; Based on the novel *Siddhartha* by Herman Hess; Director, Todd Loyd; Musical Director, Karl Mansfield; Choreographer, Jolly Abraham; Lighting, Jessica Hinkle; Costumes, Hwi-won Lee; Set, Lex Liang; Sound, Justin Stasiw; **Cast:** Michael Winther, Manu Narayan, James Harcourt, Pearl Sun, Dana Musgrove, Paolo Montalban, Howard Kaye, Sydney James Harcourt, Julianna Jaffe, Laiona Michelle; 59E59 Theater C; August 26– 30, 2009

Readings

Collaborative Series Included: *I Like You, You're Hot* by Greta Gerwig; Director, Jeremiah Maestas; Assistant Director, Nicole Lane; **Cast:** Zoey Martinson, Aleque Reid, Luke Robertson, Leah Walsh; *Don't Call it a Comeback* by Sean Kent; Director, Robyne Parrish; Assistant Director, Allison Bressi; **Cast:** Maechi Aharanwa, Matt Harrington, Andy Hassell, Anthony Wofford; *The Bank Teller* by Jim Knable; Director, Michael Lluberes; Assistant Director, Julianna Jaffe; **Cast:** Kristopher Alexander, Laura Esposito, Julie Sharbutt, Ben Yannette; Goldman-Sonnenfeldt Auditorium; July 13, 2009

Stage Left Studio

NY/XY by William LoCasto; Director, Alexander Beck; Lighting, Ellen Rosenberg; **Cast:** Brandon Bernard, Zach Harvey, Leicester Landon; June 18–August 6, 2009

Blue Lanterns by Branislav Tomich; Director, Sydnie Grosberg Ronga; Stage Manager, Abi Degay; **Cast:** Branislav Tomich; (non-resident production); September 17–November 30, 2009

The 3 Irish Widows Versus the Rest of the World by Ed Malone; Director, Rob Welsh; **Cast:** Ed Malone; January 6–April 1, 2010

First Time, Long Time by Jeremy Stuart; Presented by Cheryl King; **Cast:** Amanda Byron, Robert Sherrane, Jeremy Stuart; January 20–March 24, 2010

Stella Adler Studio

www.stellaadler.com

Decade at a Glance Written and directed by Joan Evans; Stage Manager, Emily Ciotti & Breanna Stroud; Lighting, Brian Tover; Costumes, Katja Andreive; **Cast:** Lizzi Albert, Laura Carbonell, Erika Cazeneuve, Annie Chang, Aidan Koehler, Gaja Massaro, Rafa Miguel, Tommy Nelms, Sean Powell, Lulu Rossbacher, Melanie Siegel, Margaux Susi, Elise Toscano, Cynthia Vazquez, Sarah Wharton; February 12–March 7, 2010

Storm Theatre

The Satin Slipper by Paul Claudel; Director, Peter Dobbins; Set, Ken Larson; Lighting, Michael Abrams; Costumes, Laura Taber Bacon; Sound, Amy Alta Donna; Stage Manager, Charles Casano; **Cast:** Erin Teresa Beirnard, Dan Berkey, Gabe Bettio, Cheryl Burek, Ross DeGraw, Joshua Dixon, Dihn Q. Doan, Megan Doyle, Merel Julia, Michelle Kafel, Maury Miller, Meredith Napolitano, Cassandra Palacio, Anthony Russo, Christopher Tocco, Harlan Work; January 8–February 6, 2010

Strike Anywhere Performance Ensemble

Artistic/Producing Director, Leese Walker; www.strikeanywhere.info

Macbeth Variations by Shakespeare; Directors, Leese Walker and Christophe Cagnolari; Set, Kate Foster; Costumes, Camille Assaf; Lighting, Nolan Kennedy; Education Coordinator/Stage Manager, Amanda Hinkle; **Cast:** Donna Bouthillier, Bob Bowen, Christophe Cagnolari, Maud Ivanoff, Michel Gentile, Rob Henke, Thierry Joze, Nolan Kennedy, Maxime Nourissat, Damen Scranton, Rolf Sturm, Leese Walker; Irondale Center: October 1–3, 2009

!! FreEpLaY !! Devised by the ensemble; Director, Leese Walker; Lighting, Nolan Kennedy; Interns, Ian Axness and Timothy Pracher-Dix; Box Office, Amanda Hinkle; **Cast:** Donna Bouthillier, Bob Bowen, Michel Gentile, Rob Henke, Nolan Kennedy, Damen Scranton, Rolf Sturm, Leese Walker; Brecht Forum; Ongoing

The R&D Wing A showcase of ensemble theatres; included: *Macbeth Variations; Loup Garou* Presented by Artspot Productions and Mondo Bizarro; *Floating Brothel* Presented by Purefinder; *The Ladies Aide Society Invites You To A Poverty Party To Benefit The Foundation Of Ethical Art And Culture* Presented by Wreckio Ensemble; January 10, 2010

Subjective Theatre Company

Jump Jim Crow: How to Produce Your Own Minstrel Show Book by Jesse Cameron Alick, music and lyrics by Justin Levine; Director, Donya K. Washington; Stage Manager, Hyatt Michaels; Dramaturg, Stephanie Vellahor; Choreographer, Steven Gillenwater; **Cast:** Haas Regan, Rusty Buehler, Jill Knox, Kimberlee Walker, Brandon Jones, Lynneisha Ray, Eddie Wardel; The Ukrainian Center, December 8–20, 2009

Suspended Cirque

Swingin' at Jack's Director, Brian Rardin; Music Director, Peter Kiesewalter; **Cast:** Joshua Dean, Ben Franklin, Michelle Dortignac, Angela Jones, Kristin Olness; Galapagos Art Space; April 4–25, 2010

Swandive Studio

www.strikeanywhere.info

Blackouts by J. Anthony Roman; Director, Jill DeArmon; Set, Jen Price Fick; Lighting, Joshua Rose; Costumes, Hollie Nadel; Sound, Shane Rettig; Stage Manager, Shannon O'Neil; **Cast:** Zachary Fletcher, Jamie Klassel, Lisa Snyder, and Max Woertendyke; Center Stage NY; October 7–24, 2009

T. Schreiber Studio

www.tschreiber.org

Rosencrantz and Guildenstern are Dead by Tom Stoppard; Director, Cat Parker; Set, George Allison; Costumes, Karen Ann Ledger; Lighting, Eric Cope; Sound, Andy Cohen; Stage Manager, Michael Denis; Dramaturg, Page Clements; Production Coordinator, Barb Kielhofer; Assistant Director, Cristina Lundy; Production Assistant, Oliver Sterlacci; Press, Lanie Zipoy; **Cast:** Aki Tsuchimoto, Diane Terrusa, Doug Williford, Eric Percival, Erik Jonsun, Esteban Benito, Horacio Lazo, James O'Brien, Janine Pangburn, Julian Elfer, Marguerite Forrest, Meghan Brown, Rodney Allen Umble, Therese Tucker, Tim Wienert, Tom Lawson Jr., Tootie Larios; Gloria Maddox Theatre; October 15–November 22, 2009

The Cherry Orchard by Anton Chekhov, adapted by Carol Rocamora; Director, Terry Schreiber; Set, Hal Tine´; Costumes, Dawn Nancy Testa; Lighting, Dennis Parichy; Sound, Chris Rummel; Stage Manager, Liz Richards; Technical Director,

Jason Dale Pickens; Magic Coordinator, Thomas Solomon; Producing Director, Barb Kielhofer; Assistant Director, Laura Sisskin-Fernandez; Assistant Technical Director, John W. Rhea; Assistant Set, Diem Hoang; **Cast:** Julie Garfield, Laine Bonstein, Julie Szabo, Aleksandra Stattin, Ina Marie Smith, Jamie Kirmser, Rick Forstmann, Marcus Lorenzo, Robert Pusilo, Alec A. Head, Parker Dixon, Peter Judd, Kelly Haran, Adam Swartz, David Donahoe, Rivka Borek, Marija Stajic-Sal; Gloria Maddox Theatre; February 25–April 4, 2010

Joking Apart by Alan Ayckbourn; Director, Peter Jensen; Set, Matt Brogan; Costumes, Anne Wingate; Lighting, Eric Cope; Sound, Andy Cohen; Stage Manager, Liz Richards; Dialect Coach, Page Clements; Technical Director, Andy Knauff; Producing Director, Barb Kielhofer; Assistant Director, Julia Kelly; Press, Lanie Zipoy; **Cast:** Michael Murray, Aleksandra Stattin, Michael J. Connolly, Alison Blair, James Liebman, Stephanie Seward, Sebastian Montoya, Anisa Dema; Gloria Maddox Theatre; May 20–June 27, 2010

Take Wing And Soar Productions, Inc.

Artistic Director, Debra Ann Byrd; www.takewingandsoar.org

Forgive Me? by Esther Armah; Director, Trezana Beverley; Set, Debra Ann Byrd; Lighting, James Carter; Stage Manager, Mercedes Ayala; Producer, Debra Ann Byrd; Producing Assistants, Flora Gillaird & David Weaver; House Manager, LaZette McCants; Marketing/Promotions, Centric Productions; **Cast:** Beverley Prentice, Gilbert Glenn Brown; Presented as part of the Midtown International Theatre Festival; WorkShop Theater; July 23–August 1, 2009

A Midsummer Night's Madness Adapted from William Shakespeare by The Youth Company; Director, Suzie McKenna; Lighting, James Carter; Producers, Debra Ann Byrd and Susie McKenna; Musical Director, Orphy Robinson; Choreographer, Samantha Francis; Assistant Director, Patrick Miller; Youth Producer, Coco Jackson; **Cast:** Chantelle Masuku, Debbie Ogunbodede, Isabella Adutwim, Jessica Symonds, Kate Cox, Rashmika Torchia, Scarlett Scanlon, Bradley Cumberbatch, Enrico Delves, Jordan Blake-Klein, Kofi Boateng, Mekel Edward; National Black Theatre; August 17, 2009

Pecong by Steve Carter; Directors, Arthur French and Timothy D. Stickney; Stage Manager, William J. Vila; Lighting, James Carter; Set, Pavlo Bosyy; Costumes, David Withrow; Sound, David D. Wright; Producers, Debra Ann Byrd and Jackie Jeffries; Associate Producer, Flora Gillard; House Manager, LaZette McCants; Press Agent, Penny Landau; Marketing/Promotions, Natalie Clarke; ASM, Leila Okafor; **Cast:** Phyllis Yvonne Stickney, Joyce Sylvester, Kim Weston Moran, David Heron, Natalie Clarke, Warren Jackson, Daralyn Jay, Aixa Kendrick, Lily Robinson, Albert Eggleston, Norman Anthony Small Jr., Karl O'Brian Williams, Lorna Haughton, David D. Wright; National Black Theatre; March 12–28, 2010

Readings

Le Triomphe De L'amour by Marivaux; Director, Kevin Connell; Lighting, James Carter; Stage Manager, Danielle Szabo; **Cast:** The TWAS Classical Actors of Color; October 19, 2009; *The African Company Presents Richard II* by Carlyle Brown; Director, Chuck Patterson; **Cast:** The TWAS Classical Actors of Color; November 12, 2009; *Macbeth* by William Shakespeare; Director, Timothy D. Stickney; Lighting Desig, James Carter; Stage Manager, Danielle Szabo; House Manager, LaZette McCants; **Cast:** Timothy D. Stickney, Stephanie Berry and The TWAS Classical Actors of Color; December 14, 2009

Teatro Círculo

Artistic Director, José Cheo Oliveras; Associate Artistic Directors, Beatriz Córdoba and Luis Caballero; www.teatrocirculo.org

7 Veces Siete by 7 Contemporary Playwrights; Director, Iliana García; October 23–25, 2009

El caballero del milagro by Lope de Vega; Director, Dean Zayas; Stage Manager, Edna Lee Figueroa; Choreographer, Manny Ortiz-Oliveras; Music Director, Pablo Zinger; Set, Jorge Dieppa; Lighting, Maria Cristina Fuste; Costumes, Gloria Saez; **Cast:** Juan Luis Acevedo, Iiana Garcia, Gerardo Gudino, Mario Mattei, Jose Cheo Oliveras, Manny Ortiz-Oliveras, Rita Ortiz, Jerry Soto, Fermin Suarez, Eva Cristina Vasquez; October 28–November 15, 2009

Non-resident Productions

Way To Heaven (Himmelweg) by Juan Mayorga; Presented by Equilicua Producciones US Inc.; Director, Matthew Earnest; Lighting, Derek Wright; Set, Matthew Farnest; Costumes, Patrick Johnson; Sound, Patrick Johnson; Producer, Puy Navarro; Translator, David Johnston; **Cast:** Francisco Reyes, Shawn Parr, Mark Farr, Ben Elgart, Trae Hicks, Trey Gerrald, Beth Baker, Jessica Amara Beaudry, Sal Bardo, Samantha Rahn; May 7–August 23, 2009

teaser cow by Clay Mcleod Chapman; Presented by One Year Lease Theater Company; Director, Ianthe Demos; Set, James Hunting; Costumes, Kay Anna Lee; Lighting, Mike Riggs; Sound, Nathan Leigh; Stage Manager, Rosy Garner; Choreographer, Austin McCormick; Dramaturgs, Jessica Kaplow Applebaum, Amanda Culp; Graphics, Brian Michael Thomas; Video Director, Nick Flint; Press, Sarah Parvis; Assistant Set, Kira Nehmer; **Cast:** Danny Bernardy, Sarah-Jane Casey, Nick Flint, Babis Gousias, Jim Kane, Christina Bennett Lind, Gregory Waller; January 14– February 4, 2010

The Tender Mercies by Sladjana Vujovic; Presented by One Year Lease Theater Company; Director, Jessi D. Hill; Set, James Hunting; Costumes, Paul Carey; Lighting, Mike Riggs; Sound, Nathan Leigh; Stage Manager, Colleen M. Sherry; Producer, Ianthe Demos; Dramaturgs, Jessica Kaplow Applebaum, Amanda Culp; Graphics, Brian M. Thomas; Press, Sarah Parvis; **Cast:** Jim Kane, Christina Bennett Lind, Gregory Waller; April 14– May 1, 2010

Teatro IATI (International Theater Arts Institute)

Artistic & Executive Director, Vivian Deangelo; Associate Artistic Director, Winston Estevez; Marketing & Production Manager, Germán Baruffi; Outreach, Luz Cazeneuve; Development, Liza Melanie Ostolaza; Education, Laura Spalding; Financial Manager, James Figueroa; Play Reading Program, Fabián González; www.teatroiati.org

Forbidden Love Inspired by Federico García Lorca's Blood Wedding; Adaptation by Pati Doménech; Directors, Pati Doménech and Jorge López; **Cast:** Maria Vidal; Teatro IATI Theater; March 25–April 3, 2010

I Want You By My Side by Tere Martínez; Director, Arian Blanco; Stage Manager, Karina Alos; Set, Yanko Bakulic; Audio/Visual, Walter Ventosilla; Photographer, Gabriela Luiz; **Cast:** Howard Collado, Anita Kalathara, Miriam Morale; March 27–April 3, 2010

The Brave Calf Written and directed by Walter Ventosilla; Original Music, Carrol Luna; Mask Design, Erika Rojas; **Cast:** German Baruffi, Gillian Hurst, Pedro Mir, Winston Estevez; Tour; April 23–June 30, 2010

Second Annual Performing Arts Marathon *July 9–26, 2009*

ACTion: Ecuador 2009 Presented by Dramatic Adventure Theatre; July 19

Barceloneta, de noche Written and directed by Javierantonio González; Presented by Caborca Theatre; Stage Manager, Erin Koster; Lighting, Erin Koster; **Cast:** David Skeist, Ricardo J. Hinoa, Tania Molina, Jorge Luna, Marcos Toledo, Yaremis Felix, Luis Alberto Gonzales; July 9–12

Cama para dos/Bed for Two by Alex Vásquez Escaño; Director, Diana Chery; **Cast:** Eva Vásquez, Fabián González, Yanko Bakulic; July 11–12

Fotomatón by Gustavo Ott; Director, Alfonso Rey; Lighting, Alfonso Rey; Costumes, Maria Brites; **Cast:** Felipe Tútuti; Producer, Fernando Then; July 15–18

Fragments Director, Rene Migliaccio; Presented by Black Moon Theatre Company Audio/Visual, India Evans; Choreographer, Ximena Garnica; **Cast:** Patricia Becker; July 10–18

Latin Choreographers Festival 2009 Founded and curated by Ursula Verduzco; Choreographers, Roman Baca, Benjamin Briones, Yesid López, Annabella González, Jesús Pacheco, Minou Lalleman, Cecilia Marta, Orlando Peña, Robert Spin Olivera, Pedro Ruíz, Ursula Verduzco; July 23–26

Loisaida Kathak: Home at Last Created by Janaki Patrik and Anup Kumar Das; Presented by The Kathak Ensemble & Friends; July 18, 2010

Silence & (((PHONATION))) featuring *Dialogues of Silence* by Sabrina Lastman and *(((PHONATION)))* by Bora Yoon; July 16–17, 2009

Too Much Light Makes the Baby Go Blind Written and Performed by the New York Neo-Futurists; July 12, 2009

Readings

Cotton Candy (For an Insipid Sunset) by Diana Chery Ramírez; Director, Fabián González; September 28; *No se vale llorar (Not Worth Crying Over)* by Cristian Cortez; Director, Martin Balmaceda.; November 18; *Open up, Hadrian* by Javierantonio González; June 29; *Passing Judgment* by Jason Ramírez; October 12; *Pretty September Day* by Alejandro Latorre; Director, Jennifer Ortega; March 30; *The Day a Mariachi Band Followed Charlie Home* by Carlos J. Serrano; Director, José Esquea; March 29; *Women-HOOD (La Flaca y La Gorda)* by José Antonio Goicuria; Director, Claudia Acosta; March 24

TeatroStageFest

Long Island Iced Latina by Marga Gomez; Director, David Schweizer; **Cast:** Marga Gomez; 47th Street Theatre; June 18–21, 2009

Terra Incognita

terraincognitatheater.org

Capital Fringe Festival; Pebble-and-Cart Cycle by Terra Incognita Ensemble; Director Polina Klimovitskaya; **Cast:** Dolly Williams, Natalia Krasnova, Jeremy Goren, Michael Moscoso, Dinne Kopelevich, Ellen Lanese, Anthony Spaldo, Sofia Oppenheim; Warehouse Mainstage; July 17–19, 2009

Thalia Spaish Theatre

Artistic/Executive Director, Angel Gil Orrios; Founder, Silvia Brito; www.thaliatheatre.org

Alma Flamenca/Flamenco Soul Director, Yloy Ybarra; Lighting, Angel Gil Orrios; Set, Angel Gil Orrios; Sound, Jaime Castillo; Stage Manager, Maria Aleñar; Technical Director, Fabricio Saquicela; **Cast:** Yloy Ybarra, Lia Ochoa, Ricky Santiago, Sol La Argentinita, Alfonso Cid, Cristian Puig, Jed Miley, Sean Kupisz; Co-produced with Andrea Del Conte Danza España; September 18–October 18, 2009

The Best of the Best of Mestizo Director, Armando Moreno; Set/Lighting, Angel Gil Orrios; Costumes, Armando Moreno & Fernando Mesa; Sound, Jaime Castillo; Stage Manager, Fernando Mesa; Technical Director, Fabricio Saquicela; Makeup, Alex Fernandez; **Cast:** Solanlly Jimenez, Michelle Jimenez, Yuri Pacheco, Vanessa Ascanio, Amalfi Sanchez, Suleyvi Florez, Dayana Lozano, Natalia Jimenez, Sheila Genao, Jhuliana Lopez, Gilma Agudelo, Maria Flores, Alexander Gonazles, Julian Amezquita, Jeffrei Londoño, Manuel Paq; November 6, 2009

Borges & Piazzolla Tango by Jorge Luis Borges; Director, Angel Gil Orrios; Set/Lighting, Angel Gil Orrios; Costumes, Soledad Lopez & America Barrera;

Sound, Jaime Castillo; Stage Manager, Armando Moreno; Audio/Visual, Angel Gil Orrios & Abraham Pacheco; Composer/Musical Director, Raul Jaurena; Technical Director, Fabricio Saquicela; Group Choreographers, Ivan Terrazas & Sara Grdan; **Cast:** Marga Mitchell, Francisco Fuertes, Soledad Lopez, Ivan Terrazas, Sara Grdan, Eduardo Goytia, Jennifer Wesnousky, Ed Johnson, Laure Lion, Maestro Raul Jaurena, Pablo Aslan, Maurizio Najt, Emilio Teubal, Sergio Reyes, Mauro Satalino; January 29–March 21, 2010

Mexico 200 Years/Años Director, Yloy Ybarra; Set/Lighting, Angel Gil Orrios; Costumes, Yloy Ybarra; Sound, Jaime Castillo; Technical Director, Fabricio Saquicela; Stage Manager, Armando Moreno; **Cast:** Yloy Ybarra, Natalia Brillante, Lizette Palacios, Alda Reuter, Judith Shapiro Gonzalez, Noe Dominguez, Mireya Ramos, Shae Fiol, Julie Acosta, Megan Coiley, Daniel Soberanes; April 30–May 9, 2010

The Prostitutes Will Precede You Into the Kingdom of Heaven by Jose Luis Martin Descalzo; Director, Angel Gil Orrios; Set/Lighting, Angel Gil Orrios; Costumes, Soledad Lopez; Sound, Jaime Castillo; Stage Manager, Armando Moreno; Translator, Daniel Sherr; Sculptor, William Saquicela; Technical Director, Fabricio Saquicela; **Cast:** Kathy Tejada, Soledad Lopez; May 28–June 27, 2010

Theater for the New City

www.theaterforthenewcity.net

Belle of the Ball Bearings: The Bike Shop Musical by Elizabeth Battersby, Caroline Murphy and Youn Young Park; Presented by Charles Battersby; Director, Caroline Murphy; Lighting, Alexander Bartenieff; Set, Mark Marcante; Costumes, Anne Hanavin; Sound, Richard Reta; Choreographer, Caroline Murphy; Original Music, Youn Young Park; **Cast:** Elizabeth Battersby; June 4–21, 2009

A Promise Best Kept by Edward Miller; Co-production with Little Rascals Theater Company; Director/Set, Mark Marcante; Assistant Director/Set, Jessica Hart; Sound, Joy Linscheid; Lighting, Alexander Bartenieff; **Cast:** Dan Patrick Bray, Evander Duck Jr., Kyle Fowler, Alexandra Grossi, Tina Mavrikidis, Austin Mitchell, Nick Ruggeri, Jack Tynan, April Woodall; Community Space Theater; June 10–27, 2010

Tally Ho!, or Navigating the Future Written and directed by Crystal Field; Music & Lyrics, David Tice; Set, Mary Blanchard, Walter Gurbo; Costumes, Susan Gittens, Erin Belanger, Zen Mansley, Pamela Mayo, Myrna Duarte; Sound, Joy Linscheid, David Nolan; Masks, Candice Burridge; **Cast:** Mark Marcante, Primi Rivera, Michael David, Alexander Bartenieff; Various locations throughout NYC; August 1–13, 200

Hecuba Presented by Ego Actus; Community Space Theater; August 10–23, 2009

Swimming In The Shallows Presented by Alec Turnbull; Cino Theater; August 24–30, 2009

To Love And To Cherish by Gene Ruffini; Director, Jessica Zweiman; **Cast:** Bruce Colbert, Thesa Loving, Andrew Langton, Jessica Pohly, Jake Green, Kelly Campbell, Bethany Braun and Kimberlee Walker; Cino Theater; September 3–20, 2009

EN Written and performed by Cobu; Johnson Theater; September 15–20, 2009

Paso Del Norte & Tell Them Not To Kill Me by Juan Rulfo; Director, German Jaramillo; Community Space Theater; September 17–October 4, 2009

Asian-American Theater Festival Presented by the Asian-American Theater Festival; Cino Theater; October 12–18, 2009

Sharif Don't Like It / Assimilation Written and directed by Shishir Kurup; **Cast:** Shishir Kurup; October 13–18, 2009

70/70 Horovitz Project Presented by Barefoot Theatre Company; Cabaret Theater; November 5–22, 2009

The Supper Club of Lost Causes Written and directed by Jim Farmer; Set and Costumes, Victoria Imperioli; **Cast:** Audrey Rapoport, Richard Brundage, Siho Ellsmore, Jeff Pucillo, Brian Linden, Darcie Sicilano, Bernard Bygott, Steve Greenstein, Blaire Stauffer; Community Space Theater; November 6–29, 2009

Kitch, or Two for the Price of One by Trav S.D.; Produced by Mountebanks; Director/Lighting, Ian W. Hill; Set, David Brune; Costumes, Karen Flood; Sound, Ian W. Hill; Stage Manager, Berit Johnson; Audio/Visual, Ian W. Hill; Original Music, Trav S.D.; **Cast:** Trav S.D., Kate Valentine, Audrey Crabtree, Josh Mertz, Pete Macnamara, Roger Nasser, Avery Pearson, Esther Silberstein, Gavin Starr Kendall, Betsy Head, Gyda Arber, Aaron Baker, Tom Bibla, Lily Burd, William Kahn, John Kelly, Brian Mott, Michele Cwiklik, Jillian Tully; Johnson Theater; November 12–29, 2009

Nonviolent Executions Written and directed by Steve Ben Israel; Cabaret Theater; November 27–28, 2009

Bread & Puppet Theater Presetned by Bread & Puppet Theater; Johnson Theater; December 3–13, 2009

Angry Young Women in Low Rise Jeans with High Class Issues Written and directed by Matt Morillo; **Cast:** Nick Coleman, Tom Pilutik, Angelique Letizia, Lauren Murphy, Poppi Kramer, Erika Helen Smith, Vi Flaten, Gage Cass; Community Space Theater; December 3–20, 2009

Voice 4 Vision Puppet Festival Curated by Sarah Provost and Jane Catherine Shaw; *Hobo No No* by Billy Burns; *The Mud Angels* by Luis Tentindo, live performance by Valerie Opielski; *Next to the Last Poem* and *La Mome Bijoux* by Patti Bradshaw; *Folktales of Asia & Africa* created, designed and performed by Jane Catherine Shaw; *Puppets on Film* featuring selections from Heather Henson's *Handmade Puppet Dreams Vol. IV*; *Puppet Art Attacks Puppet Slam*; Artists: Alissa Hunnicutt, Serra Hirsch, Spica Wobbe, Caitlin Lainoff, Howie Liefer, Caroline Reck, Sally Fisher, Hillary Spector; Supported by the Jim Henson Foundation; Cino Theater; December 3–13, 2009

Nutcracker: Rated R Conceived, Choreographed and directed by Angela Harriell; Additional Choreography, Katrin Hoffmann; **Cast:** Jennifer Carlson, Hyosun Choi, Sarah Conrad, Amy Daulton, Gregory Dubin, Glenn Giron, Eddie Gutierrez, Angela Harriell, Denis Hyland, Valton Jackson, Christina Johnson, Rachael Ma, Michael MacLaren, Joseph Schles, Ryan Schmidt, David F. Slone, Juliana Smith, Clare Tobin; Johnson Theater; December 17–31, 2009

Flahooley Book by E.Y. Harburg and Fred Saidy, lyrics by E.Y. Harburg, music by Sammy Fain; Co-Production with Harlem Repertory Theatre, in conjunction with the Yip Harburg Foundation; Director/Choreographer, Keith Lee Grant; Lighting, Brian Aldous; Set, Mary Myers; Costumes, Ann-Marie Wright; Audio/Visual, Daniel Fergus Tamulonis; **Cast:** Alexandra Bernard, Daniel Fergus Tamulonis, Roman Urbanski; December 18, 2009–January 3, 2010

A Colony of Artists Written and directed by Bina Sharif; Lighting, Alex Bartenieff; Light Board Operator, Bill Bradford; **Cast:** Shyla Idris, Juan-Elias Lopera, Manny Manhattan, Kevin Mitchell Martin, Angelique Rose, Bina Sharif, Joe Ulam, Serious Bob; Community Space Theater; December 31, 2009–January 17, 2010

American Soldiers Written and directed by Matt Morillo; **Cast:** Mark Marcante and Nick Coleman; Cino Theater; January 7–31, 2010

If This Ain't It! Written and directed by Don Arrington; Music Director, Rick Cutler; **Cast:** Michael Lynch, Ellen Scarsella, Andy Weiss, Erik Stevens, Luisa Bradshaw, Lauren Lindsey, Bradley Wantz, Alena Acker, Kyle T. Cheng, Alissa Stahler, Christian Harmon, Don Arrington, Camille Tibaldeo; Cabaret Theater; January 7–24, 2010

American Soldiers by Matt Morillo; Presented by KADM Productions; Director, Matt Morillo; Lighting, Amith A. Chandrashaker; Set, Mark Marcante; **Cast:** Nick Coleman, Julia Giolzetti, Tom Pilutik, Kate Reilly, Stu Richel; January 14–31, 2010

Tarantella! Spider Dance Written and directed by Alessandra Belloni; Set, Donald L.Brooks and Arden H. Mason; **Cast:** Alessandra Belloni, Joe Deninzon, John La Barbera, Vinnie Sciala, Alessandra Tartivita, Caterina Rago,Antonio Fini, Mark Mindek; Johnson Theater; January 15–24, 2010

The Fake History of George The Last by Misha Shulman; Director, Meghan Finn; Set, Czerton Lim; Lighting, Liam Billingham; Audio/Visual, Jared Mezzocchi; Original Music, Misha Shulman and Kevin Farrell; **Cast:** Jared Mezzocchi, Sarah Painter, Ben Jaeger-Thomas, Erika Helen Smith, Priscilla Flores; Community Space Theater; January 21–February 7, 2010

Duet for Solo Voice by David Scott Milton; Director, Stanley Allan Sherman; **Cast:** Jonathan Slaff, Rachel Krah, Zen Mansley; Cabaret Theater; January 28–February 14, 2010

Thunderbird American Indian Dancers Presented and performed by Thunderbird American Indian Dancers; Johnson Theater; January 29–February 7, 2010

The Divine Sister by Charles Busch; Director, Carl Andress; Stage Manager, Angela Allen; **Cast:** Charles Busch, Alison Fraser, Julie Halston, Amy Rutberg, Jennifer Van Dyck, Jonathan Walker; Cino Theater; February 6–March 7, 2010

Lotus Feet Written and directed by Michael Domitrovich; Set, Nathaniel Deverich; Lighting, Maruti Evans; Sound, Brian McCorkle; Stage Manager, Michael Alifanz; Choreographer, Stefanie Sertich; **Cast:** Christina Pumariega, Quinlan Corbett, Lori McNally, Mary Dana Abbott, Nityda Coleman, April Martucci, Haley Roth; Community Space Theater; February 11–28, 2010

Moments and Lemons by Fred Giacinto; Presented by M&L Productions; Director, Thom Fogarty; **Cast:** Tony King, Jessica Day; February 18–March 7, 2010

Revolut¿on!? written and directed by Pavel Dobruský and Vít Horejš; Co-production with the Czechoslovak-American Marionette Theater; Set/Lighting, Pavel Dobruský; Stage Manager, Michael Collins; Producers, Tereza Hofbauerova and Bonnie Stein; **Cast:** Adéla Jirá ková, Hana Kalousková, Theresa Linnihan, Sergej Šanza, Ronny Wasserstrom, Pavel Strouhal, Vít Ho ejš; Community Space Theater; March 4–21, 2010

Living In A Musical by Tom Attea; Director, Mark Marcante; Original Music, Arthur Abrams; Stage Manager, Rachel Krah; Lighting, Alexander Bartenieff; Set, Mark Marcante; Costumes, Pauline Colon; Sound, Richard Reta **Cast:** Kyle Fowler, Alexandra Grossi, Sal Mannino, Robb Gibbs, Clare Tobin, Bob Homeyer, Andrea Andert, Rachael Ma, Julie Megan Smith, Valton Jackson, David Mansley, David F. Slone, Sheira Feuerstein, Gladys Maldonado; Johnson Theater; March 4–21, 2010

Wonder Bread Written and performed by Danusia Trevino; Director, Aleksey Burago; Cabaret Theater; March 11–28, 2010

The Pomology of Sweetness & Light Presented by Black Forest Fancies; Cino Theater; March 22–April 4, 2010

Seduction of Mind (x3) *The Seduction of Time* by Lissa Moira; Original Music, Chris Wade; Choreographers, Patrick L. Salazar and Harmony Livingston; *Subterranean Skydive* written and performed by Richard West; *Such Sweet Sorrow Music* Book and concept by Chris Wade; Director, Lissa Moira; Choreographer, Harmony Livingston; Music Supervision, Dave Albulario; Community Space Theater; March 25–April 11, 2010

Havana Journal, 2004 by Eduardo Machado; Director, Stefanie Sertich; Stage Manager, Michael Alifanz; **Cast:** Crystal Field, Liam Torres, Juan Javier Cardenas, David Skeist; Johnson Theater; March 26–April 18, 2010

Stops (Along The Road) by Walter Corwin; Director, Jonathan Weber; Lighting, Mark Marcante; **Cast:** Rachel Krah, Kate McGrath, Joey Mintz, Jonathan Weber; Cabaret Theater; April 1–11, 2010

Downtown Urban Theater Festival; Downtown Urban Theater Festival; Johnson and Cino Theaters; April 15–29, 2010

Denial! Time To Face The Musical Book, music and lyrics by Nikki Jenkins; Director, Aaron Pratt; Music Director/Pianist, Brad Gardner; Stage Manager, Erin Person; Orchestrations, Brad Gardner, Michael Ross; Choreography, Camille Theobald; Hair/ Makeup, Amanda Ochoa; Set/Technical Director, Mark Marcante; Costumes, Rachel Soll; Lighting, Tim Greeson; Advertising/Program Design, Christopher Villanueva; **Cast:** Nikki Jenkins, Kristin Mularz, Jonathan Grunert, Hayley Raphael, Jenna Bitow, Matthew Corr-Addington, Eileen Faxas, Brandon Hightower, Jerome Amanquiton; Cabaret Theater; April 15–May 2, 2010

The Spring And Fall Of Eve Adams Written and directed by Barbara Kahn; Set, Mark Marcante; Lighting, Alexander Bartenieff; Costumes, Deanna R. Frieman; Stage Manager, Bill Bradford; Producers, Crystal Field; **Cast:** Jon Dalin, Marisa Petsakos, Jimmy Heyworth, Anna Podolak, Micha Lazare, Steph Van Vlack, Michelle Cohen, Martha Lee as Margaret Leonard; Community Space Theater; April 15–May 2, 2010

Generation buY & Lysistrata's Children Two plays written and directed by Philip Suraci; Set, Mark Marcante; Lighting, Alex Bartenieff; Costumes, Kat Martin; Choreographer, Barry Blumenfeld; Original Music, Joseph Albano Feiger; Mask/Puppets, Spica Wobbe; Graphics, Fred Sullivan; Art Design, Reinaldo Felix; **Cast:** Lola Buncher, Eli Cauley, Ty Cotton, Priscilla Delmoral, Jackie Donnaruma, Leila Eliot, Sheira Feuerstein, Mykel Macedon, Will Mairs, Malcolm McKenzie, Tom O'Connor, Tiffany Otero, Valentine Petrillo, Willa Pittman, Frances Raybaud, Collin Rhyins, Kendrick Shoji, Mitchel Thomas, Jason Vazquez, Michell Wolinsky, Malcom Zelaya; Cino Theater; May 6–16, 2010

Lower East Side Festival of the Arts Featuring: Kenny Lockwood and Red Road; Alpha Omega Theatrical Dance Company; Lindsay Davis; John Grimaldi, NY Lyric Circus; JT Lotus Dance Company; Richard West; Bleeker Street Opera; Andre Brown; Longing (Oh Well); Katherine Adamenko and Tomato Hands/Knife Feet; RWM Playwrights Lab; David Amram; Yangtze Repertory Theatre of America; Desipina & Company; Judy Gorman; The Love Show; Nikki Jenkins; Joe Franklin; Gary Corbin; Lissa Moira; Elizabeth Ruf; Matt Morillo; Inma Heredia; Michael Vazquez; Misha Shulman; Zero Boy; Randy Credico; Adam Wade; Infallibility; Rapscallion Theatre Collective; Human Kinetics Movement Arts; May 28–30, 2010

My Boyfriend is a Zombie Written and directed by William Electric Black; Choreographer, Jeremy Lardieri; Lighting, Federico Restrepo; Costumes, Tilly Grimes; Makeup, Kate Tsang; Musicians: Gary Schreiner, Saadi Zain, James Mussen; **Cast:** Nicole Patullo, Cara S. Liander, Allison Troesch, Macah Coates, Jamaal Kendall, Jeremy Lardieri, Lenin Alevante, Matthew Hooper, Erin Salm, Verna Hampton; Cino Theater; June 3–27, 2010

Readings

Negrophobia by Arthur French III; September 21, 2009; *The Iron Heel* written and directed by Elizabeth Ruf-Maldonado, adapted from the novel by Jack London; Johnson Theater; September 24–October 11, 2009; *Macaire* by Thomas G. Waites; October 19, 2009; *Soldier Boys* by Lazarre Seymour Simckes; November 9, 2009; *House Red* by Sean Pomposello; December 21, 2009; *Round The Night Park* by Maria Micheles; January 11, 2010; *Divinity* by Bill Wright; Februry 1, 2010; *Pamela Precious* by Matt Moses; February 22, 2010; *The Caretakers* by Michael R. McGuire; April 5, 2010; *The Naked Side of Grace* by Lucile Scott; June 7, 2010; *The Chrysalis* by Various; June 6–13, 2010

Theater Mitu

Artistic Director, Rubén Polendo; Company Manager Hilary Austin; Associate Artists, Jenni-Lynn Brick, Aysan Celik, Adam Cochran, Emily Davis, Jef Evans, Ben Fox, Chris Mills, Justin Nestor, Lori Petermann, Ryan West; www.theatermitu.org

Dr. C (Or How I Learned to Act in Eight Steps) Conceived and directed by Rubén Polendo; Text Collage, Rubén Polendo and Jocelyn Clarke; Dramaturgy, Jocelyn Clarke; Choreography, Scott Spahr; Original Music, Ellen Reid; Set, Amy

Rubin; Costumes, Candida K. Nichols; Lighting, Kate Ashton; Video, Jake Witlen; Sound, Alex Hawthorn; Stage Manager, Hilary Austin; Musicians, Jef Evans, Ellen Reid, William Thomason; Assistant Directors, John Robichau, Ben Gullard, Judi Olson; **Cast:** Matthew Carlson, Ay an Çelik, Adam Cochran, Emily Davis, Nathan Elam, Marc LeVasseur, Justin Nestor, Laura Stinger, Judi Olson; 3LD Art & Technology Center; June 4–14, 2009

Death of a Salesman by Arthur Miller; Director, Rubén Polendo; Original Music, Ellen Reid, Music Adaptation, Adam Cochran; Stage Manager, Olivia Castillon; Set, Kate Ashton, Leighton Mitchell, Rubén Polendo; Costumes, Candida K. Nichols; Masks, Lori Petermann; Object Design, Sanaz Ghajarrahimi; Lighting, Kate Ashton; Sound, Alex Hawthorn; Dramaturgy, Chris Mills; Musician, Adam Cochran; **Cast:** Justin Nestor, Emily Davis, Nathan Elam, Nikki Calonge, Ryan Conarro, Bryce D. Howard, Jenni-Lynn Brick, Ryan West, Ben Fox, Ayşan Çelik, Nathan Baesel, Mark D. Schultz, Jason Lew, Adam Cochran, Jenny Donoghue; A Theater Mitu collaboration on tour at Brigham Young University; Fall 2009

A Play on War by Jenny Connell, inspired by Brecht's *Mother Courage and Her Children*; Presented in collaboration with the NAATCO; Conceived and Directed by Rubén Polendo; Set, Justin Nestor; Lighting, Kate Ashton; Costumes, Candida K. Nichols; Original Compositions and Live Music, Adam Cochran; **Cast:** Mia Katigbak, Jon Norman Schneider, Nikki Calonge, Orville Mendoza, Marcus Ho, Brian Hirono, Nathan Elam and Bushra Laskar; The Connelly Theater; February 13–March 6, 2010

Medea by Euripedes, adapted and directed by Rubén Polendo; Dramaturgy, Chris Mills; Set, Czerton Lim; Costumes, Candida K. Nichols; Lighting, Kate Ashton; Sound, Alex Hawthorn; Company Manager, Hilary Austin; Production Manager, Danny Thomas; Assistant Director, Nick Minas; **Cast:** Justin Nestor, Ay an Çelik, Nathan Elam, Jenna Gabriel, Judi Olson, Steven Olender, Nikki Calonge, Mia Katigbak; Access Theatre; May 13–23, 2010

Theater Ten Ten

Producing Artistic Director, Judith Jarosz; www.theater1010.com

Arms and The Man by George Bernard Shaw; Director, Leah Bonvissuto; Set, David Fuller; Costumes, Mira Veikley; Lighting, Zack Brown; Sound, Leah Bonvissuto; Stage Manager, Sarah M. Wilson; Choreographer, David Fuller; **Cast:** James Arden, Ramona Floyd, Tatiana Gomberg, Sheila Joon, Timothy John McDonough, Scott Michael Morales, Mickey Ryan; October 8–November 1, 2009

The Cradle Will Rock by Marc Blitzstein; Director, David Fuller, Choreographer, Judith Jarosz; Musical Director, Eric Thomas Johnson; Set, David Fuller; Costumes, Viviane Galloway; Lighting, Zack Brown; Stage Manager, Elisabeth Salisch; **Cast:** Damron Russel Armstrong, Michael Baxter, Douglass Anne Cartwright, Sara DeLaney, Tessa Faye, Matthew James Gray, Dan Hermann, Greg Horton, David Janett, Elizabeth Kensek, Bellavia Mauro, Christopher Michael McLamb, Robert Meksin, Bill Newhall, Michael C. O'Day, Josh Powell, Sarah Rebekah, Chris Vaughn, D. Zhonzinsky, February 12–March 14, 2010

Twelfth Night by William Shakespeare; Director, Judith Jarosz; Set/Lighting, Giles Hogya & Ernesto Mier; Costumes, Deborah Wright Houston; Sound, Jason Wynn; Stage Manager, Shelby Taylor Love; Choreographers, Judith Jarosz and David Fuller; Original Music, Jason Wynn; Fight Director, David Fuller; **Cast:** Richard Brundage, Andrew Clateman, David Fuller, Elizabeth Kensek, Annalisa Loeffler, Lynn Marie Macy, Robert Meksin, Kristopher Monroe, Scott Micheal Morales, Josh Powell, David Weinheimmer; April 29–May 23, 2010

Special Events

Seth Sings More Bisen-Hersh Composed and performed by Seth Bisen-Hersh; November 8, 2009; **Annual Holiday Concert with RPM: A World of Joy** Featuring Mary Lou Barber, John Canary, Kate Canary, Paula Hoza, Jerry Nelson, Luisa Tedoff, Tim Weiss; December 6, 2009; **Sammie**

and Tudie's Imagination Playhouse January 23–March 6, 2010
The Walt Whitman Project Poetry, prose, and music of Walt Whitman; May 26, 2010

Theaterlab

www.theaterlabnyc.com

Three Sisters Come and Go by Anton Chekhov, Samuel Beckett & Julia Kristeva; Director, Orietta Crispino; Set, Taylor Ruckel & Orietta Crispino; Lighting, Drew Vanderburg; Costumes, Sara Baldocchi-Byrne; Sound/Assistant Director, Marco Casazza; Stage Manager, Dahee Kim; Dramaturg, Orietta Crispino and Marco Casazza; Technical Assistance, Jason Howard; Cast: Liza Cassidy, Claire Helene, Jackie Lowe; Theaterlab; May 12–27, 2010

TheaterSmarts

Much Ado About Nothing by William Shakespeare; Cast: Adam Ewer, Adam Ioele, Stephanie Di Pilla, Vince Ingrisano, Charlie Baker, Jeremy Weber, Matthew Garner, Lance Camarillo, Eileen Townsend, Lisa Anderson; Parks in Queens, Brooklyn and NYC; June 4–28, 2009

Theatre 3

The Most Radiant Beauty Written, designed, directed and performed by Tanya Khordoc & Barry Weil; Presented by Evolve Company as part of the Festival of Jewish Theater and Ideas; Theatre 3; Stage Manager, Kat Manion; Lighting, Jeff Nash; Original Music, Adam Bernstein; May 24–June 13, 2009

Hard Love by Motti Lerner; Director, Susan Reid; Presented by Genesis Stage as part of the Festival of Jewish Theater & Ideas; Cast: Mira Hirsch, David Silverman; June 5–11, 2009

Bird Machine Presented by Concrete Temple Theatre; Director, Renee Philippi; Lighting, Renee Molina; Costumes, Danielle Breitenbach; Sound, David Pinkard; Puppets, Carlo Adinolfi; Cast: Carlo Adinolfi, Brian Carson, Ayako Dean, Jo Jo Hristova, Leat Klingman, Megan O'Brien, Zdenko Slobodnik, Michael Tomlinson, Stacey Weingarten; June 19–July 5, 2009

Bird House by Kate Marks; Presented by The KNF Company; Director, Heidi Handelsman; Set, Sara C. Walsh; Costumes, Jessica Pabst; Lighting, Rebecca M.K. Makus; Sound, Quentin Chiappetta; Stage Manager, Shannon O'Neil; Video Projections, Alex Koch and Andy Toad; Original Music, Quentin Chiappetta; Cast: Ora Fruchter, Kylie Goldstein, Wendy Scharfman, Christina Shipp, Anthony Wills Jr., Cotton Wright; Theater 3; July 10–26, 2009

Down Range by Jeffrey Skinner; Presented by Delano Celli Productions; Director, Trish Minskoff; Set, Tim McMath; Costumes, Anne Sherwood; Lighting, John Tees III; Sound, Daniel Kluger; Stage Manager, Douglas Shearer; Projections, Alex Koch; ASM, Aaron Jaros; Fight Director, Teel James Glenn; Photographer, Scott Wynn; Graphics, Laura Skinner; Press, Paul Siebold; Cast: Bob Celli, Thaddeus Daniels, Rachel Parker, Steve Sherman, Tracy Weller; October 28–November 14, 2009

Theatre HAN

Light in the Dark: Chekhov Shorts by Anton Chekhov; Translated by Paul Schmidt, Director, Frederick Waggoner; Cast: LB Williams, Mark Thomas, Ivan De Leon, Alice Oh, Frederico Trigo, Seung Hee Lee, Insuk Kim, Sue-Yeon Park; Theatre 54 at Shetler; December 4–20, 2009

Theatre Row

Beckett Theatre

Race Music by Warren Bodow; Presented by Diverse City Theater Company; Director, Victor Lirio; Set, Maruti Evans; Lighting, Maruti Evans; Costumes, Arnulfo Maldonado; Sound, Elizabeth Rhodes; Stage Manager, Chandra LaViolette; Cast: Chris Ceraso, Brandon Jones, Teresa Stephenson, Penelope Lowder, Kevin Kelleher, Julia Sun; September 3–19, 2009

Underground by James McManus; Presented by Clockwork Theatre; Director, Owen W. Smith; Set, Jay Rohloff; Costumes, Jocelyn Melechinsky; Lighting, Vincent Vigilante; Sound, Dale Bigall; Original Music, Joe Pepe; Technical Director, Vincent Vigilante; PSM, Michelle Hines; Cast: Jay Rohloff, Doug Nyman, Marianna McClellan, Tina Alexis Allen, Phil Cutrone, Larry Greenbush, Peter Iasillo; October 4–17, 2010

Clurman Theatre

Dial 'N' For Negress by Travis Kramer; Director/Producer, Jake Hirzel; Set, Nick Francone; Lighting, Bill Sheehan; Costumes, Sidney Shannon; Sound, Carl Cassella; Stage Manager, Brian D. Gold; Choreographer, Jennifer Mudge; Original Music, Tom Oster & Kevin Smith Kirkwood; Cast: Pilin Anice, Tamala Baldwin, J. Cameron Barnett, James Solomon Benn, Katie Boren, Jimmy Brooks Jr., Bree Daniels, Kevin Smith Kirkwood, James LaRosa, Emily McNamara, Eric Roediger, and Julius Thomas III; September 10–26, 2009

Remembering Mr. Maugham by Garson Kanin; Director, Tony Speciale; Produced by Philip Margaman, Emily Miller, and Frankie J. Grade; Set/Costumes, Daniel Zimmerman; Lighting, Natalie Robin; Cast: Robert Emmet Lunney, Sam Tsoutsouvas; March 4–13, 2010

Stuck by Jessica Goldberg; Presented by the scarlett theater/film project; Director, Marshall Pailet; Set, Brandon Giles; Lighting, Robert Lilly; Sound, Drew Fornarola, John Fontein; PSM, Andrea Wales; ASM, Megan Griffith; Casting, Erica Jensen; Marketing, Katie Riegel; Press, Shane Marshall Brown; Assistant Director, Bryce Norbitz; Producer, Robert E. Schneider; Jack Thomas/Bulldog Theatrical; Cast: Anthony Alessandro, Steven Hauck, Kate Kearney-Patch, Kate MacCluggage, Athen Masci, February 11–21, 2010

The Master Builder by Henrik Ibsen; Presented by Resonance Ensemble; Director, Eric Parness; Set, Jo Winiarski; Costumes, Sidney Shannon; Lighting, Pamela Kupper; Sound, Nick Moore; Stage Manager, Sean McCain; Projections, Daniel Heffernan; Props, Sarah B. Brown; Production Manager, Joe Doran; Technical Director, Gary Levinson; Master Electrician, Flora Vassar; Press, Joe Trentacosta/Springer Associates; Cast: Pun Bandhu, Chris Ceraso, Brian D. Coats, Susan Ferrara, Jennifer Gawlik, Peter Judd, Sarah Stockton; May 9–June 5, 2010

The Glass House by June Finfer; Presented by Resonance Ensemble; Director, Evan Bergman; Set, Jo Winiarski; Costumes, Valerie Marcus Ramshur; Lighting, Pamela Kupper; Sound, Nick Moore; Stage Manager, Geoffrey Nixon; Projections, Daniel Heffernan; Props, Sarah B. Brown; Production Manager, Joe Doran; Technical Director, Gary Levinson; Master Electrician, Flora Vassar; Press, Joe Trentacosta/Springer Associates; Consultant, Kyle Bergman; Cast: David Bishins, Gina Nagy Burns, Harris Yulin, Janet Zarish, Joie Bauer, James Patterson, Chris Skeries; May 9–June 5, 2010

Kirk Theatre

Eye of God by Tim Blake Nelson; Presented by Theatre East; Director, Lisa Devine; Stage Manager, Cameron Vokey; Lighting, Jessica M. Burgess; Set, Robin Vest; Costumes, Benjamin Taylor Ridgway; Sound, Scott O'Brien; Production Manager, Amber Estes; Dialect Coach, Matthew Herrick; Producers, Christa Kimlicko Jones, Joseph Parks, Daryl Wendy Strauss, Judson Jones; Cast: Morgan Baker, Ehad Berisha, Benard Cummings, William Franke, Judson Jones, Richard Mawe, Helen Merino, Valerie Redd, Matt Savins, Douglas Sheppard, Shorey Walker; October 2–17, 2009

The Picture of Dorian Gray by Daniel Mitura; Presented by N.O.M.A.D.S. (New and Original Material Authored and Directed by Students); Director, Henning Hegland; **Cast:** Kaolin Bass, Christina Broccolini, Leif Huckman, Vayu O'Donnell, Wil Petre, Jade Rothman; January 25–February 6, 2010

The Wonder by Susanna Centlivre; Presented by Queen's Company; Director, Rebecca Patterson; **Cast:** Virginia Baeta, Maryam Benganga, Julia Campanelli, Amy Driesler, Abbi Hawk, Natalie Lebert, Annie Paul, Jacquelyn Poplar, Valerie Redd; February 27–March 14, 2010

G.B.S. by Jason Hall; Presented by Clockwork Theatre; Director, Jay Rohloff; Set/Lighting, Taryn Kennedy & Josh Windhausen; Costumes, Mary Hunt; Sound, Dale Bigall; Production Supervisor/Technical Director, Vincent Vigilante; PSM, Michelle Hines; Dramaturg, Russel Dembin; **Cast:** Curran Connor, Jason Jacoby; March 20–April 10, 2010

Lion Theatre

A Bicycle Country by Nilo Cruz; Presented by east 3rd productions; Director, Gil Ron; Lighting, Scott Hali; Set, Michael Mallard; Sound, James Bigbee Garver; **Cast:** Luca Pierucci, Lorraine Rodriguez, Francisco Solorzano; July 8–25, 2009

Al's Business Cards by Josh Koenigsberg; Presented by At Play; Director, Lauren Keating; Set, Jian Jung; Costumes, Melissa Trn; Lighting, Tito Fleetwood Ladd; Sound, Amy Altadonna; Stage Manager, Amanda Kate Joshi; **Cast:** Azhar Khan, Lauren Hines, Bobby Moreno, Malcolm Madera, Gabriel Gutierrez; August 9–22, 2009

Fathers & Sons by Richard Hoehler; Presented by Deep End Productions; Director, Chris Dolman; Set, Todd Edward Ivins; Lighting, Michael Abrams; Costumes, Jonathon Knipscher; Sound, Scott O'Brien; **Cast:** Richard Hoehler, Edwin Matos Jr.; September 17–October 4, 2009

King Lear by William Shakespeare; Presented by ShakespeareNYC; Director/Costumes, Beverly Bullock; Fight Director, Al Foote III; Lighting, Maryvel Bergen; Sound, John D. Ivy; Text Coach, Steven Eng; PSM, Steve Barrett; Assistant Director, Mary Beth Smith; **Cast:** Bill Fairbairn, Carol Jacobanis, Nicholas Stannard, Patricia McNamara, Michael Sean McGuinness, Katherine Kelly Lidz, Andrew Firda, Nathan Carlos Clifford, Peter Herrick, Jonathan Holtzman, Zack Calhoon, Joseph Mitchell Parks, Joseph Hamel, Joseph Small, Benjamin Rishworth, October 9–31, 2009

True West by Sam Shepard; Presented by Athena Theatre Company; Director, Jen Forcino; Set, Stefan Depner; Costumes, Susan Voelker; Lighting, Ross Graham; Original Music, Andrew Edwards; Stage Manager, Susan Sunday; Fight Director, Robert Tuftee; **Cast:** Brionne Davis, Ryan Spahn, Shawn Shafner, Sally Burtenshaw; January 28–February 14, 2010

Studio Theatre

Too Far Gone Out in the Middle of Nowhere by Todd Pate; Presented by The Straddler; Director, Marty Brown; Set, Jay Rohloff; Costumes/Makeup, Ben Philipp; Technical Director, Nicole Press; Sound, Jeanne Travis; Key Art Design, Monica Donovan; Marketing, Isabel Sinistore; **Cast:** Christopher Hurt, Jordan Kamp, Marianna McClellan; March 3–13, 2010

Tuesday Night Poker by Jon McCormick; Original Music, Aaron Rockers; Presented by SANDRep; **Cast:** Jon McCormick, Mike Hauschild, Adam Couperthwaite, Matt Brown, Nick Hulstine; March 24–April 4, 2010

Voice Lesson by Justing Tanner; Director, Bart DeLorenzo; **Cast:** Laurie Metcalf, French Stewart, Maile Flanagan; May 22–31, 2010

Those Indian Guys

www.thoseindianguys.com

D'Arranged Marriage by Rajeev Varma & Tarun Mohanbhai; Director, Tarun Mohanbhai with additional direction by Jim Duff; **Cast:** Rajeev Varma; The Triad NYC; April 16–July 23, 2010

Threads Theater Company

www.threadstheatercompany.org

Afterlight by Monica Flory; Director, Misti Wills; Stage Managers, Jessica Pecharsky, Amanda Gwin; Set/Lighting, Bobby Bradley; Costumes, Kimberly Prentice; Sound, Kim Fuhr; Marketing, Erin Layton; Press, Sam Morris; Props, Rachel Harrington-Davis; Crew, Jarel Lynch; Photographer, Christopher Davis; Graphics, Brenda Storer; **Cast:** Kimberly Prentice, Tyler Merna, Frank Mihelich, Angus Hepburn, Kim Carlson, Allyson Morgan, Davi Santos; Presented as part of the NY International Fringe Festival; Cherry Lane Theatre; August 14–25, 2009

Babette's Feast by Rose Courtney, conceived and developed by Abbie Killeen, adapted from the short story by Isak Dinesen; Produced in conjunction with International Arts Movement;Director, Quin Gordon; Set/Lighting, Bobby Bradley; Costumes, Kimberly Prentice; Stage Manager, Jessica Pecharsky; ASM, Jarel Lynch; Assistant to the Director, Annie Feld; Production Assistant, Kevin Gomez; Press, Sam Morris; Marketing, Anna Katherine Montgomery, Amanda Bailey, Courtney Schiessl; Graphics, Bobby Bradley; **Cast:** Abbie Killeen, Rose Courtney, Rachel Wallace, Kamel Boutros, Hal Robinson, James Russell, William Connell, Matteo Echerle, Darrie Lawrence; International Arts Movement; June 16–July 15, 2010

Throwing Bones

irttheater.org

Anaphylaxis by Mary Jane Gibson; Director, Sheila Daniels; Sound, Mark Valadez; Video Design, Scott Nath; **Cast:** Mary Jane Gibson, Scott Nath; IRT Theater; March 10–21, 2010

Tin Lily Productions

www.tinlily.org

EAT by Matin Van Veldhuizen; Director, Jillian Johnson; Stage Manager, Carrie Brown; Lighting, Jillian Johnson; Set, Annie Branson; Costumes, Melinda Huff; Audio/Visual, Jason Covert; **Cast:** Annie Branson, Tai Verley, Hollis Witherspoon; Embody Studios; January 21–February 6, 2010

Authenticating Eileen Written by the Cast; Director, Jillian Johnson; Stage Manager, Carrie Brown; Lighting, Jillian Johnson; Audio/Visual, Jillian Johnson; **Cast:** Annie Branson, Ryan Feyk, Katie Middleton, Jared Miller, Karim Muasher, Monica Rounds, Nora Jane Williams, and Hollis Witherspoon; TheaterLab; March 26–April 11, 2010

Tongue in Cheek Theater Productions

www.tictheater.com

Up a River/Down the Aisle by Jake Lipman; Director, Brian W. Seibert; Lighting/Stage Manager, Laura Schuman; Sound, Philip Rothman; **Cast:** Jake Lipman; Presented as part of the Midtown International Theatre Festival at Where Eagles Dare Blackbird Studio Theatre; July 28–August 1, 2010; Presented at the Strawberry One-Act Festival at Theatre at St. Clements August 16–18, 2010

Psych by Evan Smith; Director, Jason Bohon; Lighting, Kacie Hultgren; Set, Kacie Hultgren; Sound, Philip Rothman; Stage Manager, Margaret Reed; House Manager, Travis Kendrick; **Cast:** Jake Lipman, Brynne Kraynak, Mary Ruth Baggott, Maryll Botula, Bill Bria, Tele Durham, Kerri Ford, David Lanson, Ambien Mitchell, Susanne Nelson, Brian W. Seibert; Theatre 54 at Shetler Studios; September 9–19, 2009

Plus 1 Solo Show Festival 2009 by Sarah Kauffman, Glynn Borders, Robin Gelfenbien; Director, Christine Renee Miller, Heather Guthrie, Suzanne Agins; Stage Manager, Margaret Reed; Set/Lighting, Kacie Hultgren; House Manager/Associate Producer, Travis Kendrick; **Cast:** Sarah Kauffman, Glynn Borders, Robin Gelfenbien; Theatre 54 at Shetler Studios; September 13–14, 2009

Proof by David Auburn; Director, Kristen Kentner; Stage Manager, Allison Lemel; Lighting, Allison Lemel; Sound, Philip Rothman; **Cast:** Daryl Brown, Jake Lipman, Deirdre MacNamara, Brian W. Seibert; Bridge Theatre at Shetler Studios; April 28–May 8, 2010

Plus 1 Solo Show Festival 2010 by Fara Greenbaum, Aizzah Fatima, Bronwen Prosser; Director, Matt Hoverman, Dipti Mehta, Kathryn Walsh; Stage Manager, Allison Lemel; Lighting, Allison Lemel; **Cast:** Fara Greenbaum, Aizzah Fatima, Bronwen Prosser; Bridge Theatre at Shetler Studios; May 1–2, 2010

Toy Box Theatre Company

www.toyboxtheatre.org

'Tis Pity She's a Whore by John Ford, adapted by Toy Box Theatre Company; Director, Jonathan Barsness; Set, Gian Marco Lo Forte; Costumes, Jennifer Paar; Lighting, Simon Cleveland; Stage Manager, Sara Troficanto; Music Director, James Sparber; Fight Choreographer, Wyatt Kuether; Musicians, Brady Bagger, Christian Serramalara, James Sparber; Graphic Design, Bianca Barattini; Marketing; Producers, David Michael Holmes, Ryan Colwell; **Cast:** Ron Bopst, John Buxton, Ryan Colwell, Sarah Hankins, David Michael Holmes, Andrew Krug, Michael Nathanson, Jessica Rothenberg, Zenon Zeleniuch; Teatro IATI; September 26–October 16, 2010

Tutti Stronzi Productions

Rat Bastards by Julia Pearlstein; Director, Eureka; Lighting, Meagan Miller-McKeever; Costumes, Ramona Ponce; Sound, Aldo Perez; **Cast:** Grant Neale, Jenny Lee Mitchell. David Berent, Gregory Couba, Carol Lee Sirugo, Charles Geyer, Brian Mott, Cory Antiel, Kennedy Wiltshire; Dixon Place; June 3–7, 2009

Undergroundzero Festival

Presented by East River Commedia; Curator, Paul Bargetto; Producer, Jennifer Conley Darling; Line Producer, Allison Prouty; Associate Producer, Valentine Lysikatos; www.eastriver.org; various location; Third annual; P.S. 122; July 7–26, 2009

3! Directed by Doris Mirescu; Presented by Dangerous Ground; **Cast:** Zahraa Alzubaidi, Zoe Anastassiou, Jennifer Blair-Bianco, Patrick Flynn, Gayle Greene, Zack Helwa, Anthony LaForgia, Mark Lechner, Katie McConaghy, Florin Penisoara, Joel Repman, Zehra Tas, JC Vasquez, David White

AOI! by Yukio Mishima adapted by Ivana Catanese; Presented by The South Wing Theatre Company;Director, Kameron Steele; **Cast:** Gillian Chadsey, Craig Dolezel, Catherine Friesen, Nathan Guisinger, Sophie Nimmannit, Kristine Lee, Harold German, Rachael Richman, Brian Nishii

Evanston: A Rare Comedy by Michael Yates Crowley; Presented byWolf 359Director, Michael Rau; **Cast:** Bodine Alexander, Michael Yates Crowley, Sam West

Nick by Laura Wickens; Director, Jessica Burr; Presented by Blessed Unrest **Cast:** Zenzelé Cooper, Anna Kepe, Eunjee Lee, Nick Micozzi, John Peery, Peter Richards, Matthew Sincell, Darrell Stokes, Laura Wickens, Hannah Wilson

Pretención: un cirque de burlesque by Porkpie; Presented by Pinchbottom; **Cast:** Nasty Canasta and Jonny Porkpie, Naughtia Nice, Arrogant Mick and Tigger, Amber Ray, Angie Pontani, Bambi the Mermaid, Clams Casino, Creamy Stevens, Darlinda Just Darlinda, Dirty Martini, Gal Friday, Gigi La Femme, Harvest Moon, Jo Boobs, Julie Atlas Muz, Legs Malone, Leroi the Girl Boi, Little Brooklyn, Madame Rosebud, Mat Fraser, Ms. Tickle, Peekaboo Pointe, Ruby Valentine

I Am Trying to Hear Myself and Vandam Goodbar by Jack Ferver; **Cast:** Reid Bartelme, Tony Orrico, Chad Tolson

Tales from Bordertown (prologue) Written and performed by Eric Dean Scott; Director, Erika Latta; Presented by Wax Factory and Eric Dean Scott

Winter Journey Written and directed by Alec Duffy; Presented by Hoi Polloi; **Cast:** Jordan Coughtry; Musicians, Eugene Rohrer, Ryan Andes

We Are Being Held by Delaney Britt Brewer; Presented by Coffee Cup (a theater co.); Director, Brad Krumholz; **Cast:** Ishah Janssen-Faith, Rob O'Hare, Ike Ufomadu

The Misanthrope by Moliere translated by Tony Harrison; Presented by Columbia University School of the Arts Director, Anna Brenner; **Cast:** Matt Biagini, Elisa Matula, Michael Guagno, Maylin Murphy, Fatih Gençkal, Johanna Weller-Fahy, Mike James, Wil Petre, Ross Cowan, Rachael Richman, James Rutherford

The Jamal Lullabies by Emily Conbere; Presented by East River Commedia; Director, Paul Bargetto; **Cast:** Bekah Coulter, Debbie Friedman, Nicole Stefonek, Kristina Teschner

She of the Voice Adapted by Eliza Bent from Hari Kunzru; Presented by Thinking Person's Theatre; Director, Jose Zayas; **Cast:** Nnadi Harriott, Michael James, LeeAnet Noble, Nikaury Rodriguez, Julia Sirna-Frest, Sam Sogur; Special appearance by Bunkweave (Greg Portz and Julie Galorenzo)

Selling Splitsville Written and performed by Christine Witmer & Nora Woolley; Director, Rachel Cion

Replikas of Apocalypsis Cum Figuris & The Constant Prince by Calderon de la Barca, Ramon Lull, T.S.Eliot, St. John, Buddha, Barryman, C.S.Lewis, F.Kafka, Rumi, Lou Reed; Presented by Nu Classic Theater Director, Niky Wolcz; **Cast:** Laura Butler, Sanam Erfani, Susan Hyon, Jon Froehlich, Kyle Knauf, Daniel Irizarry, David Skeist, Isaac Woofter

Unity Stage Company

www.unitystage.org

Loyalties by John Galsworthy; Director, Sofia Landon Geier; Stage Manager, M.J. Geier; Lighting, Glenn Rivano; Sound, Cohlie Brocato; Composer, George Andoniadis; Crew, Elisa Garcia and Gabriel Decker-Lee; Box Office Manager, Evelyn Hernandez; **Cast:** Jennifer Angela Bishop, Celia Montgomery, David Sedgwick, Mac Brydon, Amelia Randolph Campbell, Ray Chao, Matt W. Cody, Jon Freda, Alfred Gingold, Graciany Miranda, John Rawlinson, Jaike Foley-Schultz, Evan Thompson; The Parlor at Cassino Restaurant; January 7–30, 2010

Untitled Theater Co. #61

www.untitledtheater.com

Velvet Oratorio by Edward Einhorn; Director, Henry Akona; Stage Manager, Marissa Bea; Lighting, Jeff Nash; Costumes, Carla Gant; Audio/Visual, Jared Mezzochi; Composer, Henry Akona; Dramaturg, Karen Ott; Musical Director, James Kennerley; Concert Master, Michael Midlarsky; **Cast:** Members of the Choir of Saint Mary the Virgin Times Square, Craig Anderson, Timothy Babcock, Danny Bowes, Peter Brown, Jonathan Farmer, Andrea Gallo, Joe Gately, Josh Hartung, Uma Incrocci, Eric Oleson, Yvonne Roen, Tony Torn; Walter Bruno Auditorium at Lincoln Center Library; November 19–30, 2009

Rudolf II by Edward Einhorn; Director, Henry Akona; Stage Manager, Berit Johnson; Lighting, Ian W. Hill; Costumes, Carla Gant; Assistant Director, Tom Berger; ASM, Lindsey Carter; Assistant Costumes, Candace Lawrence; Assistant Lighting, Romo Halladay; **Cast:** Adriana Disman, Joe Gately, James Isaac, Romo Halladay, Eric Oleson, Shelley Ray, Timothy McCown Reynolds, Yvonne Roen, Jack Schaub; Bohemian National Hall; March 5–28, 2010

Doctors Jane and Alexander Written and directed by Edward Einhorn; Lighting, Jeff Nash; Costumes, Garla Gant; Sound, Henry Akona; Choreographers, Henry Akona and Danielle Quisenberry; Original Music, Alexander S. Wiener and Henry Akona; **Cast:** Timothy Babcock, Peter Bean, Talaura Harms, Jason Liebman, Josh Mertz, Phoebe Silva, Alyssa Simon; Theater 3; May 23–June 14, 2010

Scenes from a Misunderstanding by Carey Harrison; Director, Henry Akona; Stage Manager, Marissa Bea; Lighting, Jeff Nash; Costumes, Carla Gant; **Cast:** Eric Oleson, Mick O'Brien, Kris Lundberg; Presented as part of the Festival of Jewish Theater and Ideas; Theatre 3; May 24–June 13, 2009

Vital Theatre Company
www.vitaltheatre.org

Perfect Wedding by Robin Hawdon; Director, Teresa K. Pond; Set, Daniel ZS Jagendorf; Costumes, Cherie Cunningham; Stage Manager, Kristin Orlando; Lighting, Perchik Kreiman-Miller; Fight Choreograper, Jeffrey M. Bender; **Cast:** Amber Bela Muse, Fabio Pires, Matt Johnson, Dayna Grayber, Ghana Leigh, Kristi McCarson; 45 Bleecker Street; July 8–August 2, 2009

The Bully Book by David L. Williams, music and lyrics by John Gregor; Director, Troy Miller; Stage Manager, Shani Murfin; Design, Mary Hamrick; Costumes, Cherie Cunningham; Musical Director, Jad Bernardo; **Cast:** Stephen Stocking, Jesse R. Tendler, Abigail Taylor, Frank Paiva, Josh Beyers, Anthony Johnson, Patti DeMatteo, Greg Kalafatas. Scott Lilly, Jay Paranada, Janelle Mims, Nate Gray, Carlos Avilas; McGinn/Cazale Theatre; 45 Bleecker and the McGinn/Cazale; July 6–August 2, 2009and September 12–October 12, 2009

Matthew Takes Mannahattan Book by Aurin Squire, music by Daniel S. Acquisto, lyrics by Sammy Buck; Based on the book *Matthew's Secret Door* by Christopher Moore; Director, Carlos Armesto; Stage Manager, Nicholas Rainey; Lighting, Christina Watanabe; Set, Adam Koch; Costumes, Sarita Fellows; Music Director, Martin Landry; Choreography, Tiffany Rachelle Stewart; Puppet Design, Emily DeCola; **Cast:** Kai Chapman, Daniel Cibener, Larissa Laurel, Kila Packett, Erikamari Rumore, Lareysa Smith; McGinn/Cazale Theatre; October 17–November 29, 2009

The Klezmer Nutcracker Book by Ellen Kushner, music by The Shirim Klezmer Orchestra; Based on the book *The Golden Dreydl* by Ellen Kushner; Director, Linda Ames Key; Stage Manager, Leah McVeigh; Set, Kyle Dixon; Costumes, Kate Mincer; Bethany White; Lighting, Lois Catanzaro; Choreography; Puppet Designer, Hunter Kaczorowski; **Cast:** Allison Beler, Laurabeth Breya, Kiri Chapman, Lauren Gray, Ashley Marinelli, Chris Ryan, Luke Tudball, Elizabeth Maria Walsh, Andrew Wheeler, Bethany White; McGinn/Cazale Theatre; December 5–January 3, 2010

Uncle Pirate Book by Ben H. Winters, music and lyrics by Drew Fornarola, Based on the book *Uncle Pirate* by Douglas Rees; Director, Jeremy Dobrish; Stage Manager, Nicholas Rainey; Lighting, Michael Gottlieb; Set, Alexis Distler; Costumes, Bobby Pearce; Choreographer, Christine O'Grady; Musical Director, Julie McBride; **Cast:** Ronn Burton, Lauren Kampf, Beth Kuhn, Joshua Nicholson, Steve Trzaska, Amanda Yachechak; McGinn/Cazale Theatre; January 16–February 28, 2010

Isabelle and The Pretty-Ugly Spell by Music and lyrics by Steven Fisher, book by Joan Ross Sorkin and Steven Fisher; Director, Vic DiMonda; Stage Manager, Robert Funk; Lighting, Lois Catanzaro; Set, Kyle Dixon; Costumes, Sarah Reever; Musical Director, Steven Fisher; **Cast:** Melissa Bayern, Matt DuMont, Mark Epperson, Tara Novie, Elyssa Samsel, Evan Schultz, Andrew Wheeler; McGinn/Cazale Theatre; March 13–April 25, 2010

Vortex Theater Company
www.vortextheater.com

NYC Halloween Haunted House Director/Design, Josh Randall and Kristjan Thor; Sound, Josh Randall; **Cast:** Marc Ginsburg, DL Sams, Aleksandr Petrov, Alley Scott; Sanford Meisner Theater; October 3–31, 2009

Midsummer Nightmare Haunted House Director/Design, Josh Randall and Kristjan Thor; Sound, Josh Randall; **Cast:** Alisabeth, Justin Holcomb, Bill Bria, Brandon Schraml, Sara Oliva, Cory Siegel; Sanford Meisner Theater; May 22–June 14, 2010

Walkerspace

Into the Hazard [Henry 5] by William Shakespeare, adapted and directed by Jessica Bauman; Set, Christopher Akerlind; Lighting, Christopher Akerlind; Costumes, Emily Pepper; Sound, Jeremy J. Lee; Audio/Visual, Austin Switser; Original Music, Jeremy J. Lee; Stage Manager, Emily Paige Ballou; Fight Director, Scott Barrow; **Cast:** Nick Dillenburg, David McCann, Erin Moon, Luis Moreno, Trevor Vaughn, Scott Whitehurst; June 4–20, 2009

Nesting by Caitlin Saylor Stephens; Presented by Token Collective; Director, Jennifer Sandella; **Cast:** Melissa Wolff, Caitlin Saylor Stephens, Happy Anderson, Geoff Schuppert; September 9–20, 2009

Peter-Wendy by J.M. Barrie, adapted by Jeremy Bloom; Presented by Vagabond Theatre Ensemble; Director, Jeremy Bloom; Costumes, Becca Jubelirer; Original Music, The Books; **Cast:** Laila Alj, Maite Alvarez, Amanda Bloom, Catherine Brookman, Starr Busby, Florent Chauvin, Holly Chou, Jesse Garrison, Camille Harris, Christopher Heiji, Sarah Ann Masse, Jessica Mckenna, Joyce Miller, Claire Neumann, Mike Placito, Kyle Wa; November 5–8, 2009

The Real Thing by Tom Stoppard; Presented by Out of Line Productions; Director, Greg Taubman; Set, Jeremy C. Doucette; Costumes, Nina Lourie; Lighting, Melissa Mizell; Sound, Pitr Strait; Stage Manager, Allison Hersh; Assistant Director Kate Stahl; **Cast:** Justin Badger, Sullivan Corey, Ross Degraw, Jessica Howell, Frederique Nahmani, Kristin Stewart Chase, Jonathan Tindle; November 11– 23, 2009

Where Eagles Dare

Numbers by Kieron Barry; Director, Dan Chen; Producer, Cristina Aguirre and Pink Bulb Productions; Photographer, Meagan Cignoli; **Cast:** Kristen Lewis, Christine Donlon, Gemma Fearn, Ella Jane New; Produced as part of the Midtown International Theatre Festival; Blackbox; July 14–19, 2009

Around The Block by Nelson Diaz-Marcano; Presented by Strike 38! Productions; Director, Dan De Jesus; **Cast:** Nelson Diaz-Marcano, Danielle Guidi; January 15–17, 2010

Return to Mellow Falls by Cilque Brown; Presented by Faith in God Theater Group; Director, Cilque Brown and Ben Black; Stage Manager, Michele Marinace; Lighting, Arno Austin; **Cast:** Ben Black, Jordashe Braxton, Terrell Brown, Andrew R. Cooksey, Paula Flynn, Bonnie Jones, Michael J. Kelly, Michele Marinace, Denise Collins, Sisteretta Henry; Where Eagles Dare; February 16–March 13, 2010

Play/War by Ben Spatz and Maximilian Balduzzi; Presented by Urban Research Theater; **Cast:** Ben Spatz and Maximilian Balduzzi; March 12–14, 2010

White Horse Theater Company

www.whitehorsetheater.com

Clothes for a Summer Hotel by Tennessee Williams; Director, Cyndy A. Marion; Stage Manager, Elliot Lanes; Lighting, Debra Leigh Siegel; Set, John C. Scheffler; Costumes, Adam Coffia; Sound, David Schulder; Choreographers, Liz Vacco, Vittoria Natale & Guillermo Elkouss; Original Music, Joe Gianono; **Cast:** Peter J. Crosby, Montgomery Sutton, Tom Cleary, Kristen Vaughan, Lisa Riegel, Rod Sweitzer, Chris Johnson, Kyle Lamar Mitchell, Julie Kelderman, Ambien Mitchell, Mary Goggin, Sarah Levine; Hudson Guild Theatre; February 5–21, 2010

Wide Eyed Productions

www.wideeyedproductions.com

A World Elsewhere! Arias in the Key of Clown Written and directed by Ben Newman; Stage Manager, Megan Jupin; Costumes, Antonia Ford-Roberts; Producer, Kristin Skye Hoffmann; Assistant Director, Cassandra Schwanke; **Cast:** Justin Ness, Lucy McRae, Melissa Johnson, Andrew Harriss, Trevor Dallier, Monica Moreau, Neil Fennell; Presented as part of the Fringe Festival; Cherry Lane Theatre; August 15–27, 2009

Jack and the Soy Beanstalk Written and directed by Jerrod Bogard; Set/Puppets, Jerrod Bogard; Costumes, Sabrina Kahn; Music Directors, Sky Seals and Emily Fellner; Percussion, Peter Saleh; **Cast:** Sky Seals, Jake Paque, Brianne Mai, Carlos Avilas, Laura Hall, Okieriete Onaodowan; Presented as part of the Fringe Jr. Festival; Dixon Place; August 15–21, 2009

The Last Days of Judas Iscariot by Stephen Adly Guirgis; Director, Rebecca Hengstenberg; Stage Manager, Sarah Troficanto; Lighting, Joe Novak; Set, Joshua David Bishop; Costumes, Jill Wetzel; Sound, Trevor Dallier; Producer, Kristin Skye Hoffmann; Assistant Director, Melissa Johnson; ASM, Chad Erickson; **Cast:** Jonny Beauchamp, Sebastian Citron, Joshua David Bishop, Trevor Dallier, Billy Dutton, Ali Gilbertson, Andrew Harriss, Lincoln L. Hayes, Jason Loverde, Brianne Mai, Lisa Mamazza, Mavis Martin, Colin McFadden, Okieriete Onaodowan, Sage Seals; Richmond Shepard Theatre; January 14–February 7, 2010

Noah's Arkansas by Jerrod Bogard; Director, Neil Fennell; Stage Manager, Megan Jupin; Lighting, Ryan Metzler; Set, Joshua David Bishop; Costumes, Antonia Ford-Roberts; Sound, Trevor Dallier; Props Master, Billy Dutton; ASM, Amy Bradley; Original Score, Michael Sorrentino; **Cast:** Justin Ness, Kristin Skye Hoffmann, Michael Komala, Erik Frandsen, Bennett W. Harrell, Judy Merrick, Lucy McRae, Brianne Mai; Wings Theatre; April 21–May 14, 2010

Wild Project

Mother by Lisa Ebersole; Presented by Evil July Productions; Director, Andrew Grosso; Set, Sandra Goldmark; Lighting, Brian Jones; Costumes, Becky Laskey; **Cast:** Buck Henry, Holland Taylor, Lisa Ebersole, Haskell King, Keith Randolph Smith; Wild Project; July 15–August 1, 2009

The Bereaved by Thomas Bradshaw; Presented by Partial Comfort Productions; Director, May Adrales; Set, Lee Savage; Costumes, Whitney Locher; Lighting, Jason Jeunnette; Sound, Ryan Maeker; Stage Manager, Tara Nachtigall; Fight Director, Qui Nguyen; **Cast:** Andrew Garman, McKenna Kerrigan, Jenny Seastone Stern, KK Moggie, Brian D. Coats, Vincent Madero, Christopher T. VanDijk, Brian J. Maxsween; September 9–26, 2009

The Lemon Tree by Maria Logis; Director, Mahayana Landowne; Stage Manager, Stephanie Shecter; Lighting, Les Dickert; Set, Les Dickert & Mahayana Landowne; Costumes, Mahayana landowne; Video Projections, Conzia Sarto; Mucisians & Vocalists, Justin Flynn, Pete Smith, Makaria Psiliteli Kazakos, Maria Logis; Original Music, Maria Logis, Alan Turry, Makaria Psiliteli Kazakos, Original Music; **Cast:** Zina Anaplioti, Demetrios Bonaros, Leo Giannopoulos, Maria Niora, Yury Lomakin, Olivia Roric; November 6–15, 2009

Blue Surge by Rebecca Gilman; Presented by Extant Arts; Director, Kat Vecchio; **Cast:** Pete Caslavka, Lauren Nordvig, Justin Gallo, Louise Flory, Bridget Durkin; January 21–February 7, 2010

Woodshed Collective

Artistic Directors, Teddy Bergman, Gabriel Evansohn, Stephen Squibb; Director of Development, Emily Fishbaine; Development Consultant, Sarah Rulfs; www.woodshedcollective.com

The Confidence Man by Paul Cohen; Director, Stephen Brackett, Lauren Keating and Michael Silverstone; Stage Manager, Colin Miller, Caitlin Orr, Janice Acevedo, Caley Clocksin and Gretchen Davis; Lighting, Zack Brown; Set, Sara Walsh and Daniel Zimmerman; Costumes, Jessica Pabst; Sound, Daniel Kluger and Brandon Wolcott; Associate Producer, Tara Schuster; Press/Development Intern, Rachel Begelman; Artwork and Graphic Design; **Cast:** Ben Beckley, Kate Benson, Pepper Binkley, Felipe Bonilla, Rusty Buehler, Juliette Clair, Eric Clem, Dan Cozzens, Todd D'Amour, Danny Deferrari, Aaron Dias, Matt Dickson, Nicholas Feitel, Emmitt George, Chris Gliege, Lara Gold, Jacob Grigolia-Rosenbaum, Laurel Holland, Jocelyn Kuritsky, Jane Lee, Roger Lirtsman, Brendan McDonough, Moti Margolin, Melissa Miller, Heidi Niedermeyer, Emily Perkins, Michael R. Piazza, Mallory Portnoy, Kate Cullen Roberts, Hugh Sinclair, Gina Vetro, Lee Zarrett; U.S.S. Lilac; September 1–20, 2009

WorkShop Theater Company

www.workshoptheater.org

From Russia With Angst Adaptations of short stories by Anton Chekhov; Stage Manager, Jason Healy; Lighting, Duane Pagano; Set, John Scheffler; Costumes, Alexandra Devin; Sound, David Schulder; Coordinating Producers, Carrie Edel Isaacman and Christina Romanello; included: *Death of a Government Worker* by Jonathan Pereira, directed by Katrin Hilbe; *We'll Take a Cup of Kindness Yet* by Scott C. Sickles, directed by David Gautschy; *Joy* by Robert Strozier, directed by Elena Araoz; *In Country* written and directed by Timothy Scott Harris; *Misery, Apathy & Despair* by John McKinney, directed by Richard Kent Green; **Cast:** Sutton Crawford, James Davies, Jed Dickson, Liz Forst, Joseph Franchini, Dee Dee Friedman, Stephen Girasuolo, Michael Gnat, Carrie Edel Isaacman, Noah Keen, Carolinne Messihi, Mike Mihm, David M. Pincus, Amanda Sayle, Tracy Shar, Sean Singer; Main Stage; June 11–27, 2009

FaceSpace Written and presented by Talia Gonzalez and Bisanne Masoud; Director, Daniel Winerman; Stage Manager, Jana Mattioli; Lighting and Sound, Jana Mattioli; Costumes, Chloe Demrovsky; **Cast:** Ilana Becker, Mike Carlsen, Sharon Freedman, Jon Levenson, Lindsay Ryan, Thomas F. Walsh; Presented as part of the Midtown International Theatre Festival; MainStage Theater (non-resident produciton; July 18–August 1, 2009

Next Year in Jerusalem by Dana Leslie Goldstein; Director, Robert Bruce McIntosh; Stage Manager, Michael Palmer; Set/Lighting, Duane Pagano; Costumes, Anne E. Grosz; Sound, David Schulder; Coordinating Producer, Anne Fizzard; Assistant Producer, Laura Hirschberg; **Cast:** Jodie Bentley, Burt Edwards, Dee Dee Friedman, Timothy Scott Harris, Elyse Mirto, Jake Robards, Sara Romanello; Main Stage; October 8–31, 2009

Cold Snaps by WorkShop Playwrights; Director, WorkShop Directors; Stage Manager, Michael Palmer; Set, Duane Pagano; Supervising Director/Coordinating Producer, Kathleen Brant; Assistants, Loren Dunn and Laurie Schroeder; Props Master, Mick Bleyer; **Cast:** Trey Albright, Ellen Barry, Tom Berdik, Jeff Berg, Tom Bozell, Kelly Anne Burns, Ellen Dolan, Burt Edwards, Charlotte Hampden, Abigail Hardin, Heather Massie, Elyse Mirto, Patricia O'Connell, Sean Singer, Paul Singleton, Ben Sumrall, Fred Velde; Jewel Box; December 9–19, 2009

Demon Bitch Goddess by Scott C. Sickles; Director, Thomas Coté; Lighting, Sarah Tundermann; Set, Craig Napoliello; Light/Sound Board Operator, Nelson Lugo; Coordinating Producer, Lynda Berge; Sound, David Schulder; **Cast:** Mick Bleyer, Caitlin Davies, Loren Dunn, Ken Glickfeld, Cam Kornman, Marylee Martin, Lucy McMichael, Gerrianne Raphael; Jewel Box; February 3–13, 2010

Miss Lulu Bett by Zona Gale; Director, Kathleen Brant; Stage Manager, Patrick Clayton; Lighting, Diana Duecker; Set, Craig Napoliello; Costumes, Anna Gerdes; Sound, Jeffrey Swan Jones; Coordinating Producer, Richard Kent Green; Press, Scotti Rhodes; ASM/Assistant Director, Bob Stewart; Technical Director, David M. Mead; Props Master, Mick Bleyer; **Cast:** Mary Ruth Baggott, Dan Patrick Brady, Kate Castañeda-La Mar, Anne Fizzard, Michael Gnat, Maya Jasinska, David M. Mead, Gerrianne Raphael, Laurie Schroeder, Ben Sumrall; MainStage; March 18–April 3, 2010

Special Events

Humble Pie by Leslie Gwyn; Director, Elise Marenson; **Cast:** Leslie Gwyn, Jonathan Marten, Tanya Marten, Clare Patterson; July 15, 2009

12 Angry Men by Reginald Rose; A Performance To Benefit The WorkShop Theater Company; Director, Tom Herman; September 20, 2009

Black Voice –Celebrating the Work of African American Playwrights Today and Yesterday by Various Playwrights; Coordinating Producer, Cecily Benjamin; February 6–27, 2010

The 7th Annual Will-A-Thon by William Shakespeare, conceived and directed by Charles E. Gerber; **Cast:** Mick Bleyer, Donte Bonner, Cherrye Davis, Letty Ferrer, Andy Fitzpatrick, Charles E. Gerber, Cordis Heard, Brit Herring, Susan Izatt, David M. Mead, Elyse Mirto, Natalie Smith, Jonathan Weber; April 19–24, 2010

Verbatim: Verboten Director, Jonathan Pereira; Conceived by Michael Martin, Coordinating Producer, Tracy Shar; **Cast:** Dan Patrick Brady, Cecily Benjamin, KellyAnne Burns, Anne Fizzard, Richard Kent Green, Mike Smith Rivera Loren Dunn, Amanda Sayles, Tracy Shar; WorkShop; Theater; Ongoing

Vaudeville Nouveau Director, Nelson Lugo and Richard Kent Green; Produceers, Nelson Lugo and Richard Kent Green; Ongoing

Staged Readings at the Jewel Box

On An August Eve by Linda SeagleCrawley; Original Songs, Sean Hartley and by Jeff Woodman; Musical Director, Erica Kaplan; Coordinating Producer, Paul Singleton; **Cast:** Mick Bleyer, Emme Bonilla, Justin Brill, Caitlin Davies, Bob Manus, Heather Massie, Ben Sumrall, Chris Vasquez; August 22–24, 2009

Life and Death Take On Mary And St. Theresa by Alexandra Devin; Board Operator, Amanda Sayle; Coordinating Producer, Kathleen Brant; **Cast:** David M. Mead, Gerrianne Raphael, Jane Lincoln Taylor; August 29–September 1, 2009

The Navigator by Eddie Antar; Coordinating Producer, Nelson Lugo; **Cast:** Kelly Anne Burns, Joseph Franchini, Jeff Paul, Nicole Taylor; October 15–17, 2009

Interchange by Ken Jaworowski; Board Operator, Mary Ruth Baggot; Coordinating Producer, Cecily Benjamin; **Cast:** Sean Singer, Liz Amberly, Cecily Benjamin, Kelly Campbell, Alexandra Devin, Loren Dunn, Stephen Girasuolo, Gerry Goodstein, Riley Jones-Cohen; October 28–30, 2009

Fabulous Darshan by Bob Stewart; Board Operator, Kathleen Brant; Coordinating Producer, Elyse Mirto; **Cast:** Spencer Barros, Jeff Berg, Tim Cain, Mike Smith Rivera; November 11–13, 2009

Phil by Frederic Glover; Board Operator, Stefania Diana Schramm; Coordinating Producer, Kelly Campbell; **Cast:** Kelly Campbell, Dee Dee Friedman, Timothy Scott Harris; November 20–21, 2009

Protected by Timothy Scott Harris; Stage Manager, Stefania Diana Schramm; Coordinating Producer, Chrsitina Romanello; **Cast:** Dee Dee Friedman, Cam Kornman, Jeff Paul, Bill Tatum, Matt Walker; January 14–16, 2010

The Chekhov Dreams by John McKinney; Director, Nancy Chu; Coordinating Producer, Tracy Shar; **Cast:** Clay Adams, Sutton Crawford, Jeff Paul, Gregory Waller, Maeve Yore; February 19–20, 2010

Beneath the Hush, a Whisper by Abigail Somma; Director, Tom Herman; Assistant Director, Virginia Roncetti; Coordinating Producer, Shaun Bennet Wilson; **Cast:** Greg Oliver Bodine, Jed Dickson, Joseph Franchini, Mia Moreland, Wende O' Reilly, Carey Urban; March 11–13, 2010

Tarragona by Gary Giovannetti; Director, Elysa Marden, Director; **Cast:** C.K. Allen, Lynda Berge, Lori Faiella, Brian C. Homer, Shelley McPherson, Matt Walker; March 27–31, 2010

Orange Alert by Stephen Girasuolo; Director, Maxwell Williams; **Cast:** Jodie Bentley, Burt Edwards, Lori Faiella, Joseph Faranda, Frank Piazza, P.J. Sosko, Shaun Bennet Wilson, Matthew Wise; April 8–1

Sundays@Six Reading Series

Bone to Pick by Bob Stewart; June 14; *The End of the Weak* by Ken Jaworowski; June 28; *Recession Special: Plays Inspired by the Economic Downturn* by WorkShop Playwrights; Part 1: August 23; Part II: August 30; Part III: November 22; *Excised* by Larry Brenner; September 13; *WorkShop One-Acts* by WorkShop Playwrights; September 27; *Orange Alert* by Stephen Girasuolo; October 4; *Finders Seekers and other selected scenes* by Ken Jaworowski; October 11; *With Bated Breath* by Bryden MacDonald; October 18; *The Grapes of Wrath* by John Steinbeck; October 25; *Bleached Blond Betty and the Brokenhearted* by Tom Kelly; November 1; *Figments: Fragments* by Robert Frazier; November 8; *The Chekhov Dreams* by John McKinney; December 6; *Sundays at Six Salute the Classics: Tartuffe* by Moliere; December 13; *The Garden* by Loren Dunn; December 20; *Playing Doctor* by Rich Orloff; January 10; *The Brighter Burn* by Herb Donaldson; January 17; *Beat Chick* by Prudence Holmes; January 24; *Grace Notes* by Donald Steele; January 31; *Bone Cage* by Catherine Banks; February 7; *Chimes of My Lovely* by Bob Manus; February 14; *Mother's Day* by Jennifer Fell Hayes; February 21; *The Heiress* by Ruth and Augustus Goetz; February 28; *The Silent Exile* by The Silent Exile; March 14; *Figments: Fragments* by Robert Frazier; March 21; *Derridia* by Nancy Chu; March 28; *Faith in Humanity* by Jen Makholm; April 11; *The Dishonorable Discharge of Private Pitts* by Daniel Damiano; April 18; *Song* by Frederic Glover; April 25; *Dime Heroes* by Eric Kingrea; May 2; *Flip a Coin* by Dirk Burrows; May 23

Non-resident Productions

A Night of Shorts Presented by The Wellesley Project; Main Stage; June 4–9, 2010

De Insomnio y Medianoche Presented by La Micro Theater, Inc.; Jewel Box; June 22–28, 2009

A Little Potato and Hard to Peel by David Harrell; Presented by ADH Enterprises; Director, Jayd McCarty; Stage Manager, Megan Jupin; **Cast:** David Harrell; Jewel Box Theatre; September 24–October 11, 2009

Penang Presented by Madison Street Theater; Main Stage; November 5–22, 2010

Almost Exactly Like Us by Alan M. Berks; Presented by Theatre of the Expendable; Director, Jesse Edward Rosbrow; Stage Manager, Stefania Diana Schramm; Lighting, Victoria Miller; Set, Elisha Schaefer; Costumes, Lauren Gaston; Sound, Ann Warren; Props, Jesse Louis Hathaway; ASM, Geoffrey Roecker; Fight Choreographer, Autumn Horne; Graphics, Duncan Pflaster; Photographer, Dorian Nisinson; Audience Development, Michael Roderick; Press, Emily Owens; **Cast:** Seth Austin, Timothy Fannon, Julie Fitzpatrick, Anna O'Donoghue; April 22–May 1, 2010

Xoregos Performing Company

www.xoregos.com

Brief Shorts Director/Choreography, Shela Xoregos; Stage Manager, Ryan Keough; Costumes, Yuliya Bogdanova; Original Music, James Barry; **Cast:** Daniel Broadhurst, Ralph Coppola, Omar Cruz, Carlita V. Ector, Tracy Espiritu, Naomi McDougall Jones, Joshua Warr; Various Parks and Libraries; June 6–July 20, 2009

Harlem on My Mind Director, Shela Xoregos; Stage Manager, Ashley Nelson; Costumes, Meg Zeder; **Cast:** Crystal Boyd, Phillip Burke, Allura Leggard, Tony Mitchell, Karlyma Jo Ann Nelson, Qualis Tarkington; Various venues in NYC, February 13–March 20, 2010

Yangtze Repertory Theatre of America, Inc.

www.yangtze-rep-theatre.org

Traces: Variations In A Foreign Land #10 Choreographers, David Chien Hui Shen, Mica Bernas, Kyla Barkin, Aaron Selissen; Stage Manager, Jake Witlen; Lighting, Jake Witlen; Sound, Sam SU Sheng, Ginger Burden, Lindsey Boise; Audio/Visual, Lindsey Boise; Production Manager, Jason HaoWen Wang; **Cast:** Katti Aggen, Novy Bereber, Esme Boyce, Beth Edwards, Marielis Garcia, Hayan Kim, Ashley Liang, Jorden Morley, Robert M. Valdez Jr., Anna Woolf, Sen Yang; Flushing Town Hall; September 25–26, 2009

Laughing In The Wind, a martial arts epic Written and directed by Joanna Chan; Stage Manager, Laura Archer; Lighting, Joyce Liao; Set, YoKi Lai; Costumes, David ChienHue Shen and YoKi Lai; Fight Choreographer, David ChienHui Shen; Sound/Composer/Accompanist, Sam SU Sheng; Prop Master, Jin Xin; **Cast:** Wayne Chang, Rachel Filsoof, Zane Haynes, Carl Ka-Ho Li, Ashley Liang, Ajia Maximillian, Phillip Redmond, Adrian Sinclair, Derrick St. Hill, Peter Song, Rashawn Strife, Steven Sun, Stephanie Willing, Sen Yang, Cedric Yau, Sarah Yu, Jie Zhuang; Theater For The New City-Johnson Theatre; April 30–May 23, 2010

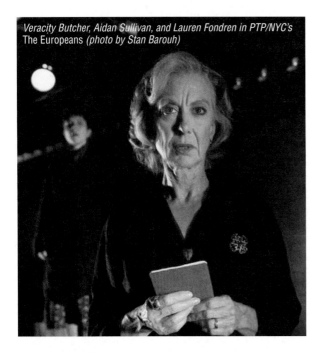

Veracity Butcher, Aidan Sullivan, and Lauren Fondren in PTP/NYC's The Europeans *(photo by Stan Barouh)*

Yara Arts Group

www.brama.com/yara

Yara 20 Years of Theatre Festival included: *A Light from the East; Blind Sight; Yara's Forest Song; Waterfall/Reflections; Virtual Souls; Flight of the White Bird; Circle; Song Tree; The Warrior's Sister; Still the River Flows;* Ukrainian Institute of America; January 22–24, 2010

Readings

Architecture by Christina Lillian Turczyn; Director, Virlana Tkacz; **Cast:** Nina Arianda, Stefka Nazarkewycz, Olga Shuhan; November 7; *Kuruma Ningyo in Translation* Conducted by Koryu Nishikawa V and Tom Lee; **Cast:** Karen Kandel, Matthew Acheson, Tom Lee; March 25; *Scythian Stones* created by Virlana Tkacz with Yara Arts Group, Ukrainian and Kyrgyz artists; Stage Manager, Nadia Sokolenko; **Cast:** Nina Matvienko, Kenzhegul Satybaldieva, Ainura Kachkynbek Kyzy, Tonia Matvienko, Lisa Shyvilova, Olia Danylchenko; March 26; *Song from Scythian Stones* Director, Virlana Tkacz; **Cast:** Kenzhegul Satybaldieva, Ainura Kachkynbek Kyzy, Nurbek Serkebaev

York Shakespeare Company

www.yorkshakespeare.org

The Merchant of Venice & **The Jew of Malta** by William Shakespeare and Christopher Marlowe; Director, Seth Duerr; **Cast:** Alexander Harvey, Antony Raymond, Brian Morvant, Daryl Brown, David Allison DeWitt, Emily Robin Fink, Emily Rose Prats, Evan Beskin, Graciany Miranda, Gustavo Obregon, Jed Charles, Jeff Topf, Jesse Michael Mothershed, Joe Hamel, John Curtis, Luis de Amechazurra, Maba Ba, Matthew Foster, Michelle Sims, Nate Washburn, Paul Rubin, Richard Zekaria, Rob Gaines, Samuel Muniz, Slavik Milberg, Steven Olender, Tyler Fischer, Valerie O'Hara, Victoria Prescott, Whitney Kimball Long; Jewish Community Center; November 28–December 20, 2009

The Punishing Blow by Randy Cohen; Director, Seth Duerr; Stage Manager, Angie McCormack; **Cast:** Seth Duerr; JCC & Museum of Jewish Heritage; January 7–8, 2009& March 25, 2009

Long Day's Journey Into Night by Eugene O'Neill; Director, Seth Duerr; Stage Manager, Angie McCormack; Lighting, Driscoll Otto; Set, Stephen K. Dobay; Costumes, Sean Sullivan; Sound, John D. Ivy; Fight Choreographer, Brian Morvant; Graphics, Ehren Ziegler; Properties, Elyse Handelman; Press, Katie Rosin/Kampfire Films PR; **Cast:** Bill Fairbairn, Rebecca Street, Seth Duerr, Alexander Harvey, Julie Jesneck; Lion Theatre on Theatre Row; May 28–June 12, 2010

Seth Duerr in the York Shakespeare Company production of Long Day's Journey Into Night *(photo by Michelle Sims)*

A scene from Oh, Those Beautiful Weimar Girls!, presented by The New Stage Theatre Company (photo by Jonathan Slaff)

The Company in Hell and High Water, or Lessons for When the Sky Falls, presented by MultiStages (photo by Ellie D'Eustachio)

Anna Nugent, Allie Darden, Brian Hampton, and Beverly Lauchner in Checking In, presented at the June Havoc Theatre as part of the Midtown International Theater Festival (photo by Roy Chicas)

Kristen Vaughan and Matthew Trumbull in Retro Productions' The Desk Set (photo by Jordana Zeldin)

Christine Donlon, Ella Jane New, Gemma Fearn, and Kristen Lewis in Numbers, presented by Pink Bulb Productions (photo by Meagan Cignoli)

Kenny Wade Marshall and David Perlman in Top of the Heap at The Gallery Players (photo by Jen Maufrais Kelly)

Andrew Loren Resto, John Philip, and Mariah Bonner in All That Might Happen, presented at Manhattan Theatre Source (photo by Tom Zuback)

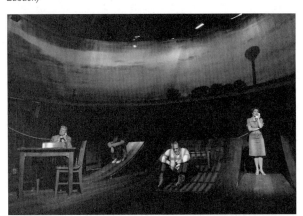

Richard Mawe, Ehad Berisha, Judson Jones, and Shorey Walker in Theatre East's Eye of God (photo by Jen Maufrais Kelly)

The Company in teaser cow, presented by One Year Lease Theater Company (photo by Amanda Culp)

The Company in Monstrosity, presented by 13P (photo by Jim Baldassare)

Haskell King in Afterclap, presented by Rising Phoenix Repertory (photo by Daniel Talbott)

PROFESSIONAL REGIONAL COMPANIES

Top: *Trista Moldovan and Michael Ellison in the Arkansas Repertory Theatre's production of* Cat on a Hot Tin Roof *(photo by Stephen B. Thornton)*

Center: *The Cast of Goodspeed Opera House's production of* 42nd Street *(photo by Diane Sobolewski)*

Bottom: *Wes Hart, Tyler Foy, Kevin Munhall, and Kimberly Fauré in* Kiss Me, Kate *at Music Theatre of Wichita (photo by Squid Ink Creative)*

Regional Roundup

By Nicole Estvanik Taylor

Adapt, adapt, adapt. That could have been the motto of professional theatre companies nationwide in the 2009–10 season. Most had to adapt to harsh financial realities: In 2009, for the second year running, more than half of theatres responding to Theatre Communications Group's annual fiscal survey reported a negative bottom line. A stroll through the season's schedules reveals theatres' unflagging enthusiasm for another kind of adaptation: retooling well-known stories for the stage.

The Greeks certainly maintained their hold on the modern theatrical imagination with such new takes as Anne Washburn's *Orestes: A Tragic Romp* at D.C.'s Folger Theatre and New Jersey's Two River Theater Company; David Catlin's gravity-defying *Icarus* and J. Nicole Brooks' *Fedra: Queen of Haiti* at Chicago's Lookingglass Theatre Company; Luis Alfaro's *Oedipus El Rey*, a three-city National New Play Network rolling premiere which—like his previous *Electricidad*—molded Greek drama for an L.A. Latino cast of characters; a ninety-minute, one-man *Iliad* adapted at Seattle Repertory Theatre by Denis O'Hare and Lisa Peterson; and Jeremy Menekseoglu's *Agon Trilogy*, a riff on Aeschylus at Chicago's Dream Theatre Company. In San Francisco, Cutting Ball Theater and the Playwrights Foundation co-produced *...And Jesus Moonwalks the Mississippi*, a new play by Marcus Gardley that blends the Greek myths of Demeter and Persephone with the history of slavery in America.

For his farewell project at Milwaukee Repertory Theater, departing artistic director Joseph Hanreddy put his own stamp on George M. Cohan's 1913 Broadway farce *Seven Keys to Baldpate* (itself a book-to-stage conversion). Hanreddy kept the original concept of a hack novelist trying to bang out a book in 24 hours, but retitled it *Seven Keys to Slaughter Peak* and transposed it to rural Wisconsin.

American lit got its due: Word for Word Performing Arts Company, a San Francisco endeavor devoted to adaptation, helped develop a new version by Octavio Solis and Jonathan Moscone of John Steinbeck's *The Pastures of Heaven*, which Moscone directed for California Shakespeare Theater. A Seattle company with a similar mission, Book-It Repertory Theatre, brought John Kennedy Toole's *A Confederacy of Dunces* alive; meanwhile, Atlanta's Theatrical Outfit went into summer 2010 with its own version. In Chicago, Tanya Saracho added *The House on Mango Street*, from the novel by Mexican-American writer Sandra Cisneros, to Steppenwolf Theatre Company's series for young adults. Composer Paul Gordon's *Daddy Long Legs*, co-written with director John Caird, turned another coming-of-age classic into a sweet two-hander for the Bay Area's TheatreWorks, Cincinnati Playhouse in the Park, and Southern California's Rubicon Theatre Company. Caridad Svich's adaptation of *La casa de los espíritus* (*The House of the Spirits*)—which has been captivating NYC's Spanish-speaking community at Repertorio Español—debuted in Svich's own English translation for Houston audiences at Main Street Theater. Svich's task was to condense Isabel Allende's sprawling family epic for a small stage, but Chicago's Building Stage faced the opposite challenge in fleshing out a spare Raymond Carver short story, "Gazebo," into a sixty-five-minute modern opera by Joshua Dumas called *One Thing, and Everything Else*.

During a nationwide centennial observance of Mark Twain's death, Hartford Stage commissioned a new *Tom Sawyer* from writer/director Laura Eason; in St. Louis, a cast of mostly disabled actors performed That Uppity Theatre Company's *The Assorted Short Adventures of Tom, Huck, and Becky*; and the Coterie Theatre of Missouri and American Folklore Theatre of Wisconsin both staged Douglas M. Parker's adaptation of Twain's memoir *Life on the Mississippi*, newly musicalized by composer Denver Casado. With 2009 marking the bicentennial of his birth, Edgar Allan Poe also inspired a spate of projects this season—at Single Carrot Theatre (*The Poe Project*) in Baltimore, where the writer is buried; plus at the Coterie (*Tell-Tale Electric Poe*), Philadelphia's Brat Productions (*Haunted Poe*), Montana Repertory Theatre (*The Poe Project*), and Alabama Shakespeare Festival (*The Fall of the House*). That last production, a 150-year-spanning tale by Robert Ford, was a commission for ASF's Southern Writers' Project—as was *Nobody* by Richard Aellen, based on the true story of African-American vaudevillians Bert Williams and George Walker.

Indeed, why stop at literature when you can adapt the lives of entertainers? "Bio" is a practical major in Hollywood and in the theatre world too, if the ongoing nationwide popularity of *Always...Patsy Cline*, *Ella*, *Lady Day at Emerson's Bar and Grill*, and *Buddy: The Buddy Holly Story* are any indication. On New Year's Eve, *Ella: The American Dream* entered the bio-revue genre at Petaluma, California's Cinnabar Theater, penned by and starring jazz singer Kim Nalley. New Jersey's Passage Theatre Company brought back actor Demetria Joyce Bailey to star in a newly conceived version of Larry Parr's *Ethel Waters: His Eye Is on the Sparrow*. San Diego's Old Globe premiered the new Rat Pack musical *Sammy*, by Leslie Bricusse, a real-life friend of Sammy Davis Jr. Other theatres staged debuts or revivals rooted in the lives and catalogues of Pearl Bailey, Woody Guthrie, Will Rogers, Ginger Rogers, Mae West, and Sophie Tucker.

Ready-made soundtrack or no, famous names from RFK to Picasso sprinkled the season's schedules. The American Theatre Critics Association put its 2010 Steinberg Award stamp of approval on Bill Cain's *Equivocation*, in which the Bard himself is a main player; it premiered at Oregon Shakespeare Festival and Seattle Rep under the direction of Bill Rauch; in the ensuing months directors David Esbjornson, Jasson Minadakis, and Garry Hynes staged their own versions around the U.S.

Chicago audiences got juicy stories this season inspired by the social circles of writers Friedrich Nietzsche (Ken Prestininzi's *Chaste*, at Trap Door Theatre) and Sir Arthur Conan Doyle (Eric Simonson's *Fake*, a premiere at Steppenwolf). In Vermont, the Weston Playhouse awarded its New Musical Award, complete with two concert readings and funds for a cast recording, to *Saint-Ex*, a musical-in-progress by Jenny Giering and Sean Barry about the author of *The Little Prince*, who was also a famous aviator. The venerable musical-writing team of Richard Maltby Jr., David Shire, and John Weidman preferred, in the U.S. premiere of *Take Flight* at New Jersey's McCarter Theatre Center, to tackle the whole pantheon of aeronautical pioneers, from Wright to Lindbergh to Earhart. Clarence Darrow (as portrayed by Paul Morella in an ever-evolving, decade-old performance) took center stage in *A Passion for Justice* at Olney Theatre Center and Everyman Theatre, both in Maryland. Laurence Fishburne reprised his 2008 Tony-nominated turn as another legal eagle in *Thurgood* to close out the season at L.A.'s Geffen Playhouse. Andy Warhol was the main player in Yale Repertory Theatre's *POP!* Abolitionist Harriet Tubman anchored a touring thirty-character solo, *Harriet's Return*, by Karen Meadow Jones. Muhammad Ali was at the center of Will Power's *Fetch Clay, Make Man* at the McCarter, and locally revered sports figures were featured at Pittsburgh Public Theater (*The Chief*, about Steelers founder Art Rooney Sr.) and Honolulu Theatre for Youth (*The Three Year Swim Club*, profiling Olympic coach Soichi Sakamoto). Not to say the spotlight was always rosy: President Lincoln once described himself as "the most miserable man living," and his depression drove Free Street Theater of Chicago's *Abe's in a Bad Way*. *Chicago Reader*'s critic named the production—featuring a cast of adolescent amateur actors—the 2010 "Best Play I Saw by Mistake."

In the category of modern legends, former Czech president Václav Havel premiered his first play in two decades, a portrait of a recently retired politician titled *Leaving*, at Philadelphia's Wilma Theater. Elaine May, famous for her comedy routines with Mike Nichols as well as her screenplays, wrote and directed a new comedy, *George Is Dead*—expanded from a 2006 one-act—for Tucson and Phoenix's Arizona Theatre Company. And Lynn Redgrave, who succumbed to cancer this year, made some of her last public appearances at Arizona's Invisible Theatre Company in her fourth and final solo show to draw on her illustrious family history, *Rachel and Juliet*.

• • •

Some of the season's work seemed engineered for national buzz. That was surely the goal for prolific composer Frank Wildhorn in giving the musical treatment to infamous duo *Bonnie and Clyde*. Laura Osnes and Stark Sands, both fresh off

Broadway, assayed the title roles at La Jolla Playhouse, Next season, the musical will undergo further fine-tuning at Florida's Asolo Repertory Theatre. Meanwhile, Wildhorn's *Wonderland*—in which a grown-up Alice is a kids' book writer with issues—will proceed from runs at the Alley Theatre in Houston and Tampa's Straz Center for the Performing Arts to a spring 2011 Broadway engagement. A third Wildhorn musical (written with Pulitzer-winner Nilo Cruz), *Havana*, had been scheduled to debut at the Pasadena Playhouse in California this season—but those plans were put on hold when, from February through the summer, the Playhouse temporarily shuttered to undergo Chapter 11 proceedings.

Glencoe, Illinois' Writers' Theatre drew enviable attention for its production of *A Streetcar Named Desire*. Point one: It was directed by David Cromer, whose high-profile successes with *Adding Machine: A Musical* and *Our Town*, both of which transferred from Chicago to New York, far outweigh the untimely closing of his Neil Simon plays on Broadway. Plus, consider that the same Tennessee Williams play recently thrilled U.S. audiences when Sydney Theatre Company toured a version starring Cate Blanchett. Throw in critical raves for Cromer's intimate production—from Chicagoans plus from out-of-towners Terry Teachout (*Wall Street Journal*) and Christopher Isherwood (*New York Times*)—and you've got a veritable recipe for buzz.

Kansas City Repertory Theatre, in a co-production with L.A.'s Center Theatre Group, also garnered favorable publicity with *Venice*, by energetic writer/performer Matt Sax and Kansas City Rep artistic director Eric Rosen. *TIME* magazine named *Venice* the best musical of the year, praising its rock-rap score and ambitious narrative about political exiles in a futuristic post-war city.

Berkeley Repertory Theatre mined its iPod for hits, beginning the season with the Green Day rock musical *American Idiot*, which transferred to Broadway, and heading into the spring with *Girlfriend*, titled after the iconic 1991 Matthew Sweet album. Todd Almond's libretto set Sweet's songs in Nebraska—from which both librettist and composer hail—and evoked the euphoria and awkwardness of first love, as experienced by two young men.

The Old Globe mounted an intriguing tuner: *Whisper House*, indie pop-rocker Duncan Sheik's spooky follow-up to his Tony and Grammy Award–winning *Spring Awakening*. The *Los Angeles Times* blog Culture Monster hailed the musical, directed by Peter Askin and featuring a book by Kyle Jarrow, for its "revivifying freshness." The Old Globe also programmed a new musical version of *The First Wives Club*, clearly aimed at Broadway. But as the 2010 Pulitzer honor for Broadway's *Next to Normal* shows, sometimes it's a new story and a fresh perspective that soars to big-time success.

Still, many of those who care about the professional U.S. theatre are concerned, and rightly so, that all that *adapting, adapting, adapting* going on—to financial realities, to marketing research, to tried-and-true source material, however creatively—must not squeeze out diverse voices and untold stories. Theatre Development Fund released a new book written by Todd London with Ben Pesner, *Outrageous Fortune*, that ignited nationwide conversations about how playwrights get through theatres' gates, and how much they're paid when they do. Last year graduating Princeton economics student Emily Glassberg Sands also put forth controversial findings that fueled an ongoing debate about the underrepresentation of female voices on U.S. stages.

In such a competitive landscape, it might appear there's scant room for a play that lacks a nationally recognizable name, topic, or star. But local stories have a special kind of draw for audiences, too, and theatre's great at doing "local." For example, Bruce Graham, dubbed by the *Philadelphia Inquirer* "the dean of Philadelphia dramatists," continued his streak of popular Pennsylvania-set comedies at Theatre Exile and Act II Playhouse with *Any Given Monday*. In Chicago, playwright James Sherman and Victory Gardens Theater artistic director Dennis Zacek built on a collaboration that dates back to 1985 and encompasses more than a dozen new plays by staging Sherman's latest, *Jacob and Jack*. Virginia Stage Company premiered VSC regular Kenny Finkle's *Alive and Well*, about a Civil War reenactor trekking through Virginia, as part of its American Soil series. PURE Theatre of Charleston staged South Carolina–flavored *Lowcountry Boil*, written by

hometown scribe R. W. Smith. Seattle's Intiman Theatre produced local playwright Sonya Schneider's *The Thin Place*, based on interviews conducted by local radio journalist Marcie Sillman, in which a crop of locals discussed religious faith. Actor/writer Jeff Daniels, founder of Purple Rose Theatre Company, completed his *Escanaba* trilogy set in the Upper Peninsula of the theatre's state of Michigan. American Repertory Theater of Cambridge, Massachusetts, gifted the Red Sox Nation with Richard Dresser's *Johnny Baseball*. In Minneapolis, Mu Performing Arts teamed writer Zaraawar Mistry with frequent Mu performer Iris Shiraishi to tell Shiraishi's story (*Becoming*) about moving to the Twin Cities from Hawaii. In an unusual collaboration with San Francisco Ballet, American Conservatory Theater created a new piece about a Bay Area landmark, the Tosca Café, the same year it celebrated the centennial of its own landmark venue, the Geary Theater. And in September 2009, Cyrano's Theatre Company of Alaska premiered Dick Reichman's *The Big One: A Chronicle of the Valdez Oil Spill*. Unfortunately, by April, that particular bit of local history had new resonance across the continent, once oil started leaking from BP's rig into the Gulf of Mexico.

Dobama Theatre in Cleveland and San Francisco Mime Troupe both turned fifty this year and celebrated in appropriate hometown style: Dobama commissioned *Ten More Minutes from Cleveland* from Eric Coble. The Mime Troupe performed *Too Big to Fail*, a scathing look at the credit crisis, in a number of the area's public parks. Still, top prize for local adaptability goes to Chicago's legendary Second City, which has been celebrating its own half-century mark by touring the country's regional houses with a show that is reinvented—as befits an improv troupe—for each locale (e.g., *Can You Be More Pacific?* and *The Second City Does Arizona, Or Close But No Saguaro*).

• • •

TDF's *Outrageous Fortune* revealed that most playwrights make significantly less money from royalties than from one-time grants, commissions, and awards. Quite a few theatres are relying on windfalls at this juncture, too. Philadelphia's Pig Iron Theatre Company was thrust into the national spotlight this year by senators John McCain and Tom Coburn, who listed a grant Pig Iron had received from the American Recovery and Reinvestment Act, administered by the National Endowment for the Arts, among stimulus projects they considered frivolous. On the plus side, Pig Iron became (one assumes) the first offbeat physical-theatre ensemble to have a snippet of its work aired on Fox News (though the artists might have preferred a less patronizing headline than "Cash for Clowns?"), and *Philly Weekly* tagged its *Welcome to Yuba City* the best new play of the season.

Too bad no one from the Edgerton Foundation was invited onto Fox to explain why theatres deserve support in a tough economy. Instead—along with other arts-minded foundations—Edgerton weighed in with its wallet, passing out twenty-seven New American Play Awards in 2009. At California's Marin Theatre Company, one such Edgerton-supported writer, Sharr White, also snagged the $10,000 Sky Cooper Prize for the political drama *Sunlight*, assuring itself a production there—followed by New Jersey and Indiana rolling premieres, thanks to the aforementioned National New Play Network. Steven Dietz's mystery-thriller *Yankee Tavern*, another NNPN beneficiary, is a clear success story for the organization's "continued life" mission, with eight productions and counting since its first staging in May 2009.

At Virginia's Signature Theatre, Musical Theatre Composer Grants funded by the Shen Family Foundation most recently saw Ricky Ian Gordon through to a premiere of his autobiographical *Sycamore Trees*. Gordon's $25,000-per-year gig includes four years of health coverage—a need also tended to by Arena Stage of D.C.'s American Voices New Play Institute, supported by the Mellon Foundation. The institute just activated playwrights' envy nationwide by announcing five lucky writers in residence: Amy Freed, Katori Hall, Lisa Kron, Charles Randolph-Wright and Karen Zacarías. Kron was in arts news this year for her much-anticipated *In the Wake*, about the disputed 2000 U.S. presidential election. When it debuted at Center Theatre Group and Berkeley Rep, the *San Francisco Chronicle*'s Robert Hurwitt suggested it has a shot of becoming "the *Angels in America* of the Bush II decade." Hall is another timely choice, fresh off the high of an unexpected best-play win at England's Olivier Awards for her play *The Mountaintop*, which imagines Martin Luther King Jr.'s final evening. (Yes, another dip into the bottomless biographical well.) That laurel will catapult her to Broadway next season; in the meantime visitors to the Inge Festival in Kansas were among the first U.S. audiences to hear the play, in a concert reading this past April, when she was presented with the festival's Otis Guernsey Award. (New Yorkers in the know also caught a workshop of it during Hall's residency at New York's Lark Play Development Center.)

Also file under sneak peek: A reading of the newest work by inaugural Greenfield Prize recipient Craig Lucas was enjoyed by Florida theatregoers, when Asolo Rep previewed the outcome of his $30,000 commission, *Love & Irony*. While a lucky few got to see Kevin Kline participate in a Manhattan Theatre Club reading of David Auburn's *The Columnist* in June 2010, audiences in Nashville caught it even sooner at the Ingram New Works Festival, where the Pulitzer-winner was the Ingram New Works Fellow. Julia Cho's Susan Smith Blackburn Prize–winning *The Language Archive*, about a linguist's marital woes, was featured in South Coast Repertory of California's Pacific Playwrights Festival. Cho and her play—commissioned by NYC's Roundabout Theatre Company and headed there in fall 2010—also summered at the 2009 National Playwrights Conference at the latest regional theatre Tony winner, Connecticut's Eugene O'Neill Theater Center. And in other festival news: Kentucky's Humana Festival of New American Plays helped to answer the question of what alumni of Jeune Lune (the recently folded Twin Cities physical theatre bastion) plan to do next—in this case, make an ensemble piece called *Fissures (lost and found)* with members of the Workhaus Playwrights Collective.

A 2010 Pulitzer nomination was good timing for Rajiv Joseph, whose *Bengal Tiger at the Baghdad Zoo* got a return engagement at Center Theatre Group; Joseph also introduced his new two-actor dysfunctional romance, *Gruesome Playground Injuries*, at Houston's Alley Theatre and Washington, D.C.'s Woolly Mammoth Theatre Company. Meanwhile, last year's Pulitzer win for Lynn Nottage's *Ruined* set the stage this year for a number of productions about Africa. Writer/actor Sahr Ngaujah, known to NYC crowds for his electric performance in *Fela!*, visited his hometown of Atlanta to give 7 Stages his play *Conversations with ICE*, which links Sierra Leone's child soldiers to the bling culture of hip-hop. Lonnie Carter's *The Lost Boys of Sudan*, first seen at Children's Theatre Company of Minneapolis, played this year at Victory Gardens, and Winter Miller's *In Darfur* traveled to D.C.'s Theater J. South African–born director Liesl Tommy, who staged *Ruined* for Oregon Shakespeare Festival—and will do so again next season for Berkeley Rep, La Jolla, and Boston's Huntington Theatre Company—directed Danai Gurira's new play *Eclipsed*, which follows the wives of rebel soldiers in Liberia, for Yale Rep, Woolly Mammoth, and the McCarter. In the spring Tommy also worked at a Sundance Institute theatre lab in Massachusetts, Shailja Patel's play about the 2008 post-election violence in Kenya, and she was an advisor for Sundance's first-ever theatre lab held in East Africa. One of the participating playwrights in that lab, Odile Gakire Katese, gave another gift to her native Rwanda this year: With actress-turned-entrepreneur Jennifer Dundas, she helped open its first ice cream shop.

• • •

One play set new records this year for simultaneous productions: *The Laramie Project: Ten Years Later*, a newly written epilogue to Tectonic Theater Project of New York's famous docudrama about Matthew Shepard's murder, premiered at 150 theatres on one October 2009 evening. It became not just a play, but an event. That's a concept theatres must wrestle with as they compete for national attention. Cornerstone Theater Company of L.A. employs a thematic approach by commissioning "cycles" of plays on crucial topics. The most recent, the four-year Justice Cycle, was capped off by the customary "bridge show" *3 Truths*, penned

by Naomi Iizuka. Taking a different tack, Woolly Mammoth organized a conference called "Who's in Your Circle? Theatre, Democracy and Engagement in the 21st Century" around performances of Charles L. Mee's *Full Circle*.

Playwright Israel Horovitz became an event on his seventieth birthday: The global 70/70 Horovitz Project set in motion a production of one of his plays for every year he's lived. In the months following his death, Horton Foote's final, nine-part work, *The Orphans' Home Cycle*, was a major event at Connecticut's Hartford Stage and New York's Signature Theatre Company. Philadelphia Theatre Company premiered a new play by Terrence McNally, *Golden Age*, which in D.C. became the final piece in the Kennedy Center's *Nights at the Opera* trilogy (also comprising McNally's *Lisbon Traviata* and *Master Class*). Both Jon Kolvenbach's *Goldfish* and its sequel *Mrs. Whitney* played in repertory at San Francisco's Magic Theatre. Aficionados of French writer Bernard-Marie Koltès raised the late scribe's state-side profile with performances and symposia in Atlanta and New Haven. CalArts embarked on a yearlong celebration of Adrienne Kennedy, and Dallas Theater Center staged all three of Neil LaBute's appearance-obsessed *Beauty Plays*, packaged in repertory for the first time. Scanning the ranks of playwrights, you might call Tarell Alvin McCraney's continued meteoric rise an event unto itself: This year he snagged a prestigious Mimi Award—as did Bruce Norris and David Adjmi—from the Harold and Mimi Steinberg Charitable Trust. He was welcomed into the ensemble of Steppenwolf Theatre Company, which produced his three-part *Brother/Sister Plays*.

One play scored so many productions it might as well have anchored a national festival: San Francisco playwright Peter Sinn Nachtrieb's 2008 apocalyptic comedy *boom* exited the 2009–10 season with more than a dozen productions to its credit. Other plays seen with increasing frequency nationwide include the laugh-fests *Boeing-Boeing*, *[title of show]*, and *The 39 Steps*, along with tarter comedies such as Evan Smith's *Savannah Disputation* and Stephen Karam's *Speech and Debate*. Frank Higgins' *Black Pearl Sings!* embeds a cappella spirituals within the framework of a drama in which a 1930s academic meets a prisoner who knows the lost melodies she's searching for. The researcher is willing to shell out money for those songs, and audiences at numerous theatres proved they were, too. Intrepid monologuist Mike Daisey also made the rounds to a string of cities with his newest piece, *The Last Cargo Cult*, tying his observations from a stay on remote Vanuatu to the role of money in American culture.

A number of writers this year plumbed the in-the-news topic of immigration: For one of its newest rolling-world-premiere projects, NNPN took on *There Are No Roosters in the Desert*, written by Kara Hartzler and based on interviews with women who have made the dangerous cross-border trek from Mexico. Octavio Solis' *Ghosts of the River*, at the Bay Area's Brava Theater Center and Teatro Visión, used shadow puppetry to tell stories from both sides of the Rio Grande. In Portland, Oregon, the bilingual *American Sueño* at Miracle Theatre Group followed four people all pursuing their version of the American Dream.

With such plays, theatre can carry us down avenues where our own experiences might never lead. At its best, it can also illuminate inaccessible corners of our hearts. Perhaps most thrilling of all is when plays dare to shine their light directly into the future. *Wilson Wants It All* at House Theatre, co-written by Phillip C. Klapperich and director Michael Rohd of Oregon's Sojourn Theatre, imagined for Chicago audiences where the American Dream might be headed in 2040: so divided by contentious political parties that the nation's fabric is tearing at the seams. The authors posit that one young woman—born, as it happens, in 2010—might leverage the ideals of her assassinated senator father to save the union. They named that character for one of theatre's most powerful tools for adaptation: Hope.

Carter J. Davis, Jennifer Sue Johnson, Anne Allgood, Billie Wildrick, and Richard Ziman in A Contemporary Theatre's Das Barbecü (photo by Chris Bennion)

Nathan Hosner and Kelley Curran in Hamlet at the Alabama Shakespeare Festival (photo by Stephen Poff)

Nikki Snelson and the Company of the Alley Theatre production of Wonderland (photo by Michal Daniel)

Anthony Fusco, Manoel Felciano, and Marcia Pizzo in Round and Round the Garden at American Conservatory Theatre (photo by Kevin Berne)

Milo Twomey and Hannah Yelland in the Kneehigh Theatre's production of Brief Encounter at American Conservatory Theatre (photo by Steve Tanner)

Colin Donnell, Burke Moses, Joe Cassidy, Jeff Brooks, Robert McClure, and Stephanie Umoh in Johnny Baseball *at the American Repertory Theatre (photo by Marcus Stern)*

The Company of Arizona Theatre Company's The Kite Runner *(photo by Tim Fuller)*

Lauren Lebowitz, Sal Sabella, Kelly McCormick, Christopher McGovern, and Stanley Bahorek in Arizona Theatre Company's [title of show] *(photo by Tim Fuller)*

Jeffrey Coon and Kristine Fraelich in Arden Theatre Company's production of Sunday in the Park with George *(photo by Mark Garvin)*

John Morrison, Michael Boudewyns, Sara Valentine, Maggie Kettering, and Ed Swidey in the Delaware Theatre Company production of It's a Wonderful Life: A Live Radio Play *(photo by Joe del Tufo)*

ACT–A Contemporary Theatre

Seattle, Washington

Forty-fifth Season

Artistic Director, Kurt Beattie

Dr. Jekyll and Mr. Hyde Adapted by Jeffrey Hatcher; Director, R. Hamilton Wright; Set, Matthew Smucker; Costumes, Marcia Dixcy Jory; Lighting, Rick Paulsen; Sound, Brendan Patrick Hogan; Assistant Lighting, Lara Wilder; Fight Choreographer, Geoffrey Alm; Stage Manager, JR Welden; ASM, Melissa Hamasaki; Dialect Coach, Alyssa Keene; Cast: Sylvie Davidson (Miss Elizabeth Jelkes), Bradford Farwell (Dr. Henry Jekyll), Deborah Fialkow (Poole/Maid/Prostitute/Police Physician/Hotel Porter/Mr. Edward Hyde/Surgical Student/Old Woman), David Anthony Lewis (Dr. H.K. Lanyon/Drunkard/Surgical Student/Mr. Edward Hyde), David Pichette (Mr. Gabriel Utterson/Mr. Edward Hyde), Brandon Whitehead (Mr. Richard Enfield/Sir Danvers Carew/Private Detective/Police Inspector/Mr. Edward Hyde); April 10–May 10, 2009

Below the Belt by Richard Dresser; Director, Pam MacKinnon; Set, Matthew Smucker; Costumes, Deb Trout; Lighting, Rick Paulsen; Sound, Brendan Patrick Hogan; Assistant Lighting, Susannah Scott; Stage Manger, Jeffrey K. Hansen; ASM, JR Welden; Cast: Judd Hirsch (Hanrahan), John Procaccino (Merkin), R. Hamilton Wright (Dobbitt); May 22–June 21, 2009

the break/s: a mixtape for stage Written and performed by Marc Bamunthi Joseph; Presented by The Hansberry Project for ACT; Director, Michael John Garcés; Executive Producer, MAPP International Productions; Dramaturg, Brian Freeman; Choreography, Stacy Printz; Video/Set, David Szlaza; Lighting, James Clotfelter; Composer, Ajayi Lumumba; June 17–July 12, 2009

Das Barbecü Book and lyrics by Jim Luigs, music by Scott Warrender; Director/Choreography, Stephen Terrell; Music Director, Richard Gray; Set/Costumes, David Zinn; Lighting, Alex Berry; Sound, Brendan Patrick Hogan; Stage Manager, Jeffrey K. Hanson; ASM, JR Welden; Cast: Anne Allgood (Fricka/Erda/Needa/more), Carter J. Davis (Siegfried/Alberich/Milam/more), Jennifer Sue Johnson (Gutrune/Freia/more), Billie Wildrick (Burnnhilde/more), Richard Ziman (Wotan/Hagen/Gunther/more); Musicians: Richard Gray (keyboard), Eric Chappelle (fiddle), Don Dieterich (drums), Jon Paul Miller (guitar); July 31–September 6, 2009

Runt of the Litter Written and performed by Bo Eason; Director, Larry Moss; September 18–October 11, 2009

Rock 'n' Roll by Tom Stoppard; Director, Kurt Beattie; Set, Matthew Smucker; Lighting, Mary Louise Geiger; Sound, Brendan Patrick Hogan; Cast: Matthew Floyd Miller (Jan), Denis Arndt (Max), Anne Allgood (Eleanor/Esme [older]), Peter Crook (Ferdinand), Andrew De Rycke (Nigel), John Farrage (Milan), Deborah Fialkow (Candida), Benjamin Harris (The Piper/Stephen), Jessica Martin (Esme [younger]/Alice), Alexandra Tavares (Lenka), Montana Von Fliss (Gillian/Magda/Deirdre); October 9–November 8, 2009

A Christmas Carol by Charles Dickens, adapted by Gregory A. Falls; Directors, Kurt Beattie & R. Hamilton Wright; Composer, Adam Stern; Set, Shelley Henze Schermer; Costumes, Deb Trout; Lighting, Michael Wellborn; Sound/Music Director, Brendan Patrick Hogan; Original Sound, Steven M. Klein; Choreography, Wade Madsen; Dialects, Alyssa Keene; Stage Manager, JR Welden; ASM, Erin B. Zatloka; Production Assistant, Verhanika Wood; Cast: Kurt Beattie or R. Hamilton Wright (Scrooge), Ian Bell (Fred/Bread Lady/Robin Crusoe/Old Joe), Mark Chamberlin (Bob Cratchit/Jonathan), Brandon Engman (Charles Cratchit/Master Fezziwig), Emily Fairbrook (Martha Cratchit/Miss Fezziwig), Chloe Forsyth (Tiny Tim/Ignorance), Benjamin Harris (Middle Scrooge/Beggar/Guest/Ali Baba/Businessman #2), Shereen Khatibloo (Belinda Cratchit/Fan), David Anthony Lewis (Spirit #2/Gent #2/Ragpicker), Jessica Martin (Spirit #1/Party Guest/Charwoman), Jenna Oratz (Elizabeth Cratchit/Lil Fezziwig/Want), Elijah Ostrow (Turkey Boy/Singing Thief/Undertaker's Assistant), Marianne Owen (Mrs. Cratchit/Elizabeth), Morgan Rowe (Mrs. Dilber/Mrs. Fezziwig/Sugar Plum Seller/Sister), Roy Stanton (Marley/Poor Man/Dick Wilkins/Spirit #3), Jennifer Lee Taylor (Belle/Niece), Brandon Whitehead (Mr. Fezziwig/Topper/Gentleman #1/Businessman #1/Grocer), Nathaniel Zang (Peter Cratchit/Young Scrooge); Understudies: Montana von Fliss, John Ulman; 34th Annual Production; November 27–December 27, 2009

Alabama Shakespeare Festival

Montgomery, Alabama

Thirty-eighth Season

Producing Artistic Director, Geoffrey Sherman; Chief Operating Instructor, Michael Vigilant

Ferdinand the Bull Based on the children's classic tale by Munro Leaf, adaptation and lyrics by Karen Zacarias, music by Deborah Wicks La Puma; Director, Nancy Rominger; Set, Peter Hicks; Costumes, Jeffrey Todhunter; Lighting, Tom Rodman; Festival Stage; November 7–December 19, 2009

A Christmas Story by Philip Grecian, based on the film distributed by Warner Brothers with a screenplay by Jean Shepherd, Leigh Brown and Bob Clark, and on the book *In God We Trust, All Others Pay Cash* by Jean Shepherd; Director, Geoffrey Sherman; Set, Peter Hicks; Costumes, Elizabeth Novak; Sound, Richelle Thompson; Lighting, Phil Monat; Stage Manager, Tanya J. Searle; Cast: Bryant Mason (The Old Man), Sandy York (Mother), Jennifer Lyon (Miss Shields), Rodney Clark (Adult Ralph), Seth Meriwether (Ralphie Parker), Hayley Covington, Claudia Hubbard, Nathan Looney, Jackson Massey, Mary Kathryn Samelson, Riley Segars, Helen Taylor; Festival Stage; November 27–December 24, 2009

Harriet's Return Written and performed by Karen Meadows Jones; Festival Stage; February 5–28, 2010

Nobody by Richard Aellen, based on the lives of African-American vaudeville performers Bert Williams and George Walker; Director, Tim Edward Rhoze; Music Director, Brett Rominger; Set, Peter Hicks; Costumes, Elizabeth Novak; Lighting, Tom Rodman; Sound, Richelle Thompson; Dramaturg, Susan Willis; Stage Manager, Jen Nelson Lane; Production Assistant, Nathan Stamper; Cast: James Bowen (Bert Williams), Sean Blake (George Walker), Erika LaVonn (Doreen Overton/Lottie Williams), Angela K. Thomas (Ada Overton Walker), Gerritt VanderMeer (Policeman Mike/Ziegfeld/Jules/Haftner/Tambo), Jonathan C. Kaplan (Danny/Policeman Jimmy/Eugene/Chief Bugaboo/Harry/Bones/Lew Docstader), Margaret Loesser Robinson (Sandy/Betty/Eva Tanguay); Octogon Stage; March 12–28, 2010

The Fall of the House by Robert Ford; Director, Nancy Rominger; Set, Peter Hicks; Costumes, Elizabeth Novak; Lighting, Tom Rodman; Sound, Richelle Thompson; Dramaturg, Susan Willis; Stage Manager, Jen Nelson Lane; Production Assistant, Nathan Stamper; Cast: Jonathan C. Kaplan (Jack/Cage/Young Janice/David Poe), Erika LaVonn (Munny), Margaret Loesser Robinson (Lucy/Judge/Eliza Poe), Angela K. Thomas (Janice Berry), Gerritt VanderMeer (Wilson/Edgar Allan Poe), Ta'Myia Narcisse-Cousarare; World Premiere; Octogon Stage; April 9–25, 2010

Lettice and Lovage by Peter Shaffer; Director, John Going; Set, Peter Hicks; Costumes, Pamela Scofield; Costumes/Lighting, Paul Wonsek; Sound, Richelle Thompson; Dramaturg, Susan Willis; Stage Manager, Tanya J. Searle; ASM, Melissa van Swol; Production Assistant, Cheryl Hansen; Cast: Diana van Fossen (Lettice Douffet), Carole Mondferdini (Lotte Schoen), Melanie Wilson (Miss Framer/Visitor), Anthony Cochrane (Mr. Bardolph), Paul Hopper (Surly Man); Visitors: Matthew Baldiga, Robert Barmettler, Matthew Bretschneider, Jordan Coughtry, Kelley Curran, Nathan Hosner, Celia Howard, Michael Pesoli, Lauren Sowa, Ricardo Vazquez; Festival Stage; Presented as part of the Spring Repertory Season; April 9–May 22, 2010

Hamlet by William Shakespeare; Festival Stage; Set, Peter Hicks; Costumes, Elizabeth Novak; Lighting, Phil Monat; Sound, Richelle Thompson; Cast: Nathan Hosner (Hamlet), Anthony Cochrane (Claudius), Paul Hopper (A Captain/

Gravedigger/Ghost of Hamlet's Father), Greta Lambert (Gertrude), Rodney Clark (Polonius), Matthew Baldiga (Third Player/Laertes), Kelley Curran (Ophelia), Matt D'Amico (Horatio), Jordan Coughtry (A Priest/Fortinbras/Rosencrantz), Michael Pesoli (Osric/Francisco/Guildenstern), Matthew Bretschneider (Fourth Player/Sailor/Barnardo/Voltemand), Ricardo Vazquez (First Player/Apprentice Gravedigger/Marcellus), Robert Barmettler (Reynaldo/English Ambassador/A Priest), Melanie Wilson (Lady), Lauren Sowa (Second Player); Presented as part of the Spring Repertory Season; April 16–May 22, 2010

All's Well That Ends Well by William Shakespeare; Director, Geoffrey Sherman; Original Music, James Conely; Set, Peter Hicks; Costumes, Elizabeth Novak; Lighting, Phil Monat; Sound, Richelle Thompson; Stage Manager, Melissa van Swol; ASM, Tanya J. Searle; Production Assistant, Cheryl Hansen; Cast: Rodey Clark (King of France), Jordan Coughtry (Bertram), Paul Hopper (Lafew), Nathan Hosner (First Lord Dumaine), Matthew Bretschneider (Second Lord of Dumaine), Matt D'Amico (Parolles), Matthew Baldiga (Second Soldier, Third Lord/French Gentleman), Michael Pesoli (Rinaldo), Anthony Cochrane (Lavatch), Carole Mondferdini (Countess of Rousillon), Kelley Curran (Helena), Celia Howard (A Widow), Lauren Sowa (Diana), Melanie Wilson (Mariana), Robert Barmettler (King's Attendant), Ricardo Vazquez (First Soldier/Fourth Lord); Festival Stage; Presented as part of the Spring Repertory Season; April 23–May 22, 2010

Cowgirls Music and lyrics by Mary Murfitt, book by Betsey Howe; Director, Karen Azenberg; Musical Director, Mary Ehlinger; Set, Peter Hicks; Costumes, Katrina Cahalan-Wilhite; Lighting, Paul Wonsek; Sound, Richelle Thompson; Stage Manager, Tanya J. Searle; Cast: Carrie Cimma (Mickey) Chelsea Lee Costa (Mo), Tamra Hayden (Lee), Angela Howell (Jo), Pear Rhein (Rita), Jessica Wright (Mary Lou); Festival Stage; June 11–July 3, 2010

Alley Theatre

Houston, Texas

Sixty-third Season

Artistic Director, Gregory Boyd; Managing Director, Dean Gladden

Sherlock Holmes and the Crucifer of Blood by Paul Giovanni; Director, Gregory Boyd; Set, Kevin Rigdon; Costumes, Blair Gulledge; Lighting, Rui Rita; Sound, Pierre Dupree; Fight Director, Brian Byrnes; Dramaturg, Lauren Halvorsen; Stage Managers, Elizabeth M. Berther and Terry Cranshaw; ASM, Rebecca R.D. Hamlin; Cast: Jeffrey Bean (Major Alistair Ross), James Black (Captain Neville St. Claire), Philip Lehl (Jonathan Small), John Tyson (Durga Dass/Inspector Lestrade), Justin Doran (Wali Dad/Birdy Johnson), James Belcher (Mohammed Singh/Hopkins/Mordecai Smith), Todd Waite (Sherlock Holmes), Chris Hutchison (John Watson M.D.), Elizabeth Bunch (Irene St. Claire) Hubbard Stage; July 15–August 16, 2009

Our Town by Thornton Wilder; Director, Gregory Boyd; Set, Kevin Rigdon; Costumes, Alejo Vietti; Lighting, Beverly Emmons; Sound, John Gromada; Movement Director, Peter Lobdell; Music Director, Michael Mertz; Dramaturgs, Mark Bly & Lauren Halvorsen; Stage Manager, Terry Cranshaw; ASM, Rebecca R.D. Hamlin; Cast: James Black (Stage Manager), Jeffrey Bean (Dr. Gibbs), Josie de Guzman (Mrs. Gibbs), Fritz Eagleton or David Heaton (Joe Crowell Jr./Si Crowell), Charlotte Booker (Mrs. Webb), Noble Shropshire (Howie Newsome), Emily Neves (Rebecca Gibbs), Elizabeth Bunch (Emily Webb), Winch Eagleton or Ashton Lambert (Wally Webb), Charles Krohn (Professor Willard), Todd Waite (Mr. Webb), John Tyson (Simon Stimson), Anne Quackenbush (Mrs. Soames), David Rainey (Constable Warren), Adam N. Gibbs, Matt Hune, Andrew Love (Baseball Players/People of the Town), Chris Hutchison (Sam Craig), James Belcher (Joe Stoddard), Melinda deKay (A Woman/People of the Town), Jay Tribble (Farmer McCarty/People of the Town), Santry Rush (Mr. Carter/People of the Town), Ellen Dyer, Jennifer Gilber, Dylan Godwin, Beth Hopp, Charles Krohn (People of the Town); Hubbard Stage; October 2–November 1, 2009

Gruesome Playground Injuries by Rajiv Joseph; Director, Rebeca Taichman; Set, Riccardo Hernandez; Costumes, Miranda Hoffman; Lighting, Christopher Akerlind; Sound, Jill BC DuBoff; Dramaturg, Mark Bly; Casting, Laura Stanczyk; Stage Manager, Elizabeth M. Berther; Cast: Selma Blair (Kayleen), Brad Fleischer (Doug); World Premiere; Neuhaus Stage; October 16–November 15, 2009

A Christmas Carol - A Ghost Story of Christmas by Charles Dickens; Adapted and originally directed by Michael Wilson; Director, James Black; Set, Tony Straiges; Costumes, Alejo Vietti; Lighting, Rui Rita; Original Music & Sound, John Gromada; Choreography, Hope Clarke; Music Director, Deborah Lewis; Dance Captain, Melissa Pritchett; Stage Manager, Terry Cranshaw; ASM, Rebecca R.D. Hamlin; Cast: Jeffrey Bean (Ebenezer Scrooge), James Black (Mrs. Dilber/Jacob Marley), Chris Hutchison (Bob Cratchit), Andrew Love (Fred/Scrooge at twenty-one), John Tyson (First Solicitor/Fiddler), Paul Hope (Second Solicitor/Mr. Fezziwig), Julia Krohn (Mary Pidgeon/Spirit of Christmas Past), Bettye Fitzpatrick (Mary Pidgeon/Spirit of Christmas Past), Melissa Pritchett (Rich Lady/Patricia/Ghostly Apparitions & Citizens of London), David Rainey (Bert/Spirit of Christmas Present), Noble Shropshire (Mr. Marvel/Spirit of Christmas Future), James Belcher (Undertaker/Old Joe), Elizabeth Bunch (Mrs. Fezziwig/Mrs. Cratchit), Beth Hopp (Wendy/Martha Cratchit/Ghostly Apparitions & Citizens of London), Charles Swan (Dick Wilkins/Mr.Topper/Ghostly Apparitions & Citizens of London), Adam N. Gibbs (Travis/Ghostly Apparitions & Citizens of London), Dylan Godwin (Party Guest/Ghostly Apparitions & Citizens of London), Emily Neves (Belle/Fred's Wife), Jennifer Gilbert (Fred's Sister-in-law/Ghostly Apparitions & Citizens of London), Sophia Jolie Groen or Artemis Melania Postolos (Tim Cratchit), Catherine Ribbeck or Sarah Swackhamer (Spoiled Child), Duncan Lambert or Cody W. Smith (Cider Boy/Cherub/Ignorance), Kyla Fleischhauer or Chantellie Wesley (Cider Girl/Cherub/Want), Liam Conner, Ashton Lambert, Dylan T. Lambert, Rock L. Morille, Marshall White (Schoolboys), Winch Eagleton or Bryn Fleischhauer (Boy Scrooge), David Heaton or Xavier Lehew (Scrooge at Fourteen/Peter Cratchit), Madeleine Ginty or Reagan Lukefahr (Fan), Marion Strauss or Evan Leigh Thornton (Claire Fezziwig/Fred Party Girl), Ally Fleischhauer or Rissa Medlenka (Belinda Cratchit), Fritz Eagleton or James Ian Wolf (Fred Party Boy/Turkey Boy); Hubbard Stage; November 20–December 27, 2009

The Santaland Diaries by David Sedaris, adapted by for the stage by Joe Mantello; Director, David Cromer; Set, Karin Rabe; Costumes, Blair Gulledge; Lighting, Kevin Rigdon; Sound, Pierre Dupree; Stage Manager, Elizabeth M. Berther; Cast: Todd Waite (Crumpet); Neuhaus Stage; November 28–December 28, 2009

Wonderland Music by Frank Wildhorn, book by Gregory Boyd & Jack Murphy, lyrics by Jack Murphy; Director, Gregory Boyd; Choreographer, Marguerite Derricks; Music Direction and Vocal Arrangements, Ron Melrose; Set, Neil Patel; Costumes, Susan Hilferty; Lighting, Paul Gallo; Sound, Jon Weston; Video and Projection, Sven Ortel; Hair and Wigs, Tom Watson; Orchestrations and Music Supervisor, Kim Scharnberg; Houston Music Director/Conductor/Additional Dance & Incidental Music Arrangements, Greg Anthony; Associate Director, Kenneth Ferrone; Associate Choreographer, Michelle Elkin; Dance Captain, Colleen Craig; Stage Manager, Kenneth J. Davis; ASM, Terry Cranshaw; Special Effects, Chic Silber; Casting, Dave Clemmons Casting; Cast: Julie Brooks (Chloe), Janet Dacal (Alice Cornwinkle), Jose Llana (Hector/El Gato), Karen Mason (Mrs. Everheart/Queen of Hearts), Darren Ritchie (Jack/White Knight), Nikki Snelson (Madeline/Mad Hatter), Edward Staudenmayer (Richard/Rabbit), Tad Wilson (Jabberwock/Ensemble), Tommar Wilson (Theo/Caterpillar); Ensemble: Sae La Chin, Carrie Cimma, Colleen Craig, Dan Domenech, Krystal Ellsworth, Mallauri Esquibel, Lori Eure, Derek Ferguson, Ashley Galvan, Laura Karklina, Mary Mossberg, Stefan Raulston, Julius Anthony Rubio, Danny Stiles; World Premiere; Hubbard Stage; January 15–February 14, 2010

Mrs. Mannerly by Jeffrey Hatcher; Director, John Rando; Set and Lighting, Kevin Rigdon; Costumes, Blair Gulledge; Sound, Tim Thomson; Dramaturg, Lauren Halvorsen; Stage Manager, Elizabeth M. Berther; Cast: James Black (Jeffrey), Josie de Guzman (Mrs. Mannerly); Neuhaus Stage; January 29–February 28, 2010

Alfred Hitchcock's The 39 Steps adapted by Patrick Barlow; Director, Mark Shanahan; Set, Hugh Landwehr; Costumes, Alejo Vietti; Lighting, Rui Rita; Sound, Ryan Rumery; Dialect Coach, Stephen Gabis; Stage Manager, Terry Cranshaw; ASM, Rebecca R.D. Hamlin; Cast: Todd Waite (Richard Hannay), Elizabeth Bunch (Annabella/Pamela/Margaret), John Tyson (Man #1), Jeffrey Bean (Man #2); Hubbard Stage; March 5–March 28, 2010

Harvey by Mary Chase; Director, Gregory Boyd; Set, Hugh Landwehr; Costumes, Judith Dolan; Lighting, Pat Collins; Original Composition and Sound, Josh Schmidt; Dramaturgs, Mark Bly and Lauren Halvorsen; New York Casting, Laura Stanczyk; Stage Manager, Elizabeth M. Berther; ASM, Rebecca R.D. Hamlin; Cast: Elizabeth Bunch (Myrtle Mae Simmons), Kristine Nielsen (Veta Louise Simmons), James Black (Elwood P. Dowd), Melissa Pritchett (Miss Johnson/Betty Chumley), Anne Quackenbush (Mrs. Ethel Chauvenet), Emily Neves (Ruth Kelly, R.N.), Jeffrey Bean (Duane Wilson), Mark Shanahan (Lyman Sanderson, M.D.), John Tyson (William R. Chumley, M.D.), James Belcher (Judge Omar Gaffney), Todd Waite (E.J. Lofgren); Hubbard Stage; April 16–May 9, 2010

Intelligence-Slave by Kenneth Lin; Director, Jackson Gay; Set and Lighting, Kevin Rigdon; Costumes, Blair Gulledge; Sound, Pierre Dupree; Dramaturg, Mark Bly; Fight Director, Brian Byrnes; Casting, Laura Stanczyk; Stage Manager, Terry Cranshaw; Cast: Andrew Weems (Curt Herzstark), James Belcher (Fritz Engelhardt), Todd Waite (Hermann Pister), Steven Louis Kane (Finn Frey), Chris Hutchison (Bruno Clemens); World Premiere; Neuhaus Stage; May 23–June 20, 2010

Boeing Boeing by Marc Camoletti, translated by Beverley Cross and Francis Evans; Director, Lisa Spirling; Production overseen and originally directed by Matthew Warchus; Set and Costumes, Rob Howell; Lighting, Michael Lincoln; Original Sound, Simon Baker; Sound, Pierre Dupree; Original Music, Clarie van Kampen; Dialect Coach, Pamela Prather; Dramaturg, Robert Shimko; Stage Manager, Elizabeth M. Berther; ASM, Rebecca R.D. Hamlin; Cast: Emily Neves (Gloria), James Black (Bernard), Josie de Guzman (Berthe), Jeffrey Bean (Robert), Elizabeth Bunch (Gabriella), Melissa Pritchett (Gretchen); Hubbard Stage; June 4–June 27, 2010

Alliance Theatre

Atlanta, Georgia

Forty-first Season

Artistic Director, Susan V. Booth; Managing Director, Thomas Pechar

Alliance Stage

Come Fly With Me Conceived, directed and choreographed by Twyla Tharp, lyrics by Frank Sinatra; Presented by Nicholas Howey by special arrangement with Frank Sinatra Enterprises and the Sinatra Family, in association with WAT Limited and Troika General Management; Set, James Youmans; Costumes, Katherine Roth; Lighting, Donald Holder; Sound, Peter McBoyle; Musical Supervision, Sam Lutfiyya; Band Leaders, Dee Daniels and Dennis Mackrel; Additional Arrangements & Orchestrations, Dave Pierce; PSM, Juliana Crawford; Cast: Laura Mead, Charlie Neshyba-Hodges, Holley Farmer, John Selya, Karine Plantadit, Keith Roberts, Rika Okamoto, Matthew Dibble, Alexander Brady, Kristine Bendul, Carolyn Doherty, Heather Hamilton, Jodi Melnick, Ashley Tuttle, Todd Burnsed, Eric Otto, Justin Peck, Joel Prouty, Matt Rivera, John Sorensen-Jolink; World Premiere; September 16–October 11, 2009

A Life in the Theatre by David Mamet; Director, Robert O'Hara; Set/Costumes, Clint Ramos; PSM, Pat A. Flora/lark hackshaw; Cast: André De Shields (Robert), Ariel Shafir (John); October 28–November 15, 2009

A Christmas Carol by Charles Dickens, adapted by David H. Bell; Director, Rosemary Newcott; Set. D. Martyn Bookwalter; Costumes, Mariann Verheyen; Lighting, Diane Ferry Williams; Music Director/Conductor, Michael Fauss; PSMs, Pat Flora, Liz Cambell; Cast: Christy Baggett (Ensemble), Elizabeth Wells Berkes (Belle/Ensemble), Ritchie Crownfield (Ensemble), Christopher DesRoches

(Young Scrooge/Ensemble), Je Nie Fleming (Mrs. Crachit/Ensemble), Neal A Ghant (Bob Crachit), Bart Hansard (Fezziwig/Christmas Present/Ensemble), David Howard (Topper/Ensemble), Jamiah Hudson (Belinda/Ensemble), Chris Kayser (Ebeneezer Scrooge), Joe Knezevich (Fred/Ensemble), Royce Mann (Tiny Tim/Ensemble), Tendal Mann (Daniel/Ignorance/Turkey Boy/Ensemble), Derek Manson (Peter/Ensemble), Daniel Thomas May (Marley/Ensemble), Bernardine Mitchell (Mrs. Dilber/Mrs. Fezziwig/Ensemble), Sinatra Osm (Dick/Ensemble), Tessa Lene Palisoc (Melinda/Ensemble), Courtney Patterson (Christmas Past/Peg/Ensemble), Jordan Shoulberg (Want/Matchgirl/Ensemble), Hanley Smith (Fan/Martha/Ensemble), James Washburn III (Wyatt/Ensemble), Laurie Williamson (Bess/Ensemble); Understudies: Corey Bradberry, Sims Lamason; November 27–December 24, 2009

Avenue X Book and lyrics byJohn Jiler, music by Ray Leslee; Director, Susan V. Booth; Choreography, Danny Pelzig; Set, Todd Rosenthal; Costumes, Mariann Verheyen; Lighting, Ken Yunker; Music Director, Darryl Jovan Williams; Sound, Clay Benning; PSM, Pat A. Flora; PSM/ASM, lark hackshaw; ASM, RL Campbell; Cast: Rebecca Blouin (Barbara), Lawrence Clayton (Roscoe), Jeremy Cohen (Chuck), Steve French (Ubazz), J.D. Goldblatt (Milton), Nick Spangler (Pasquale), Nick Spears (Julia), J.D. Webster (Julia); January 13–February 7, 2010

Lookingglass Alice Adapted by David Catlin from the novels by Lewis Carroll; Produced in association with Lookingglass Theatre Company; Director, David Catlin; Set, Daniel Ostling; Costumes, Mara Blumenfeld; Lighting, Christine Binder; Sound, Ray Nardelli; Choreography/Circus Captain, Sylvia Hernandez-Distasi; Stage Manager, Dennis Conners; Cast: Molly Brennan (Red Queen/others), Kevin Douglas (Mad Hatter/others), Anthony Fleming III (Cheshire Cat/others), Doug Hara (White Knight/others), Lindsey Noel Whiting (Alice); March 31–May 2, 2010

Hertz Stage

The Second City: Peach Drop, Stop and Roll Written and created by Matt Hovde and Seth Weitberg, additional material by the cast; Music Director/Additional Music, Lisa McQueen; PSM, Rodney Williams; Director, Matt Hovde; Cast: Randall Harr, Anthony Irons, Niki Lindgren, Amber Nash, Amy Roeder, Steven Westdahl; November 6–December 27, 2009

Tennis in Nablus by Ismail Khalidi; Director, Peggy Shannon; Set, Brian Sidney Bembridge; Costumes, Anne Kennedy; Lighting, Mike Post; Sound, Clay Benning; PSM, Rodney Williams; Cast: Andrew Benator, (Hirsh/Soldier 1/Zapata), Demosthenes Chrysan (Yusef), Suehyla El-Attar (Ambara), Bart Hansard (General Falbour), Joe Knezevich (Lieutenant Douglas Duff), Bhavesh Patel (Tariq), Jim Sarbh (Rajib), Michael Simpson (Michael O'Donegal/Radio Announcer/Reggie), Tom Thon (Hajj Waleed/Soldier 2); Understudies: David Quay (Lt. Douglass Duff/Michael O'Donegal), Khalid Robinson (Yusef); World Premiere; January 29–February 21, 2010

The Last Cargo Cult Written and performed by Mike Daisey; Director, Jean-Michele Gregory; Lighting, Pete Shinn; PSM, Pat A. Flora/lark hackshaw; March 19–April 11, 2010

Alliance Children's Theatre

Disney's Mulan Music and lyrics by Matthew Wilder and David Zippel, Stephen Schwartz, Jeanine Tesori, Alexa Junge; Music Adaptation/Additional Music & Lyrics, Bryan Louiselle; Book Adaptation/Additional Lyrics, Patrica Cotter; Based on the 1998 Disney film and the story *Fa Mulan* by Robert D. San Souci; Director, Rosemary Newcott; Choreography, Hylan Scott; Set, Kat Conley; Costumes, Syndey Roberts; Lighting, Pete Shinn; Sound, Clay Benning; Music Director, Christopher Cannon; Stage Manager, Liz Campbell; Cast: Leslie Bellair (Mulan), Blake Covington (Shang/Young Yi/Magyar), Alejandro Gutierrez (Zhang/Father/Groomer/Old Yi/Quian Po), Bethany Irby (Yun/Fa Li/Yao), Bernard Jones (Mushu/Matchmaker/Young Xiao/Emperor), J.C. Long (Laozi/Shan Yu), Brandon O'Dell (Hong/Fag Zhou/Groomer/Ling), Alecia Robinson (Lin/Grandmother Fa/Chen/Chi-Fu); Understudies: Drew Hale, Corey Mekell, Sarah Turner; Alliance Stage; February 24–March 19, 2010

American Conservatory Theatre

San Francisco, California

Forty-third Season

Artistic Director, Casey Perloff; Executive Director, Heather Kitchen

Brief Encounter by Noël Coward, directed and adapted by Emma Rice; Presented by the Kneehight Theatre; Originally produced by David Pugh & Dafydd Rogers with Cineworld; Set/Costumes, Neil Murray; Lighting, Malcolm Rippeth; Projections, Jon Driscoll, Gemma Carrington; Original Music, Simon Baker; Casting, Sam Jones; Assistant Director, Simon Harvey; Kneehigh Theatre Producer, Paul Crewes; General Manager for U.S. Tour, Michael Mushalla; Company Stage Manager, Steph Curtis; Deputy Stage Manager, Karen Habens; A.C.T. Stage Manager, Karen Szpaller; Cast: Joseph Alessi (Albert/Fred), Annette McLaughlin (Myrtle), Stuard McLoughlin (Stanley), Beverly Rudd (Beryl), Milo Twomey (Alec), Hannah Yelland (Laura), Eddy Jay (Musician), Adam Pleeth (Musician); September 11–October 17, 2009

November by David Mamet; Director, Ron Lagomarsino; Set, Erik Flatmo; Costumes, Alex Jaeger; Lighting, Alexander V. Nichols; Sound, Cliff Caruthers; Dramaturg, Michael Paller; Casting, Meryl Lind Shaw; Cast: René Augesen (Clarice Bernstein), Manoel Felciano (A Representative of the National Association of Turkey and Turkey By-products Manufacturers), Anthony Fusco (Archer Brown), Steven Anthony Jones (Dwight Grackle), Andrew Polk (Charles Smith); October 23–November 22, 2009

A Christmas Carol by Charles Dickens, adapted by Carey Perloff and Paul Walsh, music by Karl Lundeberg; Original Direction, Case11y Perloff; Director, Domenique Lozano; Music Director, Robert Rutt; Choreography, Val Caniparoli; Répétiteur, Nancy Dickson; Set, John Arnone; Costumes, Beaver Bauer; Lighting, Nancy Schertler; Sound, Jake Rodriquez; Dramaturg, Michael Paller; Stage Manager, Karen Szpaller; ASM, Danielle Callaghan; Cast: Matthew Avery, Shinelle Azoroh, Ashley Baker, Samuel Joseph Berston, James Carpenter, Bonnie Castleman, Dan Clegg, Stephanie DeMott, Penelope Devlin, Emma Rose Draisin, Marisa Duchowny, Ella Francis, Alan Frenkel-Andrade, Anthony Fusco, Cindy Goldfield, Eva Huzella, Brian Jansen, Jenna Johnson, Richardson Jones, Steven Anthony Jones, Patrick Lane, Alexandra Lee, Sharon Lockwood, Shelby Lyon, Delia MacDougall, Samantha Martin, Jarion Monroe, Nicholas Pelczar, Coroline Pernick, Richard Prioleau, Tobiah Richkind, Joshua Roberts, Max Rosenak, Julian Carlo Santos, Sadie Eve Scott, Rachel Share-Sapolsky, Tony Sinclair, William David Southall, Howard Swain, Ashley Wickett, Jack Willis; December 2–24, 2009

Phèdre by Jean Racine, translated and adapted by Timberlake Wertenbaker; Director, Carey Perloff; Presented in association with the Stratford Shakepeare Festival; Set/Costumes, Christina Poddubiuk; Lighting, James F. Ingalls; Composer, David Lang; Cast: Sean Arbuckle (Théramène), Jonathan Goad (Hippolytus), Sophia Holman (Panope), Claire Lautier (Aricie), Mairin Lee (Ismène), Roberta Maxwell (Oenone), Tom McCamus (Thesus), Seana McKenna (Phèdre); World Premiere; January 15–February 7, 2010

The Caucasian Chalk Circle by Bertolt Brecht, translated by Domenique Lozano; Director/Design, John Doyle; Composer, Nathaniel Stookey; Cast: René Augesen, Nick Childress, Manoel Felciano, Anthony Fusco, Rod Gnapp, Caroline Hewitt, Omozé Idehenre, Gregory Wallace, Jack Willis; February 18–March 14, 2010

Vigil Written and directed by Morris Panych; Set/Costumes, Ken MacDonald; Lighting, Alan Brodie; Sound, Meg Roe, Alessandro Juliani; Casting, Meryl Lind Shaw; Stage Manager, Joeseph Smelser; ASM, Danielle Callaghan; Cast: Olympia Dukakis (Grace), Marco Barricelli (Kemp); March 25–April 18, 2005

Round and Round the Garden by Alan Ayckbourn; Director, John Rando; Set, Ralph Funicello; Costumes, Lydia Tanji; Lighting, Alexander V. Nichols; Sound, Jake Rodriquez; Dramaturg, Michael Paller; Casting, Meryl Lind Shaw; Stage Manager, Elisa Guthertz; ASMs, Megan Q. Sada, Claire Zawa; Cast: René Augesen (Ruth), Manoel Felciano (Norman), Anthony Fusco (Reg), Dan Hiatt (Tom), Marcia Pizzo (Sarah), Delia MacDougall (Annie); April 29–May 23, 2010

The Tosca Project Created and staged by Carey Perloff and Val Caniparoli; Music and Sound, Darron L West; Set, Douglas W. Schmidt; Lighting, Robert Wierzel; Costumes, Robert de La Rose; Cast: Sabina Allerman, Peter Anderson, Lorna Feijoo, Sara Hogrefe, Pascal Molat, Kyle Schaefer, Nol Simonse, Rachel Ticotin, Gregory Wallace, Jack Willis; World Premiere; June 3–July 3, 2010

American Repertory Theatre

Cambridge, Massachusetts

Thirty-first Season

Artistic Director and CEO, Diane Paulus

The Donkey Show Conceived by Randy Weiner; Directors, Diane Paulus & Randy Weiner; Sets, Scott Pask; Costumes, David C. Woolard; Lighting, Evan Morris; Sound, David Remedios; Props, Tricia Green; Resident Director, Allegra Libonati; Stage manager, Taylor Adamik; Cast: Jason Beaubien (Dr. Wheelgood), Steven James DeMarco (Steve-O), Tom Fish (Moth, Tytania's Fairy), Heather Gordon (Mr. Oberon/Mia), Mike Heslin (Mustard Seed, Tytania's Fairy), Susannah Hoffman (Misty), Eric Johnson (Peaseblossom, Tytania's Fairy), Erin McShane (Helen/Vinnie #2), Cameron Oro (Cob Web, Tytania's Fairy), Cheryl Turski (Dimitri/Vinnie #1), Rebecca Whitehurst (Tytania/Sander); August 21, 2009–February 26, 2011

Sleep No More based on Shakespeare's *Macbeth*; Directed and devised by Felix Barrett and Maxine Doyle with the Company; Co-presented by Punchdrunk; Design, Felix Barrett; Choreography, Maxine Doyle; Sound & Graphics, Stephen Dobbie; Associate Designers, Livi Vaughan, Beatrice Minns; Costumes, David Israel Reynoso; Staff Director, Mikhael Tara Garver; Assistant Director, Paul Stacey; Stage Manager, Carolyn Rae Boyd; ASMs, Kyle Carlson, Alexandra McConnell-Trivelli; Cast: Phil Atkins (Duncan), Sogdiana Azhibenova (Speakeasy Bartender), Django Carranza (Annie Darcy Band), Sarah Dowling (Lady Macbeth), Conor Doyle (Witch), Stephanie Eaton (Witch), Annie Goodchild (Annie Darcy), Hector Harkness (Malcolm), Geir Hytten (Macbeth), Thomas Kee (Porter), Poornima Kirby (The Second Mrs. De Winter), Alexander LaFrance (Bellhop), Robert McNeill (Macduff), Careena Melia (Hectate), Robert Najarian (Man in Bar), Fernanda Prata (Witch), Alli Ross (Lady Macduff), Vinicius Salles (Banquo), Rusty Scott (Annie Darcy Band), Timo Shanko (Annie Darcy Band), Hayley Jane Soggin (Elsie Price), Tori Sparks (Mrs. Danvers); The Old Lincoln School; October 8, 2009–February 7, 2010

Best of Both Worlds Book and lyrics by Randy Weiner with Diane Paulus, music by Diedre Murray; Director, Diane Paulus; Sets, Riccardo Hernandez; Costumes, Emilio Sosa; Lighting, Aaron Black; Sound, Brett Jarvis; Music Director, Michael Mitchell; Associate Music Director/Choir Coordinator, David Freeman Coleman; Movement, Tracy Jack; Stage Manager, Katherine Shea; ASM, Amanda Robbins-Butcher; Cast: Gregg Baker (Ezekiel), Jeannette Bayardelle (Serena/Daughter of Joy), Mary Bond Davis (Violetta/Daughter of Joy), Nikkieli DeMone (Camillo/The Bear), Cleavant Derricks (Sweet Daddy/Narrator), Brianna Horne (Rain), Sebastien Lucien (Mamillius), Lawrence Stallings (Tariq); Loeb Drama Center; November 21, 2009–January 3, 2010

Gatz Created by Elevator Repair Service, based on *The Great Gatsby* by F. Scott Fitzgerald; Director, John Collins; Sets, Louisa Thompson; Costumes, Colleen Werthmann; Lighting, Mark Barton; Sound, Ben Williams; Stage Manager, Chris De Camillis; Cast: Laurena Allan (Myrtle), Aaron Landsman [1/7-24]/Frank Boyd [1/27-2/7] (George), Jim Fletcher (Jim), Ross Fletcher (Henry C. Gatz), Mike Iveson (Ewing), Susie Sokol [1/7-10]/Sibyl Kempson [1/12-2/7] (Jordan), Vin Knight (Chester), Annie McNamara [1/7-17]/Kristen Sieh [1/21-2/7], Kate Scelsa (Lucille), Scott Shepherd (Nick), Victoria Vazquez (Daisy), Ben Williams (Michaelis), Gary Wilmes (Tom); Loeb Drama Center; January 7–February 7, 2010

Paradise Lost By Clifford Odets; Director, Daniel Fish; Sets, Andrew Lieberman; Costumes, Kaye Voyce; Lighting, Scott Zielinski; Sound, Clive Goodwin; Video, Joshua Thorson; Stage Manager, Katherine Shea; ASM, Amanda Robbins-Butcher;

Cast: Remo Airaldi (Phil Foley), Hale Appleman (Ben), Karl Bury (Kewpie), David Chandler (Leo Gordon), Thomas Derrah (Gus Michaels), Jonathan Epstein (Sam Katz), Anthony Gaskins (Newspaper Man), Merritt Janson (Libby Michaels), Adrianna Krstansky (Bertha), Cameron Oro (Felix), Therese Plaehn (Pearl), Michael Rudko (Mr. Pike), T. Ryder Smith (Julie/Mr. May), Sally Wingert (Clara); Loeb Drama Center; February 27–March 20, 2010

Johnny Baseball Music by Robert Reale, lyrics and story by Willie Reale, book and story Richard Dresser; Director, Diane Paulus; Sets, Scott Pask; Costumes, Michael McDonald; Lighting, Donald Holder; Sound, Acme Sound Partners; Musical Arrangements, Bruce Coughlin; Vocal Arrangements/Musical Director, Wendy Bobbitt Cavett; Casting, Stephen Kopel; Associate Director, Shira Milikowski; Choreography, Peter Pucci; PSM, Chris De Camillis; Cast: Jeff Brooks (Fan 2/Wally Schang/Ed Barrow/Barker/Tom Yawkey), Charl Brown (Barman/ Porter /Tim Wyatt), Joe Cassidy (Fan 4/Manager/Sox Player/Umpire/Reporter/ Frazee's Man/Cronin), Kaitlyn Davidson (Fan 6/Razor Girl/Nurse/Booster), Colin Donnell (Johnny O'Brien), Alan H. Green (Vendor/Baron/Porter/Harold/Willie), Carly Jibson (Fan 5/Greta/Razor Girl/Booster), Paula Leggett Chase (Fan 8/Drunk Woman/Woman on the Train), Erik March (Robby), Robert McClure (Conductor/ Frazee's Man/Snodgrass/Yawkey's Crony), Burke Moses (Fan 1/Babe Ruth/ Yawkey's Crony), Charles Turner (Fan 9), Stephanie Umoh (Daisy Wyatt), Kirsten Wyatt (Fan 7/Cherie/Razor Girl/Genevieve); Loeb Drama Center; May 16–June 27, 2010

Arden Theatre Company

Philadelphia, Pennsylvania

Twenty-second Season

Artistic Director, Terrence J. Nolen

The History Boys by Alan Bennett; Director, Terrence J. Nolen; Set, David P. Gordon; Costumes, Alison Roberts; Lighting, F. Mitchell Dana; Sound & Projections, Jorge Cousineau; Musical Director & Associate Sound, Daniel Kluger; Dramaturg, Sarah Ollove; Assistant Director, Matt Ocks; Stage Manager, Katherine M. Hanley; Cast: Matthew Amendt (Irwin), Chris Bresky (Lockwood), Brian Cowden (Rudge), Ankit Dogra (Akthar), Michael Doherty (Posner), David Howey (Headmaster), Evan Jonigkeit (Dakin), Matt Leisy (Scripps), Jonathan Silver (Timms), Maureen Torsney-Weir (Mrs. Lintott), Peterson Townsend (Crowther), Frank X (Hector); F. Otto Haas Stage; September 24–November 1, 2009

Rabbit Hole by David Linsday-Abaire; Director, James J. Christy; Set, Donald Eastman; Costumes, Alison Roberts; Lighting, James Leitner; Sound/Composer, Christopher Colucci; Assistant Director, Matt Silva; Stage Manager, Alec E. Ferrell; Cast: Janis Dardaris (Nat), Grace Gonglewski (Becca), Brian Russell (Howie), Aaron Stall (Jason), Julianna Zinkel (Izzy); Arcadia Stage; October 22–December 20, 2009

Peter Pan by J.M. Barrie, adapted by Douglas Irvine; Director, David O'Connor; Set, Tom Gleeson; Costumes, Richard St. Clair; Lighting, Matt Frey; Sound/ Composer, Daniel Kluger; Puppet Design, Morgan Fitzpatrick Andrews; Fight Choreographer, J. Alex Cordaro; Assistant Director/Dramaturg, Sarah Ollove; Stage Manager, Stephanie Cook; Cast: Chris Bresky (Peter Pan), Bi Jean Ngo (Tinkerbell/Jane/Nibs/Nana/Twins), Jacqueline Real (Wendy), Sarah Sanford (Tootles/Starkey/Mrs. Darling), David J. Sweeney (Michael/Smee/Slightly), Frank X (Captain Hook); F. Otto Haas Stage; December 2, 2009–January 31, 2010

Blue Door by Tanya Barfield; Director, Walter Dallas; Set, Daniel Conway; Costumes, Alison Roberts; Lighting, Thom Weaver; Sound/Additional Music, Robert Kaplowitz; Fight Director, Charles Conwell; Dramaturg, Jacqueline E. Lawton; Assistant Director, Malika Oyetimein; Stage Manager, Alec E. Ferrell; Cast: Johnnie Hobbs Jr. (Lewis), Kes Khemnu (Simon/Rex/Jesse); Arcadia Stage; January 14–March 21, 2010

Romeo and Juliet by William Shakespeare; Director, Matt Pfeiffer; Set, Brian Sidney Bembridge; Costumes, Rosemarie E. McKelvey; Lighting, Thom Weaver; Sound, James Sugg; Fight Director, Dale Anthony Girard; Choreographer, Karen Getz; Assistant Fight Director, J. Alex Cordaro; Assistant Director, Dan Hodge; Stage Manager, Katherine M. Hanley; Cast: Krista Apple (Lady Montague/ Balthasar), Shawn Fagan (Mercutio/Friar John), Melanye Finister (Lady Capulet), Scott Greer (Lord Capulet), James William Ijames (Benvolio), Evan Jonigkeit (Romeo), Mahira Kakkar (Juliet), Sean Lally (Tybalt/Apothecary), Anthony Lawton (Friar Laurence), Matt Lorenz (Paris), Suzanne O'Donnell (Nurse), Brian Anthony Wilson (Prince), Frank X (Lord Montague/Peter); F. Otto Haas Stage; February 25–April 11, 2010

If You Give A Mouse A Cookie by Laura Numeroff, adapted by Jody Davidson; Director, Whit MacLaughlin; Set, David P. Gordon; Costume, Richard St. Clair; Lighting, Drew Billiau; Sound/Video/Original Music, Jorge Cousineau; Assistant Director, Bayla Rubin; Stage Manager, Stephanie Cook; Cast: Steve Pacek (Mouse), David Raphaely (Boy); Arcadia Stage; April 14–June 27, 2010

Sunday in the Park with George Music and lyrics by Stephen Sondheim, book by James Lapine; Director, Terrence J. Nolen; Set, James Kronzer; Costume, Rosemarie E. McKelvey; Lighting, Justin Townsend; Sound/Projection/Video, Jorge Cousineau; Musical Director, Eric Ebbenga; Choreographer, Niki Cousineau; Dramaturg, Sarah Ollove; Assistant Director, David Stradley; Stage Manager, Katherine M. Hanley; Cast: Walter Charles (Mr./Charles Redmond), Jeffrey Coon (George), Sarah Dacey-Charles (Yvonne/Naomi Eisen), Caroline Dooner (Celeste/ Waitress), Sherri L. Edelen (Mrs./Nurse/Harriet Pawling), Darren Michael Hengst (Franz/Dennis), Liz Filios (Celeste/Betty), Kristine Fraelich (Dot/Marie), Scott Greer (Jules/Bob Greenberg), Timothy Hill (Louis/Lee Randolph), Brian Hissong (Soldier/Billy Webster), Maggie Lakis (Frieda/Elaine), Michael "Tuba" McKinsey (Boatman/Alex), Danielle Standifer (Louise/A Boy), Maureen Torsney-Weir (Old Lady/Blair Daniels); F. Otto Haas Stage; May 27–July 4, 2010

Arena Stage

Washington, DC (Lincoln Theatre) and Arlington, Virginia (Crystal City)

Fifty-ninth Season

Artistic Director, Molly Smith; Executive Director, Edgar Dobie

The Quality of Life by Jane Anderson; Presented in association with Jonathan Reinis Productions and Stephen Eich; Director, Lisa Peterson; Set, Neil Patel; Costumes, Ilona Somogyi; Lighting, Alexander V. Nichols; Sound/Composer, John Gromada; Fight Choreography, David S. Leong; Stage Manager, Susan R. White; AMS, Amber Dickerson, Kurt Hall; Casting, David Caparelliotis; Dramaturg, Janine Sobeck; Cast: Johanna Day (Jeanette), Stephen Schnetzer (Neil), Annette O'Toole (Dinah), Kevin O'Rourke (Bill); Crystal City; September 17–October 18, 2009

The Fantasticks Book and lyrics by Tom Jones, music by Harvey Schmidt; Director, Amanda Dehnert; Choreographer, Sharon Jenkins; Musical Director, George Fulginti-Shakar; Set, Eugene Lee; Costumes, Jessica Ford; Hair & Makeup, Anne Nesmith; Lighting, Nancy Schertler; Sound, Timothy Thompson; Illusions, Jim Steinmeyer; Magic Consultant, Jeff Grow; Fight Choreographer, Graig Handel; Stage Manager, Martha Knight; ASM, Kurt Hall; Dramaturg, Janine Sobeck; Casting, Calleri Casting; Cast: Sebastian LaCause (El Gallo), Addi McDaniel (Luisa), Timothy Ware (Matt), Michael Stone Forrest (Huckabee), Jerome Lucas (Bellomy), Laurence O'Dwyer (Henry), Jesse Terrill (Mortimer), Nate Dendy (The Mute); Lincoln Theatre; November 20, 2009–January 10, 2010

Stick Fly by Lydia R. Diamond; Presented in collaboration with the Huntington Theatre Company; Director, Kenny Leon; Set, David Gallo; Costumes, Reggie Ray; Lighting, Allen Lee Hughes; Sound, Timothy J. Thompson; Fight Director, Robb Hunter; Stage Manager, Angelita Thomas; ASM, Jenna Henderson; Dramaturg, Janine Sobeck; Casting, Alaine Aldaffer; Cast: Rosie Benton (Kimber), Jason

Dirden (Kent), Amber Imnan (Cheryl), Billy Eugene Jones (Flip), Nikkole Salter (Taylor), Wendell W. Wright (Joe LeVay); Crystal City; January 1–February 7, 2010

The Light in the Piazza Book by Craig Lucas, music and lyrics by Adam Guettel, based on the novel by Elizabeth Spencer; Director, Molly Smith; Choreographer, Parker Esse; Musical Director, Paul Sportelli; Set, Anne Patterson; Costumes, Linda Cho; Lighting, Michael Gilliam; Sound, Timothy Thompson; Projections, Adam Larsen; Stage Manager, Susan R. White; Cast: Hollis Resnik (Margaret Johnson), Margaret Anne Florence (Clara), Nicholas Rodriquez (Fabrizio), Mary Gutzi (Signora Naccarelli), Ken Krugman (Signor Naccarelli), Ariela Morgernstern (Franca Naccarelli), Jonathan Raviv (Guiseppe Naccarelli); Ensemble: Drew Eshelman, Jennifer Irons, Michael Vitaly; Understudies: Conrad Buck, Kate Guesman; Crystal City; March 5–April 11, 2010

Duke Ellington's Sophisticated Ladies Concept by Donald McKayle, based on the music of Duke Ellington; Dance/Musical Arrangements, Lloyd Mayers, Vocal Arrangements, Malcolm Dodds and Lloyd Mayers; Original Music Direction, Mercer Ellington; Director, Charles Randolph-Wright, Choreographers, Maurice Hines and Kenneth Lee Roberson; Music Director, David Alan Bunn; Set/Projections, Alexander V. Nichols; Costumes, Reggie Ray; Lighting, Michael Gilliam; Sound, Timothy J. Thompson; Artistic Consultant, Mercedes Ellington; Stage Manager, Kurt Hall; ASM, Angelita Thomas; Dramaturg/Line Producer, Amrita Mangus; Cast: Maurice Hines, Sam Cahn, Janine DiVita, Marva Hicks, Sabra Lewis, Tony Mansker, John Manzari, Leo Manzari, Karla Mosley, Wynonna Smith, Keith Lamelle Thomas, DeMoya Watson, Hollie E. Wright, Richard Riaz Yoder; Lincoln Theatre; April 9–June 27, 2010

R. Buckminster Fuller: The History (and Mystery) of the Universe Written and directed by D.W. Jacobs; Set/Lighting, David Lee Cuthbert; Costumes, Darla Cash; Composer/Sound, Luis Perez; Projections, Jim Findlay; Dramturg, Janine Sobeck; Stage Manager, Jenna Henderson; ASM, Kurt Hall; Cast: Rick Foucheux (R. Buckminster Fuller); Crystal City; May 28–July 4, 2010

Arizona Theatre Company

Phoenix and Tucson, Arizona

Forty-third Season

Artistic Director, David Ira Goldstein; Managing Director, Kevin E. Moore; Associate Artistic Director, Samantha K. Wyer

The Kite Runner by Khaled Hosseini, adapted for the stage by Matthew Spangler; Director, David Ira Goldstein; Set, Vicki Smith; Costumes, Kish Finnegn; Lighting/Projections, David Lee Cuthbert; Sound, Scott W. Edwards; Fight Director, Ken Merckx; Dialect Coach, Lisa Anne Porter; Cultural Consultant, Humaira Ghilzai; PSM, Glenn Bruner; ASMs, Timothy Toothman, Bruno Ingram; Cast: Barzin Akhavan (Amir), Lowell Abellon (Hassan/Sohrab/Ensemble), Thomas Fiscella (Baba/Ensemble), Gregor Paslawsky (Rahim Khan/Zaman/Ensemble), James Saba (Ali/Omar Faisal/Ensemble), Rinabeth Apostol or Craig Piaget (Young Amir/Ensemble), Korken Alexander (Assef/Ensemble), Remi Sandri (General Taheri/Farid/Ensemble), Salar Nader (Tabla Player); Ensemble: Zarif Kabier Sadiqi, Lani Carissa Wong, Wahab Shayek; Tucson: September 10–October 3, 2009; Phoenix: October 8–25, 2009

George is Dead Written and directed by Elaine May; Set, John Arnone; Costumes, Sam Fleming; Lighting, Kurt Landisman; Sound, Brian Jerome Peterson; Stage Manager, Bruno Ingram; ASM, Glenn Brunner; Cast: Marlo Thomas (Doreen), Don Murray (George), Julia Brothers (Carla), Carman Lacivita (Freddie), Reese Madigan (Michael), Elizabeth Shepherd (Old Woman), Roberto Guajardo (Funeral Director); Tucson: October 17–November 7, 2009; Phoenix: November 12–December 6, 2009

Ain't Misbehavin' Conceived by Murray Horwitz & Richard Maltby Jr., music and lyrics by Thomas "Fats" Waller; Co-produced with the Cleveland Play House and San Jose Repertory Theatre; Director, Kent Gash; Musical Director/Conductor,

Darryl G. Ivey; Musical Staging/Choreographer, Byron Easley; Set, Emily Beck; Costumes, Austin K. Sanderson; Lighting, William H. Grant III; Sound, Brian Jerome Peterson; PSM, Glen Bruner; ASMs, Bruno Ingram, Timothy Toothman; Assistant to the Stage Manager, Ashley Simon; Cast: Rebecca A. Covington, Angela Grovey, Christopher L. Morgan, Ken Robinson, Aurelia Williams; Bolton Theatre; Tucson: November 28–December 20, 2009; Phoenix: December 30, 2009–January 17, 2010

[title of show] Book by Hunter Bell, music and lyrics by Jeff Bowen; Director David Ira Goldstein; Chorographer, Patricia Wilcox; Music Director, Christopher McGovern; Set, John Ezell; Costumes, Kish Finnegan; Lighting, Michael Gilliam; Sound, Abe Jacob; Projections, Jeffry Cady; Casting Telsey + Company; PSM, Glenn Bruner; ASM, Timothy Toothman; Assistant to the Stage Manager, Alena Fast; Cast: Stanley Bahorek (Hunter), Lauren Lebowitz (Susan), Kelly McCormak (Heidi) Sal Sabella (Jeff); Tucson: January 23–February 13, 2010; Phoenix: February 18–March 7, 2010

The Glass Menagerie by Tennessee Williams; Director, Juliette Carrillo; Set, Darcy Scanlin; Costumes, Emily Pepper; Lighting, Lonnie Rafael Alcaraz; Original Music & Sound, Josh Schmidt; Cast: Catalina Maynard (Amanda), Barbra Wengerd (Laura), Noel Joseph Allain (Tom), Brian Ibsen (Jim); Tucson: February 27–March 20, 2010; Phoenix: March 25–April 11, 2010

Arkansas Repertory Theatre

Little Rock, Arkansas

Thirty-fourth Season

Producing Artistic Director, Robert Hupp; Managing Director, Mike McCurdy

Always...Patsy Cline Written and originally directed by Ted Swindley; Original Music Director, Vicki Masters; Director, Robert Hupp; Music Director, Michael Heavner; Resident Set Design/Technical Director, E. Mike Nichols; Costumes, Marianne Custer; Lighting, Michael Barnett; Sound, M. Jason Pruzin; Production Manager, Rafael Colon Castanera; Stage Manager, Tara Kelly; Properties, Lynda J. Kwallek; Cast: Jessica Welch (Patsy Cline), JoAnn Robinson (Louise Seger), Sarah Haman (Understudy); September 11–October 4, 2009

The Second City Director, J. Shanoff; Musical Director, Bryan Dunn; Stage Manager, Kyle Anderson; Cast: Dana Quercioli, Edgar Blackmon, Megan Hordewilkins, Ross Bryant, Tim Robinson; October 7–18, 2009

Joseph and the Amazing Technicolor Dreamcoat Music by Andrew Lloyd Webber, lyrics by Tim Rice; Director, Alan Souza; Costumes/Production Manager, Rafael Colon Castanera; Props, Lynda J. Kwallek; Technical Director, E. Mike Nichols; Sound, M. Jason Pruzin; Cast: Austin Miller (Joseph), Shavey Brown (Gad/Butler/Ensemble), Matthew Buffalo (Issachar/Ensemble Marshal), Kennedy Carolan (Asher/Ensemble), Jenna Coker-Jones (Narrator), Kevin Crumpler (Dan/Ensemble), Todd DuBail (Jacob/Potiphar/Pharaoh), Katye Dunn (Mrs. Potiphar/Ensemble), David Garry (Reuben/Ensemble), Tony Gonzalez (Naphtali/Ensemble), Maxim Gukhman (Levi/Ensemble), Tim Hughes (Simeon/Ensemble/Assistant to the Chorographer), Cori Cable Kidder (Ensemble), Will Mann (Judah/Ensemble), Annie Mistak (Ensemble), Matthew Rickard (Swing), Nicky Romaniello (Zebulon/Ensemble), Alexandra Zorn (Ensemble); December 4, 2009–January 3, 2010

Cat on a Hot Tin Roof by Tennessee Williams; Director, Robert Hupp; Technical Director, Mike Nichols; Costumes, Margaret McKowen; Sound, M. Jason Pruzin; Stage Manager, Erin Albrecht; Production Manager, Rafael Colon Castanera; Props, Lynda J. Kwallek; Cast: Jeff Bailey (Dr. Baugh), Kathleen Doyle (Big Mama), Michael Ellison (Brick), Roger Jerome (Rev Tooker), Trista Moldovan (Maggie), Amy Tribbey (Mae), Joe Vincent (Big Daddy), Brian Wallace (Gooper); February 5–February 21, 2010

Glorious! by Peter Quilter; Director, Nicole Capri Bauer; Set, E. Mike Nichols; Costumes, Shelly Hall; Lighting, Katharine Lowery; Sound, M. Jason Pruzine; Projections, Matthew Webb; Production Manager, Rafael Colón Castanera; Stage Manager, Patrick Lanczki; Props, Lynda J. Kwallek; Cast: Lillian Castillo

(Maria), Darren Dunstan (Cosme), Patricia Kilgarriff (Florence Foster Jenkins), Laurie Pascale (Mrs. Verrinder-Gedge), Herman Petras (St. Clair), Joan Porter, (Dorothy); March 12–March 28, 2010

Frost/Nixon by Peter Morgan; Director, Gilbert McCauley; Set, Mike Nichols; Lighting, Matthew Webb; Costumes, Trish Clark; Sound, M. Jason Pruzin; Production Manager, Rafael Colón Castanera; Stage Manager, Tara Kelly; Props, Lynda J. Kwallek; Cast: Keith Langsdale (Richard Nixon), Mark Irish (Jim Reston), Brad Heberlee (David Frost), David Sitler (Jack Brennan), Nancy Noto (Evonne Goolagong), David Volin (John Birt), Maurico Leyton (Manolo Sanchez), Jay E. Raphael (Swifty Lazar), Adria Vitlar (Caroline Cushing), Jason O'Connell (Bob Zelnick); April 23–May 9, 2010

Smokey Joe's Café Music and lyrics by Jerry Leiber and Mike Stoller; Director, Ron Hutchins; Choreographer, Eric Alsford; Set, Mike Nichols; Costumes, Marianne Custer; Lighting, Kenton Yeager; Sound, M. Jason Pruzin; Stage Manager, Tara Kelly; Production Manager, Rafael Colon Castanera; Cast: Amy Miller Brennan (Pattie), Terrence Clowe (Ken), Alexander Elisa (Fred), Alltrinna Grayson (BJ), Darius Harper (Adrian), Krisha Marcano (Brenda), Matthew Ragas (Michael), Morgan Smith (DeLee), Eric LaJuan Summers (Victor); June 4–June 28, 2010

Barrington Stage Company

Pittsfield, Massachusetts

Fifteenth Season

Artistic Director, Julianne Boyd; Producing Director, Richard M. Parison Jr.

Carousel Music by Richard Rodgers, lyrics by Oscar Hammerstein II; Based on Ferenc Molnar's *Liliom*; Original Choreography, Agnes de Mille; Director, Julianne Boyd; Choreography, Joshua Bergasse; Musical Director, Darren Cohen; Cast: Aaron Ramey (Billy Bigelow), Patricia Noonan (Julie Jordan), Todd Buonopane (Mr. Snow), Sara Jean Ford (Carrie Pipperidge), Christopher Innvar (Jigger), Edmund Bagnell (2nd Heavenly Friend/Enoch Snow Jr.), Leslie Becker (Mrs. Mullin), Daniel Marcus (Dr. Selden/Captain/Starkeeper), Kristen Paulicelli (Louise), Teri Ralston (Nettie Fowler), Todd Thurston (Mr. Bascome); Ensemble: Edmund Bagnell, Al Blackstone, Daniel Garrity, Daniel Kermidas, Kaitlynn Kleinman, Hanna Koczela, Christy Morton, Ronnie Nelson, Neil O'Brien, Sarah O'Gleby, Kate Orenstein, Emelyn Theriault, Todd Thurston, Deven Walker, Peggy Pharr Wilson; June 17–July 11, 2009

Sleuth by Anthony Shaffer; Director, Jesse Berge; Cast: Charles Shaughnessy (Andrew Wyke), Jeremy Bobb (Milo Tindle); July 16–August 1, 2009

A Streetcar Named Desire by Tennessee Williams; Director, Julianne Boyd; Cast: Marin Mazzie (Blanche), Christopher Innvar (Stanley), Kim Stauffer (Stella), Kevin Carolan (Mitch), Emily Taplin Boyd (Nurse), Miles Hutton Jacoby (Young Collector), John Juback (Steve), Jeffrey Kent (Doctor), Chavez Ravine (Mexican Woman/Blues Singer), Jennifer Regan (Eunice), Thom Rivera (Pablo); August 6–29, 2009

The Fantasticks Music by Harvey Schmidt, book and lyrics by Tom Jones; Director, Andrew Volkoff; Musical Director, Christopher D. Littlefield; Choreography, Janet Watson; Set, Sam Craig; Costumes, Kristina Lucka; Lighting, Jeff Davis; Sound, Brad Berridge; Stage Manager, Renee Lutz; Casting, Pat McCorkle; Press, Charlie Sidenburg; Cast: Dana DeLisa (Luisa), Darin DePaul (Hucklebee), Jonathan Karp (The Mute), John-Charles Kelly (Bellomy), Cory Michael Smith (Matt), Bob Sorenson (Mortimer), Gordon Stanley (Henry), Steve Wilson (El Gallo); Musicians: Christopher D. Littlefield (piano), Teresa Mango (harp); October 7–18, 2009

Barrington Stage Musical Theatre Lab at BSC Stage II

Freud's Last Session by Mark St. Germain; Director, Tyler Marchant; Cast: Mark H. Dold (C.S. Lewis), Martin Rayner (Sigmund Freud); June 10–28, 2009

Underneath the Lintel by Glen Berger; Director, Andrew Volkoff; Cast: Glynis Bell; July 8–26, 2009

I'll Be Damned by Rob Broadhurst and Brent Black; August 13–29, 2009

Songs by Ridiculously Talented Composers and Lyricists You Probably Don't Know But Should hosted by William Finn; Sept 4–6, 2009

Barter Theatre

Abingdon, Virginia

Seventy-seventh Season

Producing Artistic Director, Richard Rose; Associate Artistic Director-Production, Dale F. Jordan; Associate Director, Nicholas Piper; Associate Director, Katy Brown; Director of Advancement, Jayne Duehring; Managing Director, Jeremy Wright

Forever Plaid Written and originally directed by Stuart Ross; Musical Continuity Supervision/Arrangements James Raitt, Originally Producer, Gene Wolsk; Director, Robert Randle; Assistant Choreographer, Amanda Aldridge; Musical Director, Steve Sensenig; Sets, Dale F. Jordan; Costumes, Kelly Jenkins; Lighting, Michael Barnett; Sound, Bobby Beck; Props, Chase Molden; Dance Captain, Patrick O'Neill; Casting, Paul Russell; Stage Manager, Cindi A. Raebel; ASM, Holley Housewright; Cast: Kevin Greene (Francis), Chris Vaughn (Smudge), Steven Douglas Stewart (Sparky), Patrick O'Neill (Jinx), Musicians: Steve Sensenig (piano), Brandon Story (bass); Barter Theatre; August 14–September 13, 2009

The Foreigner by Larry Shue; Director, Katy Brown; Sets/Lighting, Cheri Prough DeVol; Costumes, Colleen Metzger and Adrienne Webber; Sound, Bobby Beck; Stage Manager, Jessica Borda; Cast: Michael Poisson ("Froggy" LeSeur), Danny Vaccaro (Charlie Baker), Mary Lucy Bivins (Betty Meeks), J. Casey Barrett (Reverend David Marshall Lee), Gwen Edwards (Catherine Simms), Andrew Hampton Livingston (Owen Musser), David McCall (Ellard Simms); Barter Stage II; September 3–November 14, 2009

Little Shop of Horrors Book and lyrics by Howard Ashman, music by Alan Menken; Based on the film by Roger Corman with screenplay by Charles Griffith; Director, Evalyn Baron; Choreographer, Amanda Aldridge; Music Director, Tim Robertson; Sets/Lighting, Cheri Prough DeVol; Costumes, Amanda Aldridge; Wigs and Makeup, Ryan Fischer; Sound, Bobby Beck; Plant Design, Chase Molden; Casting, Paul Russell; Stage Manager, Jessica Borda; Cast: Lea S. Anderson (Chiffon), Taprena Augustine (Crystal), Dayna J. Dantzler (Ronnette), Michael Poisson (Mushnik), Hannah Ingram (Audrey), David McCall (Seymour), Jasper McGruder (Derelict/Audrey II), Danny Vaccaro (Orin/Bernstein/Snip/Luce et al.); Barter Stage II; September 11–November 15, 2009

Frankenstein by Mary Shelley, adapted and directed by Richard Rose; Sets, Cheri Prough DeVol; Costumes, Amanda Aldridge; Wig, Makeup and Creature Designer, Ryan Fischer; Lighting, Lucas Benjaminh Krech; Sound, Bobby Beck; Dance Choreographer, Amanda Aldridge; Fight Choreographer, Richard Rose; Fight Captain, Ezra Colón; Stage Manager, Cindi A. Raebel; Cast: Ezra Colón (Victor Frankenstein), Nicholas Piper (The Creature), Nathan Whitmer (Henry Clerval), Hannah Ingram (Elizabeth Lavenza), Jasper McGruder (Man #1), Bryan Pridgen (Man #2), Dayna J. Dantzler (Man #3), Eugene Wolf (Man #4), Lea S. Anderson (Man #5), Taprena Tricia Matthews (Woman #1), Emelie Faith Thompson (Woman #2), Carrie Smith (Woman #3), Augustine (Woman #4), McHale Parrish Bright/Lily Brock/Logan Fritz/Madison Lawson/Matthew Torbett (Youth Ensemble); Barter Theatre; September 25–November 14, 2009

Heaven Sent by Rick Whelan; Director, Mary Lucy Bivins; Sets, Dale F. Jordan; Costumes, Kelly Jenkins; Lighting, Joshua Benghiat; Sound, Bobby Beck; Props, Chase Molden; Stage Manager, Cindi A. Raebel; Cast: Eugene Wolf (Samuel Langley), Nathan Whitmer (Pastor Sims), Tricia Matthews (Mrs. Winthrop), Ezra Colón (Ralph Budleigh), Andrew Hampton Livingston (Del Cass), Julie Schroll (Nancy Flagg), J. Casey Barrett (Tom Cass/Aaron Winthrop), Carrie Smith (Molly

Stark), Savannah Grace Willis or Halle Harrison (Young Eppie), Gwen Edwards (Adult Eppie), Michael Poisson (Voice of Hugh Cass); Barter Theatre; October 8–November 14, 2009

WMKS: Christmas 1942 by Frank Higgins; Director/Lighting, Richard Rose; Vocal Arrangements, Eugene Wolf; Sets, Linda Thistle; Costumes, Amanda Aldridge; Sound, Bobby Beck; Stage Manager, Cindi A. Raebel; Cast: Eugene Wolf (Doc Carrroll), Tricia Matthews (Alma Carroll), Amy Baldwin (Cindy Turner), Nicholas Piper (Willy Turner), Andrew Leon Heil or Abigail Raye Conde (Arthel/Arthella), Cynthia Thomas (Audrey Newton), Jasper McGruder (Robert Newton), Dan Folino (Johnny Caroll); Musicians: Doug Dorschug (banjo), Claire Morison (young fiddle player), Ed Snodderly (guitar), Tim Robertson (piano), Barter Theatre; November 20–December 27, 2009

Holiday Memories by Truman Capote, adapted for the stage by Russell Vandenbroucke; Director, Katy Brown; Sets/Lighting, Cheri Prough DeVol; Costumes, Kelly Jenkins; Sound, Bobby Beck; Fight Choreographer, Ezra Colón; Stage Manager, Jessica Borda; Piano Score, Matthew Stone; Cast: Steve Sensenig (Pianist), Michael Poisson (Truman), Ezra Colón (Buddy), Mary Lucy Bivins (Aunt Sook), David McCall (Man), Gwen Edwards (Woman); Barter Stage II; November 24–December 20, 2009

Alice in Wonderland Adapted from Lewis Carroll's *Alice's Adventures in Wonderland* by Richard Rose; Director, Richard Rose; Music, Peter Yonka; Set/Lighting, Cheri Prough DeVol; Costumes, Amanda Aldridge; Puppet Designers, Krista Guffey Poisson/Ryan Fischer; Puppet Collaborators, Kelly Jenkins/Chase Molden/Adrienne Webber; Sound, Bobby Beck; Properties, Chase Molden; Stage Manager, Cindi A. Raebel; ASM, Jayme Tinti; Cast: Rebecca Reinhardt (Alice), Tricia Matthews (The White Rabbit/The Voice of the Baby), Kelly Klein (Alice's Sister/The Mouse/The Pigeon/The Dormouse/The Knave of Hearts), Ben Mackel (The Lory/Canary/Canary Chicks/The Mad Hatter/Seven of Spades), Sean Campos (The Dodo/Magpie/Eaglet/The March Hare/The Executioner), Rick McVey (The Duck/Old Crab/Little Crab/The Cook/The Cheshire Cat Head/The Mock Turtle), Danny Vaccaro (Bill, the Lizard/The Cheshire Cat Body/The Queen of Hearts), Dan Folino (The Caterpillar/The Footman/The King of Hearts), Ezra Colón (The Duchess/Five of Spades/The Dormouse), David McCall (The Cheshire Cat Head/Two of Spades/The Gryphon); Barter Theatre; February 4–April 17, 2010

Dead Man's Cell Phone by Sarah Ruhl; Director, Katy Brown; Fight Choreographer, Sean Campos; Fight Captain, Nicholas Piper; Set, Derek Smith; Costumes, Liz Whittemore; Lighting, Heather Eisenhart; Sound, Bobby Beck; Stage Manager, Holley Housewright; Cast: Ashley Campos (Jean), Michael Poisson (Gordon), Mary Lucy Bivins (Mrs. Gottlieb), Hannah Ingram (The Other Woman/The Stranger), Amy Baldwin (Hermia), Nicholas Piper (Dwight); Barter Stage II; February 12–April 11, 2010

The Diary of Anne Frank by Frances Goodrich and Albert Hackett, edited by Otto Frank; Based on the book *Anne Frank: The Diary of a Young Girl*; Director, Richard Rose; Assistant Director, Evalyn Baron; Set, Dale F. Jordan; Costumes, Amanda Aldridge; Lighting, Cheri Prough DeVol; Sound, Bobby Beck; Music, Peter Yonka; Stage Manager, Holley Housewright; Cast: Danny Vaccaro (Mr. Otto Frank), Rebecca Reinhardt (Miep Gies), Hannah Ingram (Mrs. Van Daan), Michael Poisson (Mr. Van Daan), Ben Mackel (Peter Van Daan), Tricia Matthews (Mrs. Edith Frank), Ashley Campos (Margot Frank), Kelly Klein (Anne Frank), David McCall (Mr. Kraler), Gannon McHale (Mr. Dussel); Barter Theatre; February 19–April 17, 2010

Chaps! by Jahnna Beecham and Malcolm Hillgartner; Vocal Arrangements, Malcolm Hillgartner/Chip Duford; Director, Mary Lucy Bivins; Music Director, Tim Robertson; Set, Mark DeVol; Costumes, Amanda Aldridge; Lighting, Heather Eisenhart; Sound, Bobby Beck; Stage Manager, Cindi A. Raebel; ASM, Jayme Tinti; Cast: Nicholas Piper (Archie Leitch), Ezra Colón (Stan), Rick McVey (Leslie Briggs–Stratton), Sean Campos (Miles Shadwell), Dan Folino (Clive Cooper), Amy Baldwin (Mabel Halliday); Musicians: Doug Dorschug (fiddle), Tim Robertson/Steve Sensenig (piano), Brandon Story (bass); Barter Stage II; February 26–April 22, 2010

Always . . . Patsy Cline Written and directed by Ted Swindley; Music Director, Lee Harris; Set, Matthew Evans; Costume Coordinator, Adrienne Webber; Lighting, Michael Barnett; Sound, Bobby Beck; Stage Manager, Cindi A. Raebel; ASM, Jayme Tinti; Cast: Jessica Welch (Patsy Cline), Joy Hawkins (Louise Seger); Musicians: Lee Harris (piano), Brandon Story (bass), Gill Braswell (guitar), Mark Baczynski (fiddle), Roger Rettig (steel guitar), Michael Libramento (drums); Barter Theatre; April 23–May 23, 2010

Tuesdays With Morrie by Jeffrey Hatcher and Mitch Albom (based on his book); Director, Evalyn Baron; Set/Lighting, Cheri Prough DeVol; Costumes, Kelly Jenkins; Sound, Bobby Beck; Stage Manager, Holley Housewright; Cast: Danny Vaccaro (Mitch Albom), Gannon McHale (Morrie Schwartz), Iricia Matthews (Offstage Voice of Janine); Barter Stage II; April 30–August 29, 2010

Revolutions by Richard Alfieri; Director, Arthur Allan Seidelman; Choreographer, Amanda Aldridge; Dance Captain, Amy Baldwin; Set, Dale F. Jordan; Costumes, Kelly Jenkins; Lighting, Cheri Prough DeVol; Sound, Bobby Beck; Stage Manager, Holley Housewright; Cast: Mike Ostroski (Nick Greenberg), Amy Baldwin (Maddie Marston), Dan Folino (Nick Greenberg); Barter Stage II; May 13–August 14, 2010

Annie Book by Thomas Meehan music by Charles Strouse, lyrics by Martin Charnin; Director, Richard Rose; Music Director, Steve Sensenig; Choreographer, Amanda Aldridge; Dance Captain, Ashley Campos; Set, Michael C. Allen; Costumes, Amanda Aldridge; Lighting, Joshua Benghiat; Sound, Bobby Beck; Stage Manager, Cindi A. Raebel; ASM, Jayme Tinti; Cast: Virginia Rachel Pillion or Caroline Rose Wilson (Molly), Annie Osborne or Lily Brock (Ashley), Caitlyn Cornett or Lily Brock (Tessie), Kasey Rose Crawford or Chloe Smith (Tessie), Chloe Smith or Madison Elizabeth Chandler (Phoebe), Emma Harkins or Rachel Locke (Pepper), Aria Binkley or Rachel Locke (Duffy), Alexandra Eleas or Jessica Presnell (July), Tianna Jane Stevens (Annie), Tricia Matthews (Miss Hannigan), Rick McVey (Bundles McCloskey/FDR), David McCall (Dog Catcher/Bert Healy/Henry Morgenthau Jr.), Bryan Pridgen (Dog Catcher/Honor Guard), Stanley Doodle (Sandy), Ezra Colón (Lt. Ward/Sound Effects Man/Cordell Hull), Emelie Faith Thompson (Sophie, the Kettle/Connie Boylan), Hannah Ingram (Grace Farrell), Nathan Whitmer (Drake), Roslyn Seale (Mrs. Pugh), Mary Lucy Bivins (Mrs. Greer), Eugene Wolf (Oliver "Daddy" Warbucks), Sean Campos (Rooster Hannigan), Ashley Campos (Lily St. Regis), Carrie Smith (Bonnie Boylan/Frances Perkins), Julie Schroll (Ronnie Boylan), Ben Mackel (Apple Seller/Fred McCracken/Harold Ickes), J. Casey Barrett (Louis Howe), Michael Poisson (Justice Brandeis); Hooverville–ites/Policeman/Warbuck's Servant/New Yorkers: Mary Lucy Bivins, Ezra Colón, Ben Mackel, David McCall, Michael Poisson, Rebecca Reinhardt, Roslyn Seale, J. Casey Barrett, Bryan Pridgen, Carrie Smith, Julie Schroll, Emelie Faith Thompson, Nathan Whitmer: Conductor: Steve Sensenig; Barter Theatre; May 28–August 15, 2010

Of Mice and Men by John Steinbeck; Director, Katy Brown; Sets, Cheri Prough DeVol; Costumes, Amanda Aldridge; Lighting, Lucas Benjaminh Krech; Original Music, Ben Mackel; Sound, Bobby Beck; Props, Chase Molden; Wigs/Makeup, Ryan Fischer; Fight Choreographer, Mike Ostroski; Tour Producer, Evalyn Baron; Stage Manager, Holley Housewright; Tour Manager, Rebecca Reinhardt; Tour Lead Carpenter, Michael Catalan; Tour Carpenter/Audio/Dog Handler, Mollie Slattery; Tour Lighting/Audio Engineer, Scott Padrick; Tour Wardrobe Supervisor, Marcy Bates; Cast: John Hardy (George), Mike Ostroski (Lennie), Gannon McHale (Candy), Rick McVey (The Boss), Ben Mackel (Curley), Ashley Campos (Curley's Wife), Robin Bloodworth (Slim); David Dossey, (Carlson), Sean Campos (Whit), Vince McGill (Crooks); Fall 2009 National Tour

Berkeley Repertory Theatre

Berkeley, California

Forty-second Season

Artistic Director, Tony Taccone; Managing Director, Susan Medak; Associate Artistic Director, Les Waters

American Idiot Music by Green Day (Billie Joe Armstrong, Mike Dirnt, and Tré Cool), lyrics by Billie Joe Armstrong, book by Billie Joe Armstrong and Michael Mayer; Director, Michael Mayer; Choreography, Steven Hoggett; Set, Christine Jones; Costumes, Andrea Lauer; Lighting, Kevin Adams; Sound, Brian Ronan; Video and Projections, Darrel Maloney; Musical Director, Carel Dean; Stage Manager, James Harker; ASM Michael Suenkel; Musical Coordinator, Michael Keller; Casting, Jim Carnahan, Carrie Gardner; John Gallagher Jr. (Johnny), Michael Esper (Will), Matt Caplan (Tunny), Mary Faber (Heather), Rebecca Naomi Jones (Whatsername), Tony Vincent (St. Jimmy), Christina Sajous (The Extraordinary Girl); Ensemble: Declan Bennett, Andrew Call, Gerard Canonico, Miguel Cervantes, Joshua Henry, Brian Charles Johnson, Chase Peacock, Theo Stockman, Ben Thompson, Alysha Umphress, Morgan Weed, Libby Winters; Swings: Lorin Latarro, Omar Lopez-Cepero; World Premiere; Roda Theatre; September 4–November 15, 2009

Tiny Kushner Plays by Tony Kushner; Included: *Flip Flop Fly!*, *Terminating or Sonnet LXXV or "Lass Meine Schmerzen Nicht Verloren Sein" or Ambivalence*; *East Coast Ode to Howard Jarvis: a little teleplay in tiny monologues*; *Dr. Arnold A. Hutschnecker in Paradise*; *Only We Who Guard the Mystery Shall Be Unhappy*; Director, Tony Taccone; Set, Annie Smart; Costumes, Anita Yavich; Lighting/Projections, Alexander V. Nichols; Sound, Victor Zupanc; Voice and Speech Consultant, Lynne Soffer; Movement, Marcela Lorca; Stage Manager, Kimberly Mark Webb; Assistant Director, Mina Morita; Cast: Jim Lichtscheidl, Valeri Mudek, Kate Eifrig, J.C. Cutler; West Coast Premiere; Thrust Stage; October 16–November 29, 2009

Aurélia's Oratorio Created, directed, and stage design by Victoria Thierrée Chaplin in collaboration with La Compagnie du Hanneton; Presented by Théâtre L'Avant-Scène and La Ferme du Buisson Cognac/René Marion; Lighting, Laura de Bernadis and Phillipe Lacombe; Costumes, Victoria Thierrée Chaplin, Jacques Perdiguez, Veronique Grand, Monika Schwarzl; Technical Director/Stage Manager, Gerd Walter; Company Manager, Didier Bendel; Technicians, Roberto Riegert, Nicholas Lazzaro; Crew, Tamara Prieto Arroyo, Antonia Paradsio; Cast: Aurélia Thierrée, Jaime Martinez; Roda Theatre; December 4, 2009–January 31, 2010

Coming Home by Athol Fugard; Director, Gordon Edelstein; Set, Eugene Lee; Costumes, Jessica Ford; Lighting and Projections, Stephen Strawbridge; Sound, Corrine K. Livingston; Original Compositions, John Gromada; Voice and Speech Consultant, Lynne Soffer; Stage Manager, Michael Suenkel; Assistant to the Director, Todd Yocher; Vocal Coach, Robert Rutt; Cast: Roslyn Ruff (Veronica Jonkers), Kohle T. Bolton (Mannetjie Jonkers [younger]), Jaden Malik Wiggins (Mannetjie Jonkers [older]), Thomas Silcott (Alfred Witbooi), Lou Ferguson (Oupa Jonkers); Understudies: Brandon Charles (Young Mannetjie), Victor McElhaney (Older Mannetjie); Thrust Stage; January 15–February 28, 2010

Concerning Strange Devices from the Distant West by Naomi Iizuka; Director, Les Waters; Set, Mimi Lien; Costumes, Annie Smart; Lighting, Alexander V. Nichols; Sound & Original Music, Bray Poor; Video & Projections, Leah Gelpe; Dramaturg, Madeleine Oldham; Stage Manager, Karen Szpaller; Casting, Amy Potozkin, Janet Foster; Assistant Director, Mina Morita; Cast: Kate Eastwood Norris (Isabel Hewlett), Johnny Wu, Hiro/Tattooed Man/Insect Peddler/Blind Monk), Bruce McKenzie (Andrew Farsari/Dmitri Mendelssohn), Teresa Avia Lim (Kiku/Woman in a Kimono/Servant Girl), Danny Wolohan (Edmund Hewlett); World Premiere; Roda Theatre; February 26–April 11, 2010

Girlfriend Book by Todd Almond, music and lyrics by Matthew Sweet; Director, Les Waters; Choreography, Joe Goode; Vocal Arrangements/Additional Orchestrations, Todd Almond; Set/Costumes, David Zinn; Lighting, Japhy Weideman; Sound, Jake Rodriguez; Music Director, Julie Wolf; Stage Manager, Michael Suenkel; Assistant Director, Mina Morita; Cast: Ryder Bach (Will), Jason Hite (Mike), Tyler Costin (Understudy); Musicians: Julie Wolf (guitar/keyboards/backing vocals), Shelly Doty (lead guitar/backing vocals), Jean DuSablon (bass), ieela Grant (drums); World Premiere; Thrust Stage; April 9–May 16, 2010

In the Wake by Lisa Kron; Director, Leigh Silverman; Set, David Korins; Costumes, Meg Neville; Lighting and Projections, Alexander V. Nichols; Sound,

Cricket S. Myers; Dramaturg, Pier Carlo Talenti; Casting, Bonnie Grisan, Amy Potozkin, Erika Sellin; Stage Manager, Elizabeth Atkinson; Assistant Director, Elissa Weinzimmer; Cast: Heidi Schreck (Ellen), Carson Elrod (Danny), Andrea Frankle (Kayla), Danielle Skraastad (Laurie), Emily Donahoe (Amy), Deirdre O'Connell (Judy), Miriam F. Glover (Tessa); World Premiere; Roda Theatre; May 14–June 27, 2010

Berkshire Theatre Festival

Stockbridge, Massachusetts

Eighty-first Season

Artistic Director, Kate Maguire; Administrative Producer, M. Edgar Rosenblum

Main Stage

The Einstein Project by Paul D'Andrea and Jon Klein; Director, Eric Hill; Cast: Tommy Schrider (Albert Einstein), James Barry (Werner Heisenberg); July 4–18, 2009

The Prisoner of Second Avenue by Neil Simon; Director, Warner Shook; Cast: Stephen DeRosa (Mel Edison), Veanne Cox (Edna Edison); July 25–August 8, 2009

Ghosts by Henrik Ibsen, adapted by Anders Cato and James Leverett; Director, Anders Cato; Cast: Jonathan Epstein (Engstrand), Randy Harrison (Oswald), Mia Dillon (Mrs. Alving), David Adkins (Pastor Manders), Tara Franklin (Regina); August 15–29, 2009

Unicorn Theatre

Faith Healer by Brian Friel; Director, Eric Hill; Cast: Colin Lane (Frank), Keira Naughton (Grace), David Adkins (Teddy); May 23–July 4, 2009

Candide Music by Leonard Bernstein, book adapted from Voltaire by Hugh Wheeler, lyrics by Richard Wilbur, additional lyrics by Stephen Sondheim and John LaTouche; Director, Ralph Petillo; Cast: Julian Whitley (Candide), McCaela Donovan (Cunégonde), Ben Rosenblatt (Dr. Pangloss), Kyle Schaefer (Maximilian), Matt Stern (The Governor), Becky Webber (Paquett), Julia Broder (The Old Woman), Michael Brahce (Man No. 1), Robert McFadyen (Man No. 2), Samantha Richert (Woman No. 1); July 11–August 15, 2009

Sick by Zayd Dohrn; Director, David Auburn; Cast: Rebecca Brooksher (Sarah), Lisa Emery (Maxine), Michel Gill (Sidney), Greg Keller (Jim), Ryan Spahn (Davey); August 22–September 6, 2009

Red Remembers by Andrew Guerdat; Director, John Rando; Cast: David Garrison (Red Barber); September 12–November, 2009

California Shakespeare Theatre

Berkeley/Orinda, California

Thirty-sixth Season
Artistic Director, Jonathan Moscone; Managing Director, Susie Falk

Romeo and Juliet by William Shakespeare; Director, Jonathan Moscone; Sets, Neil Patel; Costumes, Raquel M. Barreto; Lighting, Russell H. Champa; Sound, Andre Pluess; Dramaturg, Philippa Kelly; Fight Director, Dave Maier; Choreographer, Marybeth Cavanaugh; Text Coach, Nancy Carlin; PSM, Briana J. Fahey; Casting, Jessica Richards; ASM, Elizabeth Atkinson; Production Assistant, Heather Robinson; Assistant Director, Nara Dahlbacka; Assistant to the Choreographer, Marilet Martinez; Cast: Julian López-Morillas (Prince), Avery Monsen (Sampson/Peter/Balthazar), Nick Childress (Gregory/Paris' Page), Patrick Lane (Abraham/Ensemble), Thomas Azar (Benvolio), Craig Marker (Tybalt), James Carpenter (Capulet), Julie Eccles (Lady Capulet), L. Peter Callender (Montague/

A scene from Barter Theatre's Alice in Wonderland
(photo by Leah Prater)

John Gallagher Jr. in American Idiot at Berkeley Repertory Theatre
(photo by Kevin Berne)

Veanne Cox and Stephen DeRosa in Berkshire Theatre Festival's
The Prisoner of Second Avenue (photo by Lindsey Crane)

Cherene Snow in Black Pearl Sings! at the Merrimack Repertory Theatre
(photo by Meghan Moore)

Ryder Bach and Jason Hite in Girlfriend at Berkeley Repertory
Theatre (photo by Kevin Berne)

Stephen Barker Turner, Sarah Nealis, and Jud Williford in Private Lives *at California Shakespeare Theatre (photo by Kevin Berne)*

Jonathan Putnam and Geoffrey Nelson in the CATCO production of The Mystery of Irma Vep *(photo by David Alkire)*

Nicole Lowrance and Gretchen Hall in The Importance of Being Earnest *at CENTERSTAGE (photo by Richard Anderson)*

Lara Pulver and T.R. Knight in the Donmar Warehouse production of Parade *at Center Theater Group's Mark Taper Forum (photo by Craig Schwartz)*

Apothecary), Catherine Castellanos (Lady Montague/Nurse), Alex Morf (Romeo), Liam Vincent (Paris), Sarah Nealis (Juliet), Jud Williford (Mercutio/Friar John), Dan Hiatt (Friar Lawrence), Matt Hooker (Ensemble), Marilet Martinez (Ensemble), Ashley Wickett (Ensemble); Bruns Memorial Amphitheater; May 27–June 21, 2009

Private Lives by Noël Coward; Director Mark Rucker; Sets, Annie Smart; Costumes, Katherine Roth; Lighting, Scott Zielinski; Sound, Jeff Mockus; Dialect/Text Coach, Lynne Soffer; Fight Director, Dave Maier; PSM, Elizabeth Atkinson; ASM, Briana J. Fahey; Casting, Janet Foster & Jessica Richards; SDC Noël Coward Directing Fellow, Amy Anders Corcoran; Assistant Lighting, Devin S. Cruickshank; Assistant Set, Drew Kaufman; Production Assistant, Christina Hogan; Cast: Sarah Nealis (Sibyl Chase), Stephen Barker Turner (Elyot Chase), Jud Williford (Victor Prynne), Diana Lamar (Amanda Prynne), Liam Vincent (Louis); Bruns Memorial Amphitheater; July 8–August 2, 2009

Happy Days by Samuel Beckett; Director, Jonathan Moscone; Sets, Todd Rosenthal; Costumes, Meg Neville; Lighting, York Kennedy; Sound, Bradford Chapin; Dramaturg, Philippa Kelly; PSM, Briana J. Fahey; ASM, Elizabeth Atkinson; Assistant Director, Alan Patrick Kenny; Company Management Assistant, Nara Dahlbacka; Cast: Patty Gallagher (Winnie), Dan Hiatt (Willie); Bruns Memorial Amphitheater; August 12–September 6, 2009

A Midsummer Night's Dream by William Shakespeare; Director, Aaron Posner; Sets, Brian Sidney Bembridge; Costumes, Oliver Gajic; Lighting, Peter West; Sound, Andre Pluess; Dramaturg, Philippa Kelly; Fight Director, Dave Maier; Choreographer, Erika Chong Shuch; Vocal/Text Coach, Domenique Lozano; PSM, Elizabeth Atkinson; Casting, Jessica Richards & Liz Green; ASM, Briana J. Fahey; Production Assistant, Christina Hogan; Assistant Director, Kate Jopson; Cast: Ted Barker (Starveling), Patty Gallagher (P.T. Quince), Lance Gardner (Flute), Lindsey Gates (Helena), Doug Hara (Puck), Dan Hiatt (Snout/Egeus), Pegge Johnson (Titania/Hippolyta), Joan Mankin (Snug/Philostrate), Avery Monsen (Lysander), Danny Scheie (Bottom), Keith Randolph Smith (Oberon/Theseus), Richard Thieriot (Demetrius), Erin Weaver (Hermia); Bruns Memorial Amphitheater; September 16–October 11, 2009

The Contemporary American Theatre Company (CATCO)

Columbus, Ohio

Artistic Director, Geoffrey Nelson; Managing Director, T.J. Gerckens

Production Manager, T.J. Gerckens; Assistant Production Manager, Whitney W. Thiessen; Technical Director, Christopher G. Clapp; Master Electrician, Keya Myers-Alkire; Costume Studio Manager, Tatjana Longerot; Charge Scenic Artist, Edith Dinger Wadkins;

Blackbird by David Harrower; Director, Geoffrey Nelson; Sets, Jessica Trent-Secrest; Costumes, Kristine Kearney; Lighting, Jim Hutchison; Sound, Curtis A. Brown; Props, Edith Dinger Wadkins; PSM, Cheryl Ruschau; Stage Manager, Jennifer Kramer; ASM, J. Jackson; Dramaturge, Diane Rao; Fight Choreographer, Jeanine Thompson; Cast: Anna Paniccia (Una), Jonathan Putnam (Ray), Marisa Jean Riegle (Girl); Riffe Center Studio Two Theatre; June 3–21, 2009

Murderers by Jeffrey Hatcher; Director, Jonathan Putnam; Sets, Edith Dinger-Wadkins; Costumes, Mary Yaw McMullen; Lighting, Jason C. Banks; Sound, Keya Myers-Alkire; PSM, Cheryl Ruschau; ASM, Erika Prizzi; Dramaturge, Ann C. Hall; Cast: Matthew M. Moore (Gerald Halverson), Kerry Shanklin (Lucy Stickler), Jill Taylor (Minka Lupino); Riffe Center Studio Two Theatre; September 30–October 18, 2009

The Seafarer by Conor McPherson; Director, Mandy Fox; Sets, Dan Gray; Costumes, Tatjana Longerot; Lighting, Darin Keesing; Sound, Keya Myers-Alkire; Props, Stacey E. Siak; Dramaturge, C. Austin Hill; PSM, Cheryl Ruschau; ASM, Erika Prizzi; Dialect Coach, Mandy Fox; Cast: Mark Mann (James "Sharky"

Harkin), Ken Erney (Richard Harkin), Damian Bowerman (Ivan Curry), Rick Clark (Nicky Giblin), Geoffrey Nelson (Mr. Lockhart); Riffe Center Studio One Theatre; November 24–December 13, 2009

The Santaland Diaries by David Sedaris, adapted for the stage by Joe Mantello; Director, Geoffrey Nelson; Costumes, Tatjana Longerot; Sound, Keya Myers-Alkire; Stage Manager: Michael Lorr; Cast: Jonathan Putnam (David Sedaris); Riffe Center Studio Three Theatre; December 3–27, 2009

Evie's Waltz by Carter W. Lewis; Director, Ed Vaughan; Sets, Stephanie R. Gerckens; Costumes, Tatjana Longerot; Lighting, Marcus Wuebker; Sound, Keya Myers-Alkire; Props, Stacey E. Siak; PSM, Cheryl Ruschau; ASM, Erika Prizzi; Dramaturge, Nicholas Dekker; Special Effects Designer, Gregory Bell; Cast: Ralph Scott (Clay), Mandy Fox (Gloria), Caitlin Morris (Evie); Riffe Center Studio Two Theatre; February 17–March 7, 2010

Pierce to the Soul, by Chiquita Mullins Lee; Director, Geoffrey Nelson; Sets, Edith Dinger Wadkins; Costumes, Kelly McBane; Lighting, Cynthia Stillings; Sound, Keya Myers-Alkire; Props, Stacey E. Siak; PSM, Cheryl Ruschau; ASM, Erika Prizzi; Dramaturge, Bill Childs; Cast: Alan Bomar Jones (Elijah Pierce); World Premiere; Riffe Center Studio Two Theatre; April 7–25, 2010

The Mystery of Irma Vep, A Penny Dreadful, by Charles Ludlam; Directors, Geoffrey Nelson and Jeanine Thompson; Sets, D. Glen Vanderbilt; Costumes, Cynthia Turnbull; Lighting, Mary Tarantino; Sound, Keya Myers-Alkire; Props, Edith Dinger Wadkins; PSM, Cheryl Ruschau; ASM, Erika Prizzi; Dramaturge, James Bailey; Cast: Geoffrey Nelson (Nicodemus Underwood/Lady Enid Hillcrest/others), Jonathan Putnam (Jane Twisden/Lord Edgar Hillcrest/others); Riffe Center Studio Two Theatre; June 2, 2010–June 27, 2010

CENTERSTAGE

Baltimore, Maryland

Forty-seventh Season

Artistic Director, Irene Lewis; Managing Director, Michael Ross

Pearlston Series

The Importance of Being Earnest by Oscar Wilde; Director, Irene Lewis; Set, Riccardo Hernández; Costumes, Candice Donelly; Lighting, Paul Whitaker; Sound, Mark Bennett; Choreography, Nicco Annan; Dialect and Text Coach, Gillan Lane-Plescia; Production Dramaturg, Gavin Witt; Casting, Janet Foster; Stage Manager, Lori M. Doyle; ASM, Captain Kate Murphy; Cast: Luke Robertson (Algernon Moncrieff), Bill Kux (Lanel Merriman), Ben Huber (John "Jack" Worthing), Laurence O'Dwyer (Lady Bracknell), Grechen Hall (Gwendolen Fairfax), Carmen Roman (Miss Prism), Nicole Lowrance (Cecily Cardew), John Rothman (Rev. anon Chasuble); October 7–November 8, 2009

Around the World in 80 Days by Jules Verne, adapted and directed by Laura Eason; Presented in association with the Lookingglass Theatre; Set, Jacqueline & Richard Penrod; Costumes, Mara Blumenfeld; Lighting, Lee Keenan; Sound, Joshua Horvath; Composer, Kevin O'Donnell; Movement, Tracy Walsh; Dialects, Eva Breneman; Fight Director, Nick Sandys; Dramaturg, Drew Lichtenberg; Original Dramaturgy, Margot Bordelon & Cassandra Sanders; Stage Manager, Bret Torbeck; ASM, Captain Kate Murphy; Cast: Usman Ally (Mr. Naidu/others), Rom Barkhordar (Captain Speedy/others), Ravi Batista (Mrs. Aouda), John Dempsy (Inspector Fix), Kevin Douglas (Passepartout), Patrick New (Colonel Proctor/others), Ericka Ratcliff (Captain Von Darius/others), Philip R. Smith (Phileas Fogg); November 24–December 30, 2009

The Santaland Diaries by David Sedaris, adapted by Joe Mantello; Director, Irene Lewis; Set, Jennifer Stearns; Costumes, David Burdick; Lighting, Lesley Boeckman; Sound, Amy Wedel; Stage Manager, Captain Kate Murphy; Cast: Robert Dorman; December 8–20, 2009

Let There Be Love by Kwame Kwei-Armah; Director, Jeremy B. Cohen; Set, Riccardo Hernandez; Costumes, Miranda Hoffman; Lighting, Michelle Habeck; Sound, Lindsay Jones; Speech Consultant, Gillian Lane Plescia; Dramaturg, Gavin Witt; Casting, Janet Foster; Stage Mangers, Captain Kate Murphy, Laura Smith; Cast: Avery Brooks (Alfred), U.S. Premiere; February 10–March 7, 2010

Ma Rainey's Black Bottom by August Wilson; Produced in association with Philadelphia Theatre Company; Director, Ilene Lewis; Set, Riccardo Hernández; Costumes, Candice Donnelly; Lighting, Rui Rita; Sound, David Budries; Music Director, William Foster McDaniel; Cast: Ro Boddie (Sylvester), E. Faye Butler (Ma Rainey), Thomas Jefferson Byrd (Toledo), Toccarra Cash (Dussie Mae), David Fonteno (Cutler), Merwin Goldsmith (Irvin), Jeb Kreager (Policeman), Maurice McRae (Levee), Laurence O'Dwyer (Sturdyvant), Ernest Perry (Slow Drag); April 7–May 9, 2010

Short Works Series

Cyrano Adapted by Jo Rowat; Director, David Schweizer; Set, Caleb Wertenbaker; Costumes, David Burdick; Lighting, Russell Champa; Original Music and Sound, Ryan Rumery; Fight Choreography, J. Allen Suddeth; Dramaturg, Drew Lichtenberg; Casting, Janet Foster; Cast: Manu Narayan (Cyrano), Sarah Grace Wilson (Roxane/others), Luke Robertson (Christian/others); January 13–February 7, 2010

Working It Out A trio of short pieces: *Jerry & Tom* by Rick Cleveland, *Washed Up on the Potomac* by Lynn Rosen, and *Hidden in This Picture* by Aaron Sorkin; Director, Jason Loewith; Set, Neil Patel; Costumes, David Burdick; Lighting, Colin Bills; Sound, Victoria Delorio; Fight Choreography J. Allen Suddeth; Dramaturg, Kristi Banker; Casting, Janet Foster; Stage Manager, Laura Smith; Cast: *Jerry & Tom*: Vasili Bogazianos (Tom), John Ramsey (Tony/others), Luke Robertson (Jerry); *Washed Up on the Potomac*: Garrett Neergaard (Carl), Katie Jefferies (Tina), Amy Hohn (Ruth), Kate Buddeke (Deb), Joseph Wycoff (Unseen Guy); *Hidden in This Picture*: John Ramsey (Reuben), Joseph Wycoff (Robert), Garrett Neergaard (Jeff), Amy Hohn (Christine); March 3–28, 2010

Concert Readings

after the quake by Haruki Murakami, adapted by Frank Galati (April 8–11, 2010); **Wrestling with Angels**: New Perspectives on the Middle East, included: *Benedictus* by Motti Lerner, *Seven Jewish Children* by Caryl Children, *Only We Who Guard the Mystery Shall Be Unhappy* by Tony Kushner; April 15–18, 2010; **East of Berlin** by Hannah Moscovitch; April 22–25, 2010

Cabaret Series

Judy Kaye (October 15–18, 2009); Euan Morton (November 12–15, 2009); E. Faye Butler (February 11–14, 2010); Tracie Thoms and Friends (April 29–May 2, 2010)

Center Theatre Group

Los Angeles, California

Forty-third Season

Artistic Director, Michael Ritchie; Managing Director, Charles Dillingham

Ahmanson Theatre

An Evening with Patti LuPone and Mandy Patinkin Conceived by Mandy Patinkin and Paul Ford; Director, Mandy Patinkin; Production Design, David Korins; Lighting, Eric Cornwell; Sound, Daniel J. Gerhard; Choreography, Ann Reinking; Executive Producer, Staci Levine; Stage Manager/Lighting Supervisor, Matthew Aaron Stern and Peter Wolf; Assistant Stage Manager/Company Manager, Laura Skolnik; Cast: Patti LuPone (Herself), Mandy Patinkin (Himself); June 23–29, 2009

Spamalot Book and lyrics by Eric Idle, music by John DuPrez and Eric Idle; Based on the original screenplay by Graham Chapman, John Cleese, Terry Gil-liam, Eric Idle, Terry Jones, Michael Palin; Director, Mike Nichols; Choreographer, Casey Nicholaw; Associate Directors, Peter Lawrence and BT McNicholl; Associate Producers, Randi Grossman and Tisch/Avnet Financial; Musical Director, Ben Whiteley; Sets/Costumes, Tim Hatley; Lighting, Hugh Vanstone; Sound, Acme Sound Partners; Casting, Tara Rubin Casting; Wigs/Hair, David Brian Brown; Special Effects, Gregory Meeh; Projections, Elaine J. McCarthy; Musical Supervision/Vocal Arrangements, Todd Ellison; Orchestrations, Larry Hochman; Music Arrangements, Glen Kelly; Music Coordination, Michael Keller; Makeup, Joseph A. Campayno; PSM, Kenneth J. Davis; Stage Manager, Jovon E. Shuck; Cast: Matt Allen (Nun/Killer Rabbit/Ensemble), James Beaman (Sir Robin/Guard 1/Brother Maynard), Graham Bowen (Swing/Dance Captain), Nigel Columbus (Swing), Merle Dandridge (The Lady of the Lake), Lenny Daniel (Monk/French Guard/Ensemble), Ben Davis (Sir Dennis Galahad/The Black Knight/Prince Herbert's Father), Jeff Dumas (Mayor/Patsy/Guard 2), Andrew Fitch (Sir Not Appearing/Ensemble; July 22–September 6), David Havasi (French Guard/Minstrel/Ensemble), Erik Hayden (Sir Not Appearing/Ensemble; July 7–July 21), Rick Holmes (Sir Lancelot/The French Taunter/Knight of Ni/Tim the Enchanter; July 7–August 2), Matthew Greer (Sir Lancelot/The French Taunter/Knight of Ni/Tim the Enchanter; August 4–September 6), Christopher Gurr (Dennis's Mother/Sir Bedevere/Concorde/Fight Captain), Sarah Lin Johnson (Swing), John O'Hurley (King Arthur), Tera-Lee Pollin (Swing, Assistant Dance Captain), Darryl Semira (Minstrel/Sir Bars/Ensemble), Christopher Sutton (Historian/Not Dead Fred/French Guard/Minstrel/Prince Herbert), Steven Wenslawski (Monk), Paula Wise (Minstrel/Ensemble); Ensemble: Timothy Connell, Cara Cooper, Alexa Glover, Carissa Lopez, Jennifer Mathie, Vanessa Sonon; Understudies: Lyn Philistine; National Touring Company; July 7–September 6, 2009

August: Osage County by Tracy Letts; Presented by the Steppenwolf Theatre Company; Director, Anna D. Shapiro; Sets, Todd Rosenthal; Costumes, Ana Kuzmanic; Lighting, Ann G. Wrightson; Sound, Richard Woodbury; Original Music, David Singer; Casting, Stuart Howard, Amy Schecter, Paul Hardt; Fight Choreography, Chuck Coyl; Production Supervisor, Jane Grey; Technical Supervisor, Theatersmith, Inc./Smitty; PSM, William Gilinsky; Stage Manager, Cambra Overend; Cast: Shannon Cochran (Barbara Fordham), John DeVries (Beverly Weston), Libby George (Mattie Fae Aiken), Stephen Riley Key (Little Charles Aiken), Emily Kinney (Jean Fordham), Laurence Lau (Steve Heidebrecht), Marcus Nelson (Sheriff Deon Gilbeau), Paul Vincent O'Connor (Charlie Aiken), Estelle Parsons (Violet Weston), Jeff Still (Bill Fordham), DeLanna Studi (Johanna Monevata), Angelica Torn (Ivy Weston), Amy Warren (Karen Weston); Understudies: Avia Bushyhead, Stephen D'Ambrose, Barbara Kingsley, Bryn Magnus, Kim Martin-Cotton, Marcus Nelson, Cambra Overend; National Touring Company; September 8–October 18, 2009

Mary Poppins Music and lyrics by Richard M. Sherman and Robert B. Sherman, book by Julian Fellowes; New songs and additional music and lyrics by George Stiles and Anthony Drewe; Based on the stories of P.L. Travers and the Walt Disney Film; Director, Richard Eyre; Co-creator, Cameron Mackintosh; Producer, Thomas Schumacher; Music Supervisor, David Caddick; Music Director, James Dodgson; Orchestrations, William David Brohn; Sound, Steve Canyon Kennedy; Dance and Vocal Arrangements, George Stiles; Co-choreographer, Stephen Mear; Set and Costumes, Bob Crowley; Lighting, Howard Harrison; PSM, Lois L. Griffing; Stage Manager, Jimmie Lee Smith; Cast: Katie Balen (Jane Banks), Bryce Baldwin (Michael Banks), Valerie Boyle (Mrs. Brill), Ashley Brown (Mary Poppins), Michael Gerhart (Von Hussler), Bailey Grey (Jane Banks), Ellen Harvey (Miss Smythe/Katie Nanna/Miss Andrew), Wendy James (Miss Lark), Andrew Keenan-Bolger (Robertson Ay), Karl Kenzler (George Banks), Gavin Lee (Bert), Brian Letendre (Neleus), Laird Mackintosh (Policeman), Mike O'Carroll (Admiral Boom), Megan Osterhaus (Winifred Banks), Dominic Roberts (Northbrook), Nick Sanchez (Valentine), Tom Souhrada (Park Keeper), Q. Smith (Mrs. Corry), Carter Thomas (Michael Banks), Mary VanArsdel (Bird Woman); Ensemble: Tia Altinay, Carol Angeli, Gail Bennett, Kiara Bennett, Brandon Bieber, Elizabeth Broadhurst, Michael Gerhart, Geoffrey Goldberg, Emily Harvey, Tiffany Howard, Wendy James, Justin Keyes, Sam Kiernan, Brian Letendre, Laird Mackintosh, Koh Mochizuki, Shua Potter, Dominic Roberts, Nick Sanchez, Tom Souhrada; National Touring Company; November 13, 2009–February 7, 2010

Dreamgirls Book and lyrics by Tom Eyen, music by Henry Krieger, with additional material by Willie Reale; Director and Choreographer, Robert Longbottom; Sets, Robin Wagner; Costumes, William Ivey Long; Lighting, Ken Billington; Sound, Acme Sound Partners; Media Design, Howard Werner/Lightswitch; Hair, Paul Huntley; Music Direction, Sam Davis; Orchestrations, Harold Wheeler; Vocal Arrangements, David Chase & Cleavant Derricks; PSM, Ray Gin; Casting, Jay Binder/Mark Brandon; Co-choreographer, Shane Sparks; Cast: Moya Angela (Effie White), Felicia Boswell (Stepp Sister), Tallia Brinson (Stepp Sister), Patrice Covington (Pit Singer), Trevon Davis (C.C. White), Emily Ferranti (Sweetheart), Stephanie Gibson (Sweetheart), Chester Gregory (James "Thunder" Early), James Harkness (Tiny Joe Dixon), Robert Hartwell (Tru-Tone), Margaret Hoffman (Michelle Morris), Chauncey Jenkins (Tru-Tone), Jared Joseph (M.C.), Nikki Kimbrough (Stepp Sister), Douglas Lyons (Tru-Tone), Kimberly Marable (Stepp Sister), Syesha Mercado (Deena Jones), Jarran Muse (Tru-Tone), Milton Craig Nealy (Marty), Chaz Lamar Shepherd (Curtis Taylor Jr.), Adrienne Warren (Lorrell Robinson), Marc Spaulding (Little Albert), Bret Shuford (Dave); Ensemble: Ronald Duncan, Talitha Farrow, Brittney Griffin, Eric Jackson, Brittany Lewis, Amaker Smith; National Touring Company; February 25–April 4, 2010

The 39 Steps Adapted by Patrick Barlow; Based on an Original Concept by Simon Corble and Nobby Dimon; Based on the book by John Buchan; Director, Maria Aitken; Lighting, Kevin; Sound, Mic Pool; Original Movement, Toby Sedgwick; Additional Movement, Christopher Bayes; Production Manager, Aurora Productions; PSM, Harold Goldfaden; Casting, Jay Binder/Jack Bowdan; Dialect Coach, Stephen Gabis; Associate Producer, Howard Tilkin; Executive Producer, 101 Productions Ltd.; Tour Director, Nevin Hedley; Set/Costumes, Peter McKintosh; Cast: Claire Brownell (Annabella Schmidt/Pamela/Margaret), Ted Deasy (Richard Hannay), Eric Hissom (Man #1), Scott Parkinson (Man #2); Understudies: Sheffield Chastain, Allison Jean White; National Touring Company; April 27–May 16, 2010

South Pacific Music by Richard Rogers, lyrics by Oscar Hammerstein II, book by Oscar Hammerstein II and Joshua Logan; Adapted from the novel *Tales of the South Pacific* by James A. Michener; Presented by Lincoln Center Theater; Director, Bartlett Sher; Sets, Michael Yeargan; Costumes, Catherine Zuber; Lighting, Donald Holder; Sound, Scott Lehrer; Orchestrations, Robert Russell Bennett; Dance and Incidental Music Arrangements, Trude Rittmann; Casting, Tesley + Company; Music Coordination, David Lai; PSM, Brian J. L'Ecuyer; Stage Manager, Rachel Zack; Music Conduction, Lawrence Goldberg; Company Manager, Joel T. Herbst; Production Manager, Justin Reiter; General Manager, Gregory Vander Ploeg Gentry & Associates; Executive Producer, Seth C. Wenig; Music Director, Ted Sperling; Musical Staging, Christopher Gattelli; Cast: Gerry Becker (Capt. George Brackett), Genson Blimline (Stewpot/Voice over Loudspeaker), Christina Carrera (Ngana), Eric L. Christian (Kenneth Johnson), Jacqueline Colmer (Assistant Dance Captain/Swing), Carmen Cusack (Ensign Nellie Forbush), Anderson Davis (Lt. Joseph Cable), Jeremy Davis (Lt. Buzz Adams), Mike Evariste (Henry/James Hayes), Kate Fahrner (Ensign Dinah Murphy), Nicholas Galbraith (Johnny Noonan), Rod Gilfry (Emile de Becque); May 27–June 20), Alexis G.B. Holt (Bloody Mary's Assistant), Robert Hunt (Richard West), Chad Jennings (Radio Operator Bob McCaffrey), Christopher Johnstone (Thomas Hassinger), Kristie Kerwin (Ensign Sue Yaegar), Jodi Kimura (Bloody Mary's Assistant), Joe Langworth (Dance Captain/Swing), Sumie Maeda (Liat), Cathy Newman (Lt. Geneviere Marshall), CJ Palma (Jerome), Diane Phelan (Ensign Cora MacRae/Bloody Mary's Assistant), John Pinto Jr. (Yeoman Herbert Quale), David Pittsinger (Emile de Becque; June 22–July 17), Peter Rini (Cmdr. William Harbison), Travis Robertson (Tom O'Brien), Rusty Ross (Professor), Josh Rouah (Lt. Eustis), Matthew Saldivar (Luther Billis), Keala Settle (Bloody Mary), Kristen J. Smith (Ensign Connie Walewska), Matt Stokes (Swing), Gregory Williams (Swing), Victor J. Wisehart (Morton Wise); National Touring Company; May 27–July 17, 2010

Kirk Douglas Theatre

Eclipsed by Danai Gurira; Director, Robert O'Hara; Sets, Sibyl Wickersheimer; Costumes, Alex Jaeger; Lighting, Christopher Kuhl; Sound, Adam Phalen; Composer, Kathryn Bostic; Fight Direction, Steve Rankin; Dialect Coach, Joel Goldes; Casting, Bonnie Grisan; Associate Producer, Kelley Kirkpatrick; PSM,

Amy Bristol Brownewell; Stage Manager, Elle Aghabala; Cast: Edwina Findley (Number Three), Miriam F. Glover (The Girl), Michael Hyatt (Rita), Kelly M. Jenrette (Number Two), Bahni Turpin (Number One); West Coast premiere; September 13–October 18, 2009

The Wake by Lisa Kron; Director, Leigh Silverman; Co-produced with Berkeley Repertory Theatre; Sets, David Korins; Costumes, Meg Neville; Lighting and Projections, Alexander V. Nichols; Sound, Cricket S. Myers; Casting, Bonnie Grisan; Amy Potoozkin, Erika Sellin; Associate Producer, Kelley Kirkpatrick; PSM, Elizabeth Atkinson; Stage Manager, Elle Aghabala; Cast: Emily Donahoe (Amy), Carson Elrod (Danny), Andrea Frankle (Kayla), Miriam F. Glover (Tessa), Deirdre O'Connell (Judy), Heidi Screck (Ellen), Danielle Skaastad (Laurie); World Premiere; March 21–April 18, 2010

Palomino Written and directed by David Cale; Sets, Takeshi Kata; Costumes, Laura Bauer; Lighting, Beverly Emmons; Sound, Andre Pluess; Projection, Jason H. Thompson; Associate Producer, Kelley Kirkpatrick; PSM, William Joseph Barnes; Cast: David Cale; West Coast premiere; May 7–June 6, 2010

Mark Taper Forum

Oleanna by David Mamet; Director, Doug Hughes; Sets, Neil Patel; Costumes, Catherine Zuber; Lighting, Donald Holder; Fight Direction, Rick Sordelet; Associate Producer, Ann E. Wareham; PSM, Charles Means; Stage Manager, Marti McIntosh; Cast: Bill Pullman (John), Julia Stiles (Carol); Understudies: Blair Baker, Marty Lodge; May 28–July 12, 2009

Parade Music and lyrics by Jason Robert Brown, book by Alfred Uhry; Co-conceived by Harold Prince; Presented by the Donmar Warehouse; Director/ Choreographer, Rob Ashford; Musical Direction, Tom Murray; Sets/Costumes, Christopher Oram; Lighting, Neil Austin; Original London Sound, Nick Lidster and Terry Jardine for Autograph; Sound, Jon Weston; Casting, Erika Sellin; Wigs/Hair, Carol F. Doran; Associate Choreographer, Chris Bailey; Orchestrator, David Cullen; Associate Producer, Neel Keller; PSM, David S. Franklin; Stage Managers, Michelle Blair and Susie Walsh; Dance Captain, Sarah Jayne Jensen; Cast: Brad Anderson (Officer Ivey/Luther Rosser/Guard), Michael Berresse (Governor Slaton/Britt Craig/Mr. Peavy), Charlotte d'Amboise (Mrs. Phagan/ Sally Slaton), Davis Gaines (Old Soldier/Judge Roan/Guard), P.J. Griffith (Officer Starnes/Tom Watson), Curt Hansen (Young Soldier/Frankie Epps/Guard), Deidrie Henry (Minnie McKnight/Angela), Christian Hoff (Hugh Dorsey), T.R. Knight (Leo Frank), Lisa Livesay (Monteen), Hayley Podschun (Iola Stover), Lara Pulver (Lucille Frank), David St. Louis (Newt Lee/Jim Conley/Riley), Rose Sezniak (Lila/ Mary Phagan), Phoebe Strole (Essie); Ensemble: Will Collyer, Karole Foreman, Laura Griffith, Sarah Jayne Jensen, Josh Tower, Robert Yacko; September 24–November 15, 2009

Palestine, New Mexico by Richard Montoya for Culture Clash; Director, Lisa Peterson; Sets, Rachel Hauck; Costumes, Christopher Acebo; Lighting and Projections, Alexander V. Nichols; Fight Direction, Steve Rankin; Associate Producer, Kelley Kirkpatrick; PSM, Susie Walsh; Stage Manager, Elle Aghabala; Cast: LaVonne Rae Andrews (Sally 30/30), Michelle Diaz (La Megadeath), Julia Jones (Dacotah/Girl in Blue Dress), Geraldine Keams (Maria 15), Russell Means (Chief Birdsong), Richard Montoya (Top Hat), Brandon Oakes (Mountain), Robert Owens-Greygrass (Broke Arrow), Kristen Potter (Captain Catherine Siler), Kalani Queypo (Star Man) Justin Rain (Ghost of Birdsong/Suarez), Ric Salinas (Bronson), Herbert Siguenza (Farmer); World Premiere; December 3, 2009–January 24, 2010

The Subject Was Roses by Frank D. Gilroy; Director, Neil Pepe; Presented in association with Estevez Sheen Productions; Sets, Walt Spangler; Costumes, Laura Bauer; Lighting, Rui Rita; Associate Producer, Kelley Kirkpatrick; Casting, Erika Sellin; PSM, David S. Franklin; Stage Manager, Nate Genung; Cast: Frances Conroy (Nettie Cleary), Brian Geraghty (Timmy Cleary), Martin Sheen (John Cleary); Understudies: Josh Clark, Brynn Thayer, Graham Miller; February 10–March 21, 2010

Bengal Tiger at the Baghdad Zoo by Rajiv Joseph; Director, Moisés Kaufman; Sets, Derek McLane; Costumes, David Zinn; Lighting, David Lander; Music, Kathryn Bostic; Sound, Cricket S. Myers; Fight Direction, Bobby C. King;

Associate Producer, Neel Keller; Casting, Bonnie Grisan; PSM, David S. Franklin; Stage Manager, Vanessa J. Noon; Cast: Glenn Davis (Tom), Brad Fleischer (Kev), Arian Moayed (Musa), Kevin Tighe (Tiger), Hrach Titizian (Iraqi Man/Uday), Sheila Vand (Hadia/Iraqi Teenager), Necar Zadegan (Iraqi Woman/Leper); Understudies: Hend Ayoub, Corey Brill, Paul Dillon, Waleed F. Zuaiter; April 14–May 30, 2010

Cincinnati Playhouse in the Park

Cincinnati, Ohio

Fiftieth Season

Producing Artistic Director, Edward Stern; Executive Director, Buzz Ward

Sleuth by Anthony Shaffer; Director, Michael Evan Haney; Set, Paul Shortt; Costumes, Gordon DeVinney; Lighting, James Sale; Fight Director, Drew Fracher; Casting, Rich Cole; Dialect Coach, Rocco Dal Vera; PSM, Jenifer Morrow; SSM, Andrea L. Shell; ASM, Jamie Lynne Sullivan; Cast: Munson Hicks (Andrew Wyke), Michael Gabriel Goodfriend (Milo Tindle); Robert S. Marx Theatre; September 5–October 3, 2009

Victoria Musica by Michele Lowe; Director, Edward Stern; Set, Joseph P. Tilford; Costumes, Gordon DeVinney; Lighting, Thomas C. Hase; Sound, Chuck Hatcher; Casting, Rich Cole; Stage Manager, Andrea L. Shell; Music Consultant, Naomi Lewin; Dialect Coach, Rocco Dal Vera; Cast: Tommy Schrider (Jeremy Lenz), Thom Rivera (Paolo Favanti), Peter Van Wagner (Daniel Barenboim/James Glickman), Stephen Caffrey (Jonathan Wedlan), Drew Cortese (Paul Torres/Edward Fistler/Martin Laredo), Mariann Mayberry (Victoria Wedlan), Judith Hawking (Dr. Madeline Lipton/Stacey Bates/Mrs. Templeton); Evan Zes (Alex Cutty-Drake/Rudy English/Clive Rollo); World Premiere; Thompson Shelterhouse Theatre; September 26–October 25, 2009

Three Sisters by Anton Chekhov, in a new version by Sarah Ruhl, based on a literal translation by Elise Thoron, with Natalya Paramonova and Kristin Johnsen-Neshati; Director, John Doyle; Set, Scott Pask; Costumes, Ann Hould-Ward; Lighting, Jane Cox; Sound and Composer, Dan Moses Schreier; Dramaturg, Elise Thoron; Casting, Bernard Telsey; FSM, Suann Pollock; SSM, Jenifer Morrow; ASM, Jamie Lynne Sullivan; Cast: Alma Cuervo (Olga), Laila Robins (Masha), Hannah Cabell (Irina), Alexander Gemignani (Andrei), Sarah Agnew (Natasha), Keith Reddin (Kulygin), Corey Stoll (Vershinin), Frank Woods (Baron Tuzenbach), Felix Solis (Solyony), Terry Greiss (Chebutykin), Ronald Cohen (Ferapont), Lynn Cohen (Anfisa), Tim Abrahamsen (Fedotik), Joe Watts Jr. (Rode), Kelly Pekar (Maid), World Premiere; Robert S. Marx Theatre; October 24–November 21, 2009

Sanders Family Christmas: More Smoke On The Mountain by Connie Ray, conceived by Alan Bailey, musical arrangements by John Foley and Gary Fagin; Director, Alan Bailey; Set, Peter Harrison; Costumes, Jeanette deJong; Lighting, Susan Terrano; Casting, Rich Cole; PSM, Jenifer Morrow; Stage Manager, Jamie Lynne Sullivan; Cast: David Hemsley Caldwell (Reverend Mervin Oglethorpe), Tess Hartman (June Sanders), Tommy Hancock (Burl Sanders), Maryruth Barnett (Denise Sanders), Christopher Marchant (Dennis Sanders), Rhonda Coullet (Vera Sanders), Bobby Taylor (Stanley Sanders), Thompson Shelterhouse Theatre; November 7–December 31, 2009

A Christmas Carol by Charles Dickens, adapted by Howard Dallin; Director, Michael Evan Haney; Set, James Leonard Joy; Costumes, David Murin; Lighting, Kirk Bookman; Sound and Composer, David B. Smith; Lighting, Susan Terrano; Costume Coordinator, Cindy Witherspoon; Music Director, Rebecca N. Childs; Choreographer, Dee Anne Bryll; Casting, Rich Cole; Stage Manager, Andrea L. Shell; ASM, Jamie Lynne Sullivan; Cast: Bruce Cromer (Ebenezer Scrooge), Tom Ford (Mr. Cupp/Percy), Steven Michael Harper (Mr. Sosser/Topper/Man with Shoe Shine/Guest at Fezziwig's), Andy Prosky (Bob Cratchit/Schoolmaster Oxlip), Tony Roach (Fred), Gregory Procaccino (Jacob Marley/Old Joe), Dale Hodges (Ghost of Christmas Past/Mrs. Peake), Richard Lowenburg (Boy Scrooge/Guest at Fezziwig's), Julianne Fox (Fan/Guest at Fezziwig's/Streets), Keith Jochim (Mr. Fez-

ziwig/Ghost of Christmas Present), Amy Warner (Mrs. Fezziwig/Patience/Streets), Tim Abrahamsen (Poor Caroler/Dick Wilkins), Lily Blau (Scrubwoman [Mary] at Fezziwig's/Streets), Todd Lawson (Young and Mature Scrooge/Ghost of Christmas Future), Sabrina Veroczi (Belle/Catherine Margaret), Anthony Vaughn Merchant (Constable at Fezziwig's/Undertaker/Streets), Regina Pugh (Mrs. Cratchit/Laundress at Fezziwig's), Eben Franckewitz (Peter Cratchit/Gregory/Apprentice at Fezziwig's), Katie Chase (Belinda Cratchit/Guest at Fezziwig's), Maraia Reinhart (Martha Cratchit/Guest at Fezziwig's), Owen Gunderman (Tiny Tim), Kelly Pekar (Poor Caroler/Rich Mother at Fezziwig's), Joe Watts Jr. (Rich Caroler/Poulterer), Jonathan Self (Baker at Fezziwig's/Man with Pipe/Streets), Methani Ran (Ignorance/Matthew/Rich Son at Fezziwig's), Kendall Kerrington Young (Want/Guest at Fezziwig's/Streets), Kristen B. Jackson (Guest at Fezziwig's/Mrs. Dilber/Streets), Jacqueline Raposo (Rich Caroler/Guest at Fezziwig's/Rose), Darius Brown (George/Charles/Apprentice at Fezziwig's), Robert S. Marx Theatre; December 3–December 30, 2009

The Fall of Heaven by Walter Mosley, based on his novel The Tempest Tales; Director, Marion McClinton; Set, David Gallo; Costumes, Karen Perry; Lighting, Donald Holder; Sound, Rob Milburn & Michael Bodeen; Fight Director, Drew Fracher; Rake Instructor, Julia Guichard; Casting, Rich Cole; PSM, Jenifer Morrow; SSM, Andrea L. Shell; Cast: Leland Gantt (Tempest Landry), Esau Pritchett (Joshua Angel/Man #1), Anthony Marble (Basil Bob/Saint Peter/Man #2/Offstage Voices), Heather Alicia Simms (Branwyn Weeks/Woman #2), Joy C. Hooper (Alfreda/Darlene/Woman #1); World Premiere; Robert S. Marx Theatre; January 23–February 20, 2010

How? How? Why? Why? Why? by Kevin Kling; Director and Set, David Esbjornson; Stage Manager, Andrea L. Shell; Cast: Kevin Kling (Kevin), Simone Perrin (Simone); Thompson Shelterhouse Theatre; February 13–March 14, 2010

Daddy Long Legs Book by John Caird, music and lyrics and orchestrations by Paul Gordon; Based on the novel by Jean Webster; Director, John Caird; Set and Costumes, David Farley; Lighting, Paul Toben; Sound, Michael Miceli; Music Director, Laura Bergquist; Associate Director, Nell Balaban; Casting, Tara Rubin; PSM, Jenifer Morrow; SSM, Suann Pollock; ASM, Jamie Lynne Sullivan; Cast: Megan McGinnis (Jerusha Abbott), Robert Adelman Hancock (Jervis Pendleton), Laura Bergquist (Conductor/piano), Mari Thomas (violin), Mark Kosmala (cello), Ted Karas (acoustic and electric guitar), Brian Malone (percussion), Bill Jackson (bass), Jennifer Waiser (Understudy/Jerusha Abbott), Travis Poelle (Understudy/Jervis Pendleton); World Premiere; Robert S. Marx Theatre; March 13–April 10, 2010

The History of Invulnerability by David Bar Katz; Director, Michael Evan Haney; Set and Projections, David Gallo; Costumes, Anne Kennedy; Lighting, Thomas C. Hase; Sound, Jill BC DuBoff; Associate Projections, Steve Channon; Original Artwork, Joe Staton; Casting, Rich Cole; Stage Manager, Suann Pollock; Stage Management Intern, James D. Lees; Associate Lighting, Krista Billings; Additional Scenic Artist, Thomas Condon; Dialect Coach, Rocco Dal Vera; Fight Director, Drew Fracher; Rake Instructor, Julia Guichard; Cast: Steve Wilson (Superman), David Deblinger (Jerry Siegel), Joseph Parks (Joe Shuster/Benjamin/Walter Winchell/Michael Siegel/Phil Yeh/Ensemble), William Parry (Lucky Luciano/Jor-El/Perry White/Saul/Thornton Wilder/Fred Wertham/Ensemble), Eric Martin Brown (Harry Donenfeld/Nazi/Elia Kazan/Sterling North/Tom Hall/Ensemble), Alexis Jacknow (Jerry's Mother/Prostitute/Lara/Jolan/Lois Lane/Lauretta Bender/Ensemble), Richard Lowenburg (Jerry Siegel age 11/Joel), Christopher Wells (German Schoolboy/Ensemble), Ian Ferguson (German Schoolboy/Ensemble), Jonathan Self (Cossack/Artist/Guard/Ensemble), Tim Abrahamsen (Cossack/Ensemble), Lily Blau (Ukrainian Mother/Josette Frank/Ensemble), Jacqueline Raposo (Understudy/Ukrainian Mother/Josette Frank/Ensemble); World Premiere; Thompson Shelterhouse Theatre; April 3–May 2, 2010

Ain't Misbehavin' Conceived by Richard Maltby Jr. and Murray Horwitz; Created and originally directed by Richard Maltby Jr.; Original choreography and musical staging by Arthur Faria; Musical adaptations, orchestrations and arrangements by Luther Henderson; Vocal and musical concepts by Jeffrey Gutcheon and musical arrangements by Jeffrey Gutcheon and William Elliott; Director and Choreographer, Arthur Faria; Music Director, William Foster McDaniel; Co-Set Designers, John Lee Beatty and Kacie Hultgren; Original Costumes, Randy Barcelo; Costume Design Re-creation and Additional Costumes, Gail Baldoni; Lighting, Pat Collins; Sound, Matt Kraus; Stage Manager, Andrea L. Shell; SSM, Jenifer Morrow; ASM, Jamie Lynne Sullivan; Cast: Doug Eskew (Ken), Eugene Barry-Hill (Andre), Debra Walton (Charlayne), Julia Lema (Nell/Dance Captain), Cynthia Thomas (Armelia), C.E. Smith (Understudy/Andre), Jim Anderson (bass/Music Contractor), Art Gore (drums), Mike Wade (trumpet/flugelhorn), Marc Fields (trombone), Bob Carten (saxophone/clarinet); Robert S. Marx Theatre; April 30–May 29, 2010

The Fantasticks Book and lyrics by Tom Jones, music by Harvey Schmidt; Director Edward Stern; Musical Staging, Janet Watson; Music Director/Pianist Michael Sebastian; Set, Paul Shortt; Costumes, David Kay Mickelsen; Lighting, Kirk Bookman; Casting, Rich Cole; PSM, Jenifer Morrow; Cast: Ron Bohmer (The Narrator/El Gallo), Margaret-Ellen Jeffreys (The Girl/Luisa), Jon-Michael Reese (The Boy/Matt), Bill Kux (The Boy's Father/Hucklebee), Jerome Lucas Harmann (The Girl's Father/Bellomy), Joneal Joplin (The Old Actor/Henry), Dale Hodges (The Man Who Dies/Mortimer), Lily Blau (The Mute), Michelle Gwynne (at the harp), Thompson Shelterhouse Theatre; May 15–June 20, 2010

Cleveland Play House

Cleveland, Ohio

Ninety-fourth Season

Artistic Director, Michael Bloom; Managing Director, Kevin Moore

Beethoven, As I Knew Him by Hershey Felder; Director, Joel Zwick; Set, Francois-Pierre Couture; Lighting, Richard Norwood; Sound, Erik Carstensen; PSM, GiGi Garcia; Costumes, Theatr' Hall, Paris; Production Manager/Technical Director, Matt Marsden; Cast: Hershey Felder (Gerhard von Breuning/Ludwig van Beethoven); Bolton Theatre; September 15–October 4, 2009

Inherit the Wind by Jerome Lawrence & Robert Edwin Lee; Director, Seth Gordon; Set, Michael B. Raiford; Costumes, Charlene Alexis Gross; Lighting, Trad A. Burns; Sound, James C. Swonger; Stage Manager, Amanda Hartland; Cast: Lauren Cole (Melinda), Cameron McKendry (Howard), Sarah Nedwek (Rachel Brown), Mark Monday (Mr. Meeker), Tom White (Bertram Cates), Lindsay Iuen (Mrs. McClain), Leigh Williams (Mrs. Krebs), Mark Alan Gordon (Rev. Jeremiah Brown), Scott Plate (E.K. Hornbeck), Rohn Thomas (Mayor), Ed Dixon (Mathew Harrison Brady), Zac Hoogendyk (Tom Davenport), Anne McEvoy (Mrs. Brady), Scott Jaeck (Henry Drummond), Dudley Swetland (Judge), AJ Cedeno (Ensemble), Michael Flood (Ensemble), Tom Picasso (Ensemble); Drury Theatre; October 23–November 15, 2009

A Christmas Story by Philip Grecian, based on the film distributed by Warner Brothers with a screenplay by Jean Shepherd, Leigh Brown and Bob Clark, and on the book *In God We Trust, All Others Pay Cash* by Jean Shepherd; Director, Seth Gordon; Set, Michal Ganio; Costumes, David Kay Mickelson; Lighting, Richard Winkler; Sound, James C. Swogner; Stage Manager, Shannon Habenicht; Cast: Christopher Burns (Ralph), Christian Flaherty (Flick), Kole Selznick Hoffman (Schwartz), Olivia Doria (Esther Jane), Courtney Anne Nelson (Helen), Elizabeth Ann Townsend (Mother), Joey Stefanko (Ralphie), Charles Kartali (The Old Man), Matthew Taylor (Randy), Daniel Sovich (Scut Farkas), Pat Nesbit (Miss Shields); Bolton Theatre; November 27–December 20, 2009

Lost in Yonkers by Neil Simon; Director, Michael Bloom; Set, Michael Schweikhardt; Costumes, David Kay Mickelson; Lighting, Paul Miller; Sound, James C. Swonger; Stage Manager, Amanda M. Harland; Cast: Alex Wyse (Jay), Maxwell Beer (Arty), John Plumpis (Eddie), Sara Surrey (Bella), Rosemary Prinz (Grandma), Anthony Crane (Louie), Patricia Buckley (Gert); Drury Theatre; January 8–31, 2010

Ain't Misbehavin' Conceived by Murray Horwitz & Richard Maltby Jr., music and lyrics by Thomas "Fats" Waller; Co-produced with the Arizona Theatre Company and San Jose Repertory Theatre; Director, Kent Gash; Set, Emily Beck; Costumes, Austin K. Sanderson; Lighting, William H. Grant III; Sound, Brian Jerome Peterson; Stage Manager, Shannon Hebenicht; Musical Director/Conductor, Darryl G. Ivey; Musical Staging/Choreographer, Byron Easley; Cast: Rebecca A. Covington, Angela Grovey, Christopher L. Morgan, Ken Robinson, Aurelia Williams; Bolton Theatre; January 29–February 21, 2010

Emma by Michael Bloom; Director, Peter Amster; Set, Robert Mark Morgan; Costumes, Kristine Kearney; Lighting, Jeff Davis; Sound, James C. Swonger; Stage Manager, Amanda M. Harland; Composer, Joe Cerqua; Cast: Tom White (Mr. Elton), Dana Hart (Mr. Weston), Patrick Clear (Mr. Woodhouse), Sarah Nealis (Emma Woodhouse), Leigh Williams (Mrs. Weston nee Taylor), Mark L. Montgomery (Mr. Knightly), Carolyn Faye Kramer (Harriet Smith), AJ Cedeno (Robert Martin), Suzanne Lang (Miss Bates), Sarah Nedwek (Jane Fairfax), Zac Hoogendyk (Frank Churchill), Lindsay Iuen (Mrs. Elton); Ensemble: Michael Flood, Tom Picasso, Amy Pawlukiewizc, Carli Taylor Miluk (Ensemble); Drury Theatre; February 26–March 21, 2010

Bill W. & Dr. Bob by Stephen Bergman & Janet Surrey; Director, Seth Gordon; Set, Robert Mark Morgan; Costumes, Jeffrey Van Curtis; Lighting, Michael Lincoln; Sound, James C. Swonger; Stage Manager, Shannon Habenicht; Cast: Sean Patrick Reilly (Bill W.), Denise Cromier (Lois), Timothy Crowe (Dr. Bob), Margaret Daly (Anne), Charles Kartali (Man), Heather Anderson Boll (Woman); Bolton Theatre; April 9–May 9, 2010

Dallas Theater Center

Dallas, Texas

Fifty-first Season

Artistic Director, Richard Hamburger

A Midsummer Nights Dream by William Shakespeare; Set, Beowulf Boritt; Costumes, Claudia Stephens; Lighting, Tyler Micoleau; Sound, The Broken Chord Collective; Director, Kevin Moriarty; Cast: Cedric Neal (Puck), Liz Mikel (Titania), Lee Trull (Lysander), Chamblee Ferguson (Nick Bottom), Sally Nystuen Vahle (Hippolyta), Robyn Baker Flatt (Egeus), Marcus M. Mauldin (Francis Flute), Joe Nemmers (Peter Quince), Bryan Pitts (Theseus), Matthew Steven Tompkins (Oberon), Rukhmani K. Desai (Hermia), Dexter Hostetter (A Fairy), Cameron Leighton Kirkpatrick (Tom Snout), Abbey Siegworth (Helena), Matt Tallman (Demetrius), Mallory Brophy (Peaselblossom), Alexander Ferguson (Mustardseed), Josh Greenfield (Snug), Amber Pickens (Moth), Sir Young (Cobweb); Dee and Charles Wyly Theatre - Potter Rose Performance Hall; October 24–November 22, 2009

A Christmas Carol by Charles Dickens, adapted by Richard Hellesen, music by David de Berry; Director, Joel Ferrell; Set, Bob Lavalle; Costumes, Wade Laboissonniere; Lighting, Matthew Richards; Sound, Ryan Rummery; Musical Director, Heath Cabe; Cast: Sean Hennigan (Scrooge), Chamblee Ferguson (Bob Cratchit), Matthew Gray (Fred), Christina Vela (Mrs. Cratchit), Lynn Blackburn (Belle), James Crawford (Marley), Bob Reed (Fezziwig), Natalie King (Ghost of Christmas Present), Joanna Schellenberg (Ghost of Christmas Past), Andrew Bonatti (Tiny Tim); Ensemble: Deborah Brown, Jakie Cabe, Bob Hess, Beverly Johnson, Cheryl Lowber, Olubajo Sonubi; Children's Ensemble: Max Ary, Charlotte Bagwell, Christian St. John Chiles, Halle Tomlinson, Kalita Humphreys Theater; December 1–27, 2009

Give It Up! Book and lyrics by Douglas Carter Beane, music by Lewis Flynn, based on Aristophanes' *Lysistrata*; Director and Choreographer, Dan Knechtges; Set, Beowulf Boritt; Costumes, David C. Woolard; Lighting, Ben Stanton; Sound, Tony Meola; Music Supervisor, Christopher Jahnke; Music Director, Elaine Davidson; Cast: Patti Murin (Lysistrata Jones), Liz Mikel (Hetairai), Katie Boren

(Lampito), Xavier Cano (Uardo), Lindsay Nicole Chambers (Robin), Noemi del Rio (Cleonice), Carla Duren (Mhyrinne), Curtis Holbrook (Xander), Justin Keyes (Stratyllis), Telly Leung (Cinesias), Andrew Rannells (Mick), Preston Sadleir (Gustaf); World Premiere; Dee and Charles Wyly Theatre- Potter Rose Performance Hall; January 15, 2009–February 14, 2010

Death of A Salesman by Arthur Miller; Director, Amanda Dehnert; Set, Daniel Ostling; Lighting, Lap Chi Chu; Costumes, Jessica Ford; Sound, Bruce Richardson; Cast: Jeffrey DeMunn (Willy Loman), Sally Nystuen Vahle (Linda), Hassan El-Amin (Uncle Ben), Chamblee Ferguson (Howard), Matthew Gray (Biff), Sean Hennigan (Charley), Liz Mikel (The Woman), Cedric Neal (Happy), Chad Daniel (Stanley), Cliff Miller (Bernard), Sandra Dietz, Vanessa Gibens; April 16– May 22, 2010

The Beauty Plays by Neil Labute; Presented in repertory at the Dee and Charles Wyly Theatre Studio Theatre; Sets, Donna Marquet; Costumes, Ric Dreumont Leal; Lighting, Driscoll Otto; Sound, Bruce Richardson; Included: *The Shape of Things* Director, Matthew Gray; Cast: Steven Walters (Adam), Abbey Siegworth (Evelyn), Aleisha Force (Jenny), Lee Trull (Philip); March 5–May 9, 2010; *Fat Pig* Director, Kevin Moriarty; Cast: Christina Vela (Helen), Regan Adair (Tom), Aleisha Force (Jeannie), Steven Walters (Carter); March 19–May 9, 2010; *reasons to be pretty* Director, Joel Ferrell; Cast: Christina Vela (Steph), Lee Trull (Greg), Rega Adair (Kent), Abbey Siegworth (Carly); April 19–May 23, 2010

It's A Bird...It's A Plane...It's Superman Music by Charles Strouse, lyrics by Lee Adams, original book by David Newman and Robert Benton, revised book by Roberto Aguirre-Sacasa; Director, Kevin Moriarty; Music Director, Elaine Davidson; Choreographer, Joel Ferrell; Set, Beowulf Boritt; Costumes, Jennifer Caprio; Lighting, Jeff Croiter; Sound, Rob Kaplowitz; Music Supervisor, Kimberly Grigsby; Revised Orchestrations/Arrangements, Eugene Gwozdz; Flying, ZFX Inc.; Wigs, Dave Bova; Cast: Zakiya Young (Lois Lane), Matt Cavenaugh (Clark Kent/ Superman), Jenny Powers (Sydney Sharp), Patrick Cassidy (Max Mencken), Andrew Keenan Bolger (Torchy), Hassan El-Amin (Perry White), Sean Hennigan (Mayor Siegel), Cedric Neal (Cadabra), Bob Hess (Court Jester), Julie Johnson (Scarlet Widow), Matthew Kilgore (Kazam), Cara Serber (Marilyn Nessbit), Paul Taylor (Jack-in-the-Box), Kate Wetherhead (Blackbird), Kent Zimmerman (Jupiter James); Ensemble: Chris Klink; Addi McDaniel, McKenzie Warren, Steven Wenslawski; Dee and Charles Wyly Theatre- Potter Rose Performance Hall; June 18–July 25, 2010

Delaware Theatre Company

Wilmington, Delaware

Thirty-first Season

Artistic Director, Anne Marie Cammarato; Managing Director, Mary Ann Ehlslager

Fire on the Bayou Written and directed by Kevin Ramsey; Director, Kevin Ramsey; Sets, Eric Schaeffer; Costumes, Holly Payne; Lighting, Joshua Schulman; Sound, Anna Hardisty; Associate Tap Choreographer, Allie Bradley; PSM, Kari Krein; ASM, Danielle B Rose; Cast: Jeremy Cohen (Professor Short-Hair, Michael De Castro (Traps), Clinton Derricks-Carroll (Spyboy Jambalaya), Jannie Jones (Queen Marie), Tatiana Lofton (Lil' Marie), Paul "PJ" Pinkett (Flambeau), Chip Porter (Dr. Johnay); October 14–November 1, 2009

It's a Wonderful Life: A Live Radio Play by Joe Landry; Director, Anne Marie Cammarato; Sets, Eric Schaeffer; Costumes, Janus Stefanowicz; Lighting, Thom Weaver; Sound, Christopher Colucci; Composer, Christopher Colucci; Music Director, Johanna Schloss; PSM, Kari Krein; ASM, Danielle B Rose; Cast: Michael Boudewyns (Jake Laurents), Maggie Kettering (Sally Applewhite), John Morrison (Freddie Filmore), Ed Swidey (Harry "Jazzbo" Heywood), Sara Valentine (Lana Sherwood); December 2–20, 2009

My Name is Asher Lev Adapted by Aaron Posner from the novel by Chaim Potok; Co-production with Round House Theatre; Director, Jeremy Skidmore; Sets, Tony Cisek; Costumes, Ren LaDassor; Lighting, Dan Covey; Sound, Matthew

M. Neilson; Composer, Matthew M. Neilson; PSM, Danielle B Rose; ASM, Paul Jerue; Cast: Lise Bruneau (Woman), Adam Heller (Man), Alexander Strain (Asher Lev); February 10–28, 2010

10 Months: The Wilmington Voices Project Written and directed by Anne Marie Cammarato; Sets/Costumes, Beowulf Boritt; Lighting, Christopher Studley; Sound, Fabian Obispo; PSM, Danielle B Rose; ASM, Ed Swidey, Karen Decker; Cast: Ben Cherry (Actor 1), Taïfa Harris (Actor 2), Erin Moon (Actor 3); March 17–April 4, 2010

The Foocy by Anthony Lawton; Director, Matt Pfeiffer; Sets, Dave Jadico; Costumes, Mask & Puppet Design, Aaron Cromie; Lighting, Thom Weaver; Music Arrangement & Composition, Rainey Lacey; PSM, Danielle B. Rose; ASM, Paul Jerue; Cast: Aaron Cromie, Dave Jadico, Rainey Lacey, Anthony Lawton, Seth Reichgott; April 28–May 16, 2010

Denver Center Theatre Company

Denver, Colorado

Thirty-first Season

Artistic Director, Kent Thompson; Associate Artistic Director, Bruce K. Sevy

The Voysey Inheritance by Harley Granville-Barker, adapted by David Mamet; Director, Bruce K. Sevy; Set, Lisa M. Orzolek; Costumes, Bill Black; Lighting, Jane Spencer; Sound, Jason Ducat; Dialects, Kathryn G. Maes; Stage Manager, Lyle Raper; ASM, Christi B. Spann; Cast: Philip Pleasnats (Mr. Voysey), Kathleen M. Brady (Mrs. Voysey), Robert Sicular (Trenchard Voysey/Rev. Evan Colpus), Jeanne Paulsen (Honor Voysey), John Hutton (Major Booth Voysey), Sam Gregory (Edward Voysey), Shawn Fagan (Hugh Voysey), Rebecca Martin (Ethel Voysey), Dana Acheson (Alice Maitland), Randy Moore (Peacey), Michael Winters (Mr. George Booth), Sean Lyons, M. Scott McLean, Jenna Panther (Servants); Space Theatre; September 18–October 24, 2009

A Raisin in the Sun by Lorraine Hansberry; Director, Israel Hicks; Set, Michael Ganio; Costumes, David Kay Mickelsen; Lighting, Charles R. MacLeod; Sound, Craig Breitenbach; Stage Manger, Christopher C. Ewing; ASM, Kurt Van Raden; Cast: Kim Staunton (Ruth Younger), Tyler Palmer (Travis Younger), Russell Hornsby (Walter Lee Younger), Dawn Scott (Beneatha Younger), Marlene Warfield (Lena Younger), Sheldon Woodley (Joseph Asagai), Tyee Tilghman (George Merchison), Harvy Blanks (Bobo), Mike Hartman (Karl Lindner), Cajardo Rameer Lindsay, Doug Bynum (moving men); Stage Theatre; October 1–31, 2009

Well by Lisa Kron; Director, Christy Montour-Larson; Set, Lisa M. Orzolek; Costumes, Meghan Anderson Doyle; Lighting, Jane Spencer; Sound, Kimberly Fuhr; Dramaturg, Douglas Langworthy; Fight Director, Geoffrey Kent; Stage Manager, A. Phoebe Sacks; Production Assistant, D. Lynn Reiland; Cast: Kate Levy (Lisa Kron), Kathleen M. Brady (Ann Kron); Ensemble: Rachel Fowler, Shauna Miles, Robert Jason Jackson, Erik Sandvold; Ricketson Theatre; November 6– December 19, 2009

Absurd Person Singular by Alan Ayckbourn; Director, Sabin Epstein; Set, Bill Forrester; Costumes, Angela Balogh Calin; Lighting, Charles R. MacLeod; Sound, Jason Ducat; Fight Director, Geoffrey Kent; Vocal Coach, Michael Cobb, Stage Manager, Christi B. Spann; Cast: Megan Byrne (Jane Hopcroft), Chris Mixon (Sidney Hopcroft), John Hutton (Ronald Brewster-Wright), Jeanne Paulsen (Marion Brewster-Wright), Kathleen McCall (Eva Jackson), David Ivers Geoffrey Jackson); Space Theatre; November 13–December 19, 2009

A Christmas Carol by Charles Dickens, adapted by Richard Hellesen, music by David de Berry; Director, Bruce K. Sevy; Set, Vicki Smith; Costumes, Kevin Copenhaver; Lighting, Don Darnutzer; Sound, Craig Breitenbach; Music Director/ Orchestrator Gregg Coffin; Choreographer, Christine Rowan; Dialect, Kathryn G. Maes; Stage Manager, Lyle Raper; ASMs, Christopher C. Ewing, Kurt Van Raden; Cast: Christine Rowan (Street Singer/Fezziwig Daughter/Wire's Sister),

Corey Stoll, Laila Robins, Hannah Cabell, Terry Greiss, Frank Wood, and Kelly Pekar in Three Sisters at Cincinnati Playhouse in the Park (photo by Sandy Underwood)

Katie Boren, Patti Murin, Andrew Rannells, and Carla Duren in Give It Up! at Dallas Theater Center (photo by Brandon Thibodeaux)

Sandra Reeves-Phillips, Mississippi Charles Bevel, Felicia Fields, and Gregory Porter in Florida Stage's Low Down Dirty Blues (photo by Ken Jacques)

Scott Jaeck and Ed Dixon in Inherit the Wind at the Cleveland Play House (photo by Roger Mastroianni)

Aaron Tveit and the Company in Catch Me If You Can at the 5th Avenue Theatre (photo by Chris Bennion)

Javon Johnson and Patrese McClain in Two Trains Running at Geva Theatre Center (photo by Ken Huth)

Brian Dennehy in Goodman Theatre's Krapp's Last Tape (photo by Liz Lauren)

Randall Newsome in A True History of the Johnstown Flood at the Goodman Theatre (photo by Eric Y. Exit)

Erin Davie and Bradley Dean in the Goodspeed Opera House production of Camelot (photo by Diane Sobolewski)

Molly Brennan, Emanuel Ravelli, Jonathan Brody, Ora Jones, Ed Kross, and Joey Slotnick in the Goodman Theatre production of Animal Crackers (photo by Eric Y. Exit)

Ashley Pankow, Ben Hensley, Marc Liby, and Katti Powell in Are We There Yet? at Great Plains Theatre (photo by Doug Nuttelman)

Philip Pleasants (Ebenezer Scrooge), Sam Gregory (Bob Cratchit/Fiddler), M. Scott McLean (Fred/Ensemble), Harvy Blanks (Subscription Gentleman/Old Joe/Ensemble), Larry Bull (Subscription Gentleman/Ghost of Christmas Present/Ensemble), Jacob Pearce (Beggar Child/Ensemble), Mike Hartman (Ghost of Jacob Marley/Ensemble), Stephanie Cozart (Ghost of Christmas Past/Charwoman/Ensemble), Alec Farmer (Ebenezer the Child/Ensemble), Ellie Schwartz (Fan/Want/Ensemble), Jeff Cribbs (Young Ebenezer/Merchant/Ensemble), Michael Wartella (Dick Wilkins/Undertaker's Man/Ensemble), Michael Fitzpatrick (Fezziwig/Ensemble), Leslie O'Carroll (Mrs. Fezziwig/Party Guest/Laundress, Ensemble), Courtney Capak (Daughter/Ensemble), Dawn Scott (Daughter/Ensemble), Doug Bynum (Suitor/Ensemble), Andy Jobe (Suitor/Ghost of Christmas Yet to Come), Sean Lyons (Suitor/Merchant/Ensemble), Renée Brna (Belle/Martha/Ensemble), Augustus Lane Filholm (Peter/Ensemble), Zoe Miller (Belinda/Ensemble), Jack Lilley (Edward/Ensemble), Charlie Korman (Tiny Tim), Melinda Parrett (Fred's Wife/Ensemble), Jeffrey Roark (Topper/Ensemble), Connor Nguyen Erickson (Ignorance/Ensemble), Orion Pilger (Boy in the Street); Stage Theatre; November 27–December 26, 2009

When Tang Met Laika by Rogelio Martinex; Director, Terrence J. Nolen; Set, Kames Kronzer; Costumes, David Kay Mickelsen; Lighting, Charles R. MacLeod; Composer, Jorge Cousineau, Projections, Charlie Miller; Dramaturg, Douglas Langworthy; Dialects, Kathryn G. Maes; Stage Manager, Christi B. Spann; Production Assistant, D. Lynn Reiland; Cast: Ian Merrill Peakes (Patrick), Jessica Love (Elena), Megan Byrne (Samantha), Randy Moore (Foma and others), Richard Thieriot (Young Communist and others), M. Scott McLean (Young Capatalist and others), R. Ward Duffy (Yuri Gagarin and others); World Premiere; Space Theatre; January 22–February 27, 2010

Eventide Adapted by Eric Schmiedl from the novel by Kent Haruf; Director, Kent Thompson; Set, Vicki Smith; Costumes, Susan Branch Towne; Lighting, Don Darnutzer; Sound, Craig Breitenbach; Composer, Gary Grundei, Fight Director, Geoffrey Kent; Dialects, Michael Cobb; Dramaturg, Allison Horsley; Stage Manager, Christopher C. Ewing; ASMs, Kurt Van Raden, A. Phoebe Sacks; Assistant to the Director, Stephen Weitz; Cast: Philip Pleasnats (Harold McPheron), Mike Hartman (Raymond McPheron), Tonantzin Carmelo (Victoria Roubideaux), David Ivers (Luther Wallace), Leslie O'Carroll (Betty June Wallace), Augustus Lane Filholm (DJ Kephart), Ron Crawford Walter Kephart, Lauren Klein (Rose Tyler), Sam Gregory (Oscar Strelow, Judge, Cecil Walton), Geoffrey Kent (Auctioneer, Deputy), William Zielinski (Hoyt Raines), Kathleen McCall (Maggie Jones), John Hutton (Tom Guthrie), Carole Healey (Linda May, Waitress), Ellie Schwartz (Joy Rae Wallace), Thomas Russo (Richie Wallace), Rebecca Martin (Tammy), Joseph Yeargain (Bartender), Jenna Panther (Donna Lawson), Del Guitierrez (Drew Cortese); Ensemble: Sean Lyons, Chris Mazza, Joseph Yeargain (Ensemble); World Premiere; Stage Theatre; January 29–February 27, 2010

Mama Hated Diesels by Randal Myler and Dan Wheetman, with additional material by Charles Weldon; Director, Randal Myler; Musical Director, Dan Wheetman; Original Photography, Jim Steinberg; Set, Vicki Smith; Costumes, Kevin Copenhaver; Lighting, Don Darnutzer; Sound, Craig Breitenbach; Projections, Charlie I. Miller; Stage Manager, Lyle Raper; ASM, Christopher C. Ewing; Cast: Brad Bellamy, Kathleen M. Brady, Mike Hartman, Charles Weldon, Jan Leslie Harding, Augustus Lane Filholm; Singers: Rhonda Coullet, Jason Edwards; Musicians: James Cruce, David Miles Keenan, David P. Jackson; World Premiere: Stage Theatre; March 19–May 9, 2010

Othello by William Shakespeare; Direcotor, Kent Thompson; Set, Lisa M. Orzolek; Costumes, Bill Black; Lighting, Charles R. MacLeod; Sound, Jason Ducat; Composer, Gregg Coffin; Fight Director, Geoffrey Kent; Dramaturg, Douglas Langworthy; Stage Manager, Christi B. Spann; ASM, Kurt Van Raden; Cast: David Ivers (Roderigo), John Hutton (Iago), Philip Pleasants (Brabantio), Lincoln Thompson (Servant, Fighter), Caitlin Wise (Servant, Wench), Robert Jason Jackson (Othello), Harry Carnahan (Cassio), Randy Moore (The Duke), John Arp (Senator/Gratiano/Fighter), Geoffrey Kent (Senator/Lodovico/Fighter), Meghan Wolf (Desdemona), Stephen Weitz (Montano), Kathleen McCall (Emilia), Chad Callaghan, Tom Coiner, John DiAntonio (Soldiers), Allison Pistorius (Wench/Bianca); Space Theatre; March 26–May 1, 2010

Mariela in the Desert by Karen Zacarías; Director, Bruce K.Sevy; Set, Vicki Smith; Costumes, Clint Ramos; Lighting, Don Darnutzer; Sound, William Burns; Projections, Charlie I. Miller; Dramaturg, Douglas Langworthy; Stage Manager, A. Phoebe Sacks; Production Assistant, D. Lynn Reiland; Cast: Yetta Gottesman (Mariela), Robert Sicular (Jose), Franca Sofia Barchiesi (Oliva), Vivia Font (Blanca), Jean-Pierre Serret (Carlos), Sam Gregory (Adam); Ricketson Theatre; April 2–May 15

Eugene O'Neill Theater Center

Waterford, Connecticut

Forty-Sixth Season

Artistic Directors, Wendy C. Goldberg (National Playwrights Conference), Paulette Haupt (National Music Theater Conference), Pam Aciero (National Puppetry Conference), Michael Bush (Cabaret and Performance Conference); Executive Director, Preston Whiteway

National Puppetry Conference – June 18–19, 2009 at the Dina Merrill Theatre

20 Year Remix: A Retrospective by Richard Termine, Marianne Kubik and Lenny Pinna, music by Larry Siegel with assistance by Melissa Dunphy and Bradley Kemp; Producer & Ensemble Assistant, Honey Goodenough; Developed and performed by Mark Saltzman, Bonnie Berkowitz, Jean Minuchin, Populoh Valeska, Chase Woolner, Mike Horner, Katie McClenahan, Alisa Sikora Kleckner, Matt Laird, Sarah Skinner-Probst, David McTier, Steve Mark, Ian Sweetman, Brad Shur, Jeanine Padgett, Sebastienne Mundhein, Kyle Igneczi, Ben Durocher, Ed Valentine, Honey Goodenough

Calling Occupants of Interplanetary Craft by Tim Lagasse with Martin P. Robinson; Lighting, Natalie George; Follow Spots, Rachel Roccoberton, Bart Roccoberton Jr.; Developed and performed by David Karle, Jonathan Little, Spencer Lott, Paul McGinnis, Marta Mac Rostie, Marsian DeLellis, Liz Hara, Artie Poore, Amanda Maddock, Alex Griffin, Brodrick Jones, April Warren, Amanda Weiss, Brendan Yi-Fu Tay, Aaron Cromie, Morgan Lane-Tanner, Larie Berenhaus

The Little Prince by Richard Cummins and John Scoullar, conceived and directed by Scott Hitz; Puppet Design, Michael Shupbach; Cast: Michael Hinton (Aviator), Roxanna Myhrum (Little Prince), Gabriella Geisinger (Rose), Marc Petrosino, Michael Shupbach (Puppeteers)

Marionettes Composed by Melissa Dunphy and Bradley Kemp; Marionette Participants: Alisa Hunnicutt, Janice Grimaldi, Colette Nickola, Molly Light, Rolande Duprey, Caroline Reck, Thomas Getchell, Ellen Turner-Scott, Anna Vargas, Mary Nagler, Matt Brooks

A Dream Play by Joseph Jonah Therrien, music by Melissa Dunphy, Invaluable Collaborator, Josh Kigner; Cast: Derron Wood, Dan Bergeron, Isabelle Redman, Victor Chiburis, Madeline Sayet, Constancia Malahias; Silken Veils by Leila Ghaznavi, music by Hamed Nikpay & Houman Pourmehdi; Puppeteers: Leila Ghaznavi, Michael Langlois, Jane Martineau, Gita Hassin

We All Scream Written and directed by Aaron Lanthrop, puppets by Aaron Lanthrop and Gina Leigh, music by Bradley Kemp, special thanks to Tears of Joy Theater and Sarah Frechette; Puppeters: Amy Rush, Danielle McGuire, Sharon Challenger, Ian Shulz, Benjamin Shafer, Warren Mason

National Music Theater Conference

Buddy's Tavern Music by Kim Oler, lyrics by Alison Louise Hubbard, book by Raymond De Felitta; Based on the film *Two Family House*; Director, Warren Carlyle; Music Director/Pianist, Ray Fellman; PSM, Robert Bennett; ASM, Veronica Aglow; Dramaturg, Allison Horsley; Cast: Allison Briner (Marie/Miss Diminjuk), Darius De Haas (The Barkeep/Brancaccio/Sales Clerk), Jordan Gelber (Buddy), Michaela Koerner (Laura), Jodie Langel (Estelle), William Parry (Angelo/Jim/Sales Clerk/

Monahan), Steve Routman (Chip/Sales Clerk), Lindsie VanWinkle (Mary), Peter Travis (Stage Directions); Rose Barn Theater; June 26–July 2, 2009

Clear: A New Musical Experience Book, music and lyrics by Paul Oakley Stovall, additional music by Stew, Irv Johnson, Stephen Goers, Brad Simmons, Ryan Link, and Christo Willis; Director, Daniel Goldstein; Musical Director/Arranger/Pianist, Brad Simmons; PSM, Robert Bennett; ASM, Veronica Aglow; Dramaturg, Martin Kettling; Cast/Musicians: Clifton Duncan (Anthony/others/percussion), Paul Oakley Stovall (Lawson/percussion), Yassmin Alers (Rae/Mom/percussion), George Farmer (Hilmi/Brandon/others/bass/keyboard), Leenya Rideout (Alev/Senator/others/guitar/fiddle), Ryan Link (Kenny/Magnus/Marco/Jared/drums/guitar), Ken Barnett (Jake/Cameron/keyboard/percussion), Brad Simmons (Jason/Ryan/Roger/others/piano/keyboard/percussion); Rose Barn Theater; July 3–9, 2009

Eden Music by Mel Marvin, book and lyrics by Jonathan Levi; Director, Stuart Ross; Music Director/Arrangerement/Pianist, Vadim Feichtner; PSM, Robert Bennett; ASM, Veronica Aglow; Assistant Director, Hansol Jung; Dramaturg, Allison Horsley; Cast: Jerry Dixon (Rashid), Celisse Henderson (Chantal), Angel Desai (Amira), Matthew Scott (Jamie), Bob Stillman (Buddy), Janine LaManna (Thalia); Rose Barn Theater; July 10–16, 2009

National Playwrights Conference

Writers in Residence: Alfred Uhry, Chris D'Arienzo, Yaroslava Alexandrovna Pulinovich

Creation by Kathryn Walat; Director, Lisa Peterson; Dramaturg, Adrien-Alice Hansel; Set, Rachel Hauck; Lighting, Brian Lilienthal; Sound, Matt Hubbs; Props, Shaun Hart; Stage Manager, Danielle Monica Long; ASM, Alec Ferrell; Cast: John Preston (Ian Baker), Mia Barron (Sarah Frankel), Piter Marek (Amal Balhas), Nick Westrate (Zachary Owen); Dina Merrill Theater; July 9–10, 2009

The Dream of the Burning Boy by David West Read; Director, Evan Cabnet; Dramaturg, Josh Fiedler; Set, Rachel Hauck; Lighting, Raquel Davis; Sound, Matt Hubbs; Props, Shaun Hart; Stage Manager, Alec Ferrell; Cast: Reed Birney (Larry), JD Taylor (Steve), Ben Gunderson (Dane), Jessica Cummings (Chelsea), Libby Woodbridge (Rachel), Ben Morrow (Kyle), Caitlin O'Connell (Andrea); Edith Oliver Theater; July 14–15, 2009

Follow Me to Nellie's by Dominique Morisseau; Director, Seret Scott; Dramaturg, Madeleine Oldham; Set, Rachel Hauck; Lighting, Brian Lilienthal; Sound, Elisheba Ittoop; Props, Shaun Hart; Stage Manager, Danielle Monica Long; Cast: Lynda Gravátt (Nellie), Kelly McCreary (Na Rose), Nyahale Allie (Marla), Michelle Wilson (Ree Ann), Amirah Vann (Sandy), Warner Miller (Ossie), Peter Jay Fernandez (Rollo), Nick Westrate (Tom Jr.); Dina Merrill Theater; July 16–17, 2009

Natashina Mechta (Natasha's Dream) by Yaroslava Pulinovich; Director, Kyle Donnelly; Dramaturg, Christine Drew Benjamin; Stage Manager, Jana Jarret; Interpreter, Sasha Suvorkov; Cast: Mattie Hawkinson (Natasha); Rose Barn Theater; July 18, 2009

Close Up Space by Molly Smith Metzler; Director, Sheryl Kaller; Dramaturg, Annie MacRae; Set, Rachel Hauck; Lighting; Brian Lilienthal; Sound; Matt Hubbs; Props, Shaun Hart; Stage Manager, Alec Ferrell; Cast: David Adkins (Paul Barrow), Laila Robins (Vanessa Finn Adams), Libby Woodbridge (Harper), Michael Chernus (Steve), Jessica DiGiovanni (Bailey); Edith Oliver Theater; July 21–22, 2009

The Burden of Not Having a Tail by Carrie Barrett; Director, Suzanne Agins; Dramaturg, Martin Kettling; Set, Rachel Hauck; Lighting, Raquel Davis; Sound, Elisheba Ittoop; Props, Shaun Hart; Stage Manager, Danielle Monica Long; Cast: Alison Weller (Woman); Rose Barn Theater; July 23–24, 2009

A Devil at Noon by Anne Washburn; Director, Steve Cosson; Dramaturg, Martin Kettling; Set, Rachel Hauck; Lighting, Raquel Davis; Sound, Matt Hubbs; Props, Shaun Hart; Stage Manager, Alec Ferrell; Cast: Gordon Clapp (Chet Ellis), Rebecca Hart (Lois), Scott Drummond (Colin McAdams/Alien Guy), Walter Charles (Bob

Seward/The Moon Man), Scott Lowell (Tom/Don Larkin), David Ross (Dennis/Phillip Hutche); Amphitheater; July 28–29, 2009

Comes a Faery by James McLindon; Director, Sean Daniels; Dramaturg, John Baker; Set, Rachel Hauck; Lighting, Brian Lilienthal; Sound, Elisheba Ittoop; Props, Shaun Hart; Stage Manager, Danielle Monica Long; Cast: Nicole Lowrance (Siobhan), Rob Campbell (Seaneen), Danielle Slavick (Katie), Ryan King (Raphael), Barbara Walsh (Dr. Neery); Dina Merrill Theater; July 30–31, 2009

Cabaret & Performance Conference – Dina Merrill Theatre

Leslie Uggams: Uptown Downtown Conceived and directed by Michael Bush; Music Director, Don Rebic; Lighting, Seth Reiser; Sound, Kristine Eckerman; Stage Manager, Danielle Monica Long; Musicians: Steve Bargonetti (guitar), Buddy Williams (drums), Ray Kilday (bass), Walt Weiskopf (woodwinds); August 5, 2009

Penny Fuller and Anita Gillette: Sin Twisters Director, Barry Kleinbort, Music Director, Paul Greenwood, Lighting, Seth Reiser; Sound, Benji Inniger; Stage Manager, Danielle Monica Long; August 6, 2009

2010 Cabaret Fellows Showcase: Evening One Music Directors, Bruce Barnes, Beth Falcone, David Gaines, Paul Greenwood; Lighting, John Alexander, Austin Dangrove, Gareth Burghes, Cara Guglielmino, Greg Hurd, Tom Klonowski, Forrest Tallbull; Sound, Kristine Eckerman; Stage Manager, Suzanne Spicer; Featuring: Brittany Hamilton, Maggie Lacey, Kila Packett, Rebecca Pitcher, Gretchen Reinhagen, Scott Sussman; August 7, 2009

The O'Neill Follies Host, Michael Bush; Lighting, Raquel Davis and Seth Reiser; Sound, Kristine Eckerman; Stage Managers, Danielle Monica Long and Jerome Kyle Lewis; Featuring: Joel Silberman, Jay Rogers in *Bubbas, Baptists and Bells* (Music Director, Steven Ray Watkins); *The Junior Fellows*: Ed Donovan, Dalton Harrod, Kira Helper, & Victoria Zaro (Music Director, Brad Simmons); Lois Robbins in *What is a Woman?* (Music Director, Joel Silberman); Aja Nisenson in *Déjà Vu* (Music Director Joel Silberman); Nicki Parrott with John di Martino; Allan Harris in *Too Hot: The Tale of Billy Eckstein* (Music Director, Joel Silberman); August 8, 2009

Peggy Lee, Big Instruments, and Other Weapons of Mass Distraction Written and directed by Michael Bush; Lighting, Rosie Cruz; Sound, Kristine Eckerman; Stage Manager, Suzanne Spicer; Featuring: Nicki Parrot with John di Martino; August 10, 2009

Brent Barrett: Night Songs Director, Barry Kleinbort; Musical Director, Christopher Denny; Lighting, Seth Reiser; Sound, Kristine Eckerman; Stage Manager, Jana Jarrett; August 11, 2009

2010 Cabaret Fellows Showcase: Evening Two Music Directors, Bruce Barnes, Beth Falcone, David Gaines, Paul Greenwood, Brad Simmons; Lighting, John Alexander, Rosie Cruz, Austin Bansgrove, Gareth Burghes, Cara Guglielmino, Greg Hurd, Tom Klonowski, Forrest Tallbull; Sound, Kristine Eckerman; PSM, Danielle Monica Long; Stage Manager, Jerome Lewis; Featuring: Brittany Hamilton, Maggie Lacey, Kila Packett, Rebecca Pitcher, Gretchen Reinhagen, Scott Sussman; Special Added Distraction: *The Junior Fellows*: Ed Donovan, Dalton Harrod, Kira Helper, & Victoria Zaro; August 12, 2009

Stoned Soul Picnic: The Songs of Laura Nyro Based on an idea by Michael Bush and Frank Dalrymple; Directors, Michael Bush and Joel Silberman; Music Director, Steven Ray Watkins; Lighting, Raquel Davis; Sound, Kristine Eckerman; Stage Manager, Danielle Monica Long; Featuring: Celisse Henderson, Sheri Sanders and Toni Trucks; August 13, 2009

Grand Finale Cabaret Lighting, Seth Reiser; Sound, Kristine Eckerman; Stage Manager, Danielle Monica Long; Featuring: Bruce Barnes, Michael Bush, Ed Donovan, Beth Falcone, Penny Fuller, David Gaines, Paul Greenwood, Brittany Hamilton, Dalton Harrod, Kira Helper, Celese Henderson, Barry Kleinbort, Aja Nisenson, Kila Packett, Rebecca Pitcher, Gretchen Reinhagen, Lois Robbins, Sheri Sanders, Joel Silberman, Brad Simmons, Scott Sussman, Donna Trinkoff, Toni Trucks, Steven Ray Watkins, Victoria Zaro; August 14, 2009

The 5th Avenue Theatre

Seattle, Washington

Twenty-first Season

Producing Artistic Director, David Armstrong; Managing Director, Marilynn Sheldon

Catch Me If You Can Book by Terrence McNally, music by Marc Shaiman, lyrics by Scott Wittman & Marc Shaiman; Based on the DreamWorks Motion Picture; Director, Jack O'Brien; Choreographer, Jerry Mitchell; Music Director/Conductor, John McDaniel; Set, David Rockwell; Costumes, Bob Mackie; Lighting, Kenneth Posner; Sound, Walter Trarbach; Associate Set, Dick Jaris; Associate Projections, Bob Bonniol; Associate Costumes, Joe McFate; Hair and Makeup, Mary Pyanowski; Associate Lighting, Aaron Spivey; Associate Sound, Cassandra Givens; Video Technology, Sennova INC.; Production Supervisor, Andrew G. Luft; Technical Director, Mark Schmidt; Associate Musical Director, Keith Cotton; Casting, Telsey + Company; Orchestrations, Larry Blank & Marc Shaiman; Associate Director, Matt Lenz; Associate Choreographer, Joey Pizzi; PSM, Frank Lombardi; ASMs, Amy Gornet & Bret Torbeck; Cast: Aaron Tveit (Frank Abagnale Jr.), Norbert Leo Butz (Carl Hanratty), Tom Wopat (Frank Abagnale Sr.), Rachel de Benedet (Paula Abagnale), Felicia Finley (Cheryl Ann), Kerry Butler (Brenda Strong), Linda Hart (Carol Strong), Nick Wyman (Roger Strong/Family Court Judge/Frank Taylor/Bank Officer/Mr. Collins), Timothy McCuen Piggee (FBI Agent Bill Cod/Railroad Agent/Bartender/Ensemble), Clarke Thorell (FBI Agent Todd Branton/Ensemble), Brandon Wardell (FBI Agent Johnny Dollar/Ensemble), Romelda Teron Benjamin (Stewardess/Next Available Teller/Pediatrics Nurse/Ensemble), Matt Wolfe (Tailor/Motel Manager/Dr. Griffith, Bartender/Ensemble), Angie Schworer (Pan Am Stewardess/Starlet #2/Apartment Manager/Ensemble), Jason Kappus (Pan Am Pilot/Dr. Slaughter/Ensemble), Shanna Marie Palmer (Lou Anne/Flight Attendant/Ensemble), Taryn Darr (Third Teller/Starlet #1/Ensemble), Karl Warden (Auctioneer/Dr. Feldman/Ensemble/Dance Captain), Jillana Laufer (Starlet #3/Ensemble), Mo Brady (Ensemble), Anastacia McCleskey (Ensemble), Kyle Vaughn (Ensemble), David Alewine (Ensemble/Swing), Nikki Long (Swing); July 23–August 16, 2009

Joseph and the Amazing Technicolor Dreamcoat Music by Andrew Lloyd Webber, lyrics by Tim Rice; Director/Musical Staging, James Rocco; Choreographer, Jayme McDaniel; Music Director/Conductor, RJ Tancioco; Set, Martin Christoffel; Lighting, Tom Sturge; Costumes, Mark Thompson; Sound, Zach Williamson; Hair and Makeup, Mary Pyanowski; Stage Manager, Bret Torbeck; Production Supervisor, Andrew G. Luft; Technical Director, Mark Schmidt; Music Supervision, Ian Eisendrath & Albert Evans; Megamix Producers, Davee C & Dave Pascal; ASMs, Lori Amondson & Jessica C. Bomball; Cast: Anthony Fedorov (Joseph), Jennifer Paz (Narrator), Billy Joe Huels (The Pharaoh), David Alewine (Issachar), Heather Apellanes (Female Ensemble), Logan Benedict (Simeon), Charissa Bertels (Female Ensemble), Mo Brady (Zebulun), Gabriel Corey (Benjamin), Taryn Darr (Female Ensemble), Marc Dela Cruz (Gad), Michael Dela Cruz (Judah), Ben Gonio (Dan), Richard Gray (Potiphar), Hugh Hastings (Jacob), Brittany Jamieson (Female Ensemble), Daniel C. Levine (Napthali), Nikki Long Female Ensemble), Trina Mills (Female Ensemble), Kasey Nusbickel (Female Ensemble), Brandon O'Neill (Asher), Shanna Marie Palmer (Female Ensemble), Kat Ramsburg (u/s Narrator), Dane Stokinger (Rueben), Pamela Turpen (Female Ensemble), Troy L. Wageman (Levi), Lauren P. Warnke (Female Ensemble), Children's Chorus: Noah Barr, Keenan Barr, Kaitlyn Bartlett, Kevin Beall, Amelia Brummel, Andy Burnstein, Alexis Capestany, Joey Capestany, Olivia Capestany, Walker Caplan, Trinity Conn, Brayden Daher, Madeline Dalto, Sarah Dennis, Jacob Espling, Drea Gordon, Annika Summer Gustafson, Bryan Hanner, Lily Hansen, Jordan Harris, Shaye Hodgins, Brianna Jason, Shereen Khatibloo, Daniel Kranseler, Paige Lawson, Rachel Lau, Matthew Lewis, Eliza Ludlam, Eli Lotz, Mariah Lotz, Skye McCaw, Malik Muellion, Dekker O'Farrell, Jenna Oratz, Ayana Pagan, Maddy Payment, Kasey Percich, Brenna Power, Morgan Pullom, Elizabeth Rice, Mary Rising, Alexander Robertson, Emily Rudolph, Jack Sbragia, Hana Shiozaki, Ricky Spaulding, Cameron Washington, Deche Washington, Olivia

Weber, Lydia Weir, Elijah Williams, Elisabeth Williams; October 10–November 1, 2009

White Christmas Music and lyrics by Irving Berlin, book by David Ives & Paul Blake; Based on the Paramount Picture film written for the screen by Norman Krasna, Norman Panama, and Melvin Frank; Directors, James A. Rocco & David Armstrong; Choreographer, James A. Rocco; Music Director/Conductor, James May; Set, Anna Louizos; Costumes, Carrie Robbins; Lighting, Tom Sturge; Orchestrations, Larry Blank; Vocal/Dance Arrangements, Bruce Pomahac; Sound, Ken Travis; Hair and Makeup, Mary Pyanowski; Stage Manager, Jeffrey K. Hanson; Production Supervisor, Andrew G. Luft; Technical Director, Mark Schmidt; Associate Director, Aaron Tuttle; Associate Choreographer, Jayme McDaniel; ASMss, Stina Lotti & Michael B. Paul; Cast: Michael Gruber (Bob Wallace), Christina Saffran Ashford (Betty Haynes), Greg McCormick Allen (Phil Davis), Taryn Darr (Judy Haynes), Carol Swarbrick (Martha Watson), Frank Corrado (General Henry Waverly), Clayton Corzatte (Ezekiel), Lauren Carlos (Susan Waverly), Drea Gordon (Susan Waverly), Allen Galli (Ed Sullivan Announcer/Mr. Snoring Man/Mike), Richard Gray (Ralph Sheldrake), Cheryl Massey-Peters (Tessie/Mrs. Snoring Woman/Sheldrake's Secretary/Martha u/s), Pamela Turpen (Rhoda/Ensemble), Billie Wildrick (Rita/Betty u/s), Krystle Armstrong (Ensemble/Judy u/s), Gabriel Corey (Ensemble), Ross Cornell (Ensemble), Dannul Dailey (Regency Room Announcer/Train Conductor/Ensemble/Swing), Michael Ericson (Ensemble), Brittany Jamieson (Ensemble), Nikki Long (Ensemble), Jayme McDaniel (Associate Choreographer/Jimmy/Dance Captain), Trina Mills (Ensemble/Swing), Kasey Nusbickel (Ensemble), Matt Owen (Ensemble/Bob u/s), James Scheider (Ensemble/Phil u/s), Lauren P. Warnke (Ensemble); November 28–December 30, 2009

South Pacific Music by Richard Rodgers, lyrics by Oscar Hammerstein II, book by Oscar Hammerstein II & Joshua Logan; Adapted from the Pulitzer Prize-winning novel Tales of the South Pacific by James A. Michener; Original stage production directed by Joshua Logan; Director, Bartlett Sher; Musical Staging, Christopher Gattelli; Music Director, Ted Sperling; Set, Michael Yeargan; Costumes, Catherine Zuber; Lighting, Donald Holder; Sound, Scott Lehrer; Orchestrations, Robert Russell Bennett; Dance/Incidental Music Arrangements, Trude Rittmann; Casting, Telsey + Company; Music Coordinator, David Lai; Stage Manager, Brian J. L'ecuyer; Music Conductor, Lawrence Goldberg; Technical Director, William J. Pate; Company Manager, Joel T. Herbst; Production Manager, Justin Reiter; Touring Booking/Engagement Management/Press & Marketing, Broadway Booking Office NYC; General Manager, Gregory Vander Ploeg and Gentry & Associates, Executive Producer, Seth C. Wenig; Cast: Rod Gilfry (Emile de Becque), Carmen Cusack (Ensign Nellie Forbush), Gerry Becker (Capt. George Brackett), Genson Blimline (Stewpot, Voiceover Loudspeaker), Christina Carrera (Ngana), Anderson Davis (Lt. Joseph Cable), Sumie Maeda (Liat), CJ Palma (Jerome), Peter Rini (Cmdr. William Harbison), Rusty Ross (Professor), Matthew Saldivar (Luther Billis), Keala Settle (Bloody Mary), Christopher Carl (Richard West), Eric L. Christian (Kenneth Johnson), Jacqueline Colmer (Asst. Dance Captain, Swing), Jeremy David (Swing), Mike Evariste (Henry, James Hayes), Kate Fahrner (Ensign Dinah Murphy), Nicholas Galbraith (Johnny Noonan), Alexis G.B. Holt (Bloody Mary's Assistant), Chad Jennings (Radio Operator Bob McCaffrey), Christopher Johnstone (Thomas Hassinger), Kristine Kerwin (Ensign Sue Yaeger), Jodi Kimura (Bloody Mary's Assistant), Cathy Newman (Lt. Genevieve Marshall), Diane Phelan (Ensign Cora MacRae/Bloody Mary's Assistant), John Pinto Jr. (Yeoman Herbert Quale), Travis Robertson (Tom O'Brien), Josh Rouah (Lt. Eustis Carmichael/Petty Officer Hamilton Steeves), Tally Sessions (Lt. Buzz Adams), Kristen J. Smith (Ensign Connie Walewska), Matt Stokes (Dance Captain, Swing), Gregoru Williams (Swing), Victor J. Wisehart (Morton Wise); January 29–February 21, 2010

Legally Blonde Music and lyrics by Laurence O'Keefe & Nell Benjamin, book by Heather Hach; Based upon the novel by Amanda Brown and the Metro-Goldwyn motion picture; Director/Choreographer, Jerry Mitchell; Produced for Fox Theatricals by Kristin Caskey & Mike Isaacson; Set, David Rockwell; Costumes, Gregg Barnes; Lighting, Ken Posner & Paul Miller; Sound, Acme Sound Partners; Casting, Telsey + Company; Hair, David Brian Brown; Associate

Director, Marc Bruni; Associate Choreographer, Denis Jones; Production Manager, Theatersmith, INC.; Animal Trainer, Bill Berloni; Stage Manager, Tom Bartlett; General Management, Nina Lannan Associates/Maggie Brohn & Amy Jacobs; Marketing/Publicity, Allied Live; Exclusive Tour Direction, The Booking Group & Meredith Blair; Associate Producers, PMC Productions & Yasuhiro Kawana; Orchestrations, Christopher Jahnke; Arrangements, Laurence O'Keefe & James Sampliner; Music Direction/Conductor, Kyle Norris; Music Contractor, Michael Keller; Music Supervision, James Sampliner; Cast: Becky Gulsvig (Elle Woods), D.B. Bonds (Emmett Forrest), Natalie Joy Johnson (Paulette), Michael Rupert (Professor Callahan), Jeff McLean (Warner Huntington III), Megan Lewis (Vivienne Kensington), Coleen Sexton (Brooke Wyndham), Tiffany Engen (Serena/u/s Brooke), Rhiannon Hansen (Margot/u/s Elle Woods), Lucia Spina (Enid, u/s Paulette), Candice Marie Woods (Pilar), Barry Anderson (Ensemble/u/s Emmett, Callahan, Dad, Winthrop), Sara Andreas (Dance Captain/u/s Brooke, Serena, Margot, Pilar), Kyle Brown (Assistant Dance Captain/Carlos), Liberty Cogen (Ensemble/Kate/Chutney/u/s Vivienne, Enid), Ven Daniel (Kyle/Dewey/Grandmaster Chad), Brooke Leigh Engen (Ensemble/u/s Pilar, Kate/Chutney), Spencer Howard (Swing/u/s Kyle/Dewey/Grandmaster Chad), Paul Jackel (Dad/Winthrop/u/s Callahan), Jason Kappus (Ensemble/u/s Warner, Dad/Winthrop), Ashley Moniz (Swing/u/s Elle, Serena, Enid), Kathleen Elizabeth Monteleone (Ensemble/u/s Elle Woods, Margot), Brian Patrick Murphy (Ensemble/u/s Kyle/Dewey/Grandmaster Chad), Cjay Hardy Philip (Store Manager/Judge/u/s Paulette), Alex Puette (Swing), Jonathan Rayson (Aaron/u/s Emmett), Constantine Rousouli (Padamadan/Nikos/u/s Warner, Kyle/Dewey/Grandmaster Chad), J.B. Wing (Courtney/Mom/Whitney/u/s Paulette, Vivienne); February 23–March 14, 2010

On The Town Music by Leonard Bernstein, book and lyrics by Betty Comden and Adolph Green; Based on an idea by Jerome Robbins; Director, Bill Berry; Choreographer, Bob Richard; Music Director/Conductor, Ian Eisendrath; Set, Walt Spangler; Costumes, David C. Woolard; Lighting, Tom Sturge; Sound, Zach Williamson; Hair and Makeup, Mary Pyanowski; Stage Manager, Amy Gornet; Production Supervisor, Andrew G. Luft; Technical Director, Mark Schmidt; Associate Director, Brandon Ivie; Associate Choreographer, David Alewine; Associate Music Director, Faith Seetoo; Assistant Stage Managers, Jessica C. Bomball & Julie Haber; Cast: Joe Aaron Reid (Gabey), Greg McCormick Allen (Ozzie), Matt Owen (Chip), Billie Wildrick (Claire), Sarah Rudinoff (Hildy), Courtney Iventosch (Ivy), Allen Fitzpatrick (Judge Pitkin), Suzy Hunt (Madame Dilly), Jennifer Sue Johnson (Lucy Schmeeler), Richard Gray (Workman/Bill Poster/Announcer/Figment/MC), Ekello Harrid Jr. (First Workman/Uperman/Nedicks/Attendant), Frances Leah King (Old Lady/Nun), David Alewine (Rajah Bimmy/Ensemble); Ensemble: Jeffrey Alewine, Kelly Ann Barton, Ty Alexander Cheng, Gabriel Corey, Brittany Jamieson, Geneva Jenkins, Kylie Lewallen, Nikki Long (Assistant Choreographer), Vincent Lopez, Amber Nicole Mayberry, Mia Monteabaro, Joel Myers, Kasey Nusbickel, Tory Peil, Patrick Pulkrabek, Marissa Quimby, Dane Stokinger; Performance Interns: Dana Blasingame, Brian Kerrick, Arwen Morgan, Sage Price; April 11–May 2, 2010

Candide (The Royal National Theatre Version) Music by Leonard Bernstein, book adapted from Voltaire by Hugh Wheeler, in a new version by John Caird, lyrics by Richard Wilbur, additional lyrics by Stephen Sondheim, John La Touche, Lillian Hellman, Dorothy Parker, & Leonard Bernstein Director, David Armstrong; Music Director/Conductor, Joel Fram; Set, Matthew Smucker; Costumes, Lynda L. Salsbury; Lighting, Tom Sturge; Sound, Ken Travis; Hair and Makeup, Mary Pyanowski; Fight Director, Geoffrey Alm; Associate Director, Aaron Tuttle; Stage Manager, Jeffrey K. Hanson; Production Supervisor, Andrew G. Luft; Technical Director, Mark Schmidt; ASM, Bret Torbeck; Cast: David Pichette (Voltaire/Dr. Pangloss), Stanley Bahorek (Candide), Laura Griffith (Cunegonde), Anne Allgood (The Old Woman), Mike McGowan (Maximillian/Vanderdendur/Agent of Inquisition), Allen Fitzpatrick (Martin/The Minister/Grand Inquisitor), Brandon O'Neill (Cacambo/Sailor), Billie Wildrick (Paquette), Timothy McCuen Piggee (King/James, the Anabaptist/Slave/Achmed), Eric Polani Jensen (Baron/Don Issacar/The Governor/King Stanislaus); Ensemble: Jeffrey Alewine, Greg McCormick Allen, Jadd Davis, Mary Jo DuGaw, Anne Eisendrath, Corinna Lapid

Munter, Karen Skrinde, Dane Stokinger, Cayman Ilika; Performance Interns: Dana Blasingame, Emily Cawley, Sean Glynn, Arwen Morgan, Sage Price, Lauren Smith; May 25–June 13, 2010

Florida Stage

Manalapan, Florida

Twenty-forth Season

Artistic Director, Louis Tyrrell; Managing Director, Nancy Barnett

The Laramie Project: Ten Years Later (An Epilogue) by Moisés Kaufman, Leigh Fondakowski, Greg Pierotti, Andy Paris, Stephen Belber and the Tectonic Theater Project; Part of the world premiere international reading of the play presented at over 100 theatres; October 12, 2009

Two Jews Walk Into a War... by Seth Rozin; Director, Louis Tyrell; Set/Lighting, Richard Crowell; Sound, Matt Kelly; Costumes, Erin Amico; PSM, Jame Danford; Cast: Avi Hoffman (Zeblyan), Gordon McConnell (Ishaq); World Premiere; October 21–November 29, 2009

The Storytelling Ability of a Boy by Carter W. Lewis; Director, Louis Tyrell; Set, Victor Becker; Costumes, Erin Amico; Lighting, John McFadden; Sound, Matt Kell; PSM, Suzanne Clement Jones; Cast: Marshall Pailet (Peck), Bethany Anne Lind (Dora), Laura Carbonell (Caitlin); World Premiere; December 9, 2009–January 17, 2010

Sins of the Mother Written and directed by Israel Horovitz; Set, Richard Crowell; Lighting, Suzanne M. Jones; Costumes, Erin Amico; Sound, Matt Kelly; PSM, James Danford; Cast: Gordon McConnell (Bobby Maloney), Francisco Solorzano (Dougie Shimmatarro), Brian Claudio Smith (Frankie Verga/Philly Verga), David Nail (Dubbah Morrison); January 27–March 7, 2010

Dr. Radio Book by Bill Castellino, music & lyrics by Christopher McGovern; Director/Choreography, Bill Castellino; Music Director, Christopher McGovern; Set, Timothy R. Mackabee; Lighting, Michael Gilliam; Sound, Matt Kelly; Costumes, Mark Pirolo; PSM, Suzanne Clement Jones; Cast: Irene Adjan (Penny McAdams), Elizabeth Dimon (Madame Agnieska Pilchowa), Nick Duckart (Rudolph Garcia), Wayne LeGette (Benjamin Weitz/Announcer), Margot Moreland (Kate Cuorecantare/Catherine Weitz); World Premiere; March 24–May 2, 2010

When the Sun Shone Brighter by Christopher Demos-Brown; Director, Louis Tyrrell; Set, Kent Goetz; Lighting, Richard Crowell; Sound, Matt Kelly; Costumes, Michiko Kitayama Skinner; PSM, James Danford; Cast: Dan Domingues (Jose "Joe" Sanchez-Fors Jr.), Natasha Sherritt (Liz Sanchez-McGovern), John Herrera (Manny Arostegui), Bill Schwartz (Jose Sanchez Sr.), Brandon Morris (Detective Dwayne Grant), Cliff Burgess (Anthony "Tony" Rinaldi); World Premiere; May 12–June 20, 2010

Low Down Dirty Blues by Randal Myler & Dan Wheetman; Presented in association with Northlight Theatre; Director, Randal Myler; Music Director, Dan Wheetman; Set, Jack Magaw; Lighting, Don Darnutzer; Sound, Victoria Delorio; Costumes, Rachel Laritz; PSM, Suzanne Clement Jones; Cast: Mississippi Charles Bevel, Felicia P. Fields, Gregory Porter, Sandra Reaves-Phillips; Rinker Playhouse at Kravis Center for the Performing Arts (Florida Stage's new home); July 17–September 5, 2010

Geva Theatre Center

Rochester, New York

Thirty-seventh Season

Artistic Director, Mark Cuddy; Managing Director Greg Weber

Souvenir *A Fantasia on the life of Florence Foster Jenkins* by Stephen Temperley; Director Vivian Matalon; Sets, R. Michael Miller; Costumes, Tracy Christensen; Lighting, Ann G. Wrightson; Assistant Lighting, Nelson Emig; Sound, David Budries; Stage Manager, Jack Gianino/Kirsten Brannen; Cast: Donald Corren (Cosme McMoon), Judy Kaye (Florence Foster Jenkins); Mainstage Theatre; September 8–October 4, 2009

The Clean House by Sarah Ruhl; Director Emma Griffin; Sets, Jo Winiarski; Costumes, Jessica Trejos, Lighting, Raquel Davis; Sound, Lindsay Jones; Assistant Sound, Scotty Iseri; Dramaturg, Jean Gordon Ryon; Stage Manager, Janine Wochna; Cast: Tania Santiago (Matilde), Anne-Marie Cusson (Lane), Lynne McCollough (Virginia), Tuck Milligan (Charles), Judith Delgado (Ana); Mainstage Theatre; October 13–November 8, 2009

A Christmas Story by Philip Grecian, based on the film distributed by Warner Brothers with a screenplay by Jean Shepherd, Leigh Brown and Bob Clark, and on the book *In God We Trust, All Others Pay Cash* by Jean Shepherd; Director Mark Cuddy; Sets, Robert Koharchik; Costumes, B. Modern; Lighting, Kirk Bookman; Sound, Dan Roach; Associate Director, Melissa Rain Anderson; Dramaturg, Jean Gordon Ryon; Stage Manager, Kirsten Brannen; Cast: William Parry (Ralph), Michael Motkowski or Sean Ryon (Schwartz), Alana Silber or Annaleigh York (Helen Weathers), Alison Banks or Alizabeth York (Esther Jane Alberry), Johnathan Mueller (Flick), Maia Guest (Mother), Gavin Flood or Jordan McNees (Ralphie), Kyle Mueller or Chase Boss (Randy), Remi Sandri (The Old Man), Matt Shill (Scut Farkas), Brigitt Markusfeld (Miss Shields); Mainstage Theatre November 19–December 27, 2009

Almost, Maine by John Cariani; Director Skip Greer; Sets, Dipu Gupta; Costumes, Pamela Scofield; Lighting, Kendall Smith; Sound, Dan Roach; Original Music, John Zeretzke; Dramaturg, Jean Gordon Ryon; Stage Manager, Kirsten Brannen; Cast: David Mason (Pete/Steve/Lendall/Chad/Dave), Regan Thompson (Ginette/Sandrine/Gayle), Patrick Noonan (East/Jimmy/Randy/Phil), Alexis McGuinness (Glory/Waitress/Marvalyn/Marci/Suzette/Rhonda); Mainstage Theatre; January 12–February 7, 2010

Underneath the Lintel by Glen Berger; Director, Padraic Lillis; Sets, Lea Umberger; Costumes, Amanda Doherty; Lighting, Derek Madonia; Sound, Ian Hildreth; Dramaturg, Marge Betley; Stage Manager, Kirsten Brannen; Cast: Daniel Pearce (The Librarian); Nextstage Theatre; February 5–March 7, 2010

The Price by Arthur Miller; Co-produced with Syracuse Stage; Director Timothy Bond; Sets, Scott Bradley; Costumes, Laurie Churba Kohn; Lighting, Thomas C. Hase; Sound, Jonathon R. Herter; Associate Sound, Ian Hildreth; Dramaturg, Kyle Bass; Stage Manager, Christine Lomaka; Cast: Richard McWilliams (Victor), Carmen Roman (Esther), Kenneth Tigar (Gregory Solomon), Tony DeBruno (Walter); Mainstage Theatre; February 23–March 21, 2010

Convenience *Original Cast Reunion Concert* Book, music and lyrics by Gregg Coffin; Director, Mark Cuddy; Music Director, Don Kot; Vocal Arrangements/ Orchestration, Gregg Coffin and Michael Gribbin; Lighting, Derek Madonia; Sound, Ian Hildreth; Stage Manager, Kirsten Brannen; Cast: Jim Poulos (Vince), Mary Jo McConnell (Liz), Ron DeStefano (Ethan/Young Vince), Martin Vidnovic (Abe/Traitor King), Melissa Rain Anderson (Young Liz), Mainstage Theatre; March 15, 2010

Two Trains Running by August Wilson; Director Ron OJ Parson; Sets, Shaun Motley; Costumes, Myrna Colley-Lee; Lighting, Kathy A. Perkins; Sound, Ian Hildreth; Dramaturg, Marge Betley; Stage Manager, Janine Wochna; Cast: Ronald Conner (Wolf), A.C. Smith (Memphis Lee), Patrese D. McClain (Risa), Alfred Wilson (Holloway), David Shakes (Hambone), Javon Johnson (Sterling), Allen Edge (West); Mainstage Theatre; March 30–April 25, 2010

Five Course Love Book, music and lyrics by Gregg Coffin; Director Mark Cuddy; Choreography, Peggy Hickey; Musical Director, Don Kot; Sets, Adam Koch; Costumes, Devon Painter; Lighting, Robert Wierzel; Sound, Daniel Erdberg; Stage Manager, Kirsten Brannen; Cast: Troy Britton Johnson (Matt/Gino/Klaus/ Guillermo/Clutch); Kevin Ligon (Dean/Carlo/Heimlich/Ernesto/Pops); Kristen Mengelkoch (Barbie/Sofia/Gretchen/Rosalinda/Kitty); Understudies: Brad Greer, Jessica Vosk; Mainstage Theatre; May 5–June 12, 2010

Goodman Theatre

Chicago, Illinois

Eighty-fifth Season

Artistic Director, Robert Falls; Managing Director, Roche Schulfer

Albert Theatre

Animal Crackers Book by George S. Kaufman and Morrie Ryskind, music and lyrics by Bert Kalmar and Harry Ruby; Adaptor/Director, Henry Wishcamper; Choreography, John Carrafa; Clowing, Paul Kalina; Music Director/Additional Arrangements & Orchestrations, Doug Peck; Set, Robin Vest; Lighting, Matthew Richards; Costumes, Jenny Mannis; Sound, Richard Woodbury; Dramaturg, Neena Arndt; PSM, Joseph Drummond; Stage Managers, T. Paul Lynch, Alden Vasquez; Cast: Stanley Wayne Mathis (Roscoe W. Chandler/Hives), Ora Jones (Mrs. Rittenhouse), Mara Davi (Arabella Rittenhouse/Mrs. Whitehead), Tony Yazbeck (Wally Winston/M. Doucet), Jessie Mueller (Grace Carpenter/Mary Stewart), Ed Kross (John Parker/Horatio Jamison), Joey Slotnick (Captain Jeffey T. Spaulding), Jonathan Brody (Emanuel Ravelli), Molly Brennan (The Professor); September 18–November 1, 2009

A Christmas Carol by Charles Dickens, adapted by Tom Creamer; Director, William Brown; Set, Todd Rosenthal; Lighting, Robert Christen; Costumes, Heidi Sue McMath; Sound, Cecil Averett; Original Music, Andrew Hansen; PSM, Alden Vasquez; Stage Manager, Jamie Wolfe: Cast: Justin Amolsch (French Horn), John Francis Babbo (Tiny Tim Cratchit/Ignorance), Behzad Dabu (Dick Wilkins/ Young Man), Susan Felder (Charwoman/Mrs. Fezziwig), Tim Gittings (Poulterer/ Schoolmaster/Topper), Matthew Gold (Turkey Boy), Caroline Heffernan (Child in Doorway/Emily Cratchit/Want), Greg Hirte (Mr. Spinet/Violin/Fiddle), Katie Jeep (Abby, Fred's Wife/Mrs. Dilber), Anish Jethmalani (Ghost of Jacob Marley/ Old Joe), Bethany Jorgensen (Philomena/Violin), Ann Joseph (Miss Crumb), Jessie Mueller (Belle/Catherine), Lauren Patten (Martha Cratchit/Young Woman), Michael Perez (Mr. Ortle), Adam Poss (Percy/Undertaker), Ron Rains (Bob Cratchit), Malcolm Ruh (Accordian/Guitar), Nathan Sabo (Scrooge as a Boy/ Peter Cratchit), Matt Schwader (Fred), Christine Sherrill (Mrs. Cratchit), Andy Truschinski (Young Scrooge/Tree Seller/Ghost of Christmas Future), Bret Tuomi (Mr. Fezziwig/Chestnut Seller), Penelope Walker (Ghost of Christmas Present), Alex Weisman (Ghost of Christmas Past/Stephen), Mackenzie Wilkin (Fan/Belinda Cratchit), Larry Yando (Ebenezer Scrooge) 32nd Annual Production; November 20–December 31, 2009

Hughie/Krapp's Last Tape *Hughie* by Eugene O'Neill, directed by Robert Falls; *Krapp's Last Tape* by Samuel Beckett, directed by Jennifer Tarver; Set, Eugene Lee; Lighting, Robert Thomson; Costumes, Patrick Clark; Sound, Richard Woodbury; PSM, Joseph Drummond; Cast: *Hughie*: Joe Grifasi (Night Clerk), Brian Dennehy (Erie Smith); *Krapp's Last Tape*: Brian Dennehy (Krapp); January 16–February 28, 2010

A True History of the Johnstown Flood by Rebecca Gilman; Director, Robert Falls; Set, Walt Spangler; Lighting, James F. Ingalls; Costumes, Ana Kuzmanic; Original Music & Sound, Richard Woodbury; Dramaturgs, Neena Arndt and Tanya Palmer; PSM, Alden Vasquez; Stage Manager, Jamie Wolfe; Cast: Janet Ulrich Brooks (Mrs. Lippincott/Lituanian Woman/Clara Barton/Actress), Cliff Chamberlain (Richard), Sarah Charipar (Colleen), Stephen Louis Grush (James), Lucas Hall (Walter), Cedric Mays (Nathan), Randall Newsome (Fisherman/ Lituanian Man/Porter/Mill Worker/Mr. Barrett/Reporter/Actor), Heather Wood (Fanny); March 13–April 18, 2010

The Good Negro by Tracey Scott Wilson; Director, Chuck Smith; Set, Riccardo Hernandez; Lighting, Robert Christian; Costumes, Birgit Rattenborg Wise; Sound, Ray Nardelli & Joshua Horvath; PSM, Joseph Drummond; Stage Manager, T. Paul Lynch; Cast: Karen Aldridge (Corinne), Teagle F. Bougere (Henry), Tory O. Davis (Pelzie), John Hoogenakker (Paul), Billy Eugene Jones (James), Nambi E. Kelley (Claudette), Demetrios Troy (Rutherford), Dan Waller (Rowe), Mick Weber (Steve); May 1–June 6, 2010

The Sins of Sor Juana by Karen Zacharías; Director, Henry Godinez; Music, Gustavo Leone; Set, Todd Rosenthal; Lighting, Joseph Appelt; Costumes, Mina Hyun-Ok Hong; Sound, Ray Nardelli And Joshua Horvath; PSM, Alden Vasquez; Stage Manager, Jamie Wolfe; Cast: Amy J. Carle (Sor Sara/Vicereine), Laura Crotte (Xochitl/Sor Filothea), Malaya Rivera Drew (Sor Juana Inés de la Cruz), Joe Miñoso (Don Pedro), Dion Mucciacito (Silvio), Christina Nieves (Novice), Tony Plana (Padre Nuñez/Viceroy); Ensemble: Ilana Faust, Kevin Fugaro, Elly Lachman, Isabel Quintero; Presented as part of the 5th Biennial Latino Theatre Festival; June 19–July 25, 2010

Owen Theatre

Stoop Stories Written and performed by Dael Orlandersmith; Director, Jo Bonney; Set, Collette Pollard; Lighting, Keith Parham; Costumes, Anita Yavich; Sound, Eric Shimelonis; PSM, Jamie Wolfe; September 12–October 11, 2009

High Holidays by Alan Gross; Director, Steve Robman; Steven Robman; Set, Kevin Depinet; Lighting, Michael Philippi; Costumes, Birgit Rattenborg Wise; Sound, Ray Nardelli, Joshua Horvath; Dramaturg, Tanya Palmer; PSM, Kimberly Osgood; Cast: Max Zuppa (Billy), Rengin Altay (Essie), Keith Kupferer (ate), Ian Paul Custer (Rob); World Premiere; October 31–November 29, 2009

The Long Red Road by Brett C. Leonard; Director, Philip Seymour Hoffman; Set, Euguene Lee; Costumes, Janice Pytel; Original Music & Sound, Ray Nardelli & Johua Horvath; Dramaturg, Tanya Palmer; PSM, Kimberly Osgood; Cast: Tom Hardy (Sam), Greta Honold (Annie), Chris McGarry (Bob), Fiona Robert (Tasha), Katy Sullivan (Sandra), Marcos Akiaten (Clifton); February 13–March 21, 2009

5th Biennial Latino Theatre Festival Events at the Goodman included: *La Visita de la Vieja Dama* based on Friedrich Durrenmatt's *The Visit*, adapted by Raquel Carrió; Presented by Presented by Teatro Buendía (Cuba); Director, Flora Laute; July 8–11; *Charenton* by Raquel Carrió; Presented by Presented by Teatro Buendía (Cuba); Director, Flora Lauten; July 15–18; *El Nogalar* by Tanya Saracho; Presented by Teatro Vista (Chicago); Director, Cecilie Keenan; July 17; *Las Soldaderas* based on texts by Elena Poniatowska; Presented by Aguijón Theater Company; Director, Marcela Muñoz; July 21; *The Leader* Composed by Gustavo Leone and *On "Sor Juana"* a new opera by Elbio Rodríguez Barilari; July 22; *Our Dad is in Atlantis* by Javier Malpica, translated by Jorge Cortiñas; Presented by 16th Street Theater (Chicago); Director, Ann Filmer; July 23; *Of Princes, Princesses and Other Creatures* by Paola Izquierdo, translated by Susana Cook; Presented by Teatro Luna (Chicago); Director, Miranda Gonzalez; July 24; *Deserts* by Hugo Alfredo Díaz, translated by Caridad Svich; Presented by Aguijón Theater Company (Chicago); Director, Rosario Vargas (Spanish), Julieanne Ehre (English); July 24; *A Lover's Dismantling: Fragments of a Scenic Discourse* by Elana Guiochins, translated by Andy Bragen; Presented by Urban Theater Company (Chicago); Director, Marti Lyons; July 2; *Yamaha 300* by Cutberto López Reyes, translated by Mando Alvarado; Presented by Teatro Vista (Chicago); Director, Ricardo Gutierrez; July 25

Goodspeed Musicals

East Haddam and Chester, Connecticut

Forty-sixth Season

Executive Director, Michael P. Price; General Manager, Harriett Guin-Kittner; Associate Producer, Bob Alwine; Line Producer, Donna Lynn Cooper Hilton; Music Director, Michael O'Flaherty; General Manager, Harriett Kittner

Goodspeed Opera House (East Haddam)

42nd Street Music by Harry Warren, lyrics by Al Dubin, book by Michael Stewart and Mark Bramble; Director, Ray Roderick; Set, Howard Jones; Costumes, David H. Lawrence; Lighting, Charlie Morrison; Choreographer, Rick Conant; Music Director, William J. Thomas; Cast: Erick Devine (Abner Dillon), Jenifer Foote (Ann Reilly), Dale Hensley (Bert Barry, u.s. Julian Marsh), Kristen Martin (Peggy Sawyer), Austin Miller (Billy Lawlor), James Lloyd Reynolds (Julian Marsh), Dorothy Stanley (Maggie Jones, u.s. Dorothy Brock), Jonathan Stewart (Pat Denning, u.s. Abner Dillon), Laurie Wells (Dorothy Brock), Alissa Alter (Ensemble), Brandon Davidson (Ensemble), Kelly Day (Ensemble), Erin Denman (Ensemble), Tim Falter (Ensemble/Lee/Ensemble), Joe Grandy (Ensemble), Chad Harlow (Ensemble/u.s. Billy Lawlor/Pat Denning), Elise Kinnon (Phyllis Dale/Ensemble/u.s. Maggie Jones/Ann Reilly), Ashley Peacock (Ensemble), Kristyn Pope (Ensemble), Colin Pritchard (Ensemble/u.s. Bert Barry/Andy Lee), Ernie Pruneda (Ensemble), Tara Jeanne Vallee (Ensemble/Assistant Choreographer/Dance Captain), Erin West (Lorraine Fleming/Ensemble/u.s. Peggy Sawyer), Tyler Albright (Swing), Emily Thompson (Swing); April 17–July 4, 2009

Camelot Book and lyrics by Alan Jay Lerner, music by Frederick Loewe; Director, Rob Ruggiero; Set, Michael Schweikardt; Costumes, Alejo Vietti; Lighting, John Lasiter; Choreographer, Ralph Perkins; Music Director, Michael O'Flaherty; Cast: Ronn Carroll (Pellinore), Charles Everett Crocco (Tom of Warwick), Erin Davie (Guenevere), Maxime de Toledo (Lancelot), Bradley Dean (Arthur), Herman Petras (Merlyn/u.s. Pellinore), Adam Shonkwiler (Mordred), Brandon Andrus (Sir Lionel/Ensemble), Michael Deleget (Sir Clarius/Ensemble/u.s. Lancelot), Matt Faucher (Squire Dap/Ensemble, u.s. Mordred), Steve French (Sir Sagramore/Ensemble/u.s. Merlyn), Andrew Hubacher (Ensemble), Marissa McGowan (Ensemble/u.s. Guenevere), Rachel Alexa Norman (Ensemble), Rebecca Pitcher (Nimue/Ensemble), Rachel Rincione (Ensemble/u.s. Nimue), Allan Snyder (Sir Dinadan/Ensemble/u.s. Arthur), Matthew C. Thompson (Sir Angus/Ensemble), Mollie Vogt-Welch (Ensemble), Shawn Pennington (Swing), Amanda Salvatore (Swing), Ben Swimmer (u.s. Tom of Warwick); July 10–September 19, 2009

A Funny Thing Happened On the Way to the Forum Music and lyrics by Stephen Sondheim, book by Burt Shevelove and Larry Gelbart; Director and Choreographer, Ted Pappas; Set, James Noone; Costumes, Martha Bromelmeier; Lighting, Kirk Bookman; Music Director, Michael O'Flaherty;; Cast: Mark Baker (Erronius/u.s. Senex), Nat Chandler (Miles Gloriosus), Mary Gutzi (Domina), Adam Heller (Pseudolus), Sam Pinkleton (Hero), John Scherer (Hysterium), Emily Thompson (Philia), Ron Wisniski (Marcus Lycus/u.s. Pseudolus), David Wohl (Senex), Jason Babinsky (Protean/u.s. Erronius/Marcus Lycus), Kurt Domoney (Protean/u.s. Miles Gloriosus), Semhar Ghebremichael (Panacea), Laura Keller (Gymnasia), Kara Kimmer (Vibrata), Steve Konopelski (Protean), Stephanie Lynn Nelson (Tintinabula/u.s. Domina), Abbey O'Brien (Geminae), Krista Saab (Geminae), Michael Biren (Swing/u.s. Hero/Hysterium), Emily Susanne Franklin (Swing/u.s. Philia/Gymnasia/Tintinabula/Vibrata/Geminae/Panacea); September 25–November 29, 2009

Emmet Otter's Jug Band Christmas Book by Timothy Allen McDonald and Christopher Gattelli, music and lyrics by Paul Williams, based on the book by Russell and Lillian Hoban and the original television special produced and directed by Jim Henson, and written by Jerry Juhl; Produced in association with The Jim Henson Company (Executive Producer, Brian Henson); Director/Choreography, Christopher Gattelli; Set, Anna Louizos; Costumes, Gregg Barnes; Lighting, Brian MacDevitt; Music Director, Larry Pressgrove; Cast: Justin Bohon (Emmet Otter), Kathy Fitzgerald (Mrs. Alice Otter), Jill Abramovitz (Mrs. Mink/Hetty Muskrat), Stanley Bahorek (Will Possum/Charlie Muskrat), Scott Barnhardt (Wendell Porcupine/u.s. Emmet Otter), Jennifer Barnhart (Madame Squirrel/Scatfish/u.s. Old Lady Possum) Jenna Berloni (Jane understudy), Stephen Bienskie (Russ/Stan Weasel), Thomas Cannizzaro (Mayor Harrison Fox), Leo Daignault (Doc Bullfrog/Chuck Stoat), Jessica Elovsson (Swing/u.s. Mrs. Gretchen Fox/Mrs. Mink/Madame Squirrel/Scatfish/Hetty Muskrat), Craig Glenn Foster (Swing/u.s. Puss/Wendell Porcupine/Mayor Harrison Fox/Will Possum/Stan Weasel/Harvey Beaver/Charlie Muskrat), Matthew Furtado (Harvey Beaver/

Tracey Maloney and Angela Timberman in the Guthrie Theater production of Circle Mirror Transformation *(photo by Michal Daniel)*

Colman Domingo and Forrest McClendon in The Scottsboro Boys *at the Guthrie Theater (photo by Paul Kolnik)*

Bill Raymond and Bill Kux in the Hartford Stage Company annual production of A Christmas Carol–A Ghost Story of Christmas *(photo by T. Charles Erickson)*

Nikkole Salter, Jason Dirden, Billy Eugene Jones, and Rosie Benton in the Huntington Theatre Company and Arena Stage production of Stick Fly *(photo by Scott Suchman)*

Frank Roberts, Kelly Anne Clark, and Ernest W. Ray in Archy and Mehitabel *at the Illinois Theatre Center (photo courtesy of Jonathan R. Billig)*

Jeff Cummings, Minita Gandhi, La Shawn Banks, and John Lister in Indiana Repertory Theatre's Around the World in Eighty Days *(photo by Julie Curry)*

Reginald André Jackson and Erik Lochtefeld in the Intiman Theatre production of Abe Lincoln in Illinois *(photo by Chris Bennion)*

Stark Sands and Laura Osnes in Bonnie and Clyde *at La Jolla Playhouse (photo by Craig Schwartz)*

John Leguizamo in Diary of a Madman at La Jolla Playhouse *(photo by Craig Schwartz)*

u.s. Yancy Woodchuck/Doc Bullfrog/Chuck Stoat/Howard Snake/Fred Lizard/Pa Otter), Meg Guzulescu (Jane), Lisa Howard (Gretchen Fox/u.s. Mrs. Alice Otter), Anney Ozar (Old Lady Possum), James Silson (Howard Snake), David Stephens (Yancy Woodchuck/Fred Lizard/Pa Otter); December 5, 2009–January 3, 2010

The Norma Terris Theatre (Chester) - Twenty-sixth Season

Lucky Guy Book, music and lyrics by Willard Beckham; Director/Choreography, Warren Carlyle; Musical Supervision and Orchestrations, Todd Ellison; Set, Walt Spangler; Costumes, William Ivey Long; Lighting, Ken Billington; Music Director, Antony Geralis; Sound, Jay Hilton; Stage Manager, Kim Vernance; Technical Director, Jason Grant; Associate Director/Choreographer, Parker Esse; Cast: Josh Grisetti (Billy Ray), Katie Adams (Chicky), Autumn Hurlbert (Wanda), Gary Beach, (Big Al), John Bolton (GC), Stacia Fernandez (Jeannie), Stephen Carrasco, Robert H. Fowler, James Gray, Gavin Lodge (The Lucky Guy Buckaroos); May 14–June 14, 2009

Great Plains Theatre

Abilene, Kansas

Fourteenth Season

Artistic Director, Marc Liby; Production Manager, Doug Nuttleman; Technical Director, Jimilee Rempe; Education Director, Greg Kumins

South Pacific Music by Richard Rodgers, lyrics by Oscar Hammerstein; Director, Marc Liby; Musical Director, Joe Markley; Stage Manager, Doug Nuttelman; Lighting, Jimilee Rempe; Costumes, Andrea Huckaba; Cast: Laura Ernst (Nellie Forbush), Charles Fugate (Emile de Becque), Rhianna Jordan (Ngana), Caleb Jordan (Jerome), Kolby Kelly (Henry), Delali Potakey (Bloody Mary), Stephanie Henderson (Liat), Jeff Haffner (Luther Billis), Nathan Dibben (Abner), Kyle Chamberlin (Stewpot), Robert Wighs (Professor), James Jelkin (Lt. Cable), Nathan Grant (Capt. Brackett), Monte Dibben (Commander Harbison), Adam Loyd (Buzz Adams), Dylan Jost (Herbert Quale), Keegan Cole (Bob McCaffrey), Greg Krumins (Sailor); Nurses: Melissa Ford, Stephanie Gerry, Brenna Fulton, Meghan Newman, Lisa Kranz; June 5–21, 2009

Rumors by Neil Simon; Director, Marc Liby; Stage Manager, Sherri Minick; Set/Lighting, Jimilee Rempe, Costumes, Doug Nuttelman; Cast: Ashley Pankow (Chris Gorman), Greg Krumins (Ken Gorman), Katti Powell (Claire Ganz), Ben Hensley (Lenny Ganz), Bryan Benware (Ernie Cusack), Nicole Savitt (Cookie Cusack), Robert Wighs (Glenn Cooper), Lucy Lockamy (Cassie Cooper), Kyle Chamberlin (Officer Welch), Jimilee Rempe (Officer Pudney); July 10–19, 2009

You're A Good Man, Charlie Brown Music and lyrics by Clark Gesner; Director, Doug Nuttelman; Choreography, David Ollington; Musical Director, Heather Luellen; Set/Lighting, Jimilee Rempe; Costumes, Andrea Huckaba; Stage Manager, Sherri Minick; Cast: Bryan Benware (Charlie Brown), Ben Hensley (Snoopy), Katti Powell (Lucy), Robert Wighs (Linus), Doug Nuttelman (Schroeder), Ashley Pankow (Sally); July 24–August 2, 2009

Are We There Yet? by Garth Wingfield; Director, Marc Liby; Musical Director, Joe Markley; Set/Lighting, Jimilee Rempe; Costumes, Maggie Hoffman; Stage Manager, Doug Nuttelman; Cast: Ben Hensley, Katti Powell, Marc Liby, Ashley Pankow; August 7–16, 2009

Arsenic and Old Lace by Jospeh Kesselring; Director, Marc Liby; Stage Manager/Costumes, Doug Nuttelman; Set/Lighting, Jimilee Rempe; Cast: Carolyn Lowery (Abby Brewster), Bonita Hanson (Martha Brewster), Michael Misko (Teddy Brewster), Samantha Cistulli (Elaine Harper), Charles Fugate (Mortimer Brewster), Dylan Paul (Jonathan Brewster), Herman Johansen (Dr. Einstein), Edwin Hanson (Officer O'Hara/Rev. Dr. Harper), Larry Divel (Mr. Gibbs/Mr. Witherspoon), Joe Markley (Officer Brophy), Monte Dibben (Officer Klein), Kim Riley (Lieutenant Rooney); October 23–November 1, 2009

Moon Over Buffalo by Ken Ludwig; Director, Marc Liby; Set/Light Design, Jimilee Rempe; Stage Manager/Costumes, Doug Nuttelman; Cast: Herman Johansen (George Hay), Anna Gangai (Charlotte Hay), Bonita Hanson (Ethel), Samantha Cistulli (Rosiland), Michael Misko (Howard), Nicole Nicastro (Eileen), Dylan Paul (Paul), Charles Fugate (Richard); November 6–15, 2009

Joseph and the Amazing Technicolor Dreamcoat Music by Andrew Lloyd Webber, lyrics by Tim Rice; Director, Marc Liby; Musical Director, Joe Markley; Assistant Musical Director/Choreography, Ashley Pankow; Stage Manager/Costumes Doug Nuttelman; Cast: Delali Potakey (Narrator), Sean Thompson (Joseph), Larry Divel (Jacob), Dylan Paul (Napthali), Andy Brown (Levi), Michael Misko (Reuben), Sean Riley (Zebulun), Greg Krumins (Gad/Potiphar's Wife), Matt Payne (Judah), Brady Blevins (Asher), Kolby Kelly (Dan), Bryan LaFave (Benjamin), Greg Pragel (Isaachar/Potiphar), Will Amato (Simeon), Marc Liby (Pharaoh); Childrens Chorus: Brendon Dalton, Gracie Dautel, Maggie Hoffman, Ben Luty, Jordan Luty, Jauni Reeves, Raelynn Reeves, Fiona Tokach, Sage Tokach, Sarah Veach, Cassidy Woodard, Katie Zuercher; December 4–20, 2009

Guthrie Theater

Minneapolis, Minnesota

Forty-seventh Season

Director, Joe Dowling

Wurtele Thrust Stage

The Importance of Being Earnest by Oscar Wilde; Director, Joe Dowling; Set, Walt Spangler; Costumes, Mathew J. LeFebvre; Lighting, Allen Lee Hughes; Music Consultant, Adam Wernick; Sound, Scott W. Edwards; Props, Patricia Olive; Wigs, Ivy Loughborough; Dramaturg, Michael Lupu; Voice and Dialect Coach, Lucinda Holshue; Movement, Marcela Lorca; PSM, Russell W. Johnson; ASM, Michele Harms, Justin Hossle; Assistant Director, Dionne Laviolette; Cast: Heidi Armbruster (Gwendolen Fairfax), Richard S. Iglewski (Rev. Canon Frederick Chasuble), Erin Krakow (Cecily Cardew), Nick Mennell (John "Jack" Worthing), Kris L. Nelson (Lane/Merriman), John Skelley (Algernon Moncrieff), Linda Thorson (Lady Bracknell), Suzanne Warmanen (Miss Laetitia Prism); September 12–November 8, 2009

A Christmas Carol by Charles Dickens, adapted by Barbara Field; Director, Gary Gisselman; Set, Neil Patel; Costumes, Jess Goldstein; Additional Costumes, David Kay Mickelsen; Lighting, Marcus Dilliard; Musical Director, Anita Ruth; Sound, Scott W. Edwards; Dramaturg, Michael Lupu; Voice and Dialect Coaches, Elisa Carlson, Lucinda Holshue; Associate Director/Movement Coach, Myron Johnson; Stage Manager, Jason Clusman; AMS, Justin Hossle, Elizabeth R. MacNally; Assistant Director, Rob Goudy; Cast: Robert O. Berdahl (Fred/Dick Wilkins), Elizabeth Pryce Davies (Marigold Fezziwig/Sophia), Steven Epp (Jacob Marley/Ghost of Christmas Yet to Come), Laura Esping (Mrs. Cratchit), Nathaniel Fuller (Blakely/Edwards), Peter Michael Goetz (Ebenezer Scrooge), Emily Gunyou Halaas (Mrs. Fred/Petunia Fezziwig), Richard S. Iglewski (Mr. Fezziwig/Cecil/Grasper), Charity Jones (Ghost of Christmas Past/Mrs. Dilber), Michael Kissin (Fiddler/Snarkers), Lee Mark Nelson (Bob Cratchit), Richard Ooms (Forrest/Mr. Queeze/Joe), James Ramlet (Ghost of Christmas Present/Squeeze), John Skelley (Young Scrooge/Mr. Grub/Topper), Prentiss Standridge (Belle), Angela Timberman (Mrs. Fezziwig/Mrs. Grigsby/Dorothea); 35th Annual Production; November 19–December 31, 2009

Macbeth by William Shakespeare; Director, Joe Dowling; Set/Costumes, Monica Frawley; Lighting, Frances Aronson; Composer, Adam Wernick; Sound, Scott W. Edwards; Fight Director, John Stead; Voice and Language Coach, Andrew Wade; Dramaturg, Carla Steen; Movement, Marcela Lorca; PSM, Russell W. Johnson; ASMs, Chris A. Code, Michele Harms; Assistant Director, Annelise Christ; Cast: Barbara Bryne, (A Weird Sister), Raye Birk (Duncan), John Skelley (Malcolm), Benjamin Rosenbaum (Donalbain), J.C. Cutler (Lenox), Bob Davis (Rosse), James

Noah (Angus), Peter Christian Hansen (Menteth), Tyson Forbes (Cathness), Erik Heger (Macbeth), Michelle O'Neill (Lady Macbeth), Bill McCallum (Banquo), Nicholas Saxton or Graham Zima (Fleance), Robert O. Berdahl (Macduff), Sun Mee Chomet (Lady Macduff), Noah Coon or Charlie Lincoln (Macduff's Son), Elizabeth McCormick or Nina Moschkau (Macduff's Daughter), Sam Bardwell (A Sergeant in Duncan's Army/Seyton), Kris L. Nelson (A Porter in the Macbeth household), Benjamin Rosenbaum (Servant to Macbeth), Suzanne Warmanen (A Weird Sister/Gentlewoman to Lady Macbeth), Isabell Monk O'Connor (A Weird Sister/Doctor); January 30–April 3, 2010

M. Butterfly by David Henry Hwang; Director, Peter Rothstein; Set, Allen Moyer; Costumes, Linda Cho; Lighting, Marcus Dilliard; Sound, Scott W. Edwards; Dramaturg, Jo Holcomb; Movement, Marcela Lorca; Voice and Dialect Coach, Elisa Carlson; Asian Discipline Consultant, David Furumoto; Stage Manager, Martha Kulig; ASMs, Jason Clusman, Elizabeth R. MacNally; Assistant Director, Dionne Laviolette; Casting, Pat McCorkle; Cast: Andrew Long (Rene Gallimard), Randy Reyes (Song Liling), Lee Mark Nelson (Marc/Consul Sharples/Man #2), Katie Guentzel (Renee/Girl in Magazine), Tina Chilip (Suzuki/Shu-Fang/Comrade Chine), Charity Jones (Helga/Woman at Party), Nathaniel Fuller (M. Toulon/Judge/Man #1), Sherwin F. Resurreccion, Eric Sharp, Momoko Tanno (Kurogo Dancers); April 17–June 6, 2010

A Streetcar Named Desire by Tennessee Williams; Director, John Miller-Stephany; Set, Todd Rosenthal; Costumes, Mathew J. LeFebvre; Lighting, Peter Mumford; Composer, Adam Wernick; Sound, Scott W. Edwards; Dramaturgy, Michael Lupu; Voice and Dialect Coach, Elisa Carlson; Fight Director, Robin H. McFarquhar; Movement, Marcela Lorca; Stage Manager, Chirs A. Code; ASM, Elizabeth R. MacNally; Casting, Pat McCorkle; Assistant Director, Sarah Gioia; Cast: Ricardo Antonio Chavira (StanleyKowalski), Stacia Rice (Stella Kowalski), Regina Marie Williams (Negro Woman), Ann Michels (Eunice Hubbell), Gretchen Egloff (Blanche DuBois), Steve Sweere (Steve Hubbell), Brian Keane (Harold "Mitch" Mitchell), Dario Tangelson (Pablo Gonzales), Liam Benzvi (A Young Collector), Yolanda Cotterall (Mexican Woman), Raye Birk (Doctor), Beth Gilleland (Nurse); Ensemble: Joshua Allen, Phineas J. Clark, Ashley Dubose, Bryce Jasper, Tesha Keller, Richard Reeder, Roger Wayne; July 3–August 29, 2010

McGuire Proscenium Stage

Ella Book by Jeffrey Hatcher, conceived by Rob Ruggiero and Dyke Garrison; Director, Rob Ruggiero; Musical Director, George Caldwell; Music Supervision/Arrangements, Danny Holgate; Set, Michael Schweikardt; Costumes, Alejo Vietti; Lighting, John Lasiter; Sound, Michael Miceli; Wigs, Charles LaPointe; Stage Manager, Richard Costabile; ASM, Elizabeth R. MacNally; Assistant Director, Nick Eilerman; Cast: Tina Fabrique (Ella Fitzgerald), Harold Dixon (Norman Granz), Ron Haynes (Trumpet Player/Louis Armstrong), George Caldwell (Piano/Conductor), Rodney Harper (Percussionist), Clifton Kellem (Bass Player); July 21–September 6, 2009

The Laramie Project: Ten Years Later (An Epilogue) by Moisés Kaufman, Leigh Fondakowski, Greg Pierotti, Andy Paris, Stephen Belber and the Tectonic Theater Project; Director, Ben McGovern; Cast: Mark Benninghofen, Michael Booth, Bob Davis, Melissa Hart, Charity Jones, Tracey Maloney, Kris L. Nelson, Michelle O'Niell; Part of the world premiere international reading of the play presented at over 100 theatres; October 12, 2009

Faith Healer by Brian Friel, Director, Joe Dowling, Associate Director, Benjamin McGovern; Set, Frank Hallinan Flood; Costumes, Christine A. Richardson; Lighting, Marcus Dillard; Sound, Scott W. Edwards; Dramaturg, Jo Holcomb; Voice and Dialect Coach, Lucinda Holshue; Stage Manager, Martha Kulig; ASM, Chris A. Code; Props, Patricia Olive; Cast: Joe Dowling (Frank Hardy), Sally Wingert (Grace Hardy), Raye Birk (Teddy); October 17–December 6, 2009

Romeo and Juliet by William Shakespeare; Co-presented with The Acting Company (Margot Harley, Producing Director); Director, Penny Metropulos; Set, Neil Patel; Costumes, Mathew J. LeFebvre; Lighting, Michael Chybowski; Music Composition and Direction, Victor Zupanc; Fight Director, Felix Ivanov; Voice and Text Consultant, Andrew Wade; Sound, Scott W. Edwards; Casting, Pat

McCorkle; Text Preparation, Dakin Matthews; Propmaster, Scott Brodsky; PSM, Karen Parlato; Choreography, Marcela Lorca; Production Manager, Scott Palmer; Staff Repertory Director, Corey Atkins; ASM, Nick Tochelli; Company Manager, Joseph Parks; Cast: Jesse Bonnell (Abraham/Friar John/Watch); Raymond L. Chapman (Friar Laurence), Laura Esposito (Juliet), Hugh Kennedy (Benvolio), Jason McDowell-Green (Lord Montague/Capulet Guest), Jamie Smithson (Paris/Gregory), Elizabeth Stahlmann (Nurse), William Sturdivant (Mercutio/Prince), Chris Thorn (Lord Capulet), Myxolydia Tyler (Perrin), Sonny Valicenti (Romeo), Christine Weber (Lady Capulet), Isaac Woofter (Tybalt/Apothecary/Watch); January 9–31, 2010

Brief Encounter by Noël Coward, directed and adapted by Emma Rice; Presented by the Kneehight Theatre; Originally produced by David Pugh & Dafydd Rogers with Cineworld; Set/Costumes, Neil Murray; Lighting, Malcolm Rippeth; Projections, Jon Driscoll, Gemma Carrington; Original Music, Simon Baker; Casting, Sam Jones; Assistant Director, Simon Harvey; Kneehigh Theatre Producer, Paul Crewes; General Manager for U.S. Tour, Michael Mushalla; Company Stage Manager, Steph Curtis; Deputy Stage Manager, Karen Habens; A.C.T. Stage Manager, Karen Szpaller; Cast: Joseph Alessi (Albert/Fred), Annette McLaughlin (Myrtle), Stuard McLoughlin (Stanley), Beverly Rudd (Beryl), Milo Twomey (Alec), Hannah Yelland (Laura), Eddy Jay (Musician), Adam Pleeth (Musician); February 11–April 3, 2010

Dollhouse by Rebecca Gilman, based on *A Doll's House* by Henrik Ibsen; Director, Wendy C. Goldberg; Set, Alexander Dodge; Costumes, Anne Kennedy; Lighting, Josh Epstein; Sound, Reid Rejsa; Dramaturg, Carla Steen; Vocal Coach, Elisa Carlson; Movement, Marcela Lorca; Stage Manager, Michele Harms; ASM, Justin Hossle; Assistant Director, Ellen Fenster; Casting, Pat McCorkle; Cast: Sarah Agnew (Nora Helmer), Peter Christian Hansen (Terry Helmer), Matt Guidry (Pete), Norah Long (Kristine Linde), Bhavesh Patel (Raj Patel), George A. Keller (Marta), Nora Montañez (Iris), Oralia Cecena or Alaina Lucy Rivera (Skyler), Alexander Cecena or Zel Weilandgruber (Max), Piper Gallivan or Emily Marceau (Macey); May 22–July 11, 2010

The Scottsboro Boys Music and lyrics by John Kander and Fred Ebb, book by David Thompson; Presented by the Vineyard Theatre; Director/Choreography, Susan Stroman; Set, Beowulf Boritt; Costumes, Toni-Leslie James; Lighting, Kevin Adams; Sound, Peter Hylenski; Music Direction/Vocal Arrangements, David Loud; Orchestrations, Larry Hochman; Conductor/Associate Musical Director, Paul Masse; Arrangements, Glen Kelly; Music Contractor, Andrew Cooke; PSM, Megan Smith; ASM, Martha Kulig; Casting, Jim Carnahan, Stephen Kopel; Fight Director, Rick Sordelet; Associate Director/Choreographer, Jeff Whiting; Assistant Choreographer, Eric Santagata; Dance Captain, Josh Breckenridge; Props Manager (N.Y.), Jessica Provenzale; Cast: Sharon Washington (The Lady), Colman Domingo (Mr. Bones), Forrest McClendon (Mr. Tambo), David Anthony Brinkley (Interlocutor); *The Scottsboro Boys*: Sean Bradford (Ozie Powell), Josh Breckenridge (Olen Montgomery), Derrick Cobey (Andy Wright), Jeremy Gumbs (Eugene Williams), Joshua Henry (Haywood Patterson), Rodney Hicks (Clarence Norris), Kendrick Jones (Willie Roberson), Julius Thomas III (Roy Wright), Christian Dante White (Charles Weems); *And*: Sean Bradford (Ruby Bates), David Anthony Brinkley (Judge/Governor of Alabama), Colman Domingo (Sheriff Bones/Lawyer Bones/Guard Bones/Attorney General/Clerk), Jeremy Gumbs (Little George), Rodney Hicks (Preacher), Kendrick Jones (Electrofied Charlie), Forrest McClendon (Guard Tambo/Samuel Leibowitz), Julius Thomas III (Electrofied Isaac/Billy/Cook), Christian Dante White (Victoria Price); Swings: E. Clayton Cornelious, JC Montgomery; Musicians: Paul Masse (Conductor/piano/harmonium), Ernie Collins (upright bass/tuba), Bruce Doctor (drums/percussion), Dave Jensen (trumpet/coronet), Dave Graf (trombone), Carolyn Boulay (violin), Mark Henderson (flute/clarinet/piccolo/bass clarinet), Kent Saunders/David Singley (guitar/banjo/mandolin); July 31–September 25, 2010

Dowling Studio

Super Monkey Created and presented by Jon Ferguson Theater Ensemble; Director, Jon Ferguson; Cast: Jason Ballweber, Tyson Forbes, Sophie Gori, Rebecca Hurd, Emily King, Elsie Langer, Sara Richardson, Anthony Sarnicki, Paul Sommers, Dario Tangleson; World Premiere; September 17–October 4, 2009

Tales from the Book of Longing Conceived, directed and featuring Stuart Pimsler with Suzanne Costell; Presented by Stuart Pimsler Dance & Theater; Set, Joe Stanley; Lighting, Karin Olson; Company: Brian Evans, Cade Holmseth, Kari Mosel, Laura Selle Virtucio, Roxane Wallace-Patterson, Kurt Bloomberg; World Premiere; October 8–18, 2009

Northern Lights/Southern Cross: Tales from the Other Side of the World by Kevin Kling; Presented by Interact Theater in collaboration with Tutti Ensemble (Australia); Director, Jeanne Calvit; Music, Pat Rix; Set, Brad Dahlgaard; Lighting, Karin Olson; PSM, Caitlin Schaeffer; Featuring: Kevin Kling, Catherine Campbell, Larry Yazzie, Stephen Goldsmith, Lac Courte Oreilles, Alvin Baker, Sherry Lorentz, Richard Millwood, Malcolm Warner, Mother Mary Thomas, Yeon Ju, Jackie Saunders, Robert Robertson's Twin Cities Community Gospel Choir; U.S. Premiere; October 22–November 8, 2009

Singled Out: A Festival of Emerging Artists Curated by Benjamin McGovern; Included: *Mortem Capiendum* by Jason Ballweber, Brant Miller, Nick Ryan and Matt Spring; Presented by Four Humors Theater; *June of Arc* by Ryan Hill; Presented by Sandbox Theatre; *The Black Arts* Directed by Jeremey Catterton; Presented by Lamb Lays with Lion; *American Sexy* by Trista Baldwin, directed by Brian Balcom; Presentede by The New Theatre Group; January 13–24, 2010

Yellow Face by David Henry Hwang; Presented by Mu Performing Arts; Director, Rick Shiomi; Set, Joe Stanley; Lighting, Wu Chen Khoo; Costumes, Cana Potter; Props, Heidi Berg; Sound, Forest Godfrey; Stage Manager, Lisa Smith; Cast: Randy Reyes (DHH), Matt Rein (Marcus G. Dahlman), Kurt Kwan, Erika Crane, Don Eitel, Kim Kivens, Allen Malicsi, Rose Tran, Wade Vaughn; February 4–21, 2010

Coward's Women Music by Noël Coward, conceived and directed by Michael Todaro; Presented by The Producing House; Cast: Erin Schwab, Maud Hixson, Rick Carlson; March 30–April 3, 2010

Circle Mirror Transformation by Annie Baker; Director/Set, Benjamin McGovern; Costumes, Kalere A. Payton; Lighting, Karin Olson; Sound, Scott W. Edwards; Dramaturg, Jo Holcomb; Stage Manager, Tree O'Halloran; ASM, Ashley Zednick; Cast: Chris Carlson (James), Ali Rose Dachis (Lauren), Tracey Maloney (Theresa), Bill McCallum (Schultz), Angela Timberman (Marty); May 20–June 13, 2010

Walker Art Center

The Walworth Farce by Enda Walsh; Presented by Druid (Ireland); Sponsored by the Guthrie and Walker Arts; Director, Mikel Murfi; Set/Costumes, Sabine Dargent; Lighting, Paul Keogan; Production Manager, Eamonn Fox; Company Stage Manager, Sarah Lynch; U.S. Stage Manager, Paula Tierney; Cast: Michael Glenn Murphy (Dinny), Tadhg Murphy (Sean), Raymond Scannell (Sean), Mercy Ojelade (Hayley); World Touring Production; October 21–25, 2009

Hartford Stage Company

Hartford, Connecticut

Forty-fifth Season

Artistic Director, Michael Wilson; Managing Director, Michael Stotts

SummerStage 2009 Included: Betty Buckley Broadway By Request (July 8–11); The Umbilical Brothers in *THWAK!* (July 15–August 2); *Yesterdays–An Evening with Billie Holiday* by Reenie Upchurch, directed by Woodie King Jr., featuring Vanessa Rubin (August 15–22)

The Orphans' Home Cycle by Horton Foote; Part 1: *Roots in a Parched Ground, Convicts, Lily Dale*; Part 2: *The Widow Cycle, Courtship, Valentine's Day*; Part 3: *1918, Cousins, The Death of Papa*; Produced in association with Signature Theatre Company; Director, Michael Wilson; In repertory September 3–October 24, 2009 (see complete credits under the Signature Theatre Company on page 249).

Mistakes Were Made by Craig Wright; Director, Jeremy B. Cohen; Set, Walt Spanger; Lighting, Marcus Doshi; Costumes, Alejo Vietta; Sound, Obadiah Eaves; Puppets, Stefano Brancato; Cast: Will LeBow (Felix Artifex), Susan Greenhill (Esther), Stefano Brancato (Denise); October 29–November 29, 2009

A Christmas Carol–A Ghost Story of Christmas by Charles Dickens, adapted and directed by Michael Wilson; Associate Director, Jeremy B. Cohen; Choreography, Hope Clark; Set, Tony Straiges; Costumes, Zack Brown; Lighting, Robert Wierzel; Original Music and Sound, John Gromada; Dialect Coach, Gillian Lane-Plescia; Music Director, Ken Clark; Youth Director, Carleigh Cappetta; Cast: Bill Raymond (Scrooge), Bill Kux (Mrs. Dilber/Jacob Marley), Robert Hannon Davies (Bob Cratchit), Michael Bakkensen (Fred/Scrooge at 30), Nathan Johnson (Lamplighter/Party Guest), Nafe Katter (First Solicitor/Undertaker), Gustave Johnson (Second Solicitor), Johanna Morrison (Bettye Pidgeon/Spirit of Christmas Past), April Glick (Rich Lady), Alan Rust (Bert/Fezziwig/Spirit of Christmas Present), Robert Patrick Sheire (Mr. Marvell), Patrick Morrisey (Scrooge at 15), Natalie Brown (Mrs. Fezziwig/Fred's sister-in-law/Old Jo), Chelsea Farthing (Nichola), Sarah Killough (Wendy), Andrea Rice (Fiddler), Salvatore Mitson (Dick Wilkings), Alex Shamas (Party Guest), Michelle Henrick (Belle), Rebecka Jones (Mrs. Cratchit), Shaylan Ske Glezjar (Martha Cratchit), Brock Harris (Fred's wife), Evan John Works Gonzalez or Emily Weiner (Tim Cratchit), Gillian Colbath or Kristen Fitzpatrick (Spoiled Child), Tai-Anthony Nigro or Thomas Beebe (Boy Scrooge/Party Guest), Alisha Kapur or Josie Kulp (Fan), Grace Gentile or Caitlin Becker (Claire), Rachele Dalton or Hollis Long (Belinda Cratchit), Zachary Scott Zavalick or Jacob Entenman (Peter Cratchit), Jacrhys Dalton or Rodney Edwards Jr. (Ignorance/Cider Child), Trisha Kapur or Katie Rice (Want/Fruit Child), Michael Foley Griffin or Jordan Cyr (Turkey Boy), Burns Kowalski or Amina Starr Edwards (Urchin); Ghostly Apparitions/Citizens of London: Natalie Brown, Kyle Brand, Brock Harris, Sarah Killough, Patrick Morrisey, Nathan Johnson; Schoolboys: Andrew Holland, Zachary Cyr, Grace Lillian Works Gonzalez, Abbi Roce, Abigail McMillan, Jordan Tyler Virtue; 12th Annual Production; December 3–30, 2009

Gee's Bend by Elyzabeth Gregory Wilder; Director, Hana S. Sharif; Set, Scott Bradley; Costumes, Linda Cho; Lighting, Lap Chi-Chu; Sound, Daniel Baker; Cast: Kimberly Hébert Gregory (Sadie), Teagle F. Bougere (Macon), Tamela Aldridge (Nella), Miche Braden (Alice/Asia); January 14–February 14, 2010

Motherhood Out Loud Co-conceived by Susan Rose and Joan Stein; Pieces written by Leslie Ayvazian, David Cale, Pat Candaras, Jessica Goldberg, Rinne Groff, Beth Henley, Lameece Issaq, Deborah Zoe Laufer, Lisa Loomer, Michele Lowe, Brett Paesel, Marco Pennette, Theresa Rebeck, Luanne Rice, Adriana Trigiani, Annie Weisman, Cheryl West, Christine Zander, and Mark Nutter; Director, Lisa Peterson; Set, Rachel Hauck; Costumes, David Woolard; Lighting, Howell Binkley; Sound, Jill BC DuBoff; Animation, Emily Hubley; Cast: Amy Irving, Randy Graff, April Yvette Thompson, James Lecesne; February 24–March 21, 2010

The Adventures of Tom Sawyer by Mark Twain, adapted by Laura Eason; Director, Jeremy B. Cohen; Set, Daniel Ostling; Lighting, Robert Wierzel; Costumes, Ilona Somogyi; Sound, Broken Chord Collective; Cast: Chris Bowyer (Sid Sawyer), Teddy Canez (Injun Joe), Louisa Krause (Becky Thatcher), Nancy Lemenager (Aunt Polly), Eric Lochtefeld (Muff Potter), Tim McKiernan (Tom Sawyer), Joe Paulik (Joe Harper), Casey Predovic (Huckleberry Finn); World Premiere Adaptation; April 1–May 9, 2010

Huntington Theatre Company

Boston, Massachusettes

Twenty-eighth Season

Artistic Directors, Peter DuBois, Norma Jean Calderwood; Managing Director, Michael Maso

Fences by August Wilson; Director, Kenny Leon; Sets, Marjorie Bradley Kellogg; Costumes, Mariann Verheyen; Lighting, Ann Wrightson; Sound, Ben Emerson;

Music Direction/Original Music, Dwight D. Andrews; Casting, Alaine Alldaffer; PSM, Leslie Sears; Stage Manager, Vanessa Coakley; Cast: John Beasley (Troy Maxson), Eugene Lee (Bono), Crystal Fox (Rose), Brandon J. Dirden (Lyons), Bill Nunn (Gabriel), Warner Miller (Cory), Faith Lambert or Hyacinth Tauriac (Raynell); Boston University Theatre; September 11–October 11, 2009

Maureen McGovern in *A Long and Winding Road* Conceived by Philip Himberg and Maureen McGovern; Presented in collaboration with Arena Stage; Director, Philip Himberg; Musical Director, Jeffrey Harris; Set, Cristina Todesco; Costumes, Chip Schoonmaker; Lighting, David Lander; Projections, Maya Ciarrocchi; Sound, Ben Emerson; PSM, Kathryn Most; Calderwood Pavilion at the Boston Center for the Arts; October 9–November 15, 2009

A Civil War Christmas: An American Musical Celebration by Paula Vogel; Director, Jessica Thebus, Music Supervisor/Arrangements/Orchestrations/Incidental Music, Daryl Waters; Music Director/Conductor, Andrew Resnick; Set, Dan Ostling; Costumes, Miranda Hoffman; Lighting, T.J. Gerckens; Sound, Ben Emerson; Casting, Alaine Alldaffer; PSM, Gail P. Luna; Stage Manager, Leslie Sears; Cast: Uzo Aduba (Hannah/Rose/Aggy/Matron), Chris Bannow (Chester Manton Saunders/Hay/John Surratt/Union Soldier), Jason Bowen (Willy Mack/Walker Lewis/Jim Wormley), Gilbert Glenn Brown (Decatur Bronson/James Wormley/Philip Ree); Ken Cheeseman (Abraham Lincoln/Walt Whitman/Silver); Ed Hoopman (John Wilkes Booth/Robert E. Lee/William Tecumseh Sherman/Raider 2/Mary Surratt/Union Solder), Karen MacDonald (Mary Todd Lincoln/Secretary of War Stanton/Widow Saunders), DeLance Minefee (Ely Parker/George's Ghost/Frederick Wormley/Moses Levy/Louis J. Wiechmann/Reverend Brown), Jacqui Parker (Elizabeth Keckley/Mrs. Thomas), Stephen Russell (Henry Wadsworth Longfellow/Ulysses S. Grant/Ward Hill Lamon/Lewish Payne/Raider 1/Burwell/Minister), Molly Schreiber (Raz/Anna Surratt/Nicolay/Clara Barton/Mule), Alanna T. Logan or Hyacinth Tauriac (Jessa); Student Ensemble: Aaron Parker Fouhey, Alicia Lyn Hunt, Sarajane Mullins, Blake Pfeil, Rebekah Vega Romero; Children's Ensemble (at select performances): Grace Brakeman, Oliver Jay, Cameron Kelly, Savannah Koplow, Lauren Sabbag, Jeffrey Sewell, Abby Spare, Lily Steven, Amari Veale, Gabriele Lyman-von Steiger, Jonah Yannis; Musicians: Andrew Resnick (piano), Morgan Evans-Weiler (fiddle); Boston University Theatre; November 13–December 13, 2009

All My Sons by Arthur Miller; Director, David Esbjornson; Set, Scott Bradley; Costumes, Elizabeth Hope Clancy; Lighting, Christopher Akerlind; Original Music and Sound, John Gromada; Projections, Maya Ciarrocchi; Casting, Alaine Alldaffer; PSM, Carola Morrone; Stage Manager, Leslie Sears; Cast: Ken Cheeseman (Dr. Jim Bayliss), Will Lyman (Joe Keller), Owen Doyle (Frank Lubey), Dee Nelson (Sue Bayliss), Stephanie DiMaggio (Lydia Lubey), Lee Aaron Rosen (Chris Keller), Andrew Cekala or Spencer Evett (Bert), Karen MacDonald (Kate Keller), Diane Davis (Ann Deever), Michael Tisdale (George Deever); Boston University Theatre; January 8–February 7, 2010

Stick Fly by Lydia R. Diamond; Presented in collaboration with Arena Stage; Director, Kenny Leon; Set, David Gallo; Costumes, Reggie Ray; Lighting, Allen Lee Hughes; Sound, Timothy J. Thompson; Casting, Alaine Alldaffer; PSM, Kathryn Most; Stage Manager, Josiane L. Lemieux; Cast: Nikkole Salter (Taylor), Jason Dirden (Kent "Spoon"), Amber Iman (Cheryl), Billy Eugene Jones (Flip), Wendell W. Wright (Joe LeVay), Rosie Benton (Kimber); Calderwood Pavilion at the Boston Center for the Arts; February 19–March 28, 2010

Becky Shaw by Gina Gionfriddo; Director, Peter DuBois; Set, Derek McLane; Costumes, Jeff Mahshie; Lighting, David Weiner; Sound, Walter Trarbach; Casting, Alaine Alldaffer; PSM, Lori Ann Zepp; Stage Manager, Carola Morrone; Cast: Keira Naughton (Suzanna Slater), Seth Fisher (Max Garrett), Maureen Anderman (Susan Slater), Eli James (Andrew Porter), Wendy Hoopes (Becky Shaw); Boston University Theatre; March 5–April 4, 2010

Prelude to a Kiss by Craig Lucas; Director, Peter DuBois; Set, Scott Bradley; Costumes, Elizabeth Hope Clancy; Lighting, Japhy Weideman; Original Music and Sound, David Remedios; Projections, Maya Ciarrocchi; Casting, Alaine Alldaffer; PSM, Leslie Sears; Stage Manager, Carola Morrone; Cast: Brian Sgambati (Peter),

Timothy John Smith (Taylor), Cassie Beck (Rita), Jason Bowen (Tom/Jamaican Waiter), Nancy E. Carroll (Mrs. Boyle), Michael Hammond (Dr. Boyle), Ted Hewlett (Minister), Cheryl McMahon (Aunt Dorothy/Leah), Ken Cheeseman (Uncle Fred), MacIntyre Dixon (Old Man); Ensemble: Georgette Lockwood, Alex Schneps; Boston University Theatre; May 14–June 13, 2010

Illinois Theatre Center

Park Forest, Illinois

Thirty-forth Season

Producing Artistic Director, Etel Billig; Associate Director, Jonathan R. Billig; Production Manager, James Corey

A Shayna Maidel by by Barbara Lebow; Director, Etel Billig; Cast: Angela Beyer (Luisa Weiss Pechenik), Jacquie Beyer (Rose Weiss), Samuel Hicks (Duvid Pechenik), Bernard Rice (Mordechai Weiss), Judy Rossignuolo-Rice (Mama), Jeny Wasilewski (Hana); September 25–October 11, 2009

Copenhagen by Michael Frayn; Director, David Perkovich; Cast: Si Osborne (Warner Heisenberg), Mary Mulligan (Margrethe Bohr), David Perkovich (Niels Bohr); October 30–November 15, 2009

Archy and Mehitabel Book by Mel Brooks & Joe Darion, music by George Klinsinger, lyrics by Joe Darion; Director, Etel Billig; Cast: Frank Roberts (Archy), Kelly Anne Clark (Mehitabel), David Boettcher (The Newspaperman), Ernest Ray (Big Bill/Tyrone T. Tattersall), Jeny Wasilewski, Jessica Lauren Fisher, Christine Ronna; December 4–20, 2009

Crumbs from the Table of Joy by Lynn Nottage; Director, Etel Billig; Cast: Ethan Henry (Godfrey Crump), Vallea E. Woodbury (Ernestine Crump), Kona N. Burks (Ermina Crump), Makeba Pace (Lily Ann Green), Amanda-Claire Lowe (Gerte Schulte); January 29–February 14, 2010

Last of the Red Hot Lovers by Neil Simon; Director, Etel Billig; Cast: Bill Bannon (Barney), Allison Moody (Elaine), Shelley Crawford (Bobi), Kristie Berger (Jeanette); March 5–21, 2010

No Way to Treat a Lady Book, music and lyrics by Douglas J. Cohen, adapted from William Goldman's novel; Director, David Boettcher; Cast: Peter Robel (Morris Brummel), Joe Lehman (Christopher "Kit" Gill), Regina Leslie (Sarah Stone), Debra Criche Mell (Flora/Mrs. Sullivan/Carmella/Alexandra/Sadie); April 16–May 2, 2010

Indiana Repertory Theatre

Indianapolis, Indiana

Thirty-eighth Season

Artistic Director, Janet Allen; Managing Director, Steven Stolen

Mainstage

The Heavens Are Hung in Black by James Still; Director, Peter Amster; Set, Russell Metheny; Costumes, Tracy Dorman; Lighting, Lap Chi Chu; Composer & Sound, Victoria Delorio; Dramaturg, Richard J. Roberts; Stage Manager, Nathan Garrison; Cast: Nicholas Hormann (Abraham Lincoln), Anthony Prostyakov (Tad Lincoln), Jason Bradley (John Hay), Adam Crowe (Ward Hill Lamon), David Alan Anderson (Dred Scott/Servant/Old Soldier/Uncle Tom), Ryan Artzberger (Walt Whitman), Martin Yurek (Edwin Booth/Union Officer), Robert Neal (John Brown/Billy Brown), Mary Beth Fisher (Mary Todd Lincoln), Robert Elliott (Edwin Stanton/Stephen Douglas), Patrick Clear (William Seward/Jefferson Davis), Diane Kondrai (Mrs. Winston/Young Woman), Nick Abeel (Thomas Haley), Gus Leagre (Willie Lincoln/Newsboy); October 6–25, 2009

A Christmas Carol by Charles Dickens, adapted by Tom Haas; Director, Priscilla Lindsay; Set, Russell Metheny; Costumes, Murell Horton; Lighting, Michael Lincoln; Composer, Andrew Hopson; Choreographer, David Hochoy; Musical Director, Christopher Ludwa; Dramaturg, Richard J. Roberts; Stage Manager, Nathan Garrison; Cast: Charles Goad (Ebenezer Scrooge), Ben Tebbe (Bob Cratchit/Postboy/Young Marley), Matthew Brumlow (Fred/Young Scrooge/Undertaker), Cora Vander Broek (Felicity/Ghost of Christmas Past/Laundress), David Alan Anderson (Portly Gentleman/Mr. Fezziwig/Ghost of Christmas Present), Milicent Wright (Sister of Mercy/Mrs. Fezziwig/Plump Sister/Charwoman), Constance Macy (Mrs. Cratchit/Roses Sister), Bethany Ulrey (Belinda Cratchit/Young Fan/Want), Tessa Buzzetti (Belinda Cratchit/Young Fan/Want), Mauricio Suarez (Peter Cratchit/Teen Scrooge/Lamplighter), Aaron Huey (Peter Cratchit/Teen Scrooge/Lamplighter), Sydney Miller (Tiny Tim/Boy Scrooge/Ignorance/Turkey Boy), Elijah Bush (Tiny Tim/Boy Scrooge/Ignorance/Turkey Boy), Mark Goetzinger (Marley's Ghost/Topper/Old Joe), Ryan Artzberger (Schoolmaster/Nutley/Ghost of Christmas Future/Poulterer's Man), Lilia Vassileva (Fan/Belle/Martha Cratchit/Fred's Maid); November 21–December 27, 2009

Romeo and Juliet by William Shakespeare; Director, Tim Ocel; Set, Gordon R. Strain; Costumes, Linda Pisano; Lighting, Peter West; Composer, Gregg Coffin; Sound, Todd Mack Reischman; Fight Choreographer, Rob Johansen; Dramaturg, Richard J. Roberts; Stage Manager, Nathan Garrison; Casting, Claire Simon; Cast: David Alan Anderson (Capulet), Cynthia Kaye McWilliams (Lady Capulet), Claire Aubin Fort (Juliet), Wayne T. Carr (Tybalt), Karen Aldridge (Nurse), Erik Hellman (Romeo), Ryan Artzberger (Mercutio), Ben Tebbe (Benvolio), Robert Neal (Friar Laurence), Brandon Miller (Paris); January 19–February 27, 2010

Becky's New Car by Steven Dietz; Director, James Still; Set, Kate Sutton-Johnson; Costumes, Nan Zabriskie; Lighting, Michael Lincoln; Sound, Todd Mack Reischman; Dramaturg, Richard J. Roberts; Stage Manager, Nathan Garrison; ASM, Amy K. Denkmann; Cast: Constance Macy (Becky Foster), Adriano Gatto (Chris Foster), Robert Neal (Joe Foster), Michael Shelton (Steve), Nicholas Hormann (Walter Flood), Lisa Ermel (Kenni Flood), Cindy Phillips (Ginger); March 23–April 11, 2010

Around the World in 80 Days Adapted from the Jules Verne novel by Mark Brown; Director, William Brown; Set, Kevin Depinet; Costumes, Rachel Anne Healy; Lighting, Charles Cooper; Original Music & Sound, Andrew Hansen; Dramaturg, Richard J. Roberts; Stage Manager, Nathan Garrison; Casting, Claire Simon Casting; Cast: Jeff Cummings (Phileas Fogg), La Shawn Banks (Passepartout/others), John Lister (Detective Fix/others), Minita Gandhi (Aouda/others), Zack Buell (Speedy/others); April 27–May 16, 2010

Upperstage

The Giver Adapted by Eric Coble from the novel by Lois Lowry; Director, Richard J. Roberts; Set, James Schumacher; Costumes, Linda Pisano; Lighting, Betsy Cooprider-Bernstein; Sound, Todd Mack Reischman; Stage Manager, Amy K. Denkmann; Cast: Robert K. Johansen (Father), Anna Miller (Lily), Jennifer Johansen (Mother/Chief Elder), Garrett McKenna (Jonas), Reilly Crouse (Asher), Maggie Williams (Fiona/Rosemary), Fred Marshall (The Giver); October 23–November 21, 2009

Love Letters by A. R. Gurney; Director, Janet Allen; Set, Gordon R. Strain; Costumes, Beth Bennett; Lighting, Betsy Cooprider-Bernstein; Sound, Todd Mack Reischman; Dramaturg, Richard J. Roberts; Stage Manager, Amy K. Denkmann; Cast: Patrick Clear (Andrew Makepeace Ladd III), Priscilla Lindsay (Melissa Gardner); December 15, 2009–January 17, 2010

Pretty Fire by Charlayne Woodard; Director, Richard J. Roberts; Set, Robert M. Koharchik; Costumes, Wendy Meaden; Lighting, Ryan Koharchik; Sound, Ryan Peavey; Stage Manager, Amy K. Denkmann; ASM, Joel Grynheim; Cast: Milicent Wright (Charlayne); February 9–28, 2010

The Year of Magical Thinking by Joan Didion; Director, Priscilla Lindsay; Set, Robert M. Koharchik; Costumes, Wendy Meaden; Lighting, Ryan Korharchik; Sound, Michael Lamirand; Dramaturg, Richard J. Roberts; Stage Manager, Delia Neylon; Cast: Fontaine Syer (Joan); Feburary 16–March 7, 2010

After Paul McCartney by David Hoppe; Director, John Green; Set, Robert M. Koharchik; Costumes, Wendy Meaden; Lighting, Ryan Korharchik; Sound, Ryan Peavey; Dramaturg, Richard J. Roberts; Stage Manager, Amy K. Denkmann; Cast: Rob Johansen (Philip); February 24–March 14, 2010

Intiman Theatre

Seattle, Washington

Thirty-seventh Season

Artistic Director, Bartlett Sher; Managing Director, Laura Penn

Crime and Punishment by Marilyn Campbell & Curt Columbus, based on the novel by Fyodor Dostoevsky; Director, Sheila Daniels; Set, Carey Wong; Costumes, Melanie Taylor Burgess; Lighting, Dans Maree Sheehan; Sound, Joseph Swartz; Fight Choreographer, Peter Dylan O'Connor; Stage Manager, Marianne C. Wunch; ASM, Courtney Scott; Cast: Hana Lass (Sonia), Todd Jefferson Moore (Porfiry), Galen Joseph Osier (Raskolnikov); March 29–May 3, 2009

A Thousand Clowns by Herb Gardner; Director, Sari Ketter; Set, Nayna Ramey; Costumes, Marcia Dixcy Jory; Lighting, Marcus Dilliard; Sound, Joseph Swartz; Dialect Coach, Judith Shahn; Ukulele Coach, John Ackermann; New York Casting, Janet Foster; Stage Manager, Kandra L. Payne; ASM, Chris M. Roberson; Cast: Matthew Boston (Murray Burns), Bradford Farwell (Albert Amundson), Tim Hyland (Leo Herman), Julie Jesneck (Sandra Markowitz), David Pichette (Arnold Burns), Nick Robinson (Nick Burns); May 15–June 17, 2009

Othello by William Shakespeare; Presented by Theatre for a New Audience; Director, Arin Arbus; Set, Peter Ksander; Costumes, Miranda Hoffman; Lighting, Marcus Doshi; Sound, Matt O'Hare; Composer, Sarah Pickett; Voice/Text Consultant, Robert Neff Williams; Dramaturg, Benjamin Nadler; Fight Choreographer, B.H. Barry; Choreographer, Doug Elkins; Casting Director, Deborah Brown; Stage Manager, Stina Lotti; ASM, Whitney Meredith Breite and Ayisha Hunt; Cast: Dennis Butkus (Roderigo), John Campion (Iago), Stevie Ray Dallimore (Brabantio/Lodovico), Kate Forbes (Emilia), Lucas Hall (Cassio), Robert Langdon Lloyd (The Duke/Gratiano), Elizabeth Meadows Rouse (Bianca), Christian Rummel (Montano), Lucas Steele (Senator/Gentleman/Musician), Sean Patrick Thomas (Othello), Elisabeth Waterston (Desdemona); July 2–August 9, 2009

The Year of Magical Thinking by Joan Didion based on her memoir; Director, Sarna Lapine; Set and Costumes, Mikiko Suzuki MacAdams; Lighting, L.B. Morse; Sound, Leon Rothenberg; New York Casting, Janet Foster; Stage Manager, Michael B. Paul; ASM, Lisa Stahler; Cast: Judith Roberts (Joan Didion), Lori Larsen (Joan Didion alternate); August 21–September 20, 2009

Abe Lincoln in Illinois by Robert E. Sherwood; Director, Sheila Daniels; Set, Mikiko Suzuki MacAdams; Costumes, Melanie Taylor Burgess; Lighting, L.B. Morse; Composer/Arrangements/Sound, Gretta Harley; Music Director, John Ackermann; Dialect Coach, Lisa Norman; New York Casting, Janet Foster; Stage Manager, Amy Poisson; ASM, Shellie Stone; Cast: John Ackermann (Soldier), Hans Altwies (Joshua Speed), Clayton Corzatte (Ben Mattling/Barrick), Susan Corzatte (Nancy Bowling Green), Angela DiMarco (Ann Rutledge/Maid), Allen Galli (Judge Bowling Green/Sturveson), Mary Jane Gibson (Mary Todd Lincoln), Langston Emerson Guettinger (Willie Lincoln), Russell Hodgkinson (Trum Cogdal/Crimmin/Soldier), Reginald André Jackson (Ninian Edwards), Erik Lochtefeld (Abe Lincoln), Peter Dylan O'Connor (Billy Herndon), Hannah Robinson (Tad Lincoln/Jimmy Gale), Jose Rufino (Bab/Gobey/Kavanaugh), Matt Shimkus (Jack Armstrong/Phil/Soldier), Richard Nguyen Sloniker (Seth/Jed/Soldier), Adam Standley (Fergus/Robert Lincoln), Kate Wisniewski (Elizabeth Edwards/Aggie Gale), R. Hamilton Wright (Mentor Graham/Stephen Douglas/Major); October 2–November 19, 2009

Black Nativity by Langston Hughes; Director, Jacqueline Moscou; Musical Direction and Arrangements, Pastor Patrinell Wright; Choreography, Kabby Mitchell III; Set, Dana Perreault; Costumes, Doris Black; Lighting, Allen Lee Hughes; Sound, Joseph Swartz; Dramaturg, Elizabeth Heffron; Stage Manager, Jessica C. Bomball; ASM, Rachel Bury; Cast: Pastor Patrinell Wright (The Woman), Bryson D. Conley (Joseph), Rev. Joseph E. Connor (Narrator), Josephine Howell (Narrator), Jimi Ray Malary (Narrator), Pamela Yasutake (Mary), The Total Experience Gospel Choir, The Black Nativity Choir; Musicians: Timothy E. Davis (drums), Walter Finch (lead guitar), Matthew D.L. Montgomery (piano), Rick Pitts (bass guitar); December 1–December 30, 2009

Kansas City Repertory Theatre

Kansas City, Missouri

Forty-sixth Season

Artistic Director, Eric Rosen; Managing Director, Cynthia Rider; Producing Director, Jerry Genochio

Spencer Theatre

Into the Woods Music & lyrics by Stephen Sondheim, book by James Lapine; Director, Moisés Kaufman; Choreograpy, Daniel Pelzig; Cast: Kip Niven (Mysterious Man/Cinderella's Father), Michelle Ragusa (Witch), Lauren Worsham (Cinderella), Tina Stafford (Jack's Mother/Cinderella's Mother/Granny/Giant Voice), Melinda MacDonald (Cinderella's Stepmother), Claybourne Elder (Cinderella's Prince/Wolf), Dana Steingold (Little Red Riding Hood), KC Comeaux (Jack), Brynn O'Malley (Baker's Wife), Brandon Sollenberger (Rapuzel's Prince), Zachary Prince (Baker), Lauren Braton (Rapunzel), Katie Kalahurka (Florinda), Katie Karel (Lucinda), Patrick DuLaney (Steward/Father), Zackary Hoar (Boy), Euan Morton (Narrator); September 12–October 4, 2009

A Christmas Story Book by Joseph Robinette, music and lyrics by Scott Davenport Richards; Director, Eric Rosen; Producers, Gerald Goehring, Michael F. Mitri & Michael Jenkins; Cast: Becky Barta (Miss Shields/others), John Bolton (The Old Man), Aaron Dwight Conley (Flick/others), Troy Doherty (Scout Farcus/others), Patrick DuLaney (Santa/others), Karen Errington (Radio Quartet/others), Seth Golay (Jimbo/others), Jennie Greenberry (Radio Quartet/others), Dakota Hoar (Schwartz/others), James Judy (Jean Shepherd), Katie Kalahurka (Elf/others), Katherine McNamara (Esther Jane/others), Alexiya Lourdes Mendez (Mary Beth/others), Orville Mendoza (Elf/Radio Quartet/others), Alan Mingo Jr. (Radio Quartet/others), Anne L. Nathan (Mother), Kip Niven (Tree Salesman/others), Zach Rand (Grover Dill/others), Zachary Carter Sayle (Ralphie Parker), Vanessa Severo (Mrs. Schwartz/others), Jake Bennett Siegfried (Randy Parker); November 20, 2009–January 3, 2010

Around The World In 80 Days Written and directed by Laura Eason, adapted from the novel by Jules Verne; Co-Production with CenterStage; Cast: Usman Ally (Mr. Naidu/others), Lance Baker (Phileas Fogg), Rom Barkhordar (Captain Speedy/others), Ravi Batista (Mrs. Aouda), Joe Dempsey (Inspector Fix), Kevin Douglas (Passepartout), Patrick New (Colonel Proctor/others), Ericka Ratcliff (Captain Von Darius/others/Dance Captain); January 22– February 14, 2010

Bus Stop by William Inge; Director, Steve Cosson; Cast: Blair Baker (Elma), David Fritts (Carl), Jim Gall (Will), Gary Neal Johnson (Virgil), Mark Robbins (Dr. Lyman), Jedadiah Schultz (Bo), Adria Vitlar (Cherie), Cheryl Weaver (Grace); March. 12– April 4, 2010

Copaken Stage

Palamino Written, directed and performed by David Cale; World Premiere; October 9–November 15, 2009

Broke-Ology by Nathan Louis Jackson; Director, Kyle Hatley; Cast: Shamika Cotton (Sonia), Larry Powell (Malcolm King), Postell Pringle (Ennis King), David Emerson Toney (William); February 19– March 21, 2010

Venice - A New Musical by Matt Sax & Eric Rosen; Director, Eric Rosen; Cast: Uzo Aduba (Anna Monroe), Clifton Duncan (Markos Monroe), J.D. Goldblatt (Theodore Westbrook), Andrea Kiyo Goss (Willow Turner), Colin Hanlon (Michael Victor), Javier Muñoz (Venice Monroe), Angela Wildflower Polk (Hailey Daisy), Matt Sax (Clown MC (Clay), Jasmin Walker (Emilia Monroe); Ensemble: Anna Eilinsfeld, Jay Garcia, Brandon Sollenberger; April 9–May 9, 2010

La Jolla Playhouse

La Jolla, California

Fortieth Season

Artistic Director, Christopher Ashley; Managing Director, Michael Rosenberg; Director of Play Development, Shirley Fishman

Mandell Weiss Theatre

Unusual Acts of Devotion by Terrence McNally; Director, Trip Cullman; Set, Santo Loquasto; Costumes, Jess Goldstein; Lighting, Ben Stanton; Sound, John Gromada; Stage Manager, Kelly Glasgow; Assistant Director, Milana Vayntrub; ASM, Jenny Slattery, Amy Bristol Brownewell; Dramaturgy, Shirley Fishman; Casting, Telsey + Company; Production Manager, Peter J. Davis; Cast: Maria Dizzia (Nadine Choate), Harriet Harris (Josie Shelton), Joe Manganiello (Leo Belraggio), Evan Powell (Man), Doris Roberts (Mrs. Darnell), Richard Thomas (Chick Hogan); West Coast Premiere; June 2–28, 2009

The 39 Steps Adapted by Patrick Barlow, based on the book by John Buchan and the film by Alfred Hitchcock; Original concept by Simon Corble and Nobby Dimon; Director, Maria Aitken; Set/Costumes, Peter McKintosh; Lighting, Kevin Adams; Sound, Mic Pool; Movement, Toby Sedgwick and Christopher Bayes; Stage Manager, Harold Godfaden; ASM, Jara Jaramillo; Dialects, Stephen Gabis; Casting, Jay Binder and Jack Bowdan; Cast: Claire Brownell (Anabella Schmidt/Pamela/Margaret), Ted Deasy (Richard Hannay), Ertic Hissom (Man #1), Scott Parkinson (Man #2); August 11–September 13, 2009

Bonnie and Clyde Book by Ivan Menchell, music by Frank Wildhorn, lyrics by Don Black; Director and Musical Staging, Jeff Calhoun; Music Supervision & Direction/Orchestrations/Vocal Arrangements/Incidental Music, John McDaniel; Set/Costumes, Tobin Ost; Lighting, Michael Gilliam; Sound, Brian Ronan; Projections, Aaron Rhyne; Dramaturg, Shirely Fishman; PSM, Paul J. Smith; Wigs/Hair, Carol Doran; Fight Director, Steve Rankin; Vocal and Dialect Coach, Robert Barry Flemeing; ASM, Sarah Marshall; Production Mananger, Peter J. Davis; Casting, Telsey + Company; Cast: Stark Sands (Clyde), Laura Osnes (Bonnie), Mare Winningham (Emma), Melissa Van Der Schyff (Blanche), Wayne Duvall (Sheriff), Claybourne Elder (Buck), Chris Peluso (Ted); Ensemble: Leslie Becker, Daniel Cooney, Courtney Corey, Michael Covert, Victor Hernandez, Micahel Lanning, Carly Nykanen, Mike Sears, Jessica Watkins; World Premiere; November 10–December 20, 2009

No Child... Written and performed by Nilaja Sun; Director, Hal Brooks; January 30, 2010

Aurélia's Oratorio Created, directed, and stage design by Victoria Thierrée Chaplin in collaboration with La Compagnie du Hanneton; Presented by Théâtre L'Avant-Scène and La Ferme du Buisson Cognac/René Marion; Lighting, Laura de Bernadis and Phillipe Lacombe; US Tour Producer, ArKtype, Thomas O. Kriegsmann; Costumes, Victoria Thierrée Chaplin, Jacques Perdiguez, Veronique Grand, Monika Schwarzl; Technical Director/Stage Manager, Gerd Walter; Company Manager, Didier Bendel; Technicians, Roberto Riegert, Nicholas Lazzaro; Crew, Tamara Prieto Arroyo, Antonia Paradsio; Cast: Aurélia Thierrée, Jaime Martinez; February 3–28, 2010

John Leguizamo's Diary of a Madman Written and performed by John Leguizamo; Presented by special arrangement with WestBeth Entertainment; Director, Fisher Stevens; A Page to Stage Workshop Production; March 4–14, 2010; Encore at the Shank Theatre May 18–29, 2010

Mandell Weiss Forum

Restoration by Claudia Shear; Director, Christopher Ashley; Set, Scott Pask; Costumes, David C. Woolard; Lighting, David Lander; Sound, Dan Moses Schreier; Projections, Kristin Ellert; Dramaturg, Gabriel Greene; Stage Manager, Lisa Porter; Wigs, Mark Adam Rampmeyer; Vocal and Dialect Coach, Eva Barners; ASM, Hanna Wichmann; Dramaturg, Gabriel Greene; Production Manager, Peter J. Davis; Casting, Heidi Levitt; Cast: Claudia Shear (Giulia), Alan Mandell (Professor Williams), Natalija Nogulich (Marciante/Beatrice/Nonna), Daniel Serafini-Sauli (Max), Kate Shindle (Daphne); World Premiere; June 23–July 19, 2009

HOOVER COMES ALIVE! by Sean Cunningham, Songs by Michael Freidman; Presented by Les Freres Corusier; Director, Alex Timbers; Music Director/Conductor, Cris O'Bryon; Set, Kristin Ellert; Costumes, Paloma Young; Lighting, Stephen Sakowski; Sound, Toby Algya; Projections, Jake Pinholster; Dramaturg, Gabe Green; Stage Manager, Amy Blatt; Cast: Damian Baldet (Herbert Hoover), Jim Mooney (Harry S. Truman), Marshel Adams (Lucille), Maren Bush (Sheila), Ross Crain (Scotty), Patrick Riley (DJ); A Page to Stage/EDGE series presentation; September 8–13, 2009

The Laramie Project: Ten Years Later (An Epilogue) by Moisés Kaufman, Leigh Fondakowski, Greg Pierotti, Andy Paris, Stephen Belber and the Tectonic Theater Project; Director, Jarko Tresnjak; Cast: Doug Wright, Sam Woodhouse, Anne Marie Welsh, Mare Winningham, Robert Foxworth, Amanda Naughton, James Newcomb, Stark Sands, T. Ryder Smith, James Sutorius, San Diego Mayor Jerry Sanders; Part of the world premiere international reading of the play presented at over 100 theatres; October 12, 2009

Sheila and Hughes Potiker Theatre

Dogugaeshi Created and performed by Basil Twist; Original shamisen compositions created and performed by Yumiko Tanaka; Video Projections, Peter Flaherty; Lighting, Andrew Hill; Sound, Greg Duffin; Technical Director, Mike Kerns; Tour Technical Director, Chelsea Mylett; Puppeteers: Kate Brehm, Oliver W. Dazell, Jessica Scott; Presented as part of the EDEGE series; June 10–14, 2009

Herringbone Book by Tom Cone, music by Skip Kennon, lyrics by Ellen Fitzhugh; Director, Roger Rees; Music Director/Conducor, Dan Lipton; Choreography, Darren Lee; Set, Eugune Lee; Costumes, William Ivey Long; Lighting, Christopher Akerline; Sound, Leon Rothenberg; Dramaturg, Shirley Fishman; Stage Manager, Anjee Nero; Production Manager, Peter J. Davis; Cast: BD Wong (George/others); August 1–30, 2009

Creditors Adapted by Doug Wright from the play by August Strindberg, translated by Anders Casto; Director, Doug Wright; Set, Robert Brill; Costumes, Susan Hilferty; Lighting, Japhy Weideman; Sound, Jill BC DuBoff; Dramaturg, Shirley Fishman; Stage Manager, Jennifer Teel Wheeler; Wigs, Tom Watson; Composition, David Van Tieghem; ASM, Erin Giola Albrecht; Casting, Telsey + Company; Cast: Kathryn Meisle (Tekla), Omar Metwally (Adolf), T. Ryder Smith (Gustav); World Premiere September 29–October 25, 2009

The Rao and Padma Makineni Play Development Center

Chile Pod by Rhiana Yazzie; Original Music, Gary Rue; Director, Sarah Rasmussen; March 20–21, 2010

Long Wharf Theater

New Haven, Connecticut

Forty-fifth Season

Artistic Director, Gordon Edelstein; Managing Director, Joan Channick

The Fantasticks Music by Harvey Schmidt, book and lyrics by Tom Jones; Director, Amanda Dehnert; Set, Eugene Lee; Costumes, Jessica Ford; Lighting, Nancy Schertler; Sound, David Budries; Choreogrtaphy, Sharon Jenkins; Musical Director, Bill Corcoran; Stage Manager, Lori Lundquist; Cast: Michael Sharon (El

Gallo), Jessica Grové (Luisa), Nathan Parlow (Matt), Dan Sharkey (Hucklebee), Ray DeMattis (Bellomy), William Parry (Henry), Joseph Tisa (Mortimer), Jonathan Randell Silver (The Mute); Mainstage; October 7–November 1, 2009

Have You Seen Us? by Athol Fugard; Director, Gordon Edelstein; Set, Eugene Lee; Costumes, Jennifer von Mayrhauser; Lighting, Stephen Strawbridge; Sound, Corrine Livingston; Cast: Sam Waterston (Henry Parsons), Liza Colon-Zayas (Adela), Sol Frieder (Solly), Elaine Kussack (Rachel); World Premiere; November 24–December 30, 2009

Lil's 90th by Darci Picoult; Director, Jo Bonney; Music Director, Erin Hill; Set, Frank L. Aberino; Costumes, Ilona Somogyi; Lighting, Lap Chi Chu; Sound, Jill BC Duboff; Cast: Lois Smith (Lil), David Marguiles (Charlie), Nick Blaemire (Tommy), Lucy Walters (Deirdre), Kristine Nielsen (Stephie); World Premiere; Stage II; January 6–February 7, 2010

Sylvia by A.R. Gurney; Director, Eric Ting; Sets, Frank J. Alberino; Costumes, Valerie Webster; Lighting, Ben Stanton; Sound, Jill BC DuBoff; Stage Manager, Charles M. Turner III; Dramaturg, Erin Treat; Cast: Erica Sullivan (Sylvia), John Procaccino (Greg), Karen Ziemba (Kate), Jacob Ming-Trent (Tom/Phyliss/Leslie); Mainstage; February 17–March 14, 2010

No Child... Written and performed by Nilaja Sun; Director, Hal Brooks; Stage II; March 17–April 18, 2010

A Doll's House by Henrik Ibsen, adapted and directed by, Gordon Edelstein; Set, Michael Yeargan; Costumes, Jessica Ford; Lighting, Russell H. Champa; Sound, David Budries; Cast: Tim Hopper (Rank), Mark Nelson (Nils Krogstad), Maegan Pachomski (Helene), Linda Powell (Christine), Ana Reeder (Nora), Adam Trese (Torvald); World Premiere Adaptation; Mainstage; April 28–May 23, 2010

Lyric Stage

Irving, Texas

Eighteenth Season

Founding Producer, Steven Jones; Managing Director, Valerie Galloway-Chapa

The King and I Music by Richard Rodgers, book and lyrics by Oscar Hammerstein II, based on the novel *Anna and the King of Siam* by Margaret Landon; Director, Cheryl Denson, Choreography, Ann Nieman, Musical Director, Jay Dias; Cast: : Greg Dulcie (Captain Orton), Jack Vangorden (Louis Leonowens), Luann Aronson (Anna Leonowens), Edward Biley Andrion (The Interpreter), Brian Mathis (The Kralahome), Joe Nemmers (The King), Edward Andrion (Phra Alack), Adrian Li Donni (Lun Tha), Jung Eun Kim (Tuptim), Ya Han Chang (Lady Thiang), Bryse Burris (Prince Chulalongkorn), Chamblee Ferguson (Sir Edward Ramsay), Ashley Fong (Princess Ying Yaowalak) Kelly Mccain (Uncle Thomas), Addison Faith Reed (Little Eva), Mary Mcelree (Topsey), Angela Nicole Moore (Eliza), Molly Welch (Simon of Legree), Amanda Brown (Angel/George), Anthony Carillo (Buddha); Royal Princes & Princesses: Bryse Burris, Anthony Carrillo, Alison Fong, Ashley Fong, Christy Fong, Ashton Miramontes, Chet Monday, Lily Monday, Addie Morales, Tyler Rouse, Lana Staggers, Meili West; The Royal Dancers: Souk Burrowns, Sergio Antonio Garcia, Katharine Gentsch, Kyle Hughes, Tino Jalomo, Jason Mayfield, Pamela Langton, Kelly Mccain, Thomas Nanthavongdouangsy, Robert Patrick Paterno, David Staggers, Amy Wells, Justin Preece (Onstage percussion); Priests of Siam: Souk Burrowns, Ben Giddings, Robert Patrick Paterno, Greg Dulcie; Royal Wives: Kathryn Frady, Rachel Legaspi, Jackie Lengfelder, Erin Nishimura, Lauren Paige Patterson, Hani Jihyun Park, Vernicia Vernon, Lucia Welch; Amazons: Kyle Hughes, Pamela Langton; Palace Guards: Ben Giddings, Thomas Nanthavongdouangsy, Edgar "Souk" Burrowns, Sergio Antonio Garcia; June 19–28, 2009

Funny Girl Music by Jule Styne, lyrics by Bob Merrill, book by Isobel Lennart; Director, Cheryl Denson, Choregraphy, Tracy Jordan, Musical Director, Jay Dias; Cast: Kristin Dausch (Fanny Brice), Babakayode Ipaye (John/Stage Manger),

Carleen Kirksey (Emma), Lois Sonnier Hart (Mrs. Brice), Connie Coit (Mrs. Strakos), Jackie Lengfelder (Mrs. Meeker), Jane Willingham (Mrs. O'Malley), Mike Gallagher (Tom Keeney), Jeremy Dumont (Eddie Ryan), Ben Giddings (Heckie), Sarah Harder (Bubbles), Kristi Rowan (Polly), Lee Jamison Wadley (Maude), Christopher Pinnella (Nick Arnstein), Angela Nicole Moore, Addison Faith Reed (Nick's Girls), J. Alan Hanna (Stage Director), Mark Oristano (Florenz Ziegfeld Jr.), Jilian Brown (Mimsey), Alexander Ross (Ziegfeld Tenor), Jason Thomas Mayfield (Jody, Ziegfeld's Lead Dancer), Angela Moore (Vera), Kristi Rowan (Jenny), Carlos Gomez (Adolph), Lon D. Barerra (Mr. Renaldi); Ensemble: Mikey Abrams, Lon D. Barrera, Jilian Brown, Ben Giddings, Carlos Gomez, J. Alan Hanna, Sarah Harder, Babakayode Ipaye, Summer Rose Kenny, Jason Thomas Mayfield, Joy Mckay, Angela Nicole Moore, Brittany Lauren Nance, Addison Faith Reed, Alexander Ross, Kristi Rowan, Jordan Vaughan, Lee Jamison Wadley, Keith Warren; September 11–20, 2009

The Road to Qatar Music by David Krane, book and lyrics by Stephen Cole; Director, Phillip George, Musical Director, David Caldwell ; Cast: Brian Gonzales (Michael), Lee Zarrett (Jeffrey), Bill Nolte (Mansour), Jill Abramovitz (Nazirah), Bruce Warren (Farid/Claudio); World Premiere; October 9–24, 2009

Show Boat in Concert Music by Jerome Kern, Lyrics by Oscar Hammerstein II; Director/Choreography, Ann Nieman, Music Director, Jay Dias; Cast: Ebony Marshall Oliver (Queenie), Lois Sonnier Hart (Parthy Ann Hawks), David Coffee (Cap'n Andy), Megan Woodall (Ellie May Chipley), Andy Baldwin (Frank Schultz), Laurie Bulaoro (Julie Laverne), Martin Fox (Gaylord Ravenal), Cecily Ellis-Bills (Magnolia Hawks), Keron Jackson (Joe), Bill Buchanan (Windy Mclain), Alexander Ross (Steve Baker), Greg Dulcie (Vallon), Nicolette Doke (Kim Young Child), Scott Eckert (Jake); Ensemble: Laura Jill Baker, Philip Bentham, Feleceia Benton, Jillian Brown, Bill Buchanan, Sarah Chason, Kristen Cramer, Sarah Comley, Stormi Demerson, Whitney Dewell,Dayton Dobbs, Randy Dobbs, Tyler Donahue, Paul Doucet, Greg Dulcie, Mike Gallagher, Sarah Lindsay Geist, Katherine Gentsch, Ben Giddings, Carlos Gomez, Martin Antonio Guerra, Amber Nicole Guest, J. Alan Hanna, Sarah Harder, Doris Roddy Howard, Babs Ipaye, Tino Jalomo, Maurice Johnson, Neeley Jonea', Cameron Leighton Kirkpatrick, Carleen Constance Kirksey, Nancy Lamb, Gabe Lawson, Heidi Lewis, Cary Litchford, Jennifer Pyron, Mandy Rausch, Addison F. Reed, Rachael Joy Robertson, Alexander Ross, Kristin Spires, Laurie Spohn, David Staggers, Noelle Stanley, Shane Strawbridge, Dana Taylor, Jay Taylor, Octavia Y. Thomas, Vernicia Vernon, Lee Jamieson Wadley, Alicia Wallace, Keith Warren, Lucia A. Welch, Tom De Wester, James Williams, Jodi C. Wright; January 28–31, 2010

Julie Johnson Sings Written and performed by Julie Johnson; Additional Cast: Steve Barcus and Catherine Carpenter-Cox; March 26–28, 2010

McCarter Theatre Center

Princeton, New Jersey

Eightieth Season

Artistic Director, Emily Mann; Managing Director, Timothy J. Shields

Having Our Say Written and directed by Emily Mann, adapted from the book by Sarah L. Delany and A. Elizabeth Delany with Amy Hill Hearth; Set, Daniel Ostling; Costumes, Karen Perry; Lighting, Stephen Strawbridge; Original Music and Sound, Rob Milburn & Michael Bodeen; Projections, Wendall K. Harrington; PSM, Cheryl Mintz; Cast: Yvette Freeman (Dr. Bessie Delany), Lizan Mitchell (Miss Sadie Delany); Berlind Theatre; September 11–October 18, 2009

She Stoops to Conquer by Oliver Goldsmith; Director, Nicholas Martin; Set, David Korins; Costumes, Gabriel Berry; Lighting, Ben Stanton; Sound, Drew Levy; Dialect Coach, Louis Colaianni; PSM, Stephen M. Kaus; Stage Manager, Lauren Kurinskas; Cast: Brooks Ashmanskas (Tony Lumpkin), Rebecca Brooksher (Constance Neville), Francesca Choy-Kee (Pimple), Rich Dreher (Stingo/Jeremy), Zackary Grady (Thomas/Fellow), Brent Langdon (Diggory/Fellow), Adam Lerman

(Roger/Fellow), Kristine Nielsen (Mrs. Hardcastle), John O'Creagh (Sir Charles Marlow), Jessica Stone (Kate Hardcastle), Jon Patrick Walker (Charles Marlow), Jeremy Webb (George Hastings), Paxton Whitehead (Mr. Hardcastle); Matthews Theatre; October 13–November 1, 2009

A Christmas Carol by Charles Dickens, adapted by David Thompson; Director, Michael Unger; Set, Ming Cho Lee; Costumes, Jess Goldstein; Lighting, Stephen Strawbridge; Sound, Brian Ronan; Original Music & Lyrics, Michael Starobin; Choreography, Rob Ashford; Musical Director, Charles Sundquist; Choreography Supervisor, Jennifer Paulson Lee; Dialect Coach, Gillian Lane-Plescia; Supervising Stage Manager, Cheryl Mintz; Stage Manager, Hannah Woodward; Cast: Lisa Altomare (Mrs. Dilber), Justin Blanchard (Jacob Marley/Mr. Stocks), Bill Buell (Mr. Fezziwig/Old Joe), David Furr (Bob Cratchit), Richard Gallagher (Young Scrooge/Mr. Bonds), Karron Graves (Fan/Mrs. Bonds), Simon Kendall (Fred/Schoolmaster/Undertaker), Angela Lin (Lily/Belle), Janet Metz (Mrs. Cratchit), Ronica Reddick (Christmas Present), James A. Stephens (Ebenezer Scrooge), Michele Tauber (Mrs. Fezziwig/Mrs. Stocks/Laundress); Matthews Theatre; December 6–27, 2009

Fetch Clay, Make Man by Will Power; Director, Des McAnuff; Set, Riccardo Hernandez; Costumes, Paul Tazewell; Lighting, Howell Binkley; Projections, Peter Nigrini; Soundscape, Darron L West; PSM, Alison Cote; Cast: John Earl Jelks (Brother Rashid), Sonequa Martin (Sonji Clay), Richard Masur (William Fox), Evan Parke (Muhammad Ali), Ben Vereen (Stepin Fetchit); Ensemble: Ray Fisher, Kenric Green; World Premiere; Berlind Theatre; January 8–February 14, 2010

American Buffalo by David Mamet; Director, Amy Morton; Presented in association with the Steppenwolf Theatre Company; Set, Kevin Depinet; Costumes, Nan Cibula-Jenkins; Lighting, Pat Collins; Original Music & Sound, Rob Milburn & Michael Bodeen; Fight Choreographer, Rich Sordelet; PSM, Christine D. Freeburg; Cast: Patrick Andrews (Bob), John Judd (Don), Tracy Letts (Teach), Kurt Ehrmann (u/s Don); Matthews Theatre; March 9–28, 2010

Take Flight Book by John Weidman, music and orchestrations by David Shire, lyrics by Richard Maltby Jr.; Director, Sam Buntrock; Set & Costumes, David Farley; Lighting, Ken Billington; Sound, Ken Travis; Music Director, Kevin Stites; Musical Staging, Lisa Shriver; Music Coordinator, John Miller; PSM, Cheryl Mintz; Stage Manager, Alison Cote; Cast: Carey Rebecca Brown (Myra/others), Jenn Colella (Amelia Earhart), Michael Cumpsty (George Putnam), Bobby Daye (Ray Page/others), Claybourne Elder (Charles Lindbergh), Linda Gabler (Gladys/others), Marya Grandy (Brenda/others), Todd A. Horman (Banker/others), Stanton Nash (Wilbur Wright), Benjamin Schrader (Orville Wright), Price Waldman (Burke/others), William Youmans (Don Hall/others); Musicians: Kevin Stites (Conductor), Jamie Schmidt (Associate Conductor), Todd Groves, Jeff Nichols, Timothy Schadt, Will de Vos, Gregory Dlugos, Bob Renino, Charles Descarfino, John Miller; Berlind Theatre; April 30–June 6, 2010

Merrimack Repertory Theatre

Lowell, Massachusettes

Thirty-first Season

Artistic Director, Charles Towers; Executive Director, Tom Parrish

Flings & Eros by The Flying Karamazov Brothers; Director, Paul Magid; Costumes, Arthur Oliver; Lighting, David Hutson; Choreography, Douglas Elkins; Cast: Paul Magid (Dmitri), Mark Ettinger (Alexei), Rob Kimball (Pavel), Stephen Bent (Zossima); World Premiere; Liberty Hall Stage; September 10–October 4, 2009

The Seafarer by Conor McPherson; Director, Charles Towers; Set, Bill Clarke; Costumes, Deborah Newhall; Lighting, Matthew Adelson; Cast: David Adkins (Sharky), Allyn Burrows (Nicky), Jim Frangione (Ivan), Gordon Joseph Weiss (Richard), Mark Zeisler (Mr. Lockhart); Liberty Hall Stage; October 15–November 8, 2009

Heroes by Gerald Sibleyras, adapted by Tom Stoppard; Director, Carl Forsman; Set, Beowulf Boritt; Costumes, Theresa Squire; Lighting, Josh Bradford; Cast: Ron Holgate (Gustave), Kenneth Tigar (Henri), Jonathan Hogan (Phillippe); November 19–December 13, 2009

Fabuloso, A Play by John Kolvenbach; Director, Kyle Fabel; Set, Campbell Baird; Costumes, Deborah Newhall; Lighting, Paul Hackenmueller; Cast: Ed Jewett (Arthur), Rebecca Harris (Kate), Amy Kim Waschke (Samantha); Liberty Hall Stage; January 7–31, 2010

Black Pearl Sings! by Frank Higgins; Director, Benny Sato Ambush; Set, Robin Vest; Costumes, Deborah Newhall; Lighting, Brian Lilienthal; Music Director, Eugene Wolf; Cast: Cherene Snow (Pearl), Valerie Leonard (Susannah); Liberty Hall Stage; February 11–March 7, 2010

The Last Days of Mickey & Jean by Richard Dresser; Director, Charles Towers; Set, Bill Clarke; Costumes, Deborah Newhall; Lighting, Dan Kotlowitz; Cast: Jack Wetherall (Mickey), Rae C. Wright (Jean), Chris McHale (Bobby/Dr. Shockley/Tinsel); World Premiere; Liberty Hall Stage; March 18–April 11, 2010

The Blonde, the Brunette and the Vengeful Redhead by Robert Hewett; Director, Melia Bensussen; Set, Judy Gailen; Costumes, Arthur Olivier; Lighting, Dan Kotlowitz; Sound, David Remedios; Cast: Karen MacDonald; Liberty Hall Stage; April 22–May 16, 2010

Music Theatre of Wichita

Wichita, Kansas

Thirty-eighth Season

Producing Artistic Director, Wayne Bryan

The Producers Book by Mel Brooks and Thomas Meehan, music and lyrics by Mel Brooks; Original Direction and Choreography by Susan Stroman; Presented by permission of StudioCanal; Director, Mark Madama; Choreographer, Linda Goodrich; Musical Director, Thomas W. Douglas; Sets, Robin Wagner; Costumes, William Ivey Long; Sets and Costumes provided by NETworks Presentations; Lighting, David Neville; Hair and Wigs, Raymond J. Torres; Properties, Arthur Ridley; Sound, David Muehl; Technical Director, Kyle Longwell; PSM, Emily F. McMullen; Stage Manager, Kelly K. Irwin; Company Manager/Producing Associate, Nancy Reeves; Production Manager, David Neville; Cast: Michael Kostroff (Max Bialystock), Larry Raben (Leo Bloom), James Anest (Franz Liebkind), Kimberly Fauré (Ulla), Kilty Reidy (Roger DeBris), Aaron Umsted (Carmen Ghia), Daxton Bloomquist (Jack Lepidus/Guard/Ensemble), Kaleigh Cronin (Ensemble), Cody Davis (Donald Dinsmore/O'Riley/Ensemble), Tyler Foy (Ensemble), Ian Gibb (Production Tenor/Trustee/Ensemble), Kelcy Griffin (Dance Captain/Ensemble), Ryan Koss (Scott/Sergeant/Ensemble), Sam Lips (Dance Captain/Swing), Emily Mechler (Usherette/Kiss-Me Feel-Me/Ensemble), Karen L. Robu (Hold-Me Touch-Me), Paul Sabala (Mr. Marks/Bryan/Jason Green/Judge/Ensemble/Leo u.s.), Natasha Scearse (Ensemble), Melissa Steadman (Court Stenographer/Ensemble), Johnny Stellard (Kevin/O'Rourke/Ensemble), Mackenzie Warren (Usherette/Ensemble), Paige A. Williams (Ensemble), Borris York (Most Tired Accountant/O'Houlihan/Ensemble), Dani Young (Shirley/Lick-Me Bite-Me/Jury Forewoman/Ensemble); June 10–14, 2009

Camelot Book and lyrics by Alan Jay Lerner, music by Frederick Loewe; Original production directed and staged by Moss Hart; based on The Once and Future King by T.H. White; Director, Wayne Bryan; Choreographer, Amy Baker; Musical Director, Thomas W. Douglas; Sets, Bruce Brockman; Costumes, George Bacon; Lighting, David Neville; Sound, David Muehl; Hair/Wigs/Makeup, Raymond J. Torres; Properties, Arthur Ridley; Technical Director, Kyle Longwell; PSM, Kelly K. Irwin; Stage Manager, Emily F. McMullen; Company Manager/Producing Associate, Nancy Reeves; Production Manager, David Neville; Cast: Damon

Kirsche (Arthur), Laura Griffith (Guenevere), Edward Watts (Lancelot), Justin Robertson (Pellinore), Paul Sabala (Mordred), Kevin Reese (Merlin), Mackenzie Warren (Nimue/Ensemble), Kevin Munhall (Sir Sagramore), Jacob Gutierrez (Sir Dinadan), Ian Gibb (Sir Lionel), Gavin Myers (Tom of Warwick), Michael Joseph Parker (Dap/Priest), Emily Mechler (Lady Anne/Ensemble): Ensemble: Gilbert L. Bailey II, Daxton Bloomquist, Erin Clemons, Cody Davis, Kaleigh Cronin, Kimberly Fauré, Tyler Foy, Kelcy Griffin, Ryan Koss, Sam Lips, Paul H. Miller, Natasha Scearse, Melissa Steadman, Johnny Stellard, Aaron Umsted, Paige A. Williams, Borris York, Dani Young, Emily Reese (Servant), Nicholas Reese (Servant); June 24–28, 2009

Kiss Me, Kate Music and lyrics by Cole Porter, book by Sam and Bella Spewack; Director, James Brennan; Choreographer, Patti Colombo; Musical Director, Thomas W. Douglas; Sets and Properties, Arthur Ridley; Costumes, Martin Pakledinaz, provided by Goodspeed Opera; Lighting, David Neville; Sound, David Muehl; Hair/Wigs/Makeup, Raymond J. Torres; Technical Director, Kyle Longwell; PSM, Emily F. McMullen; Stage Manager, Kelly K. Irwin; Company Manager/Associate Producer, Nancy Reeves; Production Manager, David Neville; Cast: Mike McGowan (Fred/Petruchio), Jessica Wright (Lilli/Kate), Kimberly Fauré (Lois/Bianca), Wes Hart (Bill/Lucentio), Gordon Joseph Weiss (Gangster # 1), James Larsen (Gangster # 2), Darryl Reuben Hall (Paul), Nedra Dixon (Hattie), John Boldenow (Harry/Baptista), Richard Campbell (Harrison Howell), Tyler Foy (Hortensio), Kevin Munhall (Gremio), Paul Sabala (Ralph), Michael Joseph Parker (Pops/Haberdasher), Johnny Stellard (Cab Driver); Ensemble: Gilbert L. Bailey II, Daxton Bloomquist, Marisha Castle, Natalie Chung, Erin Clemons, Cody Davis, Kaleigh Cronin, Ian Gibb, Kelcy Griffin, Jacob Gutierrez, Ryan Koss, Sam Lips, Emily Mechler, Paul H. Miller, Chanee Park, Natasha Scearse, Marcus Shane, Melissa Steadman, Johnny Stellard, Aaron Umsted, Mackenzie Warren, Paige A. Williams, Borris York, Dani Young; July 8–12, 2009

Miss Saigon Music by Claude-Michel Schönberg, lyrics by Richard Maltby Jr. and Alain Boublil; Additional material by Richard Maltby Jr.; Orchestrations, William D. Brohn; Director-Choreographer, Darren Lee; Associate Director-Choreographer, Melanie Tojio Lockyer; Musical Director, Thomas W. Douglas; Sets, Dustin J. Cardwell; Costumes, Mela Hoyt-Heydon; Sets and Costumes provided by Fullerton Civic Light Opera; Lighting, David Neville; Sound, David Muehl; Hair/Wigs/Makeup, Raymond J. Torres; Properties, Arthur Ridley; Technical Director, Kyle Longwell; PSM, Kelly K. Irwin; Stage Manager, Emily F. McMullen; Company Manager/Producing Associate, Nancy Reeves; Production Manager, David Neville; Cast: Kevin Gray (Engineer), Shannon Tyo (Kim), Chris Peluso (Chris), Josh Tower (John), Doan MacKenzie (Thuy), Melissa Steadman (Ellen), Erin Clemons (Gigi/Ensemble), Sage Belen Goco or Aiden Keovixay (Tam), Kelcy Griffin (Mimi/Ensemble), Marisha Castle (Yvette/Ensemble), Ashley Jini Park (Yvonne/Ensemble); Ensemble: Gilbert L. Bailey II, Daxton Bloomquist, Marisha Castle, Natalie Chung, Cody Davis, Jim Diego, Tyler Foy, Ian Gibb (Chris u.s.), Jacob Gutierrez, Tanner Lee Hanley, Ryan Koss, Joyee Lin, Sam Lips, Emily Mechler, Paul H. Miller, Kevin Munhall, Chanee Park, Harry Perrin, Paul Sabala, Marcus Shane (Engineer u.s.), Johnny Stellard, Mami Sugita, Miller Tai, Aaron Umsted, Mackenzie Warren, Paige A. Williams, Borris York; July 22–26, 2009

The Drowsy Chaperone Music and lyrics by Lisa Lambert and Greg Morrison, book by Bob Martin and Don McKellar; Original Direction and Choreography by Casey Nicholaw, restaged by Casey Hushion; Associate Director-Choreographer, Jennifer Taylor; Musical Director, Thomas W. Douglas; Sets, J Branson; Costumes, George Mitchell; Lighting, David Neville; Hair and Wigs, Raymond J. Torres; Properties, Arthur Ridley; Sound, David Muehl; Technical Director, Kyle Longwell; PSM, Emily F. McMullen; Stage Manager, Kelly K. Irwin; Company Manager/Producing Associate, Nancy Reeves; Production Manager, David Neville; Cast: Danny Bolero (Aldolpho), Wayne Bryan (Man in Chair), Kathel Carlson (Mrs. Tottendale), Andrea Chamberlain (Janet Van De Graaff), Tyler Foy (George), Ryan Koss (Gangster # 2), Tracy Lore (Chaperone), Emily Mechler (Kitty), Betti O. (Aviatrix), Kilty Reidy (Underling), Timothy W. Robu (Feldzieg), Johnny Stellard (Robert Martin), Aaron Umsted (Gangster # 1), Kevin Munhall (Superintendent/Ensemble); Ensemble: Paul Sabala, Melissa Steadman, Mackenzie Warren; August 5–9, 2009

Disney's High School Musical 2–On Stage Book by David Simpatico, songs by Matthew Gerrard & Robbie Nevil/David N. Lawrence & Faye Greenberg/ Randy Peterson & Kevin Quinn/Jamie Houston, Bryan Louiselle, Andy Dodd, and Adam Watts/Antonina Armato & Tim James; Music Adapted, Arranged and Produced by Bryan Louiselle; Based on a Disney Channel Original Movie written by Peter Barsocchini; Director-Choreographer, Roger Castellano; Musical Director, Jesse Warkentin; Associate Choreographer, Gilbert L. Bailey II; Sets, J Branson; Costumes, Jeffrey Meek, created by Lyric Theatre of Oklahoma; Lighting, David Neville; Sound, David Muehl; Hair/Wigs/Makeup, Raymond J. Torres; Properties, Arthur Ridley; Technical Director, Kyle Longwell; Paint Shop Charge, Tara Houston; PSM, Kelly K. Irwin; Stage Manager, Emily F. McMullen; Company Manager/Producing Associate, Nancy Reeves; Production Manager, David Neville; Cast: Cooper Rowe (Troy), Caitlin Marrero (Gabriella), Sophie Menas (Sharpay), Paul Sabala (Ryan), Gilbert L. Bailey II (Chad), Janet Wiggins (Taylor), Kelly Ufford (Kelsi), Ryan Ehresman (Jack Scott), Jacob Gutierrez (Zeke/Troy u.s.), Samantha Davison (Martha), Michael Joseph Parker (Mr. Fulton), Audra Bryant (Blossom/Ensemble), Teresa Offerman (Peaches/Ensemble), Nicole Tucker (Violet/Ensemble), Jacob Aaron Cullen (Pool Boy/Ensemble), Joel Domenico (Pool Boy/Ensemble), Jordan Slusher (Pool Boy/Ensemble), Karen L. Robu (Ms. Darbus–voice), Lynn Stephan (Country Club Assistant); Ensemble: Hope Astle, Bethany Berry, Connor Bourland, Zach Bush, Maddy Campbell, Carlin Castellano, Donnie Chauncey, Joe Consiglio, Whitney Cooper, Sam Corridoni, Ian DePriest, Madeline Dreher, Natalie Farha, Kyle Gallegos, Claire Gerig, Mason Holmes (Zeke u.s.), Landon Jackson, Keaton Jadwin, Jacob January (Ryan u.s.), Cora Kilgour, Jacob Locke, Stevie Mack, Kassiani Menas, Julia Miller, Gavin Myers, Logan Moore, Ryan Neville, Josh Obermeyer, Amanda Pickett, Sarah Quinn, Colleen Richey, Lindsey Roesti, Mattie Sharp, Alyssa Schoenwald, Parker Smitherman, Eric Stephens, Ian Sutton, Alyssa Page Tedder, Mycah Westhoff, Jenny Wine (Gabriella & Sharpay u.s.), Amanda Yoder, Alasyn Zimmerman, Chris Zimmerman; August 20–23, 2009

North Carolina Theatre

Raleigh, North Carolina

Twenty-sixth and Twenty-seventh Season

Artistic Director, Casey Hushion

Disney's High School Musical 2–On Stage by David Simpatico; Director, Casey Hushion; Choreographer, Bobby Pestka; Set, Kenneth Foy; Lighting, Craig Stelzenmuller, Sound, Duncan Edwards; Costumes, Ann M. Bruskiewitz; Hair/ Wigs/Makeup,, Patricia DelSordo; Technical Director, Bill Yates Jr.; PSM, Sarah Marshall; Musical Director, Edward G. Robinson; Cast: Chase Peacock (Troy), Renée Albulario (Gabriella), Gretchen Bieber (Sharpay), Jason Edward Cook (Ryan), Josh Breckenridge (Chad), Krystal Joy Brown (Taylor), Kaitlin Rose Mercurio (Kelsi), Christopher Spaulding (Zeke), Meredith Davis (Martha), Hailey Best (Sharpette), Chandon Jones (Sharpette), Heather Shaw (Sharpette), Jeffrey Scott Vizcaino (Jack Scott), Jeffrey "JR" Richardson (Mr. Fulton); Ensemble: Amarachi Anakaraonye, Clayton Bailey, Todd Beasley, Allison Bonner, Alex Bowers, Curtis Scott Brown, Paige Kimball Burhans, Nick DeVito, Kassy Edwards, Emily Gardenhire, Elgin Giles, Robert Green, Caroline Jordan, Aaron Pratt, Jordan Sasser, Kelsey Walston, Corey Warren; Raleigh Memorial Auditorium; June 13–21, 2009

The Sound of Music Music by Richard Rodgers, lyrics by Oscar Hammerstein II, book by Howard Lindsay and Russell Crouse; Director/Choreographer, Richard Stafford; Assistant Director/Choreographer, Jonathan Stahl; Set, Kenneth Foy; Sound, Brian L. Hunt; Lighting; Craig Stelzenmuller; Costumes, Ann M. Bruskiewitz; Hair/Wigs/Makeup, Patricia DelSordo; Technical Director, Bill Yates Jr.; PSM, William Alan Coats; ASM, Candace E. Hoffman; Musical Director, Alfred E Sturgis; Cast: Kate Fisher (Maria), Tom Galantich (Captain von Trapp), Susan Ishee (Mother Abess), Vinny Genna (Max Detweiler), Christine Hunter

(Elsa Shraeder), Alex Bowers (Liesl), Daniel Marhelko (Friedrich), English Brewer Bernhardt (Louisa), Trey Fitts (Kurt), Roxanna Demers (Brigitta), Gabby Simone (Marta), Mary Kate Englehardt (Gretl), Aaron Young (Rolf), Karen Dear (Sister Berthe), Heather Patterson-King (Sister Margaretta), Mary Adamek (Sister Sophia), Danny W. Norris (Franz) Judy Long (Frau Schmidt), Monique Argent (Ursula), Chris King (Herr Zeller), Jonathan Stahl (Baron Elberfield), J. Michael Beech (Admiral von Schreiber): Ensemble: Katherine Anderson, Larry Cox, Jason Mark Durst, Emily Feuerstein, Tal Fish, Chantal Sosa Hollatschek, Alison Lawrence, Kathleen Lynch, Hilary Russo, Alexa Wildish (Ensemble). Raleigh Memorial Auditorium; July 25–August 2, 2009

West Side Story Music by Leonard Bernstein, lyrics by Stephen Sondheim, book by Arthur Laurents; Director/Choreographer, Joshua Bergasse; Set, Leo Meyer; Sound, Shannon Slaton; Lighting; John Bartenstein; Costumes, Ann M. Bruskiewitz; Hair/Wigs/Makeup, Patricia DelSordo; Technical Director, Bill Yates Jr.; PSM, William Alan Coats; ASM, Candace E. Hoffman; 2nd ASM, Eric Tysinger; Musical Director, Edward G. Robinson; Cast: Josh Young (Tony), Catherine Cheng Jones (Maria), Asmeret Ghebremichael (Anita), Leo Ash Evens (Riff), Freddy Ramirez (Bernardo), Joey Calveri (Action), Eric Mann (A-Rab), Mikey Winslow (Baby John), Todd Michel Smith (Snowboy), Patrick Mullen II (Big Deal), Brandon Rubendall (Diesel), Kiira Schmidt (Graziella/Dance Captain), Kristin Sears (Velma), Sara Edwards (Minnie), Allison Nock (Anybodys), Adrian Peña (Chino), Mathew DeGuzman (Pepe), Mario Martinez (Indio), Elgin Giles (Anxious), Cedric Stapleton (Nibbles), Vanessa Van Vrancken (Rosalia), Michelle Marmolejo (Consuelo), Christine LaDuca (Teresita), Nicole Batalias (Francisca), Caroline Jordan (Margarita), Tim Caudle (Officer Krupke), Chris King (Lt. Schrank/Gladhand), Danny W. Norris (Doc); Raleigh Memorial Auditorium; October 17–25, 2009

The Full Monty by Terrence McNally; Director, Matt Lenz; Choreographer, Josh Rhodes; Set, John Arnone; Sound, Shannon Slaton; Lighting, John Bartenstein; Costumes, Ann M. Bruskiewitz; Hair/Wigs/Makeup, Patricia DelSordo; Technical Director, Bill Yates Jr.; PSM, William Alan Coats; ASM, Candace E. Hoffman; Musical Director, Michael Horsley; Cast: Ira David Wood III (Harold Nichols), Sally Struthers (Jeanette Burmeister), Jarrod Emick (Jerry Lukowski), Joe Coots (Dave Bukatinsky), Kingsley Leggs (Noah [Horse] T. Simmons), Thomas Cannizzaro (Ethan Girard), Stephen Schellhardt (Malcolm MacGregor), Julie Reiber (Georgie Bukatinsky), Angie Schworer (Vicki Nichols), Jennifer Schrader (Pam Lukowski), Trey Fitts (Nathan Lukowski), Ken Griggs (Teddy Slaughter), Mary Adamek (Molly MacGregor), John Carroll (Buddy [Keno] Walsh), Jeremy Mills (Reg Willoughby), Vinny Genna (Tony Giordano), Tracy J. Wholf (Estelle Genovese), Anne Karner (Susan Hershey), Cessalee Stovall (Joanie Lish); Ensemble: Philip Royston Burgess, Jonathan Elliot Coarsey, Ken Griggs, Joshua Stalls; Raleigh Memorial Auditorium; February 27–March 7, 2010

Cinderella Music by Richard Rodgers, book and lyrics by Oscar Hammerstein II, adapted by Tom Briggs; Director, Gabriel Barre; Choreographer, Jennifer Paulson Lee; Associate Choreographer, Lee A. Wilkins; Set, James Youmans; Sound; Shannon Slaton; Lighting, John Bartenstein; Costumes, Ann M. Bruskiewitz; Hair/ Wigs/Makeup, Patricia DelSordo; Technical Director, Bill Yates Jr.; PSM, William Alan Coats; ASM, Corey Croughn; 2nd ASM, Helen A. Barnes, Musical Director, Edward G. Robinson; Cast: Jessica Rush (Cinderella), Paolo Montalban (Prince Christopher), Harriet D. Foy (Fairy Godmother), Everett Quinton (Stepmother), Jennifer Frankel (Joy), Louise Stewart (Grace), Stephen Schellhardt (Lionel), C.E. Smith (King Maximilian), Christine Hunter (Queen Constantina), Alexa Robertson (Young Cinderella); Ensemble: English Brewer Bernhardt, Jimmie Lee Brooks III, Jennifer Cannon, Andrew Chappelle, Joseph Cullinane (Dance Captain), Leah Darby, Stacey Harris, Caroline Jordan, Robert Mark Kaufman, Peyton Royal, Mary Simmons, Lee A. Wilkins; Raleigh Memorial Auditorium; April 10–18, 2010

Erica Sullivan and John Procaccino in the Long Wharf Theater production of Sylvia (photo by T. Charles Erickson)

Lizan Mitchell and Yvette Freeman in Having Our Say at the McCarter Theatre (photo by T. Charles Erickson)

A scene from The Drowsy Chaperone at Music Theatre of Wichita (photo by Squid Ink Creative)

Sonequa Martin, Ben Vereen, and Evan Parke in the McCarter Theatre's production of Fetch Clay, Make Man (photo by T. Charles Erickson)

Troy Britton Johnson, Obba Babatundé, and Adam James in
The Old Globe's Sammy (photo by Craig Schwartz)

Will Chase, Amy Spanger, and the Company of Robin and the 7 Hoods
at The Old Globe (photo by Craig Schwartz)

Peggy Yates, Jeffries Thaiss, and Julie-Ann Elliott in Is He Dead?
at the Olney Theatre Center (photo by Stan Barouh)

David Elias, Carter Jahnckei, Norman Aronovic, Peter B. Schmitz,
Timmy Ray James, and Harry Winter in King of the Jews at
Olney Theatre Center (photo by Stan Barouh)

Sherri Edelen and Whitney Bashor in Philadelphia Theatre Company's
The Light in the Piazza (photo by Mark Garvin)

Jeffery Carlson and Marc Kudisch in Golden Age at the Philadelphia
Theatre Company (photo by Mark Garvin)

The Old Globe

San Diego, California

Seventy-fifth Season

Executive Producer, Louis G. Spisto; Resident Artistic Director, Darko Tresnjak/ Adrian Noble; Artistic Director Emeritus, Jack O'Brien; Founding Director, Craig Noel

Lowell Davies Festival Theatre

Cyrano de Bergerac by Edmond Rostand; Director, Darko Tresnjak; Set, Ralph Funicello; Costumes, Anna R. Oliver; Lighting, York Kennedy; Sound & Music, Christopher R. Walker; Voice & Speech, Claudia Hill-Sparks; Prosthetics, Scott Ramp; Stage Manager, Mary K. Klinger; Celeste Ciulla (Roxanne's Duenna), Ashley Clements (Son/Sister Claire), Vivia Font (Fruitseller/Nun), Grant Goodman (Le Bret), Dana Green (Roxanne), Sloan Grenz (Page/Cadet), Brendan Griffin (Christian), Eric Hoffmann (Ragueneau), Kevin Hoffmann (Musketeer/ Musician/Sentry), Brian Lee Huynh (Thief/Cook/Cadet), Charles Janasz (Ligniere/ Capuchin/Bertrandou), Katie MacNichol (Lady/Lise/Mother Marguerite), Kern McFadden (Montfleury/Cook/Cadet), Patrick Page (Cyrano), Bruce Turk (Comte de Guiche), Tony von Halle (Vicomte de Valvert/Poet/Cadet), Barbara Wengerd (Thief's Apprentice/Cook/Sister Marthe); June 13–September 27, 2009 (end of seventy-fourth season)

Twelfth Night by William Shakespeare; Director, Paul Mullins; Set, Ralph Funicello; Costumes, Linda Cho; Lighting, York Kennedy; Sound & Music, Christopher R. Walker; Voice & Speech Coach, Claudia Hill-Sparks; Stage Manager, Mary K. Klinger; Cast: Ashley Clements (Benigna), Greg Derelian (Antonia), Vivia Font (Teresa), Dana Green (Viola), Eric Hoffman (Sir Toby Belch), Kevin Hoffmann (Sebastian), Brian Lee Huynh (Giuseppe/Priest), Katie MacNichol (Olivia), Kern McFadden (Sea Captain/Reynaldo), James Newcomb (Feste), Patrick Page (Malvolio), Bruce Turk (Sir Andrew Aguecheek), Gerritt VanderMeer (Orsino), Tony von Halle (Vanilio); June 13–September 27, 2009 (end of seventy-fourth season)

Coriolanus by William Shakespeare; Director, Darko Tresnjak; Set, Ralph Funicello; Costumes, Anna R. Oliver; Lighting, York Kennedy; Sound & Music, Christopher R. Walker; Voice & Speech, Claudia Hill-Sparks; Stage Manager, Mary K. Klinger; Cast: Celeste Ciulla (Volumnia), Greg Derelian (Coriolanus), Vivia Font (Roman Citizen/Volscian Partygoer), Grant Goodman (Sicnius Velutus), Sloan Grenz (Roman Soldier/Citizen/Volscian Servant), Brendan Griffin (Aufidius/ Roman Citizen), Kevin Hoffmann (Roman Senator/Soldier/Citizen/Volscian Servant), Brian Lee Huynh (Roman Citizen/Soldier), Charles Janasz (Meneius Agrippa), Kern McFadden (Roman Citizen/Soldier), James Newcomb (Junius Brutus), Gerritt VanderMeer (Cominius), Tony von Halle (Volscian General/Roman Citizen/Bodyguard); June 13–September 27, 2009 (end of seventy-fourth season)

King Lear by William Shakespeare; Director, Adrian Noble; Set, Ralph Funicello; Costumes, Deirdre Clancy; Lighting, Alan Burrett; Sound, Christopher R. Walker; Original Music, Shaun Davey; Fight Director, Steve Rankin; Vocal and Dialect Coach, Claudia Hill-Sparks; Stage Manager, James Latus; ASMs, Erin Gioia Albrecht, Moira Gleason, Annette Yé; Casting, Samantha Barrie; Cast: Robert Foxworth (King Lear), Emily Swallow (Goneril), Aubrey Saverino (Regan), Catherine Gowl (Cordelia), Donald Carrier (Duke of Albany), Michael Stewart Allen (Duke of Cornwall), Ben Diskant (King of France), Christian Durso (Duke of Burgundy), Charles Janasz (Earl of Gloucester), Jay Whittaker (Edgar), Jonno Roberts (Edmund), Joseph Marcell (Earl of Kent), Bruce Turk (Fool), Steven Marzolf (Curan/Herald), Adrian Sparks (Old Man), Craig Dudley (Doctor); Ensemble: Shirine Babb, Andrew Dahl, Grayson DeJesus, Ben Diskant, Craig Dudley, Christian Durso, Kevin Hoffmann, Andrew Hutcheson, Steven Marzolf, Jordan McArthur, Brooke Novak, Ryman Sneed, Adrian Sparks, Bree Welch; June 12–September 23, 2009

The Taming of the Shrew by William Shakespeare; Director, Ron Daniels; Set, Ralph Funicello; Costumes, Deirdre Clancy; Lighting, Alan Burrett; Sound/ Original Music, Christopher R. Walker; Fight Director, Steve Rankin; Movement,

Tony Caligagan; Vocal and Dialect Coach, Claudia Hill-Sparks; Stage Manager, James Latus; ASMs, Erin Gioia Albrecht, Moira Gleason, Annette Yé; Casting, Samantha Barrie; Cast: Adrian Sparks (Baptista Minola), Emily Swallow (Katherine), Bree Welch (Bianca), Jay Whittaker (Lucentio), Michael Stewart Allen (Tranio), Jordan McArthur (Biondello), Craig Dudley (Vincentio/A Tailor), Jonno Roberts (Petruchio), Bruce Turk (Grumio), Donald Carrier (Hortensio), Charles Janasz (A Pedant/Curtis), Shirine Babb (A Widow), Steven Marzolf (A Haberdasher); Servants Lads: Andrew Dahl, Grayson DeJesus, Ben Diskant, Christian Durso, Kevin Hoffmann, Andrew Hutcheson, Steven Marzolf; June 16– September 23, 2010

The Madness of George III by Alan Bennett; Director, Adrian Noble; Set, Ralph Funicello; Costumes, Deirdre Clancy; Lighting, Alan Burrett; Sound, Christopher R. Walker; Fight Director, Steve Rankin; Vocal and Dialect Coach, Claudia Hill-Sparks; Stage Manager, James Latus; ASMs, Erin Gioia Albrecht, Moira Gleason, Annette Yé; Casting, Samantha Barrie; Cast: Miles Anderson (George III), Emily Swallow (Queen Charlotte), Andrew Dahl (Prince of Wales), Kevin Hoffmann (Duke of York), Shirine Babb (Lady Pembroke), Jay Whittaker (William Pitt), Craig Dudley (Henry Dundas), Charles Janasz (Edward Thurlow), Michael Stewart Allen (Charles James Fox), Donald Carrier (Richard Brindsley Sheridan), Adrian Sparks (Sir Boothby Skrymshir/Sir Lucas Pepys), Grayson DeJesus (Ramsden), Joseph Marcell (Sir George Baker), Bruce Turk (Dr. Richard Warren), Robert Foxworth (Dr. Francis Willis), Steven Marzolf (Captain Fitzroy), Ben Diskant (Greville), Christian Durso (Braun), Andrew Hutcheson (Fortnum), Jordan McArthur (Papandiek), Brooke Novak (Margaret Nicholson (Brooke Novak), Catherine Gow, Aubrey Saverino, Ryman Sneed, Bree Welch (Maids); June 19–September 24, 2010

Old Globe Theatre – The Donald and Darlene Shiley Stage

The First Wives Club Book by Rupert Holmes, music & lyrics by Brian Holland, Lamont Dozier, Eddie Holland; Director, Francesca Zambello; Choreography, Lisa Stevens; Music Director/Vocal Arrangements/Incidental Music, Ron Melrose; Set, Peter J. Davison; Costumes, Paul Tazewell; Lighting, Mark McCullough; Sound, Jon Weston; Orchestrations, Harold Wheeler; Conductor, John Gentry Tennyson; Dance Arrangements, Zane Mark; Fight Director, Steve Rankin; Casting, Tara Rubin; Stage Manager, Kim Vernace; ASM, Anette Yé; Cast: Michelle Aravena (Ensemble/Brenda u.s), Mark Campbell (Swing/Morty u.s.), Sara Chase (Leslie/ Shelley/Feebee), John Dossett (Aaron), Thursday Farrar (Ensemble/Elyse u.s.), Jenifer Foote (Dance Captain/Swing), Bob Gaynor (Thad/Ensemble/Aaron u.s.), Sam Harris (Duane), Matthew LaBanca (Auctioneer/Ensemble/Duane u.s.), Ari Lerner or Austyn Myers (Jason), Victoria Matlock (Cynthia/Ensemble/Annie u.s.), Kevyn Morrow (Bill), Brad Oscar (Morty), Kat Palardy (Chris/Ensemble/Leslie-Shelley-Feebee u.s.), Sheryl Lee Ralph (Elyse), Martin Samuel (Ensemble), Richard E. Waits (Ensemble/Bill u.s.), Barbara Walsh (Brenda), Karen Ziemba (Annie); July 17–August 30, 2009 (end of seventy-fourth season)

Sammy Book, music and lyrics by Leslie Bricusse, additional songs by Anthony Newley; Director, Keith Glover, Choregraphy, Keith Young; Music Supervisor, Ian Fraser; Set, Alexander Dodge; Costumes, Fabio Toblini; Lighting, Chris Lee; Sound, David Patridge; Orchestrations, Ned Paul Ginsburg; Music Director/ Conductor/Dance Arrangements, Rahn Coleman; Casting, Tara Rubin; Stage Manager, David Sugarman; ASM, Jess Slocum; Cast: Obba Babatundé (Sammy Davis Jr), Heather Ayers (May Britt/Ensemble), Ann Duquesnay (Rosa Davis), Mary Ann Hermansen (Kim Novak/Ensemble), Adam James (Frank Sinatra), Troy Britton Johnson (Dean Martin/Cohn/Jennings/Ensemble), Ted Louis Levy (Sammy Davis, Sr.), Keewa Nurullah (Lola Folana/Ensemble), Perry Ojeda (Eddie Cantor/Ensemble), Victoria Platt (Altovise Gore/Ensemble), Lance Roberts (Will Mastin), Alonzo Saunders (Murphy/Ensemble); Ensemble: Jenelle Engleson, Stephanie Girard, Lauren Haughton, Anise Ritchie, Sarrah Strimel World Premiere; September 17–November 1, 2009

Dr Seuss' How the Grinch Stole Christmas Music by Mel Marvin, books and lyrics by Timothy Mason; Original production conceived and directed by Jack O'Brien; 12th Annual Production; November 21–December 27, 2009

Whisper House Music and lyrics by Duncan Shiek, book and lyrics by Kyle Jarrow; Director, Peter Askin, Music Director, Jason Hart, Dance Director,

Wesley Fata; Set, Michael Schweikardt; Costumes, Jenny Mannis; Lighting, Matthew Richards; Sound, Dan Moses Schreier; Projections, Aaron Rhyne; Stage Manager, Richard Costabile; ASM, Moira Gleason; Cast: Arthur Acuña (Yasuhiro), Holly Brook (Female Ghost), Celeste Ciulla (Lilly), Ted Koch (Charles), Kevin Hoffman (Lieutenant Rando), David Poe (Lead Singer Ghost), A.J. Foggiano (Christopher); World Premiere; January 13–February 21, 2010
Boeing-Boeing by Marc Camoletti and Beverly Cross; Director, Mark Schneider, based on the West End and Broadway production directed by Matthew Warchus; Set, Rob Howell, Lighting, Chris Rynne; Sound, Paul Peterson; Stage Manager, Daniel S. Rosokoff; ASM, Annette Yé; Cast: Rob Breckenridge (Bernard), Stephanie Fieger (Gabriella), Caralyn Kozlowski (Gretchen), Nancy Robinette (Berthe), Liv Rooth (Gloria), Joseph Urla (Robert); March 13–April 18, 2010

Golda's Balcony by William Gibson; Director/Production Consultant, Scott Schwartz; Scenic Consultant, Anna Louizos; Costume Consultant, Jess Goldstein; Lighting, Jeff Croiter; Sound, Alex Hawthorn; Original Broadway Sound, Mark Bennett; Props, Kathy Fabian; Projections, Batwin and Robin Productions; Wig, Paul Huntley; General Manager, KL Management, Richard Martini, Sharon Tinari Pratt; Assistant Director, Nell Balaban; PSM, Michael Joseph Ormond; Cast: Tovah Feldshuh; April 28–May 30, 2010

Robin and the 7 Hoods Book by Rupert Holmes, lyrics by Sammy Cahn, Music by Jimmy Van Heusen, based on the original screenplay by David R. Schwartz; Director and Choreopgraphy, Casey Nicholaw; Music Supervision/Vocal & Incidental Arrangements, John McDaniel; Set, Robert Brill; Costumes, Gregg Barnes; Lighting, Kenneth Posner; Sound, John Shivers, David Patridge; Orchestrator, Bill Elliott; Music Director, Mark Hummel; Dance Music, David Chase; Hair & Wigs, Josh Marquette; Casting, Tara Rubin; Stage Manager, Peter Wolf; ASMs, Brian Bogin, Jess Slocum; Cast: Eric Schneider (Robbo Ortona), Brian Shepard (Shoeshine Guy/Joey/Terrified Man/Waiter/Ensemble), Clyde Alves (Tommy/Waiter/Ensemble), Tally Sessions (Doorman/Larry/Ensemble), Stephanie Gibson (Connie/Jettsetter/Ensemble), Beth Johnson Nicely (Doreen/Jetsetter/Ensemble), Sam Prince (Showbiz Manager/Sonny/Ensemble), Adam Heller (Lieutenant Nottingham), Timothy J. Alex (Georgie/Ensemble), Andrew Cao (Stockboy/Huey/Waiter), Aleks Pevec (Mikey/Waiter/Ensemble), Anthony Wayne (Nunzie/Ensemble), Jeffrey Schecter (Willie Scarlatti), Cara Cooper, Paige Faure, Lisa Gajda, Vasthy Mompoint (Jetsetters/Ensemble), Will Chase (Little John Dante), Amy Spanger (Alana O'Dell), Rick Holmes (P.J. Sullivan), Kelly Sullivan (Marian Archer), Graham Bowen (Swing/Dance Captain), Carissa Lopez (Swing); World Premiere; July 14–August 22, 2010

Old Globe Arena Stage – The Sheryl and Harvey White Theatre

The Mystery of Irma Vep by Charles Ludlam Director, Henry Wishcamper; Set, Robin Vest; Costumes, Jenny Mannis; Lighting, Jason Bieber; Sound, Paul Peterson; Fight Director, Steve Rankin; Stage Manager, Kathryn Davies; Cast: Jeffrey M. Bender (Lady Enid/Nicodemus Underwood/Alcazar/Pev Amri), John Cariani (Lord Edgar Hillcrest/Jane Twisden/An Intruder), Chris Wollman (The Third Man); July 31–September 6, 2009 (end of seventy-fourth season)

The Savannah Disputation by Evan Smith; Director, Kim Rubinstein; Set, Deb O; Costumes, Judith Dolan; Lighting, Alan Burrett; Sound, Paul Peterson; Stage Manager, Anjee Nero; Cast: Kimberly Parker Green (Melissa), Nancy Robinette (Mary), Mikel Sarah Lambert (Margaret), James Sutorius (Father Murphy); September 26–November 1, 2009

I Do! I Do! Book & lyrics by Tom Jones, music by Harvey Schmidt; Director, Richard Jay-Alexander; Choreography, James Kinney; Music Director, Ben Toth; Cast: Patrick Page (Him), Paige Davis (Her); December 11–20, 2009

Lost in Yonkers by Neil Simon; Director, Kent Paul; Set, Ralph Funicello; Costumes, Alejo Vietti; Lighting, Matthew McCarthy; Sound, Paul Peterson; Stage Manager, Diana Moser; Cast: Jeffrey M. Bender (Louie), Steven Kaplan (Jay), Judy Kaye (Grandma Kurnitz), Austyn Myes (Arty), Amanda Naughton (Gert), Jennifer Regan (Bella), Spencer Rowe (Eddie); January 23–February 28, 2010

Alive and Well by Kenny Finkle; Co-world premiere with the Virginia Stage Company; Director, Jeremy Dobrish; Set, Robin Sanford Roberts; Costumes,

Shelly Williams; Lighting, Michael Gottlieb; Sound, Paul Peterson; Stage Manager, Moira Gleason; Casting, Samantha Barrie; Cast: Kelly McAndrew (Carla Keenan), James Knight (Zachariah Clemenson); March 20–April 25, 2010

The Whipping Man by Matthew Lopez; Director, Giovanna Sarddelli; Set, Robert Mark Morgan; Costumes, Denitsa D. Blinznakova; Lighting, Lap Chi Chu; Sound, Jill BC DuBoff; Vocal and Dialect Coach, Claudia Hill-Sparks; Stage Manager, Diana Moser; Fight Choreographer, George Yé; Cast: Mark J. Sullivan (Caleb), Charlie Robinson (Simon), Avery Glymph (John); May 8–June 13, 2010

The Last Romance by Joe DiPietro; Director, Richard Seer; Set, Alexander Dodge; Costumes, Charlotte Devaux; Lighting, Chris Rhynne; Sound, Paul Peterson; Stage Manager, Lavinia Henley; Original Music Supervisor, Mark Ferrell; Voice and Dialect Coach, Jan Gist; Cast: Joshua Jeremiah (The Young Man), Paul Michael (Ralph Bellini), Patricia Connolly (Rose Tagliatelle), Marion Ross (Carol Reynolds), Stewart (Peaches); July 30–September 5, 2010

Olney Theatre Center

Olney, Maryland

Seventy-first Season

Artistic Director, Jim Petosa; Managing Director, Amy Marshall

Is He Dead? by Mark Twain, adapted by David Ives; Director, Halo Wines; Sets, Jon Savage; Costumes, Kathleen Geldard; Lighting, Charlie Morrison; Sound, Jarett C. Pisani; Wigs, Nicole Paul; Stage Manager, William E. Cruttenden III; Technical Director, Daniel Patrick Parker; Company Manager, Sean Cox; Cast: Carlos Bustamante (Hans Von Bismark), Nick DePinto (Basil Thorpe/Claude Riviere/Charlie/The King of France), John Dow (Papa Leroux), Julie-Ann Elliott (Madame Bathilde/The Sultan of Turkey), David Frankenburger Jr. (Phelim O-Shaughnessy), Tara Giordano (Cecile LeRoux), Elizabeth Jernigan (Marie LeRoux), Eric M. Messner (Agamemnon), Richard Pilcher (Bastien Andre), Jeffries Thaiss (Jean-Francois Miller/Widow Daisy Tillou), Peggy Yates (Madam Caron/The Emporer of Russia); Mainstage; February 11–March 8, 2009

King of the Jews by Leslie Epstein; Director, Cheryl Farone; Sets, Jon Savage; Costumes, Howard Kurtz; Lighting, Colin K. Bills; Sound, Jarett C. Pisani; Wigs, Anne Nesmith; Stage Manager, Carey Stipe; Technical Director, Daniel Patrick Parker; Company Manager, Sean Cox; Cast: Norman Aronovic (Verble), David Elias (Schotter), Carter Jahncke (Martini), Timmy Ray James (M.M. Schpitalnick), James Konicek (F.X. Wohltat), Valerie Leonard (Madam Rievesaltes), David Little (Trumpelman), Justin Pereira (Nisel Lipiczany), Peter B. Schmitz (Ferdinand Philosoff), Cherie Weinert (Dorka Kleinweiss), Delaney Williams (Fried Rievesaltes), Harry A. Winter (Herman Gutfreind); World Premiere; Mulitz-Gudelsky Theatre Lab; March 11–April 12, 2009

Call of the Wild Book and lyrics by John Lipsky, music by Bill Barclay; Director, Clay Hopper; Musical Director, Christopher Youstra; Movement Director, Leslie Felbain; Sets, Jeremy W. Foil; Costumes, Pei Lee; Lighting, Nicholas Houfek; Sound, Jarett C. Pisani; Stage Manager, Brandy H. Wyont; Technical Director, Daniel Patrick Parker; Company Manager, Sean Cox; Cast: Evan Casey (Weedon Scott), William Diggle (Spitz), Gwynne Flanagan (She-Wolf/Fleabait), James Gardiner (Buck/Straggletooth), Judith Ingber (Queenie), Deborah Lubega (Pup), Joe Peck (Johnny Boy/Lord Alfred), Kieran Welsh-Phillips (White Fang/Mercedes), Stephen F. Schmidt (Francois), Thomas Adrian Simpson (Thornton/Judge), Andrew Sonntag (Blackjack Davey), Jim Zidar (Beauty Smith); Orchestra: Michaela Cohoon (Bass), Emily Holden (Violin), Mike Ranelli (Percussion), Kimberly Spath (Guitar), Christopher Youstra (Piano); World Premiere; Mainstage; April 8–May 3, 2010

The Glass Menagerie by Tennessee Williams; Director, Jim Petosa; Sets, James Kronzer, Jeremy W. Foil; Costumes, Nicole V. Moody; Lighting, Daniel McLean Wagner; Sound, Matthew Nielson; Stage Manager, Jocelyn Henjum;

Technical Director, Daniel Patrick Parker; Company Manager, Sean Cox; Cast: Briel Banks (Laura Wingfield), Michael Kaye (Tom Wingfield), Paula Langton (Amanda Wingfield), Jeffries Thaiss (Jim O'Connor); Mulitz-Gudelsky Theatre Lab; May 29–July 12, 2009

The Millionairess by George Bernard Shaw; Director, John Going; Sets, James Wolk; Costumes, Liz Covey; Lighting, Dennis Parichy; Sound, Christopher Baine; Wigs, Nicole Paul; Stage Manager, Renee E. Yancey; Technical Director, Daniel Patrick Parker; Company Manager, Sean Cox; Cast: James Denvil (Alastair Fitzfassenden), Nick DePinto (Julius Sagamore), John Dow (The Man), Julie-Ann Elliott (Epifania Ognisanti Di Parerga); David Frankenberger Jr. (Hotel Manager), Michael McKenzie (Adrian Blenderbland), Paul Morella (The Doctor), Tonya Beckman Ross (Patricia Smith), Cherie Weinert (The Woman); Mainstage; June 17–July 19, 2009

A Passion For Justice: An Encounter With Clarence Darrow by Jack Marshall, Paul Morella; Artistic Coordinator, Jim Petosa; Sets, Cristina Todesco; Lighting, Andrew Cissna; Sound, Jarett C. Pisani; Stage Manager, Renee E. Yancey; Technical Director, Daniel Patrick Parker; Company Manager, Sean Cox; Cast: Paul Morella (Clarence Darrow); Mulitz-Gudelsky Theatre Lab; August 12–September 13, 2009

Night Must Fall by Emlyn Williams; Director, John Going; Sets, James Wolk; Costumes, Liz Covey; Lighting, Dennis Parichy; Sound, Jarett Pisani; Wigs, Nan Flanagan; Dialect Coach, Leigh Smiley; Music Arranger, Christopher Youstra; Stage Manager, Jenna Henderson; Technical Director, Daniel Patrick Parker; Company Manager, Sean Cox; Cast: Kathleen Akerley (Nurse Libby), Briel Banks (Dora Parkoe), Julie-Ann Elliott (Olivia Grayne), Tim Getman (Dan), Paul Morella (Inspector Belsize), Rosemary Prinz (Mrs. Bramson), Carl Randolph (Hubert Laurie), Anne Stone (Mrs. Terence); Mainstage; September 30–October 25, 2009

Camelot Book and lyrics by Alan Jay Lerner, music by Frederick Lowe; Director/Choreographer, Stephen Nachamie; Musical Director/Arranger, Christopher Youstra; Associate Choreographer, Tara Jeanne Vallee; Sets, Jeremy W. Foil; Costumes, Eric Propp; Lighting, Charlie Morrison; Sound, Jarett Pisani; Wigs, Nan Flanagan; Dialect Consultant, Lynn Watson; Fight Choreographer, Casey Kaleba; Stage Manager, Renee E. Yancey; Technical Director, Eric Knauss; Company Manager, Sean Cox; Cast: Sharen Camille (Lady Anne), Evan Casey (Mordred/Male Ensemble), James Chatham (Tom of Warwick), Caitlin Diana Doyle (Ensemble), Maria Egler (Lady in Waiting), Jarid Faubel (Sir Dinidan), William Goniprow (Tom of Warwick), Patricia Hurley (Queen Guenevere), Carrie A. Johnson (Nimue), Todd Alan Johnson (King Arthur), Bill Largess (Merlyn/Pellinore), Deborah Lubega (Lady in Waiting), Don Kenneth Mason (Sir Sagramore), Tommy McNeal (Sir Lionel), Michael Nansel (Knight of the Round Table), Carl Randolph (Knight of the Round Table), Kirstin Riegler (Lady in Waiting), Aaron Ramey (Sir Lancelot), Andrew Sonntag (Knight of the Round Table/Dap), Ryan Speakman (Knight of the Round Table), Kara Tameika Watkins (Lady Sybil); Mainstage; November 18, 2009–January 17, 2010

Oregon Shakespeare Festival

Ashland, Oregon

Seventy-fifth Season

Artistic Director, Bill Rauch; Executive Director, Paul Nicholson

Angus Bowmer Theatre

Hamlet by William Shakespeare; Director, Bill Rauch; Sets, Christopher Acebo; Costumes, Deborah M. Dryden; Lighting, Christopher Akerlind; Composer/Sound, Paul James Prendergast; Projections Designer, William Cusick; Choreographer, Rokafella; Dramaturg, Alan Armstrong; Voice/Text, David Carey; Fight Director, U. Jonathan Toppo; Stage Manager, Amy Miranda Warner; ASM, Mara Filler; Cast: Dan Donohue (Hamlet), Jeffrey King (Claudius), Greta

Oglesby (Gertrude), Armando Durán (Horatio), Howie Seago (Ghost), Richard Elmore (Polonius), Susannah Flood (Ophelia), David DeSantos (Laertes), Brad Whitmore (Voltemand/Priest/English Ambassador), Vilma Silva (Rosencrantz), Jeany Park (Guildenstern), Christopher Livingston (Osric), Bill Geisslinger (Marcellus/Gravedigger), Josiah Phillips (Barnardo/Second Gravedigger), Khatt Taylor (Francisco/Player/Queen), Ramiz Monsef (Fortinbras/Player/King), Orion Bradshaw (Player/Lucius); February 19–October 30, 2010

Pride and Prejudice by Jane Austen, adapted for the stage by Joseph Hanreddy and J.R. Sullivan; Director, Libby Appel; Sets, William Bloodgood; Costumes, Mara Blumenfeld; Lighting, Robert Peterson; Composer/Sound, Todd Barton; Choreographer, Art Manke; Dramaturg, Lue Morgan Douthit; Voice/Text, Cynthia Bassham; Stage Manager, Jeremy Eisen; Production Assistant, Dylan Marks; Cast: Mark Murphey (Mr. Bennet), Judith-Marie Bergan (Mrs. Bennet), Nell Geisslinger (Jane Bennet), Kate Hurster (Elizabeth Bennet), Christine Albright (Mary Bennet), Kimbre Lancaster (Kitty Bennet), Susannah Flood (Lydia Bennet), Michael J. Hume (Sir William Lucas/Mr. Gardiner), Linda Alper (Lady Lucas/Mrs. Reynolds), Lisa McCormick (Charlotte Lucas), Christian Barillas (Charles Bingley), Brooke Parks (Caroline Bingley), Elijah Alexander (Mr. Darcy), James Newcomb (Mr. Collins), John Tufts (George Wickham), Demetra Pittman (Lady Catherine de Bourgh), Kevin Kenerly, Rex Young (Colonel Fitzwilliam), Robin Goodrin Nordli (Mrs. Gardiner), Meryn May MacDougall (Georgiana Darcy/Anne de Bourgh), Jonathan Dyrud (Ensign Denny), Eymard Meneses Cabling (Officer/Servant/Ensemble), Nicholas Walker (Officer/Servant/Ensemble), Kay Hilton (Singer); February 21–October 31, 2010

Cat on a Hot Tin Roof by Tennessee Williams; Director, Christopher Liam Moore; Sets, Christopher Acebo; Costumes, Alex Jaeger; Lighting, Christopher Akerlind; Composer/Sound, Andre J. Pluess; Dramaturg, Lydia G. Garcia; Voice/Text, Scott Kaiser; Movement/Fights, U. Jonathan Toppo; Stage Manager, Gwen Turos; Production Assistant, Karl Alphonso; Cast: Stephanie Beatriz (Margaret), Danforth Comins (Brick), Kate Mulligan (Mae), Rex Young (Gooper), Catherine E. Coulson (Big Mama), Julia Hogan Laurenson (Dixie), Audrey Cirzan (Trixie), Corin Elmore (Buster), Michael Winters (Big Daddy), Brad Whitmore (Reverend Tooker), Bill Geisslinger (Doctor Baugh), Gina Daniels (Daisy), Khatt Talor (Sookey); February 20–July 4, 2010

She Loves Me Book by Joe Masteroff, music by Jerry Bock, lyrics by Sheldon Harnick; Director, Rebecca Taichman; Choreographer, John Carrafa; Music Director, Darcy Danielson; Sets, Scott Bradley; Costumes, Miranda Hoffman; Lighting, Christopher Akerlind; Sound, Kai Harada; Dramaturg, Lydia G. Garcia; Voice/Text, Evamarii Johnson; Music Supervisor, Daniel Gary Busby; Orchestrations, Don Walker; Arrangements/Orchestral Reductions, Andy Einhorn; Stage Manager, D. Christian Bolender; Production Assistant, Karl Alphonso; Cast: Lisa McCormick (Amalia Balash), Eymard Meneses Cabling (Arpad), Robert Vincent Frank (Ladislav Sipos), Miriam A. Laube (Ilona Ritter), Michael Elich (Stephen Kodaly), Mark Bedard (Georg Nowack), Michael J. Hume (Mr. Maraczek), Dan Donohue (Waiter/Shopper/Optometrist/Ensemble), G. Valmont Thomas (Mr. Keller/Caroler/Ensemble), Kimbre Lancaster (Shopper/Customer/Ensemble), Terri McMahon (Shopper/Customer/Nurse/Ensemble), Emily Sophia Knapp (Customer/Tango Dancer/Shopper/Ensemble), Greta Oglesby (Customer/Caroler/Ensemble), Kate Hurster (Customer/Caroler/Ensemble), René Millán (Tango Dancer/Caroler/Ensemble), K.T. Vogt (Customer/Shopper/Ensemble), Eddie Lopez (Busboy/Shopper/Ensemble); Musicians: Darcy Danielson, Lori Calhoun, Bruce McKern, Michal Palzewicz, Jacob Phelps-Ransom, Randy Scherer, Arlene Tayloe; April 21–October 30, 2010

Throne of Blood Adaptation by Ping Chong, based on the film with original screeplay directed by Akira Kurosawa (original screenplay by Akira Kurosawa, Hideo Oguni, Shinobu Hashimoto and Ryuzo Kikushima); Director, Ping Chong; Sets, Christopher Acebo; Costumes, Stefani Mar; Lighting, Darren McCroom; Video/Projections, Maya Ciarrocchi, Composer/Sound, Todd Barton; Dramaturgs, Lue Morgan Douthit, Gina Pisasale; Voice/Text, Sara Phillips; Movement/Fight Director, John Sipes; Stage Manager, Amy Miranda Warner; ASM, Mandy Younger; Cast: Kevin Kenerly (Washizu), Ako (Lady Asaji), Danforth Comins (Yoshiako Miki/

Forest Spirit), Jonathan Haugen (Lord Kuniharu/Soldier), JaMario Stills (Prince Kunimaru/Koken), Richard Howard (Noriyasu Odagura/Forest Spirit), Michael Winters (Old General), Cristofer Jean (Forest Spirt/Soldier), Gregory Linington (First Quartet/Retainer), Peter Macon (Second General/Second Quartet), James Newcomb (Third General/Third Quartet), Elijah Alexander (Fourth General/Second Retainer), Kacy-Earl David (First Soldier/First Messenger/Second Retainer), Emily Sophia Knapp (Koken/Old Woman), Eddie Lopez (Koken), Alonzo Lee Moore IV (Koken), Daniel Marmion (Yoshiteru/Second Messenger); World Premiere; July 21–October 31, 2010

New Theatre

Well by Lisa Kron; Director, James Edmondson; Sets, Richard L. Hay; Costumes, Candice Cain; Lighting, Dawn Chiang; Composer/Sound, Joe Romano; Dramaturg, Lue Morgan Douthit; Voice/Text, Cynthia Bassham; Fight Director, U. Jonathan Toppo; Stage Manager, Jill Rendall; ASM, D. Christian Bolender; Cast: Terri McMahon (Lisa), Dee Maaske (Ann), Brent Hinkley (Head Nurse/Howard Norris/Himself), G. Valmont Thomas (Nurse 2/Jim Richardson/Little Oscar/Big Oscar/Himself), Gina Daniels (Kay/Mrs. Price/Lori Jones/Cynthia/Herself), K. T. Vogt (Joy/Dottie/Herself); February 25–June 18, 2010

Ruined by Lynn Nottage; Director, Liesl Tommy; Sets, Clint Ramos; Costumes, Christal Weatherly; Lighting, Robert Peterson; Composer/Sound, Broken Chord Collective; Choreography, Randy Duncan; Dramaturg, Lue Morgan Douthit; Voice/Text, Eva Marii Johnson; Fight Director, U. Jonathan Toppo; Stage Manager, Randall K. Lum; ASM, Mandy Younger; Phil Killian Directing Fellow, Sarah Rasmussen; Cast: Kimberly Scott (Mama Nadi), Chinasa Ogbuagu (Salima), Dawn-Lyen Gardner (Sophie), Victoria Ward (Josephine), Tyrone Wilson (Christian), Jimonn Cole (Jerome Kisembe/Ensemble), Kenajuan Bentley (Osembenga/Ensemble), Armando Durán (Mr. Harari), JaMario Stills (Simon/Aide Worker/Ensemble), Peter Macon (Fortune/Ensemble), Kelvin Underwood (Percussion/Ensemble), Chic Street Man (Guitar/Ensemble); West Coast Premiere; March 27–October 31, 2010

American Night: The Ballad of Juan José by Richard Montoya and Culture Clash; Director, Jo Bonney; Sets, Neil Patel; Costumes, Emilio Sosa; Lighting, David Weiner; Projections, Shawn Sagady; Composer/Sound, Darron L West; Choreographer, Ken Roht; Dramaturg, Judith Rosen; Voice/Text, Sara Phillips; Fight Director, U. Jonathan Toppo; Stage Manager, Randall K. Lum; Production Assistant., Karl Alphonso; Cast: René Millán (Juan José), Stephanie Beatriz (Lydia/Ensemble), Rodney Gardiner (Ben Pettus/Ensemble), David Kelly (Harry Bridges/Ensemble), Richard Montoya (Mexican Revolutionary/Ensemble), Kate Mulligan (Mrs. Finney/Ensemble), Kimberly Scott (Viola Pettus/Ensemble), Herbert Siguenza (Doña Tencha/Ensemble), Daisuke Tsuji (Johnny/Ensemble); World Premiere; June 30–October 31, 2010

Elizabethan Stage/Allen Pavilion

Twelfth Night by William Shakespeare; Director, Darko Tresnjak; Sets, David Zinn; Costumes, Linda Cho; Lighting, Jane Cox; Composer/Sound, Paul James Prendergast; Associate Costumes, Josh Pearson; Dramaturg, Gina Pisasale; Voice/Text, Ursula Meyer; Fight Director, U. Jonathan Toppo; Stage Manager, Jeremy Eisen; Production Assistant, Dylan Marks; Cast: Brooke Parks (Viola), Kenajuan Bentley (Orsino), Miriam A. Laube (Olivia), Christopher Liam Moore (Malvolio), Michael Elich (Feste), Michael J. Hume (Sir Toby Belch), Rex Young (Sir Andrew Aguecheek), Robin Goodrin Nordli (Maria), Tony DeBruno (Fabian), Christian Barillas (Sebastian/Sailor), Jimonn Cole (Antonio/Sailor), Mark Murphey (Sea Captain/Priest), Jorge Claudio Paniagua (Valentine/Officer), Fune Tautala Jr. (Curio), Kimbre Lancaster (Lady), Victoria Ward (Lady) Gregg Land (Officer/Sailor); Musicians: Aaron Moffatt, Daryl Fjeldheim; June 1–October 8, 2010

Henry IV, Part One by William Shakespeare. Director, Penny Metropulos; Sets, Michael Ganio; Costumes, Deborah M. Dryden; Lighting, Robert Peterson; Composer/Sound, Michael Keck; Dramaturg, Alan Armstrong; Voice/Text, Ursula Meyer; Fight Director, U. Jonathan Toppo; Stage Manager, Jill Rendall; ASM, Mara Filler; Cast: Cristofer Jean (Richard II/Innkeeper/Sir Richard Vernon),

Richard Howard (King Henry IV), Richard Elmore (Earl of Westmoreland/Sheriff), Daniel Marmion (Prince John of Lancaster/Servant to Hotspur), U. Jonathan Toppo (Sir Walter Blunt/Traveler), John Tufts (Prince Hal), David Kelly (Sir John Falstaff), Nell Geisslinger (Wench/Lady Mortimer), Howie Seago (Edward Poins), James Newcomb (Earl of Worcester), Josiah Phillips (Earl of Northumberland), Kevin Kenerly (Henry "Hotspur" Percy), Jeffrey King (Carrier/Earl of Douglas), Christopher Liam Moore (Gadshill/Messenger), Christopher Livingston (Peto/Ensemble), Brent Hinkley (Bardolph), Daisuke Tsuji (Traveller/Francis), Russell Lloyd (Traveller/Ensemble), Christine Albright (Lady Percy), Judith-Marie Bergan (Mistress Quickly), Elijah Alexander (Lord Mortimer), Anthony Heald (Owen Glendower); June 2–October 9, 2010

The Merchant of Venice by William Shakespeare; Director, Bill Rauch; Sets, Richard L. Hay; Costumes, Shigeru Yaji; Lighting, Jane Cox; Composer/Sound, Andre J. Pluess: Dramaturg, Judith Rosen; Voice/Text, Scott Kaiser; Creative Consultant, Lenny Neimark; Fight Director, U. Jonathan Toppo; Stage Manager, Gwen Turos; ASM, D. Christian Bolender; Phil Killian Directing Fellow, Sarah Rasmussen; Cast: Michael Winters (The Duke of Venice/Old Gobbo/Balthazar), Jonathan Haugen (Antonio), Danforth Comins (Bassanio), Vilma Silva (Portia), Dawn-Lyen Gardner (Nerissa), Anthony Heald (Shylock), Emily Sophia Knapp (Jessica), Howie Seago (Tubal/Ensemble), David DeSantos (Solanio/Ensemble), Cristofer Jean (Salerio/Ensemble), Gregory Linington (Gratiano), Daniel Marmion (Lorenzo), Mark Bedard (Launcelot Gobbo), Peter Macon (The Prince of Morocco), Armando Durán (The Prince of Arragon), Roberta Burke (Fátima/Ensemble), Ramiz Monsef (Arragon's Attendant/Ensemble), Erin Claxton (Ensemble), Zach Meyers (Ensemble); June 3–October 10, 2010

Paper Mill Playhouse

Millburn, New Jersey

Founded in 1934

Executive Director, Mark W. Jones; Artistic Director, Mark S. Hoebee

Little House on the Prairie The Musical Book by Rachel Sheinkin, music by Rachel Portman, lyrics by Donna Di Novelli; Based on the "Little House" books by Laura Ingalls Wilder; Director, Francesca Zambello; Musical Staging, Michelle Lynch; Music Supervision, Kevin Stites; Orchestrations, Larry Hochman; Set, Adrianne Lobel; Costumes, Jess Goldstein; Lighting, Mark McCullough; Sound, Carl Casella, Dominic Sack; Hair/Wigs, Charles LaPointe; PSM, Michael Danek; Cast: Melissa Gilbert (Ma), Steve Blanchard (Pa), Kara Lindsay (Laura), Kate Loprest (Nellie Olsen), Kevin Massey (Almanzo), Alessa Neeck (Mary), Anastasia Korbal (Carrie); Ensemble: Michael Boxleitner, Megan Campanile, Kurt Engh, Shawn Hamilton, Jessica Hershberg, Meredith Inglesby, Caroline Innerbichler, Lizzie Klemperer, Camille Mancuso, Lori Eve Marinacci, Garen McRoberts, Brian Muller, Will Ray, Tyler Rhodes, Gayle Samuels, Dustin Sullivan, Todd Thurston, Tony Vierling, Christian Whelan; September 10–October 10, 2009

On the Town Music and lyrics by Leonard Bernstein; Director, Mark S. Hoebee; Choregraphy, Patti Colombo; Music Director, Tom Helm; Set, Walt Spangler; Costumes, David C. Woolard; Lighting, Tom Sturge; Sound, Randy Hansen; Hair/Wigs, Mark Adam Rampmeyer; PSM, Richard C. Rauscher; Casting, Alison Franck; Cast: Tyler Hanes (Gaby), Jeffrey Schecter (Ozzie), Brian Shephard (Chip), Jennifer Cody (Hildy), Kelly Sullivan (Claire DeLoone), Yvette Tucker (Ivy), Harriet Harris (Madame Dilly), Bill Nolte (Judge Pitkin); Ensemble: Steven Ted Beckler, Paige Faure, Tyler Foy, Cameron Henderson, Tari Kelly, Logan Keslar, Dana Maddox, Lindsay Moore, Casey Muha, Caitlin Mundth, Philip Northington, James A. Pierce III, Catherine Ricafort, Rod Roberts, Ryan Sandberg, Michael Scirrotto, Molly Tynes, Kyle Vaughn, Jacob Widman, Paige Williams; November 11–December 6, 2009

The Company of Oregon Shakespeare Festival's She Loves Me (photo by Jenny Graham)

Steve Blanchard, Melissa Gilbert, and the Company in Little House on the Prairie at Paper Mill Playhouse (photo by Carol Rosegg)

Helena Ruotia, John Shepard, Chris Landis, and Ross Bickell in The Little Foxes at Pittsburg Public Theater (photo by Michael Henninger)

Chinasa Ogbagu and Kimberly Scott in Ruined at the Oregon Shakespeare Festival (photo by Jenny Graham)

Harris Doran in Pittsburgh Public Theater's production of A Midsummer Night's Dream (photo by Michael Henninger)

Leif Norby in The 39 Steps at Portland Center Stage
(photo by Owen Carey)

Mathew Shawlin, Daniel Noel, and Larry Nicks in The Drawer Boy
at Portland Stage (photo by Darren Setlow)

Aurelia Williams, Christopher L. Morgan, Angela Grovey, Rebecca
Covington, and Ken Robinson in San Jose Repertory Theatre/Arizona
Theatre Company/Cleveland Play House production of
Ain't Misbehavin' (photo by Kevin Berne)

Gavin Gregory in Portland Center Stage's Ragtime
(photo by Owen Carey)

Amy Justman, Benjamin Howes, Ben Nordstrom, Stephanie D'Abruzzo
in the Repertory Theatre of St. Louis production of [tile of show]
(photo by Jerry Naunheim Jr.)

Dwight Huntsman and Scott Coopwood in San Jose Repertory
Theatre's production of Groundswell (photo by Kevin Berne)

Lost in Yonkers by Neil Simon; Director, Michael Bloom; Set, Michael Schweikhardt; Costumes, David Kay Mickelsen; Lighting, Paul Miller; Sound, Keith Kohrs; PSM, Barbara Reo; Casting, Paul Fouquet; Cast: Rosemary Prinz (Grandma), J. Anthony Crabe (Louis), John Plumpis (Eddie), Sara Surrey (Bella), Patricia Buckley (Gert), Alex Wyse (Jay), Maxwell Beer (Arty); February 17–March 14, 2010

Smokey Joe's Cafe The songs of Jerry Leiber and Mike Stoller; Director, Mark S. Hoebee; Choreographer, Denis Jones; Music Director, Tom Helm; Set, Jonathan Spencer; Costumes, Brian Hemesath; Lighting, Charlie Morrison; Sound, Randy Hansen; Hair/Wigs, Mark Adam Rampmeyer; PSM, Andrea Cibelli; Casting, Alison Franck; Cast: Jackie Burns, Clayton Cornelius, Bernard Dotson, Felicia Finley, Carly Hughes, Andrew Rannells, Dennis Stowe, Eric Lajuan Summers, Maia Nkenge Wilson; April 7–May 2, 2010

Peter Pan Based on J.M. Barrie's play; Music by Mark Charlap, additional music by Jule Styne, lyrics by Carolyn Leigh, additional lyrics by Betty Comden and Adolph Green; Director, Mark S. Hoebee; Choreographer, Patti Colombo; Music Director, Tom Helm; Set, John Iacovelli; Costumes, Thom Heyer; Lighting, F. Mitchell Dana; Sound, Randy Hansen; Hair/Wigs, Rob Green, Jared Janas; PSM, John M. Atherlay; Casting, Alison Franck; Cast: Nancy Anderson (Peter Pan), Douglas Sills (Mr. Darling/Captain Hook), Glory Crampton (Mrs. Darling), Jessica Lee Goldyn (Tiger Lily), Hayley Podschun (Wendy), John O'Creagh (Smee); Ensemble: Randy Aaron, J. David Anderson, Adrian Arrieta, Jordan Barrow, Jack Broderick, Ryan Chotto, Dustin Clodfelter, Lauren Decierdo, Taurean Everett, Julian Farinas, Casey Garvin, Lewis Grosso, Justin Henry, Zachary Infante, Sarah Marie Jenkins, Josh Pins, Kathryn Raskin, Kyle Vaughn, Dane Wagner, Todd A. Walker, and Stephen Williams; June 2–27, 2010

Philadelphia Theatre Company

Philadelphia, Pennsylvania

Thirty-sixth Season

Producing Artistic Director, Sara Garonzik; Managing Director, Diane Claussen

Humor Abuse by Lorenzo Pisoni and Erica Schmidt; Director, Erica Schmidt; Set, John Lee Beatty; Sound, Bart Fasbender; Lighting, Ben Stanton; Cast: Lorenzo Pisoni; September 25–October 25, 2009

The Light in the Piazza Music & lyrics by Adam Guettel, book by Craig Lucas; Director, Joe Calarco; Music Director, Eric Ebbenga; Set, Michael Fagin; Costumes, Anne Kennedy; Lighting, R. Lee Kennedy; Sound, Ryan Rumery; Cast: Whitney Bashor (Clara), Sherri Edelen (Margaret), Joe Guzman (Roy/Priest), Charles Pistone (Signor Naccarelli), Kyra Miller (Franca/Tour Guide), Fran Prisco (Guiseppe), Matthew Scott (Fabrizio), Maureen Torsney-Weir (Signora Naccarelli); November 13–December 13, 2009

Golden Age by Terrence McNally; Director, Austin Pendleton; Set, Santo Loquasto; Costumes, Richard St. Clair; Lighting, Jason Lyons; Sound, Ryan Rumery; Cast: Rebecca Brooksher (Grisi), Jeffery Carlson (Bellini), Roe Hartrampf (Florimo), Marc Kudisch (Tamburini), Hoon Lee (La Blache), Christopher McFarland (Rubini), Dante Mignucci (Page), George Morfogen (Gioachino Rossini), Amanda Warren (Malibran); World Premiere; January 22–February 14, 2010

Red Hot Patriot: The Kick-Ass Wit of Molly Ivins by Margaret Engel and Allison Engel; Director, David Esbjornson; Set, John Arnone; Costumes, Elizabeth Hope Clancy; Lighting, Russell Champa; Sound, Rob Milburn; Projections, Maya Ciarrocchi; Cast: Kathleen Turner (Molly Ivins); World Premiere; March 19–April 25, 2010

Ma Rainey's Black Bottom by August Wilson; Presented in association with CENTERSTAGE; Director, Irene Lewis; Music Director, William McDaniels; Set, Riccardo Hernandez; Costumes, Candice Donnelly; Lighting, Rui Rita; Sound,

David Budries; Cast: Ro Boddie (Sylvester), E. Faye Butler (Ma Rainey), Thomas Jefferson Byrd (Toledo), Toccarra Cash (Dussie Mae), David Fonteno (Cutler), Merwin Goldsmith (Irvin), Jeb Kreager (Policeman), Maurice McRae (Levee), Laurence O'Dwyer (Sturdyvant), Ernest Perry (Slow Drag); May 21–June 13, 2010

Pittsburgh Public Theater

Pittsburgh, Pennsylvania

Thirty-fifth Season

Artistic Director, Ted Pappas; Managing Director, Mark R. Power

Ella by Jeffrey Hatcher, conceived by Rob Ruggiero and Dyke Garrison; Director, Rob Ruggiero; Musical Supervision & Arrangements, Danny Holgate; Sets, Michael Schweikardt; Costumes, Alejo Vietti; Lighting, John Lasiter; Sound, Michael Miceli; Wigs, Charles LaPointe; Stage Manager, Richard Costabile; Cast: Tina Fabrique (Ella Fitzgerald); Band: George Caldwell, Harold Dixon, Rodney Harper, Ron Haynes, Clifton Kellem; October 1–November 1, 2009

The Little Foxes by Lillian Hellman; Director, Ted Pappas; Sets, James Noone; Costumes, David R. Zyla; Lighting, Kirk Bookman; Sound, Zach Moore; Stage Manager, Fred Noel; Cast: Linda Haston (Addie), Wali Jamal (Cal), Deirdre Madigan (Birdie Hubbard), John Shepard (Oscar Hubbard), Chris Landis (Leo Hubbard), Helena Ruoti (Regina Giddens), Philip Winters (William Marshall), Ross Bickell (Ben Hubbard), Lara Hillier (Alexandra Giddens), Michael McKenzie (Horace Giddens); November 12–December 13, 2009

A Midsummer Night's Dream by William Shakespeare; Director, Ted Pappas; Sets, James Noone; Costumes, Gabriel Berry; Lighting, Kirk Bookman; Sound, Zach Moore; Stage Manager, Ruth E. Kramer; Cast: David Whalen (Theseus/Oberon), Bianca Amato (Hippolyta/Titania), Harris Doran (Puck), Alex Coleman (Egeus/Peter Quince), Lindsey Kyler (Hermia), J.T. Arbogast (Demetrius), Lucas Near-Verbrugghe (Lysander), Beth Wittig (Helena), John Ahlin (Nick Bottom), Daniel Krell (Francis Flute/Mustardseed), James Fitzgerald (Robin Starveling/Peaseblossom), Tony Bingham (Tom Snout/Cobweb), Jeremy Czarniak (Snug/Moth), Meggie Booth or Alex Lindsay Roth (Page/First Fairy); January 21–February 21, 2010

The Price by Arthur Miller; Director, Tracy Brigden; Sets, Luke Hegel-Cantarella; Costumes, Michael Krass; Lighting, Frances Aronson; Sound, Zach Moore; Stage Manager, Fredric H. Orner; Cast: Joseph Adams (Victor Franz), Chandler Vinton (Esther Franz), Noble Shropshire (Gregory Solomon), Sherman Howard (Walter Franz); March 4–April 4, 2010

Time of My Life by Alan Ayckbourn; Director, John Tillinger; Sets, James Noone; Costumes, Laurie Churba Kohn; Lighting, Rui Rita; Sound, Zach Moore; Stage Manager, Fred Noel; Cast: Paxton Whitehead (Gerry Stratton), Ann McDonough (Laura), Tim McGeever (Glyn), Jeffrey Withers (Adam), Leah Curney (Stephanie), Sarah Manton (Maureen), Tom Beckett (Ernesto Calvinu/The Waiters); April 15–May 16, 2010

Art by Yasmina Reza; Director, Ted Pappas; Sets, Anne Mundell; Costumes, Ted Pappas; Lighting, Phil Monat; Sound, Zach Moore; Stage Manager, Ruth E. Kramer; Cast: Darren Eliker (Serge) Rob Breckenridge (Marc), Harry Bouvy (Yvan); May 27–June 27, 2010

PlayMakers Repertory Company

Chapel Hill, North Carolina

Thirty-fourth Season

Producing Artistic Director, Joseph Haj; Managing Director, Hannah Grannemann

Mainstage

Opus by Michael Hollinger; Director, Brendon Fox; Sets, James Kronzer; Costumes, Marion Williams; Lighting, Pat Collins; Sound, Sarah Pickett; Stage Manager, Charles K. Bayang; Cast: Jimmy Kieffer (Carl), Jeffrey Blair Cornell (Alan), Marianne Miller (Grace), Scott Ripley (Elliot), Ray Dooley (Dorian); September 23–October 11, 2009

The Life and Adventures of Nicholas Nickleby, Parts I & II, by David Edgar; Directors, Joseph Haj, Tom Quaintance; Sets, McKay Coble; Costumes, Jan Chambers; Lighting, Tyler Micoleau; Sound, Sarah Pickett; Stage Managers, Charles K. Bayang, Sarah Smiley; Cast: Justin Adams (Nicholas Nickleby), David Adamson (Wagstaff/Linkinwater/Col. Chowser/Ensemble), Allison Altman (Madeline/Fanny/Belvawny/Ensemble), Sarah Berk (Phib/Mobbs/Infant Phenomenon/Ensemble), Prince T. Bowie (Coates/Hetherington/Ensemble), Weston Blakesley (Newman Noggs/Handsaw/Crummles Company), James E. Brinkley (Bolder/Wilbur/William/Crummles Company/Ensemble), John Brummer (Jennings/Scaley/Pyke/Frank Cheeryble/Crummles Company/Ensemble), Jeffrey Blair Cornell (Vincent Crummles/Ned Cheeryble/Snawley/Ensemble), Dede Corvinus (Mrs. LaCreevy/Mrs. Crummles/Mrs. Squeers/Ensemble), Ray Dooley (Ralph Nickleby/Crummles Company), Lenore Field (Miss Knag/Mrs. Curdle/Mrs. Lenville/Mrs. Wittiterly/Ensemble), Julie Fishell (Mrs. Nickleby/Mrs. Grudden/Peg Sliderskew), Kahlil Gonzalez-Garcia (Belling/Mr. Tix/Mr. Bane/Mr. Pluck/Ensemble), Joy Jones (Mrs. Mantalini/Miss Snevellicci/Ensemble), Jimmy Kieffer (Browdie/Pailey/Curdle/Hawk), Derrick Ledbetter (Cobbey/Verisopht/New Smike/Milliner/Crummles Company), David McClutchey (Pupker Jackson/Lenville/Brooker/Gride), Jeffrey Meanza (Mantalini/Young Wackford/Mr. Folair/Ensemble), Marianne Miller (Kate Nickleby/Miss Ledrook), Matthew Murphy (Walter Bray/Snawley Sr./Master Crummles/Mr. Wittiterly/Ensemble), Flor De Liz Perez (Hannah/Miss Bravassa/Snawley Jr./Ensemble), Jason Powers (Smike/Croupier), Scott Ripley (Squeers/Fluggers/Charles Cheeryble/Flunkey), Alice Whitley(Tilda/Master Percy Crummles/Wanda/Ensemble); November 11–December 20, 2009

All My Sons by Arthur Miller; Director, Davis McCallum; Sets, Mimi Lien; Costumes, Junghyun Georgia Lee; Lighting, Jane Cox; Sound, Sarah Pickett; Stage Manager, Sarah Smiley; Cast: John Brummer (George Deever), Christian Conn (Chris Keller), Jeffrey Blair Cornell (Jim Bayliss), Julie Fishell (Sue Bayliss), Lucas Griffin (Bert), Jimmy Kieffer (Frank Lubey), Ellen McLaughlin (Kate Keller), Marianne Miller (Ann Deever), Paul O'Brien (Joe Keller), Flor De Liz Perez (Lydia Lubey); January 27–February 14, 2010

The Importance of Being Earnest by Oscar Wilde; Director, Mathew Arbour; Sets, Marion Williams; Costumes, Anne Kennedy; Lighting, Charlie Morrison; Sound, Sarah Pickett; Stage Manager, Charles K. Bayang; Cast: John Brummer (Algernon Moncreiff), Julia Coffey (Gwendolen Fairfax), Jeffrey Blair Cornell (Reverend Chasuble), Ray Dooley (Lady Bracknell), Julie Fishell (Miss Prism), Jimmy Kieffer (Lane/Merriman), Marianne Miller (Cecily Cardew), Jeremy Webb (Jack Worthing); March 3–21, 2010

PRC ² Second Stage

The Last Cargo Cult by Mike Daisey; Director, Jean-Michelle Gregory; Cast: Mike Daisey; September 16–20, 2009

The Big Bang by Universes; Cast: Gamal Abdel Chasten, Ninja, Mildred Ruiz, Steven Sapp; January 13–17, 2010

I Have Before Me a Remarkable Document Given to Me by a Young Lady from Rwanda by Sonja Linden; Director, Raelle Myrick-Hodges; Sets, McKay Coble; Costumes, Rachel E. Pollock; Lighting, Cecilia R. Durbin; Sound, Sarah Pickett; Stage Manager, Sarah Smiley; Cast: Joy Jones (Juliette), Garth Petal (Simon); March 24–28, 2010

Portland Center Stage

Portland, Oregon

Twenty-second Season

Artistic Director, Chris Coleman

Mainstage

Ragtime Book by Terence McNally, lyrics by Lynn Ahrens, music by Stephen Flaherty; Director, Chris Coleman; Music Director/Conductor, Rick Lewis; Choreographer, Joel Ferrell; Set, G.W. Mercier; Original Costume Designer, Santo Loquasto; Additional Costumes, Jeff Cone; Lighting, Peter Maradudin; Sound, Casi Pacilio; Associate Sound, Sam Kusnetz; Fight Director, John Armour; Dialect Coach, Mary MacDonald-Lewis; Cast: Anna Jane Bishop (Little Girl), Rachael Ferrera (Sarah), Gavin Gregory (Coalhouse Walker), Tiffany Haas (Evelyn Nesbit/Kathleen/Brigit/Clerk/Ensemble), Todd A. Horman (Henry Ford/Willie/Conklin/Admiral Perry/Ensemble), Alicia Irving (Emma Goldman/Ensemble), Marty Austin Lamar (Black Attorney/Matthew Henson/Ensemble), Christine Lyons (Baron's Assistant/Ensemble), Dan Maceyak (Harry Houdini/Fireman/Bureaucrat 2/Policeman/Reporter/Ensemble/Tateh u.s), Robert Mammana (Father), Susannah Mars (Mother), Jesse Means (Booker T. Washington/Ensemble/Coalhouse u.s), Lacretta Nicole (Sarah's Friend/Ensemble), Leif Norby (Tateh/Baron Askenazy), Danny Rothman (Younger Brother), Steven Stein-Grainger (Grandfather/Charles Whitman/Ensemble), Lawrence Street (Ensemble/Booker T u.s), Alex Thede (Little Boy), Tom Treadwell (JP Morgan/Fireman/Policeman/Ensemble), Sara Catherine Wheatley (Welfare Official/Bureaucrat 1/Ensemble/Mother u.s), Kent Zimmerman (Conductor/Reporter/Policeman/Fireman/Jury Foreman/Reporter/Ensemble/Houdini u.s./Dance Captain); September 22–November 1, 2009

A Christmas Carol Adapted by Mead Hunter from the novella by Charles Dickens; Director, Rose Riordan; Composer/Arranger, Rick Lewis; Choreographer, Kent Zimmerman; Musical Director, Reece Marshburn; Set, Dex Edwards; Costumes, Jeff Cone; Lighting, Daniel Ordower; Sound, Casi Pacilio; Dialect Coach, Mary McDonald-Lewis; Cast: Ebbe Roe Smith (Ebenezer Scrooge); Christine Calfas (Dora's Sister/Miss Fezziwig #2/Gentlewoman), Kallan Dana (Martha Cratchit/Child), James Langston Drake (Peter Cratchit/Middle Ebenezer/Ghost of Christmas Past 2), Laura Faye Smith (Fan/Belle/Mrs. Belle's Daughter/Party Guest #1/Street Person), Michael Fisher-Welsh (Bob Cratchit/Suitor#2/Mrs. Belle's Husband/Thug), Hallie Jean Frost (Girl/Want & Ignorance/Miss Fezziwig #3), Debbie Hunter (Dora/Miss Fezziwig #1/Laundress/Parent), Julianna Jaffe (Ghost of Christmas Present/Shop Keeper/Suitor #1), Aimee Martin (Mary Cratchit/Schoolhouse Belle/Want & Ignorance/Turkey Boy), Henry Martin (Tiny Tim/Ghost of Christmas Past #1/Young Ebenezer), Sharonlee McLean (Mrs. Cratchit/Mrs. Belle/Mrs. Fezziwig/Charwoman), Darius Pierce (Gentleman #1/Old Fezziwig/Topper/Undertaker Man/Parent), Ted Roisum (Jacob Marley/Old Joe), Kelsey Tyler (Fred/Ebenezer/Ghost of Christmas Past 3), Kent Zimmerman (Laborer/Young Jacob Marley/Party Guest #2/Ali Baba/Dance Captain); November 24–December 27, 2009

Snow Falling on Cedars Adapted by Kevin McKeon from the book by David Guterson; Director, Chris Coleman; Set, William Bloodgood; Costumes, Jeff Cone; Lighting, Diane Ferry Williams; Sound, Casi Pacilio; Composer, Randall Tico; Dialect Coach, Mary McDonald-Lewis; Fight Director, John Armour; Cast: Vince Nappo (Ishmael, Olivia Oguma (Hatsue), Casey McFeron (Abel/Busdriver/Koenig/George Leonard), Jayne Taini (Etta Heine/Mrs. Chambers), Tom Bloom (Alvin Hicks/Fisherman3/Picker/FBI #3/Mate), Tobias Andersen (Nels), Amanda Soden (Susan Marie), William Peden (Carl Heine Jr./Coroner/Picker/FBI #2/Harvey), Scott Coopwood (Art Moran/Bureaucrat/Jackson/Officer Powell), Mia Tagano (Fujiko/Mrs. Nitta/Dr Whitman), Allan Barlow (Carl Heine Sr/Fisherman 2/FBI #1/Army Driver/Sgt. Maples/Checker), Bruce Locke (Kabuo), Alan Ariano (Zenhichi/Fisherman 1/Hisao/Mr. Nitta/Family), Connor Johnston (Boy/Will/Family); January 12–February 7, 2010

The 39 Steps Adapted by Patrick Barlow from the book by John Buchan and the movie of Alfred Hitchcock; Original concept by Nobby Dimon and Simon

Corble; Director, Nancy Keystone; Set/Lighting, Justin Townsend; Costumes, Jeff Cone; Sound, Casi Pacilio; Shadow Puppets, Sarah Frechette; Dialect Coach, Mary McDonald-Lewis; Fight Director, John Armour; Cast: Leif Norby (Richard Hannay), Christine Calfas (Annabella/Margaret/Pamela), Darius Pierce (Man 1), Ebbe Roe Smith (Man 2); February 23–March 21, 2010

The Chosen by Aaron Posner from the novel by Chaim Potok; Director, Chris Coleman; Set, Michael Olich; Lighting, Kimberly J. Scott; Costumes, Lindsay Kleinman; Sound, Casi Pacilio; Video, Patrick Weishampel; Cast: Matthew Boston (Reuven Malter), Carter Hudson (Young Reuven Malter), David Margulies (Reb Saunders), Jonathan David Martin (Danny Saunders), John Rothman (David Malter); April 6–May 2, 2010

The 25th Annual Putnam County Spelling Bee Music and lyrics by William Finn, book by Rachel Sheinkin; Conceived by Rebecca Feldman; Additional Material by Jay Reiss; Director, Rose Riordan; Music Director, Rick Lewis; Choreographer, Amy Beth Frankel; Set, Christopher Rousseau; Costumes, Jeff Cone; Lighting, Daniel Ordower; Sound, Casi Pacilio; Cast: Connor Bond (Leaf Coneybear), Ka-Ling Cheung (Marcy Park), Gavin Gregory (Mitch Mahoney), Isaac Lamb (William Barfee), Raymond J. Lee (Chip Tolentino), Susannah Mars (Rona Lisa Peretti), Ellie Mooney (Logainne "Schwarzy" Schwartzandgrubenierre), Darius Pierce (Douglas Panch), Sara Catherine Wheatley (Olive Ostrovsky); May 25–June 27, 2010

Ellyn Bye Studio

Josh Kornbluth's Ben Franklin: Unplugged by Josh Kornbluth; Director, David Dower; Set, Annie Smart; Lighting, Jim Cave; Original Music Compositions, Joshua Raoul Brody; Costumes, Sara L. Sato and Laura Hazlett; Cast: Josh Kornbluth (Himself/Ben Franklin); September 29–November 21, 2009

The Santaland Diaries by David Sedaris, adapted by Joe Mantello; Director, Wendy Knox; Set/Costumes, Jessica Ford; Lighting, Don Crossley; Original Sound, Sarah Pickett; Cast: Wade McCollum; December 3 –27, 2009

The Receptionist by Adam Bock; Director, Rose Riordan; Set/Costumes, Rose Riordan; Lighting, Don Crossley; Sound, Jen Raynak; Cast: Laura Faye Smith (Lorraine Taylor), Chris Harder (Martin Dart), Sharonlee McLean (Beverly Wilkins), Robert M. Thomas (Edward Raymond); January 26–March 21, 2010

Mike's Incredible Indian Adventure by Mike Schlitt; Director, Nancy Keystone; Set/Lighting, Daniel Meeker; Sound, Sam Kusnetz; Costumes, Jeff Cone; Cast: Mike Schlitt (Himself); April 20–June 13, 2010

The Repertory Theatre of St. Louis

St. Louis, Missouri

Forty-third Season

Artistic Director, Steven Woolf; Managing Director, Mark Bernstein

Virginia Jackson Browning Mainstage

Amadeus by Peter Shaffer; Director, Paul Mason Barnes; Sets, Bill Clarke; Costumes, Dorothy Marshall Englis; Lighting, Peter E. Sargent; Sound, Rusty Wandall; Music Supervisor, Henry Palkes; Casting, Rich Cole; Stage Manager, Glenn Dunn; ASM, Shannon B. Sturgis; Cast: Craig Baldwin (Venticello 1), Michael Dean Morgan (Venticello 2), Andrew Long (Antonio Salieri), Jeffrey Hayenga (Count Johann Kilian von Strack), Richmond Hoxie (Count Franz Orsini-Rosenberg), Walter Hudson (Baron Gottfried van Swieten), Elizabeth Stanley (Constanze Weber), Jim Poulos (Wolfgang Amadeus Mozart), Joe Hickey (Emperor Joseph II); Ensemble: Jenn Bock, Jon Breeden, Joseph Garner, Cale Hauper, Michael Monsey, Maggie Murphy, Michael B. Perkins, Khnemu Menu-Ra, Brian White; September 9–October 4, 2009

Sleuth by Anthony Shaffer; Director, Michael Evan Haney; Sets, Paul Shortt; Costumes, Gordon DeVinney; Lighting, James Sale; Fight Director, Drew

Fracher; Casting, Rich Cole; Stage Manager, T.R. Martin; ASM, Tony Dearing; Cast: Munson Hicks (Andrew Wyke), Michael Gabriel Goodfriend (Milo Tindle); October 14–November 8, 2009

A Christmas Story by Philip Grecian, based on the film distributed by Warner Brothers with a screenplay by Jean Shepherd, Leigh Brown and Bob Clark, and on the book *In God We Trust, All Others Pay Cash* by Jean Shepherd; Director, John McCluggage; Sets, Robert Mark Morgan; Costumes, Dorothy Marshall Englis; Lighting, Lap Chi Chu; Sound, Rusty Wandall; Casting, Rich Cole; Child Casting, Carrie Houk; Stage Manager, Glenn Dunn; ASM, Shannon B. Sturgis; Cast: Jeff Talbott (Ralph), Jonathan Savage (Ralphie), Marnye Young (Mother), Jeff Gurner (The Old Man), Caden Self (Randy), Susie Wall (Miss Shields), Taylor Edlin (Flick), Jarrett Harkless (Schwartz), Julia Schweizer (Esther Jane), Sarah Koo (Helen), Drew Redington (Scut Farkas); December 2–27, 2009

The 39 Steps Adapted by Patrick Barlow from the novel by John Buchan and the film of Alfred Hitchcock; Orignal concept by Simon Corble and Nobby Dimon; Director, Martha Banta; Sets, James Wolk; Costumes, Lou Bird; Lighting, Matt Frey; Sound, Mic Pool; Associate Sound, Rusty Wandall; Casting, Rich Cole; Stage Manager, T.R. Martin; ASM, Tony Dearing; Cast: Michael Keyloun (Man #1), Marina Squerciati (Annabella/Pamela/Margaret), Tyrone Mitchell Henderson (Man #2), Paul DeBoy (Richard Hannay); January 6–31, 2010

The Diary of Anne Frank by Frances Goodrich and Albert Hackett, adapted by Wendy Kesselman; Director, Steven Woolf; Sets, John Ezell; Costumes, Elizabeth Covey; Lighting, Phil Monat; Sound, Rusty Wandall; Casting, Rich Cole; Stage Manager, Glenn Dunn; ASM, Shannon B. Sturgis; Cast: Lauren Orkus (Anne Frank), Ann Talman (Edith Frank), John Rensenhouse (Otto Frank), Maura Kidwell (Miep Gies), Andrew Stroud (Peter van Daan), Maggie Wetzel (Margot Frank), Jerry Vogel (Mr. Kraler), Peggy Billo (Mrs. van Daan), Peter Van Wagner (Mr. van Daan), Gary Wayne Barker (Mr. Dussel), Cale Haupert (Nazi Officer), Jared Lotz (Police), Carl Schneider (Police); February 10–March 7, 2010

The Fantasticks Book and lyrics by Tom Jones, music by Harvey Schmidt; Director, Victoria Busset; Choreographer, Martin Céspedes; Musical Director, David Horstman; Sets, Gary M. English; Costumes, Dorothy Marshall Englis; Lighting, Peter E. Sargent; Sound, Rusty Wandall; Casting, Rich Cole; Stage Manager, Glenn Dunn; ASM, Tony Dearing; Cast: Brian Sutherland (El Gallo), Stella Heath (Luisa), Cory Michael Smith (Matt), Scott Schafer (Bellomy), Dan Sharkey (Hucklebee), Joneal Joplin (Henry), John Woodson (Mortimer), Sara M. Bruner (The Mute); March 17–April 11, 2010

Emerson Studio Theatre

Secret Order by Bob Clyman; Director, Risa Brainin; Sets and Lighting, Mark Wilson; Costumes, Lou Bird; Sound, Rusty Wandall; Casting, Rich Cole; Stage Manager, Champe Leary; Cast: Todd Lawson (William Shumway), Richmond Hoxie (Robert Brock), Angela Lin (Alice Curiton), Stan Lachow (Saul Roth); October 28–November 15, 2009

[title of show] Music and lyrics by Jeff Bowen, book by Hunter Bell; Director and Choreographer, Victoria Bussert; Musical Director, David Horstman; Sets, Scott C. Neale; Costumes, Betsy Krausnick; Lighting, John Wylie; Sound, Rusty Wandall; Casting, Rich Cole; Stage Manager, Champe Leary; Cast: Benjamin Howes (Jeff), Ben Nordstrom (Hunter), Amy Justman (Heidi), Stephanie D'Abruzzo (Susan); January 13–31, 2010

Crime and Punishment by Marilyn Campbell and Curt Columbus, based on the novel by Fyodor Dostoyevsky; Director, Stuart Carden; Sets, Gianni Downs; Costumes, Garth Dunbar; Lighting, Brian Sidney Bembridge; Sound, Andre Pluess; Casting, Rich Cole; Stage Manager, Champe Leary; Cast: Triney Sandoval (Inspector Porfiry/others), Jimmy King (Raskolnikov), Amy Landon (Sonia/others); March 10–28, 2010

The Imaginary Theatre Company

A Peter Rabbit Tale by Sarah Brandt, music & lyrics by Neal Richardson, based on the works of Beatrix Potter; Director, Kat Singleton; Sets, Scott Loebl; Costumes, Betsy Krausnick; Stage Manager, Danny Maly; Director of Education,

Marsha Coplin; Cast: Ann Ashby (Flopsy/Nutkin/Mice 2/Simpkin), Lakeetha Blakeney (Mother/Benjamin Bunny/Twinkleberry/Thomasina/Mrs. Tiggy-Winkle), Chauncy Thomas (Mopsy/Mr. McGregor/Owl/Mice 1/Tailor), Amanda Williford (Peter Rabbit); World Premiere; Touring Company; October 19, 2009–April 3, 2010

Bah! Humbug! Book, music and lyrics by Jack Herrick, adapted from A Christmas Carol by Charles Dickens; Director, Bruce Longworth; Musical Director, Neal Richardson; Sets & Costumes, Lou Bird; Stage Manager, Danny Maly; Director of Education, Marsha Coplin; Cast: Chauncy Thomas (Do-Gooder/Scroogette/Bob Cratchit/Marley's Ghost/Ghost of Christmas Past--Young Scrooge/Announcer/Doctor), Ann Ashby (Little Beggar Girl/Scroogette/Little Polly/Ghost of Christmas Present/Ma Cratchit/Nurse), Lakeetha Blakeney (Scrooge), Amanda Williford (Do-Gooder/Scroogette/Mama/Tiny Tim/Ghost of Christmas Future); Touring Company; November 9–December 31, 2009

Amelia Earhart by Kathryn Schultz Miller; Director, Jeffery Matthews; Sets, Scott Loebl; Costumes, Betsy Krausnick; Stage Manager, Danny Maly; Director of Education, Marsha Coplin; Cast: Ann Ashby (Reporter/Itasca Radio Operator), Lakeetha Blakeney (Reporter/Paul Mantz), Chauncy Thomas (George Putnam), Amanda Williford (Amelia Earhart); Touring Company; January 19–April 3, 2010

San Jose Repertory Theatre

San Jose, California

Twenty-ninth Season

Artistic Director, Rick Lombardo; Managing Director, Nick Nichols

The 25th Annual Putman County Spelling Bee Music & lyrics by William Finn, book by Rachel Sheinkin; Director, Timothy Near; Lighting, David Lee Cuthbert; Sound, Jeff Mockus; Costumes, Shigeru Yajl; PSM, Laxmi Kumaran; Cast: Alison Ewing (Rona Lisa Peretti), Marc de la Cruz (Chip Tolentino), Molly Bell (Logainne Schwartzandgrubenierre), Alex Moggridge (Leaf Coneybear), Mark Farrell (William Barfee), Sophie Oda (Marcy Park), Dani Marcus (Olive Ostrovsky), Steve Irish (Douglas Panch), Berwick Haynes (Mitch Mahoney); May 9–June 7, 2009

Forbidden Broadway by Gerard Alessandrini; Director, Gerard Alessandrini; Musical Director, Catherine Stornetta; Costumes, Alvin Colt; PSM, Catherine Bloch; Cast: Gina Kreiezmar, Jeanne Montano, William Selby, Michael West; July 7–12, 2009

The Second City Director, T.J. Shanoff; Musical Director, Chuck Malone; PSM, Kyle Anderson; Cast: Cody Dove, Niki Lindgren, Megan Hovde Wilkins, Dana Quercioli, Mark Raterman, Tim Robinson; July 14–19, 2009

As You Like It by William Shakespeare; Director, Rick Lombardo; Lighting, Daniel Meeker; Sound, Haddon Givens Kime; Costumes, B. Modern; PSM, Laxmi Kumaran; Cast: Anna Bullard (Rosalind), James Carpenter (Old Adam/Jaques), Blake Ellis (Orlando), Steve Irish (Touchstone), Craig Marker (Charles/Silvius/Lord), Cristi Miles (Celia), Sepideh Moafi (Audrey/Amiens/Lord), Andy Murray (Duke Senior/Duke Frederick/Corin), Jeanette Penley (Phebe/Lord), Alexander Prather (LeBeau/William/Lord), Jonathan Shue (Dennis/Martext/Jaques de Boys/Lord), Adam Yazbeck (Oliver/Lord); August 29–September 27, 2009

Groundswell by Ian Bruce; Director, Kirsten Brandt; Lighting, David Lee Cuthbert; Sound, Steve Schoenbeck; Costumes, Maggie Morgan; PSM, Joshua M. Rose; Cast: Dwight Huntsman (Thami), Scott Coopwood (Johan), Peter Van Norden (Smith); October 10–November 8, 2009

A Christmas Story by Philip Grecian, based on the film distributed by Warner Brothers with a screenplay by Jean Shepherd, Leigh Brown and Bob Clark, and on the book In God We Trust, All Others Pay Cash by Jean Shepherd; Director, Chris Smith; Lighting, Lap Chi Chu; Sound, Jeff Mockus; Costumes, B. Modern; PSM, Laxmi Kumaran; Cast: Nancy Carlin (Miss Shields), Emilio Fuentes

(Randy Parker), Dan Hiatt (Adult Ralph), Leah Kolchinsky (Esther Jane Alberry), Garrett Meyer (Ralphie Parker), Max Mifsud (Scut Farkus/Black Bart), Ali Molaei (Schwartz/Desperado), Elara Rivers (Helen Weathers), Nicolas Sancen (Flick/Desperado), Howard Swain (The Old Man); November 21–December 20, 2009

The Weir by Conor McPherson; Director, Rick Lombardo; Lighting, Dawn Chiang; Sound, Rick Lombardo; Costumes, Annie Smart; PSM, Laxmi Kumaran; Cast: Robert Sicular (Jack), Alex Moggridge (Brenden), Mark Anderson Phillips (Jim), Andy Murray (Finbar), Zillah Glory (Valerie); January 23–February 21, 2010

Ain't Misbehavin' Conceived by Murray Horwitz & Richard Maltby Jr., music by Thomas "Fats" Waller; Co-Produced with Arizona Theatre Company and Cleveland Play House; Director, Kent Gash; Lighting, William H. Grant III; Sound, Brian Jerome Peterson; Costumes, Austin K. Sanderson; PSM, Laxmi Kumaran; Cast: Rebecca Covington, Angela Grovey, Christopher L. Morgan, Ken Robinson, Aurelia Williams; Orchestra: Darryl G. Ivey (keyboards), Peter Barshay (upright bass), Thomas A. Fries (percussion), Mark Wright (trumpet), Dean Hubbard (trombone), Matt Morrish (tenor Saxophone/clarinet), Alan Close/Michael Corner (alto saxophone/clarinet); March 13–April 18, 2010

Sonia Flew by Melinda Lopez; Director, Richard Seer; Lighting, Trevor Norton; Sound, Paul Peterson; Costumes, Cathleen Edwards; PSM, Laxmi Kumaran; Cast: Ivonne Coll (Sonia/Marta), Julian Lopez-Morillas (Sam/Orfeo), Kwana Martinez (Nina/Pilar), Michael Santo (Daniel/Tito), Tiffany Ellen Solano (Jen/Young Sonia), Miles Gaston Villanueva (Zak/Jose); May 8–June 6, 2010

Seattle Repertory Theatre

Seattle, Washington

Forty-seventh Season

Producing Artistic Director, Jerry Manning; Managing Director, Benjamin Moore

The 39 Steps Adapted by Patrick Barlow from the book by John Buchan and the film by Alfred Hitchcock; Based on an original concept by Simon Corble & Nobby Dimon Director, Maria Aitken; Set/Costumes, Peter McKintosh; Lighting, Kevin Adams; Sound, Mic Pool; Stage Manager, Harold Goldfaden; Cast: Claire Brownell (Annabella/Pamela/Margaret), Ted Deasy (Richard Hannay), Eric Hissom (Man #1), Scott Parkinson (Man #2); Bagley Wright Theatre; September 25–October 24, 2009

Opus by Michael Hollinger; Director, Braden Abraham; Set, Etta Lilienthal; Lighting, L.B. Morse; Sound, Matt Starritt; Music Consultants, Melia Watras & Michael Jinsoo Lim; Costumes, Frances Kenny; Stage Manager, Anne Kearson; Cast: Charles Leggett (Carl), Allen Fitzpatrick (Elliot), Shawn Belyea (Alan), Chelsey Rives (Grace), Todd Jefferson Moore (Dorian); Leo Kreielsheimer Theatre; October 30–December 6, 2009

Equivocation by Bill Cain; Director, Bill Rauch; Set, Christopher Acebo; Lighting, Christopher Akerlind; Costumes, Deborah M. Dryden; Composer, Andre Pluess; Stage Manager, Randall K. Lum; Cast: Anthony Heald (Shag), Richard Elmore (Richard/Ensemble), Jonathan Haugen (Cecil/Nate/Ensemble), John Tufts (Sharpe/Ensemble), Gregory Linington (Armin/Ensemble), Christine Albright (Judith); Bagley Wright Theatre; November 18–December 13, 2009

Speech & Debate by Stephen Karam; Director, Andrea Allen; Set/Projections, Matthew Smucker; Lighting, Robert Aguilar; Sound, Matt Starritt; Costumes, Christine Meyers; Movement, Diana Cardiff; Vocal Consultant, Judith Shahn; Stage Manager, Joseph Smelser; Cast: Trick Danneker (Howie), Erin Stewart (Diwata), Justin Huertas (Solomon), Amy Thone (Teacher/Reporter); Leo Kreielsheimer Theatre; January 15–February 2, 2010

Glengarry Glen Ross by David Mamet; Director, Wilson Milam; Set, Eugene Lee; Lighting, Geoff Korf; Sound, Matt Starritt; Costumes, Deb Trout; Dialect Coach, Judith Shahn; Stage Manager, Amy Poisson; Cast: John Aylward (Shelly Levene), MJ Sieber (John Williamson), Charles Leggett (Dave Moss), Russell

Hodgkinson (George Aaronow), R. Hamilton Wright (Richard Roma), Ian Bell (James Lingk), Shawn Belyea (Baylen); Bagley Wright Theatre; February 5–28, 2010

Fences by August Wilson; Director, Timothy Bond; Set, William Bloodgood; Lighting, Geoff Korf; Composer; Michael G. Keck; Costumes, Constanza Romero; Stage Manager, Stina Lotti; Cast: James A. Williams (Troy Maxson), William Hall Jr. (Jim Bono), José A. Rufino (Lyons), Craig Alan Edwards (Gabriel), Kim Staunton (Rose), Stephen Tyrone Williams (Cory), Shiann Rush or Esmé DeCoster (Raynell); Bagley Wright Theatre; March 26–April 18, 2010

An Iliad Created by Denis O'Hare and Lisa Peterson; Director, Lisa Peterson; Set, Rachel Hauck; Lighting, Scott Zielinski; Sound/Composer, Paul James Prendergast; Costumes, Marcia Dixcy Jory; Stage Manager, Michael B. Paul; Cast: Hans Altwies (The Poet); Leo Kreielsheimer Theatre; April 9–May 16, 2010

Shakespeare Theatre Company

Washington, D.C.

Twenty-forth Season

Artistic Director, Michael Kahn; Managing Director, Chris Jennings

Phèdre by Jean Racine, adapted by Ted Hughes; Presented by The National Theatre of Great Britain; Director, Nicholas Hynter; Design, Bob Crowley; Lighting, Paule Constable; Music, Adam Cork; Cast: Helen Mirren (Phèdre), Dominic Cooper (Hippolytus), Margaret Tyzack (Oenone), Ruth Negga (Aricia), Chipo Chung (Ismene), Stanley Townsend (Theseus), Wendy Morgan (Panope/Phèdre Understudy); Ensemble: Portia Booroff, Alexander D'Andrea, Elizabeth Nestor, Tristam Wymark; Premiere and only North American engagement; Sidney Harman Hall; September 17–26, 2009

The Alchemist by Ben Johnson; Director, Michael Kahn; Set, James Noone; Costumes, Murell Horton; Lighting, Peter West; Composer, Adam Wernick; Sound, Martin Desjardins; Fight Choreography, Robb Hunter; Voice and Text Coach, Ellen O'Brien; Cast: David Manis (Subtle), Michael Milligan (Face), Kate Skinner (Dol Common), Jeff Biehl (Drugger), Nick Cordileone (Dapper), Robert Creighton (Ananias), Kyle Fabel (Pertinax Surly), Nicole Halmos (Neighbor), Wynn Harmon (Lovewit), Cameron McNary (Neighbor), Alex Morm (Kastril), David Sabin (Sir Epicure Mammon), Timothy Thomas (Tribulation); Ensemble: Felipe Cabezas, Chris Dinolfo, Brit Herring, Rachel Holt, Brian MacDonald; Lansburgh Theatre; October 6–November 22, 2009

As You Like It by William Shakespeare; Director, Maria Aitken; Original Music, Michael John LaChiusa; Sets, Derek McLane; Costumes, Martin Pakledinaz; Lighting, Japhy Weideman; Sound, Martin Desjardins; Projectoins, Jeff Sugg; Choreography, Daniel Pelzig; Music Director, Barbara Irvine; Fight Choreography, Brad Waller; Voice and Dialect Coach, Gary Logan; Cast: John Behlmann (Orlando), Francesca Faridany (Rosalind), Floyd King (Touchstone), Andrew Long (Jaques), Miriam Silverman (Celia), Anjali Bhimani (Phebe), Mark Capri (Duke Frederick/Duke Senior), Barbaby Carpenter (Oliver), Eliot Dash (William/ Charles), Aubrey K. Deeker (Silvius), Beth Glover (Audrey), Lawrence Redmond (1st Frederick Lord), Todd Scofield (Le Beau), Raphael Nash Thompson (Corin), Ted van Griethuysen (Sir Oliver Mar-Text/Adam); Ensemble: Meredith Burns, McKennah Edmunds, Julia Ferrara, Catherine LeFrere, Sarah Mollo-Christensen, Charlie Francis Murphy, Adam Navarro, Todd Quick, David Joseph Regelmann, Jon Reynolds, Patrick Vaill; Sidney Harman Hall; November 17–December 20, 2009

Richard II by William Shakespeare; Director, Michael Kahn; Set, Lee Savage; Costumes, Jennifer Moeller; Lighting, Mark McCullough; Original Music & Sound, Martin Desjardins; Voice and Text Coach, Ellen O'Brien; Fight Choreography, Rick Sordelet; Cast: Michael Hayden (Richard II), Charles Borland (Henry Bolingbroke), Conrad Feininger (Keeper/Welsh Captain/Abbot of Westminster), Philip Goodwin (Gardener/John of Gaunt), Rachael Holmes (Queen Isabel), Naomi Jacobson (Duchess of York), Stephen Paul Johnson (Lord Ross), Floyd King (Bishop of Carlisle/Woodstock, Duke of Gloucester), Dan Kremer (Lord Willoughby), John Lescault (Earl of Salisbury), Louis A. Lotorto (Sir William Bagot), Darren Matthias (Sir Stephen Scroop/Thomas Mowbray), Larry Paulsen (Groom/2nd Gardener/ Cheney), Robynn Rodriguez (Lady/Duchess of Gloucester), Tom Story (Duke of Aumerle), Ted van Griethuysen (Edmund of Langley), Scott Whitehurst (Sir Henry Green); Ensemble: Meredith Burns, Sun King Davis, Joesph Ibanez, Devon Jackson, William LeDent, Jason Marr, Sarah Moll-Christensen, Charlie Francis Murphy, Adam Navarro, Todd Quick, David Joseph Regelmann, Patrick Vaill; Sidney Harman Hall; February 2–April 11, 2010

Henry V by William Shakespeare; Director, Michael Kahn; Set, Lee Savage; Costumes, Elizabeth Hope Clancy; Lighting, Mark McCullough; Original Music, Fabian Obispo; Sound, Martin Desjardins; Choreography, Daniel Pelzig; Voice and Text Coach, Ellen O'Brien; Fight Choreography, Rick Sordelet; Music Director, George Fulginiti-Shakar; Cast: Michael Hayden (King Henry V), Charles Borland (Gower), Conrad Feininger (Earl of Westmoreland), Philip Goodwin (King of France/Archbishop of Canteury), Rachel Holmes (Katherine), Naomi Jacobson (Isabel/Hostess Quickly), Stephen Paul Johnson (Bishop of Ely/Fluellen), Floyd King (Duke of Burgandy/Bardolph), Dan Kremer (Constable of France), John Lescault (Montjoy), Louis A. Lotorto (Rambures/Nym), Darren Matthias (Ensign Pistol), Larry Paulsen (Chorus 3), Robynn Rodriguez (Alice), Tom Story (Lewis the Dauphin), Ted van Griethuysen (Sir Thomas Erpingham/Chorus 2), Derrick Lee Weeden (Duke of Exeter), Scott Whitehurst (Bishop of Norwich), Michael Williams (Soldier); Ensemble: Meredith Burns, Sun King Davis, Joseph Ibanez, Devon Jackson, William LeDent, Jason Marr, Sarah Mollo-Christensen, Charlie Francis Murphy, Adam Navarro, Todd Quick, T. Anthony Quinn, David Joseph Regelmann, Jakob Stalnaker, Patrick Vaill; Sidney Harman Hall; February 4–April 10, 2010

Aurélia's Oratorio Created, directed, and stage design by Victoria Thierrée Chaplin in collaboration with La Compagnie du Hanneton; Presented by Théâtre L'Avant-Scène and La Ferme du Buisson Cognac/René Marion; Lighting, Laura de Bernadis and Phillipe Lacombe; US Tour Producer, ArKtype/Thomas O. Kreigsmann; Costumes, Victoria Thierrée Chaplin, Jacques Perdiguez, Veronique Grand, Monika Schwarzl; Technical Director/Stage Manager, Gerd Walter; Company Manager, Didier Bendel; Technicians, Roberto Riegert, Nicholas Lazzaro; Crew, Tamara Prieto Arroyo, Antonia Paradsio; Cast: Aurélia Thierrée, Jaime Martinez; Lansburgh Theatre; March 4–7, 2010

The Liar by Pierre Corneille, translated and adapted by David Ives; Director, Michael Kahn; Set, Alexander Dodge; Costumes, Murell Horton; Original Music, Adam Wernick; Sound, Martin Desjardins; Lighting, Jeff Croiter; Text Coach, Ellen O'Brien; Stage Manager, M. William Shiner; ASM, Elizabeth Clewley; Cast: Christian Conn (Dorante), Adam Green (Cliton), Erin Partin (Clarice), Miriam Silverman (Lucrece), Tony Roach (Alcippe), Aubrey K. Deeker (Philiste), Colleen Delany (Sabine/Isabelle), David Sabin (Geronte); World Premiere; Lansburgh Theatre; April 6–May 23, 2010

Mrs. Warren's Profession by George Bernard Shaw; Director, Keith Baxter; Set, Simon Higlett; Costumes, Robert Perdziola; Original Music/Music Director, Kim D. Sherman; Lighting, Peter West; Sound, Martin Desjardins; Choreography, Karma Camp; Voice and Text Coach, Ellen O'Brien; Cast: Elizabeth Ashley (Mrs. Kitty Warren), Amanda Quaid (Vivie Warren), Ted van Griethuysen (Mr. Praed), Andrew Boyer (Sir George Crofts), Tony Roach (Frank Gardner), David Sabin (Rev. Samuel Gardner), Caitlin Diana Doyle (Ghost of Kitty Vavasour), Michael Grew (Cockney Bruiser); Sidney Harman Hall; June 8–July 11, 2010

Signature Theatre

Arlington, Virginia

Twentieth Season

Artistic Director, Eric Schaeffer; Managing Director, Maggie Boland

Dirty Blonde by Claudia Shear, conceived by Claudia Shear and James Lapine; Original song "Dirty Blonde" by Bob Stillman; Director, Jeremy Skidmore; Music Director, Gabriel Mangiante; Musical Staging, Matthew Gardiner; Sets, Daniel Conway; Costumes, Helen Huang; Lighting, Dan Covey; Sound, Matt Rowe; PSM, Julie Meyer; Assistant Director, Clementine Thomas; Production Manager, Timothy H. O'Connell; Cast: Emily Skinner (Jo/Mae West), Hugh Nees (Charlie/Others), J. Fred Shiffman (Fred Wallace/Joe Frisco/Others); ARK Theatre; August 11–October 4, 2009

First You Dream: The Music of Kander & Ebb Music by John Kander, lyrics by Fred Ebb; Director, Eric Schaeffer; Choreographer, Karma Camp; Scenic Concept, Eric Schaeffer; Costume Coordination, Kathleen Geldard; Lighting, Mark Lanks; Sound, Matt; PSM, Kerry Epstein; Production Manager, Timothy H. O'Connell; Conductor, Jon Kalbfleisch; Orchestrations, William David Brohn; Music Supervision and Vocal Arrangements, David Loud; Cast: Heidi Blickenstaff, James Clow, Eleasha Gamble, Norm Lewis, Julia Murney, Matthew Scott; MAX Theatre; September 10–27, 2009

Show Boat Music by Jerome Kern, book and lyrics by Oscar Hammerstein II, based on the novel Show Boat by Edna Ferber; Director, Eric Schaeffer; Choreographer, Karma Camp; Music Director, Jon Kalbfleisch; Sets, James Kronzer; Costumes, Kathleen Geldard; Lighting, Mark Lanks; Sound, Matt Rowe; New York Casting, Stuart Howard Casting; PSM, Kerry Epstein; ASM, Julie Meyer; Production Manager, Timothy H. O'Connell; Assistant Music Director, Jonathan Tuzman; Associate Choreographer/Assistant Director, Matthew Gardiner; Orchestrations, Jonathan Tunick; Cast: Delores King Williams (Queenie), VaShawn McIlwain (Joe), Jim Newman (Steve), Chris Sizemore (Pete/Drunk/Ensemble), Kimberly Schraf (Parthy), Harry A. Winter (Cap'n Andy), Sandy Bainum (Ellie), Bobby Smith (Frank/Charlie), Terry Burrell (Julie), Will Gartshore (Gaylord Ravenal), Stephanie Waters (Magnolia), Mardee Bennett (Worker/Ensemble), Yolanda Denise Bryant (Worker/Ethel/Ensemble), Sean Maurice Lynch (Worker/Ensemble), Kevin McAllister (Worker/Ensemble), Aaron Reeder (Worker/Ensemble), Tiffany Wharton (Worker/Ensemble), Susan Derry (Belle/Lottie/Ensemble), Helen Hedman (Belle/Landlady/Mother Superior/Old Lady/Ensemble), Hannah Willman (Belle/Dottie/Older Kim/Ensemble), Sam Ludwig (Beaux/Rubberface/Jeb/Leroy/Ensemble), J. Fred Shiffman (Beaux/Vallon/Backwoods Man/Jim/Ensemble), Matt Conner (Windy/Jake/Ensemble), Rachel Boyd (Young Kim), Anna Nowalk (Young Kim); MAX Theatre; November 10, 2009–January 17, 2010

I Am My Own Wife by Doug Wright; Director, Alan Paul; Sets, Wilson Chin; Costumes, Kathleen Geldard; Lighting, Colin K. Bills; Sound, Veronika Vorel; PSM, William E. Cruttenden III; Production Manager, Timothy H. O'Connell; Dialects, Gary Logan; Cast: Andrew Long (Doug Wright/John Marks/Charlotte Von Mahlsdorf/Tante Luise/SS Officer/SS Commander/Young Lothar Berfelde/Herr Berfelde/Prison Guard/Minna Mahlich/Cultural Minister/Stasi Official/Alfred Kirschner/Young Homosexual Man/American Soldier/Customs Official/Stasi Agent/Nurse/Prison Official/German News Anchor/Politician Markus Kaufmann/Ulrike Liptsch/Josef Rudiger/Ziggy Fluss/First Neo-Nazi/Second Neo-Nazi/Brigitte Klensch/Karl Henning/François Gardiner/Shirley Blacker/Daisuke Yamagishi/Mark Finley/Pradeep Gupta/Clive Twimbley/Dieter Jorgensen); ARK Theatre; January 12–March 7, 2010

Sweeney Todd Book by Hugh Wheeler, music and lyrics by Stephen Sondheim, from an adaptation by Christopher Bond; Director, Eric Schaeffer; Music Director, Jon Kalbfleisch; Sets, James Kronzer; Costumes, Kathleen Geldard; Lighting, Chris Lee; Sound, Matt Rowe; PSM, Kerry Epstein; ASM, Katherine C. Mielke; Production Manager, Timothy H. O'Connell; Orchestrations, Zak Sandler; Musical Staging, Matthew Gardiner; Cast: Gregory Maheu (Anthony), Edward Gero (Sweeney Todd), Channez McQuay (Beggar Woman), Sherri L. Edelen (Mrs.

Lovett), Chris Van Cleave (Judge Turpin), Chris Sizemore (Beadle), Erin Driscoll (Johanna), Sam Ludwig (Tobias), Michael Bunce (Pirelli), Ensemble: Matt Conner, Jean Cantrell, Sean Maurice Lynch, Kevin McAllister, Katie McManus, Chris Mueller, Russell Sunday, Hannah Willman, Weslie Woodley; MAX Theatre; February 9–April 4, 2010

[title of show] Book by Hunter Bell, music and lyrics by Jeff Bowen; Director and Choreographer, Matthew Gardiner; Music Director, Gabriel Mangiante; Sets, Adam Koch; Costumes, Kristopher Castle; Lighting, Mark Lanks; Sound, Matt Rowe; PSM, Julie Meyer; Assistant Music Director, Jonathan Tuzman; Assistant Director, Clementine Thomas; Production Manager, Timothy H. O'Connell; Cast: Sam Ludwig (Jeff), James Gardiner (Hunter), Jenna Sokolowski (Susan), Erin Driscoll (Heidi); ARK Theatre; April 6–June 27, 2010

Sycamore Trees Music and lyrics by Ricky Ian Gordon, book by Ricky Ian Gordon and Nina Mankin; Director, Tina Landau; Music Director, Fred Lassen; Sets, James Schuette; Costumes, Kathleen Geldard; Lighting, Scott Zielinski; Sound, Matt Rowe; PSM, Kerry Epstein; ASM, Karen Currie; Production Manager, Timothy H. O'Connell; Orchestrations, Bruce Coughlin; Cast: Diane Sutherland (Edie), Marc Kudisch (Sydney), Jessica Molaskey (Myrna), Judy Kuhn (Theresa), Farah Alvin (Ginnie), Tony Yazbeck (Andrew), Matthew Risch (The Man/David); World Premiere, MAX Theatre; May 18–June 13, 2010

South Coast Repertory

Costa Mesa, California

Forty-sixth Season

Producing Artistic Director, David Emmes; Artistic Director, Martin Benson; Managing Director, Paula Tomei; Associate Artistic Director, John Glore

Putting It Together Music and lyrics by Stephen Sondheim, devised by Stephen Sondheim and Julia McKenzie; Director, Nick DeGruccio; Musical Director, Dennis Castellano; Sets, Thomas Buderwitz; Lighting, Steven Young; Sound, Drew Dalzell; Costumes, Soojin Lee; Dramaturg, Linda Sullivan Baity; Stage Manager, Jamie A. Tucker; Cast: Dan Callaway, Harry Groener, Matt McGrath, Mary Gordon Murray, Niki Scalera; Segerstrom Stage; September 11–October 11, 2009

The Happy Ones by Julie Marie Myatt; Director, Martin Benson; Associate Director, Oanh Nguyen; Sets, Ralph Funicello; Lighting, Tom Ruzika; Composition and Sound, James Prendergast; Costumes, Angela Balogh Calin; Dramaturg, John Glore; Stage Manager, Jennifer Ellen Butler; Cast: Raphael Sbarge (Walter Wells), Geoffrey Lower (Gary Stuart), Greg Watanabe (Bao Ngo), Nike Doukas (Mary-Ellen Hughes); World Premiere; Julianne Argyros Stage; September 27–October 18, 2009

Saturn Returns by Noah Haidle; Director, David Emmes; Assistant Director, Nelson T. Eusebio; Sets, Ralph Funicello; Lighting, Lonnie Rafael Alcarez; Sound, Kimberly Egan; Costumes, Nephelie Andonyadis; Dramaturg, Kelly L. Miller; Stage Manager, Chrissy Church; Cast: Conor O'Farrell (Gustin at 58), Graham Michael Hamilton (Gustin at 28), Kristen Bush (Suzanne/Zephyr/Loretta), Nick Ullett (Gustin at 88); West Coast Premiere; Segerstrom Stage; October 23–November 22, 2009

Junie B. Jones and a Little Monkey Business Book, music and lyrics by Joan Cushing, adapted from the book by Barbara Park, illustrated by Denise Brunkus; Director, Casey Stangl; Original Orchestrations and Musical Direction, Deborah Wicks La Puma; Sets, Keith Mitchell; Lighting, Jaymi Lee Smith; Sound, Kimberly Egan; Costumes, Sara Ryung Clement; Stage Manager, Jennifer Ellen Butler; Cast: Dawn-Lyen Gardner (That Grace), Jamey Hood (Junie B. Jones), Brian Hostenske (Principal/Junie's Father/Crybaby William), Nicholas Mongiardo-Cooper (Grampa Miller/Meanie Jim), Jennifer Parsons (Mrs./Grandma Miller), Erika Whalen (Lucille/Junie's Mother); Julianne Argyros Stage; November 6–22, 2009

Anthony Heald and John Tufts in Equivocation at Seattle Repertory Theatre (photo by Chris Bennion)

Scott Parkinson and Ted Deasy in Seattle Repertory Theatre's The 39 Steps (photo by Chris Bennion)

Edward Gero and Sherri L. Edelen in the Signature Theatre production of Sweeney Todd (photo by Scott Suchman)

Conor O'Farrell, Graham Michael Hamilton, Kristen Bush, and Nick Ullett in South Coast Repertory's Saturn Returns (photo by Henry DiRocco)

Matt McGrath, Mary Gordon Murray, Niki Scalera, Harry Groener, and Dan Callaway in Putting It Together at South Coast Repertory (photo by Henry DiRocco)

David Schmittou in the Stages St. Louis production of The Drowsy Chaperone (photo by Whitney Curtis)

Alan Wilder, Kate Arrington, and Larry Yando in Fake at Steppenwolf Theatre Company (photo by Michael Brosilow)

Glenn Davis, Phillip James Brannon, and K. Todd Freeman in The Brothers Size at Steppenwolf Theatre Company (photo by Michael Brosilow)

Jamie Farmer and Jeff Boyet in Tennessee Repertory Theatre's A Christmas Story (photo by Harry Butler)

Bakari King and Patrick Waller in Big River at the Tennessee Repertory Theatre (photo by Harry Butler)

Rod Gilfry, CJ Palma, Christina Carrera, and Carmen Cusack in the national touring company of South Pacific, presented at Theatre Under the Stars (photo by Peter Coombs)

Fred Sullivan Jr., Brian McEleney, Anne Scurria, and Mauro Hantman in Trinity Repertory Company's Twelfth Night (photo by Mark Turek)

A Christmas Carol by Charles Dickens, adapted by Jerry Patch; 30th Annual Production; Director, John-David Keller; Vocal Director, Dennis Castellano; Assistant Director, Hisa Takakuwa; Sets, Thomas Buderwitz; Lighting, Donna and Tom Ruzika; Music Arrangement and Composer, Dennis McCarthy; Sound, Drew Dalzell; Costumes, Dwight Richard Odle; Choreographer, Sylvia C. Turner; Stage Manager, Jamie A. Tucker; Cast: William Francis McGuire (Fred/Gentleman), Daniel Blinkoff (Bob Cratchit), Jennifer Chu (Lena/Belle/Scavenger), Richard Doyle (Solicitor/Spirit of Christmas Past/Gentleman), Karen Hensel (Mrs. Fezziwig/Solicitor), John-David Keller (Mr. Fezziwig/Gentleman), Art Koustik (Joe/Ensemble), Timothy Landfield (Spirit of Christmas Present), Hal Landon Jr. (Ebenezer Scrooge), Ann Marie Lee (Toy Lady/Sally/Scavenger), Jennifer Parsons (Mrs. Cratchit), Jaycob Hunter (Undertaker/Young Ebenezer), Tom Shelton (Marley/Spirit of Christmas Yet-to-Come); Ensemble and Children: Christopher Hyde, Elizabeth Nolan, Oscar Gubelman, Whitney Brooks, Juli Biagi, Nicole Dumbeck, Hamilton Sparks, Evan J. P. Green, Alisha Ambe, Benjamin Dilsisian, Alex Theologides Rodriguez, Billur Foley, Andy Vargas, Angeliki Katya Harris, Valentina Gehley, Charlene J. Geisler, Congher Shomberg, Julia Jech, Karl Schreyer; Segerstrom Stage; November 28–December 26, 2009

Ordinary Days by Adam Gwon; Director, Ethan McSweeney; Musical Director, Dennis Castellano; Sets, Fred Kinney; Lighting, Lonnie Rafael Alcarez; Sound, Kimberly Egan; Costumes, Angela Balogh Calin; Projections, Jason H. Thompson; Stage Manager, Kathryn Davies; Cast: Nick Gabriel (Warren), Deborah S. Craig (Deb), David Burnham (Jason), Nancy Anderson (Claire); West Coast Premiere; Julianne Argyros Stage; January 3–24, 2010

Fences by August Wilson; Director, Seret Scott; Sets, Shaun Motley; Lighting, Peter Maradudin; Sound, Jim Ragland; Costumes, Dana Rebecca Woods; Fight Consultant, Ken Merckx; Dramaturg, Kelly L. Miller; Stage Manager, Jamie A. Tucker; Cast: Gregg Daniel (Bono), Charlie Robinson (Troy), Juanita Jennings (Rose), Brandon J. Dirden (Lyons), Baron Kelly (Gabe), Larry Bates (Cory), Skye Whitebear or Sofya Ogunseitan (Raynell); Segerstrom Stage; January 22–February 21, 2010

A Wrinkle in Time Adapted by John Glore, from the book by Madeleine L'Engle; Director, Shelley Butler; Sets, Fred Kinney; Lighting and Video, Jason H. Thompson; Original Music and Sound, Toby Algya; Costumes, Paloma H. Young; Dramaturg, Kimberly Colburn; Stage Manager, Amy Bristol Brownewell; Cast: Tessa Auberjonois (Mother/Mrs. Who/Camazotz Woman/Aunt Beast), Daniel Blinkoff (Father/Mrs. Which/Camazotz Man), Stewart Calhoun (Charles Wallace), James Michael Lambert (Calvin), William Francis McGuire (Mrs. Whatsit/Man with Red Eyes), Rebecca Mozo (Meg); World Premiere; Julianne Argyros Stage; February 5–28, 2010

In a Garden by Howard Korder; Director, David Warren; Sets, Christopher Barreca; Lighting, Lap Chi Chu; Original Music and Sound, Vincent Olivieri; Costumes, David Kay Mickelson; Dramaturg, John Glore; Stage Manager, Jennifer Ellen Butler; Cast: Mark Harelik (Othman), Matt Letscher (Hackett), Jarion Monroe (Najid), Phillip Vaden (Prudhomme); World Premiere; Julianne Argyros Stage; March 7–28, 2010

The Language Archive by Julia Cho; Director, Mark Brokaw; Sets, Neil Patel; Lighting, Mark McCullough; Original Music and Sound, Steven Cahill; Costumes, Rachel Myers; Dialect Coach, Philip D. Thompson; Dramaturg, John Glore; Stage Manager, Chrissy Church; Cast: Leo Marks (George), Betsy Brandt (Mary), Laura Heisler (Emma), Linda Gehringer (Alta), Tony Amendola (Resten); World Premiere; Segerstrom Stage; March 26–April 25, 2010

Doctor Cerberus by Roberto Aguirre-Sacasa; Director, Bart DeLorenzo; Sets, Keith Mitchell; Lighting, Rand Ryan; Original Music and Sound, Steven Cahill; Costumes, Shigeru Yaji; Projections and Video, Christopher Ash; Dramaturg, Kelly L. Miller; Stage Manager, Kathryn Davies; Cast: Jamison Jones (Doctor Cerberus/others), Brett Ryback (Franklin Robertson), Candy Buckley (Lydia Robertson), Steven Culp (Lawrence Robertson), Jarrett Sleeper (Rodney Robertson); World Premiere; Julianne Argyros Stage; April 11–May 2, 2010

2010 Pacific Playwrights Festival Included: *Completeness* by Itamar Moses; Director, Pam MacKinnon; Staged Reading; Segerstrom Stage; April 23, 2010; *Happy Face* by David West Read; Director, Art Manke; Staged Reading; Julianne Argyros Stage; April 23, 2010; *Between Us Chickens* by Sofia Alvarez; Director, Casey Stangl; Staged Reading; Nicholas Studio; April 23–24, 2010; *Right to the Top* by Amy Freed; Director, Doug Hughes; Staged Reading; Segerstrom Stage; April 24, 2010; *Kin* by Bathsheba Doran; Director, Sam Gold; Staged Reading; Julianne Argyros Stage; April 25, 2010

Crimes of the Heart by Beth Henley; Director, Warner Shook; Sets, Tom Buderwitz; Lighting, Peter Maradudin; Sound, Jim Ragland; Costumes, Angela Balogh Calin; Dramaturg, Kimberly Colburn; Stage Manager, Jamie A. Tucker; Cast: Tessa Auberjonois (Chick Boyle), Nathan Baesel (Doc Porter), Jennifer Lyon (Meg Magrath), Kasey Mahaffy (Barnette Lloyd), Kate Rylie (Babe Botrelle), Blair Sams (Lenny Magrath); Segerstrom Stage; May 7–June 6, 2010

Ben and the Magic Paintbrush by Bathsheba Doran; Director, Stefan Novinski; Sets, Keith Mitchell; Lighting, Tom Ruzika; Original Music, Dennis McCarthy; Sound, Kimberly Egan; Costumes, Sara Ryung Clement; Dramaturg, Kelly L. Miller; Stage Manager, Jennifer Ellen Butler; Cast: Gloria Garayua (Megan), Stewart Calhoun (Ben), Shannon Holt (Cynthia Crawly), Richard Doyle (Harold Crawley/Taxman), Veralyn Jones (The Queen of Bohemia/Old Woman, Policeman) and Bill Brochtrup (Pierre Robelinsky/Grumpy Man/Cleaning Woman/Prison Guard); World Premiere; Julianne Argyros Stage; May 21–June 6, 2010

Stages St. Louis

St Louis, Missouri

Twenty-third Season

Artistic Director, Michael Hamilton; Executive Producer, Jack Lane; Managing Director, Ron Gibbs

Little Shop of Horrors by Howard Ashman & Alan Menken; Director, Michael Hamilton; Sets, Richard Ellis; Costumes, John Inchiostro; Lighting, Matthew McCarthy; Orchestration, Stuart Elmore; Musical Direction, Lisa Campbell Albert; Choreography, Stephen Bourneuf; Stage Manager, Stacy A. Blackburn; Cast: Ben Nordstrom (Seymour), Maria Couch (Audrey), Darin De Paul (Mushnik), Todd DuBail (Orin/Bernstein/Snip/Luce), Valisia Lekae (Chiffon), Lisa M. Ramey (Ronnette), Rashidra Scott (Crystal), Geno Segars (Audrey II Voice), Marc A. Petrosino (Audrey II Pupeteer), Shaun Sheley, Monte J. Howell (Puppeteers); Standby: Katy Tibbets; May 29–June 28, 2009

The Drowsy Chaperone Book by Bob Martin and Don McKellar, music and lyrics by Lisa Lambert and Greg Morrison; Director, Michael Hamilton; Sets, James Wolk; Costumes, Lou Bird; Lighting, Matthew McCarthy; Orchestration, Stuart Elmore; Musical Direction, Lisa Campbell Albert; Choreography, Dana Lewis; Stage Manager, Stacy A. Blackburn; Cast: David Schmittou (Man in Chair), David Elder (Robert Martin), Tari Kelly (Janet Van De Graaff), Christianne Tisdale (Drowsy Chaperone), Edward Juvier (Aldolpho), Ed Romanoff (Feldzieg), Kari Ely (Mrs. Tottendale), John Alban Coughlan (Underling), Brian Ogilvie (George), Melinda Cowan (Kitty), Ben Nordstrom (Gangster 1), Michael Baxter (Gangster 2), Zoe VonderHaar (Trix), Patrick Martin (Super/Ensemble), Laura Ernst (Ensemble), Andrew Kruep (Ensemble), Katy Tibbets (Ensemble); Swings: Nathan Garland, Taylor Pietz; July 17–August 16, 2009

Guys & Dolls Music and lyrics by Frank Loesser, book by Jo Swerling and Abe Burrows; Director, Michael Hamilton; Sets, Mark Halpin; Costumes, Lou Bird; Lighting, Matthew McCarthy; Orchestration, Stuart Elmore; Musical Direction, Lisa Campbell Albert; Choreography, Dana Lewis; Stage Manager, Stacy A. Blackburn; Cast: Edward Watts (Sky Masterson), David Foley Jr. (Nathan Detroit), Kate Fisher (Sarah Brown), Julie Cardia (Miss Adelaide), Edward Juvier (Nicely Nicely Johnson), John Flack (Arvide Abernathy), Jason Cannon (Lieutenant Brannagan), Paul Pagano (Harry the Horse), Steve Isom (Benny Southstreet), Herschel Sparber

(Big Jule), Zoe VonderHaar (General Cartwright), Ben Nordstrom (Rusty Charlie), Becca Kloha (Agatha/Doll), Mathias Anderson (Brandy Bottle Bates/Calvin), Ellen Isom (Martha/Doll), Andrew Lebon (Angie the Ox/Hot Box MC), Michael Baxter (Scranton Slim/Drunk), Michael Ramey (Society Max/Havana Specialty), Lois Enders (Mimi/Doll), Nathan Garland (Hot Horse Herbie), Andrew Kruep (Joey Perhaps), Tara Sweeney (Doll/Havana Specialty), Stephanie Caplin (Doll), Sara Nischwitz (Doll); September 4–October 4, 2009

Steppenwolf Theatre Company

Chicago, Illinois

Artistic Director, Martha Lavey; Artistic Director, David Hawkanson

End of Thirty-third Season*

The Walls by Lisa Dillman; Presented by Rivendell Theatre Ensemble; Director, Megan Carney; Costumes, Kat Doebler; Lighting, Diane Fairchild; Sound, Chris Kriz; Stage Manager, Stephanie Hurovitz; ASM, Keri Godsey-Mack; Dramaturg, Martha Wade Steketee; Cast: Lacy Campbell, Meighan Gerachis, Mierka Girten, Danica Ivancevic, Tara Mallen, Joe Mazza, Ashley Neal, Mark Ulrich, John Zinn; Steppenwolf Visiting Company Initiative; Garage Theatre; May 13–June 20, 2009

500 Clown and The Elephant Deal Text and original music by John Fournier; Presented by 500 Clown; Director, Lisa Buxbaum Danzig; Cast: Molly Brennan, Adrian Danzig, Gerald Dowd, John Fournier, Matt Hawkins, Jessica Hudson, Paul Kalina, Matt Thompson; Steppenwolf Visiting Company Initiative; Upstairs Theatre; June 20–July 11, 2009

Honest Written and directed by Eric Simonson; Set, Kevin Depinet; Costumes, Myron Elliott; Lighting, J.R. Lederle; Sound, Joseph Fosco; Stage Manager, Jonathan Templeton; Cast: Katherine Cunningham, Erik Hellman, Martin McClendon, Lucas Neff, Kelly O'Sullivan; Garage Theatre; July 22–August 9, 2009

5th Annual First Look Repertory of New Work Program Director, Edward Sobel; Program Director, Kimberly Senior; Program Coordinator, Whitney Dibo; Set, Kevin Depinet; Costumes, Myron Elliott; Lighting, J.R. Lederle; Sound, Joseph Fosco; Stage Managers, Lauren V. Hickman, Jonathan Nook, Jonathan Templeton; *Honest* written & directed by Eric Simonson; Cast: Katherine Cunningham, Erik Hellman, Martin McClendon, Lucas Neff, Kelly O'Sullivan; *Sex with Strangers* by Laura Eason; Director, Jessica Thebus; Cast: Amy J. Carle, Stephen Louis Grush; *Ski Dubai* by Laura Jacqmin; Director, Lisa Portes; Cast: James Vincent Meredith, Cliff Chamberlain, Hilary Clemens, Jennifer Coombs, Sadieh Rifai, Rani Waterman; Garage Theatre; July 22–August 9, 2009

Sex with Strangers by Laura Eason; Director, Jessica Thebus; Set, Kevin Depinet; Costumes, Myron Elliott; Lighting, J.R. Lederle; Sound, Joseph Fosco; Stage Manager, Jonathan Nook; Cast: Amy J. Carle, Stephen Louis Grush; Garage Theatre; July 23–August 9, 2009

Ski Dubai by Laura Jacqmin; Set, Kevin Depinet; Costumes, Myron Elliott; Lighting, J.R. Lederle; Sound, Joseph Fosco; Stage Mangager, Lauren V. Hickman; Director, Lisa Portes; Cast: James Vincent Meredith, Cliff Chamberlain, Hillary Clemens, Jennifer Coombs, Sadieh Rifai, Rani Watherman; Garage Theatre; July 24–August 9, 2009

Thirty-forth Season

Fake Written and directed by Eric Simonson; Set, Todd Rosenthal; Costumes, Karin Kopischke; Lighting, Joe Appelt; Original Music & Sound, Barry G. Funderburg; Stage Manager, Michelle Medvin; ASM, Kathleen Petroziello; Cast: Kate Arrington (Rebecca Eastman/Katarina Meras), Francis Guinan (Sir Arthur Conan Doyle/Jonathan Cole), Alan Wilder (Arthur Woodward/Paul Moody), Coburn Goss (Pierre Teilhard de Chardin/Doug Arnt/Voice of Sherlock Holmes), Larry Yando (Charles Dawson/Henry Billings/Voices of Dr. Watson and BBC Radio Announcer); Downstairs Theatre; September 10–November 8, 2009

The House on Mango Street by Tanya Saracho, based on the novel bySandra Cisneros; Director, Hallie Gordon; Set, Collette Pollard; Costumes, Christine

Pascual; Lighting, J.R. Lederle; Original Music, Tamara Roberts; Sound, Kevin O'Donnell; Stage Manager, Christine D. Freeburg; ASM, Deb Styer; Choreographer, Joel Valentin-Martinez; Cast: Belinda Cervantes, Gina Cornejo, Sandra Delgado, Liza Fernandez, Ricardo Gutierrez, Christina Nieves, Tony Sancho, Mari Stratton; Steppenwolf for Young Adults; Upstairs Theatre; October 13–November 8, 2009

American Buffalo by David Mamet; Director, Amy Morton; Set, Kevin Depinet; Costumes, Nan Cibula-Jenkins; Lighting, Pat Collins; Original Music & Sound, Rob Milburn and Michael Bodeen; Fight Choreography, Rick Sordelet; Dialects, Cecilie O'Reilly; Stage Manager, Malcolm Ewen; ASM, Christine D. Freeburg; Cast: Francis Guinan (Don), Patrick Andrews (Bob), Tracy Letts (Teach); Understudies: Kurt Ehrmann (Don, Teach), Josh Schecter (Bob); Downstairs Theatre; December 13, 2009–February 14, 2010

The Brother/Sister Plays *In the Red and Brown Water* and *The Brothers Size/Marcus; Or the Secret of Sweet* by Tarell Alvin McCraney; Director, Tina Landau; Set & Costumes, James Schuette; Lighting, Scott Zielinski; Sound, Rob Milburn & Michael Bodeen; Musical Supervisor, Zane Mark; Fight Choreography David Blixt; Stage Manager, Deb Styer; ASM, Rose Marie Packer; Cast: *In the Red and Brown Water*: Alana Arenas (Oya), Phillip James Brannon (Egungun), Rodrick Covington (Shango), Glenn Davis (Elegba), K. Todd Freeman (Ogun Size), Ora Jones (Mama Moja, Nia, The Woman Who Reminds You), Jeff Parker (The Man From State, O Li Roon), Jacqueline Williams (Aunt Elegua); *The Brothers Size*: Philip James Brannon (Oshoosi Size), Glenn Davis (Elegba to 3/21), K. Todd Freeman (Ogun Size); *Marcus; Or the Secret of Sweet*: Alana Arenas (Shaunta Iyun), Phillip James Brannon (Oshoosie Size, Terrell), Rodrick Covington (Shua), Glenn Davis (Marcus to 3/21), K. Todd Freeman (Ogun Size), Ora Jones (Oba), Jeff Parker (Ensemble), Tamberla Perry (Osha), Jacqueline Williams (Shun, Aunt Elegua); Understudies: Kiplan Dooley, Betty Gabriel, Aaron Holland, Lily Mojekwu, Josh Odor, Michael Pogue; Upstairs Theatre; Three plays performed in repertory; January 21–May 23, 2010

Garage Rep Included: *Adore* Written and directed by Stephen Louis Grush; Presented by XIII Pocket; Set, Grant Sabin, Lighting, Tim Shane; Stage Manager, Jacob Lorenz; Cast: Eric Leonard, Paige Smith; *punkplay* Gregory S. Moss; Presented by Pavement Group; Director, David Perez; Set, Grant Sabin; Costumes, David Hyman; Lighting, Tim Schoen; Sound, Jeff Kelley; Stage Manager, Mary Krupka; Cast: Matt Farabee, Alexander Lane, Tanya McBride, Keith Neagle; *The Twins Would Like to Say* Written and directed by Seth Bockley and Devon de Mayo; Presented by Dog & Pony Theatre Company; Set, Grant Sabin; Costumes, Cathy Tantillo, Mieka Van der Ploeg; Lighting, Aaron Weissman; Sound, Stephen Ptacek; Stage Manager, John Rooney; ASM, Jessica Lind; Choreography, Dan Stermer; Cast: Brandon Boler, Paige Collins; Rob Fenton, Kasey Foster, Kathryn Hribar, Teeny Lamothe, Mildred Marie Langford, Ashleigh LaThrop, Nick Leininger; Steppenwolf Visiting Company Initiative; February 18–April 25, 2010

A Separate Peace by John Knowles, adapted by Nancy Gilsenan; Director, Jonathan Berry; Set, Chelsea Warren; Costumes, Alison Siple; Lighting, Heather Gilbert; Sound, Rick Sims; Assistant Director, Morgan Maher; Cast: Alan Wilder, Will Allan, Chance Bone, Jake Cohen, Curtis M. Jackson, Damir Konjicija, Govind Kumar; Steppenwolf for Young Adults; Upstairs Theatre; February 23–March 14, 2010

Louder Than a Bomb 10–The Real Chicago Renaissance Semi-Finals Presented by Young Chicago Authors; Upstairs and Downstairs Theatres; March 1, 2010

Joe Frank in "Just and Ordinary Man" Downstairs Theatre; March 13, 2010

Endgame by Samuel Beckett; Director, Frank Galati; Set & Costumes, James Schuette; Lighting, James F. Ingalls; Sound, Andre Pluess; Stage Manager, Malcolm Ewen; ASM, Michelle Medvin; Casting, Erica Daniels; Cast: Ian Barford (Clov), William Petersen (Hamm), Francis Guinan (Nagg), Martha Lavey (Nell); Understudies: Joan Merlo (Nell), Kipp Moorman (Nagg, Clov), Gary Simmers (Hamm); Downstairs Theatre; April 1–June 6, 2010

An Evening with David Sedaris Upstairs Theatre; June 8–June 13, 2010

A Parallelogram by Bruce Norris; Director, Anna D. Shapiro; Set, Todd Rosenthal; Costumes, Mara Blumenfeld; Lighting, James F. Ingalls; Sound, Michael Bodeen, Rob Milburn; Stage Manager, Laura D. Glenn; ASM, Christine D. Freeburg; Cast: Kate Arrington (Bee), Tom Irwin (Jay), Tim Bickel (JJ), Marylouise Burke (Bee 2, 3, 4); Downstairs Theatre; July 1–August 29, 2010

This Train by Tony Fitzpatrick; Presented by 16th Street Theater; Director, Ann Filmer; Cast: Kat Eggleston, Tony Fitzpatrick, Buzz Kilman, Stan Klein, John Rice; Garage Theatre; July 15–August 1, 2010

*Editors Note: The first six listings are final shows from Steppenwolf's thirty-third season that were omitted in Volume 65, which also was incorrectly listed as the thirty-eigth season. We regret the errors.

Tennessee Repertory Theatre

Nashville, Tennessee

Twenty-fifth Season

Producing Artistic Director, René D. Copeland

Steel Magnolias by Robert Harling; Director, René D. Copeland; Set, Gary C. Hoff; Costumes, Trish Clark; Technical Director, Andrew Bevaqua; Lighting, Michael Barnett; Stage Manager, David Wilkerson; Cast: Brooke Bryant (Annelle), Ruth Cordell (Caliree), Mary Jane Harvill (M'Lynn), Denice Hicks (Ouiser), Marin Miller (Shelby), and Martha Wilkinson (Truvy), Andrew Johnson Theater; October 3–24, 2009

A Christmas Story by Phillip Grecian, based upon the Warner Brothers film by Jean Shepherd, Leigh Brown and Bob Clark, and the novel *In God We Trust: All Others Pay Cash* by Jean Shepherd; Director, René D. Copeland; Assistant Director, Lauren Shouse; Set, Gary C. Hoff; Costumes, Trish Clark; Technical Director, Andrew Bevaqua; Lighting, Michael Barnett; Stage Manager, Erin Whited; Cast: Jeff Boyet (The Old Man/Ensemble), Shane Bridges (Scut Farkas/Ensemble), Jamie Farmer (Mother/Ensemble), Andrew Kanies (Randy/Ensemble), Eric D. Pasto-Crosby (Scwartz/Ensemble), Samuel Whited (Ralphie), David Wilkerson (Flick/Ensemble); Andrew Johnson Theater; November 21–December 19, 2009

Proof by David Auburn; Director, René D. Copeland; Set, Gary C. Hoff; Costumes, Trish Clark; Technical Director, Andrew Bevaqua; Lighting, Karen Palin; Stage Manager, David Wilkerson; Cast: Chip Arnold (Robert), Anna Felix (Catherine), Eric D. Pasto-Crosby (Hal), Erin Whited (Claire); Andrew Johnson Theater; February 6–20, 2010

Big River Music and lyrics by Roger Miller, book by William Hauptman; Director, René D. Copeland; Musical Director, Paul Carrol Binkley; Set, Gary C. Hoff; Costumes, Trish Clark; Technical Director, Andrew Bevaqua; Choreographer, Richard Browder; Stage Manager, David Wilkerson; Lighting, Michael Barnett; Cast: Jeff Boyet (Young Fool/Ensemble), Rona Carter (Widow Douglas), Henry Haggard (King/Ensemble), Bakari King (Jim), Aleta Myles (Alice/Ensemble), Carrie Tillis (Mary Jane Wilkes/Ensemble), Larry Tobias (Pap/Ensemble), Peter Vann (Tom Sawyer/Ensemble), Patrick Waller (Huckleberry Finn), Samuel Whited (Mark Twain/Ensemble), Bobby Wyckoff (Duke/Ensemble), Andrew Johnson Theater; March 20–April 17, 2010

Theatre Under the Stars

Houston, Texas

Forty-second Season

Founder/Producing Artistic Director, Frank M. Young; Associate Artistic Director, Roy Hamlin; Company Manager, Nicole A. Young

Grease Book, music and lyrics by Jim Jacobs and Warren Casey; Director/Choreographer, Kathleen Marshall; Cast: Eric Schneider (Danny Zuko), Emily Padgett (Sandy Dumbrowski), David Ruffin (Keneckie), Nick Verina (Sonny LaTierri), Will Blum (Roger), Brian Crum (Doody), Allie Schulz (Betty Rizzo), Kelly Felthous (Marty), Bridie Carroll (Jan), Kate Morgan Chadwick (Frenchie), Erin Henry (Patty Simcox), Scot Patrick Allan (Eugene Florczyk), Roxie Lucas (Miss Lynch), Dominic Fortuna (Vince Fontaine), Dayla Perkins (Cha-Cha DiGregorio), Taylor Hicks (Teen Angel); Ensemble: Joseph Corella, Preston Ellis, Ruby Lewis, Dayla Perkins, Mark Raumaker, Matthew William Schmidt, Christina Sivrich, Elizabeth Stacey; Swings: Preston Ellis, Lisa Maietta, Mike Russo, Elizabeth Stacey, Amber Stone; September 8–20, 2009

Meet Me in St Louis Music and lyrics by Hugh Martin and Ralph Blane, book by Hugh Wheeler; Director, Mark S. Hoebee; Choreographer, Denis Jones; Music Director, Jeff Rizzo; Cast: Jacqueline Touchet (Tootie Smith), Ed Romanoff (Postman/Motorman/Clinton Badger), Abigail Moorhead (Agnes Smith), Zach Frank (Lon Smith), Lynee Wintersteller (Anna Smith), Patti Mariano (Katie), J.B. Adams (Grandfather Prophater), Julie Osborne (Rose Smith), Anneliese Van Der Pol (Esther Smith), Brian Hissong (John Truitt), Joseph Kolinski (Alonso Smith), Dana Domenick (Eve), Colin Israel (Warren Sheffield), Dani Spieler (Lucille Ballard), Dennis O'Bannion (Peewee Drummond), Elliott Bradley (Sidney Purvis); Ensemble: Ashley Arcement, Tommy Berklund, Elliott Bradley, Monica Bradley, Monica Brown, Barry Busby, Alicia Charles, Sydney Crofton, Dana Domenick, Colin Israel, Kristina Kee, Tony Neidenbach, Dennis O'Bannion, Ed Romanoff, Dani Spieler, Kristin Warren, Dru Peacock Wiser; September 29–October 11, 2009

The Sound of Music Music by Richard Rodgers, lyrics by Oscar Hammerstein II, book by Howard Lindsay and Russell Crouse; Director, Roy Hamlin; Choreographer, Shay Rodgers; Music Director, Jeff Rizzo; Cast: Susan Shofner (The Mother Abbess), Kayleen Clements (Sister Margaretta), Marcie Henderson (Sister Berthe), Susan O. Koozin (Sister Rafaela), Ivy Castle-Rush (Sister Sophia), Kim Huber (Maria Rainer), George Dvorsky (Captin Georg von Trapp), Steve Bullitt (Franz), Theresa Nelson (Frau Schmidt), Jessica Ferguson (Liesl), Ryne Nardecchia (Frederich), Caroline Taylor (Louisa), Ian Tonroy (Kurt), Gabby Gillespie (Brigitta), Aiden Snasdell (Marta), Mandy Miller (Gretl), Ryan Kennedy (Rolf Gruber), Doris Davis (Elsa Schraeder), Ilich Guardiola (Max Detweiler), Al Bundonis (Herr Zeller), Kevin Cooney (Admiral von Schreiber), Sam Brown, Jim Shaffer, Philip Lehl (Saengergund Trio); Ensemble: Vanessa Ballam, Mallory Bechtel, Monica Brown, Sam Brown, Ivy Castle, Mary Belle Chaney, Tiffany Chen, Kayleen Clements, Sydney Crofton, Lisa E. Harris, Marcie Henderson, Brooke Humphrey, Carlon Introligator, John Johnston, Drew Jones, Austin Karkowsky, Richard M. Keck, Kristina Kee, Susan O. Koozin, Haley Landers, Julia Laskowski, Philip Lehl, Sam Linda, Doreen Litvak, Jonathan Luna, Libby Malone, Nicole Marosis, Sophia V. Mendez, Crystal O'Brien, Adam Pena, Sydney Roberts, Jim Shaffer, Corby Sullivan, Jay Tribble, Charity Van Tassel, Jennie Welch; December 8–20, 2009

Miss Saigon Music by Claude-Michael Schönberg, lyrics by Richard Matlby Jr. and Alain Boublil; Director, Bruce Lumpkin; Choreographer, Michelle Gaudette; Music Director, Thom Culcasi; Cast: Joseph Anthony Foronda (The Engineer), Melinda Chua (Kim), Angelica-Lee Aspiras (Gigi), Nina Crupiti (Mimi), Nam Holtz (Yvette), Lindsay Gee (Yvonne), Eric Kunze (Chris), Philip Michael Baskerville (John), Steven Eng (Thuy), Jessica Rush (Ellen), Audrey & Emma Kim (Tam), Billy Bustamante (Owner of the Moulin Rouge), Michael Philip O'Brien (Schultz), Mel Sagrado Maghuyop (Assistant Commissar); Eunice Bae, Tiffany Chen, Janelle Dote, Jan Javier, Jessica Wu (Bar Girls); Joey Abramowicz, Ceasar F. Barajasm Caleb Damschroder, Joshua Denning, Rob Flebbe, Nkrumah Gatling, Trey Gillen, Richard M. Keck, Mike A. Motroni, Michael Philip O'Brien, Mark Shunock, Matthew Steffens, Cameron Mitchell Worthen (Marines); Jee Teo, Joven Calloway, Mel Sagrado Maghuyop, Enrico Rodriguez, Kelvin Moon Loh, JP Moraga (Bar Staff); Kelvin Moon Loh, JP Moraga (Guards & Siolders); February 9–21, 2010

South Pacific Music by Richard Rodgers, lyrics by Oscar Hammerstein II, book by Oscar Hammerstein II & Joshua Logan, adapted from the Pulitzer Prize-winning novel Tales of the South Pacific by James A. Michener, Original stage production directed by Joshua Logan; Director, Bartlett Sher; Musical Staging, Christopher Gattelli; Music Director, Ted Sperling; Set, Michael Yeargan; Costumes, Catherine Zuber; Lighting, Donald Holder; Sound, Scott Lehrer; Orchestrations, Robert Russell Bennett; Dance/Incidental Music Arrangements, Trude Rittmann; Casting, Telsey + Company; Music Coordinator, David Lai; Stage Manager, Brian J. L'ecuyer; Music Conductor, Lawrence Goldberg; Technical Director, William J. Pate; Company Manager, Joel T. Herbst; Production Manager, Justin Reiter; Touring Booking/Engagement Management/Press & Marketing, Broadway Booking Office NYC; General Manager, Gregory Vander Ploeg and Gentry & Associates, Executive Producer, Seth C. Wenig; Cast: Rod Gilfry (Emile de Becque), Carmen Cusack (Ensign Nellie Forbush), Gerry Becker (Capt. George Brackett), Genson Blimline (Stewpot/Voiceover Loudspeaker), Christina Carrera (Ngana), Anderson Davis (Lt. Joseph Cable), Sumie Maeda (Liat), CJ Palma (Jerome), Peter Rini (Cmdr. William Harbison), Rusty Ross (Professor), Matthew Saldivar (Luther Billis), Keala Settle (Bloody Mary), Christopher Carl (Richard West), Eric L. Christian (Kenneth Johnson), Jacqueline Colmer (Asst. Dance Captain, Swing), Jeremy David (Swing), Mike Evariste (Henry, James Hayes), Kate Fahrner (Ensign Dinah Murphy), Nicholas Galbraith (Johnny Noonan), Alexis G.B. Holt (Bloody Mary's Assistant), Chad Jennings (Radio Operator Bob McCaffrey), Christopher Johnstone (Thomas Hassinger), Kristine Kerwin (Ensign Sue Yaeger), Jodi Kimura (Bloody Mary's Assistant), Cathy Newman (Lt. Genevieve Marshall), Diane Phelan (Ensign Cora MacRae/Bloody Mary's Assistant), John Pinto Jr. (Yeoman Herbert Quale), Travis Robertson (Tom O'Brien), Josh Rouah (Lt. Eustis Carmichael/Petty Officer Hamilton Steeves), Tally Sessions (Lt. Buzz Adams), Kristen J. Smith (Ensign Connie Walewska), Matt Stokes (Dance Captain/Swing), Gregoru Williams (Swing), Victor J. Wisehart (Morton Wise); National Tour; March 9–21, 2010

Little House on the Prairie The Musical Book by Rachel Sheinkin, music by Rachel Portman, lyrics by Donna Di Novelli; Based on the "Little House" Books by Laura Ingalls Wilder; Director, Francesca Zambello; Musical Staging, Michelle Lynch; Music Supervision, Kevin Stites; Cast: Melissa Gilbert (Ma), Steve Blanchard (Pa), Kara Lindsay (Laura), Kate Loprest (Nellie Olsen), Kevin Massey (Almanzo), Alessa Neeck (Mary), Anastasia Korbal (Carrie); Ensemble: Michael Boxleitner, Megan Campanile, Kurt Engh, Shawn Hamilton, Jessica Hershberg, Meredith Inglesby, Caroline Innerbichler, Lizzie Klemperer, Camille Mancuso, Lori Eve Marinacci, Garen McRoberts, Brian Muller, Will Ray, Tyler Rhodes, Gayle Samuels, Dustin Sullivan, Todd Thurston, Tony Vierling, Christian Whelan; National Tour; April 28–May 9, 2010

Trinity Repertory Theatre

Providence, Rhode Island

Forty-sixth Season

Artistic Director, Curt Columbus; Executive Director, Michael Gennaro; Production Director, Laura E. Smith; Associate Production Director, Mark Turek; General Manager, Rachel J. Tischler; Director of External Relations, Richard Jaffe; Associate Director of Marketing and PR, Marilyn Busch

Cabaret Book by Joe Masteroff, music by John Kander, lyrics by Fred Ebb; Director, Curt Columbus; Musical Direction, Michael Rice; Choreographer, Sharon Jenkins; Set, Michael McGarty; Lighting, Russell Champa; Costumes, William Lane; Sound, Peter Sasha Hurowitz; Properties, S. Michael Getz; Stage Manager, Michael D. Domue; Cast: Stephen Berenson (Herr Schultz), Janice Duclos (Fräulein Kost), Mauro Hantman (Cliff Bradshaw), Phyllis Kay (Fräulein Schneider), Stephen Thorne (Ernst Ludwig), Rachael Warren (Sally Bowles), Joe Wilson Jr. (Emcee), Kit-Kat Klub Ensemble: Matt Clevy, Patrick Mulryan, Michael Obremski, Molly O'Neill, Lizzie Vieh, Monica Willey, Gillian Williams, Anne Francisco Worden, Lynnette R. Freeman; The Chace Theater; September 11–October 11, 2009

Shooting Star by Steven Dietz; Director, Fred Sullivan Jr.; Set, Patrick Lynch; Lighting, John Ambrosone; Costumes, William Lane; Sound, Peter Sasha Hurowitz; Properties, S. Michael Getz; Stage Manager, Robin Grady; Cast: Kurt Rhoads (Reed McAllister), Nance Williamson (Elena Carson); Sarah and Joseph Dowling Jr. Theater; October 16–November 22, 2009

A Christmas Carol by Charles Dickens, adapted by Adrian Hall and Richard Cumming; Director, Birgitta Victorson; Musical Director, Michael Rice; Set, Michael McGarty; Lighting, Dan Scully; Costumes, William Lane; Sound, Peter Sasha Hurowitz; Choreographer, Jude Sandy; Properties, S. Michael Getz; PSM, Lori Lundquist; Stage Manager, Michael D. Domue; Cast: Timothy Crowe (Ebenezer Scrooge), Angela Brazil (Lucy), Janice Duclos (Mrs. Fezziwig), Mauro Hantman (Bob Cratchit), Barbara Meek (Ghost of Christmas Past), Anne Scurria (Mrs. Partlet), Fred Sullivan Jr. (Ghost of Christmas Present) Rachael Warren (Mrs. Cratchit), Joe Wilson Jr. (Jacob Marley), Liam Clancy (Tiny Tim), Sophia Rose Diodati (Martha), Kevin Fallon (Musician), Kateryne Nelson Guerrero (The Reader), Sam Haley Hill (Topper), Eric Halvarson (Turkey Boy/Young Scrooge), Emeline Herreid (The Reader), Per Janson (Fred), Steve Jobe (Musician), Carolina King (Fan/Hunger), Virginia King (Belinda), Chris Lussier (Musician), Chris Lysik (Peter/Young Marley), Julianna McGuirl (Fan/Hunger), Teddy McNulty (Turkey Boy/Young Scrooge), Sakari Monteiro (Martha), Nigel Richards (Peter/Young Marley), Haley Schreiber (Belinda), Benjamin Thornton (Tiny Tim), Chris Turner (Musician), David Rudi Utter (Young Scrooge), Monica Willey (Belle); The Chace Theater; November 20–December 27, 2009

Twelfth Night by William Shakespeare; Director, Brian McEleney; Set, Eugene Lee; Lighting, John Ambrosone; Costumes, William Lane; Sound, Peter Sasha Hurowitz; Properties, S. Michael Getz; Stage Manager, Robin Grady; Music Direction, Jamey Grisham; Cast: Stephen Berenson (Feste), Mauro Hantman (Fabian), Brian McEleney (Malvolio), Anne Scurria (Maria), Fred Sullivan Jr. (Sir Toby Belch), Stephen Thorne (Sir Andrew Aguecheek), Joe Wilson Jr. (Duke Orsino), Christopher Berry (Ensemble), Jamey Grisham (Ensemble), Cherie Corinne Rice (Viola/Sebastian), Rich Williams (Antonio) Annie Worden (Olivia); The Chace; January 29–March 7, 2010

Dead Man's Cell Phone by Sarah Ruhl; Director, Beth F. Milles; Set, Michael McGarty; Lighting, Russell Champa; Costumes, William Lane; Sound, Peter Sasha Hurowitz; Properties, S. Michael Getz; Stage Manager, Robin Grady; Cast: Richard Donelly (Dwight/Gordon Gottlieb), Janice Duclos (Jean), Phyllis Kay (Hermia Gottlieb), Barbara Meek (Mrs. Gottlieb), Rachael Warren (Carlotta/The Other Woman); Sarah and Joseph Dowling Jr. Theater; February 19–March 28, 2010

The Odd Couple by Neil Simon; Director, Curt Columbus; Set, Eugene Lee; Lighting, Eugene Lee; Costumes, William Lane; Sound, Peter Sasha Hurowitz; Properties, S. Michael Getz; Stage Manager, Katrina Olsen; Cast: Stephen Berenson (Murray), Mauro Hantman (Speed), Phyllis Kay (Gwendolyn Pigeon), Brian McEleney (Felix Unger), Fred Sullivan Jr. (Oscar Madison), Stephen Thorne (Roy), Nance Williamson (Cecily Pigeon) Joe Wilson Jr. (Vinnie); The Chace Theater; April 9–May 9, 2010

The Syringa Tree by Pamela Gien; Director, Laura Kepley; Set, Antje Ellermann; Lighting, Brian J. Lilienthal; Costumes, William Lane; Sound, John Gromada; Properties, S. Michael Getz; Stage Manager, Barbara Reo; Cast: Tiffany Nichole Greene (Iris Kgobane/John Grace/Loeska Hattingh/Moliseng Elessebett Mashlope/Peter Mombadi), Barbara Meek (Dominee Hattingh/Dr. Isaac Grace/Salamina Mashlope), Annie Scurria (Dubike/Elizabeth/Granny Elizabeth/Pietros), Rachael Warren (Mrs. Biggs/Mrs. Eugenie Grace/Zephyr); Sarah and Joseph Dowling Jr. Theater; April 30–May 30, 2010

Westport Country Playhouse

Westport, Connecticut

Seventy-ninth Season

Artistic Director, Mark Lamos; Managing Director, Michael Ross

Around the World in 80 Days by Mark Brown, adapted from the novel by Jules Verne; Director, Michael Evan Haney; Set, Joseph Tilford; Costumes, David K. Mickelsen; Lighting, Betsy Adams; Sound, David Levy; Original Music and Sound Effects, Mark Parenti; Sound Effects Elizabeth Helitzer; Cast: Jeff Bieh (Detective Fix/Andrew Stuart/Priest/U.S. and Indian Train Conductors/Elephant Owner/Young Parsi/OysterPuff/Rev. Wilson's Servant), Andrew Grusetskie (Gauthier Ralph/British Consul/Director of Police/Priest/Sir Francis/Judge Obadiah/Chinese Broker/Ship Clerk/Bunsby/Proctor/Engineer/Mudge/Clerk/Speedy/Ship Engineer/Train Clerk); Lauren Elise McCord (James Forster/Newspaperman/Priest/Aouda), Mark Shanahan (Phileas Fogg), Evan Zes (Passepartout/John Sullivan); April 21–May 9, 2009

Children by A. R. Gurney; Director, John Tillinger; Set, James Noone; Costumes, Jane Greenwood; Lighting, Rui Rita; Composer/Sound, Scott Killian; PSM, Gregory Livoti; Cast: Mary Bacon (Jane), Katie Finneran (Barbara), Judith Light (Mother), James Waterston (Randy); May 26–June 30, 2009

tick, tick...BOOM! Book, music and lyrics by Jonathan Larson; Director, Scott Schwartz; Choreography, Christopher Gattelli; Music Director, Charles Czarnecki; Set, David Farley; Costumes, Ilona Somogyi; Lighting, Herrick Goldman; Sound, Jon Weston; PSM, Matthew Melchoirre; Cast: Wilson Cruz (Michael), Colin Hanlon (Jonathan), Pearl Sun (Susan); June 23–July 18, 2009

How the Other Half Loves by Alan Ayckbourn; Director, John Tillinger; Set, James Noone; Costumes, Laurie Churba Kohn; Lighting, Stephen Strawbridge; Sound/Music, Scott Killian; Casting, Janet Foster; Dialect Coach, Liz Smith; Fight Director, Rick Sordelet; PSM, Christine Catti; Cast: Geneva Carr (Teresa Phillips), Carson Elrod (William Featherstone), Cecilia Hart (Fiona Foster), Darren Pettie (Bob Phillips), Karen Walsh, (Mary Featherstone), Paxton Whitehead (Frank Foster); July 28–August 15, 2009

That Championship Season by Jason Miller; Director, Mark Lamos; Set, David Gallo; Lighting, Jeff Nellis; Sound, David Van Tieghem; Costumes, Cynthia Nordstrom; Fight Director, B.H. Barry; Cast: Robert Clohessy (George Sikowski), John Doman (Coach), Lou Liberatore (James Daley), Tom Nelis (Tom Daley), Skipp Sudduth (Phil Romano); August 25–September 12, 2009

The Breath of Life by David Hare; Director, Mark Lamos; Set, Michael Yeargan; Lighting, Robert Wierzel; Costumes, Martin Pakledinaz; Original Music & Sound, Greg Hennigan; Dialects, Elizabeth Smith; Casting, Janet Foster; Wigs, Paul Huntley; PSM, Lloyd Davis Jr.; Cast: Jane Alexander (Madeleine Palmer), Stockard Channing (Frances Beale); September 29–October 17, 2009

Williamstown Theatre Festival

Williamstown, Massachusetts

Fifty-fifth Season

Artistic Director, Nicholas Martin; General Manager, Gilbert Medina; Artistic Associate, Amanda Charlton; Artistic Associate, Justin Waldman

Mainstage

Children by A.R. Gurney; Director, John Tillinger; Set, James Noone; Costumes, Jane Greenwood; Lighting, Rui Rita; Original Music & Sound, Scott Killian; PSM, Gregory T. Livoti; Cast: Mary Bacon (Jane), Katie Finneran (Barbara), Judith Light (Mother), James Waterston (Randy); July 1–12, 2009
True West by Sam Shepard; Director, Daniel Goldstein; Set, Neil Patel; Costumes, Linda Cho; Lighting, Ben Stanton; Sound, Darron L West; Fight Choreographer,

Tom Schall; PSM, Paul Smith; Cast: Nate Corddry (Austin), Paul Sparks (Lee), Stephen Kunken (Saul Kimmer), Debra Jo Rupp (Mom); July 15–26, 2009

The Torch-Bearers by George Kelly, adapted and directed by Dylan Baker; Set, David Korins; Costumes, Ilona Somogyi; Lighting, Rui Rita; Original Music, Mike Garin; Sound, Alex Neumann; Dialect Coach, Stephen Gabis; PSM, Gregory T. Livoti; Cast: Becky Ann Baker (Mrs. Paula Ritter), Yusef Bulos (Mr. Spindler), John Doherty (Mr. Stage Manager), Katie Finneran (Miss Florence McCrickett), Phillip Goodwin (Mr. Ralph Twiller), Jessica Hecht (Mrs. Clara Sheppard), Edward Herrmann (Mr. Huxley Hossefrosse), Lizbeth MacKay (Jenny), Andrea Martin (Mrs. Nelly Fell), Katherine McGrath (Mrs. J. Duro Pampinelli), John Rubinstein (Mr. Frederick Ritter), James Waterston (Teddy Spearing); July 29–August 9, 2009

Quartermaine's Terms by Simon Gray; Director, Maria Aitken; Set, Derek McLane; Costumes, Martin Pakledinaz; Lighting, Kevin Adams; Sound, Drew Levy; Dialect Coach, Stephen Gabis; PSM, Stephen M. Kaus; Cast: Jefferson Mays (St. John Quartermaine), Morgan Hallett (Anita Manchip), Stephen Kunken (Mark Sackling), John Horton (Eddie Loomis), Jeremy Beck (Derek Meadle), Simon Jones (Henry Windscape), Ann Dowd (Melanie Garth); August 12–23, 2009

Blanche and Beyond by Tennessee Williams, adapted and directed by Steve Lawson; Cast: Richard Thomas August 2, 2009

Nikos Stage

Knickerbocker by Jonathan Marc Sherman; Director, Nicholas Martin; Set, Alexander Dodge; Costumes, Gabriel Berry; Lighting, Philip Rosenberg; Sound, Alex Neumann; Composer, Michael Friedman; PSM, Jillian M. Oliver; Cast: Brooks Ashmanskas (Melvin), Peter Dinklage (Chester), Bob Dishy (Raymond), Rightor Doyle (Steve), Annie Parisse (Tara), Susan Pourfar (Pauline), Reg Rogers (Jerry); World Premiere; July 8–19, 2009
What is the Cause of Thunder? by Noah Haidle; Director, Justin Waldman; Set, Alexander Dodge; Costumes, Nicole Moody; Lighting, Jeff Croiter; Original Music & Sound, Fitz Patton; PSM, Conwell Worthington; Cast: Betty Gilpin (Ophelia et. all), Wendie Malick (Ada); World Premiere; July 22–August 2, 2009

Caroline in Jersey by Melinda Lopez; Director, Amanda Charlton; Set, Andrew Boyce; Costumes, Emily Rebholz; Lighting, Jake DeGroot; Sound, Bart Fasbender; Original Music, Kyle Jarrow; PSM, Libby Unsworth; Cast: Will LeBow (Will), Matt McGrath (David), Lea Thompson (Caroline), Brenda Wehle (Mimi); World Premiere; August 5–16, 2009
Direxting Studio

After the Revolution by Amy Herzog; Director, Tamara E. Fisch; Set, David Arsenault; Costumes, Jeanette Lee Porter; Lighting, Wilburn Bonnell; Sound, Leo A. Martin; PSM, Michael Block; Cast: Lucas Kavner (Robbie), Ashton Heyl (Mel), Dominic Spillane (Leo), Daniel Hartley (Jake), Lauren Blumenfeld (Lily/Jess), Gayle Rankin (Vera), Irene Sofia Lucio (Emma), Joel Perez (Miguel), Rich Dreher (Morty); Fellowship Play; July 12–13, 2009

Golden Gate Book & lyrics by Christopher Dimond, music by Michael Kooman; Director, Dan Rigazzi; Musical Director, Christopher D. Littlefield; Set, Sarah Muxlow; Costumes, Pamela Wilcox; Lighting, Isabella F. Byrd; Sound, Samantha Weller; PSM, Frances Ines Rodriguez; Cast: Dominic Spillane (Sparky/Coop), Francesca Choy-Kee (Woman/Rachel/Maddie), Lucas Kavner (Blair), Irene Sofia Lucio (Parker), Joel Perez (Glenn), Gayle Rankin (Natalie), Rich Dreher (Derrick/Peter), Daniel Hartley (Edward), Ashton Heyl (Diane/Mom), Lauren Blumenfeld (Jesus); Fellowship Musical; August 12–13, 2009

The Wilma Theater

Philadelphia, Pennsylvania

Thirty-first Season

Artistic Directors, Blanka and Jiri Zizka; Managing Director, James Haskins

Coming Home by Athol Fugard; Director, Blanka Zizka; Set & Costumes, Anne Patterson; Lighting, Thom Weaver; Composer & Musician, Mogauwane Mahloele; Sound, Andrea Sotzing; Dramaturg, Walter Bilderback; Production Manager, Iain Campbell; Stage Manager, Patreshettarlini Adams; Cast: Antonio J. Dandridge (Mannetjie, age 9), Elijah Felder (Mannetjie, age 5), Lou Ferguson (Oupa), Patrice Johnson (Veronica), Nyambi Nyambi (Alfred Witbooi); October 14–November 15, 2009

Becky Shaw by Gina Gionfriddo; Director, Anne Kauffman; Set, Mimi Lien; Lighting, Thom Weaver; Costumes, Emily Rebholz; Sound, Christopher Colucci; Stage Manager, Patreshettarlini Adams; Production Manager, Iain Campbell; Cast: Brooke Bloom (Becky Shaw), Jeremy Bobb (Max Garrett), Janis Dardaris (Susan Slater), Armando Riesco (Andrew Porter), Danielle Skraastad (Suzanna Slater); December 30, 2009–February 7, 2010

Language Rooms by Yussef El Guindi; Director, Blanka Zizka; Set, Ola Maslik; Costumes, Janus Stefanowicz; Lighting, Russell Champa; Sound, Jorge Cousineau; Stage Manager, Patreshettarlini Adams; Dramaturg, Walter Bilderback; Production Manager, Iain Campbell; Cast: Nasser Faris (Samir), Peter Jay Fernandez (Kevin), Sevan Greene (Ahmed), Julienne Hanzelka Kim (Esther), J. Paul Nicholas (Nasser); World Premiere; March 3–April 4, 2010

Leaving by Václav Havel, translated by Paul Wilson; Director, Jiri Zizka; Set, Klara Zieglerova; Costumes, Vasilija Zivanic; Lighting, Jerold R. Forsyth; Sound, Nick Rye; Dramaturg, Walter Bilderback; Production Manager, Iain Campbell; Stage Manager, Patreshettarlini Adams; Cast: F. Murray Abraham (The Voice), Krista Apple (Monika), Janis Dardaris (Grandma), Mark Cairns (Albín), Mike Dees (Bob), Peter DeLaurier (Hanuš), Victoria Frings (Zuzanna), Leonard C. Haas (Dick), Trever Long (Klein), Mary McCool (Bea), Kathryn Meisle (Irena), Jennifer R. Morris (Vlasta), Geddeth Smith (Oswald), Luigi Sottile (Victor), David Strathairn (Dr. Vilém Rieger), H. Michael Walls (Knobloch); May 19–June 20, 2010

Yale Repertory Theatre

New Haven, Connecticut

Forty-fourth Season

Artistic Director, James Bundy; Managing Director, Victoria Nolan; Associate Artistic Director, Jennifer Kiger

The Master Builder by Henrik Ibsen, translated by Paul Walsh; Director, Evan Yionoulis; Set, Timothy Brown; Costumes, Katherine Akiko Day; Lighting, Paul Whitaker; Sound/Composer, Scott L. Nielsen; Dramaturgs, Maya Cantu, Collin Mannex; Casting, Tara Rubin, Laura Schutzel; Stage Manager, James Mountcastle; Cast: Robert Hogan (Knut Brovik), Irene Sofia Lucio (Kaja Fosli), Slate Holmgren (Ragnar Brovik), David Chandler (Halvard Solness), Felicity Jones (Aline Solness), Bill Buell (Doctor Herdal), Susan Heyward (Hilda Wangel); University Theatre; September 18–October 19, 2009

Eclipsed by Danai Gurira; Director, Liesl Tommy; Set, Germán Cardenás; Costumes, Elizabeth Barrett Groth; Lighting, Marcus Doshi; Sound/Composer, Broken Chord Collective; Dramaturg, Walter Byongsok Chon; Fight Director, Rick Sordelet; Vocal and Dialect Coach, Beth McGuire; Casting, Tara Rubin, Laura Schutzel; Stage Manager, Karen Hashley; Cast: Pascale Armand (Bessie), Stacey Sargeant (Helena), Adepero Oduye (The Girl), Zainab Zah (Maima), Shona Tucker (Rita); Yale Repertory Theatre; October 23–November 14, 2009.

POP! Book and lyrics by Maggie-Kate Coleman, music by Anna K. Jacobs; Director, Mark Brokaw; Choreographer, Denis Jones; Musical Director, Lynne Shankel; Set, Valérie Thérèse Bart; Costumes, Ying Song; Lighting, Kevin Adams; Sound, David Budries; Projections, Tal Yarden; Orchestrations, Bruce Coughlin; Casting, Tara Rubin, Laura Schutzel; Stage Manager, Jenna Woods; Cast: Randy Harrison (Andy Warhol), Brian Charles Rooney (Candy), Doug Kreeger (Ondine), Danny Binstock (Gerard), Leslie Kritzer (Valerie), Emily Swallow (Viva), Cristen Paige (Edie); World Premiere; Yale Repertory Theatre; November 27–December 19, 2009

Compulsion By Rinne Groff; Co-production with The Public Theater and Berkeley Repertory Theatre; Director, Oskar Eustis; Puppet Design and Supervision, Matt Acheson; Set, Eugene Lee; Costumes, Lisa Loen; Lighting, Marie Yokoyama; Sound, Darron L West; Dramaturg, Amy Boratko; Vocal and Dialect Coach, Thom Jones; Casting, Tara Rubin, Laura Schutzel; Stage Manager, Jessica Barker; Puppet Consultant, Basil Twist; Cast: Hannah Cabell (Miss Mermin/Mrs. Silver), Mandy Patinkin (Mr. Silver), Stephen Barker Turner (Mr. Thomas/Mr. Harris/Mr. Ferris/Mr. Matzliach); Puppeteers: Emily DeCola, Liam Hurley, Eric Wright. World Premiere; Yale Repertory Theatre; January 29–February 28, 2010

The Servant of Two Masters by Carlo Goldoni, adapted by Constance Congdon from a translation by Christina Sibul; Director, Christopher Bayes; Composers, Christopher Curtis, Aaron Halva; Set, Katherine Akiko Day; Costumes, Valérie Thérèse Bart; Lighting, Chuan-Chi Chan; Sound, Nathan A. Roberts; Dramaturgs, Emmy Miller, Hannah Rae Montgomery; Fight Director, Rick Sordelet; Vocal and Dialect Coach, Beth McGuire; Casting, Tara Rubin, Laura Schutzel; Stage Manager, Bree Sherry; Cast: Andy Grotelueschen (Silvio), Da'Vine Joy Randolph (Clarice), John Treacy Egan (Il Dottore), Liz Wisan (Smeraldina), Allen Gilmore (Pantalone), Liam Craig (Brighella, Porter), Steven Epp (Truffaldino), Sarah Agnew (Beatrice), Jesse J. Perez (Florindo), Will Cobbs (Waiter), Chris Henry (Waiter); University Theatre; March 12–April 3, 2010

Battle of Black and Dogs by Bernard-Marie Koltès; Director, Robert Woodruff; Translator and Composer, Michaël Attias; Set, Riccardo Hernandez; Costumes, Tom McAlister & Ilona Somogyi; Lighting, Stephen Strawbridge; Sound, Chad Raines; Dramaturg, Amy Boratko; Fight Director, Rick Sordelet; Vocal Coach, Walton Wilson; Casting, Tara Rubin, Laura Schutzel; Stage Manager, Jenna Woods; Cast: Andrew Robinson (Horn), Albert Jones (Alboury), Tracy Middendorf (Léone), Tommy Schrider (Cal); Yale Repertory Theatre; April 16–May 8, 2010

Special Events: Noboundaries

A Series of Global Performances presented by World Performance Project at Yale and Yale Repertory Theatre

Wormwood by Theatre of the Eighth Day (Teatr Ósmego Dnia); Iseman Theater; November 5–7, 2009

The Be(A)st of Taylor Mac Written and performed by Taylor Mac; Director, David Drake; University Theatre; January 28–30, 2010

Baby-Q's MESs by Yoko Higashino and Toshio Kajiwara; Iseman Theater; March 25–27, 2010

Stockard Channing and Jane Alexander in the Westport Country
Playhouse production of The Breath of Life
(photo by T. Charles Erickson)

Judith Light and Katie Finneran
in Children at the
Westport Country Playhouse
(photo by T. Charles Erickson)

David Strathairn and Kathryn Meisle in Leaving at the Wilma Theater
(photo by John Roese)

Doug Kreeger, Danny Binstock, Brian Charles Rooney, and Randy
Harrison in Yale Repertory Theatre's POP! (photo by Joan Marcus)

John Rubinstein, Becky Ann Baker, Andrea Martin, and Katherine
McGrath in Williamstown Theatre Festival's The Torch-Bearers
(photo T. Charles Erickson)

Top: *Theatre World and Theatre World Awards founder John Willis (center) with (left to right) Michael Viade (Theatre World Awards photographer and former student of John Willis), Scott Denny, and Ben Hodges, the current editors of* Theatre World *(photo by Konrad Brattke)*

Center: *2010 Theatre World Award Winner Scarlett Johansson and fellow* A View from the Bridge *cast member Michael Cristofer (1977 Theatre World Award Winner) greet the press (photo by Michael and Laura Viade)*

Bottom: *Viola Davis (1996 Theatre World Award Winner) presents a 2010 Theatre World Award to fellow* Fences *cast member Chris Chalk (photo by Jim Baldassare)*

Nina Arianda of Venus in Fur

Chris Chalk of Fences

Bill Heck of The Orphans' Home Cycle

Jon Michael Hill of Superior Donuts

Scarlett Johansson of A View from the Bridge

Keira Keeley of The Glass Menagerie

Sahr Ngaujah of Fela!

Eddie Redmayne of Red

Andrea Riseborough of The Pride

Heidi Schreck of Circle Mirror Transformation

Stephanie Umoh of Ragtime

Michael Urie of The Temperamentals

Dorothy Loudon Starbaby Award

Bobby Steggert of Ragtime and Yank!

66th Annual Theatre World Awards

Tuesday, June 8, 2010 at New World Stages

Originally dubbed *Promising Personalities* in 1947 by co-founders Daniel Blum, Norman MacDonald, and John Willis to coincide with the first release of *Theatre World*, the definitive pictorial and statistical record of the American theatre, the Theatre World Awards, as they are now known, are the oldest awards given for debut performances in New York City, as well as one of the oldest honors bestowed on New York actors.

Administered by the Theatre World Awards Board of Directors, a committee of current New York drama critics chooses six actors and six actresses for the Theatre World Award who have distinguished themselves in Broadway and Off-Broadway productions during the past theatre season. Occasionally, Special Theatre World Awards are also bestowed on performers, casts, or others who have made a particularly lasting impression on the New York theatre scene.

This season, the Dorothy Loudon Foundation in conjunction Theatre World Awards presented the second annual Dorothy Loudon *Starbaby* Award at the Theatre World Awards ceremony. Dorothy Loudon, a former Theatre World Award winner and repeated presenter at many past ceremonies, was an ardent supporter of the Theatre World Awards and a dear friend to John Willis. "Starbaby" was a term of endearment used by Dorothy's closest friends from her early days in the theatre and it stuck with her throughout her career. The *Starbaby* Award, presented to a performer who made an auspicious Broadway or Off-Broadway performance in the season, will be presented at future Theatre World Award ceremonies.

This year also marked the debut of a new Theatre World Award designed by Wade F. Dansby 3. The new design honors the previous Theatre World Awards' Janus statuette (created by internationally recognized artist Harry Marinsky) by keeping the Janus tradition with an etching of the original sculpture adapted from the Roman myth of Janus. Janus was the God of Entrances, Exits and All Beginnings - with one face appraising the past and the other anticipating the future.

The Theatre World Award winners are selected by a committee of New York drama critics: David Cote (*Time Out New York* and NY1's *On Stage*), Joe Dziemianowicz (*New York Daily News*), Peter Filichia (*Star-Ledger* and *TheaterMania.com*), Harry Haun (*Playbill*), Matthew Murray (*TalkinBroadway.com*), Frank Scheck (*New York Post* and *The Hollywood Reporter*), and Linda Winer (*Newsday*). The Theatre World Awards Board of Directors is: Kati Meister (President), Erin Oestreich (Vice President), Mary K. Botosan (Secretary), Tom Bloom (Treasurer), Randall Hemming, Barry Keating, Cara Lustik, Tom Lynch, and Jane Stuart. Board Emeritus: Thom Christopher, Marianne Tatum, Jamie deRoy, Ben Hodges, Walter Willison, Doug Holmes, Patricia Elliott, Leigh Giroux, Scott Denny; Advisors: Jason Cicci, Christopher Cohen, Gordon Kelly, Michael Messina, Barry Monush, Matthew Murray, Flora Stamatiades.

THE CEREMONY Writer and Host, Peter Filichia; Executive Producers, Kati Meister, Erin Oestreich, Mary K. Botosan; Director, Barry Keating; Music Director/Accompanist, Alex Rybeck; Associate Director, Jeremy Quinn; Production Manager/Program Design, Mary K. Botosan; Production Stage Manager, Kimothy Cruse; Stage Manager, Alden Fulcomer; Assistant Stage Managers, Stephen Ferri, Christina Lowe, Michael Mele; Guest Coordinator, Betsy Krouner; Volunteer Coordinator, Stephen Wilde; Press Representative and Staff Photographer, Jim Baldassare; Photographers, Scott Denny, Bruce Glikas, Walter McBride, Konrad Brattke, Tom Case, Michael Viade, Michael Riordan; Video Photographers, Richard Ridge and Bradshaw Smith; Presented on the set of the *Avenue Q*, scenic design by Anna Louizos, lighting design by Howell Binkley, sound design by Acme Sound Partners; New World Stages crew for the Theatre World Awards: Light Board Operator, Jeff Gordon; Sound Mixer/Board Op, Mike Viveros; Stage Technician, Shadow Edwards; Porter, Jana Lancaster;

WINNERS Nina Arianda (*Venus in Fur*), Chris Chalk (*Fences*), Bill Heck (*The Orphans' Home Cycle*), Jon Michael Hill (*Superior Donuts*), Scarlett Johansson (*A View from the Bridge*), Keira Keeley (*The Glass Menagerie*), Sahr Ngaujah

(*Fela!*), Eddie Redmayne (*Red*), Andrea Riseborough (*The Pride*), Heidi Schreck (*Circle Mirror Transformation*), Stephanie Umoh (*Ragtime*), Michael Urie (*The Temperamentals*); **Dorothy Loudon *Starbaby* Award:** Bobby Steggert (*Yank!* & *Ragtime*)

PRESENTERS Kate Burton – *Winners* (1983); Michael Cerveris – *The Who's Tommy* (1993); Michael Cristofer – *The Cherry Orchard* (1977); Viola Davis – *Seven Guitars* (1996); Tovah Feldshuh – *Yentl* (1976); Robert LuPone – *A Chorus Line* (1976 Special Cast Award); Michael McKean – *Accomplice* (1990); Brian Stokes Mitchell – *Mail* (1988); Alfred Molina – *Molly Sweeney* (1996); Condola Rashad – *Ruined* (2009); Vanessa Williams – *Kiss of the Spider Woman* (1995)

PERFORMERS John Tartaglia – *Avenue Q* (2004) with special appearance by *Avenue Q* cast member Jennifer Barnhart and *Avenue Q* puppets Princeton and Bad Idea Bear Cindy (introduction and special comedy material); Alli Mauzey – *Cry-Baby* (2008) ("Screw Loose" from *Cry-Baby*); Loretta Ables Sayre – *South Pacific* (2008) ("It's Not Where You Start" from *Seesaw*); Jonathan Groff – *Spring Awakening* (2007) ("Only in New York" from *Thoroughly Modern Millie*)

2010 THEATRE WORLD AWARD "JANUS" WRANGLERS Luka Kain, Laurissa Romain, and Kimber Monroe from the cast of *South Pacific*

VOLUNTEERS Michael Alsondo, Tom Bernagozzi, Tara Louise Bruno, Sarah Chalfy, Amelie Cherubin, Peter Dagger, Mike Deely, Tara Djangi, Anna Eilinsfeld, Jenna Esposito, Shana Farr, Oliver Gaag, Matt Greenstein, Jeremiah Hernandez, Sharon Hunter, Matthew Kernisky, Kristin Kotalo, John Krieger, Kelsey Maples, Jennie McMullen, Michael Messina, Barry Monush, Joanna Parson, James Sheridan, Jenny Stadler

STAFF FOR NEW WORLD STAGES Executive Director, Beverley D. MacKeen; Director of Programming, Michael Coco; Director of Finance, Rainard Rachele; Box Office Treasurer, Kenneth L. Burrows; Director of Operations, Rebecca Nichols; Bookkeeper, Joan Mitchell; House Manager, Colleen Harris; Bar Manager, Erin Fehr DePalma; Events Manager, Jennifer Jones; Events Coordinator, Philip Wilson; Office Manager, Jackie Lavanway; Production Managers, Jameson Croasdale, Zane Enloe

STAFF FOR *Avenue Q* Company Manager, Ryan Lympus; General Manager, Davenport Theatrical Enterprises; Production Manager, Travis Walker; Production Stage Manager, Christine M. Daly; Production Electrician, Tom Dyer; Sound Engineer, Dave Horowitz

SUPPORT The Dorothy Loudon Foundation, School Theatre Ticket Program/ Eric Krebs; King Displays/Wayne Sapper, Alan Alda, Alec Baldwin, Susan S. Channing Foundation, Calista Flockhart, The Hugh Jackman Family Foundation, Mario Frangoulis, Joseph Pierson, Danny Aiello, John Allen, Tom Amorosi, Howard Atlee, Jordan Baker, Dylan Baker, Orson Bean, Thomas Beragozzi, Steven Bloom, Martin Brooks, Sylvia Brown-Sanders, Mrs. Michael Buckley, Pamela Burrell, Len Cariou, Esther Cohen, Paul Craffrey, John Cullum, Blythe Danner, O. David Deitz, Bambi DeJesus, Jamie deRoy, Deanna Dunagan, Lindsay Duncan, Edward Evanko, Harvey Evans, Brian Farrell, Tovah Feldshuh, William Felty, Mark Fichandler, Barbara Flood, Harry Forbes, Pat Fortunato, Bette-Lee Fox, Mario Frangoulis, Bonnie Franklin, Barbara Freitag, David Fritz, Victor Garber, Gail Gerber, Daniel Gerroll, Nancy Giles, Anita Gillette, Kathleen Giordano, Marlene J. Gould, Christopher Goutman, Harry Groener, Marvin Hamlisch, Ann Hampton Callaway, June A. Harding, Rosalind Harris, Julie Harris, The Hartman Group, Shirley Herz, Jayne Houdyshell, Bill Irwin, Jonathan Kagan, Jonathan Kaplan, Judy Kaye Green, Craig Keleman, Kevin Kilner, John Kreiger, Elisa Loti Stein, Lucie Luckinbill, Lizbeth Mackay, Dinah Manoff, Anthony Meisel, Spiro Malas, Barbara Manocherian, Kelsey Maples, Christine Marioni, Daisy Maryles, Marshall Mason, John McMartin, Kati Meister, Leslie D. Middlebrook, Antonia K. Milonas, Brian Stokes Mitchell, Susan Myerberg, James Naughton, Cynthia Nixon, Erin Oestreich, Kenneth Page, Joanna Pettet, Lonny Price, Kay Radtke, M. Kilberg Reedy, Charles Repole, Ronald Jordan Roberts, Marcia Roberts, Reva Rose, Greg Rossi, Loretta Ables Sayre, Sheila A. Smith, Susan P. Stroman, Philip Suraci, Marianne Tatum, Wesley Taylor, Jane Trese, Tracy Turner, Joan Van Ark, Jennifer Warren, Lesley Ann Warren, Jennifer Warren, Wilmore Living Trust, Caroline Winston, K. Yardley, John Lloyd Young

SPECIAL THANKS Actors' Equity Association, Michael Alsondo, Raj Atencio, Emilio Barletta (Trattoria Dopo Teatro), Miriam Berman, Boneau/Bryan-Brown, Michael Borowski, Geoff Botosan, Konrad Brattke, Broadway Beat, Amber Brockman, Tom Case, Barbara Carroll, John Cerullo (Applause Books/Hal Leonard Company), Karen Carzo (Trattoria Dopo Teatro), Scott Denny, Jamie deRoy, Discovery Times Square Exposition, Bobby Driggers, Shiva Elahi, Patricia Elliott, Brian Ferdman (TheatreMania.com), Andrew Gans (Playbill), Leigh Giroux, Bruce Glikas, Michael Goddard, Guy Gsell, Dale Heller, Barbara Hoffman, Ken Jones (Playbill), Amy Kass, Lionel Larner, Pino Manica (Trattoria Dopo Teatro), Kelsey Maples, Rosanne Martino, Kevin McAnarney, Danielle McGarry, Emily Meagher, Lindsay Meck, Michael Messina, Barry Monush, Chris Morey, Claire Moyer, Christine Olver, Gianni Onofri, Alice Playten, The Public Theater, Richard Ridge, Michael Riordan, Jeff Rose (Attitude Car Service), Wayne Sapper (King Displays), Mark Schlegel, Heath Schwartz, Bradshaw Smith, Michael Strassheim, Harriet Sternberg, Marc Thibodeau, Jack Vrtar (Custom Glass Etching), Caroline Winston, Philip Wilson, Teresa Wolf, and the agents, management, and publicity teams of the winners, presenters and performers

Gift Bags Promotions supplied by Applause Theatre and Cinema Books/Hal Leonard Publications, The Araca Group, Avon, Café Un Deux Trois, Kimara Ahnert, Jennifer Ahn/Variety, Steven Bloom, Scott Farthing/Son Masterworks, Brian Ferdman/TheaterMania, Allen L. Hubby/The Drama Book Shop, Laura Kszan/Sony Masterworks, Lisa Morris/Road Concierge Inc., Random House, Nancy Reardon, Stephen Wilde/No Cover Records, The York Theatre Company and *Yank!*, Sony/BMG

Theatre World Awards After-Party generously sponsored by **Trattoria Dopo Teatro,** 125 West 44th Street between 6th Avenue and Broadway; Transportation by **Attitude New York**

The Theatre World Awards, Inc. is a 501 (c)(3) nonprofit organization, and our annual presentation is made possible by the generous contributions of previous winners and friends. For more information please visit the website at www.theatreworldawards.org.

Tax-deductible contributions can be sent via PayPay® to info@theatreworldawards.org, or checks and money orders sent to:

Theatre World Awards, Inc.
Box 246 Radio City Station
New York, NY 10101-0246

Michael Cerveris (1993 Winner) presents to Bill Heck (MLV)

Stephanie Umoh receives her award from Brian Stokes Mitchell (1988 Winner) (JB)

Photos by Jim Baldassare (JB), Konrad Brattke (KB), Scott Denny (SD), Walter McBride (WB), and Michael & Laura Viade (MLV)

Jennifer Barnhart and John Tartaglia from Avenue Q open the ceremony (JB)

Michael McKean (1990 Winner) before presenting to Jon Michael Hill (JB)

Vanessa Williams (1995 Winner) presents to Michael Urie, her co-star on television's Ugly Betty (JB)

Scarlett Johansson (JB)

Jon Michael Hill (JB)

Alli Mauzey (2008 Winner) performs her number from Cry-Baby, the show for which she won her Theatre World Award (JB)

Host of the Awards, Peter Filichia (JB)

Nina Arianda and her presenter Tovah Feldshuh (1976 Winner) backstage at the ceremony (KB)

Keira Keeley receives her award from Condola Rashad (2009 Winner) (WM)

Loretta Ables Sayre (2008 Winner) entertains the crowd (JB)

Sherry Chastain Schreck accepts the award on her daughter Heidi's behalf (JB)

Lionel Larner, Executive of the Dorothy Loudon Foundation, and Kate Burton (1983 Winner) present the Dorothy Loudon Starbaby Award, which is now a special presentation at the Theatre World Awards ceremony (JB)

Dorothy Loudon Starbaby *Award Winner Bobby Steggert (JB)*

Robert LuPone (1976 Cast Award Winner from A Chorus Line *and Artistic Director of MCC Theater) presents and accepts the award for Andrea Riseborough who was not in attendance (JB)*

Michael Urie (JB)

Keira Keeley (JB)

Nina Arianda (MLV)

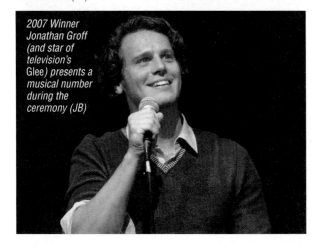

2007 Winner Jonathan Groff (and star of television's Glee) presents a musical number during the ceremony (JB)

Alfred Molina (1996 Winner) presents to his Red *co-star Eddie Redmayne (WM)*

2010 Theatre World Awards Producers Mary K. Botosan and Erin Oestreich (KB)

Bobby Steggert and Lionel Larner (MLV)

Sahr Ngaujah and Kate Burton (1983 Winner) (MLV)

Theatre World Awards photographer Laura Viade, Press Representative Jim Baldassare, and Volunteer Sharon Hunter (MLV)

2010 Theatre World Award "Janus" wranglers Luka Kain, Laurissa Romain, and Kimber Monroe from the cast of South Pacific *(KB)*

Viola Davis (1996 Winner) before presenting to Chris Chalk (JB)

Vanessa Williams (JB)

Stephanie Umoh (JB)

Michael McKean (1990 Winner) and his Superior Donuts co-star Jon Michael Hill greet the press (WM)

Chris Chalk (JB)

Bill Heck (WM)

Michael Cristofer (1977 Winner) and Scarlett Johansson backstage after he presented the award to his A View from the Bridge co-star (KB)

Sahr Ngaujah (JB)

Eddie Redmayne (JB)

Alfred Molina (1996 Winner) before presenting to Eddie Redmayne

Wesley Taylor (2009 Winner) and Jonathan Groff (2007 Winner) (MLV)

Linda Hart (1989 Winner) and John Willis (SD)

Linda Thorson (1983 Winner) and John Willis (SD)

John Willis, with (left to right) *Laura Viade* (Theatre World Awards *photographer*), *Tony Meisel* (Theatre World *publication designer*), *and* Theatre World *Co-Editors Scott Denny and Ben Hodges (MLV)*

Previous Theatre World Award Recipients

1944-45: Betty Comden (*On the Town*), Richard Davis (*Kiss Them For Me*), Richard Hart (*Dark of the Moon*), Judy Holliday (*Kiss Them for Me*), Charles Lang (*Down to Miami* and *The Overtons*), Bambi Linn (*Carousel*), John Lund (*The Hasty Heart*), Donald Murphy (*Signature* and *Common Ground*), Nancy Noland (*Common Ground*), Margaret Phillips (*The Late George Apley*), John Raitt (*Carousel*)

1945-46: Barbara Bel Geddes (*Deep Are the Roots*), Marlon Brando (*Truckline Café* and *Candida*), Bill Callahan (*Call Me Mister*), Wendell Corey (*The Wind is Ninety*), Paul Douglas (*Born Yesterday*), Mary James (*Apple of His Eye*), Burt Lancaster (*A Sound of Hunting*), Patricia Marshall (*The Day Before Spring*), Beatrice Pearson (*The Mermaids Singing*)

1946-47: Keith Andes (*The Chocolate Soldier*), Marion Bell (*Brigadoon*), Peter Cookson (*Message for Margaret*), Ann Crowley (*Carousel*), Ellen Hanley (*Barefoot Boy With Cheek*), John Jordan (*The Wanhope Building*), George Keane (*Brigadoon*), Dorothea MacFarland (*Oklahoma!*), James Mitchell (*Brigadoon*), Patricia Neal (*Another Part of the Forest*), David Wayne (*Finian's Rainbow*)

1947-48: Valerie Bettis (*Inside U.S.A.*), Edward Bryce (*The Cradle Will Rock*), Whitfield Connor (*Macbeth*), Mark Dawson (*High Button Shoes*), June Lockhart (*For Love or Money*), Estelle Loring (*Inside U.S.A.*), Peggy Maley (*Joy to the World*), Ralph Meeker (*Miser Roberts*), Meg Mundy (*The Happy Journey to Trenton and Camden* and *The Respectful Prostitute*), Douglass Watson (*Antony and Cleopatra*), James Whitmore (*Command Decision*), Patrice Wymore (*Hold It!*)

1948-49: Tod Andrews (*Summer and Smoke*), Doe Avedon (*The Young and Fair*), Jean Carson (*Bravo!*), Carol Channing (*Lend an Ear*), Richard Derr (*The Traitor*), Julie Harris (*Sundown Beach*), Mary McCarty (*Sleepy Hollow*), Allyn Ann McLerie (*Where's Charley?*), Cameron Mitchell (*Death of a Salesman*), Gene Nelson (*Lend an Ear*), Byron Palmer (*Where's Charley?*), Bob Scheerer (*Lend an Ear*)

1949-50: Nancy Andrews (*Touch and Go*), Phil Arthur (*With a Silk Thread*), Barbara Brady (*The Velvet Glove*), Lydia Clarke (*Detective Story*), Priscilla Gillette (*Regina*), Don Hanmer (*The Man*), Marcia Henderson (*Peter Pan*), Charlton Heston (*Design for a Stained Glass Window*), Rick Jason (*Now I Lay Me Down to Sleep*), Grace Kelly (*The Father*), Charles Nolte (*Design for a Stained Glass Window*), Roger Price (*Tickets, Please!*)

1950-51: Barbara Ashley (*Out of This World*), Isabel Bigley (*Guys and Dolls*), Martin Brooks (*Burning Bright*), Richard Burton (*The Lady's Not For Burning*), Pat Crowley (*Southern Exposure*), James Daly (*Major Barbara* and *Mary Rose*), Cloris Leachman (*A Story for a Sunday Evening*), Russell Nype (*Call Me Madam*), Jack Palance (*Darkness at Noon*), William Smithers (*Romeo and Juliet*), Maureen Stapleton (*The Rose Tattoo*), Marcia Van Dyke (*Marcia Van Dyke*), Eli Wallach (*The Rose Tattoo*)

1951-52: Tony Bavaar (*Paint Your Wagon*), Patricia Benoit (*Glad Tidings*), Peter Conlow (*Courtin' Time*), Virginia de Luce (*New Faces of 1952*), Ronny Graham (*New Faces of 1952*), Audrey Hepburn (*Gigi*), Diana Herbert (*The Number*), Conrad Janis (*The Brass Ring*), Dick Kallman (*Seventeen*), Charles Proctor (*Twilight Walk*), Eric Sinclair (*Much Ado About Nothing*), Kim Stanley (*The Chase*), Marian Winters (*I Am a Camera*), Helen Wood (*Seventeen*)

1952-53: Edie Adams (*Wonderful Town*), Rosemary Harris (*The Climate of Eden*), Eileen Heckart (*Picnic*), Peter Kelley (*Two's Company*), John Kerr (*Bernardine*), Richard Kiley (*Misalliance*), Gloria Marlowe (*In Any Language*), Penelope Munday (*The Climate of Eden*), Paul Newman (*Picnic*), Sheree North (*Hazel Flagg*), Geraldine Page (*Mid-Summer*), John Stewart (*Bernardine*), Ray Stricklyn (*The Climate of Eden*), Gwen Verdon (*Can-Can*)

1953-54: Orson Bean (*John Murray Anderson's Almanac*), Harry Belafonte (*John Murray Anderson's Almanac*), James Dean (*The Immoralist*), Joan Diener (*Kismet*), Ben Gazzara (*End as a Man*), Carol Haney (*The Pajama Game*), Jonathan Lucas (*The Golden Apple*), Kay Medford (*Lullaby*), Scott Merrill (*The Threepenny Opera*), Elizabeth Montgomery (*Late Love*), Leo Penn (*The Girl on the Via Flaminia*), Eva Marie Saint (*The Trip to Bountiful*)

1954-55: Julie Andrews (*The Boy Friend*), Jacqueline Brookes (*The Cretan Woman*), Shirl Conway (*Plain and Fancy*), Barbara Cook (*Plain and Fancy*), David Daniels (*Plain and Fancy*), Mary Fickett (*Tea and Sympathy*), Page Johnson (*In April Once*), Loretta Leversee (*Home is the Hero*), Jack Lord (*The Traveling Lady*), Dennis Patrick (*The Wayward Saint*), Anthony Perkins (*Tea and Sympathy*), Christopher Plummer (*The Dark is Light Enough*)

1955-56: Diane Cilento (*Tiger at the Gates*), Dick Davalos (*A View from the Bridge*), Anthony Franciosa (*A Hatful of Rain*), Andy Griffith (*No Time for Sergeants*), Laurence Harvey (*Island of Goats*), David Hedison (*A Month in the Country*), Earle Hyman (*Mister Johnson*), Susan Johnson (*The Most Happy Fella*), John Michael King (*My Fair Lady*), Jayne Mansfield (*Will Success Spoil Rock Hunter?*), Sarah Marshall (*The Ponder Heart*), Gaby Rodgers (*Mister Johnson*), Susan Strasberg (*The Diary of Anne Frank*), Fritz Weaver (*The Chalk Garden*)

1956-57: Peggy Cass (*Auntie Mame*), Sydney Chaplin (*Bells Are Ringing*), Sylvia Daneel (*The Tunnel of Love*), Bradford Dillman (*Long Day's Journey Into Night*), Peter Donat (*The First Gentleman*), George Grizzard (*The Happiest Millionaire*), Carol Lynley (*The Potting Shed*), Peter Palmer (*Li'l Abner*), Jason Robards (*Long Day's Journey Into Night*), Cliff Robertson (*Orpheus Descending*), Pippa Scott (*Child of Fortune*), Inga Swenson (*The First Gentleman*)

1957-58: Anne Bancroft (*Two for the Seesaw*), Warren Berlinger (*Blue Denim*), Colleen Dewhurst (*Children of Darkness*), Richard Easton (*The Country Wife*), Tim Everett (*The Dark at the Top of the Stairs*), Eddie Hodges (*The Music Man*), Joan Hovis (*Love Me Little*), Carol Lawrence (*West Side Story*), Jacqueline McKeever (*Oh, Captain!*), Wynne Miller (*Li'l Abner*), Robert Morse (*Say, Darling*), George C. Scott (*Richard III*)

1958-59: Lou Antonio (*The Buffalo Skinner*), Ina Balin (*A Majority of One*), Richard Cross (*Maria Golovin*), Tammy Grimes (*Look After Lulu*), Larry Hagman (*God and Kate Murphy*), Dolores Hart (*The Pleasure of His Company*), Roger Mollien (French Theatre National Populaire), France Nuyen (*The World of Suzie Wong*), Susan Oliver (*Patate*), Ben Piazza (*Kataki*), Paul Roebling (*A Desert Incident*), William Shatner (*The World of Suzie Wong*), Pat Suzuki (*Flower Drum Song*), Rip Torn (*Sweet Bird of Youth*)

1959-60: Warren Beatty (*A Loss of Roses*), Eileen Brennan (*Little Mary Sunshine*), Carol Burnett (*Once Upon a Mattress*), Patty Duke (*The Miracle*

1953 - Paul Newman, Jay Greenberg, Theatre World founder Daniel Blum, Ray Stricklyn, Peter Kelley, Johnny Steward, Eileen Heckart, Edith Adams, Geraldine Page, Richard Kiley

1957 - Top to Bottom: Jay Greenberg, Geraldine Page, Theatre World founder Daniel Blum, Bradford Dillman, Peter Palmer, Cliff Robertson, George Grizzard, Sydney Chaplin, Peter Donat, Jason Robards, Peggy Cass, Pippa Scott, Sylvia Daneel, Inga Swenson, Carol Lynley

Worker), Jane Fonda (*There Was a Little Girl*), Anita Gillette (*Russell Patterson's Sketchbook*), Elisa Loti (*Come Share My House*), Donald Madden (*Julius Caesar*), George Maharis (*The Zoo Story*), John McMartin (*Little Mary Sunshine*), Lauri Peters (*The Sound of Music*), Dick Van Dyke (*The Boys Against the Girls*)

1960-61: Joyce Bulifant (*Whisper to Me*), Dennis Cooney (*Every Other Evil*), Sandy Dennis (*Face of a Hero*), Nancy Dussault (*Do Re Mi*), Robert Goulet (*Camelot*), Joan Hackett (*Call Me By My Rightful Name*), June Harding (*Cry of the Raindrop*), Ron Husmann (*Tenderloin*), James MacArthur (*Invitation to a March*), Bruce Yarnell (*The Happiest Girl in the World*)

1961-62: Elizabeth Ashley (*Take Her, She's Mine*), Keith Baxter (*A Man for All Seasons*), Peter Fonda (*Blood, Sweat and Stanley Poole*), Don Galloway (*Bring Me a Warm Body*), Sean Garrison (*Half-Past Wednesday*), Barbara Harris (*Oh, Dad, Poor Dad, Mamma's Hung You in the Closet and I'm Feeling So Sad*), James Earl Jones (*Moon on a Rainbow Shawl*), Janet Margolin (*Daughter of Silence*), Karen Morrow (*Sing, Muse!*), Robert Redford (*Sunday in New York*), John Stride (*Romeo and Juliet*), Brenda Vaccaro (*Everybody Loves Opal*)

1962-63: Alan Arkin (*Enter Laughing*), Stuart Damon (*The Boys from Syracuse*), Melinda Dillon (*Who's Afraid of Virginia Woolf?*), Robert Drivas (*Mrs. Dally Has a Lover*), Bob Gentry (*Angels of Anadarko*), Dorothy Loudon (*Nowhere to Go But Up*), Brandon Maggart (*Put It in Writing*), Julienne Marie (*The Boys from Syracuse*), Liza Minnelli (*Best Foot Forward*), Estelle Parsons (*Mrs. Dally Has a Lover*), Diana Sands (*Tiger Tiger Burning Bright*), Swen Swenson (*Little Me*)

1963-64: Alan Alda (*Fair Game for Lover*), Gloria Bleezarde (*Never Live Over a Pretzel Factory*), Imelda De Martin (*The Amorous Flea*), Claude Giraud (*Phèdre*), Ketty Lester (*Cabin in the Sky*), Barbara Loden (*After the Fall*), Lawrence Pressman

(*Never Live Over a Pretzel Factory*), Gilbert Price (*Jerico-Jim Crow*), Philip Proctor (*The Amorous Flea*), John Tracy (*Telemachus Clay*), Jennifer West (*Dutchman*)

1964-65: Carolyn Coates (*The Trojan Women*), Joyce Jillson (*The Roar of the Greasepaint – The Smell of the Crowd*), Linda Lavin (*Wet Paint*), Luba Lisa (*I Had a Ball*), Michael O'Sullivan (*Tartuffe*), Joanna Pettet (*Poor Richard*), Beah Richards (*The Amen Corner*), Jaime Sanchez (*Conerico Was Here to Stay* and *The Toilet*), Victor Spinetti (*Oh, What a Lovely War*), Nicolas Surovy (*Helen*), Robert Walker (*I Knock at the Door* and *Pictures in the Hallway*), Clarence Williams III (*Slow Dancing on the Killing Ground_*

1965-66: Zoe Caldwell (*Slapstick Tragedy*), David Carradine (*The Royal Hunt of the Sun*), John Cullum (*On a Clear Day You Can See Forever*), John Davidson (*Oklahoma!*), Faye Dunaway (*Hogan's Ghost*), Gloria Foster (*Medea*), Robert Hooks (*Where's Daddy?* and *Day of Absence*), Jerry Lanning (*Mame*), Richard Mulligan (*Mating Dance* and *Hogan's Ghost*), April Shawhan (*3 Bags Full*), Sandra Smith (*Any Wednesday*), Lesley Ann Warren (*Drat! The Cat!*)

1966-67: Bonnie Bedelia (*My Sweet Charlie*), Richard Benjamin (*The Star-Spangled Girl*), Dustin Hoffman (*Eh?*), Terry Kiser (*Fortune and Men's Eyes*), Reva Rose (*You're A Good Man, Charlie Brown*), Robert Salvio (*Hamp*), Sheila Smith (*Mame*), Connie Stevens (*The Star-Spangled Girl*), Pamela Tiffin (*Dinner at Eight*), Leslie Uggams (*Hallelujah, Baby!*), Jon Voight (*That Summer – That Fall*), Christopher Walken (*The Rose Tattoo*)

1967-68: David Birney (*Summertree*), Pamela Burrell (*Arms and the Man*), Jordan Christopher (*Black Comedy*), Jack Crowder – a.k.a. Thalmus Rasulala (*Hello, Dolly!*), Sandy Duncan (*Ceremony of Innocence*), Julie Gregg (*The Happy Time*), Stephen Joyce (*Stephen D.*), Bernadette Peters (*George M*), Alice Playten (*Henry, Sweet Henry*), Michael Rupert (*The Happy Time*), Brenda Smiley (*Scuba Duba*), Russ Thacker (*Your Own Thing*)

1968-69: Jane Alexander (*The Great White Hope*), David Cryer (*Come Summer*), Blythe Danner (*The Miser*), Ed Evanko (*Canterbury Tales*), Ken Howard (*1776*), Lauren Jones (*Does a Tiger Wear a Necktie?*), Ron Leibman (*We Bombed in New Haven*), Marian Mercer (*Promises, Promises*), Jill O'Hara (*Promises, Promises*), Ron O'Neal (*No Place to Be Somebody*), Al Pacino (*Does a Tiger Wear a Necktie?*), Marlene Warfield (*The Great White Hope*)

1969-70: Susan Browning (*Company*), Donny Burks (*Billy Noname*), Catherine Burns (*Dear Janet Rosenberg, Dear Mr. Kooning*), Len Cariou (*Henry V* and *Applause*), Bonnie Franklin (*Applause*), David Holliday (*Coco*), Katharine Houghton (*A Scent of Flowers*), Melba Moore (*Purlie*), David Rounds (*Child's Play*), Lewis J. Stadlen (*Minnie's Boys*), Kristoffer Tabori (*How Much, How Much*), Fredricka Weber (*The Last Sweet Days of Isaac*)

1974 - Glynis Johns, Ralph Carter, and John Willis

1963 - Carol Channing presents to Dorothy Loudon

1970-71: Clifton Davis (*Do It Again*), Michael Douglas (*Pinkville*), Julie Garfield (*Uncle Vanya*), Martha Henry (*The Playboy of the Western World, Scenes From American Life*, and *Antigone*), James Naughton (*Long Days Journey Into Night*), Tricia O'Neil (*Two by Two*), Kipp Osborne (*Butterflies Are Free*), Roger Rathburn (*No, No, Nanette*), Ayn Ruymen (*The Gingerbread Lady*), Jennifer Salt (*Father's Day*), Joan Van Ark (*School for Wives*), Walter Willison (*Two by Two*)

1971-72: Jonelle Allen (*Two Gentlemen of Verona*), Maureen Anderman (*Moonchildren*), William Atherton (*Suggs*), Richard Backus (*Promenade, All!*), Adrienne Barbeau (*Grease*), Cara Duff-MacCormick (*Moonchildren*), Robert Foxworth (*The Crucible*), Elaine Joyce (*Sugar*), Jess Richards (*On The Town*), Ben Vereen (*Jesus Christ Superstar*), Beatrice Winde (*Ain't Supposed to Die a Natural Death*), James Woods (*Moonchildren*)

1972-73: D'Jamin Bartlett (*A Little Night Music*), Patricia Elliott (*A Little Night Music*), James Farentino (*A Streetcar Named Desire*), Brian Farrell (*The Last of Mrs. Lincoln*), Victor Garber (*Ghosts*), Kelly Garrett (*Mother Earth*), Mari Gorman (*The Hot l Baltimore*), Laurence Guittard (*A Little Night Music*), Trish Hawkins (*The Hot l Baltimore*), Monte Markham (*Irene*), John Rubinstein (*Pippin*), Jennifer Warren (*6 Rms Riv Vu*), Alexander H. Cohen (Special Award)

1973-74: Mark Baker (*Candide*), Maureen Brennan (*Candide*), Ralph Carter (*Raisin*), Thom Christopher (*Noel Coward in Two Keys*), John Driver (*Over Here*), Conchata Ferrell (*The Sea Horse*), Ernestine Jackson (*Raisin*), Michael Moriarty (*Find Your Way Home*), Joe Morton (*Raisin*), Ann Reinking (*Over Here*), Janie Sell (*Over Here*), Mary Woronov (*Boom Boom Room*), Sammy Cahn (Special Award)

1974-75: Peter Burnell (*In Praise of Love*), Zan Charisse (*Gypsy*), Lola Falana (*Dr. Jazz*), Peter Firth (*Equus*), Dorian Harewood (*Don't Call Back*), Joel Higgins (*Shenandoah*), Marcia McClain (*Where's Charley?*), Linda Miller (*Black Picture Show*), Marti Rolph (*Good News*), John Sheridan (*Gypsy*), Scott Stevensen (*Good News*), Donna Theodore (*Shenandoah*), Equity Library Theatre (Special Award)

1975-76: Danny Aiello (*Lamppost Reunion*), Christine Andreas (*My Fair Lady*), Dixie Carter (*Jesse and the Bandit Queen*), Tovah Feldshuh (*Yentl*), Chip Garnett (*Bubbling Brown Sugar*), Richard Kelton (*Who's Afraid of Virginia Woolf?*), Vivian Reed (*Bubbling Brown Sugar*), Charles Repole (*Very Good Eddie*), Virginia Seidel (*Very Good Eddie*), Daniel Seltzer (*Knock Knock*), John V. Shea (*Yentl*), Meryl Streep (*27 Wagons Full of Cotton*), The Cast of *A Chorus Line* (Special Award)

1976-77: Trazana Beverley (*for colored girls…*), Michael Cristofer (*The Cherry Orchard*), Joe Fields (*The Basic Training of Pavlo Hummel*), Joanna Gleason (*I Love My Wife*), Cecilia Hart (*Dirty Linen*), John Heard (*G.R. Point*), Gloria Hodes (*The Club*), Juliette Koka (*Piaf…A Remembrance*), Andrea McArdle (*Annie*), Ken Page (*Guys and Dolls*), Jonathan Pryce (*Comedians*), Chick Vennera (*Jockeys*), Eva LeGallienne (Special Award)

1977-78: Vasili Bogazianos (*P.S. Your Cat Is Dead*), Nell Carter (*Ain't Misbehavin'*), Carlin Glynn (*The Best Little Whorehouse in Texas*), Christopher Goutman (*The Promise*), William Hurt (*Ulysses in Traction, Lulu,* and *The Fifth of July*), Judy Kaye (*On the 20th Century*), Florence Lacy (*Hello, Dolly!*), Armelia McQueen (*Ain't Misbehavin'*), Gordana Rashovich (*Fefu and Her Friends*), Bo Rucker (*Native Son*), Richard Seer (*Da*), Colin Stinton (*The Water Engine*), Joseph Papp (Special Award)

1978-79: Philip Anglim (*The Elephant Man*), Lucie Arnaz (*They're Playing Our Song*), Gregory Hines (*Eubie!*), Ken Jennings (*Sweeney Todd*), Michael Jeter (*G.R. Point*), Laurie Kennedy (*Man and Superman*), Susan Kingsley (*Getting Out*), Christine Lahti (*The Woods*), Edward James Olmos (*Zoot Suit*), Kathleen Quinlan (*Taken in Marriage*), Sarah Rice (*Sweeney Todd*), Max Wright (*Once in a Lifetime*), Marshall W. Mason (Special Award)

1979-80: Maxwell Caulfield (*Class Enemy*), Leslie Denniston (*Happy New Year*), Boyd Gaines (*A Month in the Country*), Richard Gere (*Bent*), Harry Groener (*Oklahoma!*), Stephen James (*The 1940's Radio Hour*), Susan Kellermann (*Last Licks*), Dinah Manoff (*I Ought to Be in Pictures*), Lonny Price (*Class Enemy*), Marianne Tatum (*Barnum*), Anne Twomey (*Nuts*), Dianne Wiest (*The Art of Dining*), Mickey Rooney (*Sugar Babies* – Special Award)

1980-81: Brian Backer (*The Floating Light Bulb*), Lisa Banes (*Look Back in Anger*), Meg Bussert (*The Music Man*), Michael Allen Davis (*Broadway Follies*), Giancarlo Esposito (*Zooman and the Sign*), Daniel Gerroll (*Slab Boys*), Phyllis Hyman (*Sophisticated Ladies*), Cynthia Nixon (*The Philadelphia Story*), Amanda Plummer (*A Taste of Honey*), Adam Redfield (*A Life*), Wanda Richert (*42nd Street*), Rex Smith (*The Pirates of Penzance*), Elizabeth Taylor (*The Little Foxes* – Special Award)

1981-82: Karen Akers (*Nine*), Laurie Beechman (*Joseph and the Amazing Technicolor Dreamcoat*), Danny Glover (*Master Harold…and the Boys*), David Alan Grier (*The First*), Jennifer Holliday (*Dreamgirls*), Anthony Heald (*Misalliance*), Lizbeth Mackay (*Crimes of the Heart*), Peter MacNicol (*Crimes of the Heart*), Elizabeth McGovern (*My Sister in This House*), Ann Morrison (*Merrily We Roll Along*), Michael O'Keefe (*Mass Appeal*), James Widdoes (*Is There Life After High School?*), Manhattan Theatre Club (Special Award)

1982-83: Karen Allen (*Monday After the Miracle*), Suzanne Bertish (*Skirmishes*), Matthew Broderick (*Brighton Beach Memoirs*), Kate Burton (*Winners*), Joanne Camp (*Geniuses*), Harvey Fierstein (*Torch Song Trilogy*), Peter Gallagher (*A Doll's Life*), John Malkovich (*True West*), Anne Pitoniak (*'Night Mother*), James Russo (*Extremities*), Brian Tarantina (*Angels Fall*), Linda Thorson (*Streaming*), Natalia Makarova (*On Your Toes* – Special Award)

1977 Winner Michael Cristofer receives his award from Estelle Parsons (1963)

Kate Burton (1983) receives her award from her father, Richard Burton (1951)

1983-84: Martine Allard (*The Tap Dance Kid*), Joan Allen (*And a Nightingale Sang*), Kathy Whitton Baker (*Fool For Love*), Mark Capri (*On Approval*), Laura Dean (*Doonesbury*), Stephen Geoffreys (*The Human Comedy*), Todd Graff (*Baby*), Glenne Headly (*The Philanthropist*), J.J. Johnston (*American Buffalo*), Bonnie Koloc (*The Human Comedy*), Calvin Levels (*Open Admissions*), Robert Westenberg (*Zorba*), Ron Moody (*Oliver* – Special Award)

1984-85: Kevin Anderson (*Orphans*), Richard Chaves (*Tracers*), Patti Cohenour (*La Boheme* and *Big River*), Charles S. Dutton (*Ma Rainey's Black Bottom*), Nancy Giles (*Mayor*), Whoopi Goldberg (*Whoopi Goldberg*), Leilani Jones (*Grind*), John Mahoney (*Orphans*), Laurie Metcalf (*Balm in Gilead*), Barry Miller (*Biloxi Blues*), John Turturro (*Danny and the Deep Blue Sea*), Amelia White (*The Accrington Pals*), Lucille Lortel (Special Award)

1985-86: Suzy Amis (*Fresh Horses*), Alec Baldwin (*Loot*), Aled Davies (*Orchards*), Faye Grant (*Singin' in the Rain*), Julie Hagerty (*The House of Blue Leaves*), Ed Harris (*Precious Sons*), Mark Jacoby (*Sweet Charity*), Donna Kane (*Dames at Sea*), Cleo Laine (*The Mystery of Edwin Drood*), Howard McGillin (*The Mystery of Edwin Drood*), Marisa Tomei (*Daughters*), Joe Urla (*Principia Scriptoriae*), Ensemble Studio Theatre (Special Award)

1986-87: Annette Bening (*Coastal Disturbances*), Timothy Daly (*Coastal Disturbances*), Lindsay Duncan (*Les Liaisons Dangereuses*), Frank Ferrante (*Groucho: A Life in Revue*), Robert Lindsay (*Me and My Girl*), Amy Madigan (*The Lucky Spot*), Michael Maguire (*Les Misérables*), Demi Moore (*The Early Girl*), Molly Ringwald (*Lily Dale*), Frances Ruffelle (*Les Misérables*), Courtney B. Vance (*Fences*), Colm Wilkinson (*Les Misérables*), Robert DeNiro (Special Award)

1987-88: Yvonne Bryceland (*The Road to Mecca*), Philip Casnoff (*Chess*), Danielle Ferland (*Into the Woods*), Melissa Gilbert (*A Shayna Maidel*), Linda Hart (*Anything Goes*), Linzi Hateley (*Carrie*), Brian Kerwin (*Emily*), Brian Mitchell (*Mail*), Mary Murfitt (*Oil City Symphony*), Aidan Quinn *A Streetcar Named Desire*), Eric Roberts (*Burn This*), B.D. Wong (*M. Butterfly*), Tisa Chang and Martin E. Segal (Special Awards)

1988-89: Dylan Baker (*Eastern Standard*), Joan Cusack (*Road* and *Brilliant Traces*), Loren Dean (*Amulets Against the Dragon Forces*), Peter Frechette (*Eastern Standard*), Sally Mayes (*Welcome to the Club*), Sharon McNight (*Starmites*), Jennie Moreau (*Eleemosynary*), Paul Provenza (*Only Kidding*), Kyra Sedgwick (*Ah, Wilderness!*), Howard Spiegel (*Only Kidding*), Eric Stoltz (*Our*

Town), Joanne Whalley-Kilmer (*What the Butler Saw*); Pauline Collins of *Shirley Valentine* (Special Award), Mikhail Baryshnikov (Special Award)

1989-90: Denise Burse (*Ground People*), Erma Campbell (*Ground People*), Rocky Carroll (*The Piano Lesson*), Megan Gallagher (*A Few Good Men*), Tommy Hollis (*The Piano Lesson*), Robert Lambert (*Gypsy*), Kathleen Rowe McAllen (*Aspects of Love*), Michael McKean (*Accomplice*), Crista Moore (*Gypsy*), Mary-Louise Parker (*Prelude to a Kiss*), Daniel von Bargen (*Mastergate*), Jason Workman (*Jason Workman*), Stewart Granger (*The Circle* – Special Award), Kathleen Turner (*Cat on a Hot Tin Roof* – Special Award)

1990-91: Jane Adams (*I Hate Hamlet*), Gillian Anderson (*Absent Friends*), Adam Arkin (*I Hate Hamlet*), Brenda Blethyn (*Absent Friends*), Marcus Chong (*Stand-up Tragedy*), Paul Hipp (*Buddy*), LaChanze (*Once on This Island*), Kenny Neal (*Mule Bone*), Kevin Ramsey (*Oh, Kay!*), Francis Ruivivar (*Shogun*), Lea Salonga (*Miss Saigon*), Chandra Wilson (*The Good Times Are Killing Me*); Tracey Ullman (*The Big Love* and *Taming of the Shrew*), Ellen Stewart (Special Award)

1991-92: Talia Balsam (*Jake's Women*), Lindsay Crouse (*The Homecoming*), Griffin Dunne (*Search and Destroy*), Laurence Fishburne (*Two Trains Running*), Mel Harris (*Empty Hearts*), Jonathan Kaplan (*Falsettos* and *Rags*), Jessica Lange (*A Streetcar Named Desire*), Laura Linney (*Sight Unseen*), Spiro Malas (*The Most Happy Fella*), Mark Rosenthal (*Marvin's Room*), Helen Shaver (*Jake's Women*), Al White (*Two Trains Running*), The Cast of *Dancing at Lughnasa* (Special Award), Plays for Living (Special Award)

1992-93: Brent Carver (*Kiss of the Spider Woman*), Michael Cerveris (*The Who's Tommy*), Marcia Gay Harden (*Angels in America: Millennium Approaches*), Stephanie Lawrence (*Blood Brothers*), Andrea Martin (*My Favorite Year*), Liam Neeson (*Anna Christie*), Stephen Rea (*Someone Who'll Watch Over Me*), Natasha Richardson (*Anna Christie*), Martin Short (*The Goodbye Girl*), Dina Spybey (*Five Women Wearing the Same Dress*), Stephen Spinella (*Angels in America: Millennium Approaches*), Jennifer Tilly (*One Shoe Off*), John Leguizamo and Rosetta LeNoire (Special Awards)

1993-94: Marcus D'Amico (*An Inspector Calls*), Jarrod Emick (*Damn Yankees*), Arabella Field (*Snowing at Delphi* and *4 Dogs and a Bone*), Aden Gillett (*An Inspector Calls*), Sherry Glaser (*Family Secrets*), Michael Hayden (*Carousel*), Margaret Illman (*The Red Shoes*), Audra McDonald (*Carousel*), Burke Moses (*Beauty and the Beast*), Anna Deavere Smith (*Twilight: Los Angeles, 1992*), Jere Shea (*Passion*), Harriet Walter (*3Birds Alighting on a Field*)

1994-95: Gretha Boston (*Show Boat*), Billy Crudup (*Arcadia*), Ralph Fiennes (*Hamlet*), Beverly D'Angelo (*Simpatico*), Calista Flockhart (*The Glass Menagerie*), Kevin Kilner (*The Glass Menagerie*), Anthony LaPaglia (*The Rose Tattoo*), Julie Johnson (*Das Barbecü*), Helen Mirren (*A Month in the Country*), Jude Law (*Indiscretions*), Rufus Sewell (*Translations*), Vanessa Williams (*Kiss of the Spider Woman*), Brooke Shields (Special Award)

1995-96: Jordan Baker (*Suddenly Last Summer*), Joohee Choi (*The King and I*), Karen Kay Cody (*Master Class*), Viola Davis (*Seven Guitars*), Kate Forbes (*The School for Scandal*), Michael McGrath (*Swinging on a Star*), Alfred Molina (*Molly Sweeney*), Timothy Olyphant (*The Monogamist*), Adam Pascal (*Rent*), Lou Diamond Phillips (*The King and I*), Daphne Rubin-Vega (*Rent*), Brett Tabisel (*Big*), The Cast of *An Ideal Husband* (Special Award)

1996-97: Terry Beaver (*The Last Night of Ballyhoo*), Helen Carey (*London Assurance*), Kristin Chenoweth (*Steel Pier*), Jason Danieley (*Candide*), Linda Eder (*Jekyll & Hyde*), Allison Janney (*Present Laughter*), Daniel McDonald (*Steel Pier*), Janet McTeer (*A Doll's House*), Mark Ruffalo (*This Is Our Youth*), Fiona Shaw (*The Waste Land*), Antony Sher (*Stanley*), Alan Tudyk (*Bunny Bunny*), The Cast of *Skylight* (Special Award)

1997-98: Max Casella (*The Lion King*), Margaret Colin (*Jackie*), Ruaidhri Conroy (*The Cripple of Inishmaan*), Alan Cumming (*Cabaret*), Lea Delaria (*On the Town*), Edie Falco (*Side Man*), Enid Graham (*Honour*), Anna Kendrick (*High Society*), Ednita Nazario (*The Capeman*), Douglas Sills (*The Scarlet Pimpernel*), Steven Sutcliffe (*Ragtime*), Sam Trammel (*Ah, Wilderness!*), Eddie Izzard (Special Award), The Cast of *The Beauty Queen of Leenane* (Special Award)

1998-99: Jillian Armenante (*The Cider House Rules*), James Black (*Not About Nightingales*), Brendan Coyle (*The Weir*), Anna Friel (*Closer*), Rupert Graves (*Closer*), Lynda Gravátt (*The Old Settler*), Nicole Kidman (*The Blue Room*), Ciáran Hinds (*Closer*), Ute Lemper (*Chicago*), Clarke Peters (*The Iceman Cometh*), Toby Stephens (*Ring Round the Moon*), Sandra Oh (*Stop Kiss*), Jerry Herman (Special Award)

1999-2000: Craig Bierko (*The Music Man*), Everett Bradley (*Swing!*), Gabriel Byrne (*A Moon for the Misbegotten*), Ann Hampton Callaway (*Swing!*), Toni Collette (*The Wild Party*), Henry Czerny (*Arms and the Man*), Stephen Dillane (*The Real Thing*), Jennifer Ehle (*The Real Thing*), Philip Seymour Hoffman (*True West*), Hayley Mills (*Suite in Two Keys*), Cigdem Onat (*The Time of the Cuckoo*), Claudia Shear (*Dirty Blonde*), Barry Humphries (*Dame Edna: The Royal Tour* – Special Award)

2000-2001: Juliette Binoche (*Betrayal*), Macaulay Culkin (*Madame Melville*), Janie Dee (*Comic Potential*), Raúl Esparza (*The Rocky Horror Show*), Kathleen Freeman (*The Full Monty*), Deven May (*Bat Boy*), Reba McEntire (*Annie Get Your Gun*), Chris Noth (*The Best Man*), Joshua Park (*The Adventures of Tom Sawyer*), Rosie Perez (*References to Salvador Dali Make Me Hot*), Joely Richardson (*Madame Melville*), John Ritter (*The Dinner Party*), The Cast of *Stones in His Pocket* – Seán Campion & Conleth Hill (Special Awards)

2001-2002: Justin Bohon (*Oklahoma!*), Simon Callow (*The Mystery of Charles Dickens*), Mos Def (*Topdog/Underdog*), Emma Fielding (*Private Lives*), Adam Godley (*Private Lives*), Martin Jarvis (*By Jeeves*), Spencer Kayden (*Urinetown*), Gretchen Mol (*The Shape of Things*), Anna Paquin (*The Glory of Living*), Louise Pitre (*Mamma Mia!*), David Warner (*Major Barbara*), Rachel Weisz (*The Shape of Things*)

2002-2003: Antonio Banderas (*Nine*), Tammy Blanchard (*Gypsy*), Thomas Jefferson Byrd (*Ma Rainey's Black Bottom*), Jonathan Cake (*Medea*), Victoria Hamilton (*A Day in the Death of Joe Egg*), Clare Higgins (*Vincent in Brixton*), Jackie Hoffman (*Hairspray*), Mary Stuart Masterson (*Nine*), John Selya (*Movin' Out*), Daniel Sunjata (*Take Me Out*), Jochum ten Haaf (*Vincent in Brixton*), Marissa Jaret Winokur (*Hairspray*), Peter Filichia and Ben Hodges (Special Awards)

2003-2004: Shannon Cochran (*Bug*), Stephanie D'Abruzzo (*Avenue Q*), Mitchel David Federan (*The Boy From Oz*), Alexander Gemignani (*Assassins*), Hugh Jackman (*The Boy From Oz*), Isabel Keating (*The Boy From Oz*), Sanaa Lathan (*A Raisin in the Sun*), Jefferson Mays (*I Am My Own Wife*), Euan Morton (*Taboo*), Anika Noni Rose (*Caroline, or Change*), John Tartaglia (*Avenue Q*), Jennifer Westfeldt (*Wonderful Town*), Sarah Jones (*Bridge and Tunnel* – Special Award)

2004-2005: Christina Applegate (*Sweet Charity*), Ashlie Atkinson (*Fat Pig*), Hank Azaria (*Spamalot*), Gordon Clapp (*Glengarry Glen Ross*), Conor Donovan (*Privilege*), Dan Fogler (*The 25th Annual Putnam County Spelling Bee*), Heather Goldenhersh (*Doubt*), Carla Gugino (*After the Fall*), Jenn Harris (*Modern Orthodox*), Cheyenne Jackson (*All Shook Up*), Celia Keenan-Bolger (*The 25th Annual Putnam County Spelling Bee*), Tyler Maynard (*Altar Boyz*)

2005-2006: Harry Connick Jr. (*The Pajama Game*), Felicia P. Fields (*The Color Purple*), Maria Friedman (*The Woman in White*), Mamie Gummer (*Mr. Marmalade*), Jayne Houdyshell (*Well*), Bob Martin (*The Drowsy Chaperone*), Ian McDiarmid (*Faith Healer*), Nellie McKay (*The Threepenny Opera*), David Wilmot (*The Lieutenant of Inishmore*), Elisabeth Withers-Mendes (*The Color Purple*), John Lloyd Young (*Jersey Boys*)

2006–2007: Eve Best (*A Moon for the Misbegotten*), Mary Birdsong (*Martin Short: Fame Becomes Me*), Erin Davie (*Grey Gardens*), Xanthe Elbrick (*Coram Boy*), Fantasia (*The Color Purple*), Johnny Galecki (*The Little Dog Laughed*), Jonathan Groff (*Spring Awakening*), Gavin Lee (*Mary Poppins*), Lin-Manuel Miranda (*In the Heights*), Bill Nighy (*The Vertical Hour*), Stark Sands (*Journey's End*), Nilaja Sun (*No Child…*), The Actors Fund (Special Award)

2007–2008: de'Adre Aziza (*Passing Strange*), Cassie Beck (*The Drunken City*), Daniel Breaker (*Passing Strange*), Ben Daniels (*Les Liaisons Dangereuses*), Deanna Dunagan (*August: Osage County*), Hoon Lee (*Yellow Face*), Alli Mauzey (*Cry-Baby*), Jenna Russell (*Sunday in the Park with George*), Mark Rylance (*Boeing-Boeing*), Loretta Ables Sayre (*South Pacific*), Jimmi Simpson (*The Farnsworth Invention*), Paulo Szot (*South Pacific*)

2008–2009: David Alvarez (*Billy Elliot The Musical*), Chad L. Coleman (*Joe Turner's Come and Gone*), Jennifer Grace (*Our Town*), Josh Grisetti (*Enter Laughing The Musical*), Haydn Gwynne *Billy Elliot The Musical*), Colin Hanks (*33 Variations*), Marin Ireland (*reasons to be pretty*), Trent Kowalik (*Billy Elliot The Musical*), Kiril Kulish (*Billy Elliot The Musical*), Susan Louise O'Connor (*Blithe Spirit*), Condola Rashad (*Ruined*), Geoffrey Rush (*Exit the King*), Josefina Scaglione (*West Side Story*), Wesley Taylor (*Rock of Ages*); The Cast of *The Norman Conquests* (Special Award)

Michael McKean (1990)

Viola Davis (1996)

Major New York Theatrical Awards

AMERICAN THEATRE WING'S ANTOINETTE PERRY "TONY" AWARDS

Sunday, June 13, 2010 at Radio City Music Hall; 64th annual; Host: Sean Hayes. Presented for distinguished achievement in the Broadway theatre by The American Theatre Wing (Theodore S. Chapin, Chairman; Howard Sherman, Executive Director) and The Broadway League (Nina Lannan, Chairman; Charlotte St. Martin, Executive Director); Tony Awards Production General Managers, Alan Wasser and Allen Williams; Executive Producers, Ricky Kirshner and Glenn Weiss/ White Cherry Entertainment; 2009–2010 Tony Awards Nominating Committee (appointed by the Tony Awards Administration Committee): David Caddick (Music Supervisor), Ben Cameron (Program Director for the Arts, Doris Duke Charitable Foundation), Kathleen Chalfant (Actor), Hope Clarke (Stage Director/ Choreographer/Actor), Thomas Cott (Marketing Director, Alvin Ailey Dance Company), Jacqueline Z. Davis (Executive Director, The NY Public Library for the Performing Arts at Lincoln Center), Michael D. Dinwiddie (Associate Professor, Gallatin School of Individualized Study, New York University), Edgar Dobie (Managing Director, Arena Stage Washington, DC), Teresa Eyring (Executive Director, Theatre Communications Group), Paulette Haupt (Director of the Music Theatre Conference at the O'Neill Theater Center), Elena K. Holy (Founder, The International Fringe Festival), Geoffrey Johnson (Casting Director [retired]), Robert Kamlot (General Manager [retired]), Michael Kantor (Television Director/ Producer/Writer), Robert Kimball (Author), Pia Lindstrom (Arts Reporter), Howard Marren (Composer), Laurence Maslon (Associate Arts Professor, Graduate Acting Program, Tisch School of the Arts, New York), Donna McKechnie (Actor/ Choreographer), Jon Nakagawa (Producer, Contemporary Programming (Lincoln Center for the Performing Arts, Inc.), Alice Playten (Actor), Theresa Rebeck (Playwright), Donald Saddler (Choreographer), Susan H. Schulman (Director), Tamara Tunie (Actor), William Tynan (Actor/Reporter [retired]), Kimberlee Wertz (Music Contractor), Doug Wright (Playwright/Screenwriter), Andrew Zerman (Casting Director [retired])

Best Play: *Red* by John Logan, Produced by Arielle Tepper Madover, Stephanie P. McClelland, Matthew Byam Shaw, Neal Street, Fox Theatricals, Ruth Hendel/ Barbara Whitman, Philip Hagemann/Murray Rosenthal, The Donmar Warehouse

Nominees: *In the Next Room or the vibrator play* by Sarah Ruhl, Produced by Lincoln Center Theater, André Bishop, Bernard Gersten; *Next Fall* by Geoffrey Nauffts, Produced by Elton John and David Furnish, Barbara Manocherian, Richard Willis, Tom Smedes, Carole L. Haber/Chase Mishkin, Ostar, Anthony Barrile, Michael Palitz, Bob Boyett, James Spry/Catherine Schreiber, Probo Productions, Roy Furman, Naked Angels; *Time Stands Still* by Donald Margulies, Produced by Manhattan Theatre Club, Lynne Meadow, Barry Grove, Nelle Nugent/ Wendy Federman

Best Musical: *Memphis* Produced by Junkyard Dog Productions, Barbara and Buddy Freitag, Marleen and Kenny Alhadeff, Latitude Link, Jim and Susan Blair, Demos Bizar Entertainment, Land Line Productions, Apples and Oranges Productions, Dave Copley, Dancap Productions Inc., Alex and Katya Lukianov, Tony Ponturo, 2 Guys Productions, Richard Winkler, Lauren Doll, Eric and Marsi Gardiner, Linda and Bill Potter, Broadway Across America, Jocko Productions, Patty Baker, Dan Frishwasser, Bob Bartner/Scott and Kaylin Union, Loraine Boyle/ Chase Mishkin, Remmel T. Dickinson/Memphis Orpheum Group, ShadowCatcher Entertainment/Vijay and Sita Vashee

Nominees: *American Idiot* Produced by Tom Hulce & Ira Pittelman, Ruth and Steven Hendel, Vivek J. Tiwary and Gary Kaplan, Aged in Wood and Burnt Umber, Scott Delman, Latitude Link, HOP Theatricals and Jeffrey Finn, Larry Welk, Bensinger Filerman and Moellenberg Taylor, Allan S. Gordon/Elan V. McAllister, Berkeley Repertory Theatre, Awaken Entertainment, John Pinckard and John Domo; *Fela!* Produced by Shawn "Jay-Z" Carter and Will Smith & Jada Pinkett Smith, Ruth & Stephen Hendel, Roy Gabay, Sony Pictures Entertainment, Edward Tyler Nahem, Slava Smolokowski, Chip Meyrelles/Ken Greiner, Douglas G. Smith, Steve Semlitz/Cathy Glaser, Daryl Roth/True Love Productions, Susan

Dietz/Mort Swinsky, Knitting Factory Entertainment, Alicia Keys; *Million Dollar Quartet* Produced by Relevant Theatricals, John Cossette Productions, American Pop Anthology, Broadway Across America, James L. Nederlander

Best Book of a Musical: *Memphis* by Joe DiPietro

Nominees: *Everyday Rapture* by Dick Scanlan and Sherie Rene Scott; *Fela!* by Jim Lewis & Bill T. Jones; *Million Dollar Quartet* by Colin Escott and Floyd Mutrux

Best Original Score (music and/or lyrics) Written for the Theatre: *Memphis* Music by David Bryan, Lyrics by Joe DiPietro, David Bryan

Nominees: *The Addams Family* Music & Lyrics by Andrew Lippa; *Enron* Music by Adam Cork, Lyrics by Lucy Prebble; *Fences* Music by Branford Marsalis

Best Revival of a Play: *Fences* by August Wilson, Produced by Carole Shorenstein Hays and Scott Rudin

Nominees: *Lend Me a Tenor* by Ken Ludwig, Produced by The Araca Group, Stuart Thompson, Carl Moellenberg, Rodney Rigby, Olympus Theatricals, Broadway Across America, The Shubert Organization, Wendy Federman/Jamie deRoy/Richard Winkler, Lisa Cartwright, Spring Sirkin, Scott and Brian Zeilinger; *The Royal Family* by George S. Kaufman and Edna Ferber, Produced by Manhattan Theatre Club, Lynne Meadow, Barry Grove; *A View from the Bridge* by Arthur Miller, Produced by Stuart Thompson, The Araca Group, Jeffrey Finn, Broadway Across America, Olympus Theatricals, Marisa Sechrest, The Weinstein Company, Jon B. Platt, Sonia Friedman Productions/Robert G. Bartner, Mort Swinsky/ Joseph Deitch, Adam Zotovich/Ruth Hendel/Orin Wolf, Shelter Island Enterprises, The Shubert Organization

Best Revival of a Musical: *La Cage aux Folles* Produced by Sonia Friedman Productions, David Babani, Barry and Fran Weissler and Edwin W. Schloss, Bob Bartner/Norman Tulchin, Broadway Across America, Matthew Mitchell, Raise The Roof 4 Richard Winkler/Bensinger Taylor/Laudenslager Bergrère, Arelene Scanlan/John O'Boyle, Independent Presenters Network, Olympus Theatricals, Allen Spivak, Jerry Frankel/Bat-Barry Productions, Nederlander Presentations, Inc/Harvey Weinstein, Menier Chocolate Factory

Nominees: *Finian's Rainbow* Produced by David Richenthal, Jack Viertel, Alan D. Marks, Michael Speyer, Bernard Abrams, David M. Milch, Stephen Moore, Debbie Bisno/Myla Lerner, Jujamcyn Theaters, Melly Garcia, Jamie deRoy, Jon Bierman, Richard Driehaus, Kevin Spirtas, Jay Binder, StageVentures 2009 Limited Partnership; *A Little Night Music* Produced by Tom Viertel, Steven Baruch, Marc Routh, Richard Frankel, The Menier Chocolate Factory, Roger Berlind, David Babani, Sonia Friedman Productions, Andrew Fell, Daryl Roth/ Jane Bergere, Harvey Weinstein/Raise the Roof 3, Beverly Bartner/Dancap Productions, Inc., Nica Burns/Max Weitzenhoffer, Eric Falkenstein/Anna Czekaj, Jerry Frankel/Ronald Frankel, James D. Stern/Douglas L. Meyer; *Ragtime* Produced by Kevin McCollum, Roy Furman, Scott Delman, Roger Berlind, Max Cooper, Tom Kirdahy/Devin Elliott, Jeffrey A. Sine, Stephanie P. McClelland, Roy Miller, Lams Productions, Jana Robbins, Sharon Karmazin, Eric Falkenstein/ Morris Berchard, RialtoGals Productions, Independent Presenters Network, Held-Haffner Productions, HRH Foundation, Emanuel Azenberg, The John F. Kennedy Center for the Performing Arts, Michael Kaiser, Max Woodward

Best Performance by a Leading Actor in a Play: Denzel Washington, *Fences*

Nominees: Jude Law, *Hamlet*; Alfred Molina, *Red*; Liev Schreiber, *A View from the Bridge*; Christopher Walken, *A Behanding in Spokane*

Best Performance by a Leading Actress in a Play: Viola Davis, *Fences*

Nominees: Valerie Harper, *Looped*; Linda Lavin, *Collected Stories*; Laura Linney, *Time Stands Still*; Jan Maxwell, *The Royal Family*

Best Performance by a Leading Actor in a Musical: Douglas Hodge, *La Cage aux Folles*

Nominees: Kelsey Grammer, *La Cage aux Folles*; Sean Hayes, *Promises, Promises*; Chad Kimball, *Memphis*; Sahr Ngaujah, *Fela!*

Best Performance by a Leading Actress in a Musical: Catherine Zeta-Jones, *A Little Night Music*

Nominees: Kate Baldwin, *Finian's Rainbow*; Montego Glover, *Memphis*; Christiane Noll, *Ragtime*; Sherie Rene Scott, *Everyday Rapture*

Best Performance by a Featured Actor in a Play: Eddie Redmayne, *Red*

Nominees: David Alan Grier, *Race*; Stephen McKinley Henderson, *Fences*; Jon Michael Hill, *Superior Donuts*; Stephen Kunken, *Enron*

Best Performance by a Featured Actress in a Play: Scarlett Johansson, *A View from the Bridge*

Nominees: Maria Dizzia, *In the Next Room or the vibrator play*; Rosemary Harris, *The Royal Family*; Jessica Hecht, *A View from the Bridge*; Jan Maxwell, *Lend Me a Tenor*

Best Performance by a Featured Actor in a Musical: Levi Kreis, *Million Dollar Quartet*

Nominees: Kevin Chamberlin, *The Addams Family*; Robin De Jesús, *La Cage aux Folles*; Christopher Fitzgerald, *Finian's Rainbow*; Bobby Steggert, *Ragtime*

Best Performance by a Featured Actress in a Musical: Katie Finneran, *Promises, Promises*

Nominees: Barbara Cook, *Sondheim on Sondheim*; Angela Lansbury, *A Little Night Music*; Karine Plantadit, *Come Fly Away*; Lillias White, *Fela!*

Best Scenic Design of a Play: Christopher Oram, *Red*

Nominees: John Lee Beatty, *The Royal Family*; Alexander Dodge, *Present Laughter*; Santo Loquasto, *Fences*

Best Scenic Design of a Musical: Christine Jones, *American Idiot*

Nominees: Marina Draghici, *Fela!*; Derek McLane, *Ragtime*; Tim Shortall, *La Cage aux Folles*

Best Costume Design of a Play: Catherine Zuber, *The Royal Family*

Nominees: Martin Pakledinaz, *Lend Me a Tenor*; Constanza Romero, *Fences*; David Zinn, *In the Next Room or the vibrator play*

Best Costume Design of a Musical: Marina Draghici, *Fela!*

Nominees: Paul Tazewell, *Memphis*; Matthew Wright, *La Cage aux Folles*

Best Lighting Design of a Play: Neil Austin, *Red*

Nominees: Neil Austin, *Hamlet*; Mark Henderson, *Enron*; Brian MacDevitt, *Fences*

Best Lighting Design of a Musical: Kevin Adams, *American Idiot*

Nominees: Donald Holder, *Ragtime*; Nick Richings, *La Cage aux Folles*; Robert Wierzel, *Fela!*

Best Sound Design of a Play: Adam Cork, *Red*

Nominees: Acme Sound Partners, *Fences*; Adam Cork, *Enron*; Scott Lehrer, *A View from the Bridge*

Best Sound Design of a Musical: Robert Kaplowitz, *Fela!*

Nominees: Jonathan Deans, *La Cage aux Folles*; Dan Moses Schreier and Gareth Owen, *A Little Night Music*; Dan Moses Schreier, *Sondheim on Sondheim*

Best Direction of a Play: Michael Grandage, *Red*

Nominees: Sheryl Kaller, *Next Fall*; Kenny Leon, *Fences*; Gregory Mosher, *A View from the Bridge*

Best Direction of a Musical: Terry Johnson, *La Cage aux Folles*

Nominees: Christopher Ashley, *Memphis*; Marcia Milgrom Dodge, *Ragtime*; Bill T. Jones, *Fela!*

Best Choreography: Bill T. Jones, *Fela!*

Nominees: Rob Ashford, *Promises, Promises*; Lynne Page, *La Cage aux Folles*; Twyla Tharp, *Come Fly Away*

Best Orchestrations: Daryl Waters & David Bryan, *Memphis*

Nominees: Jason Carr, *La Cage aux Folles*; Aaron Johnson, *Fela!*; Jonathan Tunick, *Promises, Promises*

Special Tony Award for Lifetime Achievement in the Theatre: Alan Ayckbourn, Marian Seldes

Regional Theatre Tony Award: The Eugene O'Neill Theater Center, Waterford, Connecticut

Isabelle Stevenson Award for Service: David Hyde Pierce

Tony Honor for Excellence in the Theatre: Alliance of Resident Theatres/New York; B.H. Barry; Tom Viola; Midtown North and South New York City Police Precincts

PAST TONY AWARD-WINNING PRODUCTIONS Awards listed are Best Play followed by Best Musical, and, as awards for Best Revival and the subcategories of Best Revival of a Play and Best Revival of a Musical were instituted, they are listed respectively.

1947: No award given for musical or play **1948:** *Mister Roberts* (play) **1949:** *Death of a Salesman*; *Kiss Me, Kate* (musical) **1950:** *The Cocktail Party*; *South Pacific* **1951:** *The Rose Tattoo*; *Guys and Dolls* **1952:** *The Fourposter*; *The King and I* **1953:** *The Crucible*; *Wonderful Town* **1954:** *The Teahouse of the August Moon*; *Kismet* **1955:** *The Desperate Hours*; *The Pajama Game* **1956:** *The Diary of Anne Frank*; *Damn Yankees* **1957:** *Long Day's Journey into Night*; *My Fair Lady* **1958:** *Sunrise at Campobello*; *The Music Man* **1959:** *J.B.*; *Redhead* **1960:** *The Miracle Worker*; *Fiorello!* & *The Sound of Music* (tie) **1961:** *Becket*; *Bye Bye Birdie* **1962:** *A Man for All Seasons*; *How to Succeed in Business Without Really Trying* **1963:** *Who's Afraid of Virginia Woolf?*; *A Funny Thing Happened on the Way to the Forum* **1964:** *Luther*; *Hello, Dolly!* **1965:** *The Subject Was Roses*; *Fiddler on the Roof* **1966:** *The Persecution and Assassination of Marat as Performed by the Inmates of the Asylum of Charenton Under the Direction of the Marquis de Sade*; *Man of La Mancha* **1967:** *The Homecoming*; *Cabaret* **1968:** *Rosencrantz and Guildenstern Are Dead*; *Hallelujah Baby!* **1969:** *The Great White Hope*; *1776* **1970:** *Borstal Boy*; *Applause* **1971:** *Sleuth*; *Company* **1972:** *Sticks and Bones*; *Two Gentlemen of Verona* **1973:** *That Championship Season*; *A Little Night Music* **1974:** *The River Niger*; *Raisin* **1975:** *Equus*; *The Wiz* **1976:** *Travesties*; *A Chorus Line* **1977:** *The Shadow Box*; *Annie* **1978:** *Da*; *Ain't Misbehavin'*; *Dracula* (innovative musical revival) **1979:** *The Elephant Man*; *Sweeney Todd* **1980:** *Children of a Lesser God*; *Evita*; *Morning's at Seven* (best revival) **1981:** *Amadeus*; *42nd Street*; *The Pirates of Penzance* **1982:** *The Life and Adventures of Nicholas Nickelby*; *Nine*; *Othello* **1983:** *Torch Song Trilogy*; *Cats*; *On Your Toes* **1984:** *The Real Thing*; *La Cage aux Folles*; *Death of a Salesman* **1985:** *Biloxi Blues*; *Big River*; *A Day in the Death of Joe Egg* **1986:** *I'm Not Rappaport*; *The Mystery of Edwin Drood*; *Sweet Charity* **1987:** *Fences*; *Les Misérables*; *All My Sons* **1988:** *M. Butterfly*; *The Phantom of the Opera*; *Anything Goes* **1989:** *The Heidi Chronicles*; *Jerome Robbins' Broadway*; *Our Town* **1990:** *The Grapes of Wrath*; *City of Angels*; *Gypsy* **1991:** *Lost in Yonkers*; *The Will Rogers' Follies*; *Fiddler on the Roof* **1992:** *Dancing at Lughnasa*; *Crazy for You*; *Guys and Dolls* **1993:** *Angels in America: Millenium Approaches*; *Kiss of the Spider Woman*; *Anna Christie* **1994:** *Angels in America: Perestroika*; *Passion*; *An Inspector Calls* (play revival); *Carousel* (musical revival) **1995:** *Love! Valour! Compassion!*; *Sunset Boulevard*; *The Heiress*; *Show Boat* **1996:** *Master Class*; *Rent*; *A Delicate Balance*; *King and I* **1997:** *Last Night of Ballyhoo*; *Titanic*; *A Doll's House*; *Chicago* **1998:** *Art*; *The Lion King*; *View from the Bridge*; *Cabaret* **1999:** *Side Man*; *Fosse*; *Death of a Salesman*; *Annie Get Your Gun* **2000:** *Copenhagen*; *Contact*; *The Real Thing*; *Kiss Me, Kate* **2001:** *Proof*; *The Producers*; *One Flew Over the Cuckoo's Nest*; *42nd Street* **2002:** Edward Albee's *The Goat, or Who Is Sylvia?*; *Thoroughly Modern Millie*; *Private Lives*; *Into the Woods* **2003:** *Take Me Out*; *Hairspray*; *Long Day's Journey Into Night*; *Nine* **2004:** *I Am My Own Wife*; *Avenue Q*; *Henry IV*; *Assassins* **2005:** *Doubt*; *Monty Python's Spamalot*; *Glengarry Glen Ross*; *La Cage aux Folles* **2006:** *The History Boys*; *Jersey*

Boys; *Awake and Sing!*; *The Pajama Game* **2007:** *The Coast of Utopia*; *Spring Awakening*; *Journey's End*; *Company* **2008:** *August: Osage County*; *In the Heights*; *Boeing-Boeing*; *South Pacific* **2009:** *God of Carnage*; *Billy Elliot The Musical*; *The Norman Conquests*; *Hair*

DRAMA DESK AWARDS

Sunday, May 23, 2010 at LaGuardia Concert Hall-Lincoln Center; 55th annual; Host: Patti LuPone. Originally known as the Vernon Rice Awards until 1964 (named after the former *New York Post* theatre critic); Presented for outstanding achievement in the 2009–2010 season for Broadway, Off-Broadway, and Off-Off Broadway productions, voted on by an association of New York drama reporters, editors and critics; Executive Producer, Robert R. Blume; Producer, Lauren Class Schneider; Director of Ceremony, Jeff Kalpak; Special Events Director, Randie Levine-Miller; Director of Publicity, Les Schecter; Co-Presenters, *TheatreMania.com* and Blume Media Group Ltd.; Production Associate Producers, Joseph Callari, Ellis Nassour, Les Schecter; Board of Directors: William Wolf (President), Leslie Hoban Blake (Vice President), Charles Wright (Treasurer and 2nd Vice President), Richard Ridge (Secretary), Randy Gener, Isa Goldberg, Susan Haskins, John Istel, David Kaufman, Ellis Nassour, Sam Norkin; Nominating Committee: Barbara Siegel – Chairperson (*TheaterMania.com* and *TalkinBroadway.com*), Dan Bacalzo (*TheatreMania.com*), Christopher Byrne (*Gay City News*), Patrick Christiano (*TheaterLife.com* and *Dan's Papers*), David Kaufman (freelance and author) Gerald Raymond (*Back Stage* and *The Advocate*), Richard Ridge (*Broadway Beat TV*), Pauline Simmons (*CurtainUp* and *NY Theatre-wire.com*)

Outstanding Play: *Red* by John Logan

Nominees: Alan Ayckbourn, *My Wonderful Day*; Annie Baker, *Circle Mirror Transformation*; Lucinda Coxon, *Happy Now?*; Geoffrey Nauffts, *Next Fall*; Bruce Norris, *Clybourne Park*

Outstanding Musical: *Memphis*

Nominees: *American Idiot*; *Everyday Rapture*; *The Addams Family*; *The Scottsboro Boys*; *Yank!*

Outstanding Revival of a Play: (tie) *A View from the Bridge*; *Fences*

Nominees: *Brighton Beach Memoirs*; *Hamlet*; *So Help Me God!*; *The Boys in the Band*

Outstanding Revival of a Musical: *La Cage aux Folles*

Nominees: *A Little Night Music*; *Finian's Rainbow*; *Promises, Promises*; *Ragtime*

Outstanding Actor in a Play: Liev Schreiber, *A View from the Bridge*

Nominees: Bill Heck, *The Orphans' Home Cycle*; Jude Law, *Hamlet*; Alfred Molina, *Red*; Eddie Redmayne, *Red*; John Douglas Thompson, *The Emperor Jones*; Christopher Walken, *A Behanding in Spokane*

Outstanding Actress in a Play: Jan Maxwell, *The Royal Family*

Nominees: Ayesha Antoine, *My Wonderful Day*; Melissa Errico, *Candida*; Anne Hathaway, *Twelfth Night*; Kristen Johnston, *So Help Me God!*; Laura Linney, *Time Stands Still*

Outstanding Actor in a Musical: Douglas Hodge, *La Cage aux Folles*

Nominees: Brandon Victor Dixon, *The Scottsboro Boys*; Cheyenne Jackson, *Finian's Rainbow*; Chad Kimball, *Memphis*; Nathan Lane, *The Addams Family*; Bobby Steggert, *Yank!*

Outstanding Actress in a Musical: (tie) Montego Glover, *Memphis*; Catherine Zeta-Jones, *A Little Night Music*

Nominees: Kate Baldwin, *Finian's Rainbow*; Jayne Houdyshell, *Coraline*; Christiane Noll, *Ragtime*; Sherie Rene Scott, *Everyday Rapture*

Outstanding Featured Actor in a Play: Santino Fontana, *Brighton Beach Memoirs*

Nominees: Chris Chalk, *Fences*; Sean Dugan, *Next Fall*; Adam James, *The Pride*; Hamish Linklater, *Twelfth Night*; Nick Westrate, *The Boys in the Band*

Outstanding Featured Actress in a Play: Viola Davis, *Fences*

Nominees: Victoria Clark, *When the Rain Stops Falling*; Xanthe Elbrick, *Candida*; Mary Beth Hurt, *When the Rain Stops Falling*; Scarlett Johansson, *A View from the Bridge*; Andrea Riseborough, *The Pride*

Outstanding Featured Actor in a Musical: Christopher Fitzgerald, *Finian's Rainbow*

Nominees: Kevin Chamberlin, *The Addams Family*; Robin De Jesus, *La Cage aux Folles*; Jeffry Denman, *Yank!*; Jeremy Morse, *Bloodsong of Love*; Bobby Steggert, *Ragtime*

Outstanding Featured Actress in a Musical: Katie Finneran, *Promises, Promises*

Nominees: Carolee Carmello, *The Addams Family*; Carrie Cimma, *Lizzie Borden*; Angela Lansbury, *A Little Night Music*; Kenita Miller, *Langston in Harlem*; Terri White, *Finian's Rainbow*

Outstanding Director of a Play: Michael Grandage, *Red*

Nominees: Jonathan Bank, *So Help Me God!*; Jack Cummings III, *The Boys in the Band*; Sam Gold, *Circle Mirror Transformation*; Michael Grandage, *Hamlet*; Ethan Hawke, *A Lie of the Mind*

Outstanding Director of a Musical: Michael Mayer, *American Idiot*

Nominees: Warren Carlyle, *Finian's Rainbow*; Marcia Milgrom Dodge, *Ragtime*; Igor Goldin, *Yank!*; Terry Johnson, *La Cage aux Folles*; Susan Stroman, *The Scottsboro Boys*

Outstanding Choreography: Twyla Tharp, *Come Fly Away*

Nominees: Warren Carlyle, *Finian's Rainbow*; Marcia Milgrom Dodge, *Ragtime*; Lynne Page, *La Cage aux Folles*; Susan Stroman, *The Scottsboro Boys*; Sergio Trujillo, *Memphis*

Outstanding Music: David Bryan, *Memphis*

Nominees: Michael Friedman, *Bloody Bloody Andrew Jackson*; Joe Iconis, *Bloodsong of Love*; John Kander & Fred Ebb, *The Scottsboro Boys*; Andrew Lippa, *The Addams Family*; Joseph Zellnik, *Yank!*

Outstanding Lyrics: John Kander & Fred Ebb, *The Scottsboro Boys*

Nominees: Rick Crom, *Newsical The Musical*; Kevin Del Aguila, *Click, Clack, Moo*; Dillie Keane and Adèle Anderson, *Fascinating Aïda Absolutely Miraculous!*; Andrew Lippa, *The Addams Family*; David Zellnik, *Yank!*

Outstanding Book of a Musical: Alex Timbers, *Bloody Bloody Andrew Jackson*

Nominees: Joe DiPietro, *Memphis*; Joe Iconis, *Bloodsong of Love*; Dick Scanlan & Sherie Rene Scott, *Everyday Rapture*; David Thompson, *The Scottsboro Boys*; David Zellnik, *Yank!*

Outstanding Orchestrations: Daryl Waters & David Bryan, *Memphis*

Nominees: Larry Hochman, *The Scottsboro Boys*; Tom Kitt, *American Idiot*; Tom Kitt, *Everyday Rapture*; John Oddo, *All About Me*

Outstanding Musical Revue: *Sondheim on Sondheim*

Nominations: *Fascinating Aïda Absolutely Miraculous!*; *Million Dollar Quartet*; *Newsical The Musical*; *Simon Green: Traveling Light*

Outstanding Music in a Play: Branford Marsalis, *Fences*

Nominees: Adam Cochran, *A Play on War*; Adam Cork, *Red*; Shelby Gaines and Latham Gaines, *A Lie of the Mind*; Philip Glass, *The Bacchae*; Hem, *Twelfth Night*

Outstanding Set Design: Phelim McDermott, Julian Crouch & Basil Twist, *The Addams Family*

Nominees: Sandra Goldmark, *The Boys in the Band*; Derek McLane, *Ragtime*; Christopher Oram, *Red*; Jay Rohloff, *Underground*; Karen Tennent, *Hansel and Gretel*

Outstanding Costume Design: Matthew Wright, *La Cage aux Folles*

Nominees: Antonia Ford-Roberts & Bob Flanagan, *The Emperor Jones*; Clint Ramos, *So Help Me God!*; Bobby Frederick Tilley II, *Lizzie Borden*; David Zinn, *In the Next Room or the vibrator play*

Outstanding Lighting Design: Neil Austin, *Red*

Nominees: Neil Austin, *Hamlet*; Christian M. DeAngelis, *Lizzie Borden*; Maruti Evans, *John Ball's In the Heat of the Night*; Natasha Katz, *The Addams Family*; Dane Laffrey, *The Boys in the Band*

Outstanding Sound Design in a Musical: Acme Sound Partners, *Ragtime*

Nominees: Jonathan Deans, *La Cage aux Folles*; Ashley Hanson, Kurt Eric Fischer & Brian Ronan, *Everyday Rapture*; Peter Hylenski, *The Scottsboro Boys*; Scott Lehrer, *Finian's Rainbow*; Brian Ronan, *Promises, Promises*

Outstanding Sound Design in a Play: Fitz Patton, *When the Rain Stops Falling*

Nominees: Dan Bianchi & Wes Shippee, *Frankenstein*; Dale Bigall, *Underground*; Adam Cork, *Enron*; Lindsay Jones, *Top Secret: The Battle for the Pentagon Papers*; Elizabeth Rhodes, *John Ball's In the Heat of the Night*

Outstanding Solo Performance: Jim Brochu, *Zero Hour*

Nominees: Theodore Bikel, *Sholom Aleichem: Laughter Through Tears*; Colman Domingo, *A Boy and his Soul*; Carrie Fisher, *Wishful Drinking*; Judith Ivey, *The Lady With All the Answers*; Anna Deavere Smith, *Let Me Down Easy*

Unique Theatrical Experience: *Love, Loss, and What I Wore*

Nominees: Charles L. Mee's *Fêtes de la Nuit*; *Hansel and Gretel*; John Tartaglia's *Imaginocean*; *Stuffed and Unstrung*; *The Provenance of Beauty*

Outstanding Ensemble Performances: *Circle Mirror Transformation* and *The Temperamentals*

Special Awards: Cast, creative team, and producers of Signature Theatre's *The Orphans' Home Cycle*; Jerry Herman; Godlight Theatre Company; Ma-Yi Theater Company

PAST DRAMA DESK AWARD-WINNING PRODUCTIONS From 1954–1974, non-competitive awards were presented to various artists: performers, playwrights, choreographers, composers, designers, directors, theatre companies and occasionally to specific productions. In 1975 the awards became competitive, and citations for Outstanding New Play (P) – or in some instances Outstanding New American Play (AP) and Outstanding New Foreign Play (FP), Outstanding Musical (M), Musical Revue (MR), Outstanding Revival (R)– and later, Outstanding Play Revival (RP) and Outstanding Musical Revival (RM)–were instituted and presented as the season demanded. If year or a specific category within a year is missing, no production awards were presented in that year or specific category.

1955: *The Way of the World*; *A Thieve's Carnival*; *Twelfth Night*; *The Merchant of Venice* **1956:** *The Iceman Cometh* **1963:** *The Coach with Six Insides*; *The Boys from Syracuse* **1964:** *In White America*; *The Streets of New York* **1970:** *Borstal Boy* (P); *The Effect of Gamma Rays on Man-in-the-Moon Marigolds* (AP); *Company* (M) **1975:** *Same Time, Next Year* (AP), *Equus* (FP); **1976:** *Streamers* (P); *The Royal Family* (R) **1977:** *A Texas Trilogy* (AP); *The Comedians* (FP); *Annie* (M) **1978:** *Da* (P); *Ain't Misbehavin'* (M) **1979:** *The Elephant Man* (P); *Sweeney Todd, The Demon Barber of Fleet Street* (M) **1980:** *Children of a Lesser God* (P); *Evita* (M) **1981:** *Amadeus* (P); *Lena Horne: The Lady and Her Music* (M) **1982:** *"Master Harold"…and the boys* (P); *Nine* (M); *Entertaining Mr. Sloan* (R) **1983:** *Torch Song Trilogy* (P); *Little Shop of Horrors* (M); *On Your Toes* (R) **1984:** *The Real Thing* (P); *Sunday in the Park with George* (M); *Death of a Salesman* (R) **1985:** *As Is* (P); *A Day in the Death of Joe Egg* (R) **1986:** *A Lie of the Mind* (P); *The Mystery of Edwin Drood* (M); *Lemon Sky* (R) **1987:** *Fences* (P); *Les*

Misérables (M) **1988:** *M. Butterfly* (P); *Into the Woods* (M); *Anything Goes* (R) **1989:** *The Heidi Chronicles* (P); *Jerome Robbins' Broadway* (M); *Our Town* (R) **1990:** *The Piano Lesson* (P); *City of Angels* (M); *Gypsy* (R) **1991:** *Lost in Yonkers* (P); *The Secret Garden* (M); *And the World Goes Round* (MR); *A Little Night Music* (R) **1992:** *Lips Together, Teeth Apart* (P); *Crazy for You* (M); *Guys and Dolls* (R) **1993:** *Jeffrey* (P); *Kiss of the Spider Woman* (M); *Anna Christie* (R) **1994:** *Angels in America: Perestroika* (P); *Passion* (M); *Howard Crabtree's Whoop-Dee-Doo* (MR); *An Inspector Calls* (RP); *She Loves Me* (RM) **1995:** *Love! Valour! Compassion!* (P); *Showboat* (M); *The Heiress* (RP) **1996:** *Master Class* (P); *Rent* (M); *A Delicate Balance* (RP); *The King and I* (RM) **1997:** *How I Learned to Drive* (P), *The Life* (M); *Howard Crabtree's When Pigs Fly* (MR); *A Doll's House* (RP); *Chicago* (RM) **1998:** *The Beauty Queen of Leenane* (P); *Ragtime* (M); *A View from the Bridge* (RP); *1776* (RM) **1999:** *Wit* (P); *Parade* (M); *Fosse* (MR); (tie) *Death of a Salesman* and *The Iceman Cometh* (RP); *You're a Good Man, Charlie Brown* (RM) **2000:** *Copenhagen* (P); *Contact* (M); *The Real Thing* (RP); *Kiss Me, Kate* (RM) **2001:** *Proof* (P); *The Producers* (M); *Forbidden Broadway 2001: A Spoof Odyssey* (MR); *The Best Man* (RP); *42nd Street* (RM) **2002:** (tie) *The Goat, or Who Is Sylvia?* and *Metamorphoses* (P); *Private Lives* (RP); *Into the Woods* (RM) **2003:** *Take Me Out* (P); *Hairspray* (M); *Long Day's Journey Into Night* (RP); *Nine* (RM) **2004:** *I Am My Own Wife* (P); *Wicked* (M); *Henry IV* (RP); *Assassins* (RM) **2005:** *Doubt* (P); *Monty Python's Spamalot* (M); *Forbidden Broadway: Special Victims Unit* (MR); *Twelve Angry Men* (RP); *La Cage aux Folles* (RM) **2006:** *The History Boys* (P); *The Drowsy Chaperone* (M); *Awake and Sing!* (RP); *Sweeney Todd, The Demon Barber of Fleet Street* (RM) **2007:** *The Coast of Utopia* (P); *Spring Awakening* (M); *Journey's End* (RP); *Company* (RM) **2008:** *August: Osage County* (P); *Passing Strange* (M); *Forbidden Broadway: Rude Awakening* (MR); *Boeing-Boeing* (RP); *South Pacific* (RM) **2009:** *Ruined* (P); *Billy Elliot The Musical* (M); *The Norman Conquests* (RP); *Hair* (RM)

VILLAGE VOICE OBIE AWARDS

Monday, May 17, 2010 at Webster Hall; 55th annual; Hosts: Michael Cerveris and Anika Noni Rose. Presented for outstanding achievement in Off- and Off-Off-Broadway theater in the 2009–2010 season; Founded in 1955 by Village Voice cultural editor Jerry Tallmer; Judges: Michael Feingold (Committee Chair and *Village Voice* chief theatre critic), Alexis Soloski (*Village Voice* theatre critic), Eric Grode (*New York Sun*), Andy Probst (*AmericanTheatreWeb.com*), Kristin Marting (Artistic Director/Co-founder of HERE Arts Center), Ralph B. Peña (Artistic Director of Ma-Yi Theater Company), Martha Plimpton (actor); Producer, Eileen Phelan; Publicity, Gail Parenteau.

Best New American Play: ($1,000): *Circle Mirror Transformation* (Playwrights Horizons) and *The Aliens* (Rattlestick Playwrights Theater) by Annie Baker

Performance: Ensemble of *Circle Mirror Transformation*: Reed Birney, Tracee Chimo, Peter Friedman, Deirdre O'Connell, Heidi Schreck (Playwrights Horizons); Dane DeHaan, *The Aliens* (Rattlestick Playwrights Theater); Jonathan Hammond, *The Boys in the Band* (Transport Group); Marc Damon Johnson, *The Brother/Sister Plays* (Public Theater); Laurie Metcalf, *A Lie of the Mind* (The New Group); Wendell Pierce, sustained excellence of performance; Juliet Rylance, *As You Like It* (Bridge Project at BAM); Rocco Sisto, sustained excellence of performance

Playwrighting: Enda Walsh, *The New Electric Ballroom* (Druid Theater/St. Ann's Warehouse)

Direction: Sam Gold, *Circle Mirror Transformation* (Playwrights Horizons) and *The Aliens* (Rattlestick Playwrights Theater); Pam McKinnon, *Clybourne Park* (Playwrights Horizons)

Design/Music: Steven Dufala and Billy Blaise Dufala (machine design), *Machines Machines Machines Machines Machines Machines Machines* (rainpan 43/HERE Arts Center); Stephin Merritt (music & lyrics), *Coraline* (MCC Theater); Tyler Micoleau, sustained excellence of lighting design; Design team of Neil Murray (sets & costumes), Malcom Rippeth (lighting), Gemma Carrington & Jon Driscoll (projections), *Brief Encounter* (Kneehigh Theatre/St. Ann's Warehouse)

Special Citations: Ariane Mnouchkine & Théâtre du Soleil, *Les Éphémères* (Lincoln Center Festival); Taylor Mac, *The Lily's Revenge* (HERE Arts Center); The Ohio Theatre; Hoi Polloi [Alec Duffy, Dave Malloy, and Rick Burkhardt] and Rachel Chavkin, *Three Pianos* (Ontological Theater); Philippe Quesne and Gaëtan Vourc'h, *L'Effet De Serge* (Vivarium Studio/Under the Radar); Chris Wells, *Secret City*

Ross Wetzsteon Memorial Award ($2,000): Foundry Theatre

Sustained Achievement: David Greenspan

Obie Theater Grants ($10,000 divided among winners): Harlem School of the Arts, Ontological Incubator, Vampire Cowboys Theater Company

PAST OBIE AWARD-WINNING BEST NEW PLAYS If year is missing, no award was given that season; multiple plays were awarded in some seasons.

1956: *Absalom, Absalom* **1957:** *A House Remembered* **1959:** *The Quare Fellow* **1961:** *The Blacks* **1962:** *Who'll Save the Plowboy?* **1964:** *Play* **1965:** *The Old Glory* **1966:** *The Journey of the Fifth Horse* **1970:** *The Effect of Gamma Rays on Man-in-the-Moon Marigolds* **1971:** *The House of Blue Leaves* **1973:** *The Hot L Baltimore* **1974:** *Short Eyes* **1975:** *The First Breeze of Summer* **1976:** *American Buffalo, Sexual Perversity in Chicago* **1977:** *Curse of the Starving Class* **1978:** *Shaggy Dog Animation* **1979:** *Josephine* **1981:** *FOB* **1982:** *Metamorphosis in Miniature; Mr. Dead and Mrs. Free* **1983:** *Painting Churches; Andrea Rescued;* *Edmond* **1984:** *Fool for Love* **1985:** *The Conduct of Life* **1987:** *The Cure; Film Is Evil, Radio Is Good* **1988:** *Abingdon Square* **1990:** *Prelude to a Kiss; Imperceptible Mutabilities in the Third* Kingdom; *Bad Benny, Crowbar, Terminal Hip* **1991:** *The Fever* **1992:** *Sight Unseen; Sally's Rape, The Baltimore Waltz* **1994:** *Twilight: Los Angeles, 1992* **1995:** *Cryptogram* **1996:** *Adrienne Kennedy* **1997:** *One Flea Spare* **1998:** *Pearls for Pigs and Benita Canova* **2001:** *The Syringa Tree* **2004:** *Small Tragedy* **2009:** *Ruined*

OUTER CRITICS CIRCLE AWARDS

Thursday, May 27, 2010 at Sardi's Restaurant; 60th annual. Presented for outstanding achievement for Broadway and Off-Broadway productions during the 2009–2010 season. Winners are voted on by theatre critics of out-of-town periodicals and media. Executive Committee: Simon Saltzman (President), Mario Fratti (Vice President), Rosalind Friedman (Recording Secretary), Louis A. Rachow (Treasurer), Patrick Hoffman (Corresponding Secretary), Aubrey Reuben, Glenn M. Loney, Thomás Gentile (Members-at-Large), Marjorie Gunner (President Emeritus)

Outstanding New Broadway Play: *Red*

Nominees: *Next Fall; Superior Donuts; Time Stands Still*

Outstanding New Broadway Musical: *Memphis*

Nominees: *American Idiot; Come Fly Away; Fela!; Sondheim on Sondheim*

Outstanding New Off-Broadway Play: *The Orphans' Home Cycle*

Nominees: *Clybourne Park; The Pride; The Temperamentals*

Outstanding New Off-Broadway Musical: (tie) *The Scottsboro Boys; Bloody Bloody Andrew Jackson*

Nominees: *Tin Pan Alley Rag; Yank!*

Outstanding New Score (Broadway or Off-Broadway)**:** *Memphis*

Nominees: *Bloody Bloody Andrew Jackson; The Scottsboro Boys; Yank!*

Outstanding Revival of a Play: *Fences*

Nominees: *Lend Me a Tenor; The Royal Family; A View from the Bridge*

Outstanding Revival of a Musical: *La Cage aux Folles*

Nominees: *Finian's Rainbow; A Little Night Music; Promises, Promises*

Outstanding Director of a Play: Michael Wilson, *The Orphans' Home Cycle*

Nominees: Doug Hughes, *The Royal Family*; Kenny Leon, *Fences*; Stanley Tucci, *Lend Me a Tenor*

Outstanding Director of a Musical: Terry Johnson, *La Cage aux Folles*

Nominees: Christopher Ashley, *Memphis*; Susan Stroman, *The Scottsboro Boys*; Alex Timbers, *Bloody Bloody Andrew Jackson*

Outstanding Choreography: Sergio Trujillo, *Memphis*

Nominees: Rob Ashford, *Promises, Promises*; Bill T. Jones, *Fela!*; Susan Stroman, *The Scottsboro Boys*

Outstanding Actor in a Play: Denzel Washington, *Fences*

Nominees: Bill Heck, *The Orphans' Home Cycle*; Jude Law, *Hamlet*; Liev Schreiber, *A View from the Bridge*; Christopher Walken, *A Behanding in Spokane*

Outstanding Actress in a Play: Viola Davis, *Fences*

Nominees: Nina Arianda, *Venus in Fur*; Laura Benanti, *In the Next Room, or the vibrator play*; Laura Linney, *Time Stands Still*; Jan Maxwell, *The Royal Family*

Outstanding Actor in a Musical: Douglas Hodge, *La Cage aux Folles*

Nominees: Brandon Victor Dixon, *The Scottsboro Boys*; Sean Hayes, *Promises, Promises*; Chad Kimball, *Memphis*; Nathan Lane, *The Addams Family*

Outstanding Actress in a Musical: Catherine Zeta-Jones, *A Little Night Music*

Nominees: Kate Baldwin, *Finian's Rainbow*; Barbara Cook, *Sondheim on Sondheim*; Montego Glover, *Memphis*; Bebe Neuwirth, *The Addams Family*

Outstanding Featured Actor in a Play: Jon Michael Hill, *Superior Donuts*

Nominees: James DeMarse, *The Orphans' Home Cycle*; David Pittu, *Equivocation*; Noah Robbins, *Brighton Beach Memoirs*; Reg Rogers, *The Royal Family*

Outstanding Featured Actress in a Play: Jan Maxwell, *Lend Me a Tenor*

Nominees: Hallie Foote, *The Orphans' Home Cycle*; Rosemary Harris, *The Royal Family*; Marin Ireland, *A Lie of the Mind*; Alicia Silverstone, *Time Stands Still*

Outstanding Featured Actor in a Musical: Levi Kreis, *Million Dollar Quartet*

Nominees: Kevin Chamberlin, *The Addams Family*; Christopher Fitzgerald, *Finian's Rainbow*; Dick Latessa, *Promises, Promises*; Bobby Steggert, *Ragtime*

Outstanding Featured Actress in a Musical: Katie Finneran, *Promises, Promises*

Nominees: Carolee Carmello, *The Addams Family*; Angela Lansbury, *A Little Night Music*; Cass Morgan, *Memphis*; Terri White, *Finian's Rainbow*

Outstanding Scenic Design (Play or Musical): Phelim McDermott & Julian Crouch, *The Addams Family*

Nominees: John Lee Beatty, *The Royal Family*; Beowulf Boritt, *Sondheim on Sondheim*; Donyale Werle, *Bloody Bloody Andrew Jackson*

Outstanding Costume Design (Play or Musical): Matthew Wright, *La Cage aux Folles*

Nominees: Jane Greenwood, *Present Laughter*; Martin Pakledinaz, *Lend Me a Tenor*; Catherine Zuber, *The Royal Family*

Outstanding Lighting Design (Play or Musical): Kevin Adams, *American Idiot*
Nominees: Kevin Adams, *The Scottsboro Boys*; Ken Billington, *Sondheim on Sondheim*; Justin Townsend, *Bloody Bloody Andrew Jackson*

Outstanding Solo Performance: Carrie Fisher, *Wishful Drinking*

Nominees: Jim Brochu, *Zero Hour*; Judith Ivey, *The Lady With All the Answers*; Anna Deavere Smith, *Let Me Down Easy*

John Gassner Playwriting Award: Geoffrey Nauffts, *Next Fall*

Nominees: John Logan, *Red*; Jon Marans, *The Temperamentals*; Bruce Norris, *Clybourne Park*

PAST OUTER CRITICS CIRCLE AWARD-WINNING PRODUCTIONS

Awards listed are for Best Play and Best Musical; as other categories were cited, they are indicated as such: (R) Best Revival; (RP) Best Play Revival; (RM) Best Musical Revival; (BP) Best Productions; (OP) Best Off-Broadway Play; (OM) Best Off-Broadway Musical. Beginning with 1990, shows listed are: Best (New) Play, Best (New) Musical, Best Play Revival, Best Musical Revival, Best Off-Broadway Play, Best New Off-Broadway Musical. In 1999, the awards were qualified as "Outstanding" instead of "Best"; if year is missing, no production awards were presented.

1950: *The Cocktail Party*; *The Consul* **1951:** *Billy Budd*; *Guys and Dolls* **1952:** *Point of No Return*; no musical award **1953:** no play award; *Wonderful Town* **1954:** *The Caine Mutiny Court-Martial*; *Kismet* **1955:** *Inherit the Wind*; *Three for Tonight* **1956:** *The Diary of Anne Frank*; *My Fair Lady* **1957:** *Long Day's Journey Into Night*; *My Fair Lady* **1958:** *Look Homeward, Angel*; *The Music Man* **1959:** *The Visit*; no musical award **1960:** *The Miracle Worker*; *Bye Bye Birdie* **1962:** *Anything Goes* (R) **1964:** *The Trojan Women* (R-classic); *The Lower Depths* (R-modern) **1965:** (BP) – *Oh What a Lovely War*; *Tartuffe* **1966:** (BP) – *Wait a Minim!*; *Mame* **1967:** (BP) – *America Hurrah*; *Cabaret*; *You Know I Can't Hear You When the Water's Running*; *You're A Good Man, Charlie Brown* **1968:** (BP) – *Rosencrantz and Guildenstern are Dead*; *The Price*; *George M!*; *Your Own Thing* **1969:** *Dames at Sea* (OM) **1970:** *Child's Play*; *Company*; *The White House Murder Case* (OP); *The Last Sweet Days of Isaac* (OM) **1971:** (BP) – *A Midsummer Night's Dream*; *Follies*; *No, No, Nanette* **1972:** *Sticks and Bones* and *That Championship Season*; no musical award **1974:** *A Moon for the Misbegotten* and *Noel Coward in Two Keys*; *Candide* **1975:** *Equus*; no musical award **1977:** *for colored girls...*; *Annie* **1978:** *Da*; no musical award **1979:** *The Elephant Man*; *Sweeney Todd, the Demon Barber of Fleet Street* **1980:** *Children of a Lesser God*; *Barnum* **1981:** *Amadeus*; *The Pirates of Penzance* (R); *March of the Falsettos* (OM) **1982:** *"Master Harold"...and the Boys*; *Nine*; *A Soldier's Play* (OP) **1983:** *Brighton Beach Memoirs*; *Cats*; *You Can't Take It With You* (RP); *On Your Toes* (RM); *Extremities* (OP); *Little Shop of Horrors* (OM) **1984:** *The Real Thing*; *La Cage aux Folles*; *Death of a Salesman* (R); *Painting Churches* (OP); *A...My Name is Alice* (Revue) **1985:** *Biloxi Blues*; *Sunday in the Park With George*; *Joe Egg* (R); *The Foreigner* (OP); *Kuni-Leml* (OM) **1986:** *I'm Not Rappaport*; *The Mystery of Edwin Drood*; *Loot* (R); *A Lie of the Mind* (OP); *Nunsense* (OM) **1987:** *Fences*; *Les Les Misérables*; *All My Sons* (R); *The Common Pursuit* (OP); *Stardust* (OM) **1988:** *M. Butterfly*; *The Phantom of the Opera*; *Anything Goes* (R); *Driving Miss Daisey* (OP); *Oil City Symphony* and *Romance, Romance* (OM) **1989:** *The Heidi Chronicles*; *Jerome Robbins' Broadway* **1990:** *The Grapes of Wrath*; *City of Angels*; *Cat on a Hot Tin Roof*; *Gypsy*; *Prelude to a Kiss*; *Closer Than Ever* **1991:** *Lost in Yonkers*; *Miss Saigon*; *Fiddler on the Roof* (R); *The Sum of Us*; *Falsettoland*; *And the World Goes Round* (Revue) **1992:** *Dancing at Lughnasa*; *Crazy for You*; *The Visit*; *Guys and Dolls*; *Marvin's Room*; *Song of Singapore* **1993:** *The Sisters Rosensweig*; *The Who's Tommy*; *Anna Christie*; *Carnival*; *Jeffrey*; *Ruthless!* **1994:** *Angels in America*; *Kiss of the Spider Woman*; *An Inspector Calls*; *She Loves Me*; *Three Tall Women*; *Annie Warbucks* **1995:** *Love! Valour! Compassion!*; *Sunset Boulevard*; *The Heiress*; *Show Boat*; *Camping with Henry and Tom*; *Jelly Roll* **1996:** *Master Class*; *Victor/Victoria*; *Inherit the Wind*; *The King and I*; *Molly Sweeney* and *Picasso at the Lapin Agile*; *Rent* **1997:** *The Last Night at Ballyhoo*; *The Life*; *A Doll's House*; *Chicago*; *How I Learned to Drive*; *Howard Crabtree's When Pigs Fly* **1998:** *The Beauty Queen of Leenane*; *Ragtime*; *A View from the Bridge*; *Cabaret*; *Never the Sinner* and *Gross Indecency: The Three Trials of Oscar Wilde*; *Hedwig and the Angry Inch* **1999:** *Not About Nightingales*; *Fosse*; *The Iceman Cometh*; *Annie Get Your Gun* and *Peter Pan* and *You're A Good Man, Charlie Brown*; *Wit*; *A New Brain* **2000:** *Copenhagen*; *Contact*; *A Moon for the Misbegotten*; *Kiss Me, Kate*; *Dinner With Friends*; *The Wild Party* **2001:** *Proof*; *The Producers*; *The Best Man* and *One Flew Over the Cuckoo's Nest*; *42nd Street*; *Jitney*; *Bat Boy: The Musical* **2002:** *The Goat, or Who Is Sylvia?*; *Urinetown the Musical* and *The Dazzle*; *Morning's at Seven*; *Oklahoma!*; *tick, tick...BOOM!* **2003:** *Take Me Out*; *Hairspray*; *A Day in the Death of Joe Egg*; *Nine*; *The Exonerated*; *A Man of No Importance* **2004:** *I Am My Own Wife*; *Wicked*; *Henry IV*; *Wonderful Town*; *Intimate Apparel*; *Johnny Guitar* and

The Thing About Men **2005:** *Doubt*; *Monty Python's Spamalot*; *Twelve Angry Men*; *La Cage aux Folles*; *Fat Pig* and *Going to St. Ives*; *Altar Boyz* **2006:** *The History Boys*; *Jersey Boys*; *Awake and Sing!*; *Sweeney Todd, the Demon Barber of Fleet Street*; *Stuff Happens*; *Grey Gardens* **2007:** *The Coast of Utopia*; *Spring Awakening*; *Journey's End*; *Company*; *Indian Blood*; *In the Heights* **2008:** *August: Osage County*; *Xanadu* and *Young Frankenstein*; *The Homecoming*; *South Pacific*; *Dividing the Estate*; *Adding Machine* **2009:** *God of Carnage*; *Billy Elliot The Musical*; *The Norman Conquests*; *Hair*; *Ruined*; *The Toxic Avenger*

LUCILLE LORTEL AWARDS

Sunday, May 2, 2010 at Terminal 5; 25th annual; Hosts: Bebe Neuwirth and Bryan Batt. Presented by the League of Off-Broadway Theatres and Producers for outstanding achievement Off-Broadway. The 2009–2010 awards voting committee consisted of Terry Berliner (SDC), John Clinton Eisner (Lark Theatre Company), Kurt Everhart (*nyconstage.org*), Peter Filichia (*TheatreMania.com*), Jerry Fiske (Fellowship for the Performing Arts), George Forbes (Off-Broadway League), Susan Gallin (Susan Gallin Productions), Eleanor Goldhar (Guggenheim Foundation), Melanie Herman (MH Productions), Linda Herring (Tribeca Performing Arts Center), Walt Kiskaddeon (Actors' Equity Association), Renee Lasher (SDC), Russell Lehrer (Actors' Equity Association), Niclas Nagler (Off-Broadway League), Barbara Pasternack (Theatreworks USA), Richard Price (Theatre Development Fund), Mark Rossler (New York Foundation for the Arts), David Savran (The Graduate Center – CUNY), and Barbara Toy (American Theatre Wing).

Outstanding Play: *The Orphans' Home Cycle* by Horton Foote (Signature Theatre Company and Hartford Stage)

Nominees: *Clybourne Park* by Bruce Norris (Playwrights Horizons); *The Brother/Sister Plays* by Tarell Alvin McCraney (The Public Theater in association with McCarter Theatre); *The Temperamentals* by Jon Marans (Produced by Daryl Roth, Stacy Shane and Martian Entertainment); *When The Rain Stops Falling* by Andrew Bovell (Lincoln Center Theater)

Outstanding Musical: *The Scottsboro Boys* Book by David Thompson, lyrics and music by John Kander and Fred Ebb (Vineyard Theatre)

Nominees: *Click, Clack, Moo* Book by Billy Aronson, lyrics by Kevin Del Aguila, music by Brad Alexander, based on the book by Doreen Cronin with illustrations by Betsy Lewin (Theatreworks USA); *Everyday Rapture* Book, lyrics, and music by Dick Scanlan and Sherie Rene Scott (Second Stage); *The Toxic Avenger* Book and lyrics by Joe DiPietro, music and lyrics by David Bryan, based on Lloyd Kaufman's "The Toxic Avenger" (Produced by Jean Cheever and Tom Polum); *Yank! A WWII Love Story* Music by Joseph Zellnik, book and lyrics by David Zellnik (York Theatre Company with Maran Berthelsen/Pamela Koslow/Stuart Wilk, Matt Schicker, Hugh Hayes, Jim Kierstead and Sondra Healy/Shidan Majidi)

Outstanding Revival: *The Glass Menagerie* (Roundabout Theatre Company)

Nominees: *A Lie of the Mind* (The New Group); *Candida* (Irish Repertory Theatre and Alexis Doyle); *Measure for Measure* (Theatre for a New Audience), *The Emperor Jones* (Irish Repertory Theatre)

Outstanding Solo Show: *A Boy and His Soul* Written and performed by Colman Domingo (Vineyard Theatre)

Nominees: *Let Me Down Easy* Written and performed by Anna Deavere Smith (Second Stage); *Nightingale* Written and performed by Lynn Redgrave (Manhattan Theatre Club); *The Lady With All the Answers* Written by David Rambo, performed by Judith Ivey Cherry Lane Theatre); *Zero Hour* Written and performed by Jim Brochu (Kurt Peterson and Edmund Gaynes, in association with The Peccadillo Theatre Company)

Outstanding Director: David Cromer, *When the Rain Stops Falling* (Lincoln Center Theater)

Nominees: Walter Bobbie, *Venus in Fur*; Gordon Edelstein, *The Glass Menagerie*; Pam MacKinnon, *Clybourne Park*; Joe Mantello, *The Pride*

Outstanding Choreography: Susan Stroman, *The Scottsboro Boys* (Vineyard Theatre)

Nominees: Jeffry Denman, *Yank! A WWII Love Story*; Ken Roberson, *A Boy and His Soul*; Wendy Seyb, *Click, Clack, Moo*; Wendy Seyb, *The Toxic Avenger*

Outstanding Lead Actor: Michael Urie, *The Temperamentals* (Produced by Daryl Roth, Stacy Shane and Martian Entertainment)

Nominees: Hugh Dancy, *The Pride*; Patch Darragh, *The Glass Menagerie*; Brandon Victor Dixon, *The Scottsboro Boys*; John Douglas Thompson, *The Emperor Jones*

Outstanding Lead Actress: Judith Ivey, *The Glass Menagerie*; (Roundabout Theatre Company)

Nominees: Nina Arianda, *Venus in Fur*; Jayne Houdyshell, *Coraline*; Cristin Milioti, *Stunning*; Sherie Rene Scott, *Everyday Rapture*

Outstanding Featured Actor: Adam James, *The Pride* (MCC Theater)

Nominees: Keith Carradine, *A Lie of the Mind*; David Pittu, *Equivocation*; Jeremy Shamos, *Clybourne Park*; C.J. Wilson, *Happy Now?*

Outstanding Featured Actress: Mary Beth Hurt, *When the Rain Stops Falling* (Lincoln Center Theater)

Nominees: Tracee Chimo, *Circle Mirror Transformation*; Laurie Metcalf, *A Lie of the Mind*; Nancy Opel, *The Toxic Avenger*; Andrea Riseborough, *The Pride*

Outstanding Scenic Design: David Korins, *When the Rain Stops Falling*; (Lincoln Center Theater)

Nominees: David Korins, *Why Torture is Wrong, and the People Who Love Them*; Derek McLane, *A Lie of the Mind*; Michael Yeargan, *The Glass Menagerie*; David Zinn, *The Pride*

Outstanding Costume Design: Clint Ramos, *So Help Me God!* (Mint Theatre)

Nominees: Miranda Hoffman, *Stunning*; Martin Pakledinaz, *The Glass Menagerie*; Ilona Somogyi, *Clybourne Park*; Anita Yavich, *Venus in Fur*

Outstanding Lighting Design: Tyler Micoleau, *When the Rain Stops Falling* (Lincoln Center Theater)

Nominees: Mark Barton, *Circle Mirror Transformation*; Paul Gallo, *The Pride*; Peter Kaczorowski, *The Brother/Sister Plays*; Rui Rita, *The Orphans' Home Cycle*

Outstanding Sound Design: Fitz Patton, *When the Rain Stops Falling* (Lincoln Center Theater)

Nominees: Kurt Fischer, *The Toxic Avenger*; John Gromada, *The Orphans' Home Cycle*; Shane Rettig, *A Lie of the Mind*; Ryan Rumery and Christian Frederickson, *The Emperor Jones*

Outstanding Body of Work: Lincoln Center Theater

Edith Olivier Award for Sustained Excellence: Daryl Roth

PAST LUCILLE LORTEL-AWARD WINNING PRODUCTIONS Awards listed are Outstanding Play and Outstanding Musical, respectively, since inception.

1986: *Woza Africa!*; no musical award **1987:** *The Common Pursuit*; no musical award **1988:** no play or musical award **1989:** *The Cocktail Hour*; no musical award **1990:** no play or musical award **1991:** *Aristocrats*; *Falsettoland* **1992:** *Lips Together, Teeth Apart*; *And the World Goes 'Round* **1993:** *The Destiny of Me*; *Forbidden Broadway* **1994:** *Three Tall Women*; *Wings* **1995:** *Camping with Henry & Tom*; *Jelly Roll!* **1996:** *Molly Sweeney*; *Floyd Collins* **1997:** *How I Learned to Drive*; *Violet* **1998:** (tie) *Gross Indecency* and *The Beauty Queen of Leenane*; no musical award **1999:** *Wit*; no musical award **2000:** *Dinner With Friends*; *James Joyce's The Dead* 2001: *Proof*; *Bat Boy: The Musical* **2002:** *Metamorphoses*; *Urinetown* **2003:** *Take Me Out*; *Avenue Q* **2004:** *Bug*; *Caroline or Change* **2005:** *Doubt*; *The 25th Annual Putnam County Spelling Bee* **2006:** *The Lieutenant of Inishmore*; *The Seven* **2007:** *Stuff Happens*; (tie) *In the Heights* and *Spring Awakening* **2008:** *Betrayed*; *Adding Machine* **2009:** *Ruined*; *Fela! A New Musical*

NEW YORK DRAMA CRITICS' CIRCLE AWARD

Monday, May 10, 2010 at the Algonquin Hotel; 75th annual. Presented by members of the press in the New York area. New York Drama Critics' Circle Committee:, Adam Feldman – President (*Time Out New York*), Hilton Als (*The New Yorker*), Melissa Rose Bernardo (*Entertainment Weekly*), David Cote (*Time Out New York*), Joe Dziemianowicz – Treasurer (*The Daily News*), Michael Feingold (*The Village Voice*), Robert Feldberg (*The Bergen Record*), Elysa Gardner (*USA Today*), John Heilpern (*The New York Observer*), Michael Kuchwara (*Associate Press*), David Rooney (*Variety*), Frank Scheck (*New York Post*), David Sheward (*Back Stage*), John Simon (*Bloomberg News*), Alexis Soloski (*The Village Voice*), Terry Teachout (*The Wall Street Journal*), Elizabeth Vincentelli (*New York Post*), Linda Winer (*Newsday*), Richard Zoglin (*Time*); Vice President (non-voting): Eric Grode (*The New York Sun*)

Best Play: *The Orphans' Home Cycle* by Horton Foote

Special Citations: Lincoln Center Festival; Viola Davis; Emerging Artists Special Citation: Annie Baker for *Circle Mirror Transformation* and *The Aliens*

PAST DRAMA CRITICS' CIRLCE AWARD-WINNING PRODUCTIONS

From 1936 to 1962, the New York Drama Critics' Circle presented awards for Best American Play, Best Foreign Play, and Best Musical, although some years no awards were given in specific categories. For entries below during those years, the first entry (unless otherwise indicated) is for Best American Play, (F) for Best Foreign Play, and (M) for Best Musical. For listings from 1962 to the present, the first listing (unless otherwise indicated) is for Best Play, and proceeding listings are as follow (depending on which awards were cited): (A) Best American Play; (F) Best Foreign Play; (M) Best Musical. Special Citations, periodically presented, are indicated as (SC).

1936: *Winterset* **1937:** *High Tor* **1938:** *Of Mice and Men*, *Shadow and Substance* (F) **1939:** *The White Steed* (F) **1940:** *The Time of Your Life* **1941:** *Watch on the Rhine*, *The Corn Is Green* (F) **1942:** *Blithe Spirit* (F) **1943:** *The Patriots* **1944:** *Jacobowsky and the Colonel* (F) **1945:** *The Glass Menagerie* **1946:** *Carousel* (M) **1947:** *All My Sons*, *No Exit* (F), *Brigadoon* (M) **1948:** *A Streetcar Named Desire*, *The Winslow Boy* (F) **1949:** *Death of a Salesman*, *The Madwoman of Chaillot* (F), *South Pacific* (M) **1950:** *The Member of the Wedding*, *The Cocktail Party* (F), *The Consul* (M) **1951:** *Darkness at Noon*, *The Lady's Not for Burning* (F), *Guys and Dolls* (M) **1952:** *I Am a Camera*, *Venus Observed* (F), *Pal Joey* (M), *Don Juan in Hell* (SC) **1953:** *Picnic*, *The Love of Four Colonels* (F), *Wonderful Town* (M) **1954:** *Teahouse of the August Moon*, *Ondine* (F), *The Golden Apple* (M) **1955:** *Cat on a Hot Tin Roof*, *Witness for the Prosecution* (F), *The Saint of Bleecker Street* (M) **1956:** *The Diary of Anne Frank*, *Tiger at the Gates* (F), *My Fair Lady* (M) **1957:** *Long Day's Journey into Night*, *The Waltz of the Toreadors* (F), *The Most Happy Fella* (M) **1958:** *Look Homeward Angel*, *Look Back in Anger* (F), *The Music Man* (M) **1959:** *A Raisin in the Sun*, *The Visit* (F), *La Plume de Ma Tante* (M) **1960:** *Toys in the Attic*, *Five Finger Exercise* (F), *Fiorello!* (M) **1961:** *All the Way Home*, *A Taste of Honey* (F), *Carnival* (M) **1962:** *Night of the Iguana*, *A Man for All Seasons* (F), *How to Succeed in Business Without Really Trying* (M) **1963:** *Who's Afraid of Virginia Woolf?*, *Beyond the Fringe* (SC) **1964:** *Luther*, *Hello Dolly!* (M), *The Trojan Women* (SC) **1965:** *The Subject Was Roses*, *Fiddler on the Roof* (M) **1966:** *Marat/Sade*, *Man of La Mancha* (M), *Mark Twain Tonight* - Hal Holbrook (SC) **1967:** *The Homecoming*, *Cabaret* (M) **1968:** *Rosencrantz and Guildenstern Are Dead*, *Your Own Thing* (M) **1969:** *The Great White Hope*, *1776* (M) **1970:** *Borstal Boy*, *The Effect of Gamma Rays on Man-in-the-Moon Marigolds* (A), *Company* (M) **1971:** *Home*, *The House of Blue Leaves* (A), *Follies* (M) **1972:** *That Championship Season*, *The Screens* (A), *Two Gentlemen of Verona* (M), *Sticks and Bones* (SC), *Old Times* (SC) **1973:** *The Changing Room*, *The Hot L Baltimore* (A), *A Little Night Music* (M) **1974:** *The Contractor*, *Short Eyes* (A), *Candide* (M) **1975:** *Equus*, *The Taking of Miss Janie* (A), *A Chorus Line* (M) **1976:** *Travesties*, *Streamers* (A), *Pacific Overtures* (M) **1977:** *Otherwise Engaged*, *American Buffalo* (A), *Annie* (M) **1978:** *Da*, *Ain't Misbehavin'* (M) **1979:** *The Elephant Man*, *Sweeney Todd* (M) **1980:** *Talley's Folly*, *Betrayal* (F), *Evita* (M), Peter Brook's *Le Centre International de Créations Théâtricales* at La MaMa ETC (SC) **1981:** *A Lesson from Aloes*, *Crimes of the*

Heart (A), *Lena Horne: The Lady and Her Music* (SC), *The Pirate of Penzance* at New York Shakespeare Festival (SC) **1982:** *The Life and Adventures of Nicholas Nickleby, A Soldier's Play* (A) **1983:** *Brighton Beach Memoirs*, *Plenty* (A), *Little Shop of Horrors* (M), Young Playwrights Festival (SC) **1984:** *The Real Thing*, *Glengarry Glen Ross* (F), *Sunday in the Park with George* (M), Samuel Beckett (SC) **1985:** *Ma Rainey's Black Bottom* **1986:** *A Lie of the Mind*, *Benefactors* (A), *The Search for Signs of Intelligent Life in the Universe* (SC) **1987:** *Fences*, *Les Liaisons Dangereuses* (F), *Les Misérables* (M) **1988:** *Joe Turner's Come and Gone*, *The Road to Mecca* (F), *Into the Woods* (M) **1989:** *The Heidi Chronicles*, *Aristocrats* (F), *Bill Irwin: Largely New York* (SC) **1990:** *The Piano Lesson*, *Privates on Parade* (F), *City of Angels* (M) **1991:** *Six Degrees of Separation*, *Our Country's Good* (F), *The Will Rogers Follies* (M) Eileen Atkins - *A Room of One's Own* (SC) **1992:** *Dancing at Lughnasa*, *Two Trains Running* (A) **1993:** *Angels in America: Millenium Approaches*, *Someone Who'll Watch Over Me* (F), *Kiss of the Spider Woman* (M) **1994:** *Three Tall Women*, *Twilight: Los Angeles, 1992* - Anna Deavere Smith (SC) **1995:** *Arcadia*, *Love! Valour! Compassion!* (A), Signature Theatre Company's Horton Foote Season (SC) **1996:** *Seven Guitars*, *Molly Sweeny* (F), *Rent* (M), New York City Center's *Encores!* (SC) **1997:** *How I Learned to Drive*, *Skylight* (F), *Violet* (M), *Chicago* - Broadway revival (SC) **1998:** *Art*, *Pride's Crossing* (A), *Lion King* (M), *Cabaret* – Broadway revival (SC) **1999:** *Wit*, *Closer* (F), *Parade* (M), David Hare (SC) **2000:** *Jitney*, *James Joyce's The Dead* (M), *Copenhagen* (F) **2001:** *The Invention of Love*, *The Producers* (M), *Proof* (A) **2002:** *Edward Albee's The Goat, or Who is Sylvia?*, *Elaine Stritch: At Liberty* (SC) **2003:** *Take Me Out*, *Talking Heads* (F), *Hairspray* (M) **2004:** *Intimate Apparel*, Barbara Cook (SC) **2005:** *Doubt*, *The Pillowman* (F) **2006:** *The History Boys*, *The Drowsy Chaperone* (M), John Doyle, Sarah Travis and the Cast of *Sweeney Todd* (SC), Christine Ebersole (SC) **2007:** *The Coast of Utopia*, *Radio Golf* (A), *Spring Awakening* (M), *Journey's End* (SC) **2008:** *August: Osage County*, *Passing Strange* (M) **2009:** *Ruined*; *Black Watch* (F); *Billy Elliot The Musical* (M); Angela Lansbury (SC); Gerard Alessandrini for *Forbidden Broadway* (SC); Matthew Warchus and the Cast of *The Norman Conquests* (SC)

DRAMA LEAGUE AWARDS

Friday, May 21, 2010; Broadway Ballroom at The Marriott Marquis; 76th annual. Co-Hosted by Vanessa Williams and Michael Urie; Presented for distinguished achievement in the New York theater; winners are selected by members of the League; Honorary Co-Chairs: Norbert Leo Butz, Kathleen Chalfant, Colman Domingo, John Gallagher Jr., David Alan Grier, Valerie Harper, Sean Hayes, Judith Ivey, Linda Lavin, Alfred Molina; Presenters: Betty Buckley, Barbara Cook, Viola Davis, Sean Hayes, Liev Schreiber, Christopher Walken, Denzel Washington, Jerry Zaks.

Play: *Red*

Musical: *Sondheim on Sondheim*

Revival of a Play: *A View from the Bridge*

Revival of a Musical: *La Cage aux Folles*

Performance: Alfred Molina, *Red*

Julia Hansen Award for Excellence in Directing: Kenny Leon

Achievement in Musical Theatre: Nathan Lane

Unique Contribution to Theater: Macy's Parade & Entertainment Group

PULITZER PRIZE AWARD WINNERS FOR DRAMA

Established in 1917; Administered by the Pulitzer Prize Board, Columbia University; Lee C. Bollinger, President. Winner is chosen by a jury, composed of three to four critics, one academic and one playwright, however the board has final authority over choice. Presented for an outstanding drama or musical presented in New York or regional theater. The award goes to the playwright but production of the play as well as the script, is taken into account.

2010 Winner: *Next to Normal* by Tom Kitt and Brian Yorkey

PAST PULITZER PRIZE WINNERS If year is missing, no award was presented that year.

1918: *Why Marry?* by Jesse Lynch Williams **1920:** *Beyond the Horizon* by Eugene O'Neill **1921:** *Miss Lulu Bett* by Zona Gale **1922:** *Anna Christie* by Eugene O'Neill **1923:** *Icebound* by Owen Davis **1924:** *Hell-Bent for Heaven* by Hatcher Hughes **1925:** *They Knew What They Wanted* by Sidney Howard **1926:** *Craig's Wife* by George Kelly **1927:** *In Abraham's Bosom* by Paul Green **1928:** *Strange Interlude* by Eugene O'Neill **1929:** *Street Scene* by Elmer Rice **1930:** *The Green Pastures* by Marc Connelly **1931:** *Alison's House* by Susan Glaspell **1932:** *Of Thee I Sing* by George S. Kaufman, Morrie Ryskind, Ira and George Gershwin **1933:** *Both Your Houses* by Maxwell Anderson **1934:** *Men in White* by Sidney Kingsley **1935:** *The Old Maid* by Zoe Atkins **1936:** *Idiot's Delight* by Robert E. Sherwood **1937:** *You Can't Take It with You* by Moss Hart and George S. Kaufman **1938:** *Our Town* by Thornton Wilder **1939:** *Abe Lincoln in Illinois* by Robert E. Sherwood **1940:** *The Time of Your Life* by William Saroyan **1941:** *There Shall Be No Night* by Robert E. Sherwood **1943:** *The Skin of Our Teeth* by Thornton Wilder **1945:** *Harvey* by Mary Chase **1946:** *State of the Union* by Howard Lindsay and Russel Crouse **1948:** *A Streetcar Named Desire* by Tennessee Williams **1949:** *Death of a Salesman* by Arthur Miller **1950:** *South Pacific* by Richard Rodgers, Oscar Hammerstein II, and Joshua Logan **1952:** *The Shrike* by Joseph Kramm **1953:** *Picnic* by William Inge **1954:** *The Teahouse of the August Moon* by John Patrick **1955:** *Cat on a Hot Tin Roof* by Tennessee Williams **1956:** *The Diary of Anne Frank* by Frances Goodrich and Albert Hackett **1957:** *Long Day's Journey Into Night* by Eugene O'Neill **1958:** *Look Homeward, Angel* by Ketti Frings **1959:** *J.B.* by Archibald MacLeish **1960:** *Fiorello!* by Jerome Weidman, George Abbott, Sheldon Harnick, and Jerry Bock **1961:** *All the Way Home* by Tad Mosel **1962:** *How to Succeed in Business Without Really Trying* by Abe Burrows, Willie Gilbert, Jack Weinstock, and Frank Loesser **1965:** *The Subject Was Roses* by Frank D. Gilroy **1967:** *A Delicate Balance* by Edward Albee **1969:** *The Great White Hope* by Howard Sackler **1970:** *No Place to Be Somebody* by Charles Gordone **1971:** *The Effect of Gamma Rays on Man-in-the-Moon Marigolds* by Paul Zindel **1973:** *That Championship Season* by Jason Miller **1975:** *Seascape* by Edward Albee **1976:** *A Chorus Line* by Michael Bennett, James Kirkwood, Nicholas Dante, Marvin Hamlisch, and Edward Kleban **1977:** *The Shadow Box* by Michael Cristofer **1978:** *The Gin Game* by D.L. Coburn **1979:** *Buried Child* by Sam Shepard **1980:** *Talley's Folly* by Lanford Wilson **1981:** *Crimes of the Heart* by Beth Henley **1982:** *A Soldier's Play* by Charles Fuller **1983:** *'night, Mother* by Marsha Norman **1984:** *Glengarry Glen Ross* by David Mamet **1985:** *Sunday in the Park with George* by James Lapine and Stephen Sondheim **1987:** *Fences* by August Wilson **1988:** *Driving Miss Daisy* by Alfred Uhry **1989:** *The Heidi Chronicles* by Wendy Wasserstein **1990:** *The Piano Lesson* by August Wilson **1991:** *Lost in Yonkers* by Neil Simon **1992:** *The Kentucky Cycle* by Robert Schenkkan **1993:** *Angels in America: Millenium Approaches* by Tony Kushner **1994:** *Three Tall Women* by Edward Albee **1995:** *Young Man from Atlanta* by Horton Foote **1996:** *Rent* by Jonathan Larson **1998:** *How I Learned to Drive* by Paula Vogel **1999:** *Wit* by Margaret Edson **2000:** *Dinner with Friends* by Donald Margulies **2001:** *Proof* by David Auburn **2002:** *Topdog/Underdog* by Suzan Lori-Parks **2003:** *Anna in the Tropics* by Nilo Cruz **2004:** *I Am My Own Wife* by Doug Wright **2005:** *Doubt* by John Patrick Shanley **2007:** *Rabbit Hole* by David Lindsay-Abaire **2008:** *August: Osage County* by Tracy Letts **2009:** *Ruined* by Lynn Nottage

Regional and Other Theatrical Awards

ACCLAIM AWARDS

May 24, 2010; Jarson-Kaplan Theater at the Aronoff Center for the Arts; 5th annual; Presented by The Cincinnati Enquirer and the League of Cincinnati Theatres and hosted by the Cincinnati Arts Association for outstanding work in Cincinnati/Northern Kentucky theatre. The non-competitive awards recognize the work of local artists as well as guest artists, and support a variety of initiatives for area theatre artists and educators. Winners by production:

33 Variations (Ensemble Theatre of Cincinnati) Outstanding Supporting Performance (Equity): Dale Hodges

7 (x1) Samurai (Cincinnati Fringe Festival) Outstanding Solo Performance (Fringe): David Gaines

Angels in America: Millennium Approaches (Know Theatre of Cincinnati) Outstanding Direction (Non-Equity): Brian Isaac Phillips; Outstanding Ensemble (Non-Equity): The Cast; Outstanding Supporting Performance (Non-Equity): Michael Bath

Breaking Up is Hard to Do (Covedale Center for the Performing Arts) Outstanding Supporting Performance in Independent Production: Joshua Steele

Bury the Dead (Carnegie Visual and Performing Arts Center) Outstanding Direction of an Independent Production: Michael Burnham; Outstanding Principal Student Cast of an Independent Production: Bennett Bradley, Michael Carr, Brian Emond, Claron Hayden, Kevin Macku, Kevin Malarkey, Catherine Prevett, Hope Shangle, Jordan Shramka, Mikayla Stanley, John Ware

Bye Bye Birdie (Northern Kentucky University Theatre & Dance) Outstanding Supporting Performance in a Musical (University): Sara Kenny; Outstanding Direction (University): Ken Jones; Outstanding Choreography (University): Jane Green and Sarah Peak; Outstanding Costume Design (University): Jeff Shearer; Outstanding Musical Supporting Performance (University): Kieran Cronin

Daddy Long Legs (Cincinnati Playhouse in the Park) Outstanding Lead Performance in Equity Production: Megan McGinnis

Dirty Rotten Scoundrels (Carnegie Visual and Performing Arts Center) Outstanding Musical Performance (Equity): Charlie Clark

The Edge (Cincinnati Fringe Festival) Outstanding Supporting Performance (Fringe): Karen Wissel

Equus (New Edgecliff Theatre) Outstanding Lead Performance (Independent): Cary Davenport; Outstanding Ensemble (Independent): The Cast; Outstanding Direction (Independent): Alan Patrick Kenny; Outstanding Lighting Design (Independent):Glen Goodwin; Outstanding Sound Design (Independent):Paul Lieber

The Fall of Heaven (Cincinnati Playhouse in the Park) Outstanding Direction: Marion McClinton; Outstanding Stage Management: Jenifer Morrow; Outstanding Set Design: David Gallo; Outstanding Lighting Design: Donald Holder; Outstanding Sound Design: Rob Milburn & Michael Bodeen; Outstanding Lead Performance (Equity): Esau Pritchett

Falsettos (UC College-Conservatory of Music) Outstanding Supporting Performance (Collegiate): Mia Gentile

The Fantasticks (Cincinnati Playhouse in the Park) Outstanding Musical Lead Performance (Equity): Ron Bohmer; Outstanding Comic Duo (Equity): Dale Hodges and Joneal Joplin

Gravesongs (Cincinnati Fringe Festival) Outstanding Direction (Fringe): Liz Maxwell; Outstanding Acting Ensemble (Fringe): Rachel Christianson, Emily Eaton, Lauren Shiveley, Rebecca Whatley, Elizabeth Worley

The History of Invulnerability (Cincinnati Playhouse in the Park) Outstanding Direction (Equity): Michael Haney; Outstanding Lead Performance (Equity): David Deblinger; Outstanding Supporting Performance (Equity): Joseph Parks; Outstanding Scenic Design and Projections (Equity): David Gallo and Steve Channon

Human Comedy (UC College-Conservatory of Music) Outstanding Direction: Aubrey Berg; Outstanding Musical/Vocal Direction (Collegiate): Anthony DeAngelis; Outstanding Musical Supporting Performance (Collegiate): Carlyn Connolly; Outstanding Vocal Ensemble (Collegiate): The Cast

I Love a Piano (Commonwealth Theatre Company) Outstanding Musical Ensemble (Independent): Matt Bohnert, Sarah Drake, Roderick Justice, Edwin Large, Rachel Perin & Laura Wacksman

The Marvelous Wonderettes (Ensemble Theatre of Cincinnati) Outstanding Supporting Performances in a Musical (Non-Equity): Mia Gentile and Brooke Rucidlo

The Musical of Musicals - The Musical! (Showboat Majestic) Outstanding Musical Ensemble (Independent): Mark Femia, Lesley Hitch, Brooke Rucidlo, Michael Shawn Starks, Mike Sherman

Orpheus Descending (UC College-Conservatory of Music) Outstanding Direction (Collegiate): Ashton Byrum; Outstanding Set Design (Collegiate): John Barisonek

Othello (Cincinnati Shakespeare Company) Outstanding Supporting Performance in Equity Production: Kelly Mengelkoch

Picnic (UC College-Conservatory of Music) Outstanding Set Design (University): Tammy Honesty

Poe (Cincinnati Shakespeare Company) Outstanding Theatrical Special Event: Giles Davies

Rhinoceros (Northern Kentucky University Theatre & Dance) Outstanding Wig Design: Jeff Shearer

Sideways Stories from Wayside School (Know Theatre of Cincinnati) Outstanding Direction (Independent): Jason Ballweber; Outstanding Choreography (Independent): Lindsey Jones & Kim Popa; Outstanding Ensemble (Independent): Darnell Benjamin, Breona Conrad, Annie Kalahurka, Joshua Murphy, Kim Popa, Catherine Prevett, Dylan Shelton, Alison Vodnoy, Liz Vosmeier, Chris Wesselman

Sleuth (Cincinnati Playhouse in the Park) Outstanding Set Design/Décor (Equity): Paul Shortt, Anna C. Goller, Ingrid Heithaus, Scott Hubert, Thomas C. Nader Jr.

Three Sisters (Cincinnati Playhouse in the Park) Outstanding Ensemble (Equity): The Cast; Outstanding Direction: John Doyle; Outstanding Script Adaptation: Sarah Ruhl; Outstanding Performances (Equity): Laila Robins, Corey Stoll, Frank Wood; Outstanding Set Design: Scott Pask; Outstanding Lighting Design: Jane Cox; Outstanding Sound Designer/Composer: Dan Moses Schreier; Outstanding Costume Design: Ann Hould-Ward

Titanic the Musical (Northern Kentucky University Theatre & Dance) Outstanding Vocal Direction (Collegiate): Jamey Strawn; Outstanding Vocal Performance (Collegiate): The Cast

Victoria Musica (Cincinnati Playhouse in the Park) Outstanding Ensemble (Equity): Stephen Caffery, Drew Cortese, Judith Hawking, Mariann Mayberry, Thom Rivera, Tommy Schrider, Peter Van Wagner, Evan Zes

You Can't Take It with You (UC College-Conservatory of Music) Outstanding Set Design (Collegiate): Thomas Umfrid; Outstanding Properties (Collegiate): Kayleigh Baird & Thomas Umfrid; Outstanding Performance (Collegiate): Hope Shangle

Enquirer/Fifth Third Bank Theater Educator Award: Michele Mascari (St. Xavier High School); Judges Prize ($1,000): Lisa Bodollo (Mother of Mercy High School); Special Recognition ($500 each): Mark Femia (Cincinnati Country Day School) & Michael Sherman (Colerain High School)

Rising Star Awards ($1,000): Stephanie Brain (CCM), Lauren Spriague (CCM), Matt Bohnert (NKU)

Trailblazer Award: Dee Anne Bryll and Ed Cohen

Acclaim MVPs: Joshua Steele, Steve Goers, Mark Halpin, Patti James, Brooke Rucidlo, Liz Vosmeier, Ed Stern

AMERICAN THEATRE CRITICS ASSOCIATION AWARDS

Steinberg New Play Award and Citations

March 27, 2010; Ceremony at the Humana Festival at Actors Theatre Louisville; founded in 1977. The Harold and Mimi Steinberg/ATCA Awards honor new plays that had their world premieres in the previous year in professional productions outside New York City. From 1977–1984 ACTA gave only one play a citation. After 1985, three citations were awarded. Currently the new play award comes with a $25,000 prize and the two other citations are awarded a $7,500 prize.

2010 New Play Award: *Equivocation* by Bill Cain (premiered at the Oregon Shakespeare Festival); **Citations:** *Time Stands Still* by Donald Margulies (premiered at Geffen Playhouse, Los Angeles, CA); *Legacy of Light* by Karen Zacarias (premiered at Arena Stage, Washington, DC)

Past Recipients (after 1986, first entry is the principal citation): **1977:** *And the Soul Shall Dance* by Wakako Yamauchi **1978:** *Getting Out* by Marsha Norman **1979:** *Loose Ends* by Michael Weller **1980:** *Custer* by Robert E. Ingham **1981:** *Chekhov in Yalta* by John Driver and Jeffrey Haddow **1982:** *Talking With* by Jane Martin **1983:** *Closely Related* by Bruce MacDonald **1984:** *Wasted* by Fred Gamel **1985:** (no principal citation) *Scheherazade* by Marisha Chamberlain, *The Shaper* by John Steppling, *A Shayna Maidel* by Barbara Lebow **1986:** *Fences* by August Wilson; *Fugue* by Lenora Thuna; *Hunting Cockroaches* by Januscz Glowacki **1987:** *A Walk in the Woods* by Lee Blessing; *The Film Society* by John Robin Baitz; *Back to the World* by Stephen Mack Jones **1988:** *Heathen Valley* by Romulus Linney; *The Voice of the Prairie* by John Olive; *The Deal* by Matthew Witten **1989:** *The Piano Lesson* by August Wilson; *Generations* by Dennis Clontz; *The Downside* by Richard Dresser **1990:** *2* by Romulus Linney; *Pick Up Ax* by Anthony Clarvoe; *Marvin's Room* by Scott McPherson **1991:** *Two Trains Running* by August Wilson; *Sincerity Forever* by Mac Wellman; *The Ohio State Murders* by Adrienne Kennedy **1992:** *Could I Have This Dance* by Doug Haverty; *American Enterprise* by Jeffrey Sweet; *Miss Evers' Boys* by David Feldshuh **1993:** *Children of Paradise: Shooting a Dream* by Steven Epp, Felicity Jones, Dominique Serrand, and Paul Walsh; *Black Elk Speaks* by Christopher Sergel; *Hurricane* by Anne Galjour **1994:** *Keely and Du* by Jane Martin **1995:** *The Nanjing Race* by Reggie Cheong-Leen; *Rush Limbaugh in Night School* by Charlie Varon; *The Waiting Room* by Lisa Loomer **1996:** *Amazing Grace* by Michael Cristofer; *Jungle Rot* by Seth Greenland; *Seven Guitars* by August Wilson **1997:** *Jack and Jill* by Jane Martin; *The Last Night of Ballyhoo* by Alfred Uhry; *The Ride Down Mount Morgan* by Arthur Miller **1998:** *The Cider House Rules, Part II* by Peter Parnell; *Jitney* by August Wilson; *The Old Settler* by John Henry Redwood **1999:** *Book of Days* by Lanford Wilson; *Dinner With Friends* by Donald Margulies; *Expecting Isabel* by Lisa Loomer **2000:** *Oo-Bla-Dee* by Regina Taylor; *Compleat Female Stage Beauty* by Jeffrey Hatcher; *Syncopation* by Allan Knee **2001:** *Anton in Show Business* by Jane Martin; *Big Love* by Charles L. Mee; *King Hedley II* by August Wilson **2002:** *The Carpetbagger's Children* by Horton Foote; *The Action Against Sol Schumann* by Jeffrey Sweet; *Joe and Betty* by Murray Mednick **2003:** *Anna in the Tropics* by Nilo Cruz; *Recent Tragic Events* by Craig Wright; *Resurrection Blues* by Arthur Miller **2004:** *Intimate Apparel* by Lynn Nottage; *Gem of the Ocean* by August Wilson; *The Love Song of J. Robert Oppenheimer* by Carson Kreitzer **2005:** *The Singing Forest* by Craig Lucas; *After Ashley* by Gina Gionfriddo; *The Clean House* by Sarah Ruhl; *Madagascar* by J.T. Rogers **2006:** *A Body of Water* by Lee Blessing; *Red Light Winter* by Adam Rapp; *Radio Golf* by August Wilson **2007:** *Hunter Gatherers* by Peter Sinn Nachtrieb; *Opus* by Michael Hollinger; *Guest Artist* by Jeff Daniels **2008:** *33 Variations* by Moises Kaufman; *End Days* by Deborah Zoe Laufer; *Dead Man's Cell Phone* by Sarah Ruhl **2009:** *Song of Extinction* by E.M. (Ellen) Lewis; *Great Falls* by Lee Blessing; *Superior Donuts* by Tracy Letts

M. Elizabeth Osborn Award

March 27, 2010; Ceremony at the Humana Festival at Actors Theatre Louisville; established in 1993. Presented by the American Theatre Critics Association in memory of Theatre Communications Group and American Theatre play editor M. Elizabeth Osborn to an emerging playwright who has not received other major national awards, has not had a significant New York production, and whose work has not been staged widely in regional theatres; $1,000 prize and recognition in the *Best Plays Theater Yearbook* edited by Jeffrey Eric Jenkins.

2010 Winner: Jason Wells for *Perfect Mendacity* (premiered at Asolo Repertory Theatre, Sarasota, FL)

Past Recipients: 1994: *Hurricane* by Anne Galjour **1995:** *Rush Limbaugh in Night School* by Charlie Varon **1996:** *Beast on the Moon* by Richard Kalinoski **1997:** *Thunder Knocking On the Door* by Keith Glover **1998:** *The Glory of Living* by Rebecca Gilman **1999:** *Lamarck* by Dan O'Brien **2000:** *Marked Tree* by Coby Goss **2001:** *Waiting to Be Invited* by S.M. Shephard-Massat **2002:** *Chagrin Falls* by Mia McCullough **2003:** *The Dinosaur Within* by John Walch **2004:** *The Intelligent Design of Jenny Chow* by Rolin Jones **2005:** *Madagascar* by J.T. Rogers **2006:** *American Fiesta* by Steven Tomlinson **2007** *Vestibular Sense* by Ken LaZebnik **2008:** *Gee's Bend* by Elyzabeth Wilder **2009:** *Our Enemies: Lively Scenes of Love and Combat* by Yusseff El Guindi

THE ASCAP FOUNDATION AWARDS

The ASCAP Foundation provides Awards to emerging composers and songwriters and recognition to honor the achievements of established composers and songwriters in 2009.

Champion Award: Arlo Guthrie

Harold Adamson Lyric Award: Adam Gwon (Musical Theatre); Shawn Pander (Pop)

Robert Allen Award: Nick Howard

Harold Arlen Film & TV Award: Joe Trapanese

Louis Armstrong Scholarship: Danny Rivera

Louis Armstrong Jazz Scholarship Honoring Duke Ellington: Richard Glaser

Louis Armstrong Scholarship at Aaron Copland School of Music, Queens College: LaRon Land

Louis Armstrong Scholarship Honoring W.C. Handy: Pierre Joseph

Louis Armstrong Scholarship at the University of New Orleans: Meghan Swartz

Charlotte V. Bergen Scholarship: Graham Cohen

Irving Berlin Summer Camp Scholarship: Joshua Clampitt

Boosey & Hawkes Young Composer Award Honoring Aaron Copland: Naom Gavriel Londy

Leon Brettler Award: Lizzy McAvoy

Irving Burgie Scholarship: Clynton Cox

Irving Caesar Scholarship: Matija Budisin, Daniel Lofaso, Michael Lofaso, Kelvin Ma, Elvis Vanterpool-Krajnak

Sammy Cahn Award: Oren Lavie and Devon Sproule

Cherry Lane Foundation/Music Alive! Scholarship in honor of Quincy Jones: Allen M. Jones

Desmond Child Anthem Award: Josué Garcia

Cy Coleman Award: Erica Stenquist

Eunice & Hal David Instructor-in-Residence Award: Pat Bass

Fran Morgenstern Davis Scholarship: Andrea Carroll, Yuma Sung

John Denver Music Scholarships supported by Music Alive!/Cherry Lane Foundation: Eyeshia McSwain, Maria Slye

Jamie deRoy & Friends Award: Christine Lavin

Louis Dreyfus Warner/Chappell City College Scholarship Honoring George & Ira Gershwin: Matthew Smith

Max Dreyfus Scholarship: Joel Waggoner

Fellowship for Composition & Film Scoring: Christopher Heckman

Ira Gershwin Scholarship at LaGuardia High School: Deiran Manning

Jay Gorney Award: Christina Lord & John Munnelly

Leo Kaplan Award: Joe Trapani

Steve Kaplan TV & Film Studies Scholarship: Miles Hankins

Leiber & Stoller Music Scholarship: Lauren Desberg, Vincent Yang

Livingston & Evans Music Scholarship: Marley Eder

Frederick Loewe Scholarship: Dewey Fleszar

Henry Mancini Music Scholarship: Stephen Guerra, Stephen Wheeler

Michael Masser Scholarship: Mellisa Andrea Batallé, Simon Wiskowski, Max Wang

Rudolf Nissim Prize: Roger Zare

Rudy Perez Songwriting Scholarship: René G. Boscio

Cole Porter Award: John Mercurio

Joan & Irwin Robinson Scholarship: Brittany Easterling

Richard Rodgers New Horizons Award: Brendan Milburn and Valerie Vigoda

David Rose Scholarship: Sunna Wehrmeijer

AUDELCO AWARDS - THE "VIVS"

November 16, 2009; Harlem Stages/Aaron Davis Hall – Marion Anderson Theatre; 37th annual. Presented for excellence in Black Theatre for the 2008–2009 season by the Audience Development Committee, created by Vivian Robinson. Co-Chairs: Starletta DuPois and Rajendra Ramoon Hahar; Co-hosts: Kim Brockington and Ted Lange; Music, Tevin Thomas

Outstanding Dramatic Production of the Year: *Ruined* (Manhattan Theatre Club)

Outstanding Revival: *Zooman and the Sign* (Signature Theatre Company)

Outstanding Musical Production of the Year: *Archbishop Supreme Tartuffe* (Classical Theatre of Harlem)

Outstanding Director/Dramatic Production: Marion McClinton, *Pure Confidence* (59E59 and Mixed Blood Theatre Company)

Outstanding Director/Musical Production: Keith Lee Grant, *The Wiz* (Harlem Repertory Theatre)

Outstanding Choreographer: Keith Lee Grant, *The Wiz* (Harlem Repertory Theatre)

Outstanding Playwright: Lynn Nottage, *Ruined* (Manhattan Theatre Club)

Outstanding Lead Actor: Gavin Lawrence, *Pure Confidence* (59E59 and Mixed Blood Theatre Company)

Outstanding Lead Actress: Saidah Arrika Ekulona, *Ruined* (Manhattan Theatre Club)

Outstanding Supporting Actor: Russell G. Jones, *Ruined* (Manhattan Theatre Club)

Outstanding Supporting Actress: Quincy Tyler Jones, *Ruined* (Manhattan Theatre Club)

Outstanding Performance in a Musical/Female: Kim Brockington, *Archbishop Supreme Tartuffe* (Classical Theatre of Harlem)

Outstanding Performance in a Musical/Male: André DeShields, *Archbishop Supreme Tartuffe* (Classical Theatre of Harlem)

Outstanding Ensemble Performance: Kevin Carroll, Tracey Bonner, and January Lavoy, *Home* (Signature Theatre Company)

Outstanding Solo Performance: Khalil Ashanti, *Basic Training* (Produced by Josephson Entertainment, Erich Jungwirth/VoiceChair Productions and Richard Jordan Productions Ltd)

Outstanding Musical Director: Kelvyn Bell, *Archbishop Supreme Tartuffe* (Classical Theatre of Harlem)

Outstanding Set Design: Derek McLane, *Ruined* (Manhattan Theatre Club)

Outstanding Costume Design: Paul Tazewell, *Ruined* (Manhattan Theatre Club)

Outstanding Lighting Design: Matthew Frey, *Zooman and the Sign* (Signature Theatre Company)

Outstanding Sound Design: C. Andrew Mayer, *Pure Confidence* (59E59 and Mixed Blood Theatre Company)

Pioneer Award: Kojo Ade, Ray Aranha, Patricia White, Robin Williams

Board of Directors Award: Michael Green, LaZette McCants, Veona Thomas, Dwayne Trottman

Rising Star Honoree: Solomon Hicks

Special Achievement Award: Van Dirk Fisher (Riant Theatre)

BARRYMORE AWARDS

October 5, 2009; Walnut Street Theatre; 15th annual. Presented by the Theatre Alliance of Greater Philadelphia for excellence in theatre in the greater Philadelphia area for the 2008-2009 season.

Outstanding Production of a Play: *Something Intangible* (Arden Theatre Company)

Outstanding Production of a Musical: *Cinderella* (The People's Light & Theatre Company)

Outstanding Direction of a Play: Terrence J. Nolen, *Something Intangible* (Arden Theatre Company)

Outstanding Direction of a Musical: Pete Pryor, *Cinderella* (The People's Light & Theatre Company)

Outstanding Musical Direction: Dan Kazemi, *Avenue X* (11th Hour Theatre Company)

Outstanding Leading Actor in a Play: Ian Merrill Peakes, *Something Intangible* (Arden Theatre Company)

Outstanding Leading Actress in a Play: Kate Eastwood Norris, *Rock 'n' Roll* (The Wilma Theater)

Outstanding Leading Actor in a Musical: Michael Philip O'Brien, *Avenue X* (11th Hour Theatre Company)

Outstanding Leading Actress in a Musical: Jennie Eisenhower, *Forbidden Broadway's Greatest Hits* (Walnut Street Theatre, Independence Studio on 3)

Outstanding Supporting Actor in a Play: Jered McLenigan, *It's a Wonderful Life! A Live Radio Play* (Prince Music Theater)

Outstanding Supporting Actress in a Play: Janis Dardaris, *Scorched* (The Wilma Theater)

Outstanding Supporting Actor in a Musical: Forrest McClendon, *Avenue X* (11th Hour Theatre Company)

Outstanding Supporting Actress in a Musical: Mary Martello, *Candide* (Arden Theatre Company)

Outstanding Set Design: James Kronzer, *Something Intangible* (Arden Theatre Company)

Outstanding Lighting Design: F. Mitchell Dana, *Something Intangible* (Arden Theatre Company)

Outstanding Costume Design: Rosemarie E. McKelvey *Something Intangible* (Arden Theatre Company)

Outstanding Sound Design: Jorge Cousineau, *Scorched* (The Wilma Theater)

Outstanding Original Music: Michael Ogborn, *Cinderella* (The People's Light & Theatre Company)

Outstanding Choreography/Movement: Christopher Gattelli, *Alter Boyz* (Bristol Riverside Theatre)

Outstanding New Play: *Something Intangible* by Bruce Graham (Arden Theatre Company)

Outstanding Ensemble in a Play: *Scorched* (The Wilma Theater)

Outstanding Ensemble in a Musical: *Cinderella* (The People's Light & Theatre Company)

Ted & Stevie Wolf Award for New Approaches to Collaborations: Delaware Theatre Company & The Ferris School for Boys (*No Child...*)

Excellence in Theatre Education/Community Service Prize: Lantern Theatre Company for "Classroom Connections"

F. Otto Haas Award for Emerging Philadelphia Theatre Artist: Charlotte Cloe Fox Wind

Lifetime Achievement Award: Dugald MacArthur

Special Recognition Award: Deen Kogan

BAY AREA THEATRE CRITICS CIRCLE AWARDS

May 3, 2010; Palace of the Fine Arts Theatre Lobby; Founded in 1977. Presented by members of the print and electronic media for outstanding achievement in theatre in the San Francisco Bay Area for the 2009 calendar year.

Theatres Over 300 Seats: Drama

Entire Production: *The Kite Runner* (San Jose Repertory Theatre)

Principal Performance, Female: Judy Kaye, *Souvenir* (American Conservatory Theater)

Principal Performance, Male: Danny Scheie, *You, Nero* (Berkeley Repertory Theatre)

Supporting Performance, Female: Catherine Castellanos, *Romeo and Juliet* (California Shakespeare Theater)

Supporting Performance, Male: Adam Farabee, *The Lieutenant of Inishmore* (Berkeley Repertory Theatre)

Director: Sharon Ott, *You, Nero* (Berkeley Repertory Theatre)

Set Design: Vicki Smith, *The Kite Runner* (San Jose Repertory Theatre)

Costume Design: David Zinn, *In the Next Room or the vibrator play* (Berkeley Repertory Theatre)

Lighting Design: David Lee Cuthbert, *The Kite Runner* (San Jose Repertory Theatre)

Sound Design: Scott Edwards, *The Kite Runner* (San Jose Repertory Theatre)

Specialties (Fight choreographer, video, music directors, original score): Dave Maier (Fight Director), *The Lieutenant of Inishmore* (Berkeley Repertory Theatre)

Original Script: Matthew Spangler, *The Kite Runner* (San Jose Repertory Theatre)

Solo Performance: Rick Reynolds, *Love God Sex* (LGS Productions)

Ensemble: *The Lieutenant of Inishmore* (Berkeley Repertory Theatre)

Theatres Over 300 Seats: Musicals

Entire Production: *It Ain't Nothin' But the Blues* (TheatreWorks)

Principal Performance, Female: C. Kelly Wright, *It Ain't Nothin' But the Blues* (TheatreWorks)

Principal Performance, Male: (tie) Ray Drummond, *The Producers* (Diablo Theatre Company); Zachary Franczak, *The Who's Tommy* (Ray of Light Theatre)

Supporting Performance, Female: Allison Briner, *Tinyard Hill* (TheatreWorks)

Supporting Performance, Male: James Moye, *Tinyeard Hill* (TheatreWorks)

Director: Randal Myler, *It Ain't Nothin But the Blues* (TheatreWorks)

Music Director: (tie) Attilio Tribuzi, *Crazy for You* (Broadway by the Bay); Ben Prince, *The Who's Tommy* (Ray of Light Theatre)

Set Design: (tie) Angelo Benedetto, *The Who's Tommy* (Ray of Light Theatre); Mark Mendelson, *Hello, Dolly* (Diablo Theatre Company)

Costume Design: Mark Koss, *The Who's Tommy* (Ray of Light Theatre)

Lighting Design: (tie) Dustin Snyder, *The Who's Tommy* (Ray of Light Theatre); Michael Ramsaur, *Crazy for You* (Broadway by the Bay)

Sound Design: Cliff Caruthers, *It Ain't Nothin But the Blues* (TheatreWorks)

Original Script: Michael Mayer and Billy Joe Armstrong, *American Idiot* (Berkeley Repertory Theatre)

Specialties (Fight choreographer, video, music directors, original score): Ellyn Marie Marsh (Choreography), *The Who's Tommy* (Ray of Light Theatre); Lawrence Pech (Choreography), *Hello, Dolly* (Diablo Theatre Company); Robin Tribuzi (Choreography), *Crazy for You* (Broadway by the Bay)

Solo Performance: No award presented this season

Ensemble: *It Ain't Nothin But the Blues* (TheatreWorks)

Touring Production: *Wicked* (Best of Broadway)

Theatres 100 – 300 Seats: Drama

Entire Production: (tie) *Jack Goes Boating* (Aurora Theatre Company); *Mauritius* (Magic Theatre)

Principal Performance, Female: Zehra Berkman, *First Day of School* (San Francisco Playhouse)

Principal Performance, Male: Jud Williford, *Fat Pig* (Aurora Theatre Company)

Supporting Performance, Female: Beth Deitchman, *Miss Julie* (Aurora Theatre Company)

Supporting Performance, Male: Rod Gnapp, *Mauritius* (Magic Theatre)

Director: Loretta Greco, *Mauritius* (Magic Theatre)

Set Design: Bill English, *First Day of School* (San Francisco Playhouse)

Costume Design: Fumiko Bielefeldt, *Miss Julie* (Aurora Theatre Company)

Lighting Design: Jim Cave, *Jack Goes Boating* (Aurora Theatre Company)

Sound Design: Chris Houston, *Jack Goes Boating* (Aurora Theatre Company)

Specialties (Fight choreographer, video, music directors, original score): Lynne Soffer (Dialect Coach), *My Children! My Africa!* (Marin Theatre Company)

Original Script: Billy Aronson, *First Day of School* (San Francisco Playhouse)

Solo Performance: no award presented this season in this category

Ensemble: *Jack Goes Boating* (Aurora Theatre Company)

Theatres 100 – 300 Seats: Musicals

Entire Production: *Dames at Sea* (New Conservatory Theatre Center)

Principal Performance, Female: Rena Wilson, *Dames at Sea* (New Conservatory Theatre Center)

Principal Performance, Male: David Sattler, *All Shook Up* (Center Repertory Company)

Supporting Performance, Female: Leanne Borghesi, *Dames at Sea* (New Conservatory Theatre Center)

Supporting Performance, Male: Jarion Monroe, *Cabaret* (Center Repertory Company)

Director: Robert Barry Fleming, *All Shook Up* (Center Repertory Company)

Musical Director: G. Scott Lacy, *Dames at Sea* (New Conservatory Theatre Center)

Set Design: (tie) David Lear, *In the Mood* (6th Street Playhouse); Kuo-Hao Lo, *Dames at Sea* (New Conservatory Theatre Center)

Costume Design: Victoria Livingston Hall, *Cabaret* (Center Repertory Company)

Lighting Design: John Kelly, *Dames at Sea* (New Conservatory Theatre Center)

Sound Design: Lewis Mead, *All Shook Up* (Center Repertory Company)

Specialties (Fight choreographer, video, music directors, original score): Tom Segal (Choreography), *Wildcat* (42nd Street New Moon)

Original Script: no award presented this season in this category

Solo Performance: Mark Nadler, *My Wife Ira* (The Rrazz Room)

Ensemble: *Cabaret* (Center Repertory Company)

Theatres Under 99 Seats: Drama

Entire Production: *Who's Afraid of Virginia Woolf?* (Actors Theatre of San Francisco)

Performance, Female: Abigail Van Alyn, *The Unexpected Man* (Spare Stage Company)

Performance, Male: Ken Ruta, *The Unexpected Man* (Spare Stage Company)

Director: (tie) Rob Melrose, *The Creature* (Black Box Theatre); Stephen Drewes, *The Unexpected Man* (Spare Stage Company)

Original Script: William Bivins, *Pulp Scripture* (Original Sin Productions & Piano Fight at SF Fringe and Off-Market Theatre)

Solo Performance: no award presented this season in this category

Ensemble: *Who's Afraid of Virginia Woolf?* (Actors Theatre of San Francisco)

Theatres Under 99 Seats: Musicals

Entire Production: *SF Follies* (Produced by John Bisceglie)

Performance, Female: no award presented this season in this category

Performance, Male: J. Conrad Frank, *Katya's Holiday Spectacular!* (New Conservatory Theatre Center)

Director: John Bisceglie, *SF Follies* (Produced by John Bisceglie)

Musical Director: no award presented this season in this category

Specialties (Fight choreographer, video, music directors, original score): Kayvon Kordestani (Choreography), *SF Follies* (Produced by John Bisceglie)

Ensemble: *SF Follies* (Produced by John Bisceglie)

Special Awards

Paine Knickerbocker Award: PlayGround

Barbara Bladen Porter Award: Octavio Solis

Gene Price Award: San Francisco Playhouse

BISTRO AWARDS

April 13, 2010; Gotham Comedy Club; 25th annual. Presented by *Back Stage* for outstanding achievement in the cabaret field; Winners selected by a committee consisting of Elizabeth Ahlfors (*Cabaret Scenes*), David Finkle (*Back Stage*'s "Bistro Bits" columnist), Rob Lester (*Cabaret Scenes* & *TalkinBroadway.com*), Erv Raible (Executive/Artistic Director of the Cabaret Conference – Yale University), Roy Sander (former "Bistro Bits" columnist) and Sherry Eaker (*Back Stage* Editor at Large); Produced by Sherry Eaker; Originally created by the late *Back Stage* cabaret critic Bob Harrington.

Outstanding Vocalists: Anne Steele (Metropolitan Room)

Outstanding Jazz Vocalist: Nicole Henry (Metropolitan Room)

Outstanding Entertainers: Loli Marquez-Sterling (The Triad/Metropolitan Room); Lee Summers (The Triad)

Outstanding Debut:

Ira Eaker Special Achievement Award: Danielle Grabianowski (Metropolitan Room/Don't Tell Mama)

Outstanding Major Engagement: Liz Callaway (Metropolitan Room)

Outstanding CD: Alan Cumming, "I Bought a Blue Car Today"; Julie Reyburn, "Live at Feinstein's"

Outstanding Duo: Michael Feinstein and Cheyenne Jackson/Christine Ebersole/David Hyde Pierce (Feinstein's at Loews Regency)

Outstanding Theme Show: Sarah Rice, *Screen Gems – Songs of Old Hollywood* (Laurie Beechman Theatre at the West Bank Café)

Outstanding Tribute Show: Gretchen Reinhagen, *Special Kaye: A Tribute to the Incomparable Kaye Ballard* (Metropolitan Room)

Outstanding Comedy Series: *Celebrity Autobiography: In Their Own Words* created by Eugene Pack (The Triad)

Outstanding Songwriter: Brett Kristofferson

Outstanding Special Material: Richard Eisenberg, "Two Again"

BMI Award for Outstanding Director: Peter Napolitano

Special Awards: *I've Got a Little Twist* by David Auxier, Mark York, and Albert Bergeret (The Triad/Laurie Beechman Theatre at the West Bank Café); The Concerts at Tudor City Greens, created and produced by Raissa Katona Bennett; The Salon, created and hosted by Mark Janas (The Algonquin/Etcetera Etcetera)

Silver Anniversary Awards for Ongoing Artistic Accomplishment: Tovah Feldshuh, Paul Trueblood, Ronny Whyte

Extraordinary Cabaret Artist: Elaine Stritch

Bob Harrington Lifetime Achievement Award: Mitzi Gaynor

BROADWAY.COM AUDIENCE AWARDS

May 21, 2010; 11th annual. The Broadway.com Audience Awards give real theatergoers a chance to honor their favorite Broadway and Off-Broadway shows and performers.

New Broadway Musical: *The Addams Family*

New Broadway Play: *Next Fall*

Broadway Musical Revival: *Promises, Promises*

Broadway Play Revival: *Lend Me a Tenor*

New Off-Broadway Musical: *Bloody Bloody Andrew Jackson*

New Off-Broadway Play: *Love, Loss, and What I Wore*

Leading Actor in a Broadway Musical: John Gallagher Jr., *American Idiot*

Leading Actress in a Broadway Musical: Kristin Chenoweth, *Promises, Promises*

Leading Actor in a Broadway Play: Jude Law, *Hamlet*

Leading Actress in a Broadway Play: Laura Benanti, *In the Next Room or the vibrator play*

Featured Actor in a Broadway Musical: Kevin Chamberlin, *The Addams Family*

Featured Actress in a Broadway Musical: Angela Lansbury, *A Little Night Music*

Featured Actor in a Broadway Play: Brian d'Arcy James, *Time Stands Stil*

Featured Actress in a Broadway Play: Scarlett Johansson, *A View from the Bridge*

Diva Performance: Kristin Chenoweth, *Promises, Promises*

Solo Performance: Carrie Fisher, *Wishful Drinking*

Onstage Pair: Nathan Lane and Bebe Neuwirth, *The Addams Family*

Ensemble Cast: *American Idiot*

Breakthrough Performance (Male): Sean Hayes, *Promises, Promises*

Breakthrough Performance (Female): Krysta Rodriguez, *The Addams Family*

Replacement (Male): Kyle Dean Massey, *Next to Normal*

Replacement (Female): Mandy Gonzalez, *Wicked*

New Broadway Song: "Memphis Lives in Me" (*Memphis*)

Long-Running Broadway Show: *Wicked*

Long-Running Off-Broadway Show: *Blue Man Group*

CARBONELL AWARDS

April 12, 2010; Broward Center for the Performing Arts – Amaturo Theatre; 34th annual. Presented for outstanding achievement in South Florida theater during the 2009 calendar year. (Awards for stock and road show productions were not presented this year.)

Best New Work: *Cagney* by Peter Colley, Robert Creighton, and Christopher McGovern (Florida Stage)

Best Ensemble: *Farragut North* (GableStage)

Best Production of a Play: *Speed-the-Plow* (GableStage)

Best Director of a Play: Joseph Adler, *Speed-the-Plow* (GableStage)

Best Actor in a Play: Paul Tei, *Speed-the-Plow* (GableStage)

Best Actress in a Play: Barbara Bradshaw, *Why Torture is Wrong, and the People Who Love Them* (Mosaic Theatre)

Best Supporting Actor in a Play: Greg Weiner, *Farragut North* (GableStage)

Best Supporting Actress in a Play: Elena Maria Garcia, *Summer Shorts: Signature Shorts* (City Theatre)

Best Production of a Musical: *Les Misérables* (Actors' Playhouse at Miracle Theatre)

Best Director of a Musical: David Arisco, *Les Misérables* (Actors' Playhouse at Miracle Theatre)

Best Actor in a Musical: Brad Oscar, *Barnum* (Maltz Jupiter Theatre)

Actress in a Musical: Holly Shunkey, *Vices: A Love Story* (Caldwell Theatre Company)

Best Supporting Actor in a Musical: Gary Marachek, *Les Misérables* (Actors' Playhouse at Miracle Theatre)

Best Supporting Actress in a Musical: Gwen Hollander, *Les Misérables* (Actors' Playhouse at Miracle Theatre)

Best Musical Direction: Eric Alsford, *Les Misérables* (Actors' Playhouse at Miracle Theatre)

Best Choreography: AC Ciulla, *Vices: A Love Story* (Caldwell Theatre Company)

Best Scenic Design: Sean McClelland, *Les Misérables* (Actors' Playhouse at Miracle Theatre)

Best Lighting Design: John Manzelli, *Macon City: A Comic Book Play* (The Naked Stage)

Best Costume Design: Brian O'Keefe, *A Doll's House* (Palm Beach Dramaworks)

Best Sound Design: Matt Corey, *Broadsword* (Mad Cat Theatre Company)

George Abbott Award for Outstanding Achievement in the Arts: Robert M. Heuer, CEO and General Director of Florida Grand Opera

Bill Von Maurer Award for Theatrical Excellence: GableStage

CONNECTICUT CRITICS' CIRCLE AWARDS

June 14, 2010; 20th annual. Presented for outstanding achievement in Connecticut theater, selected by statewide reviews, feature writers, columnists, and broadcasters, for 2009–2010 season.

Outstanding Production of a Play: *Eclipsed* (Yale Repertory Theatre)

Outstanding Production of a Musical: *POP!* (Yale Repertory Theatre)

Outstanding Actress in a Play: Nilaja Sun, *No Child…* (Long Wharf Theatre)

Outstanding Actor in a Play: Bill Heck, *The Orphans' Home Cycle* (Hartford Stage)

Outstanding Actress in a Musical: Jenn Gambatese, *Annie Get Your Gun* (Goodspeed Musicals)

Outstanding Actor in a Musical: Brian Charles Rooney, *POP!* (Yale Repertory Theatre)

Outstanding Direction of a Play: Michael Wilson, *The Orphans' Home Cycle* (Hartford Stage)

Outstanding Direction of a Musical: Mark Lamos, *She Loves Me* (Westport Country Playhouse)

Outstanding Choreography: Noah Racey, *Annie Get Your Gun* (Goodspeed Musicals)

Outstanding Set Design: Jeff Cowie & David Barber, *The Orphans' Home Cycle* (Hartford Stage)

Outstanding Lighting Design: (tie) Kevin Adams, *POP!* (Yale Repertory Theatre); Robert Wierzel, *The Adventures of Huckleberry Finn* (Hartford Stage)

Outstanding Costume Design: Candice Donnelly, *She Loves Me* (Westport Country Playhouse)

Outstanding Sound Design: Chad Raines, *Battle of Black and Dogs* (Yale Repertory Theatre)

Outstanding Ensemble Performance: Tamela Aldridge, Teagle F. Bougere, Miche Brade, & Kimberly Gregory in *Gee's Bend* (Hartford Stage)

Outstanding Touring Production: *In the Heights* (Bushnell Auditorium, Hartford)

Outstanding Debut Awards: Jenilee Simons Marques, *The Miracle Worker* (Ivoryton Playhouse)

Tom Killen Memorial Award: Eugene O'Neill Theater Center, Waterford, CT

Special Award for Extraordinary Theatrical Experience: *The Orphans' Home Cycle* (Hartford Stage)

CRAIG NOEL AWARDS

January 25, 2010; Museum of Contemporary Art; 8th annual. Presented by the San Diego Theatre Critics Circle for outstanding achievement in the greater San Diego theatre in the 2009 calendar year.

New Musical: *Bonnie & Clyde* (La Jolla Playhouse)

Dramatic Production: *Cyrano de Bergerac* (The Old Globe)

Musical Production: *42nd Street* (Moonlight Stage Productions)

Special Theatrical Event: *Looking for an Echo* (Ira Aldridge Repertory Players)

Direction of a Play: Darko Tresnjak, *Cyrano de Bergerac* (The Old Globe)

Direction of a Musical: Jeff Calhoun, *Bonnie & Clyde* (La Jolla Playhouse)

Adaptation of a Play: Doug Wright, *Creditors* (La Jolla Playhouse)

Choreography: Keith Young, *Sammy* (The Old Globe)

Musical Direction: (tie) John McDaniel, *Bonnie & Clyde* (La Jolla Playhouse); Mark Danisovsky, *The Threepenny Opera* (San Diego Rep)

Music for a Play: (tie) Christopher R. Walker, *Twelfth Night* (The Old Globe); David Van Tieghem, *Creditors* (La Jolla Playhouse)

Lead Performance in a Play, Female: (tie) Karson St. John, *The Little Dog Laughed* (Diversionary); Dana Hooley, *Frozen* (ion theatre company)

Lead Performance in a Play, Male: Patrick Page, *Cyrano de Bergerac* (The Old Globe)

Featured Performance in a Play, Female: (tie) Amanda Sitton, *Doubt* (San Diego Repertory Theatre); Harriet Harris, *Unusual Acts of Devotion* (La Jolla Playhouse)

Featured Performance in a Play, Male: Armin Shimerman, *The Seafarer* (San Diego Repertory Theatre)

Lead Performance in a Musical, Female: (tie) Colleen Kollar Smith, *Bed and Sofa* (Cygnet Theatre); Laura Osnes, *Bonnie & Clyde* (La Jolla Playhouse)

Lead Performance in a Musical, Male: Obba Babatundé, *Sammy* (The Old Globe)

Featured Performance in a Musical, Female: (tie) Sara Chase, *The First Wives Club* (The Old Globe); Melissa van der Schyff, *Bonnie & Clyde* (La Jolla Playhouse)

Featured Performance in a Musical, Male: Jordan Miller, *Bed and Sofa* (Cygnet Theatre)

Ensemble: (tie) *Noises Off* (Cygnet Theatre); *The Dresser* (North Coast Repertory Theatre); *Opus* (The Old Globe)

Touring Production: *The 39 Steps* (La Jolla Playhouse)

Set Design: (tie) Michael McKeon, *Killer Joe* (Compass Theatre); Robert Brill, *Creditors* (La Jolla Playhouse)

Lighting Design: Japhy Weideman, *Creditors* (La Jolla Playhouse)

Costume Design: Linda Cho, *Twelfth Night* (The Old Globe)

Sound Design: Lindsay Jones, *Opus* (The Old Globe)

Lifetime Achievement: D.J. Sullivan (actor/teacher/labor organizer)

Special Achievement: Darko Trenjak, for his vivid re-imagining of the classics

Young Artist: Ian Brininstool, *Over the Tavern* (North Coast Repertory Theatre)

DRAMATIST GUILD AWARDS

November 2, 2009; The Players; Host: Christopher Durang. Established in 2000, these awards are presented by the Dramatists Guild of America to outstanding writers at the Dramatists Guild Annual Benefit and Awards Gala. **2009 Winners:**

Elizabeth Hull-Kate Warriner Award (to the playwright whose work deals with social, political or religious mores of the time): David Ives

Frederick Loewe Award for Dramatic Composition: Tom Kitt

Flora Roberts Award: Polly Pen

Lifetime Achievement: Lanford Wilson

ED KLEBAN AWARD

June 21, 2010; BMI; 20th annual. Presented by New Dramatists in honor of Edward Kleban; award is given annually to both a librettist and a lyricist ($100,000 to each recipient payable over two years); Board of Directors: Andre Bishop, Sheldon Harnick, Richard Maltby Jr., Francis Neuwirth (Treasurer), Alan J. Stein (Secretary), John Weidman, Maury Yeston (President); Judges: Craig Carnelia, Susan Drury, Jeffrey Sweet.

2010 Winners: Peter Mills (lyricist), Barry Wyner (librettist)

ELLIOT NORTON AWARDS

May 17, 2010; Paramount Theatre; 28th annual. Presented for outstanding contribution to the theater in Boston from April 2009 to March 2010; selected by a Boston Theater Critics Association selection committee comprising of Don Aucoin, Jared Bowen, Terry Byrne, Carolyn Clay, Iris Fanger, Louise Kennedy, Joyce Kullhawik, Sandy MacDonald, Robert Nesti, Ed Siegel and Caldwell Titcomb.

Visiting Production: *Gatz* (Elevator Repair Service at American Repertory Theater)

Outstanding Production, Large Company: *Fences* (Hunting Theatre Company)

Outstanding Production, Midsized Company: *The Savannah Disputation* (SpeakEasy Theatre Company)

Outstanding Production, Small Company: *Entertaining Mr. Sloan* (Publick Theatre Boston)

Outstanding Production, Fringe Company: *The Complete Works of William Shakespeare (Abridged)* (Orfeo Group)

Outstanding Musical Production: *Adding Machine* (SpeakEasy Stage Company)

Outstanding Ensemble: *The Savannah Disputation* (SpeakEasy Stage Company)

Outstanding New Script: *The Salt Girl* by John Kuntz

Outstanding Director, Large Company: John Collins, *Gatz* (Elevator Repair Service at American Repertory Theater)

Outstanding Director, Midsized Company: Paul Malone, *Adding Machine* (SpeakEasy Stage Company)

Outstanding Director, Small/Fringe Company: Larry Cohen, *Phantom of the Oprah* (Gold Dust Orphans)

Outstanding Actor, Large Company: Scott Shepherd, *Gatz* (Elevator Repair Service at American Repertory Theater)

Outstanding Actor, Small/Midsized Company: Nigel Gore, *Who's Afraid of Virginia Woolf?* (Publick Theatre Boston)

Outstanding Actress: Large Company: Crystal Fox, *Fences* (Huntington Theatre Company)

Outstanding Actress, Small/Midsized Company: Sandra Shipley, *Entertaining Mr. Sloan* (Publick Theatre Boston)

Outstanding Musical Performance: Jeffrey Roberson, *Phantom of the Oprah* (Gold Dust Orphans)

Outstanding Design, Large Company: Jon Savage (set), David Israel Reynoso (costumes), Scott Pinkney (lighting), *The Comedy of Errors* (Commonwealth Shakespeare Company)

Outstanding Design, Small/Midsize Company: Susan Zeeman Rogers (set), Gail Astrid Buckley (costumes), Jeff Adelberg (lighting), *Adding Machine* (SpeakEasy Stage Company)

Norton Prize for Sustained Excellence: Karen MacDonald

Special Citation: Gamm Theatre (Providence, Rhode Island)

Outstanding Theatrical Experience: *Sleep No More* (Punchdrunk and American Repertory Theater)

THE EQUITY AWARDS

St. Clair Bayfield Award Established in 1973 in memory of Equity member St. Clair Bayfield, the Award honors the best performance by an actor in a Shakespearean play in the New York metropolitan area. **2009 Winner:** David Pittu, *Twelfth Night* (The Public Theater Shakespeare in the Park)

Joe A. Callaway Award Established by Equity member Joe A. Callaway in 1989 to encourage participation in the classics and non-profit theatre. **2009 Winners:** Kate Forbes, *Othello* (Theatre for a New Audience); John Douglas Thompson, *Othello* (Theatre for a New Audience) and *The Emperor Jones* (Irish Repertory Theatre)

Clarence Derwent Awards 66th annual; Presented to honor the most promising female and male performers on the New York metropolitan scene. **2010 Winners:** Nina Arianda, *Venus in Fur* (Classic Stage Company), Bill Heck, *The Orphans' Home Cycle* (Signature Theatre Company)

Alan Eisenberg Award 2nd annual; created by former AEA Executive Director, this award is presented to an outstanding graduating senior of the University of Michigan Musical Theatre program, Mr. Eisenberg's alma mater. **2009 Winner:** Cary Tedder, University of Michigan Class of 2009

Lucy Jordan Award Established in 1992 to honor the legacy of Lucy Finney Jordan, a former ballerina and chorus "gypsy" who, for many years, was the "face" of Actors' Equity in the Western Region as the Union's Outside Field Rep. The award is given to those who demonstrate a lifetime commitment to the theatre and especially, helping other theatre artists. **2009 Winner:** Diane Ronnenberg, New York wardrobe mistress and dresser

Rosetta LeNoire Award Established in 1988, the award was named in honor of the actress Rosetta LeNoire, who was also the first recipient, not only because of her body of work in the theatre - and her work with the then titled Actors' Equity Association's Ethnic Minorities Committee - but also for founding the AMAS Repertory Theatre Company. **2010 Winners:** Jackie Taylor, Founder and Executive Director of Chicago's Black Ensemble Theater

Patrick Quinn Award 3rd annual; Established in memory of beloved actor, humanitarian and former AEA President, Patrick Quinn who passed away in September, 2006; presented to a person who has worked tirelessly for the betterment of actors. **2009 Winner:** Conrad Fowkes, actor and co-founder of Volunteer Income Tax Assistance Program at AEA

Paul Robeson Award Established in 1974 to recognize a person who best exemplified the principles by which Mr. Robeson lived. It was created by donations from members of the acting profession. **2009 Winner:** Micki Grant, actress/composer/lyricist

Richard Seff Award Established in 2003, this annual award is given to a male and female character actor who is 50 years old or older and who has been a member of the Actors' Equity for 25 years or longer, for the best performance in a featured or unfeatured supporting role in a Broadway or Off-Broadway production. **2010 Winners:** Helen Stenborg, *Vigil* (DR2), Stephen McKinley Henderson, *Fences* (Broadway)

Roger Sturtevant Musical Theatre Award 6th annual; established in 2005 in memory of Roger Sturtevant, a beloved box office treasurer and part-time casting director. This award is presented to Equity Membership Candidates who have demonstrated outstanding abilities in the musical theatre field. **2010 Winners:** Jessica Taige, Isaac Benelli

ACCA Award 4th annual; Presented to an outstanding Broadway chorus. **2009 Winner:** *West Side Story*

Diversity on Broadway Award Presented by AEA's Equal Employment Opportunity Committee for extraordinary excellence in diversity on Broadway. **2010 Winner:** The creative team and producers of *Billy Elliot The Musical*

FRED EBB AWARD

November 30, 2009; American Airlines Theatre Penthouse Lounge; 5th annual. The Fred Ebb Award recognizes excellence in musical theatre songwriting, by a lyricist, composer, or songwriting team that has not yet achieved significant commercial success. The award is meant to encourage and support aspiring songwriters to create new works for the musical theatre. The selection panel includes Mitchell S. Bernard, Sheldon Harnick, David Loud, Marin Mazzie, Tim Pinckney and Arthur Whitelaw. Presenter, Eric Schaeffer; The prize includes a $50,000 award.

2009 Winner: Marcy Heisler and Zina Goldrich

Past Recipients: 2005: John Bucchino **2006:** Robert L. Freedman and Steven Lutvak **2007:** Peter Mills **2008:** Adam Gwon

GEORGE FREEDLEY MEMORIAL AWARD

Established in 1968 to honor the late George Freedley, theatre historian, critic, author, and first curator of the New York Public Library Theatre Collection, this award honors a work about live theatre published in or distributed in the United States during the previous year. Presented by authors, publishers and members of the Theatre Library Association.

2009 Winner: Jayna Brown, *Babylon Girls: Black Women Performers and the Shaping of the Modern* (Duke University Press, 2008)

GEORGE JEAN NATHAN AWARD

With his preamble "it is my object and desire to encourage and assist in developing the art of drama criticism and the stimulation of intelligent playgoing," the late George Jean Nathan provided in his will for a prize known as the George Jean Nathan Award for Dramatic Criticism. The prize consists of the annual net income of half of Mr. Nathan's estate, which "shall be paid to the American who has written the best piece of drama criticism during the theatrical year (July 1 to June 30), whether it is an article, an essay, treatise, or book. The award now amounts to $10,000 and in addition, the winner receives a trophy symbolic of, and attesting to, the award. **2010 Winner for 08-09:** Marc Robinson (*The American Play 1787-2000*)

GLAAD MEDIA AWARDS

New York: March 13, 2010 at the Marriott Marquis; Los Angeles: April 17, 2010 at the Hyatt Regency Century Plaza; 21st annual. Presented by the Gay and Lesbian Alliance Against Defamation for fair, accurate and inclusive representations of gay individuals in the media as a means of eliminating homophobia and discrimination based on gender identity and sexual orientation.

2010 Winners in Theater: New York Theater – Broadway & Off-Broadway: *A Boy and His Soul* by Colman Domingo; Outstanding New York Theater – Off-Off Broadway: *She Likes Girls* by Claire Hutchinson; Los Angeles Theater: *Lydia* by Octavio Solis

GRAMMY AWARDS

January 31, 2010; Staples Center, Los Angeles; 52nd annual. Presented by the Recording Academy for excellence in the recording industry for albums released October 1, 2008–September 30, 2009.

Nominees: *Ain't Misbehavin'* 30th Anniversary recording (Rhino); *Hair* (Razor & Tie Entertainment/Ghostlight Records); *9 to 5 The Musical* (Dolly Records/Artist2Market Distribution); *Shrek The Musical* (Decca Broadway)

HELEN HAYES AWARDS

April 5, 2010; The Warner Theatre; 26th annual. Presented by the Washington Theatre Awards Society in recognition of excellence in Washington, D.C. for the 2009 season; Witten by Renee Calarco; Director, Jerry Whiddon; Producer/Design, Daniel MacLean Wagner; Music Director, George Hummel; Choreography, Michael J. Bobbitt; Scenic Design, Carl Gudenis; Sound, Alan H. Perry; PSM, Martha Knight.

Outstanding Resident Play: *King Lear* (Shakespeare Theatre Company)

Outstanding Resident Musical: *Ragtime* (The Kennedy Center)

Outstanding Lead Actress, Resident Musical: Christiane Noll, *Ragtime* (The Kennedy Center)

Outstanding Lead Actor, Resident Musical: Parker Drown, *Rent* (The Keegan Theatre)

Outstanding Lead Actress, Resident Play: Holly Twyford, *The Little Dog Laughed* (Signature Theatre)

Outstanding Lead Actor, Resident Play: (tie) Stacy Keach, *King Lear* (Shakespeare Theatre Company); Karl Miller, *Angels in America: Millennium Approaches* (Forum Theatre)

Outstanding Supporting Actress, Resident Musical: Eleasha Gamble, *The Civil War* (Ford's Theatre)

Outstanding Supporting Actor, Resident Musical: Laurence O'Dwyer, *The Fantasticks* (Arena Stage)

Outstanding Supporting Actress, Resident Play: Erin Weaver, *Arcadia* (Folger Theatre)

Outstanding Supporting Actor, Resident Play: Eric Hissom, *Arcadia* (Folger Theatre)

Outstanding Director, Resident Play: Robert Falls, *King Lear* (Shakespeare Theatre Company)

Outstanding Director, Resident Musical: Marcia Milgrom Dodge, *Ragtime* (The Kennedy Center)

Outstanding Set Design, Resident Production: James Noone, *Design for Living* (Shakespeare Theatre Company)

Outstanding Costume Design, Resident Production: Jimm Halliday and Santo Loquasto, *Ragtime* (The Kennedy Center)

Outstanding Lighting Design, Resident Production: Colin K. Bills, *Angels in America: Millenium Approaches* (Forum Theatre)

Outstanding Sound Design, Resident Production: Tom Teasley, *Crazyface* (Constellation Theatre Company)

Outstanding Musical Direction, Resident Production: William Knowles, *Cool Papa's Party* (MetroStage)

Outstanding Choreography: Maurice Hines, *Cool Papa's Party* (MetroStage)

Outstanding Ensemble, Resident Musical: *Rent* (The Keegan Theatre)

Outstanding Ensemble, Resident Play: (tie) *A Midsummer Night's Dream* (Synetic Theater); *Heroes* (MetroStage)

Outstanding Non-Resident Production: *A Streetcar Named Desire* (The Kennedy Center)

Outstanding Production, Theatre for Young Audiences: *The Tale of the Fisherman and the Golden Fish* (Synetic Family Theater)

Outstanding Lead Actress, Non-Resident: Cate Blanchett, *A Streetcar Named Desire* (The Kennedy Center)

Outstanding Lead Actor, Non-Resident: Jim Brochu, *Zero Hour* (Theater J)

Outstanding Supporting Performer, Non-Resident: Robin McLeavy, *A Streetcar Named Desire* (The Kennedy Center)

Charles MacArthur Award for Outstanding New Play or Musical: (tie) *Eclipsed* by Danai Gurira (Woolly Mammoth Theatre Company); *Antebellum* by Robert O'Hara (Woolly Mammoth Theatre Company)

John Aniello Award for Outstanding Emerging Theatre Company: 1st Stage

Helen Hayes Tribute: Edward Albee

Washington Post Award for Innovative Leadership in the Theatre Community: Andy Shallal

HENRY HEWES DESIGN AWARDS

December 11, 2009; Sardi's Restaurant; 45th annual. Sponsored by the American Theatre Wing, these awards are presented for outstanding design originating in the U.S. for the 2008–2009 theatre season. The award (formerly known as the Maharam Theatre Design Award up until 1999) is named after the former theatre critic for the *Saturday Review* who passed away July 20, 2006. The awards are selected by a committee comprising of Jeffrey Eric Jenkins (chair), Dan Bacalzo, David Barbour, David Cote, Glenda Frank, Mario Fratti, and Joan Ungaro; Presenters: Mark Wendland, Donald Holder, David Gallo

Scenic Design: David Korins, *Why Torture is Wrong, and the People Who Love Them* (The Public Theater); Derek McLane, *33 Variations* (Broadway); Louisa Thompson, *Blasted* (Soho Rep)

Lighting Design: Kevin Adams, *Hair* (Broadway); Tyler Micoleau, *Blasted* (Soho Rep)

Costume Design: Clint Ramos, *Women Beware Women* (Red Bull Theater)

Notable Effects: Jeff Sugg (projections), *33 Variations* (Broadway); Matt Tierney (sound design), *Blasted* (Soho Rep)

IRNE AWARDS

April 19, 2010; Boston Center for the Arts. Founded in 1997 by Beverly Creasey and Larry Stark. Presented by The Independent Reviewers of New England for extraordinary theatre in the Boston area during the 2009 calendar year.

Large Theatre

Best New Play: *The Miracle at Naples* by David Grimm (Huntington Theatre Company)

Best Play: *Fences* (Huntington Theatre Company)

Best Musical: *La Cage aux Folles* (Reagle Players)

Best Director, Play Kenny Leon, *Fences* (Huntington Theatre Company)

Best Director, Musical: Diane Paulus, *Best of Both Worlds* (American Repertory Theater)

Best Music Director: Daniel Rodriguez and Jeffrey P. Leonard, *Hello, Dolly* and *La Cage aux Folles* (Reagle Players)

Best Choreography: David Scala, *La Cage aux Folles* (Reagle Players)

Best Solo Performance: Maureen McGovern, *A Long and Winding Road* (Huntington Theatre Company)

Best Ensemble: *Dividing the Estate* (Hartford Stage)

Best Actress, Play: Crystal Fox, *Fences* (Huntington Theatre Company)

Best Actor, Play: John Beasley, *Fences* (Huntington Theatre Company)

Best Supporting Actress, Play: Jacqui Parker, *A Civil War Christmas* (Huntington Theatre Company)

Best Supporting Actor, Play: Will Lebow, *Romance* (American Repertory Theater)

Best Actress, Musical: Rachel York, *Hello, Dolly* (Reagle Players)

Best Actor, Musical: David Engel, *La Cage aux Folles* (Reagle Players)

Best Supporting Actress, Musical: Angela Robinson, *The Color Purple* (National Tour at Citi PAC)

Best Supporting Actor, Musical: R. Glen Michell, *Mame* and *La Cage aux Folles* (Reagle Players)

Best Set Design: Frances O'Connor, *Two Men of Florence* (Huntington Theatre Company)

Best Lighting Design: Ann Wrightson, *Fences* (Huntington Theatre Company)

Best Costume Design: Anita Yavich, *The Miracle at Naples* (Huntington Theatre Company)

Best Sound Design: Ben Emerson, *Fences* (Huntington Theatre Company)

Most Promising Performance by a Child Actor: Sebastian Lucien, *Best of Both Worlds* (American Repertory Theater)

Best Visiting Production: *The Color Purple* (National Tour at Citi PAC)

Small Theatre

Best New Play: *Sins of the Mother* by Israel Horovitz (Gloucester Stage Company)

Best Play: *Spring Awakening* (Zeitgeist Stage Company)

Best Musical: *Grey Gardens* (Lyric Stage Company)

Best Director, Play: David Miller, *Spring Awakening* (Zeitgeist Stage Company)

Best Director, Musical: Spiro Veloudos, *Kiss Me, Kate* and *Grey Gardens* (Lyric Stage Company)

Best Music Director: Jonathan Goldberg, *Grey Gardens* and *Kiss Me, Kate* (Lyric Stage Company)

Best Choreography: Laurel Conrad, *Seussical* (Wheelock Family Theatre)

Best Solo Performance: Tim Ruddy, *Swan Song* (Tir Na Theatre Company)

Best Ensemble: *Dark Play, or Stories for Boys* (Apolinaire Theatre)

Best Actress, Play: Marianna Bassham, *Reckless* & *Blackbird* (SpeakEasy Stage Company) and *Little Black Dress* (Boston Playwright's Theatre)

Best Actor, Play: Robert Pemberton, *Speed-the-Plow* (New Rep) and *The Random Caruso* (Centastage)

Best Supporting Actress, Play: Kate Donnelly, *Bash* (Theatre on Fire)

Best Supporting Actor, Play: Gabriel Kuttner, *Speed-the-Plow* (New Rep)

Best Actress, Musical: Shana Dirik, *Sweeney Todd* (Metro Stage)

Best Actor, Musical: Ben DiScipio, *Sweeney Todd* (Metro Stage)

Best Supporting Actress, Musical: Jennifer Beth Glick, *Seussical* (Wheelock Family Theatre)

Best Supporting Actor, Musical: (tie) Timothy John Smith, *Jerry Springer the Opera* (SpeakEasy Stage Company) and *Kiss Me, Kate* (Lyric Stage Company); James Fitzpatrick, *The Producers* (Turtle Lane Playhouse)

Best Set Design: Dalia Al-Habieli, *Humble Boy* (Publick Theatre Boston)

Best Lighting Design: Jeff Adelberg, *The Duchess of Malfi* (Actors' Shakespeare Project)

Best Costume Design: (tie) Stacey Stephens, *Funny Girl* (Fiddlehead Theatre); Greg Maraio, *The Superheroine Monologues* (Phoenix-Company One)

Best Sound Design: Nathan Leigh, *Strangers on a Train* (Stoneham Theatre)

Best Promising Performance by a Child Actor: Sirena Abalian, *Seussical* (Wheelock Family Theatre)

Best Visiting Production: *The Remarkable Rooming House of Madame Le Monde* (Beau Jest Moving Theatre)

Special Recognition

Kenneth A. MacDonald Award for Theater Excellence: Marshal Hughes, Roxbury Community College

Special Citations – Partnership in Performance Award: Nancy E. Carroll and Paula Plum

Theatre Icon Award: Theodore Kazanoff, Life of Commitment to Boston Theatre

ITBA AWARDS

Second Year; Founded by Ken Davenport, the Independent Theater Bloggers Association was created to provide structure to the quickly growing theatrical blogosphere, and give the new media voices a chance to recognize excellence for Broadway, Off-Broadway, and Off-Off-Broadway productions. 2009 Members included: Bill Brown (creatingtheater.com), Linda Buchwald (pataphysicalscience. blogspot.com), Donald Butchko (me2ism.blogspot.com), Chris Caggiano (ccagiano.typepad.com), Zack Calhoon (zackcalhoon.blogspot.com), Jodi Schoenbrun Carter (off-stage-right.com), Corine Cohen (corinescorner.com), Kevin Daly (theatreaficianado.blogspot.com), Ken Davenport (theproducers perspective.com), Ryan J. Davis (ryanjdavis.blogspot.com), Jeremy Dobrish (JeremysGreenRoom.com), Donell James Foreman (thedjf.blogspot.com), Michael Gilboe (broadwaybullet.com), Diana Glazer (lezbehonest.tumblr.com), Byrne Harrison (stagebuzz.com), Leonard Jacobs (clydefitch.com), Patrick Lee (justshowstogoyou.com), James Marino (broadwaystars.com), Tulis McCall (ushernonsense.com), Jesse North (stagerush.blogspot.com), Aaron Riccio (thatsoundscool.blogspot.com), Sarah Roberts (sarahbsadventures.blogspot. com), Michael Roderick (oneproducerinthecity.typepad.com), Adam Rothenberg (adaumbellesguest.com), David Spencer (ailsesay.com), Ethan Stanislawski (tynansanger.com), Gil Varod (BroadwayAbridged.com), Kim Weild (kimweild. com)

Outstanding New Broadway Play: *Red*

Outstanding Broadway Play Revival: *A View from the Bridge*

Outstanding New Broadway Musical: *American Idiot*

Outstanding Broadway Musical Revival: *La Cage aux Folles*

Outstanding New Off-Broadway Play: *Circle Mirror Transformation* (Playwrights Horizons)

Outstanding New Off-Broadway Musical: *Yank!* (York Theatre Company)

Outstanding Off-Broadway Revival (Musical or Play): *The Glass Menagerie* (Roundabout Theatre Company)

Outstanding Off-Off-Broadway Show: *Viral* (NY Fringe Festival and Soho Playhouse)

Outstanding Off-Off-Broadway Unique Theatrical Experience: *The Lily's Revenge* (HERE Arts Center)

Outstanding Solo Show: *A Boy and His Soul* by Coleman Domingo (Vineyard Theatre)

Outstanding Ensemble Performance: *Circle Mirror Transformation* (Playwrights Horizons)

Citation for Excellence in Off-Off-Broadway Theatre: Company XIV

Citations for Excellence by Individual Performances: Nina Arianda, *Venus In Fur*; Kate Baldwin, *Finian's Rainbow*; Desiree Burch, *The Soup Show*; Rebecca Comtois, *Viral*; Viola Davis, *Fences*; Jon Michael Hill, *Superior Donuts*; Douglas Hodge, *La Cage Aux Folles*; Sarah Lemp, *The Pied Pipers of the Lower East Side & Happy In The Poorhouse*; Laura Linney, *Time Stands Still*; Jan Maxwell, *The Royal Family* & *Lend Me A Tenor*; Bobby Steggert, *Ragtime* & *Yank!* \Amy Lynn Stewart, *Viral*

JONATHAN LARSON PERFORMING ARTS FOUNDATION AWARDS

March 9, 2010; Touch. Jonathan Larson's dream was to infuse musical theatre with a contemporary, joyful urban vitality. After 12 years of struggle as a classic "starving artist," his dream came true with the phenomenal success of *Rent*. To celebrate his creative spirit and honor his memory, Jonathan's family and friends created the Jonathan Larson Performing Arts Foundation. The mission of the Foundation is to provide financial support and encouragement to a new generation of musical theatre composers, lyricists and bookwriters, as well as nonprofit theatre companies that develop and produce their work.

2010 Recipients: Peter Lerman, Daniel Maté, and songwriting team Michael Kooman & Christopher Dimond

JOSEPH JEFFERSON AWARDS

Equity Wing Awards

October 19, 2008; North Shore Center for Performing Arts, Skokie, Illinois; 41st annual. Presented for achievement in Chicago Equity theater from August 1, 2008–July 31, 2009; given by the Jefferson Awards Committee. Director, Michael Weber; Producer, Diane Hires; Hosts, Elizabeth Ledo and Rob Lindley.

Production – Play – Large: (tie) *Ruined* (Goodman Theatre and Manhattan Theatre Club); *The Seafarer* (Steppenwolf Theatre Company)

Production – Play – Midsize: *The History Boys* (TimeLine Theatre Company)

Production – Musical – Large: *Caroline, or Change* (Court Theatre)

Production – Musical – Midsize: *Tomorrow Morning* (Hilary A. Williams, LLC)
Production – Revue: *Studs Terkel's Not Working* (The Second City e.t.c.)

Ensemble: *The History Boys* (TimeLine Theatre Company)

Director – Play: Nick Bowling, *The History Boys* (TimeLine Theatre Company)

Director – Musical: Charles Newell, *Caroline, or Change* (Court Theatre)

Director – Revue: Matt Hovde, *Studs Terke's Not Working* (The Second City e.t.c.)

New Work – Play: *Ruined* by Lynn Nottage (Goodman Theatre and Manhattan Theatre Club)

New Adaptation – Play: *Jon* by Seth Bockley (Collaboraction)

New Work or Adaptation – Musical: *A Minister's Wife* by Josh Schmidt, Jan Tranen, and Austin Pendleton (Writers' Theatre)

Solo Performance: Max McLean, *Mark's Gospel* (Fellowship for the Performing Arts)

Actress in a Principal Role – Play: Saidah Arrika Ekulona, *Ruined* (Goodman Theatre and Manhattan Theatre Club)

Actor in a Principal Role – Play: (tie) Larry Neumann Jr., *A Moon for the Misbegotten* (First Folio Theatre); William L. Petersen, *Blackbird* (Victory Gardens Theater)

Actress in a Supporting Role – Play: Spencer Kayden, *Don't Dress for Dinner* (The British Stage Company)

Actor in a Supporting Role – Play: Alex Weisman, *The History Boys* (TimeLine Theatre Company)

Actress in a Principal Role – Musical: E. Faye Butler, *Caroline, or Change* (Court Theatre)

Actor in a Principal Role – Musical: Joseph Anthony Foronda, *Miss Saigon* (Drury Lane Oakbrook)

Actress in a Supporting Role – Musical: (tie) Liz Baltes, *A Minister's Wife* (Writers' Theatre); Summer Smart, *The Light in the Piazza* (Marriott Theatre)

Actor in a Supporting Role – Musical: Max Quinlan, *The Light in the Piazza* (Marriott Theatre)

Actress in a Revue: Amanda Blake Davis, *Studs Terkel's Not Working* (The Second City e.t.c.)

Actor in a Revue: Mark David Kaplan, *Forbidden Broadway: Dances with the Stars* (John Freedson, Harriet Yellin)

Scenic Design – Large: Lucy Osborne, *Twelfth Night* (Chicago Shakespeare Theater)

Scenic Design – Midsize: Brian Sidney Bembridge, *The History Boys* (TimeLine Theatre Company)

Costume Design – Large: Mara Blumenfeld, *The Arabian Nights* (Lookingglass Theatre Company)

Costume Design – Midsize: Rachel Laritz, *The Voysey Inheritance* (Remy Bumppo Theatre Company)

Lighting Design – Large: Christopher Akerlind, *Rock 'n' Roll* (Goodman Theatre)

Lighting Design – Midsize: Jesse Klug, *Hedwig and the Angry Inch* (American Theater Company)

Sound Design – Large: Ray Nardelli and Joshua Horvath, *Miss Saigon* (Drury Lane Oakbrook)

Sound Design – Midsize: Lindsay Jones, *The K of D: An Urban Legend* (The Route 66 Theatre Company)

Choreography: David H. Bell, *The Boys from Syracuse* (Drury Lane Oakbrook)

Original Incidental Music: Dominic Kanza, *Ruined* (Goodman Theatre and Manhattan Theatre Club)

Musical Direction: Doug Peck, *Caroline, or Change* (Court Theatre)

Outstanding Achievement in Special Effects: Steve Tolin, *The Lieutenant of Inishmore* (Northlight Theatre)

Outstanding Achievement in Video Design: Mike Tutaj, *Tomorrow Morning* (Hillary A. Williams)

Tribute Award: The Second City for its 50th Anniversary

Special Award: William Pullinsi, for his 50 year career of presenting theatre

Non-Equity Awards

June 7, 2010; Park West; 37th annual. Formerly called the Citations, the Non-Equity Awards are for outstanding achievement in professional productions which played at Chicago theaters not operating under union contracts from April 1, 2009–March 31, 2010; given by the Jefferson Awards Committee.

Production – Play: *Killer Joe* (Profiles Theatre)

Production – Musical or Revue: *Chess* (Theo Ubique Cabaret Theatre & Michael James)

Ensemble: *Twelve Angry Men* (Raven Theatre)

Director – Play: Rick Snyder, *Killer Joe* (Profiles Theatre)

Director – Musical or Revue: Fred Anzevino & Brenda Didier, *Chess* (Theo Ubique Cabaret Theatre & Michael James)

New Work: (tie) Ellen Fairey, *Graceland* (Profiles Theatre); Michael Rohd & Phillip C. Klapperich, *Wilson Wants It All* (The House Theatre of Chicago)

New Adaptation: Frances Limoncelli, *Busman's Honeymoon* (Lifeline Theatre)

Actress in a Principal Role – Play: Kendra Thulin, *Harper Regan* (Steep Theatre Company)

Actor in a Principal Role – Play: Darrell W. Cox, *Killer Joe* (Profiles Theatre)

Actress in a Supporting Role – Play: (tie) Nancy Friedrich, *The Crucible* (Infamous Commonwealth Theatre); Vanessa Greenway, *The Night Season* (Vitalist Theatre with Premiere Theatre & Performance)

Actor in a Supporting Role – Play: Peter Oyloe, *The Pillowman* (Redtwist Theatre)

Actress in a Principal Role – Musical or Revue: Maggie Portman, *Chess* (Theo Ubique Cabaret Theatre & Michael James)

Actor in a Principal Role – Musical or Revue: Courtney Crouse, *Chess* (Theo Ubique Cabaret Theatre & Michael James)

Actress in a Supporting Role – Musical or Revue: Kate Garassino, *Bombs Away!* (Bailiwick Repertory Theatre)

Actor in a Supporting Role – Musical or Revue: John B. Leen, *Chess* (Theo Ubique Cabaret Theatre & Michael James)

Scenic Design: John Zucker, *I Am My Own Wife* (Bohemian Theatre Ensemble)

Costume Design: (tie) Theresa Ham, *The Glorious Ones* (Bohemian Theatre Ensemble); Joanna Melville, *St. Crispin's Day* (Strawdog Theatre Company)

Lighting Design: Sean Mallary, *St. Crispin's Day* (Strawdog Theatre Company)

Sound Design: Mike Polaski, *Mouse in a Jar* (Red Tape Theatre)

Choreography: Brenda Didier, *Chess* (Theo Ubique Cabaret Theatre & Michael James)

Original Incidental Music: Trevor Watckin, *The Black Duckling* (Dream Theatre Company)

Musical Direction: Ryan Brewster, *Chess* (Theo Ubique Cabaret Theatre & Michael James)

Artistic Specialization: (tie) Lucas Merino (Video Design), *Wilson Wants It All* (The House Theatre of Chicago); James T. Scott (Puppets), *Evolution/Creation* (Quest Theatre Ensemble)

Fight Choreography: Geoff Coates, *Treasure Island* (Lifeline Theatre

Special Award for Outstanding Achievement: Circle Theatre

KENNEDY CENTER

Honors 32nd annual; December 6, 2009 (broadcast on CBS December 29, 2009); for distinguished achievement by individuals who have made significant contributions to American culture through the arts: Mel Brooks, Dave Brubeck, Grace Bumbry, Robert DeNiro, Bruce Springsteen

Mark Twain Prize 12th annual; October 26, 2009 (Broadcast on PBS November 4, 2009); for American humor: Bill Cosby

KEVIN KLINE AWARDS

March 22, 2010; Loretto-Hilton Center for the Performing Arts; 5th annual. Presented for outstanding achievement in professional theatre in the Greater St. Louis area for the 2009 calendar year; produced by The Professional Theatre Awards Council (Steve Isom, Executive Director); Winners were selected by a floating pool of 45 judges.

Outstanding Production of a Play: (tie) *Souvenir* (Repertory Theatre of St. Louis); *Amadeus* (Repertory Theatre of St. Louis)

Outstanding Director of a Play: Michael Evan Haney, *Souvenir* (Repertory Theatre of St. Louis)

Outstanding Production of a Musical: (tie) *The Drowsy Chaperone* (Stages St. Louis); *Guys and Dolls* (Stages St. Louis)

Outstanding Director of a Musical: Matt Lenz, *Hairspray* (The Muny)

Outstanding Lead Actress in a Play: Neva Rae Powers, *Souvenir* (Repertory Theatre of St. Louis)

Outstanding Lead Actor in a Play: (tie) John Contini, *Barrymore* (Avalon Theatre Company); Jason Cannon, *Doubt* (Dramatic License Productions)

Outstanding Lead Actress in a Musical: Joline Mujica, *Hairspray* (The Muny)

Outstanding Lead Actor in a Musical: David Schmittou, *The Drowsy Chaperone* (Stages St. Louis)

Outstanding Supporting Actress in a Play: (Stray Dog Theatre)

Outstanding Supporting Actor in a Play: (tie) Cathy Simpson, *A Song for Coretta* (The Black Rep); Kirsten Wylder, *Wonder of the World* (The Orange Girls)

Outstanding Supporting Actress in a Musical: Christine Tisdale, *The Drowsy Chaperone* (Stages St. Louis)

Outstanding Supporting Actor in a Musical: (Mustard Seed Theatre)

Outstanding Musical Direction: (tie) Ross Rawlings, *Hairspray* (The Muny); Dr. Diane White-Clayton, *Black Nativity* (The Black Rep)

Outstanding Choreography: Michele Lynch, *Hairspray* (The Muny)

Outstanding Costumes Design: Dorothy Marshall Englis, *Amadeus* (Repertory Theatre of St. Louis)

Outstanding Lighting Design: Tyler Duenow, *The Trial* (Stray Dog Theatre)

Outstanding Set Design: Mark Wilson, *Secret Order* (Repertory Theatre of St. Louis)

Outstanding Sound Design: Chuck Harper, *Neighborhood 3: Requisition of Doom* (HotCity Theatre)

Outstanding Ensemble in a Play: (tie) *Souvenir* (Repertory Theatre of St. Louis); *Secret Order* (Repertory Theatre of St. Louis)

Outstanding Ensemble in a Musical: *The Drowsy Chaperone* (Stages St. Louis)

Production for Young Audiences: *Quick-Brewed Macbeth* (Shakespeare Festival St. Louis)

Outstanding New Play or Musical: *Woyzeck* (Upstream Theatre)

LOS ANGELES DRAMA CRITICS CIRCLE

March 22, 2010; Colony Theatre; 41st annual; Hosts: Jason Graae and Wenzel Jones. Presented for excellence in theatre in the Los Angeles and Orange County during the 2009 calendar year.

Productions: *Life Could Be a Dream*, produced by David Elzer, Peter Schneider & Roger Bean, (Hudson Mainstage); *Parade* (Center Theatre Group–Mark Taper Forum/Donmar Warehouse); *Stick Fly* (Matrix Theatre Company)

T.H. McCulloh Award for Best Revival: *Equus* (The Production Company at Chandler Studio Theatre)

Direction: Shirley Jo Finney, *Stick Fly* (The Matrix Theatre), Marilyn Fox, *The Browning Version* (Pacific Resident Theatre)

Writing: Brian Christopher Williams, *Anita Bryant Died for Your Sins* (West Coast Ensemble at the El Centro Theatre)

Adaptation: Kitty Felde, *Gogol Project* (Rogue Artists Ensemble at Bootleg Theater)

Musical Direction: David O, *The Wasps* (The Lost Studio); Michael Paternostro, *Life Could Be a Dream* (Hudson Mainstage); Phil Reno, *Minsky's*, (Center Theatre Group at the Ahmanson Theatre)

Musical Score: Susan Birkenhead and Charles Strouse, *Minsky's*, (Center Theatre Group–Ahmanson Theatre)

Choreography: Matthew Bourne, Stephen Mear, and Geoffrey Garratt, *Mary Poppins* (Disney and Cameron Mackintosh at the Ahmanson Theatre)

Lead Performance: Sam Anderson, *The Bird and Mr. Banks* (The Road Theatre Company at the Lankershim Arts Center); Bruce French, *The Browning Version* (Pacific Resident Theatre); Jim Hanna, *Equus* (The Production Company at The Chandler Studio Theatre); Deidrie Henry, *Coming Home* (The Fountain Theatre); Laurie Metcalf, *Voice Lessons* (Zephyr Theater); Samantha Sloyan, *Munched* (Buzzworks Theater Company at the El Centro Theatre)

Featured Performance: Hugo Armstrong, *Land of the Tigers* (The Sacred Fools Theater Company & Burglars of Hamm in association with Frantic Redhead Productions); P.J. Griffith, *Setup & Punch* (The Blank Theatre Company at the 2nd Stage Theatre); Andrea Hutchman, *Munched* (Buzzworks Theater Company at the El Centro Theatre); Sally Smythe, *The Browning Version* (Pacific Resident Theatre)

Ensemble Performance: *Hunter Gatherers* (Furious Theatre Company at the Carrie Hamilton Theatre); *Life Could Be a Dream* (Hudson Mainstage); *Stick Fly* (The Matrix Theatre)

Solo Performance: Danny Hoch, *Taking Over* (Center Theatre Group–Kirk Douglas Theatre)

Set Design: Jeff McLaughlin, *A Skull in Connemara* (Theatre Tribe)

Lighting Design: Haylee Freeman, *Gogol Project* (Rogue Artists Ensemble at Bootleg Theater); David Lander, *Bengal Tiger at the Baghdad Zoo* (Center Theatre Group–Kirk Douglas Theatre)

Costume Design: Gregg Barnes, *Minsky's* (Center Theatre Group–Ahmanson Theatre)

Sound Design: Ron Klier, *Blackbird* (VS. Theatre Company at the Elephant Studio Space)

CGI/Video Design: Brian White, *Gogol Project* (Rogue Artists Ensemble at Bootleg Theater)

Fight Choreography: Victor Warren, *Stranger* (Bootleg Theater)

Makeup Design: Ann Closs-Farley, *Land of the Tigers* (The Sacred Fools Theater Company & Burglars of Hamm in association with Frantic Redhead Productions)

Puppet Design: Wes Crain, Lena Garcia, Lynn Jeffries, Elizabeth Luce, and Brian White, *Gogol Project* (Rogue Artists Ensemble at Bootleg Theater)

Margaret Harford Award (for Sustained Excellence in Theatre): Rubicon Theatre Company

Polly Warfield Award (for outstanding single season by a small to mid-sized theatre): Celebration Theatre

Angstrom Award (for career achievement in lighting design): Luke Moyer

Joel Hirschhorn Award (for outstanding achievement in musical theatre): Jason Robert Brown

Bob Z Award (for career achievement in set design): Sibyl Wickersheimer

Milton Katseals Award (for career or special achievement in direction): Richard Israel

Special Award: Kirk Douglas for his lifetime contribution to Los Angeles Theatre

MAC AWARDS

May 4, 2010; B.B. King's; 24th annual. Presented by the Manhattan Association of Cabarets and Clubs to honor achievements in cabaret, comedy, jazz, and live entertainment in the previous year. Producer, Julie Miller; Director, Lennie Watts; Musical Director, Tracy Stark; Host, Sharon McNight

Female Vocalist: Anne Steele, *Strings Attached* (Metropolitan Room)

Male Vocalist: Hector Coris, *Life Is Wonderful* (Don't Tell Mama)

Jazz Vocalist: Mary Foster Conklin, *Moon & Sand: Songs of Salty Days and Sultry Nights* (Metropolitan Room/Nios Hotel/Silverleaf Tavern, North Square Lounge, Caffe Vivaldi)

Major Artist: Baby Jane Dexter, *All About Love* (Metropolitan Room)

New York Debut–Female: Danielle Grabianowski, *Old, New, Borrowed and Blues* (Metropolitan Room/Don't Tell Mama)

New York Debut–Male: Tom Rocco, *My Big, Fat, Proposition 8 Wedding* (Metropolitan Room)

Celebrity Artist: Marilyn Maye, *Mercer the Maye Way/Maye Presents More Mercer/An Evening with Marilyn Maye* (Metropolitan Room/Birdland)

Stand-up Comic–Female: Mary Dimino, *Cannoli and Cabbage* & *Crystal's Comedy Hour* (Broadway Comedy Club/Don't Tell Mama)

Stand-up Comic–Male: Danny Cohen (Stand-Up New York/Caroline's Comedy Club)

Musical Comedy: Gretchen Reinhagen, *Special Kaye: A Tribute to the Incomparable Kaye Ballard* (Metropolitan Room)

Vocal Duo/Group: Marquee Five, *We Can Make It: The Songs of Kander & Ebb* (Metropolitan Room/Don't Tell Mama)

Special Production: *Ricky Ritzel Has Hysterical Blondness* starring Ricky Ritzel; directed and co-written by Jim Luzar (Metropolitan Room)

Variety Production/Recurring Series: Wednesday Night at the Iguana produced and hosted by Dana Lorge and Richard Skipper

Open Mic: *Algonquin Salon/Oak Room Salon/Salon* Artistic & Musical Director/Host, Mark Janas; Executive Producer, Peter Napolitano; Associate Producer; Tanya Moberly; (Algonquin Lobby and the Oak Room/Etcetera Etcetera)

Host – Variety Show/Series or Open Mic: Dana Lorge and Richard Skipper, Wednesday Night at the Iguana

Piano Bar/Restaurant Singing Entertainer: Anne Steele (Don't Tell Mama/Brandy's)

Piano Bar/Restaurant Instrumentalist: Jerry Scott

Technical Director: Jean-Pierre Perreaux (Metropolitan Room for Marilyn Maye, Jason Graae, Baby Jane Dexter)

Director: Lennie Watts (Anne Steele at Metropolitan Room; Jenna Esposito at Metropolitan Room; Uptown Express at Metropolitan Room; 2009 MAC Awards at B.B. King's; Danielle Grabianowski at Metropolitan Room and Don't Tell Mama)

Musical Director: Tracy Stark (Rob Langeder: *Undead in Hell's Kitchen* at Don't Tell Mama; Gretchen Reinhagen: *Almost Blue* at Metropolitan Room; Kathleen France at Metropolitan Room; Delivery Girls at Feinstein's; Joshua Warr at Laurie Beechman)

Major Recording: Daryl Sherman, "Johnny Mercer: A Centennial Tribute"

Recording: Susan Winter, "Love Rolls On...Live!"

Song: "Things That Haunt Me" (Music and Lyrics by Brett Kristofferson)

Special Musical Material: "Identity Theft" (Music and Lyrics by Ray Jessel)

2009 Board of Directors Awards: Peter Leavy (Cabaret Scenes); Playbill.com

Hanson Award: Angela Schultz

Time Out New York Special Achievement Award: Brandon Cutrell

Lifetime Achievement Award: Leslie Uggams

MARGO JONES CITIZEN OF THE THEATER MEDAL

Presented by the Ohio State University Libraries and College of the Arts to a citizen of the theater who has made a lifetime commitment to the theater in the United States and has demonstrated an understanding and affirmation of the craft of playwriting. The Medal Committee is comprised of Deborah Robison for the family of Jerome Lawrence, Janet Waldo Lee and Lucy Lee for the family of Robert E. Lee, Alan Woods, Mary Taratino and Nena Couch (from the Jerome Lawrence Institute).

2010 Winner: No award was presented in 2010.

Past Recipients: 1961: Lucille Lortel **1962:** Michael Ellis **1963:** Judith Rutherford Marechal; George Savage (university award) **1964:** Richard Barr; Edward Albee; and Clinton Wilder; Richard A. Duprey (university award) **1965:** Wynn Handman; Marston Balch (university award) **1966:** Jon Jory; Arthur Ballet (university award) **1967:** Paul Baker; George C. White (workshop award) **1968:** Davey Marlin-Jones; Ellen Stewart (workshop award) **1969:** Adrian Hall; Edward Parone and Gordon Davidson (workshop award) **1970:** Joseph Papp **1971:** Zelda Fichandler **1972:** Jules Irving **1973:** Douglas Turner Ward **1974:** Paul Weidner **1975:** Robert Kalfin **1976:** Gordon Davidson **1977:** Marshall W. Mason **1978:** Jon Jory **1979:** Ellen Stewart **1980:** John Clark Donahue **1981:** Lynne Meadow **1982:** Andre Bishop **1983:** Bill Bushnell **1984:** Gregory Mosher **1985:** John Lion **1986:** Lloyd Richards **1987:** Gerald Chapman **1988:** no award **1989:** Margaret Goheen **1990:** Richard Coe **1991:** Otis L. Guernsey Jr. **1992:** Abbot Van Nostrand **1993:** Henry Hewes **1994:** Jane Alexander **1995:** Robert Whitehead **1996:** Al Hirschfield **1997:** George C. White **1998:** James Houghton **1999:** George Keathley **2000:** Eileen Heckart **2001:** Mel Gussow **2002:** Emilie S. Kilgore **2003-2004:** Christopher Durang and Marsha Norman **2005-2006:** Jerome Lawrence and Robert E. Lee **2007-2008:** David Emmes and Martin Benson **2009:** Bill Rauch

MUSICAL THEATER HALL OF FAME

This organization was established at New York University on November 10, 1993. Inductees: Harold Arlen, Irving Berlin, Leonard Bernstein, Eubie Blake, Abe Burrows, George M. Cohan, Betty Comden, Dorothy Fields, George Gershwin, Ira Gershwin, Adolph Green, Oscar Hammerstein II, E.Y. Harburg, Larry Hart, Jerome Kern, Burton Lane, Alan Jay Lerner, Frank Loesser, Frederick Loewe, Mary Martin, Ethel Merman, Cole Porter, Jerome Robbins, Richard Rodgers, Harold Rome.

NATIONAL ARTS CLUB AWARDS

Joseph Kesselring Fellowship and Honors

National Arts Club member Joseph Otto Kesselring was born in New York in 1902. He was an actor, author, producer, and playwright. Mr. Kesselring died in 1967, leaving his estate in a trust, which terminated in 1978 when the life beneficiary died. A bequest was made to the National Arts Club "on condition that said bequest be used to establish a fund to be known as the Joseph Kesselring Fund, the income and principal of which shall be used to give financial aid to playwrights, on such a basis of selection and to such as the National Arts Club may, in its sole discretion, determine." A committee appointed by the president and the governors of the National Arts Club administers the Kesselring Prizes. It approves monetary prizes annually to playwrights nominated by qualified production companies whose dramatic work has demonstrated the highest possible merit and promise and is deserving of greater recognition, but who as yet has not received prominent national notice or acclaim in the theater. The winners are chosen by a panel of judges who are independent of the Club. In addition to a cash prize, the first-prize winner also receives a staged reading of a work of his or her choice. In the fall of 2007, the Club redefined the award to consist of the Kesselring Fellowship, and created a new category called the Kesselring Honors. As of publication deadline, there were no recipients for the 2009–2010 theatre season.

Previous Fellowship Recipients: 1980: Susan Charlotte **1981:** Cheryl Hawkins **1982:** No Award **1983:** Lynn Alvarez **1984:** Philip Kan Gotanda **1985:** Bill Elverman **1986:** Marlane Meyer **1987:** Paul Schmidt **1988:** Diane Ney **1989:** Jo Carson **1990:** Elizabeth Egloff, Mel Shapiro **1991:** Tony Kushner **1992:** Marion Isaac McClinton **1993:** Anna Deavere Smith **1994:** Nicky Silver **1995:** Amy Freed, Doug Wright **1996:** Naomi Wallace **1997:** No Award **1998:** Kira Obolensky **1999:** Heather McDonald **2000:** David Auburn **2001:** David Lindsay-Abaire **2002:** Melissa James Gibson **2003:** Bridget Carpenter **2004:** Tracey Scott Wilson **2005:** Deb Margolin **2006:** Mark Schultz **2007:** Jordan Harrison **2009:** Rajiv Joseph, David Adjmi

Previous Honors Recipients (if year is missing none were presented): **1980:** Carol Lashof **1981:** William Hathaway **1983:** Constance Congdon **1985:** Laura Harrington **1986:** John Leicht **1987:** Janzsz Glowacki **1988:** Jose Rivera, Frank Hogan **1989:** Keith Reddin **1990:** Howard Korder **1991:** Quincy Long, Scott McPherson **1992:** José Rivera **1993:** Han Ong **1996:** Nilo Cruz **1997:** Kira Obolensky, Edwin Sanchez **1998:** Erik Ehn **1999:** Steven Dietz **2000:** Jessica Hagedorn **2001:** Dael Orlandersmith **2002:** Lydia Diamond **2003:** Lynn Nottage **2004:** John Borello **2005:** Tanya Barfield **2006:** Bruce Norris **2007:** Will Eno, Rinne Groff, Marcus Gardley **2009:** Jenny Schwartz, Tarrel Alvin McCraney

NATIONAL MEDALS OF THE ARTS

February 25, 2010; East Room at the White House. Presented to individuals who and organizations that have made outstanding contributions to the excellence, growth, support, and availability of the arts in the United States, selected by the President of the United States from nominees presented by the National Endowment of the Arts. **2009 Individual Winners**: Bob Dylan, singer/songwriter (Duluth, MN); Clint Eastwood, director/actor (San Francisco, CA); Milton Glaser, graphic designer (New York, NY); Maya Lin, artist/designer (Athens, OH); Rita Moreno, singer/actress/dancer (Humacao, PR); Jessye Norman, soprano (Augusta, GA); Hon. Joseph P. Riley Jr., arts patron/design advocate (Charleston, SC); Frank Stella, painter/sculptor (Malden, MA) Michael Tilson Thomas, conductor (Los Angeles, CA); John Williams, conductor/composer (Queens, NY) **2009 Organization Winners:** The Oberlin Conservatory of Music (Oberlin, OH); The School of American Ballet (New York, NY)

NEW DRAMATISTS LIFETIME ACHIEVEMENT AWARD

May 18, 2010; Marriott Marquis; 61st annual. Presented to an individual who has made an outstanding artistic contribution to the American theater. **2010 Winner:** Julie Taymor

NEW YORK INNOVATIVE THEATRE AWARDS

September 21, 2009; New World Stages; 5th annual; Host: Julie Halston. Presented to honor individuals and organizations who have achieved artistic excellence in Off-Off-Broadway theatre for the 2008-2009 season. The New York IT Awards committee recognizes the unique and essential role Off-Off-Broadway plays in contributing to American and global culture, and believes that publicly recognizing excellence in independent theatre will expand audience awareness and appreciation of the full New York theatre experience. Staff: Jason Bowcutt, Shay Gines, Nick Micozzi, Executive Directors; Awards Committee: Paul Adams (Emerging Artists Theatre), Dan Bacalzo (*TheatreMania.com*), Christopher Borg (Actor/Director), Jason Bowcutt (IT Awards), Tim Errickson (Boomerang Theatre Company), Thecla Farrell (Castillo Theatre), Constance Congdon (Playwright), Shay Gines (New York IT Awards), Ben Hodges (*Theatre World*), Leonard Jacobs (*Back Stage*), Ron Lasko (Spin Cycle P.R.), Blake Lawrence, Bob Lee, Nick Micozzi (IT Awards), Risa Shoup, (chashama), Nicky Paraiso (La MaMa E.T.C.), Jeff Riebe (The January Initiative), Akia Squiterri (Rising Sun Performance Company). Presenters: Jackie Hoffman, Nilo Cruz, John Patrick Shanley, Elizabeth Swados, Andrew Lippa, Casey Nicholaw, Charles Busch, Austin Pendleton, Taylor Mac, James Scruggs, Beverly Emmons, Magie Dominic, Bod Dahdah, Tom Wojtunik, Taryn Drongowski, Kate D. Levin.

Outstanding Ensemble: Christopher Borg, Jeffrey Cranor, Kevin R. Free, and Eevin Hartsough, *(Not) Just A Day Like Any Other* (NY Neo-Futurists)

Outstanding Solo Performance: Jeff Grow, *Creating Illusion* (soloNOVA Arts Festival)

Outstanding Actor in a Featured Role: William Apps IV, *Amerissiah* (The Amoralists)

Outstanding Actress in a Featured Role: Constance Parng, *Lee/gendary*

Outstanding Actor in a Lead Role: Julian Elfer, *Twelfth Night, or What You Will* (T. Schreiber Studio)

Outstanding Actress in a Lead Role: Elyse Mirto, *Any Day Now* (InGenius Festival at Manhattan Theatre Source)

Outstanding Choreography/Movement: Austin McCormick, *The Judgment of Paris* (Company XIV at the Duo Theatre)

Outstanding Director: Suzi Takahashi, *Lee/gendary*

Outstanding Set Design: Michael P. Kramer, *Ragtime* (Astoria Performing Arts Center)

Outstanding Costume Design: Michelle Beshaw, *The Very Sad Story of Ethel & Julius* (Theater for the New City)

Outstanding Lighting Design: Bruce Steomberg, *Blue Before Morning* (terraNOVA Collective at the DR2)

Outstanding Sound Design: Asa Wember, *Angel Eaters* (Flux Theatre Ensemble)

Outstanding Original Music: Kimmy Gatewood, Andy Hertz, Rebekka Johnson, Sarah Lowe, and Jeff Solomon, *The Apple Sisters*

Outstanding Original Full-Length Script: Nat Cassidy, *The Reckoning of Kit & Little Boots* (Gallery Players/Engine37)

Outstanding Original Short Script: Nico Vreeland, *The Interview* (Elephants on Parade 2009/EBE Ensemble)

Outstanding Performance Art Production: *Creating Illusion* (soloNOVA Arts Festiva)

Outstanding Production of a Musical: *Like You Like It* (The Gallery Players)

Outstanding Production of a Play: *Lee/gendary* (HERE Arts Center)

Artistic Achievement Award: Maria Irene Fornes

Stewardship Award: Harriet Taub and Materials for the Arts

Caffe Cino Fellowship Award ($1,000 grant): The Brick Theater Company

OTTO RENÉ CASTILLO AWARDS

May 23, 2010; Castillo Theatre All Stars Project; 12th annual. Presented to artists for and theatres from around the world in recognition for contributions to Political Theatre. The Otto Award is named for the Guatemalan poet and revolutionary Otto Rene Castillo, who was murdered by that country's military junta in 1968. **2010 Winners:** Melvin Van Peebles (director, actor, novelist and musician), Ruth Maleczech (co-founder/co-artistic director of Mabou Mines), David Diamond (artistic/managing director of the Headlines Theatre, Vancouver, Canada), Carlyle Brown (playwright and actor); The Working Classroom (Albuquerque, New Mexico); Black Tent Theatre (Tokyo, Japan)

OVATION AWARDS

January 10, 2010; Redondo Beach Performing Arts Center; 20th annual. Established in 1989, the L.A. Stage Alliance Ovation Awards are Southern California's premiere awards for excellence in theatre. Winners were selected by a 190 member voting pool of theatre professionals working in the Los Angeles theatre community for productions that played September 1, 2008–August 31, 2009.

Best Season: Troubadour Theater Company (*Alice in One-Hit Wonderland 2: Through the Looking Glass; As U2 Like It; It's a Stevie Wonderful Life*)

Production of a Musical–Intimate Theatre (Franklin R. Levy Memorial Award): *Kiss of the Spider Woman* (Havok Theatre Company)

Production of a Play–Intimate Theatre: *Family Planning* (Chalk Repertory Theatre)

Production of a Musical–Large Theatre: *Louis & Keely, Live at the Sahara* (Produced by Stuart Benjamin, Jake Broder, Taylor Hacford, Sarabeth Schedeen, Vanessa Claire)

Play–Large Theatre: *Two Trains Running* (Ebony Repertory Theatre)

Book/Lyrics/Music for an Original Musical: *Divorce! The Musical* by Erin Kamler (Produced by Rick Culbertson in association with Lynn Marks and Paradox Entertainment)

Playwrighting for an Original Play: *The Idea Man* by Kevin King (Elephant Theatre Company)

Director of a Musical: Matt Walker, *As U2 Like It* (Troubadour Theater Company)

Director of a Play: Larissa Kokernot, *Family Planning* (Chalk Repertory Theatre)

Musical Direction: Darryl Archibald, *Smokey Joe's Café* (El Portal Theatre & Corky Hale)

Choreographer: Lee Martino, *Kiss of the Spider Woman* (Havok Theatre Company)

Ensemble Performance: *Stick Fly* (The Matrix Theatre Company)

Lead Actor in a Play: Glynn Turman, *Two Trains Running* (Ebony Repertory Theatre)

Lead Actress in a Play: Julie White, *The Little Dog Laughed* (Center Theatre Group)

Lead Actor in a Musical: Jake Broder, *Louis & Keely, Live at the Sahara*

Lead Actress in a Musical: Vanessa Claire Smith, *Louis & Keely, Live at the Sahara*

Featured Actor in a Play: Hugo Armstrong, *Land of the Tigers* (Sacred Fools, Burglars of Hamm & Frantic Redhead Productions)

Featured Actress in a Play: Tasha Ames, *Rabbit Hole* (Malibu Stage Company)

Featured Actor in a Musical: Michael Paternostro, *The Producers* (Musical Theatre West)

Featured Actress in a Musical: Sarah Cornell, *The Producers* (Musical Theatre West)

Set Design–Intimate Theatre: Jeff McLaughlin, *A Skull in Connemara* (Theatre Tribe)

Set Design–Large Theatre: Allen Moyer, *The Little Dog Laughed* (Center Theatre Group)

Costume Design–Intimate Theatre: Ann Closs-Farley, *Ken Roht's Calendar Girl Competition* (Bootleg Theater)

Costume Design–Large Theatre: Sharon McGunigle, *Alice in One Hit Wonderland 2: Through the Looking Glass* (Troubadour Theater Company)

Lighting Design–Intimate Theatre: Luke Moyer, *Dracula* (NoHo Arts Center Ensemble)

Lighting Design–Large Theatre: Donald Holder, *The Little Dog Laughed* (Center Theatre Group)

Sound Design–Intimate Theatre: Ken Sawyer, *Dracula* (NoHo Arts Center Ensemble)

Sound Design–Large Theatre: (tie) Erik Carstensen, *Beethoven as I Knew Him* (Geffen Playhouse); Chris Webb & David Molina, *Lydia* (Center Theatre Group)

PITTSBURGH CIVIC LIGHT OPERA'S RICHARD RODGERS AWARD

Founded in 1988. Recognizes the lifetime contributions of outstanding talents in musical theatre; Presented by The Pittsburgh Civic Light Opera in conjunction with the families of Richard Rodgers and Oscar Hammerstein II. No award was presented this year.

Past Recipients: 1988: Mary Martin **1989:** Dame Julie Andrews **1991:** Harold Prince **1992:** Sir Cameron Mackintosh **1993:** Stephen Sondheim **1996:** Lord Andrew Lloyd Webber **2000:** Gwen Verdon **2002:** Bernadette Peters **2007:** Shirley Jones **2008:** Rob Marshall and Kathleen Marshall **2009:** Stephen Schwartz

PRINCESS GRACE AWARDS

October 21, 2009; Cipriani on 42nd Street, New York; 24th annual. Presented by the Princess Grace Foundation – USA for excellence in theatre, dance, and film across the United States. **2010 Awards:** *Statue Awards:* Brian Kulick (Artistic Director of Classic Stage Company) & Gillian Murphy (Principal Dancer at American Ballet Theatre); *Awards in Theatre and Playwrighting:* **Pierre Cardin Theater Award:** Ann Bartek (Theatre Fellowship – The Milk Can Theatre Company); **Fabergé Theater Award:** Colin K. Billis (Wooly Mammoth Theatre Company –Theatre Fellowship); **Robert and Gloria Houseman Theater Award:** James Darrah (UCLA Department of Theater – Theater Scholarship); **Gant Gaither Theater Award:** Nicolette Robinson (UCLA Department of Theater – Theater Scholarship); **Grace Le Vine Theater Award:** Lily Whitsitt (California Institute of the Arts – Theater Scholarship); Craig Bazan (The Shakespeare Theatre of New Jersey – Theatre Apprenticeship); Branden Jacobs-Jenkins (New Dramatists Inc. – Playwrighting Fellowship); *Theater Honoraria:* Denise Quinones (Repertorio Espanol), Meghan Raham (Kansas City Repertory Theatre), Tony Speciale (Classic Stage Company); *Special Projects Awards in Theater:* Scott Turner Schofield (7 Stages)

RICHARD ROGERS AWARDS

For staged readings of musicals in nonprofit theaters, administered by the American Academy of Arts and Letters and selected by a jury including Stephen Sondheim (chairman), Lynn Ahrens, John Guare, Sheldon Harnick, David Ives, Richard Maltby Jr., and Lin-Manuel Miranda.

2010 Winners: *Buddy's Tavern* by Raymond De Felitta, Alison Louise Hubbard, Kim Oler; *Rocket Science* by Patricia Cotter, Jason Rhyne, Stephen Weiner

ROBERT WHITEHEAD AWARD

March 9, 2010; Sardi's Restaurant; Founded in 1993. Presented for outstanding achievement in commercial theatre producing, bestowed on a graduate of the fourteen-week Commercial Theatre Institute Program who has demonstrated a quality of production exemplified by the late producer, Robert Whitehead. The Commercial Theatre Institute (Jed Bernstein, Director) is the nation's only formal program that professionally trains commercial theatre producers. It is a joint project of the League of American Theatres and Producers, Inc., and Theatre Development Fund. **2010 Winner:** Stuart Thompson

Previous Recipients: 1993: Susan Quint Gallin; Benjamin Mordecai **1994:** Dennis Grimaldi **1995:** Kevin McCollum **1996:** Randall L. Wreghitt **1997:** Marc Routh **1998:** Liz Oliver **1999:** Eric Krebs **2000:** Anne Strickland Squadron **2001–2003:** No Award **2004:** David Binder **2005–2007:** No Award **2008:** Nick Scandalios **2009:** Dori Bernstein

STAGE DIRECTOR AND CHOREOGRAPHERS (SDC) FOUNDATION AWARDS*

Mr. Abbot Award

Named in honor of the legendary director George Abbot, this award is presented exclusively for directors and choreographers in recognition of lifetime achievement in the American Theatre.

2009 Recipient: Donald Saddler

Previous Recipients: 1985: Harold Prince **1986:** Bob Fosse **1987:** Mike Nichols **1988:** Agnes de Mille **1989:** Michael Bennet **1990:** Gene Saks **1991:** Tommy Tune **1992:** Arvin Brown **1993:** Trevor Nunn **1994:** Jerry Zaks **1995:** Gordon Davidson **1996:** Lloyd Richards **1997:** Garson Kanin **1998:** Graciela Daniele **1999:** Vinnette Carrol, Zelda Fichandler, Peter Gennaro, Gillian Lynne, Marshall W. Mason, Andrei Serban **2000:** Cy Feuer **2001:** Susan Stroman **2002:** Jack O'Brien **2003:** Lynne Meadow **2005:** Kathleen Marshall and Rob Marshall **2007:** Daniel Sullivan

Joe A. Callaway Awards

Also known as the "Joey," this award, created in 1989, is issued for excellence in the craft of direction and/or choreography for Off-Broadway and Off-Off-Broadway.

2009 Winners: Garry Hynes (Director), *The Cripple of Inishmaan* (Atlantic Theater Company); Martha Clarke (Choreography), *The Garden of Earthly Delights* (Minetta Lane Theatre)

Previous Winners: 1989: Gloria Muzio **1990:** Frank Galati **1991:** Susan Stroman **1992:** George C. Wolfe, Hope Clark **1993:** Harold Prince **1994:** Gerald Gutierrez **1995:** Joe Mantello, Scott Elliott **1996:** Julie Taymor **1997:** Moisés Kaufman **1998:** Frank Galati, Graciela Daniele **1999:** Trevor Nunn **2000:** Gabriel Barre, Mark Dendy **2001:** Jack O'Brien **2002:** Bartlett Sher **2003:** Devanand Janki, Doug Hughes **2004:** Daniel Sullivan **2005:** Doug Hughes, Christopher Gattelli **2006:** Bill T. Jones, Peter DuBois **2007:** Thomas Kail, Andy Blankenbuehler **2008:** Giovanna Sardelli, Lynne Taylor-Corbett

*Previously known as the Society of Stage Directors and Choreographers (SSDC) Awards

STEINBERG PLAYWRIGHT AWARD

October 26, 2010; Vivian Beaumont Theatre; Premiere Year. Created by the Harold and Mimi Steinberg Charitable Trust, this award recognizes playwrights at various stages of their early careers whose profession works show great promise. This award is presented on alternate years with the Steinberg Distinguished Playwright Award which recognizes an established American playwright whose body of work has made significant contributions to the American theater. Nominating and Selection Committee: André Bishop (Artistic Director, Lincoln Center Theater), David Emmes (Producing Artistic Director, South Coast Repertory), Oskar Eustis (Artistic Director, The Public Theater), Polly K. Carl (Producing Artistic Director, Playwrights Center), Martha Lavey (Artistic Director, Steppenwolf Theatre Company), Eduardo Machado (playwright/Artistic Director, INTAR Theatre), and Marc Masterson (Artistic Director, Actors Theatre of Louisville). The winners receive 'The Mimi,' a statue designed by David Rockwell, and a cash prize (a share of $100,000 for playwrights in early stages of their careers and $200,000 for established playwrights), making the award the largest ever created to honor and encourage artistic achievement in the American Theatre.

2010 Recipients: Bruce Norris ($50,000), Tarell Alvin McCraney & David Adjmi ($25,000 each)

Previous Distinguished Recipient: 2009: Tony Kushner

SUSAN SMITH BLACKBURN PRIZE

March 3, 2010; New York City; 32nd annual; Presenter: Doug Hughes. Presented to women who have written works of outstanding quality for the English-speaking theater. The Prize is administered in Houston, London, and New York by a board of directors who choose six judges each year. 2009–2010 Judges: Hope Davis, Doug Hughes, Mark Lawson, Todd London, Indhu Rubasingham, Fiona Shaw. The winner receives a $20,000 cash prize and a signed and numbered print by artist Willem de Kooning. The Special Commendation winner receives a $5,000 cash prize, and each finalist receives $1,000.

2010 Winner: Julia Cho, *The Language Archive* (U. S.)

Special Commendation: Not presented this year

Finalists: Annie Baker, *The Aliens* (U.S.); Melissa James Gibson, *This* (U.S.); Lucy Kirkwood, *it felt empty when the heart went at first but it is alright now* (U.K.); Young Jean Lee, *The Shipment* (U.S.); Rebecca Lenkiewicz, *The Nature of Love* (U.K.); Hannah Moscovitch, *East of Berlin* (Canada); Lizzie Nunnery, *The Swallowing Dark* (U.K.); Lucy Prebble, *Enron* (U.K.); Abbie Spallen, *Strandline* (Ireland)

THEATRE DEVELOPMENT FUND AWARDS

Fred and Adele Astaire Awards

June 7, 2010; Gerald W. Lynch Theater at John Jay College; Established in 1982; Host: Ben Vereen. Originally known as the Astaire Awards these awards were founded by the Anglo-American Contemporary Dance Foundation and have been administered by Theatre Development Fund since 1991. These awards recognize outstanding achievement in dance on Broadway and in film. 2010 Nominating Committee: Anna Kisselgoff (former *New York Times* Chief Dance Critic), Wendy Perron (*Dance Magazine* Editor-in-Chief), Sylviane Gold (*Dance Magazine*), Damian Woetzel (former principal dancer, New York City Ballet). Chairman Emeritus, Douglas Watt; Honorary Chairs, Roberta Flack, Countess LuAnn de Lesseps, and Bruce Michael; Benefit Co-Chairs, Robin Cofer, Cassandra Seidenfeld-Lyster, Sara Johnson, Carolyn Kendall Buchter, and Joe Lanteri; Producers, Ron Glucksman and Patricia Watt; Gala Director, Lee Roy Reams; Writer, Randall David Cook; Choreography, Tricia Brouk.

Best Broadway Choreographer: Bill T. Jones, *Fela!*

Excellence in Dance on Film: Choreographer (Fictional Film): Marguerite Derricks, *Fame*; Director (Documentary Dance Film): Adam Del Deo and James D. Stern, *Every Little Step*

Best Female Dancer: Nicole Chantal de Weever and the female ensemble of *Fela!* (Hettie Vyrine Barnhill, Lauren de Veaux, Elasea Douglas, Rujeko Dumbutshena, Catherine Foster, Shaneeka Harrell, Chanon Judson, Shakira Marshall, Afi McClendon, Jill Vallery, Iris Wilson, Aimee Graham

Best Male Dancer: Charlie Neshyba-Hodges, *Come Fly Away*

Douglas Watt Lifetime Achievement Award: Kenny Ortega

Irene Sharaff Awards

April 23, 2010; Hudson Theatre; 15th annual. Founded in 1993, this award has become an occasion for the costume design community to come together to honor its own and pays tribute to the art of costume design. Named after the revered costume designer, the awards are decided upon by the TDF Costume Collection Advisory Committee (Gregory A. Poplyk–Chairman, Gregg Barnes, Suzy Benzinger, Dean Brown, Linda Fisher, Lana Fritz, Rodney Gordon, Desmond Heeley, Allen Lee Hughes, Holly Hynes, Carolyn Kostopoulous, Kitty Leech, Anna Louizos, Mimi Maxmen, David Murin, Sally Ann Parsons, Robert Perdziola, Carrie Robbins, Tony Walton, Patrick Wiley, David Zinn).

Lifetime Achievement Award: Albert Wolsky

Young Master Award: Alejo Vietti

Artisan Award: John David Ridge

The Robert L.B. Tobin Award: Ming Cho Lee

Memorial Tribute: Randy Barcelo

THE THEATER HALL OF FAME

January 25, 2010; Gershwin Theatre North Rotunda; 39th annual; Host: Pia Lindstrom. The Theater of Hall of Fame was created in 1971 to honor those who have made outstanding contributions to the American theater in a career spanning at least twenty-five years, with at least five major credits. Producer, Terry Hodge Taylor; Presenters: John Guare, Frank Dunlop, Joseph Hardy, Michael Montel, Everett Quinton, Paul Libin, David Stone, Marc Platt, Nick Scandalios (Inductees), Liz Smith (Founder's Award).

2010 Inductees (for the year 2009)**:** Roger Berlind, Jim Dale, Charles Ludlam, Ted Mann, John McMartin, Lynn Redgrave, Stephen Schwartz, Andrew Lloyd Webber

Previous Inductees: George Abbott, Maude Adams, Viola Adams, Stella Adler, Edward Albee, Theoni V. Aldredge, Ira Aldridge, Jane Alexander, Mary Alice, Winthrop Ames, Judith Anderson, Maxwell Anderson, Robert Anderson, Julie Andrews, Margaret Anglin, Jean Anouilh, Harold Arlen, George Arliss, Boris Aronson, Adele Astaire, Fred Astaire, Eileen Atkins, Brooks Atkinson, Alan Ayckbourn, Emanuel Azenberg, Lauren Bacall, Pearl Bailey, George Balanchine, William Ball, Anne Bancroft, Tallulah Bankhead, Richard Barr, Philip Barry, Ethel Barrymore, John Barrymore, Lionel Barrymore, Howard Bay, Nora Bayes, John Lee Beatty, Julian Beck, Samuel Beckett, Brian Bedford, S.N. Behrman, Barbara Bel Geddes, Norman Bel Geddes, David Belasco, Michael Bennett, Richard Bennett, Robert Russell Bennett, Eric Bentley, Irving Berlin, Sarah Bernhardt, Leonard Bernstein, Patricia Birch, Earl Blackwell, Kermit Bloomgarden, Jerry Bock, Ray Bolger, Edwin Booth, Roscoe Lee Brown, Junius Brutus Booth, Shirley Booth, Philip Bosco, Dion Boucicault, Alice Brady, Bertolt Brecht, Fannie Brice, Peter Brook, John Mason Brown, Robert Brustein, Billie Burke, Abe Burrows, Richard Burton, Mrs. Patrick Campbell, Zoe Caldwell, Eddie Cantor, Len Cariou, Morris Carnovsky, Mrs. Leslie Carter, Gower Champion, Frank Chanfrau, Carol Channing, Stockard Channing, Ruth Chatterton, Paddy Chayefsky, Anton Chekhov, Ina Claire, Bobby Clark, Harold Clurman, Lee. J. Cobb, Richard L. Coe, George M. Cohan,

Alexander H. Cohen, Jack Cole, Cy Coleman, Constance Collier, Alvin Colt, Betty Comden, Marc Connelly, Barbara Cook, Thomas Abthorpe Cooper, Katherine Cornell, Noel Coward, Jane Cowl, Lotta Crabtree, Cheryl Crawford, Hume Cronyn, Rachel Crothers, Russel Crouse, John Cullum, Charlotte Cushman, Jean Dalrymple, Augustin Daly, Graciela Daniele, E.L. Davenport, Gordon Davidson, Ossie Davis, Owen Davis, Ruby Dee, Alfred De Liagre Jr., Agnes DeMille, Colleen Dewhurst, Howard Dietz, Dudley Digges, Melvyn Douglas, Eddie Dowling, Alfred Drake, Marie Dressler, John Drew, Mrs. John Drew, William Dunlap, Mildred Dunnock, Charles Durning, Eleanora Duse, Jeanne Eagles, Richard Easton, Fred Ebb, Ben Edwards, Florence Eldridge, Lehman Engel, Maurice Evans, Abe Feder, Jose Ferber, Cy Feuer, Zelda Fichandler, Dorothy Fields, Herbert Fields, Lewis Fields, W.C. Fields, Harvey Fierstein, Jules Fisher, Minnie Maddern Fiske, Clyde Fitch, Geraldine Fitzgerald, Henry Fonda, Lynn Fontanne, Horton Foote, Edwin Forrest, Bob Fosse, Brian Friel, Rudolf Friml, Charles Frohman, Daniel Frohman, Robert Fryer, Athol Fugard, John Gassner, Larry Gelbart, Peter Gennaro, Grace George, George Gershwin, Ira Gershwin, Bernard Gersten, William Gibson, John Gielgud, W.S. Gilbert, Jack Gilford, William Gillette, Charles Gilpin, Lillian Gish, Susan Glaspell, John Golden, Max Gordon, Ruth Gordon, Adolph Green, Paul Green, Charlotte Greenwood, Jane Greenwood, Joel Grey, Tammy Grimes, George Grizzard, John Guare, Otis L. Guernsey Jr., A.R. Gurney, Mel Gussow, Tyrone Guthrie, Uta Hagen, Sir Peter Hall, Lewis Hallam, T. Edward Hambleton, Marvin Hamlisch, Oscar Hammerstein II, Walter Hampden, Otto Harbach, E.Y. Harburg, Sheldon Harnick, Edward Harrigan, Jed Harris, Julie Harris, Rosemary Harris, Sam H. Harris, Rex Harrison, Kitty Carlisle Hart, Lorenz Hart, Moss Hart, Tony Hart, June Havoc, Helen Hayes, Leland Hayward, George Hearn, Ben Hecht, Eileen Heckart, Theresa Helburn, Lillian Hellman, Katharine Hepburn, Victor Herbert, Jerry Herman, James A. Herne, Henry Hewes, Gregory Hines, Al Hirschfeld, Raymond Hitchcock, Hal Holbrook, Celeste Holm, Hanya Holm, Arthur Hopkins, De Wolf Hopper, John Houseman, Eugene Howard, Leslie Howard, Sidney Howard, Willie Howard, Barnard Hughes, Henry Hull, Josephine Hull, Walter Huston, Earle Hyman, Henrik Ibsen, William Inge, Dana Ivey, Bernard B. Jacobs, Elise Janis, Joseph Jefferson, Al Jolson, James Earl Jones, Margo Jones, Robert Edmond Jones, Tom Jones, Jon Jory, Raul Julia, Madeline Kahn, John Kander, Garson Kanin, George S. Kaufman, Danny Kaye, Elia Kazan, Gene Kelly, George Kelly, Fanny Kemble, Jerome Kern, Walter Kerr, Michael Kidd, Richard Kiley, Willa Kim, Sidney Kingsley, Kevin Kline, Florence Klotz, Joseph Wood Krutch, Bert Lahr, Burton Lane, Frank Langella, Lawrence Langner, Lillie Langtry, Angela Lansbury, Nathan Lane, Charles Laughton, Arthur Laurents, Gertrude Lawrence, Jerome Lawrence, Eva Le Gallienne, Canada Lee, Eugene Lee, Ming Cho Lee, Robert E. Lee, Lotte Lenya, Alan Jay Lerner, Sam Levene, Robert Lewis, Beatrice Lillie, Howard Lindsay, John Lithgow, Frank Loesser, Frederick Loewe, Joshua Logan, William Ivey Long, Santo Loquasto, Pauline Lord, Lucille Lortel, Dorothy Loudon, Alfred Lunt, Patti LuPone, Charles MacArthur, Steele MacKaye, Judith Malina, David Mamet, Rouben Mamoulian, Richard Mansfield, Robert B. Mantell, Frederic March, Nancy Marchand, Julia Marlowe, Ernest H. Martin, Mary Martin, Raymond Massey, Elizabeth Ireland McCann, Ian McKellen, Siobhan McKenna, Terrence McNally, Sanford Meisner, Helen Menken, Burgess Meredith, Ethel Merman, David Merrick, Jo Mielziner, Arthur Miller, Marilyn Miller, Liza Minnelli, Helena Modjeska, Ferenc Molnar, Lola Montez, Victor Moore, Robert Morse, Zero Mostel, Anna Cora Mowatt, Paul Muni, Brian Murray, Tharon Musser, George Jean Nathan, Mildred Natwick, Alla Nazimova, Patricia Neal, James M. Nederlander, Mike Nichols, Elliot Norton, Jack O'Brien, Sean O'Casey, Clifford Odets, Donald Oenslager, Laurence Olivier, Eugene O'Neill, Jerry Orbach, Geraldine Page, Joseph Papp, Estelle Parsons, Osgood Perkins, Bernadette Peters, Molly Picon, Harold Pinter, Luigi Pirandello, Christopher Plummer, Cole Porter, Robert Preston, Harold Prince, Jose Quintero, Ellis Rabb, John Raitt, Tony Randall, Michael Redgrave, Ada Rehan, Elmer Rice, Lloyd Richards, Ralph Richardson, Chita Rivera, Jason Robards, Jerome Robbins, Paul Robeson, Richard Rodgers, Will Rogers, Sigmund Romberg, Harold Rome, Billy Rose, Lillian Russell, Donald Saddler, Gene Saks, Diana Sands, William Saroyan, Joseph Schildkraut, Harvey Schmidt, Alan Schneider, Gerald Shoenfeld, Arthur Schwartz, Maurice Schwartz, George C. Scott, Marian Seldes, Peter Shaffer, Irene Sharaff, George Bernard Shaw, Sam Shepard, Robert F. Sherwood, J.J. Shubert, Lee Shubert, Herman

Shumlin, Neil Simon, Lee Simonson, Edmund Simpson, Otis Skinner, Lois Smith, Maggie Smith, Oliver Smith, Stephen Sondheim, E.H. Sothern, Kim Stanley, Jean Stapleton, Maureen Stapleton, Joseph Stein, Frances Sternhagen, Roger L. Stevens, Isabelle Stevenson, Ellen Stewart, Dorothy Stickney, Fred Stone, Peter Stone, Tom Stoppard, Lee Strasburg, August Strindberg, Elaine Stritch, Charles Strouse, Jule Styne, Margaret Sullivan, Arthur Sullivan, Jessica Tandy, Laurette Taylor, Ellen Terry, Sada Thompson, Cleon Throckmorton, Tommy Tune, Jonathan Tunick, Gwen Verdon, Robin Wagner, Nancy Walker, Eli Wallach, James Wallack, Lester Wallack, Tony Walton, Douglas Turner Ward, David Warfield, Wendy Wasserstein, Ethel Waters, Clifton Webb, Joseph Weber, Margaret Webster, Kurt Weill, Orson Welles, Mae West, Robert Whitehead, Richard Wilbur, Oscar Wilde, Thorton Wilder, Bert Williams, Tennessee Williams, August Wilson, Elizabeth Wilson, Lanford Wilson, P.G. Wodehouse, Peggy Wood, Alexander Woollcott, Irene Worth, Teresa Wright, Ed Wynn, Vincent Youmans, Stark Young, Florenz Ziegfeld, Patricia Zipprodt

Theater Hall of Fame Founders Award

Established in 1993 in honor of Earl Blackwell, James M. Nederlander, Gerald Oestreicher and Arnold Weissberger. The Theater Hall of Fame Founders Award is voted by the Hall's board of directors and is presented to an individual for his of her outstanding contribution to the theater.

2009 Recipient: Shirley Herz

Past Recipients: (if year is missing, no award was presented) **1993:** James M. Nederlander **1994:** Kitty Carlisle Hart **1995:** Harvey Sabinson **1996:** Henry Hewes **1997:** Otis L. Guernsey Jr. **1998:** Edward Colton **2000:** Gerard Oestreicher; Arnold Weissberger **2001:** Tom Dillon **2003:** Price Berkley **2004:** No Award **2005:** Donald Seawell **2007:** Roy Somlyo

UNITED STATES INSTITUTE FOR THEATRE TECHNOLOGY (USITT) AWARDS

Presented at the 50th annual USITT Conference and Stage Expo, March 21–April 3, 2010 at the Kansas City Convention & Entertainment Facilities, Kansas City, Missouri.

USITT Golden Anniversary Award Dr. Joel E. Rubin

USITT 50th Gala Awards Jennifer Tipton, Sally Struthers, François Leroux (Walt Disney Entertainment)

USITT Award First presented in 1967, this award recognizes a lifetime contribution in the performing arts community in any capacity. Recipients of this award do not need to be members of the Institute nor must they have any connection to USITT. No award presented this year.

Thomas DeGaetani Award First presented in 1983, this award honors an outstanding lifetime contribution to the performing arts community by an individual or a performing arts/entertainment-focused organization living and/or working in the area where the Annual Conference & Stage Expo is Held. **2010 Recipient:** University of Missouri-Kansas City

Joel E. Rubin Founder's Award First Presented in 1970, this award is presented to a USITT member in recognition of outstanding and continued service to the Institute. No award presented this season.

Distinguished Achievement Awards First presented in 1998, this award recognizes achievement by designers and technicians with established careers in the areas of scenic design, lighting design, technical direction, costume design, theatre architecture, theatrical consulting, production management, sound design, arts management, and costume direction. The recipient, who does not have to be a member of USITT. No awards presented this year.

International Health & Safety Award First presented in 1985, this award is recognizes outstanding contribution towards health and safety in the performing arts. It is only given in those years where there is important activity in the area of the Conference and Expo, and can be presented to an individual for career-long dedication as well as for specific initiatives. No award presented this year.

Golden Pen Award First presented in 1986, this award is presented to an author of an outstanding major, recent publication in the field of design and production for the performing arts. **2010 Recipient:** Oscar Brockett, Margaret Mitchell, and Linda Hardberger, *Making the Scene: A History of Stage Design and Technology in Europe and the United States*

Herbert D. Greggs Awards First presented in 1979 and 1998, respectively, the Herbert D. Greggs Award (highest honor) and the Herbert D. Greggs Merit Award promote innovative, in-depth writing about theatre design and technology in *TD&T*. **2010 Greggs Award Recipient:** Holly Poe Durbin for her three-part series "Seeing with Three Eyes" (Winter, Spring, and Fall 2008) **2010 Greggs Merit Award:** Patrick Atkinson for "In the Wings: Eugene Camille Fitch's Images of the Theatre" (Summer 2009)

Architecture Awards Created in 1994 and sponsored by the USITT Architecture Commission, these awards honors excellence in the design of theatre projects. Honor Awards (the highest designation) and Merit Awards are evaluated by a panel of distinguished jurors for creative image, contextual resonance, community contribution, explorations in new technologies, and functional operations. **2009 Honor Awards:** The Royal Conservatory of Music, TELUS Centre for Performance and Learning (Toronto, Canada) designed by Kuwabara Payne McKenna Blumberg Architects; **2010 Merit Awards:** Vukovich Center for Communication Arts (Meadville, PA) designed by Polshek Partnership Architects; Henry Miller's Theatre (New York, NY) designed by Cook and Fox Architects; Winspear Opera House (Dallas, TX) designed by Foster + Partners; Theatre De Quat'sous (Montreal, Canada) designed by Le Architectes Fab G; Renée and Henry Segerstrom Concert Hall and Samueli Theater (Costa Mesa, CA) designed by Pelli Clarke Pelli; Iwaki Performing Arts Center (Fukushima, Japan) designed by Naomi Sato Architects & Shimizu Corporation

Special Citations Special Citations recognize outstanding achievement in any area of the performing arts by an individual or an organization. The initial Special Citation was presented in 1963. No citations presented this year.

International Travel Awards for Individual/Professionals and Students Established in 2004 to provide USITT members with funding for international travel for advanced research and education in theatre related fields. The student award was established in 2003 to assist USITT student members. Awards are presented to Individual/Professionals on even years, and to Students on odd years. **2010 Individual/Professional Travel Award Recipient:** Rusty Cloyese

Rising Star Award Established by LDI and *LiveDesign* magazine in 2005, this award is given annually to a young professional at the beginning of his or her career; recipients must be in the first four years of professional (non-academic) work following the completion of his or her highest degree. **2010 Recipient:** Ben Pilat (lighting designer)

Tech Expo Winners The Theatre Technology Exhibition, popularly known as Tech Expo, is mounted in alternate years at USITT's Annual Conference. Projects that demonstrate developments and creative solutions in all technical areas are juried by a distinguished panel of theatrical technicians. Prizes are awarded to the most inventive exhibitions; all entries that are accepted appear in the *Tech Expo Catalog*. 2010 was not an award year.

YD & T Awards These awards are presented to young designers and technicians for recognition at the beginning of their careers, and made possible by gifts to USITT. **2010 Recipients:**

KM Fabrics Technical Production Award: Amanda Haley

Robert E. Cohen Sound Achievement Award: David Hunter

USITT Barbizon Lighting Award: James Tan Khoon Song

USITT Rose Brand Scene Design Award: G. Warren Stiles

USITT Zelma H. Weisfeld Costume Design & Technology Award: Ariana Schwartz

USITT Kryolan Corporation Makeup Design Award: Beauty Thibodeau

USITT Frederick A. Buerki Golden Hammer Scenic Technology Award: Chris Swetcky

USITT Clear-Com Stage Management Award: Bekah Wachenfeld

USITT W. Oren Parker Scene Design Award: Caitlin Ayer

USITT Stage Technology Lighting Design Award: no award presented

WILLIAM INGE THEATRE FESTIVAL AWARDS

April 21–24, 2010; 29th annual. The Inge Festival brings some of the world's most beloved playwrights to America's heartland in Independence, Missouri. During the four-day festival, honorees are chosen for distinguished achievement in American theater. Also, the festival selects a winner of the Otis Guernsey New Voices Playwriting Award, which recognizes contemporary playwrights whose voices are helping shape the American theater of today. It is named for the late Otis L. Guernsey Jr., beloved theater writer and editor who was a frequent guest at the William Inge Theatre Festival and a champion of exciting new plays.

2010 Honoree: Paula Vogel

18th Annual Otis Guernsey New Voices in Playwrighting Award: Katori Hall

Previous Festival Honorees: 1982: William Inge Celebration; **1983:** Jerome Lawrence **1984:** William Gibson **1985:** Robert Anderson **1986:** John Patrick **1987:** Garson Kanin **1988:** Sidney Kingsley (in Independence), Robert E. Lee (on the road) **1989:** Horton Foote **1990:** Betty Comden & Adolph Green **1991:** Edward Albee **1992:** Peter Shaffer **1993:** Wendy Wasserstein **1994:** Terrence McNally **1995:** Arthur Miller **1996:** August Wilson **1997:** Neil Simon **1998:** Stephen Sondheim **1999:** John Guare **2000:** A.R. Gurney **2001:** Lanford Wilson **2002:** John Kander & Fred Ebb **2003:** Romulus Linney **2004:** Arthur Laurents **2005:** Tina Howe **2006:** 25th Anniversary retrospective **2007:** Jerry Bock & Sheldon Harnick **2008:** Christopher Durang **2009:** Tom Jones and Harvey Schmidt

Previous New Voices Recipients: 1993: Jason Milligan **1994:** Catherine Butterfield **1995:** Mary Hanes **1996:** Brian Burgess Cross **1997:** Joe DiPietro **1998:** David Ives **1999:** David Hirson **2000:** James Still **2001:** Mark St. Germain **2002:** Dana Yeaton **2003:** Theresa Rebeck **2004:** Mary Portser **2005:** Lynne Kaufman **2006:** Melanie Marnich **2007:** JT Rogers **2008:** Adam Bock **2009:** Carlos Murillo

LONGEST-RUNNING SHOWS

Top: *Brian Stokes Mitchell and the original cast of* Ragtime *(1998) (photo by Catherine Ashmore)*

Center: *Zeljko Ivanek and Matthew Broderick in* Brighton Beach Memoirs *(1983) (photo by Jay Thompson)*

Bottom: Front Row: *Jacqueline Mayro, Steve Skiles;* back row: *Walter Willison, Ron Tannas, and Gregg Stump in* Your Own Thing *(1968) (photo by Bert Andrews)*

Longest-Running Shows on Broadway

The Phantom of the Opera*
9,292 performances
Opened January 26, 1988

Cats
7,485 performances
Opened October 7, 1982
Closed September 10, 2000

Les Misérables
6,680 performances
Opened March 12, 1987
Closed May 18, 2003

A Chorus Line
6,137 performances
Opened July 25, 1975
Closed April 28, 1990

Oh! Calcutta (revival)
5,959 performances
Opened September 24, 1976
Closed August 6, 1989

Chicago* (revival)
5,621 performances
Opened November 19, 1996

Beauty and the Beast
5,464 performances
Opened April 18, 1994
Closed July 29, 2007

The Lion King*
5,205 performances
Opened November 13, 1997

Rent
5,124 performances
Opened April 29, 1996
Closed September 7, 2008

Miss Saigon
4,097 performances
Opened April 11, 1991
Closed January 28, 2001

Mamma Mia!*
3,568 performances
Opened October 12, 2001

42nd Street
3,486 performances
Opened August 25, 1980
Closed January 8, 1989

Grease
3,388 performances
Opened February 14, 1972
Closed April 13, 1980

Fiddler on the Roof
3,242 performances
Opened September 22, 1964
Closed July 2, 1972

Life With Father
3,224 performances
Opened November 8, 1939
Closed July 12, 1947

Chita Rivera and Dick Van Dyke in Bye Bye Birdie *(1960)*
(photo by Friedman-Abeles)

Tobacco Road
3,182 performances
Opened December 4, 1933
Closed May 31, 1941

Hello, Dolly!
2,844 performances
Opened January 16, 1964
Closed December 27, 1970

Wicked*
2,726 performances
Opened October 30, 2003

My Fair Lady
2,717 performances
Opened March 15, 1956
Closed September 29, 1962

Hairspray
2,641 performances
Opened August 15, 2002
Closed January 4, 2009

Avenue Q
2,534 performances
Opened July 31, 2003
Closed September 13, 2009

The Producers
2,502 performances
Opened April 19, 2001
Closed April 22, 2007

Cabaret (1998 revival)
2,378 performances
Opened March 19, 1998
Closed January 4, 2004

Annie
2,377 performances
Opened April 21, 1977
Closed January 22, 1983

Man of La Mancha
2,328 performances
Opened November 22, 1965
Closed June 26, 1971

Abie's Irish Rose
2,327 performances
Opened May 23, 1922
Closed October 21, 1927

Oklahoma!
2,212 performances
Opened March 31, 1943
Closed May 29, 1948

Smokey Joe's Café
2,036 performances
Opened March 2, 1995
Closed January 16, 2000

Pippin
1,944 performances
Opened October 23, 1972
Closed June 12, 1977

South Pacific
1,925 performances
Opened April 7, 1949
Closed January 16, 1954

The Magic Show
1,920 performances
Opened May 28, 1974
Closed December 31, 1978

Jersey Boys*
1,881 performances
Opened November 6, 2006

Patty Duke in The Miracle Worker *(1959)*
(photo by Fred Fehl)

Aida
1,852 performances
Opened March 23, 2000
Closed September 5, 2004

Gemini
1,819 performances
Opened May 21, 1977
Closed September 6, 1981

Deathtrap
1,793 performances
Opened February 26, 1978
Closed June 13, 1982

Harvey
1,775 performances
Opened November 1, 1944
Closed January 15, 1949

Dancin'
1,774 performances
Opened March 27, 1978
Closed June 27, 1982

La Cage aux Folles
1,761 performances
Opened August 21, 1983
Closed November 15, 1987

Hair
1,750 performances
Opened April 29, 1968
Closed July 1, 1972

The Wiz
1,672 performances
Opened January 5, 1975
Closed January 29, 1979

Born Yesterday
1,642 performances
Opened February 4, 1946
Closed December 31, 1949

**The Best Little
Whorehouse in Texas**
1,639 performances
Opened June 19, 1978
Closed March 27, 1982

Crazy for You
1,622 performances
Opened February 19, 1992
Closed January 7, 1996

Ain't Misbehavin'
1,604 performances
Opened May 9, 1978
Closed February 21, 1982

Monty Python's Spamalot
1,574 performances
Opened March 17, 2005
Closed January 11, 2009

Mary, Mary
1,572 performances
Opened March 8, 1961
Closed December 12, 1964

Evita
1,567 performances
Opened September 25, 1979
Closed June 26, 1983

The Voice of the Turtle
1,557 performances
Opened December 8, 1943
Closed January 3, 1948

Jekyll & Hyde
1,543 performances
Opened April 28, 1997
Closed January 7, 2001

Barefoot in the Park
1,530 performances
Opened October 23, 1963
Closed June 25, 1967

Brighton Beach Memoirs
1,530 performances
Opened March 27, 1983
Closed May 11, 1986

42nd Street (revival)
1,524 performances
Opened May 2, 2001
Closed January 2, 2005

Dreamgirls
1,522 performances
Opened December 20, 1981
Closed August 11, 1985

Mame
1,508 performances
Opened May 24, 1966
Closed January 3, 1970

Grease (1994 revival)
1,505 performances
Opened May 11, 1994
Closed January 25, 1998

Mary Poppins[*]
1,477 performances
Opened November 16, 2006

Same Time, Next Year
1,453 performances
Opened March 14, 1975
Closed September 3, 1978

Arsenic and Old Lace
1,444 performances
Opened January 10, 1941
Closed June 17, 1944

The Sound of Music
1,443 performances
Opened November 16, 1959
Closed June 15, 1963

Me and My Girl
1,420 performances
Opened August 10, 1986
Closed December 31, 1989

**How to Succeed in Business
Without Really Trying**
1,417 performances
Opened October 14, 1961
Closed March 6, 1965

Hellzapoppin'
1,404 performances
Opened September 22, 1938
Closed December 17, 1941

The Music Man
1,375 performances
Opened December 19, 1957
Closed April 15, 1961

Funny Girl
1,348 performances
Opened March 26, 1964
Closed July 15, 1967

Mummenschanz
1,326 performances
Opened March 30, 1977
Closed April 20, 1980

Movin' Out
1,303 performances
Opened October 24, 2002
Closed December 11, 2005

Angel Street
1,295 performances
Opened December 5, 1941
Closed December 30, 1944

Lightnin'
1,291 performances
Opened August 26, 1918
Closed August 27, 1921

Promises, Promises
1,281 performances
Opened December 1, 1968
Closed January 1, 1972

The King and I
1,246 performances
Opened March 29, 1951
Closed March 20, 1954

Cactus Flower
1,234 performances
Opened December 8, 1965
Closed November 23, 1968

Mary Alice and James Earl Jones in Fences *(1987)*
(photo by Ron Scherl)

The original cast of A Little Night Music *(1973)
(photo by Martha Swope)*

Sleuth
1,222 performances
Opened November 12, 1970
Closed October 13, 1973

Torch Song Trilogy
1,222 performances
Opened June 10, 1982
Closed May 19, 1985

1776
1,217 performances
Opened March 16, 1969
Closed February 13, 1972

Equus
1,209 performances
Opened October 24, 1974
Closed October 7, 1977

Sugar Babies
1,208 performances
Opened October 8, 1979
Closed August 28, 1982

Guys and Dolls
1,200 performances
Opened November 24, 1950
Closed November 28, 1953

Amadeus
1,181 performances
Opened December 17, 1980
Closed October 16, 1983

Cabaret
1,165 performances
Opened November 20, 1966
Closed September 6, 1969

Mister Roberts
1,157 performances
Opened February 18, 1948
Closed January 6, 1951

Annie Get Your Gun
1,147 performances
Opened May 16, 1946
Closed February 12, 1949

Guys and Dolls (1992 revival)
1,144 performances
Opened April 14, 1992
Closed January 8, 1995

The Seven Year Itch
1,141 performances
Opened November 20, 1952
Closed August 13, 1955

The 25th Annual Putnam County Spelling Bee
1,136 performances
Opened May 2, 2005
Closed January 20, 2008

Bring in 'da Noise, Bring in 'da Funk
1,130 performances
Opened April 25, 1996
Closed January 19, 1999

Butterflies Are Free
1,128 performances
Opened October 21, 1969
Closed July 2, 1972

Pins and Needles
1,108 performances
Opened November 27, 1937
Closed June 22, 1940

Plaza Suite
1,097 performances
Opened February 14, 1968
Closed October 3, 1970

Fosse
1,093 performances
Opened January 14, 1999
Closed August 25, 2001

They're Playing Our Song
1,082 performances
Opened February 11, 1979
Closed September 6, 1981

Grand Hotel (musical)
1,077 performances
Opened November 12, 1989
Closed April 25, 1992

Kiss Me, Kate
1,070 performances
Opened December 30, 1948
Closed July 25, 1951

Don't Bother Me, I Can't Cope
1,065 performances
Opened April 19, 1972
Closed October 27, 1974

The Pajama Game
1,063 performances
Opened May 13, 1954
Closed November 24, 1956

Shenandoah
1,050 performances
Opened January 7, 1975
Closed August 7, 1977

Annie Get Your Gun (1999 revival)
1,046 performances
Opened March 4, 1999
Closed September 1, 2001

The Teahouse of the August Moon
1,027 performances
Opened October 15, 1953
Closed March 24, 1956

Damn Yankees
1,019 performances
Opened May 5, 1955
Closed October 12, 1957

Contact
1,010 performances
Opened March 30, 2000
Closed September 1, 2002

Never Too Late
1,007 performances
Opened November 26, 1962
Closed April 24, 1965

Big River
1,005 performances
Opened April 25, 1985
Closed September 20, 1987

The Will Rogers Follies
983 performances
Opened May 1, 1991
Closed September 5, 1993

Any Wednesday
982 performances
Opened February 18, 1964
Closed June 26, 1966

Sunset Boulevard
977 performances
Opened November 17, 1994
Closed March 22, 1997

Urinetown the Musical
965 performances
Opened September 20, 2001
Closed January 18, 2004

A Funny Thing Happened on the Way to the Forum
964 performances
Opened May 8, 1962
Closed August 29, 1964

The Odd Couple
964 performances
Opened March 10, 1965
Closed July 2, 1967

Anna Lucasta
957 performances
Opened August 30, 1944
Closed November 30, 1946

Kiss and Tell
956 performances
Opened March 17, 1943
Closed June 23, 1945

Show Boat (1994 revival)
949 performances
Opened October 2, 1994
Closed January 5, 1997

In the Heights*
928 Performances
Opened March 9, 2008

Dracula (1977 revival)
925 performances
Opened October 20, 1977
Closed January 6, 1980

Bells Are Ringing
924 performances
Opened November 29, 1956
Closed March 7, 1959

The Moon Is Blue
924 performances
Opened March 8, 1951
Closed May 30, 1953

Beatlemania
920 performances
Opened May 31, 1977
Closed October 17, 1979

Proof
917 performances
Opened October 24, 2000
Closed January 5, 2003

The Elephant Man
916 performances
Opened April 19, 1979
Closed June 28, 1981

The Color Purple
910 performances
Opened December 1, 2005
Closed February 24, 2008

Kiss of the Spider Woman
906 performances
Opened May 3, 1993
Closed July 1, 1995

Thoroughly Modern Millie
904 performances
Opened April 18, 2002
Closed June 20, 2004

Luv
901 performances
Opened November 11, 1964
Closed January 7, 1967

South Pacific* (revival)
901 performances
Opened April 3, 2008

The Who's Tommy
900 performances
Opened April 22, 1993
Closed June 17, 1995

Chicago
898 performances
Opened June 3, 1975
Closed August 27, 1977

Applause
896 performances
Opened March 30, 1970
Closed July 27, 1972

Can-Can
892 performances
Opened May 7, 1953
Closed June 25, 1955

Carousel
890 performances
Opened April 19, 1945
Closed May 24, 1947

I'm Not Rappaport
890 performances
Opened November 19, 1985
Closed January 17, 1988

Hats Off to Ice
889 performances
Opened June 22, 1944
Closed April 2, 1946

Fanny
888 performances
Opened November 4, 1954
Closed December 16, 1956

Children of a Lesser God
887 performances
Opened March 30, 1980
Closed May 16, 1982

Follow the Girls
882 performances
Opened April 8, 1944
Closed May 18, 1946

Kiss Me, Kate (revival)
881 performances
Opened November 18, 1999
Closed December 30, 2001

City of Angels
878 performances
Opened December 11, 1989
Closed January 19, 1992

Camelot
873 performances
Opened December 3, 1960
Closed January 5, 1963

I Love My Wife
872 performances
Opened April 17, 1977
Closed May 20, 1979

The Bat
867 performances
Opened August 23, 1920
Unknown closing date

My Sister Eileen
864 performances
Opened December 26, 1940
Closed January 16, 1943

No, No, Nanette (revival)
861 performances
Opened January 19, 1971
Closed February 3, 1973

Song of Norway
860 performances
Opened August 21, 1944
Closed September 7, 1946

Spring Awakening
859 performances
Opened December 10, 2006
Closed January 18, 2009

Chapter Two
857 performances
Opened December 4, 1977
Closed December 9, 1979

A Streetcar Named Desire
855 performances
Opened December 3, 1947
Closed December 17, 1949

Barnum
854 performances
Opened April 30, 1980
Closed May 16, 1982

Comedy in Music
849 performances
Opened October 2, 1953
Closed January 21, 1956

Raisin
847 performances
Opened October 18, 1973
Closed December 7, 1975

Blood Brothers
839 performances
Opened April 25, 1993
Closed April 30, 1995

You Can't Take It With You
837 performances
Opened December 14, 1936
Unknown closing date

La Plume de Ma Tante
835 performances
Opened November 11, 1958
Closed December 17, 1960

Three Men on a Horse
835 performances
Opened January 30, 1935
Closed January 9, 1937

Ragtime
861 performances
Opened January 18, 1998
Closed January 16, 2000

The Subject Was Roses
832 performances
Opened May 25, 1964
Closed May 21, 1966

Black and Blue
824 performances
Opened January 26, 1989
Closed January 20, 1991

The King and I (1996 revival)
807 performances
Opened April 11, 1996
Closed February 22, 1998

Inherit the Wind
806 performances
Opened April 21, 1955
Closed June 22, 1957

Anything Goes (1987 revival)
804 performances
Opened October 19, 1987
Closed September 3, 1989

Titanic
804 performances
Opened April 23, 1997
Closed March 21, 1999

*George Hearn and Les Cagelles in
La Cage aux Folles (1984)
(photo by Martha Swope)*

No Time for Sergeants
796 performances
Opened October 20, 1955
Closed September 14, 1957

Fiorello!
795 performances
Opened November 23, 1959
Closed October 28, 1961

Where's Charley?
792 performances
Opened October 11, 1948
Closed September 9, 1950

The Ladder
789 performances
Opened October 22, 1926
Unknown closing date

Fiddler on the Roof (2004 revival)
781 performances
Opened February 26, 2004
Closed January 8, 2006

Forty Carats
780 performances
Opened December 26, 1968
Closed November 7, 1970

Lost in Yonkers
780 performances
Opened February 21, 1991
Closed January 3, 1993

The Prisoner of Second Avenue
780 performances
Opened November 11, 1971
Closed September 29, 1973

M. Butterfly
777 performances
Opened March 20, 1988
Closed January 27, 1990

The Tale of the Allergist's Wife
777 performances
Opened November 2, 2000
Closed September 15, 2002

Oliver!
774 performances
Opened January 6, 1963
Closed November 14, 1964

The Pirates of Penzance
(1981 revival)
772 performances
Opened January 8, 1981
Closed November 28, 1982

The 39 Steps
771 performances
Opened January 15, 2008
Closed January 10, 2010

The Full Monty
770 performances
Opened October 26, 2000
Closed September 1, 2002

Woman of the Year
770 performances
Opened March 29, 1981
Closed March 13, 1983

My One and Only
767 performances
Opened May 1, 1983
Closed March 3, 1985

Sophisticated Ladies
767 performances
Opened March 1, 1981
Closed January 2, 1983

Bubbling Brown Sugar
766 performances
Opened March 2, 1976
Closed December 31, 1977

Into the Woods
765 performances
Opened November 5, 1987
Closed September 3, 1989

State of the Union
765 performances
Opened November 14, 1945
Closed September 13, 1947

Starlight Express
761 performances
Opened March 15, 1987
Closed January 8, 1989

The First Year
760 performances
Opened October 20, 1920
Unknown closing date

A Chorus Line (revival)
759 performances
Opened October 5, 2006
Closed August 17, 2008

Broadway Bound
756 performances
Opened December 4, 1986
Closed September 25, 1988

You Know I Can't Hear You When the Water's Running
755 performances
Opened March 13, 1967
Closed January 4, 1969

Two for the Seesaw
750 performances
Opened January 16, 1958
Closed October 31, 1959

Joseph and the Amazing Technicolor Dreamcoat
747 performances
Opened January 27, 1982
Closed September 4, 1983

Death of a Salesman
742 performances
Opened February 10, 1949
Closed November 18, 1950

for colored girls who have considered suicide/when the rainbow is enuf
742 performances
Opened September 15, 1976
Closed July 16, 1978

Sons o' Fun
742 performances
Opened December 1, 1941
Closed August 29, 1943

Candide (1974 revival)
740 performances
Opened March 10, 1974
Closed January 4, 1976

Gentlemen Prefer Blondes
740 performances
Opened December 8, 1949
Closed September 15, 1951

The Man Who Came to Dinner
739 performances
Opened October 16, 1939
Closed July 12, 1941

Nine
739 performances
Opened May 9, 1982
Closed February 4, 1984

Call Me Mister
734 performances
Opened April 18, 1946
Closed January 10, 1948

Victor/Victoria
734 performances
Opened October 25, 1995
Closed July 27, 1997

West Side Story
732 performances
Opened September 26, 1957
Closed June 27, 1959

High Button Shoes
727 performances
Opened October 9, 1947
Closed July 2, 1949

Finian's Rainbow
725 performances
Opened January 10, 1947
Closed October 2, 1948

Claudia
722 performances
Opened February 12, 1941
Closed January 9, 1943

Clint Allmon, Carlin Glynn and Henderson Forsythe in The Best Little Whorehouse in Texas *(1978) (photo by Ilene Jones)*

Sandra Church and Ethyl Merman in the original production of Gypsy
(1959) (photo by Friedman-Abeles)

The Gold Diggers
720 performances
Opened September 30, 1919
Unknown closing date

Jesus Christ Superstar
720 performances
Opened October 12, 1971
Closed June 30, 1973

Carnival!
719 performances
Opened April 13, 1961
Closed January 5, 1963

The Miracle Worker
719 performances
Opened October 19, 1959
Closed July 1, 1961

The Diary of Anne Frank
717 performances
Opened October 5, 1955
Closed June 22, 1955

**A Funny Thing Happened
on the Way to the Forum** (revival)
715 performances
Opened April 18, 1996
Closed January 4, 1998

I Remember Mama
714 performances
Opened October 19, 1944
Closed June 29, 1946

Tea and Sympathy
712 performances
Opened September 30, 1953
Closed June 18, 1955

Junior Miss
710 performances
Opened November 18, 1941
Closed July 24, 1943

Footloose
708 performances
Opened October 22, 1998
Closed July 2, 2000

Last of the Red Hot Lovers
706 performances
Opened December 28, 1969
Closed September 4, 1971

The Secret Garden
706 performances
Opened April 25, 1991
Closed January 3, 1993

Company
705 performances
Opened April 26, 1970
Closed January 1, 1972

Seventh Heaven
704 performances
Opened October 30, 1922
Unknown closing date

Gypsy
702 performances
Opened May 21, 1959
Closed March 25, 1961

That Championship Season
700 performances
Opened September 14, 1972
Closed April 21, 1974

The Music Man (2000 revival)
698 performances
Opened April 27, 2000
Closed December 30, 2001

Da
697 performances
Opened May 1, 1978
Closed January 1, 1980

Cat on a Hot Tin Roof
694 performances
Opened March 24, 1955
Closed November 17, 1956

Li'l Abner
693 performances
Opened November 15, 1956
Closed July 12, 1958

The Children's Hour
691 performances
Opened November 20, 1934
Unknown closing date

Purlie
688 performances
Opened March 15, 1970
Closed November 6, 1971

Dead End
687 performances
Opened October 28, 1935
Closed June 12, 1937

The Lion and the Mouse
686 performances
Opened November 20, 1905
Unknown closing date

White Cargo
686 performances
Opened November 5, 1923
Unknown closing date

The Little Mermaid
685 performances
Opened January 10, 2008
Closed August 30, 2009

Dear Ruth
683 performances
Opened December 13, 1944
Closed July 27, 1946

East Is West
680 performances
Opened December 25, 1918
Unknown closing date

Come Blow Your Horn
677 performances
Opened February 22, 1961
Closed October 6, 1962

The Most Happy Fella
676 performances
Opened May 3, 1956
Closed December 14, 1957

The Drowsy Chaperone
672 performances
Opened May 1, 2006
Closed December 30, 2007

Defending the Caveman
671 performances
Opened March 26, 1995
Closed June 22, 1997

The Doughgirls
671 performances
Opened December 30, 1942
Closed July 29, 1944

The Impossible Years
670 performances
Opened October 13, 1965
Closed May 27, 1967

Irene
670 performances
Opened November 18, 1919
Unknown closing date

Boy Meets Girl
669 performances
Opened November 27, 1935
Unknown closing date

The Tap Dance Kid
669 performances
Opened December 21, 1983
Closed August 11, 1985

Beyond the Fringe
667 performances
Opened October 27, 1962
Closed May 30, 1964

Who's Afraid of Virginia Woolf?
664 performances
Opened October 13, 1962
Closed May 16, 1964

Blithe Spirit
657 performances
Opened November 5, 1941
Closed June 5, 1943

A Trip to Chinatown
657 performances
Opened November 9, 1891
Unknown closing date

The Women
657 performances
Opened December 26, 1936
Unknown closing date

Bloomer Girl
654 performances
Opened October 5, 1944
Closed April 27, 1946

The Fifth Season
654 performances
Opened January 23, 1953
Closed October 23, 1954

August: Osage County
648 performances
Opened December 4, 2007
Closed June 28, 2009

Rain
648 performances
Opened September 1, 1924
Unknown closing date

Witness for the Prosecution
645 performances
Opened December 16, 1954
Closed June 30, 1956

Call Me Madam
644 performances
Opened October 12, 1950
Closed May 3, 1952

Janie
642 performances
Opened September 10, 1942
Closed January 16, 1944

Billy Elliot The Musical*
644 performances
Opened November 13, 2008

The Green Pastures
640 performances
Opened February 26, 1930
Closed August 29, 1931

Auntie Mame
639 performances
Opened October 31, 1956
Closed June 28, 1958

A Man for All Seasons
637 performances
Opened November 22, 1961
Closed June 1, 1963

Jerome Robbins' Broadway
634 performances
Opened February 26, 1989
Closed September 1, 1990

The Fourposter
632 performances
Opened October 24, 1951
Closed May 2, 1953

Dirty Rotten Scoundrels
627 performances
Opened March 3, 2005
Closed September 3, 2006

The Music Master
627 performances
Opened September 26, 1904
Unknown closing date

Two Gentlemen of Verona
(musical)
627 performances
Opened December 1, 1971
Closed May 20, 1973

The Tenth Man
623 performances
Opened November 5, 1959
Closed May 13, 1961

The Heidi Chronicles
621 performances
Opened March 9, 1989
Closed September 1, 1990

Robert Lindsay and the cast of Me and My Girl *(1987) (photo by Nathaniel Kramer)*

Is Zat So?
618 performances
Opened January 5, 1925
Closed July 1926

Anniversary Waltz
615 performances
Opened April 7, 1954
Closed September 24, 1955

The Happy Time (play)
614 performances
Opened January 24, 1950
Closed July 14, 1951

Separate Rooms
613 performances
Opened March 23, 1940
Closed September 6, 1941

Affairs of State
610 performances
Opened September 25, 1950
Closed March 8, 1952

Oh! Calcutta!
610 performances
Opened June 17, 1969
Closed August 12, 1972

Star and Garter
609 performances
Opened June 24, 1942
Closed December 4, 1943

The Mystery of Edwin Drood
608 performances
Opened December 2, 1985
Closed May 16, 1987

The Student Prince
608 performances
Opened December 2, 1924
Unknown closing date

Sweet Charity
608 performances
Opened January 29, 1966
Closed July 15, 1967

Bye Bye Birdie
607 performances
Opened April 14, 1960
Closed October 7, 1961

Riverdance on Broadway
605 performances
Opened March 16, 2000
Closed August 26, 2001

Irene (revival)
604 performances
Opened March 13, 1973
Closed September 8, 1974

Sunday in the Park With George
604 performances
Opened May 2, 1984
Closed October 13, 1985

Adonis
603 performances
Opened circa 1884
Unknown closing date

Broadway
603 performances
Opened September 16, 1926
Unknown closing date

Peg o' My Heart
603 performances
Opened December 20, 1912
Unknown closing date

Master Class
601 performances
Opened November 5, 1995
Closed June 29, 1997

Street Scene (play)
601 performances
Opened January 10, 1929
Unknown closing date

Flower Drum Song
600 performances
Opened December 1, 1958
Closed May 7, 1960

Kiki
600 performances
Opened November 29, 1921
Unknown closing date

A Little Night Music
600 performances
Opened February 25, 1973
Closed August 3, 1974

Art
600 performances
Opened March 1, 1998
Closed August 8, 1999

Agnes of God
599 performances
Opened March 30, 1982
Closed September 4, 1983

Don't Drink the Water
598 performances
Opened November 17, 1966
Closed April 20, 1968

Wish You Were Here
598 performances
Opened June 25, 1952
Closed November 28, 1953

Sarafina!
597 performances
Opened January 28, 1988
Closed July 2, 1989

A Society Circus
596 performances
Opened December 13, 1905
Closed November 24, 1906

Legally Blonde
595 performances
Opened April 29, 2007
Closed October 19, 2008

Absurd Person Singular
592 performances
Opened October 8, 1974
Closed March 6, 1976

A Day in Hollywood/A Night in the Ukraine
588 performances
Opened May 1, 1980
Closed September 27, 1981

The Me Nobody Knows
586 performances
Opened December 18, 1970
Closed November 21, 1971

The Two Mrs. Carrolls
585 performances
Opened August 3, 1943
Closed February 3, 1945

Robert Redford and Elizabeth Ashley in the original production of Barefoot in the Park *(1963) (photo by Sabinson)*

Kismet (musical)
583 performances
Opened December 3, 1953
Closed April 23, 1955

Gypsy (1989 revival)
582 performances
Opened November 16, 1989
Closed July 28, 1991

Brigadoon
581 performances
Opened March 13, 1947
Closed July 31, 1948

Detective Story
581 performances
Opened March 23, 1949
Closed August 12, 1950

No Strings
580 performances
Opened March 14, 1962
Closed August 3, 1963

Brother Rat
577 performances
Opened December 16, 1936
Unknown closing date

Blossom Time
576 performances
Opened September 29, 1921
Unknown closing date

Pump Boys and Dinettes
573 performances
Opened February 4, 1982
Closed June 18, 1983

Show Boat
572 performances
Opened December 27, 1927
Closed May 4, 1929

The Show-Off
571 performances
Opened February 5, 1924
Unknown closing date

Sally
570 performances
Opened December 21, 1920
Closed April 22, 1922

Jelly's Last Jam
569 performances
Opened April 26, 1992
Closed September 5, 1993

Golden Boy (musical)
568 performances
Opened October 20, 1964
Closed March 5, 1966

One Touch of Venus
567 performances
Opened October 7, 1943
Closed February 10, 1945

The Real Thing
566 performances
Opened January 5, 1984
Closed May 12, 1985

Happy Birthday
564 performances
Opened October 31, 1946
Closed March 13, 1948

Look Homeward, Angel
564 performances
Opened November 28, 1957
Closed April 4, 1959

Morning's at Seven (revival)
564 performances
Opened April 10, 1980
Closed August 16, 1981

The Glass Menagerie
561 performances
Opened March 31, 1945
Closed August 3, 1946

I Do! I Do!
560 performances
Opened December 5, 1966
Closed June 15, 1968

Wonderful Town
559 performances
Opened February 25, 1953
Closed July 3, 1954

The Last Night of Ballyhoo
557 performances
Opened February 27, 1997
Closed June 28, 1998

Rose Marie
557 performances
Opened September 2, 1924
Unknown closing date

Strictly Dishonorable
557 performances
Opened September 18, 1929
Unknown closing date

Sweeney Todd, the Demon Barber of Fleet Street
557 performances
Opened March 1, 1979
Closed June 29, 1980

The Great White Hope
556 performances
Opened October 3, 1968
Closed January 31, 1970

A Majority of One
556 performances
Opened February 16, 1959
Closed June 25, 1960

The Sisters Rosensweig
556 performances
Opened March 18, 1993
Closed July 16, 1994

Sunrise at Campobello
556 performances
Opened January 30, 1958
Closed May 30, 1959

Toys in the Attic
556 performances
Opened February 25, 1960
Closed April 8, 1961

Jamaica
555 performances
Opened October 31, 1957
Closed April 11, 1959

Stop the World—I Want to Get Off
555 performances
Opened October 3, 1962
Closed February 1, 1964

Grease (2007 revival)
554 performances
Opened August 19, 2007
Closed January 4, 2009

Florodora
553 performances
Opened November 10, 1900
Closed January 25, 1902

Noises Off
553 performances
Opened December 11, 1983
Closed April 6, 1985

Ziegfeld Follies (1943)
553 performances
Opened April 1, 1943
Closed July 22, 1944

Dial "M" for Murder
552 performances
Opened October 29, 1952
Closed February 27, 1954

Good News
551 performances
Opened September 6, 1927
Unknown closing date

Peter Pan (revival)
551 performances
Opened September 6, 1979
Closed January 4, 1981

How to Succeed in Business Without Really Trying (revival)
548 performances
Opened March 23, 1995
Closed July 14, 1996

Let's Face It
547 performances
Opened October 29, 1941
Closed March 20, 1943

Milk and Honey
543 performances
Opened October 10, 1961
Closed January 26, 1963

Within the Law
541 performances
Opened September 11, 1912
Unknown closing date

Pal Joey (revival)
540 performances
Opened January 3, 1952
Closed April 18, 1953

The Sound of Music (revival)
540 performances
Opened March 12, 1998
Closed June 20, 1999

What Makes Sammy Run?
540 performances
Opened February 27, 1964
Closed June 12, 1965

The Sunshine Boys
538 performances
Opened December 20, 1972
Closed April 21, 1974

What a Life
538 performances
Opened April 13, 1938
Closed July 8, 1939

Crimes of the Heart
535 performances
Opened November 4, 1981
Closed February 13, 1983

Damn Yankees (revival)
533 performances
Opened March 3, 1994
Closed August 6, 1995

The Unsinkable Molly Brown
532 performances
Opened November 3, 1960
Closed February 10, 1962

The Red Mill (revival)
531 performances
Opened October 16, 1945
Closed January 18, 1947

Rumors
531 performances
Opened November 17, 1988
Closed February 24, 1990

A Raisin in the Sun
530 performances
Opened March 11, 1959
Closed June 25, 1960

Godspell
527 performances
Opened June 22, 1976
Closed September 4, 1977

Fences
526 performances
Opened March 26, 1987
Closed June 26, 1988

The Solid Gold Cadillac
526 performances
Opened November 5, 1953
Closed February 12, 1955

Doubt
525 performances
Opened March 9, 2005
Closed July 2, 2006

Biloxi Blues
524 performances
Opened March 28, 1985
Closed June 28, 1986

Irma La Douce
524 performances
Opened September 29, 1960
Closed December 31, 1961

The Boomerang
522 performances
Opened August 10, 1915
Unknown closing date

Follies
521 performances
Opened April 4, 1971
Closed July 1, 1972

Rosalinda
521 performances
Opened October 28, 1942
Closed January 22, 1944

The Best Man
520 performances
Opened March 31, 1960
Closed July 8, 1961

Chauve-Souris
520 performances
Opened February 4, 1922
Unknown closing date

Blackbirds of 1928
518 performances
Opened May 9, 1928
Unknown closing date

The Gin Game
517 performances
Opened October 6, 1977
Closed December 31, 1978

Side Man
517 performances
Opened June 25, 1988
Closed October 31, 1999

Sunny
517 performances
Opened September 22, 1925
Closed December 11, 1926

Victoria Regina
517 performances
Opened December 26, 1935
Unknown closing date

Xanadu
512 Performances
Opened July 10, 2007
Closed September 28, 2008

Curtains
511 Performances
Opened March 22, 2007
Closed June 29, 2008

Fifth of July
511 performances
Opened November 5, 1980
Closed January 24, 1982

Half a Sixpence
511 performances
Opened April 25, 1965
Closed July 16, 1966

The Vagabond King
511 performances
Opened September 21, 1925
Closed December 4, 1926

The New Moon
509 performances
Opened September 19, 1928
Closed December 14, 1929

The World of Suzie Wong
508 performances
Opened October 14, 1958
Closed January 2, 1960

The Rothschilds
507 performances
Opened October 19, 1970
Closed January 1, 1972

On Your Toes (revival)
505 performances
Opened March 6, 1983
Closed May 20, 1984

Sugar
505 performances
Opened April 9, 1972
Closed June 23, 1973

The Light in the Piazza
504 performances
Opened March 17, 2005
Closed July 2, 2006

Shuffle Along
504 performances
Opened May 23, 1921
Closed July 15, 1922

Up in Central Park
504 performances
Opened January 27, 1945
Closed January 13, 1946

Carmen Jones
503 performances
Opened December 2, 1943
Closed February 10, 1945

Saturday Night Fever
502 performances
Opened October 21, 1999
Closed December 30, 2000

The Member of the Wedding
501 performances
Opened January 5, 1950
Closed March 17, 1951

Panama Hattie
501 performances
Opened October 30, 1940
Closed January 13, 1942

Personal Appearance
501 performances
Opened October 17, 1934
Unknown closing date

Bird in Hand
500 performances
Opened April 4, 1929
Unknown closing date

Room Service
500 performances
Opened May 19, 1937
Unknown closing date

Sailor, Beware!
500 performances
Opened September 28, 1933
Unknown closing date

Tomorrow the World
500 performances
Opened April 14, 1943
Closed June 17, 1944

West Side Story* (2009 revival)
500 performances
Opened March 19, 2009

* Production is still running as
of May 31, 2010; count includes
performances up to and including
that date.

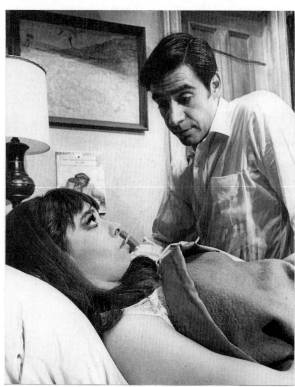

Jill O'Hara and Jerry Orbach in Promises, Promises *(1968)*
(photo by Friedman-Abeles)

Longest-Running Shows Off-Broadway

The Fantasticks
17,162 performances
Opened May 3, 1960
Closed January 13, 2002

Blue Man Group*
10,060 performances
Opened November 17, 1991

Perfect Crime*
9,448 performances
Opened April 18, 1987

Stomp*
6,854 performances
Opened February 27, 1994

Tony 'n' Tina's Wedding*
5,899 performances
Opened February 6, 1988

I Love You, You're Perfect, Now Change
5,003 performances
Opened August 1, 1996
Closed July 29, 2008

Nunsense
3,672 performances
Opened December 12, 1985
Closed October 16, 1994

Naked Boys Singing*
2,898 performances
Opened July 22, 1999

The Threepenny Opera
2,611 performances
Opened September 20, 1955
Closed December 17, 1961

De La Guarda
2,475 performances
Opened June 16, 1998
Closed September 12, 2004

Forbidden Broadway (original)
2,332 performances
Opened January 15, 1982
Closed August 30, 1987

Little Shop of Horrors
2,209 performances
Opened July 27, 1982
Closed November 1, 1987

Godspell
2,124 performances
Opened May 17, 1971
Closed June 13, 1976

Altar Boyz
2,032 performances
Opened March 1, 2005
Closed January 10, 2010

Vampire Lesbians of Sodom
2,024 performances
Opened June 19, 1985
Closed May 27, 1990

Jacques Brel is Alive and Well and Living in Paris
1,847 performances
Opened January 22, 1968
Closed July 2, 1972

Forever Plaid
1,811 performances
Opened May 20, 1990
Closed June 12, 1994

Vanities
1,785 performances
Opened March 22, 1976
Closed August 3, 1980

The Donkey Show
1,717 performances
Opened August 18, 1999
Closed July 16, 2005

Menopause the Musical
1,712 performances
Opened April 4, 2002
Closed May 14, 2006

You're A Good Man, Charlie Brown
1,597 performances
Opened March 7, 1967
Closed February 14, 1971

The Fantasticks* (revival)
1,472 performances
Opened August 23, 2006

The Blacks
1,408 performances
Opened May 4, 1961
Closed September 27, 1964

The Vagina Monologues
1,381 performances
Opened October 3, 1999
Closed January 26, 2003

One Mo' Time
1,372 performances
Opened October 22, 1979
Closed 1982–83 season

Grandma Sylvia's Funeral
1,360 performances
Opened October 9, 1994
Closed June 20, 1998

The Gazillion Bubble Show*
1,334 performances
Opened February 15, 2007

Let My People Come
1,327 performances
Opened January 8, 1974
Closed July 5, 1976

Late Nite Catechism
1,268 performances
Opened October 4, 1995
Closed May 18, 2003

Driving Miss Daisy
1,195 performances
Opened April 15, 1987
Closed June 3, 1990

The Hot L Baltimore
1,166 performances
Opened September 8, 1973
Closed January 4, 1976

I'm Getting My Act Together and Taking It on the Road
1,165 performances
Opened May 16, 1978
Closed March 15, 1981

Little Mary Sunshine
1,143 performances
Opened November 18, 1959
Closed September 2, 1962

Steel Magnolias
1,126 performances
Opened November 17, 1987
Closed February 25, 1990

El Grande de Coca-Cola
1,114 performances
Opened February 13, 1973
Closed April 13, 1975

The Proposition
1,109 performances
Opened March 24, 1971
Closed April 14, 1974

Our Sinatra
1,096 performances
Opened December 8, 1999
Closed July 28, 2002

Beau Jest
1,069 performances
Opened October 10, 1991
Closed May 1, 1994

Jewtopia
1,052 performances
Opened October 21, 2004
Closed April 29, 2007

Tamara
1,036 performances
Opened November 9, 1989
Closed July 15, 1990

One Flew Over the Cuckoo's Nest (revival)
1,025 performances
Opened March 23, 1971
Closed September 16, 1973

Front row: *Ted LaPlat, Michael Lipton, Christopher Brenau;* back row: *Matthew Tobin, Leon Russon, Harold Scott, Wayne Tippet, and David Daniels in* The Boys in the Band *(1968) (photo by Friedman-Abeles)*

Slava's Snowshow
1,004 Performances
Opened September 8, 2004
Closed January 14, 2007

The Boys in the Band
1,000 performances
Opened April 14, 1968
Closed September 29, 1970

Fool For Love
1,000 performances
Opened November 27, 1983
Closed September 29, 1985

Forbidden Broadway:
20th Anniversary Celebration
994 performances
Opened March 20, 2002
Closed July 4, 2004

Other People's Money
990 performances
Opened February 7, 1989
Closed July 4, 1991

Cloud 9
971 performances
Opened May 18, 1981
Closed September 4, 1983

Fuerza Bruta: Look Up*
957 performances
Opened October 24, 2007

Secrets Every Smart Traveler
Should Know
953 performances
Opened October 30, 1997
Closed February 21, 2000

Sister Mary Ignatius
Explains It All for You &
The Actor's Nightmare
947 performances
Opened October 21, 1981
Closed January 29, 1984

Your Own Thing
933 performances
Opened January 13, 1968
Closed April 5, 1970

Curley McDimple
931 performances
Opened November 22, 1967
Closed January 25, 1970

Leave It to Jane (revival)
928 performances
Opened May 29, 1959
Closed 1961–62 season

The Mad Show
871 performances
Opened January 9, 1966
Closed September 10, 1967

Hedwig and the Angry Inch
857 performances
Opened February 14, 1998
Closed April 9, 2000

Forbidden Broadway Strikes
Back
850 performances
Opened October 17, 1996
Closed September 20, 1998

When Pigs Fly
840 performances
Opened August 14, 1996
Closed August 15, 1998

Scrambled Feet
831 performances
Opened June 11, 1979
Closed June 7, 1981

The Effect of Gamma Rays on
Man-in-the-Moon Marigolds
819 performances
Opened April 7, 1970
Closed June 1, 1973

Forbidden Broadway SVU
816 performances
Opened December 16, 2004
Closed April 15, 2007

Over the River and
Through the Woods
800 performances
Opened October 5, 1998
Closed September 3, 2000

A View from the Bridge (revival)
780 performances
Opened January 28, 1965
Closed December 11, 1966

The Boy Friend (revival)
763 performances
Opened January 25, 1958
Closed 1961–62 season

True West
762 performances
Opened December 23, 1980
Closed January 11, 1981

Forbidden Broadway
Cleans Up Its Act!
754 performances
Opened November 17, 1998
Closed August 30, 2000

Robert Duvall and Jeanne Kaplan in A View from the Bridge *(1965) (photo by Henry Grossman)*

Isn't It Romantic
733 performances
Opened December 15, 1983
Closed September 1, 1985

Dime a Dozen
728 performances
Opened June 13, 1962
Closed 1963–64 season

The Pocket Watch
725 performances
Opened November 14, 1966
Closed June 18, 1967

The Connection
722 performances
Opened June 9, 1959
Closed June 4, 1961

The Passion of Dracula
714 performances
Opened September 28, 1977
Closed July 14, 1979

Love, Janis
713 performances
Opened April 22, 2001
Closed January 5, 2003

Adaptation & Next
707 performances
Opened February 10, 1969
Closed October 18, 1970

Oh! Calcutta!
704 performances
Opened June 17, 1969
Closed August 12, 1972

Scuba Duba
692 performances
Opened November 11, 1967
Closed June 8, 1969

The Foreigner
686 performances
Opened November 2, 1984
Closed June 8, 1986

The Knack
685 performances
Opened January 14, 1964
Closed January 9, 1966

My Mother's Italian, My Father's
Jewish & I'm in Therapy
684 performances
Opened December 8, 2006
Closed August 24, 2008

Fully Committed
675 performances
Opened December 14, 1999
Closed May 27, 2001

The Club
674 performances
Opened October 14, 1976
Closed May 21, 1978

The Balcony
672 performances
Opened March 3, 1960
Closed December 21, 1961

Penn & Teller
666 performances
Opened July 30, 1985
Closed January 19, 1992

Dinner With Friends
654 performances
Opened November 4, 1999
Closed May 27, 2000

America Hurrah
634 performances
Opened November 7, 1966
Closed May 5, 1968

Cookin'
632 Performances
Opened July 7, 2004
Closed August 7, 2005

Oil City Symphony
626 performances
Opened November 5, 1987
Closed May 7, 1989

The Countess
618 performances
Opened September 28, 1999
Closed December 30, 2000

The Exonerated
608 performances
Opened October 10, 2002
Closed March 7, 2004

The Dining Room
607 performances
Opened February 11, 1982
Closed July 17, 1983

Hogan's Goat
607 performances
Opened March 6, 1965
Closed April 23, 1967

Drumstruck
607 performances
Opened June 16, 2005
Closed November 16, 2006

Beehive
600 performances
Opened March 30, 1986
Closed August 23, 1987

Criss Angel Mindfreak
600 performances
Opened November 20, 2001
Closed January 5, 2003

The Trojan Women
600 performances
Opened December 23, 1963
Closed May 30, 1965

The Syringa Tree
586 performances
Opened September 14, 2000
Closed June 2, 2002

**The Musical of Musicals
(The Musical!)**
583 Performances
Opened December 16, 2003
Closed November 13, 2005

**Krapp's Last Tape &
The Zoo Story**
582 performances
Opened August 29, 1960
Closed May 21, 1961

Three Tall Women
582 performances
Opened April 13, 1994
Closed August 26, 1995

**The Dumbwaiter &
The Collection**
578 performances
Opened January 21, 1962
Closed April 12, 1964

Forbidden Broadway 1990
576 performances
Opened January 23, 1990
Closed June 9, 1991

Dames at Sea
575 performances
Opened April 22, 1969
Closed May 10, 1970

The Crucible (revival)
571 performances
Opened 1957
Closed 1958

The Iceman Cometh (revival)
565 performances
Opened May 8, 1956
Closed February 23, 1958

**Forbidden Broadway 2001:
A Spoof Odyssey**
552 performances
Opened December 6, 2000
Closed February 6, 2002

The Hostage (revival)
545 performances
Opened October 16, 1972
Closed October 8, 1973

David Drake, Carole Monferdini, and Roy Cockrum in Vampire Lesbians
of Sodom *(1985) (photo by T.L. Boston)*

The Marvelous Wonderettes
545 performances
Opened September 14, 2008
Closed January 3, 2010

Wit
545 performances
Opened October 6, 1998
Closed April 9, 2000

**What's a Nice Country Like You
Doing in a State Like This?**
543 performances
Opened July 31, 1985
Closed February 9, 1987

Forbidden Broadway 1988
534 performances
Opened September 15, 1988
Closed December 24, 1989

**Gross Indecency: The Three
Trials of Oscar Wilde**
534 performances
Opened September 5, 1997
Closed September 13, 1998

**Frankie and Johnny
in the Claire de Lune**
533 performances
Opened December 4, 1987
Closed March 12, 1989

**Six Characters in Search
of an Author** (revival)
529 performances
Opened March 8, 1963
Closed June 28, 1964

All in the Timing
526 performances
Opened November 24, 1993
Closed February 13, 1994

Our Town* (revival)
525 performances
Opened February 26, 2009

Oleanna
513 performances
Opened October 3, 1992
Closed January 16, 1994

Making Porn
511 performances
Opened June 12, 1996
Closed September 14, 1997

The Dirtiest Show in Town
509 performances
Opened June 26, 1970
Closed September 17, 1971

**Happy Ending &
Day of Absence**
504 performances
Opened June 13, 1965
Closed January 29, 1967

Greater Tuna
501 performances
Opened October 21, 1982
Closed December 31, 1983

A Shayna Maidel
501 performances
Opened October 29, 1987
Closed January 8, 1989

The Boys from Syracuse (revival)
500 performances
Opened April 15, 1963
Closed June 28, 1964

*Production is still running as
of May 31, 2010; count includes
performances up to and including
that date.

OBITUARIES

GENE BARRY

DAVID BROWN

DAVID CARRADINE

ALAINA REED-AMINI (Bernice Reed, Alaina Reed Hall), 63, Springfield, Ohio-born actress, died Dec. 17, 2009, at St. John's Health Center in Santa Monica, California, following a two-year battle with breast cancer. She was perhaps best known for her work on television in *Sesame Street* from 1976 until 1988, playing photographer Olivia, and on *227* as Rose Lee Holloway to Marla Gibbs' Mary Jenkins. Her Broadway theatre credits interspersed with an accomplished cabaret career include *Chicago; Hair;* and *Eubie!* Off-Broadway credits include *Sgt. Pepper's Lonely Hearts Club Band on the Road* (an adaptation of the Beatle's album); *In Trousers*, by William Finn (the first in the trilogy the latter two parts would become *Falsettos*); and *A...My Name is Alice*. Her other television credits include those on *A Different World; Ally McBeal; Friends; The Drew Carey Show; E.R.;* and her film credits include *Death Becomes Her* and *Cruel Intentions*. While working on *227* she met and married cast member Peter Hall, who died in 1991. Her husband, Tamim Amini, and two children from a previous marriage survive her.

GENE BARRY (Eugene Klass), 90, New York, New York-born actor, died Dec. 9, 2009, in Woodland Hills, California, at an assisted-living facility, of congestive heart failure. His Broadway credits include *La Cage Aux Folles* (1984, Tony nomination); *New Moon; Rosalinda; The Merry Widow; Catherine Was Great; The Would-Be Gentleman; Happy as Larry; The Perfect Setup;* and *Bless You All.* Having made his nightclub debut in the Latin Quarter in 1962, in 1999 he performed at the Oak Room at the Algonquin Hotel in Manhattan. His television credits include *Bat Masterson* from 1958-1961; *Burke's Law* from 1963-1966; *The Name of the Game* from 1968-1971; and *The Adventurer* in the 1972-73 season. His other and numerous television credits include those in *Playhouse 90; General Electric Theater; Our Miss Brooks; The Twilight Zone; Fantasy Island; The Love Boat; Charlie's Angels;* and *Murder She Wrote*. His film credits include *War of the Worlds* (1953 and 2005); *The Atomic City; The Girls of Pleasure Island; Those Redheads from Seattle; Red Garters; The Purple Mask; Soldier of Fortune; The Houston Story; Forty Guns; Hong Kong Confidential; Thunder Road; Maroc 7;* and *The Second Coming of Suzanne* (which he also executive produced). His wife of fifty-eight years, Betty (who acted under the name Julie Carson), died in 2003. His daughter, Elizabeth; two sons, Michael L., and Frederick J., of Topanga, California; three grandchildren; and two great-children survive him.

PINA BAUSCH (Phillipine Bausch), 68, Solingen, Germany-born choreographer, died June 30, 2009, of cancer. A regular at the Brooklyn Academy of Music since 1984, her company's base was in Wuppertal, Germany, but the company was often at Sadler's Wells Theater in London and the Théâtre de la Ville in Paris, as well as other festivals around the world. Arriving in the United States from Germany in 1958, she worked with José Limon, Antony Tudor, and others at Juilliard School, and eventually joined Tudor's company at the Metropolitan Opera. She also worked with Paul Taylor. In 1962 she returned to Germany and worked with Kurt Jooss, with whom she had studied in her youth at the Folkswang School in Essen. On her return she joined Jooss's Folkswang Ballet as a soloist. Her many works include *Café Müller; Fritz;* and *Rite of Spring;* and she staged two Gluck operas, *Iphigénie en Tauride* and *Ofgeo ed Euridice*. Her several film appearances include Fellini's *And the Ship Sails On*. Her companion, Ronald Kay; and a son, Salomon Bausch, survive her.

MARJORIE BEDDOW, 72, Grosse Point, Michigan-born actress/choreographer/author, died Jan. 3, 2010, at her home in New York, New York. Her Broadway credits include *Two on the Aisle;* followed by *Redhead; Fiorello!; Show Boat; The Conquering Hero; We Take the Town; Take Me Along; Little Me; Almanac; Here's Love; Ulysses in Nighttown,* and as a choreographer she created the Broadway musicals *Dear Oscar* and *Wind in the Willows*. Her Off-Broadway credits include *Sing Melancholy Baby; Second Summer; Wit & Wisdom; Anyone Can Whistle;* and *Johnny on a Spot,* as well as having served as show doctor and production supervisor for *Menopause The Musical* Off-Broadway. Her tour credits include *Pajama Game; Sweet Charity; Damn Yankees; On Your Toes; Ready When You Are C.B.; Ballroom; No, No Nanette; Fashion; El Grande De Coca-Cola;* and *Chicago*. On film she portrayed a Little Old Lady in *The Producers* (and later appeared in the musical version). Other film credits include *Waltzing Anna; Enchanted;* and *Doubt*. Her book, *Bob Fosse's Broadway* (Heinemann Drama) is in its fourth printing. Earlier in her career she was a dancer with the Ballet Russe de Monte Carlo as well as with the Metropolitan Opera Ballet. She is survived by her daughter, Pamela Jeanette Saunders; nieces Laura Parry and Margery Parry Colucci; and nephews David and Daniel Parry.

MINA BERN (Mina Bernholtz), 98, Polish-born actress, died Jan. 10, 2010, in New York, New York, of heart failure. Fleeing the Nazis in 1939 during World War II, she first landed in the Soviet Union, then Palestine, and finally, in 1949, New York, performing with the revue *Shalom, Tel Aviv*. Her Broadway credits include *Let's Sing Yiddish; Light Lively and Yiddish; Sing Israel Sing;* and *Those Were the Days*. Her Off-Broadway credits include *The Special; Old Lady's Guide to Survival; Blacksmith's Folly; Sweet Dreams;* and *A Klezmer's Tale*. She and her second husband, Ben Bonus, helped maintain Yiddish theatre well after its decline began in the 1950s, touring the U.S., Canada, and Latin America with an assortment of Yiddish revues. Her other stage credits include *Yentl*. Her film credits include *Crossing Delancey; Avalon;* and *I'm Not Rappaport*. Mr. Bonus died in 1984. In 1999 she received an Obie Award for Sustained Excellence. Her daughter, Renya Pearlman of Israel; two granddaughters; and four great-grandchildren survive her.

JOHN EDWARD BLANKENCHIP, 89, Independence, Kansas-born director/designer/professor, died Apr. 1, 2010, at a healthcare facility in Los Angeles, California, of age-related causes. Having taught at the University of Southern California School of Theatre for more than half a century, his stage credits

DIXIE CARTER

JOHN FORSYTHE

MORTON GOTTLIEB

include *Vivien Leigh: The Last Press Conference*, in productions in Edinburgh, London, and New York, as well as having his students and alumni perform at the Edinburgh Fringe Festival, mounting productions there for twenty-three seasons between 1966-2005. He also designed for La Jolla Playhouse and for the Guild Opera Company in Hollywood, California. Ray Bradbury's designer of choice for productions of his plays, he designed fifteen of them, including *Something Wicked This Way Comes*. He also designed for the Tanglewood Music Festival in Massachusetts. There were no immediate surviving family members.

DAVID BROWN, 93, New York, New York-born producer, died Feb. 1, 2010, at his home in Manhattan, of kidney failure, following a long illness. Following a highly successful film production career (most notably with his frequent partner Richard Zanuck), his Broadway credits include *Tru; A Few Good Men; The Cemetery Club; Sweet Smell of Success;* and *Dirty Rotten Scoundrels*. His film credits both with Zanuck and on his own with The Manhattan Project Ltd., include *The Sugarland Express; Jaws; The Sting* (Academy Award); *The Player; Chocolat; Driving Miss Daisy* (Academy Award); *Cocoon; The Verdict; Kiss the Girls; Along Came a Spider;* and *Angela's Ashes*. He was a veteran of World War II and prior to his film career worked for the *Wall Street Journal* and *Women's Wear Daily*, the *Saturday Evening Post*, *Harper's*, and *Collier's*, before becoming an editor himself and including managing editor of *Cosmopolitan* magazine. His first two marriages having ended in divorce, his third marriage (in 1959) was to Helen Gurley Brown, editor in chief of *Cosmopolitan* for thirty-two years and for which he continued—once she assumed the editorship—to contribute cover blurbs over the years. Ms. Brown and a half-brother, Edward, of Montecito, California, survive him.

CARMEN CAPALBO (Carmen Charles Capalbo), 84, Harrisburg, Pennsylvania-born director, died Mar. 14, 2010, in New York, New York, of emphysema. As director of *The Threepenny Opera* in 1950—which was one of the most triumphant Off-Broadway productions in theatre history, he convinced Lotte Lenya, the widow of author Kurt Weill, to take the role of Jenny—the role she had originally played twenty-four years earlier in Berlin, Germany. Opening on Mar. 10, 1954, the production received rave reviews and ran originally for ninety-six performances. After a campaign to have it revived, it reopened on Sept. 20, 1955, and ran for 2,611 performances—a record that stood until *The Fantasticks* overtook it on Aug. 4, 1966. The American Theatre Wing departed from its practice of only honoring Broadway productions and bestowed a Special Tony Award to the production as well as a Tony Award for Best Featured or Supporting Actress in a Musical upon Lenya. His other Broadway credits include *Moon for the Misbegotten* (1957); *The Potting Shed; The Cave Dwellers;* and *Seidman and Son*. His Broadway credits as a production stage manager include *Les Fausses Confidences/Baptiste; Occupe-toi d'Amelie;* and *Hamlet*. His *The Rise and Fall of the City of Mahagonny*, with Estelle Parsons and Barbara Harris, was poorly received, and thus began a string of less successfully executed productions, including attempts to mount Cole

Porter's *Nymph Errant* and the Nelson Algren novel *A Walk on the Wild Side* with music by Lou Reed (although Reed had a hit from the show with the song *Walk on the Wild Side*). He received a Bronze Star for bravery as well as a Purple Heart in World War II before founding the Spur, a repertory company for which he directed four plays at the Cherry Lane Theater in 1946, including *Juno and the Paycock* and *Awake and Sing!* His credits also include a story editor for the CBS drama series *Studio One*. His marriage to Patricia McBride, a dancer with the Ballet Society (now the New York City Ballet), ended in divorce. His son Marco, of Manhattan; sister, Jenny First, of Harrisburg, Pennsylvania; and daughter, Carla, of Pollino, Italy, survive him.

DAVID CARRADINE (John Arthur Carradine), 72, Hollywood-born actor, best remembered for his starring role on the 1970s series *Kung Fu*, was found dead on June 4, 2009, in his Bangkok, Thailand hotel room, having accidentally hanged himself. A 1966 Theatre World Award winner for his role in *The Royal Hunt of the Sun*, his other Broadway credits include *The Deputy*. His many films include *Bus Riley's Back in Town; The Violent Ones; Young Billy Young; The Good Guys and the Bad Guys; Macho Callahan; Boxcar Bertha; Mean Streets; Death Race 2000; Cannonball; Bound for Glory* (as Woody Guthrie); *The Serpent's Egg; Gray Lady Down; Circle of Iron; The Long Riders; Q; Lone Wolf McQuade; Sonny Boy; Bird on a Wire; Roadside Prophets; Kill Bill: Vol. 2; How to Rob a Bank; The Golden Boys;* and *Crank: High Voltage*. He was the eldest son of the late actor John Carradine. His fifth wife, Annie; five daughters, Kansas, Calista, Amanda, Madeline, and Olivia; two sons, Free and Max; four half-brothers, including actors Keith and Robert Carradine and another brother Bruce; and several grandchildren and great-grand children survive him.

DIXIE CARTER, 70, McLemoresville, Tennessee-born actress/singer, died Apr. 10, 2010, in a Houston, Texas, hospital, of complications from endometrial cancer. She lived in Beverly Hills, California. A 1976 Theatre World Award winner for her role in *Jesse and the Bandit Queen*, her other Broadway credits include *Sextet; Pal Joey; Master Class;* and *Thoroughly Modern Millie*. Other New York stage credits include Perdita in a Joseph Papp production of *The Winter's Tale* in Central Park; *Buried Inside Extra; Taken in Marriage; Carousel; Merry Widow; Fathers and Sons;* and *A Couple of White Chicks*. She also performed in revues at the Upstairs at the Downstairs nightclub, alongside Lily Tomlin and Madeline Kahn. Perhaps best known for her role as Julia Sugarbaker on the television sitcom *Designing Women* that ran from 1986-1993. Her numerous other television credits include *The Killing of Randy Webster; Diff'rent Strokes; Filthy Rich;* and *On Our Own*. She received her sole Emmy Award nomination for her work in 2007 on the television show *Desperate Housewives*. Her feature films include *That Evening Sun*. She also had a very successful cabaret career, performing at—among other venues—Café Carlyle in New York, New York. Her two prior marriages to New York investment banker and newspaper scion Arthur L. Carter as well as to actor George Hearn ended in divorce. She married her third husband, actor Hal Holbrook, in 1984. He, as well as two daughters, Ginna Carter of Los Angeles, California, and Mary Dixie Carter of Brooklyn, New York; sister, Melba Helen Heath of San Anselmo, California; and several nieces and nephews survive her.

MERCE CUNNINGHAM (Mercier Philip Cunningham), 90, Centralia, Washington-born choreographer, died July 24, 2009, at his home in Manhattan. Over a career of nearly seven decades, he, along with Isadora Duncan, Serge Diaghilev, Martha Graham, and George Balanchine, were the top flight of choreographers rethinking dance in America. And along with Jerome Robbins and Paul Taylor he is considered to have founded the New York School of Dance. He shared a belief with frequent collaborator and his companion John Cage that music and dance were independent of each other, which is probably his most celebrated achievement. The Merce Cunningham Dance Company gave its first performance in 1953, at the Black Mountain College in North Carolina, and designers for it over the years included Robert Rauschenberg, Jasper Johns, Frank Stella, and Andy Warhol. His many creations include *Totem Ancestor* (1942); *The* Seasons (1947); *Changeling* (1957); *Antic* Meet (1958); *RainForest* (1968); *Borst Park* (1972); *Inlets* (1977); *Inlets 2* (1983); *Minutiae* (1954); *Springweather and People* (1955); *Pond Way* (1998); *Solo* (1975); *Biped* (1999); and *Trackers* (1991). In the 1960s he and his company began to tour internationally. Beginning his career at George Washington University in Washington, D.C., he also studied early at the Cornish School in Seattle and studied with Alexander Koriansky and Bonnie Bird. In the 1940s he studied with the previously all-female Martha Graham Company, where he appeared in such works as *El Penitente* (1940); *Letter to the World* (1941); and *Appalachian Spring* (1944). Until 1989 he appeared in every single performance given by his ensemble. And in 1999, at eighty years of age, he danced a duet with Michail Baryshnikov at the New York State Theater in *Occasion Piece* (1980). His last work was the ninety-minute *Nearly Ninety* at the Brooklyn Academy of Music. In his last years he was widely considered the greatest living dancer. His companion John Cage died in 1992.

T. SCOTT CUNNINGHAM (Timothy Scott Cunningham), 47, Los Angeles, California-born and Shelbyville, Tennessee-raised actor, died June 26, 2009, in Manhattan, of complications from pneumonia and acute respiratory distress syndrome. A founding member in 1994 of the Drama Department theatre company as well as The Vineyard Community of Artists, his roles there include *As Bees in Honey Drown* and *Music From a Sparkling Planet*. His other Off-Broadway credits include *Pterodactyls; New England; Stand-In; Wally's Ghost; What You Get and What You Expect; The Country Club; Don Juan in Chicago; Fit to Be Tied;* and *The Eros Trilogy*. His Broadway credits include *Love! Valour! Compassion!; Tartuffe: Born Again;* and *Design for Living*. Other New York stage credits include *Wintertime; Dear Boy;* and *New England*. He toured nationally in *Twelve Angry Men* and his numerous regional production credits include *Cat on a Hot Tin Roof* and *At Home at the Zoo*. His numerous television and film credits include *The Out of Towners; Our Very Own; People I Know; The Boys of Sunset Ridge; Law and Order: Criminal Intent; Maximum Bob; Cybill;* and *Central Park West*. His parents, Tim and Judy Cunningham; brother, Kevin, all of Shelbyville, Tennessee; and partner Harvy Bouvy, of Manhattan, survive him.

ART D'LUGOFF (Arthur Joshua Dlugoff), 85, Harlem, New York and Brooklyn, New York-raised owner of the famous Village Gate venue, died Nov. 3, 2009, at New York-Presbyterian Hospital, after experiencing shortness of breath. As act impresario and owner of the New York institution the Village Gate for over thirty years, Off-Broadway productions that opened there include *Let My People Come; Macbird; Jacques Brel is Alive and Well and Living in Paris;* and *One Mo' Time*. The theatre productions were in addition to presenting more regular and traditional nightclub fare for which it was renowned including acts such as Nina Simone, Jimi Hendrix, Aretha Franklin, and jazz acts like Miles Davis and John Coltrane. The Village Gate closed its doors in 1994. Before becoming a nightclub owner, he enjoyed professions from an encyclopedia salesman to a cab driver in Los Angeles, California, as well as a concert promoter. He also helped conceived the National Jazz Museum in Harlem and he served with the Army Air Forces in China in World War II. His brother, Burt, of Baltimore, Maryland; wife,

the former Avital Achai; son, Raphael; three daughters, Sharon D'Lugoff Blythe, Dahlia D'Lugoff, and Rashi D'Lugoff; and five grandchildren survive him.

MAX EISEN, 91, Bronx, New York-born press agent, died Nov. 23, 2009, at his home in Manhattan, of natural causes. The numerous productions that Eisen promoted over his nearly fifty-year career include *Stockade; The Matchmaker; The Best House in Naples; Li'l Abner; The Subject Was Roses; Wiener Blut; The World of Charles Aznavour; Inadmissible Evidence; First One Asleep, Whistle; Manuela Vargas; Gilbert Becaud on Broadway; Let's Sing Yiddish; Les Ballets Africains; The Apparation Theatre of Prague; Sing Israel, Sing; The Trial of Lee Harvey Oswald; A Day in the Death of Joe Egg; I'm Solomon; Woman Is My Idea; Her First Roman; A Way of Life; Butterflies Are Free; Minnie's Boys, Look to the Lilies; The Engagement Baby; Light, Lively and Yiddish; Les Blancs; 70, Girls, 70; You're a Good Man, Charlie Brown; Wild and Wonderful; The Sign in Sidney Brustein's Window; Wise Child; The Love Suicide at Schofield Barracks; Children! Children!; Elizabeth I; Heathen!; Mother Earth; Raisin; Find Your Way Home; The Freedom of the City; Tubstrip; Goodtime Charley; The Fifth Season; Lamppost Reunion; Very Good Eddie; Bubbling Brown Sugar; Zalmen or The Madness of God; Guys and Dolls* (1976); *Going Up* (1976); *Wheelbarrow Closers; Don't Step on My Olive Branch; Ipi-Tombi; The Basic Training of Pavlo Hummel; Some of My Best Friends; Cold Storage; Long Day's Journey Into Night; The Effect of Gamma Rays on Man-in-the-Moon Marigolds; Eubie!; Whoopee!* (1979); *Manny; King Richard III; Horowitz and Mrs. Washington; Your Arms Too Short to Box With God* (1980); *Fifth of July; A Lesson from Aloes; Marlowe; The Babe; The Wiz* (1984); *Corpse!; The Mikado* (1987); *Those Were the Days;* and *Gypsy Passion*. He was a veteran of the U.S. Army during World War II and for several years after the war he worked in the circulation department of what was then the *Paris Herald Tribune*. His wife of forty-four years, the former Barbara Glenn; son, Glenn; daughter, Lee Kittay; and five grandchildren survive him.

RUTH FORD, 98, Brookhaven, Mississippi-born actress, died Aug. 11, 2009, at her home in New York, New York. Her Broadway credits include *The Shoemaker's Holiday; Danton's Death; Swingin' The Dream; No Exit; This Time Tomorrow; Clutterbuck; The House of Bernarda Alba; Island of Goats; Miss Julie and The Stronger; Requiem for a Nun* (in the role of Temple Drake, written for her by author and friend William Faulkner); *The Milk Train Doesn't Stop Here Anymore; Dinner at Eight; The Ninety Day Mistress; The Grass Harp; Poor Murderer;* and *Harold and Maude*. Her other stage credits include Mart Crowley's *A Breeze From the Gulf*. Her film roles included *Truck Busters; The Gorilla Man;* and *Lady Gangster*. A model following her arrival in New York from Mississippi for publications such as *Harper's, Vogue,* and *Mademoiselle,* she was also considered a great salonniere for hosting artists of all types for over forty years in her apartment in the Dakota building—the storied apartment house on West 72nd Street built in the 1880s. There she hosted such luminaries as Edward Albee; Leonard Bernstein; Truman Capote; William Faulkner; Arthur Laurents; Terrence McNally; and Tennessee Williams. Her first marriage, to actor Peter van Eyck, ended in divorce, and her second, to Zachary Scott, ended with his death in 1965. Her daughter, Shelly Scott of Santa Barbara; a granddaughter; and two great-grandchildren survive her.

JOHN FORSYTHE (John Lincoln Freund), 92, Penns Grove, New Jersey-born actor, died Apr. 1, 2010, at his home in Santa Ynez, California, of complications from pneumonia, following a yearlong battle with cancer. Perhaps best remembered as Blake Carrington on the long-running evening television soap opera *Dynasty* from 1981-1989, it was a role that brought him two Golden Globe Awards along with two other nominations, as well as two Emmy Award nominations. His Broadway credits include *Yankee Point; Vickie; Winged Victory; Yellow Jack; It Takes Two; All My Sons; The Teahouse of the August Moon; Mister Roberts, Weekend;* and *Sacrilege*. His other television roles include that of Bentley Gregg on *Bachelor Father* from 1957-1962, as well as the voice of Charlie in *Charlie's Angels*, from 1976-1981. His film roles include *Destination Tokyo; The Trouble With Harry; Kitten With a Whip; Madame X; In Cold Blood;* and *Scrooged*. His numerous other television credits include *The John Forsythe Show; To Rome With Love; The Powers That Be; What Makes Sammy Run?; The Captive City;* and *It Happens Every Thursday*. His first marriage (from 1938-1940) to Parker McCormick ended in divorce. His second marriage, to Julie Warren, lasted for more than fifty years, until her death in 1994. His third wife, Nicole Carter; son, Dall; daughters, Page Courtemanche and Brook Forsythe, all of Southern California; six grandchildren; and five great-grandchildren survive him.

RAY FRY, 86, Hebron, Indiana-born and Gary, Indiana-raised actor, died May 4, 2009, in Louisville, Kentucky, following a brief illness. His Broadway credits include *Hickory Stick; The Cradle Will Rock; Danton's Death; The Country Wife; The Caucasian Chalk Circle; The Alchemist; The Little Foxes; Saint Joan; Tiger at the Gates; Cyrano de Bergerac; A Cry of Players; The Miser; Operation Sidewinder; Beggar on Horseback; The Good Woman of Setzuan; The Playboy of the Western World; Mary Stuart; Narrow Road to the Deep North; Twelfth Night; Enemies; The Plough and the Stars; The Merchant of Venice;* and *A Streetcar Named Desire.* He was a founding member of the acting companies of the American Conservatory Theater in San Francisco, California, and the Repertory Theatre at New York's Lincoln Center. Credits at Lincoln Center Repertory include *Galileo; Bananas; Birthday Party;* and *Antigone.* He was also a twenty-four year veteran of Actors Theatre of Louisville, where he reprised the role of Scrooge in *A Christmas Carol* for ten years. He also appeared at Indiana Repertory Theatre; Guthrie Theater; O'Neill Theatre Center; Dallas Shakespeare Festival; Sundance Institute, and four summers with the New Harmony Project in Indiana. He performed on U.S.O. tours during the Korean War in Germany, France, and England.

LARRY GELBART, 81, Chicago, Illinois-born writer, died Sept. 11, 2009, at his home in Beverly Hills, California, of cancer. His Broadway credits include *The Conquering Hero; A Funny Thing Happened on the Way to the Forum* (1962 Tony Award Best Author of a Musical, 1962 Tony Award Best Musical, 1972, 1996); *Sly Fox* (1976, 2004); *Jerome Robbins' Broadway; Mastergate;* and *City of Angels* (1990 Tony Award, Drama Desk Award). He helped to produce, create, and write the series adaptation of *M*A*S*H,* and his other television credits include *AfterMASH; Barbarians at the Gate; Weapons of Mass Distraction;* and *And Starring Pancho Villa as Himself.* He worked on such other screenplays as *The Notorious Landlady; The Thrill of it All; The Wrong Box; Not with My Wife You Don't!; Movie Movie; Blame it on Rio;* and *Bedazzled* (2000). He earned Oscar nominations for scripting the hit comedies *Oh, God!* and *Tootsie.* In the beginning of his career he wrote jokes for the Jack Paar, Eddie Cantor, and Bob Hope radio shows, among others. *Laughing Matters,* a collection of his essays and reminiscences about writing *M*A*S*H, Tootsie, Oh, God!,* and a few other things was published by Random House in 1998. His wife of fifty-three years, Pat; two children, Becky Gelbart-Barton and Adam; two stepsons, Gary and Paul Markowitz, all of Los Angeles, California; six grandchildren; and two great-grandchildren survive him.

MORTON GOTTLIEB, 88, Brooklyn, New York-born producer, died June 24, 2009, in Englewood, New Jersey, of natural causes. A Tony Award winner for *Sleuth* in 1971, his other Broadway credits include *Edward, My Son; Gigi; Caesar and Cleopatra; Antony and Cleopatra; His and Hers; The Sleeping Prince; Time Remembered; The Rope Dancers; Handful of Fire; The Gazebo; Look After Lulu; Much Ado About Nothing* (1959); *Chéri, Five Finger Exercise; The Best Man; Romulus; The Hollow Crown; Enter Laughing; Chips With Everything; The White House; P.S. I Love You; The Killing of Sister George* (Tony nomination); *Come Live With Me; The Promise; Lovers* (Tony nomination); *We Bombed in New Haven; The Mundy Scheme; Veronica's Room; Same Time, Next Year* (1975 Drama Desk Award, Tony nomination); *Tribute; Faith Healer; Romantic Comedy; Special Occasions;* and *Dancing in the End Zone.* His niece, the talent agent Hildy Gottlieb Hill, of Beverly Hills, California; sister-in-law, Claire Gottlieb of Manhattan; and another niece, Wendy Gottlieb, of Southampton, New York, survive him.

SHELLY GROSS (Sheldon Harvey Gross), 88, Philadelphia, Pennsylvania-born producer, died June 25, 2009, in Palm Beach Gardens, Florida, of bladder cancer. With childhood friend Lee Guber as business partners for over thirty years, together their Broadway credits include *Catch Me if You Can; Sherry!; The Grand Music Hall of Israel; Inquest; Lorelei* (1974); *Charles Aznavour on Broadway; Tony & Lena Sing; Barry Manilow on Broadway; The King and I* (1977); *Murder at the Howard Johnson's; Bruce Forsyth on Broadway; Englebert Humperdinck*

on Broadway; Bring Back Birdie; Shirley MacLaine on Broadway; Patti La Belle on Broadway; Patti La Belle; Peter, Paul, & Mary "From Bleecker to Broadway"; The Temptations/The Four Tops; The Victor Borge Holiday Show on Broadway; Peter, Paul, & Mary "A Holiday Celebration"; Stephanie Mills Comes "Home" to Broadway; and *Camelot* (1993). Broadway productions that the duo took on the road include *Fiddler on the Roof; Gypsy; Cabaret;* and *Man of La Mancha.* Together Gross and Guber also founded the Westbury Music Fair on Long Island and the Valley Forge Music Fair outside Philadelphia, as well as the Shady Grove Music Fair outside Washington and the Painters Mill Music Fair in suburban Baltimore. They also operated the Deauville Hotel in Miami Beach and the American Wax Museum in Philadelphia. Their concert division booked acts in theaters around the country, and stars they toured ranged from Judy Garland to Bill Cosby to Bruce Springsteen, as well as a pop, folk, rock and country bands; and childrens' theatre. Mr. Guber died in 1988. Mr. Gross was a veteran of World War II, serving in the South Pacific. His wife of sixty-three years, the former Joan Seidel; three sons, Byron, Rick, and Dan; and four grandchildren survive him.

JUNE HAVOC (Ellen Evangeline Hovick), 97, Vancouver, British Columbia-born actress, died Mar. 28, 2010, in Stamford, Connecticut. The child vaudeville star known as "Baby June" who sometimes earned up to $1,500 a week in touring those venues lived to see her early accomplishments overshadowed by those of her more famous sibling, Gypsy Rose Lee. Based on Lee's memoir Arthur Laurents penned the book for Ethel Merman that became the iconic *Gypsy*–one of the most revered Broadway musicals of all time. Her own Broadway credits include *Forbidden Melody; Pal Joey* (1940); *Mexican Hayride; Sadie Thompson; The Ryan Girl; Dunnigan's Daughter; Dream Girl; Affairs of State; The Infernal Machine; The Beaux Strategem* (1959); *The Warm Peninsula; Marathon '33* (Tony nomination as Best Director); *Dinner at Eight* (1966); and *Habeas Corpus* (1976 Drama Desk Award nomination Outstanding Featured Actress in a Play). Off-Broadway credits include *The Old Lady's Guide to Survival.* Her film roles include those in *Four Jacks and a Jill; Gentleman's Agreement; My Sister Eileen; When My Baby Smiles at Me; Intrigue;* and *Lady Possessed.* In addition, she was artistic director of the New Orleans Repertory Theater in 1970 and also toured with a stage show, *An Unexpected Evening With June Havoc.* She published her memoir, *More Havoc,* in 1980, and in 2003, a ninety-nine-seat performance space in an office building on West 36th St. in New York was dedicated as the June Havoc Theater. Marriages to Bobby Reed, Donald S. Gibbs, and William Spier all ended in divorce. Her daughter, April Hyde, died in 1998. There are no immediate survivors.

LENA HORNE (Lena Calhoun Horne), 92, Brooklyn, New York-born actress/singer, died May 9, 2010, at New York Presbyterian/Weill Cornell Medical Center in New York, New York. She lived in Manhattan. The first black performer to be signed to a long-term contract by a major Hollywood studio, her Broadway theatre credits include *Dance With Your Gods; Lew Leslie's Blackbirds of 1939; Jamaica* (1959 Tony Award nomination); *Tony & Lena Sing* (with Tony Bennett); and *The Lady and Her Music* (1981 Special Tony Award); Drama Desk Award Outstanding Actress in a Musical). A pioneer for a woman of color in cinema, her many credits in that medium include *The Duke Is Tops; Panama Hattie; Thousands Cheer; Broadway Rhythm; Two Girls and a Sailor; Ziegfeld Follies; Words and Music; Til the Clouds Roll By; Stormy Weather; Cabin in the Sky; Death of a Gunfighter;* and *The Wiz.* Her numerous television credits include *Your Show of Shows* and her many successful nightclub performances include *Lena Horne at the Waldorf-Astoria,* which was recorded and became the best-selling album by a female singer in RCA Victor's history. During World War II she appeared over a dozen times on the U.S. Army radio program *Command Performance* as well as toured with the U.S.O. Her first marriage to Louis Jones ended in divorce and her second husband, Lennie Hayton, died in 1971. A son died of kidney failure also in 1971. Her daughter, Gail Lumet Buckley, survives her.

LOU JACOBI (Louis Harold Jacobovitch), 95, Toronto, Canada-born character actor, died of natural causes on Oct. 23, 2009, at his Manhattan home. His Broadway credits include *The Diary of Anne Frank;* followed by *The Tenth Man; Come Blow Your Horn; Fade Out–Fade In; Don't Drink the Water; A Way of Life; Norman, Is That You?; Unlikely Heroes; Come Blow Your Horn; The Sunshine*

LOU JACOBI

LENA HORNE

KARL MALDEN

Boys; and *Cheaters.* His London, England, theatre credits include *Guys and Dolls* and *Pal Joey.* His film roles include that of the philosophical bar owner Moustache in the 1963 comedy hit *Irma La Douce; Is Your Honeymoon Really Necessary?; A Kid for Two Farthings; The Diary of Anne Frank* (repeating his Broadway role); *The Last of the Secret Agents?; Little Murders; Penelope; Everything You Always Wanted to Know about Sex* But Were Afraid to Ask; Next Stop Greenwich Village; Roseland; Arthur; My Favorite Year; Amazon Women on the Moon; Avalon;* and *I.Q.* His television credits include *Playhouse 90; The Man From U.N.C.L.E.; That Girl; Ivan the Terrible;* and as a regular on *The Dean Martin Show.* His regional theatre credits include *Rocket to the Moon.* He made a series of comedy recordings including *The Yiddish Are Coming! The Yiddish Are Coming!* and *Al Tijuana and His Jewish Brass.* His wife of over forty years, Ruth Ludwin, died in 2004. A brother, Avrom Jacobovitch and a sister, Rae Gold, both of Toronto, Canada, survive him.

H.M. "HARRY" KATOUKAS (Haralambos Monroe Koutoukas), 72, Endicott, New York-born playwright who, along with Sam Shepard, Tom Eyen, Robert Patrick, Doric Wilson, and Lanford Wilson, was of the foremost proliferators of the Off-Off-Broadway theatre movement in the early 1960s, died Mar. 6, 2010, at his home in Manhattan, of complications from diabetes. Katoukas helped to establish Off-Off-Broadway theatre at venues like La MaMa ETC and Café Cino. Calling his surreal works "camps," pieces such as *Medea at the Laundromat* and *Awful People Are Coming Over So We Must Be Hard at Work and Hope They Will Go Away* presented warped situations and dialogue. Other playwriting credits include *Afamis Notes; The Brown Book; Butterfly Encounter; Turtles Don't Dream;* and *Disarming Attachments.* His School of Gargoyles theatre workshop included alumni such as Gerome Ragni and James Rado, who wrote *Hair!;* Tom O'Horgan, its director; and the actor and playwright Harvey Fierstein. He was the recipient of a 1966 Village Voice Obie Award for "Assaulting Established Tradition." His film credits include *Naked in New York.* His sister, Jean Ann Davidson, of Enwell, New York, survives him.

GRACE KEAGY, 87, Youngstown, Ohio-born actress, died Oct. 4, 2009, in Rochester New York, of ovarian cancer. Her Broadway credits include *Goodtime Charley; The Grand Tour; Carmelina* (Drama Desk Award nomination); *I Remember Mama; Musical Chairs;* and *Woman of the Year.* Off-Broadway credits include *Call Me Madam* and *D.* Her regional theatre credits include *The Shoemaker's Holiday* at the Guthrie Theater and *How to Succeed in Business Without Really Trying* at the Chanhassen Dinner Theatres. She also made appearances at the former Friar's Dinner Theater, Old Log Theatre, and the Minnesota Opera, all located in Minnesota. She made her television soap opera debut at the age of sixty-three in shows like *As the World Turns; One Life to Live; The Doctors; Ryan's Hope;* and *Search for Tomorrow.* Her other television credits include *Mrs. Santa Claus* starring Angela Lansbury. Two sons; a stepson; three daughters; twelve grandchildren; and eleven great-grandchildren survive her.

JOHN KENLEY (John Kremchek), 103, Denver, Colorado-born theatre impresario, died Oct. 23, 2009, in Cleveland, Ohio, of complications from pneumonia. Beginning his career as a song-and-dance man in New York in the 1920s, he eventually performed with Martha Graham as a dancer in John Murray Anderson's Greenwich Village Follies. He then worked as a play reader for the Shuberts before segueing into an assistant for Lee Shubert. His Kenley Players, founded in the 1940s, became a fixture on summer stock circuit in Ohio and elsewhere, and he was perhaps best known for casting unconventional celebrities with high popular appeal. At its height the company played to audiences of 5,000 throughout the Midwest. Billing top names at top pay in hundreds of productions, performers he coaxed to often small town venues ranged from the 1940s through the 1970s included Gloria Swanson; Arthur Godfrey; Ethel Merman; Mae West; Burt Reynolds; Florence Henderson; Robert Goulet; and William Shatner. Anomalies he purveyed were Hugh Downs in *Under the Yum Yum Tree;* Merv Griffin in *Come Blow Your Horn;* and Joe Namath in *Picnic.* He was a veteran of World War II. No immediate family members survive.

MICHAEL KUCHWARA, 63, Scranton, Pennsylvania-born drama critic, died May 22, 2010, at Beth Israel Hospital in Manhattan, of idiopathic ischemic lung disease. As longtime drama critic for the Associated Press from 1984 until his death, he had a worldwide following of readers for over twenty-five years. He received his master's degree in journalism from the University of Missouri, and before being named drama critic at the Associated Press worked as general assignment editor and reporter for the AP in Chicago and in New York at its main editing desk for national news. As print journalism periodicals diminished in the 1990s and particularly as drama critic posts at news outlets diminished along with them, the remaining outlets increasingly picked up the Associated Press and consequently his reviews of productions. Scoops he broke include the death of Lynn Redgrave earlier this year as well as the fact that the 2010 failed Times Square bombing did *not,* in fact, cause *The Lion King* to go dark. His last review was published May 10, 2010, and he was listening to music from *Gypsy,* his favorite show, when he died. His wife, Johnnie Kay Kuchwara; and sister, Pat Henley, survive him.

GEORGE MACPHERSON, 78, Elrama, Pennsylvania-born theatre producer, died June 2, 2009, in Orangeburg, South Carolina, of lung cancer. As partner, with Tom Mallow in American Theater Productions, where MacPherson served as executive director, he proliferated tours as well as helped create the overall environment of touring productions that allowed them to boom during the 1980s and 1990s. Touring productions he coproduced include *The Secret Garden; Guys and Dolls; Big River; The Who's Tommy;* and *Angels in America.* He was a veteran of the Korean War and worked as a veterinarian for circus productions such as Ringling Brothers and Barnum & Bailey Circus and managed movie theaters and public relations for them before segueing into becoming a Los Angeles policeman.

JACK MANNING

NAN MARTIN

ZAKES MOKAI

In the 1960s and 1970s he worked as a press agent and manager, representing Victor Borge, Harry Belafonte, and the National Ballet of Canada, among others. Also in the 1970s he was the founding general manager of Hamilton Place in Hamilton, Ontario, and immediately prior to his partnership with Tom Mallow he helped start the Roy Thomson Hall in Toronto, Canada. American Theater Productions merged with Dodger Productions in 1990 and dissolved in 1996. He ran the theatrical management for a Dutch theatrical and television production company following the dissolution of Dodger Productions and in 1997 became the president of Masque Sound, a company started by three stagehands in 1936 that provides sound systems for Broadway musicals and concerts. Mr. Mallow died in 2002. His wife, the former Judith Winter; daughter, Morag; sons, Duncan, of Hartford, and Malcolm, of Toronto; sister, Dee Deibel of San Rafael, California; and two grandchildren survive him.

KARL MALDEN (Mladen Sekulovich), 97, Chicago, Illinois-born actor, died July 1, 2009, at his Brentwood, California, home of natural causes. In a highly successful stage and screen career that lasted for over sixty years, his Broadway credits–usually portraying the archetypal "everyman" include *Golden Boy; How to Get Tough About It; Missouri Legend; The Gentle People; Key Largo; Journey to Jerusalem; Flight to the West; Uncle Harry; The Sun Field; Counterattack; Sons and Soldiers; Winged Victory; The Assassin; Truckline Café; All My Sons; A Streetcar Named Desire; Peer Gynt; Desire Under the Elms* (1952)*; Tea and Sympathy; The Desperate Hours;* and *The Egghead.* An Academy Award winner for repeating his Broadway role of Mitch in *A Streetcar Named Desire,* following his debut in *They Knew What They Wanted,* he was seen in such movies as *Winged Victory; Kiss of Death* (1947); *Boomerang!* (1947); *The Gunfighter; Halls of Montezuma; Where the Sidewalk Ends; I Confess; Ruby Gentry; Phantom of the Rue Morgue; On the Waterfront* (Oscar nomination); *Baby Doll; Fear Strikes Out; The Hanging Tree; Pollyanna* (1960)*; Parrish; One-Eyed Jacks; All Fall Down; Birdman of Alcatraz; Gypsy; How the West Was Won; Dead Ringer; Cheyenne Autumn; The Cincinnati Kid; Nevada Smith; Murderers' Row; Hotel; The Adventures of Bullwhip Griffin; Hot Millions; Patton* (as Gen. Omar N. Bradley); *Wild Rovers; Twilight Time;* and *Nuts.* He also directed the 1957 film *Time Limit.* His numerous television credits include Lt. Mike Stone in *The Streets of San Francisco; Skag; Fatal Vision,* for which he won an Emmy Award; and *The Hijacking of the Achille Lauro.* But he was perhaps best known to later generations of television viewers as the long-running pitchman for American Express travelers' checks in the 1970s, encouraging audiences to "Don't leave home without them." He graduated from the Goodman Theatre in Chicago and worked initially with The Group Theatre, studying there as well as Actors Studio upon moving to New York in the 1940s. He was a veteran of World Ward II, and he also served as the president of the Academy of Motion Picture Arts and Sciences from 1989-1992. His wife of seventy years; two daughters; three granddaughters; and four great- grandchildren survive him.

JACK MANNING (Jack Wilson Marks), 93, Cincinnati, Ohio-born actor/director/ teacher, died Aug. 31, 2009, at his home in Rancho Palo Verdes, California, of natural causes. His Broadway credits include *Junior Miss; The Great Big Doorstep; Harriet; Othello; The Streets Are Guarded; The Mermaids Singing; O'Daniel; Alice in Wonderland; Man and Superman; Billy Budd; The Tender Trap; Say, Darling; Do I Hear a Waltz?;* and *The Boyfriend.* His radio credits include *The Aldrich Family; The Green Hornet; The Shadow;* and *The Goldbergs.* With Helen Hayes, with whom he had appeared in *Harriet,* he was the founder of the Helen Hayes Repertory Company, a touring ensemble, in 1964. He also taught acting at his own studios, first in New York and later in Los Angeles, as well as at HB Studios in New York and colleges and universities throughout the country. His television credits include a one-man serial version of *Hamlet,* broadcast in ten installments of fifteen minutes on the DuMont network in 1953; *The Paper Chase; Studio One; The Mary Tyler Moore Show; Here's Lucy; Kojak;* and *The Waltons.* His film credits include *Walk East on Beacon; Where's Poppa?; The Owl and the Pussycat; The Great Northfield Minnesota Raid;* and *The Great Waldo Pepper.* A first marriage to Virginia Schuchardt, ended in divorce. His second wife, the former Frances Ann Smith; son, Colin; daughters, Brook Manning and Gale Nichols; three grandchildren; and a great-grandchild survive him.

NAN MARTIN (Nan Clow Martin), 82, Decatur, Illinois-born actress, died Mar. 4, 2010, at her home in Malibu, California, of complications from emphysema. Her Broadway credits include *A Story for a Sunday Evening; The Constant Wife; Makropoulos Secret; J.B.* (Tony nomination); *The Great God Brown; Lysistrata; Henry IV, Part I; Under the Yum-Yum Tree; Come Live With Me; Summer Brave;* and *The Eccentricities of a Nightingale.* Her Off-Broadway credits include *Saturday Night Kid; Sweet Confession; Much Ado About Nothing; Phaedra; Merchant of Venice; Taming of the Shrew;* and *The Old Boy.* She had been a regular at Joseph Papp's Shakespeare in the Park in the early 1960s. Her film credits include *Goodbye, Columbus; Toys in the Attic;* and *A Nightmare on Elm Street 3: Dream Warriors,* and her numerous television credits include a notable recurring role in the 1990s on *The Drew Carey Show; The Twilight Zone; The Untouchables; NYPD Blue;* and *CSI: Crime Scene Investigation.* Her late stage career consisted mostly of performances with South Coast Repertory in Costa Mesa, California, where credits include *Road to Mecca.* She began her career modeling for fashion designer Adrian in Los Angeles, California, before moving to New York to embark upon an acting career. Her first marriage to screen composer Robert Emmet Dolan ended in divorce. Her husband, Harry Gesner; sons, Casey Dolan, of Los Angeles, and Zen Gesner, of Malibu; and three grandsons survive her.

JUDI ANN MASON, 54, Shreveport, Louisiana-born pioneering young, female African-American playwright/screenwriter, died July 8, 2009, in Los Angeles, California of a ruptured aorta. Her credits include *Livin' Fat,* produced in 1976 Off-Broadway at the Negro Ensemble Company, followed by *The Daughters of* the Mock and Jonah and the Wonder Dog. Her A Star Ain't Nothin' But a Hole in Heaven won the first Kennedy Center Lorraine Hansberry Award for plays about the African-American experience. Her small screen credits include Good Times; Sanford and Son; A Different World; Cosby Show; Beverly Hills 90210; and I'll Fly Away, and her film credits include Sister Act 2: Back in the Habit. Her daughter, Mason Synclaire Williams; a son, Austin Barrett Williams; and three siblings survive her.

RODGER MCFARLANE, 54, Mobile, Alabama-born gay activist/producer, died May 15, 2009, in Truth or Consequences, New Mexico, of suicide brought on by complications from a broken back in 2002. In 1993 he produced Larry Kramer's The Destiny of Me, the Pulitzer Prize nominated play that was the sequel to Kramer's The Normal Heart. He was the founding executive director Gay Men's Health Crisis from 1982-1985, and was the executive director of Broadway Cares/Equity Fights AIDS from 1989-1994, and also served as president of Bailey House, a nonprofit organization that provides shelter for homeless people with AIDS. From 2004-2008 he served as the executive director of the Gill Foundation, that provides grants and operating support for nonprofit and community foundations. He was also a founding member of the New York branch of the AIDS Coalition to Unleash Power (ACT UP). He was a veteran of the U.S. Navy.

CAROLINE MCWILLIAMS (Caroline Margaret McWilliams), 64, Seattle, Washington-born and Barrington, Rhode Island-raised actress, died Feb. 11, 2010, at her home in Los Angeles, California, of complications from multiple myeloma. Best know for her work on the television series Soap (from 1978-79) and its spinoff Benson (from 1979-81), her Broadway credits include The Rothschilds; Cat on a Hot Tin Roof (1974); and Boccaccio. Credits as a director include Divorcons (Let's Get a Divorce); You Haven't Changed a Bit and Other Lies; and The Smoke and Ice Follies. Her other television credits include Guiding Light; Nearly Departed; Beverly Hills 90210; and Judging Amy, and her film roles include Mermaids. Her son, Sean Douglas; sisters, Kelly-Jo Dvareckas, Norma Liedtke, and Patti McWilliams survive her. A previous marriage to actor Michael Keaton ended in divorce.

JAMES MITCHELL (Jimmy Mitchell), 89, Sacramento, California-born actor/dancer, died Jan. 22, 2010, in Los Angeles, California, of chronic obstructive pulmonary disease complicated by pneumonia. A 1947 Theatre World Award winner for Brigadoon, his other Broadway credits include Bloomer Girl; Billion Dollar Baby; Come Summer (assistant director); Paint Your Wagon; Livin' The Life; Carousel; First Impressions; Carnival!; The Deputy; and Mack & Mabel, before settling into a highly successful thirty-year run as Palmer Cortlandt on the daytime soap opera All My Children, for which he is best known, and which garnered him seven Daytime Emmy Award nominations. His Off-Broadway credits include Winkelberg; The Threepenny Opera; Livin' the Life; The Father; and L'Histoire du Soldat. His national tours include The Rainmaker; The King and I; Funny Girl; and The Threepenny Opera. His other television credits include Omnibus; Bloomer Girl; Gold Rush; Ford Startime; The Perry Como Show; and The 38th Academy Awards. Initially a principal dancer for Agnes de Mille from 1953-54, his numerous dance credits include those with the American Ballet Theatre from 1950-51, 1955, and 1956), where he performed in Rodeo and Fall River Legend. His direction credits include those at the Paper Mill Playhouse; Mark Taper Forum; and The Muny, among other theatres. His film credits include Brigadoon; The Toast of New Orleans; Deep in My Heart; Colorado Territory; Border Incident; Stars in My Crown; The Band Wagon; The Prodigal; The Peacemaker; and The Turning Point. His partner, Academy Award-winning costume designer Albert Wolsky, survives him.

ZAKES MOKAE, 75, South African actor, died Sept. 11, 2009, in Las Vegas, Nevada, from complications of a stroke. A 1982 Tony Award winner as Best Featured Actor in a Play and Drama Desk Award nominee for his role in Athol Fugard's Master Harold ... and the Boys, his other Broadway credits include A Lesson from Aloes; Blood Knot; and The Song of Jacob Zulu (Tony Award nomination). His Off-Broadway credits include Boesman and Lena, followed by Fingernails Blue as Flowers; The Cherry Orchard; Trial of Vessey; and Last Days of British Honduras. He was seen in such films as The Comedians; The River

Niger; The Island (1980); Cry Freedom; The Serpent and the Rainbow; A Dry White Season; Dad; A Rage in Harlem; Outbreak; and Waterworld. His wife, Madelyn; two sisters; two brothers; a daughter; and grandchildren survive him.

THARON MUSSER (Tharon Myrene Musser), 84, Virginia-born prolific lighting designer, died Apr. 20, 2009, in Newtown, Connecticut, of complications from Alheizemer's disease. A Tony Award winner for her work on Follies; A Chorus Line; and Dreamgirls; her other Broadway credits include Long Day's Journey Into Night; Li'l Abner; Shinbone Alley; Monique; Madropoulos Secret; The Chairs and The Lesson; The Infernal Machine; The Entertainer; The Firstborn; The Shadow of a Gunman; J.B.; The Rivalry; The Beaux Stratagem (1959); Once Upon a Mattress; The Great God Brown; Only in America; Five Finger Exercise; Peer Gynt; The Long Dream; The Tumbler; The Garden of Sweets; Giants, Sons of Giants; Calculated Risk; Nowhere to Go But Up; Andorra; Mother Courage and Her Children; Here's Love; Marathon '33; Any Wednesday; The Seagull; The Crucible (1964); Golden Boy; Alfie!; Kelly; All in Good Time; Flora, The Red Menace; Minor Miracle; Malcolm; The Great Indoors; The Lion in Winter; Mame; A Delicate Balance; Breakfast at Tiffany's; Hallelujah, Baby!; The Imaginary Invalid (1967); A Touch of the Poet (1967); Tonight at 8:30; The Birthday Party; After the Rain; The Promise; Everything in the Garden; Lovers; Maggie Flynn; The Fig Leaves Are Falling; A Way of Life; The Gingham Dog; Blood Red Roses; Applause (Tony nomination); The Boy Friend (1970); The Trial of the Catonsville Nine; On the Town (1971); The Prisoner of Second Avenue; Night Watch; The Creation of the World and Other Business; The Great God Brown; Don Juan (1972); The Sunshine Boys; A Little Night Music (Tony nomination); Sondheim: A Musical Tribute; The Good Doctor (Tony nomination); Candide (1974); Scapino (1974); God's Favorite; Good News (1974); The Wiz, Same Time, Next Year; Me and Bessie; Pacific Overtures (Tony nomination);1600 Pennsylvania Avenue; California Suite; The Act (Tony nomination); Chapter Two; Tribute; Ballroom (Tony nomination, Drama Desk Award nomination); They're Playing Our Song (Drama Desk Award nomination); Whose Life is it Anyway? (1979, 1980); The 1940's Radio Hour; Romantic Comedy; Last Licks; Children of a Lesser God; I Ought to Be in Pictures; The Roast; 42nd Street; Fools; The Moony Shapiro Songbook; Special Occasions; Merlin; Brighton Beach Memoirs; Private Lives (1983); The Real Thing (Tony nomination); Open Admissions; Biloxi Blues; The Odd Couple (1985); Jerry's Girls; Broadway Bound; A Month of Sundays; Dreamgirls (1987); Teddy & Alice; Rumors; Welcome to the Club; Artist Descending a Staircase (Tony nomination); Lost in Yonkers; The Secret Garden (Tony nomination); The Goodbye Girl; Laughter on the 23rd Floor; Uncle Vanya; The Lonesome West; and A Chorus Line (2006). She also received a Drama Desk Award for Dreamgirls. Her lighting design for 1975's A Chorus Line helped revolutionize lighting and that production was the first to use a computerized console. For thirteen seasons she designed the lighting for the American Shakespeare Festival in Stratford, Connecticut. She was honored as a USITT Distinguished Lighting Designer in 1996; honored with an Eddy Award from Entertainment Design in 2000; and received a tribute at the 2007 United States Institute for Theatre Technology conference in Phoenix, Arizona. Her longtime partner, Marilyn Rennagel, survives her.

CRAIG NOEL, 94, Deming, New Mexico-born theatre founder/producer of the Old Globe Theatre in San Diego, California, died Apr. 3, 2010, in San Diego. Affiliated with the Old Globe from its inception in 1937 (named the Old Globe in 1958), he served as artistic director from 1949-1981, and then as executive director with title of founding director, he directed more than 200 productions and produced nearly 300 others over forty years. Currently the Old Globe is one of the oldest nonprofits in the country, with 20,000 subscribers and a $20 million annual budget. It produces fifteen plays and musicals annually on its three stages in Balboa Park. Noel also inaugurated the San Diego Shakespeare Festival in 1949. He was a veteran of World War II, where he served in the Army in the South Pacific, and he was assigned to special services and became director of the Ernie Pyle Theater in Tokyo, Japan, providing entertainment to occupation troops. He also worked at 20th Century Fox directing screen tests for a time before embarking on his regional theatre career. In 2007 he was awarded a National Medal of the Arts by President George W. Bush. His partner of thirty-seven years, Hamzda Houidi, survives him.

CHARLES NOLTE, 87, Duluth, Iowa-born and Wayzata, Minnesota-raised actor/director/educator, died Jan. 14, 2010, in Minneapolis, of prostate cancer. A 1950 Theatre World Award winner for *Design for a Stained Glass Window* (with Charlton Heston), his other Broadway credits include *Uniform of Flesh; Mister Roberts; Antony and Cleopatra; Billy Budd;* and *The Caine Mutiny Court Martial.* His other New York credits include *Tin Top Valley* with Julie Harris in 1946. His touring production credits include *Antony and Cleopatra* (with Katherine Cornell). His European theatre credits include *Under Ten Flags* (again with Katherine Cornell) in Rome; *Medea* (with Judith Anderson) in Paris; and *The Summer People* in London. A professor at the University of Minnesota from the 1960s to the late 1990s, a group of his former students started the Playwrights' Center, and he also taught acting at the Guthrie Theater drama school. His *Do Not Pass Go* was produced at the Cherry Lane Theatre Off-Broadway in 1965. He directed more than a twelve productions at the local Theatre-in-the-Round Players, and the University of Minnesota honored him in 1997 by naming a theatre space within its Rarig Center the Charles Nolte Experimental Theatre. He served in the U.S. Navy from 1943-1945. Mr. Nolte was a close personal friend of the founder of this publication, Daniel Blum, in the 1940s and 1950s.

LEE PELTY (Isaac Peltynovich), 74, Chicago, Illinois actor who portrayed Tevye in *Fiddler on the Roof* over 2000 times in the Chicago area, died Nov. 29, 2009, in Chicago, of lung cancer. Theatres at which he played Tevye include the Candlelight Dinner Playhouse in Summit, Illinois, in 1971, 1977, 1980, and 1990, respectively. The first run lasted nearly two years. By his own estimate he had belted out the word "Tradition" some 56,000 times. Other roles included Don Quixote in *Man of La Mancha.* His wife, Barbara; son, Adam; and grandson, Noah, survive him.

DAVID POWERS, 88, Bristol, Tennessee-born press agent, died Oct. 4, 2009, at the Lillian Booth Actors Home in Englewood, New Jersey. Beginning his career as a press agent in 1948, he began working with Harvey Sabinson in the 1950s, and then the both of them teaming up with Lee Solters in the early 1960s, his credits alone or with his partners include *Red Gloves; Wonderful Town; By the Beautiful Sea; The Desperate Hours; The Wayward Saint; Tiger at the Gates; A Hatful of Rain; The First Gentleman; The Egghead; Romanoff and Juliet; Jamaica; The Dark at the Top of the Stairs; A Shadow of My Enemy; Oh Captain!; Interlock; The Man in the Dog Suit; Epitaph for George Dillon; Maria Golovin; Ages of Man; Triple Play; Destry Rides Again; Heartbreak House* (1959); *Take Me Along; The Tenth Man; A Loss of Roses; A Mighty Man Is He; The Deadly Game; Period of Adjustment; Little Moon of Alban; Rhinoceros; Big Fish, Little Fish; Carnival!; I Can Get It for You Wholesale; Stop the World–Want to Get Off; Mother Courage and Her Children; Luther; 110 in the Shade; Hello, Dolly!; Fade Out-Fade In; Ben Franklin in Paris; The Roar of the Greasepaint-The Smell of the Crowd; The Yearling; The Persecution and Assasination of Marat as Performed by the Inmates of the Asylum of Charenton under the Direction of the Marquis de Sade; Happily Never After; Mark Twain Tonight; Breakfast at Tiffany's; Henry, Sweet Henry; How Now, Dow Jones; The Happy Time; Promises, Promises; Hadrian VII; Celebration; Billy; A Patriot for Me; Gantry; The Incomparable Max; Different Times; 6 Rms Riv Vu; Good Evening; Ulysses in Nighttown; Words & Music; Doctor Jazz; We Interrupt This Program; Kennedy's Children; Sweet Bird of Youth; Piaf…A Remembrance; Annie; The Gin Game; A History of the American Film; I Remember Mama; Barnum; Billy Bishop Goes to War; Medea; Seven Brides for Seven Brothers; Foxfire; Peg; The Golden Age; Take Me Along* (1985); *The Iceman Cometh* (1985); *Lillian; Sweet Sue; Eastern Standard; Metamorphosis; A Few Good Men;* and *The Speed of Darkness.*

HARVE PRESNELL (George Harvey Presnell), 75, Modesto, California-born actor/singer, best known for his role as Leadville Johnny Brown in the original Broadway production of *The Unsinkable Molly Brown* and its film adaptation, died of pancreatic cancer on June 30, 2009, in Santa Monica, California. His other Broadway productions include *Annie.* Other stage credits include *Annie 2: Miss Hannigan's Revenge* and the baritone in the 1960 recording of Carl Orff's *Carmina Burana,* with Eugene Ormandy conducting the Philadelphia Orchestra. His national tours included *Annie* and *On a Clear Day You Can See Forever.* His other movies include *When the Boys Meet the Girls; The Glory Guys; Paint Your Wagon; Fargo; The Chamber; The Whole Wide World; Face/Off; Saving Private Ryan; Patch Adams; Old School; Flags of Our Fathers;* and *Evan Almighty.* His television credits include *The Pretender; Andy Barker, P.I.; Larger Than Life; Face/Off;* and *The Legend of Bagger Vance.* In the 1950s he performed on recordings with the Roger Wagner Chorale for Capitol Records. His second wife, Veeva; six children; Stephanie, Taylor, Etoile, Tulley, Shannon, and Raine; and several grandchildren survive him.

CORIN REDGRAVE (Corin William Redgrave), 70, London, England-born actor and member of the famous English dynasty of Redgrave actors and actresses, died Apr. 6, 2010, in London, England. He had suffered a heart attack and from prostate cancer in recent years. His thirty-five year interregnum between Broadway appearances occurred between *Chips with Everything* in 1963, and *Not About Nightingales,* in 1999, for which he received Best Actor in a Play Tony and Drama Desk Award nominations. His other London stage credits include Lysander in *A Midsummer Night's Dream* at the Royal Court Theatre; *King Lear* with the Royal Shakespeare Company; *Antony and Cleopatra;* and *The Tempest.* His film credits include *A Man for All Seasons; Excalibur; In the Name of the Father; Four Weddings and a Funeral;* and *Persuasion.* His British television credits include *Ultraviolet; The Vice; Trial & Retribution; Shameless;* and *Foyle's War.* He founded the Moving Theater, dedicated to political works, with his sister, Vanessa Redgrave, who shared many of his far left-wing political views, and it was with the Alley Theater of Houston that they produced the premiere of *Not About Nightingales* at the Royal National Theater in 1998. It would earn him his Tony nomination the following year. In 1995 he published a book about his relationship with his father–famed English actor Michael Redgrave, entitled *Michael Redgrave–My Father.* His wife, Kika Markham; daughter, Jemma; son, Luke, from a previous marriage to Deidre Hamilton-Hill; sons, Harvey and Arden from his marriage to Markham; sister, actress Vanessa Redgrave; and grandchildren survive him. His niece, actress Natasha Richardson, died Mar. 18, 2009, and his sister, actress Lynn Redgrave, died on May 2, 2010.

LYNN REDGRAVE (Lynn Rachel Redgrave), 67, London, England-born actress and member of the famous English dynasty of Redgrave actors and actresses, died May 2, 2010, at her home in Kent, Connecticut, of complications from breast cancer. Her Broadway credits include *Black Comedy/White Lies; My Fat Friend; Mrs. Warren's Profession* (Tony Award nomination); *Knock Knock; Saint Joan; Aren't We All* (Drama Desk Award nomination); *Sweet Sue; Love Letters; A Little Hotel on the Side; The Master Builder; Shakespeare for My Father* (Tony Award and Drama Desk Award nomination); *Moon Over Buffalo;* and *The Constant Wife* (Tony Award and Drama Desk Award nominations). She won a Drama Desk Award for *Talking Heads* in 2003. She also appeared in *Strike Up the Band* at Encores! She joined the National Theater of Britain during its inaugural season of 1963, and eventually she performed there in productions directed by Laurence Olivier; Franco Zeferelli; and Noël Coward; and performed with the likes of Peter O'Toole; Maggie Smith; as well as her father, famed actor Michael Redgrave. Her numerous other British stage credits include *Billy Liar; Three Sisters;* and *A Midsummer Night's Dream* at the Royal Court Theater. Her film credits include *Georgy Girl* (Academy Award nomination); *Shine; Gods and Monsters* (Academy Award nomination); and *The Happy Hooker.* An equally prolific television actress, she appeared in *House Calls; Kojak; The Love Boat; Murder She Wrote;* and as a television spokesperson for Weight Watchers. In her later years she authored several plays based on the members of her family. The first was in 1993 and entitled *Shakespeare for My Father,* followed by *The Mandrake Root; Nightingale;* and *Rachel and Juliet,* in which she had performed last in fall 2009. Her marriage to actor/director John Clark, ended in divorce in 2000. Her sister, actress Vanessa Redgrave; son, Benjamin Clark; two daughters, Annabel and Pema Clark; and five grandchildren survive her. Her niece, actress Natasha Richardson, died Mar. 18, 2009, and her brother, actor Corin Redgrave, died less than a month earlier than she, on Apr. 6, 2010.

FRANCES REID, 95, Wichita Falls, Texas-born actress, died Feb. 3, 2010, in Beverly Hills, California. Best known as the matriarch Alice Horton on the daytime soap opera *Days of Our Lives* for more than forty years, her Broadway credits prior to that engagement include *The Dream of Sganarelle; Revenge with Music;*

CRAIG NOEL

HARVE PRESNELL

LYNNE REDGRAVE

Where There's a Will; The Rivals; Bird in Hand; The Patriots; Listen, Professor; A Highland Fling; Little Women (1944); *Star-Spangled Family; The Wind is Ninety; Hamlet* (1945, 1946); *Cyrano de Bergerac* (1946); *King Richard III* (1949); and *Twelfth Night* (1949). Her other television credits include *Portia Faces Life; As The World Turns; The Edge of Night; Hallmark Hall of Fame; Wagon Train; Dr. Kildare; Perry Mason;* and *Mr. Novak.* She received a Daytime Emmy Lifetime Achievement Award in 2004.

M. EDGAR ROSENBLUM (Morton Edgar Rosenblum), 78, Brooklyn, New York-born regional theatre producer of Long Wharf Theatre in New Haven, Connecticut, and teacher, died Apr. 18, 2010, in Woodstock, New York, of a heart attack. As half of one of the longest-running partnerships with an artistic director (Arvin Brown) of the last half-century of regional theatre, for twenty-six years the partners purveyed regional theatre and productions to Broadway that included *The Changing Room* and *The Gin Game.* The Long Wharf's annual budget was $400,000 when Rosenblum arrived at the Long Wharf. When he left it was $5.5 million. And subscribers in the 1980s numbered $18,000. Additionally he taught theatre management at Yale University and served as the president of the League of American Theaters and the American Arts Alliance (now known as Performing Arts Alliance). Following his tenure at the Long Wharf, he served as executive director for Theater for a New Audience in New York, and at his death he was the director of the California International Theater Festival, whose second season was presented in Calabasas, California, in July 2010. His wife, Cornelia; brother, Robert, of Manhattan; and daughter, Jessica, of Manhattan and Miami, Florida survive him.

ARNOLD STANG, 91, New York, New York-born character player, instantly recognizable by his horn-rimmed glasses and his squawking voice, died Dec. 20, 2009, in Newton, Massachusetts, of pneumonia. His Broadway credits include *All in Favor; Sailor Beware; Same Time Next Week; Wallflower; Wedding Breakfast; A Funny Thing Happened on the Way to the Forum; You'll See Stars;* and *The Front Page.* His radio roles were numerous and included *Top Cat; The Horn and Hardart Children's Hour; Let's Pretend; The Goldbergs;* and *The Henry Morgan Show.* His voice work credits include *Pinocchio in Outer Space.* Television credits include *The Henry Morgan Show* (transplanting his character from the radio medium); *Broadside; McHale's Navy; Bonanza; Batman;* and *The Cosby Show.* He could be seen in such motion pictures as *Seven Days Leave; So This is New York; The Man with the Golden Arm; Dondi; The Wonderful World of the Brothers Grimm; It's a Mad Mad Mad Mad World; Skidoo; Hello Down There; Ghost Dad;* and *Dennis the Menace.* His wife of sixty-one years, JoAnne; his son David, of Cambridge, Massachusetts; his daughter, Deborah Stang, of Brighton, Massachusetts; and two grandchildren survive him.

ALLEN SWIFT (Ira Stadlen), 87, Washington Heights, New York-born and Brooklyn-raised actor, died Apr. 18, 2010, in Manhattan. His Broadway credits

include: *How to Make a Man; The Student Gypsy; Checking Out; My Old Friends;* and *The Iceman Cometh* (1985). His multitude of voiceover credits includes those of the voices Mighty Mouse, Dinky Duck, and Howdy Doody (for one year, as host Bob Smith recovered from a heart attack). His other *Howdy Doody* characters included Phineas T. Buster, Flub-a-Dub, and the live character Chief Thunderchicken. His voice over characters included an Eveready battery and a toilet plunger, among others. At one point he recorded over thirty radio and television commercials a day, including those for beer, laundry detergent, Jell-O, and Hostess Ho Hos. Other characters included Simon Bar Sinister and Riff Raff on *Underdog,* most of the *Tom and Jerry* cartoons made from 1960-62, and *Popeye the Sailor* from 1956-60 on WPIX in New York. He was a veteran of the Army Air Corps in World War II. As a stand-up comedian and magician he appeared on television in programs such as *The Bob Hope Show* and *Texaco Star Theater.* His first marriage, to Vivienne Chassler, ended in divorce. His wife, Lenore Loveman; son, the actor Lewis J. Stadlen; two daughters, Maxime, of Vallecito, California, and Clare, of Durham, North Carolina; and five grandchildren survive him.

DORIS EATON TRAVIS, 106, Norfolk, Virginia-born actress/dancer/author and the last surviving Ziegfeld Girl, died May 11, 2010, in Commerce, Michigan. Her Broadway credits include *Mother Carey's Chickens; Ziegfeld Follies of 1918; Ziegfeld Midnight Frolic* [1919]; *Ziegfeld Follies of 1920; No Other Girl; The Sap; Excess Baggage; Cross My Heart; Page Pygmalion;* and *Merrily We Roll Along.* Other stage credits include *The Blue Bird* at the Shubert Belasco Theatre in Washington (with her sisters Mary and Pearl Eaton); various plays and melodramas for the Poli Stock Company; and the *Hollywood Box Revue* and the *Gorham Follies* in Los Angeles, California. Her film credits include *At the Stage Door; Tell Your Children;* and *Egypt.* Following her stage career, she taught dance as an Arthur Murray dance instructor for three decades, eventually owning and managing a chain of nearly twenty schools. Following that second career, she began a third as a horse ranch manager and earned a degree from the University of Oklahoma. As the last surviving Ziegfeld Girl, she was in demand as an interview subject for books and documentaries, and appeared nearly every year for over a decade in Easter Bonnet Competition benefit performances for *Broadway Cares/ Equity Fights AIDS.* On May 12, 2010, the lights of Broadway marquees were dimmed in her honor.

HELEN WAGNER, 91, Lubbock, Texas-born actress, who spoke the first words ("Good morning, dear.") of the CBS soap opera *As the World Turns* and performed the role of matriarch Nancy Hughes for more than fifty years, died May 1, 2010, in Mount Kisco, New York. Her Broadway credits include *Sunny River; Oklahoma!;* and *The Winter's Tale.* She is acknowledged by the Guinness Book of Records as having the longest-running role in the history of television, and it was a scene in which she was performing that was interrupted by Walter Cronkite on Nov. 22, 1963, to announce that President John F. Kennedy had been shot. She was presented with a Daytime Emmy Lifetime Achievement Award in 2004.

ARNOLD STANG

DORIS EATON TRAVIS

EDWARD WOODWARD

DOUGLAS WATT (Douglas Benjamin Watt), 95, Bronx-born theatre critic, died Sept. 28, 2010, of complications from pneumonia. He lived in Southampton, Long Island, and Manhattan. Beginning his career as a copy boy in the drama department of the *New York Daily News* in 1934, he worked there nearly sixty years, retiring as critic at-large in 1993. He was influential in bringing *Porgy and Bess* back to Broadway in September 1942, after a first unsuccessful prior run, by highly praising and advocating an out-of-town production in New Jersey. Additionally he wrote about New York nightlife in columns for the *New Yorker* as well as the *Daily News*. He graduated from Cornell University at age nineteen and was a veteran of World War II, having written from Okinawa, Japan, for *Stars and Stripes*. He was a dedicated member of the Theatre World Awards voting committee, chaired by Peter Filichia, for decades, and a dedicated friend as well to longtime *Theatre World* editor John Willis. His wife of fifty-eight years, Ethel Madsen Watt; daughters, Patricia, and Katherine, of Brooklyn; and two sons, Richard, of Pleasantville, New York, and James of Atlanta; and eight grandchildren survive him.

COLLIN WILCOX (Collin Wilcox-Horne, Collin Wilcox Paxton), 74, Cincinnati, Ohio-born and Highlands, North Carolina-raised actress, died Oct. 14, 2009, in Highlands, North Carolina, of brain cancer. She studied at the Goodman School of Drama in Chicago, Illinois, as well as performed there with the Compass Players improvisational troupe–a precursor to Second City comedy troupe. Her Broadway credits include *The Day the Money Stopped* (Actors' Equity Clarence Derwent Award as the year's most promising performer); *Look, We've Come Through; Strange Interlude* (1963); and *The Family Way*. Her Off-Broadway credits include *Season of Choice; Camino Real; The Good Soup;* and *Too True To Be Good*. Her numerous television credits include *The Untouchables; The Twilight Zone; The Defenders; Gunsmoke; Dr. Kildare; The Fugitive; Ironside; Columbo; The Waltons; Little House on the Prairie; A Member of the Wedding;* and *The Autobiography of Miss Jane Pittman*. Her film roles include Mayella Ewell, the young white woman who falsely accuses a black man of rape in *To Kill a Mockingbird;* and those in *Catch-22* and *Jaws 2*. Her two previous marriages, to Walter Beakel, and Geoffrey Horne, ended in divorce. Her third husband, Scott Paxton; daughter, Kimberly Horne; sons, Michael G. Paxton and William Horne; and three grandchildren survive her.

EDWARD WOODWARD, 79, Croyden, Surrey, England-born actor, best known in America for his starring role on the CBS series *The Equalizer*, for which he received five Emmy Award nominations and a Golden Globe Award, died in Truro, Cornwall, England, on Nov. 16, 2009, after suffering from a series of illnesses. His Broadway credits include *Rattle of a Simple Man; High Spirits;* and *The Best Laid Plans*. His British theatre credits with the Royal Shakespeare Company include *Romeo and Juliet; Hamlet; Pericles;* and *Much Ado About Nothing*. His other West End credits include *Cyrano de Bergerac* and The *White Devil*. His other American television credits include *Over My Dead Body*. He was seen in such motion pictures as the 1973 cult horror film *The Wicker Man; Becket; The File of the Golden Goose; Young Winston; Breaker Morant; King David; Mister Johnson;* and *Hot Fuzz*. His British television credits include *Callan*. He also recorded twelve solo albums as a singer and won an Emmy Award as host of the 1989 documentary, *Remembering World War II*. He was made an officer of the Order of the British Empire. His second wife, actress Michele Dotrice; their daughter, Emily Woodward Wakem; two sons, Tim, and Peter; and daughter, Sarah Woodward, from his first marriage, survive him.

GILBERTO ZALDIVAR, 75, Deleyte, Cuba-born theatre founder, died Oct. 5, 2009, at his home in Manhattan, of complications of Lewy body disease, a form of dementia. Co-founder (with fellow Cuban René Buch) of the Repertorio Español, he oversaw the production of more than 250 plays over a span of forty years. Productions ranged from Seventeenth century Spanish-language classics to original, commissioned works by emerging American-born Hispanic playwrights and performers who worked there include Raul Julia and Miriam Colón. Playwrights whose works Zaldivar was responsible for producing include García Lorca; Calderón de la Barca; and Unamuno; as well as translations of novels by writers such as Gabriel Garcia Márquez and Mario Vargas Llosa. Prior to founding his company he worked in corporate accounting and eventually became an executive at Diners Club. In 1972 Repertorio Español moved into the 140-seat Gramercy Arts Theater on East 27th Street, which is its current home. On behalf of the Repertorio Español Zaldivar accepted Obies, Drama Desks, as well as the New York State Governor's Award. His companion, Robert Weber Federico, who succeeded him as Repertorio Español's executive director in 2005; sister, Nancy Zaldivar, of Miami, Florida; and numerous cousins who remain in Cuba survive him.

Index

P

P.S. 122 135, 269, 313, 314, 330
Paar, Jennifer 310, 311, 330
Paauwe, Heather 295
Pabst, Jessica 75, 236, 255, 256, 282, 293, 328, 332
Pace University 155
Pace, Allyson 270
Pace, Jenna 185
Pace, Makeba 373
Pacek, Steve 347
Pacent, Nicole 271
Pacheco, Abraham 325
Pacheco, Jesús 111, 325
Pacheco, Omar 140
Pacheco, Yuri 325
Pachomski, Maegan 376
Pachtman, Matthew 36, 44, 75
Pacific Resident Theatre 442
Pacilio, Casi 389, 390
Pacino, Al 418
Pack, Eugene 434
Packard, Geoff 104, 107
Packawallop Productions Inc. 311
Packer, Rose Marie 397
Packett, Kila 289, 331, 363
Packett, Kilan 261
Packman, Glenn 277
Padden, Michael 41, 222
Padgett, Emily 107, 117, 398
Padgett, Jeanine 362
Padilha, Zeca 174
Padmore, Mark 199
Padovano, Shayna 174, 270
Padrick, Scott 350
Paesel, Brett 372
PaGAGnini 230
Pagan, Alejandro 132
Pagan, Ayana 364
Pagano, Chris 259
Pagano, Duane 152, 291, 332
Pagano, Frank 237
Pagano, Paul 396
Page 121 Productions 267
Page 73 Productions 145, 184, 302, 311
Page, Anthony 110
Page, Geraldine 417, 418

Page, Jeffrey 48
Page, Ken 408, 419
Page, Lynne 51, 69, 423, 424
Page, Michael 190
Page, Patrick 165, 382, 383, 436
Pageant Wagon Productions 290
Paget, Ian 99, 113
Pagliano, Jeff 320
Paglino, Francesco 196
Paglino, Nick 268
Pagnol, Marcel 214
Paguia, Marco 80
Pai, Ian 186
Paice, Jill 81
Paige, Amanda Ryan 185
Paige, Cristen 401
Paige, Dylan 285
Pailet, Janet 29
Pailet, Marshall 328, 365
Paine, Carolyn 298
Paine, Rebekah 232
Painkillers 131
Paint Your Wagon 301
Painter, Devon 178, 235, 366
Painter, Sarah 270, 326
Paisner, Caryl 109
Paiva, Frank 144, 331
Pajama Game, The 452
Pak, Joy 36, 40, 53, 80
Pak, Susan H. 299
Pakenham, Kate 103
Pakledinaz, Martin 64, 87, 141, 209, 214, 246, 378, 392, 400, 423, 426, 428
Pal Joey 458
Pal, Anjili J. 217
Pal, Anuvab 318
Pal, Daniela Ruth 272
Palace Theatre 69, 111, 258
Palacio, Cassandra 323
Palacios, Lizette 325
Palamino 375
Palance, Jack 417
Palardy, Kat 382
Palasthy, April 270
Pale Fire 311
Palestine 162, 163
Palestine, New Mexico 356
Paley, Petronia 281
Palijaro, Roy 114
Palileo, Maia Cruz 279
Palin, Karen 398
Palin, Michael 355
Palisoc, Tessa Lene 345

Palitz, Michael 58, 422
Palkes, Henry 390
Palladino, Nick 297
Pallanck, Rodney 309
Pallas, Ted 48, 284
Paller, Michael 346
Pallister, Carolyn 272
Palm Beach Dramaworks 435
Palm, Michael 114, 116, 198, 199
Palma, CJ 356, 364, 395, 399
Pálmai, Anna 195
Palmatier, Nancy 91, 173
Palmer, Byron 417
Palmer, Jeremy 47
Palmer, Jessica 278
Palmer, Kristen 283
Palmer, Masaya 116
Palmer, Michael 267, 272, 276, 332
Palmer, Peter 417, 418
Palmer, Rachael 299
Palmer, Ryan 284
Palmer, Scott 163, 371
Palmer, Sean 98
Palmer, Sean Jeremy 276
Palmer, Shanna Marie 364
Palmer, Stephanie 221, 242
Palmer, Tanya 179, 366, 367
Palmer, Todd 109
Palmer, Tyler 359
Palmieri, Gayle 41, 92
Palmieri, Marc 132, 271, 315
Palombo, Rose 150
Palomino 356
Palumbo, Antonio 32, 36, 40, 53, 80, 245
Palyk, Roman 30
Palzewicz, Michal 384
Pamatmat, A. Rey 243, 271
Pamela Precious 327
Pampin, Edi 188
Pan Asian Repertory Theatre 234
Panama Hattie 459
Panama, Norman 47, 364
Pancholy, Maulik 201
Pander, Shawn 431
Pandibulan 295
Pando, Nicole 94, 165
Pandolfo, Nicole 280
Pandya, Rohi Mirza 278
Pang, Andy 302

Pangallo, Jill 279
Pangburn, Janine 323
Paniagua, Jorge Claudio 385
Paniccia, Anna 354
Panicked Productions 268, 300
Pankow, Ashley 361, 370
Pankow, John 208, 226
Panoply Performance Laboratory, The 311
Panovski, Naum 317
Panter, Howard 89, 91
Panther, Jenna 359, 362
Pantuso, Chris 35, 56, 64
Panych, Morris 138, 346
Papaelias, Lucas 184
Papais, John 301
Paparone, Frankie 108
Papathanassiou, Thomas 305
Pape, Florence 316
Pape, Jeremy 135, 168, 269, 314
Paper Mill Playhouse 385, 386, 388
Papermoon Puppet Theatre 278
Papp, Joseph 419
Pappas, Alex 274, 275, 286
Pappas, Ted 367, 388
Pappas, Victor 207
Paq, Manuel 325
Paque, Jake 332
Paquin, Anna 421
Parade 353, 356, 442
Paradine, Jason 241, 265, 283
Paradise Factory 266, 275, 311
Paradise Lost 346
Paradise, Grace 109
Paradise, Sandy 42
Paradox of the Urban Cliché 221
Paradsio, Antonia 351, 375, 392
Paraiso, Nicky 294
Parallel Exit 230
Parallelogram, A 398
Paramonova, Natalya 357
Paramount Pictures 47
Paranada, Jay 331
Paranosic, Milica 273
Pardo, Diego Daniel 128
Pardue, Scott 299
Paremski, Natasha 115
Parental Guidance

Suggested 322
Parenti, James 319
Parenti, Mark 297, 400
Parents' Evening 179
Pareschi, Brian 60, 82
Parham, Bryonha 44, 45
Parham, Keith 367
Parham, Timothy 257
Parichy, Dennis 323, 384
Parillo, Erick 191
Paris, Andy 197, 256, 365, 371, 376
Paris, Anika 301
Paris, Patrick 276
Pariseau, Pam 31, 190
Parish, Lauren 283
Parisien, Pierre 183
Parison, Richard M. Jr. 349
Parisse, Annie 237, 400
Park Avenue Armory 195, 196
Park Side Productions 299
Park, Ashley Jini 378
Park, Barbara 393
Park, Chanee 378
Park, Hani Jihyun 376
Park, Jeany 384
Park, Joshua 421
Park, Kina 237, 277, 317
Park, Kyoung H. 282
Park, Michael 237
Park, Ryan 228
Park, Sue-Yeon 328
Park, Youn Young 325
Parke, Evan 377, 380
Parker, Alecia 69, 88
Parker, Alfie Jr. 109, 116
Parker, Cat 323
Parker, Christian 208
Parker, Daniel Patrick 383, 384
Parker, Dorothy 365
Parker, Douglas M. 338
Parker, Ellen 223
Parker, Gloria 178
Parker, Griffin 280, 319
Parker, Jacqui 373, 439
Parker, Jeff 397
Parker, Jerome 44
Parker, John Eric 39, 213
Parker, Katey 297, 298
Parker, Kristin 191
Parker, Lisa 295
Parker, Mary-Louise 420
Parker, Michael Joseph 378, 379
Parker, Nicole 112
Parker, Rachel 328

Parker, Robert Ross 270, 282, 289
Parker, Timothy Britten 112
Parkin-Ring, Josh 311
Parkins, Zeena 314
Parkinson, Scott 190, 356, 375, 391, 394
Parkinson, Steve 154
Parkman, Russell 257
Parks, Brooke 384, 385
Parks, Derrick 259
Parks, Jessica 159, 182
Parks, Jim 269
Parks, Joseph 163, 232, 328, 357, 371, 430
Parks, Joseph Mitchell 329
Parks, Suzan-Lori 240, 242
Parlato, Dennis 188
Parlato, Karen 163, 371
Parlow, Nathan 376
Parmeggiani, Frida 210
Parmele, Owen E. 103
Parnassus Enterprise 78
Parnes, Joey 92
Parness, Alaina 133
Parness, Eric 143, 328
Parng, Constance 291, 444
Parpan, Morgan 319
Parquet, Lori 280
Parr, Larry 338
Parr, Shawn 324
Parra, Maria 274
Parrett, Melinda 362
Parris, Mamie 45
Parrish, Lauren 308
Parrish, Robyne 323
Parrish, Tom 377
Parrott, Catherine A. 59, 214, 247
Parrott, Nicki 363
Parry, A. Scott 284
Parry, Charlotte 226, 285
Parry, Evalyn 290
Parry, Natasha 252
Parry, William 258, 357, 362, 366, 376
Parsekian, Aaron 77
Parson, Joanna 270, 273, 283, 408
Parson, Ron OJ 366
Parson, Wendy 42, 254
Parsons, Estelle 355, 418
Parsons, Jennifer 393, 396
Parsons, Nathan 200
Parsons, Randeil 302
Part Time Productions

Ben Hodges (Editor in Chief) served as an editorial assistant for seven years on the 2001 Special Tony Honor Award-winning *Theatre World*, becoming the associate editor to John Willis in 1998 and editor in chief in 2008. *Theatre World*–at sixty-six–is the most complete annual pictorial and statistical record of the American theatre, including Broadway, Off-Broadway, Off-Off-Broadway, and regional theatre productions, and is referenced daily by students, historians, and industry professionals worldwide.

Also an assistant for seven years to John Willis for the prestigious Theatre World Awards given for Broadway and Off-Broadway debut performances, Ben was elected to the Theatre World Awards board of directors in 2002 and served as executive producer for the annual ceremony from 2002-2007. In 2003 he was presented with a Special Theatre World Award in recognition of his ongoing stewardship of the event. He also served as executive producer for the 2005 LAMBDA Literary Foundation "Lammy" Awards, given for excellence in LGBT publishing.

The Commercial Theater Institute Guide to Producing Plays and Musicals, which Hodges co-edited with late Commercial Theater Institute director Frederic B. Vogel, was released by Applause Theatre and Cinema Books in 2007, and with contributions by twenty-eight Broadway producers, general managers, attorneys, and publicists, is in its second printing and has become the definitive resource in its field. It has also been adopted as a course book by North Carolina School for the Arts, among other colleges and universities.

Forbidden Acts, the acclaimed first collected anthology of gay and lesbian plays from the span of the twentieth century, edited and with an introduction by Hodges, was published by Applause Theatre and Cinema Books in 2003 and became a finalist for the 2003 LAMBDA Literary Award for Drama, and is in its second printing. It has been adopted as a course book by New York University, Cornell University, Salisbury University, University of Las Vegas, and University of Louisville, among other high schools, colleges and universities.

His *Out Plays: Landmark Gay and Lesbian Plays from the Twentieth Century*, edited and with an introduction by Hodges, featuring a foreword by Harvey Fierstein and a new introduction to *The Boys in the Band* by Mart Crowley, was released by Alyson Books in spring 2008. With *Out Plays*, Hodges became the most prolific single anthologist of published gay and lesbian American plays.

His highly acclaimed *The American Theatre Wing Presents The Play That Changed My Life: America's Foremost Playwrights on the Plays That Influenced Them*, with essays by scores of America's foremost American playwrights including David Auburn, Christopher Durang, Lynn Nottage, and John Patrick Shanley, was released by Applause Theatre and Cinema Books in fall 2009 and is currently in its third printing.

As an actor, director, and/or producer, Ben has appeared in New York with The Barrow Group Theater Company, Origin Theater Company, Daedalus Theater Company, Monday Morning Productions, the Strawberry One-Act Festival, Coyote Girls Productions, Jet Productions, New York Actors' Alliance, and Outcast Productions. Additionally, he has appeared in numerous productions presented by theatre companies that he founded, including the Tuesday Group and Visionary Works. On film, he can be seen in *Macbeth: The Comedy*.

In 2001, Ben became director of development and then served as executive director for Fat Chance Productions Inc. and the Ground Floor Theatre, a New York-based nonprofit theatre and film production company. *Prey for Rock and Roll* was developed by Fat Chance from their stage production (the first legit production to play CBGBs) into a critically acclaimed feature film starring Gina Gershon and *The Sopranos'* Emmy winner Drea de Matteo. *Prey for Rock and Roll* debuted at the Sundance Film Festival in 2003 and won Best Feature at the 2003 Santa Cruz Film Festival. Additionally, Fat Chance produced the American premiere of award-winning Irish playwright Enda Walsh's *Misterman* Off-Broadway, and a host of readings, workshops, and productions in their Ground Floor Theatre, their mission statement being to present new works by new artists.

In 2003, frustrated with the increasingly daunting economic prospects involved in producing theatre on a small scale in New York, Ben organized NOOBA, the New Off-Off Broadway Association, an advocacy group dedicated to representing the concerns of expressly Off-Off-Broadway producers in the public forum and in negotiations with other local professional arts organizations; their chief objective the reformation of the Actors' Equity Basic Showcase Code.

He also serves on the New York Innovative Theatre Awards Committee, selecting outstanding individuals for recognition Off-Off-Broadway, and as vice-president of Summer Stage New York, a professional summer theatre program in Fayetteville, New York, and as executive producer of the annual Fire Island Pines Literary Weekend.

In 2005 Ben founded and served for two years as executive director of The Learning Theatre Inc., a 501(c)(3) nonprofit organization incorporating theatre into the development and lives of learning disabled and autistic children. He currently serves on the board of directors.

In support of his projects and publications, Ben has appeared on nationwide radio on *The Joey Reynolds Show*, *The Michael Dresser Show*, *Stage and Screen with Mark Gordon*, and on television on New York 1 and *Philly Live* in Philadelphia, PA–the only live televised LGBT call-in show in the United States. Reviews and articles on Ben, his projects, or publications have appeared in *The New York Times*, *The New Yorker*, *GQ*, *Elle*, *Genre*, *Back Stage*, *Time Out New York*, *Playbill*, *Next*, *New York Blade*, *Library Journal*, *The Advocate*, *Chicago Free Press*, *Philadelphia Gay News*, *Houston Voice*, *Stage Directions*, *Between the Lines*, *The Flint Journal*, and *Citizen Tribune*, as well as the web sites CurtainUp.com and in Peter Filichia's Diary on Theatermania.com. He has made guest appearances in support of his publications at the Good Beans Café in Flint, Michigan, at the Common Language Bookstore in Ann Arbor, Michigan, at A Different Light in both Los Angeles and San Francisco, The Open Book in Sacramento, and at Giovanni's Room in Philadelphia, as well as at the DR2 Theatre D-2 Lounge in New York City.

He holds a BFA in Theatre Acting and Directing from Otterbein College in Westerville, Ohio, is an alumnus of the Commercial Theater Institute, and is a candidate for a 2012 Juris Doctor degree from Seton Hall University School of Law in Newark, New Jersey. He lives in New York City. For more information or to schedule speaking engagements, please visit benhodges.com, or e-mail benjamin hodges@e-mail.com.

Scott Denny (Co-Editor) is an actor and singer who has worked professionally for over twenty years. Originally from Terre Haute, Indiana, he attended Western Kentucky University in Bowling Green, Kentucky and holds a degree in performing arts.

Most recently he appeared in the Irish Repertory Theatre's gala *Brigadoon* concert at the Shubert Theatre in June 2010 and at the 2010 MAC Awards.

His professional theatrical credits include Richard Henry Lee in the Big League Theatricals national tour of *1776*, Uncle Wes in the Las Vegas and national touring production of *Footloose*, and the assistant company manager and swing on the 2001-2002 national tour of Susan Stroman's production of *The Music Man*. While on tour he arranged several cast benefit cabarets for local charities.

Regionally he has appeared in *Evita*, *The Wizard of Oz*, and *The King and I* at Houston's Theatre Under the Stars, *The Mikado* starring Eric Idle at Houston Grand Opera, and in the regional premieres of *Silver Dollar* and *Paper Moon* at Stage One in Wichita,

Kansas. He performed frequently at the Broadway Palm Dinner Theatre in Fort Myers, Florida, as well as Beef and Boards Dinner Theatre (Indianapolis, Indiana), Fireside Theatre (Fort Atkinson, Wisconsin), Miami Valley Dinner Theatre (Springboro, Ohio), Dutch Apple Dinner Theatre (Lancaster, Pennsylvania), Circa 21 (Rock Island, Illinois), and the Crown Uptown (Wichita, Kansas). He worked six summers the Galveston Island Outdoor Musicals and at Sullivan Illinois' historic Little Theatre on the Square. Credits at those theatres include *Me and My Girl*, *Gypsy*, *She Loves Me*, *The Best Little Whorehouse in Texas*, *The Music Man*, *Some Like It Hot*, *Man of La Mancha*, *The Odd Couple*, *South Pacific*, *Oklahoma*, *Grease*, *Wonderful Life! The Musical*, *How to Succeed…*, among several others

In New York he has appeared Off-Off-Broadway in *Election Day The Musical*, *Like You Like It*, *Vanity Fair*, and in several readings, workshops, and cabaret shows. His screen credits include the independent films *Red Hook*, *Clear Blue Tuesday*, and *Illegally Yours*.

Scott worked as an assistant editor on *Theatre World* Volume 60, and has been an associate editor on Volumes 61-65. In the fall of 2006 Scott served as Treasurer on the Board of Directors of the Theatre World Awards and was the associate producer for the 2006 Awards and co-producer for the 2007, 2008, and 2009 Awards.

Seasonally Scott works for the Macy's Thanksgiving Day Parade and Macy's Annual Events in the production office, and spent one season in the costume operations for the Parade. Since 2003 Scott has also worked as an outside group sales manager specializing in incentive groups for Cruise Everything, a travel agency located in Fort Myers, Florida. He coordinated the entertainment and sales operations for four cruises with two of QVC's most known and loved personalities, the Quacker Factory host Jeanne Bice, and Jenniefer Kirk of Kirks Folly Jewelry, as well as three New York Theatre vacations. In addition to his other many hats, he bartends at the Duplex Cabaret and Piano Bar.

He is honored to help continue the astounding work of the late John Willis, and would like to thank his high school drama teacher Jean Shutt for introducing him to the wonderful theatre world, as well as the former theatre faculties of Western Kentucky University and Indiana State University: Bill Leonard, Jackson Kessler, Beverly Veenker, Steve Probus, Jim Brown, Larry Ruff, Lew Hackleman, Gary Stewart, Glenn and Patti Harbaugh, Don Nigro, David DelColletti, and the late Whit Combs.

Shay Gines (Associate Editor) graduated from the Actors Training Program at the University of Utah. Since then she has done everything from spackling walls at the Pasadena Playhouse and running follow-spot for the Pioneer Theatre Company to serving as the Artist in Residence for Touchstone Theatre. She has performed in theatres of all sizes from 30 to 1,000 seats and across the country, from Los Angeles to New York City. She is an award-winning producer whose Off and Off-Off-Broadway shows include: *Home Again Home Again Jiggity Jig*, *What the F**k?!*, *Hamlet*, and *Muse of Fire*. She was a founding member and the Producing Director for Esperance Theatre Company, served for five years as the Managing Director for Emerging Artists Theatre Company, and is an Executive Director for the Innovative Theatre Foundation.

Adam Feldman (Contributing Editor: Broadway Review) is the Associate Theater Editor at *Time Out New York*, where he is also Cabaret Editor. Since 2005, he has served as president of the New York Drama Critics' Circle, making him both the youngest and the longest-serving president in the group's 75-year history. His essays and reviews have appeared in Canada's *Globe and Mail* and *National Post*, as well as Broadway.com, *Time Out London*, *Time Out New York Kids* and *The Gay & Lesbian Review*. He is a frequent commentator on New York's NPR station, WNYC, and has been interviewed on ABC's Nightline, CNN and CBS News. He has hosted panel events at the 92nd Street Y, the Brooklyn Academy of Music, the Public Theater and Theater Row, among others. He is a graduate of Harvard University, where he received the Helen Choate Bell prize for essays on American literature.

Linda Buchwald (Contributing Editor: Off-Broadway Review) is a graduate of the Goldring Arts Journalism Program at Syracuse University. Currently, she is the assistant editor for *Scholastic MATH Magazine*. She is a regular contributor to TDF Stages and StageGrade. Her writing has appeared in *The Village Voice, The Sondheim Review*, and other publications. She also runs a (mostly) theater blog, *Pataphysical Science*, and is a member of the Independent Theater Bloggers Association (ITBA).

Nicole Estvanik Taylor (Contributing Regional Editor) is the managing editor of *American Theatre* magazine, published by Theatre Communications Group, and her byline appears frequently in its pages. She has also written about the arts for *TheatreForum* and the Creative Capital Foundation. She was born into a family whose home phone number doubled as the box office for a community theatre troupe, which accounts for the role of theatre in her life; her taste for magazine work came later, during a stint as an *Atlantic Monthly* intern and a post-college editorial gig at her alma mater's quarterly publication, *Boston College Magazine*. She is a graduate of the Columbia Publishing Course and has also worked as a freelance copy editor on several books.

Kelley Murphy Perlstein (Assistant Editor) has been working professionally in the theatre for over 20 years. She has her B.A. in Theatre from the University of Science and Arts of Oklahoma and an M.F.A. in Music Theatre Performance from Roosevelt University in Chicago. From 2000-2007, she was the Development Director and eventually Managing Director of Praxis Theatre Project, an Off-Off Broadway company in New York City. She currently resides in Dallas, TX.

Cristina Politano (Assistant Editor) graduated from Barnard College, where she edited the French Literary Review and drew cartoons for a variety of publications, including the Columbia Daily Spectator. She currently lives in New York and gives lessons in French.